THE ROUGH GUIDE TO

New Zealand

There are more than two hundred Rough Guide titles
covering destinations from Alaska to Zimbabwe
and subjects from Accoustic Guitar to Travel Health

Forthcoming travel guides include
The Algarve • The Bahamas • Cambodia • Caribbean Islands
Costa Brava • New York Restaurants • Bolivia • Zanzibar

Forthcoming Reference guides include
Elvis • Online Travel • Internet Radio • Cult TV

Rough Guides on the Internet
www.roughguides.com

ROUGH GUIDE CREDITS

Text editors: Claire Fogg and Sam Thorne
Series editor: Mark Ellingham
Editorial: Martin Dunford, Jonathan Buckley, Jo Mead, Kate Berens, Amanda Tomlin, Ann-Marie Shaw, Paul Gray, Helena Smith, Judith Bamber, Orla Duane, Olivia Eccleshall, Ruth Blackmore, Geoff Howard, Claire Saunders, Gavin Thomas, Alexander Mark Rogers, Polly Thomas, Joe Staines, Lisa Nellis, Andrew Tomičić, Richard Lim, Duncan Clark, Peter Buckley (UK); Andrew Rosenberg, Mary Beth Maioli, Don Bapst, Stephen Timblin (US)
Production: Susanne Hillen, Andy Hilliard, Link Hall, Helen Ostick, Julia Bovis, Michelle Draycott, Katie Pringle, Robert Evers, Mike Hancock, Robert McKinlay
Cartography: Melissa Baker, Maxine Repath, Ed Wright
Picture research: Louise Boulton, Sharon Martins
Online: Kelly Cross, Anja Mutić-Blessing (US)
Finance: John Fisher, Gary Singh, Edward Downey, Mark Hall, Tim Bill
Marketing & Publicity: Richard Trillo, Niki Smith, David Wearn, Jemima Broadbridge (UK); Jean Marie Kelly, Simon Carloss, David Wechsler (US)
Administration: Tania Hummel, Demelza Dallow, Julie Sanderson

ACKNOWLEDGEMENTS

This book is dedicated to Guy Harper

The authors would like to thank our editor, Claire Fogg; her last-minute stand-in, Sam Thorne; and Paul Gray and Kate Berens for being there to make sure everything went as smoothly as possible. Thanks also go to all the readers who wrote in, emailed or just accosted us out in the field, sometimes with great suggestions, other times just to tell us they disagreed with our opinions; and all the staff of visitor centres around the country who gave up their time to help. Thanks too to Gordon Burrow at the YHA in New Zealand, Chris McKellar for advice on the Kiwi gay scene and Roy Colbert for his help on the Dunedin Sound. Finally thanks go to Maxine Repath and Mandy Muggridge Geographic Services Ltd for cartography, Rob McKinlay and Katie Pringle for typesetting, Elaine Pollard for proofreading, and Sharon Martins and Louise Boulton for picture research.

Tony and Laura: Thanks to Peter Hawes and Elizabeth Barker for their invaluable input; Singapore Airlines; Topcat; Southern Air; Suzanne Miller, Ann Shepherd, Catherine Connew and Richard Maloney of the DOC; David Hindley; Stephen ONeil; Peter Kitchen (Kitch); Evan Bloomfield, Barbara Hughes (ENABLE); Jennifer Beaston and Bronwyn Grant. Mention must also be made of the wonderful Tony at ACE Rentals (Auckland); Renny Rentals (Christchurch) who were fantastically helpful; Rae White of the Saltmarsh Partnership; Hamish (you know who you are) for giggles and a guiding hand; all the people who helped us, took us in, looked after our home while we were away and to anyone who walked, talked or supped with us and generally made their feelings known on how to improve the book. Special thanks to to Anne, Violet and Don for their kindness and support.

Paul: Thanks to Lynda Heard at Fullers Auckland; Tainui Stephens at TVNZ's Maori Department for improvements to the History and Maoritanga sections; Jules Brown for his epicurean insights; Annie and Mel for boozy nights around the Auckland bars; Catarina de Nave for Auckland restaurant advice; Diana Pahors at the Sydney Flight Centre; Niki and Alex in Christchurch; and Wendy and Phil in Queenstown for walks and oenological deliberations. Cheers, too, to all those who shared experiences and huts on numerous tramps throughout the country, helped pass long bus journeys and shared meals across the land. Special thanks too to Susan Wood for giving us a good plug on her show; and all the friends and acquaintances around New Zealand and elsewhere who have pointed out areas of weakness in the first edition, suggested great restaurants, waxed lyrical about everything from hostels to luxurious retreats and generally helped make this second edition what it is. And most of all thanks to Irene for continued support and forbearance over my long evenings spent at the computer and even longer research trips down-country.

PUBLISHING INFORMATION

This second edition published October 2000 by
Rough Guides Ltd, 62–70 Shorts Gardens,
London WC2H 9AH. Reprinted February & December 2001 and February 2002
Distributed by the Penguin Group:
Penguin Books Ltd, 27 Wrights Lane, London W8 5TZ
Penguin Putnam, Inc. 375 Hudson Street, NY 10014, USA
Penguin Books Australia Ltd, 487 Maroondah Highway, PO Box 257, Ringwood, Victoria 3134, Australia
Penguin Books Canada Ltd, 10 Alcorn Avenue, Toronto, Ontario, Canada M4V 1E4
Penguin Books (NZ) Ltd, 182–190 Wairau Road, Auckland 10, New Zealand
Typeset in Linotron Univers and Century Old Style to an original design by Andrew Oliver.
Printed in England by Clays Ltd, St Ives PLC
Illustrations in Part One and Part Three by Edward Briant.
Illustrations on p.1 & p.843 by Henry Iles
© Laura Harper, Tony Mudd and Paul Whitfield 2000
No part of this book may be reproduced in any form without permission from the publisher except for the quotation of brief passages in reviews.
928pp – Includes index
A catalogue record for this book is available from the British Library
ISBN 1-85828-555-0

THE ROUGH GUIDE TO

New Zealand

written and researched by

Laura Harper, Tony Mudd
and Paul Whitfield

ROUGH
GUIDES

We set out to do something different when the first Rough Guide was published in 1982. Mark Ellingham, just out of university, was travelling in Greece. He brought along the popular guides of the day, but found they were all lacking in some way. They were either strong on ruins and museums but went on for pages without mentioning a beach or taverna. Or they were so conscious of the need to save money that they lost sight of Greece's cultural and historical significance. Also, none of the books told him anything about Greece's contemporary life – its politics, its culture, its people, and how they lived.

So with no job in prospect, Mark decided to write his own guidebook, one which aimed to provide practical information that was second to none, detailing the best beaches and the hottest clubs and restaurants, while also giving hard-hitting accounts of every sight, both famous and obscure, and providing up-to-the-minute information on contemporary culture. It was a guide that encouraged independent travellers to find the best of Greece, and was a great success, getting shortlisted for the Thomas Cook travel guide award,

and encouraging Mark, along with three friends, to expand the series.

The Rough Guide list grew rapidly and the letters flooded in, indicating a much broader readership than had been anticipated, but one which uniformly appreciated the Rough Guide mix of practical detail and humour, irreverence and enthusiasm. Things haven't changed. The same four friends who began the series are still the caretakers of the Rough Guide mission today: to provide the most reliable, up-to-date and entertaining information to independent-minded travellers of all ages, on all budgets.

We now publish more than 150 titles and have offices in London and New York. The travel guides are written and researched by a dedicated team of more than 100 authors, based in Britain, Europe, the USA and Australia. We have also created a unique series of phrasebooks to accompany the travel series, along with an acclaimed series of music guides, and a best-selling pocket guide to the Internet and World Wide Web. We also publish comprehensive travel information on our Web site:

www.roughguides.com

HELP US UPDATE

We've gone to a lot of effort to ensure that the second edition of *The Rough Guide to New Zealand* is accurate and up-to-date. However, things change – places get "discovered", opening hours are notoriously fickle, restaurants and rooms raise prices or lower standards. If you feel we've got it wrong or left something out, we'd like to know, and if you can remember the address, the price, the time, the phone number, so much the better.

We'll credit all contributions, and send a copy of the next edition (or any other Rough Guide if you prefer) for the best letters. Please mark letters: "Rough Guide New Zealand Update" and send to:
Rough Guides, 62–70 Shorts Gardens, London WC2H 9AH, or Rough Guides, 4th Floor, 345 Hudson St, New York, NY 10014.
Or send email to: mail@roughguides.co.uk
Online updates about this book can be found on Rough Guides' Web site at www.roughguides.com

THE AUTHORS

Laura Harper first visited New Zealand during a year out from book editing in the UK. She quickly fell in love with the place and its people and stayed for four months. Back in the UK, she updated the *Rough Guide to Florida* with Tony Mudd before co-writing this book. She keeps her hand in as a freelance writer and editor for a number of book publishers, covering a broad range of topics including, of course, travel. When not writing newspaper or magazine articles about New Zealand, the rest of her working life is spent as a freelance copywriter for advertising and marketing agencies in her home county of Suffolk.

After several years as a freelance editor, researcher and writer, **Tony Mudd** travelled round the world with Laura Harper in 1994, later returning to the land of the long white cloud to research the *Rough Guide to New Zealand*. He has also contributed to the *Rough Guide to Florida*, Yahoo's Internet site (writing text for various destinations around

the world), and produced pieces for newspapers, magazines, radio and other Net sites. He dovetails this work with giving talks on New Zealand, writing fiction, poetry, reviews and exploring the Suffolk coast.

Paul Whitfield emigrated from Britain to New Zealand aged thirteen and spent ten formative years there, little suspecting that a decade or so on he would be writing this Rough Guide to his adopted land. After ten years back in Britain, he went out to research the first edition of this book. Catching up with old friends and meeting new ones re-awakened a desire to live in Godzone, and in 1998 he moved back to Auckland. With this second edition now firmly tucked away, he's busy researching and writing the *Rough Guide to Alaska*, and doing regular Rough Guide update work in Wales, California and Mexico. Spells back home allow time for climbing, whitewater kayaking and tramping the Kiwi backcountry.

READERS' LETTERS

Thanks to all the readers who took the trouble to write in with their comments on the first edition (apologies for any omissions or misspellings):

Judy Ablow, David Allan, Michelle Allnutt, Colin Babb, Alison Birch, Frances Bland, Liz Boot, Kylie Booth, Graeme Brown, Katarina Cartwright, C.G., Metsada and Benny Chor, Andrew Clifford, Sally Coutts, Rachel Day, John Deeks, Judy Doyle, Mark Ellingham, Helen Elphick, Carol Flux, Michael Genton, Mike Gepp, Gail Gibbons, Brian Gilberthorpe, Kay Gordon, the Hall Family, Pete Hanson, Graham Hawkyard, Jenny Hoskins, Trevor Hoskins, Lauragaye Jackson, James and

Eileen, Jason and Beata, Darren Jones, Davina Lavery, Monique Leerschool, Jurgen Maerschond, Roger Madge, David Masters, Jamie McArdle, Charlie McFeely, A. McLeod, Peter McNamara, Helen Midwinter, Clive Mitchell, Natasha Montgomery, Kim Morton, Benjamin Needham, Cathy Nolan, John Palmer, Mike Pennell, Fiona Pereira, Helen Reynolds, Leonna Sanderson, Katya Scholtz, Tim Searle, Julia Smith, Niki Smith, Vanessa Smith Holburn, Tom Stainer, Julie Thomas, Elen Van Haaften, Louis Van Wyk, Vicky Wallwork, David Wearn, Martin White, Sandra Whitlock, Alan Whittaker, W. Wood, Andrea Yates.

CONTENTS

Introduction x

PART THREE CONTEXTS   843

LIST OF MAPS

MAP SYMBOLS

▬▬	Railway	⌃⌃	Mountains
⎯◇⎯	State Highway	▲	Peak
══	Road	⬐	Viewpoint
-----	Path	⼞	Cliff
– – –	Ferry route	ⵙ	Lighthouse
▬▬	Waterway	⥁	Waterfall
▬▬▬	Chapter division boundary	⥽	Marshland
◆	Places of Interest	⋎	Spring
◼	Restaurant	✕	Airport
◉	Hotel	P	Parking
⚊	Campsite	★	Bus stop
⚑	Hut	T	Toilet
⛴	Shelter	⊞	Hospital
⚲	Church (regional maps)	ⓘ	Tourist office
♖	Castle	✉	Post office
⚑	Museum	⒞	Telephone
⚕	Public Gardens	◼	Building
⚘	Winery	⊣	Church
⊕	Swimming pool	⊹	Cemetery
⛷	Ski area	▒	Park
⚐	Golf course	▓	National Park
⌂	Cave	░	Beach
		⧄	Glacier

INTRODUCTION

New Zealand comes with a reputation as a unique land packed with magnificent, raw **scenery**: craggy coastlines, sweeping beaches, primeval forests, snow-capped alpine mountains, bubbling volcanic pools, fast-flowing rivers and glacier-fed lakes, all beneath a brilliant blue sky. Even **Kiwis** themselves – named after the endearing, if decidedly odd, flightless bird that has become the national emblem – seem to be filled with astonishment at the stupendous vistas of what they like to think of as "Godzone" (God's own country). All of this provides a canvas for boundless **diversions**, from moody strolls along windswept beaches and multi-day tramps over alpine passes to the adrenalin-charged adventure activities of bungy jumping and whitewater rafting; in fact, some visitors take on New Zealand as a kind of large-scale assault course, aiming to tackle as many adventures as possible in the time available. The one-time albatross of isolation – even Australia is over a thousand kilometres away – has become a boon, bolstering New Zealand's clean, **green** image, which is, in truth, more an accident of geography than the result of past government policy.

To a large extent New Zealand lives up to these expectations, and remains unfettered by the crowds you'd find elsewhere. What's more, everything is easily accessible, packed into a land area little larger than Britain and with a population of just 3.8 million, over half of it tucked away in the three largest **cities**: Auckland, the capital Wellington, and the South Island's Christchurch. Elsewhere, you can travel miles through steep-hilled farmland and rarely see a soul, and there are even remote spots which, it's reliably contended, no human has ever visited.

Geologically, New Zealand split off from the super-continent of Gondwanaland early, developing a unique **ecosystem** in which birds adapted to fill the role normally held by mammals, many becoming flightless through lack of predators. That all changed around 1200 years ago when the arrival of Polynesian navigators made this the last major land mass to be settled by humans. On sighting the new land from their canoes, Maori named it **Aotearoa** – "the land of the long white cloud" – and proceeded to radically alter the fragile ecosystem, dispatching forever the giant ostrich-sized moa, which formed a major part of their diet. A delicate ecological balance was achieved before the arrival of *pakeha* – white Europeans, predominantly of British origin – who swarmed off their square-rigged ships full of colonial zeal.

The subsequent uneasy coexistence between **Maori** and **European** societies informs both recorded history and the current wrangles over cultural identity, land and resource rights. The British didn't invade as such, and were to some degree reluctant to enter into the 1840 **Treaty of Waitangi**, New Zealand's founding document, which effectively ceded New Zealand to the British Crown while guaranteeing Maori hegemony over their land and traditional gathering and fishing rights. As time wore on and increasing numbers of settlers demanded to buy ever larger parcels of land from Maori, antipathy soon surfaced, eventually escalating to hostility. Once Maori were subdued, a policy of partial integration ensured the rapid dilution of their cultural heritage and all but destroyed **Maoritanga** – the Maori way of doing things. Maori, however, were left well outside the new European order, where difference was perceived as tantamount to a

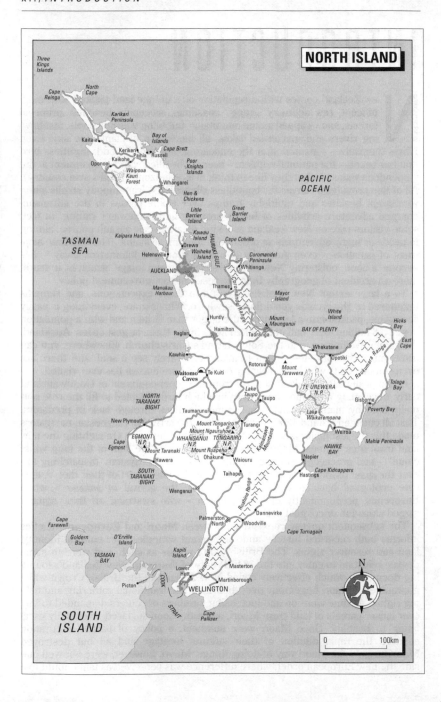

NORTH ISLAND

Three Kings Islands

Cape Reinga
North Cape

Karikari Peninsula

Kaitaia
Bay of Islands
Cape Brett
Kerikeri
Paihia
Russell
Kaikohe
Opononi
Waipoua Kauri Forest

Poor Knights Islands

Whangarei

Hen & Chickens

Dargaville

Little Barrier Island

Great Barrier Island

PACIFIC OCEAN

Kaipara Harbour

Kawau Island
Orewa
Waiheke Island

Cape Colville

HAURAKI GULF

TASMAN SEA

Helensville

AUCKLAND

Coromandel Peninsula
Whitianga

Manukau Harbour

Thames

Coromandel Range

Mayor Island

White Island

Huntly
Hamilton
Mount Maunganui

BAY OF PLENTY

Hicks Bay

Raglan
Tauranga
Whakatane
Opotiki

East Cape

Kawhia

Waitomo Caves
Te Kuiti

Rotorua
Mount Tarawera

Raukumara Range

TE UREWERA N.P.

Tolaga Bay

NORTH TARANAKI BIGHT

Lake Taupo
Taupo

Gisborne
Poverty Bay

Taumarunui

Lake Waikaremoana

New Plymouth

Mount Tongariro
Mount Ngauruhoe
Turangi

Wairoa

EGMONT N.P.

WHANGANUI N.P.

TONGARIRO N.P.

Kaimanawa Mountains

Mahia Peninsula

Cape Egmont
Mount Taranaki
Mount Ruapehu
Ohakune
Waiouru

Napier

HAWKE BAY

Hawera

Cape Kidnappers
Hastings

SOUTH TARANAKI BIGHT

Taihape

Wanganui

Ruahine Range

Dannevirke

Cape Farewell

Palmerston North
Woodville

Cape Turnagain

Golden Bay
D'Erville Island

TASMAN BAY

Kapiti Island

Tararua Range

Lower Hutt
Masterton

Picton

COOK STRAIT

Martinborough

WELLINGTON

SOUTH ISLAND

Cape Palliser

N

0   100km

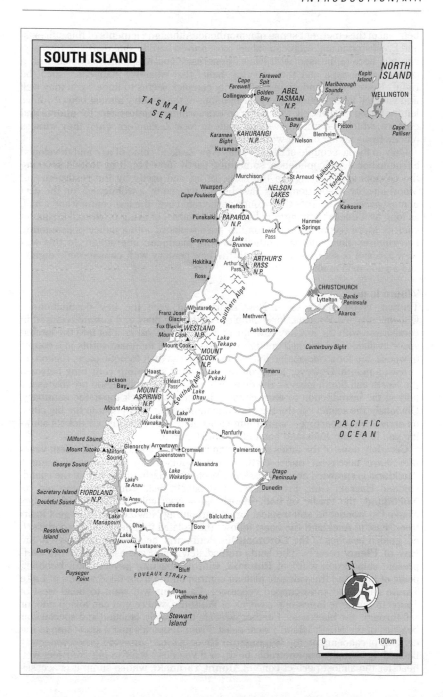

SOUTH ISLAND

NORTH ISLAND

TASMAN SEA

Cape Farewell
Farewell Spit
Collingwood
Golden Bay
ABEL TASMAN N.P.
Kapiti Island
Marlborough Sounds
WELLINGTON

Karamea Bight
KAHURANGI N.P.
Karamea
Tasman Bay
Nelson
Picton
Blenheim
Cape Palliser

Murchison
St Arnaud
Kaikoura Ranges

Westport
Cape Foulwind
NELSON LAKES N.P.

Reefton
Punakaiki
PAPAROA N.P.
Lewis Pass
Hanmer Springs
Kaikoura

Greymouth
Lake Brunner

Hokitika
Arthur's Pass
ARTHUR'S PASS N.P.

Ross
CHRISTCHURCH
Lyttelton
Banks Peninsula

Whataroa
Southern Alps
Methven
Akaroa

Franz Josef Glacier
Fox Glacier
WESTLAND N.P.
Mount Cook
Ashburton

Mount Cook
Lake Tekapo
MOUNT COOK N.P.

Haast
Lake Pukaki
Timaru

Jackson Bay
Haast Pass
MOUNT ASPIRING N.P.
Southern Alps
Lake Ohau

Mount Aspiring
Lake Hawea
Canterbury Bight

Lake Wanaka
Lake Hawea
Oamaru

Milford Sound
Wanaka
Ranfurly
PACIFIC OCEAN

Mount Tutoko
Milford Sound
Glenorchy
Arrowtown
Cromwell
Palmerston

George Sound
Queenstown
Alexandra

Secretary Island
Lake Te Anau
FIORDLAND N.P.
Lake Wakatipu
Otago Peninsula

Doubtful Sound
Te Anau
Manapouri
Dunedin

Resolution Island
Lake Manapouri
Ohai
Lumsden
Balclutha

Dusky Sound
Lake Hauroko
Tuatapere
Gore

Puyseger Point
Riverton
Invercargill
Bluff

FOVEAUX STRAIT
Oban (Halfmoon Bay)

Stewart Island

0   100km

betrayal of the emergent sense of nationhood. Although elements of this still exist and Presbyterian and Anglican values have proved hard to shake off, the Kiwi psyche has become infused with Maori generosity and hospitality, coupled with a colonial mateyness and the unerring belief that whatever happens, "she'll be right". However, an underlying inferiority complex seems to linger: you may well find yourself interrogated as to your opinions of the country almost before you've left the airport. Balancing this out is an extraordinary enthusiasm for **sports** and **culture**, which generate a swelling pride in New Zealanders when they witness plucky Kiwis taking on the world.

Only in the last couple of decades has New Zealand come of age and developed a true national self-confidence, something partly forced on it by Britain severing the colonial apron strings in the early 1970s, and partly by the resurgence of Maori identity. Maori demands have been nurtured by a willingness on the part of most *pakeha* to redress the wrongs perpetrated over the last century and a half, as long as it doesn't impinge on their high standard of living or overall feeling of control. More recently, integration has been replaced with a policy of promoting two cultures alongside each other, but with maximum interaction. In this way New Zealand is set to forge through the new century with considerable dignity and a good deal of uncertainty.

Where to go

Tourism is big business in New Zealand but even the key destinations – Queenstown and Rotorua, for example – only seem busy and commercialized in comparison with the low-key Kiwi norm. New Zealand packs a lot into the limited space available and is small enough that you can visit the main sights in a couple of weeks, but for a reasonable look around at a less than frenetic pace, reckon on at least a month. However long you've got, look at spreading your time between the North and South islands: the diverse attractions of each region are discussed fully in the introduction to each chapter, but here's a quick top-to-toe summary. Obviously, the scenery is the big draw and most people only pop into the big cities on arrival and departure – something easily done with open-jaw air tickets allowing you to fly into Auckland and out of Christchurch.

Certainly none of the cities ranks on an international scale, but in recent years they have taken on more distinct and sophisticated identities. Go-ahead **Auckland** is sprawled around sparkling Waitemata Harbour, an arm of the island-studded Hauraki Gulf. From here, most people head south, missing out on **Northland**, the cradle of both Maori and *pakeha* colonization, which comes cloaked in wonderful sub-tropical forest harbouring New Zealand's largest kauri trees. East of Auckland the coast follows the isolated greenery and long, deserted, golden beaches of the **Coromandel Peninsula**, before running down to the **Bay of Plenty** resorts. The lands immediately south are assailed by the ever-present sulphurous whiff of **Rotorua**, with its spurting geysers and bubbling pools of mud, and the volcanic plateau centred on the trout-filled waters of **Lake Taupo** and three snow-capped volcanoes. Cave fans will want to head west of Taupo to the eerie limestone caverns of **Waitomo**, where you can abseil into, or raft through, the blackness. Further west are the moody, isolated and spectacular beaches of the North Island's west coast. From Taupo it's just a short hop to the delights of canoeing on the **Whanganui River**, a broad, emerald green waterway banked by virtually impenetrable bush, or if you don't want to get your feet wet, head for the almost perfect cone of **Mount Taranaki**, whose summit is accessible in just one day. East of Taupo lie the ranges that form the North Island's backbone, and beyond them the **Hawke's Bay wine country**, centred on the Art Deco city of Napier, and the up-and-coming wine region of Martinborough. Only an hour or so away is the capital, **Wellington**, the most self-contained of New Zealand's cities, with its centre squeezed onto reclaimed harbourside land and the suburbs slung over steep hills overlooking glistening bays. Politicians and bureaucrats give it well-scrubbed and urbane sophistication, enlivened by a burgeoning café society and after-dark scene.

The **South Island** kicks off with **Nelson**, a pretty and compact spot surrounded by lovely beaches and within easy reach of the world-renowned wineries of Marlborough. From there you've a choice of nipping around behind the 3000-metre summits of the Southern Alps and following the West Coast to the fabulous **glaciers** at Fox and Franz Josef, or sticking to the east, passing the whale-watching territory of **Kaikoura** en route to the South Island's largest centre, straight-laced **Christchurch**, a city with its roots firmly in the traditions of England. From Christchurch it's possible to head across country to the West Coast via the famous **Arthur's Pass** scenic railway, or shoot southwest across the patchwork Canterbury Plains to the foothills of the **Southern Alps** and **Mount Cook** with its distinctive drooping-tent summit.

The flatlands of Canterbury run down, via the grand architecture of **Oamaru**, to the unmistakably Scottish-influenced city of **Dunedin**, birthplace of some of the country's best rock bands and base for exploring the teeming wildlife of the **Otago Peninsula**. In the middle of the nineteenth century prospectors arrived here and rushed inland to gold strikes throughout central Otago and around stunningly set **Queenstown**, now a highly commercialized activity centre where bungy jumping, rafting, jetboating and skiing hold sway. This is also the tramping heartland, with the **Routeburn Track** linking Queenstown to the rain-sodden fiords, lakes and mountains of **Fiordland**, and the world-renowned **Milford Track**. The further south you travel, the more you'll feel the bite of the Antarctic winds, which reach their peak on New Zealand's third land mass, the tiny and isolated **Stewart Island**, covered mostly by dense coastal rainforest and famous for testing the patience of even the most avid trampers with its almost permanently muddy tracks.

When to go

With over a thousand kilometres of ocean in every direction, it comes as no surprise that New Zealand has a maritime climate: warm through the southern summer months of December to March and never truly cold, even in winter.

Weather patterns are strongly affected by the prevailing westerlies, which suck up moisture from the Tasman Sea and dump it on the western side of both islands. The South Island gets the lion's share, with the West Coast and Fiordland ranking among the world's wettest places. The mountain ranges running the length of both islands cast long rain shadows over the eastern lands, making them considerably drier, though the south is a few degrees cooler than elsewhere, and sub-tropical Auckland and Northland are appreciably more humid. In the North Island, warm, damp summers fade almost imperceptibly into cool, wet winters, but the further south you go the more the year divides into four distinct seasons.

Such regional variation makes it viable to visit at any time of year, provided you pick your destinations. The **summer** months are the most popular and you'll find everything open, though often packed with holidaying Kiwis from Christmas to the end of January. Accommodation at this time is at a premium. In general, you're better off joining the bulk of foreign visitors during the **shoulder seasons** – October to Christmas and February to April or May – when sights and attractions can be a shade quieter, and rooms easier to come by. **Winter** (June–Sept) is the wettest, coldest and consequently least popular time, though Northland can still be relatively balmy. The switch to prevailing southerly winds tends to bring periods of crisp, dry and cloudless weather to the West Coast and heavy snowfalls to the fine, under-utilized and plentiful skiing pistes of the Southern Alps and Central North Island.

CLIMATE CHART

	Jan	Feb	March	April	May	June	July	Aug	Sept	Oct	Nov	Dec
Auckland												
av. max. temp. (°C)	23	23	22	19	17	14	13	14	16	17	19	21
av. min. temp. (°C)	16	16	15	13	11	9	8	8	9	11	12	14
av. rainfall (mm)	79	94	81	97	17	137	145	117	102	102	89	79
Napier												
av. max. temp. (°C)	24	23	22	19	17	14	13	14	17	19	21	23
av. min. temp. (°C)	14	14	13	10	8	5	5	6	7	9	11	13
av. rainfall (mm)	74	76	74	76	89	86	102	84	56	56	61	58
Wellington												
av. max. temp. (°C)	21	21	19	17	14	13	12	12	14	16	17	19
av. min. temp. (°C)	13	13	12	11	8	7	6	6	8	9	10	12
av. rainfall (mm)	81	81	81	97	117	117	137	117	97	102	89	89
Christchurch												
av. max. temp. (°C)	21	21	19	17	13	11	10	11	14	17	19	21
av. min. temp. (°C)	12	12	10	7	4	2	2	2	4	7	8	11
av. rainfall (mm)	56	43	48	48	66	66	69	48	46	43	48	56
Hokitika												
av. max. temp. (°C)	19	19	18	16	14	12	12	12	13	15	16	18
av. min. temp. (°C)	12	12	11	8	6	3	3	3	6	8	9	11
av. rainfall (mm)	262	191	239	236	244	231	218	239	226	292	267	262
Queenstown												
av. max. temp. (°C)	21	21	20	7	11	9	9	11	14	18	19	20
av. min. temp. (°C)	10	10	9	7	3	1	0	1	3	5	7	10
av. rainfall (mm)	79	72	74	72	64	58	59	63	66	77	64	62
Dunedin												
av. max. temp. (°C)	19	19	17	15	12	9	9	11	13	15	17	18
av. min. temp. (°C)	10	10	9	7	5	4	3	3	5	6	7	9
av. rainfall (mm)	86	71	76	71	81	81	79	76	69	76	81	89

PART ONE

THE

BASICS

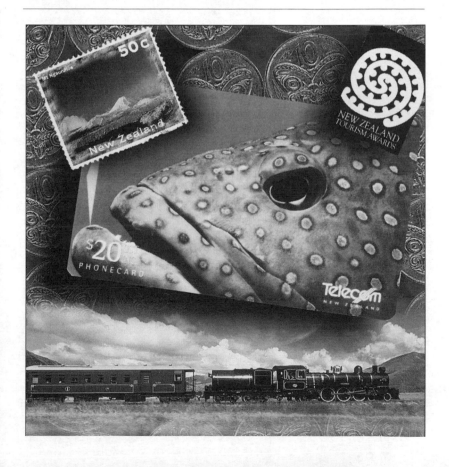

BASICS

GETTING THERE FROM BRITAIN AND IRELAND

Over a dozen airlines compete to fly you from Britain to New Zealand for as little as £450–1000, remarkably cheap considering the distances involved but prices depend upon the time of year and rocket around Christmas. Going for the cheapest flight typically means sacrificing some comfort, which you may regret, given that your journey will last at least 24 hours, longer if your flight makes more than the obligatory refuelling stop. There are no direct flights to New Zealand from Ireland, and prices are proportionately higher, since the short hop to London (around £75 return) has to be added on to the fare.

No matter how keen you are to arrive in New Zealand, it makes sense to break the journey, and most **scheduled flights** allow multiple **stopovers** either in North America and the Pacific, or Asia and Australia. The vast majority of direct scheduled flights to New Zealand depart from London's Heathrow, though Garuda Indonesia fly from London Gatwick (1 weekly), and Singapore Airlines use Manchester (5 weekly) as well as Heathrow. There are few overseas flights into Wellington, so the only real choice is between the main international airport at **Auckland**, in the north of the North Island, and the second airport at **Christchurch**, midway down the South Island. Christchurch receives fewer direct flights, but most scheduled airlines have a code-share shuttle from Auckland at no extra cost. The most desirable option, an **open-jaw ticket** (flying into one and out of the other), usually costs no more than an ordinary return and means not retracing your steps to get out of the country.

Charter flights to Auckland and Christchurch from London Gatwick with Britannia are currently suspended, but may subsequently be reinstated. Contact Austravel (see box on p.5) for latest details.

If you are planning on doing a lot of **travelling within New Zealand**, especially between the North and South islands, it may be worth looking into **air passes** offered by both Air New Zealand and Ansett Australia (see "Getting Around", p.25). In addition, if you are **combining Australia and New Zealand**, there are handy airpasses covering internal travel in each country and the joining flight. Qantas's **Boomerang Pass** is available to all international travellers (not just Qantas ticket holders), and comprises between two and ten coupons, each valid for a flight within Australasia: a one-zone coupon to fly within New Zealand or short hops in Oz costs £100, a two-zone trans-Tasman coupon costs £125. Air New Zealand/Ansett's **G'day Pass** is fundamentally the same, but has a larger number of travel zones and a wider range of prices: within single zones in New Zealand and Australia, £95; multi zones, £120; and mega zones (New Zealand to Perth or Cairns), £215.

FARES

The surest way to land a flight at a reasonable price is to book as far ahead as possible through a **travel agent**, or one of the many **Internet** agencies offering rock bottom flights, although you won't necessarily know who you're flying with. These are almost invariably cheaper than buying direct from the airline, though we've given a rundown of all the carriers to show the variety of routes (see box overleaf). In the end you'll find the available flights at much the same price everywhere, the main differential being between the plusher airlines like Air New Zealand and British Airways (BA) – which offer more leg-room, movies and comforting accessories – and Singapore, Thai, Garuda Indonesia and United, which are generally the least expensive.

AIRLINES FLYING FROM THE UK TO NEW ZEALAND

Aerolineas Argentinas (☎0845/601 1915). Twice-weekly flights from London Heathrow via Madrid and Buenos Aires to Auckland.

Air New Zealand (☎020/8741 2299). Daily to Auckland, via Los Angeles and the popular South Pacific route with a choice of stopovers in Honolulu, Fiji, Western Samoa, the Cook Islands, Tahiti and Tonga. Easy connections to Christchurch.

British Airways (UK reservations ☎0345/222 111, in the Republic of Ireland ☎1800/626 747). Daily flights from London Heathrow to Auckland and Christchurch, with stopovers in Australia or America, LA or Brisbane.

Canadian Airlines International (UK reservations ☎0345/616 767, in the Republic of Ireland ☎1800/709 900). Daily flights from London Heathrow to Auckland via Vancouver and Honolulu.

Cathay Pacific (☎0345/581 581). Daily flights from Heathrow and Manchester to Auckland via Hong Kong.

Garuda Indonesia (☎020/7486 3011). London Gatwick to Auckland via Bangkok and Bali.

Japanese Airlines (☎0345/747 700). Three flights weekly from Heathrow to Auckland, via Tokyo.

Korean Air (☎0800/413 000; in the Republic of Ireland ☎01/799 7990). Flights a week vary at different times of the year, running from Heathrow to Auckland and Christchurch via Seoul.

Malaysian Airlines (MAS) (UK reservations ☎020/7341 2020, in the Republic of Ireland ☎01/676 1561). Two flights weekly from Heathrow to Auckland and Christchurch via Kuala Lumpur.

Qantas (☎0345/747 767). Daily scheduled flights from Heathrow to Auckland and Christchurch, via LA, Bangkok, Singapore, Sydney and Melbourne.

Singapore Airlines (UK reservations ☎0870/6088 886, in the Republic of Ireland ☎01/671 0722). Flights from Heathrow (daily) and Manchester (daily) to Auckland and Christchurch via Singapore, long wait at Singapore on Manchester flights.

Thai Airways International (☎0870/606 0911). Four flights weekly from Heathrow to Auckland, via Bangkok and Sydney.

United Airlines (☎0845/844 4777). Daily flights from Heathrow to Auckland, with various US stopovers, usually LA or Chicago.

Tourists and those on short-term working visas (see p.13) are generally required by New Zealand immigration to arrive with a ticket out of the country, so **one-way tickets** are really only viable for Australian and New Zealand residents. If you've purchased a return ticket and find you want to stay longer or head off on a totally different route, it's sometimes possible to cash in the return half of your ticket (though you'll make a loss on the deal) at the same travel agent where you bought it. Alternatively, you could try flogging it on the Internet but don't hold your breath.

The cheapest **scheduled fare** you're likely to find is around £450–500 return, available during the low-season months of April, May and June; if you insist on flying with Air New Zealand, Qantas, BA or Singapore, expect to pay upwards of £650 for a flight in this off-peak period. The most expensive time to fly is in the two weeks before **Christmas**, when you'll be lucky to find anything for less than £1000 return: to stand a chance of getting one of the cheaper tickets, aim to book at least six months in advance. In between times

(the **shoulder seasons** of July–Nov and Jan–March), you should expect to pay £750–850 (nearer £1000 with the prestige airlines).

The lowest **charter fares** are for stays of two weeks and start at £600 return. Standard fares for four- to eight-week stays hover around £750–850 in November, early December and most of January, rising through £900–1000 over Christmas.

STOPOVERS AND RTW TICKETS

An excellent alternative to a direct flight is a **multi-stopover ticket**, often for little more than an ordinary return. Unusual routes combining the resources of two or more airlines in a **round-the-world (RTW) ticket** (usually valid for 12 months) are more expensive, but are almost infinitely variable. The best deals are along fixed routes such as the Aerolineas Argentinas/Thai combo that takes you from London through Buenos Aires, Auckland, Sydney, Perth and Bangkok from around £1100, or Alitalia/Air New Zealand's London-

FLIGHT AND TRAVEL AGENTS

Austravel, 5th Floor, 50–51 Conduit St, London W1R 9FB (☎020/7287 0212, *www.austravel.net*), plus branches in Bournemouth, Bristol, Edinburgh, Leeds and Manchester. Offers stopovers in Tokyo, Seoul, Singapore, LA or Fiji from as little as £499 return, rising to £969 at Christmas. Austravel also lays on "Focus Downunder" audio-visual presentations all over the UK to help you plan your trip.

Bridge the World, 1–3 Ferdinand St, London NW1 8ES (☎020/7911 0900, *www.b-t-w.co.uk*). Round-the-world ticket specialist, with good deals aimed at the backpacker market. A second office, at 4 Regents Place, Regent St, London W1R 6BH (☎020/7734 7447), concentrates on swankier arrangements and tours specifically to New Zealand and Australia. Agents for Kiwi Experience.

Campus Travel, 52 Grosvenor Gardens, London SW1W 0AG (national call line ☎0870/240 1010, *www.usitcampus.co.uk*), plus branches in Birmingham, Brighton, Bristol, Cambridge, Coventry, Edinburgh, Leeds, Liverpool, Manchester, Nottingham, Oxford, Sheffield and many more. Student/youth travel specialists, with branches in YHA shops and on university campuses all over Britain.

Cresta World Travel, 32 Victoria St, Table Court, Altrincham, WA14 1ET (☎0161/927 7000, *www.shoppingcentre.com*). Comprehensive range of flights and round-the-world tickets to New Zealand and Australia, with good backpacker deals.

Destination Group, 14 Eville St, London EC1N 8SB (☎020/7400 7000, *www.destination-group.co.uk*). Good discount fares, especially on Garuda flights; Far East and USA inclusive packages.

Flightbookers, 177–178 Tottenham Court Rd, London W1P 9LF (☎020/7757 2000, *www.tmn.com/wwwanderer*). Low fares on scheduled flights.

Joe Walsh Tours, 34 Grafton St, Dublin 2 (☎01/671 8751); 69 Upper O'Connell St, Dublin 2 (☎01/872 2555); 8–11 Baggot St, Dublin 2 (☎01/676 3053); 117 St Patrick St, Cork (☎021/277 959). General budget fares agent (*reservations@joewalshtours.ie*).

Jupiter Travel, 46 Victoria Rd, Surbiton, Surrey KT6 4JL (☎020/8296 0309, or 8339 9929). Cheap and reliable agent with multi-stopover and RTW tickets to New Zealand.

London Flight Centre, 131 Earls Court Rd, London SW5 9RH (☎020/7244 6411, *www.topdecktravel.co.uk*). Long-established agent dealing in discount flights; visas and vaccinations are also on offer.

North South Travel, Moulsham Mill Centre, Parkway, Chelmsford, Essex CM2 7PX (☎01245/608 291, *nstravel@demon.co.uk*). Friendly, competitive travel agency, offering discounted fares worldwide. Profits go to support projects in the developing world, especially the promotion of sustainable tourism.

Quest Worldwide Travel and Tours, Quebec House, 4–10 Richmond Rd, Kingston, Surrey KT2 5HL (☎020/8547 0403). Specialists in round-the-world and Australasian discount fares, with plenty of round-the-world ideas, plus car and motorhome rental, guided Great Walks and bus tours, including Magic Bus.

STA Travel, Priory House, 6 Wrights Lane, London W8 6TA (☎020/7361 6100), plus branches in Birmingham, Bristol, Cambridge, Canterbury, Cardiff, Coventry, Durham, Glasgow, Leeds, Loughborough, Manchester, Nottingham, Oxford, Warwick and Sheffield; Web site *www.sta-travel.com*. Worldwide specialists in low-cost flights and tours; also good deals for students and under-26s. Experts on New Zealand travel with branches in major Kiwi cities.

Thomas Cook, PO Box 2, 13–14 Coningsby Road, Peterborough, Cambridge, PE3 8AB (☎0990/666 222, Flights Direct ☎0990/101 520); 11 Donegall Place, Belfast (☎028/9024 2341) 118 Grafton St, Dublin 2 (☎01/677 1721), plus branches nationwide. Long-established one-stop travel agency for package holidays and scheduled flights; other services include exchange and travellers' cheques, travel insurance and car rental.

Trailfinders, 194 Kensington High St, London, W8 7RG (☎020/7938 3939, *www.trailfinders.com*), 42–50 Earls Court Rd, London W8 6FT (☎020/7938 3366); 4–5 Dawson St, Dublin 2 (☎01/677 7888), plus branches in Manchester, Glasgow, Birmingham and Bristol. One of the most efficient agents for independent travellers; their quarterly magazine is worth scrutinizing for round-the-world routes (call ☎020/7938 3366 for a free copy).

Travel Bag, 52 Regent St, London W1R 6DX (☎020/7287 4522). Discount flights to New Zealand, plus tours and adventure trips; agents for Kiwi Experience.

Travel Mood, 214 & 246 Edgeware Rd, London W2 1DH (☎020/7258 1234) and branches in Leeds and Dundee. Discount fares and round-the-world tickets; also car rental and bus tours, including Kiwi Experience.

based circuit through Bangkok, Singapore, Bali, Auckland, Christchurch, Sydney/Cairns, Los Angeles or New York for a little under £780–880; though Trailfinders will usually knock a little off this using a slightly amended route. It is also possible to reduce your flight costs by incorporating an **overland section** into your round-the-world ticket: common land sectors include Delhi to Kathmandu, Brisbane or Sydney to Cairns, and Buenos Aires to São Paulo.

ORGANIZED TOURS

The rapid increase in long-haul package tourism in recent years hasn't passed New Zealand by, and there are now well over a dozen companies offering everything from flexible backpacker-orientated excursions through mainstream bus **tours** to no-expense-spared extravaganzas. Of course, they're not for everyone, but if time is limited and you have a fairly clear idea of what it is you want to do, there are good deals going. Even if an all-in package doesn't appeal, there may be some mileage in **pre-booking** some accommodation, tours or a rental vehicle – all things most agents listed in the box on p.5 can arrange.

Full "see-it-all" packages can work out quite expensive – to say nothing of being rather tame and controlled – but aren't bad value, considering what you'd be spending anyway. Basic **bus tours** range from 6 days around Northland for about £900 to 17–21 day nationwide tours staying in four-star hotels with all meals, and various cruises and sightseeing included, costing around £3500. A number of companies, most notably Kiwi Experience and Magic Bus (see "Getting Around", p.28, for details), operate **flexible bus tours**, which you can hop off whenever you like and rejoin a day or two later when the next bus comes through.

Pretty much all the major tour operators can also book you onto **tramping trips**, including some of the guided Great Walks (see p.51); you'll still need to book way in advance, though. Mount Cook organize **skiing** holidays in the South Island, based either at Queenstown for Coronet Peak and The Remarkables or at Methven for Mount Hutt, costing around £380–400 for 6 days, including accommodation, transport from there to the field, ski passes and bus travel from Christchurch. It's also possible – and usually cheaper – to contact ski clubs at the fields direct: check out the contacts at *www.snow.co.nz*.

PACKAGE TOUR AND SPECIALIST OPERATORS

Most flight and travel agents can also arrange tours and accommodation – see box on p.5.

Australian Pacific Tours (☎020/8879 7444). Massive range of fully-inclusive bus tours, a variety of 15-day national tours costing from £2070 with meals, £1735 without.

Connections (☎020/8747 0333, fax 8742 3045). Minibus tours for 18–35s, including all transport and most meals, but not international flights (6–16 days; £275–625).

Contiki (☎020/8290 6777). Bus tours for 18–35s "thriving on good times and loads of fun". Itineraries range from 3 days around the Bay of Islands (£99) to a 15-day grand tour (£585 from Christchurch; £615 from Auckland), with accommodation and most meals included.

Explore Worldwide (☎01252/319 448). Small-group tours, staying in small hotels and including treks, canoeing and rafting (18 days on South or North islands £1690; 32 days for both £2695).

Journeys of Distinction (☎01695/578 140). Sedate and exclusive, fully-escorted tours (27 days £3445; 28 days £3495).

Kuoni Worldwide (☎01306/741 111, *australasia.sales@kuoni.co.uk*). A 15- to 17-night bus tour inclusive of flights from Britain and all luxurious accommodation, plus some meals (£2508–2335), as well as more flexible holidays ranging from 3 to 10 days.

Mount Cook Line (☎020/8741 5652, fax 8741 2125). Major New Zealand holiday and travel company offering tame, planned-itinerary tours as well as flight and bus passes, motorhome rental and ski holidays.

Sunbeam Tours (☎01483/454 455). Bus tours, self-drive car and motorhome holidays, guided Great Walks, semi-independent tours at mid-range prices.

GETTING THERE FROM THE USA AND CANADA

Auckland is the only city in New Zealand that has direct, non-stop flights from North America. From there you will find several connections a day to the two other major airports, Wellington and Christchurch. The flying time from Los Angeles to Auckland is approximately 12 hours 45 minutes.

The low season for fares is currently April 17 to August 23; shoulder season runs from August 24 to December 8 and through most of March and April; high season is December 9 to March 5.

SHOPPING FOR TICKETS

Barring special offers, the cheapest of the airlines' published fares is usually an **Apex** ticket, although this will carry certain restrictions: you'll most likely have to book – and pay – at least 21 days before departure, spend a minimum of seven days and a maximum of one month, fly early or mid-week, and you tend to get penalized if you change your schedule.

You can normally cut costs further, and possibly avoid some of the APEX restrictions, by going through a **specialist flight agent** – either a **consolidator**, who buys up blocks of tickets from the airlines and sells them at a discount, or a **discount agent**, who in addition to dealing with discounted flights may also offer special student and youth fares and a range of

DISCOUNT FLIGHT AGENTS, TRAVEL CLUBS & CONSOLIDATORS

Air Brokers International, 150 Post St, Suite 620, San Francisco, CA 94108 (☎1-800/883-3273, *www.airbrokers.com*). Consolidator and specialist in RTW and Circle Pacific tickets.

Airtech, 588 Broadway, Suite 204, New York, NY 10012 (☎1-800/575-TECH, *www.airtech.com*). Standby seat broker; also deals in consolidator fares and courier flights.

AirTreks.com, 442 Post St, Suite 400, San Francisco, CA 94102 (☎1-800/350-0612, *www.airtreks.com*). Round-the-world and Circle Pacific tickets. The Web site features an interactive database that lets you build your own RTW itinerary.

Council Travel, 205 E 42nd St, New York, NY 10017 (☎1-800/226-8624, *www.counciltravel.com*), and branches in many other US cities. Student and budget travel agency.

Now Voyager, 74 Varick St, Suite 307, New York, NY 10013 (☎212/431-1616, *www.*

nowvoyagertravel.com). Courier flight broker and consolidator.

Skylink, 265 Madison Ave, Suite 500, New York, NY 10016 (☎1-800/AIR-ONLY, *www.skylinktravel.com*), plus branches in Chicago, Los Angeles, Montreal, Toronto, and Washington DC. Consolidator.

STA Travel, 10 Downing St, New York, NY 10014 (☎1-800/777-0112, *www.sta-travel.com*), plus branches in the Los Angeles, San Francisco and Boston areas. Worldwide discount travel firm; also student IDs, insurance, car rental and travel passes.

Travel CUTS, 243 College St, Toronto, ON M5T 1P7 (☎416/979-2406 or (Canada only) ☎1-800/667-2887, *www.travelcuts.com*), and other branches all over Canada. Agent specializing in student fares, IDs and other travel services.

Worldtek Travel, 111 Water St, New Haven, CT 06511 (☎1-800/243-1723). Discount travel agency.

other travel-related services such as travel insurance, rail passes, car rentals, tours and the like. Bear in mind, though, that penalties for changing your plans can be stiff. If you travel a lot, **discount travel clubs** are another option – the annual membership fee may be worth it for benefits such as cut-price air tickets and car rental.

Remember that these companies make their money by dealing in bulk – don't expect them to answer lots of questions, and don't automatically assume that tickets from a travel specialist will be cheapest – once you get a quote, check with the airlines and you may turn up an even better deal. Be advised also that the pool of travel companies is swimming with sharks – exercise caution and *never* deal with a company that demands cash up front or refuses to accept payment by credit card.

FLIGHTS FROM THE USA

Air New Zealand, Qantas and United have daily non-stop flights **from Los Angeles** to Auckland, with connections to Christchurch and Wellington, for a midweek round-trip Apex fare of $925, rising to $1491 in peak season. Expect to pay an extra $50–100 for weekend travel. Singapore Airlines fly daily from LA to Auckland via Singapore, and 3 days a week to Christchurch, again via Singapore, but their fares are significantly higher, ranging from $1500 to $1900. And don't forget the discount travel companies, which sometimes offer fares for up to $200 less than those quoted above.

Flights from all **other US cities** are routed via Los Angeles. Air New Zealand and United quote **add-on fares** of $422–657 (from New York) or $397–632 (from Chicago), but shopping around the discount agents or checking out the newspapers for special offers could save you more than a few bucks.

FLIGHTS FROM CANADA

Canadian Airlines flies daily **from Vancouver** and **from Toronto** to Auckland via Hawaii, and **from Montreal** to Auckland via LA. United has daily flights from Vancouver, Toronto and Montreal to Auckland via LA, with Air Canada connections from other Canadian cities. Depending on the season, sample Apex midweek fares are in the following ranges: from Vancouver

---

AIRLINES IN THE USA AND CANADA

Air Canada, ☎1-888/247-2262, *www.aircanada.ca*
Air New Zealand, ☎1-800/262-1234, in Canada ☎1-800/663-5494, *www.airnz.com*
Canadian Airlines, ☎1-800/426-7000; in Canada ☎1-800/665-1177, *www.cdnair.com*
Qantas, ☎1-800/227-4500, *www.qantas.com*
Singapore Airlines, ☎1-800/742-3333, *www.singaporeair.com*
United, ☎1-800/538-2929, *www.ual.com*

CAN$1512–2264; from Toronto CAN$1970–2722; from Montreal CAN$2154–2466. Finally, discount travel companies have been known to track down fares from Vancouver for CAN$1004, or from Toronto for CAN$1378.

RTW AND CIRCLE-PACIFIC ROUTES

If New Zealand is only one stop on a longer journey, you might want to consider buying a **Round-the-World (RTW)** ticket. A sample itinerary of LA–Tahiti–Cook Islands–Fiji–Auckland–Sydney–Kuala Lumpur–Istanbul–London–LA would cost $2295 (low-season departure). An equally exotic option is a **Circle Pacific** ticket. Air New Zealand offer a "Pacific Escapade" ticket for $2600, valid for six months, originating from LA and with no limit to stopovers as long as you follow an onward circular route (no backtracking) and do not exceed 20,000 miles. However, a discount agent should be able to put together cheaper itineraries by combining sectors from different airlines, such as LA–Bangkok–Bali–Auckland–LA, starting from $1350.

ORGANIZED TOURS

Tour operators offer everything from luxury all-inclusive vacations to straightforward car-rental and accommodation **packages** (starting from around $50 a day) and simple home stays (from $50 per night). There's also a seemingly infinite range of **activities** to indulge in, from wine-tasting to hanging out with miniature penguins (see box opposite); flights, unless otherwise stated, are from Los Angeles.

SPECIALIST AGENTS AND TOUR OPERATORS

Abercrombie and Kent (☎1-800/323-7308, *www.abercrombiekent.com*). Upmarket operator with customized tours and set packages. Their 9-day cultural/historical sightseeing package is priced at $3880 (land costs and internal flights only).

Australian Pacific Tours (☎1-800/290-8687, *www.aptours.com*). Various land-only packages, including eco-tours of the national parks from $2190 (10 days) or $4465 (21 days).

Collette Tours (☎1-800/832-4656, in Canada ☎1-800/468-5955, *www.collettetours.com*). Specialists in Australia and New Zealand travel. Their 16-day fully escorted tour of the Bay of Islands, North and South islands, including trips to glaciers and rainforests, starts at $1499 (land only).

Contiki Holidays (☎1-800/CONTIKI, *www.contiki.com*). Specialists in travel for 18–35s. Their several land packages range from a 3-day Bay of Islands tour ($155) to an 11-day Grand Adventurer ($645).

Elderhostel (☎617/426-8056, *www.elderhostel.org*). Educational and activity programmes for senior travellers. In addition to joint Australia/New Zealand packages, specialist month-long tours include the Great New Zealand Train Trek and Land of Geysers and Greenstone ($4428–5192, including return flights).

Inta-Aussie Tours (☎1-800/531-9222, *www.inta-aussie.com*). North American agents catering to the cost-conscious, free-wheeling traveller: escorted land tours, such as their Essential New Zealand (10 days; $873–1044), customized packages, transport and accommodation passes, etc.

Inta-G dAY Tours (☎1-888/429-9667, *www.inta-gday.com*). A division of Inta-Aussie

that offers customized tours and travel information for gay travellers.

Newmans South Pacific Vacations (☎1-800/421-3326, *www.newmansvacations.com*). Specialists in New Zealand vacations, with around 50 different package options in addition to fully independent tours. Their tours include a 14-day bus tour (from $1595, land only) and a 5-day walking tour through the Fiordland National Park (from $890, also land only).

New Zealand Travellers (☎1-800/362-2718). Backpacking and day-hiking tours of the South Island from around $2200 (12 days, airfares extra).

Qantas Vacations (☎1-800/641-8772, in Canada ☎1-800/268-7525, *www.qantas.com*). Highly flexible packages, including fly-drives out of LA, with accommodation and one internal flight for $1635 (10 days) or $2200 (21 days).

Skylink Women's Travel (☎1-800/225 5759, *www.skylinktravel.com*). Specialists in tours for lesbian travellers.

Swain Tours (☎1-800/22-SWAIN, *www.swainaustralia.com*). South Pacific specialists offering customized individual and group itineraries including walking/trek tours through several national parks for $540–890 (3–5 days, land only).

Sunbeam Tours (☎1-800/955-1818, *www.sunbeamtours.com*). Customized tours, along with several set packages. Their 16-day sightseeing tour of the North and South Islands starts at $2199 (land only).

United Vacations (☎1-800/328-6877, *www.unitedvacations-sp.com*). Variety of fly-drives, excursions and escorted tours. A 12-day land/air package starts at $2100.

GETTING THERE FROM AUSTRALIA

Australia–New Zealand routes are busy and competition is fierce, resulting in an ever-changing range of deals and special offers; your best bet is to check the latest with a specialist travel agent (see box opposite). It's a relatively short hop across the Tasman: flying time from Sydney to Auckland is around 3 hours.

All the fares quoted below are for travel during low or shoulder seasons; flying at **peak times** (primarily December to mid-January) can add substantially to these prices. Ultimately, the price you pay for your flight will depend on how much flexibility you want; many of the cheapest deals are hedged with restrictions – typically a maximum stay of thirty days, and an **advance-purchase** requirement. Qantas and Air New Zealand each have daily direct flights from most Australian cities to Auckland. Flights **from the eastern states** cost around A$550, while flights **from Perth** start at A$949; flying to Wellington or Christchurch can add an extra A$150–200, though Qantas and Air New Zealand don't add any premium. Look out for occasional **promotional fares**, which can bring down prices to as low as A$379 for a 30-day return from Sydney to Auckland.

Open-jaw tickets – which let you fly into one city and out of another, making your own way between – can save a lot of backtracking, and don't add hugely to the total fare, if at all. For example, flying from eastern Australia into

AIRLINES

Air New Zealand ☎13 2476.
Ansett Australia ☎13 1414.
Qantas ☎13 1211.

Singapore Airlines ☎13 1011.
Thai Airways ☎13 1223.
United Airlines ☎13 1777.

TRAVEL AGENTS

Anywhere Travel, 345 Anzac Parade, Kingsford, Sydney (☎02/9663 0411 & 018 401 014, *anywhere@ozemail.com.au*).

Flight Centres, 82 Elizabeth St, Sydney, plus branches nationwide (☎02/9235 3522, nearest branch ☎13 1600, *www.flightcentre.com.au*).

Northern Gateway, 22 Cavenagh St, Darwin (☎08/8941 1394, *oztravel@norgate.com.au*).

STA Travel, 855 George St, Sydney; 256 Flinders St, Melbourne; other offices in state capitals and major universities (nearest branch ☎13 1776, fastfare telesales ☎1300/360 960, *www.statravel.com.au, traveller@statravelaus.com.au*).

Student Flights, a budget-oriented subsidiary of Flight Centres (☎1800/069 063).

Student Uni Travel, 92 Pitt St, Sydney (☎02/9232 8444) plus branches in Brisbane, Cairns, Darwin, Melbourne and Perth.

Thomas Cook, 175 Pitt St, Sydney (☎02/9231 2877); 257 Collins St, Melbourne; plus branches in other state capitals (local branch ☎13 1771, Thomas Cook Direct telesales ☎1800/801 002, *www.thomascook.com.au*).

Trailfinders, 8 Spring St, Sydney (☎02/9247 7666); 91 Elizabeth St, Brisbane (☎07/3229 0887); Hides corner, Shield St, Cairns (☎07/4041 1199).

Travel.com.au, 76-80 Clarence St, Sydney (☎02/9262 3555, *www.travel.com.au, consultant@travel.com.au*).

Auckland and out of Christchurch, or vice versa, with Qantas or Air New Zealand costs from A$699. There are also various **air passes** for internal flights available (see "Getting Around", p.25, for details).

Cruise **ships** do pass through the Pacific between November and January, but not on a regular basis; travel agents should be able to advise on which vessels are operating each season.

RTW TICKETS

If you're taking in New Zealand at the beginning (or end) of your **grand tour**, you can usually add a New Zealand stop at negligible extra cost, since most routes to the USA go via New Zealand gateway airports anyway. There's a vast range of **RTW routes** and your choice will largely depend on where you plan to travel after the Antipodes: sample routes from Sydney might take in Manila, Bangkok, Frankfurt, Honolulu, Fiji, Auckland and back to Sydney (from A$1700); or, starting from Adelaide, flying to Bangkok, Munich and Mexico City, then travelling overland to San Francisco, before picking up the homeward leg via Honolulu and Auckland back to Adelaide (from A$2699).

PACKAGES AND TOURS

There's a huge variety of holidays and tours to New Zealand available in Australia. The holiday subsidiaries of airlines such as Air New Zealand, Ansett and Qantas package short **city-breaks** (flight and accommodation) and **fly-drive** deals for little more than the cost of the regular airfare.

If serious exploring, kayaking and tramping are high on your list, check out some of the **adventure tours**; these can be a good way of covering a lot of ground in a short time, and getting you to remote places that would otherwise be inaccessible without your own transport. A more economical option is offered by **backpacker-orientated companies** such as Magic Bus (see "Getting Around", p.28), whose tours can be booked through STA and several other agents if you want to plan ahead.

In winter, Australians flock to the reliable snow of New Zealand's skifields, which are near enough to the eastern cities to allow for short breaks. Basic four-day airfare and accommodation **skiing** packages from Sydney start from A$799, rising to A$1099 for a seven-day trip to Queenstown, including return airfare, accommodation, lift passes and transport to the skifields.

SPECIALIST AGENTS AND TOUR OPERATORS

Adventure World (☎02/9956 7766 & 1300/363 055, *syd@adventureworld.com.au*). Agents for Explore Worldwide's hotel and camping tours (15–29 days, A$2740–5295; airfares extra).

Qantas Holidays (☎1300/360 347). Fly-drive packages and campervan holidays in summer (3–5 days, A$600–800), plus all-inclusive tours and winter ski deals.

The Ski & Snowboard Travel Company (☎02/9955 5201, fax 9922 4679,

www.ozemail.com.au/~skitrav/, *skitrav @ozemail.com.au*). Good deals on custom designed skiing trips to Queenstown, Wanaka and Mount Hutt. Rates vary with dates, standard of accommodation etc.

Value Tours (☎1300/ 361 322 & 02/9262 5611). Skiing and snowboarding holidays throughout New Zealand, plus airfares, car and campervan rental and accommodation passes.

VISAS AND RED TAPE

All visitors to New Zealand must have a passport and it must be valid for at least three months beyond the time you intend to stay, although if your home country has an embassy or consulate in New Zealand that can renew your passport, you can get away with one month.

On arrival, British citizens are automatically issued with a **permit** to stay for up to six months, and a three-month permit is granted to citizens of most other European countries, Southeast Asian nations, Japan, the USA and Canada. Australian citizens and permanent residents can stay indefinitely.

Other nationalities need to obtain a **visa** from a New Zealand Embassy; a tourist visa costs the local equivalent of NZ$61 and is normally valid for three months. You will also have to pay a visitor application fee of $65.

The granting of a visitor permit or tourist visa is dependent upon your having evidence of **sufficient funds** to support yourself without working (about NZ$1000 a month, or NZ$400 a month if your accommodation is prepaid), in the form of a bank draft, cash, travellers' cheques, a statement from a New Zealand bank account, one of the major credit cards, or a friend or relative who is prepared to guarantee your accommodation and maintenance (although you are rarely asked to prove these things when you get off the plane). You must also have a confirmed **onward ticket** and right of entry (including any necessary visas) to your proposed destination.

NEW ZEALAND EMBASSIES AND CONSULATES ABROAD

AUSTRALIA

High Commission: Commonwealth Avenue, Canberra, ACT 2600 (☎02/6270 4211, fax 6273 3194).

Consulates: Level 14, 1 Alfred St, Circular Quay, Sydney (☎02/9247 8567); 60 Albert Rd, Melbourne (☎03/9696 0501); Watkins Place Building, 288 Edward St, Brisbane (☎07/3221 9933).

CANADA

High Commission: Suite 727, 99 Bank St, Ottawa, Ontario K1P 6G3 (☎613/238 5991).

Consulate: Suite 1200, 888 Dunsmuir St, Vancouver, British Columbia, V6C 3K4 (☎604/684 7388).

IRELAND

Embassy: 46 Upper Mount Street, Dublin 2 (☎01/676 2464).

JAPAN

Embassy: 20–40 Kamiyama-cho, Shibuya-ku, Tokyo 150 (☎03/3467 2271/5).

NETHERLANDS

Embassy: Carnegielaan 10, 2517 KH The Hague (☎70/346 9324).

UK

High Commission: The Haymarket, London SW1Y 4TQ (☎020/7973 0363).

Consulate: The Ballance House, 118a Lisburn Rd, Glenavy, Co. Antrim (☎028/9264 8098).

USA

Embassy: 37 Observatory Circle NW, Washington, DC 20008 (☎202/328 4848, visa enquiries ☎202/328-4835).

Consulates: Suite 1150, 12400 Wilshire Boulevard, Los Angeles (☎310/207 1605); Suite 1904, 780 Third Ave, New York (☎212/832 4038).

Tourist visas, visitor permits and short-term work permits and study permits can be extended in three-month chunks up to nine months, and "genuine tourists" may be able to get extensions up to a maximum stay of twelve months. Apply for extensions (each costing NZ$61) though the New Zealand Immigration Service, which has offices in Auckland, Christchurch, Dunedin, Hamilton, Manukau, Palmerston North and Wellington. The immigration **Web site** *www.immigration.govt.nz* offers up-to-date information on all these matters.

WORKING AND STUDYING

If working or studying is part of your plan, you're better off obtaining the **relevant visa** before entering the country. You can apply for a **short-term** work or study permit after you have entered New Zealand, but if it is granted, it will only cover the time left on your visitor permit.

British, Canadian and Japanese citizens between the ages of 18 and 30 may be able to obtain a **Working Holiday Visa**. This entitles you to undertake short-term work as you travel around the country for up to twelve months. Only two thousand such permits are granted each year, beginning in July, and are allocated on a first-come, first-served basis, so apply early.

A **long-term work permit** must be obtained before you enter New Zealand and will be granted only if you have a confirmed job offer and no New Zealand citizen is suitable and available for the post. These permits stipulate the type of employment in which you can engage and are normally valid for up to three years.

You can **study** for up to three months on a visitor permit, but to study longer you will need to obtain a study permit before you enter the country. For **further information** on the various permits and visas available, consult the *Visiting New Zealand* leaflet, which is stocked by all New Zealand embassies and consulates (see box opposite).

CUSTOMS

In a country all too familiar with the damage that can be caused by the import of non-native plants and animals, New Zealand customs take particular care to minimize the chance of destructive foreign bodies being introduced to the delicate environment of the country. Aircraft cabins are often sprayed with **insecticide** before passengers are allowed to disembark, to kill off any stowaway insects or micro-organisms; the spray is apparently harmless to humans.

It is prohibited to import certain goods into New Zealand. The following must be **declared** at customs and will either be treated or confiscated: fresh food, plants or parts of plants (dead or alive), animals (dead or alive), equipment used with animals, camping gear, golf clubs, used bicycles, biological specimens, and footwear (specifically walking boots). If your camping stuff or boots have soil deposits from other countries, they will be cleaned before being returned to you. The **duty-free allowance** is 200 cigarettes, or 250 grams of tobacco, or 50 cigars; alcohol allowances are a generous 4.5 litres of wine or beer, plus one bottle of not more than 1125ml of spirits. It is possible for people from the UK to take an extra two bottles of spirits and 200 cigarettes under the Dover Allowance Provision.

There are restrictions on the **export** of wildlife, plantlife, antiquities and works of art. If you're unsure, contact the nearest customs office; there are offices in Auckland, Christchurch, Dunedin, Invercargill, Napier, Nelson, New Plymouth, Tauranga, Mount Maunganui, Timaru, Wellington and Whangarei. A more detailed rundown on these provisions is available on *www.quarantine.govt.nz.*

INSURANCE

New Zealand's accident compensation scheme no longer provides preferential treatment for touring Brits so you'll probably need some travel insurance. Insurance premiums vary according to the level of coverage: pricier policies tend to be more comprehensive while others may cover only certain risks (accidents, illnesses, delayed or lost luggage, cancelled flights, etc). In particular, ask whether the policy pays medical costs up front or reimburses you later, and whether it provides for medical evacuation to your home country. Note also that very few insurers will arrange on-the-spot payments in the event of a major loss; you will usually be reimbursed only after going home. In all cases of loss or theft of goods, you will have to contact the local police to have a report made out so that your insurer can process the claim.

While in New Zealand you are quite likely to be participating in what are considered to be "**dangerous activities**" (skiing, mountaineering – even tramping qualifies under some policies), so be sure to ask whether these activities are covered: most companies have supplementary policies covering you for pretty much everything except bungy jumping.

Some insurance companies refuse to cover travellers **over 65**, and most that do charge hefty premiums; some of the best policies for older travellers, and some indispensable advise, are offered by Age Concern (☎01883/834 887).

Before buying an insurance policy, **Americans and Canadians** should check that they're not already covered. Canadian provincial health plans typically provide some overseas **medical coverage**, although they are unlikely to pick up the full tab in the event of a mishap. Holders of official student/teacher/youth cards are entitled to accident coverage and hospital in-patient benefits – the annual membership is far less than the cost of comparable insurance. **Students** may also find that their health coverage extends during the vacations and for one term beyond the date of last enrolment, and **homeowners'** or **renters'** insurance often covers theft or loss of documents, money and valuables while overseas.

ROUGH GUIDES TRAVEL INSURANCE

Rough Guides now offer their own **travel insurance**, customized for our readers by a leading UK broker and backed by a Lloyds underwriter. It's available for anyone, of any nationality, travelling anywhere in the world, and we are convinced that this is the best-value scheme you'll find.

There are two main Rough Guide insurance plans: **Essential**, for effective, no-frills cover, starting at £11.75 for 2 weeks; and **Premier** – more expensive but with more generous and extensive benefits. Each offer European or Worldwide cover, and can be supplemented with a "Hazardous Activities Premium" if you plan to indulge in sports considered dangerous, such as skiing, scuba-diving or trekking. Unlike many policies, the Rough Guides schemes are calculated by the day, so if you're travelling for 27 days rather than a month, that's all you pay for. You can alternatively take out annual **multi-trip insurance**, which covers you for all your travel throughout the year (with a maximum of 60 days for any one trip).

For a **policy quote**, call the Rough Guides Insurance Line on UK freefone 0800/015 0906, or, if you're calling from outside Britain on (+44) 1243 621 046. Alternatively, get an online quote at *www.roughguides.com/insurance*.

TRAVELLERS WITH DISABILITIES

New Zealand is disabled-traveller-friendly, but that does not mean everything is rosy. Many public buildings, galleries and museums are accessible to disabled travellers, but as a rule restaurants and local public transport make few concessions.

Long-distance transport companies will generally offer disabled travellers help with boarding, but on-board access to toilets and other amenities can be difficult for wheelchair users. All accommodation in New Zealand should have at least one room or unit suitable for disabled trav-

ellers but the level of facilities and access varies considerably, often depending on the age of the building in question. On the plus side, many tour operators are prepared to go to that extra bit of trouble to enable travellers with disabilities to participate in activities.

PLANNING A TRIP

There are **organized tours and holidays** specifically for people with disabilities – the contacts in the box below will be able to put you touch with

---

BEFORE YOU LEAVE: USEFUL ORGANIZATIONS

UK

Access Travel, 16 Haweswater Ave, Astley, Lancashire M29 7BL (☎01942/888 844). Tour operator that can arrange flights and transfers.

Holiday Care Service, 2nd floor, Imperial Building, Victoria Rd, Horley, Surrey RH6 7PZ (☎01293/774535). Provides free list of accessible accommodation in New Zealand.

RADAR (Royal Association for Disability and Rehabilitation), 12 City Forum, 250 City Rd, London EC1V 8AF (☎020/7250 3222; Minicom ☎020/7250 4119). Produces a holiday guide *Getting There* to long-haul destinations (£5, including p&p) every two years, devoting several pages to New Zealand.

Tripscope, Alexandra House, Albany Rd, London TW8 ONE (☎020/8580 7021, fax 8580 7022, *tripscope@cableinet.co.uk*). This registered charity provides a national telephone information service offering free advice on international transport and travel for those with a mobility problem.

IRELAND

Irish Wheelchair Association, Blackheath Drive, Clontarf, Dublin 3 (☎01/833 8241). Provides information for wheelchair travellers intending to go to New Zealand, including travel, accommodation and activities.

USA

Directions Unlimited, 720 N Bedford Rd, Bedford Hills, NY 10507 (☎914/241-1700). Travel

agency specializing in custom tours for people with disabilities.

Society for the Advancement of Travel for the Handicapped (SATH), 347 5th Ave, Suite 610, New York, NY 10016 (☎212/447-7284, *www.sittravel.com*). Non-profit travel-industry referral service that passes queries on to its members as appropriate; allow plenty of time for a response.

Travel Information Service (☎215/456-9600). Telephone information and referral service.

Twin Peaks Press, Box 129, Vancouver, WA 98666 (☎360/694-2462 or 1-800/637-2256). Publisher of the *Directory of Travel Agencies for the Disabled* ($19.95), listing more than 370 agencies worldwide; *Travel for the Disabled* ($19.95); the *Directory of Accessible Van Rentals* ($9.95); and *Wheelchair Vagabond* ($14.95), loaded with personal tips.

CANADA

Jewish Rehabilitation Hospital, 3205 Place Alton Goldbloom, Chomedy Laval, Quebec H7V 1RT (☎514/688-9550, ext 226). Guidebooks and travel information.

AUSTRALIA

ACROD (Australian Council for Rehabilitation of the Disabled), PO Box 60, Curtin, ACT 2605 (☎02/6282 4333). Provides lists of useful organizations, plus specialist travel agencies and tour operators.

any specialists for trips to New Zealand. If you want to be more **independent**, it's important to become an authority on where you must be self-reliant and where you may expect help, especially regarding transport and accommodation. It is also vital to be honest – with travel agencies, insurance companies and travel companions. Know your limitations and make sure others know them. If you do not use a wheelchair all the time but your walking capabilities are limited, remember that you are likely to need to cover greater distances while travelling (often over rougher terrain and in hotter temperatures) than you are used to. If you use a wheelchair, have it serviced before you go and carry a repair kit.

Read your travel **insurance** small print carefully to make sure that people with a pre-existing medical condition are not excluded. And use your travel agent to make your journey simpler: airline or bus companies can cope better if they are expecting you, with a wheelchair provided at airports and staff primed to help. A **medical certificate** of your fitness to travel, provided by your doctor, is also extremely useful; some airlines or insurance companies may insist on it. Make sure that you have extra supplies of drugs – carried with you if you fly – and a prescription including the generic name in case of emergency. Carry spares of any clothing or equipment that might be hard to find; if there's an association representing people with your disability, contact them early in the planning process.

Once you're **in New Zealand**, several organizations provide information for travellers with disabilities and give practical advice on where to go and how to get there (see box below for contact details).

ACCOMMODATION

The New Zealand Tourism Board's *Where to Stay Guide* provides a few useful pointers on disabled-friendly accommodation, with **countrywide listings**, in which disabled facilities are indicated by a wheelchair symbol.

Current New Zealand **law** stipulates that any newly built hotel, hostel or motel must have at least one room modified for disabled access and use. Many pre-existing accommodation establishments have also **converted rooms** to meet these requirements, including most YHA hostels, some motels, campsites and larger hotels. Older buildings, homestays and B&Bs are the least likely to lend themselves to such conversions.

TRAVELLING

Few airlines, trains, ferries and buses allow complete independence. Air New Zealand provides a special wheelchair narrow enough to move

USEFUL CONTACTS IN NEW ZEALAND

Disability Information – Project Enable ☎0800/801 981. Information service that can help with advice on travel, accommodation and activities.

Disability Resource Centre, PO Box 24-042, Royal Oak, Auckland (☎09/625 8069, fax 624 1633).

Disabled Persons Assembly (DPA), 5th Floor, Central House, 26 Brandon St, Wellington (☎04/472 2626). Worth contacting for local information on access.

Enable Tourism, 34 Whittaker Street, Shannon (☎06/362 7163, fax 362 7162, *enabletour@xtra.co.nz*). Provides a comprehensive service of contacts and advice.

Galaxy Motors, Frank Hall, 274 Great South Road, Takanini, Auckland (☎07/826 4020, *fhall@xtra.co.nz*), Personalized tours with a tour guide, companion, carer or translator.

New Zealand Disabilities Resource Centre, Bennet St, PO Box4547, Palmerston North (☎06/952 0011, 0800/171 1981, *www.nzdrc.govt.nz, nzdrc@nzdrc.govt.nz*); Petone Office, PO Box 38847, Petone, Wellington; Christchurch Office, PO Box 33054, Christchurch.

Physical Freedom and Manawatu Jet Tours, 235 Cambridge Avenue, Ashhurst (☎ & fax 06/329 4060, *mjt@clear.net.nz*). Specialize in outdoor pursuits (bungy, white water rafting, kayaking, absailing) and have an accessible bus that accommodates five wheel chairs and offer personalized tours.

The Paraplegic and Physically Disabled Association, PO Box 610, Hamilton. Provides information (postal enquiries only) on sporting activities across New Zealand.

The Saints Host Service, 55 Leaver Terrace, North Beach, Christchurch (☎ & fax 03/388 6283). Provides tours and request hosts.

around in the plane, and the rear toilet cubicles are wider than the others to facilitate access; other **domestic airlines** will provide help, if not always extra facilities. Cook Strait **ferries** have reasonable access for disabled travellers, including physical help while boarding, if needed, and adapted toilets. If given advance warning, **trains** will provide attendants to get passengers in wheelchairs or sight-impaired travellers on board, but moving around the train in a standard wheelchair is impossible and there are no specially adapted toilets; the problems with long-distance **buses** are much the same.

Some specifically adapted taxis (for wheelchairs) are available in the cities, but must be prebooked; otherwise taxi drivers obligingly deal with wheelchairs by throwing them into the boot and their occupant onto a seat. The New Zealand Total Mobility Scheme also allows for anyone unable to use public transport to use taxis at a subsidized rate (50 percent); a list of participating areas and companies is available from the Disabled Persons Assembly (see box opposite), who will also arrange for the necessary vouchers to be issued. There is also a parking concession for people with mobility problems, assuming they bring the relevant medical certificates with them. For more details email *enabletour@xtra.co.nz*. The staff on public buses will endeavour to lend a hand, but buses are difficult to board. Some small minibus conversions are available and shuttle buses will help you board and stow your chair, but it pays to let the operator know beforehand of your particular needs. Enable Tourism can provide lists of companies with rental cars adapted for disabled travellers, while some car rental operators will fit hand controls if they are given advance notice.

HEALTH

New Zealand is relatively free of serious health hazards and the most common pitfalls are not taking precautions or simply underestimating the power of nature. No vaccinations are required to enter the country, but you should make sure you have adequate health cover in your travel insurance, especially if you plan to take on the Great Outdoors (see p.54 for advice on tramping health and safety).

New Zealand has a fine health service, despite recent government cuts, and medical services are reasonably cheap by world standards. Although all visitors are covered by the **accident compensation scheme**, under which you can claim some medical and hospital expenses in the event of an accident, without full accident cover in your travel insurance (see p.14), you could still face a hefty bill. For more minor ailments, you can visit a **doctor** for a consultation around ($35) and, armed with a prescription, buy any required medication at a reasonable price.

AIDS is as much of an issue in New Zealand as elsewhere but official attitudes are reasonably enlightened, and there are no restrictions on people with HIV or AIDS entering the country.

Support organizations include the New Zealand AIDS Foundation, 76 Grafton Rd, Grafton, Auckland (☎09/303 3124) and the 24-hour HIV/AIDS National Hotline (☎0800/802 437).

THE SUN

The biggest health problem for visitors to New Zealand is over-exposure to the **sun**, which shines more fiercely here than in the northern hemisphere, its damaging ultra-violet rays reaching a far greater intensity. You should take extra care, especially at first, to avoid burning. New Zealand has a high rate of **skin cancer**, so it makes sense to slap on maximum-protection **sunblock**. Remember to **re-apply** every few hours as well as after swimming, and you should avoid sunbathing altogether between 11am and 3pm, when the sun is at its strongest. Keep a check on any moles on your body and if you notice any changes, during or after your trip, see a doctor right away.

BUGS AND CRITTERS

Something worth avoiding is **giardia**, a parasite that inhabits rivers and lakes in some national parks. Infection results from drinking contaminated water, with symptoms appearing several weeks later: a bloated stomach, cramps, explosive diarrhoea and wind. The Department of Conservation advises on the likely presence of giardia in national parks around the country. To minimize the risk of infection, purify **drinking water** by using iodine-based solutions or tablets (regular chlorine-based tablets aren't effective against giardia); by fast-boiling water for at least seven minutes; or by using a giardia-rated filter (obtainable from any outdoors or camping shop).

The relatively rare **amoebic meningitis** is another water-borne hazard, this time contracted from hot thermal pools. The amoeba enters the body via the nose or ears, lodges in the brain, and weeks later causes severe headaches, stiffness of the neck, hypersensitivity to light, and eventually coma. If you experience any of these symptoms, seek medical attention immediately, but to avoid contamination in the first place, simply don't put your head underwater in thermal pools.

Virtually without exception, New Zealand **wildlife** is harmless. Even **shark attacks** are rare; you are more likely to be carried away by a strong tide than a great white, though it still pays to be sensible and obey any local warnings when swimming.

The country is free of snakes, scorpions and other nasties, and there's only one poisonous creature: the **little katipo spider**. Mercifully rare, this 6mm-long critter (the biting female is black with a red patch), is found in coastal areas – except in the far south – and only bites if disturbed. The bite can be fatal, but antivenin is available in most hospitals, is effective up to three days after a bite and no one has died from an encounter with the spider for many years. The West Coast of the South Island in the summer is the worst place for **mosquitoes** and **sandflies**, though they appear to a lesser degree in many other places across the country. They are more irritating than dangerous and a liberal application of repellent keeps most of them at bay, albeit briefly.

GEOLOGICAL HAZARDS

Although common in New Zealand, **earthquakes** are usually minor. If the worst happens, the best advice is to stand in a doorway or crouch under a table. If caught in the open, try to get inside; failing that, keep your distance from trees and rocky outcrops to reduce the chances of being injured by falling branches or debris. New Zealand's **volcanoes** also have a habit of making their presence felt: vulcanologists are often able to predict periods of eruptive activity, and if warnings are issued, get at least as far away as they suggest.

INFORMATION, MAPS AND INTERNET SITES

New Zealand promotes itself heavily and enthusiastically abroad through the New Zealand Tourism Board (see box below), where enquiries will trigger a deluge of glossy brochures. Much of it comprises inspirational, if rose-tinted, images of the country but is of limited practical use; specific requests can prove far more fruitful.

Many of the information centres listed below, as well as some cafés, bars and hostels, keep a supply of **free newspapers** and **magazines** orientated towards backpackers and usually filled with promotional copy, but informative nonetheless. Two of the best are the *New Zealand* *Backpackers News* and *TNT* (which has stacks of information available on their Web site at *www.tntmag.com.au*).

VISITOR CENTRES

Once you arrive you'll soon be weighed down with leaflets advertising just about everything in the country. Every town of any size will have an **official visitor centre**, signified by the green Visitor Information Network (VIN) logo. These are invariably well-stocked, staffed by helpful and knowledgeable personnel and sometimes offer some form of video or slide presentation on the area. Apart from dishing out local maps and leaflets, they'll book you into accommodation, get you on trips and activities, and book onward travel, all at no extra charge. In the more popular tourist areas, you'll also come across all manner of places presenting themselves as independent **information centres**, which always follow a hidden agenda, typically promoting a number of allied adventure companies. While these can be useful, it's worth remembering that their advice won't be impartial.

Other useful resources are the **Department of Conservation (DOC)** offices and field centres, usually sited close to wilderness areas and popular tramping tracks, and often serving as the local visitor centre as well. Again these are highly informative and well geared to trampers' needs,

---

NEW ZEALAND TOURISM BOARD OFFICES

The **New Zealand Tourism Board** head office can be contacted at PO Box 95, Wellington, New Zealand (☎04/ 917 5400, fax 915 3817, *www.purenz.com*).

Australia 8/35 Pitt St, Sydney, NSW 2000 (☎02/9247 5222, fax 9241 1136).

Canada Use USA offices; Canada Information Line ☎1800/888 5494.

Germany Rossmarkt 11, 60311 Frankfurt am Main (☎069/971 2110, fax 971 2113); handles Western European and Nordic enquiries.

Japan World Trade Centre Building 12F, 2–4–1 Hamamatsu-cho, Minato-ku, Tokyo 105-6112 (☎03/5400 1311, fax 5400 1312).

South Africa Holiday House, 158–169 Hendrik Verwoerd Drive, Randburg 2125 (☎011/289 8186, fax 289 8023).

United Kingdom New Zealand House, Haymarket, London, SW1Y 4TQ (☎020/7930 1662, fax 7839 8929, premium rated information line ☎0906/364 0650); also handles enquiries from Ireland.

USA Suite 300, 501 Santa Monica Blvd, Santa Monica, CA 90401 (☎310/395 7480 & 1800/388 5494, fax 395 5453); 780 3rd Ave, Suite 1904, New York, NY 10017-2024 (☎212/832 8482, fax 832 7602).

with local weather forecasts, intentions forms and maps.

Finally, drivers who are already members of motoring associations at home can generally make use of New Zealand's **Automobile Association** (AA), which provides many useful services to drivers (see p.30) and supports a nationwide network of offices (see "Listings" throughout the Guide), stocking excellent maps and providing information on accommodation.

MAPS

Specialist booksellers (see box below) should have a reasonable stock of **maps of New Zealand**. The best available is the two-sided 1:1,000,000 edition produced by *International Travel Maps*, with all the important roads, and an attractive and instructive colour scheme giving a good sense of the country's terrain. The 1:2,000,000 maps produced by *GeoCentre* and *Bartholemew* come a distant joint second. **Road atlases** are widely available in New Zealand bookshops and service stations; the best are those produced by the AA, all of which indicate the type of road surface – though some roads marked as unsealed have since been tar-sealed. The AA also provide their members with simple but effective strip maps of major touring routes free of charge.

With a road atlas and our city plans you can't go far wrong on the roads, but more detailed maps may be required for **tramping**. All the major walks are covered by the *Trackmap* and *Parkmap* series, complete with photos ($13.50 from DOC

MAP OUTLETS

BRITAIN

Stanfords in London is the UK's largest map seller, and operates a **mail-order service**, as do most bookshops. By far the best outlet for **New Zealand books, maps and periodicals** in Britain is Kiwifruits: The New Zealand Shop, 7 Royal Opera Arcade, Pall Mall, London SW1Y 4UY (☎020/7930 4587, fax 7839 0592), who also run a mail-order service.

London Daunt Books, 83 Marylebone High St, W1M 3DE (☎020/7224 2295), and 193 Haverstock Hill, NW3 4QL (☎020/7794 4006); National Map Centre, 22–24 Caxton St, SW1

(☎020/7222 2466, *www.mapsworld.com*); Stanfords, 12–14 Long Acre, WC2E 9LH (☎020/7836 1321), 52 Grosvenor Gardens, SW1W 0AG (☎020/7730 1314), and within the British Airways offices at 156 Regent St, W1R 5TA (☎020/7434 4744); The Travel Bookshop, 13–15 Blenheim Crescent, W11 2EE (☎020/7229 5260).

Cardiff Blackwell's, 13–17 Royal Arcade, CF1 2PR (☎029/2039 5036).

Glasgow John Smith and Sons, 57–61 St Vincent St, G2 5TB (☎0141/221 7472).

IRELAND

Belfast Waterstone's, Queens Building, 8 Royal Ave, BT1 1DA (☎028/9024 7355).

Dublin Easons Bookshop, 80 Middle Abbey St, Dublin 1 (☎01/873 3811); Fred Hanna's

Bookshop, 27–29 Nassau St, Dublin 2 (☎01/677 1255); Hodges Figgis Bookshop, 56–58 Dawson St, Dublin 2 (☎01/677 4754).

USA

Rand McNally (*www.randmcnallystore.com*) have 24 locations throughout North America. Call ☎1-800/333-0136 (ext 2111) for the location of your nearest store, or for **direct mail** maps.

Chicago Rand McNally, 444 N Michigan Ave, IL 60611 (☎312/321-1751); The Savvy Traveller, 310

S Michigan Ave, IL 60604 (☎312/913-9800, *www.thesavvytraveller.com*).

Los Angeles Rand McNally, 10250 Santa Monica Blvd, Suite 681, CA 90067 (☎310/556-2202).

New York The Complete Traveler Bookstore, 199 Madison Ave at 35th St, NY 10016

offices and bookshops in New Zealand), or go for the larger scale *Topo* maps ($12.50), which cover the whole country.

NEW ZEALAND ON THE NET

Perhaps because of its geographical isolation, New Zealand has embraced the **Internet** with a vengeance, so a little time spent surfing is a good way to familiarize yourself with the place, book transport and accommodation, and gather travel tips. Throughout the guide we've listed relevant **Web sites**; listed here are some of the most useful general sites.

TRAVEL SITES

New Zealand Tourism Board *www.purenz.com*
New Zealand's official tourism site. Lightweight and short on hard facts but a fair starting point, with useful links to other Kiwi-related Web sites.

Department of Conservation *www.doc.govt.nz*
DOC's web presence with a motherlode of stuff on the environment and the latest conservation issues plus details on national parks and Great Walks.

ACCOMMODATION SITES
AA Accommodation Guide
www.nz-accommodation.co.nz
A huge range of accommodation around NZ; mostly motels and campsites.

Budget Backpacker Hostels .
www.backpack.co.nz
Net version of the "Blue Book" backpacker hostels guide, with details of all the hostels.

(☎212/685-9007); Rand McNally, 150 E 52nd St, NY 10022 (☎212/758-7488); Traveler's Choice Bookstore, 2 Wooster St, NY 10013 (☎212/941-1535).
San Francisco The Complete Traveler Bookstore, 3207 Fillmore St, CA 92123 (☎415/923-1511, *info@completetraveler.com*); Phileas Fogg's Books & Maps, 87 Stanford Shopping Center, Palo Alto, CA 94304 (☎1-800/533-FOGG); Rand McNally, 595 Market St, CA 94105 (☎415/777-3131); Sierra Club Bookstore, 85 Second St, CA 94105 (☎415/977-5600).
Seattle Elliot Bay Book Company, 101 South Main St, WA 98104 (☎206/624-6600).
Washington DC Rand McNally, 7101 Democracy Blvd, Bethesda, MD 20817 (☎301/365-6277).

CANADA

Montreal Ulysses Travel Books, 4176 St-Denis (☎514/843-9882, fax 843-9448, *guiduly@ulysses.ca*).
Toronto Open Air Books and Maps, 25 Toronto St, ON, M5C 2R1 (☎416/363-0719).

Vancouver International Travel Books and Maps, 552 Seymour St, BC, V6B 3J5 (☎604/687-3320).

AUSTRALIA

Adelaide The Map Shop, 6-10 Peel St, SA 5000 (☎08/8231 2033, fax 8231 2373, *mercator @mapshop.net.au, mapshop.net.au*).
Brisbane Worldwide Maps and Guides, 187 George St (☎07/3221 4330, fax 3211 3684, *enterprise.powerup.com.au*).
Melbourne Map Land, 372 Little Bourke Street (☎03/9670 4383, fax 9670 7779, *mapland @lexicon.net.au*); Melbourne Map Centre, 738-740 Waverley Road, Chadstone, Victoria, and PO Box 55, Holmesglen, Victoria, 3148 (03/9569-5472, fax 9569-8000, *info@melbmap.com.au, melbmap.com.au*).
Perth Perth Map Centre, First Floor Shaft Lane, 884 Hay St, WA 6000 (☎09/9322-5733, fax 9322 5733, *sales@perthmap.com.au, www.q-net.net.au/perthmap*).
Sydney Dymocks, 350 George St, New South Wales (☎02/9223 5974, fax 9232 3061); Travel Bookshop, 6 Bridge St, NSW 2000 (☎02/9241-3554, fax 9241-3159, *www.blueskies.com.au/travelbook*).

Friars' Guide *www.friars.co.nz*
Complete on-line listing of this guide to some of New Zealand's finer B&Bs and lodges.

New Zealand Bed & Breakfast Book
www.bnb.co.nz
Electronic listing of this handy guide to most of New Zealand's B&Bs.

VIP Hostels *www.vip.co.nz*
Straightforward list of member hostels with an online reservation facility.

YHA *www.yha.org.nz*
Official YHA site with everything you need to know about membership and the hostels themselves.

ADVENTURE TOURISM AND SPORTS SITES

Hiking *www.hike.co.nz*
Excellent tramping site covering all the Great Walks. There's track notes, altitude profiles photos of flora and you can even listen to birdsong; links to guided walks.

Mountain Biking *www.mountainbike.co.nz*
Hook into the scene with events calendar, biking e-zines, lists of bike shops and clubs and a buy-and-sell room.

Skiing *www.snow.co.nz*
Everything you need to know, with links to fields, shops, snow reports and webcams.

Surfing *www.surf.co.nz*
Surfing news, surf reports, weather and even webcams at key beaches.

Rugby *www.newzealandrugby.com*
Great starting point for everything to do with Rugby Union in NZ.

MISCELLANEOUS SITES

Beer *www.brewing.co.nz*
Kiwi microbrewers' collective Web site with regional listings of brewers.

Maori Culture *www.culture.co.nz*
Labour-of-love site dedicated to all things Maori with everything from personal profiles and Maori history to an online cookbook.

Nature & Co *www.environment.co.nz*
Stacks of material on NZ's natural environment, biodiversity issues, wildlife, eco-travel and adventure.

New Zealand Herald *www.herald.co.nz*
Auckland's answer to The Press site. All the Kiwi news and sports you could hope for.

New Zealand Wine *www.nzwine.com*
Official site of NZ wine and grape industry. Lots of great background on wine styles and wineries, and plenty of links to more opinionated sites.

NZ Music *www.nz-music.co.nz*
Basic portal to Web sites of most of the more popular and important current Kiwi acts.

Nzoom *nzoom.co.nz*
TVNZ's "homepage for New Zealanders" with excellent coverage of news, sport entertainment, weather and much more.

The (Christchurch) Press *www.press.co.nz*
Excellent site belonging to one of New Zealand's best daily papers: includes the latest news and reviews, plus a good subject search facility.

Search NZ *www.searchnz.co.nz*
Leading NZ-specific search engine.

Soda *www.soda.co.nz*
Site Of the Day Award: site promoting the best Kiwi Web sites, with hot links to recent award-winners in various categories. Something for everyone.

COSTS, MONEY AND BANKS

After a few years riding the crest of an economic wave, New Zealand has recently seen a downturn in the economy and a resulting dive in the value of the New Zealand dollar. Consequently, most things will seem fairly cheap by European and North American standards. The quality of goods and standards of service you can expect are high and, on balance, the country offers very good value for money, though the instability of exchange rates introduces some uncertainty.

New Zealanders are a straightforward bunch and the price quoted is what you pay. In almost all cases, the 12.5 percent Goods and Service Tax (GST) is included in the listed price, and no tip is expected.

The **currency** is the Kiwi dollar, or "buck", divided into 100 cents. There are $100, $50, $20, $10 and $5 notes made of a sturdy plastic material, and coins in denominations of $2 and $1, and 50¢, 20¢, 10¢ and 5¢; grocery prices are given to the nearest cent, but the final bill is rounded up or down to the nearest five cents.

SOME BASIC COSTS

New Zealand is well set up for all visitors, but **budget travellers** are especially well catered for, with an extensive network of backpackers' hostels and discounts on travel and the all-too-tempting array of adventure activities that can easily wreak havoc with your spending money.

The **minimum expenditure** if you are camping, hitching or cycling, preparing most of your own

food and keeping a tight rein on tours and activities would be in the region of $30 a day, rising to $40–60 if you stay in hostels, use public transport and indulge in the odd meal out. Couples staying in hostel rooms or homestays, eating at unpretentious restaurants and not skimping on attractions and activities are looking at around $70–90 each per day; and if you rent a car for at least some of your stay, sleep in comfortable B&Bs and eat well, you should reckon on at least $100 a day. All these figures can be ramped up dramatically once you start bungy jumping and jetboat riding, though this can be offset by abstemious tramping days. With the prevalence of good hostels, **single travellers** can live almost as cheaply as couples, though you'll pay around thirty percent more if you insist on having a room to yourself.

Accommodation costs from as little as a couple of dollars for a basic campsite, but an $8 per-person pitch or a $14–18 dorm bed in a hostel is more common. Simple double rooms start from as little as $35, though you'll pay $70–90 for a motel unit, $70–120 for homestays and B&Bs, $150–300 for flash international-standard hotels, and anything up to $1000 a person for exclusive retreats. **Food** is good quality and great value; supermarkets are reasonably priced and you can usually find a filling plateful at a pub or café for under $10. A reasonable three-course meal will cost upwards of $30, though you can save on drinks by patronizing **BYO** (Bring Your Own) restaurants, where you can drink wine you've brought with you. Though still common in smaller places, these are harder to find in the cities. **Drinking** in pubs and restaurants is substantially more expensive than buying from a bottle shop or from a supermarket.

Given New Zealand's compact size, **transport** costs shouldn't be prohibitive, but if you find yourself moving on every couple of days it can soon add up. Though you are unlikely to return from New Zealand laden with souvenirs, you can completely blow your budget on **adventure trips** – such as a bungy jump (around $130) or tandem parachuting ($170 and up). If you've got the money, by all means spend it; if not, think carefully about how best to get the maximum enjoyment from your visit.

Student **discounts** are few and far between, but you can make substantial savings on accommodation and travel if you buy either the YHA or VIP cards (see box p.38); kids and seniors enjoy reductions of around fifty percent on most trains, buses and entry to many sights.

TRAVELLERS' CHEQUES, CREDIT AND DEBIT CARDS

There are **no exchange controls** in New Zealand, so you can bring in as much in cash and travellers' cheques as you like.

The safest way to carry your money is still as **travellers' cheques**, which can be exchanged efficiently at banks and bureaux de change all over New Zealand, will be replaced if they are lost or stolen, and usually offer a slightly better exchange rate. Recognized brands – American Express, Thomas Cook, Mastercard and Visa – are accepted in all major currencies and, though cheques in New Zealand dollars relieve the uncertainty of fluctuating exchange rates, they aren't generally accepted as cash. You usually pay one to two percent commission when you buy travellers' cheques but there is seldom an additional charge when you cash them.

As a back-up, or even a primary source of funds, **credit cards** are extremely useful: Visa, Mastercard, Bankcard and, to a lesser extent, American Express and Diners Club cards are widely accepted. You'll find more resistance at some supermarkets, and many hostels, campsites and homestays will only accept cash, though YHAs do accept cards. You'll also find credit cards useful for advance booking of accommodation and trips, and with the appropriate PIN you can obtain **cash advances** through 24-hour ATMs found almost everywhere. You should be aware that such withdrawals may accrue interest immediately or be subject to a two percent premium – check with your bank before you go too wild. Most ATMs also have the facility for **international debit card** transactions using the Plus and Cirrus networks.

CREDIT CARD HOTLINES

To report **lost** or **stolen** cards in New Zealand, call:

American Express	☎0800/656 660
Bankcard (Access/Mastercard)	☎0800/449 140
Diners Club	☎0800/652 582
Visa	☎0508/445 594

BANKS AND EXCHANGE

The best **exchange rates** are usually from **banks** – BNZ, ANZ, Westpac, Postbank and The National Bank have branches in towns of any size and are open from Monday to Friday 9.30am to 4.30pm except for public holidays, while some city branches stay open on Saturday until around noon. Outside banking hours, you'll have to rely on **bureaux de change** in the big cities and tourist centres, which are typically open from 8am to 8pm daily. If you get caught short, the larger hotels will often change travellers' cheques at any time, but rates tend to be poor.

EXCHANGE RATES

Exchange rates tend to be fairly stable in relation to the Australian and US dollars, less so against European currencies. The **New Zealand dollar** currently trades at NZ$3 for £1, NZ$1.9 for US$1 and NZ$1.25 for A$1.

If you are spending some time in New Zealand – say a couple of months or more – you may want to open a **bank account**. The ease of doing so can depend largely on the whim of the bank clerk, so shop around: having a New Zealand address you can use for statements helps (though isn't always necessary), and you'll need a couple of pieces of ID. The ANZ and BNZ banks seem particularly helpful and maintain an extensive network of branches and accessible ATMs.

The big advantage of having an account is that you can get money from branches and ATMs using a **cash card**, the same piece of plastic doubling as an **EFTPOS** (Electronic Funds Transfer at Point of Sale) card. This enables you to pay for stuff at shops, service stations, restaurants, in fact just about anywhere, by swiping the card and punching in your PIN (Personal Identification Number). Almost everywhere will also give you cash, so you can go for weeks without visiting a bank, which has to be a good thing.

EMERGENCY CASH

If you run out of cash, or there is some kind of emergency, the best way to get money sent out is to get in touch with your bank at home and have them wire money to the nearest bank. This is often time consuming (it may take a week) and inconvenient, though relatively cheap. You'll probably pay twice as much to have cash sent through

Western Union (see box) or through the Moneygram service used by American Express (cardholders only) and Thomas Cook: contact the nearest office or in the US call (☎1-800/543-4080). In all cases, the fees charged are independent of source or destination, and only depend on the amount being transferred: wiring US$1000, or equivalent, to New Zealand will cost US$70. The funds should be available for collection at the company's local office within minutes of being sent, and by using this service the sender can dispatch cash by phone by using their credit card.

GETTING AROUND

New Zealand is a relatively small country and getting around is easy, with some form of transport going to most destinations.

Although it is possible to **fly** to many of the major destinations in New Zealand, you need to consider whether the time you save outweighs the substantial expense involved. With time to spare you will appreciate the scenery better by travelling more slowly and at ground level. The **rail** service is fairly limited and is also quite expensive, while the Interislander **ferries** connecting the North and South islands are subject to stiff competition and thus quite good value. The cheapest and easiest way to get around is by **bus** or **shuttle bus** but this is also the most

Regular long-distance bus, train and plane services can be found under **Travel details** at the end of each chapter, with local buses and trains covered in the main text.

time-consuming mode of travel. With careful planning, you can reduce your costs by **booking in advance** and taking advantage of the many special offers and **reduced fares** (see box on p.26).

For getting off the beaten track, you'll need a car. **Rental cars** are fine for short periods, but if you are staying in the country for more than a month, it's more economical to **buy** a car, provided you're not averse to some haggling and paperwork. New Zealand is renowned for its green countryside and some travellers prefer to **cycle** their way around – a fine way of seeing the country, so long as you're fit and in no great hurry.

However, you'll still need to take to the air or the water (or your feet) to reach the **offshore islands** and the more **remote** parts of the country that remain stubbornly impenetrable by road, such as Fiordland.

DOMESTIC FLIGHTS

Domestic flights are generally **expensive**, but may well be worth it if you have limited time in the country – especially if you can bag a **standby bargain** or tag one on to your international flight for a little extra. The stranglehold of the major carriers, Air New Zealand and Ansett Australia, results in the absurd situation whereby it is sometimes cheaper to fly from New Zealand to Australia than to fly between the North and South islands. There are, however, a number of small companies (most wholly or partly owned by ANZ and Ansett) flying specific routes that offer good deals from time to time; check the latest with local visitor centres.

Air New Zealand and Ansett offer a broad range of **fares** for domestic flights, from the usual business and economy classes to cheaper, limited-availability **advance-purchase tickets** that are only bookable in New Zealand; see box below for more on these and **concessionary fares** available to backpackers and seniors. A full-fare economy-class flight from Auckland to Christchurch is currently about $250–360. Two of the most **useful short hops** are the very scenic Southern Air flights from Invercargill to Stewart Island ($80–120) and the cheap trip over Cook Straight from either the North or South islands for about the same cost as a ferry ticket but taking only half an hour.

Flights can be **booked** through travel agents, some visitor centres or direct with an airline; special offers are widely promoted at airports or in visitor centres around the country.

FERRIES

The ferries you're most likely to use are those plying the **Cook Strait** between the North and South islands, but there are also ferries to Stewart Island from the South Island and from Auckland across the Hauraki Gulf and over to Coromandel. Information about these short ferry trips is included in our accounts on Invercargill (see p.683) and Auckland (see p.75).

The Interislander fleet that shuttles between **Wellington** on the North Island and **Picton** on the South Island consists of three ferries and the quicker wave-piercing catamaran called the *Lynx* (nicknamed the Vomit Comet, for all-too-obvious reasons). These days they have stiff competition from the smooth ride of the even faster catamaran, *Topcat*, which along with other planned carriers means the prices stay down. All the ferries run seven days a week year-round, take around three hours, are very reliable and surprisingly comfortable in most conditions. The standard fare is around $46 one-way, though this can be reduced by as much as half if you book in advance or take

FARE CONCESSIONS

Backpacker discounts of thirty to fifty percent are available on many forms of transport to holders of YHA or VIP cards (see box on p.38). Fare concessions are also available to **children** on provision of proof of age, as are **seniors'** discounts – with the exception of over-60s airfares, which are only available to New Zealand residents.

FLIGHTS

Advance-purchase fares (14–21 days) give 30–65 percent discount on all Air New Zealand, Ansett and Mount Cook flights, booked in NZ.

Standby fares (50 percent off) are available on some Air New Zealand and Ansett flights to holders of YHA and VIP cards.

FERRIES

Advance-purchase fares (7 days) give 15–50 percent discount on selected sailings.

TRAINS

Advance-purhase fares (economy, saver and super saver), offering discounts of 25–50 percent, are available in limited numbers; **day-excursion** fares are discounted by 30 percent.

No Frills tickets are available in limited numbers, offering significant reductions (around 50

percent) for travelling in older, non-air-conditioned carriages; call ☎0800/802 802 for details.

A discount of 30 percent is available to **YHA** and **VIP** card holders.

Over 60s are entitled to a 30 percent reduction on all services.

Blind and other **disabled travellers** are entitled to a 50 percent discount if they present authorization (from the DPA; see p.16).

BUSES

YHA and **VIP** cardholders get 30 percent off fares with all three of the major companies (InterCity, Newmans and Mount Cook); and 5 percent off with Kiwi Experience.

Advance-purchase fares offer 30 percent discount for tickets bought 5 days ahead of travel, and there are a limited number of 50 percent discounts available on a first-come, first-served basis.

NEW ZEALAND TRAVEL PASSES

Travel passes generally offer unlimited travel within a specified period. You'll probably get your money's worth if you're determined to see a lot in a limited amount of time, but if you prefer a more leisurely pace, think carefully before you buy. Most can be bought either before you leave or after you arrive, but **air passes** are usually restricted to **non-residents** of New Zealand.

FLIGHTS
Air New Zealand and Ansett **air passes** both work out at around $150 per flight; good value if you are flying between the main islands but otherwise not a great saving; Air New Zealand's pass is also valid on Mount Cook Airline services. For both passes, the minimum purchase is **3 coupons** ($450) and the maximum is **8** ($1140), each redeemable for one flight. You can get a refund on any leftover coupons, so long as you apply before you leave the country.

BUSES
InterCity offer **fixed-route passes**, with seasonal variations in pricing, such as the **Coromandel Loop Pass** (Thames to Coromandel, Whitianga and back; all year $37); **Pacific Coast Traveller** (around the east coast to Gisborne and Napier via Rotorua; May–Sept $142, Sept–May $149); **North Island Value Pass** (any route between Auckland and Wellington; May–Sept $95, Sept–May $99); and the **Forests, islands and geysers** (which combines bits of the above for a whole island experience; May–Sept $255, Sept–May $260). Prices for their **South Island** passes are also seasonal: options include the **West Coast Passport** (Nelson to Queenstown; May–Sept $109, Sept–May $125); the **East Coast Explorer** (Te Anau to Picton, via Dunedin and Christchurch; $119/$132); and the **Milford Bound** (Christchurch to Milford, via Mount Cook

and Queenstown; $119/$132); a combination of the best bits of these is available as a **Pathfinder** ($340/$370). A combined North and South islands pass will cost $340–549.

Of the other passes available, Newmans **stopover passes** are good value. The deal is for either of the two islands – $95 for a comprehensive look around the North or $129 for a more limited visit to the South. You simply break your journey where you choose and book buses for the next stage, usually $3 per sector. Although it's an independent way of getting about without a car, you'll find yourself restricted by well-defined routes.

COMBINED TRAVEL PASSES
Tranz Rail's range of travel passes combine trains, buses and planes. The **3 in 1 pass** is valid for travel on trains and InterCity buses and for one Interislander ferry crossing (5 days' travel over 10 days, £144; 22 days in 8 weeks, £284). The **4 in 1** version offers all the above plus one domestic flight on Ansett or Air New Zealand (5 travel days £192, 8 days £241).

Tranz Rail Scenic Throughfares are a range of fixed-itinerary tickets that connect the North and South islands, combining trains with the Interislander ferries and selected bus services, for example Wellington to Christchurch ($85), Wellington to Waitomo ($75), Auckland to Waitomo ($38), or Christchurch to Auckland ($165).

---

a night or early morning crossing; add $10 each way for a bike, $140 for a car. The *Lynx* operates between Wellington and Picton from December to April, but is cancelled if the swell is greater than half a metre (the other ferries keep running). *Topcat*'s wave-piercing technology makes it less susceptible to bad weather and it runs most of the time.

Reservations can be made for both Interislander services at travel agents or by phone or fax (☎0800/802 802, fax 0800/101 525); you'll generally get the best deal by booking direct. Reservations for the *Topcat* are on ☎0800/486 7228.

TRAINS

Tranz Rail **trains** are a fast method of travel to a limited number of destinations in New Zealand, despite the fact that they seem to have been kept largely as a **tourist attraction**, with the exception of the **commuter services** that run into Wellington from the Hutt Valley and Palmerston North.

Most carriages are air-conditioned, with on-board phones and huge picture windows; airline-style meals (including vegetarian options) are served at your seat, and there's also a buffet car. Passengers check in on the platform before boarding (a ticket guarantees a seat) and bags are carried in a luggage van. As a contrast to the trains, stations tend to be in a depressingly run-down state.

These days **services** are limited. On the North Island, trains run from Auckland to Wellington; from Hamilton to Tauranga and Rotorua; from Palmerston North to Gisborne; from Napier to Palmerston North and on to Wellington; and from Masterton to Wellington. On the South Island, the main service operates between Picton and Invercargill along the east coast only. From Christchurch, a branch line runs to Greymouth on the west coast, while further south at Dunedin another service cuts inland to Middlemarch. These last two services are scenic trips run almost entirely for the benefit of tourists and are priced accordingly.

Tranz Rail have a multi-tier **fare** structure, with advance-purchase and concessionary fares available only within New Zealand (see box on previous page). The minimum fare is $14, no matter how short your journey, and a standard, non-discounted ticket from Auckland to Wellington is $122; Picton to Christchurch will set you back $73.

Tranz Rail also offers a range of **passes** for unlimited travel for a certain number of days within a specified period and **fixed-itinerary tickets** (see box on previous page). For further information and advance **bookings**, call Tranz Rail on ☎0800/802 802 or fax on 0800/101 525, *www.tranzrail.co.nz*.

BUSES

Buses and **shuttle buses** (minibuses) are, because of stiff competition, the cheapest form of public transport and will get you to most places. In general, they are reliable and reasonably comfortable: the larger buses are usually air-conditioned; some have toilets and show feature films and New Zealand promotional material to while away longer journeys. The **main bus companies** are InterCity *www.intercitycoach.co.nz* (who operate on both islands) and Newmans (with services concentrated on the North Island); Mount Cook Landlines (who run between Auckland and Wellington, via Rotorua, on the North Island and serve most destinations on the South Island) are now part of the Intercity set-up. One other competitor who offers an excellent service around the top half of the North Island is Northliner Express (☎09/402 7857).

One fact worth remembering is that the big bus operators charge more for South Island journeys than for North, so you might want to try different modes of transport in the South. Standard fares with most bus companies from Auckland to Wellington are in the region of $94; Christchurch to Queenstown, $118; Queenstown to Nelson, $176; Christchurch to Picton, $46; though prices often plummet during off-peak periods and a range of discounted fares is available (see box on p.26). Bus bookings can be made by phone: InterCity (Mon–Fri 7am–8pm & Sat–Sun 7am–7pm; in Auckland ☎09/357 8400, in Wellington ☎04/472 5111, in Christchurch ☎03/379 9020); and Newmans (☎0800/777 707), or at most visitor centres and travel agents. Note that once you've bought your ticket or pass, you may incur an agent's reservation fee of $3 unless you book bus seats direct.

SHUTTLE BUSES

A host of **shuttle bus** companies fill in the gaps around the country – more on the South Island than the North – linking with the services of the major operators to take you off the beaten track. An ever-growing number of shuttle operators also compete with the big companies on the main routes; though generally cheaper, they're not as comfortable over long distances. Most major bus companies don't operate on unsealed roads, so in areas such as the remoter parts of the Coromandel Peninsula and the Catlins you'll have to resort to shuttle buses.

Most visitor centres carry shuttle-bus timetables, so you can compare destinations and fares. **Fares** can be as low as half the price of standard (but not discounted) bus fares, for example Christchurch to Queenstown ($40), Picton to Christchurch ($25), or Queenstown to Dunedin ($25), though these vary with supply and demand.

BACKPACKER BUSES AND TOURS

One of the cheapest ways to cover a lot of ground is on a **backpacker bus**, which combines the flexibility of independent travel with the convenience of a tour. The deal is that you purchase a ticket for a fixed route (valid for up to 6 months), then either stick with the one bus, or stay in some places longer and hop on a later bus. Unlike more conventional tours, the ticket does not cover the cost of accommodation, adventure activities (although these are often discounted), side-trips or food.

The best backpacker buses and deals are run by **Magic Bus** a subsidiary of YHA whose service is pretty comprehensive on both islands, reliable and flexible. Trips are generally less gung-ho and target the more independently minded travellers (Auckland ☎09/358 5600, Wellington ☎04/387 2018, Christchurch ☎03/377 0951, *www.magicbus.co.nz*) offering thirteen, well-planned options (3–18 days; $165–673). They also offer a travel pass, Go, which includes travel and discounted accommodation but is only available through travel agents outside New Zealand. Best known of the backpacker buses is the "Great Green Drunken Bus" run by **Kiwi Experience** (Auckland ☎09/366 1665, Wellington ☎04/385 2153, Christchurch ☎03/377 0550, *enquiries @kiwiex.co.nz*), offering fifteen trips with a reputation for rowdy group-bonding and drinking (1–25 days; $119–925).

Probably one of the best and most complete wilderness experiences available for anyone who is reasonably fit, takes their environment seriously, wants to see things that few others will, and doesn't mind making the effort is available from **New Zealand Nature Safaris**, 52 Holborn Drive, Wellington (☎0800/697 232, fax 04/563 7324, *www.nzsafari.co.nz*). Good-humoured and informative guides take small groups tramping, climbing and wilderness camping in virtually untouched country, almost everything included (3–10 days; $295–850). More upmarket tours are organized by **Kiwi Wildlife Tours**, 24 Polkinghorne Drive, Manly, Whangaparaoa (☎09/424 2505, *www.kiwi-wildlife.co.nz*, *info@kiwi-wildlife.co.nz*). These minibus-based birding tours usually feature boat excursions, and up-scale accommodation and meals are included. Rates for the 11- and 18-day tours range from $3400 for the more stripped down affairs to luxurious $17,000 packages.

Along more traditional lines and are the lighter weight backpacker tours of **Flying Kiwi** (☎03/573 8126, *flyingkiwi@xtra.co.nz*) who offer **budget bus tours** where participants muck in with the cooking and dishes. Vehicles are equipped with bikes, canoe, windsurfer, kitchen, awning, fridge, beds, tents and hot shower. Aiming to get off the beaten track a little, their trips operate all year, with eight options available (2–28 days; around $150–1125); it works out at about $70 per day, plus a bit more for eating out with the team and hiring extra bikes or kayaks.

For cyclists **Pedaltours** (☎09/302 0968 & 0800/302 0968, US freephone ☎1-888/222 9187, fax 302 0967, *www.pedaltours.co.nz*, *info @pedaltours.co.nz*) offer guided road and mountain biking tours of both islands, from a gentle 3-day jaunt around the Marlborough wine country ($470), to a full 19-day Grand Tour of the South Island ($5200). High-standard accommodation and hearty meals are included, and bikes can be rented from them if needed (for around $100 extra a week); there is also often luggage transfer and/or mini-bus support, though this depends on the trip. Customized tours can be arranged for groups. Motorcycle tours can be organized through **Adventure New Zealand Motorcycle Tours**, 82 Achilles Avenue, Nelson (mobile ☎021/969 071, *www.thunderbike.co.nz/anzmtr*, *mctours@thunderbike.co.nz*), who provide boutique tours of the South Island with small groups (max 8); itineraries can often be tweaked to suit. Bikes are all late-model, tours are accompanied by a luxury coach and everything is done to the highest standard. Rates range from $4500 for a standard 10-day trip to $7000 for a 14-day deluxe ride.

Tours for women-only groups are run by **Wanderwomen**, PO Box 68058, Newton, Auckland (☎09/360 7330, fax 360 7333, *www.wanderwomen.co.nz*, *lizzie@wanderwomen.co.nz*), who provide safe, enriching and environmentally aware outdoor activities. Trips range from a few hours kayaking or caving ($30–60) to multi-day adventure holidays (roughly $100 a day including accommodation and food) taking in tramping, rock climbing, ice climbing, snorkelling, surfing and other sports. They also do some family excursions.

> **New Zealand** domestic **travel arrangements** can be made in advance from abroad through most **travel agents** (see boxes on pp.6, 9 and 11); some also act as agents for Kiwi Experience and others bus and train travel.

DRIVING

If your budget will stretch to it, driving is the best way to go, enabling you to get to places beyond the reach of public transport and to set your own timetable, although it's worth being conscious of the damage to the environment cars cause and using more eco-friendly transport wherever possible.

In order to **drive** in New Zealand you need a valid **licence** from Australia, Britain, Canada, Fiji,

Germany, Namibia, The Netherlands, Switzerland or South Africa; citizens of other countries need to obtain an International Driver's Licence before they leave (available from national motoring organizations).

Road rules are similar to those in the UK, Australia and the US, but if you plan to do much driving, you should pick up a copy of *The Road Guide* from AA offices or selected bookshops and newsagents for about $14.95. The one variation peculiar to New Zealand is that you must **give way** to all traffic crossing or coming from your right; this means that if you are turning left and another car coming from the opposite direction wants to turn right into the same side-road, you must let them go first. Most importantly, **drive on the left**, and remember that **seatbelts** are compulsory for all occupants. Always **park** in the same direction as that in which you are travelling; roadside parking facing oncoming traffic is illegal.

The **speed limit** for the open road is 100km/hr, reduced to 50km/hr in built-up areas and in limited speed zones (signposted **LSZ**) when road conditions are deemed unsafe – owing to bad weather, poor visibility, crossing pedestrians, cyclists, or excessive traffic. The fine for speeding is currently $120; some drivers warn others of lurking police patrols by flashing their headlights at oncoming cars. **Drink driving** is a major problem in New Zealand: as part of a campaign to cut the death-toll, random breath tests have been introduced, and offenders are dealt with severely.

Unleaded and super unleaded **petrol** and **diesel** are available in New Zealand. Prices hover around 97¢ a litre for unleaded, $1.02 for super unleaded, and 75¢ for diesel, with predictably higher prices in more out-of-the-way places.

The New Zealand **Automobile Association (AA)** has reciprocal rights with motoring organizations from lots of other countries, so check with your home service before you leave. If you don't qualify and you'll be driving your own vehicle, consider joining the AA as an overseas visitor ($54, plus $25 joining fee, *www.aa.org.nz*), valid for six months, or as a full member ($66, plus $25 joining fee), valid for a year. Apart from free 24-hour emergency **breakdown service** (☎0800/500 222) – excluding vehicles bogged on beaches – membership entitles you to free maps, accommodation guides and legal assistance, discounts on some rental cars and accommodation, plus access to insurance and pre-purchase vehicle inspection services.

Road conditions are generally good: most roads are sealed, although a few have a "**metalled**" surface composed of an aggregate of loose chippings. Obviously, these are slower to drive along, are prone to wash-outs and landslides after heavy rain, and demand considerably more care and attention from the driver. Metalled roads are clearly marked on most maps, so plan your route carefully beforehand. Some car-rental companies **prohibit** the use of their cars on the worst metalled roads – typically those along Ninety Mile Beach, Skippers Canyon and around the Coromandel Peninsula. Always **check conditions locally** before setting off on these routes.

Compared with most parts of the world, there are relatively few cars on New Zealand's roads, but **traffic** can still be a problem around the major cities and on public holidays. Other **hazards** include flocks of sheep and slow, wide farm equipment on country roads, as well as monstrous logging trucks in forested regions.

RENTING A CAR OR CAMPERVAN

Although you can get good **rental deals** with the major international companies (Avis, Budget and Hertz all operate in NZ – see opposite for reservation numbers) before you leave home, if you have a few days to spare when you arrive you'll usually get cheaper rates from **local firms**. Competition is fierce, so there are always deals to be had. Your best bet is to go for mid-range firms (we've listed the more reliable outfits throughout the Guide), rather than the sometimes-unscrupulous outfits that appear to offer rock-bottom rates.

Renting a **car** in New Zealand is fairly simple: you need a full, clean driver's licence and you must be over 21; drivers under 25 often have to pay more for insurance. For most roads you won't need **4WD** and, since 4WD rental rates are steep (usually $10–20 extra per day), you'll do best to rent for specific areas rather than long term. **Daily rates** with the major companies are in the region of $80 for a small two-door hatchback, or $90 for a medium-sized four-door saloon. With mid-range and smaller companies you can get a car on the road for about $55 a day, although many advertise deceptively cheap rates, then add on extra charges for insurance and mileage up to this level. **Weekly rates** should save you around $5 or $10 per day – keep your eyes peeled for deals.

One-way rental is handy but usually incurs a large drop-off fee, which can be as much as

$100–120. However, since most one-way rentals seem to go from north to south, if you're travelling in the opposite direction, you may be able to sweet-talk your way out of drop-off charges. In particular, there is often a glut of cars in Queenstown or Christchurch which the company would be glad to get dropped off in Picton; the same applies in Wellington, if you're heading upcountry to Auckland. Also by using the cars on the journey you're ensuring that they don't just get driven by one disgruntled rental car employee who is just fowling up the environment.

Remember that car rental is a **seasonal** business: from December to February business is good and prices are at their highest, but for the rest of the year the companies will be prepared to make deals rather than leave their vehicles idle, so shop around and don't be afraid to haggle. **Before signing** on the dotted line, always **check** the following points:

● The accident cover and bond. Before giving you a car, rental companies take a credit-card slip or a cash bond from you for anything up to $1000 (usually between $500 and $750). If you have an accident, the bond is used to pay for any damage: in some cases you pay anything up to the value of the bond; in others you pay the entire bond, no matter how slight the damage.

● A Value of Collision Damage Waiver will cost extra but means that if you have an accident, you won't automatically forfeit your bond.

● Check exactly how much damage you'll be liable for in the event of an accident. Although some companies only charge a $500 bond, the contract might stipulate that you are in fact liable for the first $1000 worth of damage.

● Check the car for any visible defects, so you won't end up being charged for someone else's mistakes.

● Check whether there are any restrictions on driving along certain roads

● If you'll be driving a fair distance, avoid limited-mileage deals whereby you pay for each kilometre in excess of a set daily allowance.

● Check that insurance cover is adequate, bearing in mind any existing travel or vehicle insurance you may have.

RENTAL RESERVATIONS

CARS

For general information and special offers, check out the Avis, Budget and Hertz Web sites: www.avis.com, www.budgetrentacar.com and www.hertz.com.

UK
Avis ☎0990/900 500
Budget ☎0800/181 181
Hertz ☎0990/996 699

USA and Canada
Avis ☎1-800/331-1084
Budget ☎1-800/527-0700
Hertz (USA) ☎1-800/654-3001
Hertz (Canada) ☎1-800/263-0600

Australia
Avis ☎1800/225 533
Budget ☎13 2727
Hertz ☎13 3039

CAMPERVANS

UK
Brits: NZ, ☎0990/143 607
Freedom Campervans ☎0993/823 363
Maui ☎01737/842 735

Australia
Brits: NZ ☎1800/331 454
Maui ☎64/9/275 3529

New Zealand
Adventure Campervans ☎0800/844 255,
www.nzmotorhomes.co.nz,
sales@nzmotorhomes.co.nz
Backpackers Campervans ☎0800/422 267,
www.kiwicampa.co.nz, campanz@mustbuy.co.nz
Brits ☎0800/831 900, www.britz.com,
info@britz.com
Kea Campers ☎0800/404 888, www.kea.co.nz,
keacampa@xtra.co.nz
Maui Motorhomes ☎0800/651080; www.
maui-rentals.com, nzinfo@maui-rentals.com
Paradise ☎0800/800 987, www.paradise.co.nz,
info@paradise.co.nz

A rented **campervan** provides independence, accommodation and a mobile kitchen. The disadvantages are its potential for isolating you from Kiwis and fellow travellers, the risk of theft – and the expense, though this is offset by savings on accommodation, especially for families and groups. Campervan-rental **rates** average about $150 a day during the high season (Oct–April), dropping to $100 the rest of the year. The two most popular rental firms are Maui and Brits: NZ (see box on previous page), but a few smaller companies in New Zealand offer campervans and converted delivery vans at slightly cheaper rates. Freedom Campervans (☎09/275 3034 in Auckland, ☎03/379 3822 in Christchurch), who also have an office in the UK (see box), offer vans for $74–124 a day, depending on season, and Greentours (☎0800/399 935) have converted Toyota vans for about $55 a day or $330 a week, year round.

Although no special licence is required to drive a campervan, some caution is needed, especially in high winds and when climbing hills and going around tight corners. Bear in mind, too, that you are not allowed to **park** a campervan in a lay-by **overnight** – though you're unlikely to be hassled in isolated areas. Finally have some consideration for other road users, in a campervan you are the slowest thing on the road so let people pass wherever possible.

BUYING A USED CAR

Buying a used car in New Zealand can be **cost-effective** if you are staying in the country for more than eight weeks or so. Reselling can recoup enough of the price to make it a cheaper option than using public transport or renting a car long term, though reselling without a guaranteed buy-back can be a lengthy process.

A decent car bought privately will **cost** anything from $1500, whereas one bought from a garage will begin at around $4000; if you pay less than this, chances are you'll be buying a petrol- and oil-guzzling disaster. Check over vehicles carefully, taking into account their age and the number of previous owners. Since the majority of people buy cars in Auckland and then try to sell them in Christchurch, as a buyer in Christchurch you often have more choice and are in a better bargaining position. For general pointers, call the premium-rated AA Techline (Mon–Fri 8.30am–5pm; ☎0900/58324, but only from private phones – this service does not work on public phones, 99¢ per minute), who can fill you in on

the good and bad points about a range of vehicles and their running costs, and advise on maintenance and approximate value, or get the AA to check the vehicle (☎0800/ 222 4325, see below).

The major points of entry (Auckland, Christchurch and Wellington) have plenty of **garages** falling over themselves to sell you a used car so bargain; some also offer a **buy-back service** at the end of your trip, usually paying about fifty percent of the original purchase price. This is only useful if you are returning to the city of purchase; some garages guarantee to buy back the car but also give you the option to try to sell it privately first for a better price.

If you're mechanically minded and confident of your ability to spot a lemon, you can try to pick up a cheap car at an **auction** or **fair**; they're held weekly in Auckland and Christchurch, and are advertised in the local press. Buying a car in a **private sale** is a good compromise if you don't know your big end from your steering column. Trawl the local papers or noticeboards at supermarkets and hostels for likely candidates. If you buy from a **fellow traveller**, you might be able to negotiate a canny price if their flight is imminent or get some useful extras (camping equipment and the like) thrown in. Just make sure you arrange a **vehicle inspection**, either from the AA (contact the local technical centre; numbers listed in *AA Services Handbook* or call 0800 AACHECK, costs range between $80–120) or from Car Inspection Services of Auckland (☎09/309 8084); this will set you back around $75–80, but may save you buying a wreck and/or give you enough ammunition to negotiate a significant price reduction. Finally, before you close a private sale, call **Autocheck** (☎0800/658 934), which will warn you if there's money owing on a vehicle being sold privately, a **debt** that a buyer would inherit.

Before they're allowed on the road, all vehicles must have a **Warrant of Fitness** (WOF), which is a test of its mechanical worthiness and safety, just like an MOT in the UK. WOFs are carried out and issued by specified garages and last for a year. Always check the expiry date, as the test must have been carried out no more than 28 days before you apply to register the car.

When you buy a car you have to **transfer** the vehicle **ownership** by filing a form (filled in by buyer and seller) at the post office, but it should already be registered. If it isn't, or in any case when it runs out, you'll have to pay for **registra-**

tion (6 months, $110; 12 months, $206). Next you'll need **insurance** (approximately $150 for 6 months) – shop around or use the AA if you're a member. Although it's not compulsory to have insurance in New Zealand, you'll pay through the nose if you risk it and are involved in an accident, whether it's deemed to be your fault or not.

HITCHING AND CAR SHARES

Although many travellers enthuse about **hitching** in New Zealand – and it does enjoy a reputation of relative safety – the official advice is don't. Sadly, New Zealand has its share of unpleasant individuals and, with an extensive network of affordable transport and tours at your disposal, there's really little reason to take unnecessary **risks**. If you're determined to do it regardless, hitch in pairs (no guarantee of avoiding trouble but safer than going solo). **Women**, especially, should trust their instincts: it's better to refuse a lift than regret it later; there will always be another car. Always ask the driver where they are going, rather than telling them where you're headed, and keep your gear with you so you can make a quick get away if it becomes necessary.

Finding the best **hitching spots** around the country is generally a matter of common sense, or common knowledge on the travellers' grapevine. Some town and city hostels drop their guests at hitching spots as a matter of course; pick a spot where you can be clearly seen and drivers can stop safely.

A good compromise is **car share**, where the cost of travel is shared. You can organize this formally through organizations such as Travelpool in Auckland (daily 9am–8pm; ☎09/307 0001) and Travelshare in Wellington (daily 8am–9pm; ☎04/473 5558), to whom you pay a commission for the introduction service, before signing a contract with the driver to split the cost of the journey; obviously the more of you there are, the cheaper it gets. Casual car shares are also advertised on hostel noticeboards, which saves on commission but demands more trust on both sides.

MOTORBIKING

Although motorbikes are generally cheaper to buy than cars and more economical from a fuel point of view, bear in mind that you'll also be more **exposed** to the elements and be able to carry considerably less stuff with you. Be prepared for riding on **unsealed roads**, which can be a far-from-pleasant experience, and be sure you know what you're doing – there's nothing worse than having to push a broken-down bike a few kilometres to the nearest town. Note also that to ride a motorbike your international licence must specify motorbikes.

A worthwhile **secondhand bike** will set you back approximately $1000, and the registration procedure is the same as for cars (see opposite). Motorbikes can be **rented** or bought (outright or on a buy-back basis) from Graham Crosby Motorcycles Ltd, 299 Great North Rd, Grey Lynn, Auckland (☎09/376 2711, fax 376 5033), or through the same channels as cars (see pp.30-31).

CYCLING

Cycling is an excellent way of appreciating the countryside, especially if you're reasonably fit and keep your time on the main highways to a minimum. Disadvantages are dealing with **unsealed roads**, which become irksome if you're on them all day and wreak havoc with your tyres (fat tyres limit the damage).

Contrary to what you might think, cycling in New Zealand's mountainous **South Island** is easier than in the North Island. The South Island's north–south alpine backbone presents virtually the only geographical barrier, while the eastern two-thirds of the island comprise a flat plain. By contrast, in the **North Island** you can barely go 10km without encountering significant hills – and you have to contend with a great deal more traffic, including overbearing logging trucks. If you do get sick of pedalling, you can always hoick your bike onto a **bus, shuttle** or **train** for around $10–12 per trip.

Most people seem to prefer using mountain **bikes** but since the majority of riding is on roads, touring bikes are just as good; **helmets** are required by law. If all you want to do is explore locally, some **hostels** and guesthouses have pre-loved bikes you can use for a nominal sum, or even for **free**. **Renting** bikes for more than the odd day can be an expensive option, costing anything from $15–35 a day, depending whether you want a bike with little more than pedals and brakes, a tourer, or a state-of-the-art mountain bike. Specialist cycle shops also do economical monthly rental for around $200 for a touring bike, $300 for a full-suspension superbike.

If you plan on any long-distance cycle-touring, it's generally cheaper to **buy**, though you have to factor in the cost of transporting the bike by bus or train (see previous page) if you shirk the longer hauls. Hostel noticeboards are the place to look for bargains (between $150 and $300 is a reasonable deal), often accompanied by extras like wet-weather gear, lights, helmet and a pump; some cycle shops will guarantee **buy back** at the end of your trip for about fifty percent of the purchase price.

It is possible to bring **your own bike** to New Zealand by plane and if you intend to cycle a lot this is the cheapest option. On most airlines, assuming you prepare and package them appropriately, bikes simply count as a piece of luggage and don't incur any extra cost so long as you don't exceed your baggage limit. It's easy enough

to find **spares** in cities and larger country towns but in the more out-of-the-way places you may have to wait some time for spares to be delivered.

Visitors with extensive cycling in mind should get in touch with **Adventure Cycles** (☎09/309 5566) or **Cycle Xpress** (☎09/379 0779), both in Auckland. If you're bringing your own bike they'll let you store the bike box you transported your machine in, help you organize an emergency package of spare parts and extra clothing to be forwarded at your request, and give your bike a final once over before you set off, all for around $20. They also operate buy-back schemes (see above), which are good value for anything longer than a two-month tour.

ACCOMMODATION

Accommodation will make up a fair chunk of your spending while in New Zealand, though the expense is ameliorated by excellent standards. Almost every town has a motel or hostel of some description, so finding accommodation is seldom a problem – though it's advisable to book in advance from Christmas through to the end of January when Kiwis take their summer holidays, and a couple of months either side when places fill with international visitors.

Kiwis travel widely at home, most choosing to self-cater at the country's huge number of well-equipped motor camps (or holiday parks, as they now prefer to be known) and motels, shunning

hotels, which cater mainly to package holiday-makers and the business community. An appealing alternative is the range of guesthouses, bed & breakfasts, homestays and farmstays, which cover the whole spectrum from a room in someone's suburban home to pampered luxury in a country mansion.

In the last decade or so, New Zealand has, together with Australia, pioneered the backpacker hostel, a less-regimented alternative to traditional YHAs, which have transformed themselves dramatically to compete. Found all over the country, hostels offer superb value to budget travellers.

Wherever you stay, you can expect unstinting hospitality and a truckload of valuable advice on local activities and onward travel. As far as facilities go, there is almost always some form of laundry, low-cost Internet access, and tea and coffee are often provided free.

HOTELS AND MOTELS

In New Zealand, a "hotel" may not be quite what you expect. The term is frequently used to describe old-style pubs, which were once legally obliged to provide rooms for drinkers to recuperate from their excesses. Many no longer provide accommodation, but some have transformed themselves into backpacker hostels, while others are dedicated to preserving the tradition. At their best, hotels offer comfortable rooms in characterful, historic buildings, though just as often lodgings are rudimentary. Hotel bars are frequently at the centre of smalltown social life and, at weekends in particular, they can be pretty raucous; for the asking price of around $50 a double, you may find a budget room at a hostel a better bet.

In the **cities** and **major resorts**, you'll also come across hotels in the conventional sense, predominantly business- or tourbus-orientated places with all the usual trappings of international-style establishments. Priced accordingly, they're seldom good value, usually costing $150–300 a room, though at quiet times and weekends there can be substantial discounts; it's always worth asking.

Most Kiwi families on the move prefer the astonishingly well-equipped **motels**, which congregate along the roads running into town, making them more convenient for drivers than for those using trains or buses. They come provided with bed linen, towels, TV (usually with Sky), a full kitchen and tea and coffee, but are often depressingly functional concrete-block places with little to distinguish one from another. Rooms range from all-in-one-room **studios** ($60–90 for two), with beds, kettle, toaster and a microwave; through **one-bedroom units** ($70–100 for two), usually with a full and separate kitchen; to two- and three-bedroom **suites**, sleeping six or eight. Suites generally go for the same basic price as a one-bedroom unit, with each additional adult paying $12–18, making them an economical choice

for groups travelling together. Anything calling itself a **motor inn** or similar will be quite luxurious, with a bar, restaurant, swimming pool and sauna but no cooking facilities.

GUESTHOUSES AND B&BS

While families might prefer the freedom and adaptability of a motel, couples are generally better served by a guesthouse, homestay or bed and breakfast (B&B). These terms are used almost interchangeably in New Zealand, though the cheaper places are more likely to call themselves **guesthouses**, offering simple rooms, usually with a bathroom down the hall and a modest continental breakfast included in the price.

A **B&B** may be exactly the same as a guesthouse, but the term also encompasses luxurious colonial homes with well-furnished en-suite rooms and sumptuous home-cooked breakfasts. Those at the top end are now fashioning themselves as "**boutique hotels**" and "exclusive retreats", where standards of service and comfort are raised to extraordinary levels, with prices to match.

Roughly speaking, **rates** for a double room are around $60–80 at guesthouses, $70–120 at B&Bs, $120–250 at boutique hotels and reach stratospheric levels when it comes to the exclusive retreats, where $800 per person per night is not unheard of, though that includes all meals and drinks. Rates drop in the low season, when these places can often be exceptionally good value. If you're travelling alone and don't fancy hostels, B&Bs can also be a viable alternative, usually charging **lone travellers** 60–80 percent of the

double room rate, though some only ask fifty percent.

HOMESTAYS AND FARMSTAYS

Homestays usually offer a guest room or two in
an ordinary house where you muck in with the
owners and join them for breakfast the following
morning. Staying in such places can be an excellent way to meet ordinary New Zealanders; you'll
be well looked after, sometimes to the point of
being overwhelmed by your hosts' generosity.
Always try to book ahead, and bear in mind you'll
usually have to pay in cash. Rural versions often
operate as **farmstays**, where you're encouraged
to stay a couple of nights and are welcome to
spend the intervening day trying your hand at
farm tasks: rounding up sheep, milking cows,
fencing, whatever might need doing. Both homestays and farmstays charge $60–80 for a double
room, including breakfast; some cook dinner on
request for $15–25 per person, and you'll pay a
small fee for lunch if you spend the day at the
farm.

There are also places where you can **work for
your keep**, typically toiling for four hours a day
in return for board and lodging. FHiNZ, PO Box 99,
Woodville (☎ & fax 06/376 4582), organize stays
on farms, orchards and horticultural holdings for
singles, couples and families, and no experience
is needed. Over 120 places are listed in their
booklet ($15) and accommodation ranges from
basic to quite luxurious. An organization run
along the same lines is the international
WWOOF (Willing Workers on Organic Farms, PO
Box 1172, Nelson; ☎ & fax 03/544 9890,
www.wwoof.co.nz wwoof-nz@xtra.co.nz), which
coordinates some five hundred properties (membership and booklet $30), mostly farms but also
orchards, market gardens and self-sufficiency
orientated smallholdings, all using organic methods to a greater or lesser degree. They'll expect
a stay of at least two nights, though much longer
periods are common; armed with the booklet, you
then **book direct** (preferably a week or more in
advance). Most hosts will work you three to four
hours a day and vary the tasks to keep you interested, but there have been occasional reports of
taskmasters; make sure you discuss what will be
expected of you before you commit yourself.
Property managers are vetted but **lone women**
may feel happier seeking placements with couples or families.

HOSTELS AND BACKPACKERS

New Zealand is awash with budget, self-catering
places, pretty much interchangeably known as
hostels or **backpackers** and offering a bed or
bunk for around $15–18. As often as not they're in
superb locations – bang in the centre of town,
beside the beach, close to a ski field or amid magnificent scenery in a national or forest park – and
are invariably great places to meet others, hook-
up to the travellers' grapevine and pick through
the mass of local information, aided by genuinely
helpful managers. Wherever you stay, you'll find a
fully-equipped kitchen, laundry, TV and games
room, a travellers' noticeboard, and a stack of
tourist information. Often there'll also be a pool,
barbecue area, bike and/or canoe rental and information on local work opportunities. If you **book
ahead** – essential in January and February, and
preferable in December and March – hostels may
even pick you up from the nearest public transport.

Many hostels allow you to pitch a tent in the
grounds for $10–12 a person, but generally the
most basic and **cheapest accommodation** is in
a 6–12 bunk dorm ($13–18), with 3–4 bed shares
usually priced a dollar or two higher. Most hostels
nowadays also have double, twin and family
rooms ($18–25 per adult), the more expensive
ones with en-suite bathrooms. Unless you are
planning on only using YHA hostels (where all
bedding is provided), you can save money by carrying your own sleeping bag or sleeping sheet.

The odd **YMCA** and **YWCA** does exist but with
plenty of other choices and the tendency of Ys to
cater to long-termers, they are rarely the most
appealing option.

YHAS

New Zealand's **YHA hostels** are some of the best
of their kind in the world. They're clean, secure,
well-equipped, run by trained staff, and frequently beautifully sited, though despite their best
modernizing efforts some still retain an institutional feel. They've now abandoned daily chores,
arcane opening hours (but office hours are still
generally limited to 8–11am, 1–3pm & 5–10pm)
and strict segregation of the sexes, though there's
almost always a dorm solely for women. Newer
hostels have been purpose-built to reflect the
YHA's environmental concerns, promoting recycling and energy conservation; older places are
likely to be converted schools or large houses.

HOSTELLING INTERNATIONAL OFFICES

Australia PO Box 314, Camperdown, New South Wales 1450 (02/9565 1699, fax 9565 1325, *yha@yha.org.au*)

Canada Suite 400, 205 Catherine St, Ottawa, ON K2P 1C3 (☎1-800/663 5777 & 613/237-7884, fax 237-7868, *info@hostellingintl.ca*).

England and Wales Trevelyan House, 8 St Stephen's Hill, St Albans, Herts, AL1 2DY (☎01727/855 215,fax 844 126, *www.yha.org.uk*, *customerservices@yha.org.uk*); London shop and information office: 14 Southampton St, London WC2 7HY (☎020/7836 1036).

Ireland 61 Mountjoy St, Dublin 7 (☎01/830 4555, fax 830 5808, *www.irelandyha.org*, *anoige@iol.ie*).

New Zealand PO Box 436, 193 Cashel St, Christchurch 1 (☎03/379 9970, fax 365 4476, *info@yha.org.nz*).

Northern Ireland 22 Donegall Rd, Belfast BT12 5JN (☎028/9031 5435, fax 9043 9699, *info@hini.org.uk*).

Scotland 7 Glebe Crescent, Stirling, FK8 2JA (☎01786/891 400, fax 891 333, *www.syha.org.uk*, *info@syha.org.uk*).

USA 733 15th St NW, Suite 840, Washington, DC 20005 (☎202/783 6161, fax 703 0171, *www.hiayh.org*, *hiayhsev@hiayh.org*).

Fifty-five hostels are listed in the annual *YHA Hostel Accommodation Guide* and the condensed *Quick Guide* version (both free to all). Over half of these are **full YHA hostels** open only to members: either obtain a Hostelling International Card in your own country (see box above), stump up the $30 annual membership or go with the introductory DownUnder Card (also valid in Australia) which achieves full membership by allowing you to pay an additional $3 for each of your first ten YHA stays. The rest of the hostels are affiliated **associate hostels**, where no membership card is required, though there is often a discount of a dollar or so for members. At full YHAs all bedding is supplied, whereas associate hostels usually charge a small additional fee if you are not using your own sleeping bag or sheet.

At the cheapest hostel, you can pay as little as $10, and in some city places as much as $20, though the majority of beds fall into the $15–18 range. You can book ahead either from another hostel (they charge $1 for the phone call) or through the YHA National Reservations Centre, PO Box 436, Christchurch (☎03/379 9808, fax 379 4415, *www.yha.org.nz*, *book@yha.org.nz*) using a credit card or bank draft; you can also make advance bookings before you leave through Hostelling International offices in your home country (see box above).

BACKPACKER HOSTELS

YHAs are outnumbered six-to-one by independent **backpacker hostels**. Quality is more variable than in YHAs: a few fall well short of expected standards, with disinterested staff and cramped rooms, but the majority have excellent facilities and a warm atmosphere; some are friendly and relaxed, others are more free-spirited and raucous. Many of the best places have been specially built or converted, though some are substantially less appealing, wedged into former hotel rooms above pubs. On average, **prices** are comparable with YHAs, with the basic rate often a dollar or two less, but offset by having to supply your own bedding or renting it for $1–2 a time.

Around eighty hostels are members of VIP Backpacker Resorts (PO Box 80021, Green Bay Auckland; ☎09/827 6016, fax 827 6013, *www.vip.co.nz*, *backpack@vip.co.nz*), an umbrella organization that offers a dollar off each night's stay to people who buy the annual **VIP backpacker discount card** ($30, valid in New Zealand, at 130 hostels in Australia and a few others dotted across Pacific islands). Others have aligned themselves with Nomads (38 Fort St, Auckland ☎0800/666 237, *www.nomads-backpackers.com*, *bookings@nomads-backpackers.com*), a smaller but growing organisation working on a similar basis who have their Nomads Adventure Card, a kind of phone card that also offers discounts on hostel accommodation and travel.

The best **guide** to backpackers throughout the country is the free *Budget Backpacker Hostels* booklet (BBH or simply "Blue Book"), which details the majority of non-YHA hostels in New

Zealand (including some VIP and Nomads places), currently numbering over 250. The entries don't pretend to be impartial, but each hostel is given a rating based on an annual survey of guests, and these are fairly reliable assessments of the overall tone and general appeal of the place. Brandishing the Blue Book at the VIP hostels listed will get you VIP's dollar discount. Obtain one at visitor centres, all participating hostels, direct from Budget Backpackers Hostels NZ Ltd (c/- Rainbow Lodge, 99 Titiraupenga, St, Taupo; ☎ & fax 07/377 1568), or through their Web site, *www.backpack.co.nz* where there are also full hostel listings.

MOTORCAMPS, CAMPSITES AND CABINS

New Zealand has some of the world's best camping facilities, so even if you've never been camping before, you may well find yourself using **motor camps** (also known as **holiday parks**), which are geared up for Kiwi families on holiday, with space to pitch tents, hook-ups for campervans and usually a broad range of rooms and dorms. Elsewhere there is more down-to-earth camping at wonderfully located DOC sites.

Camping is largely a **summer activity** (Nov–May), especially in the South Island where winters can get very cold. At worst, New Zealand is very wet, windy and plagued by voracious winged insects, so the first priority for tent campers is good-quality gear with a fly sheet which will repel the worst that the elements can dish out, and an inner tent with enough bug-proof ventilation for those hot mornings.

Busy times at motor camps fall into line with the school holidays, making Easter and the summer period from Christmas to the end of January the most hectic. **Book** as far in advance as possible at this time and a day or two before you arrive

anytime through February and March. DOC sites are not generally bookable, and while this is no problem through most of the year, Christmas can be a mad free-for-all.

MOTOR CAMPS AND CABINS

Motor camps are typically located on the outskirts of towns and are invariably well-equipped, with communal kitchen, TV lounge, games area, laundry, and sometimes a swimming pool; non-residents can often get showers for $2–3. **Campers** usually get the quietest and most sylvan corner of the site and are charged $7–9 per person; there is often no distinction between tent pitches and **powered sites** set aside for campervans, which are charged an extra dollar or so per person for the use of power hook-ups and dump station.

In addition, most sites have some form of onsite accommodation: the basic dorm-style **lodge** ($10–15 per person); 2–4 berth **standard cabins** ($30–35 for two, plus $10 for each extra person), often little more than a shed with bunks; larger **tourist cabins** and **tourist flats** ($45–60 for two, plus $12–15 each extra person), all with cooking facilities and some with bathrooms; and fully self-contained **motel units** ($60–90 for two, plus $13–18 per extra person), usually with a separate bedroom and a TV. In all but the motel units, blankets, sheets and towels are not generally included, so bring a sleeping bag or be prepared to pay $2–3 a night to rent bed linen.

DOC CAMPSITES

Few motor camps can match the idyllic locations of the two hundred and fifty **campsites** operated by the **Department of Conservation** (DOC) in national parks, reserves, maritime and forest parks, the majority beautifully set by sweeping beaches or deep in the bush. This is back-to-nature camping, low-cost and with simple facilities, though sites almost always have running water and toilets of some sort. Listed in the DOC's free *Conservation Campsites* leaflet, the sites fall into one of three categories: **informal** (free), often accessible only on foot and with nothing but a water supply; the more common **standard** ($2–6 per person), all with vehicular access and many with barbecues, fireplaces, picnic tables and refuse collection; and rare **serviced** ($6–9 per person), which are similar in scope to the regular motor camps described above. At any site children aged 5–15 are charged half price, and only the serviced sites can be booked in advance.

Other possibilities for using your tent include pitching in the grounds of many backpackers (see p.36) and along backcountry tramps (see p.52). **Free camping** is not generally a viable option, though with huge areas of thinly populated land you can probably get away with a dusk-to-dawn stay pretty much anywhere outside the cities, though this is not strictly legal. Parking your campervan overnight in roadside rest areas is also proscribed, though many do and suffer no adverse consequences.

> For advice on **backcountry camping** and **trampers' huts**, see the "Outdoor Activities" section on p.51.

FOOD AND DRINK

Forget any preconceptions you may have about "slam in the lamb" Kiwi cuisine with a pavlova for dessert, New Zealand's food scene has forged ahead in recent years – both in terms of the quality of the food and the places where it's served.

New Zealand's **gastronomic roots** were nurtured in the British tradition of overcooked meat and two nuked vegetables, an unfortunate heritage which still informs the cooking patterns of older Kiwis and hasn't been completely displaced at some farmstays and guesthouses. Indeed, it is

only in the last decade or so that New Zealand's chefs have really woken up to the possibilities presented by a fabulous larder of super-fresh, top-quality ingredients, formulating what might be termed **Modern Kiwi** cuisine. Taking its culinary cues from Californian and contemporary Australian cuisine, it combines traditional elements such as steak, salmon and crayfish with flavours drawn from the **Mediterranean**, **Asia** and the **Pacific Rim**: sun-dried tomatoes, lemongrass, basil, ginger, coconut and many more. Restaurateurs feel duty-bound to fill their menu with as broad a spectrum as possible, lining up seafood linguini, couscous, sushi, Thai venison meatballs and a chicken korma alongside the rack of lamb and gourmet pizza. Sometimes this results in gastronomic overload, but more often the results are sensational.

NEW ZEALAND INGREDIENTS

New Zealanders have a taste for meat. The quality of New Zealand lamb is matched by that of other **meats**, beef, chicken and, more recently, farmed venison, which appears on menus as cervena. Farmed ostrich is also gaining fans for its leanness and superb taste, though the greasy charms of **muttonbird** remain a mystery to most.

FOOD AND DRINK TERMS

butternut	type of pumpkin	*muttonbird*	gull-sized sooty shearwater that was a major component of the pre-European Maori diet and is said to taste like oily and slightly fishy mutton – hence the name
capsicum	bell peppers		
cervena	farmed venison		
crayfish	a slightly sweeter and pincer-less type of lobster		
eggplant	aubergine	*paua*	the muscular foot of the abalone, often minced and served as a fritter
entree	appetizer		
feijoa	fleshy, tomato-sized fruit with melon-like flesh and a tangy, perfumed flavour	*pavlova*	sickly meringue confection topped with cream and fruit that's claimed by Kiwis as adamantly as it is by Aussies
hogget	the meat from a year-old sheep. Older and more tasty (though less succulent) than lamb, but not as tough as mutton		
		pikelets	small, thick pancakes served cold with butter and jam or whipped cream
hot dog	a rather disgusting-looking battered sausage on a stick, dipped in tomato ketchup. What the rest of the world knows as a hot dog is known here as an American hot dog	*puha*	type of watercress traditionally gathered by Maori
		saveloy	particularly revolting but popular kind of sausage served boiled
kiwifruit	hairy brown egg-sized fruit with a juicy green centre which swept the world in the 1980s to become the garnish of choice. The New Zealand-grown variety is now market ed as *Zespri*	*silverside*	top-grade corned beef, cured in honey and often served with tangy mustard
		swede	rutabaga
		tamarillo	slightly bitter, deep-red fruit, often known as a tree tomato
kumara	particularly delicious type of sweet potato and a long-standing Maori staple; often served as kumara chips with sour cream	*Vegemite*	a dark savoury yeast-extract spread that mystifies most people but is much loved by antipodeans, who insist it is far superior to its British equivalent, Marmite
lamington	sponge cake coated in choco-late or pink icing and rolled in desiccated coconut		

A traditional source of sustenance for Maori, each April and May these birds of the shearwater family are still plucked from their burrows on the Titi Islands, off the southwest tip of Stewart Island, and sold through fishmongers in areas with substantial Maori populations.

With the country's long coastline, it's no surprise that **fish and seafood** loom large on the culinary horizon. The white, flaky flesh of the **snapper** is the most common saltwater fish, though you'll also come across tuna, John Dory, groper (often known by its Maori name of hapuku), flounder, blue cod (a speciality from the Chatham Islands), the firm and delicately flavoured terakihi and the moist-textured **orange roughy**. You'll also see a lot of **salmon** – but not trout, which cannot be bought or sold, though some hotel restaurants will cook your catch for you. One much-loved delicacy is **whitebait**, a tiny silvery fish mostly caught on the West Coast and eaten whole in fritters during the August to November season. Shellfish are a real New Zealand speciality, and the king of them all is the **toheroa**, a type of clam dug from the sands of Ninety Mile Beach on the rare occasions when numbers reach harvestable levels. They are usually made into soups and are sometimes substituted by the inferior and sweeter **tuatua**, also dug from Northland beaches. On menus you're more likely to come across the fabulous **Bluff oysters**, scallops and sensational **green-lipped mussels**, which have a flavour and texture that's hard to beat and are grown in the cool clear waters of the Marlborough Sounds, especially around Havelock. Pricey **crayfish** is also delicious and if you get a chance, try **smoked eel** and **smoked marlin**.

Vegetables too are generally fresh and delicious. British favourites – potatoes, carrots, peas, cabbage – along with pumpkin and squash are common in Kiwi homes but on restaurant menus you're far more likely to encounter aubergines (eggplant), capsicums (bell peppers) and tomatoes. Pacific staples to look out for are **kumara** (sweet potato), which crops up in hangi and deep-fried as kumara chips, and the starchy taro and sweeter yam, both much more rarely seen.

New Zealanders eat a lot of **cheese**, yoghurt and ice cream, and all are first-rate. Small producers springing up all over the country – but especially around the Kapiti Coast (north of Wellington), Blenheim and Banks Peninsula (east of Christchurch) – are turning out some gorgeous individual cheeses, from the traditional hard cheddar-style to spicy pepper brie. **Ice cream** of the firm, scooped variety is something of a New Zealand institution, and is available in a vast range of flavours, including intensely fruity ones and the indulgent hokey pokey – vanilla ice cream riddled with chunks of caramel.

Fruit too is a winner, especially at harvest time when stalls line the roadsides selling apples, pears, citrus and stonefruits for next to nothing. Top-quality fruit and dairy products are the starting point for some delicious **desserts** traditionally variations on the themes of ice cream, cheesecake and pavlova, though now supplemented by rich cakes and modern twists on British-style steamed puddings.

This abundance of fresh vegetables and superb dairy food means that self-catering **vegetarians** will eat very well, though those who eat in restaurants are less well served. Outside the major centres you'll find few dedicated vegetarian restaurants, and will have to rely on the token meat-free dishes served at most regular restaurants and cafés. Pretty much everywhere you'll be able to get a salad, sandwich, or vegetarian pizza and pasta – but it can get a bit monotonous. **Vegans** can always ask for a simple stir-fry if all else fails. In terms of snacks, you may find yourself developing an unhealthy reliance on nachos (a plateful of tortilla chips with a dollop of refried beans, grilled cheese and a hearty helping of sour cream), and the ubiquitous vegeburger.

If you are taking a rafting expedition or 4WD **tour** on which food is provided, give them plenty of notice of your dietary needs – otherwise you might be left with bread and salad.

RESTAURANTS, CAFES AND BARS

The quality of **restaurants** in New Zealand is typically superb, the portions are respectable, and with the current low value of the NZ dollar will seem wonderful value for money – especially at **BYO** establishments, where the cost is eased if you "bring your own" wine, sometimes for a small corkage fee (typically $2–5). In most restaurants you can expect to pay upwards of $15 for a main course, perhaps $30 for three courses without wine. Service tends to be unpretentious and helpful without being forced, and there is no expectation of a tip, though a reward for exceptional service is always welcomed.

New Zealand's range of **ethnic restaurants** is meagre by international standards, with only the major influx of east Asian immigrants enervating the scene and lending a strong Chinese and Japanese flavour to the larger cities, alongside a smattering of Mexican places. **Maori food** is barely represented in restaurants at all, but you shouldn't miss the opportunity to sample the contents of a hangi (see box overleaf), an earth oven producing delectable, fall-off-the-bone meat and delicately steamed vegetables.

Often there is little common ground between restaurants and the better **café/bars** which have sprung up all over the land and offer food that's just as good and a few dollars cheaper. Here, dining is less formal and you may well find yourself elbow to elbow with folk only there for the beer or coffee, but dining is very much part of the café/bar scene. Simpler **cafés** may only stretch to breakfasts, grilled focaccias stuffed with Italian-inspired fillings, salads and cakes but always produce good coffee and keep long hours.

Though common in the more cosmopolitan cities, cafés are less prevalent in the country towns, which are still ruled by traditional **tearooms**, daytime (most close around 5pm), self-service places that are low on atmosphere but high on value. Most are now equipped with a coffee machine, though espresso incompetence may

---

THE HANGI

In New Zealand restaurants you'll find little or no representation of **Maori** or Polynesian cuisines, but you can sample traditional cooking methods at a **hangi** (pronounced nasally as "hungi"), where meat and vegetables are steamed for hours in an earth oven then served to the assembled masses. The ideal way to experience a hangi is as a guest at a private gathering of extended families, but most people have to settle for one of the commercial affairs in Rotorua or Christchurch. Though you'll be a paying customer rather than a guest, the hangi will be no less authentic.

First the men light a **fire** and place river stones in the embers. While these are heating, they dig a suitably large pit, place the **hot stones** in the bottom and cover them with **wet sacking**. Meanwhile the women prepare lamb, pork, chicken, fish, shellfish and vegetables (particularly kumara), wrapping the morsels in leaves then arranging them in baskets (originally of flax, but now most often of steel mesh). The baskets are lowered into the cooking pit and covered with earth so that the steam and the flavours are sealed in. A couple of hours later, the baskets are disinterred, revealing fabulously tender **steam-smoked** meat and vegetables with a faintly earth flavour. A suitably reverential silence, broken only by munching and appreciative murmurs, descends.

---

mean you're better sticking with the staple of tea, usually accompanied by a cellophane-wrapped sandwich, uninspiring savouries and either "Devonshire (cream) Teas" or home-style cakes – the carrot cake and ginger crunch are generally good bets. On main tourist routes, long-distance buses usually make their comfort stops at tearooms.

Some of the more civilized bars serve **pub meals**, often the best budget eating around with straightforward plates of steak and chips, lasagne or burritos, all served with salad for around $10. One to look out for here is the nationwide *Cobb & Co.* chain, formerly used as waystations by stagecoaches and now offering reliable, if uninspired, meals and good last-all-day breakfasts.

BREAKFAST, SNACKS AND TAKEAWAYS

New Zealanders generally take a fairly light "continental" **breakfast** of juice, cereals, toast and tea or coffee. Visitors staying at a homestay or B&B may well be offered an additional "cooked breakfast" probably along the lines of the traditional English breakfast of bacon and eggs; if you're staying in motels, hostels or campsites, you'll generally have to fend for yourself. In the bigger towns, you'll often find a **bakery** selling fresh croissants, bagels and focaccia, but increasingly New Zealanders are going out for breakfast or brunch, aided by the proliferation of cafés serving anything from a bowl of fruit and muesli ($5) to stupendous platefuls of Eggs Florentine and smoked salmon ($12–14).

In the cities you'll also come across **food courts**, usually in shopping malls where a central seating area is surrounded by a dozen or so stalls selling bargain plates of all manner of ethnic dishes. Some have outlets for **fast food**, a market dominated by the ubiquitous *McDonald's, Pizza Hut, KFC* and *Burger King*. Meat **pies** are a stalwart of Kiwi snacking: sold in bakeries and from warming cabinets in pubs everywhere, the traditional steak and mince varieties are now supplemented by bacon and egg, venison, steak and cheese, steak and oyster and many others, though there is seldom a vegetarian version.

Undeterred by US fast-food hegemony, traditional **burger bars** continue to serve constructions far removed from the limp franchise offerings: weighty buns with juicy patties, thick ketchup, a stack of lettuce and tomato and that all-important slice of beetroot. At one stage, *McDonald's* even succumbed to consumer pressure and produced a Kiwiburger laden with beetroot and not a pickle in sight.

Fish and chips (or "greasies") are also rightly popular – the fish is often shark (euphemistically called lemon fish) and the chips (fries) are invariably thick and crisp. Look out too for paua fritters, a battered slab of minced abalone that's something of an acquired taste.

SELF-CATERING

If you're **self-catering** your best bet for supplies is the local supermarket: the warehouse-style Pak 'n Save is cheap and found in most large towns and usually stays open until at least 8pm every day. The less common Big Fresh is also good with many products available loose in bins so you can pick as much as you need. Failing that, you'll notice a marked drop in scope and an appreciable hike in prices at the neighbourhood superette – IGA and Four Square are the biggies. Convenient corner shops (or dairies), stock the essentials, but along with shops at campsites, also tend to have inflated prices, more so if located in isolated areas or anywhere with a captive market.

DRINKING

New Zealand boasts many fine wines and beers, which can be sampled in cafés and restaurants all over the land. But for the lowest prices and a genuine Kiwi atmosphere you can't go past the **pub**, often known as a **hotel** from the days when all drinking establishments were required to have rooms for revellers to sleep off a skinful. The pub is a place where folk stop off on their way home from work, the emphasis being on consumption and back-slapping camaraderie, with ambience and decor taking a back seat. In the cities, where competition from cafés is strong, pubs are sharpening up their act and comfortable, relaxed bars are more common, but in country areas little has changed. Rural pubs can initially be daunting for strangers, but once you get chatting, barriers soon drop. Some pubs are still divided into the **public bar**, a joyless Formica and linoleum place where overalls and work boots are the sartorial order of the day, and the **lounge bar**, where you are expected to dress up and are charged more for the privilege.

There is barely any limitation on the **hours** you can drink, most bars shutting up around midnight on weeknights if it is quiet, more like 3am at weekends. Until December 1999, arcane Sunday licensing laws forbade the sale of alcohol in shops and pretty much anywhere else unless it was accompanied by a meal. However, on Sundays you can now buy beer as well as wine in supermarkets, and get a drink without eating. The **drinking age** has been lowered to 18 (from 20) and anyone looking under 25 can expect to be asked for identification.

BEER

Beer is drunk everywhere and often in New Zealand. Nearly all beer is produced by two huge conglomerates – New Zealand Breweries and DB – who market countless variations on the lager and Pilsener theme, as well as insipid, deep-brown liquid dispensed from taps and in bottles as "draught" – a distant and altogether feebler

relation of British-style bitter. Increasingly, Kiwi beer drinkers are turning to lager, especially their beloved Steinlager, which regularly bags international awards, as well as the newfangled cold-filtered and ice beers. There really isn't a lot to choose between them except for alcohol content, normally around four percent though five percent is common for premium beers usually described as "export".

To find something truly different, seek out **boutique beers** such as those brewed near Nelson by Mac's. Try their dark and delicious stout-like Black Mac, or wait around for the Oktober Mac, a light and fresh concoction brewed in September and only available until it runs out. Nelson's Pink Elephant brewery also produces a wonderful naturally brewed bitter of the same name which is delicious and packs a punch. Small, regional brewers and in-house micro-breweries are increasingly establishing themselves on the scene – look out for the *Loaded Hog* and *One Red Dog* restaurant/bars. Most bottle shops stock a fair range of foreign brews and the flashier bars are always well stocked with the best of international bottled beers – at a price. On tap, you will only find New Zealand beer, except for the odd ersatz Irish bar pouring Guinness. A good source of information about all things beery in New Zealand is *www.brewing.co.nz*.

Measures are standard throughout the country: traditionalists buy a one-litre **jug** which is then decanted into the required number of glasses, usually a **seven** (originally seven fluid ounces, or 200mls), a **ten**, or even an elegantly fluted **twelve**. Despite 25 years under the metric system, handled "**pints**" (roughly half a litre) have now become widespread. Prices vary enormously, but you can expect to pay around $4–5 for a pint. It is much cheaper to buy in bulk from a bottle shop where beer is either sold in six-packs or cartons of a dozen ($14–18); serious drinkers go for refillable half-gallon **flagons** (2.25 litres) or their metricated variant, the two-litre **rigger**; these can be bought for around a dollar and filled for $7–9 at taps in bottle shops.

WINES AND SPIRITS

Kiwis are justifiably loyal to New Zealand winemakers, who have made great strides in recent years and now produce wines which rank alongside some of the best in the world. New Zealand is rapidly encroaching on the Loire's standing as the world benchmark for Sauvignon Blanc, and there is an increasing band of fans for the bold fruitiness of its Chardonnay and the apricot and citrus palate of its Riesling. Certainly wine menus feature few non-Kiwi **whites**, but reds are often of the broad-shouldered Aussie variety. Nevertheless, New Zealand **reds** are rapidly improving and there are some very fine young-drinking varietals using Cabernet Sauvignon, Merlot and, the great red hope, Pinot Noir. A liking for **champagne** no longer implies "champagne tastes" in New Zealand: you can still buy the wildly overpriced French stuff, but good Kiwi Methode Traditionelle (fermented in the bottle in the time-honoured way) starts at around $12 a bottle: Montana's Lindaur Brut is widely available, and justly popular. The latest drinking trend is **dessert wines** (or "stickies") typically made from grapes withered on the vine by the botrytis fungus, the so-called "noble rot".

Most bars and licensed restaurants will have a tempting range of wines, many sold by the glass ($3–6, $8 for dessert wine), while in shops the racks are groaning with bottles starting from $8 ($12–15 for reasonable quality). Nowadays, the "chateau cardboard" wine bladders are considered passé, so do yourself (and your hosts) a favour and buy a decent bottle if invited to a barbecue or dinner.

If you want to try before you buy, visit a few **wineries**, where you are usually free to sample half a dozen different wines. Among the established wine-growing areas, **Henderson** and the **Kumeu Valley**, 15km west of Auckland, is one of the more accessible though its urban nature makes it perhaps the least appealing to tour. On the east coast of the North Island, the area around **Gisborne** is good for a tasting afternoon, but wine connoisseurs are better off in **Hawke's Bay**, where Napier and Hastings are surrounded by almost thirty vineyards open to the public. Further south, **Martinborough** has the most accessible cluster of vineyards, many within walking distance. The colder climate of the South Island effectively limits wine production to the northern part, though there are a few vineyards in **Central Otago** near Queenstown and Alexandra. The best though are in **Marlborough**, close to Blenheim, which competes with Hawke's Bay for the title of New Zealand's top wine region. A good starting point for information on the Kiwi wine scene is *www.nzwine.com*.

New Zealand also produces fruit **liqueurs**; some are delicious, though few visitors develop an enduring taste for the sickly sweet kiwifruit or feijoa varieties, which are mostly sold through souvenir shops. International **spirits** are widely available and their dominance is only challenged by a couple of South Island whiskies, the blended Wilson's and the ten-year-old single malt Lammelaw.

SOFT DRINKS

New Zealand coolers are stocked with just about every international brand of carbonated soft drink, but one home-grown brand to look out for is L&P – originally **Lemon and Paeroa** after the Hauraki Plains town where it was first made – a genuinely lemon-flavoured pop. **Milkshakes**, thickshakes (usually with a dollop of ice cream) and smoothies made with blended fruit are popular thirst quenchers, and almost any café worth its salt serves glasses of **spirulina**, a thick, green goo made from powdered seaweed and often mixed with the likes of apple juice and avocado. Advocates claim restorative properties when drunk the morning after a bender.

TEA AND COFFEE

Tea is usually a down-to-earth Indian blend (sometimes jocularly known as "gumboot"), though you may also have a choice of a dozen or so flavoured, scented and herbal varieties. **Coffee** drinking has been elevated to an art form with a specialized terminology: an Italian-style espresso is known as a **short black**; a weaker and larger version is a **long black**, which with the addition of milk becomes a **flat white**; **cappuccinos** come regular or chocolate-laced as a **mochaccino**; while a milky **café latte** is usually sold in a glass but sometimes in a gargantuan bowl. Better places will serve all these decaffeinated, skinny and even made with soya milk. Flavoured syrups are occasionally available, but are not common.

COMMUNICATIONS AND MEDIA

Communications services in New Zealand are generally first-rate, and excellent international networks make it pretty easy to keep in touch. The standard of media coverage sometimes leaves a little to be desired, but for the most part this is a well informed country with relatively sophisticated tastes.

MAIL

Post boxes are white, black and red and found everywhere, usually with some indication of when and how often their contents are collected. Most New Zealand towns used to boast rather grand Victorian or Edwardian **post offices** in or near their centres but these days the majority have been sold off and postal services are now operated from much less picturesque, multi-purpose **post shops** (Mon–Fri 9am–5pm, plus Sat 9am–12.30pm in large towns and cities).

The extremely efficient mail service operates two forms of **domestic** delivery: **Standard** (40¢, or 80¢ for larger envelopes), delivered to any destination within 2–3 days; and **FastPost** (80¢, or $1.20 for larger envelopes), delivered in 1 day from cities and 2 from rural areas. **International air mail** takes 3–6 days to reach Australia ($1.10), and 6–12 days to Europe ($1.80), Asia and the United States ($1.50), depending on where it's posted; prices are higher for larger envelopes. **Aerogrammes** cost $1.10 to anywhere in the world, as do air-mail **postcards**. Make sure you send your missives by air mail, or the recipients could be in for a long wait. **Stamps** are sold at some newsagents, garages and general stores, as well as at post offices and post shops. For further information, phone the NZ Post **information line** (℡0800/501 501), call into any post shop, or consult their Web site at *www.nzpost.co.nz*. There is also the competing National Post service (blue boxes) which is marginally cheaper but operates only within New Zealand and is best ignored.

One post office in each major town operates a **Poste Restante** service, where you can receive mail; we've listed the major ones in the "Listings" section of each town account, and you can get hold of a list of their addresses from the New Zealand Embassy or Tourism Board in your home country or any Central Post Office in New Zealand. You need a passport or other ID to collect mail, which is returned to the sender after three months – though if you change your plans you can get it redirected (at a charge of $7 within New Zealand, $10–20 internationally) by filling in a form at any post office. Most **hostels** and **hotels** will also keep mail for you, preferably marked with your expected date of arrival. Holders of an American Express card or travellers' cheques can have letters (not packages) sent to **American Express** offices, which will hold it for thirty days; addresses are given in the "Listings" sections throughout the Guide – and you can pick up a booklet of all their locations from any American Express office.

FAX AND EMAIL

Most post offices offer a **fax sending** service, charging a basic transaction fee of $2.50 plus a per page fee of $1.50 within New Zealand, $1.60 to Australia, $3 to North America and $4 to Europe and Asia. Faxes can also be sent from the vast majority of hostels and motels, and most hotels, but are not cheap, usually costing around $5 a page overseas and $1 a page within New Zealand. The average charge for receiving a fax is $1 a page.

Increasingly faxes are being supplanted by **email**, and almost everywhere you go in New Zealand you'll find someone offering **Internet access**. We've mentioned places in most town accounts but more are springing up all the time – visitor centres should be able to point you in the right direction. The best bet is usually one of the **Internet cafés** which continue to spring up all over the place. Rates are usually $2–3 for a fifteen minute session, $6–8 for an hour; the cafés often let you do a free email check, though they'll expect you to pay if you want to read or reply to any. In smaller towns, visitor centres sometimes offer Net access. Many backpacker hostels also offer access via a coin-operated machine, and the better B&Bs and lodges will usually allow guests to use their machine to check email; increasingly places have sockets so you can plug in your own modem-equipped computer. Internet access is less common at the cheaper B&Bs and still fairly rare at motels, though this will undoubtedly change very soon.

PHONES

There are two **phone companies** in New Zealand: the formerly state-run **Telecom**, which still has a monopoly on public payphones and local calls, and **Clear**, which competes for long-distance and international business. There is a huge discrepancy between the rates that apply to calls made from public and private phones in New Zealand, and if at all possible you should try to use **private phones**. On a private phone, depending on the type of line rental, local calls are either free or cost 20¢ for as long as you want. Long-distance and international calls from New Zealand cost between a third and a half the day-time rate when dialled outside peak hours (Mon–Fri 8am–6pm).

Public telephones are pretty easy to find. The most common accept both credit cards (Visa, Mastercard, AmEx and Diners; minimum call charge $2, 75¢ additional fee) and slot-in phonecards ($5, $10, $20 and $50), which can be bought at post offices, newsagents, dairies,

garages, visitor centres and supermarkets. You'll also see phones which accept these cards and coins (10¢, 20¢, 50¢, $1 and $2; no change given); and, rarely, phones which only accept coins.

COSTS AND CODES

A **local call** on a public payphone costs 50¢ flat rate. Calls outside the local area made during peak time are charged according to distance, from 40¢ to the maximum **nationwide** rate of $1.40 a minute; off-peak calls are half price. Any ☎0800 and ☎0508 numbers are a **free call** nationwide, and require no coins or cards. Calls to **mobile phones** (numbers prefixed ☎025 and ☎021) are charged at $1.20 per minute; calls to **premium-rated** information lines (prefixed ☎0900) cannot be made from payphones.

You can make **international calls** from any phone box, though it's a good deal cheaper using account-based phonecards (see below) which can be used on any phone. From a **public phone**, calls to Australia cost $1.80 a minute peak ($1.10 off-peak), to the USA, Canada and UK $3 a minute ($2.40 off-peak); international dialling codes are listed in the box opposite.

On a **private phone**, you can dial ☎013 before you make a national call (☎0160 for international) and the operator will call you back when you've finished to tell you the **cost**; however they will add $2.80 ($5–9 internationally) for the service.

There are only five **area codes** in New Zealand. The North Island is divided into four area codes, while the South Island makes do with just one; all numbers in the Guide are given with their area code. Even within the same area, you may have to dial the code if you're calling another town some distance away.

PHONECARDS AND CALLING CARDS

For **long-distance and international calling** you are best off with pre-paid **phonecards**, which come in denominations from $5 to $50. These can be used on any phone. To make a call you dial the access number, the card number and your password (you choose it when you first use the card) followed by the number you are calling; the cost of the call is then deducted from your account which can be topped up using your credit card. There are numerous such cards around offering highly competitive rates, but the two biggest players are NetTel (☎0800/279 666, *www.nettel-group.com*), and Telecom's Yabba (☎0800/922 224, *www.telecom.co.nz*). Both are

---

USEFUL PHONE NUMBERS

National operator ☎010 (additional $2.80 for collect or price-required calls)

International operator ☎0170 (additional $5–9 for collect or price-required calls)

National directory assistance ☎018 (50¢ for up to two numbers)

International directory assistance ☎0172 ($1.50 for up to two numbers)

Emergency services (police, ambulance and fire brigade) ☎111 (no charge)

INTERNATIONAL DIALLING CODES

To **call New Zealand** from overseas, dial the international access code (☎00 from the UK, ☎011 from the USA and Canada, ☎0011 from Australia), followed by ☎64, the area code minus its initial zero, and then the number.

To **dial out** of New Zealand, it's ☎00, followed by the country code (see below), then the area code (without the initial zero if there is one) and the number. Remember that there'll be a time difference between your country and New Zealand, which can be substantial (check out p.66 to avoid rude awakenings).

COUNTRY CODES

Remember to dial ☎00 first, then:

Australia: 61	**Netherlands**: 31
Canada: 1	**UK**: 44
Ireland: 353	**USA**: 1

HOME COUNTRY DIRECT

The **Home Country Direct** system enables you to talk to an operator in your own country and then to make a collect call (reverse the charges) or charge your call to a credit card.

Australia: Optus ☎000996, Telstra ☎000961 for Telstra.
Canada: Canada Direct ☎000919, AT&T Canada ☎000926.
Ireland: ☎000953.
Netherlands: ☎000931.

UK: British Telecom ☎000950, CWC ☎000940.
USA: Ameritech ☎000913, AT&T ☎000911, Bell South ☎0009011, Hawaiian Tel ☎000918, MCI ☎000912, Southwestern Bell ☎0009013, Sprint ☎000999, Teleglobe USA ☎000917, Worldcom ☎000910.

widely available through hostels, campsites, corner stores and visitor centres, and both offer similar rates (roughly 30¢ a min nationally and 30–50¢ to Australia, the UK and North America). Yabba's rates are usually slightly higher, but in compensation they offer an off-peak maximum per-call charge of $5 nationally, $10 to Australia and $15 to the UK, Ireland, the US and Canada. There are also **discount phone centres** springing up in major cities and popular tourist destinations, though rates are little better than those offered by the phonecards.

MOBILE PHONES

For sheer convenience you can't do better than a **mobile phone**, and it needn't cost the earth. If you're thinking of bringing your phone from home then you'll find both analogue and digital networks: check with your service to see if your phone needs adapting for use in New Zealand. A simpler approach is to buy a **pre-paid phone** when you get there. There is no account involved, just buy the phone and a pre-paid card which can then be topped up using your credit card. If you

are careful and make mostly off-peak calls it can work out to be very good value, though there is usually some clause which requires you to make say $10 of calls per month, which isn't hard to do. Telecom (*www.telecom.co.nz*) and Vodafone run the two networks and have outlets in main streets of major towns. They'll both sell you a phone for under $100, and (depending on the special offers at the time) you may even get a pre-paid card thrown in. Shop around for other features like text messaging and voicemail, and if you are planning to spend time in remote areas you might appreciate the wider coverage of Telecom's analogue network.

MEDIA

New Zealand has no **national daily newspaper** but it does have three pretenders: Auckland's *New Zealand Herald*, which can be found throughout the northern half of the North Island, Wellington's *The Dominion* which covers the rest of the North Island, and Christchurch's *The Press* which has widespread readership in the South Island. Each contains local and national stories, editorial comment and limited international news – usually gleaned from news agencies, with only a limited amount of original journalism. Of the three, *The Press* is probably the most highly regarded, though the difference between them is negligible. Most areas also have their own regional paper with extensive (and often entertainingly parochial) local detail but international coverage that ranges from fair to woeful. There are two nationwide **Sunday papers**: the tabloid *Sunday News*, and the broadsheet *Sunday Star-Times*, which usually has a few worthwhile articles, music and film reviews. Foreign weekly news digests (such as *The Guardian Weekly*, *The Weekly Telegraph* and one or two incarnations of the less esteemed UK tabloids) are reasonably widely available through newsagents and supermarkets, though most **international dailies** aren't stocked outside big-city specialist shops. The bigger city libraries usually have a good selection.

For more in-depth analysis of international news, pick-up a copy of *Newsweek Time* or *The Economist* **magazines**, which are all widely available in New Zealand. To keep abreast of Kiwi current affairs, pick up *The Listener*, which carries in-depth articles as well as international and national news, entertainment reviews, and TV and radio listings. Visiting **nature** buffs might want to take a look at the quarterly *New Zealand Geographic*, and outdoor enthusiasts should keep an eye out for the sporadically published *New Zealand Adventure*. To tap into the edgier end of the Kiwi fashion, music and arts scene, read the bi-monthly *Pavement*, a kind of Kiwi version of *The Face*.

TELEVISION AND RADIO

New Zealand has four free-to-air terrestrial **television** channels (all carrying a huge load of advertising and programme sponsorship) plus numerous subscription-based Sky TV channels. TV1 and TV2 are both government owned; the avowedly populist TV2 being somewhat balanced by TV1, which is slightly more high-brow and likely to become more so if the current government gets its way. **Reception** of TV1 and TV2 is pretty good throughout the country, something which can't be said of the two private channels; TV3, which pitches itself somewhere between TV1 and TV2, and TV4, which has less mainstream material – particularly comedy.

Finding your favourite programmes takes a little effort. Most of the more popular British and American comedies and dramas, along with New Zealand news and current affairs, can be found in prime time. Quality documentaries, serious discussion and even some relatively mainstream comedy can be shunted out to inconvenient timeslots. Sports and movie fans will probably want to stay in places that have Sky TV (most motels do), which also broadcasts dozens of international satellite channels.

The most informative radio station is Radio New Zealand's **National Radio** (AM band; *www.rnz.co.nz*), which gives an insight into the Kiwi mindset and concerns of the day; programmes focus on news, current affairs, talk shows, plays, book readings and short stories. Other stations that are widely broadcast include the jazz- and classics-oriented **Concert FM**, and a couple of vapid but popular talkback stations, **Newstalk ZB** and **Radio Pacific**. Most other stations are local, usually failing to penetrate the airwaves between towns. The staple diet here is current pop and classic rock, though **student radio stations** – in particular bFM (95.0 FM) in Auckland, Radio Active (89.0 FM) in Wellington and RDU (98.3 FM) in Christchurch – usually present a much more diverse playlist. Radio frequencies and reception vary throughout the country, so check for tuning details in *The Listener*.

OPENING HOURS, HOLIDAYS AND FESTIVALS

Opening hours have changed in New Zealand in the last few years, and there's now a marked trend towards Sunday opening in large towns and cities. However, the further out into the wilds you go the more conservative the opening times become, with many small towns being shut up tight from Saturday lunchtime until Monday morning. Holidays result in amiable mayhem, as Kiwis hit the roads en masse.

OPENING HOURS

Banks open Monday to Friday, 9.30am to 4.30pm, with some city branches opening on Saturday mornings (until 12.30pm). **Shops** are usually open Monday to Friday, 9am to 5pm, and until noon on Saturday. **Late-night shopping** until 8 or 9pm on Thursday and Friday nights is becoming more common, and many tourist-orientated shops are open daily until 8pm as a matter of course. In larger towns and cities, many shops stay open on Saturday afternoons and **Sundays**.

An ever-increasing number of **supermarkets** (at least one in or near each major city) now open seven days a week, 24 hours a day and

small "**dairies**" (corner shops or convenience stores) also keep long hours and open on Sundays. **Museums** and **sights** usually open around 9am, although small-town museums often open only in the afternoons and/or only on specific days.

HOLIDAYS

Christmas falls in the middle of summer in the southern hemisphere, during the school **summer holidays**, which run from mid-December until the end of January. The knock-on effects of this are that there are more people out and about, prices go up, and accommodation and travel can be difficult to book. To help you chart a path through the chaos, visitor centres are open for longer hours, as are some museums and many other tourist attractions. Other **school holidays** hit for a week in the middle of April, the second week in July and the first two weeks of October, though these have a less pronounced effect than **the main bout of summer madness**. **Public holidays** (see box overleaf) are big news in New Zealand and it can feel like the entire country has taken to the roads, so it's worth considering staying put rather than trying to travel on these days.

There are a number of **regional festivals** which celebrate characteristics of the area and are usually treated as a showcase for local businesses and artistic talent (the box overleaf lists some worth looking out for). Cities, towns and villages also take one day a year to celebrate the **anniversary** of the founding of their community. Although this isn't a good time to actually arrive in town, if you're there already, you can join in the shenanigans. Festivities usually consist of an agricultural show, horse jumping, sheep shearing, cake baking and best-vegetable contests, plus a novelty event like wellington boot throwing – all in the salubrious surroundings of the local A&P Showground and accompanied by the acrid smell of fried onions and the excessive consumption of alcohol.

HOLIDAYS AND FESTIVALS

All the festivals listed below are covered in more detail in the relevant section of the Guide; **public holidays** are in bold.

JANUARY
New Year's Day (January 1).
The Gathering, Golden Bay (three days to 1Jan), is a happening or rave fuelled by peace, loving, chemicals and booze, or so we're told.
Whaleboat Racing Regatta, Kawhia (January 1).
Public Holiday (January 2).
Mountain Rock Festival, Manawatu Gorge, between Palmerston North and Napier (second weekend).
Wellington anniversary day (January 22).
Wellington Summer Festival (January–February).
Anniversary day for Auckland, Northland, Waikato, Coromandel, Taupo and the Bay of Plenty, celebrated with a massive regatta on Auckland's Waitemata Harbour (fifth Monday in January or first Monday in February).

FEBRUARY
Nelson anniversary day (February 1).
Taste Nelson food and wine festival (first Saturday).
Garden City Festival, Christchurch (February 3–14).
Waitangi Day (February 6).
Hawke's Bay Harvest food and wine festival (Waitangi holiday weekend).
Marlborough Food and Wine Festival, Blenheim (second weekend).
Art Deco Weekend, Napier (third weekend).
Devonport Food and Wine Festival (third weekend).
International Festival of the Arts, Wellington, in even-numbered years only; roughly coinciding with this, the month-long Wellington Fringe Festival is held every year, and draws acts from all over the world (late February to early March).

MARCH
Golden Shears sheep-shearing competition in Masterton (first week).
Wildfoods Festival, Hokitika (second Saturday).
Auckland Round-the-Bays fun run (early March).
New Plymouth Festival of the Arts (throughout March).

Ngaruawahia Maori Regatta, near Hamilton (closest Saturday to March 17).
Public holiday in Dunedin, Otago and Southland, including Fiordland (third Monday).
23rd Otago and Southland anniversary day (March 23).
Taranaki Anniversary Day (March 31).

APRIL
Arrowtown Autumn Festival (week before Easter).
Good Friday and **Easter Sunday** (late March to late April).
Waiheke Jazz Festival; Royal New Zealand Easter Show, Auckland; Highland Games, Hastings (Easter week).
Gumboot day, Taihape (Easter Tuesday).
ANZAC Day (April 25).

JUNE
Queen's Birthday (first Monday).

JULY
Auckland International Film Festival (early July).

OCTOBER
Labour Day (fourth Monday).
Public holiday in Hawke's Bay, Gisborne, Marlborough, Nelson (one week after Labour Day).

NOVEMBER
Hawke's Bay and Marlborough anniversary day (November 1).
Guy Fawkes' Night fireworks (November 5).
Canterbury Show week (second week).
Toast Martinborough food and wine festival (third Sunday).

DECEMBER
Westland anniversary day (December 1).
16th Canterbury anniversary day (December 16).
Christmas Day (December 25).
Boxing Day (December 26).

OUTDOOR ACTIVITIES

Life in New Zealand is very much tied to the Great Outdoors, and no visit to the country would be complete without spending a fair chunk of your time in intimate contact with nature.

The lofty peaks of the Southern Alps are perfect for challenging **mountaineering** and great **skiing**, and the lower slopes are ideal for multi-day **tramps** which cross low passes between valleys choked with sub-tropical and temperate rainforests. Along the coasts there are sheltered lagoons and calm harbours for gentle **swimming** and **boating**, but also sweeping strands battered by some top-class **surf**.

Kiwis have long taken it for granted that within a few minutes' drive of their home they can find a deserted beach or piece of "bush" and wander freely through it, an attitude enshrined in the fabulous collection of **national**, **forest** and **maritime parks**. They are all administered by the **Department of Conservation (DOC)**, Visitor Information Centre, PO Box 5086, Wellington (☎04/472 7356, fax 471 2075, *www.doc.govt.nz*) which struggles to balance the maintenance of a fragile ecology with the demands of tourism. For the most part it manages remarkably well, providing a superb network of well-signposted paths studded with trampers' huts; operating visitor centres that present highly informative material about the local history, flora and fauna; and publishing excellent leaflets for the major walking tracks.

For some years New Zealand has been addicted to outdoor thrills and spills, and now promotes itself as the **adventure tourism** capital of the world. All over the country you will find places to go **bungy jumping**, whitewater or cave **rafting**, **jetboating**, tandem **skydiving**, **mountain biking**, stunt **flying**, **scuba diving**, in fact you name it and someone somewhere organizes it. The New Zealand DIY ethic reigns supreme and it sometimes seems as though every Kiwi in possession of a minibus and a mobile phone runs an adventure-tourism business. While thousands of people participate in these activities every day without incident, standards of **instructor training** do vary. It seems to be a point of honour for all male (and they are almost all male) river guides, bungy operators and tandem parachute instructors to play the macho card and put the wind up you as much as possible. Such bravado shouldn't necessarily be interpreted as a genuine disregard for **safety**, but the fact remains that there have been quite a few well publicized injuries and deaths in recent years – a tragic situation that's finally being addressed by industry-regulated codes of practice and an independent system of **accreditation**.

Before engaging in any adventure activities, check your **insurance cover** (see p.14).

TRAMPING

Tramping, trekking, bushwalking, hiking – call it what you will, it is one of the most compelling reasons to visit New Zealand, and for many the sole objective. Even if the concept sounds appalling, you should try it once; reluctant trampers are frequently bitten by the bug.

Tramps are multi-day walks, normally taking three to five days and following a well-worn trail through relatively untouched wilderness, more often than not in one of the country's national parks. Along the way you'll be either camping out or staying in idyllically located trampers' huts, and will consequently be lugging a pack over some pretty rugged ground, so a moderate level of **fitness** is required. If this sounds daunting, you can sign up with one of the **guided tramping** companies, which maintain more salubrious huts, provide meals and carry much of your gear, but at a price, details of these are given throughout the Guide.

The main **tramping season** is in summer, from October to May. Some of the most popular tramps – the Milford, Routeburn and Kepler – are in the cooler southern half of the South Island, where the season is shorter by a few weeks at either end.

THE TRAMPS

Rugged terrain and a history of track-bashing by explorers and deer hunters has left New Zealand with a web of tramps following river valleys and linking up over passes, high above the bushline. As far as possible, we've indicated the degree of difficulty of all tramps covered in the Guide, broadly following the DOC's classification system: a **path** is level, well-graded and often wheelchair-accessible; **walking tracks** and **tramping tracks** (usually marked with red and white or orange flashes on trees) are respectively more arduous affairs requiring some fitness and proper walking equipment; and a **route** requires considerable tramping experience to cope with an ill-defined trail, frequently above the bushline. The DOC's estimated **walking times** can trip you up: along paths likely to be used by families, for example, you can easily find yourself finishing in under half the time specified, but on serious routes aimed at fit trampers you might struggle to keep pace. We've given estimates for moderately fit individuals and, where possible, included the distance and amount of climbing involved to further aid route planning.

Invaluable information on walking directions, details of access, huts and an adequate map are contained in the excellent DOC **tramp leaflets** (usually $1 apiece); as long as you stick to the designated route, there's really no need to fork out for specialized **maps** (see pp.20–21), unless you're keen to identify features along the way. In any case, most trampers' huts have a copy of the local area map pinned to the wall or laminated into the table. In describing tramps we have used – "**true directions**" in relation to rivers and streams, whereby the left bank (sometimes referred to as the – "true left") is the left-hand side of the river looking downstream.

Eight of New Zealand's finest and most popular tramps (and a river journey) have been classified by the DOC as **Great Walks**; all are covered in detail in the text. On the North Island, the gentle **Lake Waikaremoana Circuit** (3–4 days) circumnavigates one of the country's most beautiful lakes; and the **Tongariro Northern Circuit** (3–4 days) takes in the magnificent volcanic and semi-desert scenery of the central part of the island. The popular **Abel Tasman Coastal Track** (2–3 days) skirts the pristine beaches and crystal-clear bays of the northern half of the South Island and avoids the difficult logistics of the **Heaphy Track** (4–5 days), which passes through the Kahurangi National Park, balancing sub-alpine tops and surf-pounded beaches. The tramping heartland is around Queenstown and Fiordland, where there are three magnificent, alpine Great Walks: the world-famous **Milford Track** (4 days) passing through stunning glaciated scenery; the equally superb **Routeburn Track** (3 days), which spends much longer above the bushline; and the **Kepler Track** (4 days), intended to take the pressure off the other two, but no less appealing for that. Finally, there's the **Rakiura Track** (3 days) on Stewart Island, conveniently circular and partly along the coast.

Great Walks get the lion's share of DOC track spending, resulting in relatively smooth, broad walkways, with boardwalks over muddy sections and bridges over almost every stream. In short, they represent the slightly **sanitized** side of New Zealand tramping and are sometimes disparagingly referred to as hikers' highways. This is somewhat unfair since, even on the busiest tramps, by judiciously picking your departure time each morning, you can go all day hardly seeing anyone.

Access to tracks is seldom a problem in the most popular tramping regions, though it does require some planning. Most tramps finish some distance from their start, so taking your own vehicle is not much use; besides, cars parked at trailheads are an open invitation to thieves. Great Walks always have transport from the nearest town, but there are often equally stunning and barely used tramps close by which just require a little more patience and tenacity to get to – we've included some of **the best of the rest** in the Guide, all listed under "Tramps" in the index.

BACKCOUNTRY ACCOMMODATION: HUTS AND CAMPING

Going bush needn't involve too much discomfort as New Zealand's backcountry is strung with a network of almost nine hundred **trampers' huts**, sited less than a day's walk apart, frequently in beautiful surroundings. They fall into five distinct categories as defined by the DOC, which maintains the majority of them, though all are fairly simple, communal affairs.

The simplest huts are the crude **Category 4** (free), mostly used by hunters and rarely encountered on the major tramps. Next up in luxury is **Category 3** ($5 per person per night), basic, weatherproof huts usually equipped with individual bunks or sleeping platforms accommodating a dozen or so, an external long-drop toilet and a water supply. There is seldom any heating and there are **no cooking facilities**. **Category 2** huts ($10) tend to be larger, sleeping twenty or more in bunks with mattresses; water is piped indoors to a sink – and flush toilets are occasionally encountered. Again, you'll need to bring your own stove and cooking gear, but heating is provided; if the fire is a wood-burning one, you should replace any firewood you use. More sophisticated still are **Category 1** huts (typically $14), though these are extremely rare as most have been converted to **Great Walk Huts**, found in the most popular walking areas and along the Great Walks. These tend to have separate bunkrooms, gas rings for cooking (but no utensils), gas stoves for heating, a drying room and occasionally solar-powered lighting. Most cost a modest $12–15 a night, though fees are substantially higher on the Milford and Routeburn tracks ($35), reflecting the extra costs involved in maintaining these fragile areas. In winter (May–Sept), these huts are often stripped of their heating and cooking facilities and revert to Category 3 status.

Hut fees are usually paid in advance at the local DOC office, visitor centre or other outlet close to the start of the track. For most tramps you buy a quantity of $5 tickets (valid for 15 months) and give the warden the appropriate number (one for a Category 3 hut, two for a Category 2 hut and so on) or post them in the hut's honesty box. You can sometimes buy tickets direct from wardens, but there is often a 25 percent premium on the price (60 percent on the Milford and Routeburn tracks). If you are planning a lot of tramping outside the Great Walks system, it may be worth buying an **Annual Hut Pass** ($65), which allows you to stay in all Category 2 and 3 huts; in winter it can also be used in the downgraded Great Walk huts. With the exception of the Milford and Routeburn tracks, having a ticket or an annual hut pass doesn't guarantee you a place: bunks are allocated on a **first-come, first-served** basis, so at busy times you may find yourself in an undignified gallop along the trail to stake your claim.

All the Great Walks operate under a separate system of **accommodation passes**, and in addition, the oversubscribed Milford and Routeburn tracks require **reservations** as far in **advance** as possible. The easiest way to do this from overseas is to use a booking agent or send a letter or fax, with payment, to the relevant DOC office (see Guide accounts of the major tramps), stating where you intend to spend each night.

Camping is allowed on all tracks except the Milford, and costs one hut ticket ($5) per night. Rules vary, but in most cases you're required to minimize environmental impact by camping close to the huts, whose facilities you're welcome to use (toilets, water and gas rings where available, but obviously not bunks).

EQUIPMENT

Tramping in New Zealand can be a dispiriting experience unless you're equipped for both hot, sunny days and wet, cold and windy weather. The best Kiwi tramps pass through some of the world's wettest regions, with parts of the Milford Track receiving over six metres of rain a year. It is essential to carry a good **waterproof**, preferably made from breathable fabric and fitted with a good hood. Keeping your lower half dry is less crucial and most Kiwis tramp in **shorts**. Early starts often involve wading through long, sodden grass, so a pair of knee-length gaiters can come in handy. Comfortable **boots** with good ankle support are a must; take suitably broken-in leather boots or lightweight walking boots, and some comfortable footwear for day's end. You'll also need a **warm jacket** or jumper and a windproof shell, plus a good sleeping bag; even the heated huts are cold at night. All this, along with lighter clothing for sunny days, should be kept inside a robust **backpack**, preferably lined with a strong **waterproof liner** such as those sold at DOC offices ($4).

Once on the tramp, you need to be totally self-sufficient. On Great Walks, you need to carry a **pan** or two, a **bowl** or plate, a **mug** and **cutlery**; on other tramps you also need a **cooking stove** and **fuel**, both available in New Zealand. **Food** can be your heaviest burden; freeze-dried meals (available from all outdoors shops) are light and reasonably tasty, but they are expensive, and many cost-conscious trampers just carry quantities of pasta or rice, dried soups for sauces, a handful of fresh vegetables, muesli (granola), milk powder, and bread or crackers for lunch. Also consider taking biscuits, trail mix (known in New Zealand as "scroggin"), tea, coffee and powdered fruit drinks (the *Raro* brand is good), and jam, peanut butter or Vegemite. All huts have a drinkable **water** supply, but the DOC advise treating water taken from lakes and rivers to protect yourself from **giardia**; see pp.17–18 for more on this and suitable water-purification methods.

You should also carry a basic **first aid kit**, moleskin to prevent blisters, **sunscreen**, **insect repellent**, a **torch** (flashlight) with spare battery and bulb, **candles**, **matches** or a lighter, and a **compass** (though few bother on the better-marked tracks). Don't forget your **camera**, and if you've an interest in New Zealand's flora and fauna you might also want to take relevant guides (see Contexts for some recommendations).

In the most popular tramping areas you can **rent** stoves, pans, sleeping bags and waterproofs. Most important of all, remember that you'll have to carry all this stuff for hours each day. Hotels and hostels in nearby towns will generally let you leave your **surplus gear** either free or for a small fee, perhaps $1 a day.

SAFETY

Most people spend days or weeks tramping in New Zealand with nothing worse than stiff legs and a few irritating sandfly bites, but **safety** is nonetheless a serious issue and every year there are cases of individuals failing to return from tramps. The culprit is usually New Zealand's **fickle weather**. It cannot be stressed too strongly that within an hour (even in high summer) a warm, cloudless day can turn bitterly cold, with high winds driving in thick banks of track-obscuring cloud. Heeding the weather forecast (posted in DOC offices) is some help, but there is no substitute for carrying warm, windproof and waterproof clothing.

Failed **river crossings** are one of the most common causes of tramping fatalities. If you are confronted with something that *looks* too dangerous to cross, then it *is*, and you should wait until the level falls (usually as quickly as it rose) or backtrack. If the worst happens and you get swept away while attempting a crossing, don't try to stand up in fast-flowing water; you may trap your leg between rocks and drown. Instead, face downstream on your back and float feet first until you reach a place where swimming to the bank seems feasible.

If you do get lost or injured, your chances of being found are better if you left word of your whereabouts either with a friend or with the near-

est DOC office, which stock **intention forms** for you to declare your planned route and estimated finishing time. While on the tramp, fill in the hut logs as you go, so that your movements can be traced, and when you return, *don't forget* to check in with your contact or with the DOC.

Animals are not a problem in the New Zealand bush. Kiwis never tire of reminding you there are no snakes, and there are only two poisonous spiders, very rarely encountered. You might stumble upon the odd irate wild pig but the biggest irritants are likely to be **kea**, boisterous green parrots that delight in sliding down hut roofs, pinching anything they can get their beaks into then tearing it apart. If you want to keep your boots, don't leave them outside when kea are around.

SWIMMING, SURFING AND WINDSURFING

Kiwi life is inextricably linked with the **beach** and from Christmas to the end of March (longer in the warmer northern climes) a weekend isn't complete without a dip or a waterside barbecue – though you should never underestimate the ferocity of the southern sun (see p.17 for precautions). Some of the best beaches (often stretching away into the salt-spray) are open to the pounding Tasman surf or Pacific rollers. Swimming here can be very hazardous, so only venture into the water at beaches patrolled by **surf lifesaving clubs** and always swim between the flags. For more on the dangers and how best to deal with them, read our box on p.117. Spotter planes patrol the most popular beaches and warn of any **sharks** in the area: if you notice everyone heading for the safety of the beach, get out of the water.

New Zealand's tempestuous coastline offers near-perfect conditions for **surfing** and **windsurfing**. At major beach resorts there is often a kiosk or shop renting out small dinghies, catamarans, canoes and windsurfers; in regions where there is reliably good surf you might also come across boogie boards and surfboards for rent, and seaside hostels often have a couple for guests' use.

SAILING

New Zealand's numerous harbours studded with small islands and ringed with deserted bays make **sailing** one of Kiwis' favourite pursuits. Kids are often introduced to the tiny "P Class" dinghies before they're riding bikes, and many grow up to own the yachts which choke the marinas for most of the year. Unless you manage to befriend one of these fortunate folk, you'll probably be limited to commercial yacht **charters** (expensive and usually with a skipper), more reasonably priced and often excellent **day-sailing trips**, or renting a small catamaran for some inshore antics along the bay. Most of what's available is in the northern half of the North Island with Auckland's Hauraki Gulf and the Bay of Islands being the main focal points.

SCUBA DIVING AND SNORKELLING

The waters around New Zealand's coast offer some superb opportunities for **scuba diving** and **snorkelling**. What they lack in tropical warmth and fabulously colourful fish they make up for with the range of diving environments. Pretty much anywhere along the more sheltered eastern side of both islands you'll find somewhere with rewarding snorkelling, but much the best and most accessible spot is the **Goat Island Marine Reserve**, in Northland, where there's a superb range of habitats close to the shore. Northland also has world-class scuba diving at the **Poor Knights Islands Marine Reserve**, reached by boat from Tutukaka; wreck diving on the *Rainbow Warrior*, from Matauri Bay; other good spots lie close to Auckland in the **Hauraki Gulf Maritime Park** and off Great Barrier Island. In the South Island there are the crystal-clear **Pupu Springs**, and fabulous growths of **black and red corals** relatively close to the surface of the southwestern **fiords** near Milford.

For the inexperienced, the easiest way to get a taste of what's under the surface is to take a "**resort dive**"with an instructor. If you want to dive independently, you need to be PADI qualified, which demands classroom instruction and a series of dives over a minimum period of a week. For more information, pick up the free, comprehensive, bi-monthly *Dive New Zealand* brochure from dive shops and the bigger visitor centres, or consult their Web site at *www.divenewzealand.com*.

RAFTING

Whitewater rafting is undoubtedly one of the most thrilling of New Zealand's adventure activities, negotiating challenging rapids (see box

overleaf for details of grading) amid gorgeous scenery. Visitor numbers and weather restrict the main **rafting season** to October to May, and most companies set the **lower age limit** at twelve or thirteen. In general you'll be supplied with all the gear you need except for a swimming costume and an old pair of trainers. After safety instruction, you'll be placed in eight-seater rafts along with a guide (usually perched on the back) and directed through narrow, rock-strewn riverbeds, spending an average of a couple of hours on the water, before being ferried back for refreshments.

Thrilling though it undoubtedly is, rafting is also one of the most **dangerous** of the adventure activities, claiming a number of lives in recent years. Operators seem to be cleaning up their act with a self-imposed code of practice, but there are still cowboys out there. It might seem to be stating the obvious, but fatalities happen when people fall out of rafts: heed the guide's instructions about how best to stay on board and how to protect yourself if you do get a dunking.

Each main island has its major rafting centre – **Rotorua** on the North Island and **Queenstown** on the South Island – each with an enviable selection of river runs from mildly enervating to heart-stopping. Less frequented but equally exciting rafting areas include Turangi on the North Island, and central Canterbury and the West Coast in the South Island.

In more remote areas, **helirafting** is common, with rafts and punters airlifted to otherwise inaccessible reaches by helicopter. This can involve a lot of expense and considerable hanging around, so make sure what you are letting yourself in for and be wary of extravagant claims – the water may be no more exciting than more accessible (and cheaper) rivers. That said, if it's a wilderness experience you are after then consider basing yourself in Hokitika, Greymouth or Karamea for the best West Coast rivers.

Rafts are exchanged for inner tubes to undertake **cave tubing**, which involves a generally placid drift through underground waterways, with the emphasis on exploration and viewing glowworms.

CANOEING AND KAYAKING

New Zealand is a paddler's paradise, and pretty much anywhere with water nearby has somewhere you can **rent** either canoes or kayaks.

GRADING OF RIVERS

Both rivers and rapids are graded according to the six-level grading system below, the river grade being dictated by the grade of the most demanding rapid. This lends itself to some creative thinking, and you need to take rafting company promotional material with a pinch of salt – a river hyped as Grade V might be almost entirely Grade III with one Grade V rapid. For maximum thrills and spills, the expression to look out for is "Continuous Grade IV".

I Very easy; a few small waves.
II A flicker of interest with choppier wave patterns. Dunking potential for inexperienced kayakers but no sweat in a raft.
III Bigger but still easily ridden waves make this bouncy and fun. Good proving ground for novice rafters.
IV Huge, less predictable waves churned up by rocks midstream make this excellent fun

but dramatically increase the chance of a swim.
V Serious stuff with chaotic standing waves, churning narrow channels and huge holes ready to swallow you up. Best avoided by first-time rafters but thrilling nonetheless.
VI Dicing with death; commercially unraftable and only shot by the most experienced of paddlers.

Sometimes this is simply an opportunity to muck around in boats but often there is some kind of instruction or **guided trips** available, with the emphasis being on learning new skills and soaking up the scenery.

Grade II water is pretty much the limit for novices, making the scenic **Whanganui River** a perennial favourite. Despite its riverine nature, the **Whanganui Journey** (3–5 days) operates as a Great Walk and special arrangements apply to access and accommodation (see p.53); several companies rent out all the necessary gear, often including the DOC hut passes as part of their all-inclusive price. Far shorter trips down similar water are run on the **Matukituki River** near Wanaka and the **Dart River** from Glenorchy.

Casual paddlers are much more likely to find themselves **sea kayaking** the near-landlocked harbours in Northland or the bays along the Abel Tasman Coastal Path; a perfect way to experience

New Zealand's magnificent coastline and to encounter dolphins and seals.

JETBOATING

The shallow, braided rivers of the high Canterbury sheep country posed access difficulties for run-owner Bill Hamilton, who got around the problem by inventing the **Hamilton Jetboat**. His inspired invention could plane in as little as 100mm of water, reach prodigious speeds (up to 80km per hour) and negotiate rapids while maintaining astonishing turn-on-a-sixpence manoeuvrability.

The jetboat carried its first fare-paying passengers on a deep and glassy section of the Shotover River, which is still used by the pioneering Shotover Jet. Over half a dozen companies now run similar deep-water trips around Queenstown, while at nearby Glenorchy there's a wonderful wilderness trip along the shallow and twisting Dart River. Other key sites include the Wilkin River at Makarora and the Waikato River immediately below Taupo's Huka Falls.

Thrills-and-spills rides ($60–70) tend to last for around thirty eye-streaming minutes, time enough for as many 360-degree spins as anyone really needs. **Wilderness trips** ($50–100) can last two hours or longer, pacing their antics.

BUNGY JUMPING, BRIDGE SWINGING AND RAP JUMPING

For maximum adrenalin, minimum risk and greatest expense, you can't go past **bungy**

WHEN IS A KAYAK A CANOE?

In New Zealand, **canoe** seems to be the generic term for any small craft, whether it be fitted with a closed cockpit – elsewhere known as a kayak – or of the open variety paddled with a single-bladed paddle, sometimes differentiated by the term **Canadian canoe**.

To further confuse matters, some rafting companies run small **inflatable** boats akin to **mini-rafts** and paddled with a double-bladed paddle, which tend to be called **kayaks**.

jumping. Not only is New Zealand the birth-place of commercial bungy jumping, it also has some of the world's finest jump sites – bridges over deep canyons and platforms cantilevered out over rivers. It is a complete head game; there's really nothing to fear but a massive rush of wind that lasts for ten seconds and a huge surge of adrenalin that can linger in the system for days.

The craze was kicked off by Kiwi A.J. Hackett who, after a spectacular and highly-publicized jump from the Eiffel Tower in 1986, set up the first commercial operation just outside Queenstown on the **Kawerau Suspension Bridge** (43m). Its location beside the Queenstown–Cromwell high-way, and the chance to be dunked in the river make this the most popular jump site, but there are now four other local sites, two above the Shotover River in **Skippers Canyon**, and a hand-ful of other sites around the country.

Wherever you jump, there'll be a boom-box cranking out Limp Bizkit or suchlike while they strap the bungy cord to your legs. You'll be fed the jocular spiel about the bungy breaking (it won't) or not being attached properly (it will be) then you'll be chivvied into producing a cheesy (or wan) grin for a camera or three before shuffling out onto the precipice for the countdown. A swan dive is the traditional first jump, but there is often a sub-stantial discount for second and subsequent jumps on the same day, giving jump veterans the opportunity to try The Elevator (just hopping off the platform, either forwards or backwards) or any number of variations. The pleasure is greatly enhanced by pre-jump banter and post-jump analysis, making the longer trips involving a drive into the site – the Skippers Canyon and Nevis sites in particular – all the more appealing. To show how brave you've been, this will all have been captured on video; there are also souvenir strips of used bungy cord to buy and a T-shirt, sometimes included in the jump package. **Prices** range from $90–150.

There have been a couple of injuries in the past but, on balance, bungy jumping is **one of the safest** adventure activities. The bungy cords are made from latex rubber (if it's good enough for condoms...) and only used 600 times, a quarter of their expected life. Some folk have been known to notch up over 1500 jumps without adverse effects, though bloodshot eyes aren't uncommon and there have been isolated reports of detached retinas and aggravated back injuries.

A couple of close relatives of bungy jumping have hit the scene in recent years. A couple of places are now offering **bridge swinging**, which involves a gut-wrenching fall and super-fast swing along a gorge while harnessed to a cable.

CANYONING AND MOUNTAINEERING

The easiest way to get your hands on New Zealand rock is to go **canyoning**, which involves following a steep and confined river gorge or streambed down chutes and over waterfalls for a few hours, sliding, jumping and abseiling all the way. This is currently only commercially available in a handful of places, the most accessible being in **Auckland, Queenstown, Wanaka,** and **Hanmer Springs**, though there are bound to be more places in the near future.

In the main, New Zealand is better suited to **mountaineering** than rock climbing, though most of what is available is fairly serious stuff, suitable only for well-equipped parties with a good deal of experience. For most people the only way to get above the snow line is to tackle the easy summit of **Mount Ruapehu**, the North Island's highest point, or pay for a guided ascent of one of New Zealand's classic peaks. Prime can-didates here are the country's highest mountain, **Mount Cook** (3754m), accessed from the climbers' heartland of Mount Cook Village, and New Zealand's single most beautiful peak, the pyramidal **Mount Aspiring** (3030m), approached from Wanaka. In both areas there is a compre-hensive system of climbers' huts used as bases for what are typically twenty-hour attempts on the summit.

FLYING, SKYDIVING AND PARAGLIDING

Almost every town in New Zealand seems to har-bour an airstrip or a helipad, and there is inevitably someone happy to get you airborne for half an hour's **flightseeing**. The best of these cross the truly spectacular mountain scenery of the Southern Alps or the ice-sculpted terrain of Fiordland, either from Fox Glacier, Franz Josef Glacier, Mount Cook, Wanaka or Queenstown. Half an hour in a plane will set you back around $100; helicopters cost around fifty percent more and can't cover the same distances but score on manoeuvrability and the chance to land. If money is tight, you could always take a regular flight to somewhere you want to go anyway. First choice here would have to be the journey from either

Wanaka or Queenstown to Milford Sound, which overflies some of the very best of Fiordland.

In **tandem skydiving**, a kind of double harness links you to an instructor, who has control of the parachute. After suitable instruction, the plane circles up to around 2500m and you leap out together, experiencing around thirty seconds of eerie freefall before the instructor pulls the ripcord. Again the Southern Alps and Fiordland are popular jumping grounds, and Taupo seems to be establishing itself as a low-cost and reliable venue, charging as little as $165 a shot; elsewhere $180–200 is more common though you may get more personal attention.

A hill, a gentle breeze and substantial tourist presence and you've all the ingredients for **tandem paragliding**, where you and an instructor jointly launch off a hilltop, slung below a manoeuvrable parachute. For perhaps ten minutes of graceful gliding and stomach-churning banked turns, you pay a little over $100; Queenstown, Wanaka and Nelson are prime spots.

SKIING AND SNOWBOARDING

New Zealand's **ski season** (roughly June to October or November) starts as snows on northern hemisphere slopes finally melt away. This, combined with the South Island's backbone of 3000m peaks and the North Island's equally lofty volcanoes, make New Zealand an increasingly popular international ski destination. Most fields, though, are geared to the domestic downhill market, and the eastern side of the Southern Alps is littered with **club fields** sporting a handful of rope tows, simple lifts and a motley collection of private ski lodges. They're open to all-comers, but some are only accessible by 4WD vehicles, others have a long walk in, and ski schools are almost unheard of. Conversely, lift tickets are only $20–40, queues are short and there's usually a gear-rental shop not too far away. Throughout the country, there are also a dozen exceptions to this norm: **commercial resorts**, with high-speed quad chairs (lift tickets around $55), ski schools, gear rental and groomed wide-open slopes. What you won't find are massive on-site resorts of the scale found in North America and Europe; skiers commute daily to the slopes from nearby après-ski towns. **Gear rental**, either from shops in the nearest town or on the field, ranges from around $30 a day for a full set of decent equipment to around $40–50 for the fancy stuff or for snowboarding tackle.

The best up-to-date source of skiing information is the free, annual **Ski & Snowboard Guide** published by Brown Bear Publications, PO Box 22630, Christchurch (☎03/365 4792, fax 365 4797, *info@brownbear.co.nz*). For each field it gives a detailed rundown of facilities, expected season, lift ticket prices and an indication of suitability for beginners, intermediates and advanced skiers. Heliskiing is also dealt with and there's brief coverage of the main ski towns. Their Web site (with the guide in downloadable, ready-to-print format), and the best starting point for all things skiing in New Zealand, is *www.snow.co.nz*.

The main **North Island** fields include the country's two largest and most popular destinations, **Turoa** and **Whakapapa**, both on the volcanic Mount Ruapehu, which erupted during the 1995 and 1996 seasons but has remained quiet since. The Southern Alps give the **South Island** a great deal more scope, with the greatest concentration of commercial fields being around Queenstown – **Coronet Peak** and **The Remarkables** – and Wanaka – **Treble Cone**, **Cardrona** and the **Waiorau Nordic Ski Area**, New Zealand's only organized cross-country site. Further north, **Porter Heights** and **Mount Hutt** are within two hours' drive of Christchurch, and the Nelson region is home to New Zealand's newest commercial field, **Mount Lyford**. All these ski areas are covered in the relevant chapters of the Guide.

At weekends and school holidays the tow queues at the major fields can become unfeasibly long, and the ideal solution is **heliskiing**. Guides conversant with the routes and skilled in reading avalanche danger take small parties onto virgin slopes high among the sparkling peaks of the Southern Alps. Provided you are an intermediate skier and are reasonably proficient at skiing powder you should be able to pass the ability questionnaire, but at around $500 a day it isn't for everyone. If you can't resist, places to consider are the usual suspects of Fox Glacier, Wanaka and Queenstown; in Canterbury, you can ski the wonderful Tasman Glacier from Mount Cook Village or get a taster from the Mount Hutt skifield car park.

FISHING

Kiwis grow up fishing: virtually everyone seems to have fond memories of long days out on a small boat trailing a line for snapper, if only to stock the beachside barbecue. All around the New Zealand **coast**, but particularly in the north of the North Island, there are low-key canoe, yacht and launch trips on which there is always time for a little **casual fishing**, but you'll also find plenty of trips aimed at more dedicated anglers. Most sea trips aim to land something of modest size with good flavour: snapper, kahawai, moki and flounder being common catches. Bigger boats might hope for hapuku, then there's a step up to the **big-game fishing** boats. From December to May these scout the seas off the northern half of the North Island for marlin, shark and tuna. This is serious business and you're looking at around $200 per person per day to go out on a boat with three others, but on the smaller boats, a day out fishing might cost as little as $60, with all tackle supplied.

Inland, the **rivers** and **lakes** are choked with rainbow and brown trout, quinnat and Atlantic salmon, all introduced for sport at the end of the nineteenth century. Certain areas have gained enviable reputations: the waters of the Lake Taupo catchment are world-renowned for the abundance and fighting quality of the rainbow trout; South Island rivers, particularly around Gore, boast the finest brown trout in the land; and braided gravel-bed rivers draining the eastern slopes of the Southern Alps across the Canterbury Plains bear superb salmon. Archaic laws prohibit the sale of **trout**, so if you want to eat some you've got to go out and catch it.

A national **fishing licence** ($65 for the year from Oct 1 to Sept 30; $25 for 7 days; and $13 for 24 hours) covers all New Zealand's lakes and rivers except for those in the Taupo catchment area, where a local licensing arrangement applies (see p.299).

Wherever you fish, the **rules** are taken very seriously and are rigidly enforced. If you're found with an undersize catch or an over-full bag, heavy fines may be imposed and equipment confiscated. Be sure to find out the **local regulations** before you set out.

HORSE TREKKING

New Zealand's highly urbanized population leaves a huge amount of countryside available for **horse trekking**, occasionally along beaches, often through patches of native bush and tracts of farmland; there may even be an opportunity to swim the horses. There are schools everywhere and all levels of experience are catered for, but more experienced riders might prefer the greater scope of full-day or even week-long wilderness treks. We've highlighted some of the more noteworthy places and operators throughout the Guide.

MOUNTAIN BIKING

If you prefer a smaller saddle, you'll find a stack of places renting out **mountain bikes**. For a quality machine, you might be paying over $40 a day, but for that you get a bike, a helmet and a headful of advice about local routes. The main trail-biking areas around Rotorua, Queenstown, Mount Cook and Hanmer Springs will often have a couple of companies willing to take you out on **guided rides** (the going rate is about $100 a half-day), usually dropping you at the top of the hill and picking you up at the bottom. For general information about the Kiwi **off-road biking** scene consult *www.mountainbike.co.nz*.

Mountain bikes aren't allowed off-road in national parks and reserves, and elsewhere you must respect the enjoyment of others by letting walkers know of your presence, avoiding skid damage to tracks and keeping your speed down. For more information, consult the specific biking guides available in New Zealand.

POLICE, TROUBLE AND HARASSMENT

Violent crime is still sufficiently novel in New Zealand that it is reported with relish by the media. As long as you use your common sense and don't drop your guard just because you're on holiday, you're unlikely to run into any trouble.

There are a few areas, like K' Road in Auckland, where it is unwise for **lone women** to walk late at night, and obviously the more isolated a spot the less chance of getting help but as long as you are reasonably careful you should be OK. Although this is by no means a rule, another area of difficulty for lone women involves taking up work in exchange for board and lodging **not** arranged through recognized organizations like the WWOOFing set-up (see p.36). Travellers pay good money for a number of different leaflets and booklets listing farms where people need help, not realizing that the only criteria for a listing, in most cases, is handing over cash. This means that single, unscrupulous types get promoted and you could find yourself stuck on a farm in the middle of nowhere resisting the unwanted advances of the randy owner, or being exploited by doing hours of heavy labour for a plate of beans and a shit-hole to sleep in. The point is that in such situations it's your word against theirs and they're the locals so you might not always get a fair deal even if you complain to the authorities. The best way to avoid this, if you want to taste the country life, is to stick with the WWOOFing booklet when organizing your trip and remember that although it's very good, even so it's not a complete guarantee.

The main source of crime in New Zealand is vehicles. **Car break-ins** are common in cities, or in car parks at the beginning of short or long walks, or even just on the roadside while you go to take a picture of a waterfall. Campervans are particularly vulnerable, since they contain all your possessions and make obvious and easy pickings. When you leave your vehicle, take your valuables with you, and put packs and bags in the boot or out of sight. If you have a particularly vulnerable vehicle, whether because of age or make, invest in a steering lock or in some way of beefing up the boot lock. When setting out on long walks use a **secure car park** if possible, where your car will be kept safe for a small sum. There is rarely any **stealing** in hostels apart from the odd case of mistaken identity when it comes to food in the fridge, although it doesn't do any harm to lock away stuff if you can.

Nude and topless **sunbathing** is not something you will see in New Zealand except at naturist camps and recognized nudist beaches. Assuming someone takes the trouble to complain, naked sun worshippers on a crowded public beach may even be arrested, and **topless** women may well find themselves being asked to cover up or made to feel uncomfortable. There are, however, hundreds of isolated beaches and beauty spots in New Zealand that are so remote you can pretty much do what you like.

☎111 is the free **emergency telephone number** to summon the police, ambulance or fire service.

POLICE AND THE LAW

The **police** are still perceived as friendly, mostly incorruptible and helpful which, generally speaking, they are. If you do get arrested, you will be allowed one phone call; a solicitor will be appointed if you cannot afford one and you may be able to claim legal aid. It is unlikely that your consulate will take more than a passing interest unless there is something strange or unusual about the case against you.

The laws regarding **alcohol** consumption in New Zealand are pretty lenient, and unless you are actively causing trouble, the police will give you a wide berth. The same does not apply to **drink driving** (see p.30), which is taken very seriously. Home-grown **marijuana** or "electric *puha*" (taken from the Maori, *puha* meaning watercress) has a reputation for being very potent and is pretty easily available. It is, however, **illegal** and although a certain amount of tolerance is sometimes shown towards personal use, the police and courts take a dim view of any tangles with **hard drugs**, handing out long custodial sentences. The general folk lore has it that all marijuana supply is handled by one of two warring gangs, the Mongrel Mob or Black Power, which is over simplifying the situation but it's worth bearing in mind that extreme violence erupts between them from time to time and in general it's best to avoid members of either group **Gangs** tend to be easily identifiable, most of them like to wear black, sport traditional tattoos and wrap around sunglasses, as well as seriously deficient hair cuts. Of course not all gang members look exactly like this but if you come across someone who does you probably wouldn't want to talk to them anyway.

PREJUDICE

Most New Zealanders welcome foreign visitors with open arms and, as a traveller, you're unlikely to experience overt **discrimination** to any great degree. There are few places in New Zealand where you will be refused service because of your race, colour or gender, although on rare occasions you may feel slightly **uneasy**. This can be the case for lone women in out-of-the-way **country pubs**, or for tourists who stray into predominantly Maori pubs. More often than not, the locals will be friendly but you might end up feeling like the cowboy who stops all the music and conversation when he walks through the door.

Despite constant efforts to maintain good relations between **Maori** and *pakeha* (Europeans), tensions do exist – inflamed by disproportionately high rates of unemployment and imprisonment among the Maori population. **Asian** immigrants, meanwhile, often bear the brunt of prejudice from both Maori and *pakeha* due to their high profile success in education and business and the perception that they are relative newcomers.

GAY AND LESBIAN NEW ZEALAND

New Zealand has in recent years become a broadly gay-friendly place, defying the odds in what has always been perceived as a fairly macho country. Certainly there remains an undercurrent of redneck intolerance, particularly in rural areas, but it generally stays well below the surface.

All this has partly come about in response to New Zealand's admirable recent history of resistance to anti-gay bigotry. Homosexuality was decriminalized in 1986 and the **age of consent** was set at sixteen (the same as for heterosexuals). The human rights section of the **legislation**, making it illegal to discriminate against gays and people with HIV or AIDS, was passed in 1993, with none of the usual exceptions made for the military or the police. There are officially no restrictions on people with HIV or AIDS entering the country; see "Health", p.17, for details of support organizations.

Such is the mainstream **acceptance** that the New Zealand Symphony Orchestra is quite upfront about one of its most prominent composers, Gareth Farr, doubling as a drag queen – though not mid-concert.

WHERE TO GO

This tolerant attitude has conspired to de-ghettoize the gay community; even in **Auckland** and **Wellington**, the only cities with genuinely vibrant gay scenes, there aren't any predominantly gay areas and most venues have a mixed clientele. Auckland's gay community celebrates its existence with a glam, over-the-top parade and associated revelry known as the **Hero Parade**. Perennially cash-strapped it isn't happening in 2000 but should re-surface in February 2001 for a two-week celebration of film, theatre, dance and sport that culminates in a street parade along Ponsonby Road and an all-night dance party.

Outside the festival season, places slip back into the groove of easy-going clubbing. Auckland's scene is generally the largest and most lively, but the intimate nature of Wellington makes it more accessible and welcoming. **Christchurch** has a small number of predominantly gay venues in the inner city and the fledgling **Freedom dance party** each February; and **Nelson** has a moderately active gay community centred on Spectrum,

GAY AND LESBIAN CONTACTS

Publications *Express* (fortnightly, $2.50; ☎ & fax 09/361 0190, *express@outnet.co.nz*), sold in almost any decent bookstore, graces the magazine racks of gay-friendly cafés and is often distributed free at gay venues; it is the best source of on-the-ground information and a good way to make contacts. Also keep your eyes skinned for the national bi-monthly *OUT!* ($5), and the Wellington-based *Lesbian Quarterly*. The *New Zealand Gay & Lesbian Guide* ($6) is available from R Harris, No2 RD, Palmerston, Otago (☎03/465 1742).

Travel information The non-profit *New Zealand Gay and Lesbian Tourism Association*, Private Bag, Auckland (☎09/379 0776, fax 303 4262, *secretariat@nzglta.org.nz*) provides travel information aimed at gay, lesbian and bisexual visitors, and vets businesses for standards of service and hospitality, working closely with the New Zealand Tourism Board. *Gaytravel Net*, PO Box 11–584, Wellington (☎04/384 1865 & 0800/429

872, fax 882 8246, *reznz@gaytravel.net.nz*, *www.gaytravel.net.nz/nz*) run a nationwide gay and lesbian accommodation and travel reservation service and also have a branch in Auckland.

Web sites One of the best is *www.nz.com/glb/* which gives direct access to all manner of gay, lesbian, bisexual and transgender information including a virtual gay tour of NZ and the *New Zealand Pink Pages*, essentially a collection of linked pages including what's on in the gay community and a calendar of events all over the country. Almost all sites of interest can be reached from here, though you may want to go directly to *www.hero.org.nz* for the Hero Festival, *www.womenz.org.nz* for the Auckland Women's Centre site with links to lesbian pages, or *www.our.net.nz*, an increasingly extensive site with easy access to hot-linked gay accommodation around the country, chat rooms, restaurants, travel agents and much more.

42 Franklyn St (☎03/547 2827). Elsewhere it is hard to find a gay network to plug into; even Queenstown is quiet, though this is beginning to change.

Out in the sticks you'll be relying on the gay press (see box opposite) to make contacts – unless you can time your visit to coincide with the annual **Vinegar Hill Summer Camp**, held just outside the small town of Hunterville, in the middle of the North Island, from Boxing Day to just after New Year. It is a very laid-back affair with perhaps a couple of hundred gay men and women camping out, mixing and partying. There's no charge (except a couple of dollars for camping), no tickets and no hot water, but a large river runs through the grounds and everyone has a great time. Around the same time Takaka hosts the broadly similar annual gay men's **Summer Camp**, which runs for two weeks from December 27 and draws around eighty gay men. Some camp on site, others stay at B&Bs nearby. Check the gay press for details – or just turn up.

WORK

Australians don't need to undergo any formalities to work in New Zealand, but just about everyone else needs a Work Visa: apply at New Zealand embassies or consulates before you leave home (see p.12).

But be warned: given persistent **unemployment**, these are almost impossible to obtain unless you have an offer of employment from a prospective employer who can prove there are no New Zealanders available to take the job. The only significant exception is the **Working Holiday Scheme** (details at *www.immigration.govt.nz/work/*), for those aged 18 to 30, which gives you a temporary work permit valid for twelve months. Four thousand Brits (plus 250 Irish citizens, 400 Canadians, 250 Dutch and assorted French, Japanese, Koreans and Malaysians) are eligible each year on a first-come-first-served basis starting on July 1, so apply as far in advance as you can: you'll need a passport, £30, evidence of a return ticket to New Zealand (or the funds to pay for it), and the equivalent of NZ$4200 (sponsorship from a New Zealand citizen is not accepted in place of this sum). Visitors who choose to work illegally run the risk of being caught in one of the periodic crackdowns.

Once in New Zealand there are plenty of opportunities for **casual** paid work, and in addition there are organized **work programmes** – both paid and voluntary. If you are thinking of working, one of the best contacts is New Zealand Job Search (☎09/358 4874, *jobs@acb.co.nz*) located at Auckland Central Backpackers, 16 Shortland St, Auckland.

CASUAL WORK

One of the main sources of casual work is **picking fruit** or related **orchard work** such as packing or pruning and thinning. The main areas to consider are Kerikeri in the Bay of Islands for citrus and kiwifruit, Hastings in Hawke's Bay for apples, pears and peaches, Tauranga and Te Puke for kiwifruit, and Alexandra and Cromwell in Central Otago for stonefruit. Most work is available during the autumn **picking season**, which runs roughly from January to May, but this is also when there are most people looking for work so you can often find something just as easily in the off-season. In popular working areas, some hostels cater to short-term workers and these are usually the best places to find out what's going.

Picking can be hard and heavy work and is usually **paid** by the quantity gathered, rather than by the hour. When you're starting off, the poor returns can be frustrating but with persistence and application you can soon find yourself pulling in a decent wage. Don't expect to earn a fortune, but in an eight-hour day you should gross $70–100. Rates do vary considerably so it's worth asking around, factoring in any meals and accommodation which are sometimes included.

Finding other types of casual work is more ad hoc, with no recognized channels other than newspapers, and hostel noticeboards; just keep your ear to the ground, particularly in popular tourist areas – Rotorua, Nelson, Queenstown – where people running **cafés**, **bars** and **hostels** often need extra staff during peak periods. If you have no luck, try your chances in more out of the way locales, where there'll be fewer travellers clamouring for work. Bar and restaurant work usually pays around $8 an hour and tips are negligible. **Ski resorts** occasionally employ people during the July to October season, usually in catering roles. The traditional $8 an hour may be supplemented by a lift pass and subsidized food and drink, though finding affordable accommodation can be difficult and may offset a lot of what you gain. Hiring clinics for ski and snowboard instructors are usually held at the beginning of the season at a small cost, though if you are experienced it is better to apply directly to the resort beforehand.

Your earnings will be taxed and your employer will require you to obtain a tax number: pop along to the nearest tax office with your passport and they should issue one on the same day. The tax department rakes in twenty-four per cent of your earnings and you probably won't be able to reclaim any of this.

WORKING PROGRAMMES

One way to reduce your travelling costs without transgressing the terms of your visitor permit is to **work for your board**, most easily achieved doing farm work through Willing Workers On Organic Farms (WWOOF; see p.36). No money changes hands, but in exchange for four hours work a day, you get free board and lodging.

The Department of Conservation's **Conservation Volunteer Programme** (*www.doc.govt.nz/commu/involv/consvol2.htm*) provides an excellent way to spend time out in the New Zealand bush while putting something back into the environment. Often you will get into areas most visitors never see and learn some skills while you're at it. Projects include bat surveys, kiwi monitoring and nest protection, as well as more rugged tasks like track maintenance, tree planting and hut repair – all detailed in a booklet available from DOC offices nationwide or direct from head office at PO Box 10-420, 59 Boulcott St, Wellington (☎04/471 0726, fax 471 1082). You can muck in for just a day or up to five days; for longer outings a small fee (around $60 for the duration, but sometimes as much as $200) may be levied to cover food and transport.

DIRECTORY

CHILDREN New Zealand is a child-friendly place: nearly every town of any size has Plunket Rooms, which can be used for changing nappies and sometimes host play groups; family rooms are commonly available in motels, and children are welcomed in most restaurants.

CIGARETTES AND SMOKING Smoking is outlawed on most public transport and in many public buildings, and smoking in restaurants is strongly discouraged if not banned. Cigarette advertising has long been outlawed and now sponsorship has gone the same way, with the cigarette-tax-funded Smokefree organization standing in where Rothman's and others have been ousted. Consequently cigarettes are expensive and best bought duty-free on arrival.

DATES New Zealand follows Britain's lead with dates, and 1/4/2000 means April 1 not January 4.

DEPARTURE TAX A departure tax (to be paid in NZ currency) is charged to everyone over the age of 12. If you are leaving from Auckland this is $20, while Wellington and Christchurch charge $25. This is occasionally included in the air-ticket price, but more often you have to pay at the airport; keep some cash handy or pay by credit card.

ELECTRICITY New Zealand operates a 230/240volt, 50Hz AC power supply, and sockets take a three-prong, flat-pin type of plug. North American appliances require both a transformer and an adaptor, British and Irish equipment needs only an adaptor and Australian appliances need no alteration. Suitable adaptors are widely available in New Zealand and at most international airports.

EMERGENCIES Dial ☎111

FLOORS What would be called the first floor in the US is the *ground* floor in NZ, the one above is known as the first, and so on.

GST A Goods and Services Tax is charged at 12.5 percent on almost all items and services and is included in the price quoted, except for some business hotels where rates will be clearly marked GST-exclusive. GST exemption is available on more expensive items bought at shops bearing the "Duty-Free Shopping" sticker which are to be sent or taken out of the country.

MEASUREMENTS New Zealand uses the metric system of measurements. Distances are in kilometres, petrol is bought in litres, and food is

METRIC CONVERSION TABLE		
	1 centimetre (cm) = 0.394in	1 inch (in) – 2.54cm 1 foot (ft) = 30.48cm
1 metre (m) = 100cm 1 kilometre (km) = 1000m	1 metre = 39.37in 1 kilometre = 0.621 miles	1 yard (yd) = 0.91m 1 mile = 1.610km
1 hectare = 10,000 square metres	1 hectare = 2.471 acres 1 litre = 0.22 UK gallons 1 litre = 0.26 US gallons	1 acre = 0.4 hectares 1 UK gallon (gal) = 4.55 litres 1 US gallon (gal) = 5.46 litres
1 kilogramme (kg) = 1000g	1 gramme (g) = 0.035oz 1 kilogramme = 2.2lb	1 ounce (oz) = 28.57g 1 pound (lb) = 454g

weighed in kilos (see conversion table on previous page if you're struggling).

PHOTOGRAPHY Film is widely available, but at a price – and processing is expensive, too. For transparencies, Fujichrome Velvia seems to be particularly good at capturing New Zealand's intense blues and greens and costs around $27 for 36 exposures, plus $15 for processing.

SEASONS Don't forget that in the southern hemisphere the seasons are reversed. Summer lasts from November to March, and winter from June to September, with a couple of transitional months in between that pass for spring and autumn.

TIME New Zealand Standard Time (NZST) is 12 hours ahead of Greenwich Mean Time, so at noon in New Zealand, it's midnight in London, 7pm in New York, 4pm in Los Angeles, and 10am in Sydney. From the first Sunday in October to the third Sunday in March, Daylight Saving puts the clocks one hour further forward.

TIPPING There is never an expectation of a tip, though reward for exceptional service is always welcomed.

CHAPTER 2
NORTHLAND

CHAPTER 1
AUCKLAND
& AROUND

CHAPTER 5
THE COROMANDEL,
BAY OF PLENTY
& EASTLAND

CHAPTER 3
WESTERN
NORTH ISLAND

CHAPTER 4
CENTRAL
NORTH
ISLAND

CHAPTER 6
POVERTY BAY,
HAWKE'S BAY &
THE WAIRARAPA

TASMAN SEA

CHAPTER 8
MARLBOROUGH,
NELSON &
KAIKOURA

CHAPTER 7
WELLINGTON
& AROUND

CHAPTER 12
THE WEST COAST

CHAPTER 10
CENTRAL
SOUTH
ISLAND

CHAPTER 9
CHRISTCHURCH &
SOUTH TO OTAGO

CHAPTER 13
QUEENSTOWN,
WANAKA &
THE GOLD COUNTRY

CHAPTER 14
FIORDLAND

PACIFIC OCEAN

CHAPTER 11
DUNEDIN TO
STEWART ISLAND

CHAPTER ONE

AUCKLAND AND AROUND

Auckland is New Zealand's largest and most cosmopolitan city and, as the site of the major international airport, is likely to be your introduction to the country. As planes bank high over the island-studded **Hauraki Gulf**, bright-spinnakered yachts tack through the glistening waters towards this "City of Sails". Indeed, Auckland looks its best from the water, the high-rise downtown dwarfed by the Skytower and backed by the low, grassy humps of some of the fifty-odd extinct volcanoes which ring the **Waitemata Harbour**. Beyond the central business district it is a low-slung city, rarely rising above two stories with prim wooden villas, each surrounded by a substantial garden, spreading off into the distance. As a consequence it is one of the least densely populated cities in the world; occupying twice the area of London and almost that of Los Angeles, it has barely a million inhabitants. With its attractive harbour, warm climate and the country's most exciting and vibrant cultural life, Auckland's fans rank it alongside Sydney, though it fails to live up to the claim on most counts. Look beyond the glitzy shopfronts and there's a modest small-town feel and a measured pace, though this can seem frenetic enough in comparison with the rest of the country.

Where Auckland stakes its claim to fame is as the **world's largest Polynesian city**. Almost twenty percent of the city's population declare Maori descent or are the families of migrants who arrived from Tonga, Samoa, the Cook Islands and other South Pacific islands during the 1960s and 1970s. Nevertheless, the Polynesian profile has traditionally been confined to small pockets, notably the nexus of **Karangahape Road** (universally abbreviated to K' Road), and it is only fairly recently, as the second generation reaches maturity, that Polynesia is making its presence felt in mainstream Auckland life, notably in the arts.

Auckland is often regarded very much as a transit place, and many visitors only stay long enough for a quick zip around the smattering of key sights before moving on to far less metropolitan locales. You could be forgiven for doing the same, but don't miss the **Auckland Museum**, with its matchless collection of Maori and Pacific Island carving and artefacts. With more time, dip into the country's strongest collection of New Zealand fine art at the **Auckland Art Gallery**, and delve into the perspex shark tunnels of **Kelly Tarlton's Underwater World**. Beyond these, the pleasure is in ambling around the fashionable inner-city suburbs of Ponsonby, Parnell and Devonport, and using the city as a base for exploring what's **around Auckland** – the wild and desolate West Coast **surf beaches** less than an hour's drive from downtown, and the **wineries** nearby. Ferries based in the centre of the city open up the **Hauraki Gulf islands**: the botanically and geologically fascinating Rangitoto Island, the sophisticated city retreat of Waiheke Island and the time-warped and isolated Great Barrier Island.

Auckland's **climate** is often described as muggy; it is never scorching hot, and the heat is always tempered by a sea breeze. Winters are generally mild but rainy.

AUCKLAND

AUCKLAND's urban sprawl completely smothers the North Island's wasp waist, a narrow isthmus where the island is all but severed by river estuaries probing inland from the city's two harbours. To the west, the shallow and silted **Manukau Harbour** opens out onto the Tasman Sea at a rare break in the long string of black-sand beaches continually pounded by heavy surf. Maori named the eastern anchorage the **Waitemata Harbour** for its "sparkling waters", which constitute Auckland's deep water port and a focus for the heart of the city. Every summer weekend the harbour and adjoining Hauraki Gulf explode into a riot of brightly-coloured sails.

There could hardly be a more appropriate venue for the **Americas Cup**, which was held in the Hauraki Gulf with great fanfare over the summer of 1999–2000 (see box on p.85). Team New Zealand's emphatic victory brings the event back to the Waitemata Harbour over the summer of 2002–2003, and with the infrastructure now firmly in place – there seem to be pavement cafés and trendy restaurants everywhere – Auckland seems set to consolidate its position as New Zealand's most progressive city. Despite Auckland's cosmopolitan bustle and harbourside setting, few fall in love with the city on short acquaintance or stick around long enough to scratch below the surface. Those who persist might just find themselves as enthusiastic about the place as Aucklanders.

Some history
The earth's crust between the Waitemata and Manukau harbours is so thin that every few thousand years, magma finds a fissure and bursts onto the surface, producing yet another volcano. The most recent eruption, some six hundred years ago, formed Rangitoto Island, to the horror of some of the region's earliest Maori inhabitants settled on adjacent Motutapu Island. Legend records their ancestors' arrival on the Tamaki Isthmus, the narrowest neck of land between the Waitemata and Manukau harbours. With plentiful catches from two harbours and rich volcanic soils on a wealth of highly defensible volcano-top sites, the land, which they came to know as *Tamaki-makau-rau* ("the spouse sought by a hundred lovers"), was the prize of numerous battles over the centuries. By the middle of the eighteenth century it had fallen to **Kiwi Tamaki**, who established a three-thousand-strong pa or fortified village on *Maungakiekie* ("One Tree Hill"), and a satellite pa on just about every volcano in the district, but was eventually overwhelmed by rival *hapu* (sub-tribes) from Kaipara Harbour to the north.

With the arrival of musket-trading **Europeans** in the Bay of Islands around the beginning of the nineteenth century, Northland Ngapuhi were able to launch successful raids on the Tamaki Maori which, combined with the predations of smallpox epidemics, left the region almost uninhabited, a significant factor in its choice as the new capital after the signing of the Treaty of Waitangi in 1840. Scottish medic **John Logan Campbell** was one of few European residents when this fertile land, with easy access to major river and sea-borne trading routes, was purchased for £55 and some blankets. The capital was roughly laid out and Campbell took advantage of his early start, wheeling and dealing to achieve control of half the city, eventually becoming mayor and "the father of Auckland". After 1840, immigrants boosted the population to the extent that more land was needed, a demand which partly precipitated the **New Zealand Wars** of the 1860s (see Contexts, p.850).

During the depression that followed, many sought their fortunes in the Otago goldfields and, as the balance of European population shifted south, so did the centre of government. Auckland lost its **capital status** to Wellington in 1865 and the city slumped further, only seeing the glimpse of a recovery when prospectors flooded through on their way to the gold mines around Thames in the late 1860s. Since then Auckland has never looked back, repeatedly ranking as New Zealand's fastest growing city and absorbing waves of migrants, initially from Britain then, in the 1960s and 1970s from the Polynesian Islands of the South Pacific and, most recently, from Asian countries. Rising with its head high after the depression years of the early 1990s, and a brief slump after the Asian financial melt down, Auckland is confidently leading New Zealand's renaissance as a modern nation, accepted on its own terms.

Arrival and information

As New Zealand's major gateway city, Auckland receives the bulk of **international arrivals**, a few disembarking from stately cruise ships at the dock by the Ferry Building, but the vast majority arriving by air.

Auckland International Airport (☎09/275 0789) is located 20km south of the city centre in the suburb of Mangere. The international terminal is connected to two domestic terminals – one operated by Air NZ, the other by Ansett NZ – by a shuttle bus (every 15min) but if you've a light load it is only a ten-minute walk. Before leaving the international terminal you can grab a free shower (in most toilets; towels $5), and if you've got a few hours to kill there are even single and double day rooms ($30/40 for up to 4 hours, $40/50 for longer) with bed, shower, TV and tea and coffee making facilities. The well-stocked and helpful **visitor centre** (☎09/275 6467) stays open for all international arrivals and will book you into a city hotel free of charge, or you can make use of the bank of courtesy phones nearby. There's also a branch of the BNZ **bank** which changes money at poor rates, and some **duty-free shops**, where inbound passengers can top up their quota.

A **taxi** into the city will set you back close to $40, but there are plenty of **minibuses** vying for trade after each arrival, and most offer discounts to backpackers in possession of a YHA or student card. The Airbus (every 20min 4.40am–8.30pm; $12 one-way, $20 return) follows a fixed route into the city (roughly 50min), stopping in Newmarket and Parnell. Other buses are more or less door-to-door services and charge around $18 for the first person to any one central destination and $6 for each accompanying person; for Devonport the rates start at around $35. Door-to-door services include Johnston's Shuttle Link (☎09/275 1234 & 0800/727 747) and Super Shuttle (☎09/307 5210).

InterCity and Newmans operate most of the **long-distance bus services** that use the **Inter City Bus Terminal** under Auckland's Sky City casino complex on Hobson Street. Northland's Northliner arrives at the Downtown Tourist Centre on Quay Street, opposite the Ferry Building, a site also used by many of the major tour bus operators and minor companies like The Little Kiwi who run services to Hamilton and Rotorua. For additional information see "Listings" on p.112.

Trains pull in ten minutes' walk east of the centre of the city at the station on Beach Road.

Information

Auckland's main **visitor centre**, 287 Queen St (daily 9am–5pm; ☎09/979 2333, fax 979 2334, *www.aucklandnz.com, reservations@aucklandnz.com*), though often crowded, is fairly efficient at booking and organizing pretty much anything you might want to do in New Zealand. It is often easier to get attention at the second **visitor centre** on the wharf close to the Maritime Museum, Viaduct Basin (daily 9am–5pm), which shares the same contact details as the former and is equally well stocked with leaflets from around the country.

Both visitor centres, as well as booking agents, hotels and hostels, stock a number of advertisement-heavy **free publications**; the best of which are the quarterlies, the *Auckland A–Z Visitors Guide* and the *Auckland What's On*. Both have sketch **maps** that are adequate for most purposes, or you could splash out on Wises' *Greater Auckland* fold-out sheet ($10).

The compact **Department of Conservation (DOC) office**, in the Ferry Building at 99 Quay St (☎09/379 6476, fax 379 3609, *jhart@doc.govt.nz*; Mon–Fri 10am–6pm, plus Nov to mid-March Sat & Sun 10am–3pm), stocks DOC material for the whole country but specializes in the Auckland and Hauraki Gulf region.

City transport

Auckland's public transport is in a sorry state and periodic moves to improve it are hampered by the city's vast spread and low population density. That said, you'll find you can get to most places **on foot** (see box opposite), by local **bus**, or with one of the city tour buses that shuttle between the major sights. Out on the harbour, **ferries** connect the city to the inner suburb of Devonport and numerous islands. **Taxis** are plentiful and can be flagged down, though they seldom cruise the streets and are best contacted by phone (see "Listings", p.114, for numbers). Few visitors will find much

---

AUCKLAND WALKS

The most ambitious walking normally attempted in Auckland is a stroll through The Domain or a more demanding hike up to one of the volcano-top viewpoints. The best of these have been threaded together as the well-marked **Coast to Coast Walkway**, a four-hour, 13-kilometre route straddling the isthmus from the Ferry Building on the Waitemata Harbour to Onehunga on the Manukau Harbour. By devoting a full day to the enterprise you can take in much of the best Auckland has to offer, including excellent harbour views from The Domain and the summits of Mount Eden and One Tree Hill, the Auckland Museum, Albert Park, and numerous sites pivotal to the development of the city. All is revealed in the free Coast to Coast Walkway leaflet, which includes an indication of where the walkway intersects with bus routes for walkers who want to tackle shorter sections.

---

use for the Tranz Metro suburban **train** services (for enquiries ☎0800/103 080), which start from the station on Beach Road and call at graffiti-covered and inhospitable stations in places that are low on most visitors' must-see lists; the two lines run south through Newmarket and Ellerslie, and west through Henderson then north to Waitakere. **Parking** isn't a major headache, but Auckland **drivers** aren't especially courteous and really you're better off renting a car once you're ready to leave the city. Hilly terrain and motorists' lack of bike-awareness render **cycling** an unrealistic option through city streets, but the situation is redeemed by a few dedicated routes.

Buses

The majority of **local buses** are run by Stagecoach Auckland, who also staff the Rideline **timetable** helpline (☎09/366 6400). The useful *Auckland Busabout Guide* leaflet is available free from visitor centres; other sources of bus **information** include newsagents and the Information Kiosk (Mon–Fri 7.15am–6.45pm, Sat & Sun 9.15am–4.45pm) at the **Downtown Bus Terminal** on Commerce Street.

The single most useful **route** is The Link (Mon–Thurs 6am–10pm, Fri 6am–11.30pm, Sat & Sun 7am–11pm; $1); these flashy white buses ply a continuous loop through the city, Parnell, Newmarket, K' Road and Ponsonby every ten minutes during weekdays and every twenty minutes in the evening and at weekends. Of the remaining services, city-bound buses will be marked "Downtown" if terminating at the Downtown Bus Terminal, or "Midtown" if ending their run at the corner of Victoria Street and Queen Street.

For buses other than The Link, **fares** are charged according to a zonal system: the inner city, Parnell, Mount Eden and Ponsonby are covered by one zone ($1.10 per journey), from the city to Newmarket is two zones ($2.20), Henderson is five zones ($4.50), and so on. You can save ten percent by buying a **Ten-trip Ticket** (price determined by the number of zones covered), which is also valid on the trains; for short-stay visitors, a better deal is the one-day **Auckland Pass** ($7 from bus drivers), which gives all-day unlimited travel on the entire bus network (including The Link) and includes the Devonport ferry. The same ground is covered with the **three-day Rover** ($17), excellent value if you want to get about a bit.

Tourist buses

To avoid dealing with complex timetables and numerous routes, you'll find it easier to get around the main sights on the hop-on-hop-off United Airlines **Explorer Bus** (☎0800/439 756, *www.explorer-bus.co.nz*; $20 1-day or $30 for a 2-day ticket), which runs every half-hour between 10am and 4pm, and comes with an en-route commentary. The

EXPLORING AUCKLAND'S WATERWAYS

Auckland is so water-focused that it would be a shame not to get out on the harbour at some point; and there is a welter of ways to do just that. The easiest and cheapest way is to hop on one of the **ferries** (see opposite), but for prolonged forays, consider one of the many **cruises** available; for a close-up perspective, a **sea-kayaking** trip offers a more intimate experience.

CRUISES

Fullers, of ferries fame, also offer a range of **inexpensive cruises**, the most useful being their Coffee Cruise Harbour Explorer (3 daily; 2hr; $20 all day) which tours the inner harbour calling at Devonport, Rangitoto and Kelly Tarlton's wharf. You can stay on board for the full circuit, or by starting on the earliest boat you can make two 2hr stops at two out of these three destinations, even joining the Volcanic Explorer to the summit of Rangitoto (extra charge; see p.124).

Romantics might prefer a trip **under sail** with Pride of Auckland (☎09/373 4557, fax 377 0459, *pride.of.akl@xtra.co.nz*) who are based at the Maritime Museum and run a variety of cruises with coffee or a meal served on board: try the City of Sails (hourly; 45min; $40), the Luncheon Cruise (1pm; 1hr 30min; $60), or the Dinner Cruise (7pm; 2hr 30min; $85).

On most **summer weekends** (though not over the 2000–01 summer) you can help sail the *Søren Larsen* (☎09/411 8755, fax 411 8484; Nov–March Sat 1–4pm, $49 & Sun 10am–3pm, $89), a Danish Baltic trader built of oak in 1949 and later fitted with a nineteenth-century sailing rig. This majestic vessel starred in the 1970s TV series *The Onedin Line* and led the First Fleet re-enactment that formed a part of the Australian bicentennial celebrations in 1987. Passengers are free to participate – steering, hauling sheets and climbing the rigging – though maritime instruction tends to be a larger component of the mid-week trips to Hauraki Gulf and Coromandel (2–5 nights; $450–1000).

KAYAKING

Several companies around Auckland will take you **kayaking**. One of the most popular trips is with Fergs Kayaks (☎ & fax 09/529 2230), kayaking the 7km across to Rangitoto Island (see p.124), watching sundown, hiking to the summit, then paddling back by the light of your torch, and perhaps that of a silvery moon (Oct–March daily 5.30pm; 5–6hr; $60). They also do day-trips to Rangitoto and both day and evening trips 3km to Devonport, stopping for a fish-and-chip supper (Oct–March daily 6pm; 4hr; $50).

The Devonport-based Little Adventure Co (☎09/446 6335, *www.littleadventure.co.nz, littleadventure@paradise.net.nz*) arranges less ambitious trips, guiding you along the coastline (1hr for $25, half-day $55, full-day $80), or on a twilight or moonlit tour ($50/40), while highly-regarded paddling trips with an ecological bent are organized by Auckland Wilderness Kayaking (☎09/813 3399, *www.nzkayak.co.nz, gowild@nzkayak .co.nz*), who offer half- and full-day paddles on the Hauraki Gulf ($50 & $95) along with night paddles ($60) and overnight trips (price dependent on numbers).

circuit starts from the Ferry Building on Quay Street and goes along Tamaki Drive to Kelly Tarlton's Underwater World, up to Parnell and the Auckland Museum, out to the Auckland Zoo and MOTAT, and back via Victoria Park Market and the America's Cup Village, and during the summer months (Oct–April) there's a second loop taking in Mount Eden and the Auckland Art Gallery.

If you're really pressed for time, and don't mind the highly structured nature of a fully-fledged **bus tour**, there are plenty of companies willing to oblige (see "Listings", p.112, for details).

Ferries

The Waitemata Harbour was once a seething mass of ferries bringing commuters in from the suburbs. Services have been rationalized over the years, but the harbour **ferries** remain a fast, pleasurable and scenic way to get around. The main destinations are the Hauraki Gulf islands (see p.123), but there are also services calling at Devonport and the Orakei Wharf, run by Fullers, the principal ferry company (℡09/367 9111, timetable information ℡09/367 9102, *www.fullers.co.nz, enquiries@fullersakl.co.nz*). The **Devonport Ferry** (daily 6am–11pm; every 30min; $7 return, bikes free) is the cheapest of the ferries, takes around fifteen minutes to cross the harbour, and forms part of the Auckland Pass and Rover (see p.73). To explore further afield, invest in a **Coffee Cruise Harbour Explorer** (see box opposite).

Driving

With many of the Auckland region's sights conveniently accessible on foot or by public transport, there isn't a huge advantage in having a car while you're in the city, though you'll need one to explore far-flung gems like the Kumeu wineries and the surf beaches of the West Coast. As the main point of entry, Auckland is awash with places to **rent a car** (see "Listings", p.113 for details of outfits in the city); and if you're planning on some serious touring, you may be interested in **buying a car** – see Basics, p.32, for some advice on the pros and cons, as well as the potential pitfalls.

With relatively tame rush hours, **driving** around Auckland isn't especially taxing, though drivers are sometimes aggressive and inconsiderate. On first acquaintance, Auckland's urban freeways can be unnerving, with frequent junctions and vehicles overtaking on all sides. If you are used to driving on the right, it takes that much longer to go with the flow; if you've just arrived after a long flight, consider waiting a day or so before driving. Inner-city streets are metered, which means that parking is best done in multi-storey **car parks** which are dotted all over the central city and reasonably well signposted; none are open 24 hours, so check the latest exit time – usually around midnight.

Cycling

Cycling around Auckland's hills can be a tiring and dispiriting exercise. However, a few areas lend themselves to pedal-powered exploration, most notably the harbourside Tamaki Drive east of the city centre, which forms part of a 50km **cycle route** around the city and isthmus – detailed in a free leaflet available from visitor centres. **Rental bikes** cost around $15–25 per day ($70–120 a week), depending on the sophistication of the model; see "Listings", p.112, for details of outlets. In addition, there are several companies that offer monthly rental and **buy-back schemes** for long-stayers (see Basics, pp.33-4).

Accommodation

Auckland has a broader range of accommodation than anywhere else in the country, but that doesn't stop everywhere filling up through December, January and February, when you should definitely **book ahead**. At other times this is less critical, and through the quiet winter months from June to September you'll be spoiled for choice and will find significant discounts on room rates, particularly if you're staying for a few days; it's always worth asking.

| **ACCOMMODATION PRICES** |

Accommodation listed in this guide has been categorized into one of nine price bands, as set out below. The rates quoted represent the **cheapest available** double or twin **room** – except for category ①, which are per-person rates for a dorm bed. Note that fees for **tent sites** and **DOC huts** (quoted in dollars) are also per-person, unless otherwise stated.

① under $20 per person	④ $60–80	⑦ $140–180
② under $40 per room	⑤ $80–100	⑧ $180–240
③ $40–60	⑥ $100–140	⑨ over $240

For more on accommodation, see p.34.

Perhaps more than anywhere else in New Zealand, Auckland is a place where you might choose to stay outside the **city centre**. Unless you have a mind to hit the clubs or have arrangements to make in the centre, you may have little cause to spend much time there, and sightseeing can be done just as easily from the **suburbs**. Inner-city suburbs such as **Parnell**, 2km east of the centre; **Ponsonby**, a similar distance west of the centre; **Mount Eden**, 2km south of the central city; and peaceful and salubrious **Devonport**, a short ferry journey across the harbour, all make excellent alternatives. Besides, all four suburbs are well supplied with places to eat and drink, Ponsonby and Parnell's main streets ranking as the city's most vibrant.

The city centre remains the place to find international four- and five-star **hotels**, mostly geared towards business travellers and tour groups; walk-in rates are usually prohibitively high, though there are sometimes tempting weekend deals. Backpacker **hostels** also congregate in the city centre inner suburbs, particularly Parnell; **B&Bs** and **guesthouses** are strongest in Devonport and the southern suburbs of Epsom and Remuera; and the widest selection of **motels** is just south of Newmarket in Epsom.

Predictably, **campsites** are much further out.

Hotels and motels

As befits New Zealand's largest city, the range of **hotels** and **motels** is second to none. Hotels pepper the city centre and inner suburbs, ranging from places little more salubrious than the hostels up to swanky five-star affairs. High city rents force motels further out and you'll see them just about everywhere, but nowhere more so than the stretch of Great South Road in Epsom, immediately south of the Newmarket shops, where there are at least a dozen places in a kilometre. We've stuck to recommending places that are relatively convenient to the centre and the main sights.

City centre

All the following hotels and motels are marked on the map opposite.

Aspen Lodge, 62 Emily Place (☎09/379 6698, fax 377 7625, *www.spenlidge.co.nz, aspenlodge@xtra.co.nz*). Compact hotel right in the heart of the city but surprisingly quiet and with a small garden and deck. Rooms aren't big and don't have private facilities but it's great value and a continental breakfast is included. ④.

City Life, 171 Queen St (☎09/379 9222 & 0800/368 888, fax 379 9223, *reser@dynpac.co.nz*). Classy modern high-rise hotel where suites come equipped with full kitchens, a separate living room, stereo, video, and even a washer and drier. Standard rooms are simpler but still very tastefully done. Rooms ⑧, suites ⑧–⑨.

De Brett, 2 High St, at cnr with Shortland St (☎09/377 2389, fax 377 2391, *www.acb.co.nz/debrett, debrett@acb.co.nz*). Built in the Thirties, this international-standard hotel still retains some Art-Deco features in the public areas and en-suite rooms which are modernized but slightly faded. A continental breakfast is included in the price. ⑤.

First Imperial, 131–139 Hobson St (☎09/355 1500, fax 357 6793, *www.firstimperial.co.nz, res@firstimperial.co.nz*). Spacious, modern and surprisingly quiet business hotel with on-site bar and restaurant and quality rooms, all with private facilities and some with good harbour views. Rooms ⑦, apartments. ⑧.

Heritage, 35 Hobson St (☎09/379 8553 & 0800/368 888, fax 379 8554, *res.heritageak@dynasty.co.nz*). Top class hotel fashioned from the original Farmers department store – once the city's grandest. Occasional bits of aged planking and wooden supports crop up in public areas, but it has had a major refit to a very high standard and many rooms have views across the harbour or into the glassed-in atrium. There's tennis courts, a health club, and indoor and outside pools, the latter with views over the city rooftops. ⑧–⑨.

Kiwi International, 411 Queen St (☎09/379 6487 & 0800/100 411, fax 379 6496, *kiwihotel@xtra.co.nz*). A rather characterless and ageing warren of rooms that compensates with off-street parking and low rates. The standard rooms are fairly comfortable, economy rooms come without a bathroom and there are bunks in dorms, though no self-catering facilities. Dorms ①, economy rooms ③, standard rooms ⑤.

Park Towers, 3 Scotia Place (☎09/309 2800 & 0800/809 377, fax 302 1964, *parktowr@ihug.co.nz*). One of the best-value hotels in the city with smallish modern rooms, many having expansive views. There's the full range of hotel facilities including bar, brasserie and off-street parking. ⑥.

AIRPORT ACCOMMODATION

With a choice of several efficient door-to-door shuttle services into central Auckland there is little reason to stay near the airport except if you arrive at midnight or have a hideously early flight to catch. There is no accommodation actually at the airport site, but a dozen places line Kirkbride Road in Mangere, some 5km away at the end of the approach road and close to many of the car-rental pick-up points. All the places listed below provide their own free shuttle service to the airport (either on a fixed schedule or to order), and have a freephone at the airport: just give them a call and they'll pick you up. Alternatively, a taxi will cost $12–15. There isn't much of interest around the airport hotels, but the better hotels have bars and restaurants, and there are couple of cheap restaurants and takeaways nearby.

Airport Pensione, 1 Westney Rd (☎ & fax 09/275 0533). Nine rooms (some en suite) in a converted suburban house well placed for the airport and with a continental breakfast thrown in with the very reasonable price. ③.

Jet Inn, 63 Westney Rd (☎09/275 4100 & 0800/538 466, fax 275 3291, *reservations@jetinn.co.nz*). New business hotel with all the expected facilities – Sky TV, minibars, lovely outdoor pool – and décor attractively supplemented with traditional arts and crafts from the owners' native South Africa. Rates include a continental breakfast in the hotel restaurant. ⑥.

Pacific Inn, 210 Kirkbride Rd (☎09/275 1129 & 0800/504 800, fax 275 1128, *info@ pacific-mn.co.nz*). Somewhat run-down but reasonably priced hotel with fairly spacious studio rooms, TV and tea- and coffee-making facilities, and a restaurant and bar downstairs. ④.

Skyway Lodge, 30 Kirkbride Rd (☎09/275 4443, fax 275 5012, *skyway@ihug.co.nz*). Several grades of budget accommodation in friendly and relaxed surroundings with a refreshing pool, guests' kitchen and free luggage storage. Accommodation is in 4-bunk dorms, double and twin rooms and self-catering motel units. Dorms ①, doubles ③, en-suite doubles & units ④.

Sky City, cnr Victoria St & Federal St (☎09/912 6000 & 0800/777 711, fax 912 6032, *www.skycity.co.nz*). Part of the casino complex, with all the facilities that entails: rooftop pool, gym, sauna, bars and restaurants. Rooms are standard, international-hotel style but nicely done, many with good harbour views. Rack rates start high and rise through the stratosphere, but walk-in rates (including breakfast and valet parking) are often lower, especially at weekends and in the winter. Specials ⑧, otherwise ⑨.

Whitaker Lodge, 21 Whitaker Place (☎09/377 3623, fax 377 3621, *kmclaren@clear.net.nz*). Very central motel tucked down in Grafton Gully and right by the motorway but surprisingly appealing. Choice of smallish rooms without cooking facilities or regular motel units. Rooms ⑤, units ⑥.

Parnell
All the following hotels and motels are marked on the map on p.105.

Parnell Inn, 320 Parnell Rd (☎09/358 0642, fax 367 1032, *parnelin@ihug.co.nz*). Compact and simple hotel attached to *The Other Side* café right in the heart of Parnell. Rooms are fairly small, some having cooking facilities, and off-street parking is available. ⑤.

Parnell Rise, 73 Parnell Rd (☎09/358 1178, fax 357 0518, *parnell.motel@xtra.co.nz*). Ageing but functional, clean and super-cheap motel right in Parnell and an easy walk from the city. ④.

Parnell Village, 2 St Stephen's Ave (☎09/377 1463, fax 373 4192, *parnellvillage@clear.net.nz*). Well maintained motor inn opposite the cathedral with studios and large one- and two-bedroom self-catering units. Studios ⑤, units ⑥.

Epsom
All the following hotels and motels are marked on the map opposite.

Green Park, 66 Great South Rd (☎09/520 3038, fax 520 1384, *green.park@xtra.co.nz*). Renovated motel with standard and executive suites, all with separate bedrooms and full facilities. ⑤–⑥.

Hansen's, 96 Great South Rd (☎09/520 2804, fax 524 7597). One of the cheapest motels in town with small but perfectly formed self-contained studios and a nice swimming pool. ④.

Newmarket Motel off Broadway, 11 Alpers Ave (☎09/529 3550, fax 529 3551). Business-orientated hotel with air-conditioned, soundproofed en-suite rooms. Plump for the much larger suites if your budget allows. Studios ⑥–⑦, suites ⑧.

Siesta, 70 Great South Rd (☎09/520 2107, fax 522 4413, *siesta@newnet.co.nz*). Good modern motel with kitchenless studios and self-catering units. Studios ④, units ⑤.

Tudor Court, 108 Great South Rd (☎09/523 1069, fax 523 3970, *stayattudor@tudor.co.nz*). Compact motel with small hotel-style rooms and slightly larger ones with kitchenettes. ④.

Ponsonby, Herne Bay and Freeman's Bay

All the following hotels and motels are marked on the map on p.106.

Abaco Spa, 59 Jervois Rd (☎09/376 0119 & 0800/220 066, fax 378 7937, *abacospa@xtra.co.nz*). Mainstream motel close to Herne Bay and Ponsonby shops and restaurants, with budget kitchenless rooms, and larger motel units, some with private spas and distant harbour views. Budget rooms ④, units ⑥.

Harbour Bridge, 6 Tweed St (☎09/376 3489, fax 378 6592). Excellent-value modern motel units based around a century-old house with a peaceful garden and located in a quiet street. ⑤.

Unicorn, 31 Shelley Beach Rd (☎09/376 2067, fax 376 0685, *unicorn.motel@pin.co.nz*). Top-quality, modern, air-conditioned motel with spacious fully-equipped units; there's a private spa and a pool. ⑥.

B&Bs and guesthouses

Auckland's stock of B&Bs and guesthouses is rapidly expanding. New places are continually opening, many pitching for the upper end of the market, with just a few rooms and an almost obsessive attention to the finest detail. Places are scattered widely around the **inner suburbs** on the south side of the harbour, but in recent years the choice in the North Shore suburb of **Devonport** has mushroomed. At last count there were over two dozen high-standard places, not all of them close to the ferry but all willing to pick up and drop off if you arrive that way. Note that airport shuttle buses will drop you in Devonport for only a few dollars more than the central Auckland fare.

> ### GAY-FRIENDLY ACCOMMODATION
> Although Auckland doesn't have any exclusively gay or lesbian hotels, neither does it have a reputation for homophobic proprietors, so you can stay pretty much where you like. There is, however, some gay-friendly accommodation, including *Aspen Lodge*, a compact **hotel** in the city centre, and several small **guesthouses**: check out *Bavaria B&B* in Mount Eden; *The Great Ponsonby B&B* in Ponsonby; and *Herne Bay B&B* in Herne Bay – all reviewed in our main "B&Bs and guesthouses" listings, starting below.

Parnell
All the following guesthouses are marked on the map on p.105.

Chalet Chevron, 14 Brighton Rd, Parnell (☎09/309 0291, fax 373 5754, *chaletchevron@xtra.co.nz*). Comfortable B&B with cheery and colourful en-suite rooms, some with distant sea views, and several well geared for singles. A full breakfast is served and there's free tea and coffee all day. ⑥.

St Georges Bay Lodge, 43 St Georges Bay Rd, Parnell (☎09/303 1050, fax 303 1055, *enquiry @stgeorge.co.nz*). Gorgeous and welcoming B&B in one of the four original St Georges Bay villas, built in the 1890s and since tastefully and authentically renovated, fitted out in native timbers and hung with New Zealand artworks. Complimentary port and wine, and a full breakfast are all part of the package. ⑧.

Mount Eden, Epsom and Remuera
All the following guesthouses are marked on the map on p.79.

Aachen House, 39 Market Rd, Remuera (☎09/520 2329 & 0800/222 436, fax 524 2898, *www.aachenhouse.co.nz, info@aachenhouse.co.nz*). Elegant boutique B&B in an Edwardian house sumptuously decorated with antiques. Every comfort is catered for: rooms are spacious, beds are huge, bathrooms are beautifully tiled and breakfasts are delicious. ⑧.

Bavaria, 83 Valley Rd, Mount Eden (☎09/638 9641, fax 638 9665, *bavaria@xtra.co.nz*). Spacious, comfortable ninety-year-old B&B villa that's popular with German speakers, and boasts a pleasant deck and garden. Buses numbered in the 250s and 260s run along Dominion Road close by. ⑥.

Pentlands, 22 Pentlands Ave, Mount Eden (☎ & fax 09/638 7031, *www.pentland.co.nz, hoppy. pentland@xtra.co.nz*). Peaceful, low-cost B&B ten minutes' walk from Mount Eden shops with plain bathless rooms but spacious lounges and a tennis court and barbecue area out back. Continental breakfast is served. ④.

Taurima, 18 Epsom Ave, Epsom (☎ & fax 09/630 7710, *tychen@ihug.co.nz*). Friendly B&B in an attractive suburban villa fifteen minutes' walk from Mount Eden and Newmarket. Only one of the rooms and the self-catering cottage in the garden are en suite, but all are nicely decorated and a formidable cooked breakfast is served. ⑤.

Devonport
All the following guesthouses are marked on the map on p.98.

Cheltenham-by-the-Sea, 2 Grove Rd (☎09/445 9437, fax 445 9432, *mossman@clear.net.nz*). One of Devonport's cheapest B&Bs, right by Cheltenham Beach, twenty minutes' walk from the ferry. Rooms are spacious and simple, in a comfortable, modern home run by friendly folk. ⑤, en suite ⑥.

Devonport Villa, 46 Tainui Rd (☎09/445 8397, fax 445 9766, *dvilla@ihug.co.nz*). Luxurious, top-class B&B near Cheltenham Beach in a lovingly restored Edwardian villa decorated with contemporary Kiwi art. There's a tastefully restrained feel to both the very comfortable en-suite rooms in the house and the colonial style cottages in the garden. Sumptuous breakfasts are served. Queen rooms ⑧, king suites ⑨.

The Garden Room, 23 Cheltenham Rd (☎ & fax 09/445 2472, *b.hall@clear.net.nz*). One room inside the house and a lovely private cottage in a leafy garden, all done to a very high standard; sumptuous breakfasts can be served under an arbour or in your room. ⑥.

Karin's Garden Villa, 14 Sinclair St (☎ & fax 09/445 8689, *homepages.ihug.co.nz/~karins*, *karins@ihug.co.nz*). Very good-value B&B with a self-catering kitchen and pleasant rooms, some with private verandas overlooking the large garden. It is all run by a personable German woman who injects a warm, communal atmosphere. Continental breakfast is served, it is only fifteen minutes' walk from the ferry and there is Internet access. Rooms ⑥, s/c cottage ⑦.

Peace and Plenty Inn, 6 Flagstaff Terrace (☎09/445 2925, fax 445 2901, *nz.com/heritaeinns/peace&plenty*, *peaceandplenty@xtra.co.nz*). One of New Zealand's finest B&Bs. Elegantly restored kauri floorboards lead through to a lovely veranda, past exquisite rooms filled with fresh flowers and equipped with sherry and port. If you can bear to venture outside the bounds of the inn, you're right in the heart of Devonport. The communal breakfast is a major event, and the hosts will even take you sailing. ⑧.

Villa Cambria, 71 Vauxhall Rd (☎09/445 7899, fax 446 0508, *www.villacambria.co.nz*, *villacambria@xtra.co.nz*). Beautifully decorated Victorian villa close to Cheltenham beach and fifteen minutes' walk from Devonport with friendly and attentive hosts who provide lovely breakfasts and are relaxed enough to refer to their guests as inn-mates. All rooms en suite with complimentary port. Rooms ⑦, large loft room ⑧.

Ponsonby and Herne Bay
All the following guesthouses are marked on the map on p.106.

Freeman's B&B, 65 Wellington St, Ponsonby (☎09/376 5046, fax 376 4052). Good-value B&B well-placed midway between the city and Ponsonby with doubles, spacious self-contained apartments (without breakfast) and a secluded garden. Rooms ⑤, apartments ⑥.

The Great Ponsonby B&B, 30 Ponsonby Terrace, Ponsonby (☎09/376 5989, fax 376 5527, *www.dmd.co.nz/pons/*, *great.ponsonby@xtra.co.nz*). Boutique hotel in a restored 1898 villa three minutes' walk from Ponsonby Road, boldly decorated in ocean tones using native timbers and Pacific artworks and furnishings. All rooms are en suite (some with baths) and come with Sky TV, there are several self-catering studio units. Everyone has use of the sunny lounge and shaded garden. Rooms ⑥, studios ⑧.

Herne Bay B&B, 4 Shelly Beach Rd, Herne Bay (☎09/360 0309, fax 360 0389, *briarross@xtra.co.nz*). Relaxed and very low key, if dowdily decorated, B&B in a large Edwardian house converted to accommodate three classes of room, and with a rooftop turret which is great for watching the sunset. Some rooms share facilities and have access to a small communal kitchen, some have their own kitchen, and the larger ones have a separate living area. Continental breakfast is served. Room ④, s/c room ⑤, s/c suite ⑥.

Hostels

Auckland has stacks of **backpacker hostels**. The scene is highly competitive, and most are very well set up for assisting new arrivals in planning their onward travel, even to the extent of having a fully staffed on-site travel service – sometimes pushing favoured trips and activities, but generally offering fair and impartial advice.

There's a definite trade-off between proximity to the facilities offered by **downtown** hostels, and the relative quiet and comfort of places outside the centre. Those in the centre tend to cram in the beds and, with bars and clubs only a short stagger away, cater to party animals. The emphasis is firmly on having a wild time and the larger places have a reputation for being noisy at night; self-catering facilities seem like an afterthought and serve to encourage guests to eat out or patronize the on-site café. Hostels in the **inner suburbs** – Parnell, Ponsonby and Mount Eden – tend to be less boisterous affairs often in old, converted houses, sometimes with gardens and always with easy parking.

As you'd expect, **prices** are a touch higher than at hostels in the rest of the country, though by squeezing ten or twelve into a dorm, hostels are still able to offer beds around the $15 mark. Small dorms and four-shares hover around $18 and most doubles and twins just edge over $40. If you are arriving during the peak summer season, try to book a couple of days in advance to be sure of getting a bed.

City centre

All the following hostels are marked on the map on p.77.

Albert Park, 27–31 Victoria St East (☎09/309 0336, fax 309 9474, *bakpak@albertpark.co.nz*). Probably the best of the city centre backpackers; clean and fairly spacious with some large and several smaller dorms, comfortable doubles, reasonable cooking facilities, bar and pool table. Dorms ①, rooms ③.

Auckland Central, 9 Fort St (☎09/358 4877, fax 358 4872, *www.acb.co.nz, backpackers@acb.co.nz*). Auckland's biggest and rowdiest hostel, located in an eight-storey building just off Queen St. Facilities run to a cinema, a well-stocked rooftop bar and café with good-value daily specials, pool tables and video games, an outdoor-gear shop, Internet access and a big travel centre. The ten-bed dorms are some of the cheapest in the centre, though the marginally more expensive four-shares are a better bet. Dorms ①, rooms ③.

Auckland City YHA, cnr City Rd & Liverpool St (☎09/309 2802, fax 373 5083, *yhaauck@yha.org.nz*). Large and central YHA with seven floors of mostly twin and double rooms – some with fine city views – plus well-equipped common areas and a large travel centre; even a bistro on site. Dorms ①, rooms ③.

Auckland International YHA, 5 Turner St (☎09/302 8200, fax 302 8205, *yhaakint@yha.org.nz*). Just down the hill and even larger than its brother, this purpose-built YHA is thoroughly modern with excellent cooking facilities, spacious rooms, separate TV and smoking lounges, Internet access and a travel centre. Dorms ①, rooms ③, en-suite rooms ④.

Central City, 26 Lorne St (☎09/358 5685, fax 358 4716, *ccbnz@xtra.co.nz*). Large, busy and ever-popular hostel just off Queen Street with a lively atmosphere and stacks of local information plus a travel agency and bar downstairs. Four floors of ten-bunk dorms, four-shares and doubles are well-equipped and fairly spacious. Dorms ①, rooms ③.

Constitution Hill, 6 Constitution Hill (☎09/303 4768, fax 379 9422, *bed@backpackers.co.nz*). The smallest of Auckland's central backpackers fills a couple of houses close to the city and train station and mid-way to Parnell. It is friendly, homely, has a small garden and fairly cramped four- and six-bunk dorms and double rooms. Dorms ①, rooms ③.

Parnell, Newmarket and Grafton

All the following hostels are marked on the map on p.105.

City Garden Lodge, 25 St Georges Bay Rd, Parnell (☎09/302 0880, fax 309 8998). One of the city's finest backpackers in a spacious, well-organized villa surrounded by expansive lawns. For an extra dollar or two, the three- and five-person dorms have beds rather than bunks, and there are some lovely double and twin rooms. Dorms ①, rooms ③.

Georgia Parkside, 189 Park Rd, Grafton (☎ & fax 09/309 8999, ☎0508/436744, *bacpacgeorgia@xtra.co.nz*). Low cost beds squeezed into twelve-bunk dorms and four-shares in an ageing house, but with good facilities for the price. Dorms ①, rooms ③.

International Backpackers (Alan's Place), 2 Churton St, Parnell (☎ & fax 09/358 4584, *international.bp@xtra.co.nz*). Clean, peaceful hostel in a former YHA on a quiet street three minutes' from Parnell with parking and a nice fenced garden. Internet access. Dorms ①, rooms ③.

Lantana Lodge, 60 St Georges Bay Rd, Parnell (☎09/373 4546). Small, spotlessly clean and friendly hostel with good facilities and a homely feel. Dorms ①, rooms ③.

Mount Eden

All the following hostels are marked on the map on p.79.

Bamber House, 22 View Rd, Mount Eden (☎ & fax 09/623 4267, *bamber@ihug.co.nz*). Well-run, spacious and very clean hostel with all the facilities you could ask for, lawns right around the house and a great new outdoor pool. The cheapest beds are in a cramped bunkhouse outside, but there are better dorms inside and well-priced doubles. Catch bus #274 or #275 from the Downtown Bus Terminal. Dorms ①, rooms ③.

Oaklands Lodge, 5a Oaklands Road, Mount Eden (☎ & fax 09/638 6545, *info@oaklands.co.nz*). Former YHA in a big old house right by Mount Eden shops. Beds come in a large dorms, four-shares and doubles. Catch buses #274 or #275 from the Downtown Bus Terminal. Dorms ①, rooms ③.

Ponsonby and Grey Lynn

All the following hostels are marked on the map on p.106.

Brown Kiwi, 7 Prosford St (☎09/378 0191, *www.brownkiwi.co.nz*). Lovely little hostel in a recently restored colonial home right in the thick of the Ponsonby café zone but with a peaceful patio and tiny garden at the back. This, along with Internet access and laundry facilities help justify slightly higher rates than at some other hostels for the 4–8 bunk rooms and comfortable doubles. Poor daytime parking but it is accessible by the Link bus. Dorms ①, rooms ②.

Ponsonby Backpackers, 2 Franklin Rd, Ponsonby (☎0800/476 676, fax 09/360 1365, *www.ponsonby-backpackers.co.nz, info@ponsonby-backpackers.co.nz*). Rambling hostel in a large Victorian house with off-street parking, Internet access and $12 tent pitches. The rooms are nothing special but prices are low, the place is a good deal more peaceful than the city hostels and you're right by the Ponsonby bars and restaurants. Catch the Link bus from Queen Street. Dorms ①, rooms ②.

Campsites and motor parks

You'd have to travel a long way to find anywhere genuinely attractive to pitch a **tent**, but there are numerous well-equipped motor camps within the city limits which are fine for **campervans** and often have bargain **cabins**. However, without your own vehicle, you'll find yourself spending a lot of time and money on buses, the costs outweighing any saving you may make over staying in town.

Avondale Motor Park, 46 Bollard Ave, Avondale (☎09/828 7228, fax 828 3344, *avondalemotorpark@xtra.co.nz*). Restful and fairly central site 6km southwest of the city and accessible by Stagecoach buses #210–29 from Victoria St. Tent sites $9, on-site vans ②, cabins & flats ③.

North Shore Motels & Holiday Park, 52 Northcote Rd, Takapuna (☎09/418 2578, fax 480 0435). Well-appointed site on the North Shore, just off the northern motorway, with indoor swimming pool and extensive barbecue areas. Catch Stagecoach buses #921 and #922 from the corner of Victoria and Hobson streets. Tent sites $15, cabins & motel units ③–⑥.

Remuera Motor Lodge and Inner City Camping Ground, 16 Minto Rd (☎09/524 5126 & 0508/244244, fax 524 5639, *remlodge@ihug.co.nz*). About the most central, convenient and appealing site, 6km east of the city in a quiet, sylvan residential area. There's even a swimming pool. Buses #645 and #655 from the Downtown Bus Terminal will get you here. Sites $13, tourist flats ④, motel units ⑤.

Takapuna Beach Caravan Park, 22 The Promenade, Takapuna (☎ & fax 09/489 7909, *takabeach@kiwi-camps.co.nz*). Beachside caravan park on the North Shore overlooking Rangitoto and within five minutes' walk of the Takapuna shops and restaurants. Stagecoach buses numbered in the 800s and 900s from the cnr Victoria St & Hobson St pass nearby. Tent sites $11, flats & cabins ③–④.

Tui Glen Motor Park, 56 Edmonton Rd, Henderson (☎09/838 8978, fax 837 3080, *gmichael@xtra.co.nz*). Well-equipped and pleasant site in a residential area at the foot of the Waitakere Ranges, 12km west of the city and accessible on the Henderson train line, Stagecoach buses from the Downtown Bus Terminal and express Whenuapai Buses from Lower Albert St. Tent sites $8, campervan sites $15, flats & cabins ②–③.

The City

Auckland's city centre clings to the southern shores of the **Waitemata Harbour**, with **Queen Street**, the main drag, striking south through a downbeat business district largely sustained by banks and insurance companies, as the ascendant inner-city suburbs – trendy Ponsonby, affluent Parnell and go-ahead Newmarket – continually erode its mercantile dominance.

Queen Street meets the harbour at the Ferry Building, hub of ferry services to the North Shore, the maritime suburb of **Devonport** and to the islands of the Hauraki Gulf. One of the best ways to begin your exploration of the city is on foot, following the **Coast-to-Coast Walkway** which starts here and winds up through the city past many sights (see box on p.73). Skirting **Albert Park**, wedged between the **University** and the **Auckland Art Gallery**, the route then veers towards **The Domain**, an extensive blanket of parkland that represents Auckland's premiere green space, laid out around the city's most-visited attraction, the **Auckland Museum**. The Domain divides the city from the inner-eastern suburb of **Parnell**, ecclesiastical heart of the city with the **Cathedral**, one of Auckland's oldest churches and a couple of historical houses, both associated with clergymen. The walkway finishes beside the Manukau Harbour, after climbing to two of Auckland's highest points, **Mount Eden** and its more diverting kin, **One Tree Hill** with its encircling **Cornwall Park**.

To the east of Parnell, the harbourside **Tamaki Drive** runs past **Kelly Tarlton's Underwater World** to the city beaches of Mission Bay and St Heliers. West of the centre, the suburbs spread out beyond the reclaimed basin of Freeman's Bay to Auckland's most concentrated cluster of superb restaurants and cafés along **Ponsonby Road**, and out to Western Springs, home to the **Auckland Zoo** and the transport museum commonly referred to by its abbreviated name, **MOTAT**.

Aucklanders with time on their hands and a penchant for thundering breakers leave the stresses of city behind and head to the surf **beaches** of the West Coast (see p.116) but there are local spots for a more impulsive dip, particularly compact and often-crowded coves along **Tamaki Drive** and the more expansive strands on the North Shore near **Takapuna**.

Downtown and The Domain

Auckland's central city street names represent a roll call of prime movers in New Zealand's early European history. The city's backbone, Queen Street, along with attendant royal acolytes, Victoria and Albert streets, forms a central grid bedded with thoroughfares commemorating the country's first Governor-General, William Hobson; Willoughby Shortland, New Zealand's first colonial secretary; and William Symonds, who chivvied along isthmus Maori chiefs reluctant to sign the Treaty of Waitangi.

The central business district butts up against the **Waitemata Harbour**, formerly divorced form the city by docks, but now reconnected through the development of the **Maritime Museum** and the adjacent waterside rejuvenation of **Viaduct Basin** and Princes Wharf, essentially flashy restaurants around a marina.

There's little of abiding interest right in the city centre except for the **Auckland Art Gallery**, the country's foremost showcase for fine art. The highbrow theme continues to the east at the excellent **Auckland Museum**, packed with superb Maori and Pacific Island artefacts, which dominates **The Domain**, a vast swathe of trees and lawns sweeping down towards the harbour.

The waterfront

Auckland's waterfront is dominated by the Neoclassical 1912 **Ferry Building**, which is still the hub of the Waitemata Harbour ferry services, though the chaotic bustle of the days before the construction of the harbour bridge is now a distant memory. Nonetheless, there's a constant ebb and flow of commuters and sightseers boarding speedy catamarans to Devonport, the Coromandel Peninsula and offshore to Rangitoto, Waiheke and Great Barrier islands.

In the wake of the 1999–2000 America's Cup challenge, the majority of the waterfront activity has shifted a couple of hundred metres west to Viaduct Basin, until recently a moribund yacht harbour, often referred to as the **America's Cup Village**. Run down wharves have been re-paved, strung with elegant lighting and lined by the endless outdoor seating of the new restaurants. At present it is all just a little too shiny and pleased with itself, a situation that will probably change as the America's Cup euphoria winds down. For the moment it is fine for a couple of hours strolling past the super-yachts

THE AMERICA'S CUP

For a few glorious days in May 1995 **yacht-racing** eclipsed rugby as New Zealand's premiere sport as Peter Blake, skipper of the *Black Magic* crew, wrested yachting's most valuable prize, the America's Cup, from the Americans (for only the second time in the race's 144-year history). Blake was feted as a national hero and the crew were welcomed down Queen Street with a ticker-tape parade; scenes repeated in March 2000 as Team New Zealand retained the trophy on the Hauraki Gulf.

The cup was **first contested** as the "One Hundred Guinea Cup", with fifteen British boats and one American racing to circumnavigate the Isle of Wight, off the south coast of England, as part of imperial Britain's self-congratulatory Great Exhibition in 1851. The schooner *America* romped away with the trophy and the New York Yacht Club held on to it through 23 defences, during which time the race became a battlefield for some of the world's most experienced crews and a proving ground for the latest boat designs, using space-age composite materials.

Finally, in 1983, the Perth Yacht Club's controversial winged-keel *Australia II*, showed that the Americans didn't have an inalienable right to the silverware. The America's Cup became something of a holy grail for Kiwis, and everything eventually came together in 1995, with *Black Magic* losing only one race in the challenger series. Kiwis went nuts. When Peter Blake declared that the **red socks** he had been wearing were his lucky charm, the entire nation – Prime Minister Jim Bolger and Governor-General Catherine Tizard included – donned red socks, the proceeds of sales going to fund the *Black Magic* crew, who went on to trounce the Americans five–nil in the final series.

The victory in the seas off San Diego earned New Zealand the right to **defend the trophy** on home turf, in what was to be a five-month jibe-fest through the summer of 1999–2000. Over the next four years Auckland's waterfront – particularly the former fishing harbour of Viaduct Basin – was given a complete makeover with the construction of new yacht berths, several apartment blocks going up, and dozens of flash restaurants opening. It didn't come without controversy and **Maori** groups with claims to the development sites struggled to get some remuneration from the event. For one disgruntled Maori, things came to a head in February 1997 when, driven by frustration, he smashed the cup – then on display in the Royal New Zealand Yacht Squadron's clubhouse – with a sledge hammer.

Nonetheless, by November 1999 half the world's multi-million-dollar super-yachts were filling the berths and the frenetic activity around the Viaduct Basin had become the buzz of the nation. Meanwhile on the waters of the **Hauraki Gulf**, a dozen overseas challengers (five from the United States alone) competed to find who would win the Louis Vuitton Cup, and with it the right to challenge the Kiwi defender. The relatively inexperienced (but well funded) Italian *Prada* team eventually saw off such seasoned competition as Dennis Connor's *Stars and Stripes*. They did it with such grace and style that they gained a place in the hearts of Kiwis who even hoisted the Italian flag next to the New Zealand ensign on the harbour bridge. There was no love lost at sea, and when *Prada* took on the "black boat" of Russell Coutts' *Team New Zealand* they were trounced 5–0 in the best of nine series.

The Waitemata Harbour will once again host the America's Cup over the summer of 2002–2003 and as the developers and restaurant owners rub their hands in glee, *Team New Zealand* struggles to hold itself together in the face of huge cash offers from rival syndicates. To keep abreast of the lead-up to the America's Cup, surf *www. americascup.org* which relives past triumphs and charts the countdown to the next contest.

moored alongside, maybe signing up for one of the harbour cruises, and idling away the afternoon over a cappuccino or chardonnay.

The only specific sight is the **National Maritime Museum**, Viaduct Basin, on the corner of Quay Street and Hobson Street (daily: Nov–Easter 9am–6pm; Easter–Oct

9am–5pm; $12) which pays homage to the maritime history of an island nation reliant on the sea for Maori and *pakeha* colonization, trade and sport. Outrigger and double-hulled canoes from all over the South Pacific illustrate the huge variety of designs employed for fishing, lagoon sailing and ocean voyaging – the last represented by the huge 23m-long *Taratai*, which carried New Zealand photographer and writer James Siers and a crew of thirteen over 2400km from Kiribati to Fiji in 1976. Made entirely from traditional materials and propelled by an oceanic lateen sail, its intriguing method of operation is neatly demonstrated on a rig nearby. The creaking and rolling innards of a migrant ship and displays on New Zealand's coastal traders and whalers lead on to a collection of just about every class of yacht, culminating in the devotional exhibits on yacht racing – in particular, comprehensive coverage of the **America's Cup** (see box on previous page), its history and detailed scale replicas of key entrants. Other high-lights include a very early example of the Hamilton Jetboat, which was designed for shallow, braided Canterbury rivers, and a replica of a classic 1950s holiday *bach* and milk bar, with great archival film footage adding to the nostalgic flavour.

The city centre
The windswept **Queen Elizabeth II Square**, opposite the Ferry Building, makes an inauspicious and scruffy introduction to the city centre – not helped by the gradually decaying Neoclassical frontage of the 1910 former post office, now lying idle. South, across Customs Street lies the city's main axis, **Queen Street**, an inelegant canyon lined by shops, banks and offices threaded by arcades – notably Queen's Arcade and The Strand Arcade – running through to the parallel High, Lorne and Elliot streets. The foot of Queen Street once had a three-hundred-metre-long wharf extending out to deep water, but progressive reclamation has shifted the shoreline away from Fort Street (originally Fore Street), which, in keeping with its port-of-call past, is now downtown's red-light district. Jean Batten Place runs south off Fort Street, becoming **High Street**, which is energized by bookshops and trendy clothes shops, and is one of the liveliest places to be on Friday and Saturday nights. Most of the action happens around the junc-tion with the former blacksmithing street of **Vulcan Lane**, now equally well-equipped with bars and swanky stores.

The city centre is dominated by the concrete **Skytower**, on the corner of Victoria Street and Federal Street (Sun–Thurs 8.30am–11pm, Fri & Sat 8.30am–midnight; $15, plus $3 for upper viewing deck), built in the mid-1990s as a potent symbol for the city in the run-up to the millennium. At 328m, it is New Zealand's tallest structure (just pip-ping the Eiffel Tower and Sydney's Centrepoint), and has the obligatory observation decks with stupendous views right over the city and Hauraki Gulf. It sprouts from **Harrah's Sky City Casino**, another newcomer to the city that's struggling to carve a niche for itself in a country where temperance is still revered. If you can demonstrate that you are over eighteen and eschew shorts, singlets and thongs (flip-flops), you can get on to a gaming floor awash in deep blue and green decor that's supposed to repre-sent Polynesian demi-god Maui's underwater realm. All the usual distractions intended to separate you from your money are here, along with cafés, bars, a high-roller room and Alto Casino and Bar for those who prefer the jacket-and-tie approach. Learner classes are held most mornings.

One of Queen Street's few buildings of any distinction is the Art Nouveau **Civic Theatre**, on the corner of Wellesley Street. The talk of the town when it opened in 1929, the management went as far as to import a small Indian boy from Fiji to complement the ornate Moghul-style decor. After a couple of years of intense renovation it has now reopened in its full splendour complete with a star-strewn artificial sky and the ornate proscenium arch and flanking lions with blazing red eyes. It is well worth a look, but unless you happen to strike one of the infrequent open days, the only way to get inside is to see a performance (see p.110).

The Force Entertainment Centre is bang next door, but an architectural mile away; its chunky post-modern form adding little to the block's recent rejuvenation. The multiplex inside includes what is currently the world's largest **Imax cinema** ($15) with a changing selection of films screening throughout the day. The Imax complex flanks **Aotea Square**, overlooked on its other sides by the recently refurbished Town Hall and the city's foremost concert hall, the Aotea Centre, which opened in a blaze of glory in 1990, with Kiri Te Kanawa honouring a longstanding promise to perform on the inaugural night.

The Art Gallery and Albert Park

Moving east of Queen Street, Victoria Street runs up to the **Auckland Art Gallery**, which comes in two parts – one predominantly traditional, the other resolutely contemporary – which jointly make up the world's most important collection of Kiwi art. In recognition of this, the fee for any exhibition in the Heritage Gallery that contains mainly New Zealand works is waived on Monday, as is the entry fee to the New Gallery.

The elaborate mock-French-styled **Heritage Gallery**, on the corner of Wellesley Street and Kitchener Street (daily 10am–5pm; free, special exhibitions $5–12; free guided tours daily at 2pm; infoline ☎09/309 0831), includes a small but respectable collection of quality works by internationally renowned artists – Brueghel, Corot, Maillol, Liechtenstein – but this is essentially a place to come to appreciate New Zealand art. Works change frequently, but you can expect to find original drawings by the artists on James Cook's expeditions setting the scene for overwrought and often crass oils depicting Maori migrations. These romantic and idealized images of Maori life seen through European eyes frequently show composite scenes that could never have happened, contributing to a mythical view that persisted for decades. Two works show contrasting but equally misleading views: Kennett Watkins' 1912 *The Legend of the Voyage to New Zealand*, with its plump, happy natives on a still lagoon; and Charles Goldie's 1898 *The Arrival of the Maoris in New Zealand*, modelled on Géricault's *Raft of the Medusa* and showing starving, frightened voyagers battling tempestuous seas.

Much of the rest of the early collection is devoted to works by two of the country's most loved artists – both highly respected by Maori as among the few to accurately portray their ancestors. Bohemian immigrant **Gottfried Lindauer** emigrated to New Zealand in 1873 and spent his later years painting lifelike, almost documentary, portraits of *rangatira* (chiefs) and high-born Maori men and women. In the early part of the twentieth century, **Charles F. Goldie** became New Zealand's resident "old master" and earned international recognition for his painterly portraits of elderly Maori subjects regally showing off their traditional tattoos, or *moko* – though they were in fact often painted from photographs (sometimes after the subject's death).

Contemporary landscape painters largely projected their European visions of beauty onto New Zealand landscapes, reducing vibrant visions of shimmering colour into subdued scenes reminiscent of English parkland, drab north European seas and Swiss Alps. It took half a century for more representative images to become the norm – an evolutionary process which continued into the 1960s and 1970s, when many works betray an almost cartoon-like quality, with heavily delineated spaces daubed in shocking colours. Look out for works by **Rita Angus**, renowned for her images of Central Otago in the 1940s, and **Tony Fomison** (1939–90), painter of one of the gallery's most expensive works, *Study of Holbein's "Dead Christ"*. Completed in 1973, it is typical of his later, more obsessive period, combining the artist's passion for art history and his preoccupation with mortality.

Across the street, the **New Gallery**, on the corner of Wellesley Street and Lorne Street (daily 10am–5pm; $4), has two light and spacious floors, signalling its more youthful and approachable nature. The exhibitions and site-specific installations by predominantly New Zealand, and particularly Maori artists vary constantly. One name to look out for is **Colin McCahon**, who died in 1987, but whose fascination with the power and beauty of New Zealand landscape informs so much recent Kiwi art; indeed, there is a whole room set aside for his work. Others, such as **Gordon Walters**, draw their inspiration from Maori iconography, in Walters' case controversially employing vibrant, graphic representations of traditional Maori symbols – spirals, fern-root emblems and stylized human forms (for more on Maori design, see "Maoritanga" in Contexts, p.859).

The gallery's works spill outside, with George Rickey's stainless-steel 1984 *Double L Gyratory* and Neil Dawson's monumental semicircular *Throwback* sculpture creeping into **Albert Park**. These formal Victorian-style gardens spread uphill to the university, and are generally thronged with sunbathing students and office workers. Originally the site of a Maori pa, the land was successively conscripted into service as Albert Barracks in the 1840s and 1850s, and then as a labyrinthine network of air-raid shelters during World War II, before relaxing into its current incarnation as peaceful parkland. It comes filled with a century's worth of memorials, a floral clock, some beautiful oaks and Morton Bay Fig trees and the 1882 former gatekeeper's cottage containing the **Bruce Wilkinson Collection** (daily 10am–4pm; free), a small display of ornate clocks and figurines amassed by an Auckland businessman and donated to the city.

Karangahape Road

At its southern end, Queen Street climbs to the ridge-top **Karangahape Road**, universally known as K' Road, formerly an uptown residential area for prosperous nineteenth-century merchants, and long associated with Auckland's Polynesian community. For twenty years now, planners have hailed a K' Road shopping renaissance but it remains determinedly downmarket. Groovy cafes, and clothes shops selling budget designer garb and clubbing gear have gradually gained a toehold, ousting some of the more dowdy shops, and Pacific culture remains strong – evidenced by a couple of agents specializing in Pacific Island travel, the Niuean consulate and a Samoan Church.

K' Road is much loved by those who know it and much maligned, even feared, by those who don't – chiefly on account of the notoriety associated with its western end, a two-hundred-metre-long corridor of massage parlours, strip clubs and gay cruising clubs. It is certainly one of the seedier parts of town, but the raunchy places are interspersed with more mainstream nightclubs and there is always a vibrant feel that is seldom intimidating, though the usual precautions should be exercised at night.

Further east, K' Road crosses Symonds Street by the little-known and somewhat neglected **Symonds Street Cemetery**, one of Auckland's earliest burial grounds, with allocations for Jewish, Presbyterian, Wesleyan, Roman Catholic and Anglican faiths – the last two areas largely destroyed by the motorway cut through Grafton Gully in the 1960s. A patch of deciduous woodland shades the grave of New Zealand's first Governor, William Hobson (tucked away on the eastern side of Symonds Street almost under the vast concrete span of Grafton Bridge).

The Domain

Grafton Gully separates the city centre from **The Domain**, a vast swathe of semi-formal gardens draped over the low, irregular profile of an extinct volcano known to Maori as *Pukekawa* or "hill of bitter memories", a reference to the bloodshed of ancient inter-tribal fighting. In the 1840s, when Auckland was the national capital, Governor Grey set aside the core of The Domain as the city's first park, and it remains the finest, furnished with all the obligatory mid-nineteenth-century accoutrements: a band rotunda, phoenix palms, formal flower beds and spacious lawns. In summer, the scores of rugby pitches metamorphose into cricket ovals and softball diamonds, and every few weeks marquees and stages are erected in the crater's shallow amphitheatre for outdoor musical extravaganzas.

The Domain's volcanic spring was one of Auckland's original water sources and was used to farm the country's first rainbow trout in 1884, and by the Auckland Acclimatisation Society to grow European plants, thereby promoting the rapid Europeanization of the New Zealand countryside. The spirit of this enterprise lingers on in the **Winter gardens** (Nov–March 9am–7.30pm; April–Oct daily 9am–4.30pm; free), a shallow fishpond in a formal sunken courtyard flanked by two elaborate barrel-roofed glasshouses – one temperate, the other heated to mimic tropical climes – filled with neatly tended botanical specimens. Next door, a former scoria quarry has been transformed into the **Fernz Fernery** (same hours; free), a verdant dell with over a hundred types of fern in dry, intermediate and wet habitats.

Auckland Museum

The highest point on the domain is crowned by the imposing Greco-Roman-style **Auckland Museum** (*Te Papa Whakahiku*; daily 10am–5pm; $5 donation expected and valid for repeated entry on one day, *www.akmuseum.org.nz*). Built as a World War I memorial in 1929, the names of World War II battles were duly added to those of earlier bloodbaths around the outer walls. The contents of Auckland's original city museum were moved here and the holdings expanded to form one of the world's finest collections of Maori and Pacific art. For decades the stuffy glass cases were sadly neglected but a major revamp has just been completed. The museum remains traditional in its approach, but its execution is thoroughly contemporary, with each of the three floors taking on an individual identity – the people (ground), the place (middle), and New Zealand at War (top). Kids are catered for with the **Children's Discovery Centre** on the middle floor – and, if you're interested in buying Maori crafts while you're in New Zealand, check out the high-quality traditional and contemporary work in the museum **shop**.

Auckland Museum is on the route of the Coast-to-Coast Walkway, and both the city tour **buses** and regular buses with numbers beginning #63- and #65- from the Downtown Bus Terminal stop outside the museum. The Link bus stops on Parnell Road, five minutes' walk away.

GROUND FLOOR

The museum's entrance is flanked by rooms containing the Pacific Island collections, notably the **Pacific Masterpieces** room arrayed with Polynesian, Melanesian and Micronesian shields high on the walls and filled with exquisite works. Look out for the shell-inlaid ceremonial food bowl from the Solomon Islands; ceremonial clubs; and a wonderfully resonant slit-gong from Vanuatu. The textiles are fabulous too with designs far more varied than you'd expect considering the limited raw materials: the Hawaiian red feather cloak is especially fine. The entrance to the **Pacific Lifeways** room is dominated by a simple yet majestic, breadfruit-wood statue from the Caroline Islands depicting **Kave**, Polynesia's malevolent and highest-ranked female deity whose menace is barely hinted at in this serene form. In the main, this room concentrates on the daily life of Pacific peoples, characterized by an elegant vessel for holding kava (a mildly narcotic drink brewed from roots), polished with years of use; stunning tooth and shell necklaces; New Guinean and Solomon Island equipment for preparing betel nuts for chewing; and fine examples of patterned tapa cloth, made from the bark of the mulberry tree. If you're lucky they may even have folk sitting on rush mats and demonstrating the processes involved.

The highlight of the ground floor collection is **He Taonga Maori**, the extensive Maori collection. As traditional Maori villages started to disappear towards the end of the nineteenth century, some of the best examples of carved panels, meeting houses and food stores were rescued. Many are currently displayed here, though some of the exhibits are claimed by Maori groups throughout the country and may ultimately be returned to their traditional owners. He Taonga Maori is dominated by the intricately carved prow- and stern-piece of **Te Toki a Tapiri**, a 25m-long war canoe (*waka taua*), the only surviving specimen from the pre-European era. Designed to seat a hundred warriors, it was hewn from a single totara log near Wairoa in Hawke's Bay, in 1836, and donated to the museum in 1885. The canoe stands outside **Hotunui**, a large and wonderfully restored carved meeting house (*whare whakairo*), built near Thames in 1878, late enough to have a corrugated iron rather than rush roof, and re-erected here in 1929. Once again the craftsmanship is superb; the house's exterior is all grotesque faces, lolling tongues and glistening paua-shell eyes, while the interior is lined with wonderful geometric *tukutuku* panels. Elsewhere you are bombarded with magnificent work in the shape of storehouses and stand-alone statues, many of them the work of the renowned Te Arawa carvers from the Rotorua district.

Maori artistry is the subject of the opposite end of the gallery, with the transition from purely Polynesian motifs to an identifiably Maori style exemplified in the **Kaitaia Carving**. This two-and-a-half-metre-wide totara carving is thought to have been designed for a ceremonial gateway – guarded by the central goblin-like figure with sweeping arms that stretch out to become lizard forms at their extremities: Polynesian in style but Maori in concept. It was found around 1920 near Kaitaia (see p.185) and is estimated to date from the twelfth or thirteenth century, predating most Maori art so far discovered. To round out the experience, head along to the 45-minute Maori cultural performance (11am & 1.30pm; $8) of song and dance, heralded by a conch-blast echoing through the building.

A couple of smaller but no less interesting galleries are tucked around the back: **Wild Child**, which explores the more entertaining aspects of growing up in the young colony; and **City**, covering how Auckland has grown from a tiny trading post to a million-strong city in the space of two long lifetimes.

MIDDLE FLOOR

The middle floor of the museum comprises the **natural history galleries**, an unusual combination of modern thematic displays and stuffed birds in cases. It delineates the progress from the "Big Bang" through an exploration of plate tectonics and the break up of Gondwanaland, the geology and seismology of New Zealand and its flora and fauna. Dinosaur skeletons allude to their presence here until 65 million years ago, something scientists had discounted until recently when fossils started turning up. Displays like the three-metre Giant Moa can't be missed, but there's a lot of stuff virtually hidden so be prepared to take your time. Armed with the knowledge of how New Zealand came to be, you proceed to a series of ecosystems such as a reconstruction of a cave in Waitomo complete with stuffed beasts and live animals in tanks and aquariums. Move on to a three-storey-high model of a kauri complete with lighting and sound that compresses a day of birdsong and animal chatter into a few minutes. The live animal theme follows through to the sealife section where you can walk across a tank full of crabs before learning more about how introduced species have effected New Zealand's unique environment.

TOP FLOOR

A multi-levelled approach is used on the top floor in the **Scars on the Heart** exhibition, an emotional exploration of how New Zealanders' involvement in war has helped shape national identity. At any time you are able to divert from the main timeline and explore specific topics in more detail via interactive displays concentrating on personal accounts of the troops' experiences and the responses of those back home. Artefacts aren't completely abandoned, but most of the uniforms, arms and memorabilia are neatly worked into the greater fabric of the exhibition, with the exception of the boldly displayed armoury. You enter through a slightly incongruous mock-up of an 1860s

Auckland street that sets the scene for the New Zealand Wars, interpreted from both Maori and *pakeha* perspectives. World War I gets extensive coverage, particularly the Gallipoli campaign in Turkey, when botched leadership led to a massacre of ANZAC – Australian and New Zealand Army Corps – troops in the trenches. Powerful visuals and rousing martial music accompany newsreel footage of the Pacific campaigns of World War II, and finally New Zealand's foray into Vietnam is documented.

East of the city

The Auckland Domain separates the city from the fashionable inner suburbs of **Parnell** and **Newmarket**, the former an established, moneyed district of restaurants, boutiques and galleries with a modest line in churches and historical houses, the latter a relative upstart. To the east lies Auckland's prime waterfront, traced by **Tamaki Drive**, a twisting thoroughfare that skirts eight kilometres of some of Auckland's most popular city beaches – **Mission Bay**, Kohimarama and **St Heliers** – and some of the city's most expensive real estate. Throughout the summer it is the favoured hangout of roller-bladers and recreational cyclists, all jockeying for position. **Kelly Tarlton's Underwater World** is the only specific sight, but the harbour views out to Rangitoto and the Hauraki Gulf are excellent both from shore level and from a couple of headland viewpoints. The gentle hills behind are dotted with the secluded mansions of leafy **Remuera**, Auckland's old-money suburb. Further east you're well into the suburban heartland of Panmure, Pakuranga and the former "fencible" settlement of **Howick**.

Buses numbered #63- and #65- strike through the Domain to Parnell, while the 65-buses head for Newmarket.

Parnell

Forty years ago, few would have predicted the transformation of run-down **PARNELL**, 2km east of Queen Street, into one of New Zealand's most sought-after addresses with restored kauri villas clamouring around the fashionable shops of the main thoroughfare, Parnell Road.

In fact, the district narrowly escaped the high-rise-concrete fate of many an inner-city suburb in the mid-1960s. Just as the bulldozers were closing in on the quaint but dilapidated shops and houses, eccentric dreamer **Les Harvey** managed to raise enough money to buy the properties, whisking them from under the developers' noses. In the guise of the now somewhat dated, ersatz-Victorian **Parnell Village**, the area blossomed, with rent from the shops and restaurants funding much-needed restoration. Meanwhile, Harvey successfully campaigned against New Zealand's strict trading laws, with the result that during the 1970s and much of the 1980s Parnell was the only place in Auckland where you could shop on a Saturday. Parnell Road soon established an enviable reputation for chic clothes shops, swanky restaurants and dealer art galleries.

Even if you are not buying, Parnell makes an appealing place to spend half a day browsing, sipping cappuccinos at pavement cafés and exploring some of the marks left by Parnell's long history. At the southern end of Parnell Road stands one of the world's largest wooden churches, the **Cathedral Church of St Mary** (Mon–Sat 10am–4pm, Sun 1–5pm; free), built from native timbers in 1886. Inside, the most interesting feature is a series of photos taken on the dramatic day in 1984 when the church was rolled from its original site across Parnell Road to join its more modern (and more messy) kin, the **Auckland Cathedral of the Holy Trinity** (same hours; free). The original Gothic chancel was started in 1959 then left half-finished until the late 1980s, when an airy nave with a Swiss chalet-style roof was grafted on, supposedly in imitation of the older church alongside. The result is shambolic. Nevertheless, it is worth admiring the new stained-glass windows; the bold and bright side panels symbolize Maori and *pakeha* contributions to society. The Maori window has sea creatures frolicking in ribbed

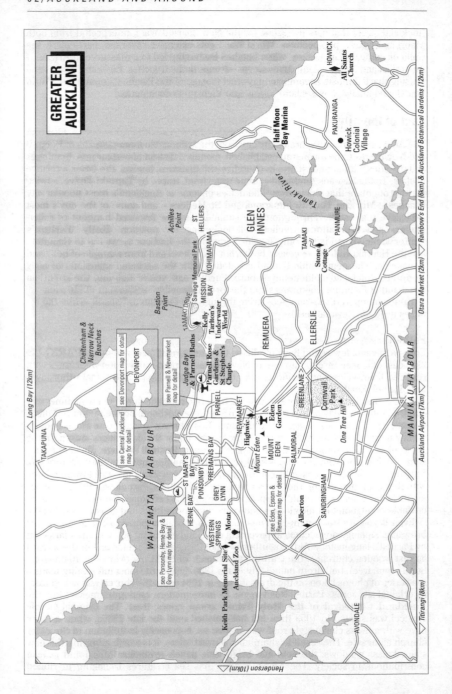

waves, while on the shore a basket of kumara is surrounded by shellfish, native birds and flowers. European influence is seen through Cook's arrival and the settlement that followed in his footsteps: the city skyline, sunbathing citizens on St Heliers Beach and cars careening along Tamaki Drive.

The Gothic flourishes of the nineteenth-century church show the influence of New Zealand's prominent missionary bishop, George Selwyn. With his favoured architect, Frederick Thatcher, Selwyn left behind a trail of trademark wooden **"Selwyn" churches**, distinguished by vertical timber battens – examples include St Stephen's Chapel, down the hill at Judges Bay (see below) and All Saints' at Howick (see p.95). In 1857, Selwyn commissioned Thatcher to build the nearby **Kinder House**, at 2 Ayr St (Mon–Sat 11am–3pm; $2), for the headmaster of the new grammar school – a post filled by John Kinder, an accomplished watercolourist and documentary photographer. Built of rough-hewn Rangitoto volcanic rock, the house contains some interesting photos and reproductions of Kinder's paintings of nineteenth-century New Zealand. Enthusiastic volunteers will flesh out the details both here and down the road at **Ewelme Cottage**, 14 Ayr St (Wed–Sun 10.30am–noon & 1–4.30pm; $3, $10 joint ticket with Highwic in Newmarket and Alberton), a pioneer kauri house built as a family home in 1864 for the wonderfully-named Howick clergyman Vicesimus Lush, who wanted his sons to live close to the grammar school. The appeal of the place lies not so much in the house itself but in its contents: the furniture, fittings and possessions have been left just as they were when Lush's descendants finally moved out in 1968, the family heirlooms betraying a desire to replicate the home comforts of their native Oxfordshire.

Judges Bay and Newmarket

From here, you can continue south to Newmarket (see below) or north past the cathedral and down Gladstone Road to Dove-Myer Robinson Park and the **Parnell Rose Gardens** (unrestricted entry; free), where five thousand bushes are at their glorious best from October to April. The park sweeps from the rose beds down to **Judges Bay**, named for three officers of the colony's Supreme Court who lived here from 1841, commuting to the courts on Symonds Street by rowboat. Bishop Selwyn used to stay with his friend, the Chief Justice William Martin, and had **St Stephen's Chapel** (usually closed) built nearby on a prominent knoll overlooking the harbour; the waterside Judges Bay Road leads to the open-air saltwater Parnell Baths (see p.114).

The southern continuation of Parnell Road runs into Broadway, the main drag through **NEWMARKET**, a formerly run-down suburb on the eastern flanks of Mount Eden which, over the last decade, has re-invented itself with scores of fashionable shops, several excellent restaurants and numerous motels. Specific sights are few, but if you are staying over this way there are a couple of things to do.

The Gothic timber mansion of **Highwic**, 40 Gillies Ave (Wed–Sun 10.30am–noon & 1–4.30pm; $5, $10 joint ticket with Ewelme Cottage in Parnell and Alberton; ☎09/524 5729), lies at the far end of Newmarket shops, almost buried under a motorway overpass. Built as a "city" property by a wealthy rural auctioneer and landowner in 1862, the estate, complete with its outbuildings and servants' quarters, gives a fair indication of the contrasting lives of the aristocracy and the less fortunate. From here it is a short walk to **Eden Garden**, 24 Omana Ave (daily 9am–4.30pm; $5; *www.edengarden.co.nz*), a verdant enclave created in a former quarry and tended by volunteers. There's year-round interest with a little of everything from watergardens, cacti and proteas to Australasia's largest and most varied collection of camellias, in full bloom from April to October.

Along the Tamaki Drive waterfront

Quay Street runs east from the foot of Queen Street, soon becoming **Tamaki Drive**, which separates Waitemata Harbour from Judges Bay. Crossing the causeway to

Okahu Bay brings you to one of the city's foremost attractions, **Kelly Tarlton's Underwater World and Antarctic Encounter**, 23 Tamaki Drive (daily: Nov–March 9am–9pm; April–Oct 9am–6pm; $20).

Underwater World was the brainchild of Kiwi diver, treasure hunter and salvage expert, Kelly Tarlton, who wanted to share the undersea wonders off New Zealand's shores with the non-diving public. Having failed to secure a location in his home town of Paihia in the Bay of Islands, he settled on these huge tanks which, from 1910 until 1961, flushed the city's effluent into Waitemata Harbour on the outgoing tides. Opened in 1985, the aquarium pioneered the walk-through acrylic tunnels (which have since become de rigueur for all self-respecting aquariums), a novelty which lured 100,000 visitors in the seven weeks before Tarlton's untimely death from a heart attack at the age of 47. A moving walkway glides you through two tanks, both sculpted into the gnarled rock walls: the first is dominated by flowing kelp beds, colourful reef fish and twisting eels; the second with graceful rays and smallish sharks, all appearing alarmingly close in the crystal-clear water. You can step off the walkway for closer inspection at any time.

The remaining tanks have since been converted into the **Antarctic Encounter**, a synthesis of Antarctic history and penguin-arium. An earnest video welcome from Sir Edmund Hillary introduces you to an accomplished replica of the prefabricated hut used by Robert Falcon Scott and his team on their ill-starred 1911 attempt to be the first to reach the South Pole and plant the British flag there; the original hut still stands at Scott Base, New Zealand's Antarctic foothold. Other Kiwi connections derive from the fact that Scott departed for the ice from Port Chalmers, near Dunedin, after first picking up a pianola donated by the people of Christchurch. Nor is a pianola the only unexpected thing you'll encounter in this capacious shelter. Fittings include a fully-functional laboratory and a printing press – from which the *South Polar Times* rolled every few months throughout the three long years of the expedition. Contemporary footage and tales of their exploits add to the haunting atmosphere. Seamlessly moving from the sublime to the ridiculous, the **Snow Cat** is an inept attempt at a Disney-esque ride made bearable by the close-up views of King and Gentoo penguins shooting through the water and hopping around on fake icebergs.

City tour **buses** and Yellow Buses numbered #74- to 76- from the Downtown Bus Terminal all stop outside and the Harbour Explorer **ferry** stops at the end of Orakei Wharf, opposite the entrance.

A little further along Tamaki Drive, Hapimana Street leads up onto the grassy range of Bastion Point and the **M.J. Savage Memorial Park**, the nation's austere Art Deco homage to its first Labour prime minister, who ushered in the welfare state in the late 1930s. More recently, **Bastion Point** was the site of a seventeen-month stand-off between police and its traditional owners, the Ngati Whatua, over the subdivision of land for housing. The occupiers were finally removed in May 1977, but the stand helped to galvanize the land-rights movement, and paved the way for a significant change in government attitude. Within a decade, the Waitangi Tribunal recommended that the land be returned, along with a compensatory cash payment.

Bastion Point looks down on **MISSION BAY**, the closest of the truly worthwhile city **beaches**, where a grassy waterside reserve is backed by an enticing row of cafés and restaurants. Swimming is best here close to high tide; at other times the water remains shallow a long way out. Similar conditions prevail at the sheltered beaches of **Kohimarama** and **St Heliers Bay**, both a short way further along Tamaki Drive, which finishes on a high note with excellent harbour views from **Achilles Point**.

Panmure and Howick

With your own transport it is easy enough to wind south from St Heliers through the low-rent suburbs of Glen Innes and Tamaki to **PANMURE**, one of four **fencible settlements** – Panmure and Howick in the east, Onehunga and Otahuhu in the south – set up around the young capital as a defence against disgruntled Maori and ambitious French. So-called "fencibles" (pensioned British soldiers) were re-enlisted to defend these sites for seven years, in return for free passage and a block of land. Skirmishes were few, and the original shipments of men and their families formed the basis of small towns, all of which were subsequently engulfed by the Auckland conurbation. Panmure has its relocated and restored **Stone Cottage**, at the corner of King's Road and Queen's Road (Fri & Sun 1–3pm; free), but the best place to get a sense of fencible life is at the **Howick Historical Village**, Bells Road, Lloyd Elsmore Park (daily admission 10am–5pm, last admission 4pm; $9; *www.fencible.org.nz*), ten kilometres east of downtown through the numbing suburb of Pakuranga. Over thirty buildings dating from the 1840s and 1870s have been restored and re-sited from the four fencible settlements, and arranged in a believable village setting complete with a pond, a working blacksmith and market gardens. Volunteers role-play the diligently researched lives of real 1850s characters as they amble between the tents and makeshift Maori-style *raupo* huts used on arrival, the officers' cottages, the hostelry, school hall and flower mill.

The colonial village is one kilometre off Pakuranga Road, plied by all Howick & Eastern **buses**, which take about forty minutes to get out here from the Downtown Bus Terminal.

In the last ten years, droll Kiwis have dubbed the suburb of **HOWICK**, a further 5km east, "Chowick" – on account of its Chinese inhabitants' weakness for huge, florid mansions, which have gradually marched across the former farmland to the south of town. For Aucklanders, these have become almost an attraction in their own right, mounting a challenge to Howick's more traditional sight, the distinctive, square-turreted **All Saints' Church**, the country's oldest active "Selwyn" church (see p.93), built in 1847.

West of the city

The suburbs of West Auckland developed later than their eastern counterparts, a consequence of their distance from the sea in the days when almost all travel was by ferry. The exceptions were the inner suburbs of Freeman's Bay, **Ponsonby** and Herne Bay, now enjoying renewed desirability for their proximity to the city and an unsurpassed array of the city's best restaurants, cafés and bars. Except for the flagging **Victoria Park Market**, sights are scarce until you get out to **Western Springs**, infant Auckland's major water source. The site of the springs is now part of **MOTAT**, a less than thrilling transport and technology museum, and the small but go-ahead **Auckland Zoo**. To the south stands **Alberton**, once one of the city's grandest residences, but now just a brief distraction before you hit the wineries and West Coast beaches (see "Around Auckland", p.115).

Freeman's Bay, Ponsonby and Herne Bay

Victoria Street climbs the ridge west of Queen Street and descends into **Freeman's Bay**, a flat basin long-since reclaimed from the Waitemata Harbour to accommodate early saw-milling operations. The land is now given over to the popular rugby and cricket fields of Victoria Park, all overshadowed by the 38m-high chimney of Auckland's defunct incinerator, occupied since 1984 by **Victoria Park Market** (daily 9am–7pm), a knot of stalls and restaurants. Despite having lost some of its more aspirational patrons to Ponsonby up the road, it's still an interesting enough place to mooch about for reasonably priced clothes and crafts, and a good place to break your walk out to Ponsonby. The **Link bus** passes on its way to Ponsonby, and city tour buses also stop here.

Victoria Park Market is the starting point of the **Historic Ponsonby Heritage Walk** (pick up a free leaflet at the market), which winds past wisteria-draped kauri clapboard villas and grandiose civic buildings in the neighbouring suburbs of St Mary's Bay and **PONSONBY**. Early in Auckland's European history these became fashionable neighbourhoods, only moving downmarket with the arrival of trams at the turn of the century. Inner-city living conditions deteriorated dramatically in the Depression of the 1930s, and the resulting low rents attracted large numbers of Pacific Islanders during the 1950s. Ponsonby took a bohemian turn in the Seventies and before long young professionals were moving in, restoring old houses and spending fistfuls of dollars in the cafés, restaurants and boutiques along Ponsonby Road. The street itself may not be beautiful, but the people sure are: musicians, actors and media folk congregate to lunch, schmooze and be seen in the latest fashionable haunt. There's good reason to brave the poseurs, though, for some of New Zealand's classiest shopping (particularly clothes and ceramics) and eating.

Beyond St Mary's Bay and Ponsonby lies **HERNE BAY**, which followed its neighbours' economic ebb and flow and now ranks as Auckland's most expensive suburb, the merchants' water-view villas fetching astronomical prices. There's little to see out this way, but you may find yourself staying here or indulging at one of the restaurants and cafés along Jervois Road.

Western Springs: MOTAT and the zoo

In the late nineteenth century the burgeoning city of Auckland, with its meagre supply of unreliable streams, was heavily reliant on the waters of **Western Springs**, 4km west of the city.

The area is now devoted to attractive parkland, a major music venue and two of Auckland's more significant sights, the most prominent of which is the **Museum of Transport, Technology and Social History** (MOTAT), on Great North Road (info-line ☎09/846 7020; daily 10am–5pm; $10). This trawl through New Zealand's vehicular and industrial past in a jumble of sheds and halls feels half-baked and incomplete – and it's all too obvious that some of the displays haven't been updated in over twenty years. However it might be just the thing if you're newly arrived and have kids to entertain: hidden among the shiny cars and jet-black steam engines are a reconstruction of a Victorian Village, and the Western Springs' pumphouse whose original engine still slowly turns, albeit by electricity rather than steam. Next door, the aviation section includes a replica of the home-built plane first flown near Timaru by Richard Pearse (see p.582).

Admission includes entry to the **Sir Keith Park Memorial Site** (same hours), a kilometre away and linked to the main site by ancient rattling trams (every 10–20min; $2 return). This is one for aeroplane buffs, with a couple of dozen lovingly restored examples slotted into a hangar around the star attractions – one of the few surviving World War II Lancaster bombers, plus a double-decker flying boat, all decked out for dining in a more gracious age, which was used on Air New Zealand's South Pacific "Coral Route" until the mid-1960s.

The tram between the two sites also stops outside the **Auckland Zoo**, Motions Road (daily 9.30am–5.30pm; $12), which has all but overturned the ancient regime of caged bears, replacing them with naturalistic habitats and captive breeding programmes. The centrepiece is the trailblazing Pridelands development with lions, hippos, baboons, rhinos, giraffes, zebras and gazelles all roaming across mock savannah behind enclosing moats. Naturally, New Zealand's wildlife is well represented, with a nocturnal kiwi house, a group of tuatara which form part of conservation work on offshore islands, and a large walk-through aviary. One of the best displays features the desert-dwelling meerkats: plastic domes placed at ground level enable you to observe their super-cute behaviour at close quarters. Elsewhere, the "rainforest walk" threads its way among artificial islands inhabited by colonies of monkeys, and you can even walk through the wallaby enclosure unhindered. On overcast days, when the animals tend to be more active, it is particularly good for kids who can also have fun at Kinder Surprise, a small farm with keeper talks and animal-feeding sessions held throughout the day.

Western Springs is reached by Stagecoach bus #045 from Custom Street East and is also on city tour **bus** routes.

Alberton

The only other diversion in the western suburbs proper is the imposing mid-Victorian mansion of **Alberton**, 100 Mount Albert Rd (Wed–Sun 10.30am–noon & 1–4.30pm; $5, $10 joint ticket with Highwic in Newmarket and Ewelme Cottage in Parnell), 3km south of the zoo, which began life as a farmstead built in 1863 by Allan Kerr-Taylor. This grand old house achieved its current form – replete with turrets and verandas – through a series of late-nineteenth-century additions befitting the centrepiece for an estate which once stretched over much of western Auckland. The last of Kerr-Taylor's daughters died in 1972 leaving a house little changed in decades: the family furniture and possessions remain surrounded by peeling century-old wallpaper.

The North Shore

Until the 1960s there was very little to the **North Shore**, just a handful of scattered communities linked to each other and the rest of Auckland by a web of ferries criss-crossing the harbour. The completion of the harbour bridge in 1959 provided the catalyst for development. By the early 1970s, the volume of traffic to the booming suburbs log-jammed the bridge – until a Japanese company attached a two-lane extension (affectionately dubbed "the Nippon Clip-ons") to each side. The vast urban sprawl marches inexorably towards the Hibiscus Coast (see p.120), with only the maritime village of **Devonport** to keep you from the string of excellent, calm swimming **beaches** which stretch the length of this coast. At the southern end the pick are the quiet coves of **Cheltenham** and **Narrow Neck**, both a short walk from Devonport. Further north try the more open and busier **Takapuna**, a short stroll from dozens of good cafés and reached by buses #80- and #90-, and **Long Bay** (buses #83- & 85-), with a grassy reserve and barbecue areas. All to some degree suffer from the Auckland curse of being shallow at low tide but beaches tend to be well attended throughout the summer days.

Devonport

DEVONPORT is one of Auckland's oldest suburbs, founded in 1840 and still linked to the city by a fifteen-minute ferry journey. The naval station was one of Devonport's earliest tenants, soon followed by wealthy merchants, who built fine kauri villas. Some of these are graced with little turrets ("widows' watches") which served as lookouts where the traders could watch for the arrival of their precious cargoes, and wives could watch hopefully for their returning husbands. Wandering along the peaceful streets and the tree-fringed waterfront past grand houses is the essence of Devonport's appeal, and there's no shortage of tempting cafés and restaurants along the main street to punctuate your amblings.

On the main street, you can't fail to notice what was once Devonport's post office, and later **Jackson's Muzeum**, bedecked in old New Zealand and British telephone boxes. Longstanding wrangles with the local council over the museum's somewhat unorthodox use of a listed building have seen the museum close and much of Bryan Jackson's lifetime "collection of collections" has been sold off, but it is worth spending a few minutes reading Jackson's impassioned anti-council diatribes (some almost libellous) posted on the building's walls.

Unless you have a soft spot for lifeless collections of uniforms and guns, you can blithely skip the **Navy Museum**, Spring Street (daily 10am–4.30pm; free) in favour of a stiff walk up one of the two ancient volcanoes that back Devonport. The closest,

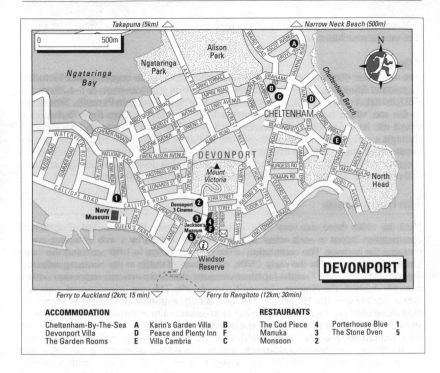

Takapuna (5km)   Narrow Neck Beach (500m)

Ngataringa Bay

Ngataringa Park

Alison Park

CHELTENHAM

Cheltenham Beach

DEVONPORT

Mount Victoria

North Head

Navy Museum

Devonport 3 Cinema

Jackson's Museum

Windsor Reserve

DEVONPORT

Ferry to Auckland (2km; 15 min)   Ferry to Rangitoto (12km; 30min)

ACCOMMODATION				RESTAURANTS			
Cheltenham-By-The-Sea	A	Karin's Garden Villa	B	The Cod Piece	4	Porterhouse Blue	1
Devonport Villa	D	Peace and Plenty Inn	F	Manuka	3	The Stone Oven	5
The Garden Rooms	E	Villa Cambria	C	Monsoon	2		

about fifteen minutes' walk, is **Mount Victoria** (*Taka-a-ranga*; unrestricted access for pedestrians; closed to vehicles from dusk on Thurs, Fri & Sat), from where you get fabulous city, harbour and gulf views. The hill was once the site of a Maori pa and fortified village, and the remains of terraces and kumara pits can still be detected on the northern and eastern slopes. A kilometre east, the grass- and flax-covered volcanic plug of **North Head** (*Maungauika*; daily 6am–10pm, vehicles 8am–8pm; free) guards the entrance to the inner harbour, a strategic site for Maori before it was coopted to form part of the young nation's coastal defences. In the wake of the "Russian Scares" of 1884–86, which were precipitated by the opening of the port of Vladivostok, North Head became Fort Cautley, riddled with an extensive system of concrete tunnels linking gun emplacements. Most of the tunnels remain closed to the public, but you are free to poke around some of the peripheral remains and the gulf views are unbeatable.

Devonport is best reached on the **Devonport Ferry** (daily 6am–11pm, every 30min; $7 return, bikes free) which forms part of the Auckland Pass (see p.73). The ferry is met by Fullers' hour-long "Devonport Explorer Tour" (☎09/367 9111; daily 10am–3pm; $15), but really you're better off calling in to the **visitor centre**, Windsor Reserve, Victoria Rd (daily 9am–5pm; ☎09/446 0677, fax 446 0698, *visitorinfo@nthshore.govt.nz*), picking up the free *Old Devonport Walk* leaflet, or a free map, and exploring at your own pace.

If you happen to be here around the middle of February, head for the **Devonport Food and Wine Festival**, where for $10 you can buy the festival glass and spend the day sampling (for a small additional sums) the food and drink on offer from winemakers, market gardeners and restaurateurs.

South of the city

The southern tranche of Auckland, arching around the eastern end of Manukau Harbour, is the most neglected by visitors, though the airport at Mangere is where most arrive. In the main there are few unmissable attractions but the city's most lofty volcano, **Mount Eden**, offers superb views, and its near-identical twin, **One Tree Hill**, has some of the best surviving examples of the terracing undertaken by early Maori inhabitants. Further south, Auckland's Polynesian community plies its wares early each Saturday morning at the **Otara Market**.

Mount Eden and One Tree Hill

At 196m, **Mount Eden** (*Maungawhau*), is Auckland city's highest volcano and is named for George Eden, the first Earl of Auckland. The extensive views from the summit car park, just 2km south of the city, make it extraordinarily popular with tour buses which grind up the steep slope through the day and well into the evening, though you can walk up from Mount Eden Road or take buses #274 or #275 from Custom Street East.

More rewarding, though, is the area around **One Tree Hill** (*Maungakiekie*; 183m), 5km to the southeast. One of the city's most distinctive landmarks, One Tree Hill is indeed topped by a single ageing pine tree – and a twenty-metre-tall granite obelisk. For a century, until just before the arrival of Europeans, *Maungakiekie* ("mountain of the kiekie plant") was one of the largest pa sites in the country; an estimated 4000 people were drawn here by the proximity to abundant seafood from both harbours and the rich soils of the volcanic cone, which still bears the scars of extensive earthworks – the remains of dwellings and kumara pits. The site had already been abandoned when it was bought by the Scottish medic and "father of Auckland", Sir John Logan Campbell, who was one of only two European residents when the city was granted capital status in 1840. Through widespread land purchases and the founding of numerous shipping, banking and insurance companies, Campbell prospered, eventually becoming mayor in time for the visit of the heirs to the British throne, the Duke and Duchess of Cornwall, in 1901. To commemorate the event, he donated his One Tree Hill estate to the people of New Zealand and named it **Cornwall Park** (daily 7am–dusk; free) in honour of his distinguished guests. The park puts on its best display around Christmas time, when avenues of pohutukawa trees erupt in a riot of red blossom. Campbell is buried at the summit, next to the obelisk, which bears inscriptions in Maori and English lauding Maori–*pakeha* friendship. The summit is known in Maori as *Te Totara-i-ahua*, a reference to the single totara which originally gave One Tree Hill its name. Early settlers cut it down in 1852, and Campbell planted several pines as a windbreak; a lone pine survives, heavily stayed after a 1994 attempt by a Maori activist to avenge the loss of the totara by attacking its usurper with a chainsaw. A similar attack in 1999 probably sealed the tree's fate; for the moment it lives on as plans for a replacement totara take shape.

Free leaflets outlining a trail around the archeological and volcanic sites of the hill are available from the **visitor centre** (daily 10am–4pm), which is housed in **Huia Lodge**, originally built on the northern slopes by Campbell as a gatekeeper's house and now containing displays on the park and the man. Immediately opposite is **Acacia Cottage** (dawn–dusk; free), Campbell's original home and the city's oldest building, resited from central Auckland in the 1920s. Over the years, it has been heavily restored, but it's worth sticking your head in to see the simple construction and plain furnishings. Campbell devotees can round off their homage with a visit to the magisterial statue of him in mayoral garb at the northern end of the park by Manukau Road.

Fans of astronomy are better served on the southern side of One Tree Hill at the **Auckland Observatory**, on Manukau Road, where a frequently changing schedule of 45-minute multimedia programmes on the moon, and the crystalline stars and distant galaxies of the southern skies is played out on the ceiling of the **StarDome Planetarium** (☎09/625 6945, *www.stardome.org.nz*; Wed–Sat 8pm & 9pm; $10). Weather and darkness permitting, the shows are followed by thirty minutes or so of telescope viewing; what you see obviously varies, but the moons of Jupiter, binary stars and Saturn's rings are all possibilities.

Most of Cornwall Park is closed after dark but the observatory and the summit are accessible from the southern entrance off Manukau Road, which can be reached on **buses** numbered #300–#319 from the corner of Queen and Victoria streets.

South Auckland

Head much beyond Cornwall Park and you are venturing into **South Auckland**, the city's poorest sector and the less-then-flatteringly-depicted gangland setting for Lee Tamahori's film *Once were Warriors*. There isn't a great deal to see down here, but neither is it a no-go zone and the **Otara Market** is certainly worth a look. Each Saturday morning, stalls sprawl across the car park of the Otara Town Centre, 18km south of central Auckland. Plausibly billed as the largest Maori and Polynesian market in the world, its authenticity has been somewhat diluted by an influx of market traders flogging cheap clothes and shoddy trinkets. The tat is alleviated by displays of island-style floral print fabrics, reasonably priced Maori carvings and truckloads of cheap fruit and veg, including many varieties peculiar to the islands like taro and yams. Your best bet for a bargain is the food: there are stalls where you can buy home-made cakes and Maori bread, and there's even a van ingeniously kitted out to produce an ersatz hangi. The market gets going around 5am and runs through to noon, though by 10am things are winding down, so get there early. Take the Otara exit off the southern motorway or catch buses #487 or #497 for the fifty-minute journey from the Downtown Bus Terminal.

Parents with kids may well want to push on a few kilometres further south to **Rainbow's End**, Great South Road, Manukau City (24hr infoline ☎09/262 2044; Christmas–Jan daily 10am–6pm, Feb–Christmas daily 10am–5pm), New Zealand's largest theme park, with a few mega-rides – corkscrew roller coaster, log flume – supplemented by the likes of pirate ships, go-karts and flight simulators. The most taxing decision you'll be required to make is whether to go for the Minipass (any 3 rides; $15 for adults & kids) or go the whole hog with the Superpass (as many rides as you can handle; $30, kids $20). Buses numbered #3-7, #4-7, #45 and #70 all come out this way.

If you have your own transport, consider a jaunt to the **Auckland Botanic Gardens**, 102 Hill Road (daily 9am–dusk; free), just by the Manurewa motorway turn-off, 27km south of the city centre. This extensive but relatively young collection of native and exotic plants opened in 1982, but came of age in 1998 when New Zealand's top horticultural show, the **Ellerslie Flower Show** (held annually in mid-Nov), was relocated here. The gardens come complete with interpretative visitor centre (daily 9am–4pm), a reference library, a café and a network of walks centred on two ornamental lakes.

Eating

Aucklanders take their eating seriously and there is no shortage of wonderful **restaurants** (as detailed in Mark Graham's *Auckland Restaurants: the Rough Guide*), with ever more adventurous places opening all the time. They may only be following the trends of Australia or California but they're close behind and easily as good. If you're after a more casual eating experience, don't overlook the **pubs** (see "Pubs and bars" listings, starting on p.108), many offering a decent meal for under $10.

For several years, the best areas for grazing have been the inner-city suburbs, chiefly along **Ponsonby Road**, Auckland's culinary crucible; **Parnell Road**, the other main eat street; and **Devonport**, with a more modest but still tempting selection. In the wake of the 2000 America's Cup defence the **city waterfront** has been rejuvenated, with about fifty eating places opening up in six months: just how many can last the distance remains to be seen. The full range of culinary styles is represented, though many serve excellent seafood.

Central Auckland and Viaduct Basin

The centre of Auckland is undoubtedly the best place to grab something quick during the day with dozens of places geared up to cope with the **lunchtime** press of office workers and bank staff. Among the most popular are the **food halls**, seating plazas surrounded by numerous vendors, often tucked away in the basements of the shopping arcades which spur off Queen Street. For a broad choice and a bustling atmosphere, check out the ones under the BNZ Tower at 125 Queen St; Centre at 280 Queen St, the Atrium on Elliot Street, or the Downtown Shopping Centre at the foot of Queen Street. There's a stronger Asian influence in the spartan and spotless Food Alley, 9 Albert St, with Indonesian, Thai, Chinese and Indian offerings; and all manner of stuff at Victoria Park Market in Freeman's Bay. **K' Road** is less influenced by the daytime crowds and its selection of quirky places can be lively at any hour.

In the evening, parts of the city can feel pretty dead, but if you know where to look – **High Street** and **Lorne Street** are both good hunting grounds – there are plenty of places to eat. Nowhere are the restaurants so densely packed as around the **America's Cup Village** – essentially Viaduct Basin and Princes Wharf – where virtually all the waterside spots are occupied. The restaurants are out to impress just as much as the clientele, though this isn't reflected in the prices which are a dollar or two above the city average.

Cafés and takeaways

Art Gallery, Kitchener St. Two excellent cafés, one in each section of the gallery, both providing sandwiches, quiches, cakes and coffee in airy and relaxing surroundings. No entry fee to reach the cafés.

Brazil, 256 K' Rd. Quirky super-slim café in a mosaiced and barrel-vaulted former theatre entrance that vibrates to heavy beats and jazz grooves. Eggs Benedict, Thai chicken salad and cakes are eased down by shakes or industrial-strength espressos made from beans roasted in the basement.

Café Aroma, 18 Lorne St. Another slender establishment, this time with a fine line in exceptionally tasty all-day breakfasts, sandwiches, panini and cakes.

Café Verona, 169 K' Rd. Longstanding muso hangout and general place-to-be-seen in the booths supping good coffee and tucking in to low-cost quiches, salads and pasta dishes.

Hare Krishna: Food for Life, 423 Queen St. Serene restaurant serving wholesome vegetarian weekday lunches costing $3–6.

Khmer Satay Noodle House, 10 Vulcan Lane. Burmese eat-in and takeaway that's always thronged with lunching city types and is excellent for a quick cheap meal of chicken satay. Most dishes $5–7.

Melba, 33 Vulcan Lane. Reliable café in the heart of the shopping and clubbing district that's justifiably popular for all-day breakfasts (from French toast to sautéed kidneys), delicious muffins, coffee and light meals (chicken sandwich, Cajun tarakihi for example) all day every day.

Middle East Café, 23a Wellesley St. Tiny camel-themed eat-in or take-out café that's become an Auckland institution, justly celebrated for its shawarma and felafel, all ready to be cloaked in creamy garlic and spicy tomato sauce.

Peter's Pies, 484 Queen St. Eat-in and takeaway pie shop – steak and mushroom, lasagne and vegetable, smoked fish – that also does bargain breakfasts, burgers and coffee.

Rasoi, 211 K' Rd. Budget south Indian vegetarian café dishing up dosas, uttappams and thalis for $5–10 and there's an all-you-can-eat Maharajah thali for $14. Great sweets too.

RESTAURANTS, CAFÉS, BARS & CLUBS:
CENTRAL AUCKLAND

RESTAURANTS, CAFÉS, BARS & CLUBS

Aotea Centre	35	Centre	32	Harbourside		Merchant Mezze Bar	39	Simple Cottage	23
Art Gallery	34	Civic Tavern	31	Seafood Bar & Grill	3	Middle East Café	28	Sinners	49
Atrium	26	D-72	17	Hare Krishna	44	Mogul	27	Superfly	8
Belgian Beer Café	12	Ding How	18	Kamo	51	Ottos	24	Tabac	9
BNZ Tower	11	Downtown		Khmer Satay		Papa Jack's		Temple	43
Box/Cause Celebre	16	Shopping Centre	5	Noodle House	13	Voodoo Lounge	14	Teppan Yaki	41
Brazil	46	Dynasty Chinese		Kiwi Tavern	7	Peter's Pies	42	Tony's	33
Café Aroma	29	Restaurant	40	Legends	45	The Power Station	53	Toto'	21
Café Verona	48	Euro	1	Loaded Hog	4	Rasoi	47	Victoria Park Market	20
Caravanserai		Food Alley	6	Manifesto	36	Roots	50	White Lady Diner	10
Tea House	38	Galbraith's Alehouse	54	Mekong Café	30	Sake Bar Rikka	19	Wofem Bros Bagelry	25
Classic	37	Galatos	52	Melba	15	Shakespeare Tavern	22	Wildlife	2

Simple Cottage, 50 High St (☎09/303 4599). Even the vegetarian restaurants in Auckland have had the modern café/bar treatment, this sleek establishment selling good coffee alongside herbal teas, tofu burgers ($9), salads and daily selections of lasagne, ratatouille, felafel and moussaka. Ingredients are often organic, vegans are well served and, with advance notice, they'll cater to those with special diets. Licensed.

Teppan Yaki, 456 Queen St. Cheap and cheerful fried rice and noodles bar with main dishes for under $10.

White Lady Diner, cnr Queen St & Shortland St. Kerbside caravan in the club zone, open for refuelling throughout the night. Toasted sandwiches and burgers, notably the pack-in-the-works Aucklander, fit the bill – and the staff understand fluent drunk.

Wofem Bros Bagelry, 54 High St (☎09/366 7359). Auckland's best bagel café serving variously flavoured bagelwiches piled with tempting combinations – chicken, cranberry and camembert; Mediterranean; tuna; vegetarian – along with coffee and juices, inside or out.

Restaurants

Belgian Beer Café, 8 Vulcan Lane. The infatuation with all things Belgian has hit New Zealand and is best manifest in this former pub convincingly converted into a Belgian bar where bargain pots of mussels come dressed with lobster bisque and brandy, mustard and cream, or coconut cream and lemongrass. The expected Hoegaarden, Stella and Leffe are supplemented by bottled fruit beers and a selection of Kiwi wines. Licensed.

Caravanserai Tea House, 430 Queen St. Relaxed Middle Eastern place decked out in Turkish rugs and cushions, some around knee-high tables. The extensive range of mezze, moussaka and kebabs go for around $12, or there are lighter snacks for half that. Licensed.

D72, Freyberg Place. A Kiwi angle on the traditional American diner with designer plastic chairs outside and booths within where you can tuck into burgers, waffles, Caesar salad, eggs Benedict and much more at slightly inflated prices. Licensed.

Ding How, 2nd floor, 55 Albert St, entrance, St Patrick's Square (☎09/358 4838). Intimate Cantonese restaurant (reservations advised) with terrific dim sum (11.30am–2.30pm) carried around on trays as the waiters shout out the options; peer under the lids and dive in. There's a full dinner menu too. Open daily until 10.30pm. Licensed and BYO.

Dynasty Chinese Restaurant, 57–59 Wakefield St. Large restaurant always popular with Auckland's Chinese community especially for Sunday morning yum cha. Licensed.

Euro, Princes Wharf (☎09/309 9866). The talk of the town when it opened in time for the America's Cup defence, and still very much the place to be seen, this in no way detracts from the very high quality food and service. Their signature dish of rotisserie chicken on a bed of mashed potato and peanut slaw is superb, and the appetizers are all pretty fantastic too. Licensed.

Harbourside Seafood Bar & Grill, 99 Quay St (☎09/307 0556). Classy but none-too-formal, award-winning Pacific Rim seafood restaurant upstairs in the Ferry Building. If it's warm, reserve a table on the harbour-view terrace, and feast on beautifully prepared and presented fish and crustaceans. Expect to part with at least $50 for a full meal. Licensed.

Kamo, 382 K' Rd (☎09/377 2313). Stripped-down, rowdy restaurant which is one of the very few that serves Pacific-influenced dishes alongside Mediterranean and Pacific Rim favourites, all at reasonable prices. Try the *ika mata* (literally "fish prepared and eaten"), fresh fish marinated in coconut cream and finely diced vegetables. Licensed.

Kermadec, 1st Floor, Viaduct Basin, cnr Lower Hobson St & Quay St (restaurant ☎09/309 0412, brasserie and bars ☎09/309 0413). Fashionable and imaginatively decorated seafood emporium, with a large bustling brasserie for classy versions of bistro favourites and the more formal, and expensive, Pacific Room for fine dining. Licensed.

The Mekong Café, 38 Wellesley St West (☎09/303 4345). Few decorative frills but excellent meals turned out in this friendly Vietnamese restaurant. Most mains run $13–17 – the crispy-skin chicken is amazingly good – or try the authentic sugarcane prawns ($21). BYO (and there's a wine shop next door).

Merchant Mezze Bar, 430 Queen St, cnr Mayoral Drive (☎09/307 0349). Buzzing café with a small deck outside and Turkish rugs strewn within. Specializes in dishes from around the Mediterranean, the Middle East and beyond – anything from Spanish tortilla and grilled mushroom on polenta to ceviche and Thai green curry. Soups, salads, mezze ($6–9) and mains ($12–16) are served until 11pm, then drinks and coffee until midnight or later. Licensed.

Moghul, 2 Lorne St (☎09/366 0885). Good value Indian curry restaurant that's great at any time but especially notable for $13 lunches comprising five dishes plus rice and naan. Another good bet is the $25 Moghul banquet (minimum two). Licensed & BYO.

Ottos, 40 Kitchener St (☎09/300 9595). Among the most exalted of Auckland's fine dining restaurants, converted from a former magistrate's court and tastefully decked out in taupe and cream with huge potted palms. You might try a starter of duck confit dressed with coconut and palm sugar and a green paw paw salad, then follow with pan seared venison, onion ravioli and black fig chutney. Expect $80–100 for three courses with wine. Licensed.

Sake Bar Rikka, Victoria Park Market (☎09/377 8239). Excellent Japanese restaurant: settle down to their formidable platter of tempura, miso, sushi, chicken teriyaki and more for two people (under $40) and every kind of sake known to mankind including chilled versions. Licensed.

ToTo', 53 Nelson St (☎09/302 2665). One of the city's finest modern Italian restaurants whose airy white, opera-filled room and terrace have become a lunchtime stable for TV execs from across the road. Kick off with exquisite *ripieno* "stuffed breads" ($5) and follow up with roasted scallops with an eggplant puree ($21), lobster and garlic risotto ($30) or a supremely thin *prosciutto e funghi* pizza ($21). Closed Sat & Sun lunch. Licensed.

Tony's, 32 Lorne St (☎09/373 2138). Traditional steak restaurant highly regarded for its juicy slabs of prime meat ($25–30), plus cheaper lunches. Licensed.

Wildfire, Princes Wharf (☎09/377 6869). Flashy new Mediterranean-influenced place with tables by the water or inside where a massive fiery grill flares up from time to time. Gourmet pizzas are overshadowed by the nightly rotisserie specials (quail, duck cervena; $26–28) and the *churrascaria*, a vast selection of meats and seafood marinated in herbs and roasted over manuka coals. It is served after tapas and the whole shebang costs $40. Licensed.

Parnell

Parnell's eating places split into two camps; established **restaurants** with the accent on fine dining, and trendier, cheaper places catering to younger devotees, and backpackers from the nearby hostels.

Antoine's, 333 Parnell Rd (☎09/307 9875). Fancy French dining consistently rated among the best in Auckland and much favoured by Parnell and Remuera blue bloods. It's all very professionally, if somewhat conservatively, done. Try top-quality lamb and salmon dishes, at top-notch prices.

Chocolate Café, 323 Parnell Rd. Compact chocolate emporium selling handmade choccies and a range of chocolate (and coffee) drinks. Tables inside and out, and it stays open late for that post-dinner dessert.

Iguaçu, 269 Parnell Rd (☎09/358 4804). Flashy conservatory-style brasserie frequented by a young corporate crowd and wannabes, but worth a look in for a light meal or just a glass of wine. Sunday lunchtime jazz. Licensed.

Java Room, 317 Parnell Rd (☎09/366 1606). Intimate restaurant serving loosely Indonesian-influenced dishes but stretching to dim sum, spicy fish cakes, Szechwan prawns and whole snapper in sambal. Licensed & BYO.

The Other Side, 320 Parnell Rd. Bright, breezy and reasonably priced café serving good breakfasts and a typical range of Kiwi café food with German additions like bratwurst and schnitzel.

Pandoro, 427 Parnell Rd. Bakery specializing in Italian-style loaves, stuffed pizza bread – and chocolate brownies.

Portofino, 156 Parnell Rd (☎09/373 3740). Basic but reliable trattoria without the pretensions of much of this street, but with pasta and pizza favourites all exceptionally well done. Licensed & BYO.

Strawberry Alarm Clock, 119 Parnell Rd. Low-key café popular with Parnell's bright young things and perfect for breakfasts, a snack, or just hanging out over good coffee either inside or out in the rear courtyard.

Toto, 259 Parnell Rd. Smart and minuscule café with great coffee and a stack of good magazines for browsing.

▽ Highwic (200m) & Eden Garden (500m)

CAFÉS, RESTAURANTS & BARS		ACCOMMODATION	
Antoine's	8	Chalet Chevron	H
Bodrum	12	City Garden Lodge	E
Carlton	13	Georgia Parkside	I
Chocolate Café	7	International Backpackers	A
Iguaçu	4	Lantana Lodge	C
Java Room	6	Parnell Inn	F
Kebab Kid	9	Parnell Rise	B
Kenzie	14	Parnell Village	G
Pandoro	10	St Georges Bay Lodge	D
Portofino	2		
Strawberry Alarm Clock	1		
Toto	3		
The Other Side	5		
Vivo	11		

Newmarket

Newmarket is rapidly heading the same way as Parnell, with interesting new places opening up all the time, though unless you are staying nearby it isn't worth making a special effort.

Bodrum, 2 Osborne St. Boisterous Turkish restaurant open nightly for feta- and potato-stuffed filo cigars, kebabs in every style imaginable and regional favourites like felafel, moussaka and spanakopita, all at moderate prices. Licensed & BYO.

Kenzie, 17a Remuera Rd. Smart café selling pricey but delicious lunches, cakes and coffee, all beautifully presented.

Vivo, 65 Davis Crescent (☎09/522 0688). Gourmet pizza served in a capacious wood-floored interior or out on the pavement with the denizens of this trendy little street.

Tamaki Drive: Okahu Bay and Mission Bay

If you find yourself peckish while visiting Kelly Tarlton's, roller blading along Tamaki Drive or just out for a swim at Mission Bay then head along to one of Mission Bay's cafés; *Hammerheads* is best saved for a more formal lunch or dinner.

Bar Comida, 81 Tamaki Drive. Quality version of the typical Kiwi cover-all-the-bases café/restaurant/bar with wood-fired gourmet pizza, great coffee and cakes, and a strong line in *pide*, Turkish flatbreads applied to anything from BLT to *lahmejan*, a lamb, parsley and lemon juice combo from Istanbul. Licensed.

Bluefins, cnr Tamaki Drive & Aitkin Ave (☎09/528 4551). Classy terracotta-tiled seafood restaurant serving delicious seared scallops, tempura dishes and super-fresh daily specials. Mains around $25. Closed Sun & Mon. Licensed.

Hammerheads, 19 Tamaki Drive, Okahu Bay, by Kelly Tarlton's (☎09/521 4400). Popular waterfront seafood restaurant that's renowned for painfully slow service. The delectable food is worth the delay, though, and your wait is eased by dynamite cocktails and tremendous views. Licensed.

Ponsonby, Herne Bay and Grey Lynn

At the cutting edge of Auckland's foodie scene is Ponsonby Road, a street where devotion to style is as important as culinary prowess. But don't be intimidated; the food is almost invariably excellent and though prices are generally a notch above those in more downbeat parts of the city, nowhere is prohibitively expensive, and there are sev-

PONSONBY, HERNE BAY AND GREY LYNN

CAFÉS, RESTAURANTS & BARS

Atlas Power Café	D
Atomic Café	Q
Bolliwood	U
Café Cezanne	F
Dizengoff	I
Espresso Bambina	G
Fusion	C
Garage Bar	O
GPK	H
Hula Hut	J
Java Jive	E
Masala	M
Ponsonby Fresh Fish & Chip Co.	N
Ponsonby Pies	R
Santos	T
Sierra Café	B
Surrender Dorothy	L
SPQR	P
St Arnou	S
Tuatara	K
Vinnie's	A

ACCOMMODATION

Abaco Spa Motel	4
Brown Kiwi	5
Freeman's B&B	7
Harbour Bridge Motel	1
Herne Bay B&B	3
Ponsonby Backpackers	8
The Great Ponsonby B&B	6
Unicorn Motel	2

eral reasonably-priced places hanging in there. Again, popular daytime cafés frequently ease into more rumbustious drinking later on, often until the wee hours.

Atlas Power Café, 285 Ponsonby Rd, Ponsonby. Small modern café with a strong gay following, and pricey but delectable sandwiches and salads for around $14.

Atomic Café, 121 Ponsonby Rd, Ponsonby (☎09/376 4954). Atomic's own-roast coffee has become a byword for quality espresso all over town and to emphasise the point they've gathered an array of ingenious old coffee makers to grace the walls. Here, at their home base, the muffins reign supreme and macrobiotic and organic food dominates the blackboard. The sandpit in the grapevine-shaded courtyard and fluffies (cappuccino froth adorned with hundreds and thousands) make it a great place for harassed parents. Open to 5pm daily, until midnight Fri & Sat.

Bolliwood, 110 Ponsonby Rd (☎09/376 8966). The modern face of Indian restaurants in a vast room with bold colour scheme and a certain theatricality to the proceedings. The menu ranges from dairy-based north Indian dishes to lighter and spicier southern fare such as appam and dosas made from rice flour ground on the premises. Licensed.

Café Cézanne, 296 Ponsonby Rd, Ponsonby. This casual, ramshackle place is a welcome refuge from the glitz; great for reading the papers over hearty quiches, pizza slices and huge wedges of cake.

Dizengoff, 256 Ponsonby Rd, Ponsonby (☎09/360 0108). Unlicensed breakfast and lunch café specializing in wonderful bagels, Kosher meals and luscious char-grilled vegetables all at reasonable prices.

Espresso Bambina, 266 Ponsonby Rd, Ponsonby. Minimally decorated postage-stamp-sized sandwich bar, perfect for delicious panini, bruschetta and great coffee.

Fusion, 32 Jervois Rd. Wonderfully relaxed restaurant and café that's a personal favourite, despite service that can be a little inconsistent. Their Big Breakfast and berry smoothies are particularly good. Daytime and Wed–Fri evenings.

GPK, 262 Ponsonby Rd, Ponsonby (☎09/360 1113). Smart bar and restaurant wood-firing some of the tastiest pizzas in town with avant-garde toppings such as Thai green curry or octopus. They're small, considering the $19 price tag, but well worth it; eat in or take out. Licensed.

Masala, 169 Ponsonby Rd, Ponsonby (☎09/378 4500). Spartan Indian restaurant that's always bustling with diners eager to get their chapatis around tandoori dishes and succulent butter chicken. Licensed.

Ponsonby Fresh Fish and Chip Co, 127 Ponsonby Rd, Ponsonby (☎09/378 7885). One of the best basic fish, chips and burger takeaways around, frequently lauded in *Metro* magazine's annual readers' poll and always busy, so call ahead or trot across the road to the SPQR bar and wait. The vegetarian burgers are sensational.

Ponsonby Pies, 134 Ponsonby Rd, Ponsonby. Basically a takeaway with a few chairs that's great for sumptuous filled focaccia and some of the best pies in the land: apple and pork, silverbeet and cheese, pumpkin and bacon, to name but a few.

Santos, 114 Ponsonby Rd, Ponsonby. Trendy little spot serving the best cappuccinos on Ponsonby Road and panini to match.

Sierra Café, 50 Jervois Rd, Herne Bay. Excellent café with great coffee roasted on site and a tempting range of all-day breakfasts and lunches.

Tuatara, 198 Ponsonby Rd, Ponsonby (☎09/360 0098). Big, loud café and brasserie with reliable tasty food; one of the key places to see and be seen on this street full of such places. Licensed.

Vinnies 166 Jervois Rd (☎09/376 5597). Intimate restaurant with white linen table cloths that is consistently rated as one of Auckland's finest formal restaurants. Their wood-fired kitchen turns out fine dishes like braised lambs' tongues, perhaps kicked off with snapper ceviche in a raspberry citrus vinaigrette. Expensive. Licensed

Devonport

Devonport's range of places to eat is rapidly catching up with Auckland's major foodie hangouts with plenty of worthwhile **lunch stops** and a several quality restaurants for **evening dining**.

The Cod Piece, 26 Victoria Rd. Sit in and take-out fish and chip place cheekily named by the gay owners who recently earned the wrath of prim Devonport residents for the "more than a mouthful" sign which has now been removed. Gourmet burgers too.

Manuka, 49 Victoria Rd. Wood-fired piazza restaurant that's good at any time of the day for light snacks and salads or just for coffee and cake.

Monsoon, 71 Victoria Rd (☎09/445 4263). There is seldom a bad word said about this excellent value-for-money Thai/Malaysian place with tasty dishes such as fish and Tiger prawns in a red curry sauce for around $16. Evenings only. Licensed

Porterhouse Blue, 58 Calliope Rd (☎09/445 0309). Devonport's finest: white tablecloths and impeccable service provide the setting for meals which might start with lamb brains or goat's cheese and artichoke ravioli and continue with roasted ribeye with a baked tomato and mushy pea pie. Expect to pay $60 for three courses without wine. Evening only, closed Sun. Licensed.

The Stone Oven, 3 Clarence St. Large, bustling bakery and café with a solid reputation for organic sourdough, black Russian and barley rye breads; also popular for quiches, pies, sandwiches, cakes and pastries to take away or eat in, accompanied by aromatic coffee.

Drinking, nightlife and entertainment

Auckland certainly doesn't rank as a great city for nightlife but, with a million people to entertain, there is always something going on, even if it is just a night down at the local **boozer**. The best way to find out **what's on** is to pick up the *New Zealand Herald*. For gig information, the best bet is the monthly *Real Groove* ($3.50), available from most record store and magazine shops.

New Zealand produces plenty of **bands** and at any time you should be able to find some quality local acts bashing away in a club or dedicated venue; due to New Zealand's remoteness, bands from North America or Europe are less frequent visitors. One of the best ways to see local bands is to attend one of the **free summer concerts** held in Aotea Square, Albert Park and The Domain, under the *Music in Parks* banner (☎09/379 2020, *www.akcity.govt.nz/freesummer/*; mid-Dec to early Feb), mostly on Friday, Saturday and Sunday afternoons.

After a lull of a few years, Auckland's **arts scene** is picking up, and on any night of the week there should be a choice of a couple of plays, comedy and maybe some dance or opera.

Pubs and bars

In Auckland, as in much of the rest of the country, the distinction between eating and drinking places is frequently blurred, with cafés, restaurants and bars all just points along the same continuum. The factor uniting those listed below is their dedication to **drinking**: some are bars which may serve food but where drinking is the norm; others are old-time hotels in the Kiwi tradition, though even these have been dramatically smartened up and may do a sideline in inexpensive counter meals.

Drinking hours have relaxed markedly over the years to the point where they are almost unlimited and you will find places serving alcohol virtually round the clock. The exception is in Auckland's former **"dry areas"**, principally Grey Lynn, which borders Ponsonby, and Mount Eden. Both voted to relinquish their dry status in recent years, but you still won't find any pubs, and even licensed restaurants are scarce.

City centre

Civic Tavern, cnr Queen St & Wellesley St. Two-in-one pub that's good for a quick snifter before the movies up the road: choose between *Murphy's Irish Bar* downstairs and the *London Bar* upstairs with bistro meals and a hundred brands of bottled beer.

GAY AND LESBIAN AUCKLAND

New Zealand has a fairly small but progressive and proactive **gay culture**, and Auckland, the most vibrant of the cities, is at its centre. The two-week **Hero** Festival has tradition-ally taken place in February with a **Lesbian and Gay Film Festival** and a number of other events leading up to the climactic **Hero Parade**. Ponsonby Road is closed off for the Saturday night and tens of thousands – gay, straight and voyeuristic party animals alike – line the streets to egg on the lavish floats. Unfortunately, the community's rever-ential nod to Sydney's Mardi Gras stumbles financially from one year to the next and the 2000 festival was called off. The 2001 event is planned but nothing is concrete at time of writing: watch the gay press for details.

There's a heap of information about **what's happening** in the fortnightly *Express* magazine ($2.50; *guynz.com/express*), which can be bought from branches of Maggazzino and the Out! bookshop (☎09/377 7770; 45 Anzac Ave), and is available for browsing in many cafés. It's also worth tuning in to *Round the Bend*, the Sunday evening gay and lesbian interest programme (8–9pm) on 95BFM (*www.95bfm.co.nz*), preceded by an hour of *The Girls Own Show*. Look out too for *Queer Nation*, sporadi-cally on TV2 at 11pm.

Outside of festival time, the gay **scene** is fairly low-key, gently woven into the café/bar mainstream of Ponsonby, Parnell and Newmarket, with the exception of the western end of K' Road where the strip clubs mingle freely with gay bars and cruise clubs. Among the **cafés**, *Atlas Power Café* in Ponsonby (see p.107) attracts a significant gay clientele, and, in the same area, the intimate and friendly *Surrender Dorothy*, 175 Ponsonby Rd, is great for a quiet drink, though it isn't exclusively gay. Almost all the significant gay action hap-pens along a short section of K' Road, where *Legend*, 335 K' Rd (☎09/377 6062; open nightly) and *Sinners*, 373 K' Rd (☎09/308 9985; Wed–Sat only; *www.sinners.co.nz*) are two of the hottest **clubs**, both open late and often hosting live drag acts or other entertain-ment.

USEFUL CONTACTS

Budget Travel, 177 Parnell Rd, Auckland; postal address PO Box 37–259, Parnell, Auckland (☎09/302 0553, fax 358 1206, *jennyr@budgettravel.co.nz*). This branch of the nationwide chain of travel agencies has a particular interest in helping gay vis-itors plan their travels.

Pride Centre, 281 K' Rd, Auckland; postal address PO Box 5426, Wellesley St (☎09/302 0590, fax 303 2042, *www.our.net.nz/pride.htm, pride@xtra.co .nz*). The best place to tap into the scene, with a drop-in centre (generally Mon–Fri 9am–5pm) and a good events noticeboard.

See p.80 for advice on finding **gay-friendly accommodation** in the city.

Kiwi Tavern, 3 Britomart Place (☎09/307 1717). Top-floor bar with pool tables, and drink discounts that's predictably popular with backpackers especially on Tuesday nights when they do a "Drink your way around NZ" six-beers-for-$6 deal.

The Loaded Hog, Viaduct Basin. Vast, bustling, glass-walled bar with seating right on the quay, bar food, an impressive range of wines by the glass and four tantalizing micro-brewed beers; beware of the dress standards (no shorts, vests or thongs) enforced in the evenings.

Manifesto, 315 Queen St (☎09/303 4405). Fashionable, uptown evening-only wine and espresso bar with regular live jazz, particularly on Sunday-night, for $5–10.

Shakespeare Tavern, 61 Albert St. Pub with an in-house micro-brewery producing a thirst-quenching low-alcohol ginger beer and a handful of commendable, stiffer brews – also sold in two-litre bottles to take away.

Tabac, 6 Mills Lane. Cosy bar co-owned by former Crowded House singer/songwriter Neil Finn; good for a quiet-ish drink.

The suburbs

Carlton, cnr Broadway & Khyber Pass Rd, Newmarket. Pub and brasserie offering good-value meals but better known as a sports bar, especially for big games. Live music most weekends.

Garage Bar, 152 Ponsonby Rd, Ponsonby. Diminutive, smart, barstool-perching place with fine wines by the glass, plenty of top-shelf cocktails and a great window seat. Closed Sunday.

Galbraith's Alehouse, 2 Mount Eden Rd (☎09/379 3557). Former library converted into a micro-brew pub with English-style ales – the warm and flat but wondrously toothsome kind – plus hand-pulled Guinness, Orangeboom, Tuborg, Boddingtons and fifty-odd bottled varieties, plus wine by the glass and quality bar meals matched to suggested tipples.

Hula Hut, 212 Ponsonby Rd, Ponsonby. Currently the hippest place in the street with Hawaiian-style ceiling fans cooling drinkers sat around surf-board tables. Eclectic music, tasty (if pricey) cocktails and a small selection of snacky food.

SPQR, 150 Ponsonby Rd, Ponsonby. Dimly lit and eternally groovy bar with an excellent range of wines (all sold by the glass) and beers, and fine Italian food (especially the pizzas); a good venue for spotting off-duty rock stars and actors.

St Arnou, 43 Ponsonby Rd, Ponsonby. Restaurant and bar chiefly noted for its fabulous and ever-changing range of beers brewed on site, often plundering recipes from around the world.

Clubs and gigs

Auckland undoubtedly has New Zealand's largest and most exciting club scene and, by sheer weight of population, gets to see more bands than anywhere else; indeed, the bigger international acts often make it no further.

Though the area downtown around the junction of Vulcan Lane and High Street occasionally grasps the **clubbing** torch, the flame currently burns brightest along Karangahape Road, where you can join the nightly flow of bright young things surging between the bars and clubs. Unless someone special is on the decks or a band is playing, few clubs charge admission, encouraging sporadic and unpredictable exoduses to other venues – just follow the crowds.

Many of the clubs have one area set up as a stage and on any night of the week you might find top Kiwi acts and even overseas **bands** blazing away in the corner; a few pubs may also put on a band from time to time. Bigger acts understandably opt for the larger venues; tickets can be booked through Ticketek (☎09/307 5000).

All venues listed are in the **city centre** unless otherwise specified.

The Box/Cause Celebre, 35 High St (☎09/303 1336). Twin clubs, *The Box* currently noted for e-driven drum 'n' bass or Techno, while *Celebre* mixes acid jazz and smoother sounds.

Civic Theatre, cnr Queen St & Wellesley St (☎09/307 5058). Wondrously restored theatre (see p.86) worth visiting if there's anything at all on: could be dance, theatre or classic movies.

Galatos, 17 Galatos St. (☎09/303 1928). Small venue with a broad selection of DJ-led dance nights and off-beat live acts.

Java Jive, 12 Pompallier Terrace, Ponsonby (☎09/376 5870). Tiny basement bar with nightly live music. Regular acoustic, jazz and blues sessions; call or check local listings magazines for details.

Kings Arms, 59 France St, Newton (☎09/373 3240). Popular second-string venue hosting mostly local acts who can't quite fill the Power Station.

Logan Campbell Centre, 217 Greenlane West, Greenlane (☎09/638 8833). Major indoor rock venue way down south and disparagingly known as the Logan Concrete Centre for its acoustically abominable interior: avoid it unless there's someone you *really* must see.

Papa Jack's Voodoo Lounge, 9 Vulcan Lane (☎09/358 4847). Big bar with a party atmosphere that's heaving at weekends when it stays open to the small hours. Mixed dance and alternative rock DJs occasionally give way to top Kiwi touring bands when there'll be a small cover charge.

The Power Station, 33 Mount Eden Rd, Mount Eden (☎09/377 3488). Sweaty venue that's usually the most happening place for alternative rock, rap and dance acts.

Roots, 322 K' Rd (☎09/308 9667). Late-night club that's very much the place to go for DJs spinning reggae, Cuban and African beats.

Superfly, 30 Swanson St (☎09/379 0844). Dark and way-cool bar that reverberates to DJ-driven House and Techno from 11pm until early. Fitted with deep sofas, pool table and (at last visit) a Dirty Harry pinball machine. Closed Sun–Tues.

Temple, 486 Queen St (☎09/377 4866, *www.temple.co.nz*). Tiny bar and with early-evening happy hours that also sees emerging and more established Kiwi acoustic and blues acts pretty much every night. Admission ranges from free to $10, and Monday is open-mic night. Also pool tables upstairs and pool competition on Wednesday at 8pm.

Classical music, dance, theatre and comedy

Auckland's **theatre** scene is hardly vibrant at the moment; there is no professional company with a permanent venue though the Auckland Theatre Company (☎09/309 3395, *www.auckland-theatre.co.nz*) is now firmly established at both the Aotea Centre and the Maidment, with occasional performances elsewhere. The Aotea Centre doubles as the major venue for classical music, **opera** and **ballet**, but events are held only sporadically: the New Zealand Symphony Orchestra strikes up every month or so, the Wellington-based New Zealand Ballet calls in during its tours of the provinces from time to time, and the Auckland Opera puts on several shows a year. The **comedy** scene is livelier, with a dedicated venue hosting regular stand-up comedy, while in late April and early May theatres and pubs around town are alive with local stand-up comics and top-flight international acts for the two-week **comedy festival**.

Aotea Centre, Aotea Square, Queen St (☎09/307 5060). New Zealand's first purpose-built opera house, opened in 1990 and the home stage for New Zealand Symphony Orchestra and the New Zealand Ballet. The Auckland Theatre Company frequently perform in its **Herald Theatre**.

Classic, 321 Queen St (☎09/373 4321, *www.comedy.co.nz*). Bar and comedy venue hosting all the best local names and the smaller world-class acts when they're in town. Shows Wed–Sat (and sometimes other nights) but with the best line-ups at weekends when it is around $15 for the main acts and $6 for the 11pm improv show.

Silo Theatre, Lower Grays Ave (☎09/373 5151, *www.silo.co.nz*). Small venue specializing in less mainstream plays and events. Success varies, but there's usually something interesting on.

Maidment Theatre, cnr Princess St & Alfred St (☎09/308 2383). Two university theatres, with mainstream works in the larger venue and more daring stuff in the studio.

Cinema

Suburban multiplexes have virtually killed off smaller cinemas leaving central Auckland with just one twelve-screen monstrosity and one arthouse screen; **repertory** cinemas are more widely scattered, and are listed below. The annual **Auckland International Film Festival**, usually held in early July, presses many of these cinemas into service for arthouse and foreign screenings. **Admission** is around $12, though many cinemas drop their admission to $7 before 6pm on weekdays.

Academy, 64 Lorne St (☎09/373 2761). Predominantly arthouse cinema tucked underneath the main library.

Capitol Cinema, 610 Dominion Rd, Balmoral (☎09/623 2276). Tucked away in the southern suburbs, this is the place to go for off-beat art films.

Devonport 3, 56 Victoria Rd, Devonport (☎09/445 4470). First-run Hollywood movies. Accessible from the city with Fullers' Ferry & Movie Pass for much the same price you'd pay for just the movie on Queen Street.

Force Entertainment Centre, Queen St (☎09/915 2222). Twelve-screen multiplex and Imax in the heart of the city.

Hollywood, 20 St Georges Rd, Avondale, 6km southwest of the city centre (☎09/828 8393). Mainstream movies through the week and classics on weekend afternoons, often with accompaniment from the Wurlitzer organ.

Listings

Airlines Air New Zealand and Air New Zealand Link, cnr Queen St & Custom St (☎0800/737 767); Ansett New Zealand, 75 Queen St (☎0800/267 388); British Airways (see Qantas, below); Canadian, 48 Emily Place (☎09/309 0735); Garuda, 120 Albert St (☎09/366 1862); JAL, 120 Albert St (☎09/379 9906); Malaysian, 12th Floor, 12–26 Swanson St (☎09/373 2741); Qantas, 191 Queen St (flight info ☎09/306 5564, reservations ☎0800/808 767); Singapore Airlines, cnr Albert St & Fanshaw St (☎09/303 2129); Thai, 22 Fanshawe St (☎09/377 3886); United, 7 City Rd (☎09/379 3800); see also the *Yellow Pages* under "Airlines".

American Express 105 Queen St (Mon–Fri 8.30am–5.30pm & Sat 9.30am–12.30pm; ☎379 8286 & 0800/801 122); 69 Symonds St (Mon–Fri 8.30am–5pm; ☎367 4235).

Automobile Association 99 Albert St (☎09/377 4660, fax 309 2745, *www.nzaa.co.nz*).

Banks and exchange American Express (see above); Interforex, 2 Queen St (☎09/302 3031) & 99 Quay St (☎09/302 3066); Thomas Cook (see p.114); Travelex, 32 Queen St (☎09/358 9173).

Bike rental Penny Farthing, cnr Khyber Pass Rd & Symonds St (☎09/379 2524, fax 379 2002) rent entry level mountain bikes for $25 a day; Adventure Cycles, 1 Fort Lane (☎09/309 5566 & 0800/335566, *adventurecycles@xtra.co.nz*), have roadsters for $18 and mountain bikes from $15–25, and offer touring bikes at around $180 a month. Adventure Cycles also offer a service whereby you buy the equipment and they'll buy it back from you at the end of your trip for half the purchase price, a service also offered by Pack & Pedal, 436 Broadway, Newmarket (☎09/522 2161, fax 522 2163, *www.packnpedal.co.nz*, *shop@packnpedal.co.*nz).

Bookshops The biggest bookshops are downtown on Queen St: Borders, at #291 (☎09/309 3377), and Whitcoulls, 210 Queen St (☎09/356 5400). In addition, try Unity Books, 19 High St (☎09/307 0731); Hard to Find (But Worth The Effort) Quality Secondhand Books, 171–75 The Mall, Onehunga (☎09/634 4340) for a massive selection of secondhand books; Out!, 45 Anzac Ave (☎09/377 7770) for gay-interest books and magazines; and the Women's Bookshop, 105 Ponsonby Rd (☎09/376 4399), for feminist literature and women's interest books. For **maps**, make for the Auckland Map Centre, 1a Wyndham St (☎09/309 7725), or Specialty Maps, 46 Albert St (☎09/307 2217).

Bus departures InterCity (☎09/913 6100, *www.intercitycoach.co.nz*) run the most comprehensive range of services to many destinations in conjunction with their partner (☎09/913 6100, *www. newmanscoach.co.nz*). Tickets for InterCity and Newmans can be bought at the office in the Sky City terminal on Hobson St. The Little Kiwi (☎0800/759 999) run to Hamilton and Rotorua daily via Auckland Airport and offer very competitive prices.

Buying a car For general advice, consult Basics (see p.32), then peruse the noticeboards in hostels and at the main visitor centre or get along to one of the weekend car fairs, which are typically dominated by private sellers rather than dealers. The major Saturday venue is the Saturday Car Fair, Beach Road, City (☎09/636 9775); on Sunday you've a choice of the Auckland Car Fair, Ellerslie Racecourse, Greenlane (☎09/529 2233, *www.carfair.co.nz*), and the Manukau Car Fair, Manukau City Shopping Centre (☎09/358 5000). All take place in the morning from 9am to noon or 1am (gates usually open around 8am) and are well organized, with qualified folk on hand to check roadworthiness. Alternatively, glance through the page of cars for sale in the weekly *Auto Trader* or *Trade & Exchange* magazines, or pick up Wednesday's *New Zealand Herald* newspaper.

Camping and outdoor equipment Bivouac, 109 Queen St (☎09/366 1966) & 326 Broadway, Newmarket (☎09/529 2298) have a good selection of quality gear for sale or rent; Kathmandu, 350 Queen St (☎09/309 4615) stocks all the major brands; and it's also worth checking the noticeboard in Auckland's main visitor centre and around the hostels for offers of camping and tramping gear for sale.

Canyoning About the most fun you can have with a wetsuit on in these parts is to go canyoning, a combination of swimming, abseiling, jumping into deep pools and sliding down rock chutes. Two companies operate in the Waitakere Ranges, both making pick-ups in Auckland and both charging $125 for a full day out. Canyonz (☎ & fax 534 1468, *www.canyonz.co.nz*, *canyonz@xtra.co.nz*) operate on a stream close to Karekare with a good variety of all aspects including an 8m waterfall jump or abseil. Awol Canyoning Adventures (☎09/630 7100, fax 623 0505, *www.awoladventures.co.nz*, *info@awoladventures.co.nz*) run similar though steeper trips with more emphasis on abseils. Both trips often end up with a visit to one of the West Coast surf beaches.

MOVING ON FROM AUCKLAND

Moving on from Auckland is a straightforward business, with frequent **buses** following the main routes north and south to most major destinations, and **trains** (Tranzrail ☎0800/802 802, *www.tranzrail.co.nz*) leaving daily for Hamilton, Wellington, Rotorua and Tauranga. With your **own transport** you have a couple of alternatives if you're heading north. You can take SH1 directly over the harbour bridge and make for Orewa, or go west around the head of the Waitemata Harbour past the wineries, West Coast Beaches and Waitakere Ranges to meet up with SH1 at Wellsford. **Cyclists** must use the Devonport Ferry rather than the harbour bridge if heading directly north but will do well to take the western route, possibly riding a suburban train to Waitakere (bikes carried free outside peak hours). Southbound cyclists are better off following the Seabird Coast (see p.123) avoiding the Southern Motorway, the main route south out of the city for motorists.

The network of **ferries** and **flights** linking the islands in the Hauraki Gulf presents more interesting ways to get out of the city. By linking them together you can visit a few islands and continue on to Whitianga on the Coromandel Peninsula or Whangarei without returning to Auckland. The most useful combination is to take a ferry to Great Barrier Island (see p.133) and catch a flight from there, possibly adding Waiheke Island to your itinerary; contact Fullers (☎09/367 9111) and Great Barrier Airlines (☎09/275 9120 & 0800/275 912) for schedules and fares. If you are heading directly to the Coromandel Peninsula, consider Pakatoa Ferries ($32 each way; ☎09/379 0066) which run from Pier 4, near the Ferry Building, to Hannaford's Point Wharf, 10km south of Coromandel, where a bus awaits to run you into town.

Finally, if you're on your way out of New Zealand, **airline** and **travel agents** are listed below – and remember to keep $20 aside for your **airport tax**.

Car rental The international companies all have depots close to the airport and free shuttle bus to get you to them; smaller companies, frequently offering highly competitive rates in return for older cars and a poorer back-up network, are mostly based in the city or inner suburbs. Rates are highly competitive and deals come and go so call around. You'll see scores of flyers around town but don't take too much notice of the outrageously cheap offers, they almost certainly won't apply to you. Look under "Rental Cars" in the *Yellow Pages*. Reputable companies include: A2B Rentals, 11 Stanley St (☎09/377 0825 & 0800/616 888, *www.a2brentals.co.nz*, *info@a2brentals.co.nz*); Apex, 29 Beach Rd (☎09/257 0292 & 0800/500 660, *www.nzrentalcar.co.nz*, *rentals@southern.co.nz*); Avis, 17–19 Nelson St (☎09/379 2650, *www.avis.com*) & airport (☎09/275 7239); Budget, 83 Beach Rd (☎09/375 2270) & airport (☎09/256 8447); Hertz, 154 Victoria St West (☎09/367 6350) & airport (☎09/256 8690); National Car Rental, 69 Shortland St (☎09/379 5080) & airport (☎09/275 0066); NZ Rent a Car, 7 Fanshaw St (☎09/308 9004, *www.nzcars.co.nz*, *rent@nzcars.co.nz*); Rent-a-Dent, 105 Lower Cook St (☎09/309 0066) & airport (☎09/275 2044); Thrifty Car Rental, 79 Fanshaw St (☎09/366 0562) & airport (☎09/257 0562).

Consulates Australia, Union House, 32–38 Quay St (☎09/303 2429); Canada (☎09/309 8516); Netherlands, 57 Symonds St (☎09/379 5399); UK, Floor 17, 151 Queen St (☎09/303 2973); USA, cnr Shortland St & O'Connell St (☎09/303 2724).

Cruises See p.74.

Emergencies Police, fire and ambulance, ☎111; main police station, cnr Cook St & Vincent St (☎09/379 4240).

Events Auckland Anniversary Weekend, sailing regatta on the Waitemata Harbour on the last weekend in Jan; Devonport Food and Wine Festival, third weekend in Feb; Round-the-Bays Run, a 10km fun run that attracts up to 70,000 participants, early March; Pasifika Festival, a celebration of Polynesian and Pacific Island culture held in Grey Lynn Park, mid-March; Round the Bays Run, when up to 70,000 jog 10km along Tamaki drive, last Sunday in March; Waiheke Jazz Festival, Easter week; Royal New Zealand Easter Show, Easter weekend, family entertainment Kiwi-style with equestrian events, wine tasting and arts and crafts, all held at the showgrounds along Greenlane; International Comedy Festival, late April and early May; Auckland International Film Festival, early July.

Ferries See p.75.

Gay and lesbian Auckland See box on p.109.

Internet access and discount phone centres There are places all over the central city mostly charging $5–8 an hour: try Usit Beyond (see Travel agencies below); NZ Discount Phone & Email Centre, 1 Queen St (☎09/358 3000, *nzphone@Ihug.co.nz*); the 24hr *Cyber Gates*, 409 Queen St; or Cyber City, 29 Victoria St (☎09/303 3009, *ytpark@hotmail.com*), next to *Albert Park Backpackers*.

Kayak rental Ferg's Kayaks, 12 Tamaki Drive, Okahu Bay (☎ & fax 09/529 2230; $18 for 2hr); see also p.74 for details of organized kayaking trips.

Laundry Clean Green Laundromat, 18 Fort St (☎09/358 4370; Mon–Sat 9am–8pm).

Left luggage Sky City Bus Terminal, Hobson St (daily 7am–8pm); many hostels also have long-term storage for one-time guests at minimal or no charge.

Library Auckland Public Library, 44–46 Lorne St (☎09/377 0209; Mon–Thurs 9.30am–8pm, Fri 9.30am–9pm, Sat 10am–4pm).

Medical treatment Auckland Hospital, Park Rd, Grafton (☎09/379 7440); Travelcare, 5th Floor, Dingwall Building, 87 Queen St (☎09/373 4621), offers diving medicals, physiotherapy, X-rays and dental treatment. Registered medical practitioners are listed separately at the beginning of the *White Pages* phone directory.

Newspapers and magazines Auckland's morning paper is the anodyne *New Zealand Herald*, the closest New Zealand gets to a national daily. The best selection of international newspapers – mostly from Australia, UK and the US – is at Borders, 291 Queen St. This is also your best bet for specialist magazines, which are also sold at branches of Magazzino (33 Victoria St; 123 Ponsonby Rd, Ponsonby; and 3 Mortimer Passage, Newmarket). These shops also sell *Metro*, Auckland's city monthly which, if nothing else, offers an insight into the aspirations of upwardly mobile Aucklanders.

Pharmacy The most convenient late-opening pharmacy is the Auckland City Urgent Pharmacy, 60 Broadway, Newmarket (Mon–Fri 6pm–1am, Sat & Sun 9am–1am); emergency departments of hospitals (see "Medical treatment" above) have 24hr pharmacies.

Post office Auckland's main post office (☎09/379 6714; Mon–Thurs 9am–5pm, Fri 9am–6pm, Sat 9am–noon) is just off Queen St at 24 Wellesley St West. **Poste restante** (Mon–Fri 8.30am–5pm, Sat 8.30am–noon) is in the Bledisloe Building, 24 Wellesley St.

Roller blading Tamaki Drive is a favourite spot, and blades can be rented for around $10 for the first hour and $5 for each subsequent hour from Ferg's Kayaks, on Tamaki Drive across Okahu Bay from Kelly Tarlton's.

Sailing See p.85.

Swimming Central pools include the indoor Edwardian-style Tepid Baths, 102 Customs St West (☎09/379 4745), the open-air saltwater Parnell Baths, Judges Bay Rd (☎09/373 3561), and the heated outdoor Point Erin Baths, cnr Shelley Beach Rd & Sarsfield St, Herne Bay (☎09/376 6863). Otherwise, simply head for one of the beaches (see "The North Shore", p.97).

Taxis Alert (☎09/309 2000); Co-op (☎09/300 3000); Corporate (☎09/631 1111). To add a little zest to your ride, call Auckland City Tuk Tuks (☎09/360 1988), who run open sided three-seater tricycles.

Thomas Cook 159 Queen St (☎09/379 3924); and at 34 Queen St (☎09/377 2666).

Tours There's a wide choice of Auckland-based trips, ranging from short tours of the city (half-day and full-day, $36–99) to multi-day jaunts to the Bay of Islands, Rotorua and Waitomo (2–3 days, from $300); operators include Grey Line (☎09/377 0904) and Great Sights (☎09/303 1170). See also "Canyoning" p.112 – and the box on p.74 for details of cruises, sailing and kayaking trips.

Travel agencies Auckland Central Backpackers Travel Centre, 16 Shortland St (☎09/358 4877, *travel@acb.co.nz*) specializes in budget domestic travel, as does CCB Travel Shop, City Central Backpackers, 26 Lorne St (☎09/309 5742); for internal and international travel, try Budget Travel, 16 Fort St (☎09/366 0061 & 0800/808 040), STA Travel, 10 High St (☎09/309 0458), or Usit Beyond, cnr Shortland St & Jean Batten Place (☎0800/788 3368 & 09/379 4224, fax 366 6275, *www.usitbeyond.co.nz, enquiries@usitbeyond.co.nz*).

Women's centres Auckland Women's Centre, 4 Warnock St, Grey Lynn (Mon–Fri 9am–4pm; ☎09/376 3227, fax 376 1817, *www.womenz.org.nz, akcentre@womenz.org.nz*) offers counselling, health advice, massage and a library.

AROUND AUCKLAND

For many, the best Auckland has to offer lies in the immediate vicinity, with its verdant hills, magnificent beaches and appealing seaside communities. Few would argue that the **Waitakere Ranges**, to the **west** of the city, rank among New Zealand's most spectacular landscapes, but their proximity makes them a viable break from the urban bustle. The hills also serve to deflect the prevailing westerly winds, providing shelter for the **vineyards** of the Henderson Valley and Kumeu, home base for many of the country's top winemakers, most of which offer tastings.

Spectacular expanses of sand which can't be beaten for long moody strolls are found pretty much the full length of New Zealand's western seaboard, but it is only at Auckland's **West Coast beaches** that you will find surf-lifesaving patrols in reassuring numbers. Heading **north**, Auckland infringes on southern Northland, making the **Hibiscus Coast** a virtual suburb enormously popular with day-trippers and holiday-home owners. South of Auckland, the **Hunua Ranges** offer a few modest walks and again provide a windbreak, this time for the **Seabird Coast**, where low shingle banks and extensive mudflats form an excellent breeding ground for dozens of migratory species.

West of Auckland

Auckland's suburban sprawl peters out some 20km west of the centre among the enveloping folds of the **Waitakere Ranges**. Despite being the most accessible expanse of greenery for almost a million people, the hills remain largely unspoiled, with plenty of trails through native bush. On a hot summer day, thousands head up and over the hills to one of half a dozen thundering **surf beaches**, all largely undeveloped but for a few holiday homes (known to most Kiwis as *baches*) and the odd shop. The soils around the eastern fringes of the Waitakeres nurture long established **vineyards**, mainly clustered in the Henderson Valley but also stretching north to Kumeu, just short of the Kaipara Harbour town of **Helensville** and the **hot pools** at Parakai.

You'll need your own transport to do justice to the beaches and most of the ranges, unless you join one of the West Coast tours: Bush & Beach (☎0800/423 224, fax 09/478 2882, *www.bushandbeach.co.nz*) run a half-day trip out west ($60) and a more satisfying full-day tour ($99) which take in the Muriwai gannets; and GeoTours (☎09/525 3991, *murray@geotours.co.nz*) do a Gannets & Volcanics of the West trip (half-day; $59) concentrating on landforms. You can also see something of the area on canyoning trips (see "Listings", p.112) from Auckland.

As far as public transport goes, the Tranz-Metro **trains** make it as far as Henderson and Waitakere – a boon for cyclists keen to get out of the city quickly – and city **buses** with numbers beginning #06– run through Henderson to Kumeu.

The Henderson and Kumeu wineries

Much of New Zealand's enviable reputation as a producer of quality wine is the result of vintages emanating from West Auckland, the historical home of the country's viticulture. The bigger enterprises now grow most of their grapes in Marlborough, Gisborne and Hawke's Bay, but much of the production process is still centred 20km west of central Auckland around the suburban Henderson Valley, or 15km further north around the contiguous and equally characterless villages of **Kumeu** and **Huapai**.

As early as 1819 the Reverend Samuel Marsden planted grapes, ostensibly to produce sacramental wine, in Kerikeri in the Bay of Islands, but commercial winemaking didn't really get under way until Dalmatians turned their hand to growing grapes after the kauri gum they came to dig ceased to be profitable (see box on p.198 for the finer points of gum digging). Many of today's thriving businesses owe their existence to these immigrant families, a legacy evident in winery names such as Babich, Delegat, Nobilo and Selak. Today, the region is producing some quality wines and winning prestigious awards, usually with the key varietals of Cabernet Sauvignon, Merlot, Pinot Noir and Chardonnay.

The free *Winemakers of Auckland* leaflet available from Auckland visitor centres details the wineries which can be visited; most offer tastings. Give Henderson a miss and head out to the rural and broadly more appealing Kumeu where half a dozen places do tastings, notably *Coopers Creek*, SH16, Huapai (☎09/412 8560, *www.cooperscreek .co.nz*; Mon–Fri 9.30am–5.30pm, Sat 10.30am–5.30pm), *Kumeu River*, SH16, Kumeu (☎09/412 8415, *www.kumeuriver.co.nz*; Mon–Fri 9am–5.30pm, Sat 11.30am–5.30pm), *Nobilo*, Station Road, Huapai (☎09/412 6666, *www.nobilo.co.nz*; Mon–Fri 9am–5pm, Sat & Sun 10am–5pm), and *Matua Valley*, Waimauku Valley Road, Waimauku (☎09/411 8301, *www.matua.co.nz*; Mon–Fri 9am–5pm, Sat 10am–5pm, Sun 11am–4.30pm). At the last, reserve a table to eat at the wonderful, if pricey *Hunting Lodge* **restaurant** (☎09/411 8259; lunch Fri–Sun; dinner Thurs–Sun; $25–30 for main dishes), which is beautifully set beside the vines. For more modest eating, visit *Carriages*, SH15 in Huapai, where excellent café-style food is served on a large deck or inside a couple of old railway carriages.

If you plan to do some serious tasting, do yourself a favour – designate a non-drinking driver, or leave the car behind and join one of the West Coast tours run by Bush & Beach or Auckland Adventures (see previous page), both of which visit wineries as part of wider explorations.

The Waitakere Ranges and the West Coast beaches

Auckland's western limit is defined by the bush-clad **Waitakere Ranges**, which rise up to five hundred metres. At less than an hour's drive from the city, the hills are a perennially popular weekend destination for Aucklanders intent on a picnic and a bit of a stroll. The western slopes roll down to the wild, black-sand **West Coast beaches**. Pounded by heavy surf and punctuated by precipitous headlands, these tempestuous shores are a perfect counterpoint to the calm, gently shelving beaches of the Hauraki Gulf.

The Kawarau a Maki people knew the region as *Te Wao Nui a Tiriwa* or "the Great Forest of Tiriwa", aptly describing the kauri groves that swathed the hills before the arrival of Europeans. By the turn of the century, diggers had pretty much cleaned out the kauri gum, but logging continued until the 1940s, by which time the land was economically spent. The Auckland Regional Council bought the land, built reservoirs and designated a vast tract as the Centennial Memorial Park, with two hundred kilometres of walking tracks leading to fine vistas and some of the numerous waterfalls which cascade off the escarpment.

The easiest access to the majority of the walks and beaches is the **Waitakere Scenic Drive** (Route 24), which winds through the ranges from the dormitory suburb of **Titirangi**, in the foothills, to the informative **Arataki visitor centre** (daily 9am–5pm). From here, walkways forge into the second-growth forest, where panels identify kahikatea, rimu, rewarewa, nikau palms and a multitude of other species, all readily visible from the three nature trails (20min, 40min and 1hr) which loop around the centre, the longest visiting one of the few mature kauri stands to survive the loggers' onslaught. One recently felled kauri has been transformed by Kawarau a Maki carvers into a striking *pou*, or guardian post, the largest of several fine carvings around the centre. Arataki is also the place to pick up **camping** permits (call the Parksline in advance

ALWAYS SWIM BETWEEN THE FLAGS

The New Zealand coast is frequently pounded by ferocious surf and even strong swimmers can find themselves in difficulty in what may seem relatively benign conditions. Most drownings happen when people swim outside areas patrolled by volunteer lifeguards. Every day throughout the peak holiday weeks (Christmas–Jan), and at weekends through the rest of the summer (Nov–Easter), the most popular surf beaches are monitored daily from around 10am to 5pm. Lifeguards stake out a section of beach between two red and yellow flags and continually monitor that area: always **swim between the flags**.

Before entering the water, watch other swimmers to see if they are being dragged along the beach by a strong along-shore current or **rip**. Often the rip will turn out to sea at some point leaving a "river" of disturbed but relatively calm water through the pattern of curling breakers. On entering the water, feel the strength of the waves and current before committing yourself too deeply, then keep glancing back to where you left your towel to judge your drift along the shore. Look out too for **sand bars**, a common feature of surf beaches at certain tides: wading out to sea, you may well be neck deep, then suddenly be only up to your knees. The corollary is that moments after being comfortably within your depth you'll be floundering around in a **hole**, reaching for the bottom. Note that **boogie boards**, while providing flotation, can make you vulnerable to rips, and riders should always wear fins (flippers).

If you do find yourself in **trouble**, try not to panic, raise one hand in the air and yell to attract the attention of other swimmers and surf rescue folk. Most of all, don't struggle against the current; either swim across the rip or let it drag you out. Around 100–200 metres offshore the current will subside and you can swim away from the rip and bodysurf the breakers back to shore. If you have to be rescued (or are just feeling generous), a large donation is in order. Surf lifeguards are dedicated volunteers, always strapped for cash and in need of new rescue equipment.

on ☎09/303 1530) for the twelve backpacker sites ($4 per person) scattered through the ranges and located on the *Waitakere Ranges Recreation and Track Guide* map ($8, available from the visitor centre).

Beyond the visitor centre, the scenic drive swings north along the range, passing side roads to the **beaches**. Noted for their foot-scorching, golden-black sands and demanding swimming conditions, mountainous waves and strong tidal rips are par for the course here. Before entering the water, study the box (above), and heed all warning signs.

A very limited **bus** service (#159; 1 daily Mon–Fri) runs from Henderson to Piha Beach, and in summer there is the Piha Surf Shuttle (☎025/227 4000; $15–20 per person depending on numbers) which picks up in Auckland around 8am and leaves Piha for the city at 4pm; otherwise you are on your own.

Whatipu

WHATIPU is the southernmost of the West Coast surf beaches, located by the sandbar entrance to Manukau Harbour, the watery grave of many a ship. It is something of an outlier, 45km from central Auckland along the curvy Manukau Harbour shoreline. The wharf at Whatipu was briefly the terminus of the precarious coastal **Parahara Railway**, which hauled kauri from the mill at Karekare across the beach and headlands during the 1870s. The tracks were continually pounded by surf, but a second tramway from Piha covered the same treacherous expanse in the early twentieth century. Scant remains are visible, including an old tunnel which proved too tight a squeeze for a large steam engine whose boiler still litters the shore.

Over the last few decades, the sea has receded more than half a kilometre leaving a very broad beach backed by wetlands colonized by cabbage trees, tall *toe toe* grasses and waterfowl. It is a great place to explore, particularly along the base of the cliffs to the north where, in 30min, you can walk to the **Ballroom Cave**, fitted with a sprung dancefloor in the 1920s that apparently still survives, buried by five metres of sand that has drifted into the cave in the intervening years.

The only sign of civilization here now is the *Whatipu Lodge* (☎09/811 8860; tent sites $10 per site, rooms $22 per person. Occupying a 120-year-old former mill manager's house, the lodge only has electricity when the generator is fired up each evening, but has extensive communal cooking facilities, hot showers, a tennis court, a cosy library and a full-size billiard table.

Karekare, Piha and Te Henga

You can walk 5km north along the beach from Whatipu to **KAREKARE**, otherwise reached by a 17km road from Arataki visitor centre. Perhaps the most intimate and immediately appealing of the West Coast settlements, Karekare has regenerating manuka, pohutukawa and cabbage trees running down to a deep, smooth beach hemmed in by high promontories and only a smattering of houses more or less successfully integrated into the bush. In one hectic year, this dramatic spot was jolted out of its relative obscurity, providing the setting for beach scenes in Jane Campion's 1993 film *The Piano* and, at much the same time, the inspiration for Crowded House's *Together Alone* album. Spikes that once secured the Parahara railway tracks to the wave-cut platform around the headland to the south can still be seen from the **Gap Gallery Track** (15min each way), which winds around Korekau Point to the seemingly endless beach beyond – but beware, the track is submerged at high tide. The Karekare Surf Club patrols a safe swimming area on summer weekends, or there is the pool below **Karekare Falls**, a five-minute walk on a track just inland from the road. Despite the presence of the fine colonial Winchelsea House, which took guests for its first fifty years, there is nowhere to stay and no facilities at Karekare.

For decades **PIHA**, 20km west of the visitor centre at Arataki and 40km west of central Auckland, has been an icon for Aucklanders. It is the quintessential West Coast beach with its string of low-key weekend cottages and crashing surf that lures day-tripping families as well as a youthful partying set whose New Year's Eve antics hastened in a dusk-till-dawn alcohol ban on holiday weekends. Piha feels on the brink of change; in the last few years some of the quaint old-time *baches* have been displaced by condo-style developments, and gentrification seems inevitable.

For the time being, though, a 3km-long sweep of gold and black sand is hemmed in by bush-clad hills and split by Piha's defining feature, the 101m **Lion Rock**. This former pa site, with some imagination, resembles a seated lion staring out to sea; the energetic climb up the steps to the summit (30–40min return) is best done as the day cools and the sun casts a gentler light. The **Tasman Lookout Track** (30–40min return) leaves the south end of the beach, climbing up to a lookout over the tiny cove of The Gap where a spectacular blowhole performs in heavy surf.

Most **swimmers** flock to South Piha, the quarter of the beach south of Lion Rock where the more prestigious of the two surf-lifesaving clubs hogs the best **surf**. North Piha Road follows the beach north of Lion Rock for 2km to the second surf club. If battling raging surf isn't your thing, head for the cool **pool** below Kitekite Falls, a three-stage plunge reached on a loop track (1hr 30min) that starts 1km up Glen Esk Road, which runs inland opposite Piha's central Domain.

Most of Piha's visitors are day-trippers so the only **places to stay** are the poorly shaded, year-round *Piha Domain Motor Camp* (☎09/812 8815; tent sites $10; on-site vans ②), slightly set back from the beach and best booked in advance; and *Piha Adventure* Homestay, 117 Piha Rd, 3km before you reach the beach (☎ 09/812 8595, fax

812 8583, *pihaadventurehomestay@xtra.co.nz*; ⑥)), which has comfortable rooms and an outdoor pool. **Eating** possibilities are equally scanty with only a general store and a fine traditional burger bar at South Piha.

The smaller and much less popular **TE HENGA** (also known as Bethell's Beach) lies at the end of a long road from Waitakere 8km north along the coast. Less dramatic than Karekare, Piha or Muriwai, Te Henga is correspondingly less visited, making it good for escaping the crowds at the height of summer. There are no shops, but there is a surf club and **accommodation** – at either the elegant pohutukawa-shaded *Te Koinga Cottage*, which can house up to seven but comfortably sleeps two couples, or *Turehu Cottage*, a smaller studio sleeping two; both have kitchen facilities (☎ & fax 09/810 9581, *www.bethellsbeach.com*; ⑦–⑧)).

Muriwai

MURIWAI, the most populous of the West Coast beach settlements, lies 15km north of Piha, and 10km coastwards from Huapai. Again, there's wonderful surf and a long beach stretching 45km north to the heads of Kaipara Harbour (see p.197). The main attraction here, though, is at the southern end of the beach where a **gannet colony** occupies Motutara Island and Otakamiro Point, the headland between the main beach and the surfers' cove of Maori Bay. The gannets breed here between September and March before migrating to sunnier Australian climes, a few staying behind with the fur seals which inhabit the rocks below. Gannets normally prefer the protection of islands and this is one of the few places where they nest on the mainland, in this case right below some excellent viewing platforms from where you can observe them gracefully wheeling on the up-draughts. Short paths lead up here from near the surf club and off the road to Maori Bay. The beach, dunes and exotic planted forests to the north are best explored on **horse treks** run by the Muriwai Riding Centre, 290 Oaia Rd (☎09/411 8480; 2hr; $45).

The Waterfront **general** store serves coffee and light meals, and you can **stay** at either the *Muriwai Beach Motel*, 280 Motutara Rd (☎09/411 8780, fax 411 9202; ④), half a kilometre back from the beach, or the shaded *Muriwai Beach Motor Camp*, (☎09/411 9262; tent sites $10). For those without transport, Bush & Beach Ltd (see p.115) run half-day and full day trips out here.

The southern Kaipara: Helensville and Parakai

Venture beyond the vineyards of Kumeu and you'll soon find yourself in uninspiring **HELENSVILLE**, 45km from Auckland but more closely associated with Kaipara Harbour (see p.197). Like many Kaipara towns, Helensville was founded on timber which, following the completion of the rail link to Auckland in 1881, was floated here in huge rafts then loaded onto wagons. Dairying has replaced the kauri trade and, though the spread of the Auckland conurbation is threatening, Helensville just potters along. Photos of busier days are displayed at the **Helensville Pioneer Museum**, on Commercial Street (daily 1–3.30pm; $3 suggested donation) but you'll get a better idea of what the kauri logging days were like with Kaipara Tours (call ☎09/420 8466 for information; Dec to mid-March, according to demand), which ply the waters of Kaipara Harbour, visiting kauri mills and bush camps. The three-hour Historical and Nature Cruise costs a bargain $12 and leaves from Springs Road in Parakai, just north of the Aquatic Park (see overleaf), while the "Go North" Bus'n'Boat Adventure ($50) links up with a 4WD sand bus to take you into Dargaville (see p.200) along Ripiro Beach. These trips currently leave on Sunday only from **Shelly Beach wharf**, 20km north of Helensville and, with buses run by The Paradise Connexion (see box on p.190), allow you to head north from Dargaville up the West Coast.

To get to the wharf, you have to drive through **PARAKAI**, 3km north of Helensville and chiefly noted for its Aquatic Park (☎09/420 8998; daily 10am–10pm; $10, private spa $5 extra per hour), where a series of enclosed and open pools are filled by natural hot springs; entry includes free use of a couple of buffeting water chutes.

Practicalities

Richies **buses** (☎09/366 6400; Mon–Fri only) operate from Auckland's Downtown Bus Terminal to Parakai and Helensville, with one evening service continuing on to Orewa (see below). There's a **visitor centre** (Mon–Thurs 9am–5.30pm, Fri 9am–6pm, Sat 9am–1pm; ☎09/420 7468, *www.helensville.co.nz*) at 40 Commercial Rd, right in the heart of town.

The best **place to stay** is the central *Malolo House*, 110 Commercial Rd (☎ & fax 09/420 7262, *malolo@xtra.co.nz*; dorms ①, budget rooms ③–④, B&B ⑤), which operates both high-standard backpacker accommodation and a beautifully decorated B&B with lavish breakfasts; there's also an outdoor hot tub. If this doesn't suit, try the *Parakai Mineral Park Motel*, 3 Parakai Ave (☎09/420 8856; ④), where each room has its own outdoor mineral pool, or the **campsite** adjacent to Parakai's Aquatic Park (☎09/420 8998; tent sites $12 including pool entry).

Helensville is basically **takeaway** land, with the notable exception of *No. 88*, at 88 Commercial Rd (☎09/420 8894; closed Mon), a superb evening **restaurant** serving well-prepared modern dishes such as chicken filo wrap ($10) and venison on kumara and potato cake with blueberry and macadamia nut marmalade ($22).

North of Auckland

The straggling suburbs of north Auckland virtually merge into **The Hibiscus Coast**, which starts 40km north of the city and is increasingly favoured by retirees and long-distance commuters. The region centres on the suburban Whangaparoa Peninsula, the launching point for trips to Tiritiri Matangi Island (see p.142), and the pleasant beachside community of **Orewa**, now bypassed and somewhat quietened by an extension of the northern motorway. Immediately to the north, the hot springs at **Waiwera** herald the beach-and-barbecue scene of **Wenderholm** and the wonderful **Puhoi** pub. Travelling north, the account continues on p.147 with Warkworth.

Orewa

The most striking of the Hibiscus Coast beaches is the three-kilometre strand backed by **OREWA**, the region's main town, which garners just about all the accommodation and restaurants. Swimming aside, there isn't a great deal to do here, though the visitor centre can point you towards pleasant bushwalks and minor diversions such as the town's stern-looking statue of Edmund Hillary.

South of Orewa, the **Whangaparoa Peninsula** juts out 12km into the Hauraki Gulf, its central ridge traced by Whangaparoa Road, which passes the small-time, narrow-gauge **Whangaparoa Railway**, 400 Whangaparoa Rd (Sat & Sun 10am–5pm, plus school holidays Mon–Fri 10am–4pm; $5) on the way to **Shakespear Regional Park** (8am–dusk; free), a pleasant enough place to swim and wander through regenerating bush spotting pukeko, red-crowned parakeets and tui. The peninsula's most enticing diversion, though, is a trip to the bird sanctuary of **Tiritiri Matangi** (see p.142), with boats leaving from the vast Gulf Harbour Marina just before Shakespear Park. Auckland's Stagecoach bus routes #898 and #899 run along Whangaparoa Road to Shakespear Park several times a day, passing within 2km of the Tiritiri Matangi wharf.

Practicalities

Auckland's Stagecoach **buses** (☎09/366 6400) run a complex timetable from the Downtown Bus Terminal in Auckland to the Hibiscus Coast, often requiring a transfer at Silverdale, just south of Orewa. These, and more direct but less frequent services run by Main Coachlines (☎09/278 8070), stop on Puriri Street, after passing the well-stocked **visitor centre**, 214a Hibiscus Coast Highway (Mon–Fri 9am–5pm, Sat & Sun 10am–4pm; ☎09/426 0076, fax 426 0086, *hbcvic@rodney.govt.nz*).

ACCOMMODATION

Accommodation is predominantly in motels strung along Orewa's main drag, supplemented by a couple of budget places. The most convenient of the **backpackers'** places is *Pillows Travellers Lodge*, 412 Hibiscus Coast Highway (☎ & fax 09/426 6338, *pillows.lodge@xtra.co.nz*; dorms ①, rooms ②–③), has small modern dorms and Internet access, while 2km north at Hatfields Beach, *Marco Polo Backpackers*, 2d Hammond Ave (☎09/426 8455, *marcopolo@clear.net.nz*; dorms ①, rooms ②), has very nice rooms set around a lush garden and exudes a more relaxed atmosphere. People often stay at this peaceful retreat for a few days and take a tour to the marine sanctuary of Goat Island (see p.150; 5hr; $30); wetsuit and snorkelling gear can be rented from Seafriends at Goat Island.

Beachfront **motels** such as the *Edgewater Motel*, 387–89 Hibiscus Coast Highway (☎09/426 5260, fax 426 3378; ⑤) and *Golden Sands*, 381 Hibiscus Coast Highway (☎09/426 5177, fax 426 4804, *goldensands@xtra.co.nz*; ④) tend to be expensive, particularly during the summer months. Cheaper accommodation is available at the peaceful *Puriri Park Holiday Complex*, Puriri Ave (☎09/426 4648, fax 426 2680; tent sites $10, cabins & tourist flats ③). For **homestay**, try the central and cheap *Orewa* B&B, 6 Lillian Place (☎09/426 9678; ④), or one of the finest in the vicinity, *The Ambers*, 149 Pine Valley Rd, Silverdale (☎09/426 5354, fax 426 3287, *gzwier@xtra.co.nz*; ⑥), 4km south of Orewa and beautifully furnished.

EATING

Inexpensive eating centres on a number of decent **café/bars** around Orewa, including *Creole Bar Brasserie*, 310 Pacific Coast Hwy, which does good nachos and the like, and stays open late at weekends, when there is usually some live entertainment. The best of the mid-range places is *Il Veneziano*, Red Beach Shopping Centre, Red Beach Road, 2km south of Orewa (☎09/426 5444; closed Mon): about the closest you can get to a genuine Venetian **restaurant** in these parts, everything is done with great verve and the menu justifiably effuses over the modern Italian dishes, priced around the $18 mark. Top-class lunches and candlelit dinners are served at the *Walnut Cottage*, 498 Hibiscus Coast Highway (☎09/426 6523; closed Mon & Tues, & Wed lunch; BYO & licensed), a very popular restaurant in the riverside watchhouse of Orewa's oldest residence.

Waiwera and Wenderholm

The main highway north of Orewa (and bus #895) runs through the cluster of holiday and retirement homes that make up Hatfields Beach to **WAIWERA**, 6km north of Orewa, where Maori once dug holes in the sands to take advantage of the naturally hot springs. Bathing is now formalized in the **Waiwera Thermal Resort**, Waiwera Road (*www.waiwera.co.nz*; daily 9am–10pm; $14), a vast complex of suicidal water slides and over twenty indoor and outdoor pools naturally heated to between 34 and 46°C.

Occupying a high headland between the estuaries of the Puhoi and Waiwera rivers, **Wenderholm Park** was the first of Auckland's regional parks and is still one of the most celebrated. Its sweeping golden beach is backed by pohutukawa-shaded swathes of grass and is often packed with barbecuing families on summer weekends. Walking tracks ranging from twenty minutes to two hours wind up through nikau palm groves onto the headland and you can take a peek at **Coudrey House** (Jan daily 1–4pm, Feb–Dec Sat & Sun 1–4pm; $1.50 donation requested), an 1860s colonial homestead. The #895 bus terminates here on summer Sundays.

Puhoi

The village of **PUHOI**, 6km north of Waiwera, is reached on a side road that passes a Calvary – evidence of the staunchly Catholic Bohemian migrants who arrived here in 1863 from Egerland, in what was then the Austro-Hungarian Empire. Their descendants still form a small proportion of Puhoi's tiny population. As the land was found to be poor, the settlers were forced to eke out a living by cutting the bush for timber, and the horns of some of the more famed bullock teams are still ranged around the walls of the historic **Puhoi Tavern**, a single-roomed bar festooned with all manner of pioneering paraphernalia and photos of harder times. Buy a beer, charm the bartender and you may be invited to see the side room, with its kauri table laid with numerous ancient tea services and walls hung with what is claimed to be New Zealand's largest collection of paintings of Maori chiefs and princesses. Come on the second or last Friday of each month to see ageing members of a local Bohemian band playing their accordions and supping jugs of beer.

Few visitors get much further than the pub, but there is an interesting **Puhoi Historical Society Museum** (Christmas–Easter daily 1–4pm; Easter–Christmas Sat, Sun & school holidays 1–4pm; $1 donation requested) in the former Convent School, with a model of the village as it once was and a phalanx of volunteers brimming with tales of the old days. For some gentle activity, you can **kayak** along a tidal section of the river ($15 per hour) or continue downstream to Wenderholm (2hr; $30, including pickup at the far end) with Puhoi River Canoe Hire (☎09/422 0891).

Southeast of Auckland

Most southbound travellers hurry along Auckland's southern motorway to Hamilton or turn off to Thames at Pokeno – either way missing out on the (admittedly modest) attractions of the **Hunua Ranges** and **The Seabird Coast** on its eastern shore. For **cyclists** in particular the coast road is an excellent way into and out of Auckland, avoiding the worst of the city's traffic: follow Tamaki Drive from central Auckland then wind through Panmure, Howick and Whitford to Clevedon and the coast.

Even for Auckland day-trippers the older and more rounded Hunuas definitely play second fiddle to the more biologically rich Waitakeres, but there are a few decent walks – notably those around the **Hunua Falls**. There are greater rewards further south with excellent seabird viewing and hot pools at **Miranda**.

The Hunua Ranges

A considerable amount of rain dumps on the 700m-high **Hunua Ranges**, 50km southeast of Auckland, and flows down into a series of four dams which jointly supply sixty percent of the city's water. The bush surrounding the reservoirs was once logged for kauri but has largely regenerated, providing a habitat for birds; bellbirds, long since extinct in the city, can sometimes be heard here.

Access to the region is easiest through the village of **CLEVEDON**, home to Auckland's polo club (games on Sundays Dec–April; ☎09/292 8556), and with a couple of restaurants and a smattering of craft shops. Pressing on south to Hunua, you'll come across the **Hunua Ranges Park visitor centre** (daily 8am–4.30pm), which sells the *Hunua Recreation & Track Guide* ($8) – invaluable for extended walks in the ranges. The best of the walks are around the thirty-metre Hunua Falls, around 5km east, where the Wairoa River carves its way through the crater of an ancient volcano. A good half-day hike, passing some lovely swimming holes, crosses the Wairoa River at the falls and follows Massey Track to Cossey's Dam and back down the Cossey Creek Track to the falls.

The Seabird Coast and Miranda

The Hunua Ranges are bounded to the east by the Firth of Thames, a sheltered arm of the Hauraki Gulf which separates South Auckland from the Coromandel Peninsula. Its frequently windswept western littoral has become known as **the Seabird Coast**, in recognition of its international importance for migrating shorebirds; almost a quarter of all known species visit the region. During winter, the vast inter-tidal flats support huge 30,000-strong flocks of birds, with over fifty percent of the entire world population of the wrybill plover over-wintering here. During the southern summer (Sept–March), the arctic migrants are more significant – notably bar-tailed godwits and lesser knots, as well as turnstones, curlews, sandpipers and red-necked stints – who fly 15,000 kilometres from Alaska, Siberia and Mongolia.

The tidal flats butt up against the geologically significant "chenier plain" around Miranda, where the land has been built up from successive depositions of shell banks; much has been converted to farmland but newer shell banks in the making can be seen along the coast.

From Clevedon the coast road winds 35km past the small beach settlements of Kawakawa Bay and Orere Point, and the **Tapapakanga Regional Park** (primitive camping $5) to **KAIAUA**. Here you'll find the *Kaiaua Motor Camp* (☎09/232 2712; tent sites $8, cabins ②) and decent en-suite rooms at the *Bay View Hotel* (☎09/232 2717 fax 232 2658; ③), which also does a good grilled snapper. The adjacent *Kaiaua Fisheries*, has twice been voted the best **fish and chip** shop in the land, and now operates a licensed seafood restaurant in the evening.

The coast's birdlife is thoroughly interpreted at the **Miranda Shorebird Centre**, 7km south of Kaiaua (daily 9am–5pm, and often later); they'll fill you in on the current hot sightings and point you in the direction of the best viewing spots. With a sunny veranda for viewing, the centre also has a good self-catering accommodation (phone ☎09/232 2781 or see the warden in the cottage next door; dorms ①, flat ③). A further 7km south are the slightly alkaline **Miranda Hot Springs** (daily 9am–9pm; $7, private spa $3 extra per hour), with a large warm, open pool surrounded by grassy lawns and barbecue areas with private kauri spa tubs. Entry to the pool is free if you stay at the adjacent *Miranda Holiday Park* (☎ & fax 07/867 3205 & 0800/833 144; tent sites $12, dorms ①, on-site vans ③, cabins ⑤).

From here it is a twenty-minute drive to Thames (see p.334).

ISLANDS OF THE HAURAKI GULF

One of Auckland's greatest assets is the island-studded **Hauraki Gulf**, a seventy-kilometre-square patch of ocean to the northeast of the city that was recently host to New Zealand's successful defence of the America's Cup. In Maori, Hauraki means "wind from the north" – though the gulf is somewhat sheltered from the prevailing winds and ocean swells by the islands of Great Barrier and Little Barrier, creating benign conditions for Auckland's legions of yachties. Most are content just to sail but those who wish to strike land can choose from some of the 47 islands, administered by the Department of Conservation, and designated either for recreational use, with full access, or as sanctuaries for endangered wildlife, requiring permits.

Auckland's nearest island neighbour is uninhabited **Rangitoto**, a flat cone of gnarled and twisted lava which dominates the harbourscape. The most populous of the gulf islands is **Waiheke**, increasingly a commuter suburb of Auckland – but one with sandy beaches and a delightfully slow pace, enlivened by some quality wineries and an improving range of restaurants. Such sophistication is a far cry from the largest island hereabouts, **Great Barrier**, which until recently seemed trapped in a thirty-year time warp. However, the advent of fast ferries has put its sandy surf beaches, hilly tramping tracks and exceptional fishing within easy reach of holidaying Aucklanders and international visitors, many of whom continue on to the Coromandel (see p.325). DOC's happy compromise of allowing access to wildlife sanctuaries is wonderfully demonstrated at **Tiritiri Matangi**, where a day-trip gives visitors an unsurpassed opportunity to see some of the world's rarest bird species. **Little Barrier Island** resists any such interference, and is pretty much off-limits except to researchers.

Frequent **ferries** run to the more popular islands from the wharves around Auckland's Ferry Building, at the foot of Queen Street; there's a DOC **information** centre (Mon–Fri 10am–6pm, plus Nov to mid-March Sat & Sun 10am–3pm; ☎09/379 6476, fax 379 3609, *jhart@doc.govt.nz*), conveniently located in the same complex. Around the corner is the Fullers Cruise Centre (daily 8am–5pm; bookings and enquiries ☎09/367 9111, timetable information ☎09/367 9102, *www.fullers.co.nz*, *enquiries@fullersakl.co.nz*), which sells tickets for most island-bound boats. A few steps along the waterfront you'll also find the upstart Pacific Ferries who run slightly cheaper services to Waiheke, and Pakatoa Ferries (☎09/379 0066) who run to the tiny township of Coromandel on the peninsula of the same name. For more on cruising and kayaking the gulf, see our box on p.74.

Rangitoto and Motutapu islands

The distinctive, low, conical shape of **Rangitoto**, 10km northeast of the city centre, is a familiar sight to every Aucklander – yet few Aucklanders have actually set foot on the island. They miss out on a freakish land of fractured black lava, with the world's largest pohutukawa forest clinging precariously to the crevices. Alongside lies the much older and geologically quite distinct island of **Motutapu** or "sacred island", linked to Rangitoto by a narrow causeway.

A **day-trip** is enough to get a feel for Rangitoto, make the obligatory hike to the summit and tackle a few other trails, but **longer stays** are possible if you're prepared to pitch your tent at the primitive campsite at Home Bay on Motutapu.

Rangitoto is Auckland's youngest and largest **volcano**. Molten magma probably pushed its way through the bed of the Hauraki Gulf around six hundred years ago – watched by Motutapu Maori, who apparently called the island "blood red sky" after the awesome spectacle that accompanied its creation. Others attribute the name to a contraction of *Te Rangi i totongia a Tamatekapua* ("the day the blood of Tamatekapua was shed"), recalling an incident when chiefs of the Arawa and Tainui clashed at Islington Bay.

Rangitoto's youth, lack of soil and the porous nature of the rock have created unusual conditions for **plant life**, though the meagre supply of insects attracts few birds, making things eerily quiet. Pohutukawa trees seeded first, given a head start by their roots, which are able to tap underground reservoirs of fresh water up to 20 metres below the surface, then smaller and fleshier plants established themselves under the protective canopy. Harsh conditions have led to some strange botanical anomalies: both

RANGITOTO & MOTUTAPU ISLANDS

Billy Goat Point
Sandy Bay
Administration Bay
Station Bay
Mullet Bay
Motutapu Island
DOC Campsite
Boulder Bay
Gardiner Gap
Whites Beach
McKenzie Bay
Rangitoto Island
Toilets
Home Bay
Rangitoto 260m
Lava Caves
Islington Bay
Otahuhu Point
Wilsons Park
Old Quarry
Summit Track
Coastal Path
Emu Bay
Flax Point
Kidney Fern Grove
Emu Point
Swimming Pool
Kowhai Grove
Rangitoto Wharf

0   2 km

▽ Ferry to Auckland (15 km; 40 min) & Devonport (12 km; 30 min)

epiphytes and mud-loving mangroves are found growing directly on the lava, an alpine moss is found at sea level, and the pohutukawa has hybridized with its close relative, the northern rata, to produce a spectrum of blossoms ranging from pink to crimson. Sadly, the succulent pohutukawa leaves are a big hit with **possums**, which were introduced in the 1880s and proceeded to ravage the forests. Their eradication in 1990 has allowed the pohutukawa to rebounded with renewed vigour, and in fifty years' time Rangitoto will look completely different.

Europeans gave Rangitoto a wide berth until the Crown purchased the island for £15 in 1854, putting it to use as a military lookout point and a workcamp for prisoners. From the 1890s, areas were leased for camping and, in keeping with the defiantly anti-authoritarian streak that thrived in early New Zealand, unauthorized *baches* were cobbled together on the sites. By 1937, over 120 *baches* had sprouted, but subsequent legislation decreed that they could be neither sold nor handed down, and must be removed upon the expiry of the lease. Only thirty-three remain and, ironically, some of the finest examples are being preserved for posterity, their corrugated iron chimneys and cast-off veranda railings used as fenceposts capturing the make-do spirit of the times.

The moment you step across the **causeway** onto **Motutapu**, the landscape changes dramatically; suddenly, you are back in rural New Zealand with its characteristic grassy paddocks, ridge-top fencelines, corrugated iron barns and macrocarpa windbreaks. The DOC's plan is to gradually restore its cultural and natural landscape, replanting the valleys with native trees – you can join their volunteer programme (see p.64 for details)

RANGITOTO SUMMIT WALK

The best way to appreciate Rangitoto Island is on foot; but bear in mind that, though not especially steep, the terrain is rough and it can get very hot out there on the black lava. Consequently the best walks are those that follow shady paths to the summit rather than the more open roads. A favourite is the clockwise **Summit/Coastal Path loop** (12km; 5–6hr; 260m ascent) around the southeast of the island. Turn left just past the toilets at Rangitoto Wharf and follow signs for the **Kowhai Grove**, a typical Rangitoto bush area with an abundance of the yellow-flowering kowhai that blossoms in September. Turn right onto the coastal road towards Rangitoto Wharf then left into **Kidney Fern Grove**, which is packed with unusual miniature ferns that unfurl after rain. The well-worn **Summit Track** winds through patches of pohutukawa forest. Around three-quarters of the way to the summit, a side track leads to the **lava caves** (20min return), which probe deep into the side of the volcano. Further along the main track a former military observation post on the **summit** provides views down into the bush-shrouded sixty-metre-deep crater and out across Auckland city and the Hauraki Gulf.

Continue northwards to the east–west road across the island and follow it towards Islington Bay; from there, pick up the **coastal track** south, initially following the bay then cutting inland through some little-frequented forests back to Rangitoto Wharf.

– restoring wetlands and interpreting the numerous Maori sites. Currently though Motutapu is drearier than Rangitoto: about the only thing to do is walk the Motutapu Walkway to the campsite and beach at Home Bay (6km; 1hr 30min one-way), then walk back again.

Practicalities

Fullers **ferries** (Christmas–April 3 daily; May–Christmas Mon–Fri 2 daily, Sat & Sun 3 daily; $18 return), dock at Rangitoto Wharf after a thirty-minute journey from Auckland; there are also occasional departures from Devonport. At Rangitoto Wharf there is an **information kiosk**, which opens to coincide with ferry arrivals; here you'll find a few bags of potato chips, a toilet block, the island's only **drinking water**, and a sun-warmed saltwater swimming pool that's great for kids. Apart from more toilet facilities at Islington Bay there's nothing else on the island, so bring everything you need – including strong shoes to protect you from the sharp rocks, sun hat, raincoat and, if you're planning a walk, carry plenty of water. Boats are met by the only transport on the island, the **Summit Safari**, a dusty summit trip on a shaded, tractor-drawn buggy with a full and informative commentary (2hr; $17); the final 800m is on foot along a boardwalk.

The DOC have intentionally done all they can to ensure that the twin islands are the preserve of day-trippers. As a concession to the hardy and determined, there is a primitive but pleasant beachside DOC **campsite** ($6), with toilets and water, at Home Bay on the eastern side of Motutapu, over an hour's walk from Islington Bay and almost three hours' walk from Rangitoto Wharf.

Waiheke Island

Pastoral **WAIHEKE**, 20km east of Auckland, is the second-largest of the gulf islands and easily the most populous, particularly on summer weekends when Auckland day-trippers and weekenders quadruple the island's 8000 resident population. The traffic isn't all one-way, though, and a fast and frequent ferry service makes it feasible for a tenth of the islanders to leave every day for work in the city – a trend that threatens to turn Waiheke into just another suburb. For the moment Waiheke, with its chain of sandy beaches along the north coast and a climate that's slightly warmer and a lot less humid than Auckland, retains its sybaritic character – and is increasingly being discovered by international visitors in search of a peaceful spot to recover from jet lag or to idle away their last few days before flying out.

The **earliest settlers** on Waiheke trace their lineage back to the crew of the Tainui canoe who landed at Onetangi and gave the island its first name of *Te Motu-arai-Roa*, "the long sheltering island". *Waiheke*, or "cascading waters", originally referred to a particular creek but was assumed by European settlers to cover the whole island. Among the first **Europeans** to set foot on Waikehe was Samuel Marsden, who preached here in 1818 and established a mission near Matiatia. The island went through the familiar cycle of kauri logging, gum digging and clearance for farming. Gradually, the island's magnificent coastal scenery gained popularity as a setting for grand picnics, and hamper-encumbered Victorians, surreally attired in formal dress, arrived in boatloads.

Development was initially sluggish, but the availability of cheap land amid dramatic landscapes drew painters and **craftspeople** to the island's shores; others followed as access from Auckland became easier and faster. Since the mid-1980s, the city has been less than forty minutes away, and Waiheke has become increasingly **sophisticated**: dilapidated shacks have been replaced by swanky condos, cafés and restaurants are a match for many in Auckland and boutique **wineries** produce some of the finest Cabernet Sauvignon blends in the country.

Arrival, information and getting around

Fullers operate fast **ferries** (35min; $17 return, bikes free) from the Ferry Building in Auckland to the Matiatia Wharf at the western end of Waiheke, just over a kilometre from the main settlement of Oneroa, every couple of hours. Fullers have been forced to drop their fares (previously $23) to match those of Pacific Ferries (☎09/303 1741, fax 303 1742, *www.pacificferries.co.nz, admin@pacificferries.co.nz*) a new player which also runs fast ferries along an identical route to almost the same timetable ($17 return). If you're staying for a couple of days or longer, you may find it cost-effective to bring your vehicle over using the daily **car ferry**, a flat-deck barge run by Subritzky Shipping Line (☎09/534 5663; $100 return for a car and driver, plus $20 per passenger) from Half Moon Bay near Pakuranga in Auckland's eastern suburbs to Kennedy Point. With frequent fast ferries there is little advantage in **flying** here, though if you are planning to visit Great Barrier Island and don't need to return to Auckland you can fly there with Waiheke Air Services (☎09/372 5000; 2 daily; $65). The **airport** is 3km east of Ostend and is reached by taxi (see "Listings", p.133) for around $10 from Oneroa.

Information

Waiheke's main source of information is the efficient **visitor centre**, 2 Korora Rd, Oneroa (daily: Nov–Easter 9am–5pm; Easter–Oct 9am–4pm; ☎09/372 9999, fax 372 9919, *www.ki-wi.co.nz/vin.htm, waiheke@iconz.co.nz*), which can organize most things on the island, and stores bags for $2 apiece. **Shops**, a couple of **banks** and a post office are also clustered in Oneroa. The weekly *Gulf News* ($1.50) comes out on Thursday afternoons and has details of **what's on**, as well as a rundown of arts and crafts outlets. The island goes mad at Easter for the four days of the **Waiheke Island Jazz Festival**, which is held at venues and cafés all over the island.

Getting around

Ferries connect with the island's two main **bus routes** – #1 to Onetangi via Oneroa, Surfdale and Ostend, and #2 to Rocky Bay via Oneroa, Little Oneroa and Palm Beach –

which return in time for ferry departures. Tickets and a $7 day pass (which becomes worthwhile for return trips between Oneroa and Onetangi) are available on the bus. Pacific Ferries also run their own buses to the main settlements. These operate as feeder services for their ferry runs, but can be used by anyone; Palm Beach return costs $2.50. For more flexibility, rent a vehicle (see "Listings" on p.133 for details of outlets). A car will set you back $50 per day, a jeep $65, both plus 40¢ per kilometre; a scooter goes for $45, while bikes cost around $25 per day, though bear in mind that Waiheke is very undulating and you'll need to be pretty fit.

Day-trippers are well catered for by a number of **island tours**. Among those departing from Auckland, which include the return ferry trip, are Fullers Island Explorer (daily year-round; $34), which includes an hour-and-a-half island tour, plus an all-day bus pass so you can explore further on your own, and their Beyond & Back Tour (Oct–Easter daily, 10am; $40), which visits the eastern half of the island and stops for a barbecue lunch at Onetangi. If you're only here for the wine, Fullers also run a half-day Vineyard Explorer Tour (Dec–Feb daily, Nov & March Wed–Sun, April–Oct Sat & Sun; $56, $33 if you are already on the island) which starts from Auckland at noon and spends three hours sightseeing and visiting the *Mudbrick, Peninsula* and *Stonyridge* vineyards, with the option of returning on a late ferry. On balance, this is the best way to tour the wineries, some of which are otherwise only open by appointment.

Island-based operators include Waiheke Island Shuttles (☎09/372 7756) and several taxi companies (see "Listings", p.133), which all run tours and **drop-offs** at accommodation around the island, with prices depending on numbers and destination.

Accommodation

If your visit coincides with the Jazz Festival, the peak Christmas and January season, or any weekend, be sure to **reserve** a room as far **in advance** as you can, though this tends to be less critical at the backpacker hostels dotted along the north coast beaches. At other times, accommodation is fairly plentiful, especially if you follow Aucklanders' lead and go for **B&Bs**; most are registered with the visitor centre and with the Fullers Cruise Centre at the Ferry Building in Auckland. **Camping** is restricted to the grounds of the various hostels and a primitive, windswept and hard-to-reach site at *Whakanewha Regional Park* ($5, permit required from the visitor centre) on the tidal Rocky Bay, a couple of kilometres' walk from the nearest bus stop.

Though there's a lot to be said for basing yourself at one of the quieter and more relaxing **beaches** like Palm Beach and Onetangi, many people prefer to stay close to Oneroa, for the convenience of being near the buses, restaurants, shops and other facilities.

Hotels, motels and B&Bs

Appletree Cottage, 33 Kiwi St, Oneroa (☎09/372 6647). A simple but pleasant and inexpensive cottage for rent. ④.

Island View, 9 Hauraki Rd, Palm Beach (☎09/372 9000). A friendly, modern B&B with good sea views, but a fifteen-minute trek to the beach. ⑤.

Jungle's Edge, 5a Crescent Rd West, Palm Beach (☎ & fax 09/372 2283, *homepages.win .co.nz/windsors, windsors@win.co.nz*). Gay-run and gay-orientated B&B in a big modern home with a large secluded deck in the bush, ten minutes' stroll from Palm Beach. Rates include a cooked breakfast and they drop to ⑥ for subsequent nights. Includes cooked breakfast, pick up and drop off. ⑦.

Kiwi House, 23 Kiwi St, Oneroa (☎09/372 9123, *kiwihouse@clear.net.nz*). At this sociable place, several good rooms (with continental breakfast included) all have access to communal self-catering facilities, a TV lounge and barbecue. ④.

Palm Beach Lodge, 23 Tiri View Rd, Palm Beach (☎ & fax 09/372 7763, *palmbch@talk.co.nz*). Luxurious salmon-pink guesthouse with lovely rooms, each with a balcony overlooking the sea and free use of kayaks, mountain bikes and a dinghy. ⑨.

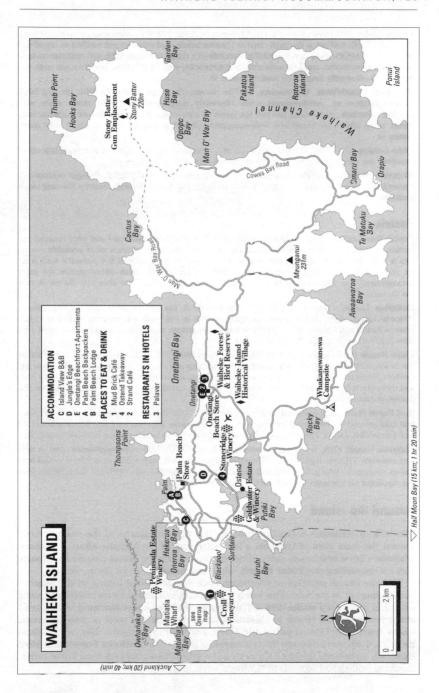

WAIHEKE ISLAND

ACCOMMODATION

C Island View B&B
D Jungle's Edge
E Onetangi Beachfront Apartments
A Palm Beach Backpackers
B Palm Beach Lodge

PLACES TO EAT & DRINK

1 Mud Brick Café
4 Ostend Takeaway
2 Strand Café

RESTAURANTS IN HOTELS

3 Palaver

◁ Auckland (20 km; 40 min)

▽ Half Moon Bay (15 km; 1 hr 20 min)

0 ⸺ 2 km

Punga Lodge, 223 Ocean View Rd, Little Oneroa (☎ & fax 372 6675, *www.ki-wi.co.nz/punga.htm*). Delightful B&B, well set in the bush close to Oneroa beach, and with tea and muffins on tap all day provided by helpful hosts. Accommodation consists of a range of comfortable and spacious en-suite doubles with verandas, and four self-catering apartments of different sizes. There's a spa pool, and good-value off-season deals. Free boat transfers. ⑥.

Onetangi Beachfront Apartments, 27 The Strand, Onetangi (☎09/372 7051, fax 372 5056, *www.onetangi.co.nz*, *info@onetangi.co.nz*). Recently upgraded waterfront motel units with kayaks, volleyball court, sauna and two spa pools all free to guests. Some units are quite old fashioned, while others are brand new, well-equipped and with sea views. Older units ⑤, new apartments ⑥.

Twin Gables, 17 Tiri Rd, Oneroa (☎09/372 9877). Another goodie, this bed and breakfast offers excellent sea views from attractive modern rooms with shared facilities. ⑤.

Women's Guesthouse, Hekerua Bay (call for directions ☎09/372 9284). Budget women-only (though not exclusively lesbian) retreat near a secluded bay with bush walks nearby. Evening meals available. ②.

Hostels

Fossil Bay Lodge, 58 Korora Rd, Oneroa (☎09/372 7569). A haphazard and very relaxed collection of huts, small dorms and self-catering units including a mud-brick affair available during Jan & Feb when it isn't being used as a Steiner school. It is all located five minutes' walk from an all-but private beach, a kilometre from town on an organic farm where guests (by prior arrangement) can often do four hours' work in return for a room. Tent sites $10, dorms ①, cabins ②, units ③.

Hekerua Lodge, 11 Hekerua Rd, Little Oneroa (☎ & fax 09/372 8990, *collrich@clear.net.nz*). Peaceful and friendly, pool-equipped backpackers set in the bush ten minutes' walk from Little Oneroa Beach and Oneroa shops, and with additional private rooms and a self-contained unit. Tent sites $12, dorms ①, rooms ③, unit ⑤.

Palm Beach Backpackers, 54 Palm Rd, Palm Beach (☎09/372 8662). Lively backpackers right by the beach with nice verandas, grassy lawns for camping and chalets divided into small dorms and doubles. Breakfast and evening barbecues are usually available, there are kayaks and bikes for rent, and there is a full programme of winery and island tours, kayaking trips and the like. Tent sites $12, dorms ①, rooms ②.

Red Earth Homestay, 6 Kennedy Rd, Surfdale (☎09/372 9975). A very peaceful and relaxed place that falls somewhere between a backpackers and a homestay with space for just five people (a twin and a three-bed dorm). There's a nice deck and easy access to beach and the Surfdale shops. ①.

Waiheke Island YHA, Seaview Rd, Onetangi (☎ & fax 09/372 8971, *robb.meg@bigfoot.com*). A well-run associate YHA set high on the hill overlooking the beach, with a host of activities available to guests – mountain-biking, kayaking and snorkelling. Call Jaguar Tours (☎09/372 7312) before leaving Auckland for transport to the hostel. Dorms ①, rooms ②.

Around the island

The bulk of Waiheke's population inhabits the western quarter of the island, chiefly around the main town of **Oneroa**, a kilometre east of the Matiatia wharf. For many, Waiheke's finest beaches lie east of Oneroa, particularly the almost circular **Enclosure Bay** for snorkelling and **Palm Beach**, while **Onetangi** is one for the surfies.

Waiheke has no shortage of diversions once you've tired of baking on the beaches and cooling off in the surf. The lovely bays and headlands lend themselves to some short but often steep **walks** detailed in the free *Waiheke Island Walkways* leaflet, available from the visitor centre in Oneroa. One of the best and most accessible coastal tracks leads from Oneroa past Little Oneroa around to Enclosure Bay, while inland there's a shady stroll through the regenerating bush of the **Waiheke Forest and Bird Reserve**, up behind Onetangi. If you're still restless, take your pick from horse riding, kayaking, sailing and so on (see "Listings" on p.133).

Oneroa and around

The settlement of **ONEROA** is draped across a narrow isthmus between the sandy sweep of Oneroa Bay – one of the best and most accessible beaches on the island – and the shallow and silty Blackpool Beach. The ridge-top main street runs up to the island's visitor centre (see p.127), where you can pick up a free leaflet about the *Arts & Crafts Trail* around the scattered **studios** of Waiheke's numerous artists and craftspeople; studio opening times tend to be erratic, so call ahead if you're set on visiting particular workshops (phone numbers are in the leaflet). Local artists' work is also displayed in the adjoining Artworks gallery (daily 10am–4pm; free). In the same building is the slightly eccentric **Whittaker's Musical Experience** (daily except Tues 10am–4pm; donations requested), a room full of flageolets, piano accordions, player pianos, xylophones and more, some dating back two hundred years – and all ably demonstrated during the "musical experience" performance (at 1pm; 1hr 30min; $7, $4 if you're on the Island Explorer tour). Two of Waiheke's **vineyards** are easily accessible from Oneroa: the *Peninsula Estate*, 52a Korora Rd, 1km northwest of town (☎09/372 7866; sales daily 1–4pm in summer; free tours and tastings by appointment only); and the more casual *Mudbrick*, 2km west on Church Bay Road (☎09/372 9050; daily in summer; tours and tasting by appointment), where you should also investigate the attached *Mudbrick Vineyard Restaurant* (see "Eating and entertainment", overleaf).

The rest of the island

What passes for a main road on Waiheke winds east from Oneroa through the contiguous settlements of Little Oneroa, Blackpool and Surfdale, and across the lagoon at Putaki Bay to **OSTEND**. The island's light-industrial heart, far from any appealing beaches, Ostend is best ignored except on Saturday mornings (8am–1pm) when the Ostend Hall, corner of Ostend Rd and Belgium St, is given over to the **Ostend Market**, a very Waiheke affair with organic produce, arts and crafts, food stalls, massage, iridology readings, and local entertainers.

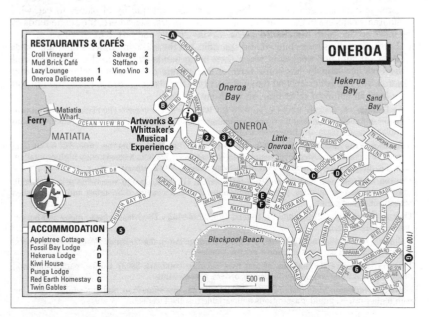

RESTAURANTS & CAFÉS

Croll Vineyard	5	Salvage	2
Mud Brick Café		Steffano	6
Lazy Lounge	1	Vino Vino	3
Oneroa Delicatessen	4		

ONEROA

ACCOMMODATION

Appletree Cottage	F
Fossil Bay Lodge	A
Hekerua Lodge	D
Kiwi House	E
Punga Lodge	C
Red Earth Homestay	G
Twin Gables	B

0   500 m

A couple of Waiheke's most reputable **wineries** lie between here and Onetangi. At *Goldwater Estate*, 18 Causeway Rd (☎09/372 7493; sales and tastings daily 11am–4pm in summer), you can picnic in style, accompanied by one of their fine wines (price range $15–30); you'll need to bring your own provisions, but glasses are lent for free if you buy wine. The organic, hand-tended vineyards of *Stonyridge*, 80 Onetangi Rd, produce the world-class Larose, one of New Zealand's top Bordeaux-style reds. Each vintage is sold out before it is even bottled so there are often no cellar-door sales, but the **tour and tasting** (by appointment, ☎09/372 8822; $10, or coordinate your visit with the Fullers tour – generally 11.30am on summer weekends) is entertaining and you can stick around for an excellent, moderately priced al fresco meal in view of the vines, olive trees and cork oaks.

Six kilometres east of Oneroa, **PALM BEACH** takes a neat bite out of the north coast, with houses tumbling down to a small sandy beach separated by a handful of rocks from the nude bathing zone at the western end. The Palm Beach Store rents boogie boards at $10 per day. Waiheke's longest and most exposed beach is **ONETANGI**, popular in summer with surfers, board riders and swimmers, and an occasional venue for beach horse races, usually Waitangi weekend at the beginning of February. The beachside Onetangi Beach Store rents waveskis ($10 an hour) and boogie boards ($5 an hour).

There are no shops or restaurants east of Onetangi, just tracts of open farm land riddled with fledgling vineyards and bordered by fine swimming beaches. One of the best of these is **Cactus Bay**, which is accessible down a short track from the end of Man O' War Bay Road, 6km east of Oneroa. Jaguar Tours (☎09/372 7312) run trips out to the road end, the start of the track (12km return; 3–4hr return) to the labyrinth of dank concrete tunnels which make up **Stony Batter**, abandoned World War II defences against the threat of Japanese attack – take a torch if you want to poke around.

Eating and entertainment

Oneroa is unchallenged on Waiheke for its **range** and **quality** of places to eat, with restaurants catering to the demands of city day-trippers. Elsewhere, the scene tends to be more ad hoc, with **beachside cafés** serving snacks and fast food.

Entertainment is more limited and sporadic, but there is sometimes something on at *Salvage* on summer weekends when they bring bands over from the mainland, and *Vino Vino* occasionally has some form of **live music** on summer weekends. Beyond Oneroa, you can generally find musical activity at the *Onetangi Beach Hotel*, though you may have an enforced quiet time on weekday nights.

Lazy Lounge, cnr Waikare Rd & Ocean View Rd. Waiheke's loosest café. The place to hang out with an endless parade of the island's more interesting characters calling in for coffee, mushroom and pumpkin lasagne, pizza or a hearty slice of cake.

Mudbrick Vineyard Restaurant, Church Bay Road, 2km west of Oneroa (☎09/372 9050). The expensive but delicious Mediterranean-inspired meals here maintain a consistently high reputation. Lunch & dinner daily in summer with mains approaching $30; licensed.

Oneroa Delicatessen, 153 Ocean View Rd, Oneroa. The best, though somewhat pricey, place in town for wholesome quiches, panini, sumptuous cakes and a range of breakfast and lunch dishes served with good coffee.

Ostend Takeaways, 30 Belgium St, Ostend (☎09/372 8463). The island's best chippy and burger bar, and they deliver.

Palaver, The Strand, Onetangi (☎09/372 8028). Lounge bar in the *Onetangi Beach Hotel* also serving fairly standard bar food at modest prices. Licensed.

Pizzeria and caffe da Stefano, Miami Ave, Surfdale (☎09/372 5309). Coffee, panini and good pizza restaurant that will deliver for larger orders. Closed Mon.

Salvage, Pendragon Mall, Oneroa (☎09/372 2273). Opposite *Vino Vino*, and in a similar vein – but with higher prices, grander aspirations and variable results. Licensed.

Strand Café, at the beach store, The Strand, Onetangi. Casual place, serving breakfasts, light meals and takeaways.

Vino Vino, 153 Ocean View Rd, Oneroa (☎09/372 9888). Hard to beat for light meals, extending to bruschetta, warm salads and daily blackboard specials. Eat inside, or out on the deck with fabulous views across to the Coromandel. Licensed.

Listings

Bike rental Wharf Rats Trading Co (☎09/372 7937) rent out regular bikes at the Matiatia wharf.

Car and motorbike rental Waiheke Rental Cars (☎09/372 8635), at Matiatia Wharf and beside the tourist office, rents cars, motorbikes and 50cc scooters and will deliver. Waiheke Auto Rentals (☎ 09/372 8998), also at Matiatia Wharf, so much the same.

Ferries Fullers (☎09/367 9111); Pacific Ferries (☎09/303 1741); Subritzky Shipping Line (☎09/534 5663).

Horse riding Shepherd's Point Riding Centre, 91 Ostend Rd, Ostend (☎09/372 8104) will take you on a two-hour beach ride ($50), or a full-day bush-and-beach session ($80, including lunch).

Internet access Waiheke Business Centre, 124 Ocean View Rd, Oneroa (Mon–Fri 9am–5pm, Sat 9am–4pm; ☎09/372 8997, *koos@shipshop.co.nz*) have Internet access.

Kayaking The one to go with is Ross Adventures (☎09/372 5550), who run from Matiatia and offer four-hour paddles ($50), moonlit evening trips ($50) and round-the-island camping trips (2–5 days; $110 per day).

Medical emergencies Waiheke Island Community Health Services, 5 Belgium St, Ostend (☎09/372 8893, after hours ☎09/372 5005).

Sailing Sailing Adventures (☎025/771704) will run half-day, full-day and overnight sailing trips, provide fishing lines and barbecue your catch. Costs roughly $70 a day with a two-person minimum.

Taxis Dial-a-Cab (☎09/372 9666); Waiheke Taxi (☎09/372 8038).

Great Barrier Island (Aotea)

Rugged and sparsely populated **GREAT BARRIER ISLAND** (*Aotea*) lies 90km northeast of Auckland on the outer fringes of the Hauraki Gulf and, though only 30km long and 15km wide, packs in a mountainous heart which drops away to deep indented harbours in the west and eases gently to golden surf beaches in the east. It is only a two-hour ferry or half-hour plane ride from the big city but seems a world apart, almost anachronistic in its lack of mains electricity or a reticulated water supply. There are no towns to speak of, no industry and no regular public transport, lending Great Barrier that sense of peace and detachment unique to island life, enhanced by **surf beaches**, **hot springs** and **tightly packed mountains** clad in bush spared the ravages of deer and possums.

Ferries arrive in **Tryphena**, the southern harbour and major settlement, some continuing up the west coast to the minuscule hamlets of **Whangaparapara** and **Port Fitzroy**, both ideal jumping-off points for tramps in the Great Barrier Forest. **Claris**, in the east, is the site of the main airport and is convenient for the best beaches at **Medlands** and **Awana Bay**.

Some history

Great Barrier is formed from the same line of extinct **volcanoes** as the Coromandel Peninsula, and shares a common geological and human past. Aotea was one of the places first populated by **Maori**, and the Ngatiwai and Ngatimaru people were occupying numerous pa sites when Cook sailed by in 1769; recognizing the calming influence of Aotea and neighbouring Hauturu on the waters of the Hauraki Gulf, Cook renamed them Great Barrier Island and Little Barrier Island. The vast stands of kauri all over the island were soon seized upon for ships' timbers, the first load being taken in 1791. Kauri **logging** didn't really get under way until the late nineteenth century but continued until 1942, outliving some early copper mining at Miners Head and sporadic attempts to extract gold and silver from a large quartz intrusion in the centre of the island. Kauri logging and gum digging were replaced by a short-lived whale-oil extraction industry at Whangaparapara in the 1950s, but the Barrier soon fell back on tilling the poor clay soils and its peak population of over 5000 dropped back to little more than 1000.

The space and tranquillity of the island appealed to budding alternative lifestylers, many of whom trickled across from the mainland in the 1960s and 1970s. Much of the Seventies idealism has been supplanted by a more modern pragmatism, but **self-sufficiency** remains. Now more of a necessity in the face of isolation than a lifestyle choice, many people grow their own vegetables; everyone has their own water supply and the load on diesel generators is eased by wind-driven turbines and solar panels. However, **agriculture** is beginning to take a back seat to **tourism** and second-home-owners – a trend resisted to some degree by islanders, who fear that the Barrier will become just another commuter suburb for Auckland. At present this seems unlikely, though the introduction of a fast ferry service in 1992 (reducing travelling time from five to two hours) and the inclusion of the Barrier within the domain of Auckland City Council in 1993 have certainly made their mark, and a new entrepreneurial spirit has resulted in dilapidated lodges being bought by ambitious owners keen to make the Barrier a real destination. An anarchic streak lingers, though: until the early 1990s, island vehicles were exempt from the usual annual mechanical checks and even today, when the Department of Transport inspectors come over, half the population stays at home and the island grinds to a halt.

Arrival, information and getting around

Points of entry are the **airport** at Claris on the east coast, the grass airstrip at Okiwi in the north, and the three main **harbours** of Port Fitzroy, Whangaparapara and Tryphena Harbour. Around the first two ports there's little more than a couple of lodges and a shop, leaving the bulk of the activity to the four main bays of Tryphena Harbour. Ferries arrive at Shoal Bay, from where shuttle buses run to Mulberry Grove, where there's a motel, or on to Stonewall Village, where there are several places to stay and eat, and a shop. Puriri Bay is a short walk along the coast from Stonewall.

The vast majority of visitors arrive from Auckland aboard Fullers **ferries** (☎09/367 9111; Nov–Easter Fri & Sun; Easter–Oct Tues, Thurs, Fri & Sun; 2hr), which call at each of the three main west coast harbours. A standard return **fare** costs $99 ($89 if booked 3 days in advance), but look out for specials such as a day-return for $50, a day-return plus a two-hour minibus tour of the island for $67, and occasional backpacker discounts. Shuttle buses meet the ferry, charging around $5–10 to Stonewall Village, $10–15 to Medlands: ask around when you arrive. Ferries are occasionally cancelled due to bad weather, but you can pre-empt the inconvenience this may cause by buying a boat/fly deal ($115), flying back.

With less urgency (or a desire to bring a car), travel with Sealink (☎09/373 4036 & ☎0800/485387, fax 307 1505), who run two comfortable barges which carry passengers, cars and just about all the island's freight, leaving Wynyard Wharf in Auckland (Christmas–Jan daily, Feb–Christmas 5 weekly; 4hr) for Tryphena, with one service a week (Tuesday) continuing to Port Fitzroy. Fares are $400 return for car and driver, $65 return for foot passengers.

To slot into the island pace as soon as you leave Auckland, travel from Marsden Wharf, close to Auckland's Ferry Building, with Great Barrier Shipping Co. (in Auckland ☎09/307 1405, on the Barrier ☎09/429 0431, fax 307 0475; $50 return) which uses an old Pacific Island trading vessel for its twice weekly six-hour service. The

Tuesday service calls at Tryphena, Whangaparapara and back to Auckland; the Thursday run goes to Tryphena, Whangaparapara and Port Fitzroy where it stays overnight, returning to Auckland via Kawau island (see p.149) the next day.

Some visitors prefer the reliability of daily **flights**. The two main players are Great Barrier Airlines (☎09/275 9120 & ☎0800/275 912, *gba@gbair.co.nz*), and Great Barrier Xpress (☎0800/222123, fax 09/325 7026, *mountain.air@xtra.co.nz*). Both operate at least three scheduled flights a day from Auckland International Airport to Claris and charge $169 return; services are met by shuttle buses which drop off in Medlands ($5 each way) and Tryphena ($7 each way). GBA also fly from the Barrier to Whangarei, Whitianga and Tauranga around three times a week. Northern Air (☎09/256 8699) is competitively priced, but runs less frequently to fewer places.

Information

The island currently has no real visitor centre though those disembarking at Tryphena can pick up a fair bit of information from the Fullers kiosk (open for all arrivals) beside the wharf. **Information** is available by phone or fax (Mon–Fri 10am–2pm; ☎09/429 0033, fax 429 0660), and there may be a **visitor centre** (same hours and numbers) in the Civil Defence Building in Claris if funding is forthcoming. The main **DOC office** is the well-stocked and informative Port Fitzroy Field Base (Mon–Fri 8am–4.30pm; ☎09/429 0044, fax 429 0071), ten minutes' walk west of the Port Fitzroy wharf, which is supported by a smaller and sporadically open field base at Whangaparapara. Note that there are **no banks** or ATMs on the island but several places have EFTPOS facilities.

Getting around

Other than a seasonal **bus** service between Tryphena and Claris (Christmas to mid-January only), there is no scheduled public transport on the island. The closest you'll get are services run by Safari Tours & Travel (☎09/429 0448) including a morning bus from Tryphena to Medlands ($10) and on to some hot springs ($15), and a good all-day island **tour** ($45). Bob's Island Tours (☎09/420 0988; $45) do a similar trip, venturing off the beaten track a little more. Both these companies also operate as the island's **taxi** services.

Many people **rent a car** for at least part of their stay, but rates are high, at around $70 for one day, dropping to $60 a day for longer rentals; note that all roads are gravel except for the run from Tryphena to Claris. **Mountain bikes** can be rented for around $20 a day, though the hills are steep and the roads dusty and hot in summer (see "Listings", p.141, for details of car- and bike-rental outfits).

Accommodation

Accommodation on Great Barrier is broad ranging. Walkers and campers are well catered for with some pleasant but basic campsites, a couple of trampers' **huts** and a cabin, which is well set up for groups. Most of these are towards the north of the island, close to the Great Barrier Forest: all six **DOC campsites** are marked on the map on p.137, and tend to be empty most of the year except for Christmas to the end of January when you should definitely book in advance (☎09/429 0044); note that camping is not permitted outside designated campsites. There are now four backpackers' **hostels** scattered across the island, but most of the rest of the accommodation is concentrated around Tryphena Harbour and ranges from comfortable guesthouses to high-class **lodges**. Some of the best of the island's **self-catering cottages** are given below, but there are many more on lists held by Fullers office; the owners often live close by and can arrange breakfast and sometimes dinner. In fact, given the dearth of places to eat, many lodges and **guesthouses** also have self-catering units.

Most places **pick up** from the harbours and airport, though those in Tryphena will expect you to catch the transport which meets each boat or plane. The island's remoteness means that accommodation is generally more **expensive** than the mainland, particularly from Labour Weekend to Easter; some places further boost their rates from Christmas to the end of January when visitor numbers are at their peak – and you'll need to **book well ahead** to stand any chance of finding a place to stay. The price codes we've given below are based on standard summer prices.

Lodges and guesthouses

Barrier Oasis Lodge, Stonewall, Tryphena (☎09/429 0021, fax 429 0034; *barrieroasislodge @xtra.co.nz*). One of the finest places on the island, with lovely en-suite rooms with great valley views and a couple of separate self-contained units. Rooms are let on a B&B basis, though you are encouraged to go full-board with delicious Asian-influenced meals included. Unit ⑦, rooms ⑧.

The Flowerhouse, Rosalie Bay (☎09/429 0464, *flowerhouse@islands.co.nz*). One beautiful guest room in a retreat tucked away in a remote valley, where the emphasis is on peace and healthy living. The room is let on a full-board basis, with meals made from home-grown organic produce. Free pick-up from Tryphena. ⑦.

Great Barrier Lodge, Whangaparapara Harbour (☎09/429 0488, fax 429 0197). This is pretty much all there is at Whangaparapara, and the comfortable harbourside lodge also serves as the local shop. Accommodation is in cottages in the grounds or rooms in the main building, where there is a bar and restaurant serving home-style meals. Mountain bikes are available for $15 per day, as are rental cars ($95). Bunkroom $25pp, rooms ⑤, cottages ⑥.

Jetty Tourist Lodge, Kairara Bay, Port Fitzroy (☎09/429 0050, fax 429 0908). Superbly sited place with bar and restaurant overlooking Kairara Bay, around 2km from Port Fitzroy Wharf. B&B accommodation is in nicely decorated, self-contained chalets. ⑥.

Medlands Lodge, Masons Rd (☎09/429 0352, fax 429 0993). Two self-contained units and a nice double room in a rural setting 2km from the beach. ⑥.

Pigeons Lodge, Shoal Bay Rd, Tryphena (☎09/429 0437, fax 429 0127, *pigeons.lodge@xtra.co.nz*). Small, comfortable and classy B&B nestled in the bush near the sea, with en-suite accommodation, a self-catering chalet and a good licensed restaurant. ⑥.

Pohutukawa Lodge, Stonewall, Tryphena (☎09/429 0211, fax 429 0117, *plodge@xtra.co.nz*). The pick of the places around Tryphena, homely, small and welcoming, with a great pub and restaurant spilling out onto the veranda and peaceful garden. It is all conveniently close to the shop; there are international newspapers on hand, and aromatherapy massage is available. Attractive rooms are let on a B&B basis, and there are compact three-bed backpacker dorms. Dorms ①, B&B ⑤.

Tipi & Bob's Waterfront Lodge, Puriri Bay Rd, Tryphena (☎ & fax 09/429 0550). Good but pricey motel rooms, some with fine sea views. Cottage and units ⑤, with sea views ⑥.

Self-catering cottages

(Note: see also "Lodges and guesthouses" above)

DOC Guest Cottage, Okiwi (☎09/429 0044). Fully-equipped cottage sleeping up to ten, with gas cooking and wood supplied for barbecues. It is a little isolated but beach and forest are only thirty minutes' walk away. ③.

DOC Guest Cottage, Port Fitzroy (☎09/429 0044). Similar set-up to Okiwi above, but beautifully sited at Port Fitzroy adjacent to the DOC office and campsite and ten minutes' walk from the wharf. ③.

Fitzroy House, Glenfern Rd, Port Fitzroy (☎09/429 0091, fax 429 0492, *ftzhouse@voyager.co.nz*). Two very comfortable self-contained cottages sleeping six, one with views over the northern shore of the inner harbour. The emphasis here is on nature tourism with free use of canoes and a dinghy (sea kayaks are extra), a lovely walkway with a bridge into the top of a kauri, and combination walks where you get dropped off by Unimog (a kind of 4WD German military truck), do a hike, then get picked up by yacht. Bring your own food. ⑥.

Hi Look Cottage, Shoal Bay Rd, Tryphena (☎09/429 0437). Quaint, simple self-contained two-bedroom set among native bush and close to the sea. ⑤.

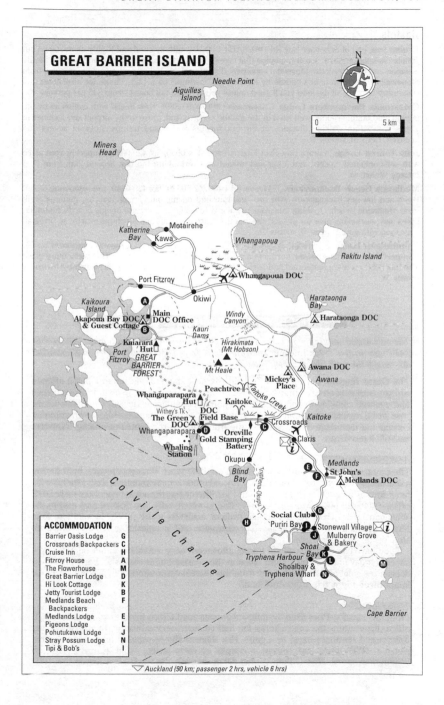

GREAT BARRIER ISLAND

0   5 km

N

Needle Point

Aiguilles Island

Miners Head

Katherine Bay
Kawa
Motairehe

Whangapoua

Rakitu Island

Port Fitzroy
Okiwi

Whangapoua DOC

Kaikoura Island

Ⓐ Main DOC Office
Akapoua Bay DOC & Guest Cottage
Ⓑ

Harataonga Bay

Harataonga DOC

Windy Canyon

Kauri Dams

Kaiarara Hut
Port Fitzroy
GREAT BARRIER FOREST

Hirakimata (Mt Hobson)

Mt Heale

Awana DOC

Awana

Mickey's Place

Peachtree
Whangaparapara Hut

Kaitoke

Withey's Tk
The Green DOC
Whangaparapara
Ⓓ

DOC Field Base

Kaitoke Creek

Ⓒ Crossroads

Kaitoke

Oreville Gold Stamping Battery

Claris
ⓘ

Whaling Station

Okupu

Medlands

Blind Bay

Ⓔ St John's
Ⓕ Medlands DOC

Tryphena-Okupu Tk

Social Club Ⓖ
Ⓗ Puriri Bay
Ⓙ Stonewall Village ⓘ
Mulberry Grove & Bakery

Shoal Bay
Ⓚ
Tryphena Harbour
Shoalbay & Tryphena Wharf
Ⓛ
Ⓝ

Ⓜ

Cape Barrier

ACCOMMODATION

Barrier Oasis Lodge	**G**
Crossroads Backpackers	**C**
Cruise Inn	**H**
Fitzroy House	**A**
The Flowerhouse	**M**
Great Barrier Lodge	**D**
Hi Look Cottage	**K**
Jetty Tourist Lodge	**B**
Medlands Beach Backpackers	**F**
Medlands Lodge	**E**
Pigeons Lodge	**L**
Pohutukawa Lodge	**J**
Stray Possum Lodge	**N**
Tipi & Bob's	**I**

▽ Auckland (90 km; passenger 2 hrs, vehicle 6 hrs)

Hostels

Cruise Inn, end of Schooner Bay Rd (☎025/534 134). Beautifully sited and highly characterful but simple backpacker dorm accommodation that takes a bit of effort to reach but is well worth it for the isolation and the alternative lifestyle it espouses. It's about three hours' walk through bushland from Stonewall or about an hour's paddle by kayak (see "Listings" on p.142). Phone for directions, and remember to bring all the food you'll need unless you arrange full board (from $45 per person). ①.

Crossroads Backpackers Lodge, Crossroads (☎09/429 0889). New hostel with cabins let by the person, and double rooms, well sited in the middle of the island, close to the airport and facilities in Claris and within walking distance of the hot springs and island tramps. Internet access and licensed. Beds ①, rooms ③.

Jetty Tourist Lodge, Kaiara Bay, Port Fitzroy (☎09/429 0050, fax 429 0086). Superbly sited place with self-contained chalets, and a bar and restaurant overlooking the bay, around 2km from Port Fitzroy Wharf. ⑥.

Medlands Beach Backpackers, 9 Mason Rd (☎09/429 0320, fax 429 0340, *tim-mbb@ihug.co.nz*). Basic and low-key backpackers with two- and four-bed dorms on a small farm ten minutes' walk from Medlands Beach – making this place popular with surfers. There are boogie boards, mountain bikes and snorkelling gear for guests' use, but there are no meals and no shops nearby, so bring all your food with you. Dorms ①, rooms ③.

Pohutukawa Lodge, Stonewall, Tryphena (☎09/429 0211, fax 429 0117, *pigeons.lodge@xtra.co.nz*). Compact three-bed backpacker dorms in a good location close to the shop. This welcoming place also has B&B rooms, a restaurant and Irish pub, and aromatherapy massage is available. Dorms ①, rooms ⑤.

THE GREAT BARRIER FOREST TRAMP

The only decent walking map is the 1:50,000 Great Barrier Island Infomap ($13.50); the DOC also print a Track Information leaflet (50¢ from DOC offices) which will just about do, though the walk timings are a little inconsistent.

The **Great Barrier Forest**, New Zealand's largest stand of possum-free bush, offers a **unique** tramping **environment**. Because the area is so compact, in no time at all you can find yourself climbing in and out of little subtropical gullies luxuriant with nikau palms, tree ferns, regenerating rimu and kauri, up onto scrubby manuka ridges with stunning coastal and mountain views. Many of the tracks follow the routes of mining tramways past old kauri dams.

ACCESS AND HUTS

The tramp can be done equally well from Port Fitzroy or Whangaparapara, both having a reasonably well-stocked shop, a campsite and other accommodation. Both also have 24-bunk **huts** (Category 2; $10) nearby, but Port Fitzroy has the advantage of the main DOC office (☎09/429 0044; Mon–Fri 8am–4.30pm), which sells hut **tickets** and **maps**; the Whangaparapara DOC residence has leaflets available in the porch. In addition, Port Fitzroy's beautifully sited *Akapoua Bay* **campsite** ($6) is superior to Whangaparapara's simple site, *The Green* ($6).

If you have come specifically to tramp, afternoon ferry arrivals at either port dictate a short first day followed by a night spent at the nearest hut or campsite. Early afternoon departures point to a short final day from the nearest accommodation, making for a min-imum **three-night trip** from Auckland.

THE TRAMP

From the wharf at **Port Fitzroy**, follow the coast road fifteen minutes south to the DOC office. From there the road climbs for half an hour over a headland with views over Kairara and Rarohara bays, to a gate. The Kairara Hut is roughly fifteen minutes on, along a 4WD track and across a couple of river fords. From **Kairara Hut to Whangaparapara Hut** (13km; 7–9hr; 800m ascent), the track soon leaves the 4WD

Stray Possum Lodge, Shoal Bay (☎ & fax 09/429 0109; *www.acb.co.nz/stray-possum, straypossumlodge@acb.co.nz*). Very much part of the backpacker circuit, this activity-orientated hostel has a bar and on-site café (with pizza oven) set in a spacious clearing in attractive bush. Beds are in four- to six-bed dorms or in well-appointed self-contained chalets ideal for groups of up to six. Daily trips visit the hot springs or drop-off for walks and horse rides, and there are mountain bikes, kayaks, snorkelling gear and surfboards for rent (see also "Tours" in Listings on p.142 for details of package deals from Auckland). Tent sites $12, dorms ①, made-up rooms ③, chalets ⑤.

Campsites

Akapoua DOC Campsite, Port Fitzroy. Harbour edge site right by the DOC office and an easy walk to the harbour and shop at Port Fitzroy. It comes equipped with coin-operated barbecues, cold showers and toilets. Tent sites $6.

Awana DOC Campsite, Awana. Exposed site with separate tent and vehicle sites, all 400m from a good surf beach. Cold showers and toilets. Tent sites $6.

The Green DOC Campsite, Whangaparapara. Basic campsite with barbecues, water and toilets but without vehicular access. No showers but it's close to the sea and there's a stream to wash in. Tent sites $6.

Harataonga DOC Campsite, Harataonga. Shady site 300m back from the beach, equipped with toilets and cold showers. Tent sites $6.

Medlands DOC Campsite, Medlands Beach. Attractive beach-back site that gets very crowded in the peak season. Cold showers, stream water and toilets. Tent sites $6.

---

track and crosses the Kairara Stream several times as it climbs steeply to the first and most impressive **kauri dam** (see overleaf), reached in under an hour. The well-defined path continues for another fifty minutes to one of the upper dams then begins a long and arduous series of boardwalks and wooden steps designed to keep trampers on the path and prevent the disturbance of nesting black petrels. It'll take a good thirty to forty minutes to reach the summit of the 621-metre **Hirakimata** (Mount Hobson), where you'll be amply rewarded by panoramic views.

Less extensive boardwalks extend south around the dramatic spire of Mount Heale towards the junction of **two paths**. To the right a path follows the south branch of the Kairara Stream **back to the Kairara Hut** in around an hour and a half, making a four-to-five-hour circuit from the hut. The leftmost path follows an undulating but gradually descending route into Kaitoke Creek No.1 eventually reaching the edge of Kaitoke Swamp right by the hard-to-locate **Peach Tree Hot Spring**. Originally dug by kauri loggers, the pools here are hotter than the more widely used **Kaitoke Hot Spring** – the latter reached along a ten-minute track which spurs off south twenty minutes ahead; the more attractive hollows are to be found upstream. Back on the main track, you soon reach the 4WD forest road: follow it south for a hundred metres or so, then join the sign-posted track to **Whangaparapara Hut**, fifteen minutes on. From here it is ten minutes' walk to the DOC residence and half an hour to the Whangaparapara Wharf.

There are two main routes from **Whangaparapara Hut to Kairara Hut**, the direct and dull route following the Pack Track due north of the hut and the 4WD forest road (11km; 5hr; 200m ascent), and the more appealing semi-coastal Kiwiriki Track (12km; 6hr; 300m ascent) which branches off the 4WD forest road just north of its junction with the Pack Track. The track cuts west from the forest road by the rocky knob of Maungapiko, leading to the picnic area at Kiwiriki Bay then climbing steeply over a ridge to Coffins Creek before a relatively gentle walk to a second picnic area at **Kairara Bay**. From here it is half an hour to Kairara Hut and another hour or so to the Port Fitzroy Wharf.

An alternative start to either route eschews the Pack Track and follows the far more interesting **Withey's Track**, which starts between the Whangaparapara DOC field base and the hut; it takes half an hour longer, but goes through some lovely bush with delightful streamside nikau groves.

Mickey's Place, Awana (☎09/429 0140). Hospitable commercial campsite 25km north of Tryphena that's less well-sited than the nearby DOC site but features hot showers, toilets and a cookhouse, all for $4.

Around the island

Places which would be regarded as sights in the usual sense are thin on the ground on Great Barrier, and most of those that do exist require some perseverance to get to. Much of the pleasure here is in lazing on the beaches and striking out on foot into the **Great Barrier Forest**, a rugged chunk of regenerating bush and kauri-logging relics that takes up almost half the island between Port Fitzroy and Whangaparapara. If you're looking for more structure to your day, there are a few small-time operators keen to keep you entertained by means of various activities and tours (see "Listings", opposite, for details). Tryphena has a particular dearth of things to do, though there is the appealing **Tryphena to Okupu Walking Track** (4hr) from Puriri Bay around coastal headlands to Okupu on Blind Bay.

Most people head straight for **Medlands Beach**, a long sweep of golden sands broken by a sheltering island and often endowed with some of the Barrier's best surf – though, be warned, there is no patrolled area. The pretty blue and white **St John's Church** looks somewhat out of place – and it is, having only been moved here in 1986, making the journey from the mainland by barge before being dragged over the dunes.

North of Medlands, the road leaves the coast for the airport at **CLARIS**, where the post office runs the gimmicky **Great Barrier Pigeon-Gram Service** (summer only; $20 to send a pigeon-gram letter) in imitation of the original pigeon-mail service – said to be the world's first airmail service – set up in 1898 after it took a sobering three days to notify Auckland that the SS *Wairarapa* had been wrecked on the northwest coast. Birds took under two hours to cover the same distance, and were used until 1908 when a telephone was finally established. One or two letters are now attached to birds which fly to Auckland, where the letters are forwarded anywhere in the world.

Crossroads, 2km north of Claris, is just that – the junction of roads to Okupu, Port Fitzroy and the north of the island, and Whangaparapara. The Whangaparapara road runs past the scant roadside remains of the **Oreville gold stamping battery** (unrestricted entry) and the start of a path to **Kaitoke Hot Springs** (4km; 1hr 20min return; also on the Great Barrier Forest Tramp – see box on previous page), sulphurous dammed pools that aren't especially pretty but are perfect for an hour's wallowing. At Whangaparapara itself, a short stroll around the bay brings you to the foundations of a whaling station built here in the 1950s.

North from Crossroads, the Port Fitzroy road passes two excellent camping spots by the surf beach at Awana Bay, then the start of a short track to **Windy Canyon** (1km; 20–30min return), a narrow defile that gets its name from the eerie sounds produced by certain wind conditions. A narrow path winds through nikau palms and tree ferns to a viewpoint that gives a sense of the island's interior, as well as fabulous coastal views.

The island's highest point, Hirakimata, can be reached in three hours from here or a similar time from **PORT FITZROY**, whose harbour remains remarkably calm under most wind conditions, a property not lost on the dozens of yachties who flock here in summer. Apart from the shop and a few places to stay there's not a lot here, but Port Fitzroy makes the best base for **tramping** or shorter day-walks to some fine **kauri dams** (see box on previous page for details of long and short routes). For three years from 1926, the Kauri Timber Company hacked trees out of the relatively inaccessible Kairara Valley, shunning the tramways and trestle bridges employed in more manageable terrain in favour of six kauri dams – wooden structures up to twenty metres high and spanning the valley floor. Logs were cut and rolled into the reservoirs as the stream built up the water level behind the dams. The upper dams were then tripped, followed seconds later by the lower dams; the combined releases sent a torrent of water and logs sluicing down to Kairara Bay, where they were lashed together in rafts and floated to Auckland.

Eating and drinking

The absence of stand-alone **restaurants** forces pretty much everywhere that provides a bed for the night to offer meals and drinks for both guests and non-residents. There's also a couple of shops where you can get snacks when you're on the move and pick up picnic provisions. **Drinking** tends to happen in bars attached to accommodation establishments or in the social clubs at Tryphena and Crossroads.

Barrier Oasis Lodge, Stonewall, Tryphena (☎09/429 0021). Delicious meals using local and home-grown produce, including olives, their own fresh pasta and delicious cheese, for around $20, while evening meals are table d'hôte and will set you back $40.

Claris Texas Café, Claris. Easily the best café on the island with a sunny deck and a grassy patch for the kids. It is open 8am–5pm daily for light meals, panini, great desserts and excellent coffee; then for à la carte evening meals (summer nightly, winter Thurs–Sat; booking essential ☎09/429 0811) which might include chargrilled calamari or pan-fried sole with ginger and chive hollandaise.

The Currach Irish Pub, Stonewall, Tryphena. An Irish Pub that's about as traditional as you can get on a South Pacific Island – a lot of the paraphernalia came from the owner's grandmother's pub, in County Kerry, which closed in 1950. What's more there's Murphy's, Kilkenny Ale and Celtic Red on tap, and there is often live acoustic music, especially on Thursday when anyone is welcome to jam. Full breakfasts are served until 9.30am, and in the evening you might expect seafood chowder ($7), sirloin steak "pohutukawa" ($17), a platter of fresh local seafood ($19), or one of the chef's daily specials.

The Flowerhouse, Rosalie Bay (☎09/429 0464). Lunches made from home-grown organic produce, including olives, their own fresh pasta and delicious cheese, for around $20. Reservations are essential and they'll pick you up from Tryphena.

Great Barrier Island Sports & Social Club, Whangaparapara Road, at the foot of the road to Medlands Beach (☎09/429 0260). Cavernous public bar with pool tables and bar meals (Wed, Fri & Sat).

Great Barrier Lodge, Whangaparapara Harbour. Bar and restaurant serving home-style meals indoors or from the spacious deck with harbour views.

Jetty Tourist Lodge, Kairara Bay, Port Fitzroy (☎09/429 0050). Spacious restaurant with a large deck and a bar overlooking the bay. Hearty Kiwi meat and seafood dishes go for around $20, and breakfasts, lunches and Devonshire teas are also served.

Pigeons Lodge, Shoal Bay Rd, Tryphena (☎09/429 0437). Guests and visitors alike can avail themselves of this guesthouse's charming licensed restaurant and eat out on the deck (mains around $20).

Tipi & Bob's Holiday Lodge, Puriri Bay, Tryphena (☎09/429 0550). The rather soulless public bar and leafy garden bar are always popular spots, as is the spartan seafood restaurant serving $20–25 mains and cheaper takeaways.

Listings

Bike rental *Stray Possum Lodge* and *Great Barrier Lodge* both rent bikes to guests, or try Great Barrier Hire Centre in Claris (☎09/429 0417) who rent machines to all comers.

Car rental On the southern half of the island, try Tryphena's Better Bargain Rental (☎09/429 0092), the 4WDs of Wheels Down Under Rentals (☎09/429 0110), or cars offered by Bob's Car Rental (☎09/429 0988). For car rental on the north of the island, call Aotea Tours (☎ & fax 09/429 0055).

Fishing To test Great Barrier's enviable reputation, head out for a day's fishing in the Colville Channel aboard any of the Tryphena-based boats who charge $400–500 a day for four people: try Hot Pursuit (☎09/429 0070), Vitamin C (☎09/429 0949) or Mokum (☎09/429 0485).

Golf Pioneer Park, Whangaparapara Rd, Claris (☎09/429 0420; green fee $10, club rental $5), is a nine-hole par-three course surrounded by bush and with pukeko strutting across the fairways; every Thursday and Sunday the lively bar serves cheap drinks and decent meals.

Horse riding Great Barrier Island Adventure Horse Treks (☎09/429 0274) will take you out onto the beach and hinterland for $25 per hour.

Internet *Crossroads Backpackers Lodge*, junction of roads to Okupu, Port Fitzroy and the north of the island, and Whangaparapara, has Internet facilities open to all.

Kayaking Aotea Kayak (☎09/429 0664) operate all year and run short paddling trips ($30), and joint 4–5hr kayak and snorkelling trips ($55).

Scuba diving Tryphena-based Destination Aotea (☎09/429 0449) run dives with all equipment included ($130) exploring some of New Zealand's best locations, with wrecks, varied undersea terrain and stacks of marine life to explore, all in conditions of good visibility (especially in autumn).

Tours *Stray Possum* (☎0800/767 786) offers the "Possum Pursuit Pass" ($45), which includes mountain biking, kayaking, trips and activities for as long as you stay at the lodge; package deals include the pass plus ferry transport to and from Auckland ($99), or a loop from Auckland to the Barrier by ferry, a flight on to Whitianga with Coromandel Air then InterCity bus back to Auckland, or vice versa ($120).

Tiritiri Matangi

No one with even the vaguest interest in New Zealand's wonderful birdlife should pass up the opportunity to visit **Tiritiri Matangi**, a low island 4km off the tip of the Whangaparoa Peninsula and 30km north of Auckland. Tiritiri Matangi is run as an "open sanctuary", and visitors are free to roam through the predator-free bush where, within a couple of hours, it is quite possible to see takahe, stitchbirds, saddlebacks, whiteheads, North Island robins, parakeets and brown teals – though to stand a chance of seeing the little spotted kiwi, you'll have to be here at night.

Judging by evidence from pa sites on the island, Tiritiri Matangi was first populated by the Kawerau **Maori** and later by the Ngati Paoa, both of whom are now recognized as the land's traditional owners. They partly **cleared the island** of bush, a process continued by Europeans who arrived in the mid-nineteenth century to graze sheep and cattle. Fortunately, **predators** such as possums, stoats, weasels, deer, cats, wallabies, rats and the like failed to get a foothold on Tiritiri, so after farming became uneconomic in the early 1970s it was singled out as a prime site for helping to restore barely viable bird populations. The cacophony of birdsong in the Tiritiri bush is stark evidence of just how catastrophic the impact of these predators has been elsewhere.

When grazing stopped, a **reafforestation** programme was implemented: a quarter of a million saplings raised from seeds found on the island have been planted out to form rapidly regenerating bush, though it is still far from mature. The **birds** seem to like it, however, and are mostly thriving – with nesting boxes standing in for decaying trees, and feeding stations equipped with video cameras and pressure-sensitive perches that weigh birds each time they alight.

Three of the species released here are among the rarest in the world, with total populations of around a couple of hundred. The most visible are the flightless **takahe**, lumbering blue-green turkey-sized birds long thought to be extinct (see Contexts p.868 for more on these ungainly critters); birds moved here from Fiordland have bred well and are easily spotted as they seem unafraid of humans and are very inquisitive. **Saddlebacks** and **stitchbirds** both stick to the bush, but often reveal themselves if you sit quietly for a few moments on some of the bush boardwalks. **Northern blue penguins** also frequent Tiritiri, and can be seen all year round – but are more in evidence in March, when they come ashore to moult, and from September to December, when they nest in specially constructed viewing boxes located along the seashore path just west of the main wharf.

Practicalities

Tiritiri Matangi is typically visited as a **day-trip**, giving almost five hours on the island; you'll need to take your own lunch, as there is **no food** available. The most reliable way to get here is with Fullers Gulf Harbour Ferries (☎09/424 5561), who depart from the Auckland Ferry Building (Thurs–Sun 9am; $30 return) for the forty-minute run up to Gulf Harbour Marina on the Whangaparoa Peninsula, 30km north of Auckland (see p.120), from where it makes the twenty-minute crossing (Thurs–Sun 9.45am; $25 return) to Tiritiri. On other weekdays (particularly Wednesday), the ferry is often chartered for school trips and you are usually welcome to tag along. Boats depart for Gulf Harbour and Auckland at 3.30pm.

Visitors arriving on scheduled ferries can join extremely worthwhile **guided walks** (1hr; $5), which leave from the wharf and are led by volunteers and DOC rangers steeped in bird-lore. Otherwise, you're free to wander the island at will or indulge in a little **swimming** from Hobbs Beach, a ten-minute walk west of the wharf (turn left as you step ashore), and the only sandy strand on Tiritiri.

It's also possible to **stay overnight** in a self-contained bunkhouse – bring a sleeping bag and food – near the lighthouse (call the rangers on ☎09/479 4490; ①), but weekends are booked months ahead and even for week nights you'll need to book at least two weeks in advance; you can also get **general information** on this phone number.

Other gulf islands

There are dozens of other islands scattered around the Hauraki Gulf, several of them privately owned but more forming part of the Hauraki Gulf Maritime Park. The most easily accessible is the DOC-managed recreation reserve of **Motuihe Island**, just 3km south of Motutapu Island, a popular day-trip destination for Aucklanders keen to laze on the sheltered sandy beaches of the northwestern peninsula and spend three or four hours exploring the easy walking trails. The majority of the island is farmland, with small patches of bush around its fringes. The northwestern end of the island, where the boats dock, has had something of a chequered history. It was used as a smallpox and influenza quarantine station from 1873 until after World War I, doubling up as prisoner-of-war camp; during World War II, the same buildings served as a naval base associated with gun emplacements built in the northern tip of the island. Motuihe is most easily visited on day-trips run on Sundays throughout the summer ($20 return) setting off from the ferry building at 9.30am and spending almost five hours on the island. If you want to **stay** longer there are boats on Wednesday and Friday evening allowing you to stop over in a well-supplied farmhouse sleeping up to twelve ($12 per person, $60 minimum nightly charge), a bunkhouse (①) and a campsite ($5). All are booked through the **kiosk** (☎09/534 8095), which is open daily in summer for groceries and takeaways.

Very few visitors make it out to **Little Barrier Island** (*Hauturu*), 80km north of Auckland, a nature reserve barred to those without the necessary DOC permit (contact the Auckland DOC office – see p.72). Although around a third of its trees were felled for timber before the government acquired the island and set it aside as a wildlife sanctuary in 1884, mountainous Little Barrier remains largely unspoiled, its vast forests unaffected by introduced pests. The island is home to fascinating creatures – including giant earthworms up to a metre long, the prehistoric tuatara and a mouse-sized version of the grasshopper-like weta – and once cats were eradicated in 1975 Little Barrier also became a refuge for birds under threat on the mainland, such as the kakapo, kaka, stitchbird and the kokako.

travel details

Trains

From Auckland to: Hamilton (4 daily; 2hr); National Park (2 daily; 5hr 30min); Ohakune (2 daily; 6hr); Palmerston North (2 daily; 8–9hr); Rotorua (1 daily; 4hr 15min); Tauranga (1 daily; 3hr 30min); Wellington (2 daily; 11hr).

Buses

From Auckland to: Cambridge (4 daily; 3hr); Dargaville (2–3 daily; 3hr); Gisborne (1 daily; 9hr 15min); Hamilton (16–20 daily; 2hr 30min); Hastings (3 daily; 8hr); Helensville (Mon-Fri 8 daily; 1hr 10min); Kaitaia (2 daily; 6hr 40min); Kerikeri (4–6 daily; 5hr); Kumeu (4–6 daily; 35min); Mangonui (2 daily; 6hr); Napier (3 daily; 7hr 30min); New Plymouth (3 daily; 6–7hr); Opononi (1 daily; 7hr); Orewa (hourly; 45–60min); Paihia via Whangarei (3–7 daily; 4hr); Paihia via Opononi (1 daily; 7hr 45min); Palmerston North (2 daily; 9hr); Piha (5 weekly; 1hr 10min); Rotorua (9 daily; 4hr); Taupo (8 daily; 4–5hr); Tauranga (7–8 daily; 3hr 30min–4hr 30min); Thames (4 daily; 2hr); Warkworth (8–10 daily; 1hr); Waipu (3–7 daily; 2hr 20min); Waitomo (3–4 daily; 3hr 30min); Whangarei (3–7 daily; 2hr 45min); Wellington (5 daily; 11–12hr).

From Helensville to: Orewa (2 Mon–Fri; 40min).

From Orewa to: Auckland (hourly; 45–60min); Helensville (2 Mon–Fri; 40min); Waiwera (hourly; 15min); Wenderholm (summer Sundays 4 daily; 15min).

Ferries

From Auckland to: Coromandel (1 daily; 2hr 15min); Devonport (every 30min; 10min); Great Barrier (5–7 weekly; 2-6hr); Motuihe (2-3 weekly; 50min); Rangitoto (2–3 daily; 40min); Tiritiri Matangi (4 weekly; 1hr 30min); Waiheke (7–10 daily; 40min).

From Gulf Harbour Marina to: Tiritiri Matangi Island (4 weekly; 20min).

From Half Moon Bay to: Waiheke (3–5 daily; 1hr).

Flights

From Auckland to: Bay of Islands, Paihia (2–4 daily; 50min); Blenheim (1-2 daily; 1hr 20min); Christchurch (14–20 daily; 1hr 20min); Dunedin (2 daily; 2hr 30min); Gisborne (4-5 daily; 1hr); Great Barrier Island (5–10 daily; 30min), Hamilton (1-2 daily; 35min); Kaitaia (1–2 daily; 1hr–1hr 30min), Napier (5–7 daily; 1hr); Nelson (2-3 daily; 1hr 30min); New Plymouth (5–7 daily; 50min); Palmerston North (5-8 daily; 1hr 10min); Queenstown (1-2 daily; 2hr 30min); Rotorua (4–6 daily; 45min); Taupo (2–3 daily; 50min); Tauranga (7 daily; 40min); Wanganui (2–3 daily; 1hr); Wellington (24–16 daily; 1hr); Whakatane (3-5 daily; 50min); Whangarei (8–10 daily; 40min).

Great Barrier Island: to Tauranga (3 weekly; 1hr); Whangarei (3 weekly; 30min); Whitianga (3 weekly; 20min).

From Waiheke Island to: Great Barrier Island (2 daily; 30min).

NORTHLAND

T he narrow and staunchly Maori province of **Northland** (*Taitokerau*) thrusts 350km out from Auckland into the sub-tropical north, separating the Pacific Ocean from the Tasman Sea – two oceans which meet in the maelstrom off Cape Reinga, the North Island's most northerly accessible point. This is the "Winterless North", a name which only really holds true in the very northernmost part but rightly suggests that palms, citrus fruit and even bananas thrive here, frosts are rare, and around its shores the waters off the myriad gorgeous beaches stay warmer than elsewhere.

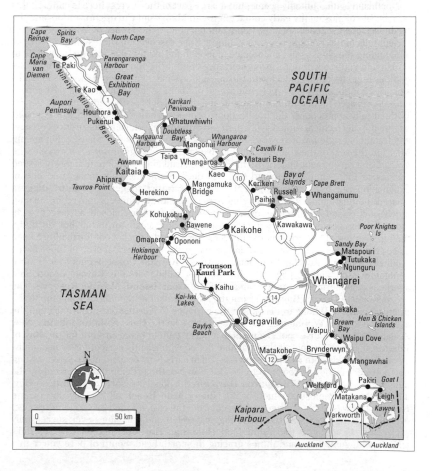

Scenically it splits down the middle. The **east coast** contorts into a labyrinth of straggling peninsulas scalloped into hidden coves between plunging headlands draped in the Christmas crimson blossom of pohutukawa trees. The beaches tend to be calm and safe, only chopping up during occasional Pacific storms, whose force is broken by clusters of protective barrier islands. The **west coast** could hardly be a greater contrast, one enormous dune-backed beach pounded by powerful Tasman breakers and occasionally broken by harbours, all with treacherous bars. Tidal rips and holes make swimming dangerous and there are no lifeguard patrols. Some beaches are even designated as roads, but are full of hazards for the unwary – and rental cars aren't insured for beach driving.

Exploration of the undulating **interior** is both hampered and enlivened by the roads: there was a time when lack of investment in infrastructure earned Northland the title of "the **roadless north**", an image it has only really shed in the last forty years or so. Furthermore, the major routes are inland and often well away from the unspoiled, deserted beaches that are the main event in these parts, leading to long forays down twisting side roads.

Northland is undoubtedly scenic, but a large part of the interest here is cultural: this was the site of most of the early contact between **Maori** and **European** settlers and the birthplace of New Zealand's most important document, the **Treaty of Waitangi**. Maori legend tells of the great Polynesian explorer Kupe discovering the Hokianga Harbour and, finding the climate and abundance of food to his liking, encouraging his people to return and settle here. But it was their ancestors in the Bay of Islands who bore the dubious honour of first contact with Europeans, as whalers plundered the seas and missionaries sought converts largely ungoverned. Maori social structure and past experience ill-prepared them for this onslaught, and their leaders petitioned Britain to step in. Without fully appreciating the implications or understanding the duplicity of the *pakeha*, the northern chiefs signed away their **sovereignty** in return for assurances on land and traditional rights, which were seldom respected. There is still a perception among Maori in the rest of the country that the five northern *iwi* gave *Aotearoa* away to the *pakeha*, and resentment lingers. As more fertile farmlands were found in newly settled regions further south, Northland fell into decline and the pattern became one of exploitation rather than development. Rapacious **kauri loggers** and **gum diggers** cleared the bush and, as extractive industries died away, pioneers moved in, turning much of the land to **dairy country**. Local dairy factories closed as larger semi-industrial complexes centralized processing, leaving small towns all but destitute, though planting of fast-growing exotic trees and sporadic pockets of horticulture keep places ticking over, aided by cultivation of marijuana, a major cash crop in these parts.

Finally escaping Auckland's urban sprawl, the **Kowhai Coast** begins to feel more genuinely rural and is popular with yachties sailing around Kawau Island, and snorkellers exploring the underwater world of **Goat Island Marine Reserve**. The broad sweep of **Bream Bay** runs from the Nova Scotian settlement of Waipu up to the dramatic crags of Whangarei Heads at the entrance to Northland's major port and the associated town of **Whangarei**. Off the coast here lie the **Poor Knights Islands**, New Zealand's premiere dive spot. Tourists in a hurry tend to make straight for the **Bay of Islands**, a jagged bite out of the coastline dotted with islands perfect for cruising, diving and swimming with dolphins, and steeped in early New Zealand history. Everything north of here is loosely referred to as **The Far North**, a region characterized by the quiet remoteness of the **Whangaroa Harbour**, the popular resorts of **Doubtless Bay**, and the Aupori Peninsula, which backs **Ninety Mile Beach** all the way up to **Cape Reinga**. The west coast feels very different from the east, marked by economic neglect over the last fifty years as the kauri logging ended and dairying never successfully replaced it. First stop is the fragmented **Hokianga Harbour**, one of New Zealand's largest, with some fine sand dunes gracing the north head. South of here you're into the **Waipoua Forest,** all that remains after the depredations of the loggers, a story best told at the excellent **Matakohe Kauri Museum** on the shores of the Kaipara Harbour.

Since so much of Northland is steeped in Maori history, spirituality and culture – increasingly evident the further north you travel – the area offers opportunities for genuine **cultural exchange**. For information on how to get involved, check out the useful Maori Tourism Association Web site at *www.taitokerau.com*.

Northland has no passenger train services so **getting around** by public transport means travelling by **bus**. Kaitaia and the Bay of Islands airports have direct **flights** to Auckland and each other, Whangarei has flights to Auckland and Great Barrier Island, and Kerikeri has flights to Auckland and Kaitaia, but distances are relatively short and high prices act as a deterrent. Details of frequencies and journey times are given in "Travel details" at the end of the chapter (see p.203).

The Kowhai Coast to Bream Bay

Auckland's influence begins to wane by the time you reach the **Kowhai Coast,** a 30km stretch of shallow harbours, beach-strung peninsulas and small islands. Freed from the shackles of the city, a more individual character becomes apparent, particularly once you pass sleepy **Warkworth** and either head out to **Kawau Island,** one-time home of Governor General George Grey, or up the coast to Leigh and the snorkelling and diving nirvana of **Goat Island Marine Reserve.**

There's little to detain you on SH1 between Warkworth and Waipu as it passes through dull Wellsford and the road junction and bus interchange at **Brynderwyn,** where SH12 loops off to Dargaville, the Waipoua Kauri Forest and the Hokianga Harbour.

Northbound voyagers are better off on the coast following **Bream Bay,** named by Cook when he visited in 1770 and his crew hauled in tarakihi, which was mistaken for bream. Gently curving 20km from the modest rocky headland of Bream Tail in the south, past the entrance to Whangarei Harbour, to the dramatic and craggy Bream Head, the bay has no sizable towns – only the small beach communities of **Mangawhai Heads** and **Waipu Cove,** looking out to the **Hen and Chicken Islands,** refuges for rare birds like the handsome wattled saddleback.

Warkworth and around

The economic focus of the **Kowhai Coast** is the easy-going small town of **WARKWORTH,** at the head of the Mahurangi Harbour, sheltered from the sea by its eponymous peninsula. For much of the year Warkworth exudes the peace and slow pace of a pleasant Kiwi rural town, only coming to life at the peak of the summer season when thousands of yachties descend, their boats moored in the numerous estuaries and coves. From the late 1820s the languid stretch of river that flows behind the town seethed with boats shipping out kauri, initially as spars for the Royal Navy and latterly as sawn planks. A high-grade limestone deposit was discovered in 1865 and cement production became important for a while, sparking furious competition to run a ferry service to Auckland. To learn more, head 3km south to the **Warkworth and Districts Museum**, on Tudor Collins Drive, 1.5km off the main road (daily: Nov–Easter 9am–4pm; Easter–Oct 9am–3.30pm; $4), which explores the region's history through re-created rooms, examples of kauri gum and a 5m-long, 130-link chain carved from a single piece of kauri. The two ancient kauri outside mark the start of two well-presented twenty-minute nature trails through the **Parri Kauri Park** (9am–dusk; donations invited), a stand of bush preserved as a public amenity at the end of the nineteenth century. A couple of kilometres further south along SH1, there's the much-touted **Satellite Earth Station Visitor Centre**, Thompson Road (daily 9am–3pm; free), a blatant promotion of Telecom's satellite networks adjacent to New Zealand's first satellite dish.

Following SH1 north, it is 5km to the entertaining **Sheepworld** (daily 9am–5pm; $10), where you can observe bottle-feeding of lambs or try your hand at a little shearing. The complex also contains **Matakana Co-op Market** (daily 10am–4pm), a quality craft, plants and produce co-op that's worth a quick peek. The **Dome Forest Walkway** begins 2km further north on SH1, leading up through native forest to a lookout point (40min return), continuing steeply to the summit (1hr 30min return) for superb views, and gently down to the twenty magnificent trees of the Waiwhiu Kauri Grove (3hr return).

Practicalities

Warkworth's **visitor centre**, 1 Baxter St (Christmas–Feb Mon–Fri 8.30am–5.30pm, Sat & Sun 9am–3pm; March–Christmas Mon–Fri 9am–5pm, Sat & Sun 9am–3pm; ☎09/425 9081, fax 425 7584, *service@warkworth-information.co.nz*) is right in the centre of town at the junction of Queen Street and Neville Street, where InterCity buses stop. Northliner buses pull up on SH1 near the ambulance station.

Central **accommodation** includes modern pub-style rooms at the *Bridge House Lodge*, Elizabeth Street (☎09/425 8351, fax 425 7410; ⑤) and *The Warkworth Inn*, 9 Queen Street (☎09/425 8569, fax 425 9696; dorms ①; rooms ④), Warkworth's original 1860 hotel, with well-priced B&B at the top end of this price category and a room-only option at the bottom end; campervans can park outside and use the facilities for $20. The *Central Motel* on Neville Street (☎09/425 8645; ④) has twelve units to choose from, plus a spa and swimming pool. Among several good **B&Bs** and homestays, one stands out: *Saltings Guest House*, 1210 Sandspit Rd (☎09/425 9670, fax 425 9674; ⑥) is a standard 1970s Kiwi home exquisitely restyled along Mediterranean lines; fine breakfasts are served. *Saltings* overlooks Sandspit, 7km from Warkworth, within walking distance of the Kawau ferry wharf and the adjacent *Sandspit Motor Camp*, 1334 Sandspit Rd (☎ & fax 09/425 8610; tent sites $9, cabins on waterfront ③).

Daytime **eating** is best done at *Ducks Crossing Café*, which serves good quiche, salads, cakes and coffee in the River View Plaza down by the languid river, the *Queen Street Corner Café*, on the corner of Queen Street and Neville Street, or the café out at the *Morris & James* pottery (see p.150). In the evening, make for the *Pizza Co*, 18 Neville St (BYO), which serves fine traditional pizza, superb vegetable soup and a spicy pepperoni Garibaldi stew.

Kawau Island

KAWAU ISLAND holds a special place in the hearts of the Hauraki Gulf yachting fraternity, as much for the safety of its rangy harbours as for the sandy coves wedged between modest cliffs. With a meagre resident population of around a hundred, the island is chiefly the preserve of **holiday homes** – some multimillion dollar affairs with helipads – which choke a shoreline bristling with jetties, virtually one for every house. And there lies the problem for the casual visitor: you can't do much without your own boat except visit the Mansion House on the unimaginatively named Mansion House Bay, and the sumptuous exotic grounds thereabouts.

Once farmed, the island is slowly reverting to kanuka scrub and is not an especially appealing place to walk. Besides, **access** is difficult to all but the DOC-managed southwestern tenth of the island, where one of New Zealand's first export industries sprang up around a briefly profitable **copper trade** in the 1840s and 1850s. Mines in Dispute Cove yielded copper ore, which was processed at Smeltinghouse Bay on Bon Accord Harbour, the inlet that nearly cuts the island in two. The industry was defunct by 1862 when George Grey, then doing his second stint as New Zealand's governor, was looking for a private home and bought the mine manager's house and adjacent assay office, linking the two with his own larger-roomed extension to form the **Mansion House** (daily 10am–3.30pm; $4). Grey was an austere man and there's little flamboyance in the construction, the rooms being simply decorated using kauri and totara panels and, the sole nod to his position, some kauri pillars sent to England for turning. Grey sold up in 1888, after which the house spent much of its life as a hotel, over the years sprouting ugly extensions which had to be stripped away during restoration. Apart from a collection of silverware, there is little in the house that belonged to Grey, but most of the furniture is contemporary with his tenure.

Grey's pursuit of the Victorian fashion for things exotic resulted in **grounds** stocked with flora and fauna imported from all over the world. Though much of it was ill-tended after his departure, the dell running back from the house is still a gracious place. Chilean wine palms, coral trees, Moreton Bay figs and a smattering of native species stud the formal lawns, where peacocks – one completely white – strut by, weka scurry around and rosellas screech overhead. Grey also brought in four species of **wallaby** – most easily seen in a large compound in the dell – which have overtaken the island to the extent that they are now regularly culled, and residents construct impenetrable fences to protect their gardens.

A **stroll** through the gardens runs to the tiny beach at **Lady's Bay** and on to a network of short tracks that drop down to coves on Bon Accord Harbour and to the ruins of the old copper mine (about 40min).

Practicalities

Boats to Kawau Island leave from **Sandspit** (all-day parking $5), a small road-end community on the Matakana Estuary, 8km east of Warkworth. Throughout the year, Kawau Kat Cruises (☎0800/888 006) operate the **Royal Mail Run** (daily 10.30am; 4hr; $39), delivering mail, papers and groceries to all the wharves on the island and giving you about two hours ashore at Mansion House Bay; their **direct service** (2pm, plus extra services Christmas–Easter; $24) gives you more time at the bay. For a cheaper and more leisurely option, try a **Coffee Cruise** on the MV *Matata* (☎0800/225 292; Christmas–Easter daily 10am & 2pm; Easter–Christmas Mon, Wed–Sat 10am, Thurs 7.15am, 10am & 2.30pm, Fri 10am, 3pm & 7pm, Sun 10am & 3pm; $25), which follows a similar itinerary to the Mail Run – though you'll need to go out on the early boat and come back on the later one (return boats are at 1pm & 4pm) if you want to linger on the island. Both companies run a range of other cruises in summer. Bring whatever you need to Kawau as there are only meagre supplies at the **kiosk** (Christmas–Easter daily 10am–4pm; rest of the year Sat & Sun only) in the Mansion House grounds.

There are several **places to stay** on Kawau, most, such as *St Clair Lodge*, Vivian Bay (☎09/422 8850, *stclair.lodge@xtra.co.nz*; ⑨), geared to romantic weekends away with all meals included in the price. More modest accommodation includes *Pah Farm Fishing Lodge*, Moores Bay (☎09/422 8765, fax 422 8794; tent sites $10, dorms ①), and a simple, self-contained **DOC house** (☎09/422 8882, *whangareivc@doc.govt.nz*; ④), *Sunny Bay Cottage*, within fifteen minutes' walk of the Mansion House and let for a minimum of two nights. Anyone keen to put in a week's **voluntary work** can stay free in a DOC bunkhouse at Mansion House Bay by contacting the volunteer coordinator at the Auckland Conservancy office (☎09/307 9279).

Matakana

MATAKANA, 8km northeast of Warkworth, is little more than a road junction at the heart of a fledgling grape-growing region dotted with craftspeople who have set up shop far enough from Auckland to discourage the weekend masses but close enough to lure interested buyers. The key player in the district is the **Morris & James Country Pottery**, Tongue Farm Road (☎09/422 7116; Mon–Fri 10am–4.30pm, Sat & Sun 10am–5pm; free 30min guided tour 11.30am Mon–Fri), which in the late 1970s exploited New Zealand's fortress economy by producing otherwise unobtainable hand-made terracotta tiles and large garden pots from the local clay. Since then, its distinctive designs, executed in lustrous multi-layered salt glaze, have infiltrated ceramics shops throughout the country. In the workshop, you can watch wall tiles being hand decorated, before tucking into sumptuous Mediterranean and Pacific Rim lunches at the café/bar. The pottery is off the Leigh road just east of Matakana and almost opposite Matakana Dairy Factory on Matakana Valley Road.

Half the valley seems to be **vineyards**, but there are currently only two retail outlets: *Heron's Flight*, 49 Sharp's Rd (☎09/422 7915; daily 10am–6pm; tastings $5), which produces reputable Cabernet Merlot, Chardonnay and other varietals; and *Hyperion Wines*, Tongue Farm Road, 1km east of Matakana (☎09/422 9375, *sales@hyperion–wines .co.nz*; Sat & Sun 11am–6pm; closed Mon–Fri; tastings free), which focuses on a Cabernet Sauvignon/Merlot, as well as Pinot Noir, Pinot Gris and Chardonnay. The attached **restaurant** does lunches daily in summer and on winter weekends.

Leigh and the Goat Island Marine Reserve

The coast-bound road runs 13km east of Matakana to **LEIGH**, a clifftop village which boasts the fine sandy bay of **Mathesons Beach**, 1km to the west, and a picturesque harbour bobbing with wooden fishing boats. The fleet's presence attests to the abundance of fish where ocean currents meet the waters of the Hauraki Gulf, though overfishing has taken its toll, something which underlines the importance of places like the **Goat Island Marine Reserve**, 4km northeast of Leigh, and so-named for its most prominent feature, a small bush-clad island 300m offshore. Established in 1975, New Zealand's first marine reserve stretches 5km along the shoreline and 800m off the coast. Two angling- and shellfishing-free decades later the undersea life is thriving, with large rock lobster and huge snapper. Feeding is discouraged but commonly practised – blue maomaos in particular seem to have developed a taste for hand-fed frozen peas and frequently mob swimmers and divers.

Easy beach access, wonderfully clear water, rock pools on wave-cut platforms, a variety of undersea terrains and relatively benign currents combine to make this an enormously popular year-round **diving** spot, as well as a summer destination for sun-seeking families. Snorkellers get a lush world of kelp forest with numerous multi-coloured fish; those who venture deeper confront more exposed seascapes with an abundance of sponges. Snorkelling **gear** – mask, snorkel and fins ($11), with wetsuit ($12), or diving gear for a single dive ($60) – can be rented from Seafriends (☎09/422 6212, fax 422 6245; daily 9am–dusk), just over a kilometre up the Goat Island access road. **Non-divers** wanting a taste of what's down there can view a series of aquariums that re-create different Goat Island ecosystems, and, in fine weather, join 45-minute tours around the island with Glass Bottomed Boat Habitat Explorer (call in advance to check times and conditions ☎09/422 6334; all year, weather permitting $18).

Heading north up the coast, it is possible to reach Mangawhai Heads via a string of dirt roads through steep green hills over boggy farmland and scrubby bush. It's not an especially striking journey, though, and you'll do as well to return to SH1 in Warkworth – unless you're drawn to the long, dune-backed white strand of **PAKIRI**, 10km from Leigh, where there are a couple of places to stay, and you can go **horse riding** with Pakiri Beach Horse Rides (☎ & fax 09/422 6275), a couple of kilometres further north on Rahuikiri Road. Trips head along the beach and into the forest behind ($30 an hour, $120 a day including lunch); multi-day safaris can also be arranged.

Practicalities

There's no public transport to Leigh, and the facilities are limited once you get here. Nevertheless, you can **stay** comfortably at the *Leigh Motel*, 15 Hill St (☎09/422 6179; ④), which has good two-night deals outside of January, or more modestly at the small and grassy *Goat Island Backpackers* (☎09/422 6185; tent sites $10, powered sites $12, bunkhouse $12, cabins ③), about 1km back from the reserve. Further north **in Pakiri**, there's beachside accommodation at the *Pakiri Beach Motor Camp*, Pakiri Beach Road (☎09/422 6199; tent sites $10.50, cabins ②, motel units ⑤), or with *Pakiri Beach Horse Rides* (☎ & fax 09/422 6275; dorms ①, beach cabins ④, full-board farmstay ⑦), a couple of kilometres further north on Rahuikiri Road.

Eating is a big surprise, with the slick *Leigh Saw Mill Café*, Pakiri Road (☎09/422 6019), a vast sawmill sensitively converted into a smart café/bar serving fine gourmet pizza and a small range of well-presented dishes, often supplemented by daily specials based around an Indian, Thai or Japanese theme; weekends typically draw touring bands. Good alternatives include the café/restaurant at *Seafriends* (Oct–Apr daily 9am–8pm, May–Sept daily 10am–4pm; BYO & licensed), just over a kilometre up the Goat Island access road, and Leigh's takeaway, both serving excellent seafood in their own way.

Mangawhai Heads and Waipu Cove

Steering shy of the dirt roads which fan off SH1, your next chance to join the coast is at **Mangawhai Heads**, 30km north of Leigh, where the Mangawhai Harbour reaches the sea. An expanding cluster of holiday homes straggles over the hillsides behind a fine surf beach. If you want to linger and sample the surf, try the well-equipped motel, *Pohutukawa Beachfront Apartments*, 72 Wintle St (☎09/431 4483; ⑤) at the lower end of this price code, or the *Mangawhai Heads Motor Camp*, Mangawhai Heads Road (☎ & fax 09/431 4675, *campnewing@xtra.co.nz*; tent sites $8), which is right on the beach. The *Naja Garden Café*, on Molesworth Drive (daily 8.30am–5pm), serves break-fasts, fine salads, quiches and good espresso.

You know you are getting close to the Scottish enclave of Waipu when you reach the delightful **Lang's Beach**, 12km north of Mangawhai Heads, with its tree-backed strand and the *Lochalsh B&B*, perched above the main road (☎ & fax 09/432 0053, *langs@xtra.co.nz*; ⑤), offering two double rooms and overlooking the beach. From here it is a further 4km to the top surf beach of **Waipu Cove**, a cluster of houses by a sweeping stretch of Bream Bay, again with limited accommodation: camping at the *Waipu Cove Reserve Camp*, 897 Cove Rd (☎09/432 0410; tent and powered sites mid-Dec to mid-Feb $12.50, rest of the year $8), and rooms at the pool-equipped *Cove Beach Motel*, 891 Cove Rd (☎09/432 0348, *ann@covebeach.co.nz*; ④, and 2-bedroom units ⑤), both right by the beach.

Waipu and around

Driving through, you wouldn't pick nondescript **WAIPU** as different from any other small Kiwi town but for an Aberdeen granite monument surmounted by a Scottish lion rampant in the middle of the main street. Erected in 1914 to commemorate the sixtieth anniversary of the town's founding, the monument recalls the Scottish home of settlers who arrived here by way of Nova Scotia, following the charismatic preacher the Reverend Norman McLeod. Like numerous other crofters dispossessed by the eighteenth-century Highland clearances and enticed by stories of the New World, McLeod left Scotland in 1817 with some 400 followers and set down roots in St Ann's, Nova Scotia, where they stayed until a series of harsh winters in the late 1850s drove them out. Some went to Australia, but most decamped to Waipu, forming a self-contained and deathly strict Calvinist community that eked a living from farming and forestry. The town is proud of its heritage, and every year someone is sponsored to study pipes, drum or Scottish country dancing at The Gaelic College of Arts and Crafts in Nova Scotia. The biggest event of the year is Waipu's annual New Year's Day **Highland Games**, in which competitors heft large stones, toss cabers and lug sheaves in the Caledonian Park. The Scottish history and genealogy of the settlers is recounted in the **Waipu House of Memories**, on the main street (daily 9.30am–4pm; $4), which is jammed full of photos of anxious first-boat arrivees and their personal effects.

Unless you happen to coincide with the Games, there's nothing much to do in Waipu, though there's a popular excursion to the **Waipu Caves** (unrestricted entry), a 200m glow-worm-filled passage forming part of an extensive underground system in the limestone country 13km to the west. Obtain a map from the visitor centre in Waipu (see "Practicalities" below), take a couple of good torches – it's pitch-black and very disorientating inside the caves – and explore: there are no guides, so use your judgement as to how far to penetrate. The cave is signposted from Waipu Caves Road and is impenetrable when wet; you'll get muddy even in dry weather.

North from Waipu, the road runs parallel to Bream Bay, though occasional turnings give access to the long white **beach** that lies to the east. The best place to head down to the sands is at **Uretiti**, 6km north of Waipu, where there is a primitive DOC camping area ($6), with water and cold showers and an adjacent nudist beach. Four kilometres north, Ruakaka marks a turn-off for the **Marsden Point Oil Refinery** (daily 10am–5pm; free), 10km to the north, where an impressively overwrought show (every half hour; 20min) focuses on a vast scale model of New Zealand's only oil refinery.

Practicalities

InterCity and Northliner **buses** drop off and pick up on request and outside Bargain Buys, on the main street, which also acts as a ticket agent (☎09/432 0046). Nearby, the Waipu House of Memories (see above) contains the **visitor centre** (daily 9.30am–4pm; ☎ & fax 09/432 0746, *waipu9@xtra.co.nz*) with **Internet access**. The best budget **accommodation** is at the super-relaxed and excellent *Ebb & Flow Backpackers*, 3km south of Waipu on Johnson Point Road (☎09/432 0217, *ebbnflow_2000@yahoo.co.uk*; dorms ①, rooms ②); perched on the edge of the Waipu Estuary wildlife reserve, it enjoys lovely sea views out to the Hen and Chicken Islands. There are cheaper dorm beds and some more appealing units at the *Clansman Motel and Restaurant*, 30 Cove

Rd (☎ 09/432 0424, fax 432 0995; budget rooms ③, units ④–⑤ depending on the size), whose varied meals are à la carte for around $20. **Meals** are also to be had at *The Pizza Barn 'n' Bar*, 2 Cove Rd (☎09/432 0737), in Waipu's former post office revamped in cosy log-cabin style, which serves not only pizzas but also a range of well-priced lunches and dinners daily in its casual dining room or out in the garden. For basic Kiwi fare, head to *Granz Café*, opposite the visitor centre, which dishes up all-day breakfasts, lunch and afternoon tea (closed Sun May–Sept).

Whangarei and around

On initial acquaintance, **WHANGAREI** is a bit of a disappointment. If you've come from the south, Bream Bay's sweeping coastline and the attractive Whangarei Harbour seem to promise more than Northland's provincial capital is able to deliver. Ranks of car sales yards and print shops edge into the central grid of streets, and even the **port** that originally brought prosperity to Whangarei is several kilometres out of town and doesn't contribute any character. But Whangarei does have redeeming features, not least the new riverside **Town Basin**, where sleek yachts are moored outside a renovated settler-style shopping and restaurant complex. Elsewhere there's a smattering of modest museums and sights and a few pleasant walks, but Whangarei is perhaps best used as a base either for a swimming and walking day-trip out to Whangarei Heads, or for diving and snorkelling around the **Poor Knights Islands**.

Arrival, information and accommodation

Though a rail line runs from Auckland to Whangarei, no passenger trains make it this far. InterCity and Northliner **buses** pull up on Rose Street, the hub of the skeletal local service which runs on weekdays only. Daily **flights** from Auckland and Sunday flights from Great Barrier Island arrive at Onerahi Airport, 5km east and linked to town by a **shuttle bus** (☎09/437 0666 & 0800/455 555; $7). The **visitor centre** lies 2km south of town on the main route from Auckland, at 92 Otaika Rd (Christmas–Jan daily 8.30am–6.30pm; Feb–Christmas Mon–Fri 8.30am–5pm, Sat & Sun 10am–4pm; ☎09/438 1079, fax 438 2943, *whangarei@clear.net.nz*), and you can gather information on local walks at the **DOC office**, in the same building (☎09/430 2007; same hours). There's also a simple café attached to the visitor centre, which overlooks a park.

It is seldom difficult to find **accommodation** in Whangarei and, though there are few places that are really special, prices are reasonable.

Hotels, motels and B&Bs

Channel Vista Homestay, 254 Beach Rd, Onerahi, 5km east of town towards Whangarei Heads (☎ & fax 09/436 5529, *tancred@igrin.co.nz*). Luxurious modern homestay with two self-contained suites overlooking Whangarei Harbour and let on a B&B basis. ⑤.

Chelsea House B&B, 83 Hatea Drive (☎0508 243573, *mel.clarke@clear.net.nz*). A pleasant double-gabled villa, 10min walk from the town centre, offering two en-suite rooms – a double with its own kitchen and a twin. ④.

Cheviot Park Motor Lodge, cnr Western Hills Drive (SH1) & Cheviot St (☎09/438 2341 & 0508/243 846, fax 438 0442, *g.jansen@xtra.co.nz*). A cheerful and well-kept motel about 1.5km southwest of the town centre, with a choice of studios or 1-bedroom suites. ⑤.

Fountain Lodge Motel, 17 Tarewa Rd (☎ & fax 09/438 3532, freephone 0800/999 944, *ghen@clear.net.nz*). Well-appointed motel close to the town centre with a couple of kitchenless studio units and several fully self-contained units. ④.

Motel Six, 153 Bank St (☎09/438 9219, fax 438 9218, *motel6@xtra.co.nz*). Standard, decent motel ten minutes' walk from the centre with spa pool and in-house video. ④.

A *(100 m)* & **B** *(6 km)* △ *Whangarei Falls (4 km) & Bay of Islands (70 km)*

ACCOMMODATION	
Alpha Caravan Park	H
Bunkdown Lodge	K
Central Backpackers (Hatea House)	C
Channel Vista Homestay	J
Chelsea House	A
Cheviot Park Motor Lodge	F
Fountain Lodge Motel	I
Motel Six	E
Settlers Hotel	D
Whangarei Falls Caravan Park	B
YHA	G

RESTAURANTS, CAFÉS & BARS	
Barfly	1
Bogart's Café	8
Dickens' Inn & Oliver's Café	5
Killer Prawn	3
Planet Earth	4
Red Iguana	7
Reva's on the Waterfront	2
Rin Chin Chilla	6

Clarke Homestead & Whangarei Museum (6 km), Bushwacka (18 km) & F (1.5 km)

WHANGAREI

Mt Parahaki on foot (1.5 km)
Mt Parahaki by car (3 km)
Whangarei Heads (25 km) & J (5 km)

Craft Quarry
Cafler Park
Whangarei Art Museum
Margie Maddren Fernery

Town Basin
Burning Issues
Clapham's Clocks
Reyburn House
Northland Breweries

Raumanga Stream

0   250 m

▽ *(i) (2 km), Auckland (170 km), The Papermakers (4 km) & K (1.5km)*

Settlers Hotel, 63 Hatea Drive (☎09/438 2699, fax 438 0794, *settlers@ihug.co.nz*). Comfortable, en-suite rooms in a complex with on-site bar, restaurant and swimming pool. (Twenty percent discount at weekends.) ⑤.

Hostels and campsites

Alpha Caravan Park, 34 Tarewa Rd (☎ & fax 09/438 9867). Compact but convenient site ten minutes' walk from town. Tent sites $9, units ③.

Bunkdown Lodge, 23 Otaika Rd (☎09/438 8886, fax 438 8826, *bunkdown@ihug.co.nz*). Close to the visitor centre, this is an attractive turn-of-the-century kauri villa that makes a spacious, well-equipped and especially friendly hostel. Dorms ①, rooms ③.

Central Backpackers (Hatea House), 67 Hatea Drive (☎09/437 6174, fax 437 6141, *centralback@xtra.co.nz*). This suburban house has been converted into a slightly cramped but clean hostel with dorms, doubles and a couple of compact units with fridge and stove. Guests can rent kayaks at bargain prices and all-comers can join coastal kayak trips ($35). Dorms ①, rooms ②, units ③.

Whangarei Falls Caravan Park, Ngunguru Rd, 6km from town near Whangarei Falls (☎ & fax 09/437 0609, *wh.falls@ihug.co.nz*). Although less convenient than the other campsites, the setting – on the edge of the countryside, with a pool and spa – compensates. Tent sites $9, dorms ①, cabins ②.

YHA, 52 Punga Grove Ave (☎ & fax 09/438 8954, *gourlie@ihug.co.nz*). Intimate hilltop hostel a fifteen-minute steep walk up from the centre, with good views over the town, 4- and 6-bed dorms, and Friday night barbecues in summer; also free bikes, and glow-worms a 10min walk away into the bush. Four twins/doubles are in a separate, brand new complex. Dorms ①, rooms ②.

The Town

Whangarei's greatest concentration of sights is around the **Town Basin**, a prettified zone of upmarket galleries, shops and restaurants based around an 1880s villa. Of the museums in the complex, few will be disappointed about missing **Di's Dolls Museum** (Mon–Sat 9am–4.30pm, Sun 10am–4.30pm; $3.50); likewise, only those desperate for a kitsch diversion should venture near the fibreglass and stuffed specimens in the **Museum of Fishes** (daily 10am–4pm; $5). Make instead for **Burning Issues Gallery** next door (daily 10am–5pm; free), a glass and ceramics studio where you can watch glass-blowing most days. Nearby is **Clapham's Clocks** (daily: Dec–April 9am–8pm; May–Nov 9am–5pm; $5), right by New Zealand's largest sundial. Inside, one long room is packed with 1500 clocks, from mechanisms taken out of church towers to cuckoo clocks, by way of work-time recorders, domestic timepieces and all manner of ornamental clocks. Nearby, Whangarei's oldest kauri villa, **Reyburn House** (Tues–Fri 10am–4pm, Sat & Sun 1–4pm; free), hosts the Northland Society of Arts' exhibition gallery, usually containing a few quality pieces. Finally, if they have time, **Northland Breweries**, 104 Lower Dent St (☎09/438 4664; Mon–Sat 9am–6pm; free) will show you around their micro-brew plant and let you sample their chemical-free brews.

On the western side of the town centre, the small but well-kept **Cafler Park** makes a pleasant place for a stroll, structured around a visit to the Rose Gardens and the adjacent **Whangarei Art Museum** (*Te Wharetaonga o Whangarei*; Tues–Fri 10am–4pm, Sat & Sun noon–4pm; donations requested), with a small permanent collection of New Zealand art and frequently changing exhibitions that showcase Kiwi artists. A footbridge crosses the stream running through Cafler Park to the restful and cool **Margie Maddren Fernery**, First Avenue (daily 10am–4pm; free), a compact collection of native ferns packed into half a dozen specially built compounds. These are flanked by two glasshouses: the **Filmy Fern House** provides a damp, draught-free environment for New Zealand's more delicate fern species, while the **Snow Conservatory** contains a steamy tropical hot-house and a desert room packed with cacti. From here, it is ten minutes' walk to the **Craft Quarry**, Selwyn Avenue (daily 10am–4pm; free), an artists' cooperative and something of a focus for the vibrant crafts community in this part of Northland. You are free to wander among anarchic shacks built from adobe, timber and corrugated iron, watch the artisans at work and, of course, to buy their handiwork.

Another collection of museums lies 6km southwest on SH14 in Maunu, occupying the grounds of the **Clarke Homestead** (daily 10am–4pm; $3 per venue, $7 to all three sites), a rare example of an unrestored original homestead. Built in 1886 for a Scottish doctor, Alexander Clarke, the house was at its most vibrant in the 1930s when Alexander's son, James, held high-society parties here. Much of what you see dates from that era, since James's bachelor son, Basil, took little interest in the upkeep of the place right up to his death in the 1980s. Among the accumulated possessions of the three generations, the highlight has to be Basil's unkempt, boys' own bedroom, complete with hunting gear, drum kit and an impressive shelf of medicines. In Basil's later years, he bequeathed the grounds to the **Whangarei Museum** (same hours; $3). Housed in a modern building, its collection of local history, flora and fauna is augmented by a small but strong Maori collection. Among the clubs, fishing lures and agricultural implements is a lovely feather cloak, but the prize exhibit is the *waka tupapuka*, a unique sixteenth-century wooden funerary chest decorated with bird-form carvings, as opposed to the more common human forms. The museum encourages appreciation of native fauna through the **Kiwi House** (same hours; $3), one of the best of its ilk, nicely laid out and with good visibility. On several Sundays through the summer the complex holds themed "live days", when $5 gets you the run of the place along with, say, vintage transport buffs, or log-skidding experts.

Further southwest on SH14, 18km from Whangarei, past Maungatapere, is **The Bushwacka Experience**, a fun outdoors adventure that takes place in some interesting geology and bush hidden away on a dairy farm (they'll pick you up from Whangarei). You tailor the trip to suit yourself (☎09/434 7839; 2–5hr; $30 per hour), choosing from a range of mostly guide-led activities that include a 4WD safari in rugged terrain; relaxing at a BBQ or on a bush walk to some giant kauri; exploring the "squeeze", just one of many deep rock crevices that opened up in the hillside during volcanic activity several hundred years ago; and, for the fit, abseiling into the "Black Hole".

A mere 4km south of town at Otaika on SH1 you can visit **The Papermakers**, who produce an interesting range of handcrafted paper from recycled materials in an 18th-century cottage (book ahead ☎09/438 2652; daily $4, or $6 to make paper). Don't let the period costumes put you off – instead have a go at making paper and cards, which you can take away with you.

Perhaps Whangarei's greatest appeal, though, is the number of small parks and easy **walks** within a few minutes of the town, most of them outlined on the *Whangarei Walks* leaflet (available free from the visitor centre). Views over the harbour and town are the reward for making it up to the ugly sheet-metal war memorial atop the 240m **Mount Parahaki**, which can be approached by car along Memorial Drive (off Riverside Drive; 3km) or on foot along the steep forty-minute Ross Track from the end of Dundas Road (1.5km). Understandably more popular is the twenty-minute stroll encircling the broad curtain of the **Whangarei Falls**, where the Hatea River cascades over a 26m basalt ridge into a popular swimming hole. The falls are 5km northeast of the town centre and Kamo-bound buses pass close by (Mon–Fri only). The road out to the falls passes Whareora Road, where **A.H. Reed Memorial Kauri Park** has shady paths through native bush and, 3km further along, the fluted and weather-worn limestone formations of **Abbey Caves** (unrestricted access) invite comparison with Henry Moore sculptures. Though the caves are open to anyone, you really need some experience and confidence to enter them; the best bet is to enrol on a **guided tour** from Whangarei, which goes into one cave (☎09/437 6174; around 1hr 15min; $12–30, depending on numbers).

Eating and drinking

Whangarei, the largest town for some distance, has more choice for eating than anywhere between Auckland and the Bay of Islands. A selection of popular **fast-food** franchises line Bank Street, while more imaginative **restaurants** cluster around the Town Basin and along Cameron Street. For **groceries**, Pak 'n' Save, on the corner of Robert Street and Curruth Street, has the best prices.

Barfly, 13 Rathbone St. Friendly all-day café/bar known locally for its excellent coffee, wood-fired pizzas, vegetarian dishes, and lavish desserts (Mon–Sat from 8am; Sun from 9am).

Bogart's Café, 84 Cameron St. Easy-going restaurant serving crispy gourmet pizzas and a range of appealing mains for around $17 in the evenings; also opens during the day on weekdays for coffee and snacks. BYO & licensed.

Dickens' Inn & Oliver's Café, 71 Cameron St. Spacious café/bar doing breakfast, enormous sourdough sandwiches and rich desserts at moderate prices.

Killer Prawn, 28 Bank St. Café/bar and restaurant that's the place to be seen in Whangarei, with a conservatory ambience. Prawns feature in all manner of dishes but not to the exclusion of a multitude of dishes from sashimi to steaks. Light snacks start at around $5, mains $15–25.

Parua Bay Tavern, Parua Bay Rd (☎09/436 5856). Waterside pub 20km out of town on the road to Whangarei Heads which frequently hosts live bands; look for fly posters around town.

Planet Earth, Bank St (near cnr Vine St). A big, colourful and kicking bar where live bands play from time to time as the mood takes them. Food is of the standard bar variety – burgers, pizzas and nachos. Closed Sun.

Reva's On The Waterfront, Town Basin (☎09/438 8969). A Whangarei institution, with breezy, quayside seating and a broad range of moderately priced daily specials from char-grilled peppers and Bream Bay seafood to gourmet pizzas.

Red Iguana, *Grand Hotel*, cnr Bank St & Rose St. Nicely modernized version of a traditional Kiwi bar mainly devoted to bar-propping, boozing and sport-watching but also serving $7 lunches and hosting live bands at weekends.

Rin Chin Chilla, 6 Vine St. Small, cheery coffee bar with a basic range of kebabs and nachos. Closed Sun & Mon.

Around Whangarei

The best reason to spend more than a night or two in Whangarei is to explore the surrounding area, principally those areas east and north of the town where the craggy, weathered remains of ancient volcanoes abut the sea. Half a day can be well spent around **Whangarei Heads**, the district's volcanic heartland where dramatic walks follow the coast to calm harbour beaches and windswept coastal strands. There are no roads running directly north, so you'll need to return to Whangarei to get back out to the coast at **Tutukaka** which, along with the neighbouring service village of Ngunguru, acts as the base for dive trips to the undersea wonderland around the **Poor Knights Islands**.

There is no public transport in either direction and the rugged terrain can make cycling a challenge, but dive-trip operators run vehicles out from Whangarei.

Whangarei Heads

The winding road around the northern side of Whangarei Harbour runs 35km southeast out to **Whangarei Heads**, a catch-all name for a series of small beach communities scattered around jagged volcanic mountains terminating in Bream Head, the northern limit of Bream Bay. Numerous attractive bays provide safe swimming, but there is really nothing special to see or do until the road leaves the harbour and climbs to a saddle, the start of an excellent **walk** (3km; 2hr–2hr 30min; 200m ascent) up the 430m **Mount Manaia**, the heads' most distinctive summit, crowned with five deeply eroded pinnacles shrouded in legend. One tells of a jealous dispute between two chiefs, Manaia, whose pa (fortified village) stood atop Mount Manaia, and the lesser chief, Hautatu, from across the water at Marsden Point, who was married to the beautiful Pito. Hautatu was sent away on a raid, leaving the coast clear for Manaia to steal Pito. Hautatu returned and was chasing Manaia, his two children and Pito across the hilltop when all five were struck by lightning, leaving the figures petrified on the summit. These pinnacles remain *tapu* but you can climb to their base through native bush, passing fine viewpoints.

Beyond Mount Manaia, a road forks north to **Pataua**, a family holiday village clustered around either side of a large lagoon, the two halves linked by a slender footbridge. A second road returns to the harbourside, passing the lovely McLeod's Bay on the way to **Urquarts Bay**, where a short walk (20min) leads to the white-sand **Smugglers Cove**, a longer trail (3hr return) continues to Peach Cove, and very keen walkers can press on to **Ocean Beach** (5hr one way), a wild surf beach that's also accessible by road.

Tutukaka and the Poor Knights

The Tutukaka coast means one of two things to New Zealanders, big game fishing or scuba diving – both based in **TUTUKAKA**, set on a lovely deeply incised harbour 30km northeast of Whangarei. This small coastal community is light on amenities, which are mainly provided by **NGUNGURU**, 5km back towards Whangarei. The largest settlement hereabouts, Ngunguru is strung along an attractive, sandy estuary that's fine for swimming if you dodge the jetskis.

Boats leave from Tutukaka for one of the world's premiere dive locations, the **Poor Knights Islands** marine reserve, 25km offshore, where the warm East Auckland current swirling around Cape Reinga and the lack of run-off from the land combine to create wonderfully clear water rich in New Zealand's most diverse range of sealife, including sub-tropical species found nowhere else around its shores. Two large and numerous smaller islands were cultivated by Maori but, after a nineteenth-century massacre, became *tapu* and were eventually turned into a safe haven for geckos, skinks and thousands of tuatara, the sole survivors of a branch of prehistoric lizards the rest of which became extinct 60 million years back.

As land access is forbidden, interest is focused below the surface, where the volcanic forces which created the islands and subsequent changes in sea level have left a marine wonderland of near-vertical rock faces dropping down almost 100m to sand floors through a labyrinth of caves, fissures and rock arches teeming with rainbow-coloured fish, crabs, soft corals, kelp forests and shellfish. The Poor Knights even lie along the migratory routes of a number of whale species, so blue, humpback, sei and minke whales, as well as dolphins, are not uncommon. There's also a wreck to explore: in February 1999, an ex-naval survey ship HMNZS *Tui* was deliberately scuttled to create an artificial reef, which is already quite well-established. At the time of writing plans are afoot to sink another ship, the *Waikato*, to further enrich these waters.

Non-divers can appreciate these waters from the safety of a **cruise** on the *Wairangi* – an ex-pilot boat skippered by a marine biologist with substantial expertise. Day-trips to the Poor Knights Islands (☎09/434 3350, *ritchie@ihug.co.nz*; $50) leave from Tutukaka Marina, stopping for snorkelling opportunities, and dolphin sightings are common. The *Wairangi* also operates overnight charters, comfortably accommodating 12 people (prices variable and negotiable).

Everything is protected within the Poor Knights reserve, but rich pickings attract free-ranging species such as marlin, shark and tuna, which stray outside the reserve and are picked off by **big game anglers** during the December to May season. Anglers

---

DIVING AND SNORKELLING THE POOR KNIGHTS

Some prior experience opens up the best the Poor Knights have to offer, but there's plenty for novices and even snorkellers. Most of the year **visibility** is 15–20m (up to 30m Jan–Sept); in spring, the water is occasionally made murky by a profusion of plankton, but usually it's clear and there's lots to see.

Both Tutukaka and Whangarei, with its greater range of amenities, can be used as **diving** bases, though the **boats** all leave from Tutukaka and offer broadly the same deal – a full day out (9am–4pm) with two dives and all the equipment you need for $135–160, including **transport from Whangarei**. Divers with their own gear can expect to pay around $90 for the same two dives, and a day's **snorkelling** starts at $75. First-time divers can experience a "Try Dive" with full gear and an instructor for around $190. Half a dozen companies run daily trips in the main season (Nov–April), and usually at least one of them goes out most days through the rest of the year. The visitor centre in Whangarei (see p.153) has a full list of current **operators**, but the most prominent and one of the most professional in Tutukaka is Dive Tutukaka, Marina Rd (☎09/434 3867 & 0800/288 882), who offer trips to the Poor Knights Islands or to the HMNZS *Tui*. In Whangarei, good deals are available at The Dive Shop, Water St (☎09/438 3521) and Sub Aqua Dive Centre, 41 Clyde St (☎09/438 1075).

wanting to rent a quarter-share of a **charter** gamefishing boat for the day will be looking at paying $200 or more: contact the Whangarei Deep Sea Anglers Club (☎09/434 3818).

PRACTICALITIES

A limited weekday **shuttle** service (Tuatara Transit ☎09/434 3092) operates between Whangarei, Tutukaka and Ngunguru, but otherwise you'll need your own wheels. Ngunguru is where you'll find the bulk of the local **accommodation**: camping and cabins at the waterside *Ngunguru Motor Camp*, Papaka Road (☎09/434 3851; tent sites $15 or $25 for two, cabins ②–③), cheap but good rooms at the *Chalet Court Motel*, Main Road (☎09/434 3786; ④), and budget rooms or B&B at *Brimar Lodge*, 1890 Ngunguru Rd (☎09/434 3951; budget rooms ①; B&B ⑤–⑦), who also supply dinners by arrangement and divers' lunches ($10 a head, for guests only). Closer to Tutukaka, try the tranquil, self-contained suites at *Pacific Rendezvous*, 73 Motel Rd, off the Tutukaka Block Road (☎09/434 3847 & 0800/999 800, fax 434 3919; ⑥), which are fabulously sited on the peninsula that forms the southern arm of Tutukaka's harbour. In the same general area, diving groups are welcome at the two spacious and fully self-contained units set in a secluded sub-tropical garden at *Malibu Mals*, Kowharewa Bay (☎09/434 3450; ④). One unit sleeps 2–4 people, the other 6–8. To get there turn off the Tutukaka Block Road, towards Whangaumu Bay for 3km.

  Eating is best done in Tutukaka at the *Schnappa Rock Café*, Marina Road (☎09/434 3774), a casual, modern place serving great burgers and seafood, gourmet sandwiches ($9), cakes and coffee plus large and tasty evening meals (around $18) daily all year round. The *Blue Marlin Restaurant* upstairs at the Whangarei Deep Sea Anglers Club beside the Tutukaka harbour offers a range of dishes for around the $20 mark – pasta, cajun chicken and, not surprisingly, seafood – as well as a cheaper bistro menu.

Beaches north of Tutukaka

Settlements get smaller north of Tutukaka, most comprising a few holiday homes ranged behind the beach and little else. Day-trippers flock from Whangarei for safe swimming in gorgeous bays tucked between headlands and dotted with numerous islets. Favourites include **MATAPOURI**, 6km from Tutukaka, which backs a curving white-sand bay bounded by bushy headlands, and the pristine **Whale Bay**, 1km further north and reached by a twenty-minute bush walk off the road. The only facilities along this stretch are at Matapouri, where there's a shop and takeaway (daily 8am–6pm). Heading inland from here the road is sealed all the way to Hikurangi, where it joins SH1.

  The coastal section between here and the Bay of Islands is most easily reached from Russell (see p.170).

The Bay of Islands

THE BAY OF ISLANDS, 240km north of Auckland, is one of the brightest stars in New Zealand's tourism firmament, luring thousands to its beautiful coastal scenery, pattern of islands and clear blue waters. It is undoubtedly an appealing place but for scenery alone, it is really no more stunning than several other spots along the Northland coast, such as Whangaroa and Hokianga harbours. What sets it apart is the ease with which you can get out among the islands, and the bay's rich history, abundantly displayed through churches, mission stations and orchards – the detritus of tentative ventures onto a new land. For this is the cradle of European settlement and a focal point for Maori, on account of the **Treaty of Waitangi** (see box on p.168) which is, despite its limitations, New Zealand's most important legal document.

It is perhaps surprising that much of your time in the Bay of Islands will in fact be spent on the mainland. There are no settlements on the islands and there is only one on which you are allowed to stay overnight. The vast majority of visitors base themselves in beachside **Paihia**, which is well geared to deal with the hordes eager to launch themselves on the various cruises, yachting trips, swimming with dolphins and the like, and is the closest town to the Treaty House at **Waitangi**. The compact town of **Russell**, a couple of kilometres across the bay by passenger ferry but distant by road, is more restrained, prettier and no less accessible to cruises. Moving away from the bay itself, **Kerikeri** is intimately entwined with early missionary history while further afield, **Waimate North** was another important mission site and still has its Mission House, though the regional focus has now moved to neighbouring **Kaikohe**.

As the main tourist centre in Northland, the Bay of Islands is forced into service as a staging post for forays further north, in particular day-long **bus tours to Cape Reinga** and Ninety Mile Beach – arduous affairs lasting eleven hours, mostly spent stuck inside. You're better off making your way up to Mangonui or Kaitaia and taking a trip from there, but if time is short, take your pick from the wide range of Paihia-based excursions (see box on pp.190-91), which include scenic flights over Northland.

Some history

A warm climate, abundant seafood and deep, sheltered harbours all contributed to dense pre-European **Maori settlement** in the Bay of Islands, with every headland seeming to support a pa site. The sheltered bay was also immediately appealing to **Captain Cook**, who anchored here in 1769 and prosaically noted in his journal, "I have named it the Bay of Islands on account of the great number which line its shores, and these help to form several safe and commodious harbours". Cook landed on Motuarohia Island at what become known as Cook's Cove, where he forged generally good relations with the inhabitants. Three years later French sailor **Marion du Fresne**, en route from Mauritius to Tahiti, became the first European to have sus-

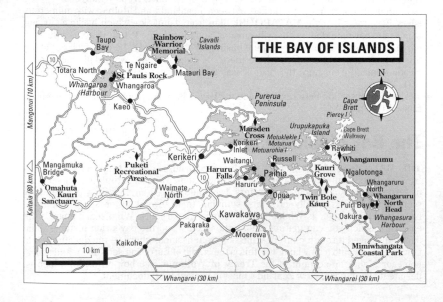

tained contact with Maori but ultimately fared less well. He stayed three months while his crew recovered their health and the ship was refitted, but a misunderstanding, probably over *tapu*, soured their initial accord and du Fresne and 26 of his crew were killed. The French retaliated, destroying a pa and killing hundreds of Maori.

Despite amicable relations between the local Ngapuhi Maori and *pakeha* whalers in the early years of the nineteenth century, the situation gradually deteriorated to the point where historian Robert Hughes described the mid-nineteenth-century Bay of Islands as "a veritable rookery of absconders ... littered with grim little communities and patriarchal clans of convicts". With increased contact, **firearms**, grog and Old World **diseases** spread and the fabric of Maori life began to break down, a process accelerated by the arrival in 1814 of Samuel Marsden, the first of many **missionaries** intent on turning Maori into God-fearing Christians. In 1833 James Busby, the British resident, was sent to secure British interests and prevent the brutal treatment meted out to the Maori by whaling captains; lacking armed back-up or judicial authority, he had little effect. The signing of the **Treaty of Waitangi** in 1840 brought effective policing, but heralded a decline in the importance of the Bay of Islands as the capital moved from its original site of Kororareka, near Russell, first to Auckland and later to Wellington.

The Bay of Islands regained some degree of world recognition in 1927 when American writer **Zane Grey** came here to fish for striped and black marlin and published photos of his exploits. Every summer since, the Bay has seen game fishing tournaments and glistening catches strung up on the jetties.

The islands

The only island to accommodate overnight guests is **Urupukapuka Island** where Zane Grey, author of best-selling westerns and avid hooker of marlin, set up his fishing resort at Otehei Bay. The resort largely burned down in 1973 but you can still stay in the accommodation units, now operating as the *Zane Grey Lodge* (☎09/403 7009, *reservations@zanegrey.co.nz*; ①), with spartan rooms, full camp kitchen and optional linen rental ($5). This is behind the *Zane Grey* restaurant, a frequent stopping point for Fullers cruises, which provide regular access; lodge guests pay the concessionary $35 return fare to get out here. There are also basic DOC **campsites** in all but the western bays and there's a range of Maori pa and terrace sites, which can be explored in a few hours following signs on the island and the free *Urupukapuka Island Archeological Walk* leaflet.

Of the remaining six large islands, by far the most popular is **Motuarohia**, more commonly known as **Roberton Island** after John Roberton, who moved here in 1839. The DOC manages the most dramatic central section, an isthmus almost severed by a pair of perfectly circular blue lagoons. Understandably, it is immensely popular with both private boaties and commercial cruises, and theDOC have even gone to the trouble of installing an undersea nature trail for snorkellers, waymarked by inscribed stainless-steel plaques. The wildlife sanctuary of **Moturua** lies adjacent, offering a network of walks through bush alive with spotted kiwi, saddlebacks and North Island robins.

There are also a couple of features that don't quite rank as islands but are often on cruise itineraries. **The Black Rocks**, bare islets formed from columnar jointed basalt, rise only 10m out of the water but plummet a sheer 30m beneath, allowing boats to inspect at close quarters. At the outer limit of the bay there's the craggy peninsula of **Cape Brett**, named by Cook in 1769 after the then Lord of the Admiralty, Lord Piercy Brett. Cruises also regularly pass through the **Hole in The Rock**, a natural tunnel through Piercy Island.

Exploring the bay

Wherever you turn in the Bay of Islands, there are people desperate to take you yachting, scuba diving, dolphin watching, kayaking or fishing. In the vast majority of cases, trips start in **Paihia** and pick up from **Russell** wharf around fifteen minutes later. Occasionally there are no pick-ups available, but the ferry between Paihia and Russell only costs $6 return. The Bay of Islands is popular and **prices** can be quite high, especially during the summer months when demand outstrips supply and everything should be **booked** at least a couple of days **in advance**. Most hotels and motels will book these trips for you and hostels can usually arrange some sort of "backpacker" discount of around ten percent.

In addition to the water-based activities covered below you can see the bay in style on traditional seaplane **flights** offered by Paihia-based Salt Air (☎ & fax 09/402 8338; 30min; $95), who also offer island stopovers.

Cruises

Without getting out onto the water you are missing the essence of the Bay of Islands. Two main companies vie for **cruise business** from the Maritime Building on Marsden Road, by the wharf in Paihia: the longstanding Fullers (☎09/402 7421; daily: Oct–May 7am–9pm; June–Sept 7am–6pm) operates large and stable craft, while the family-run King's (☎09/402 8288, fax 402 7915; daily 7am–9.30pm) run faster trips in smaller boats. In the peak season expect the boats to be full, so book in good time.

For 35 years from 1919, Fullers boats collected cream from dairy farms around the perimeter of the bay, but as the infrastructure improved, the cream took to the roads and the boats began to take passengers. By the 1950s, the cream trade had died and the boat trip had been transformed into the leisurely **Cream Trip** (Oct–May daily; June–Sep Mon, Wed, Thurs & Sat; 5hr; $65), which still delivers groceries and the mail to wharves all around the bay and includes a cream tea, for old time's sake. The **Hole in the Rock Cruise** (1–2 daily; 4hr; $50–55) is another popular excursion, speeding out through the islands to Cape Brett and, when conditions permit, edging through the hole; by splitting your journey between the two daily summer trips, you can spend a few hours on Urupukapuka. If that's still not long enough, the **Island Experience** (Oct–May daily; $35) gives you five hours ashore. Finally, the **Supercruise** (Oct–May daily; June–Sept Mon, Wed, Thurs & Sat; 6hr; $89) visits the Hole in the Rock and spends a short time at Otehei Bay, where you get to experience **Nautilus** (included on this trip, otherwise $12), a kind of deep-hulled boat with undersea viewing windows which putters out into the bay for twenty minutes to a spot where fish are fed. In partnership with Fullers is the adrenalin-pumping **Excitor** (☎09/402 7020, *excitor@ihug.co.nz*; or book through Fullers or direct at the Excitor kiosk on Paihia wharf; 6 daily in summer, 2 daily in winter; 1hr 30min; $60), an open craft a bit like a giant jetboat, which speeds across the Bay of Islands to pass several times through the Hole in the Rock.

King's, meanwhile, offers a **Hole in the Rock Scenic** cruise (1–2 daily; 3hr; $50), which makes no island stops, and the **See the Bay in a Day** trip (Dec–April daily; 6hr; $75), taking in the Hole in the Rock, an approximation of the Cream Trip and an island stop of the captain's choice. King's led the field with fast boats on the bay, introducing **Mack Attack** (mid-Dec to May; 5 daily; 1hr 30min; $50), an exhilarating blast out to the Hole in the Rock and back in an open catamaran. On fine days you're decked out in windproof and waterproof gear, protective glasses and life jacket; on rainy days it all gets too painful, so they don't go.

Sailing and kayaking

Fullers' Northland-built **schooner** in the "tall ship" tradition, *R. Tucker Thompson*, sails out into the islands and anchors for a swim and barbecue lunch (Nov–April daily; 7hr;

$75). Smaller **yachts** usually take less than a dozen passengers: competition is tight and the standards high – all have snorkelling and fishing gear on board, typically go out for six hours and include lunch. Expect to pay around $65 for the day. The pick of the bunch are *Carino* (☎09/402 8040, *carinonz@voyager.co.nz*), a catamaran skippered by a woman who also offers swimming with dolphins; 30-foot catamaran, *Straycat* (☎09/402 6130); and *She's a Lady* (☎09/402 8119, *glen@bay-of-islands.com*), a 40-foot ocean-going yacht.

Lack of previous experience is no impediment to going **kayaking** in Paihia. Coastal Kayakers, based by the Waitangi Bridge (☎09/402 8105, fax 403 8550), operate year-round and run half-day trips upstream to **Haruru Falls** ($43) and full-day trips ($65), which also includes paddling around **Motumaire Island**; longer excursions operate from November to June (2–5 days; $110–550). Island Kayaks, based at Pipi Patch Lodge, 18 Kings Rd (☎09/402 7111, *islandkayaks@acb.co.nz*) also operate all year, offering half-days trips exploring the inner islands and bays ($45–48), a full-day option beyond the inner harbour, which includes open-water kayaking, requiring some previous experience ($65–68), and an overnighter on Urupukapuka Island, again for those with experience ($150). In Waitangi, New Zealand Sea Kayaking (☎ & fax 09/402 8596, *nzkayak@clear.net.nz*) run November to April only, with a half-day trip ($40), full-day ($60), and overnighters (2–3 days, $170–240), focusing on the inner islands and bays or exploring further afield on outer coast expeditions.

If you want to go it **alone**, Bay Beach Hire, at the south end of Paihia Beach (☎09/402 7905; Oct–April) **rents** double and single open kayaks ($10 per hour, $35 a day), windsurfers ($25 per hour) and catamarans ($20 per hour); Coastal Kayakers (see above) also rent out kayaks for two or more people at a time, for safety's sake (year-round; $10 per hour, $28 per half-day, $40 a day), aquabikes ($10 per hr) and catamarans (Dec–March; $20–30 an hour).

Dolphin watching

Relatively warm water all year round and an abundance of marine mammals make the Bay of Islands one of the best places to go **dolphin watching**. You're likely to see bottlenose and common dolphins in pretty much any season, orca from May to August and Minke and Bryde's **whales** from August to January. If you don't see anything, most companies will take you out for a second chance.

Only four companies are licensed to actively search for and swim with dolphins, though that doesn't bar others from watching. Only a dozen people are allowed in the water at a time and, since most trips carry around 35 people in the peak season, you can expect to be in the water about a third of the time that the dolphins are about. The pioneers, **Dolphin Discoveries**, on the corner of Marsden and Williams roads opposite the visitor centre (☎09/402 8234, fax 402 6058, *dolphin@igrin.co.nz*; $85), are sensitive to the needs of the dolphins and claim a ninety-five percent success rate, while Fullers **Dolphin Encounters** ($85) include the option of a stopover on Urupukapuka for a few hours if you take the early boat. Finally, *Carino* (see above; $60, plus $5 for BBQ lunch), a large red catamaran based in Paihia, takes you on a day sail around the islands, with a chance to swim with the dolphins if you come across them in the right conditions.

Diving and fishing

The main people running **scuba-diving** trips are Paihia Dive, Hire & Charter (☎09/402 7551, fax 402 7110, *divepaihia@xtra.co.nz*), who will take you **snorkelling** ($50) and diving in the Bay of Islands (from $85 with no gear supplied; from $145 with gear supplied) or on the wreck of the *Rainbow Warrior* (see p.180; $135–150). Two smaller companies, who charge much the same as Paihia Dive are Octopus Divers, based in Kerikeri (π & fax 09/407 8381, *hoyle@igrin.co.nz*) and Dive North (book through Paihia visitor centre π09/402 7345, or *divenorth@xtra.co.nz*).

There is a wider range and greater choice of **fishing trips** than any other activity: everything from a little line fishing for snapper to big game boats in search of marlin, shark, tuna and kingfish. The best method is to ask around and speak to the skippers to make sure you get a trip that suits; daily charter rates range from around $60 to $500 for the big game boats.

Paihia and Waitangi

PAIHIA is where it all happens. In its own way, it is just as historically important as Russell, Waitangi and Kerikeri, but this two-kilometre-long string of waterside motels, restaurants and holiday homes has been completely over-run by the demands of tourism. Its location on three flat bays looking out towards Russell and the Bay of Islands is pleasing enough and the encircling forested hills make an attractive backdrop, but the town itself could hardly be called pretty. Nevertheless, abundant well-priced accommodation, several good restaurants, a couple of boisterous bars and endless possibilities to get out on the water make this the goal of the vast majority of the Bay of Islands' visitors. Other attractions are Paihia's **jazz festival**, usually held during the last three days of August ($25 pass, admits you to any of the venues in town), and a **food and wine festival** running over two days at the beginning of October ($16 in advance, or $25 on the day). Information and tickets are available from the visitor centre in Paihia (see below).

Legend has it that the town was named in 1823 by the less than accomplished Maori scholar, the Reverend Henry Williams, when he was looking for a site to establish the Church Missionary Society's third mission. He apparently exclaimed, "*pai* [good] here!"; unlikely, but it makes a nice story. At the time, Maori were overwhelmed by the influx of Europeans and looked to the missionaries to intercede on their behalf. A plaque outside the current St Paul's Anglican Church on Marsden Road marks the spot where, in 1831, the northern chiefs petitioned the British Crown for a representative to establish law and order. In 1833 King William IV belatedly addressed their concerns by sending the first British resident, James Busby. He built a house on a promontory 2km north across the Waitangi River in **WAITANGI** – the scene some seven years later of the signing of the **Treaty of Waitangi**, which ceded the nation's sovereignty to Britain in return for the protection Busby was ill-equipped to provide.

Arrival, information and transport

Northliner and InterCity **buses** arrive on the waterfront Marsden Road outside the Bay of Islands' main **visitor centre** (daily: Oct–Nov 8am–6pm; Dec–Feb 8am–8pm; March & April 8am–6pm; May–Sept 8am–5pm; π09/402 7345, fax 402 7301, *visitorinfo@fndc.govt.nz*). The adjacent Maritime Building contains booking desks for all the major tour operators and stays open until around 9pm in summer, a little earlier in winter. The Bay of Islands **airport** is roughly midway between Paihia and Kerikeri, and planes are met by a shuttle bus service.

Paihia isn't big, and everywhere is within walking distance. If you've got bags to carry, engage the services of the **Paihia Tuk Tuk Shuttle Service** (π025/866 071), who will drop one to three people pretty much anywhere in town for $7 and run up to Haruru Falls for $15. **Parking** in Paihia is something of a nightmare, owing to a plethora of restricted areas. Try Williams Road, where there is a section of free unlimited parking opposite the Four Square supermarket. To explore the mainland on **mountain bike**, head for the only place that rents them, Bay Beach Hire, at the south end of Paihia Beach (π09/402 7905; Oct–April; $5 per hr, $15 half day, $20 full day).

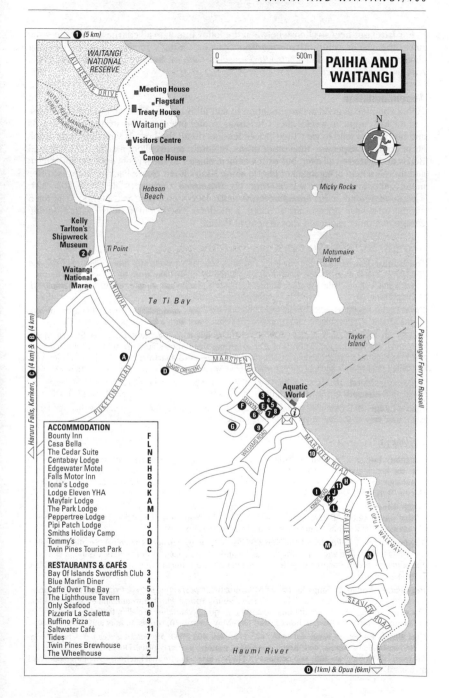

PAIHIA AND WAITANGI

0 _____ 500m

WAITANGI NATIONAL RESERVE

TAU HENARE DRIVE

HUTIA CREEK MANGROVE FOREST BOARDWALK

Meeting House
Flagstaff
Treaty House
Waitangi
Visitors Centre
Canoe House

Hobson Beach

Micky Rocks

Kelly Tarlton's Shipwreck Museum ❷

Ti Point

Motumaire Island

Waitangi National Marae

TE KARUWHA

Te Ti Bay

Taylor Island

Passenger Ferry to Russell

Haruru Falls, Kerikeri, ❻ (4 km) & ❸ (4 km)

PUKETONA ROAD

❹

❻

DAVIS CRESCENT

MARSDEN ROAD

SELWYN ROAD

Aquatic World

❺ ❹ ❺
Ⓔ
❻ Ⓔ ❼ ❽
Ⓖ
❾

ⓘ

MARSDEN ROAD

WILLIAMS ROAD

❿

KINGS ROAD

Ⓘ ⓫ Ⓗ
Ⓙ
Ⓚ
Ⓛ

SEAVIEW ROAD

PAIHIA OPUA WALKWAY

Ⓜ

Ⓝ

SEAVIEW ROAD

Haumi River

Ⓓ (1km) & Opua (6km)

ACCOMMODATION

Bounty Inn	F
Casa Bella	L
The Cedar Suite	N
Centabay Lodge	E
Edgewater Motel	H
Falls Motor Inn	B
Iona's Lodge	G
Lodge Eleven YHA	K
Mayfair Lodge	A
The Park Lodge	M
Peppertree Lodge	I
Pipi Patch Lodge	J
Smiths Holiday Camp	O
Tommy's	D
Twin Pines Tourist Park	C

RESTAURANTS & CAFÉS

Bay Of Islands Swordfish Club	3
Blue Marlin Diner	4
Caffe Over The Bay	5
The Lighthouse Tavern	8
Only Seafood	10
Pizzeria La Scaletta	6
Ruffino Pizza	9
Saltwater Café	11
Tides	7
Twin Pines Brewhouse	1
The Wheelhouse	2

For **Internet access** choose between the following, who all charge around the same rates: the visitor centre (*visitorinfo@fndc.govt.nz*); King's in the Maritime Building (*kingz@voyager.co.nz*); and *Boots Off Travellers Café* on Selwyn Road (☎09/402 6632, *paihia@bootsoff.net.nz*).

Accommodation

Paihia abounds in good accommodation to suit all budgets. That isn't to say it's cheap, and for the couple of weeks after Christmas, motel prices can be stratospheric. B&Bs and homestays tend to vary their prices less, as do all the hostels which, though a dollar or so more expensive than other areas, maintain an excellent standard. Motels and B&Bs are scattered all over, but with a central cluster in the streets opposite the wharf, and there's a kind of backpacker ghetto along Kings Road. Some backpackers also offer motel units. If you fancy self-catering, try *Brampton Cottage* (☎ & fax 09/403 7521, *www.holidayhomes.co.nz*, *brampton@xtra.co.nz*; Dec–Feb $450 for 3 nights, $750 for 5 nights; off-season prices start at $360), a modern 2-bedroomed house with a double garage in a quiet sheltered spot in central Paihia.

HOTELS, MOTELS AND B&BS

The Bounty Inn, Williams Rd, cnr Bayview Rd & Selwyn Rd (☎09/402 7088 & 0800/117 897, fax 402 7081). Pleasant central yet quiet motel, secluded by bush 100m from the beach. Each unit has either a sundeck or a balcony; other bonuses include a private spa, on-site restaurant and ample off-street parking. ⑥.

Casa Bella, MacMurray Rd (☎09/402 7387, fax 402 7166, *casa.bel@xtra.co.nz*). Plain but decent rooms around a quiet stucco-and-Spanish-arches courtyard with a heated pool and spa. ⑥.

The Cedar Suite, 5 Sullivan's Rd (☎09/402 8516, fax 402 8555, *Cdr.Swt@xtra.co.nz*). Superb, nicely furnished and very hospitable B&B in a bush setting five minutes' walk from the beach. Rooms in the house come with cooked or continental breakfast, the apartment can be bed only or self-contained, and there's a lovely cottage with bay views sleeping up to six. B&B ⑤; cottage ⑥.

Edgewater Motel, 10 Marsden Rd (☎09/402 7875, fax 402 7265, *edgewater_motel@xtra.co.nz*). Small, fully-equipped quality motel right by the beach with in-house video and a spa pool. ⑥.

Iona's Lodge, 29 Bayview Rd (☎09/402 8072). Central, self-contained B&B units with a wonderful panoramic view of the bay at very reasonable prices. ⑤.

HOSTELS

Centabay Lodge, 27 Selwyn Rd (☎09/402 7466, fax 402 8145, *centabay@xtra.co.nz*). Central hostel near the beach and shops, with decent three- to five-bunk dorms, en-suite twins and doubles and motel-style self-catering studios. Guests get free use of a rowboat and kayaks, and can rent bikes. Dorms ①, rooms ②, studios ④.

Lodge Eleven YHA, cnr Kings Rd & MacMurray Rd (☎ & fax 09/402 7487). Excellent central hostel that's good value. All dorms and rooms are en suite, and the airy motel-style doubles and twins are serviced daily. Tennis courts next door. Dorms ①, rooms ③.

Mayfair Lodge, 7 Puketona Rd (☎ & fax 09/402 7471, *mayfair.lodge@xtra.co.nz*). Smallish hostel at the Waitangi end of town with a friendly feel, some of the cheapest dorm beds around, a spa pool and a games room. Rooms range from spacious six-bunk dorms to twins and made-up doubles. Dorms ①, rooms ②.

Peppertree Lodge, 15 Kings Rd (☎ & fax 09/402 6122, *peppertree.lodge@xtra.co.nz*). Deluxe, quiet and central hostel with spacious 8-bunk dorms, 4-bunk rooms with bathroom, and en-suite doubles. The games room, TV room, quiet lounge and fully-equipped kitchen are all in tip-top condition without seeming sterile. Be sure to book ahead Oct–May. Dorms ①, rooms ③, fully self-contained ④.

Pipi Patch Lodge, 18 Kings Rd (☎09/402 7111, fax 402 8300, *pipipatch@acb.co.nz*). Central converted motel that's popular with Kiwi Experience, making it a party place. Dorms sleep up to 8, units (as twins or doubles) are fully self-contained. There's also a communal kitchen, spa, plunge pool and own bar. Dorms ①, rooms ③.

Tommy's, 44 Davis Crescent (☎09/402 8668, *tommys@xtra.co.nz*). Brand new and amiably run hostel that's quieter than some of the more central places and sports super-clean facilities. Dorms ①, rooms ②.

CAMPSITES

Falls Motor Inn and Caravan Park, Puketona Rd (☎ & fax 09/402 7816, *bookings@falls.co.nz*). Tent sites down by the river opposite Haruru Falls, 4km north of Paihia, and full-blown motel units around a nice pool with commanding views. Tent sites $12, motel units ⑤.

The Park Lodge, cnr Seaview Rd & MacMurray Rd (☎09/402 7826, fax 402 8500 *parklodge@xtra.co.nz*). Average hotel backed by Paihia's most central campsite. Tent sites $10.

Smith's Holiday Camp, Opua Rd, 3km south of Paihia (☎09/402 7678, *smithshc@xtra.co.nz*). Small and peaceful waterside site with a range of cabins, and dinghies for rent. Tent sites $10, cabins ③–⑤.

Twin Pines Tourist Park, Puketone Rd (☎ & fax 09/402 7322). Attractive, well laid out and recently upgraded site by Haruru Falls, 4km north of Paihia. Tent sites $13, cabins & motel units ⑤–⑥.

The Town

Paihia is primarily a base for exploring the bay (see p.162), but there are a couple of diverting sights on land. The most prominent of these is **Aquatic World**, Marsden Road (daily: Dec–Feb 9am–9pm; March–Nov 9am–5pm; $6.50), bang next to the wharf and filled with a series of well-presented tanks full of local sea life. Visits are guided and informative, adding greatly to what could easily be just another run-of-the-mill aquarium.

Around a kilometre north, the Waitangi River separates Paihia and Waitangi and provides a mooring for the *Tui*, a three-masted barque built as a sugar lighter in 1917 and now accommodating **Kelly Tarlton's Shipwreck Museum** (daily 10am–6pm; $6.50). Kelly Tarlton was New Zealand's foremost wreck diver and this museum demonstrates the scale of his pioneering excavations. A salty soundtrack accompanies you through the bowels of the ship, where the expected bounty of nails, pottery and tankards is spiced up with a bottle of 1903 whisky, found by laboratory testing to be almost identical to the day it was bottled, and a collection of strangely dated-looking sunglasses and calculators from the *Mikhail Lermontov*, a Soviet cruise ship that went down in the Marlborough Sounds in 1986. If feeling peckish you won't have to go far – the quirky onboard restaurant, *The Wheelhouse*, serves light lunches and full dinners (see p.170).

From Paihia you can get stuck into some **adventure activities** for the day in local native forest with Drop Down Under Adventures (book through Paihia visitor centre or hostels; around $55 for the day, and ten percent backpacker discount; free pick-up), who will take you abseiling 30-metre waterfalls, swimming in rock pools, and on a challenge course. No previous experience is necessary and they supply all the gear.

The Waitangi National Reserve

Crossing the bridge over the Waitangi River from the shipwreck museum you enter the **Waitangi National Reserve** (unrestricted access), the single most symbolic place in New Zealand for Maori and *pakeha* alike, a focal point for the modern nation's struggle for identity. For it was here in 1840 that William Hobson, Queen Victoria's representative, and nearly fifty Maori chiefs signed the Treaty of Waitangi (see box overleaf), ceding *Aotearoa*'s sovereignty to Britain and ostensibly affording the Maori protection and guaranteeing them rights over land and resources. When the area was gifted to the people of New Zealand in 1932 by Governor-General Lord Bledisloe, the Treaty House was being used as a sheep shelter and the grounds were neglected, but a sudden desire to commemorate the 1940 centennial of the signing in fitting fashion provoked a flurry of restoration. The house is now the centrepiece of the **Waitangi Visitor Centre and Treaty House** (daily Dec–Feb 9am–6pm; rest of the year 9am–5pm; $8), where a sappy and anodyne twenty-minute video setting the historical framework is bolstered by a

THE TREATY OF WAITANGI

The Treaty of Waitangi is the **founding document** of modern New Zealand, a touchstone for both *pakeha* and Maori, with implications that permeate New Zealand society. Signed in 1840 between what were ostensibly two sovereign states – the United Kingdom and the United Tribes of New Zealand, plus other Maori leaders – the treaty remains central to New Zealand's **race relations**. The Maori rights guaranteed by it have seldom been upheld, and the constant struggle for recognition continues.

THE TREATY AT WAITANGI

Motivated by a desire to staunch perceived **Pacific expansionism** of the French, who were planning a settlement on Banks Peninsula, and an obligation on the Crown to protect Maori from rapacious **land-grabbing** by settlers, the British instructed naval captain William Hobson to negotiate the **transfer of sovereignty** with "the free and intelligent consent of the natives" and to deal fairly with the Maori. Within a few days of his arrival, Hobson, with the help of James Busby and others, drew up both the English Treaty and a Maori "translation". On the face of it, it is a straightforward document, but the complications of having **two versions** (see Contexts, p.848) and the implications of striking a deal between two peoples with widely differing views on land and resource ownership and usage have reverberated down the years. The treaty was unveiled in grand style on February 5, 1840, to a gathering of some 400 representatives of the **five northern tribes** in front of Busby's residence in Waitangi. Presented as a contract between the **chiefs** and **Queen Victoria** – someone whose role was comprehensible in chiefly terms – the benefits were amplified and the costs downplayed. As most chiefs didn't understand English, they **signed** the Maori version of the treaty, which still has *mana* (prestige) among Maori today.

THE TREATY AFTER WAITANGI

The pattern set at Waitangi was repeated up and down the country, as seven copies of the treaty were dispatched to garner signatures and extend Crown authority over parts of the North Island that had not yet been covered, and the South Island. On May 21, before signed treaty copies had been returned, Hobson **claimed** New Zealand for Britain: the North Island on the grounds of **cession** by Maori, and the South Island by right of Cook's "**discovery**", as it was considered to be *in terrorium nullis* ("without owners"), despite a significant Maori population.

Maori fears were alerted from the start, and as the settler population grew and demand for land increased, successive governments passed laws that gradually stripped Maori of control over their affairs – actions which led to the **New Zealand Wars** of the 1860s (see "History" in Contexts, p.849). Over the decades, small concessions were made, but nothing significant changed until 1973, when **Waitangi Day** (February 6) became an official national holiday. From 1971, Maori groups, supported by a small but articulate band of *pakeha*, began a campaign of **direct action**, increasingly disrupting commemorations, thereby alienating many *pakeha* and splitting Maori allegiances between angry, young, urban Maori and the *kaumatua* (elders), who saw the actions as disrespectful to the ancestors and an affront to tradition. Many strands of Maori society were unified by the *hikoi* (march) to Waitangi to protest against the celebrations in 1985, a watershed year in which Paul Reeves was appointed New Zealand's first Maori Governor General and the **Waitangi Tribunal** (see Contexts, p.857) was given some teeth.

Protests have continued over the last decade – including several infamous flag-trampling, egg-pelting and spitting incidents – as successive governments have vacillated over maintaining the commemorations at Waitangi or trying to defuse the situation by promoting a parallel event at the Governor General's residence in Wellington.

small exhibition of Maori artefacts, including a musket owned by Hone Heke, the first Maori chief to sign the Treaty of Waitangi, and a portrait of him blithely entitled *Johny Heke*.

The **Treaty House** itself was built in Georgian colonial style in 1833–34; it was once described as "only a couple of rooms separated by a lobby" and is thoroughly unprepossessing, largely because James Busby's superiors in Sydney failed to supply the requisite materials. The original part of the house is furnished as it would have been in Busby's time, while the wings added in the 1880s contain displays on Busby, Waitangi life and the treaty itself. The front windows look towards Russell over sweeping lawns, where marquees were erected on three significant occasions: in 1834, when Maori chiefs chose the Confederation of Tribes flag, which now flies on one yard arm of the central flagpole; the meeting a year later at which northern Maori leaders signed the Declaration of Independence of New Zealand; and, in 1840, the signing of the Treaty of Waitangi.

The northern side of the lawn is flanked by the *whare runanga* or **Maori meeting house**, built between 1934 and 1940. Though proposed by Bledisloe and northern Maori chiefs, the construction of the house was a cooperative effort between all Maori and is unique in that it is pan-tribal. A short audio-visual presentation highlights and explains key elements on the richly-carved panels, introducing the major themes and legends depicted. Housed in a specially built shelter in the Treaty House grounds is another centennial project, the world's largest **war canoe** (*waka*) – the *Nga Toki Awhaorua* is named after the vessel navigated by Kupe when he discovered *Aotearoa*. This is undoubtedly an impressive boat, over 35m long, propelled by eighty warriors and built over two years from two huge kauri by members of the five northern tribes; it has traditionally been launched each year since 1940 on Waitangi Day, though the future of the launching, along with the Waitangi Day commemoration ceremony, remains uncertain.

The *Waitangi Resort Hotel* and the prestigious Waitangi golf course encircle the Treaty House grounds, but the Waitangi National Reserve extends beyond the fairways to the scenic viewpoint atop Mount Bledisloe, 3km away, and 2km beyond that to **Haruru Falls**, a horseshoe formed where the Waitangi River drops over a basalt lava flow. Though not that impressive by New Zealand standards, there is good swimming at the base. Haruru Falls are also accessible from outside the Treaty House grounds on the very gentle **Hutia Creek Mangrove Forest Boardwalk** (2hr).

Around Paihia

Drivers travelling between Paihia and Russell will be catching the vehicular ferry (see p.172) across the narrow Veronica Channel at **OPUA**, the Bay of Islands' major deepwater port. Fans of mangroves and estuarine scenery can tackle the gentle **Paihia–Opua Coastal Walkway** (6km; 2–3hr one-way) to get here.

The 13km stretch of railway between Opua and Kawakawa, which last carried passengers in the 1960s and saw its final freight train in 1986, is now operated as the **Bay of Islands Vintage Railway** (☎09/404 0684; Christmas–Easter 3 daily; Easter–Christmas Mon, Tues, Sat & Sat 2 daily; 45min one-way; $16 return, $10 one-way), with steam and diesel locos hauling restored 1930s rolling stock. The highlight is the final rumble down the centre of Kawakawa's main street.

Eating and drinking

Paihia's **range** of places to eat is unmatched anywhere in the Bay of Islands and competition keeps **prices** tolerable; though none is actually on the waterfront, many have sea views and salty menus by way of compensation. The **restaurants** are also good places to stick around for post-prandial drinking, though there are a couple of more downbeat bars and an out-of-town **brewhouse** that's worth the journey. There are also two *pipi* (mussel) beds at Te Ti Bay (the next one along towards Waitangi), where you can forage when the tide's out.

Bay of Islands Swordfish Club, Marsden Rd. Private club overlooking the bay, which welcomes visitors outside the peak summer season for some of the cheapest drinks in town. A temporary membership available at any time of year costs $2.50. Simple good-value food is served from 6pm.

Blue Marlin Diner, Marsden Rd. Cheap and cheerful licensed café and takeaway, serving breakfast from $6 and, later in the day, steaks and seafood platters for $16.

Caffe Over the Bay, Paihia Mall, Marsden Rd. The best place for a daytime coffee on the veranda but also worth a visit for good salmon-bagel breakfasts and reasonably priced lunches and dinners with an international slant. Dinners in summer only. Licensed.

The Lighthouse Tavern, upstairs in the Paihia Mall. Paihia's liveliest drinking spot and a traditional Kiwi bar, with entertainment (including disco) 6 nights a week all year and drinking till late. Be warned, though, this place can get rough.

Only Seafood, 40 Marsden Rd (✆09/402 6066). As the name implies it's seafood only at this popular dinner spot, upstairs in a big atmospheric villa. Main courses are around $20 and generally good value, but the expensive wine list encourages BYO ($5 corkage). Book early in summer to avoid long waits. Open all year.

Pizzeria La Scaletta, Selwyn Rd (✆09/402 7039). Gourmet pizza bar with beer on tap and outside dining, or takeaway.

Ruffino Pizza, 39 Williams Rd (upstairs; ✆09/402 7964). Pizza and pasta to eat at the café or takeaway. BYO. Open daily from 5.30pm.

Saltwater Café, 14 Kings Rd (no bookings). Award-winning café and restaurant serving some of the tastiest and best presented food in town, concentrating on NZ lamb, beef and seafood for around $25. BYO & licensed.

Tides, Williams Rd (✆09/402 7557). Highly regarded, innovative food for well-priced breakfast, lunch and dinner with the emphasis on fresh seafood and top-quality lamb, though the portions can be rather small. Licensed. Closed Tues in winter.

Twin Pines Brew House, Puketona Rd, Haruru Falls (✆09/402 7195). Fine old villa shipped from Auckland in 1980 and refitted to micro-brew a malty ale and a clean-tasting lager, and cook a good range of bar meals. A courtesy bus runs from Paihia during the peak summer season. (Oct–April daily from midday till late; rest of the year Wed & Thurs 4–11pm, Fri–Sun noon–11pm.)

The Wheelhouse, Kelly Tarlton's Shipwreck Museum, Waitangi (✆09/402 7018). Fine dining with a difference: light lunches and full-blown dinners are served either on the glassed-over exhibit tables down below or on deck among the creaking rigging. BYO & licensed.

Russell

For much of the year the small hillside village of **RUSSELL** is a sleepy place favoured by city escapees, its isolation on a narrow peninsula with poor road but good sea access giving it an island ambience. But through the summer it is swamped with day-trippers piling off the passenger ferries from Paihia, a couple of kilometres across the water, to browse around New Zealand's most **historic** village and stroll along its appealing tree-lined waterfronts. Evenings are more peaceful – the major exception being **New Year's Eve**, when half the nation's youth seem to descend and the all-night revelry harks back to the 1830s when **Kororareka**, as Russell was then known, was a swashbuckling town full of **whalers** and sealers with a reputation as the "Hell Hole of the Pacific".

Tales of **debauchery** may well have been exaggerated over the years, but one observer noted in 1836 that it was "notorious at present for containing, I should think, a greater number of rogues than any other spot of equal size in the universe" and a missionary found it "a dreadful place – the very seat of Satan". Savage and drunken behaviour served as an open invitation to **missionaries**, who gradually tamed a hostile congregation and left behind Russell's two oldest buildings, the church and a

△ *Tapeka Point Historic Reserve (1 km)*

RUSSELL

Oneroa Bay

Flagstaff

Flagstaff Hill Historic Reserve Ⓐ

Kororareka Point Scenic Reserve

Kororareka Bay

Ⓑ

Fullers Office

Ⓒ

RSA

ⓘ

Bay of Islands Swordfish Club

Ⓓ

Christ Church

Bay of Islands Maritime & Historic Park Visitor Centre

Russell Museum

Pompallier House

Ⓔ

Ⓕ

HOPE AVENUE

EATING & DRINKING

Duke of Marlborough Hotel	1
Duke of Marlborough Tavern	2
The Gables	4
Gannets	5
Quarterdeck	7
Sally's	3
Waterfront Café	6

△ Paihai

N

ACCOMMODATION

Arcadia Lodge	F
Brampton House	A
Browns Lodge	D
Motel Russell	E
Russell Holiday Park	B
Russell Lodge	C

0   500 m

Opua (8 km) ▷

printing works used for producing religious tracts. By 1840, Kororareka was the largest settlement in the country, but it was deemed far too bawdy to be worthy of capital status and, after the signing of the Treaty of Waitangi, William Hobson moved his capital progressively further south.

Meanwhile, initial **Maori** enthusiasm for the Treaty of Waitangi had become tarnished: financial benefits had failed to materialize and the Confederation of Tribes flag that flew from Flagstaff Hill between 1834 and 1840 had been replaced by the Union Jack. This came to be a symbol of the **British betrayal**, and as resentment crystallized, it found a leader in Hone Heke Pokai, Ngapuhi chief and son-in-law of Kerikeri's Hongi Hika. Between July 1844 and March 1845, Hongi and his followers cut down the flagstaff four times, the last sparking the first **New Zealand War**, which raged for nearly a year. Kororareka was sacked and all but destroyed during the fighting, and when the rebuilding began, the authorities tried to expunge its past by **renaming** it Russell.

The new town never really flourished but grew slowly around its **beachfront** into a well laid out and peaceful place that is a delight to be in. Most Bay of Islands **cruises and trips** can be joined at Russell, but far fewer people stay here on account of the limited range of motels and budget accommodation – a consequence of ordinances designed to preserve the character of the place and to limit the strain on the town's water supply and sewage disposal, both of which struggle during the peak season.

Don't let this put you off staying here, but if you are only passing through, everything can be seen comfortably in a day.

Arrival and information

Most visitors **arrive** in Russell by way of ferries. Drivers from Paihia and SH1 typically cross the narrow strait at **Opua**, 9km south of Russell, on the small **vehicle ferry**, which leaves every ten to twenty minutes (daily 7am–9pm, Fri until 10pm; every 10min until 5.30pm, every 20min 5.30–9pm; last crossing from Russell is at 8.45pm; car & driver $14 return, passengers $2). Pedestrians and cyclists can get directly from Paihia to Russell on one of three **passenger ferries** – Fullers, the *Waimarie*, and the *Waitere* – which between them manage a boat every twenty to thirty minutes (Oct–May until 10.30pm; rest of year until 7.30pm; $3 one-way, $5–6 return); tickets are bought on the boat and you must return on the same boat from which you buy.

There is no fully fledged visitor centre, but information is available from **Russell Information**, on the end of the wharf (daily 8.30am–5pm, until 7pm Christmas–Jan; ☎09/403 8020, fax 403 7868), and, to a lesser degree, from the Fullers office, Cass Street (7.30am–5pm, until 7pm in high season; ☎ & fax 09/403 7866). For specific walking and environment information, make for the DOC's **Bay of Islands Maritime & Historic Park visitor centre**, The Strand (daily: Nov–May 8.30am–5pm, June–Oct 8.30am–4pm; ☎09/403 7685, fax 403 7649), which is full of interesting displays and sells the enlightening *Russell Heritage Trails* leaflet ($1). Few places are more than half a kilometre away from the wharf, though short-stay visitors may fancy the **Russell Mini Tour** (5 daily; 1hr; $12), which leaves from outside the Fullers office and visits the major sights.

Accommodation

Accommodation in Russell is much more limited than across the water in Paihia and tends to be more upmarket, in keeping with Russell's quieter and more refined image. Beside a handful of **motels**, **hotels** and **backpacker lodges** you're in **B&B** and **homestay** territory; in addition to those listed below, King's, or the visitor centre in Paihia, can help you pick one out.

Don't expect to find many vacancies in the three weeks after **Christmas**. To stay here then, **book well ahead** and be prepared to pay a premium; **inflated rates** tend to carry on into the rest of January and February, as well.

Arcadia Lodge, Florance Ave (☎09/403 7756, fax 403 7657, *arcadialodge@xtra.co.nz*). One of Russell's gems, a rambling wooden historic house encircled by decks overlooking luxuriant English cottage gardens, and the bay. It's a 5min stroll to the village and some of the 10 romantic rooms (B&B or simply rented as doubles) enjoy sea views, while most of them have their own bathrooms (some are en suite). ⑤–⑥, B&B ⑦.

Brampton House, Wellington St (☎ & fax 09/403 7521, *brampton@xtra.co.nz*). Two spotless, well-appointed suites (with separate entrances and terraces) in the highest house in Russell, surrounded by bush and commanding fabulous views all around. Deft touches such as complimentary wine and sumptuous breakfasts make this a treat. ⑦.

Browns Lodge, Ashby St (☎09/403 7693, fax 403 7683, *brown.lodge@xtra.co.nz*). Richly furnished homestay in a modern all-timber house with three comfortable air-conditioned suites, each with a veranda overlooking Russell and the bay. ⑦.

Motel Russell, Matauwhi Bay Rd (☎09/403 7854 & 0800/240 011, fax 403 8001). Despite the lack of sea views, this is the pick of Russell's motels, with pleasant self-contained units and hotel-style rooms, and an attractive pool and spa. ⑥.

Russell Holiday Park, Longbeach Rd (☎09/403 7826, fax 403 7221, *russell.top10@xtra.co.nz*). Central, well-ordered and spotless campsite with tent and powered sites, backpacker bunks (except in the peak season) and an extensive range of high-standard cabins and motel units. Tent sites $12, dorms ①, cabins ④, units ⑥.

Russell Lodge, cnr Chapel St & Beresford St (☎09/403 7640 & 0800/478 773, fax 403 7641). Combined backpackers and motel in a garden setting right in the heart of Russell. Backpackers get four-bunk cabins, each with a bathroom, and there are studio and family units. Everyone has access to the kitchen and pool. Dorms ③, studios & units ⑤.

The Town

Several historic buildings and Flagstaff Hill constitute the main sights in Russell, supplemented by a few diverting craft shops. Arriving on the passenger ferry, the single most striking building at the western end of town is **Pompallier House** (daily 10am–5pm; $5), New Zealand's oldest industrial building, dating from 1841. It was built as a print shop for the French Roman Catholic bishop, Jean Baptiste François Pompallier, who had arrived three years earlier and found the Catholic word of God under siege from tracts in Maori, written by Anglicans and Wesleyans. Pompallier duly imported a press and paper, installed a tannery and set about printing *Ako Marama*, a book containing a pastoral letter, prayers, hymns, psalms and a burial service in Maori. Lacking money to import all the timber needed, the missionaries built a rammed-earth structure apparently modelled on a kind of French pigeon coop, but elegant nonetheless, with its hipped roof flared to form the upper verandas and its windows heavily shuttered to keep out prying eyes. For many years the press was kept secret, not out of religious protectionism but because of the great value of the contents; the lead type could be melted down for shot and the paper could be used for making cartridges. The printing operation only lasted until 1850 and the building changed hands several times as a domestic house, its original function being completely obliterated. Subsequent work has largely restored it to its 1841 state, an austere place of wooden boards and lime-washed walls where artisans are again producing handmade books. In the summer the processes are all amply explained in each room, while through the winter interesting fifty-minute guided tours are obligatory. Only four out of the original six thousand copies of *Ako Marama* survive, one of them in the small museum upstairs, which also charts the changes the house has undergone.

The only other building to survive Hone Heke's ransacking of Russell was the prim, white, weatherboard Christ Church, Robertson Road, built in 1836 and now New Zealand's oldest surviving church – earlier examples at Kerikeri and Paihia having been lost. Unlike most churches of similar vintage, it was not a mission church but was built by local settlers: an appeal for public donations loosened the purse strings of Charles Darwin, who passed through the Bay of Islands at the time, long before he fell out with the church over his theory of evolution. In the mid-nineteenth century the church was besieged during skirmishes between Hone Heke's warriors and the British, leaving several still-visible bullet holes; the neat cemetery contains some of the oldest European graves in the country and numerous headstones inscribed in Maori.

The small **Russell Museum** (*Te Whare Taonga o Kororareka*), York Street (daily: late Dec–early Feb 10am–5pm; early Feb–late Dec 10am–4pm; $2.50), contains tolerable displays on Russell's whaling days, a few Maori pieces, fishing tackle left behind by American writer Zane Grey and an impressive one-fifth scale model of Cook's *Endeavour*, which called in here in 1769. From the museum, a stroll along The Strand passes the rooms of the prestigious Bay of Islands Game Fishing Club, which was founded in 1924, and the Duke of Marlborough hotel – the original building on this site held New Zealand's first liquor licence.

At the end of The Strand, turn left into Wellington Street for a steep climb up to **Flagstaff Hill** (*Maiki*). The current flagpole was erected in 1857, some twelve years after the destruction of the fourth by Hone Heke (see Contexts, p.849), as a conciliatory gesture by a son of one of the chiefs who had ordered the original felling. The Confederation of Tribes flag, abandoned after the signing of the Treaty of Waitangi, is now flown on twelve significant days of the year, such as the anniversary of Hone Heke's death and the final day of the first New Zealand War. From Flagstaff Hill it is only a further kilometre to the **Tapeka Point Historic Reserve**, a former pa site on a headland at the end of the peninsula, a wonderfully defensible position with great views and abundant evidence of terracing. Another worthwhile one-kilometre stroll from Russell is to **Oneroa Bay** (Long Beach), a gently shelving beach sheltered from the prevailing wind and safe for swimming.

Eating and drinking

The range of restaurants in Russell is not especially varied, and prices are relatively high. Drinking options are no better, though there are a number of low-cost private clubs – the RSA on Cass Street and the Bay of Islands Swordfish Club on The Strand for example – which often welcome visitors.

The Duke of Marlborough Hotel, The Strand (☎09/403 7829). Well prepared traditional food is served in New Zealand's oldest licensed establishment, now a pricey hotel. The verandaed bar is a good place to idle over a daytime coffee.

The Duke of Marlborough Tavern, York St. Unreconstructed Kiwi pub with mainstream bar meals and a lively atmosphere.

The Gables, The Strand (☎09/403 7618). Expensive waterfront restaurant serving superb French-tinged but widely varied dishes from lamb fillets to chicken quesadilla in candlelit rooms built in 1847.

Gannets, cnr Chapel St & York St (☎09/403 7990). Award-winning airy lunch (summer only) and dinner (all year) venue serving a broad range of food indoors and outdoors. Especially popular are the pink fish chowder and other seafood. Book ahead for dinner; licensed.

Quarterdeck, The Strand (☎09/403 7761). Moderately priced, mainly seafood restaurant on the front with dining in separate booths and lively drinking at the bar. Licensed.

Sally's, 25 The Strand (☎09/403 7652). Friendly reasonably priced restaurant, predictably strong on seafood, open for lunch and dinner. Licensed & BYO. Book ahead in peak season.

Waterfront Café, The Strand. Simple café where the best coffee in town will wash down an all-day breakfast or snack. In summer it also operates as an ice-cream parlour.

Around Russell: Whangaruru Harbour

To the south and east of Russell lies the mixed kauri forest of the **Ngaiotonga Scenic Reserve** and some wonderful coastline around the **Whangaruru Harbour**. The twisting and incompletely sealed Russell Road runs through the region, closely tracing the coast from Orongo Bay, just south of Russell. Just beyond the Waikare Road turn-off for Kawakawa and Paihia, a side road leads to some fine stands of kauri visited on the **Ngaiotonga Kauri Grove Walk** (1km; 20min), the **Twin Bole Kauri Walk** (5min), and the **Ngaiotonga–Russell Forest Walkway** (21km; 9hr); the last is best tackled over two days with a tent.

Continuing along Russell Road, you'll reach the junction of the road to the scattered and predominantly Maori village of **RAWHITI**, the start of the challenging but rewarding **Cape Brett Tramping Track** (20km; 8hr; $15 fee, payable in advance; hut bookings essential at the DOC visitor centre, The Strand, Russell ☎09/403 7685). This terminates at the end of the peninsula, where you turn around and come back for another eight hours. Fortunately, there's a trampers' hut at the cape (21 beds, $12; annual hut pass not valid) with gas burners but no cooking gear. The track crosses private land and you should check with the DOC in Russell for the latest news about access to sections of the peninsula, where possum control is periodically undertaken. The base of the Cape Brett peninsula is crossed by the **Whangamumu Walking Track** (4km; 1hr), which starts close to the Rawhiti Road junction, and runs through forest to a beach where the remains of a 1920s whaling operation can be seen.

At **NGAIOTONGA**, 20km south of Rawhiti, a dirt road branches 8km through lumpy farmland until you round a corner revealing the broad isthmus sweep of **Bland Bay** with great beaches on both sides. You can camp at the simple Bland Beach Motor Camp (☎09/433 6759; tent sites $8) or press on a further 2km to **Whangaruru North Head Scenic Reserve**, with yet more lovely beaches, fine walks around the end of the peninsula and a DOC campsite (closed July–Sept; $6) with water and toilets.

The main settlement on the mainland side of the Whangaruru Harbour is **OAKURA**, 12km south of Ngaiotonga along Russell Road. Not a great deal happens here but that is exactly its appeal, with no shortage of places to swim and walk, all with lovely sea and island views. There are a few **places to stay**, including the *Whangaruru Harbour Motor Camp*, Ohawiri Road (☎09/433 6806; tent sites $8.50, cabins ②, motel units ④), and the *Oakura Bay B&B*, 24 Rapata Rd (☎ & fax 09/433 6066; dorms ①, homestay ③), which also offers evening meals for $20 and kayak rental for around $15 a day.

Kerikeri

KERIKERI, 25km northwest of Paihia, is both central to the historical development of and yet geographically removed from the Bay of Islands. On initial acquaintance it is a very ordinary service town strung along the main road, surrounded by the orchards that form Kerikeri's economic mainstay and offer abundant opportunities for casual work. Two kilometres to the east of town, the thin ribbon of the Kerikeri Inlet forces its way from the sea to its tidal limit at **Kerikeri Basin**, the site chosen by Samuel Marsden for the Church Missionary Society's second mission. John Butler, the first Anglican missionary, arrived here in 1819 but initially struggled: requiring the trust, generosity and compliance of the Ngapuhi for the mission's survival, he found himself compromised, being ethically unable to sell the Ngapuhi the muskets they so wanted. As missions opened in the new settlements that sprang up after 1840, Kerikeri's importance waned.

In the 1920s the land was planted with sub-tropical crops, which thrive here: the mainstay is citrus, supported by tamarillos, feijoas, melons, courgettes, peppers and kiwifruit. For most of the year it is possible to get **seasonal work** in the orchards, either weeding, thinning or picking the produce. Work is easiest to find during the winter (April–August), when kiwifruit and mandarins are harvested; the best contacts are the managers of the hostels (see p.177), many of which also require good weekly rates. Kerikeri's other claim to fame is the profusion of **craft shops** scattered among the orchards and frequently featuring on tour-bus itineraries. You can pick up a free *Kerikeri Art & Craft Trail* map at Ann's Travel in Kerikeri (see below).

Arrival, information and accommodation

Air New Zealand link **flights** (Eagle Air) from Auckland and Kaitaia land at Kerikeri Airport, 5km from town. Airport shuttles (operated by Paihia Taxis) charge $10 per person to Kerikeri, and $15 to Paihia. Northliner and InterCity **buses** (southbound around 8am and northbound around 1.30pm) stop outside a disused building on Cobham Road. You can make bookings through the Kerikeri Travel Shop on Fairway Drive (☎09/407 8013). There is no official visitor centre, but Ann's Travel, Hub Mall on Kerikeri Road (usually Mon–Fri 9am–5pm, Sat 9am–noon; ☎09/407 8667, *annstravel@xtra.co.nz*) dispenses bus tickets and can provide local **information**. The foyer at the library on Cobham Road (Mon–Fri 9am–5pm, Sat 10am–noon; ☎09/407 9297) also supplies local information but does not take bookings. The **DOC office**, 34 Landing Rd (☎09/407 8474), just over the river from the Stone Store, can advise on local walks and more ambitious treks into the Puketi and Omahuta forests (see p.179). For **Internet access** try Scottronic Technologies Ltd, a computer store in Hub Mall on Kerikeri Road (☎09/407 8932, *theteam@scottron.co.nz*).

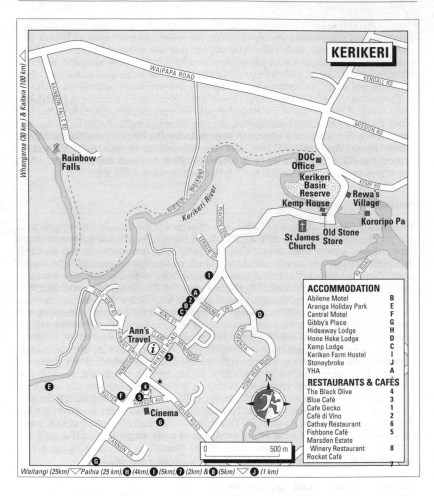

ACCOMMODATION
Abilene Motel	B
Aranga Holiday Park	E
Central Motel	F
Gibby's Place	G
Hideaway Lodge	H
Hone Heke Lodge	D
Kemp Lodge	C
Keriken Farm Hostel	I
Stoneybroke	J
YHA	A

RESTAURANTS & CAFÉS
The Black Olive	4
Blue Café	3
Cafe Gecko	1
Café di Vino	2
Cathay Restaurant	6
Fishbone Café	5
Marsden Estate Winery Restaurant	8
Rocket Café	7

Waitangi (25km) ▽ Paihia (25 km), **H** (4km), **I** (5km), **7** (2km) & **8** (5km) ▽ **J** (1 km)

Kerikeri is fairly well endowed with **accommodation** in all categories, but is particularly strong in budget places – a consequence of the area's popularity with long-stay casual workers. Seasonal **price fluctuations** are nowhere near as marked as in Paihia, though it is still difficult to find a place in January, when places are correspondingly expensive; prices quoted here are outside this post-Christmas madness.

MOTELS AND B&BS

Abilene Motel, 136 Kerikeri Rd (☎09/407 9203, fax 407 8608, *abilene@kerikeri.net.nz*). Standard, centrally located motel in a garden setting with pool and spa. ⑤.

Central Motel, 58 Kerikeri Rd (☎09/407 8921 & 0800/867 667, fax 407 8005, *ewrigley@voyager.co.nz*). Aptly named motel, with some newish and some older rooms around a pleasant pool and spa. ⑤.

Kemp Lodge, 134 Kerikeri Rd (☎ & fax 09/407 8295). Three pleasant and modern self-contained cottages close to town, and complete with TV and video, solar-heated pool and spa. ⑤.

Stoneybroke, Edmonds Rd, 1km east of town beside Kerikeri Inlet (☎09/407 7371). Pleasant homestay with a double and a twin (sharing a bathroom), and interesting hosts. ④.

HOSTELS AND CAMPSITES

Aranga Holiday Park, Kerikeri Rd (☎09/407 9326, fax 407 9897). Large streamside site on the edge of town with a spacious area for tents, well-equipped standard cabins, self-catering tourist flats and single rooms for long-stayers at a bargain $80 a week. Friday nights feature a major barbecue, served with bread and salads. Tent sites $10, dorms ①, cabins ②, flats ④.

Gibby's Place, Kerikeri Rd (☎09/407 9024, fax 407 9624, *gibbysplace@xtra.co.nz*). Cosy, quiet camp-site in a big tree-filled garden with a pool – a far cry from the usual holiday park. Tent and powered sites $8, cabins ③, en-suite doubles & en-suite family room ④.

Hideaway Lodge, Wiroa Rd, 4km west of Kerikeri (☎ & fax 09/407 9773). Large, slightly run-down but well-appointed hostel, with bikes to get into town. Reduced weekly rates are popular with folk stopping to work around Kerikeri, who also appreciate the large pool and games room after a hard day in the orange groves. Tent sites $8, dorms ①, rooms ②.

Hone Heke Lodge, 65 Hone Heke Rd (☎ & fax 09/407 8170). Central hostel with six-bed dorms, each with a fridge and cooking gear, and doubles and twins, some en suite. There's also a games room and barbecue area. Tent sites $10, dorms ①, rooms ②.

Kerikeri Farm Hostel, SH10, 5km west (☎09/407 6989). Top-class hostel on an organic citrus orchard, with comfortable dorms and rooms in a lovely wooden house. Rates are high for Kerikeri but well worth it; dinner ($10–15) and breakfast also available. Dorms ①, rooms ②

Kerikeri YHA, Main Rd (☎09/407 9391, fax 407 9328). Well-placed hostel close to the centre but showing its age. Dorms ①, rooms ②.

The Town

The only way to get a sense of Kerikeri's past importance is to make straight for **Kerikeri Basin**, nearly 2km east of the current town. It was here, in 1821, that mission carpenters started work on what is now New Zealand's oldest European-style building, **Kemp House** (daily 9.30am–5.30pm; $5, combined entry to the downstairs part of the Old Stone Store, see below), a restrained two-storey Georgian colonial affair which has miraculously survived fire and periodic flooding. The first occupants, missionary John Butler and family, soon moved on and by 1832 the house was in the hands of lay missionary and blacksmith James Kemp, who extended the three-up-three-down design.

Next door is the only other extant building from the mission station, the **Old Stone Store** (same times as Kemp House; $2 to view upstairs), which is ranked as the country's oldest stone building, constructed mostly of local stone with keystones and quoins of Sydney sandstone. Completed in 1835 as a central provision store for the Church Missionary Society, it successively served as a munitions store for troops garrisoned here to fight Hone Heke, then a kauri trading store and a shop, before being opened to the public in 1975. Flooding and the predations of heavy passing traffic have taken their toll, forcing a major restoration project which has recently been completed.

Opposite the Old Stone Store, a five-minute path along the river leads to the well-delineated site of local chief Hongi Hika's **Kororipo Pa**, passing the site where, in the 1820s, he had a European-style house built. The pa commands a hill on a prominent bend in the river, a relatively secure base from which to launch inter-tribal attacks using their newly acquired firearms. Signs help interpret the dips and humps in the ground, but you'll get a better appreciation of pre-European Maori life from **Rewa's Village**, 1 Landing Rd (daily 10am–4pm or later, honesty box entry after hours; $2.50), a 1969 reconstruction of a fishing village across the river from the pa site. It comes complete with marae, weapons and *kumara* stores, and authentic hangi site with an adjacent shell midden; the entrance kiosk screens a short video on the history of the area. Opposite is the **Kerikeri Basin Reserve** and the start of a track (1hr each way) past the swimming holes at Fairy Pools to the impressively undercut **Rainbow Falls**, which are also accessible off Waipapa Road, 3km north of the Basin.

Elsewhere Kerikeri is dominated by orchards, and the roads running between them (especially SH10 and Kerikeri Road) come studded with **craft outlets**. The free and widely available *Kerikeri Art & Craft Trail* leaflet advertises the major ones; you can easily spend a day trawling round them all. A few highly regarded establishments include The Enz of the Earth, right in town at 127 Kerikeri Rd (☎09/407 8367; daily), which combines Indian and Indonesian handicrafts with an exotic garden of wind chimes, water and tropical plants, making an appealing place to sit and relax; The Kauri Workshop, Kerikeri Rd, closer to SH10 (☎09/407 9196; daily), stocks just about everything you could conceivably make out of kauri; nearby Makana Confections (☎09/407 6800; daily 9am–5.30pm) produce tantalizing chocolates; Blue Gum Pottery (Mon–Fri 10am–5pm, Sat 10am–3pm; ☎09/407 9008), northwest of town on SH10, lets you watch the making of their mostly pastel-shaded **pots** at their shop a few metres from the co-operatively run Origin (☎09/407 9065; daily 10am–5pm). The last is probably the best of the lot, with a wide selection of **knitwear**, handmade **paper**, pottery and some fine wooden furniture.

Eating and entertainment

Kerikeri's decent eating options have increased in recent years and include one of the finest **restaurants** north of Auckland. **Entertainment** is thinner on the ground but there is always the sixty-year-old and lovingly restored Cathay Cinema, on Hobson Avenue (☎09/407 4428), which shows first-run movies and has a good café attached.

The Black Olive, Kerikeri Rd. Compact eat-in and take-out pasta restaurant open from 5pm daily, which also bakes good traditional and gourmet pizza. BYO.

Blue Café, The Village Mall. Small, laid-back café tucked away in an arcade that's fine for a daytime coffee or a range of meals, including some Malaysian-inspired rice and noodle dishes.

Café Di Vino, Kerikeri Rd (☎09/407 6606). One of Northland's best restaurants, on the outskirts of Kerikeri with an attractive veranda setting by a tranquil garden. Tuck into gorgeous European and Indonesian influenced dishes for café-style lunch and dinner, but expect to pay $40 for three courses. Closed Tues. Licensed.

Cathay Restaurant, Hobson Ave, next door to the cinema. Attractive café furbished in wood, open daily for all-day breakfasts, snacks, light meals, vegetarian food, and tasty cakes and coffee. Licensed. Oct–April open till late in the evening; rest of the year until 3pm.

Fishbone Café, 88 Kerikeri Rd (☎09/407 6065). Bright eating spot popular for its high-quality fusion food all day every day in summer, more limited hours in winter. There's outdoor eating and booking is essential for dinner. Winter: Mon–Wed until 4pm, Thurs–Sat till late in the evening. Licensed.

Café Gecko, 132 Kerikeri Rd. Reasonably priced dinners of wood-fired gourmet pizzas, fish and pasta at this small, vibrant and stylish café, open daily from 6pm in summer, with open-air decking at the back. Closed Sun & Mon in winter. Licensed.

Marsden Estate Winery & Restaurant, Wiroa Rd (towards airport; ☎09/407 9398). Relaxed outdoor and indoor dining amid the vines beside a lake, at moderate prices and with plenty of choice on the menu. Daily 10am–5pm.

Rocket Café, Kerikeri Rd, 3km west of town. Excellent modern breakfast and lunch café on the site of *Robbs Fruit Winery*, an orchard specializing in feijoa, kiwifruit and boysenberry wines and preserves. A fine range of quiches, pizzas and filo rolls stuffed with imaginative fillings, plus great coffee are served outside or in the airy interior. Open daily.

Around Kerikeri

A natural progression 15km southwest from Kerikeri's Kemp House is **WAIMATE NORTH** and **Te Waimate Mission House**, set in lush gardens (☎09/405 9734;

grounds open daily during daylight hours, free; building open Nov–April Sat–Mon 10am–12.30pm & 1.30–4.30pm or by arrangement; rest of the year by arrangement; $5), New Zealand's second-oldest European building. Now pretty much in the middle of nowhere, in the 1830s this was the centre of a vigorous Anglican mission, the first to be established on an inland site chosen for its fertile soils and large Maori population. At the time, missionaries were keen to add European **agricultural techniques** to the language and religion they were teaching the Maori, and they made use of the grounds already cultivated by the missionaries' friend and Ngapuhi chief, Hongi Hika. By 1834 locally grown wheat was being milled at the river, orchards were flourishing and crops were sprouting – all duly impressing Charles Darwin, who visited the following year. Ultimately though, transport difficulties made this first European-style farm uneconomic and the mission declined. The **house** itself was built by converts in 1831–32 and almost entirely fashioned of local kauri. Though much modified over the years, it has been restored as accurately as possible to its original design and the somewhat lifeless rooms have been stocked with furniture and effects, giving some insight into the early mission lifestyle. The modest mission **Church of St John the Baptist** just nearby is also open daily during daylight hours (free).

The nearest substantial town is **KAIKOHE**, almost equidistant from both coasts and seemingly displaced in Northland, where so much is water-focused. There's little reason to stop, but the staff at the unofficial **visitor centre**, *Curly Rock Café*, 112 Broadway (Dec–April daily 7.30am till late evening; May–Nov daily 7.30am–7pm; ☎09/401 1911), will give directions to **Ngawha Springs** (daily 7am–9.45pm; $2), 7km to the east, where naturally heated waters fill Waiariki Pools, a series of eight tanks surrounded by wooden boardwalks but otherwise unfettered by tourist trappings.

The stands of the **Puketi and Omahuta native forests**, 20km north of Kaikohe, jointly comprise one of the largest continuous tracts of kauri forest in the north. The easiest and most rewarding access is to the east of the forest: head north off SH1 at Okaihau, or west off SH10 just north of Kerikeri along Pungaere Road. Both routes bring you to the **Puketi Recreation Area**, where there's a campsite and a trampers' hut at the start of the 20-kilometre **Waipapa River Track** – best done in one short (5hr) and one long (8hr) day, camping midway. This and several other worthwhile tracks are detailed in the DOC's *Puketi and Omahuta Forests* leaflet (50¢) which, along with camping and hut details, can be obtained from the DOC office in Kerikeri.

North to Doubtless Bay

North of the Bay of Islands everything gets a lot quieter. There are few towns of any consequence along the coast and it is the peace and slow pace that attract visitors to an array of glorious beaches and the lovely Whangaroa Harbour. The first stop north of Kerikeri is tiny **Matauri Bay**, where a hilltop memorial commemorates the Greenpeace flagship, *Rainbow Warrior*, which was sunk in Auckland Harbour in 1985. The wreck now lies off the coast of Motutapere Island, a site which can be dived from here. A mostly unsealed backroad continues north by way of fabulous sea views from headlands and gorgeous beaches – **Te Ngaire**, **Wainui Bay**, **Mahinepua Bay** and **Tauranga Bay** – before delivering you to the **Whangaroa Harbour**, one of the most beautiful in Northland and an excellent place to go sailing or kayaking.

Further north is the huge bite out of the coast called **Doubtless Bay**, which had two celebrated discoverers: Kupe, said to have first set foot on *Aotearoa* in Taipa; and Cook, who sailed past in 1769 and pronounced it "doubtless, a bay". French explorer, Jean François Marie de Surville, was also close by and, a week later, became the first European to enter the bay, though he departed in an undignified hurry after a dispute with local Maori over a missing dinghy – and it was Cook's moniker that stuck.

FRENCH NUCLEAR TESTING IN THE PACIFIC

The French government has always claimed that nuclear testing is completely safe, but for decades has persisted in conducting its tests on the tiny Pacific atolls of **Mururoa** and Fangataufa, 15,000km from Paris and 4000km northeast of New Zealand. In 1966 France turned its back on the 1963 **Partial Test Ban Treaty**, which outlawed **atmospheric testing**, and relocated Pacific islanders away from their ancestral villages to make way for a barrage of tests over the next eight years. The French authorities claimed that "Not a single particle of radioactive fallout will ever reach an inhabited island" – and yet radiation was routinely detected as far away as Samoa, Fiji and even New Zealand. Increasingly antagonistic public opinion forced the French to conduct their tests **underground** in deep shafts, where another 200 detonations took place, threatening the geological stability of these fragile coral atolls. Surveys with very limited access to the test sites have since revealed severe **fissuring**; there is also evidence of radioactive isotopes in the Mururoa lagoon, as well as submarine slides and subsidence.

In 1985, **Greenpeace** coordinated a New Zealand-based protest flotilla, headed by its flagship, *Rainbow Warrior*, but before the fleet could set sail from Auckland, the French secret service sabotaged the *Rainbow Warrior*, detonating two bombs below the waterline. As rescuers recovered the body of Greenpeace photographer Fernando Pereira, two **French secret service** agents posing as tourists were arrested. Flatly denying all knowledge at first, the French government was finally forced to admit to what David Lange (then Prime Minister of New Zealand) described as "a sordid act of international state-backed terrorism". The two captured agents were sentenced to ten years in jail, but France used all its international muscle to have them serve their sentences on a French Pacific island; they both served less than two years.

In 1995, to worldwide opprobrium, France announced a further series of tests. Greenpeace duly dispatched *Rainbow Warrior II*, which was impounded by the French navy on the tenth **anniversary** of the sinking of the original *Rainbow Warrior*. In early 1996 the French finally agreed to stop nuclear testing in the Pacific and it is only now that **relations** between the French and New Zealand governments are becoming more amicable. In April 1997, the two **foreign ministers** met for the first time since the bombing of the *Rainbow Warrior*.

Bounded on the west and north by the sheltering **Karikari Peninsula**, the bay offers safe boating, a boon for **Kiwi vacationers** who enjoy the abundant fish and dolphins. In January you can barely move up here and you'll struggle to find accommodation, but the shoulder seasons can be surprisingly quiet and outside December, January and February the relatively high room prices drop to more affordable levels. Most of the bay's facilities cluster along the southern shore in a string of beachside settlements – **Coopers Beach**, **Cable Bay** and **Taipa Bay** – running west from picturesque Mangonui.

Matauri Bay

The high ridge behind **MATAURI BAY**, 20km north of Kerikeri and 10km off SH10, provides the dramatic first glimpse of a long curving sandy bay that stretches north to a stand of Norfolk pines and the offshore Cavalli Islands. The northern limit of the main bay is defined by Matauri Bay Hill, topped by a distinctive stone and steel memorial to the *Rainbow Warrior* (see box above), now scuttled off Motutapere Island, one of the Cavalli Islands.

Missionary Samuel Marsden first set foot in *Aotearoa* in 1814 at Matauri Bay, where he mediated between the Ngati Kura people – who still own the bay – and some Bay of Islands Maori, a process commemorated by the quaint wooden **Samuel Marsden**

Memorial Church on the road in, and a small memorial behind the beach. The strength of Maori culture in the bay is evident from the finely carved *Mataatua II waka* further north along the beach: constructed in the early 1990s, its name echoes the Ngati Kura's ancestral *waka*, which lies in waters nearby. The resonance of this legendary canoe partly led the Ngati Kura to offer a final resting place to the wreck of the *Rainbow Warrior*.

Sculptor Chris Booth was commissioned to design the **Rainbow Warrior Memorial**, composed of a stone arch symbolizing a rainbow and the salvaged bronze propeller of the vessel. It is reached by a well-worn path from near the holiday park at the foot of the hill. Two-tank **dive trips** out to the wreck, ten minutes by boat, can be organized through Matauri Cat Charters (☎09/405 0525), at the holiday park, who charge $145 for two dives with full gear rental; $95 if you have your own gear (they also offer a one-dive option at $90/$70 respectively). The best visibility is typically in April; from September to November plankton sometimes obscure the view.

Facilities in the bay are limited to a **shop** opposite the family-orientated *Matauri Bay Holiday Park* (☎ & fax 09/405 0525; tent sites $10, powered sites $3 extra; on-site vans ③), and, around the corner, *Ocean's Holiday Village* (☎ & fax 09/405 0417; house for 2 & units ⑦), a self-contained **resort** with spacious units, houses of up to four bedrooms, a licensed restaurant (open daily in summer, weekends only in winter), and dinghies and kayaks for guests' use. The resort is a popular family holiday spot in summer.

The pretty 24-kilometre **coastal route** from Matauri Bay to Whangaroa Harbour is mainly unsealed and occasionally used by logging trucks, which can be unnerving as you wind your way over the hills and through a series of bays.

The Whangaroa Harbour

Time spent around the virtually landlocked and sheltered **Whangaroa Harbour** is the perfect antidote to Bay of Islands commercialism. The scenery, albeit on a smaller scale, is easily a match for its southern cousin and, despite the limited facilities, you can still get out onto the water for a cruise or to join the big-game fishers. Narrow inlets forge between cliffs and steep hills, most notably two bald volcanic plugs, St Paul and St Peter, rising up behind the harbour's two settlements, **WHANGAROA** and **TOTARA NORTH**.

The harbour wasn't always so quiet though, being among the first areas to receive the attention of pioneers, most famously those on the *Boyd*, a ship which called here in 1809 to load kauri spars for shipping to Britain. A couple of days after its arrival, all 66 crew were killed and the ship burned by local Maori in retribution for the crew's mistreatment of Tara, a high-born Maori sailor who had apparently transgressed the ship's rules. A British whaler avenged the incident by burning the entire Maori village, thereby sparking off a series of skirmishes that spread over the north for five years, substantially reducing the enthusiasm of sea captains for the Whangaroa Harbour. Nonetheless, the vast stands of kauri were soon being hacked away and the harbour was said by contemporary observers to be choked with logs; some were rafted to Auckland, while others were milled at Totara North, which claims the oldest operational mill in the country.

The single best thing to do around Whangaroa is to spend a day on the *Snow Cloud* (☎09/405 0523, fax 405 0604, *snowcloud@xtra.co.nz*; 10–11hr; $65, including meals), an eleven-metre **yacht** which typically sails out to the Cavalli Islands, stopping to snorkel, sunbathe and walk. The next best bet is to **kayak** with the knowledgeable and environmentally sensitive Northland Sea Kayaking on the northeastern flank of the harbour (☎09/405 0381, *northlandseakayaking@xtra.co.nz*); day-trips start at $60, and include free self-catering accommodation for the number of days you spend paddling; camping trips are also available, as is pick-up and drop-off at Kaeo, the nearest town

($15). **Dive** trips to the *Rainbow Warrior* run from the Whangaroa Harbour Retreat Motor Camp (see below; $135 including full gear hire; $70 with your own gear), who give you two dives. Land-based activities primarily mean **walks**, two of the most rewarding being the short hike up St Paul from the top of Old Hospital Road in Whangaroa and the DOC's **Lane Cove Walk** (1hr 30min–2hr each way) from Totara North past freshwater pools, mangroves and viewpoints to the Lane Cove Cottage (①) on the Pekapeka Bay. The hut sleeps sixteen, but only opens up for a minimum of four people. It has a solar-heated shower, water, toilets and plenty of sandflies, but you'll need your own cooking gear. Book well in advance in summer.

Practicalities

No public **transport** reaches either the small community of Whangaroa, 6km off SH10 on the southern side of the harbour, or the tiny Totara North, 4km off the highway on the northern side.

Most of the harbour's limited **accommodation** clusters along the road to Whangaroa, first up being the tree-shaded *Whangaroa Harbour Retreat Motor Camp* (☎09/405 0306; tent sites $10, cabins ②–④), 3km south of the centre and with its own small grocery and takeaway food shop. Pricier is *Truant Lodge Motel* (☎09/405 0133; ⑤); and there are basic rooms with shared bathrooms at Whangaroa's longstanding **pub**, the *Marlin Hotel* (☎09/405 0347; ③), right opposite the wharf. For something different, there's the luxurious *Kingfish Lodge* (☎09/405 0164, *fish@kingfishlodge.co.nz*; ⑨), out towards the harbour heads and only accessible by boat or by air. The three **hostels** close to the harbour are all excellent in their own way. In Whangaroa, the *Sunseeker Lodge*, Old Hospital Road (☎ & fax 09/405 0496; dorms ①, rooms ③, motel units ⑤), perched on the hill overlooking the harbour, benefits from a personable host and relaxed atmosphere; sea kayaks are available for guests' use for a small fee. There's also a badminton court, and boat trips into the harbour are available for the price of the fuel. The extremely welcoming *Kahoe Farms Hostel* (☎09/405 1804, *mjoh@igrin.co.nz*; tent sites $10, dorms ①, rooms ③) is on SH10 and just over 1.5km north of the Totara North turn-off. This is a beautifully restored homestead tucked into a corner of a working cattle farm, where people come to kickback for days, fuelled by Stefano's fine pizza, bread and espresso. Guests are entertained by bushwalks, kayaking through the mangroves ($30 a day), horse riding ($15 an hour) and bike riding (free), to say nothing of free transport to a whacky little cinema called The Swamp Palace (see opposite), at Oruru near Taipa.

Small **shops** in Whangaroa and Totara North provide for self-caterers, and the *Marlin Hotel* and the *Whangaroa Big Gamefish Club* (opposite each other in Whangaroa) serve reliable, if unexceptional, **seafood** dishes.

Mangonui and around

There's an undeniably antiquated air to **MANGONUI**, an attractive and increasingly visited village strung along a sheltered half-kilometre of harbour off Doubtless Bay. A handful of two-storey buildings with wooden, street-level verandas have been preserved and a few trinket shops nestle between a clutch of cafés, but this is still very much a working village, with a lively fishing wharf and a traditional grocery perched on stilts over the water. It makes the most obvious stopping point on the way north, with excellent beaches nearby and a waterfront where you can successfully catch your supper over an afternoon beer and have it cooked up at one of the local restaurants.

Mangonui means "big shark", a name recalling an incident when the legendary chief Moehuri's *waka* was led into the harbour by such a fish. But it was whales and the business of restocking **whaling** ships with food that made the town: one apocryphal story tells of a harbour so packed with ships that folk could cross from one side to the other by leaping between boats. As whaling diminished, the kauri trade took its place, chiefly around Mill Bay, the cove five minutes' walk to the west. While ships were being repaired and restocked at Mangonui, barrels were being fixed a couple of kilometres west beside a stream crossing the strand that became known as **COOPER'S BEACH**. This glorious and well-shaded sweep is now backed by a string of motels and blighted by a rash of big new houses and construction sites, as the land is progressively bought up by developers and sold off in expensive chunks. The beach is popular in January and at weekends, but at other times you might still find you have it pretty much to yourself.

Another couple of kilometres west, the smaller settlement of **CABLE BAY** owes its existence to its short-lived role as the terminus of the 1902 trans-Pacific cable; in 1912, the telegraph station was moved to Auckland. The Taipa River separates Cable Bay from the beachside village of **TAIPA**, now the haunt of sunbathers and swimmers but historically significant as the spot where Kupe, the discoverer of *Aotearoa* in Maori legend, first set foot on the land.

Diversions in the district include **visiting the Rangikapiti Pa Historic Reserve**, off Rangikapiti Rd (unrestricted entry), chiefly noted for its fabulous bay views; **dolphin encounters** with Doubtless Bay Adventures (book through the visitor centre at Mangonui; $75); and **diving** off the Karikari Peninsula and elsewhere with Seabed Safaris (☎09/408 5885). Resort dives from the shore go for $145 for one dive (including full gear hire), and $100 for each subsequent dive; or, if you have your own gear $75 for the first dive and $45 for the second. Boat dives start at $95 (including full gear hire). For $135 (including full gear) you can dive the *Rainbow Warrior* wreck. In Mangonui you can check out a selection of handmade **woven flax** items for sale at Flax Bush, The Waterfront (Oct–April daily 10am–5pm; May–Sept Wed–Sun 10am–5pm), a small craft shop whose reasonably priced goods are all made by weavers of the far north. If you're hankering after a *kete*, for example, it's worth a look: Northland prices are the best you'll find in the country. Art of a different kind is to be found at Arterior, 11 Melody Lane (☎09/406 0455; most days 9am–5pm), a studio where Annie Tothill makes and sells vibrant wall-hangings, throws, clothes and so on from natural fabrics, including silk. Seven kilometres inland from Taipa, at Oruru Community Hall, is a quirky classic **cinema**, The Swamp Palace (☎09/408 7040 for screening info; $8, backpackers $6), catering to an eclectic mix of tastes, each film introduced with a short talk by the proprietor.

From Mangonui you can join an organized trip to Cape Reinga and Ninety Mile Beach (see box on p.190–91).

Practicalities

SH10 bypasses the Mangonui waterfront, which is reached on a 2km loop road plied once a day by southbound and northbound Northliner and InterCity services. **Buses** stop outside the Wilton's Garage, Waterfront Road (☎09/406 0024), where you can also buy tickets. The **visitor centre** (daily: Dec–May 8.30am–6pm; June–Nov 9am–5pm; ☎09/406 1190, fax 406 1197, *mangonui.info@xtra.co.nz*), a few metres before the garage, can point you to accommodation, both here and in Cooper's Beach.

ACCOMMODATION

Most prominent of Mangonui's places is the turn-of-the-century *Mangonui Hotel*, Waterfront Rd (☎09/406 0003, fax 406 0015; ⑤), right opposite the harbour and with an excellent upstairs veranda for whiling the day away. Rooms are fairly plain and the best ones with harbour views go quickly, so book ahead or arrive early. Further around the shore, the even more ancient *Old Oak Inn*, Waterfront Rd (☎ & fax 09/406 0665; dorms ①, backpacker rooms ③, hotel rooms ④), has a backpacker section with dorms and doubles, while the hotel rooms upstairs are small but characterful. Best of the **B&Bs**

are *The Abraham Lincoln*, Hihi Rd (☎09/406 0090; ④), near the water's edge about 7km from Mangonui and across the bay, accessed from SH10 (south) and the Hihi Road turn-off, which also operates as a farmstay, and *Mac 'n' Mo's*, on SH10 and north of the turnoff to Mangonui (☎ & fax 09/406 0538; ④), a little further out in Cooper's Beach.

Motels are scattered liberally among the communities. Mangonui has the *Acacia Lodge*, Mill Bay Road (☎ & fax 09/406 0417, *graemedunn@acacia.co.nz*; ⑤–⑥), with the more expensive rooms featuring balconies and spa baths; while Cooper's Beach has the luxurious *Beach Lodge*, on SH10 (☎ & fax 09/406 0068; ⑧), right by the water and with all mod cons, and the more modest *San Marino*, on San Marino Drive, off Kupe Road and also right on the beach (☎09/406 0345, fax 406 0202; ⑤–⑥). There are no **hostels** in the area.

EATING, DRINKING AND ENTERTAINMENT
Mangonui has the best range of places to eat north of Kerikeri. Besides the *Old Oak Inn*, which has a bar and a licensed and BYO **restaurant** serving tasty light lunches and evening dinners, there's good mid-priced eating at the Mangonui Hotel's *CJ's Bar & Brasserie*; fine sandwiches, soups and pizzas at reasonable prices from *Dolphin Café* on Waterfront Road; and the best meals for miles around at *The Slung Anchor Kitchen & Bar*, Beach Road (☎09/406 1233; daily 24hr), a café and restaurant which produces imaginative seafood concoctions. Mangonui boasts the finest **fish and chips** in the north – some would say in the country – at the wharfside *Mangonui Fish Shop*, also on Beach Road, where you sit on decking that overhangs the water, beside an expensive bar. Many customers bring their own sauces and relishes to the table, since the shop charges extra for these. The **bar** at the *Mangonui Hotel* (Oct–April till 10pm; rest of the year till 9pm) is the focus of the town's more rumbustious social life and occasionally hosts bands.

The Karikari Peninsula

Doubtless Bay to the east and Rangaunu Harbour to the west are both bounded by the crooked arm of the **Karikari Peninsula** as it strikes north, its flat forearm and lumpy fist swathed in unspoiled golden- and white-sand beaches which, at least outside the peak season, have barely a soul on them. There is no public transport, facilities are limited and, without diving or fishing gear, you'll have to resign yourself to lazing on the beaches and swimming from them – and there can be few better places to do just that.

The initial approach across a low and scrubby isthmus is less than inspiring, though it is worth stopping briefly at **Lake Ohia**, 1km off SH10, which has gradually drained to reveal the stumps of a 40,000-year-old kauri forest thought to have been destroyed by some prehistoric cataclysm. A kilometre on, the **Gum Hole Reserve** has a short trail past holes left by kauri gum diggers (see box on p.198 for more on their exploits). Eight kilometres later, a side road leads to the peninsula's west coast and the **Puheke Scenic Reserve**, a gorgeous dune-backed beach that's desolate outside the season but popular in January. There's another fine strand nearby at the beachside hamlet of **RANGIPUTA**, with the *White Sands Motor Lodge* (☎09/408 7080; ⑤–⑦) and, 1km back down the road, the attractive, spa-equipped *Reef Lodge*, Rangiputa Road (☎ & fax 09/408 7100, *ReefLodge@clear.net.nz*; ⑥), set among lawns and backed by a golden beach.

The peninsula's arterial road continues past the Rangiputa junction to the community of **TOKERAU BEACH**, a cluster of houses and a couple of shops at the northern end of the grand sweep of Doubtless Bay, but there is no accommodation here.

The Karikari Peninsula saves its best until last: **Maitai Bay**, 20km north off SH10, is a matchless double arc of golden sand split by a rocky knoll, all encompassed by the *Maitai Bay Campground* ($6 per adult), the largest DOC campsite in Northland. Much of the site is *tapu* to local Maori, and you are encouraged to respect the sacred areas, which is easy enough for most of the year when the site is deserted, but more problematic when the site is splitting its seams in early January.

Kaitaia and around

KAITAIA, 40km west of Mangonui, is a dilapidated town of little charm and less excitement – evidence of its unemployment rate, which is among the highest in the country – yet it plays an important role as the Far North's largest commercial centre. As the starting point for some of the best bus trips to Cape Reinga and Ninety Mile Beach (see p.188), Kaitaia is on most visitors' itineraries and makes a possible base for ventures north, though with your own transport you might want to whizz round the sights, refuel and push on. If you're planning on using Kaitaia as a springboard to the far north, it's wise to check the **road conditions** beyond Awanui (8km north of Kaitaia) with the DOC (☎09/408 6014) before you set off, as they tend to vary.

Kaitaia donned its service-town mantle once the extractive industries petered out. A Maori village already flourished here when the first European missionary, Joseph Matthews, came looking for a **mission** site in 1832. The protection of the mission encouraged pastoralists who, by the 1880s, found themselves swamped by **gum diggers** keen to plunder the underground deposits around Lake Ohia (see opposite) and **Ahipara** (15km west of Kaitaia; see p.187). Many early arrivals were young Dalmatians (mostly Croats) fleeing tough conditions in what was then part of the Austro-Hungarian Empire. The only evidence of this episode in Kaitaia's history is a telephone directory full of Croat names, a Serbo-Croat welcome sign at the entrance to town, and a cultural society which holds a traditional dance each year.

The Town

The best place to gain a sense of the area is the surprisingly good **Far North Regional Museum**, 6 South Rd (Mon–Fri 10am–5pm; $2.50), with arresting displays on pretty much every aspect of local life and history. The room of Ngati Kahu pieces is particularly strong; you enter under one of three copies of the twelfth- or thirteenth-century **Kaitaia Carving**. The carving was found around 1920 on the outskirts of Kaitaia and represents the transitional period as Polynesian art was taking on distinctly Maori elements; the original is held in the Auckland Museum (see p.89). Another rare find is a series of boards from palisades once surrounding pa sites: these were mostly burned or rotted away, but several examples survive here. Elsewhere in the room, beautifully woven and decorative flax-and-kiwi-feather cloaks contrast with utilitarian items – a carved canoe bailer, collections of clubs, spears and oratory staffs – and a complete skeleton of a juvenile kuri, the Polynesian dog brought to New Zealand by early Maori settlers that died out around a century ago. Pride of place in the main room goes to a huge one-and-a-half-tonne anchor, the earliest European artefact to be left in New Zealand and one of three left by de Surville in 1769 when he departed in haste (see p.846). The maritime theme continues through a collection of ships in glass cases, including a fine whaler made of matchsticks, and sundry bits and pieces from the *Rainbow Warrior*. Photographs of early gum-digging operations are supported by examples of the diggers' tools and polished pieces of prize gum in shades from pale amber to deep treacle.

Dalmatians steeped in viniculture grew the first grapes in the region, though the vineyards were soon abandoned and experts have long claimed that the climate is too moist for successful wine making. Nonetheless, New Zealand's northernmost winery, **Okahu Estate**, on the corner of Okahiu Road and Pukepoto Road (☎09/408 2066; daily 10am–6pm), 3km out on the road to Ahipara, has managed to produce small quantities of award-winning boutique wines – and offers free tastings.

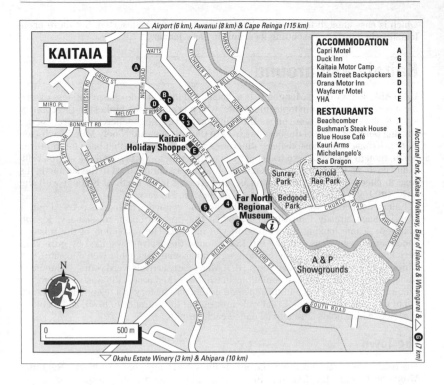

△ Airport (6 km), Awanui (8 km) & Cape Reinga (115 km)

KAITAIA

ACCOMMODATION
Capri Motel	A
Duck Inn	G
Kaitaia Motor Camp	F
Main Street Backpackers	B
Orana Motor Inn	D
Wayfarer Motel	C
YHA	E

RESTAURANTS
Beachcomber	1
Bushman's Steak House	5
Blue House Café	6
Kauri Arms	2
Michelangelo's	4
Sea Dragon	3

Nocturnal Park, Kaitaia Walkway, Bay of Islands & Whangarei & △ G (7 km)

▽ Okahu Estate Winery (3 km) & Ahipara (10 km)

As elsewhere throughout the north, Maori people make up a large proportion of the population and influence the local culture, though on a short visit this may not be particularly evident. One way around this is to join the excellent Tall Tale Travel 'n' Tours, 237a Commerce St, behind KFC (☎09/408 0870, fax 408 1100, *tall-tale-tours@xtra.co.nz*; roughly 2hr; $25, including $5 donation to the local marae) on a genuine **Maori-led visit** to the working Te Rarawa **marae**, just outside Kaitaia. Times and itineraries are flexible and the emphasis is on fostering an understanding of Maori culture, in particular marae protocol, land issues and spiritual concepts of life, death and healing. Their **Cape Reinga** tour (full day; $40) comes to life through the telling of myths and legends, and interaction with the environment via sand tobogganing and gathering shellfish on the shore. Back in Kaitaia, you can join **craft workshops** to make something from flax or bone (or join in with any of a dozen other activities), run by Peter Kitchen, the energetic and humorous owner of Tall Tale Travel 'n' Tours, who is a walking encyclopedia of all things Maori. His workshop (same contact details as above; 2hr for $10) is next door to *Main Street Backpackers* (see opposite); you can also check out the high-quality handmade bodycare and herbal remedies produced by Peter from natural New Zealand ingredients, based on Maori knowledge of native plants.

Practicalities

Once-daily InterCity and Northliner **buses** pull up outside the Kaitaia Holiday Shoppe, 170 Commerce St (☎09/408 0540), which handles ticket sales. Kaitaia has one of only three tarmacked runways in Northland, 6km north near Awanui, so you can arrive **by**

air direct from Auckland and the Bay of Islands with Air New Zealand Link Services (1 flight daily Mon–Fri & Sun), who also operate from Kerikeri (4 flights daily Mon–Fri, 3 flights daily Sat & Sun).

Kaitaia's **visitor centre** is at Jaycee Park, South Road (Oct–March daily 8.30am–5pm; April–Sept Mon–Fri 8.30am–5pm, Sat & Sun 9am–1pm; ☎ & fax 09/408 0879, *fndckta@xtra.co.nz*). Car rental is available from the Holiday Shoppe (Mon–Fri only), but is prohibitively expensive and, since **rental cars** can't be driven along Ninety Mile Beach, you're better off taking a **bus tour** to Cape Reinga (see p.188), or hiring a 4WD from the visitor centre ($99 per day plus fuel). **Internet access** is available daily at reasonable rates at *Hackers Internet Café*, 84 Commerce St (☎09/408 4999, *DaleCurrie@Hackers.co.nz*; Mon–Sat 9am till late; Sun 11am–5pm).

Accommodation

Even in the peak season it is seldom difficult to obtain accommodation in Kaitaia at prices considerably lower than at the coastal resorts to the east. Of the **motels**, try the basic but perfectly adequate *Capri Motel*, 5 North Rd (☎09/408 0224, fax 408 0086, *CapriMotel@xtra.co.nz*; ④) and the smarter *Wayfarer Motel*, 231 Commerce St (☎09/408 2600, fax 408 2601; ④–⑤), with spa and swimming pool. The *Orana Motor Inn*, 238–242 Commerce St (☎09/408 1510, fax 408 1512; ⑤), is more like a hotel, with a pool, restaurant and separate bar, but no cooking facilities; and there are a few home-stays, such as *Duck Inn*, Fryer Rd (☎09/408 0966; ③), 7km south of central Kaitaia, which operates as a B&B and farmstay.

The **budget** market is catered for by an antiquated *YHA*, 160 Commerce St (☎09/408 1840; dorms ①, rooms ②), and the *Main Street Backpackers*, 235 Commerce St (☎09/408 1275, fax 408 1100, *mainstreet@xtra.co.nz*; tent sites $10, dorms ①, rooms ②), which actively promotes itself as New Zealand's first Maori backpackers; along with a hangi once a week Oct–April and the opportunity to hand-carve bone pendants or wood, or weave flax next door at the workshop (see Tall Tale Tours opposite). *Main Street* also rent out bikes ($10 a day), provide free sand-toboggans and rent camping gear for use at Cape Reinga, and pass on local knowledge about the danger spots and tides of Ninety Mile Beach. **Campers** should head for *Kaitaia Motor Camp*, 67 South Rd (☎09/408 1212; tent sites $5; powered sites $8.50), which is mainly a campervan park.

Eating and drinking

Kaitaia's eating options are severely limited but slowly improving. For daytime **burgers**, sandwiches, **pizza** and decent coffee, make for *Michelangelo's*, 26 Commerce St, a diner where you can eat in or take away. More substantial **meals** are better at the all-day *Blue House Café*, 14 Commerce St (daily from 7am, with shorter hours in winter), which dish-es up enormous portions of simple hearty Kiwi food at great prices; the bar up one end makes this the best place for a drink. Or try the *Bushman's Steak House*, at the corner of Bank Street and Puckey Avenue, which has live music at weekends; *Sea Dragon*, 185 Commerce St, a reasonably priced BYO Chinese restaurant and takeaway; or the pricier and marginally more formal lunchtime *Beachcomber Restaurant*, the Plaza, 222 Commerce St (☎09/408 2010; licensed; dinner also on Sat, closed Sun), currently Kaitaia's pinnacle of culinary achievement and predictably strong on seafood. Apart from the *Blue House*, **drinking** happens at two pubs along the main street, of which the *Kauri Arms* is the more popular, and both drum up custom with local bands at weekends.

Ahipara and the gumfields

Bus tours along Ninety Mile Beach turn off long before its final southern curl around to **AHIPARA**, a scattered village 15km west of Kaitaia that grew up around the Ahipara gumfields. A hundred kilometres of sand recede into sea spray to the north, while to the south the high flatlands of the Ahipara Plateau tumble to the sea in a cascade of golden dunes; the northernmost bay is known as Shipwreck Bay for the paddle-shaft of the *Favourite*, wrecked in 1870, which still sticks out of the surf.

At their peak, the **gumfields**, which were worked from around 1880 until World War II, supported three hotels and two thousand people. Unlike most fields, where experimental probing and digging was the norm, here the soil was methodically excavated, washed and sieved to extract the valuable kauri gum (fossilized resin; see box on p.198). None of the machinery remains on the plateau, but gum can still be found – particularly in the stream that washes down into **Shipwreck Bay**, which you can reach along an unsealed road from Ahipara (2km). At low tide you can swim and pick mussels off the rocks. From the bay a roughly 5km walk (1hr) takes you to the big dunes – equip yourself with a sandboard from *Main Street Backpackers* in Kaitaia for surfing.

Alternatively try the **Gumfields Walk** (29.5km; 12hr round trip; simple free maps and guidelines available from *Main Street Backpackers*; tide dependent), best tackled with at least one other person and be sure to let others (such as the people you're staying with, or the visitor centre) know of your intentions. This unique trek takes you into an eerie and desolate landscape of wind-sculpted dunes and an ancient kauri forest uncovered by the sand. From Ahipara or Shipwreck Bay, you head to the terraced gumfields to the south and on towards the southern shore by way of a track through the dunes, and all the way around the point, past great beaches, back to the start. There's every chance you'll find some kauri gum on the way, which is easily transformed once polished with wet 'n' dry sandpaper.

An unsealed road crosses the tablelands south from Shipwreck Bay through the gumfields to the sand dunes, but it's pretty rough from the gumfields onwards and not advisable for most cars. Instead, head **onto the dunes** with quad bikes rented from Quad Bike Hire (☎09/409 4888; $40 1hr, $70 2hr, $90 3hr); on production of a current driver's licence you're set free to bounce around the dunes and, if the tide is right, return around the shore. A guided version with Tua Tua Tours (☎09/409 4875) costs $115 for three hours (or $150 for two sharing a bike).

Finally, if time is short consider a **scenic flight** over Shipwreck Bay and the gumfields from Kaitaia Airport with Blue Sky Scenics (☎09/406 7320; 25min; $98 for one passenger; $48 per person if more than one).

Practicalities

There are a few **places to stay** at Ahipara: the lovely *Siesta Guest House*, Tasman Heights Road (☎ & fax 09/409 2011, *ninetymile@xtra.co.nz*; ⑥), offers de luxe B&B in a Mediterranean-style home with courtesy transfers from Kaitaia and dinner with wine for an extra $30 or so per person; or there's the simple *Pine Tree Lodge Motor Camp* (☎09/409 4864, *pinetree@xtra.co.nz*; tent sites $8, cabins ②). *Adriaan Lodge*, Reefview Road (☎ & fax 09/409 4888, *wattzi@xtra.co.nz*; dorms ①, studio ③, units ⑤), has attractive self-contained units for groups, a studio and backpacker bunks, plus fine **dining** and licensed **drinking** in its *Bay View Restaurant*.

Ninety Mile Beach and Cape Reinga

Northland's final gesture is the **Aupori Peninsula**, a narrow, 100km-long finger of consolidated and grassed-over dunes ending in a lumpy knot of 60-million-year-old marine volcanoes. To Maori, it is known as *Te Hika o te Ika* ("the tail of the fish"), recalling the legend of Maui hauling up the North Island ("the fish") from the sea while in his canoe (the South Island).

The most northerly accessible point is **Cape Reinga**, a spiritually significant place for all Maori, for this is the "place of leaping", where the spirits of the dead depart. Beginning their journey by sliding down the roots of an 800-year-old pohutukawa into the ocean, they climb out again on Ohaua, the highest of the Three Kings Islands, to bid a final farewell before returning to their ancestors in Hawaiiki. The spirits reach Cape Reinga along **Ninety Mile Beach**, a wide band of sand running straight for over a hundred kilometres (actually around 64 miles) along the western side of the peninsula. Most visitors follow the spirits, but in modern buses specifically designed for belting along the hard-packed sand at the edge of the surf then negotiating the quicksands of Te Paki Stream to return to the road. The main road runs more-or-less down the centre of the peninsula, following the hilly contours and seldom glimpsing the western ocean, which is kept tantalizingly out of sight by the thin pine ribbon of the **Aupori Forest**. The forests, and the cattle farms that cover most of the rest of the peninsula, were previously the preserve of gum diggers, who worked the area intensively early this century.

If you've made it this far north, you'll already be familiar with the paucity of facilities in rural Northland so the Aupori Peninsula doesn't come as much of a surprise. **Accommodation** is sporadically scattered along the way and ranges from some superlative primitive DOC campsites (kept in good condition) to motels, lodges and hostels. All tend to be very reasonably priced, reflecting the tendency of most visitors to pass through without stopping; however, all are very busy immediately after Christmas. There are a few **places to eat**, though nothing stays open after around 8pm. Pukenui and Waitiki both have a shop and expensive **petrol**.

Awanui and the Kauri Kingdom

AWANUI, 8km north of Kaitaia on SH1, was formerly the site of an important radio transmitter to the outside world, but has become a dilapidated rural backwater notable chiefly for the convergence of the eastern and western roads north. Almost all buses to Cape Reinga stop 1km north at the **Ancient Kauri Kingdom** (daily 9am–5pm; free), a defunct dairy factory now operating as a sawmill, cutting and shaping huge peat-preserved kauri

THE LEGEND OF TE HOUTAEWA AND THE MARATHON

Each year competitors from around the world take part in a series of running and walking events on Ninety Mile Beach in mid-March, originally inspired by the tale of a great Maori athlete.

According to legend, **Te Houtaewa**, the fastest runner of his day, enjoyed playing pranks on the enemies of his people. One day his mother asked him to collect some *kumara* from the gardens at Te Kao towards the northern end of the beach, but instead Te Houtaewa ran off south over the hard sands to annoy the **Te Rarawa** people living in Ahipara. Soon after, Te Houtaewa was spotted filling two large *kete* from the Te Rarawa storehouse and a line of people gathered to block his way back to the beach. Sprinting up a hill Te Houtaewa drew his enemies in pursuit. After waiting for the Te Rarawa to draw close, Te Houtaewa (still clasping the baskets) ran back onto the beach, sending his pursuers sprawling. The Te Rarawa dispatched their best athletes in response, but despite his heavy load Te Houtaewa outran and outwitted them, arriving home to find the hangi hot, in readiness for his stolen *kumara*.

Today events range from the mammoth **Te Houteawa Challenge**, a 60km open marathon run by international competitors, to a 6km **Walk for Life**. Competitors can arrange entry via Tall Tale Promotion, part of Tall Tale Travel 'n' Tours, based in Kaitaia (☎09/408 0870, fax 408 1100; see p.186; fees are $6–70, depending on event).

GETTING TO THE CAPE

The best way to experience the phenomenal length and wild beauty of Ninety Mile Beach is to take one of the **bus tours** based in Kaitaia, Mangonui and Paihia in the Bay of Islands. Those from Paihia are the most numerous but are also the longest (11hr), and tours starting further north give you less time in the bus and more time to explore. Their **content** varies but in essence they do the same trip, a loop up the Aupori Peninsula and back, travelling SH1 in one direction and Ninety Mile Beach in the other, the order being dictated by the tide. **Highlights** include leaping or tobogganing down the sand dunes that flank Te Paki Stream, and the rambling and varied collection of the Wagener Museum.

From **Kaitaia**, there are currently two **bus** companies running trips to the cape, picking up from your accommodation around 9am, fitting in a bit of sand tobogganing and returning by 5pm. Both are in fierce competition and frequently undercut prices, so check the latest offers when you arrive. Harrison's Cape Runner, 123 North Rd (☎09/408 1033 & 0800/227 373) have informative and entertaining small-group tours for $40; if you want to do the 3-day walk at Cape Reinga, they will drop you off and pick you up later. Sand Safaris, 221 Commerce St (☎09/408 1778 & 0800/869 090), offer well-run, slightly more formal tours and charge around $5 more.

From **Mangonui**, Paradise Connexion Tours (☎09/406 0460) charge $50, including pick-up from your accommodation. They have a Landrover set aside for trips of only two people; otherwise you go up in their big bus.

From **Paihia**, the two big cruise companies dominate the Cape Reinga tour market. Most trips run daily, leaving at around 7.30am, returning about eleven hours later, and going via Kerikeri, Mangonui and Awanui in one direction and passing Kaitaia and the kauri trees of the Puketi Forest in the other. Kings (☎09/402 8288) run the all-in Cape Reinga Scenic ($77, plus $10 for picnic lunch). Fullers (☎09/402 7421) operate swanky custom-designed buses on the Cape Reinga Heritage ($89 including lunch), which includes a marae visit, and the more sightseeing-orientated Cape Reinga Wanderer (Oct–May only; $89 including lunch), with sand tobogganning, swimming and shellfish digging. Both companies offer ten percent **discounts** if you sign up for both a cruise and

---

logs hauled out of swamps where they have lain for between 30,000 and 50,000 years. You can wander around parts of the factory and watch slabs of wood being fashioned into hot tubs, Gothic furniture and table tops, but, predictably, the emphasis is on the shop, which peddles trinkets and souvenirs. There's also a licensed lunchtime café.

The main southern entrance to Ninety Mile Beach, the Waipapakauri Ramp, is about 15km north.

Houhora and Pukenui

The peninsula's largest concentration of facilities spreads through an area known as **HOUHORA**. Thirty kilometres north of Awanui, a 3km side road turns east to **Houhora Heads** and the **Wagener Museum Complex**, a golf course, campsite, café and twin museums that are on the itinerary of almost all the cape-bound tour buses. It was here in 1860 that Polish pioneers used locally hewn timbers and mortar made from powdered seashells to build the **Subritzky Homestead** (Christmas–Jan 8.30am–4.30pm; rest of year opens for bus tours by arrangement; $3). Although now largely restored to its original state, some rooms still reflect the style of later inhabitants, particularly the last resident, Uncle Fred, who lived here until 1960 in a simple room with a bed made of gum sacks. When descendants of the Subritzkys decided to restore the homestead in the late 1960s, they could only obtain the original furniture as part of a large purchase that included the makings of the ever-expanding **Wagener** a cape trip. **Smaller operators** from Paihia tend to use smaller vehicles and take a less rigid approach, letting the group fine-tune the itinerary and not fussing overly if things run past the scheduled return time: Northern Exposure Tours (☎09/402 8644 & 0800/573 875; $72) use a minibus and include a beachside picnic lunch, also picking up from **Kerikeri**; 4x4 Dune-Rider (☎09/402 8681; $75) make the cape trip in a 4WD so you can get right off the beaten track, will pick up in **Kaeo**, **Mangonui**, **Taipa** and **Awanui** too, and will also drop you off and pick you up another day at no extra cost.

If for some unfathomable reason you are intent on seeing Cape Reinga and not bothered about driving along Ninety Mile Beach, you can **drive to the Cape** via the main road (check conditions with the DOC first on ☎09/408 6014) and avoid the beach altogether. Alternatively you can **fly** there from Paihia with Salt Air Paihia (☎09/402 8338; $239pp), who land at Te Paki station and cover the last section by road and 4WD; or **overfly** the cape in a Salt Air Paihia seaplane ($1500 per group of five) or with Kaitaia-based Blue Sky Scenics (☎09/406 7320; $135pp).

GOING IT ALONE ON NINETY MILE BEACH

Rental cars are **not insured** to drive on Ninety Mile Beach – and for good reason. Vehicles frequently get **bogged** in the sand and abandoned by their occupants, who return home with salutary photos of the roof sticking out of the surf. If you are determined to take your own vehicle for a spin on the beach, **seek local advice** and prepare your long-suffering car by spraying some form of water repellent on the spark plugs – CRC is a common brand. Schedule your trip to coincide with a **receding tide**, starting two hours after high water and preferably going in the same direction as the bus traffic that day; drive close to the water's edge, avoiding any soft sand, and slow down to cross streams running over the beach – they often have deceptively steep banks. If you do get stuck in **soft sand**, lowering the tyre pressure will improve traction. There are several **access points** along the beach, but the only ones realistically available to ordinary vehicles are the ones used by the tour buses: the southern access at **Waipapakauri Ramp**, 6km north of Awanui; and the more dangerous northern one along **Te Paki Stream**, which involves negotiating 3km of quicksand – start in low gear and don't stop, no matter how tempting the dunes look.

Museum (daily: Christmas–Jan 7am–7pm; rest of year 8am–6pm; $6). This somewhat random assemblage includes one of the world's largest collection of seashells, a similarly superlative array of nearly 500 chamber pots, musical instruments, Victorian arcade games, guns, polished kauri gum, ancient washing machines and Maori artefacts. Again, there's a simple licensed café here.

A couple of kilometres north along SH1, the junction of Lambs Road and Wharf Road marks the centre of **PUKENUI**, a working fishing village where good catches are to be had off the wharf.

Practicalities

The area around Houhora and Pukenui has the greatest concentration of **places to stay** on the Aupori Peninsula. The spacious A-frame chalets of the *Houhora Chalets Motor Lodge*, on the corner of SH1 and Houhora Heads Road (☎ & fax 409 8860; ④), and the *Houhora Heads Motor Camp*, Houhora Heads Road (☎09/409 8564; tent sites $7, on-site vans ②), are both close to the Wagener Museum. **In Pukenui**, the attractive *Pukenui Lodge Motel and Backpackers Hostel*, on the corner of SH1 and Wharf Road (☎09/409 8837, fax 409 8704, *pukenui@igrin.co.nz*; dorms ①, doubles ②, motel units ⑤), has a swimming pool and **bikes for rent**. Another option is the compact *Pukenui Holiday Camp*, Lambs Road (☎ & fax 09/409 8803, *pukenuiholidays@xtra.co.nz*; tent sites $10, dorms ①, on-site vans & cabins ②–③). Some 6km north, a side road winds 6km east to the excellent *North Wind Lodge Backpackers*, Otaipango Road, **Henderson**

Bay (☎ & fax 09/409 8515; dorms ①, rooms ②), a modern house not far from a fine beach with bikes for guests' use, pick-ups from Pukenui and the possibility of joining up with Cape Reinga trips.

The only places to eat are the **cafés** at Kauri Kingdom and the Wagener Museum and the *Talk of the North* **restaurant** and takeaway at Pukenui (daily from around 11.30am–9pm), but you can always seek refuge at New Zealand's northernmost **pub**, the waterside *Houhora Tavern*, which lies 2km north of Pukenui, just off the highway.

The Parengarenga Harbour, Te Kao and Waitiki Landing

The Houhora Harbour is the last you see of the sea before the straggling arms of the **Parengarenga Harbour**, 20km further north, a place largely forgotten by most New Zealanders until 1985, when it was identified as the drop-off point for the limpet mines (delivered by yacht from New Caledonia) that were used to sabotage the *Rainbow Warrior*. Bends in the road occasionally reveal glimpses of the silica sands of the harbour's southern headland, which are pure white except in late February and early March when hundreds of thousands of bar-tailed godwits turn the vista black as they gather for their 12,000km journey to Siberia.

This whole area is intensely Maori, with the Ngati Kuri people owning much of the land and comprising the bulk of the population, particularly in the settlement of **TE KAO**, just south of the harbour on SH1. The only reason to stop here is for the twin-towered Ratana Temple, one of the few remaining houses of the Ratana religion, which combines Christian belief with elements of Maori culture and spiritual belief. There's a shady streamside DOC **campsite** nearby at *Rarawa* ($6), 4km off SH1, just back from a fine white-sand beach.

The last place of any consequence before the land sinks into the ocean is **WAITIKI LANDING**, the end of the tar seal 24km from Cape Reinga and comprising only a **café**, takeaway and **accommodation** at the *Waitiki Landing Complex*, SH1 (☎ & fax 09/409 7508, *waitiki.landing@xtra.co.nz*; tent sites $7, powered sites $18 for two, bunks ①, cabins ③). From here, one twisting 15km road runs to the DOC **campsite** at Kapowairua ($5) beside the gorgeous **Spirits Bay**, the other to Cape Reinga, passing the Te Paki Stream entrance to Ninety Mile Beach.

Cape Reinga

The last leg from Waitiki Landing to **Cape Reinga** runs high through the hills before revealing the Tasman Sea and the huge dunes that foreshadow it. Magnificent seascapes unfold – until you hit the Cape Reinga car park, which is surrounded by a shabby cluster of meteorological and DOC buildings that detract from the scenic grandeur and spirituality of the place without contributing much in the way of comfort. There's a souvenir shop and a post office that closes once the tour buses have gone (around 4pm in summer). Escape quickly down the well-trodden ten-minute path to the Cape Reinga **lighthouse**, dramatically perched on a headland 165m above Colombia Bank, where the waves of the Tasman Sea meet the swirling currents of the Pacific Ocean in a boiling cauldron of surf. On clear days, the view from here is stunning: east to the Surville Cliffs of North Cape, west to Cape Maria van Diemen and north to the rocky **Three Kings Islands** 57km offshore, which were named by Abel Tasman, who first came upon them on the eve of Epiphany 1643.

Several dramatic **walks** radiate from the car park. Only avid beach nuts are going to get much pleasure out of the long sandy trudge of the Cape Reinga Walkway (134km, can be walked in either direction, minimum 3 days), which runs the length of Ninety Mile Beach – with limited fresh water, no facilities and a cavalcade of buses passing each day, to say nothing of the sandflies, which are massive up here, especially in summer. The walkway does, however, provide the conduit for shorter strolls: west to Te Werahi Beach (30min one way), and steeply east to Sandy Bay (30min one way) and the lovely **Tapotupotu Bay** (*Ngatangawhiti*; 2hr one way), the latter also accessible by road and a common picnic stop for tour buses. For a fee, Waitiki Landing Complex (see opposite) operate pick-up and drop-off services to various walks in the Cape Reinga region, and can supply further information on the walks themselves.

This far north, the only place to stay is the beautifully located DOC **campsite** at Tapotupotu Bay ($6).

The Hokianga Harbour

The Tasman Sea burrows deep into western Northland south of Kaitaia, the narrow mangrove-flanked fissures of the **Hokianga Harbour** snaking deep inland past tiny, almost moribund, communities. For a few days' relaxation, the tranquillity and easy pace of this rural backwater are hard to beat. You are likely to spend most of your time on the southern shores, from where the striking deep blue waters beautifully set off the mountainous sand dunes of North Head. The dunes are best seen from the rocky promontory of South Head high above the treacherous Hokianga Bar, or reached by boat for a little sand tobogganing. High forest ranges immediately to the south make excellent hiking and horse-trekking territory, and the giant kauri of the Waipoua Forest are within easy striking distance, but the focus is definitely the harbour.

It was here that the great Polynesian explorer **Kupe**, guided by the stars, moon and tides, first set foot on *Aotearoa*, arriving from his homeland in Hawaiiki during the tenth century. Some years later, he went back to Hawaiiki and the harbour became known as *Hokianganui-a-Kupe*, "the place of Kupe's great return". His descendants returned to become the ancestors of the Ngapuhi. **Cook** saw the Hokianga Heads in 1770 but didn't realize what lay beyond, and it wasn't until a **missionary** crossed the hill from the Bay of Islands in 1819 that Europeans became aware of Hokianga Harbour. Catholics, Anglicans and Wesleyans weren't slow to convert the Ngapuhi, gaining their trust and frequently intermarrying, setting the tone for the well-integrated Maori and European communities that exist today. The Hokianga soon rivalled the pre-eminence of the Bay of Islands and notched up several **firsts**: European boat building was begun here in 1826, the first signal station opened two years later, and the first Catholic Mass was celebrated in the same year. When the Treaty of Waitangi was signed, it was considered to have little validity until the Hokianga chiefs added their marks a few days later.

With the demise of kauri felling and milling that afflicted much of Northland, Hokianga became an **economic backwater**, with little industry, high unemployment and limited facilities. Over the last couple of decades, however, city dwellers, artists and craftspeople have snapped up bargain properties and moved up here in a small and fairly inconspicuous way, settling in **Kohukohu** on the north shore, **Rawene**, a short ferry ride away to the south, and the two larger but still small-time resorts of **Opononi** and **Omapere**, opposite the dunes near the harbour entrance.

On a practical note, you'll need to stock up with cash before exploring the Hokianga and kauri forests: there are **no banks** between Kaitaia and Dargaville, 170km away to the south, though all towns have EFTPOS facilities and the *Omapere Tourist Hotel and Motel* in the centre of Omapere will often change money, but at poor rates.

The Hokianga region is served by a **visitor centre** in Omapere on SH12 (see p.195).

Kohukohu and the northern Hokianga

Heading south from Kaitaia, the steep and tightly twisting SH1 passes through forests draped over the Mangamuka Ranges. The alternative route follows a winding minor road via the harbourside **Herekino** (23km from Kaitaia), which has an unusual farm-stay, *Tui Inn*, Puhata Road (☎09/409 3883; ①), run by a kind of Kiwi Crocodile Dundee who offers horse trekking for around $30 for the day, as well as fishing and hunting (at Herekino turn off onto the Whangape Road for 1km). On SH1, after forty kilometres, you'll come to **Mangamuka Bridge** (the western entrance to the Omahuta Forest; see p.179), where a narrower and equally tortuous road follows the northernmost arm of the Hokianga Harbour 25km to **Narrows Landing**, the northern terminus for the Rawene Vehicular Ferry (☎09/405 2602; daily 7.45am–8pm; car and driver $13 one way, $18 return, passengers $1.50), which runs on the hour southbound and half-hour north-bound.

Four kilometres before the ferry, the road passes **KOHUKOHU**, a small waterside village where even the sole pub and grocery shop barely seem to be hanging on. Once the hub of Hokianga's kauri industry, the dairying that replaced it also lapsed, con-signing Kohukohu to years of decline only partly arrested by the recent influx of rat-race refugees. The upshot of all this is a low-key place with some attractive, century-old wooden houses where the delightful places to stay make a brief sojourn tempting.

The Kohukohu area has two excellent **places to stay**, the cheapest being *The Tree House* (☎09/405 5855, *tree.house@xtra.co.nz*; tent sites $10, campervans welcome, dorms ①, rooms ②), at **MOTUKARAKA**, 2km west of the ferry amid ultra-relaxing organic macadamia and fruit orchards, filled with birdsong. Dorms in this hideaway are spacious and well designed, as are the twins and doubles scattered around the grounds. The tasteful and aptly-named *Harbour Views Guesthouse*, Rakautapu Road, Kohukohu (☎09/405 5815; ④), makes a lovely spot for a peaceful night or two with shady veran-das, nicely decorated rooms and dinner for $15.

Rawene

The vehicular ferry shuttles from near Kohukohu across to appealing **RAWENE**, a slightly livelier village occupying the tip of Herd's Point, a peninsula roughly halfway up the harbour. Though almost isolated by the mud flats at low tide, Rawene's strategic position made it an obvious choice for the location of a timber mill, which contributed material for the town's attractive wooden buildings, some perched out on stilts over the water.

On a sunny day it is a pleasant place to saunter around, the only significant distrac-tion being **Clendon House**, Clendon Esplanade (Nov–April Sat, Sun & Mon 10am–4pm; $2), on a hillside overlooking the harbour. This was the last residence of James Clendon, a pivotal figure in the early life of the colony, serving as US honorary consul, Justice of the Peace and member of the First Legislative Council before taking up a position as resident magistrate of the Hokianga district in 1861. The house wasn't finished until 1868 and Clendon only lived there for the four years prior to his death, leaving his part-Maori second wife, Jane, and eight kids. The colonial-era contents of the two-storey house owe more to Jane than James, but nonetheless reflect the relative wealth of someone in his position with much of the stuffy furniture emanating from Britain. The upper floor has been restored as a child's playroom and schoolroom, and one room beside the veranda has been retained as the post office it once was.

Practicalities

Rawene's location at the only crossing point makes it an ideal base for exploring both sides of the harbour. Parnell Street is the main thoroughfare and passes the most con-venient **accommodation**, the *Masonic Hotel* (☎09/405 7822, *masonic@igrin.co.nz*, fax 401 1768; ②), with small but decent traditional hotel rooms. The *Rawene Motor Camp*, Marmon Street, 1.5km from Ferry Landing (☎09/405 7720; tent sites $8, on-site vans $12 and cabins ②), with tent sites and cabins tucked away in bush enclaves, and a pool.

The nearest hostel is *Senace*, 5km west on SH12 (☎09/405 7790; dorms ①, rooms ②), with basic beds and cooking facilities.

For such a small place you can **eat** well. First stop should be the relaxed, daytime *Boatshed Café*, on Clendon Esplanade, which is built on stilts over the water and offers a stack of magazines, light snacks and cakes and the best espresso for miles around. The *Masonic Hotel* does good bar meals and reasonably priced à la carte dinners, has a peaceful veranda to sup away the afternoon and puts on bands most summer weekends.

Opononi and Omapere

The two small-time resorts of **OPONONI** and **OMAPERE** run pretty seamlessly for 4km along the southern shore of the Hokianga Harbour, with great views across to the sand dunes on the north side. Kiwis of a certain age will be able tell you all about Opononi and the eventful summer of 1955–56 when a wild bottlenose dolphin, dubbed "Opo", took a shine to the local populace and started playing with the kids in the shallows and performing tricks with beach balls. At the time, New Zealand still had whaling factories on its shores, dolphin-watching trips were decades away and signs had to be erected discouraging people from shooting the precocious dolphin. And yet Opo's antics captivated the nation: Christmas holidaymakers jammed the narrow dirt roads; film crews were dispatched; protective laws were drafted; and bandwagon-jumping Auckland musicians Pat McMinn, Bill Langford and The Crombie Murdoch Trio cobbled together the novelty song, *Opo The Crazy Dolphin*. Written and recorded in a day, the tape arrived at the radio station for its first airing just as news of Opo's untimely death broke – the song was a hit nonetheless.

Opononi has dined out on its fifteen minutes of fame ever since, though the only concrete reminder is a statue of Opo outside the *Opononi Resort Hotel*. To get a better sense of the frenzied enthusiasm for Opo, head to Omapere – just a roadside string of clapboard houses and a few places to stay and eat – where the **local museum** inside the visitor centre (see below) shows a short video in the classic mould of corny-yet-charming Fifties documentary footage.

Dune trips, cruises and activities

Opononi and Omapere make good bases for exploring the surrounding area. The biggest of all the kauri trees, **Tane Mahuta**, is only 15km south of Omapere and boats ply across the harbour to the **sand dunes** – though the vistas from the south side are often so striking that it is enough to visit the **viewpoints**. The most notable are the **Arai te Uru Reserve**, reached along Signal Station Road just west of Omapere, and the magical **Pakia Hill**, by SH12 further up the hill.

The **dunes** are most easily visited by boat from the Opononi wharf. Hokianga Express (☎09/405 8872) will drop you off and pick you up a couple of hours later for around $15 and also supply sand toboggans. In addition they run **harbour cruises** (minimum four people; 1hr for $25; 3hr for $50) pretty much on demand, or you can charter the boat for $250 per half day, $500 full day. On land, Okopako Horse Trekking will take you **riding** into the bush and the hills above the treeline (☎09/405 8815; 2–3hr; $20 for first hour, $10 for each subsequent hour).

Walks

The best and most popular of the short walks in the district is the **Waiotemarama Walk** which starts 8km southeast of Opononi along Waiotemarama Gorge Road; the starting point is conveniently marked by one of the region's better craft shops, Labyrinth Woodworks (☎09/405 4581), whose wares include carved kauri pieces and excellent woodblock prints by noted local craftsman Allan Gale. The full route through the bush to SH12 takes an entire day but most people just walk the initial short section up a lovely bush-clad valley full of ferns, nikau palms and kauri. Ten minutes' walk gets you to an attractive waterfall with a small swimming hole and in another ten minutes you reach the first kauri. Beyond there you climb higher, eventually topping out on the 680m Hauturu (5–6hr return).

Another popular outing is the **Hokianga Track** (8km; 3–4hr; 300m ascent) from Hokianga South Head along Kaikai Beach and up the Waimamaku River back to SH12. More ambitious walkers should set two or three days aside for the **Waipoua Coast Walkway**, a 50km coastal trek that continues south from the Hokianga Track to Maunganui Bluff and on to Kai Iwi Lakes (see p.199), with few facilities along the way; details are available in the DOC's *Waipoua & Trounson Kauri Forests* leaflet ($1) and from visitor centres.

Practicalities

Westcoaster run daily **bus services** through the Hokianga on behalf of InterCity and Northliner, stopping by the wharf in Opononi and outside the **Hokianga visitor centre** (daily 8.30am–5pm; ☎09/405 8869, fax 405 8317, *fndchka@hotmail.com*) on the main road in Omapere, where you can book and buy tickets, and gather information on the Waipoua Kauri Forest as well as on the more immediate area. The buses also stop at the start of the track to the biggest kauri in the forests just south, giving you time to do the short walk up to it before carrying on.

ACCOMMODATION

The twin towns are well served with budget accommodation. In **Opononi** there's the small, cosy and central *House of Harmony: Te Rangimarie*, SH12 (☎ & fax 09/405 8778; tent sites $10, dorms ①, rooms ②). The beautifully sited and well-organized *Globetrekkers*, SH12 (☎ & fax 09/405 8183, *shirley@extra.co.nz*; tent sites $8, dorms ①, rooms ②), heads the field in **Omapere**; but the diminutive *Green Café Guesthouse*, SH12 (☎09/405 8193; dorms ①, rooms ②), is also appealing. For something a little more upmarket, head for either the *Omapere Tourist Hotel & Motel*, SH12 (☎09/405 8737, fax 405 8801, *icesam@ihug.co.nz*; tent and campervan sites $9, rooms ⑤–⑥), which is beautifully set opposite the dunes and has a heated pool, bar and restaurant; or the relaxed and friendly homestay run by *Alexa & Owen Whaley*, Signal Station Road (☎09/405 8641, *owen_whaley@paradise.co.nz*; ④), which is located on a smallholding with wonderful views over the harbour.

The best of the **out of town places** are *Okopako Lodge: The Wilderness Farm*, Mountain Road, on a twisting unsealed road 5km east of Opononi and 2km off SH12 (☎ & fax 09/405 8815; tent sites $9, dorms ①, YHA rooms ②; B&B ④ plus optional farmhouse dinner for $20), a combined B&B and associate YHA hostel high in the hills with panoramic views and offering modern accommodation and extremely professional horse trekking through the adjacent native bush ($20 for first hour, $10 for each subsequent hour) and up to views over the entire Hokianga Harbour; and the nearby *Taane and Karen Thomas*, on the corner of Taita Road and SH12, Waimamaku (☎09/405 8131; ④ including meals), a Maori-run homestay that offers the chance to learn some weaving and a smattering of the language, songs and legends, as well as to partake in communal meals, all included in the price. **Campers** are best served at the hostels or the spacious, harbourside *Opononi Holiday Park*, SH12, Opononi (☎ & fax 09/405 8791; tent sites $10, powered sites $10, cabins ③).

EATING

In Omapere **places to eat** are strung along SH12, where you can fill up on basic fare such as takeaway fish and chips from *Omapere Fish Supplies*; or snack in the plastic surroundings of the *Omapere Tearooms*. The classiest dining is at the *Harbourmaster's Restaurant*, in the *Omapere Tourist Hotel and Motel*, where tasty bistro-style bar meals supplement more expensive à la carte dinners concentrating on local seafood. Stunning views can be had from the *Calypso*, a trendy café open for daytime eating from Monday to Wednesday, and all day between Thursday and Sunday, 2km south on SH12, in Pakia Hill.

The Kauri Forests and the northern Kaipara Harbour

Northland, Auckland and the Coromandel Peninsula were once covered in mixed forest dominated by the mighty kauri (see box overleaf), the world's second largest tree after the Californian redwoods. By the early years of the twentieth century, rapacious Europeans had nearly felled the lot, the only extensive pockets remaining in the **Waipoua and Trounson kauri forests** south of the Hokianga Harbour. Small stands of kauri occur all over Northland, but three-quarters of all the surviving mature trees grow in these two small forests, between them barely covering 100 square kilometres. **Walks** provide access to the more celebrated examples, which dwarf the surrounding tataire, kohekohe and towai, normally some of the larger forest trees.

This land is home to the Te Roroa people who, like their kin in the north, traditionally used the kauri sparingly. Simple tools made felling and working these huge trees a difficult task, and one reserved for major projects such as large war canoes. Once the Europeans arrived with metal tools, bullock trains, wheels and winches, clear felling became more manageable and most of the trees had gone by the end of the nineteenth century. The demand for ships during World War II saw renewed interest in the kauri and sparked a corresponding campaign to save something of what was left, resulting in the creation in 1952 of the Waipoua Sanctuary, which provided limited protection, but since bolstered to the point where it is now illegal to fell a kauri except in specified circumstances such as culling a diseased or dying tree, or the construction of a new ceremonial canoe.

Driving through miles of farmland it is often hard to imagine the same landscape surrounded by dense forest. This is certainly true of the lands to the south around the muddy shores of the **Kaipara Harbour**, a labyrinth of mangrove-choked inlets and small beaches. This series of drowned valleys constitutes New Zealand's largest harbour, with the longest coastline and a catchment area that covers nearly half of Northland. The Kaipara once unified this quarter of Northland, the sailboats plying its waters linking the dairy farming and logging towns on its shores. Kauri was shipped out from the largest northern town, **Dargaville**, headed either for Helensville (see p.119) or out to sea, but the fragile boats all too often foundered on the unpredictable Kaipara Bar and were eventually washed up on **Ripiro Beach**, a fabulous salty strand which just pips Ninety Mile Beach as New Zealand's longest, running for 108km. The region declined in step with the demise of harbour traffic, and modern Dargaville survives on horticulture and a constant stream of kauri-forest-bound tourists pausing to explore the beach and the windswept Kaipara Heads. If you're pushed for time, skip the town in favour of a couple of hours at the **Matakohe Kauri Museum**, 45km south, which gives the best sense of what the kauri meant to the Northland economy and their spiritual significance for Maori.

One daily **bus** in each direction runs through the kauri forests, making a brief stop to glimpse at the biggest tree; two or three buses a day run south from Dargaville, so judicious timing should enable you to see the Kauri Museum.

THE KAURI AND ITS USES

The **kauri** (*Agathis Australis*) isn't the tallest species of tree, nor does it boast the greatest girth, but as its gargantuan trunk barely tapers from roots to crown it ranks alongside the sequoias, or redwoods, of California as one of the largest trees in existence. Unlike the redwoods, which are useless as building **timber**, kauri produce beautiful wood, thereby hastening their demise and spawning industries that dominated the economy of the young colony in the latter half of the nineteenth century.

The kauri is a type of **pine** which now grows only in New Zealand, though it once also grew in Australia and southeast Asia, where it still has close relations. Identifiable remains of kauri forests are found all over New Zealand but by the time humans arrived on the scene, its **range** had contracted to Northland, Auckland, the Coromandel Peninsula and northern Waikato. Individual trees can live up to 2000 years, reaching 50m in height and 20m in girth, finally toppling over as the rotting core becomes too weak to support its immense weight.

KAURI LOGGERS

Maori have long used mature kauri for dugout canoes, but it was the young "rickers" which first drew the attention of **European** kauri **loggers** since they formed perfect **spars** for sailing ships. The bigger trees didn't escape attention for long, soon earning an unmatched reputation for their durable, easy-to-work and blemish-free wood with a straight, fine grain. Loggers' ingenuity was taxed to the limit by the difficulty of getting such huge logs out of the bush. On easier terrain, **bullock wagons** with up to twelve teams were lashed together to haul the trunks over primitive roads or tramways, horse-turned winches were used on steeper ground and, where water could be deployed to transport the timber, dams were constructed from hewn logs. In narrow valleys and gullies all over Northland and the Coromandel, loggers constructed **kauri dams** up to 20m high and 60m across, with trap doors at the base. Trees along the sides of the valley were felled while the dam was filling, then the dam was tripped to flush the floating trunks down the valley to inlets where the logs were rafted up and towed to the mills.

GUM DIGGERS

Once an area had been logged, the **gum diggers** typically moved in. Like most pines, kauri exudes a thick resin to heal any wounds inflicted on it, and huge candle-drip accretions form on the sides of trunks and in globules around the base, further hardening off in time. In pre-European times, **Maori** had chewed it as gum, made torches to attract fish at night and burned the powdered resin to form a pigment used for *moko* (traditional tattoos). Once *pakeha* got in on the act, it was exported as a raw material for furniture **varnishes**, linoleum, denture moulds and the "gilt" edging on books. When it could no longer be found on the ground, diggers – Maori, Chinese and Malaysian, but mostly Dalmatian – thrust long poles into the earth and hooked out pieces with bent rods; elsewhere, the ground was turned over, loosened and sluiced to recover the gum. Almost all New Zealand gum was **exported**, but by the early twentieth century synthetic resins had captured the gum market. Kauri gum is still considered one of the finest varnishes for musical instruments, though prices don't justify collecting it; occasional accidental finds supply such specialist needs.

Waipoua and Trounson kauri forests

SH12 provides a unique opportunity to drive through nearly 20km of mature kauri in **Waipoua Kauri Forest**. The road twists and turns, following the contours of the hill country and skirting around the base of the big trees so as to cause minimal damage to their fragile and shallow root system. No sooner have you entered the forest than signs indicate the three-minute path to New Zealand's mightiest tree, the 1200-year-old **Tane Mahuta**, "Lord of the Forest". A vast wall of bark rises up nearly 18m to the lowest branches, where it seems that half the forest's epiphytes have lodged in the crook. A kilometre or so further south, a car park marks the beginning of a ten-minute track to a clearing where three paths lead off to notable trees. The shortest (5min return) runs to the **Four Sisters**, relatively slender kauri all growing close together on the same mound of shed bark. A second path (30min return) twists among numerous big trees to the Big Daddy of them all, **Te Matua Ngahere**, the "Father of the Forest", ranked as the second largest tree on account of its shorter stature but, if anything, more richly festooned in epiphytes than its brothers. The third, the **Yakas Track** (6km; 3hr), leads to the Waipoua Forest visitor centre (see below); even if you don't fancy the full track, walk the first thirty minutes to Cathedral Grove, a dense conglomeration of trees, the largest being the **Yakas Kauri**, named after veteran bushman Nicholas Yakas.

In the heart of the first forest, a side road leads 1km to the **Waipoua Forest visitor centre** (Oct–April Mon–Fri 8.30am–4.30pm, Sat–Sun 9am–4.30pm; May–Sept Mon–Fri 8.30am–6pm, Sat–Sun 9am–6pm; ☎09/439 0605, *akereopa@doc.govt.nz*), fount of all knowledge on the reserve. The grounds contain **Maxwell Cottage** (daylight hours; free), a woodcutter's cottage from 1900 built with vertical kauri paling, and a DOC **campsite** (book through the visitor centre; tent sites $6, 2-bed cabins ②, 4-bed cabins $10pp) with hot and cold running water. South of here the highway runs through farmland, passing the nearest formal **accommodation**, *Waipoua Lodge*, SH12 (☎ & fax 09/439 0422, *tony@waipoualodge.co.nz*; ⑤–⑥), with attractively set-up self-contained doubles in a former woolshed, stables and calfpen that are much more luxurious than they sound, and set amid landscaped gardens and bush (cut with walks); freshly baked bread is provided each morning and there's an on-site **restaurant**, which serves moderately priced lunches and fine evening meals incorporating produce from their vegetable garden (main courses $15–25). Nearby, the Aranga Coast Road branches west to the 460m **Maunganui Bluff**, the northern limit of Ripiro Beach (see p.201).

Another small but superb stand of kauri, the **Trounson Kauri Park**, lies 17km southeast of Waipoua and can be visited on a short track from the car park or from the simple DOC **campsite** ($7). There's more accommodation in the area, with a range of cabins and motel units nearby at *Kauri Coast Holiday Park*, Trounson Park Road (☎ & fax 09/439 0621, *kauricoast@clear.net.nz*; tent sites $10, dorms ①, cabins ②), and the appealing, rural *Kaihu Farm Hostel* (☎09/439 4004; dorms ①, rooms ②) on SH12 some 7km away but within easy walking distance of the forest and with good $10 meals on offer.

Kai Iwi Lakes

The **Kai Iwi Lakes**, 11km west of SH12 and 35km northwest of Dargaville, are a real change of pace, with pine woods running down to fresh, crystal-blue waters fringed by silica-white sand. All three are dune lakes – relatively common along Northland's western seaboard – fed by rainwater and with no visible outlet. Though the largest, **Taharoa**, is less than a kilometre across, and **Waikere** and **Kai Iwi** are barely a hundred metres long, they constitute the deepest and some of the largest dune lakes in the country. Families flock here in the summer to swim, fish and waterski, but outside the first week in January you can usually find a quiet spot. Around Lake Taharoa **accommodation** consists of the large and well-equipped *Kai Iwi Lakes Campground* (☎09/439 8360; tent sites $8) on the gently shelving shores of Taharoa Lake; the more intimate *Promenade Point* site (☎09/439 8360; tent sites $8), which has just water, toilet and cold showers; and the more substantial motel-style *Waterlea*, neighbouring Lake Taharoa

(☎ & fax 09/439 0727; ④–⑤), which also serves meals, rents mountain bikes and kayaks (around $8 an hour), takes folk water-skiing ($60 per hour) and trout-fishing ($45 an hour for 2 people).

Walkers can follow the beach north from here to Maunganui Bluff (2hr one way) and either walk back, follow Aranga Coast Road inland to pick up a bus on SH12, or continue north along the Waipoua Coast Walkway to the Hokianga Harbour.

No **buses** go right out to the lakes, but if you're heading north from Dargaville in summer it's worth asking around for a lift, since someone is usually travelling out there.

Dargaville and around

Sleepy **DARGAVILLE**, 30km south of Kai Iwi Lakes, is trying to shake off its cow-town image by pitching itself as the capital of the Kauri Coast, an amorphous region encompassing everywhere south from the Hokianga down and around the Kaipara. In reality, it is more a service town for the region's farming community, traditionally dairy-based but more recently burgeoning into the country's top kumara-growing district. The town was founded as a port in 1872, 64km up the strongly tidal but navigable Northern Wairoa River, by Joseph McMullen Dargaville, an Australian of Irish descent. Ships came to load kauri logs and transport gum (see box on p.198) extracted by Dalmatian settlers who, by the early part of the twentieth century, formed a sizeable portion of the community; a building on Normanby Street still proclaims itself the Yugoslav Social Hall, while from the harbour end of Hokianga Road, a statue of a jolly little gum digger commemorates their presence.

There are only two specific sights here and the biggest is 2km west of town: the **Dargaville Maritime Museum** (daily 9am–4pm; $3) is in the hilltop Harding Park and marked by two masts rescued from the *Rainbow Warrior* (see box on p.180). Space is found for a good collection of kauri gum – including an 84kg piece reputed to be the largest found – among the extensive displays of artefacts recovered from wrecks discovered off the coast. Local experts contend that the Spaniard Juan Fernandez was the first European to visit New Zealand in 1576, a full 66 years before Abel Tasman's more widely recognized "discovery". Naturally, this is highly controversial and most of the evidence is circumstantial, but Ross Wiseman in his book *The Spanish Discovery of New Zealand in 1576* (see p.877) puts a strong case. Remains from later wrecks are on show along with photos of their excavation, the only pre-European artefact being the Ngati Whatua *waka* which lay buried under the sands of the North Head of the Kaipara Harbour from 1809 until 1972, and is a rare example of a canoe hewn entirely by stone tools. Back in town, the central **Woodturners Kauri Gallery & Studio**, 4 Murdoch St (☎09/439 4975; most days from 10am till dark) shows off the magnificence and extraordinarily varied grains and colours of kauri, in pieces worked by one of New Zealand's leading woodturners, Rick Taylor; he also gives individual tuition to anyone who's prepared to have a go for a week or so, if booked ahead on the same number as above or *kauri4u@hotmail.com* ($325 per day, negotiable for longer periods).

Short **cruises** on the Northern Wairoa River take place at weekends on a fine traditional schooner, the *Te Aroha* (☎09/439 8360, *mvtearoha@xtra.co.nz*; departs Dargaville wharf Sat–Sun 10am & 2pm; 30min; $10); comfortable cruises of 2–5 days also operate by arrangement (from $80 for an overnight cruise; book well in advance), focusing on local culture, wildlife and history. To get further downriver by **jetboat**, contact Kaipara Kapers who operate from Dargaville wharf (☎ & fax 09/431 7493; *jetboat@kauricoast.co.nz*) and can tailor a trip to your needs, tying in with other local operators; options include a pretty extreme 30min journey down the Kaihu River ($35); or a trip to Ripiro Beach where you ride quad bikes over the dunes at

Pouto Point, followed by an exciting beach ride in a special truck "Big Foot", exploring shipwreck relics on the way (5hr; $155); or a 2hr trip taking in a pub lunch, where the landlord recounts some of the rich history of the area ($60 including lunch).

Ripiro Beach stretches 108km from Maunganui Bluff south to Pouto Point, the northern head of the Kaipara Harbour, and is accessible at several points, most easily at **Baylys Beach**, a conglomeration of mostly holiday homes 14km west of Dargaville. The sands of Ripiro Beach are renowned for their mobility, with several metres of beach often being shifted by a single tide, and huge areas being reclaimed over the centuries; periodically an anchor or prow of a long-lost wreck reappears through the sand. As elsewhere on the West Coast, tidal rips and holes make swimming dangerous and there are no beach patrols. Beach driving is no less fraught with danger and shouldn't be undertaken without prior local consultation; vehicles frequently get stranded. Nevertheless it's a fine place for long moody walks, digging up **tua tua**, the locally renowned shellfish (you find them with your feet – by doing a sort of twist you'll find a patch of them), and spotting seals and penguins in winter. When easterlies are blowing the shore is lined with kites flying in the wind, the sign of **kite fishing**, where lines are run out for about a kilometre, from which separate lines (traces) are hung for about twenty minutes at a time; bringing the lines back in is hard work and a free fish goes to anyone who wants to help with any of the different jobs. For adventure on the sands try **horse riding** with the excellent Dargaville-based Baylys Beach Horse Treks (☎09/439 6342; pick-ups from Dargaville; 3hr; $33). Better still, sign up for the full-day combined **jetboat** ride and **beach drive** with Kaipara Kapers (see opposite) or Taylor Made Tours (☎09/439 1576), who join forces to provide a highly informative excursion to Ripiro Beach ($155), where a specially designed 4WD truck thunders along the wild, exposed beach to the disused 1884 Kaipara lighthouse. Finally, to **quadbike** over the sand and dunes, contact Pouto 4x4 Quad Tours (☎09/439 8360; $35), who can also tie in with Kaipara Kapers and Taylor Made Tours on demand.

About 17km south of Dargaville through flat country and just off SH12 is the flat-topped **Toka Toka Peak**, an extinct volcanic core or plug (180m), which you can climb in twenty minutes from a side road, for expansive views of the whole district. In wet weather the track is extremely slippery, so caution is needed. Turn left off SH12 after the *Toka Toka* pub for 1km to the start of the track.

Practicalities

Two **bus** services stop on Kapia Street in Dargaville: InterCity (operated by Westcoast) runs between Opononi and Brynderwyn, where it connects with services to Auckland; and Mainline run direct from Dargaville to Auckland. Tickets for both are available from the **visitor centre**, 65 Normanby St (Nov–March Mon–Fri 8.30am–5.30pm & Sat–Sun 9am–4.30pm; April–Oct Mon–Fri 8.30am–5pm & Sat–Sun 10am–4.30pm; ☎09/439 8360, *info@kauricoast.co.nz*), which also has comprehensive **accommodation** listings for the region.

The best budget place to stay is *The Greenhouse Hostel*, 13 Portland St (☎09/439 6342; tent sites $8, dorms ①, rooms ②), a former 1920s schoolhouse functioning as an associate YHA **hostel**, with free use of bikes; one of the managers can show you how to polish a small piece of kauri gum to keep ($30). Traditional **pub beds** are available at the *Northern Wairoa Hotel*, on the corner of Victoria Street and Hokianga Road (☎09/439 8923; ④), and there are reasonable **motels** such as *Dargaville Motel*, 217 Victoria St (☎09/439 7734; ④). Dargaville's grandest rooms are at the engagingly low-key *Kauri House Lodge*, Bowen Street (☎ & fax 09/439 8082; ⑦), where comfortable en-suite rooms are set in a vast kauri-built house, complete with billiard room, library and swimming pool. Campers can choose between *Selwyn Park Motor Camp*, Onslow St,

Dargaville (☎09/439 8296; tent sites $9, cabins ②–③), and the *Baylys Beach Motor Camp*, Baylys Coast Road, Baylys Beach (☎ & fax 09/439 6349; tent sites $9, cabins ②–③).

Belushi's Café, 102 Victoria St, does cappuccinos, bagels, big muffins and good **breakfasts** during the day, while the *New Asian Restaurant*, 114 Victoria St (BYO & licensed), dishes up tolerable Chinese meals. The *Northern Wairoa Hotel* is locally renowned for its bargain **pub meals** and juicy Sunday roasts in an unusually elegant restaurant. Modern Kiwi cuisine is served up daily for lunch and dinner (around the $20 mark) at the licensed *Uno* on Hokianga Road, a big barn of a place that's also a popular bar; and the equally trendy *Blah Blah Blah* on Victoria St. The best value for money, though, is to be had at the *Seaview Café*, at Baylys Beach (☎09/439 4549), with shady outdoor seating for daytime coffee and tasty snacks, and an evening blackboard menu.

Matakohe and its museum

If there is one museum you must see in the north it is the **Matakohe Kauri Museum**, Church Road (Nov–Easter daily 9am–5.30pm; Easter–Oct daily 9am–5pm; $7), on the outskirts of the village of **MATAKOHE**, 45km south of Dargaville. One of the best in the country and deserving at least a couple of hours, it focuses on the way the kauri shaped the lives of pioneers in Northland, from the makeshift settlements around logging camps and on the gumfields through to the merchants who could afford to buy the fine pieces of furniture or finely carved kauri gum. A 22m-long reconstruction of a vertical slice of a cut kauri makes an impressive start, providing a canvas for a photographic essay of its felling in 1994 after being struck by lightning. Mock-ups of the various methods of transporting the huge logs – kauri dams, wooden sleds, bullock trains and winches – lead on to a pit-saw operation and a steam-driven breaking-down mill where planks were shaped. Fine examples of cut boards surround the wall, some exhibiting the dark staining of swamp kauri where water in the peat bogs has penetrated the grain, others showing blemishes where gum climbers punctured the bark, a process which eventually killed many trees. Matakohe has the most extensive display of kauri gum anywhere, with glass cases stuffed full of everything from vast lumps of the raw material to finely worked pieces in every imaginable form down to strands braided into a plait. Rather lifeless tableaux of wealthy Victorian families at leisure in kauri-panelled rooms are perhaps the only weakness among rooms groaning with magnificently detailed furniture and fascinating photos.

Several mildly diverting wooden buildings (open during museum hours) have been moved into the museum grounds from the surrounding area: a one-room schoolhouse used for nearly a century until 1972, a 1909 post office and a diminutive pioneer church dating back to 1867. By the church is the 1950 Coates Memorial Church built in honour of locally raised Joseph Gordon Coates who, in 1925, became the country's first New Zealand-born prime minister.

It is possible to visit the museum using **public transport**, most easily done if you are heading north, when timings are more amenable. Alternatively, you can **stay** nearby in the warren of rooms at the *Old Post Office Guest House*, on SH12 in the village of Paparoa, 6km east of Matakohe (☎09/431 6444; tent sites $10; dorms ①, rooms ③); one of the double rooms is located in a renovated solid kauri nineteenth-century jail. Kayaks are free for guests' use and breakfast is available. The *Travellers Lodge*, on SH16 in Ruawai, 15km west of Matakohe (☎09/439 2283; tent sites $10, dorms ①, rooms ②), is also convenient for the museum.

travel details

Buses

Two major bus companies serve Northland. The most comprehensive operation is InterCity combined with West Coaster (☎09/913 6100), who run two routes, one up the eastern side from Auckland's Sky City depot through Warkworth, Brynderwyn, Whangarei, Paihia, Kerikeri and Mangonui to Kaitaia, the other spurring off at Brynderwyn and covering Dargaville, the Waipoua Forest, Omapaere, Opononi and Kaikohe on the way to Paihia. Their **Twin Coast Kauri Discovery** pass ($85) is valid for three months and covers a loop from Auckland to Paihia and back through Opononi, the Waipoua Forest and Dargaville, or vice versa. Northliner Express (☎09/307 5873 in Auckland, ☎09/438 3206 in Whangarei) run almost identical services with a similar frequency from Auckland's Downtown Airline Terminal. They sell three useful passes, all valid for a month and all requiring some form of backpacker or student ID: the **Bay of Islands Pass** ($49) covers Auckland to Kerikeri via Paihia, the **Loop Pass** ($79) which is identical to InterCity's Twin Coast Kauri Discovery, and the **Northland Freedom Pass** ($109), which adds the leg up to Kaitaia. There is also one short-range operator: Mainline Coaches (☎09/278 8070), who also serve Warkworth and continue on to Dargaville.

From Dargaville to: Auckland (2–3 daily; 3hr 15min); Opononi (3 weekly Tues, Thurs & Sun; 2hr 10min).

From Kaitaia to: Auckland (2 daily; 7hr).

From Kerikeri to: Auckland (2 daily; 5hr).

From Mangonui to: Auckland (2 daily; 6hr 30min).

From Opononi/Omapere to: Auckland (3 weekly Mon,Wed & Fri; 6hr 30min); Paihia (3 weekly Tues, Thurs & Sun; 2hr 15min), Dargaville (3 weekly Mon, Wed & Fri; 2hr 30min).

From Paihia to: Auckland via Whangarei (3–4 daily; 4hr 30min); Auckland via Opononi and Dargaville (3 weekly Mon, Wed & Fri; 8hr 15min); Kaitaia (2 daily; 2hr 10min); Kerikeri (8 daily; 20min); Mangonui (2–3 daily; 1hr 40min).

From Waipu to: Auckland (4 daily; 2hr 30min); Whangarei (4 daily; 30min).

From Warkworth to: Auckland (7–8 daily; 1hr 15min).

From Whangarei to: Auckland (6–7 daily; 3hr); Paihia (7 daily; 1hr 15min); Warkworth (6 daily; 1hr 45min).

Ferries

From Kohukohu to: Rawene (hourly; 20min).

From Opua to: Okiato (every 10–20min; 15min).

From Paihia to: Russell by passenger ferry (every 20min; 20min); by vehicular ferry (every 10–20min; 15min).

From Rawene to: Kohukohu (hourly; 20min).

Flights

From Bay of Islands (Paihia) to: Auckland (2–3 daily; 50min); Kaitaia (1 daily; 25min).

From Kaitaia to: Auckland (1–2 daily; 1hr–1hr 30min).

From Kerikeri to: Auckland (3–4 daily; 1hr).

From Whangarei to: Auckland (5–7 daily; 40min); Great Barrier Island (1 weekly; 30min).

CHAPTER THREE

WESTERN NORTH ISLAND

M uch of the **Western North Island** is ignored by visitors, who pass through the major transit centres of Hamilton and Palmerston North in a mad dash to get somewhere else. This is to do the area a disservice, however, for it contains fascinating caves; two spectacular national parks that encompass a dormant volcano and a winding river; a number of intriguing scenic reserves; a moody, isolated and rugged coast; and an extraordinary **history** of pre-European settlement and post-European conflict. This region is deeply rooted in **Maori** legend and history, for it was on the west coast at **Kawhia** that the Tainui people first landed in New Zealand. Kawhia was also the birthplace of **Te Rauparaha**, the great Maori chief who led his people from Kawhia to escape the better-armed tribes of the Waikato down the west coast to Kapiti Island and on to the South Island, pursuing his individual road to justice, fame and glory. The Waikato's **recent history** has also been a turbulent one. Containing some of the richest and most productive land in the country, it is no surprise that both Maori and *pakeha* covet its spoils.

Spreading south from the estuary of the Waikato River is a swathe of land known as **The Waikato**, bounded to the west by the crashing waves, long beaches, bluffs and dense forests of the coast and to the east by the North Island's central plateau. Dominating the region is **Hamilton**, New Zealand's largest inland city and fourth-largest overall; poised at the intersection of two major highways (SH1 and SH3), and two rail lines, virtually everywhere on the North Island is readily accessible from this sprawling hub. The most visited seaside towns are **Raglan**, which is within easy reach of a world-class surfing beach, and **Kawhia**, the first landfall of the Tainui Maori canoe and spiritual home of its people. Both nestle in sheltered and ancient green-swathed harbours, Raglan beneath the imposing **Karioi Mountain**, just north of the dark Pirongia Forest Park, Kawhia only 4km from the black-sand of **Ocean Beach**, with its hot thermal pools. **Inland**, this rich dairying and agricultural region benefits from the fecund soil scattered by long-extinct volcanoes and the natural irrigation of plentiful streams and high rainfall, where farming settlements sit on the riverbanks, taking pride in their respective traditions. Maori cultural heritage is richest in **Ngaruawahia**, home of the Maori Queen, and **Te Awamutu**, scene of some of the bloodiest battles between Maori and *pakeha*. Nearby, tranquillity is regained at **Yarndley's Bush**, one of the few remaining stands of kahikatea trees, while **Cambridge** is redolent with the air of the English home counties.

South of the Waikato is **The King Country**, which took its name from the King Movement (see box on p.214) and was the last significant area in New Zealand to succumb to the onrush of European colonization. At one time a densely forested and inhospitable hinterland, a number of stalwart communities coexist with some extraordinary natural features – most famously the **Waitomo Caves**, which offer travellers the chance to explore unusual rock formations above and below ground and marvel at glow-worm-filled caverns. South of Waitomo is the small, historically significant settle-

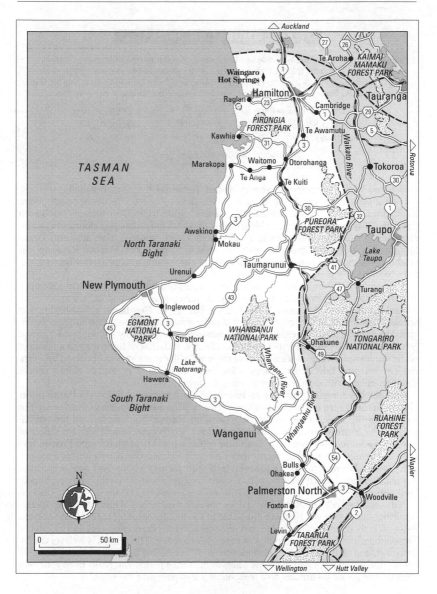

ment of **Te Kuiti,** where the leader of the King Movement sought refuge in the 1860s and these days, more prosaically, it relishes in the title of the sheep-shearing capital of New Zealand, but also has access to the lush, tall canopy of the **Pureora Forest Park**.

Further south is **Taumarunui,** a once-vibrant dairy community that now provides access to the northern end of the magnificent Whanganui River and the cross-country scenic heritage trail to the **Taranaki** region. This giant thumb-print peninsula is dominated by the symmetrical cone of **Mount Taranaki** (2518m). Perched at the centre of **Egmont National Park**, the mountain offers all but the terminal couch potato the chance to climb a long slumbering volcano, while trout-filled streams bubble up through its granular slopes, tumbling down to a dynamic coastline characterized by estuaries, black iron-sand beaches, cliffs and rocky shores. The adjacent, coast-hugging city of **New Plymouth**, with the striking **Sugar Loaf Marine Reserve** just offshore, balanced by some stimulating cultural attractions, makes a lively base for visitors to this justly popular tramping and skiing region.

The seductive **Whanganui National Park**, meanwhile, offers a gentle river adventure that makes an ideal introduction to wilderness canoeing, as you paddle past spectacular natural features and man-made follies like the **Bridge to Nowhere**, a road bridge that speaks volumes about the resistance of this unforgiving landscape to the inroads of cultivation and civilization. The estuary of the **Whanganui River** finally spills into the Tasman Sea at the city of **Wanganui**, its history intertwined with that of the river and a talisman of the successful taming of at least part of the land, with ornate streets bordered by splendid Victorian and Edwardian edifices, a fine museum and gallery, and an elderly paddle steamer, sailing with dignity and reminding the town of its past.

Another city teeming with fine architecture – and transport links – is **Palmerston North**, in the centre of the rich farming region of **Manawatu**. South of the city are the foothills of the dark, dense and moody **Tararua Range**, looming behind the coastal strip of the **Horowhenua region**, with its long windswept beaches and a string of unprepossessing retirement and commuter settlements. Museum-infested **Foxton** was once a thriving flax-weaving centre that vied with Palmerston North for regional primacy, while **Levin** is a quirky town littered with factory shops and access into the Tararua Range, which shadows the coast south towards Otaki and eventually Wellington.

Although the Western North Island does not suffer extremes of **climate**, water sports, canoeing and caving will be more enjoyable in the months leading up to Christmas and those directly after it, whereas ski and snowboard enthusiasts will want to visit Mount Taranaki during the **winter** months of June to September. The region is well served by transport, and all the major destinations are easily accessible by **bus**, **train** or **plane**. To get off the beaten track and to access walks in the forest parks, you really need your own vehicle, though local **shuttles** do a reasonable job of plugging the gaps.

Hamilton

On SH1, 136km south of Auckland and 102km northwest of Rotorua, **HAMILTON** has been dubbed "The Fountain City" owing to its predilection for water-gushing ornamentation, though a more accurate moniker might be "Transit Centre". A hub of North

Island air, rail and road routes, the town resembles nothing so much as a glorified interchange. A spread-out, predominantly suburban community on the banks of the languid green Waikato River, home to the University of Waikato, a commercial centre for local farmers, the city contains little of lasting interest to visitors. However, there is tranquillity to be found in **Hamilton Gardens** or on the riverbanks, and a rewarding half-day can easily be spent trawling the collections of the regional **Museum of Art and History**, and, as befits a city of Hamilton's size, a good deal of accommodation, diverse restaurants, nightlife and shopping.

Archeological evidence indicates that the **Tainui** settlement of **Kirikirioa** had existed on the current site of Hamilton for at least two hundred years before the **Europeans** muscled in on the act in the 1830s. The Europeans named their new settlement after **John Fane Charles Hamilton**, an officer of the Royal Navy who had died, either bravely or foolishly (depending whose interpretation you believe), at the battle of Gate Pa, near Tauranga, a few months earlier; a fictionalized account of the events leading up to his death appears in Maurice Shadbolt's excellent novel *The House of Strife* (see Contexts p.879). The **river** remained the only supply route for the city until the **railway** came in 1878, effectively opening up the country to more European immigration, farming and commercial expansion.

Arrival, information and city transport

Hamilton **airport**, 12km south, is connected to the city by Super Shuttle, which meets arrivals from Monday to Friday (Sat & Sun by arrangement; 20min; ☎07/843 7778 & 0800/727 747; $10). The **train** station is on Fraser Street in the suburb of Frankton, a twenty-minute walk west of the city centre (bus #8). Train and bus **tickets** can be bought at the Hamilton Travel Centre, on the corner of Ward Street and Anglesea Street, where InterCity and Newmans **buses** drop off.

At time of writing the Hamilton **visitor centre** is in the Hamilton Travel Centre (Mon–Fri 9am–5pm, Sat & Sun 10am–4pm; ☎07/839 3580, fax 839 3127, *www. hamiltoninfo.co.nz*) but will be moving to the corner of Anglesea Street and Bryce Street at the beginning of 2001. The **DOC office**, a few minutes' walk north at 18 London St (Mon–Fri 8.30am–4.15pm; ☎07/838 3363, fax 839 0794), like many DOC offices no longer encourages visits from the public so try to get everything you need at the visitor centre. Most of Hamilton's attractions are within walking distance of the centre, and other destinations can be reached by an extensive **local bus** network centred on Hamilton Travel Centre.

Accommodation

There is a variety of business accommodation for farm company reps in Hamilton, with **motels** clustered on Ulster and Victoria streets, and in the western and eastern suburbs of the city, but few noteworthy **B&Bs** or campsites. A dearth of inexpensive centrally located accommodation means that **hostels**, which are small to start with, fill up quickly. The YHA, now under a much–needed change of management, is the best option.

Hotels, motels and B&Bs

Bavaria Motel, 203–207 Ulster St (☎07/839 2520 & fax 839 2531, *bavaria@ihug.co.nz*). Large, comfortable units within eight minutes' walk of the city and conveniently close to a supermarket. ④.

Le Grand Hotel, cnr Victoria St & Collingwood St (☎07/839 1994, *legrandehotel@xtra.co.nz*). An elegant grand old building in the centre of town, with 38 well-designed rooms, tastefully decorated and furnished. ⑥–⑨.

Swimming Pool (1 km), Auckland (136 km) & **A**

CENTRAL HAMILTON

0   500 m

B

C

N

E   **D**

DOC Office

2

3

(From 2001)

(Current) *i*   **4**

Cinema **F**

AA Office

Waipa Delta

Museum &
Art Gallery

Train
Station

See Inset

G

St Peter's
Cathedral

Memorial
Park

*Lake
Rotoroa*

Rose Gardens &
Hamilton Gardens

i Liby

5
6
7

Wesley
Chambers

8
9
K
10

11

Anglesea
Clinic &
Pharmacy

12
14
15
16
13
19 17
18

20

Airport (12 km) & Te Awamuta (30 km)

ACCOMMODATION		RESTAURANTS, CAFÉS & BARS			
Bavaria Motel	C	The Bank Bar & Brasserie	11	Little India	16
Flying Hedgehog Backpackers	D	Barzurk	5	Loaded Hog	20
Hamilton East Tourist Court	H	Biddy Mulligan's	2	Metropolis	8
Home from Home B&B	A	Bourbon St	3	Montana	9
J's Backpackers	J	Café Hasan Baba	7	Museum Café	15
Le Grand Hotel	K	Cazbar Brasserie	10	Outback	14
Manhattan Lodge Motel	I	Cobb & Co	12	Rocket Espresso Lounge	17
Mill Lodge Motor Inn	E	Cue Bar	13	La Shiraz	1
Novotel Yainui	F	Diggers	19	Tables on the River	4
Parklands Travel Hotel/Motel	G	JBC	6	Turtle Lake Café	21
YHA Hamilton	B	Judder Bar	18		

Home from Home B&B, 12 Galbraith Ave, Beerscourt (☎ & fax 07/849 2788,). A comfortable bolt-hole in the friendly home of a South African family, deep in suburbia, about twenty minutes' walk from Victoria Street. ④.

Manhattan Lodge Motel, 218 Grey St (☎ & fax 07/856 3785). Friendly, quiet and agreeable place set well back from the road, just a couple of minutes' walk from restaurants and shops in the suburb of Hamilton East. ④.

Mill Lodge Motor Inn, 135 Ulster St (☎07/839 3143 & fax 839 4361). Restful, self-contained studio and one- and two-bedroom units near the city centre. ⑤.

Novotel Tainui, 7 Alma St (☎07/838 1366, fax 838 1367, *hamilton@novotel.co.nz*). A posh comfortable spot with all the usual facilities. ⑥.

Parklands Travel Hotel/Motel, 24 Bridge St (☎07/838 2461). Simple, inexpensive and clean hotel rooms and studio-style motel units. Rooms ③, units ④.

Hostels and campsites

Flying Hedgehog Backpackers, 8 Liverpool St (☎ & fax 07/839 3906). Small friendly hostel, with dorms and doubles (neither with lockable doors, although there's a security door into the building) but cursed with a small kitchen; free extras include an evening glass of wine or beer; videos, and lifts to hitching points. Dorms ①, rooms ②.

Hamilton East Tourist Court, 61 Cameron Rd (☎ & fax 07/856 6220). Spacious site adjacent to a food store about 3km from the city centre. Tent sites ① for two, cabins ②, tourist flats ③.

J's Backpackers, 8 Grey St (☎07/856 8934, *bookme@jsbackpackers.co.nz*). Amiable place which has now been considerably extended, run by a couple who offer highly individual tours, including kayaking on the Waikato (4hr; $40, 90min; $15, pick-ups arranged if you can't paddle back upstream). Dorms ①, rooms ③.

Parklands Travel Hotel/Motel, 24 Bridge St (☎07/838 2461). Basic backpacker dorms and doubles, alongside motel-style accommodation (see above). Dorms ①, backpacker doubles ②.

YHA Hamilton, 1190 Victoria St (☎07/838 0009, fax 838 0837). This is a much improved hostel in a large, old house with airy rooms, well-equipped kitchen, an excellent view from the terrace and superb grounds that lead down to the river. Dorms ①, rooms ②.

The City

The main drag is **Victoria Street**, which runs northwest to southeast along the west bank of the tree-lined, dawdling Waikato River, and parallel to Anglesea Street. The area immediately around Victoria Street contains almost everything of interest in Hamilton.

Much of the city is subsumed by low, suburban architecture, but a short walk along Victoria Street from its southeastern end as far as the junction with London Street reveals structures of classical splendour and endeavour. Built in 1915 of rough-cast concrete, **St Peter's Cathedral** is actually modelled on a fifteenth-century Norfolk church. As you progress north past the grand Victorian-era bank buildings (now mostly restaurants and retail outlets), the post office, some splendid old hotels and municipal buildings, you begin to discern the prosperity that farming and trade have brought to the area. The 1924 **Wesley Chambers**, on the corner of Collingwood Street, is an imposing edifice, influenced by the architecture of boom-time Chicago and embellished with wrought-iron balconies. Squeezed in between, inside or disguised by these august facades is evidence of more recent economic prosperity, with uninspiring offices, run-of-the-mill plazas, malls, shopping court-yards and car parks.

Waikato Museum of Art and History

The best thing in Hamilton is the **Waikato Museum of Art and History** (daily 10am–4.30pm; $2), which occupies a challenging modern construction on Grantham

Street, opposite Hood Street. The open airy spaces combine two previously separate institutions – the historic museum and the art gallery – in a functional and pleasing large-windowed building, stepping down to the river on five levels. The vast collection of Australasian paintings and photographs is augmented by objects relating to Tainui culture, including woven flax, domestic items, tools, ritual artefacts and fine examples of wood and stone carving. Among items relating to European settlement and development, one of the more interesting is the *Bullock Webster Diary*, which contains amusing cartoons of long-dead settlers and accounts of their dealings with the author/artist. Most exhibitions are rotated, although a magnificent war canoe (*Te Winika*), contemporary Tainui carvings plus carved elements from the entry to a meeting house, and *tukutuku* (decorative panels made from flax, leather and wood) are on permanent display. Also worth checking out is *Tainui, Ngati Koroki* the detailed wood-carved model of a *waka* by Fred Graham.

A further feature is the Excite Exhibition ($5), a hands-on series of science displays intended for children and school groups. Of more interest within the building is the **Waikato Film Theatre**, which has special screenings of arthouse films and shows connected with the exhibitions, usually advertised in the local paper, and a relaxing **café** with tasty snacks (see "Eating and drinking", below).

Parks and gardens

From the museum, a pretty riverside **walk**, via Victoria Bridge and Memorial Drive, leads to **Memorial Park**, where the pitiful remains of the *Rangiriri*, an 1864 sternwheel steamer, gaze longingly at the river. In a much healthier state, the old paddle steamer *Waipa Delta* still **cruises** sedately along the Waikato River from the jetty a little way south: midday cruises run from 12.30pm ($30, including lunch); afternoon cruises begin at 3pm ($20, including tea); and dinner cruises run from 7pm ($45, including smorgasbord); call ☎07/854 9415 for details and bookings. It's all rather leisurely and you'll probably have more fun cruising the river in a **kayak** from J's *Backpackers* (see previous page).

From Memorial Park, a footpath heads south a couple of kilometres to the extensive **Hamilton Gardens** (daily 7.30am–dusk; free), which can also be reached by road across the Cobham Bridge. The gardens' visitor centre (daily 9am–4pm), close to the Turtle Lake and opposite the café, stocks free maps. The formal gardens boast spectacular massed displays of roses, tropical plants, chrysanthemums, rhododendrons and cacti, while the authentic Japanese Garden's pavilion overlooks ordered gardens full of Zen and classic scroll features intended to encourage contemplation. Along similar lines is the intricate Chinese Scholar's Garden, which represents an idealized world characterized by walls, a courtyard, and carefully chosen combinations of plants, rock arrangements, bridges and ponds. Although equally artificial, the Turtle Lake manages to look more natural and is well worth strolling round, or at least observing from the terrace in front of the *Turtle Lake Café* (see "Eating and drinking", below).

Eating and drinking

With very few exceptions, the best places to eat and drink are concentrated on or around Victoria Street. In recent years Hamilton has accumulated a great variety of restaurants offering quality food and value for money, some small moody cafés, and one or two trendy places where you can pay an arm and a leg for a drink.

Cafés

Café Hasan Baba, 228 Victoria St. A cheap and cheerful café serving authentic Turkish and Middle Eastern dishes. Dinner daily, plus Sun lunch; BYO.

Cobb and Co., Victoria St, near junction with Collingwood St. Predictable, reliable place for inexpensive breakfasts and simple but substantial meals. Daily 7.30am–10pm; licensed.

Turtle Lake Café, Hamilton Gardens, Cobham Drive. Tasty and imaginative food, such as banana yoghurt curry, lamb shanks tagine and Cajun-style fish, for under $25. Other pluses are outdoor seating, floor-to-ceiling windows and a simple modern bar. Daily 11.30am–2pm & 6–9.30pm.

Metropolis, 211 Victoria St. A hip all-day café that serves an eclectic range of tasty food for lunch and dinner (closed Mon & Sun evenings), including a broad range of veggie and vegan options and some good coffee and liqueurs. Dished up with a depressing lip-curled surliness that can be off putting. Licensed & BYO.

Museum Café, Museum of Art and History, Grantham St. The lunches are reasonably priced, dinners more expensive; all good quality trad Kiwi, Mediterranean and Asian influenced food in a relaxed and stylish setting. Lunch & dinner daily, plus weekend brunch.

Rocket Espresso Lounge, 181 Victoria St at cnr with Hood St. This relaxed, intimate, and truly individual coffee house has an array of ugly blue chairs, excellent beverages, tasty light snacks and meals from all over the globe at reasonable prices and is considerably more friendly than the main opposition. Mon–Sat 9am–5pm. Also worth looking out for is *Circa Espresso*, 385 Greys St, run by the same people and a good watering hole if you're on the other side of the river.

Restaurants

The Bank Bar and Brasserie, cnr Hood St & Victoria St. An old bank has been given a new lease of life by a cleanly decorated interior with lots of wood, loud music and the feel of a big-city bistro. This is a firm favourite with local wage slaves, who relish the substantial snacks and main meals of steak, fish and grills. Sun–Thurs 11am–11pm, Fri–Sat 11am–3am.

Barzurk Gourmet Pizza Bar, 250 Victoria St. Excellent pizzas with a variety of toppings ($15–19). Lunch Wed–Sun, dinner daily.

Cazbar Brasserie, The Marketplace, off Hood St. Stylish, dinner/night spot with more champagne chic than its neighbours. Snacks are served all day, and globally inspired dinner mains go for under $20. Live music Tues–Sat until 3am; licensed.

Little India, 4 Alexander St (☎07/838 1620). Part of a NZ chain serving good quality Indian food including tasty veggie options, at reasonable prices in a modern airy setting. Daily for dinner, Mon–Fri for lunch, licensed & BYO.

Montana, 131 Victoria St. A traditional, value-for-money place popular with city-visiting farmers, sales reps and the blue-rinse brigade. What it lacks in finesse, it makes up for with excellent meat and seafood.

La Shiraz, 851 Victoria St (☎07/838 1960). Popular tandoori and roti restaurant (book dinner Fri & Sat), with authentic banquets for under $20. Dinner daily, lunch Thurs & Fri; licensed & BYO.

Tables on the River, 12 Alam St (☎07/839 6555). Sophisticated, expensive and popular wine bar and restaurant capitalizing on the fad for "fusion" cuisine (a melting pot of Pacific-Rim, European and Asian influences).

Nightlife and entertainment

Many of the restaurants and bars double up as **drinking** venues, some branching out into live **music** and dancing on Friday and Saturday nights, while theatres often act as concert venues for bands, travelling cabaret and classical music. The Village 7 multiplex **cinema**, in the Centreplace Mall on Ward Street, shows the usual mainstream releases, while the Waikato Film Society occasionally screens arthouse and more obscure films at the Museum of Art and History, Grantham Street. Check the daily *Waikato Times* (80¢, 90¢ Sat) for details of these and other happenings; comprehensive events and **entertainment listings** are in the Friday and Saturday editions.

The Bank Bar and Brasserie, cnr Hood St & Victoria St. A hugely popular nightspot on Fridays and Saturdays from around 10pm, when the DJ-instigated dancing starts.

Biddy Mulligans Irish Pub, 742 Victoria St. Live Irish-sounding bands on Fri, Sat & Sun nights, accompanied by imported and home-grown beer. Daily 11am–midnight.

Bourbon Street, 6 Bryce St. One of the most atmospheric drinking and dancing spots, this tardis-like place runs the gamut – with prolonged happy hours on Wednesdays (4pm–midnight), dancing and shows on Fridays, comedy and live music on Saturdays, and laid-back blues on Sunday.

Cue Bar, adjacent to the *Outback* (see below), a glorified pool hall with loud music and a big bar that stays open until 3am.

Diggers, 17 Hood St. A real drinkers' den with a long kauri bar that's open till midnight and provides welcome respite from the trendy city bars. It's also the liveliest place on a Sunday night with regular live gigs and a great atmosphere.

JBC (short for *Jazz Blues Concept Bar and Café*), 270 Victoria St, 10m up the little alley opposite Collingwood St. The most relaxed, hippest and entertaining of the night spots cum bars with a real talent for digging up alternative acts, comedy, jazz, blues and off-the-wall games as well as serving good veggie food. Plays cool music and provides a home for dreadful Seventies furniture. Open late but closed Sun.

Judder Bar, a couple of doors down from the *Rocket Espresso Lounge* on Hood St is this stylish bar that often contains lots of suits but is OK nonetheless.

Loaded Hog, 27 Hood St. One of the most attractive bars in the city, this large double-gabled building is dotted with rural New Zealand memorabilia and has tables on the street out front. The usual array of excellent home-brewed ales is supplemented by a broad selection from around the country and full menu. Dinner daily, lunch daily; DJ-cranked dancing Fri & Sat night.

Outback Inn, The Marketplace, off Hood St. Studeny drinking hole with bare wooden floors, a good selection of beers and some alcohol-absorbing snacks. DJ at weekends.

Listings

AA (Automobile Association) 295 Barton St (☎07/839 1397).

American Express Calder and Lawson Travel Ltd, 455 Grey St (☎07/856 9009).

Banks and foreign exchange Both National and Trust Bank have branches on Victoria St, as do most of the other major national banks; all offer exchange facilities (see also listings for American Express and Thomas Cook).

Bike rental R&R Sport, 943 Victoria St (☎07/839 3755 & 0800/777 767), charges about $25 a day for a mountain bike.

Bookshops Dimensions Women's Bookshop, 266 Victoria St; The Government Bookshop, 33 King St; Browsers, 221 Victoria St, Crows Nest Books, Arcadia Building, Worley Place and Nonesuch, 192 Victoria St, both buy and sell secondhand books.

Buses Local buses run from the Hamilton Travel Centre, cnr Ward St & Anglesea St (☎07/834 3457); a full timetable ($1) is available there or at the visitor centre. Local bus companies also run scheduled services to the neighbouring communities of Huntly, Paeroa, Raglan, Thames and Te Awamutu; Roadcat Transport (☎02/594 9440) runs to and from Auckland as do the Little Kiwi Bus Company (☎0800/759 999).

Car rental Budget (☎07/838 3585); Cambridge Car Rentals (☎07/823 0990); Hertz (☎07/839 4824); Rent-a-Dent (☎07/839 1049); Waikato Car Rentals (☎07/855 0094).

Glasses Eyewear, cnr Ward St & Worley Place in the Downtown Plaza where you can buy or have specs adjusted at low prices.

Internet Access Places in town include the central Hamilton library, *Central Park* (Liverpool Street) and *Houston Internet Café* (Collingwood Street), both of which operate pretty much within office hours.

Library Central Hamilton library, Garden Place on Victoria St, has Internet access.

Medical treatment Southern Cross Hospital, cnr Von Tempsky St & Beale St; Anglesea Clinic and Pharmacy, cnr Anglesea St & Thackery St (daily 7.30am–11pm) offers consultations and fills prescriptions.

Post offices The main post office is in Post Office Mall, Victoria St; in addition, post shops are located on London St and Victoria St.

Swimming Te Rapa Waterworld, Garnett Ave (Mon–Thur, 6am–9pm, Fri–Sun, 9am–9pm; $2.50).

Taxis The principal taxi rank is outside the Hamilton Travel Centre, or call Dial a Cab (☎07/847 5050 & 0800/342 522).

Thomas Cook Garden Place (☎07/838 0149).

Trains Information and tickets are available at the train station on Fraser St, Hamilton Travel Centre (see below) and the visitor centre.

Travel agents Hamilton Travel Centre, cnr Anglesea St & Ward St (☎07/856 4579), deals with national and international travel arrangements, as do the Air New Zealand Travel Centre, 25 Ward St (☎07/839 9835), and STA, 42 Ward St (☎07/839 1833).

Around Hamilton

The area north of Hamilton is largely **farmland**, with little to delay even the most inquisitive explorer, save for **Ngaruawahia**, home of the Maori monarch and scene of the signing of the Raupatu Land Settlement, whereby the New Zealand government agreed to compensate the Tainui for land confiscated in the 1860s. To the southeast of the city, the genteel English charms of **Cambridge** contrast with the turbulent history of the former garrison township of **Te Awamutu.**

The principal attraction on the sand-swathed **coast** to the west of Hamilton is **Raglan**, a surfing Mecca with a curious siren-like quality that lulls visitors into staying longer than they had intended, while further south along the robust and frowning coastline is **Kawhia**, a moribund little community on the site of the Tainui people's first landfall in *Aotearoa* – and still their spiritual home. The **beaches** south of Kawhia are typically black sand, steeped in isolation and lashed by wind and sea, though a little comfort can be taken in the **thermal pools** that bubble up at the shoreline close to Kawhia. Sandwiched between Raglan and Kawhia lies the **Pirongia Forest Park**, though the best access is on the landward side from the township of Te Awamutu. South of Raglan and within the forest park, a number of **walks** lead to viewpoints atop wind-buffeted hills, from which you can truly appreciate the grisly, rough-hewn coastline to the north and south.

Ngaruawahia and around

The most interesting and culturally significant spot north of Hamilton is **NGARU-AWAHIA**, 18km away on SH1, a farming centre at the junction of the Waikato and Waipa rivers. Both rivers were important Maori canoe routes, and the area has long held great significance for Maori: it is here that the **King Movement** (see box overleaf) has its roots, and the town is home to the current monarch, Te Arikinui Dame Te Atairangikaahu. The town's Maori character is evident in the strikingly carved and decorated **Mahinarangi House**, which houses the Maori throne; **Turongo House**, the official residence of the present queen; and the Kimi-ora Cultural Complex, with its spectacular mural and a conspicuous tetrahedral roof. It is easy to recognize the marae by the pa-like fence around it with wonderfully carved red posts every three metres along River Road. All the buildings sit within the marae's grounds, formally open to the public only on **Regatta Day** (the closest Saturday to March 17) when a unique regatta takes place at the confluence of the two rivers, featuring traditional Maori canoes, hurdle races and a parade of great war canoes before the Maori queen. You can make enquiries at the marae office, River Road on the north side of the main river bridge entering the town (☎07/824 5189), but if you're not there around the time of the regatta don't hold out too much hope of being allowed in. On the opposite side of SH1 from the marae is **Turangawaewae House**, Eyre Street, the building intended to be the Maori parliament, which was opened in 1920 and is distinctive because of its intricate, red-painted wood carvings on a cream facade.

Twenty-three kilometres west of Ngaruawahia, at the junction with SH22, are the popular though slightly run-down **Waingaro Hot Springs**, Waingaro Road (daily

---

THE KING MOVEMENT

Before Europeans arrived on the scene, Maori loyalty was solely to their immediate family and tribe, but wrangles with acquisitive European settlers led many tribes to discard age-old feuds in favour of a **common crusade** against the *pakeha*. Initially a response to poor communication and administration, **Maori nationalism** hardened in the face of blatantly unjust decisions and increasing pressure to "sell" their ancestral lands.

In 1856, the influential Otaki Maori sought a chief who might **unite** the disparate tribes against the Europeans, and in 1858 the Waikato, Taupo and some other tribes (largely originating from the Tainui canoe) chose **Te Wherowhero** as their leader. Taking the title of Potatau I, the newly elected king established himself at **Ngarauwahia** – to this day the heartland of the **King Movement**. The principal tenet of the movement was to resist the appropriation of Maori land and to provide a basis for a degree of self-government. Whether out of a genuine misunderstanding of these aims or for reasons of pure economic expediency, the settlers interpreted the formation of the movement as an act of rebellion – despite the fact that Queen Victoria was included in its prayers – and tension heightened. The situation escalated into **armed conflict** later in 1858 when the Waitara Block near New Plymouth was confiscated from its Maori owners. The fighting spread throughout the central North Island: the King Movement won a notable victory at Gate Pa, in the Bay of Plenty, but were eventually overwhelmed at Te Ranga. Seeing the wars as an opportunity to **settle old scores**, some Maori tribes sided with the British and, in a series of battles along the Waikato, forced the kingites further and further south, until a crushing blow was struck at Orakau in 1864. The king and his followers fled south of the Puniu River into an area that, by virtue of their presence, became known as the **King Country**.

They remained there, almost devoid of all European contact, until 1881, when **King Tawhiao**, who had succeeded to the throne in 1860, made peace. Gradually the followers of the King Movement drifted back to **Ngaruawahia**. Although by no means supported by all Maori, the loose coalition of the contemporary King Movement plays an important role in the current reassessment of Maori–*pakeha* relations, and the reigning Maori queen, **Te Arikinui Dame Te Atairangikaahu**, has been the recipient of many state and royal visits.

9am–10pm; $6), a large pool complex based around a series of natural springs, which tends to get busy on summer weekends. Nearby *Worsp's Farm* (☎07/825 4515; ③ self-catering), north of the springs via Matira Road, offers **accommodation** and is the base for the **Hole Adventure**, an enjoyable four-hour caving, riding the flying fox (zip wire) and abseiling trip with a "Jurassic stroll" through prehistoric caves and ancient bushland ($95, minimum 4 people). They also offer a ninety-minute caving stroll ($25, no minimum number of people).

Continuing north, SH1 cuts an almost uninterrupted straight line to Auckland, passing through the depressing and flat town of **Huntly**, 16km further north, famous for open-cast coal mines and the largest power station in the country, whose twin 150m-high chimneys dominate the townscape. There is a tour of the power station (daily on request; free) for real enthusiasts.

Cambridge

About 24km east of Hamilton on SH1 is **CAMBRIDGE**, marooned in a broad agricultural belt renowned for stud farms. With a modicum of charm, Cambridge is attractive in a bucolic sort of a way, boasting a village green, tree-lined avenues and a picturesque sunken lake, **Te Koutu Lake**, five minutes' walk from the centre. Around the lakeside, reached from Albert Street, are picnic areas and tracks through stands of tall chestnut and oak trees. The most significant building in Cambridge is **St Andrew's Anglican Church**, on the corner of Victoria Street and SH1, opposite the entrance to Te Koutu Park. A Victorian construction with a tall steeple, the church hides a fine dark-wood interior and original stained-glass windows.

Another good reason to visit Cambridge is Frank Vosper's **New Zealand Horse Magic**, 6km southeast of the town on SH1, near Karapiro. Set in lush, gently rolling countryside with lots of trees and well-manicured lawns, the stud conducts interesting and informative tours (☎07/827 8118; 10.30am; 1hr; $12; casual visits outside tour times, $5) that include a show jumping and dressage demonstration. There is also the opportunity for a short stint in the saddle.

Practicalities

Local **buses** (#20) from Hamilton stop on Duke Street in the centre of town, while both InterCity and Newmans services stop at the Cambridge Travel Centre, Alpha Street. The **visitor centre** is on Queen Street, near the Victoria Street roundabout (Mon–Fri 9am–5pm; ☎07/823 3456, fax 823 3457).

Among the many places to eat in Cambridge, four stand out. *Alphaz*, 72 Alpha St (lunch & dinner daily), is a spacious plant-strewn **restaurant** and bar with an attractive outdoor courtyard and excellent snacks and meals. Much more typical of Cambridge is the pleasant *Fran's Deli Café*, 62 Victoria St (Mon–Sat 11am–5pm), where you can grab simple **snacks** and light meals for under $10, while enjoying local art displayed on the walls. *Sazarac Café*, 35 Duke St (BYO), offers a selection of coffees and fresh juices, a snack menu for $10 and under, a big all-day breakfast for under $10, and specials such as the Big-Texburger and veggie burger for around $15. The last and by far the most swanky is *Souter House*, 19 Victoria St (Nov–Feb daily lunch & dinner, March–Oct Mon–Sat dinner only; licensed; ☎07/827 3610), a sumptuous silver-service restaurant in an elegant 1878 house.

Te Awamutu and around

The small town of **TE AWAMUTU**, 30km south of Hamilton on SH3, is a placid place, surrounded by rolling hills, hedgerowed dairy pasture and peat lakes, all overlooked by mounts Pirongia, Maungatautari and Kakepuku.

Local Maori trace their descent to the Tainui canoe and by the nineteenth century there was a heavy Maori presence on the land, as evidenced by the many pa sites in the loops of rivers and on steep hill tops – the earthwork foundations of which are still visible today. During the 1863 **New Zealand Wars**, Te Awamutu was a garrison for government forces, and one of the most famous battles of the conflict was fought at the hastily constructed Orakau pa, where 2000 soldiers were held at bay for three days by just 300 Maori, an incident touchingly remembered in the local church.

The Town

Te Awamutu is known for its extensive **rose gardens**, on the corner of Arawata Street and Gorst Avenue, which are at their best between November and May. The town also basks in reflected glory as the birthplace of Neil and Tim Finn. Fans of Split Enz and Crowded House will be unable to resist a self-guided tour (leaflet from the visitor centre) around places of significance in the **Finn brothers'** formative years.

A poignant reminder of the New Zealand Wars can be seen in **St John's Church**, on the opposite side of Arawata Street from the rose gardens and the visitor centre (where you pick up the key; free). Built as a garrison church in 1841, St John's was spared as other European buildings burned around it, because the Maori chieftainess, Te Paea Potatau, had placed her *mana* upon it. A tribute inside the church, written in Maori and

English, is from the British Regiment of Foot, the 65th, honouring their Maori enemies, many of whom crawled, under fire, onto the battlefield to give water to their wounded British foes. The church also contains one of the oldest figurative, painted stained-glass windows in New Zealand.

Te Awamutu Museum (Mon–Fri 10am–4pm, Sat & Sun 10am–1pm; free), is on Roche Street, about ten minutes' walk west of the visitor centre. Alongside an excellent collection of early Maori artefacts (tools, clothes, carving and household relics), there are displays about the European settlers and the New Zealand Wars. The museum's pride and joy is *Uenuku*, a striking darkwood carving and sacred relic of the Tainui people, said to have been carried to New Zealand from Hawaiki in the Tainui canoe; the carving is a representation of a traditional spirit or god as a rainbow.

Around Te Awamutu

There is little to stop for along the straight highway north of town, except the atmospheric **Yarndley's Bush** (dawn–dusk; free), one of the largest remaining stands of the towering kahikatea on the North Island. To reach the bush reserve, turn off SH3 3km north of Te Awamautu, on to the Ngaroto Road and continue for 1500m to the signposted entrance. A **loop walk** (20min) winds through the reserve, past huge root buttresses, and midway along, a raised platform gives you a bird's eye view of the constantly moving canopy. The drainage of marshland for farming and the use of odourless kahikatea wood to make boxes to transport butter overseas, has hastened the demise of these magnificent native trees.

Dominating the landscape to the west of Te Awamutu is **Pirongia Mountain** (959m), scarred by redoubt trenches from the New Zealand Wars. The peak lies within the **Pirongia Forest Park**, an area traversed by a series of interesting nature **walks** described in the DOC *Pirongia Forest Park* leaflet ($1, from Te Awamutu visitor centre). Of the two best **summit tracks**, the more rewarding and easier route is the Mahaukura Track (6km; 4hr), from the education centre at the end of Grey Road, 16km west of Te Awamutu. The more direct (and steeper) Wharauroa Route (5km; 3.5hr), begins at O' Shea Road, 3km west of the township of Pirongia.

Practicalities

Trains on the main Auckland–Wellington line stop at Station Road, about 2km west of the visitor centre. All the **bus** companies drop off at Law's Garage, 90 Mahoe St which also acts as a ticket office. The **visitor centre**, on Gorst Avenue, near the corner with Arawata Street (Mon–Fri 9am–4.30pm, Sat & Sun 10am–3pm; ☎07/871 3259, *www.teawamutu.gen.nz, theteam@teawamutu.co.nz*), and everything in town is within fifteen minutes' walk of here. Te Awamutu's **accommodation** and eating options are limited, to say the least. A safe bet, just a few minutes' walk from the visitor centre are the clean, comfortable serviced units at the *Road Runner Motel*, 141 Bond St (☎07/871 7420; camping $9, cabins ②, units ④) which has a campsite and cabins. Aside from the usual ranks of fast-food joints, try *Robert Harris*, Arawata Street, for a good-value **breakfast**; *Taylor's*, 414 Greenhill Drive, especially for its silver service **lunch**; *Salvador's* at 50 Alexandra St for coffee, soup and pastries; and either *Burns House*, upstairs at 55 Alexandra St, or the *Rose and Thorn*, 32 Arawata St, for inexpensive and generous **dinners**.

Raglan and around

Following the gently undulating contours of the land west of Hamilton for 48km, SH23 leads to **RAGLAN**, a tiny beach town that's as far west as you can go without getting wet. The centre of the community is on Bow Street, bordered by banks, a selection of shops and a garage, and with a central reservation lined with palm trees. These days it's much busier than of old, principally because Raglan's famed among **surfers** for having the best left-handed break in the world, creating perfect board-riding conditions: the finest waves are generally to be found at **Manu Bay** and **Whale Bay**, 8km south of town on Whaanga Road.

Most of the settlement lies around the southern side of the large and picturesque **Raglan Harbour**, with its long sandy beaches, sparkling ocean and lush green vegetation, in the shadow of **Karioi Mountain** to the southeast. **Maori** history recounts the journey of the great migratory canoe *Tainui* south along the West Coast until Mount Karioi loomed in the far distance. They travelled towards it for a very long time, but when they reached the mouth of the harbour a bar blocked their way, so they named the harbour *Whaingaroa* ("long pursuit") and paddled on to *Aotea* ("Kawhia Harbour"), where they could finally land. A derivation of Whaingaroa, Whangaroa was the name used for the harbour until 1855, when it was renamed Raglan, after the officer who led the Charge of the Light Brigade.

Housed in an old police station, the **Raglan Museum**, Wainui Street (Sat & Sun only 1–3.30pm; donation requested), has a modest local history collection. For a more colourful version of local lore, you'd do better to hop aboard a **Raglan Harbour Cruise** (☎07/825 0300; on request; 90min; $15; book ahead Dec–March), which leaves from the jetty at the bottom of Bow Street. The skipper keeps passengers amused with a seemingly endless string of amusing facts and fictions woven around the historic sites the boat passes. The trip also takes in the so-called pancake rocks, sedimentary limestone formations which appear to be made of a pliable dough. With the increased economic wealth of the town, as it exploits the regular visitors, has come an influx of alternative art, tat and jewellery outlets, of which the most worthwhile is Show Off, 2 Bow St, a harbour of handmade danglies, rings and bracelets.

Walks around Raglan

In the **Karioi Range**, there are two one-day tracks to the **summit** of Mount Karioi (755m), both steep in places but well worth it for the views of the mouth of Raglan Harbour and up and down the storm-battered coast. The best place to start is at the **Te Toto Gorge** (4km; 4hr, one-way), 12km south of Raglan, off Whaanga Road. The path starts opposite an ocean-jutting point and heads up the gorge. After a strenuous and difficult climb within a cliff-lined cut to a lookout, the final walk to the summit is considerably easier. The alternative **Wairake Track** (3.5km; 3hr one-way) is shorter, steeper, and slightly less scenic, tackling the landward side of the mountain from Karioi Road.

Inland, a much easier walk leads to the **Bridal Veil Falls**, hidden in dense native bush 23km southeast of Raglan. Water plummets 55m down a sheer rock face into a green pool; some droplets evaporate before they hit the bottom, creating a shimmering veil, adorned with ethereal rainbows in sunny weather. From the Kawhia Road, a signpost indicates the track to the falls, which is about a ten-minute stroll beside a small stream.

Practicalities

Buses (#23) from Hamilton run four times daily (Mon–Sat; 1hr; about $5; ☎07/856 7184), stopping outside the **visitor centre** at the bottom of Bow Street (April–Oct daily 10am–4pm; Nov–May Mon–Fri 9am–5pm, Sat & Sun 10am–4pm; ☎07/825 0556). Raglan Harbour Cruises run a **water taxi** service (☎07/825 0300) to various points around the bay. For explorations further afield, you can either walk or cadge a lift for despite the town's growth it no longer has a taxi or bike rental service. You can however **rent surf gear** from the Raglan Surf Company and Lift Off Surf Shop, both in the centre of town near the visitor centre. The shops are open daily (9am–5pm) and board rental prices vary according to season.

ACCOMMODATION

The best place to stay in town is the small but exceptional and friendly *Raglan Backpackers*, 6 Nero St (☎07/825 0515; dorms ①, rooms ②), a clean and comfortable **hostel** laid out around a courtyard and backing on to a beach, a mere minute's walk from the visitor centre; they also rent **kayaks** for crossing the harbour ($5 for 2hr, free if staying at the hostel) and offer **surf lessons** (90min; $15 including wetsuit and board). More idiosyncratic accommodation is on offer at *Raglan Wagon Cabins*, Whaanga Road, about 2km south of Raglan (☎07/825 8268; dorms ①, rooms ②), a collection of brightly painted, sometimes grubby, converted **train carriages** set on top of a windswept hill with panoramic views. A little off the beaten track, but with superb views, is Marcus Vernon's **farmstay** (☎07/825 6892, fax 825 6896; dorms $40 per person including breakfast, rooms ④, the house ⑦), 334 Houchen Rd. Head 8km east of Raglan on SH23 and then about 6km up Kawhia Falls Road, turn left on to Houchen Road, and the house is about another 3km up a farm track at the end of the road; pickups can be arranged from the Bridal Veil Falls. Rooms are rustic but clean, and you can either go your own way or muck in with Marcus – dinner by arrangement; **horse treks** are available (1hr $25; 2hr $35; Bridal Veil $40; moonlight trek $50) through Magic Mountain Horse Trekking, also run by Marcus. A large number of **holiday homes** are available through the visitor centre (see previous page), but they only make economic sense if you're in a large group and staying for at least a week. Otherwise quite a few **B&Bs** have opened up in town, mostly up the hill away from the bay: the best is *Luxury Retreat*, 6 Upper Wainui Rd (☎07/825 8684; ④).

EATING AND DRINKING

The explosion of surfers and travellers means visitors are spoiled for choice when it comes to eating and drinking in Raglan. Perhaps the finest place is *Vinnie's*, Wainui Road, near the junction with Bow Street (lunch & dinner daily; BYO), which trailblazed the café scene hereabouts. It has enjoyed a renaissance and is a great place to enjoy good fish, steaks and cakes at agreeable prices. Next in the pecking order is *Molasses*, 10 Bow St, a bright comfortable bar/café offering excellent coffee, muffins, fry ups and Internet access. Otherwise there's *Tongue and Groove*, Bow Street diagonally opposite *Molasses*, where they have **live music** and a snacky free-range/organic menu; or the *Black Rock Café* in the *Harbour View Hotel*, Bow Street (daily 10am–midnight, closed Mon & Tues May–Nov; licensed), a good spot to eat lunch or dinner though sometimes it's a bit dead. One really good venue for **live entertainment** at weekends, despite the fact that the outside looks like a Darby and Joan club, is the *Raglan Club*, adjacent to the garage, where they get some surprisingly good bands and very lively evenings.

Kawhia

The sleepy, unspectacular settlement of **KAWHIA**, 55km south of Raglan, can be reached via the scenic but at times hair-raising Whaanga Road – be prepared for a 30km unsealed section – which passes the Bridal Veil Falls (see previous page), or by the more widely used inland route, which detours around the eastern edge of Pirongia Forest Park, entering town on SH31. Perched on the northern side of the large Kawhia Harbour, Kawhia's resident population of 450 swells to 4000 in the summer, swamped by holidaying Kiwi families, who flock to the Ocean Beach and its **hot springs**.

Kawhia is the spiritual home of the **Tainui** people, whose *waka* (canoe) landed here in 1350, according to the legend of the Great Migration from Hawaiki. The Tainui were members of the bird cult, *Korotangi*, represented by a carved bird on the prow of their canoe, which reputedly warned of impending disaster or misfortune. As it happened, the sea in and around Kawhia Harbour was so bountiful that the Tainui lived on its shores for some three hundred years, until tribal battles over the rich fishing grounds forced them inland. In 1821, after constant attacks by the better-armed Waikato Maori, the great Tainui chief Te Rauparaha led his people to the relative safety of Kapiti Island.

With the arrival of **European** settlers and missionaries in the 1830s, Kawhia became a highly prosperous port, providing a gateway to the fertile King Country, although its fortunes declined in the early years of the twentieth century, owing to its unsuitability for deep-draft ships. These days the settlement is known throughout New Zealand for annual **whale-boat races** (January 1), when eleven-metre, five-crew whaling boats are rowed across the bay.

The Town & around

The town itself is little more than a couple of petrol stations, a handful of combined shops and cafés, and a quaint little museum, all strung along Jervois Street and SH31 (the only road into town). The **Kawhia Museum** (open by arrangement; ☎07/871 0714, 871 0808 & 871 0161; free), on the waterfront beside the wharf, at the end of Jervois Street, reveals much about Maori culture and early European settlers, augmented by an extensive photographic collection. One of the highlights of the museum is an original kauri whaleboat built in the 1880s, although the whaling station it worked from was a commercial failure.

The **Tainui canoe** is buried on a grassy knoll above the beautifully carved and painted **Maketu Marae**; *Hani* and *Puna* stones mark its stern and prow. Of particular significance to the Tainui people is the pohutukawa tree, *Tangi te Korowhiti*, to which the canoe was moored when it first landed; the tree still stands at the end of the footpath where it joins Kaora Street. Maketu Marae is a short walk (about 800m) along a waterfront footpath from the museum, where you should seek permission to enter the marae but there may be no-one willing to show you around.

On Ocean Beach, the **Te Puia Hot Springs** bubble up from beneath the black sand between half and low tides (check times at the museum or in any of the local stores). The protocol is to dig a hole to sit in: shovels can be borrowed from the general store for a $5 deposit, but be warned that the black sand gets very hot and can be uncomfortable on bare feet. The climb over the sand dunes on your way to the springs is rewarding in its own right, revealing views of Mount Karioi to the north and Albatross Point to the south. The car park is at the end of the unsealed Taunui/Kawhia Forest Road 4km from the town. If you want to **cruise** around the harbour then try Phil and Lissa Skipworth (☎07/871 0149; about $12), or Dove Charters (☎07/870 3493; $55 a day, $35 a night).

From Kawhia it is possible to continue along the coast and then cut east through the backdoor to Waitomo (see p.221) or double back to Otorohanga and continue south on SH3 to the Waitomo turn-off.

Practicalities

The only public transport is the Kawhia Bus and Freight **bus** service from Te Awamutu (Mon–Sat). The museum (see above) acts as an unofficial **visitor centre**, dispensing free maps and details of local attractions.

The best-value **accommodation** is at *Kawhia Beachside S–cape* motor camp, on the beachfront (☎07/871 0727, fax 871 0217; tent sites $7.50, dorms ①, cabins ②–③); they also rent kayaks (for use in the bay, under $5 for 30min). For a basic, spacious holiday flat/backpackers try *Wee Knot Inn*, Jervois Street (☎07/871 0778; dorm ①).

The best place to get a **drink** is the *Wee Knot Inn*, a locals' haunt with a variety of beers, snacks, coffee – and usually a story or some advice. Also on Jervois Street, there are two stores (opposite one another) that serve burgers, fish and chips, and a variety of other **snacks** during the day (daily); or when you fancy something a bit more substantial in a nice setting try *Annie's* (☎07/871 0198), adjacent to *Wee Knot Inn* – if you arrive after 6.30pm just give her a ring and she'll come and cook for you. Last but not least is the excellent **fish and chips** at *Kawhia Seafoods*, on the quay opposite the museum (Wed–Sun, closes 6.30pm).

The King Country

Now characterized by a rural landscape given over mostly to farming, gardens and dairy cattle, the **King Country** derives its name from more uncertain times when it became the refuge of King Tawhiao and members of the **King Movement** (see box on p.214), as they were driven south in defeat during the New Zealand Wars. The area soon gained a reputation as an inhospitable **Maori stronghold**, renowned for difficult terrain and the type of welcome that meant few, if any, Europeans had the nerve to enter. However, the forest's respite was short-lived: when peace was declared in 1881, eager **loggers** descended in droves.

These days the most famous place in the King Country is **Waitomo**, a tiny village that sits at the heart of a unique and dramatic landscape, honeycombed by **limestone caves** eerily illuminated by millions of **glow-worms**, and overlaid by a geological wonderland of karst features. North of Waitomo is the small dairying town of **Otorohanga**, with the unexpected pleasure of a **kiwi house** and large aviary, while to the south is **Te Kuiti**, devoted to sheep farming – and reputedly the shearing capital of the world. In the 1860s, the town provided sanctuary for Maori rebel Te Kooti, who reciprocated with a beautifully carved **meeting house**. Further south is the **Pureora Forest Park**, an enclave of rich lowland podocarp forest that was the site of a conservation battle in the late 1970s, and now provides access to some excellent **walks** and a home for the rare **kokako** bird, which seems to prefer an ungainly walk to flight. The last community in the King Country, the rather jaded town of **Taumarunui** provides access to the Whanganui River, a **historic drive** to Stratford and the spectacular **coastal road** via **Mokau**, a tiny and intriguing coastal settlement, before heading through the Taranaki coastal plains to New Plymouth.

Otorohanga

Some 30km south of Te Awamutu, **OTOROHANGA** (meaning "food for a journey") is surrounded by sheep and cattle country. Most visitors are here to see the birds at **Kiwi House Native Bird Park**, Alex Telfer Drive, off Kakamutu Road (daily: Sept–May 9.30am–5pm; June–Aug 9.30am–4pm; $8), five minutes' walk from the town centre. And if you do want to see kiwis, this is as good a place as any: a ten-minute film (hourly until 4pm), is followed by a guided tour through the kiwi enclosure. You're left to find your own way around the remainder of the park, which is given over to extensive walk-through aviaries and cages that house tuatara (lizard-like creatures) and geckoes.

Back on Kakamutu Road is the small **Otorohanga Museum** (Sun 2–4pm; other times by arrangement, ☎07/873 8849; donation appreciated). Prize exhibits include Maori flax weavings, dog-hair cloaks, and a splendid portrait of Wahanui Huatare, a one-time local elder, in traditional costume; a separate room houses the 110-year-old wheelbarrow used in the inaugural ceremony for the railway, which finally opened up the King Country to *pakeha* settlement.

Once you've had enough of the kiwis and local history, check out the **Karam and John Haddad Menswear Store**, 65–71 Manipoto St, the premier stockist of Swandri bushwear and Kiwi Stockman waxed coats, plus bucket loads of other great stuff, for men and women – vital accessories if you want to be taken seriously in rural New Zealand and considerably cheaper than anywhere else in the country.

Practicalities

The **train** station, on the Auckland–Wellington line, is just behind the main street in the centre of town, while InterCity and Newmans **buses** drop off right at the **visitor centre**, 87 Maniapoto St (Mon–Fri 9am–5pm, Sat & Sun 10am–3pm; ☎07/873 8951, fax 873 8398, *otovin@xtra.co.nz*). Bill Miller, the doyen of Otorohanga Taxis (☎07/873 8279 & 0800/808 279, fax 873 8214), runs **guided trips** as well as a **taxi** service; there's not much about Otorohanga that Bill doesn't know, and his enthusiasm is either infectious or overpowering.

Most visitors press on to Waitomo once they've crossed the kiwis off their list, but if you want to **stay**, try the *Otorohanga Backpackers*, 1 Sangro Crescent (☎07/873 6022; dorms ①, rooms ②), a small, comfortable hostel with friendly owners, or the *Otorohanga Kiwi Town Holiday Park*, Domain Road (☎07/873 8214; tent sites $7), a well-kept, sheltered campsite where you can hear the call of the kiwis at night. **Eating** in Otorohanga revolves around tearooms and takeaways all a short walk along Maniapoto Street, the main drag; the best bet for a sit-down meal is the *Otorohanga Club*, also on Maniapoto St, serving upmarket food and booze at low prices. Heading south on SH3, you can't miss the **Big Apple** (daily 10am–5pm, plus evenings Fri–Sun), set in an apple and kiwi orchard just north of the Waitomo turn-off. The Big Apple viewing tower overlooks the valley and is now showing distinct signs of wear, while next door is a four-hundred-seater restaurant, buffet, bar, and café; prices are reasonable, but it can all feel a little too much like a production line. Another option is the fruit and veg market, adjacent to the Big Apple, with wholesome produce at low prices.

Waitomo and the caves

The tiny village of **WAITOMO**, 16km south of Otorohanga, lies 6km up the Waitomo Caves Road to the west of SH3. In addition to Waitomo's famed **caves**, the region has many other features typical of eroded limestone or **karst** areas – dry valleys, streams that disappear down funnel-shaped sinkholes, craggy limestone outcrops, fluted rocks, and potholes and natural bridges caused by cave ceiling collapses – some of which lie just off the Te Anga Road as it heads towards the long black **beaches**, craggy bluffs and tiny wind-lashed communities of the coast. The features both above and below ground have been sculpted by water into eerie and extraordinarily beautiful shapes.

Appropriately enough, Waitomo means "water entering shaft" and, for over a hundred years, visitors have flocked to this diminutive village to explore the surrounding caves and to marvel at a twilight world illuminated by glow-worms. The cave passages were first discovered in 1887 by Maori chief Tane Tinorau and English surveyor Fred Mace, who built a raft of flax stems and drifted along an underground stream, with candles as their only source of light. First opened to tourists in 1888, the caves were acquired by the government in 1906, but were eventually returned, in 1989, to their traditional owners, who now receive a percentage of all the revenue generated and participate in the site's management.

Arrival, information and transport

Train travellers have to get off at Otorohanga and join connecting Newmans shuttle buses to Waitomo; Newmans shuttles also meet flights at Hamilton airport. All the major **bus** companies pass through Waitomo, stopping opposite the **visitor centre** (daily April–Sept 8.30am–5pm, Oct–March 8am–5.30pm; ☎07/878 7640, fax 878 6184, *www.waitomo-museum.co.nz*, *waitomomuseum@xtra.co.nz*), in the Waitomo Museum of Caves in the centre of the village. As well as providing information, the centre also takes bookings for cave trips and onward travel. The Waitomo Shuttle (☎0800/808 279) operates a **taxi** service and an air and rail pick-up service. **Regional connections** include

Perry's Bus to Te Kuiti (Oct–April Mon–Sat), the Waitomo Wanderer Rotorua (daily), and Otorohanga Taxis to and from Otorohanga (daily; see above; $7 one-way).

Accommodation

Although backpackers are well provided for in Waitomo, other options are **limited**. To make sure you get what you want, **book in advance**, particularly during December and January.

Cavelands Country Holiday Park, Waitomo Caves Rd, opposite the Museum of Caves (☎0800/400 104). Spacious campsite conveniently near the general store. Tent sites $10, dorms ③, cabins ②, chalets ④.

Dalziels B&B, Waitomo Caves Rd, at the eastern end of the village (☎07/878 7641). Comfortable, clean, spacious rooms and a friendly welcome. ④.

Glow-worm Motel, cnr SH3 & Waitomo Caves Rd, 8km east (☎07/873 8882). Straightforward motel with nine comfortable, fully self-contained units. ④.

Hamilton Tomo Group Lodge, 1km west (☎07/878 7442). Caving club lodge that welcomes visitors. Large and clean, if simple, dorms have access to kitchen facilities and a mine of local knowledge. ①.

Juno Hall Backpackers, Waitomo Caves Rd, 1km east (☎07/878 7649). Farmhouse-style hostel, with a courtesy bus to the village pub and THC Glow-worm Cave; the hostel is also the base for Waitomo Horse Treks (see p.224). Camping $7.50, dorms ①, rooms ③.

THL Waitomo Caves Hotel and Hostel, up the steep hill beside the Museum of Caves (☎07/878 8227). By far the most impressive building in the area, this grand old hotel was built in 1908. Many of the rooms have recently been refurbished and are very plush, but backpackers are also catered for in an associate YHA section with simple dorms and rooms (linen $5). Dorms ①, backpacker doubles ②, hotel rooms ⑤.

Woodlyn Park, 700m up Waitomo Valley Rd, off Waitomo Caves Rd (☎07/878 6666, fax 878 8866). Part of the self-built complex – including shows and a jetboat lake – are these newly converted, self-contained and comfortable rail carriages. ④.

The Village

Waitomo village is a small collection of buildings on either side of the Waitomo Caves Road. The dominant feature is the campsite, in a bowl opposite the general store and pub, while the *THL Waitomo Caves Hotel* sits atop the hill, brooding like an ancient castle over all it surveys. Passing the Glow-worm Cave, Waitomo Caves Road becomes Te Anga Road, which then forks at the Johnston Memorial Grove of trees: Te Anga Road forges west toward Te Anga and the coast; while Tumutumu Road heads southwest towards the limestone bluffs, the faultline, the Aranui Cave and the Ruakuri Natural Tunnel.

A visit to the **Museum of Caves**, on Waitomo Caves Road in the village centre (daily 8.30am–5pm; $4; included in Black Water Rafting & Waitomo Adventures trips), will greatly enhance your caves experience. The revamped museum is interactive, with tight crawl holes and intelligent displays on the geology and history of the caves and their exploration, tourism and the life cycle of glow-worms and cave wetas (an insect with an other-worldly appearance, that apparently influenced the modelmakers working on the *Aliens* films). A video shown in the reception area makes a good starting point for choosing cave trips, giving you a pretty good idea of the various options.

An alternative to cave trips and walks are the activities at the especially built **Woodlyn Park**, 700m up Waitomo Valley Road from the village (☎07/878 6666, fax 878 8866). On offer is an endearing Pioneer Heritage show (about 1hr, $10, at least 2 daily) presenting the history of logging and farming with loads of audience participation, laughs and seemingly uncontrollable animals. Although set up for families its off-the-wall slant is something travellers of any age enjoy. Another diversion, this time with kids firmly in mind, is the Pink Gum Boot Tour which involves searching for trolls, fairies and elves in magical woods and a cave (2hr; $13 adults, $10 children). Most thrilling, however, are the powerful self-drive jetboats, little single-seaters that careen around what seems an exceedingly tight course, at high speed ($35 for 7 laps).

Perched on a hill above the Ohaki Maori Cultural Centre (not open to the public) 500m west of Waitomo is the replica Ohaki Maori Village. From here the **Opapaka Pa Bush Walk** (45min) climbs past plants and trees traditionally used in Maori medicine to the original pa site, which is thought to have been established in the 1700s. Back towards the village, on the main road, is the **Shearing Shed** (daily 9.30am–4.30pm, shearings 1pm; free), where cute little Angora bunnies get sheared and their soft fur is made into heart-stoppingly expensive fluffy goods.

The caves

There are more than forty-five kilometres of cave passages around Waitomo, about three kilometres of which can be visited on **guided tours**; the only caves you can safely explore **independently** are the Piripiri Caves west of the village (see p.225). The caves were gouged out of Waitomo's ancient limestone when rainwater mixed with carbon dioxide in the air, forming a weak acid that flowed down cracks in the rock; as more carbon dioxide was absorbed from the soil the acid grew stronger, dissolving the limestone and enlarging the cracks and joints – eventually forming the varied caves you see today. The process continues, and each year a further seventy cubic metres of limestone (about the size of a double-decker bus) is dissolved; at the present rate, the caves will be entirely eroded in less than two million years.

The **Glow-worm Cave** has over 1300m of inter-connecting passages. Highlights include the amazing acoustics of the Cavern Cathedral and a boat ride through the cave grotto, where glow-worms shed pinpricks of ghostly pale-green light resembling constellations in the night sky of another planet. The best **tours** (daily 9am–5pm; every 30min; 40min; $20) are the first or the last of the day, when there are less tourists. A **glow-worm** is the larval stage of the fungus gnat, which produces light to lure unsuspecting flying food. The **larvae** are considerably more efficient than the average light bulb – ninety percent of the power they generate is light. When the adult gnats emerge, they are mouthless and so live only a few days, during which time they frantically seek out a mate and the female lays about 120 eggs.

Aranui Cave, 3.5km east of the visitor centre, is only 250m long, but is geologically more spectacular, with high-ceilinged chambers and magnificent stalactites and stalagmites. Tickets for **tours** (daily 10am, 11am, 1pm, 2pm & 3pm; 45min; $20) must be bought at the visitor centre or the kiosk at the Glow-worm Cave. A two-cave combo costs $30, and a museum-and-cave special is $22.

If you want to escape the crowds, consider heading 8km south to **Waitomo's Moa and Glow–worm Experience**, Boddies Rd, Oparure (daily, 3hr; on request with a minimum of two; $50 2-cave visit, $27 1-cave visit; closed June–Aug), a gentle trip across the farm and native bush includes a tractor drive to two very different caves, one with an impressive display of glow-worms.

Cave tubing, canoeing, climbing and abseiling

Trips can be booked at the visitor centre and operators tend to use it as their **starting point**. You'd do well to **book in advance** (*www.waitomo.com*), especially around December and January, as the area fills up quickly with curious Kiwis and foreign travellers. Adventure trips into the caves are well organized and you shouldn't find yourself in situations of real danger, though they're not really recommended for borderline claustrophobics. For **cave tubing** ("Black Water Rafting" is now a trademarked name, see overleaf) trips, you'll be kitted out with a wetsuit, caver's helmet with lamp, rubber boots and – most importantly of all – the **inner tube** from a car tyre, which enables you to float with the current through pitch-black caverns peering up at the multitude of glow-worms, unsure whether the cave roof is one or one hundred metres above your head. Heavy **rain** does sometimes lead to **cancellation**, so it pays to have a day or two to spare. The two original adventure **companies**, Black Water Rafting and Waitomo Adventures, tend to have the most experienced and well-trained staff with first aid knowledge.

Black Water Rafting (☎07/878 6219 & 0800/247 612, *www.blackwaterrafting.co.nz*) run two wetsuit-clad trips. The first (3hr, 90min underground; $65) involves a bit of climbing, a jump from an underground waterfall and an idyllic float through a glow-worm cave, while the second (5hr, 3hr underground; $125) is a little more adventurous and demanding, adding abseiling and an eerie flying fox ride into the darkness to the itinerary. Both tours end up at the *Black Water Café* for hot showers and a warming feed. A more off-beat proposition is **Longtomo Rafting** (☎07/878 7640; daily 9am & 2pm; 3–4hr; $65): cave canoeing with a 22-metre descent followed by paddling through large cave passages, with lots of glow-worms.

The most spectacular trip run by **Waitomo Adventures** (☎07/878 7788 & 0800/WAITOMO) is the **Lost World Adventure** (4hr; $195), involving a stomach-churning 100-metre tandem abseil into a spectacular pothole, followed by a walk through monstrous stone blocks that were once the ceiling in a massive cavern before climbing out on a seemingly endless ladder. The best trip is the first of the morning when the light is just beginning to break into the hole and as you descend it illuminates the rock forms, plants and waking birds – and for real cave junkies, there's also an extended version of the trip over one and a half days. The other option is Haggis Honking Holes (4hr; $125), a madcap series of abseils, climbs and crawl-throughs where you're not sure if it's the water or the adrenaline rushing in your ears.

Of the recent arrivals in Waitomo **Big Red** (contact through the visitor centre; 4hr for $100; 2hr for $55, overland section only) offer the novelty of a 4x4 bike ride procession around a farm with various karst features, taking you cave-tubing afterwards.

If you are into serious caving – and have some prior experience – you may want to contact the **Waitomo Cave Club** (via the *Hamilton Tomo Group Lodge*, see "Accommodation", p.222) as they can usually arrange contacts or a trip.

Walks and horse trekking

The **Waitomo Walkway** (10km; 3hr round-trip) starts opposite the glow-worm caves, and can be divided into three shorter walks, each with a distinct character. The last section (about 30min), from the car park near the Ruakuri Cave on Tumutumu Road, is the most spectacular, featuring the Raukuri Natural Tunnel and after dusk an impressive array of glow-worms. A free leaflet from the visitor centre outlines the various options.

Also taking advantage of the above-ground scenery, **Waitomo Horse Trekking** run through *Juno Hall Backpackers* offer various treks (☎07/878 7649; 1hr, $30; 2hr, $40; 4hr $70).

Eating and drinking

Considering the size of the town the **range** and **quality** of food in Waitomo is quite good, principally because it is such a tourist hotspot. This also means that **in winter** the options and opening times become severely restricted, though you can always adjourn to the trusty **pub**. The THL Caves organization is currently putting a café at the entrance of Glow-worm Cave to make sure that the tourist dollars – from the coach parties they cater to – don't escape into the rest of the town.

Black Water Café, 1km east of the village, opposite *Juno Backpackers Lodge*. Cooked breakfasts ($7), simple snacks and light meals are served from early morning to late evening. A comfortable, no-fuss spot (daily 6.30am–8.30pm), with mussels, spare ribs, sausages, veggie burgers, salads, quiches, pies and dessert for around $10. Licensed.

Cavelands Café, in the general store next to the Museum of Caves. Inexpensive soups, pizza, burgers, fish and salads, plus an array of other small town snack-bar nosh. Daily Oct–April 9am–9pm, May–Sept 9am–6pm.

Roselands Farm and Garden BBQ Restaurant, Fullerton Rd, five minutes drive south of the village. Splendid buffet lunches of char-grilled meat and fish with salad and dessert ($20), served in a beautiful garden setting. Lunch only (11am–2.30pm); licensed.

THL Waitomo Caves Hotel Restaurant, up the steep hill beside the Museum of Caves. Fine European-style and Asian-influenced food for lunch and dinner, usually buffet style, in old world colonial surroundings. Prices are high here and in the attached bar.

Waitomo Caves Tavern, next to the Museum of Caves. It may appear unprepossessing at first but this friendly pub is where everyone (locals and tourists alike) ends up. Exceptionally large evening meals including the likes of steak, egg and chips ($8) or veggie samosa and chips ($6), fish ($7), and a variety of other snacks as well as occasional live music.

Around Waitomo: towards the coast

There are three particularly impressive natural sights just west of Waitomo, along Te Anga Road, though there is no public transport out this way. The **Mangapohue Natural Bridge**, 21km from the village, is signposted from a lay-by on the right-hand side of the road. An easy footpath (15min one-way) winds through forest to an atmospheric steep-sided limestone gorge with a remarkable natural double bridge formed by the erosion of a collapsed cave. Just past the Mangapohue Bridge, the **Marakopa Tunnel Trek** (☎07/876 7865; Oct–March 10.30am–4pm; 4hr; $20, including torches & picnic) offers a relaxed guided walk through farmland adjacent to the Marakopa River and into a grandiose tunnel that's 270m long and 50m high.

A few kilometres further on, the **Piripiri Caves** lie a short walk (10min one-way) away, through a forested landscape full of weathered limestone outcrops. Inside the cavern (carry a torch and spare batteries), the Oyster Room contains giant fossil oysters 30 million years old. About 5km past the caves, the track to the dramatic **Marokopa Falls** (15min one-way) leads from the roadside through a forest of tawa, pukatea and kohekohe trees. The sense of anticipation is heightened by the sound of falling water, which grows gradually louder as you approach the broad, multi-tiered cascade.

If you continue west along the road towards the coast you will come across tiny **TE ANGA**, some 33km from Waitomo. Here you'll find the characterful *Te Anga Tavern*, opposite the Ngahuinga Bluff Scenic Reserve 1.5km from the falls, a sleepy locals' haunt where time has put its feet up. Have an inexpensive snack lunch and maybe a pint or two beneath the glassy-eyed stares of various wild-boar heads that decorate the walls. Continuing southwest towards the coast along the course of the river, after 16km you'll reach the hamlet of **MAROKOPA**, with its long, wild black-sand beaches – best viewed from the Marokopa Lookout, which is accessible from the Marokopa rivermouth. Stop at the Albatross Anchor, at the end of the road overlooking the beach, saved from the ship of the same name which foundered crossing the harbour bar, and take in the spot where the river meets the roaring white-capped waves – but be careful, the sea is dangerous and sometimes even fishermen get dragged in. **Kiritehere Beach**, about 3km south of Marokopa, has a variety of unusual rock formations and a number of ancient fossils scattered among the sands.

Te Kuiti

Back on SH3, the hills narrow around the plain town of **TE KUITI**, 19km south of Waitomo. At the fulcrum of road and rail routes, from Te Kuiti you can either make for the coast along SH3 or veer inland on SH30 to Pureora Forest Park.

Te Kuiti hosts the annual **New Zealand Shearing and Wool Handling Championships**, which is held in late March or early April (depending upon Easter), and the town's primacy in the competitive world of shearing is reinforced by the seven-metre-high statue of a man shearing a sheep at the southern end of Rora Street. More intriguingly Te Kuiti also has a proud Maori history, for it was here that King Tawhiao and his followers fled after the battle of Rangiriri in 1864. Eight years later, Maori rebel Te Kooti (see box on p.401) also sought refuge here and lived under the Maori King's protection until he was pardoned. In return for sanctuary, Te Kooti left a magnificently carved **meeting house**, Te Tokanganui-a-noho, opposite the south end of Rora Street, on Awakino Road; ask at the visitor centre and they'll secure you permission to look around.

Practicalities

The **train** station lies between Rora and Carroll streets and a footbridge over the tracks takes you to the **visitor centre** on Rora Street (Oct–April Mon–Sun 9am–5pm, May–Sept Mon–Fri 9am–5pm, Sat & Sun 10am–4pm; ☎07/878 8077, *thcomf@mtxlink.co.nz*), just a few minutes' walk from *Tiffany's Restaurant*. *Tiffany's* is a focal point of life in Te Kuiti: InterCity and Newmans **buses** stop opposite, at the corner of Rora Street and Lawrence Street; the smaller operators pick up and drop off right outside; and it's here that you buy bus tickets, weekdays only – overnight buses are cheaper. Perry's Bus run a regular **shuttle** to Waitomo and across to the coast.

The **DOC office**, 78 Taupiri St (Mon–Fri 8am–4.30pm), has details of the Pureora Forest Park (see below).

Good-quality **rooms** are available at the *Panorama Motor Inn,* 59 Awakino St (☎07/878 8051; ⑤), and the attached restaurant serves wholesome country food, or settle for the *Domain Motor Camp*, Hinerangi Street (☎07/878 8966; tent sites $5.50, on-site vans & cabins ②), along the bank of the Mangaokewa River. Winner of the silliest name for a **bar** contest is *How Barzarre*, on the corner of King Street and Taupiri Street, where you can get snack food, good salads, booze and liqueur coffees. The most convenient places to grab a simple **snack** or meal between buses are *Tiffany's* (daily 8am–8pm) and the *Te Kuiti Pie Cart* (Mon–Thurs 5pm–midnight, Fri & Sat noon–4am); both on Rora Street.

Pureora Forest Park

The **Pureora Forest Park** straddles the Hauhungaroa Range west of Lake Taupo. Te Kuiti provides the easiest access from the west, along SH30 via the small community of Benneydale, but there is no public transport. The park narrowly escaped logging in 1978, when it became the site of a successful tree-top protest.

Along with Little Barrier Island (see p.143) and a few pockets around Rotorua, this broad-leaf forest environment is now one of the few remaining habitats of the rare North Island **kokako**. The 38cm-tall bluish-grey birds are poor fliers, preferring to walk, climb or hop; their forest habitat enables them to clamber grumpily up through the branches, but they tend to nest closer to the ground, so an area free of introduced predators is vital for their survival – if you go looking for them, be careful where you tread.

The **DOC office** on Barryville Road (☎07/878 1080), off SH30 46km from Te Kuiti, stocks leaflets and maps describing various short walks in the park ($1) and detailing mountain-bike access. In the vicinity of the DOC office, there are several sights worth a look: the largest recorded totara tree, the **Pouakani Tree**, is just five minutes' drive east; slightly further in, 2.5km along Pikiariki Road, the **Forest Tower**, close to the site of the landmark anti-logging protest, gives a twelve-metre-high protestor's-eye view of the surrounds. The easy **Totara Walk** (30min loop track) starts at the junction of

Barryville Road and Link Road, 1km from the DOC office. This wheelchair-accessible track winds through giant podocarps, past matai, rimu, tawa, kahikatea, ferns, vines and perching plants, with a screeching accompaniment from kaka high up in the leafy canopy. A more challenging route with excellent views, the **Mount Pureora Summit Track** (2km; 3hr; 1165m ascent), starts from the Link Road car park, 10km from the DOC office.

Taumarunui

A small town in the centre of the King Country surrounded by national parks and forests, **TAUMARUNUI** sits astride SH4, 82km south of Te Kuiti, and marks the confluence of the Ongarua and Whanganui rivers. Taumarunui was one of the last places to be settled by Europeans, and didn't really take well to the invaders until 1908, when the railway came to town. Upon encountering a gradient too steep for trains, the surveyor, Rochforte, curled the rail line into the **Raurimu Spiral**, thereby easing the gradient of the climb and allowing the use of the most direct route. A lookout at Raurimu, 37km south of town on SH4, and a model in the visitor centre clearly show what an amazing idea and a remarkable feat of engineering it was. There's also an excellent one-day rail trip to the Tongariro National Park (see p.305) via the Spiral ($17 one way; bookings at the visitor centre) which is good for those pushed for time.

These days Taumarunui has a population of 5500 and dwindling industries have left it rather run-down. The only reason most travellers stop here is to visit the **Whanganui National Park** by canoe or jetboat (see p.248) or to follow the **Taumarunui–Stratford Heritage Trail**.

Practicalities

Both **buses** and **trains** use the train station on Hakiaha Street (SH4) as their stop in town, and it also contains the **visitor centre** (Mon–Fri 9am–4.30pm, Sat & Sun 10am–4pm, *www.middle-of-everywhere.co.nz, info@ruapehude.govt.nz*). The **DOC office** (Mon–Fri 8am–noon & 1–4.30pm) is in Cherry Grove, off Taumarunui Street, about fifteen minutes' walk from the visitor centre, and sells passes and hut tickets for the Whanganui National Park. For **Internet** access check out the library (Mon noon–5pm, Tues–Fri 10am–5pm, Sat 9am–noon), Hakiaha Street, opposite the ANZ Bank.

A range of **accommodation** is available at the *Taumarunui Family Inn*, an old colonial hotel on the corner of Marae Street and Miriama Street (☎07/895 3478, fax 895 6072; dorms ①, backpacker rooms ②, hotel rooms ③). On the opposite side of Marae Street, *Calverts Spa Motel*, at no. 6 (☎07/895 8500, fax 895 8400; ④–⑤), has quiet, comfortable motel rooms with free continental breakfast.

Most of the **eating** places in Tamarunui cater to the truckie trade and are lined up and down the main drag, Hakiaha Street. The 24-hour *Main Trunk Café*, a converted railway carriage at the east end of town on Hakiaha Street opposite the police, serves filling burgers, steaks, fish, exceptional toasted sandwiches and full cooked breakfasts from 10am to 10pm. The *Rivers II Café*, 43 Hakiaha St (daily, BYO after 5pm), serves excellent coffee, calzone, pies, aged steaks and various veggie options while the *Willows Restaurant*, on the first floor at 93 Hakiaha St (Tues–Fri 9am–11pm, Sat 6pm–midnight; BYO), serves a variety of steaks, seafood, pasta dishes and liqueur coffees.

Taumarunui–Stratford Heritage Trail

This rugged 155-kilometre road (SH43), is described in the *Taranaki–SH43 Heritage Trail* leaflet (free from visitor centres or accessible at *tipnet.taranaki.ac.nz/tourism*).

Skirting the Whanganui National Park, the route is bordered by farmland, **scenic reserves** and about thirty supposed points of historic and geographical interest; you'll need to allow a minimum of three hours to travel the route, some stretches of which are unsealed – considerably longer if you want to spend time at any of the **diversions** along the way. The trip's worthwhile for back-country buffs with at least a day to spare but otherwise you're better sticking to the main roads.

The first notable stop, **Maraekowhai Reserve**, is about 17km down a signposted, unsealed road. A track begins just below the car park at the road end and follows a creek to a lookout over the **Ohara Falls** (10min). Just before the falls, another track branches off to the left over a small plank bridge, climbing to a one-time stronghold of the Hau Hau (see p.379), where in 1862 they erected a war pole, **Rongo-nui**, with four arms pointing in all directions of the compass, intended to call warriors to their cause from all over the country. At the end of hostilities, a peace pole, **Rerekore**, was erected close by, and both are now preserved on this site, which is also accessible from the Whanganui River (see p.252).

Back on SH43, the road snakes through the Tangarakau Gorge, carved by the river from sedimentary limestone. Around 90km from Taumarunui is the tiny village of **WHANGAMOMONA**, a self-declared republic with a population of seventy. The centre of the community is the hotel, built in 1911, where you can get your passport stamped or buy a Whangamomonian version, while wetting your whistle. The *Whangamomona Hotel/Pub*, Ohura Road (☎06/762 5823; tent sites $8 dorms ①, cabins & rooms ②–④), also has **accommodation**, serves meals and is open daily from 11am till the barman goes to bed. This sleepy little village, which is disturbed only by one freight train a day, declared itself a republic on October 28, 1995, after the New Zealand government had altered the regional borders, taking the village out of Taranaki. The anniversary of the declaration is celebrated each year, on the closest Saturday to that date: the population swells to about 3500 (special trains run from Hamilton and Auckland), who come to witness the annual swearing in of the president, whip-cracking and gumboot-throwing competitions – and a good deal of drinking and eating.

Climbing beside steep bluffs, SH43 passes a couple of saddles with views down the valley and across the **Taranaki Plains** before descending to flat dairy pasture, eventually rolling into **Stratford** (see p.240) as the permanently snow-capped Mount Taranaki looms into view.

The coast road to Taranaki

Heading southwest from Te Kuiti, **SH3** makes a beeline for the coast, then twists its way through tiny communities, sandwiched between the spectacular **black beaches** and **cliffs** of the coast and steep inland ranges, until the scenery opens out onto **Taranaki Plains** just north of New Plymouth (see opposite).

Mokau and around

The small community of **MOKAU**, 73km from Te Kuiti, has two good surf beaches, Mokau and Rapanui (both subject to strong rips and currents so don't go swimming), a small **museum**, the **Maniaroa Marae** and pa, and some enjoyable **river cruises**. Mokau also featured in Jane Campion's film *The Piano*, particularly in the bush scenes and the fence line, seen in silhouette, along which the daughter dances.

There is an abundance of seafood on the beaches near Mokau, including mussels, cockles, pipi and – if you know where and when (Aug 15–Nov 30) to look – whitebait. For a taste of the black-beach scenery so typical of this coastline, head for the **estuary** about ten minutes' walk from town, where a cave and waterfall are set back from the beach. From the jetty near the rivermouth, the 83-year-old historic creamboat, MV

Cygnet (☎06/752 9775; daily 11am; 3hr; $25), **cruises** up river via a number of points of historic interest, old coal workings and abandoned farms; weather permitting, this veteran vessel also offers an unusual candlelight bush-dining trip. Back in town, the local **museum** (daily 10am–4pm; donation $1), on SH3 as you enter Mokau from Awakino, charts the history of the small Maori settlements on either side of the Mokau rivermouth and of the 1840 European settlement beside the coal-rich river. Nearby, the **Maniaroa Marae** and pa is the resting place of the Tainui canoe anchor stone from the alleged Great Migration, a historic *waka* and some excellent wood carvings; ask at the museum to ensure that you follow the correct protocol for entering the Marae.

Continuing south down the coast, after 18km you'll come to a fascinating **sea cave** just south of the **Tongaporutu Rivermouth**. Conveniently signalled by two rock stacks on the beach opposite the entrance, the cave bears **ancient footprints** on its upper walls, about four metres up from the floor. For many years this coastal, tide-dependent route was the only access for Maori travelling between the Waikato and Taranaki districts, and this cave provided shelter. Local lore has it that the infamous chief **Te Rauparaha**, along with his most trusted female companion, rested in a sea cave to recover from a debilitating attack of boils. When the boils were lanced, the chief braced himself against the cave wall and, due to the combination of the sudden pain and his great strength, left impressions of his hands and feet in the rock. The chief was reputed to have six toes – as do eight of the foot imprints in the cave.

One further place along SH3 is the fascinating **White Cliffs Brewery**, 487 Main North Rd, just outside Urenui, 31km from New Plymouth (Mon–Sat 10am–4pm, ☎06/752 3676). This micro brewery of international standing produces the delicious **Mike's Mild Ale**, a super brew that will make you well disposed towards the entire region even if it's raining. Mike, assuming he's not busy brewing a new batch, will give you a short tiki tour (free) before selling you some of the stuff.

PRACTICALITIES

Both InterCity and Newmans run buses between Auckland and New Plymouth via the settlement, stopping in Mokau at the side of the main road, opposite the *Mokau Roadhouse*. The museum acts as an unofficial **visitor centre**, providing maps of the local area and lists of attractions and facilities. If you're enamoured with Mokau's unassuming charms, **stay** at the *Palm House Backpackers* (☎06/752 9081; ①), a cosy, well kept hostel on SH3, at the first bend west of the museum, or at the nearby roadside *Rivieria Motor Camp and White Bait Inn Tearooms* (☎06/752 9713; tent sites $6, flats & cabins ②). **Meals** and food supplies are available at the campsite, *Mokau Roadhouse*, *White Bait Inn Tearooms*, and the general store and post office – but be warned supplies are limited.

New Plymouth and around

The city of **NEW PLYMOUTH** sits at the junction of SH3, linking it with Te Kuiti to the north and Wanganui to the south, and SH45 (named "Surf Highway" by the local tourist board), skirting the coast of the Taranaki Peninsula. Although relatively isolated, the city bustles with prosperity and bristles with a sense of its own importance: as the only deep-water international port on the west coast, **Port Taranaki**, at the edge of the city, serves as New Zealand's western gateway. Like everything else in the region, the city is dominated by **Mount Taranaki** (Egmont) – though some visitors never even glimpse the summit through its cloak of low cloud, leading local wags to quip, "If you can see the mountain, it's going to rain; if you can't, it's raining already". Your best chance of seeing the gently rising cone is either early in the morning or just before sunset.

Captain **Cook** was the first European to sight the mountain, naming it **Egmont** after the first Lord of the Admiralty, but it was not until 1828 that a trading and **whaling station** was established by John Lowe and Richard Barrett on the Ngamotu Beach, overlooked today by the modern city. They found few **Maori** living in the area because of annual raids by the northern tribes, which forced many Te Atiawa Maori to migrate with Te Rauparaha to Kapiti Island. In 1841, the **Plymouth Company** dispatched six ships of English colonists to New Zealand; mostly from the West Country, they named their community New Plymouth. From the late 1840s many Te Atiawa people returned to their homeland and disputes arose over **land sales** to settlers, which in 1860 culminated in a ten-year armed conflict, slowing the development of the town and leaving a legacy of **Maori grievances**, some of which are still being addressed today.

Although there is no danger of the city rivalling the natural architecture of Mount Taranaki, it does boast an outstanding **gallery**, an excellent **museum** and a tranquil **public park**, as well as a lively restaurant and after-hours entertainment scene. Just offshore is the **Sugar Loaf Islands Marine Reserve**, a haven for wildlife above and beneath the sea, while 17km further south along SH45 is the surfing and windsurfing hotspot of **Oakura**. On the northeastern outskirts of the city is the **Bell Block**, home of the **Fitzroy Pole**, which commemorates one of the few instances in early New Zealand history when settlers were compelled to give back land they had taken from local Maori. Further northeast along SH3 is **Waitara**, a small settlement that effectively became the catalyst for the New Zealand Wars of the 1860s. Following SH3 as it cuts inland from the city, you'll come to the small settlement of **Egmont Village**, 12km from New Plymouth and one of the main access points to the Egmont National Park, along with Stratford and SH45.

Arrival, information and transport

The **airport** is about ten minutes' drive northeast, from where Withatruck buses shuttle into the city ($8; on request; ☎06/751 1777). InterCity and Newmans **buses** both drop off at the Travel Centre, 32 Queen St, in the centre of the city. The **visitor centre**, on the corner of Leach Street and Liardet Street (Mon–Fri 8.30am–5pm, Sat & Sun 10am–3pm; ☎06/759 6080, fax 759 6073, *www.newplymouthnz.com, info@newplymouth.govt.nz*), stocks leaflets covering the many self-guided walks around the town, brochures and folders on the accommodation and restaurants in the area, as well as details of trips and sights, and a booking service. The **DOC office**, 220 Devon St West (Mon–Fri 8.30am–4.30pm), has information on Egmont National Park and sells hut tickets.

New Plymouth City Bus Lines run **local bus** services from their depot, at 32 Queen St, to all the suburbs of New Plymouth via various stops in the city; check at the visitor centre for details. There are no public buses to the mountain although some private shuttle companies do offer services (see p.238).

Accommodation

The best-value accommodation in New Plymouth is offered by the hostels and B&Bs. The majority of places are concentrated around Devon Street and climbing south from there.

Hotels, farmstays and B&Bs

Balconies B&B, 161 Powderham St (☎06/757 8866, *balconies@paradise.net.nz*). A five-minute walk from the visitor centre, this large turn-of-the-century manor house offers B&B in comfortable, high-ceilinged rooms. ④.

Devon Hotel, 390 Devon St (☎06/759 9099 & 0800/800 930, *mail@devon.co.nz*). A smart, refurbished hotel with a range of rooms from economy to luxury, and a dining room. ④–⑦.

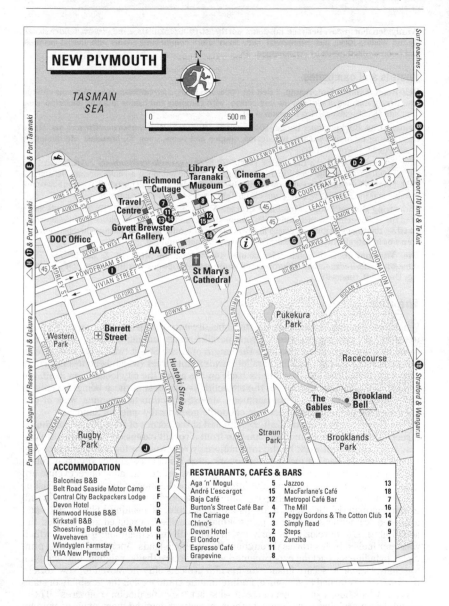

NEW PLYMOUTH

TASMAN SEA

0   500 m

Surf beaches

A
B C
D 2

Airport (10 km) & Te Kuit

E & Port Taranaki

H 17 & Port Taranaki

Pariututu Rock, Sugar Loaf Reserve (1 km) & Oakura

G F

18 Stratford & Wanganui

Library & Taranaki Museum

Richmond Cottage

Cinema

Travel Centre

Govett Brewster Art Gallery

DOC Office

AA Office

St Mary's Cathedral

Western Park

Barrett Street

Pukekura Park

Racecourse

The Gables

Brookland Bell

Rugby Park

Straun Park

Brooklands Park

Huatoki Stream

ACCOMMODATION	
Balconies B&B	I
Belt Road Seaside Motor Camp	E
Central City Backpackers Lodge	F
Devon Hotel	D
Henwood House B&B	B
Kirkstall B&B	A
Shoestring Budget Lodge & Motel	G
Wavehaven	H
Windyglen Farmstay	C
YHA New Plymouth	J

RESTAURANTS, CAFÉS & BARS			
Aga 'n' Mogul	5	Jazzoo	13
André L'escargot	15	MacFarlane's Café	18
Baja Café	12	Metropol Café Bar	7
Burton's Street Café Bar	4	The Mill	16
The Carriage	17	Peggy Gordons & The Cotton Club	14
Chino's	3	Simply Read	6
Devon Hotel	2	Steps	9
El Condor	10	Zanziba	1
Espresso Café	11		
Grapevine	8		

Henwood House B&B, 122 Henwood Rd, Bell Block, 5km east on SH3 (☎ & fax 06/755 1212, *henwoodhouse@xtra.co.nz*). Grand 1890s wooden house nestled among trees, with spacious rooms, a lounge and sun deck; dinner by arrangement ($35). ⑤–⑥.

Kirkstall B&B, 8 Baring Terrace (☎06/758 3222). An intimate and friendly B&B in a 1920s house with lovely views over a garden that slopes down to the Te Henui River, about fifteen minutes' walk from the city centre, with characterful rooms; dinner by arrangement ($30). ④–⑤.

Windyglen Farmstay, Bertrand Rd, 28km northeast (☎06/752 0603, *windyglen@netsource.co.nz*).
By the Waitara River, this commercial dairy farm offers comfortable rooms with shared facilities,
and home-cooked meals by arrangement. ⑤.

Hostels and campsites

Belt Road Seaside Motorcamp, 2 Belt Rd (☎06/758 0228, *c.parkes@xtra.co.nz*). A scenic cliff-top
site, twenty minutes' walk from the city centre, with camping and cabins in a tidy sheltered area.
Tent sites $8.50, cabins $11 per person or ②.

Central City Backpackers Lodge, 104 Leach St (☎06/758 0473, *ambercourt@xtra.co.nz*). Has a
clean dining room and kitchen, two dorms, singles and twins; linen $5, breakfast and dinner by
arrangement. Dorms ①, rooms ③.

New Plymouth YHA, 12 Clawton St (☎06/753 5720, *egmontlodge@taranaki_bakpak.co.nz*). An
ultra-friendly, comfortable hostel in a peaceful garden, reached along a gentle streamside walking
track (15min) from the city centre, or by bike (rental $5 a day from the hostel). The rooms are com-
fortable and the facilities well kept and clean. Tent sites $9, dorms ①, rooms ③.

Shoestring Budget Lodge, Motel and Cottage Mews, 48 Lemon St (☎06/758 0404). Only 350m
from the visitor centre, with a sauna ($4), roomy kitchen and dining room adorned by a long wood-
en table, this is one of the best places in town. Stay in the range of rooms within the charming old
house or in bargain motel units. Dorms ①, rooms ③, motel units ④.

The Wavehaven, 1518 South Rd, Oakura, 10km west on SH45 (☎ & fax 06/752 7800,
wave.haven@taranaki.ac.nz). Self-proclaimed home of the thrill-seeker, with clean comfortable lodging. Dorms ①, rooms ②.

The City

What New Plymouth lacks in architectural beauty it makes up for with energy. The centre of the city comprises a grid of broad parallel roads running north to west, complicated by a one-way system that runs the length of Leach Street (which becomes Vivian
Street as it heads west) and the parallel Powderham Street (which becomes Courtney
Street as it heads north). Turning its back on the coast, the city looks in on itself, the
central blocks containing most of the attractions – the best of these being the gallery
and museum – eating and entertainment, almost all within ten minutes' walk of one
another, though be warned the whole caboodle goes deadly quiet on Sundays.

The **Govett-Brewster Art Gallery**, situated at the corner of King Street and Queen
Street (daily 10.30am–5pm; free), benefits from a recent extension that allows the display of a selection of work by the internationally renowned artist and filmmaker Len
Lye: the gallery was left most of Lye's work after his death and they regularly rotate
the material on show. The remainder of the gallery, auditorium and concert venue are
given over to travelling national and international exhibitions (check with the visitor
centre) and an art and design shop containing the gallery's own publications and broader ranging material. Best known for his kinetic sculptures, paintings, photographs and
animated "cameraless" films (he painstakingly stencilled, scratched and drew on the
actual film), Lye developed an early fascination with movement and tribal art, which
was later fuelled by his travels throughout the Pacific Islands. Applying surrealist principles to indigenous art, he experimented with sculpture, batik, painting, film and photography. Unable to secure finance for his film projects after he moved to New York in
the 1950s, he returned to sculpture, finding that he could exploit the flexibility of stainless steel rods, loops and strips to create abstract "tangible motion sculptures". These
motor-driven sculptures are erratic in their movement, lending them an air of anarchy
that induces a certain primal fear – apparently, Lye was particularly delighted when his
works frightened small children, considering this a litmus test of their effectiveness.
Should you need some reassuring refreshment, the gallery also has a superb café.

At the bottom of King Street, in the public library building, is the **Taranaki
Museum**, accessed from Ariki Street (Mon–Fri 9am–4.30pm, Sat & Sun 1–5pm; free).

Exhibitions change every eight weeks, while of the permanent collection the extensive Maori section is unmissable, likewise the large collection of paintings, ranging from 1834 pen-and-ink sketches through to contemporary works, such as those of John Bevan Ford (see p.259). Highlights of the "Taonga Maori Treasures" include the anchor from the Tokomaru Canoe, which brought Taranaki Maori to New Zealand; the Tokomaru waka, an intricate Tauihu (canoe prow) thought to be one of a number carved for Te Rauparaha in the 1830s; volcanic rock carvings and wood carvings of a style unique to Taranaki with three-dimensional figures, unlike many Maori carvings which are reliefs on a flat background. There's also an amusing area dedicated to James Edward Little from Torquay in England. An ingenious and skilful forger of Polynesian artefacts, Little's work is in museums all over the world.

Diagonally opposite the museum is the **Richmond Historic Cottage**, Ariki Street (Nov–May Mon, Wed & Fri 2–4pm; Sat & Sun 1–4pm; June–Oct Fri–Sun only, same hours; $1), a stone cottage built in 1854 (moved to its current location in 1962), for the Richmond family and furnished with period artefacts. Christopher William Richmond went on to become the local member of parliament.

Straight up Liardet Street, on the hill past the visitor centre, is **Pukekura Park and Brooklands** (daily dawn–dusk; free), a green, tranquil oasis in the city. The Pukekura section is dominated by water and rich plant life, with the **King Fern Gully** and fern-clad tunnels offering welcome relief from the usual rhododendron displays. Brooklands provides a glimpse of the past in **The Gables** (Jan daily 1–4pm; Feb–Dec Sat & Sun only 1–4pm; free), one of the earliest colonial hospitals (1847), now resurrected as an art gallery and medical museum. This part of the park also contains a 2000-year-old puriri tree in a stand of native bush and the **Brooklands Bowl**, an outdoor amphitheatre used for concerts and events throughout the year. Every evening from mid-December to early February, the **light festival** creates spectacular colours and magical effects in the skies above the parks after sunset.

On Vivian Street between Brougham Street and Robe Street is **St Mary's Pro Cathedral**. Designed by Frederick Thatcher and begun in 1845, this is the oldest stone church in New Zealand, a simple austere building marred by a modern annexe but worth visiting for its imposing gabled dark-wood interior and atmospheric graveyard dotted with ancient knotted trees and gravestone testaments to disease and war. Also inside the cathedral is a striking Maori memorial with carvings by John Bevan Ford and tukutuku panels by Min Crawford; unveiled in 1972, the memorial invites forgiveness for past injustices by telling the story of Raumahora and Takarangi whose love for each other united two warring *iwi*.

Another monument to the past unease between Maori and European settlers, **Fitzroy's Pole**, lies northeast of the city centre, on the corner of Devon Street East and Smart Road, on the way to Waitara. The carved pole was erected by Maori to commemorate Governor Fitzroy's 1844 decision, which forced *pakeha* settlers to give up their properties in the Bell Block area. Also at the east end of the city are several good **surfing beaches**, at the end of Octavius Place, with access by road or by following the pathway along the sea wall.

At the western end of the city and visible from the main breakwater of Port Taranaki is the massive **New Plymouth Power Station** (tours for groups only), which is passed by the most scenic of many walks around the city and its outlying suburbs, the **Coastal Walkway** (7km). Running from Lake Rotomanu at the northeastern end of the city to the mouth of Herekawa Stream at the southwestern end, the walk passes the Fitzroy Seaside Park and takes in the port, power station and **Paritutu Rock**. The rock overlooks and is part of the Sugar Loaf Marine Reserve (see overleaf) and is of great significance to the Maori as a border between the Taranaki and Te Atiawa territories and because it makes a near-perfect natural fortress. The twenty-minute climb up the rock, which begins beside the Survivors Outdoor Training Centre, opposite the car park on

Centennial Drive, is quite arduous, with a steel rope providing guidance and support. There is another lookout point on the western side of the rock at Ngatu Road, with good views down the coast.

Around New Plymouth

With the exception of the mountain the most spectacular sight around New Plymouth is the **Sugar Loaf Marine Reserve**, opposite the Paritutu Rock and reached by boat from the southern end of the city. Further south, the pretty **Carrington Road** provides a picturesque drive to some abundant and colourful formal gardens, while wilder pleasures are to be had in the surf off **Oakura**, along the coast on SH45. Heading out of the city in the opposite direction, **Waitara**, just off SH3, offers more intellectual grist, with memorials to its seminal role in the events that led to the New Zealand Wars of the 1860s (see p.849).

Sugar Loaf Marine Reserve

The **Sugar Loaf Marine Reserve** consists of a number of steep-sided rocky islands rising sharply from the sea, the Paritutu and Mataora rocks on the mainland and the Tokamapuna Reef. The reserve is DOC-administered, and a *Sugar Loaf Marine Reserve* pamphlet (free) is available at the DOC office and the visitor centre.

The eroded remnants of an early volcanic centre, later occupied by Maori, the islands were named by Captain Cook in 1770, who was struck by Moteroa Island's similarity to sugar loaves baked in Britain at the time. These days they provide a sanctuary for rare plants, little blue penguins, petrels, sooty shearwaters and other bird species. The reserve also contains an abundance of marine life, with 67 species of fish, as well as New Zealand's most northerly breeding colony of fur seals, migrating humpback whales (Aug–Sept) and dolphins (Oct–Dec), while underwater canyons up to 30m deep are chock-full of multicoloured anemones, sponges, seaweeds and slugs.

No one is allowed to land on the islands and the best way to see the reserve is by boat. A memorable way to visit is with the eccentric but hyper-friendly **Happy Chaddy's Charters** (☎06/758 9133; 1hr; $20) in an old lifeboat launched with suitable aplomb from its shed between the Main and Lee breakwaters in the Ocean View Parade marina, off St Aubyn Street. More of a water-level view is available with **Discovery Adventure Tours** (☎06/758 0116), who offer snorkelling (2hr; $35) and scuba dives and gear rental for qualified divers ($45 for two dives with your own gear, $95 including gear rental).

Along Carrington Road

Carrington Road heads southwest out of town, skirting the mountain and passing a few attractions. At no. 548, 8km from New Plymouth, the historic **Hurworth Cottage** (not open to the public) was originally occupied by a young lawyer, Harry Atkinson, who went on to become New Zealand's Prime Minister four times and was one of the first politicians to advocate women's suffrage and welfare benefits. Built in 1856, the cottage is the only survivor of a settlement called Hurworth, which was abandoned during the New Zealand Wars.

A few kilometres further on, the **Pouakai Zoo Park**, 590 Carrington Rd (daily 9am–5pm; $4), has an interesting walk-through bird enclosure, but the rest of the enclosures are pretty lacklustre. Around 20km from New Plymouth, **Pukeiti**, 2290 Carrington Rd (open daily 10am, last entry 3pm; $8), is a rainforest garden that boasts the largest collection of rhododendrons and azaleas in New Zealand; although there are flowers in bloom all year round, the best time to visit is from November to August. There's also a restaurant in the gardens, serving light lunches, morning and afternoon teas.

Oakura

On SH45, 17km west of town, lies the surfing hotspot of **OAKURA**, with the best **windsurfing** beach in Taranaki and some good conventional boardriding. Windsurf Kiwi, 43 Pitcairn St, and Vertigo Total Surf, Main St, both **rent** learner, slalom and wave boards, and proffer information and advice on the choicest locations. While in Oakura, a visit to the **Koru pa** is well worth a brief detour: turn towards Mount Taranaki on the Wairau Road and left into Surrey Road, from which an easy walk (15min) brings you to the stronghold of the Nga Mahanga, its stone-faced ramparts now mostly strangled by native vegetation.

Around Waitara

The small coastal settlement of **WAITARA**, 15km northeast of New Plymouth and served by local buses (Mon–Sat every 2hr), marks the beginning of the **Waitara Campaign Trail**, a 19-kilometre drive which traces the culture clash that sparked the first Taranaki Land War. The self-guided tour is described in a booklet, *The Waitara Campaign Historic Trail* (available from New Plymouth Museum; $6) and by boards and plaques along the trail.

Some 8km south of Waitara, just outside the village of **LEPPERTON**, is **Sentry Hill Winery**, 152 Cross Rd (Dec & Jan daily 9am–5pm; Feb–May & Sept–Nov Wed–Sun same hours; June–Aug Sat & Sun same hours), where you can taste the kiwi fruit and boysenberry wines, some killer golden scrumpy and hair-raising regiment gin. About 5km northeast from the winery, close to the Waitara River, is **Windyglen Horse Treks**, Bertrand Road (☎06/752 0603; 30min to all day, $25–85), offering accommodation (see p.232) and horse rides over rolling country with views of the sea and Mount Taranaki.

Eating, drinking and entertainment

The majority of the cafés, **restaurants** and clubs are on what is known as the **Devon Mile**, on Devon Street between Dawson and Eliot streets. As for **drinking**, no visit to Taranaki would be complete without a taste of the local, naturally brewed Mike's Mild Ale (see p.229), a lovely drop, highly regarded throughout the world but proof that a prophet is not recognized in his own town since it's only available in a few of New Plymouth's pubs and bars.

For those of a more cultural persuasion, the **Festival of the Arts** takes over the town each March, making use of venues in Pukekura Park, the State Theatre, Govett-Brewster Art Gallery and Brooklands Bowl to showcase classical concerts, pop concerts, performance artists, comedy, parades and a searchlight tattoo. Otherwise, you can always view the natural wonders of the **night sky** on Tuesday evenings at Marshland Observatory, Marshland Hill, Robe St (summer 8–10pm, winter 7.30–9.30pm; $2). Last but not least is a visit to the **Top Town Cinema**, 119–125 Devon St (☎06/759 9077), where they have five screens of mostly Hollywood movies.

Cafés

Chino's, 117 Devon St East. An excellent spot for daily snacks, lunches and dinners with an authentic wholesome Italian flavour, and some lovely coffee. Licensed and BYO.

El Condor, 170 Devon St East. Tiny, very simple place with value-for-money pasta and pizza.

Espresso Café, Govett-Brewster Gallery, cnr Queen St & King St. One of the most stylish and imaginative spots in town for carnivores and vegetarians, with great variety (all meals under $15), a deli counter, good wine, luscious cakes and excellent coffee. Daily 8am–4pm.

MacFarlane's Café, cnr Kelly St & Matai St, Inglewood. A popular Sunday brunch ($11.50) spot, with reasonable snacks and main meals including pasta, salads, burgers and speciality hot-chocolate drinks. Daily 9am–6pm, until 10pm Thurs–Sat; licensed.

Metropol Café Bar, cnr King St & Egmont St. A lively brasserie, with French-influenced snacks, salads and main courses, most for under $20. Daily 11am to midnight.

Simply Read, 2 Dawson St. This personable café/bookshop with great views overlooking the beach is one of the very best places in town. They serve good strong coffee, a selection of teas, wholesome sandwiches and pastries, and they don't mind you browsing while you sup. Daily 9am–4pm.

Steps, 37 Gover St. Good-value toasted focaccia sandwiches, veggie meals and snacks, plus Italian and Asian main meals, followed by rich cakes or other sinful desserts. Lunch Tues–Fri, dinner Tues–Sat; BYO.

Restaurants

Aga 'n' Mogul, 103 Devon St East. Passable licensed and BYO Tandoori, lunch and dinner restaurant with tasty veggie options, large portions and light decor that is slightly spoiled by the too-loud music; though their authentic Kingfisher beer helps you tune out of the surrounding noise.

André l'Escargot, 37–43 Brougham St (☎06/758 4812). Elegant institution that serves excellent French food and wine for lunch and dinner, with classics such as onion soup gratinée, half a dozen Burgundy snails, roast rabbit or côte du boeuf coming in under the $30 mark.

Burton's Street Café/Bar, *State Hotel*, cnr Gover St & Devon St. Moderately priced breakfasts, lunches, snacks and dinners, all in fearsome portions, plus drinks served in a bar bedecked with rural memorabilia.

Devon Hotel, 390 Devon St East (☎06/759 9099). Worth a visit for its excellent evening smorgasbord ($25), with cabaret-like entertainment at the weekends, when it gets crowded.

Zanziba, 440 Devon St East (☎06/757 8147). About a kilometre from the town centre but well worth the effort is this licensed, brightly painted, lively café/restaurant famed for filling brunches, imaginative lunches and agreeable dinners including some decent veggie alternatives, all ranging from $5–$22.

Bars and clubs

Baja Café Bar, 17–19 Devon St West. Previously just another Irish bar but now a classy, cool place with a restaurant serving an excellent selection of international cuisine, including Mexican and Thai for under $22. The DJ cranked club out the back goes off Thurs–Sat nights and settles into a sports bar/pool hall for the rest of the week.

Grapevine Wine Bar, upstairs at 36c Currie St. Intimate relaxed bar occupied by laid-back night owls where the live music is often mellower than at other local haunts. Dinners served Mon–Sat; live music Fri.

Jazzoo, cnr Devon St & King St opposite *Peggy Gordon's Celtic Bar*. First floor café cum dance bar with a tasty New World mix of cuisine (both lunch and supper) and BBQs on the balcony. Live sounds dominate on Thurs, and DJ rhythms on Fri & Sat until 3am. They also have an Internet link.

The Mill, 2 Powderham St. A massive converted flour mill with many bars for the late-night crowd, a wide range of beers and snacks, and live bands or more likely a DJ at weekends.

Peggy Gordon's Celtic Bar, cnr Egmont St & Devon St. With pictures of Irish and Scottish folk heroes on the walls, an extensive range of single malt whiskies, twelve beers on tap, and live Irish music on Fri & Sat, it's no surprise that this is a popular haunt of both locals and travellers. The basement Cotton Club carries on after hours (Thurs–Sat 9pm–3am), while an annual street party, held on November 16, sees thousands of revellers taking over the surrounding area.

Listings

AA (Automobile Association) 49–55 Powderham St (☎06/757 5646).

Banks All the major banks have branches along Devon St or within one block of the city centre (see also listing for Thomas Cook).

Bike rental Coronation Cycles, 207 Coronation Ave (☎06/757 9260; $20 a day).

Camping and outdoor equipment Kiwi Outdoors, 18 Ariki St, sells work clothes, outdoor gear and camping equipment.

Car rental Avis (☎06/757 5736); Hertz (☎06/758 8189); Rent-a-dent (☎06/278 8308 & 0800/736 822).

Cinema 5 119–125 Devon St East (☎06/759 9077).

Internet Access Check out either the *Jazzoo Café* (see opposite) or the public library (see below).

Library There's a public library on Brougham St (Mon, Wed & Fri 9am–8.30pm, Tues & Thurs 9am–5.30pm, Sat 9am–noon). They have Internet access.

Medical treatment Vivian Street Pharmacy, 95 Vivian St; Southern Cross Hospital, St Aubyn St (☎06/758 2338); duty doctors are listed in the *Daily News* on Fri & Sat (70¢).

Post office The main post office, with a poste restante service, is at 21 Currie St (Mon–Fri 9am–5pm).

Swimming The Fletcher Challenge Aquatic Centre, Buckley Terrace, Kawaroa Park (☎06/758 6496), is a massive complex with indoor and outdoor pools, wave machine, gym and fitness suite.

Thomas Cook 55–57 Devon St (☎06/757 5459).

Tours Cruise New Zealand (☎06/758 3222) offer a number of bus tours to points of interest around the region; Tubby's Tours (☎06/753 6306) run guided trips around the city, as well as a shuttle to Mount Taranaki (see "Trailhead transport", p.238). MacAlpine Adventure Guides, 477 St Aubyn St (☎025/417 042, after hours 06/751 3542), offer guided tramps, climbing and abseiling down Dawson Falls (about $30); while Mountain Guides (☎06/758 8261) add photography, skiing and snowboarding. Taranaki Ecological Experiences (☎06/753 5493) offer individually tailored guided walks ($24 per hour, $45–60 per trip depending on destination). Finally there's dam dropping with Kaitiaki Adventures (☎ & fax 06/278 5555; $80 for about a 3hr trip; see p.241).

Egmont National Park

In the centre of **Egmont National Park** is **Mount Taranaki**, a dormant strato-volcano that last erupted in 1755, when the layer-cake of lava flows collapsed in on itself. The crater near the summit is always filled with snow and a climb to the top of the mountain is a journey from a sub-tropical sea to an alpine summit, crossing a treeline characterized by stunted flag-form trees, lopsidedly shaped by the constant buffeting of the wind. Standing alone in relatively flat surroundings, Mount Taranaki always looks spectacular, even when partially obscured by cloud, and it's well worth making the trip to the informative visitor centres just to experience the splendid **vistas** in all directions (if the weather cooperates) – and maybe to tackle the summit track or other **walks** on its slopes.

According to **Maori**, there was a time when all the mountains on the North Island were crowded together on the central plateau. The group was dominated by chiefs Ruapehu, Tongariro, Ngaruahoe and Taranaki, while around them clustered all the smaller mountains, including the beautiful **Pihanga**, who favoured **Taranaki** among all her suitors. Challenged by the other mountains, Taranaki knocked Tongariro to his knees, striking off the top of his head to make him the shape he is today, and defeated Ngaruahoe, but when the time came to face Ruapehu, Taranaki was exhausted and badly wounded. However, Taranaki's love for Pihanga was so great that he turned his back on the other mountains and set off in the direction of the setting sun, guided by Rauhoto Tapairu, first to **Wanganui** and then west to where he stands today. The furrow Taranaki left as he made his way to Wanganui later filled with water and became the **Whanganui River**.

Park practicalities

The boundary to the national park is almost perfectly circular, surrounded by fertile dairy farmland, and encloses a thin ribbon of **native bush** traversed by over 140km of **walking tracks**. Three sealed roads divide the mountain into three sections, each served by a DOC office: the **Egmont Road** and **Dawson Falls** sections of the park, which provide access to the two summit tracks and the **Pembroke Road** section, which provides access to the **Manganui Skifield** (see box opposite).

On the north face of the mountain, the **Egmont visitor centre**, at the top of Egmont Road (March–Sept daily 9am–4pm; rest of year Wed–Sun 9am–4pm; ☎06/756 0990), is accessible from SH3 between New Plymouth and Inglewood, with various displays about the mountain, maps of all the tracks, good viewing windows and weather updates. On the south face, the smaller **Dawson Falls visitor centre**, at the top of Upper Manaia Road (opening times same as Egmont; ☎025/430 248), is accessible from the town of Manaia on SH45, or along any of the small roads that connect with the Manaia Road between Opanuake and Stratford. There is also a **DOC field centre**, Pembroke Road (☎06/765 5144), on the lower east side of the mountain, which is accessible from Stratford.

Both the DOC office and visitor centre in New Plymouth (see p.230) also have information on the park.

Accommodation and eating

The majority of visitors base themselves in New Plymouth, but there's a smattering of luxurious **accommodation** in the park itself, catering to sightseers in summer and **skiers** in winter. The *Dawson Falls Mountain Lodge*, Upper Manaia Road (☎06/765 5457; ⑥, cooked breakfast $16), 45 minutes' drive from New Plymouth, is a quiet alpine-style lodge with Swiss ornamented, individually decorated rooms, stunning views, a restaurant, coffee lounge and bar. On a par is the *Mountain House Motor Lodge & B&B*, Pembroke Road (☎ & fax 06/765 6100, *mountainhome@xtra.co.nz*; ⑤–⑥, cooked breakfast $9), a hotel/motel, B&B and restaurant at 846m above sea level, with pleasant rooms, colourful paintings everywhere and wonderful views, all within easy reach of the skifields. A more **affordable** alternative for **trampers** wanting an early start is *The Missing Leg Backpackers*, 1082 Junction Rd (☎06/752 2570; dorms ①, rooms ⑤), a barn-like building next to the turning for Egmont Road, which is pretty basic but has bikes for rent and a shuttle service up the mountain (for guests only; $10 with a bike).

The licensed **restaurants** at the *Dawson Falls* and the *Mountain House* serve excellent, if expensive dinners; the Mountain House has a slight edge by virtue of having a Swiss chef who routinely prepares a daily choice of at least thirteen desserts. For lunch, the **coffee shop** in the *Dawson Falls* and the *Mountain House* **bar** both oblige with lighter, more snacky fare.

Tramping in the park

Mount Taranaki offers travellers a rare chance to climb to the **summit** of a mountain in one day with little real hardship. This is not to diminish the very real dangers posed by quick and violent weather changes: be sure to wear sturdy boots, and carry extra clothing and a plentiful supply of water and food. Always seek advice at DOC offices or visitor centres, record your itinerary in the intentions book or search and rescue cards before setting out, and get an early start. If you want to spend longer than a day on the mountain and are happy to forgo the goal-driven dash to the summit, the spectacular and testing **Round-the-Mountain Circuit** might fit the bill, or try any number of **shorter walks**.

Trailhead transport – and guided walks

No public **buses** run from New Plymouth to the mountain, but several shuttle operators fill the void: Carter Travel Mountain Shuttle, The Travel Centre, 32 Queen St (☎06/759 9093 & 757 5482; $30 return for one passenger, $20 for 2 or more); Year 2000

Mountain Shuttle (☎06/758 3222; $10 return, minimum 2 reservations); and Inglewood Cabs (☎06/756 6193 & 0800/320 315; about $25 return). All are bookable direct or through the New Plymouth visitor centre.

If you don't want to tackle the mountain alone or aspire to go climbing or abseiling, check out the list of approved **mountain guides** at the back of the DOC leaflet, *Walks in the Egmont National Park* ($1), which is available at local visitor centres and DOC offices. Costs depend on the number of participants, but a couple of reliable outfits to try are: MacAlpine Adventure Guides, 477 St Aubyn St (☎06/751 3542), who offer summit treks, round the mountain, and abseiling down Dawson Falls; and Mountain Guides (☎06/758 8261). Finally, if you're here in February, you can join one of the local **alpine clubs'** inexpensive day climbs to the summit; book through either the New Plymouth or the Stratford visitor centres.

Summit climbs

Of the two one-day **summit routes**, the **Northern Route** is the easier and safer option, though you should still allow about seven hours (4hr ascent, 3hr descent). The track begins at the top car park at North Egmont from which you follow a gravel road and then a wooden stairway close to Tahurangi Lodge, before heading over scoria slopes (rough surfaces of cooled lava) to the Lizard Ridge (2134m), which leads to the crater. After crossing the crater ice and a short scoria slope, it arrives at the summit rocks.

The ten-hour **Southern Route** (7hr ascent, 3hr descent) leaves Dawson Falls at the top of the Upper Manaia Road, climbing through bush and then making a rapid ascent up a staircase to the Lake Dive Track. From there on it is a steep series of zig-zags up scoria slopes. On a clear day, your efforts will be rewarded by panoramic **views** from the summit, taking in the central plateau, north to Hamilton and beyond, south to Kapiti Island, Wellington and the South Island, and out to sea across the Taranaki Bights and the Sugar Loaf Islands.

The Round-the-mountain circuit

The well marked **Round-the-mountain circuit**, accessible from all three sections of the mountain, is actually two tracks: the shorter, **high-level** summer **route** (Dec–Feb only; 3–4 days) and the longer, **low-level route** (year-round; 5 days). Note that although the five-day walk is easily manageable, you have be fit to do the shorter walk as the going is much more strenuous. The routes can be undertaken in either direction, but are described **clockwise** here, starting at the top of Pembroke Road. All **huts** on the circuit itself are classified as back-country (Category 2; $10), but the Camphouse at North Egmont and the Konini Lodge at Dawson Falls, both with 30-odd bunks, are relatively luxurious (Category 1; $16). Hut **tickets** must be bought in advance from local DOC offices or visitor centres.

Day one (6hr) of the **low-level route** involves a walk from the end of Pembroke Road over the Waingongoro swingbridge and joins the summit track before heading left at the

---

MANGANUI SKIFIELD

From the top of Pembroke Road, it's just thirty minutes' walk to the **Manganui Skifield** (June–Oct daily 9am–4pm; ☎06/765 7669). A small club field with a vertical drop of 420m, the slopes are rarely crowded and the skiing and snowboarding is suitable for all levels. There are two **lifts** at the field ($30 per day), a flying fox to get skiing gear from one side of the gorge to the other, a public shelter with toilets, and a canteen. Ski and snowboard **rental** is available at the *Mountain House Motor Lodge*, Pembroke Rd (☎06/765 7669), while taxis operated by Inglewood Cabs (☎0800/320 315) run to the fields ($25) from Stratford.

Hasties Hill Walk and then onto the Lake Dive Track, crossing water courses and through forest to the **Lake Dive Hut** (18 bunks). Day two (6–7hr), the hardest, entails a traverse across difficult terrain to the **Waiaua Gorge Hut** (18 bunks), which is reached by an aluminium ladder. Day three (7–8hr), the longest, is fairly easy-going along the Oanui Track and up to Kahui Hut, before heading through scrub and tussock to the head of the Pyramid Stream Gorges and up steps to the **Holly Hut** (30 bunks). Day four (6–7hr) heads along the ridge above the Kokowai Stream and Egmont Road to the **Maketawa Hut** (18 bunks). The last day is a three-hour stroll back to the mountain house.

The shorter **high-level route** involves leaving the plateau car park at the top of Pembroke Road and heading straight to the Holly Hut; day two to the Waiaua Gorge Hut; and day three back to the plateau.

Shorter walks

On the **south side** of the mountain, at the top of Upper Manaia Road, several tracks branch off from the Dawson Falls visitor centre to places of interest. A short track to the 17m-high **Dawson Falls** (20min), which plummet over an ancient lava flow, can be extended along the **Kapuni Walk** (1hr). Another good walk leads to **Wilkies Pool** (1hr), where the waters of the Kapuni Gorge rush through a staircase of rock pools. The tougher walk to **Hasties Hill** (2hr 30min) involves crossing the flank of the mountain to a lookout and returning via the **Kaupokponui Falls.**

Short walks round the **North Egmont** section of the park, starting from the top of Egmont Road, include the unusual and atmospheric **Ngatoro Loop Track** (1hr), which winds through the hidden valley of the Goblin Forest, with its kaikawaka trees, alpine plants and gnarled trunks hung with ferns and cushiony mosses. Alternatively, the **Veronica Loop Track** (2hr) climbs up to a ridge, through mountain forest and scrub with fine views of the ancient lava flows known as Humphries Castle, New Plymouth and the coast.

There are more good walking tracks around **East Egmont**, at the top of Pembroke Road, from where the **Enchanted Track** (3hr) heads for Jackson's Lookout before dropping through dense vegetation at lower altitudes, while the **Curtis Falls Track** (4hr) traces the Te Popo Stream, via steps and ladders, to the Manganui River Gorge, then follows the riverbed past two waterfalls.

New Plymouth to Wanganui

The swift, virtually uninterrupted progress of the **inland** SH3 to Hawera, 74km due south, is dull by comparison with the scenic coastal route (see below).

Just over halfway between New Plymouth and Hawera on SH3 is the small town of **STRATFORD**, which provides access to Mount Taranaki, especially the Manganui Skifield (see box on previous page) and a home for a truly grotesque mock-tudor clock tower (built in 1996 to hide the 1960s version). The **visitor centre** on Broadway 1km south of the clock tower (Mon–Fri 8.30am–5pm & Sat 10am–3pm; ☎06/765 6708, fax 765 7500, *stuperry@info.stratford.govt.nz*), also acts as the InterCity and Newmans **bus** stop. There are a couple of **places to stay**, mostly patronized by the ski crowd. *Stratford Holiday Park*, 10 Page St (☎ & fax 06/765 6440; tent sites $9, dorms ①, cabins ②–③, motel units ③–④), has a wide range of on-site accommodation, as well as camping, in clean, well-cared-for surroundings; bike rental is also available for $25 a day. Under the same management, *Taranaki Accommodation Lodge* (☎ & fax 06/765 6440; ②) occupies a former nurses' home, with mostly twin rooms. The only worthwhile eatery in Stratford is the *Back Stage Café*, 234 Broadway close to the clock tower, licensed and BYO. Open from Tuesday to Sunday it serves good coffee, big snacks and some thoughtful, inexpensive (under $20) and tasty main courses.

It takes about four hours to drive around the **Surf Highway** (SH45) to Hawera, including a couple of stops along the way; a free map of the route is available at the New Plymouth visitor centre. The Surf Highway tends to be about 3km from the actual surf for most of its length and is accompanied by the almost constant buffeting of strong winds off the sea. At Pungarehu, about a third of the way, Cape Road cuts west to the cast-iron tower of **Cape Egmont Lighthouse**, precariously perched on the western-most point of the cape and overlooking Taranaki's windswept coast.

Hawera

HAWERA is situated at the confluence of SH3 and SH45 and is flat, spread out and sur-rounded by gently undulating farmland. With a population of 8000, Hawera is primari-ly a service and administration centre for the district's dairy farms, but visitors are pro-vided for with spectacular cliff-lined **surfing beaches**, one of the best **museums** in these parts and the chance to go **dam dropping**.

The town itself was birthplace and home of the famous New Zealand author, **Ronald Hugh Morrieson** (see Contexts p.879) who loved jazz, wrote well-observed and amus-ing novels about small-town life and liked a drink or two – appropriate since the only memorial to his existence is a café/bar (see below) containing memorabilia rescued from his now demolished house.

The **Tawhiti Museum and Bush Railway** (Museum Sept–May, Fri–Mon 10am–4pm; June–Aug, Sun 10am–4pm, $5; Railway first Sun in the month, every Sun during school holidays, & public holidays, $3) is on Ohangi Road, near the junction with Tawhiti Road, about 4km outside Hawera. The unique exhibits really bring the past to life, recreating the social and technological heritage of both Maori and *pakeha* through the extensive use of photographs, models and dioramas. Among the most impressive are representations of pa sites, including the virtually impregnable Turuturumokai pa, and the changes to fortifications wrought by the advent of musket warfare. Other highlights include a record of the life of Chew Chong, a widely respect-ed Chinese migrant who initiated the export of local fungi to China, a working pottery and the small-scale bush railway that trundles through displays recounting the logging history of Taranaki.

The other irresistible sight in Hawera is the **Elvis Presley Record Rooms**, 51 Argyle St (visits by appointment, ☎06/278 7624; donation requested), about ten min-utes' walk from the visitor centre. K.D. Wasley's shrine to the King is his garage, which contains thousands of rare recordings, photographs and memorabilia.

Kaitiaki Adventures started **dam dropping** (whitewater sledging) in Hawera (☎0800/336 376) and although they now run slightly more trips out of Rotorua (see p.280) their original venture ($80 for about 3hr) still operates here. As long as you can swim you'll be equipped with a wetsuit, helmet and buoyant plastic sledge. First you must throw yourself off a dam, either from the centre or higher sides (and as many times as you can stand it!), thereafter the Wainongoro river is mostly docile and much of the trip involves floating and paddling along while the guide imparts local Maori his-tory and folklore. It's great fun and not as hard as it sounds: the drop is no higher than 6m or, slightly more disturbingly, over 9 metres from the dam sides.

Practicalities

InterCity **buses** stop at the Hawera Travel Centre on Glover Road, while Newmans drop off at the **visitor centre**, 55 High St (Mon–Fri 8.30am–5pm, Dec–Jan also Sat & Sun 10am–3pm; *hawvin@nzhost.co.nz*). BB Cars (☎0800/837 383) or Southern Cabs (☎0800/282 822) will run you out to the Tawhiti Museum and other local sights.

In town, there are comfortable units at the *Furlong Motor Inn*, 256 Waihi Rd (☎06/278 5136; ④); clean and simple rooms at the *Dominion Hotel*, Princes Street

(☎06/278 7385, ④); or a range of on-site **accommodation** at the *King Edward Park Motorcamp*, Waihi Road (☎06/278 8544; tent sites $9, studios & cabins ②–④). To stay in a more scenic setting, head 4km past the Tawhiti Museum, along Ararata Road, to *Wheatley Downs* (☎06/278 6523; dorms ①, rooms ②), a friendly farmstay with views of Mount Taranaki.

When it comes to **eating**, the best place in town is the eponymous *Morrieson's Café Bar* on Victoria Street (daily 11am–1am). This stylish spot contains some of the great writer's possessions and books and serves good value well-presented food and refreshing ale. If you're looking for **breakfasts**, call into *Auntie's Café*, 79 High St (closed Sun), purveyor of coffee, tea, toast, bacon and eggs from early morning to late afternoon, or the value-for-money *Whistle Stop Café,* next to the InterCity bus stop.

Hawera to Wanganui

Cutting through heavily cultivated farmland, SH3 splits **PATEA**, the only major community between Hawera and Wanganui. The township has a large model of the Aotea Canoe in the main street, commemorating the settlement of the area by Turi and his *hapu*, a good surfing beach at the mouth of the Patea River and a safe freshwater swimming hole, overlooked by the Manawapou Redoubt and pa site.

About 20km before Wanganui is the well-signposted turn-off for **Bushy Park Historic Homestead and Scenic Reserve**, 8km off the main road (daily 10am–5pm; $3). The park contains a large stand of native bush thick with vines, creepers and supplejack, the largest rata tree in New Zealand (3.5m in diameter and 43m tall) and a 1906 homestead. Notable features in the house include a striking stained-glass window, a carved over-mantle and fireplace and a huge five-metre chesterfield in the entrance hall; you can even **stay** and soak up the gracious surroundings (☎06/342 9879, *tourism@wanganui.govt.nz*; B&B ⑥).

Wanganui and around

WANGANUI nestles by the sea on the banks of the Whanganui River at the junction of SH3 and SH4. One of New Zealand's oldest cities and the largest community with access to the **Whanganui National Park**, Wanganui was the hub of early European commerce, by virtue of its access to the interior and coastal links with the ports of Wellington and New Plymouth. Today this clean and well-kept municipality has been given a facelift with an eye to the settlement's **colonial past**: the late Victorian and early Edwardian facades have been refurbished, while mock-gaslight lampposts have been installed along **cobblestone** paths. The aura of civic pride is enhanced by a profusion of flowerbeds, borders and hanging baskets. In addition to its pretty-as-a-postcard riverbank charm, Wanganui contains a pleasing **art gallery** and an excellent **museum**, both with collections of some note, along with an endearing **riverboat museum** that pays tribute to the sturdy craft that were once the city's lifeblood.

By the time **Europeans** arrived in the 1830s, the Maori population was well-established, and land rights quickly became a bone of contention. Transactions Maori perceived as a ritual exchange of gifts, the New Zealand Company took as a successful negotiation for the purchase of Wanganui and a large amount of surrounding land. Settlement went ahead regardless of the misunderstanding, and it was not until the **Gilfillan Massacre** of 1847 that trouble erupted again. When a Maori was accidentally injured, his tribesmen took *utu* (retribution), massacring four members of the Gilfillan family. Further violent incidents culminated in a full-scale but inconclusive **battle** at St John's Hill. The next year the problems were apparently resolved by a payment of £1000 to the Maori; local tribes took no action during the wars in Taranaki, even help-

---

WHANGANUI VERSUS WANGANUI

Visitors are often confused by the variant spellings of **Whanganui** (the original Maori), which is retained for the **river** and the **national park**, and **Wanganui** (the Anglicized version), which has been adopted by the **city**. Explanations of the discrepancy cite the silent "H" in spoken Maori being omitted when the name was written down, or the H being dropped over time as a result of common early English usage. A debate has been raging in the council chambers for some time about whether to restore the original Maori name to the city, but don't hold your breath.

---

ing European settlers by defeating Hauhau warriors at Moutoa Island in 1864 (see p.250).

In 1995 many of the simmering old **grievances** and one or two more recent ones reached boiling point when, on Waitangi Day, Maori occupied the Moutoa Gardens, claiming it as **Maori land**. The four-month **occupation** ended peacefully in the High Court, but created much bitterness on both sides, neither of which particularly distinguished themselves during the occupation. Now, each **Waitangi Day**, the town seems to hold its breath as Maori from all over the country congregate to commemorate the incident, which is seen as a watershed in Maori–*pakeha* relations.

Arrival, information and city transport

The **airport** is ten minutes' drive southwest of the city centre and is linked by Ash Mayor Transport shuttles (☎06/347 7444). **Buses** drop off at various places around town: InterCity stop at Taupo Quay, Newmans at 156 Ridgway St, and White Star at 161 Ingestre St.

The **visitor centre**, 101 Guyton St (March–Oct Mon–Fri 8.30am–5pm, Sat & Sun 10am–2pm; Nov–Feb Mon–Fri 8.30am–6pm, Sat & Sun 9am–3pm; ☎06/349 0508, fax 349 0509, *www.wanganui.govt.nz, infocentre@wanganui.govt.nz*), provides useful leaflets and maps and acts as a booking office for trips, travel and accommodation, as well as providing an **Internet** link. The **DOC office**, 74 Ingestre St (Mon–Fri 8am–5pm), sells leaflets on the Whanganui National Park and the Whanganui River Road, plus hut and camping tickets. The city centre is easily manageable on foot, though **Wanganui Taxi Buses** (☎06/343 5555) run a limited weekday service round the city and to the beaches at the rivermouth; a timetable is available at the visitor centre. If the buses don't suit then try **River City Cabs** (☎06/345 3333) who run a taxi service by request.

Accommodation

Accommodation in Wanganui is plentiful but hardly varied. There are lots of motels, one central hotel/pub of note, two hostels and a couple of good motorcamps but few worthy B&Bs.

Hotels, motels and B&Bs

Acacia Park Motel, 140 Anzac Parade (☎ & fax 06/343 9093). Simple, clean rooms set in extensive grounds overlooking the river. ⑤.

Arlesford House, just off SH3, 7km from Wanganui (☎06/347 7751). Situated in six acres of well tended garden, this friendly spot offers respite from the city. It's also a fine example of a 1930s house with heart rimu floors and spacious rooms boasting pastoral views. ⑦–⑧.

Avenue Motor Inn, 379 Victoria Ave (☎06/345 0907, *dot@xtra.co.nz*). A range of rooms, from clean and budget to plush spacious suites. On-site restaurant and swimming pool. ⑥.

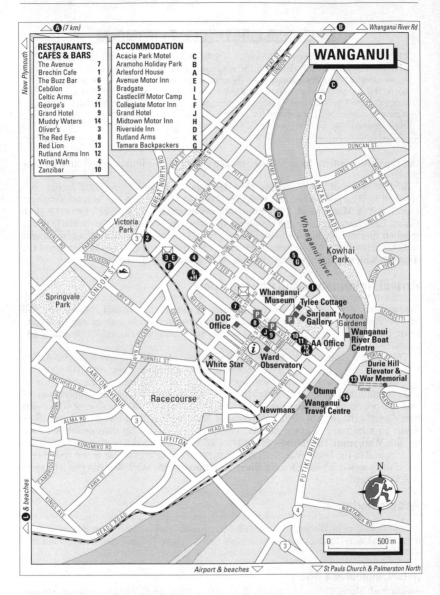

RESTAURANTS, CAFES & BARS

The Avenue	7
Brechin Cafe	1
The Buzz Bar	6
Cebōlon	5
Celtic Arms	2
George's	11
Grand Hotel	9
Muddy Waters	14
Oliver's	3
The Red Eye	8
Red Lion	13
Rutland Arms Inn	12
Wing Wah	4
Zanzibar	10

ACCOMMODATION

Acacia Park Motel	C
Aramoho Holiday Park	B
Arlesford House	A
Avenue Motor Inn	E
Bradgate	I
Castlecliff Motor Camp	L
Collegiate Motor Inn	F
Grand Hotel	J
Midtown Motor Inn	H
Riverside Inn	D
Rutland Arms	K
Tamara Backpackers	G

WANGANUI

Bradgate, 7 Somme Parade (☎06/345 3634). An agreeable spot with comfortable high-ceilinged rooms in a house overlooking the river, just eight minutes' walk from the city centre. ④.

Collegiate Motor Inn, 122 Liverpool St (☎06/345 8309). Well-appointed, spacious rooms – some fully self-contained, others with only tea- and toast-making facilities. ⑤.

Grand Hotel, 99 Guyton St (☎06/345 0955, *the-grand-hotel@xtra.co.nz*). A grand old hotel indeed: built in 1927 with a number of bars, a restaurant and clean, comfortable, good-value rooms. ④.

Midtown Motor Inn, 321 Victoria Ave (☎06/345 8408, fax 345 8406, *midtown@clear.net.nz*). Modern, comfortable motel with a variety of budget and economy rooms, a restaurant, lounge bar and café/bar. ④–⑤.

Riverside Inn, 2 Plymouth St (☎06/347 2529). A large characterful 1895 house by the river, surrounded by lawns and the occasional lemon tree, with separate backpacker accommodation (see below) and a corridor full of extremely comfortable, airy and quiet B&B rooms. ④.

Rutland Arms Inn, cnr Victoria Ave & Ridgeway St (☎06/347 7677, fax 347 7345, *enquiries @rutland-arms.co.nz*). Luxurious central accommodation in an historic building at the top end of the market. ⑥.

Hostels and campsites

Aramoho Holiday Park, 460 Somme Parade (☎06/343 8402). Well-tended site 6km from the city centre, by the river in the shade of giant trees. Tent sites $10, cabins ②–③, motel units ④.

Castlecliff Motor Camp, 1a Rangiora St, Castlecliff, 9km south (☎06/344 2227, *tokiwipark@xtra.co.nz*). Close by the beach, bus stop and general store, this site offers camping and a range of on-site accommodation. Tent sites $9, backpacker huts ①, cabins ②.

Riverside Inn Backpackers, 2 Plymouth St (☎06/347 2529). Clean, well-kept backpacker dorms and doubles at the back of this YHA-affiliated hostel, with a thoroughly equipped kitchen and cosy lounge (and B&B rooms, see above). Dorms ①, rooms ②.

Tamara Backpackers, 24 Somme Parade (☎06/347 6300, *tamarabakpak@xtra.co.nz*). A large historic building with plenty of space, pretty gardens and a friendly atmosphere just three minutes' walk from the city centre. Offers free bike rental and lots of neat, comfortable dorms and doubles and a balcony with a river view. They also provide Internet access. Dorms ①, rooms ②.

The City

The most impressive part of Wanganui is **Queens Park**, Watt Street. On a hill known to Maori as Pukenamu, the park marks the site of the last tribal war in Wanganui (1832) and now constitutes the cultural heart of the modern city, containing the Whanganui Regional Museum, Sarjeant Art Gallery, Alexander Library and Davis Library. The **Whanganui Regional Museum** (Mon–Sat 10am–4.30pm, Sun 1–4.30pm; $2), founded in 1892, has an outstanding collection of Maori artefacts, tools, weapons, tukutuku, garments, ornaments, musical instruments and three impressive canoes, all gathered in Te Ati Haunui-a-Paparangi, the central Maori court, in the shape and style of a meeting house. Hung around the collection and in smaller galleries off the main area are Lindauer's portraits of Maori in full ceremonial dress and *moko* (traditional tattoos). Though sometimes criticized for the sitters' passivity, if you look at these portraits long enough the strongest impression is of great *mana* (dignity and pride). Other exhibits include a reconstruction of an early street in the *pakeha* settlement, photographs and displays on New Zealand geology and natural history, including a large number of moa bones. To the east of the museum, at the top of the Veteran Steps, is the **Sarjeant Art Gallery** (Mon–Fri 10.30am–4.30pm & Sat–Sun 1–4.30pm; free), an engaging 1917 building of Oamaru stone, with a magnificent dome that filters natural light to illuminate the exhibits. The highly regarded permanent collection concentrates on contemporary New Zealand art and photography, and is augmented by various touring exhibitions. One of Wanganui's oldest buildings, dating from 1853, is **Tylee Cottage**, on the corner of Cameron Street and Bell Street, which now provides accommodation for the artists in residence at the Sarjeant Gallery.

Southwest of Queen's Park, on Hill Street, **Cook's Gardens** contain the 1903 **Ward Observatory**, with the largest refractor still in use in New Zealand (Monday nights during winter or by arrangement, ☎06/345 4357; donation requested). Back on Victoria Avenue, the pretty **Watt Fountain** marks the intersection of Victoria Avenue and Ridgway Street and is surrounded by a number of ornate classical buildings, including the old Post Office and the striking Rutland Building. The Cinema 3 Complex provides a welcome change of pace, in the shape of a stylish 1950s Art Deco exterior, foyer and mezzanine lounge, not to mention luxurious ladies' powder rooms.

At the southern end of SH3 as it enters the city is **St Paul's Memorial Church**, Anaua Street (donation requested). The church is sometimes locked, but you can get a key from the house on the corner or a small wooden box near the church entrance. From the outside St Paul's looks like just another small whitewashed weatherboard church, but inside it is magnificently decorated with Maori carvings adorned with *paua*, a painted rib ceiling (as in Maori meeting houses), beautiful etched-glass windows and *tukutuku* panels.

Along the riverbanks

On the west bank of the river, Taupo Quay is flanked by old warehouses, stores and at no. 1a, the admirable **Whanganui River Boat Centre** (Mon–Fri 9am–4pm, Sat 10am–4pm, Sun 1–4pm; donation requested; ☎06/347 1863 for information about excursions). Housed in an 1881 two-storey timber-framed building, the centre's museum concentrates on the river and its history in relation to the town – a centre of pre-Great War tourism when thousands of people from all over the world came to travel up the Whanganui River and stay at the hotel at Pipiriki. The Centre was established to restore the *Waimarie* **paddle steamer** which sank at its moorings in 1952. The *Waimarie*, built by Yarrow and Co. of London in 1899 and transported to New Zealand in kit form, was designed with a shallow draught and tough bottom suitable for river work. After 68,000 hours spent using skills from half a century ago the ship was finally rebuilt in 1999 and these days runs worthwhile **excursions** (1hr; $25) along the river it used to ply. With each trip a small contribution goes towards the next seemingly impossible project of the River Boat Centre: it's also involved in the restoration of *Wairua*, a 1904 raised **propeller boat** (forerunner of the modern jetboat) that was capable of progress in only 30cm of water.

Near the Whanganui River Boat Centre, at the junction of Taupo Quay and Somme Parade, lie the historic **Moutoa Gardens**, scene of the signing of the document agreeing to the sale of Wanganui and, many years later, of a significant Maori land rights protest. Traditionally Maori had lived at Moutoa during the fishing season until it was co-opted by *pakeha* settlers, who renamed the area Market Square. An ancient law prohibited the police from arresting Maori in the gardens; combined with the historical precedent, this gave the four-month occupation in 1995 great resonance.

Across the City Bridge, on the east bank of the river, is the **Durie Hill Elevator and Tower** (Mon–Fri 7.30am–6pm, Sat 10am–6pm, Sun 11am–5pm; $1), where a Maori carved gateway marks the entrance to a 213-metre tunnel at the end of which a historic 1919 elevator carries passengers up through the hill to the summit, saving a 176-step climb. Once at the top of the hill there are two excellent vantage points: the lift's machinery room or atop the **Memorial Tower** (daily 8am–dusk), both granting extensive views of the city, beaches and inland. Once you've seen enough try the walk down the steps to the river – it only takes about ten minutes, and provides some satisfying views of the surrounding area.

The beaches

Adjacent to the southern jaw of the mouth of the Whanganui River is **South Beach**, a vast desolate tract of sand accessible from the old airport road, while on the northern jaw is **Castlecliff Beach**, a broad sweep of black iron-sand, with safe swimming, good surf and the usual motley collection of driftwood. South of Castlecliff Beach and accessible by walking along the beach (2hr, but check tides at the visitor centre) or by following the Rapanui Road off SH3 north for 20km, is **Mowhanu Beach**, a spectacular swimming beach surrounded by papa cliffs (sandstone and mudstone) and renowned for good windsurfing.

Eating and drinking

Wanganui seems to have been decimated in recent years with only a few decent restaurants and stylish cafés left. Nevertheless **Italian food** remains a good bet out toward the Whanganui River Road, owing to the presence of migrant workers who stayed on after being brought in to work on the aborted hydroelectric scheme. Otherwise the city boasts one or two good **cafés**, swanky **bars**, some spit-and-sawdust **pubs** and a couple of late-night venues that gear up at weekends (check listings in the *Wanganui Chronicle*; Friday; 70¢).

Cafés and takeaways

The Avenue, cnr Victoria Ave & Ingestre St. Quite simply a great fish and chip shop. Daily except Mon, 4pm till late.

Brechin Café and Gallery, 17 Pitt St, nr cnr Dublin St. An out of the way treasure where you can get coffee, sumptuous cakes and healthy but huge meals at reasonable prices. The walls are adorned with the art of Pauline the owner – a disturbing mix of expressionist, semi-abstract colour co-ordination. Wed–Sun 9am–4pm.

Cebōlon, 25 Somme Parade. Swanky licensed café decorated in the style of Euro-Kiwi with a touch of Germanic thrown in, offering relaxing music, smooth coffees, indulgent cakes, hearty soups, salads and wholesome dinners. Closed Sun. Attached to the café is a Kiwiana "antique" shop that's best avoided.

George's, 40 Victoria Ave, next to the cinema. The only other fish and chip shop in town that's worth a visit, also selling good-value fresh fish. Mon–Fri 7am–7pm.

Muddy Waters, 9 Putiki Drive. Turn-of-the-century brick bakery overlooking the river near City Bridge, serving coffee, juices, shakes, home-made pies, sandwiches and snacks. Daily 6.30am–6.30pm.

The Red Eye, 96 Guyten St. Hippest BYO café in town with eye-brightening coffee, alternative art-student atmosphere and lovely wholesome food for lunch or dinner, including Tandoori chicken, Indonesian stir fry and trad New Zealand favourites. They occasionally have acoustic live music at weekends.

Zanzibar, Victoria Court, Victoria Ave, in a mall 10m southeast of Maria Place. Easy going licensed café serving tasty food such as Thai-style snacks, red-beet curry and Cajun chicken in bright surroundings with cool jazz. Daily; late Wed–Sat for dinners.

Restaurants

Grand Hotel, 99 Guyton St. Cobb and Co franchise, dishing up simple food in large portions. Daily 7am–9pm.

Olivers, Avenue Motel, 379 Victoria Ave. Gourmet pizzas and big dinners. Closed Sun; licensed.

Peppers Brasserie, Avenue Motel, 379 Victoria Ave. Snacks and meals served daily from 10am–9.30pm.

Riviera, Upokongaro, 11km north on SH4 (☎06/345 6459; book Fri & Sat dinner). The best and most authentic Italian restaurant in the area – fresh pasta, great coffee, home-made ice cream – and nothing on the menu costs more than $21. Lunch Thurs–Sun, dinner Wed–Sun; licensed.

Wing Wah, 330 Victoria St. Good-quality Chinese restaurant and take away offering reasonable prices, with generous banquet meals for two or more and some authentic eastern cuisine. Daily 4.30–10pm; licensed.

Bars and clubs

Celtic Arms, 437 Victoria Ave. Bargain pub food, including fry up breakfasts, fish'n'chips, pan-fried snapper or steak, plus live folk, jazz or rock on Fridays. Thurs–Sat noon–2am, Sun–Wed noon to midnight.

The Buzz Bar, Midtown Motor Inn, 321 Victoria Ave. Popular neon, mirror and chrome sports bar with big-screen TV, all-day bar snacks, daily happy hours (4.30–6.30pm) and an upstairs nightclub called Metro on Fri and Sat nights, with a DJ and dance music.

Red Lion, 45 Anzac Parade. An atmospheric pub with a wide selection of beers and bar meals and about the best place to see live music at weekends. Daily 11am–3am.

Rutland Arms Inn, 48–52 Ridgway St. A pseudo-old-style pub, with 14 beers on tap, bar snacks, and dinners featuring olde English desserts like apple and blackberry crumble served from 5.30pm. Daily 8.30am–11pm, until 1am Thurs–Sat.

Listings

Automobile Association 78 Victoria Ave (☎06/348 9160).

Banks All the major banks are situated on Victoria Ave or within one block of it.

Buses Wanganui Taxi Buses (☎06/343 5555); InterCity (☎06/345 4433); Newmans (☎06/345 5566); White Star (☎06/347 6677); Ash's Coachlines (☎06/347 7444); Rivercity Tours (☎06/344 2554).

Car rental Avis (☎06/345 7612); Hertz (☎06/345 7357); Rent-a-dent (☎06/345 1505).

Cinema Embassy 3 Cinema, 34 Victoria Ave; check local press for screenings (☎06/345 7958).

Internet Visitor's Centre, *Bit Works Web Café*, 49 Ridgeway St ($2 for 15min); the library, Queens Park.

Medical treatment Wanganui Hospital, cnr Heads Rd & Carlton Ave (☎06/348 1234); Wanganui City Doctors Clinic, 163 Wicksteed St (Mon–Fri 5–10pm & Sat–Sun 8am–10pm; ☎06/348 8333); Wicksteed After Hours Pharmacy, 214 Wicksteed St (Mon–Fri 5pm–8.30am, Sat & Sun 24hr; ☎06/345 6166).

Music Records, CDs, tapes, mags plus information on night spots from the friendly Ridgeway Records, 26 Victoria Avenue.

Post office Wanganui Central Post Office, 60 Ridgway St; Mid-Avenue Post Office, 226 Victoria Ave, between Plymouth St & Ingestre St.

Taxis Wanganui Taxis (☎06/343 5555 & 0800/500 000) have ranks on Guyton St, Maria Pl and Ridgway St; or River City Cabs (☎06/345 3333).

Whanganui National Park

The emerald-green waters of the Whanganui River tumble 329km from the northern slopes of Mount Tongariro to the Tasman Sea at Wanganui, by way of 239 listed rapids. The middle reaches of the river bisect the **Wanganui National Park**, and the flow is rarely violent, making the river excellent for **canoeing**, even for people with little or no experience. The main highway from Taumaranui, SH4, mirrors the course of the river for 166km, before joining it in Wanganui.

Traditionally, **Maori** held that each bend of the river had a *kaitiaki* (guardian), who controlled the *mauri* (life force). The *mana* of each settlement depended upon the way in which the food supplies and living areas were maintained: sheltered terraces on the riverbanks were cultivated and elaborate weirs were constructed to trap eels and lamprey. The first **European** arrivals in the valley were **missionaries** who, in the 1840s, set about converting local Maori – and leaving a legacy of biblical place names along the river road. The river's isolation also attracted recluses and visionaries fleeing the excesses of the civilized world, such as poet **James K. Baxter**, who set up a commune here in the 1970s and was held in great affection by local Maori. Right up until the early 1900s, the river was the primary route to the interior of the North Island, and by 1891 a regular **boat service** carried passengers and cargo to the settlers between Pipiriki and Taumarunui, and **tourists** between Wanganui and Mount Ruapehu (see p.316). The riverboat tourist-trade dried up during the Great War and ceased in the 1920s with the coming of the railway and better roads, though the boats still operated a cargo and passenger service until the 1950s.

European attempts to stamp their mark on this wild landscape have often been ill-fated. In 1917 the **Maungpurua Valley**, in the middle of the park, was opened up for settlement by servicemen returning from the first war, who little realized they were trading one battlefield for another. Plagued by **economic hardship**, remoteness and difficulty of access, many settlers had abandoned their farms by the 1920s. A bridge over the Maungpurua Valley was opened in 1936, but after a major flood in 1942, the government declined to make any further funds available for road maintenance and the bridge was cut off, the three remaining families ordered out and the valley officially closed. Today, the only signs that the valley was ever inhabited are the disappearing road, old fence lines, stands of exotic trees planted by the farmers, occasional brick chimneys and the poignant **Bridge to Nowhere**, which can be reached from the river or on the three-day Mangapurua Track.

Encompassing one of the largest remaining tracts of **lowland forest** in the North Island, Whanganui National Park sits on a bed of soft **sandstone** and **mudstone** (*papa*), which has been eroded to form deep gorges, sharp ridges, sheer cliffs and waterfalls. Beneath the canopy of broad-leaved podocarps and mountain beech, an understorey of tree ferns and clinging plants extends down to the riverbanks, while abundant and vociferous **birdlife** includes the kereru (native pigeon), fantail, tui, robin, grey warbler, tomtit and brown kiwi. Occupying a swathe of riverside land between Taumarunui and Wanganui, the park can be **accessed** from the west via SH43 on to the Mangaehu Road and the **Matemateaonga Track**, and from the north through Whakahoro, which is linked to SH4 by roads from Owhango and Raurimu. From **Pipiriki**, to the south, routes lead up the **Whanganui River Road** from Wanganui or down a rougher 28km from Raetihi on SH4.

Whanganui River Road

The **Whanganui River Road** between **Wanganui** and **Pipiriki** is rough, partially sealed, twisting, narrow and time consuming – all factors which mean you'd do well to join the **Whanganui River Mail Run**, run by Rivercity Tours (☎06/344 2554 & 0800/377 311; $10 one way, $25 return), rather than struggling along in your own vehicle. Starting in Wanganui at 7.30am, the trip takes in all the sights along the way and arrives in Pipiriki around four hours later. At Pipiriki you can join pre-arranged jet-boat trips further upriver ($30–60 extra) before heading for home; tea and coffee are supplied but you need to bring your own food. If you want to go it alone, note that the route is subject to floods and landslips, and has no petrol stations.

Opened in 1934, the 78-kilometre road, bordered by river, farmland and heavily forested national park, is the supply route for the four hundred people who live along the river between Wanganui and Pipiriki. Near the start of the river road, 14km from Wanganui, is an unmanned **visitor kiosk** with a map, descriptions of sights and history relating to the route.

Aramoana to Moutoa Island

After 3km the river road winds up to the summit lookout of **Aramoana**, the starting point of the Aramoana Walkway (see p.254). Some 11km further on, you will pass **Oyster Shell Bluffs**, small roadside overhangs with oyster-shell deposits embedded in them, and **Hipango Park**, a scenic reserve on the riverbank that's only accessible from the river aboard a paddle steamer or with Rivercity jetboats (see p.253). Around 35km from Wanganui are the remains of **ATENE**, a tiny village with few occupied houses, and the start of the Atene Skyline Track (see p.255). The first real settlement of note is **KORINITI**, or Corinth, site of the Ngati Pamoana pa and a 1920s meeting house but you'll have to content yourself with the view from the road as a constant flow of casual visitors have upset the locals. About 3km further up the river road is the well-preserved **Operiki pa site**, accessible via a stile on the left of the road and marked by a yellow sign. As you continue along the river road you will see the track to the **Kawana Flour Mill**, 56km from Wanganui. One of a number of water-powered flour mills that operated along the river road, the 1854 mill has recently been restored. A further 4km along is one of the larger settlements, **RANANA**, where there's a **campsite** (see p.252) and a Roman Catholic mission church that's still in use today. One kilometre from the church is **Moutoa Island**, scene of a famous and vicious battle in 1864 when the lower river Maori defeated the rebellious Hauhau warriors, thereby protecting the *mana* of the river and saving an untold number of settlers' lives.

Hiruharama (Jerusalem)

One of the most famous sites on the river is **HIRUHARAMA**, or Jerusalem, originally a Maori village and Catholic mission but now better known as the site of the **James K. Baxter** commune, which briefly flourished here in the early 1970s. Baxter, one of New Zealand's most (in)famous poets, attracted upwards of two hundred of his followers to the area. A devout Roman Catholic convert whose life followed few of the usual practices of the church, he became father to a flock of his own, the *nga moki* (fatherless ones), though they soon dispersed after his death in 1972. The main commune house is situated high on a hill to the right of the road, and Baxter is buried just below the house, though you'll have to fork out $5 to pay homage at his grave. Instead take ten minutes to look over the church and talk to the Sisters of Compassion, who still live in the **convent** and provide **accommodation** for visitors (see overleaf). The present church was built in 1892 and features a Maori-designed and carved altar; also in the church is a photo of Mother Mary Joseph Aubert (1833–1926), who established the first community of sisters in 1829, and a portrait of Baxter, looking suitably Christ-like.

After 70km on the river road you will reach its highest point, marked by a picnic site, with excellent views of the national park and the increasingly spectacular river gorge; 2km further along is the **Omorehu Waterfall Lookout**, overlooking one of many impressive waterfalls that cascade into the Whanganui River.

Pipiriki

The most important community on the river road is at its end: **PIPIRIKI**, some 78km from Wanganui, is the gateway to the Whanganui National Park. A **DOC office** (daily 10am–4pm) is maintained in the **Colonial House Museum** (same hours; $1), which is full of pictures, articles and information about the river. The other point of historical interest in the village is the 1904 MV *Ongarue*, the longest-serving **riverboat** on the middle reaches of the river, though these days the proud vessel sits high and dry on the riverbank and is in a sorry state. From the Pipiriki picnic area, beside the river, a short walk (15min) leads to the picturesque **Paparoa Waterfall** on the Kaitane Stream. Otherwise, there's little to Pipiriki besides a public shelter, toilets and a basic **campsite**.

From here, the **Pipiriki–Raetihi Road** heads off to Raetihi and SH4, another tortuous 28km east.

Park practicalities

Information on the national park and the river is most readily available from visitor centres in Taumarunui and Wanganui. Alternatively you can pick up useful leaflets, including *In and Around the Whanganui National Park* ($1), from **DOC** maintained offices in Wanganui (74 Ingestre St; Mon–Fri 8am–4.30pm), Taumarunui (Cherry Grove, off Taumarunui Street; Mon–Fri 8am–noon & 1–4.30pm) and Pipiriki (Colonial House Museum; Oct–April daily 10am–4pm).

All **overnight** visitors to the national park must buy a **DOC Facility User Pass**: these are valid for seven days (six nights) and cost $25 in advance from DOC offices (☎06/385 5022) or $35 from rangers in the park; if you are joining an organized **canoeing trip** (see box on p.253), check whether or not this is included in the price. There are no shops in the park, so you need to take all your **supplies** with you – and don't drink the river water unless you have boiled it first.

Accommodation and eating

Accommodation can be booked through *tourism@wanganui.govt.nz* or *wagvin @nzhost.co.nz*. The most unusual place to stay in the park is in **Koriniti**, where the flying fox (✆ & fax 06/342 8160; tent sites $8, self-catering in lodge ②; dinner, bed and breakfast ④) gives visitors the chance to sample the lifestyle of modern river settlers: reached across the eponymous flying fox ($2.50), which spans the river 45 minutes' drive (44km) north of Wanganui, the property offers rustic accommodation, walks, home-brewed beers, excellent meals (by arrangement) and morning or afternoon teas $5. Behind the marae at **Ranana**, the *Kauika Campsite* (✆06/342 8061; tent sites $6), adjacent to the river, has toilets, showers, fresh water and a kitchen, while further north at **Hiruharama**, accommodation is offered in the convent for $5 per person; blankets, sheets and cooking facilities are available. At the end of the Whanganui River Road, in **Pipiriki** itself, there are basic free campsites with shelter, toilets and water; during summer. If you're going to brave the area for more than a day's visit it pays to bring supplies with you.

At **Raetihi** on SH4, 28km east of Pipiriki, the *Raetihi Motor Camp* (✆06/385 4176; tent sites $10) offers camping and runs glow-worm tours (free) and canoeing trips (from $100 per person). About 17km upriver from Pipiriki, by the **Matemateaonga Walkway**, the *Ramanui Lodge and Park* (✆025/480 308; woolshed ③; dinner, bed and breakfast ④; tent sites $4; jetboat ride in & dinner, bed and breakfast $110) is only accessible by tramping or boat ($5). Set amid regenerating native lowland forest alongside the river, rates include dinner and a cooked breakfast; a number of jetboating, walking and canoeing trips are on offer; and wine and beer is available for purchase.

In addition, trampers' accommodation is provided by four **DOC huts** on the Matemateaonga Walkway (Category 2–3; $5–10) and one on the Mangapurua Track (Category 2; $10); all are basic back-country huts, with drinking-water supplies, stoves and toilets.

River trips

The best way to explore the Whanganui National Park is **from the river**, not least because tracks tend to get washed away or become otherwise impassable. The Whanganui, on the other hand, provides a safe and reliable route to the wilderness from November to April, and is well furnished with lodge, marae and farmstay accommodation or, better still, a number of good campsites close to the river's banks.

Canoeing/kayaking trips (see box opposite for operators) range from one to five days, and most include return transport (so you only have to paddle downstream) and pretty much everything you'll need – except sleeping bags and tents for longer trips. Virtually all the companies also offer canoe or kayak and gear **rentals** for independent paddlers, with daily **rates** averaging $40–60. **Guided** canoe/kayak river trips can start as high up the river as Taumarunui, but the higher up you start, the longer you'll have to paddle to reach the best of the scenery, which is why many trips start in Whakahoro at the confluence with the Retaruke River. A trip starting **from Taumarunui** takes you past several spectacular water cascades and the *niu poles* of the Hauhau warriors – the latter site is also accessible from the Stratford–Taumarunui Heritage Trail (SH43; see p.227) – before you reach Whakahoro. Heading downstream **from Whakahoro** you'll see the Mangapapa Stream Ravine, the **Man-o-war Bluff** (named for its supposed resemblance to an old iron-clad battleship) and the **Tarepokiore Whirlpool**, which once completely spun a river steamer. From the **Mangapurua Landing**, you can walk to the Bridge to Nowhere (40min) before continuing past the Puraroto Caves to Pipiriki. Trips **from Wanganui** generally involve travelling by road to Pipiriki, Whakahoro or Taumarunui and paddling downstream from there.

WHANGANUI RIVER CANOE/KAYAK, FLIGHT AND JETBOAT TOUR OPERATORS

Trips **start** from various **points** along the river between Taumarunui in the north and Pipiriki in the south; few venture beyond Pipiriki, where the river broadens and becomes tidal as it flows towards its estuary at Wanganui. Although it is not a guarantee of better equipment, training or **safety-consciousness**, membership of the Whanganui River Commercial Operators Association is a good indication. Check with companies before you book – but bear in mind that many Maori operators refuse to join the *pakeha*-controlled association on principle. The best trips are usually three-day adventures running from Whakahoro as far as Pipiriki; longer ones into Wanganui itself can be a little too much (five days), likewise trips starting from Taumarunui. Advance booking is recommended.

TAUMARUNUI- AND WHAKAHORO-BASED OPERATORS

Blazing Paddles (☎ & fax 07/895 8074). Gear rental with prices including drop-off, pick-up and looking after your vehicle (3-day canoe/kayak rental $113/142); they can also organize guides.

Plateau Outdoor Adventure Guides (☎07/892 2740, fax 892 2611). Fully inclusive guided canoe, kayak and motorized raft trips (3-day canoe/kayak trip $390; canoe/kayak rental $35/40 per day; pick-up and drop-off $50). They also offer canyoning ($50 for 4hr) and horse treks ($25 for 1hr).

Wades Landing Outdoors/Whanganui River Jet (☎07/895 5995, fax 895 7995). Jetboating and canoeing trips from Whakahoro to Pipiriki (jetboat to Bridge to Nowhere $85; 3-day guided canoe/kayak trip $390; 3-day canoe/kayak rental $100/106).

Yeti Tours (☎06/385 8197 & 0800/322 388, fax 06/385 8492, *yeti.tours@xtra.co.nz*). Guided paddling trips including gear and food (4–6 day guided canoe/kayak trips $610–715); they also offer canoe/kayak rental (canoe rental $40 per day for two; kayak $25 per day).

WANGANUI- AND PIPIRIKI-BASED OPERATORS

Baldwin Adventure Tours (☎ & fax 06/342 4717). Gentle trips aboard the fourteen-seater motorized canoe, MV *Adventurer*. The 1-day trip from Wanganui including garden visit is $25; 2-day Whakahoro to Koriniti trip including coach ride is $330; and a 5-day guided canoe adventure from Whakahoro to Pipiriki is $550. Although worthwhile these aren't run on a regular basis so check well in advance.

Bridge to Nowhere (☎ & fax 06/385 4128; $70). Popular regular jetboat tours from Pipiriki to the Bridge to Nowhere including a walk up to the bridge itself.

Canoe Safaris (☎06/385 9237 & 0800/2 PADDLE, fax 385 8758, *canoe@voyager.co.nz*). Excellent excursions on various rivers including the Whanganui, where a 4-day trip sets you back $560 but includes everything you can think of.

Remote Adventures (☎06/346 5747 & 0800/150 338, fax 346 6033). Scenic flights over the park; fly over the Bridge to Nowhere for about $130 per person with a minimum of four.

River Spirit (☎06/342 1748, fax 342 1007). Jetboat trips to the Bridge to Nowhere ($70) or a visit to the flying fox (see opposite) including lunch ($90). An overnight trip to and from Wanganui, staying at the *Ramanui Lodge* and including DB&B is $250.

Rivercity Tours (☎06/344 2554, fax 344 7462). This lot operate the mail run up the river road to Pipiriki ($25) as well as offering 4-day escorted canoe trips from Whakahoro to Pipiriki ($495), canoe/kayak rental ($55/75 per day) and jetboat trips to the Bridge to Nowhere ($65).

Wairua Hikoi Tours (☎06/345 3485). Day-trips from Jerusalem incorporating a visit to the flying fox (see opposite) and a commentary focusing on Maori folklore, stories and insights into the use of herbal medicines ($75), or self-guided tours ($45).

Jetboat trips (again, see box on previous page) range from relaxed to frenetic, and tend to be more expensive; they can begin at either end of the river and take in many of same sights, depending upon time and accessibility (power boats cannot enter some of the narrow tributaries or caves).

Walks in the park

Although the national park covers a large area, there are only two walks of more than one day that are worth doing, and even they depend upon **track conditions**. The routes are predominantly through bush, leading to lookouts. The best times to go walking in the park are from **October to April** and you must buy **passes** before setting out (see p.251).

Trampers also need to arrange jetboat pick-up *before* setting out: in Wakahoro, Wades Landing Outdoors (☎07/895 5995) offer **trailhead transport** for trampers, as do Pipiriki-based Bridge to Nowhere jetboats (☎06/385 4128).

The Mangapurua Track

Before attempting this particular track check with the DOC (☎06/385 5022 & 349 0508) as over the last three years it has often been closed. The **Mangapurua Track** (40km; 3 days; 663m ascent) starts from Whakahoro, heading up the Kaiwhakauka Valley before descending through the Mangapurua Valley to Mangapurua Landing, the jetboat pick-up point 30km upstream from Pipiriki. There is a **hut** near the start of the track at Whakahoro, but otherwise you stay overnight in clearly marked **camping** areas, with side streams providing water. Day one (8hr) follows old road routes and consists of easy riverside walking up the Kaiwhakauka Valley before dropping into the Mangapurua Valley, where you pitch camp. Day two (6hr) heads through bush and along sections hewn from sheer papa bluffs, but day three (6hr) is the highlight, taking in the atmospheric Bridge to Nowhere and beyond to the Mangapurua Landing, where signs mark the pick-up point and another camping spot.

Matemateaonga Walkway

The **Matemateaonga Walkway** (42km; 4 days; 732m ascent), pretty much always open, starts just off the Upper Mangehu Road at a turning off SH43 48km from Stratford. Matemateaonga means "isolated desolation", reflecting the rugged nature and remoteness of the bush penetrated by this walk. Using old Maori trails, you are able to push deep into the dense forest before emerging at the river for a pre-arranged pick-up.

Day one (1hr 30min) heads up the Kohi Saddle overlooking the Matemateaonga Range and along to the **Omaru Hut** (Category 2; 12 bunks; $10). On day two (5hr), the track continues along the range through dense bush with occasional small clearings; after about three hours, you can take the side-track to Mount Humphries (90min return), for spectacular views across the park to mounts Taranaki and Tongariro, before continuing along the main track to the **Pouri Hut** (Category 2; 12 bunks; $10). Day three (7hr) is an easy gradient along a well-defined track, mostly along a ridge crest, before ascending to a clearing where the **Otaraheke Hut** (Category 3; 2 bunks; $5) provides an ideal shelter for lunch, before the final descent to the **Puketotara Hut** (Category 2; 12 bunks; $10). The last day (1hr) comprises a steep descent from the hut to the river, where a large sign marks the pick-up point.

Short walks

The best short walks in the park are accessible from the **Whanganui River Road** (see p.250). The **Aramoana Walk** (closed Sept–Oct for lambing), marked from the road, heads inland for about 40min – you can only go up one side and back the same way. It's an easy enough amble, beginning and ending 17km from Wanganui at the Aramoana Summit and heading through farmland, a plantation of pine, banks and cuttings. On a clear day, there are views of the northeast horizon dominated by Mount Ruapehu and the northwest horizon dominated by Mount Taranaki.

Further along the river road, some 35km from Wanganui, the **Atene Skyline Track** (18km; 8hr) is almost a loop, with the start and finish just 2km apart on the road. The track begins at the upriver entrance, climbing up to an old road that follows a gently ascending ridge line to a clearing, where you can get fresh water (the only point on the track). Shortly after this you reach the highest point, before skirting some impressive sandstone bluffs and descending steeply back to the river road. A shorter **nature trail** (20min) shares the same starting point, taking you past examples of the flora and fauna of the region.

Palmerston North and around

On the way to Palmerston North, you really owe it to yourself to stop at **BULLS**, 44km south of Wanganui on SH3, where the locals have let their sense of humour get the better of them. Stop off for a look at the signs outside the bank, Cash-a-Bull; the police station, Const-a-Bull; the visitor centre, Inform-a-Bull; the school, Educatc-a-Bull; supermarket, Comest-a-Bull, and even the fire station, Extinguish-a-Bull; then run.

Seven kilometres on from Bulls toward Palmerston North is **OHAKEA** where the Airforce Museum (daily 9.30am–4.30pm; $8), just off SH3, forms a worthy stop for people with an aeronautical bent. Here you can browse through the remnants of old planes, make pretend on flight simulators, pick up some history or just gaze from the café window at the fully operational RNZAF base next door.

About 30km from Ohakea, sitting on the banks of the Manawatu River, **PALMERSTON NORTH** is a thriving provincial capital, with an exuberant character and plenty to explore. Its **pivotal position** on the main north–south rail line and at the junction of road routes between Wellington and Auckland and between the west and east coasts makes it one of New Zealand's biggest interchanges. After the arrival of the rail line in 1886, Palmerston North grew from little more than a crossroads to a city with an identity, reflected in some splendid **architecture**. An array of **cultural diversions** – an excellent museum and gallery, a visually stunning library and two theatres – in tandem with the young blood from **Massey University**, create a stimulating atmosphere – though things are noticeably duller when the students are on vacation (Dec–March). With its roots in commercial supply, the city also has an embarrassment of **shops**, malls and mega stores, along with some excellent restaurants and cafés – not to mention an inordinate number of car parks.

Arrival, information and city transport

Palmerston North **airport**, 3km northeast of the city, receives Air New Zealand and Ansett flights, and is linked to the centre by the Palmerston Shuttle (☎06/358 4499; $6). The **train station** is on Matthews Avenue, about 1.5km northwest of the city centre and served by local transit **buses**. InterCity and Newmans **coaches** drop off at the Palmerston North Travel Centre, on the corner of Pitt Street and Main Street.

The helpful and friendly **visitor centre**, the old Municipal Building, Church Street, at the southwest corner of The Square (Mon–Fri 9am–5pm, Sat & Sun 10am–3pm; ☎06/354 6593, *manawatu.visitor-info@xtra.co.nz*), is packed to the gills with information on the area, including an excellent weekly events sheet and a range of glossy booklets detailing various aspects of the town – including city walks (free) – as well as offering a full booking service.

The Palmerston North Travel Centre is the focal point for all **local bus** services, which run in a series of loops from the terminal to various parts of the city ($1.50); a timetable is available at the visitor centre or the travel centre. Note that services are somewhat reduced outside term time.

Accommodation

If further proof were needed that Palmerston North is a city geared to the needs of the car, then the large number of **motels**, mostly on or around Fitzherbert Avenue, and relative dearth of other good accommodation should suffice.

Hotels and motels

Acacia Court Motel, 374 Tremaine Ave (☎06/358 3471). A friendly welcome and clean, fully self-contained, ground-floor units. ③–④.

Albert Motor Lodge, 692–700 Main St (☎06/357 3115). Small hotel/motel with an in-house bar and restaurant, and plenty of en-suite single and double rooms with satellite TV. ④–⑤.

Birch Trees Lodge, 97 Tremaine Ave (☎06/356 1455). Six self-contained modern units and four well-kept studios, all spacious and agreeable. ④–⑥.

Empire Establishment Hotel, cnr Main St & Princess St (☎06/357 8002). Centrally located, recently refurbished hotel rooms. There's a Cobb and Co restaurant downstairs and a popular bar, which can be noisy at weekends. ④–⑤.

Illuzzions Motel, 127 Fitzherbert Ave (☎06/355 0050, *illuzzions@clear.net.nz*). Despite the awful name and its mock-Tudor appearance, this is a pretty classy establishment, with well-appointed units – and a free round of golf for each guest. ⑥.

Quality Hotel, 110 Fitzherbert Ave (☎06/356 8059, fax 356 8604, *quality.palmerston@cdlhrus.co.nz*). A modern comfortable hotel only five minutes' walk from the square, offering a variety of accommodation largely for corporate custom. Prices drop from May–Sept and there is a lively bar often frequented by students and a reasonably priced carvery restaurant, popular with families, attached to the hotel. ⑤–⑥.

B&Bs, hostels and campsites

Emma's B&B, 250 Fitzherbert Ave (☎06/357 5143, *emmasplace@xtra.co.nz*). Run by a friendly Dutch couple, who offer cosy, basic accommodation with full cooked breakfasts. Popular with students and often busy. ④.

Contact House, 186 Fitzherbert House (☎06/355 3653, fax 355 3687, *contract.house @clear.net.nz*). The pick of the bunch in terms of value for money with modern colourful rooms only 5min walk from the square. Breakfast is simple but it's so hospitable here that you'll feel spoiled. ③, B&B ④.

Grey's Inn B&B, 123 Grey St (☎06/358 6928, *ak1@clear.net.nz*). Very comfortable rooms with their own facilities in a friendly and welcoming house. ③–⑥.

The Pepper Tree (YHA), 121 Grey St (☎06/355 4054, *peppertree@clear.net.nz*). A comfortable hostel within easy walking distance of the central square. Run by friendly and helpful folk, this is a small place, so phone ahead. Dorms ①, rooms ②.

The City

The focal point of Palmerston North is the **central square**, bordered by Broadway Avenue and Church Street. Among the mish-mash of colonial buildings that surround the square are a number of fine examples from different architectural schools: lavish classical Victorian and Edwardian edifices, the elegant lines of Art Deco-influenced structures from the late 1920s and early 1930s, and practical modern constructions like the public library, sensitively poking its nose from behind the classical facade of a much older building.

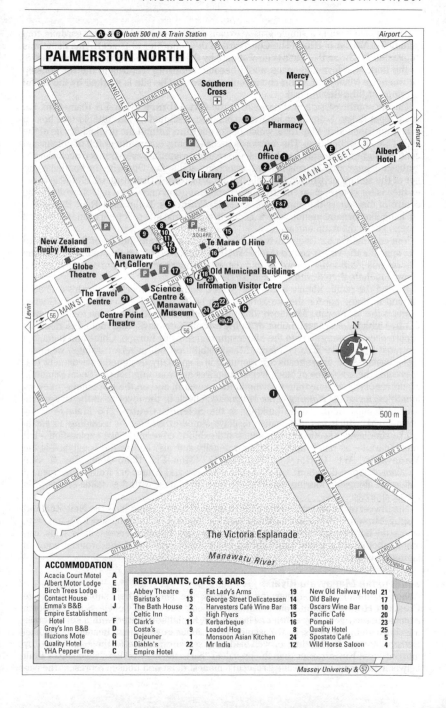

PALMERSTON NORTH

△ Ⓐ & Ⓑ (both 500 m) & Train Station

Airport △

Mercy ✚

Southern Cross ✚

Pharmacy

AA Office ❶
❷

Ⓔ

Albert Hotel

City Library

❸

Cinema

❺

F&7

❻

❽
❾ ❿
⓫
⓮ ⓬
⓭

New Zealand Rugby Museum

Manawatu Art Gallery

⓯

Te Marae O Hine

⓰

Globe Theatre

⓱

Old Municipal Buildings

❶❽
❷⓿

Science Centre & Manawatu Museum

❿❾

Infromation Visitor Cetre

The Travel Centre

㉑

㉓㉒
㉔

Ⓖ

Centre Point Theatre

H&25

N

0   500 m

Ⓘ

Ⓙ

The Victoria Esplanade

Manawatu River

Ashurst ▷

Levin ◁

Massey University & ㊗ ▽

ACCOMMODATION

Acacia Court Motel	**A**
Albert Motor Lodge	**E**
Birch Trees Lodge	**B**
Contact House	**I**
Emma's B&B	**J**
Empire Establishment Hotel	**F**
Grey's Inn B&B	**D**
Illuzions Mote	**G**
Quality Hotel	**H**
YHA Pepper Tree	**C**

RESTAURANTS, CAFÉS & BARS

Abbey Theatre	**6**	Fat Lady's Arms	**19**	New Old Railway Hotel	**21**
Barista's	**13**	George Street Delicatessen	**14**	Old Bailey	**17**
The Bath House	**2**	Harvesters Café Wine Bar	**18**	Oscars Wine Bar	**10**
Celtic Inn	**3**	High Flyers	**15**	Pacific Café	**20**
Clark's	**11**	Kerbarbeque	**16**	Pompeii	**23**
Costa's	**9**	Loaded Hog	**8**	Quality Hotel	**25**
Dejeuner	**1**	Monsoon Asian Kitchen	**24**	Spostato Café	**5**
Diablo's	**22**	Mr India	**12**	Wild Horse Saloon	**4**
Empire Hotel	**7**				

The square itself is a simple grassy expanse with trees and well-kept gardens containing **Te Marae o Hine** (The Courtyard of the Daughter of Peace). This name was suggested for the settlement's central square by the chief of the Ngati Raukawa in 1878, in the hope that love and peace would become enduring features in the relationship between the Manawatu Maori and incoming *pakeha*. The site is marked by the skilful carvings of John Bevan Ford.

On the southeast side of the square is the **City Library** (Mon–Fri 10am–6pm, Sat 10am–4pm & Sun 1–4pm), an innovative building designed by Ian Athfield (see box on p.442) and opened in May 1995, which peeks out from behind the original facade of the 1927 C.M. Ross building. The interior is a challenging environment full of colour and contrast, light and texture in which all the reading materials are arranged according to "subject living rooms" furnished with armchairs and sofas. Opposite the southern corner of the square on Church Street is the old **Municipal Building**, which today houses the visitor centre, an art centre and a couple of good cafés (see p.260), while in the centre of the square the impressive Art Deco **Women's Toilet and Rest Room** has an icing-like ornamentation and a geometric aquamarine relief surrounded by half moons above the main entrance.

You can enjoy a bird's-eye view of Palmerston North from the top of the **civic centre**, opposite the visitor centre (Mon–Fri 10am–3pm; free); from this vantage point, the city reveals itself to be sprawling and flat with a number of small green parks, like a runny omelette dotted with sprigs of parsley.

Behind the public library is **George Street**, home of Palmerston North's café society and a honey pot for the weekend-brunch bees. Around the corner from George Street is the **Manawatu Museum** (daily 10am–5pm; $6, also admits you to the Science Centre) which contains a number of highly evocative displays. One room describes the experiences of immigrants to the Manawatu region from Europe, China and India, but the most impressive area is a large Maori exhibition hall where carvings, weapons, tools, baskets and figureheads are mounted in a specially designed environment that re-creates the ambience of bush, trees, campfires and meeting houses. Local Rangitaki Maori regularly demonstrate weaving in the museum, and on the last Sunday of every month perform *The Naming of the Manawatu*; check in the foyer or at the visitor centre for details. In the same building is the **Science Centre**, 396 Main St (daily 10am–5pm), which has imaginative displays aimed at children – including an earthquake simulator, a section on volcanoes and exhibits covering space exploration – but shouldn't take as much time to explore. Finally and just across the courtyard is the **Manawatu Art Gallery**, 398 Main St (Mon–Fri 10am–5pm, Sat & Sun 11.30am–4.30pm; donation) which displays *pakeha* and Maori art from its permanent collection alongside touring exhibitions; check the latest with the visitor centre or in the local press.

Northwest of the square, on the edge of the A&P Showgrounds, is the **New Zealand Rugby Museum**, 87 Cuba St (Mon–Sat 10am–noon & 1.30–4pm, Sun 1.30–4pm; $3), where die-hard rugger fans can marvel at caps, ties, blazers, jerseys, balls, cups, cartoons, photographs, a reference library of games on video and the bronzed boots of famous players.

South to the Manawatu River

Although not on most sightseeing itineraries, the leafy garden suburb of **Savage Crescent Housing Estate**, at the junction of Cook Street and College Street, is worth a quick look on your way south to The Victoria Esplanade. Faced with a severe housing shortage in the 1930s, New Zealand's first Labour government, headed by Michael Savage, funded the building of well-made houses comparable to those inhabited by more affluent Kiwis, rather than the prevalent "barracks-like workers' dwellings". Built between 1939 and 1945, Savage Crescent's modest detached houses represent the partial fulfilment of that egalitarian dream, although sadly these days they do look a little run-down.

A couple of kilometres south of the square, the tree-filled parklands of **The Victoria Esplanade** (daily dawn to dusk; free) stretch along the north bank of the Manawutu River, with manicured lawns and flowerbeds, a miniature railway, bird aviaries, rose gardens and many excellent spots for a picnic. On the south side of the river, at the bottom of Fitzherbert Avenue, **Massey University Campus** is well worth an hour of your time. Served by local buses from the Travel Centre, the spacious leafy campus is an appealing mixture of trees, modern and old buildings that seem to blend into a dreamy academic blur.

Around Palmerston North

Near the township of Himatangi, 38km southwest on SH56, is the windswept **Himatangi Beach**. Stretching 10km in either direction, the grey sands are strewn with tangles of driftwood and in the summer water-sports fanatics, sunbathers and surf-sailers (sails on three-wheeled go-carts) occupy the flat foreshore. Deviate from the beach road down the Himatangi Block Road about 300m and you'll find one of the more bizarre activities in the area: **possum spotting** with Spot Light Tours (☎06/357 9476; $25 with own transport, $38 if picked up from Palmerston North), involving tramping round the farm and bush after dark.

Back on SH3, 13km northeast of Palmerston North, is the small town of **ASHHURST**, home to the internationally renowned **John Bevan Ford Art Studio**, 6 Lincoln St – turn right off the main road through town and follow Lincoln Street almost to the end. The Studio's workshop is open to the public (daily 11am–4pm) for viewing work in progress. Ford produces finely wrought coloured-ink drawings on handmade watercolour paper and, more famously, sculptures, large wooden carvings using traditional Maori and more contemporary techniques as well as bright designs for Dilena rugs, again innovative while retaining their native origins. His works feature in many of New Zealand's galleries and an official archive is held at the Taranaki Museum in New Plymouth, and in the Arts Centre in Christchurch; examples are also held by the British Museum, Museum of Volkerkunde in Berlin, National Art Gallery of Australia, National Maritime Museum in Holland and at least one American president.

Heading out of Ashhurst along Oxford Street then Cloyton Road, turn down North Grove Road and after about 3km you'll find the ultra-relaxing **Herb Farm and Café** (Nov–Feb Thurs & Sun 10.30am–5pm, Fri & Sat 10.30am–10pm; March–Oct Fri, Sat & Sun 11am–4.30pm; guided tour map $4). A walk around the garden of medicinal plants, herbs, grasses, trees and flowers is thoroughly worthwhile, filling your senses with lush colours and aromas. The café has excellent salads as well as pastries and hot herbal toddies, while if you want to take away some essential oils or a remedy then the shop will cater to your needs.

Still further out from Ashhurst, 3km along the Gorge Road, brings you to **Go 4 Wheels** (☎06/376 7136, *go4wheels@amcom.co.nz*) where you can experience one of North Island's better 4WD motorbike excursions (3hr; $95 includes bike tuition). The trip involves climbing modified cattle tracks to a summit where you can enjoy staggering views of the plains below and **Tararua Wind Farm**, with its 48 wind turbines, each 40m high, together producing enough electricity to supply 15,000 homes.

Eating

Palmerston North has some good value-for-money restaurants and bars, though the town's prosperity also means that there are a few corporate yuppie-bars which trade in expensive drinks and overpriced food. Happily, the student population moderates tendencies in this direction. The best and cheapest ice cream in town is available at the BP Petrol Station on Fitzherbert Avenue, while the *Albert Hotel*, corner of Albert and Church streets, has a Saturday morning food market (6–10am) full of the cheapest local produce around.

Cafés

Barista's Espresso Bar, George St. Modern minimalist café, with a corrugated-iron counter bar where they grind their own coffee and serve amazing cakes, snacky meals ($6–18), mains around the $20 mark and bagels for breakfast. Daily 8am–11pm; licensed.

Clark's, City Library, 4 The Square. Stylish café serving excellent brunches, good coffee, light snacks and more filling meals all day long.

George Street Delicatessen, cnr George St & Main St. The best espresso bar/deli in the city with sandwiches, quiches, bagels, bargain breakfasts, and mixed platters for two, spring salad, hash browns full of pumpkin and kumera, all for under $18. You can also buy cheeses, other deli goods and lovely breads at the counter. Mon–Fri 6am–6pm, Sat 6am–4pm, Sun 7am–3pm; April–Sept closed Sun.

Harvesters Café Wine Bar, in the old Municipal Building, Church St. Another stylish city venue offering café fare at reasonable prices, with a dinner menu (from 6.30pm) that includes Cajun pork and Mediterranean fish. Mon–Sat 11am–midnight; live jazz or blues every Thurs night.

Kebarbeque 84 The Square, off Fitzherbert Ave. Authentically spicy, eat in or take away and perfect for ultra hungry lovers of Turkish cuisine.

Pompeii, 353 Ferguson St. The best place to go for pizza, eat in or takeaway, with a broad range of toppings from the sublime to the ridiculous.

Restaurants

The Bath House, 161 Broadway Ave. A restaurant and lounge bar in a bathhouse wittily decorated in "fall of the Roman Empire" bacchanalia, plus courtyard dining. Food is suitably decadent – French- and Italian-influenced meals, finger food, and brunches.

Costa's, Cuba St, opposite the Wharehouse superstore (book Fri & Sat, ☎06/356 6383). Evening restaurant with arched windows looking down on the street. The food is inexpensive (mains under $20) and includes nachos, beef satay, pasta, Tex–Mex, Chinese and Thai. Licensed.

Dejeuner, 159 Broadway Ave (☎06/356 1449). Expensive French cousin of *The Bath House*, offering top-notch cuisine. Licensed & BYO.

Monsoon Asian Kitchen, 347 Ferguson St. Value-for-money Chinese, Malaysian and Singaporean cuisine. Dinner Tues–Sun; BYO.

Mr India, 79e George St (☎06/345 5075). Superb, authentic and charismatic restaraunt where you always get too much to eat without destroying your bank account. Lunches 11am–2pm, dinner 5.30pm onwards; licensed & BYO.

Spostato Café, 213 Cuba St. Charmingly decorated, relaxed Italian restaurant, with friendly service and good authentic food at sensible prices. Dinner daily; BYO.

Drinking and entertainment

Palmerston North has more than its fair share of entertainment venues. The **Centre Point Theatre**, on the corner of Church Street and Pitt Street (☎06/359 6983), is an intimate purpose-built performance space, with a pleasant pre-show and interval bar; or take in a movie at the seven-screen **Downtown Cinema**, on Broadway Avenue between Princess Street and the square. The received wisdom regarding nightlife is that there's more fun to be had in term time – and the later you start, the better.

Bars and pubs

Celtic Inn, Regent Arcade. Primarily a late-night drinking den, with Irish food and live music Fri & Sat nights.

Diablo's, 96 Fitzherbert Ave (daily 11am–late). Purporting to be a café this is more of a bar/night spot. The food's not bad but you're better off visiting late in the week or in the evening at the weekend when the party is DJ piloted and always lively.

Empire Hotel, cnr Princess St & Main St. A recently refurbished drinking hole with a lively atmosphere and cheap food in the attached *Cobb and Co* restaurant.

Fat Lady's Arms, cnr Church St & Linton St. Part of a national chain that guarantees late nights, very loud music, lots of ale, lively surroundings and affordable snacky food. Closed Mon.

Loaded Hog, cnr George St & Coleman Mall. Another Kiwiana, rural and well-managed incarnation of the chain with home-brewed natural ales and good food, always busy at weekends.

Murray's Bar, *Fielding Hotel*, Kimbolton Rd, Fielding, about 14km from Palmerston North. This most Irish of Irish bars – actually run by an Irishman and a literary one to boot – is well worth the trip out into the sticks. Amongst the usual array of trad beers and snacks there is the added bonus of plentiful books to browse and occasional live music and plays, sometimes featuring local celeb author Peter Hawes (see Contexts p.878).

Old Bailey, Grand Hotel Building, 341 Church St. A reasonable stab at an English-style pub, serving a broad range of beer and wine and generous New Zealand pub grub, always busy in the evenings.

Oscar's Wine Bar, 1 The Square, by Coleman Mall. Unpretentious little bar, with bags of character and occasional live entertainment.

Quality Hotel, 110 Fitzherbert Ave. An excellent bar frequented by students and a reasonably priced carvery restaurant (dinner daily) that's popular with families.

Clubs and music venues

Abbey Theatre, 369 Church St. Nightclub and party venue in an old stone church, where the music ranges from heavy funk and 1990s techno to 1960s, 70s and 80s disco. Thurs, Fri & Sat.

High Flyers, in the Old Post Office Building. The Square is a bouncer-fronted after office nightspot where suits sometimes dance.

New Old Railway Hotel, cnr David St & Main St. A three bar extravaganza, at least one of which has live entertainment Wed–Sat.

Wild Horse Saloon, cnr Main St & Princess St. Rough pub that transmogrifies into a riotous punk and alternative music venue on Fri and Sat nights, when things can get pretty wild.

Listings

Airlines Air New Zealand, 30 Broadway Ave (☎06/351 8800); Ansett, Shop 11 the Plaza, cnr Church St & The Square (☎06/355 5188).

AA (Automobile Association) 185 Broadway Ave (☎06/357 7039).

Banks and exchange The city has a full complement of banks on The Square or within two blocks of it (see also listing for Thomas Cook).

Bookshop Best in the region is McKenzie Book Sellers, 51 George St (Mon–Fri 9am–8pm, Sat & Sun 10am–5pm).

Car rental Avis (☎06/358 4284); Hertz (☎06/357 0921); Rent-a-dent (☎06/355 5227); Thrifty (☎06/355 4365).

Events The second week of March brings International Festival Day, with food stalls from various minority groups, performance and street art, and a parade of people representing different nations. In mid-December, the Cathedral of the Holy Spirit, 197 Broadway Ave, hosts a week-long flower and music festival, in which the aisle is carpeted with flowers and choirs give a series of recitals.

Internet/email *Internet Café*, 134 Princess St (☎06/354 2463), offers Internet access as does the public library, on The Square. The latter is slightly more expensive.

Medical treatment City Health and Pharmacy, 22 Victoria St (daily 8am–10pm; ☎06/355 5333), has doctors available for consultation ($39) and an after-hours druggist.

Newspapers The local daily is the award-winning *Evening Standard* (Mon–Sat, 70¢), which includes entertainment listings and has emergency information on Friday, but is worth buying just for a read; the Sunday paper is *The Tribune*.

Post offices The main post office is on Princess St, between Main St & Broadway Ave; a number of postal shops are scattered about the city.

Taxis Palmerston North Taxis (☎06/335 5333 & 357 6076).

Thomas Cook cnr Broadway Ave & Princes St (☎06/356 4800).

Tours Adventure Aviation (☎06/351 5020), offer scenic flights in a Tiger Moth – dress warmly (15–20min; $99); a similar service in more modern and less airy planes is offered by the Manawatu District Aero Club, at the airport (☎06/356 9793); Manawatu Wine Tours (☎06/357 1077) tour the wineries around Hawke's Bay and Martinborough; Pauline's Tours and Travel (☎06/357 0058) offer garden, mountain, wine, beach, river and volcano trips; Tui's Bus Tours (☎ & fax 06/357 4136) run half- and full-day guided tours around the area.

Travel agencies Tranz Rail, Mathews Ave (☎06/351 6828), visitor centre (see p.255).

South to Otaki

To the south of Palmerston North and the Manawatu, the peaks of the rugged and inhospitable **Tararua Mountains** corral the **Horowhenua** region into a strip along the coast. Renowned for its gentle landscape, lakes, walkways, fruit and vegetable growing, rivers and beaches, the area has a few mildly diverting settlements, but lacks any substantial attractions. Being only around ninety minutes' drive from Wellington, this is prime **commuter territory** – and also contains a high proportion of **retired** people. If you choose to stop, then the tourist-orientated **Foxton**, with a plethora of **museums** and an extraordinary long flat **beach** facing its seaside offshoot of **Foxton Beach**, and **Levin**, full of factory shops, some good eateries and with access to the mountains, are the best bets. Continuing **south to Otaki** and beyond, the natural barrier of the Tararua Mountains separates the Kapiti Coast from the Hutt Valley until you reach the outskirts of Wellington (see Chapter 7; p.434).

Archeological evidence suggests that there was a semi-nomadic **moa-hunter** culture in this area between 1400 and 1650AD, pre-dating larger tribal settlements. **Europeans** came to the area in the early 1800s and settled at the mouth of the Manawatu River, but skedaddled to Foxton owing to land-purchase problems. Foxton's early growth was based on **flax milling** and the export of flax, agricultural products and timber from its port. The opening of the Wellington–Palmerston North **rail line** in 1886 spelled the end of Foxton's commercial domination of the area; and the final ignominy was the closure of the Foxton–Palmerston North branch line in 1959.

Foxton

FOXTON is perched on the coastal plain 38km southwest of Palmerston North, reached via SH56 and SH1. The town is split in two, with the main centre beside SH1 and **Foxton Beach** 5km away on the coast, where there's a long sandy beach with good surfing, safe swimming areas and abundant birdlife around the Manawatu River estuary. The small community by the beach is full of *baches* for vacationing New Zealanders. Inland Foxton is a place where you step back in time: the town has old-style shop facades, cobblestoned paving and no less than five **museums**, along with some heritage attractions and decorative murals painted on prominent buildings.

Foxton was once the flax-stripping capital of New Zealand. Maori had long relied on handmade **flax** items for their everyday needs and European immigrants followed their lead, using it for woolpacks, binder twine, fibrous plaster lashings, upholsterers' tow and carpet. In an effort to streamline the stripping and weaving processes, mills were constructed alongside swamps and on riverbanks in Manawatu and Horowhenua in the 1880s, and the history of this industry is recounted in the pick of the town's museums, the **Flax Stripper Museum**, Main Street (Tues–Sun 1–3pm; $2). Still on the flax theme, sixty-five types of green flax and their uses are marked along the riverside **flaxwalk**, which starts in Harbour Street and is described in a free leaflet available from the visitor centre or the museum. Another way to take a trip back in time is to sign up for a cruise on the **MV Corsair** (☎06/363 8897; $10 for 35min), an old boat whose skipper will fill you in on the Maori and European history of the river and the town.

At the north end of Main Street, in Coronation Hall, the **Museum of Audio Visual Arts and Sciences**, Avenue Road (Tues–Fri 1–3pm Sat & Sun 2–4pm; $4), offers an insight into early broadcasting and home entertainment through its collection of over 14,000 records going back to the early 1890s, assorted gramophones, cameras, projectors, restored Pianola rolls, and vintage radios and televisions. Only museum addicts will want to go for a hat-trick by visiting the **Trolley Bus Museum and Gainsborough Doll Gallery**, 55 Main St (Tues–Sun 11am–4.30pm; $2), with its surreal juxtaposition of a 1953 London Bus and an assortment of ancient and modern dolls, some looking remarkably sinister.

Practicalities

The old Rail and Tram Station, 80–88 Main St, is the **bus** stop and booking office for Newmans and InterCity services. The same building houses the **visitor centre** (daily 8.30am–5pm; ☎06/363 8940), a good daytime **café** (daily 9am–4pm) and a horse-drawn tram hauled out every summer for tourist rides around town (15min; $2). When **food** cravings hit, make for the *Laughing Fox* (Mon–Wed 9.30am–3.30pm, Thurs–Sun 9.30am till last customer leaves; licensed), on SH1 as it passes the town and topped by an odd-looking turret so you can't miss it, offering filling snacks, quiches, satay, salads, curries and pastries and lavish cakes.

Levin and around

The town of **LEVIN** sits at the junction of SH1 and SH57, 19km south of Foxton and 57km southwest of Palmerston North. The principal community in the Horowhenua region, Levin makes a living from horticulture and clothes-manufacturing. The town is crammed with **factory shops** flogging discount clothing and in the orchards around town, **fruit-picking** work can often be had (Nov–May). If neither of these grab you, you need only stay long enough to take a quick spin around the nearby coast and mountains.

At the **Papaitonga Scenic Reserve**, 4km south of Levin on SH1, a gentle stroll to the Papaitonga Lookout (10min) or the Otomuiri Lookout (20min), provides great views of Lake Papaitonga and the surrounding wetlands, which provide a refuge for many rare birds, including the spotless crake, Australasian bittern, and New Zealand dabchick. Wilder scenery is the attraction at **Waitarere Beach**, 15km northwest of Levin, off SH1. This vast dune-backed, grey-sand beach boasts pounding surf and the rusted hulk of the *Hydrbad*, which was wrecked in a storm in 1878.

Tararua Forest Park

The rugged **Tararua Forest Park** is often ignored as travellers head south or north. Sandwiched between SH1 and SH2, the mountains of the Tararua Range form an almost impenetrable barrier, their exposed peaks buffeted by fog, rain, high winds and snow funnelled from the Cook Strait. The **tracks** in the area are not the broad highways of New Zealand's Great Walks, but narrow and barely distinguishable paths fraught with undulating and sometimes muddy terrain, while the **huts** on the tracks are all very basic, classified as back-country. The mountains offer a genuinely rugged and isolated experience for the keen, fit, experienced trampers, but are not for the faint-hearted – though there are some short walks accessible from Levin, Otaki (see p.466) and

Masterton (see p.425), which give a brief taste of the range. For longer tramps, get a guide or go with someone who knows the area really well.

The Levin visitor centre (see below) can put you in touch with local tramping clubs, who will recommend a **guide** for walks in the Tararua Range. **Back to Basics Guided Walks** (Maria Clements ☎06/368 6306) offer tailored trips ($50–95 a day), with an experienced guide who delights in passing on esoteric bush skills – the subtle art of navigation without benefit of a map or compass – and is also a member of the local search and rescue team. For a taste of the park, you can reach some of the **shorter walks** in the park from Levin – such as the **Mount Thompson Track** (2–4hr), which ascends one of the smaller peaks in the range, but nonetheless offers good views of the coast and Kapiti Island. The walk begins around 100m past the Panatewaewae car park on North Manakau Road, a turning off SH1 some 10km south of Levin.

Practicalities

The **train** station backs on to Oxford Street in the centre of town, and **buses** pull into the Levin Mall car park. The **visitor centre**, 93 Oxford St (Mon–Fri 9am–5.30pm, Sat & Sun 10am–3pm), is about six minutes' walk from both the station and the bus stop.

Fantails **B&B**, 44 Queen St and 40 MacArthur St (☎ & fax 06/368 9279; ⑤–⑥), provide excellent, well-appointed **rooms** in two houses. **Motel** accommodation is available at the *Mountain View*, The Avenue (☎06/368 5214, fax 368 4091; ④), where most units have cooking facilities, or in the comfortable log-cabin-like units at the *Welcome Inn*, 353a Oxford St (☎ & fax 06/368 3834; ④).

The best place to **eat** in Levin is *Italian Flame*, 104 Oxford St (closed Sun; licensed), where you can enjoy a relaxed, authentic and very filling Italian dinner without breaking the bank. A close second and open all day (open late on Thurs, Fri & Sat; licensed) is *Café Nua*, 7 Bath St where you can eat Kiwi: steaks, venison, deli sandwiches, burgers, veggie dishes and some staunch coffee. Another safe bet is the café attached to *Fantails*, 40 MacArthur St (Wed–Sun 9am–4.30pm), which is set in pretty tree-filled gardens and has a variety of snacks, light meals and excellent ice cream.

travel details

Trains

From Hamilton to: Auckland (1 daily; 2hr 5min); Rotorua (1 daily; 2hr 6min); Tauranga (1 daily; 1hr 25min); Te Awamutu (1 daily; 19min).

From Levin to: Wellington (1 daily; 1hr 39min).

From Otorohanga to: Te Kuiti (1 daily; 16min).

From Palmerston North to: Hastings (1 daily 2hr; 46min); Levin (1 daily; 38min).

From Taumarunui to: Palmerston North (1 daily; 4hr 25min).

From Te Awamutu to: Otorohanga (1 daily; 19min).

From Te Kuiti to: Taumarunui (1 daily; 16min).

Buses

From Hamilton to: Auckland (10 daily; 2hr 15min); Cambridge (10 daily; 20min); Ngaruawahia (6 daily; 50min); New Plymouth (5 daily; 4hr 20min); Otorohanga (3 daily; 1 hr 5min); Raglan (2 daily; 45min); Te Awamutu (6 daily; 40min); Te Kuiti (4 daily; 1hr 25min); Thames (3 daily; 1hr 50min); Tauranga (3 daily; 1hr 40min); Rotorua (8 daily; 1hr 45min); Wanganui (2 daily; 6hr 15min).

From Otorohanga to: Te Kuiti (4 daily; 25min); Waitomo (6 daily; 30min).

From New Plymouth to: Wanganui (3 daily; 2hr 50min).

From Palmerston North to: Hastings (4 daily; 2hr 55min); Masterton (7 daily; 1hr 35min); Rotorua (3 daily; 5hr 30min); Wellington (8 daily; 2hr 5min).

From Taumaranui to: Wanganui (2 daily; 3hr 30min).

From Te Awamutu to: Kawhia (Mon–Sat 1; 1hr 30min); Otorohanga (3 daily; 25min).

From Te Kuiti to: New Plymouth (4 daily; 2hr 55min); Taumarunui (2 daily; 1hr).

From Wanganui to: Palmerston North (3 daily; 1hr 5min).

Flights

From Hamilton to: Auckland (6 daily; 30min); Christchurch (16 daily; 2hr 5min); Napier (4 daily; 2hr 55min); Nelson (17 daily; 2hr 30min); Palmerston North (6 daily; 1hr); Wellington (15 daily; 50min).

From New Plymouth to: Auckland (11 daily; 50min); Christchurch (11 daily; 2hr 5min); Tauranga (12 daily; 2hr 10min); Wellington (10 daily; 55min).

From Palmerston North to: Auckland (24 daily; 1hr 10min); Christchurch (14 daily; 1hr 25min); Nelson (12 daily; 1hr 35min); Tauranga (12 daily; 2hr 30min); Wellington (9 daily; 35min).

CHAPTER FOUR

CENTRAL NORTH ISLAND

T he landlocked **Central North Island** contains more than its fair share of New Zealand's star attractions. The area is delineated by three defining geological features: Lake Taupo, the country's largest; the Tongariro National Park, with its trio of active volcanoes; and the volcanic field that feeds colourful and fiercely active thermal areas, principally around the Arawa heartland of **Rotorua**. If you are ticking off Kiwi icons, then time is well spent around Rotorua, where **boiling mud pools** plop next to spouting **geysers** fuelled by superheated water, which is drawn off to fill the hot pools found all over town. To complete this quintessential New Zealand experience, here you'll also find the most accessible expression of Maori culture, with highly-regarded Arawa carvings and any number of groups ready to perform traditional dances and haka, and feed you with fall-off-the-bone meat cooked in a **hangi** steam oven.

The dramatic volcanic scenery is all the more striking for its contrast with the encroaching pines of the **Kaingaroa Forest**, one of the world's largest plantation forests, with serried ranks of fast-growing conifers marching to the horizon. When the country was being carved up for farming, the central North Island was all but abandoned as cattle grazed here soon contracted "bush sickness" and died. In the 1930s, scientists discovered that the disease was caused by an easily rectified deficiency of the mineral cobalt, but by this stage the free-draining pumice soils had already been planted with millions of radiata pine seedlings by gangs of convicts and Great Depression relief workers. Since then, sylviculture has continued to consolidate its position as the region's chief earner through pulp and paper mills at Kinleith, near Tokoroa, and Kawerau.

The rest of the region is loosely referred to as the **Volcanic Plateau**, a sometimes-bleak high country that is overlaid with a layer of rock and ash expelled two thousand years back when a huge volcano blew itself apart, the resultant crater being filled by **Lake Taupo**. This serene lake, and the streams and rivers feeding it, have since become a fishing mecca for anglers keen to snag brown and rainbow trout, but the area is no less appealing for the lure of its watersports and the thundering rapids of the Waikato River, which drains the lake. South of Lake Taupo rise the three majestic volcanoes of the **Tongariro National Park**, created in 1887, since when it has become a winter playground for North Island skiers and a summer destination for trampers intent on bagging a couple of magical walks.

If you're hot-footing it to this region **from Auckland**, you've got a choice of **routes**: the direct SH1 through Hamilton; or the faster, less congested and broadly more appealing journey along SH2, which branches east at Pokeno, 50km south of Auckland, then along SH27 as it cuts south across the fringes of the Hauraki Plains. The two routes converge on the small town of Tirau, where SH1 heads almost 100km south to Taupo and SH5 crosses the Mamaku Plateau to Rotorua, 52km away to the east.

The **altitude** of the Volcanic Plateau lends Taupo, the Tongariro National Park and environs a refreshing crispness even in high summer, when it is a welcome retreat from the stickiness of Auckland and the north. Spring and autumn are tolerably warm and have the added advantage of freedom from the summer hordes, though the often freezing winter months from May to October are best left to winter-sports enthusiasts. The

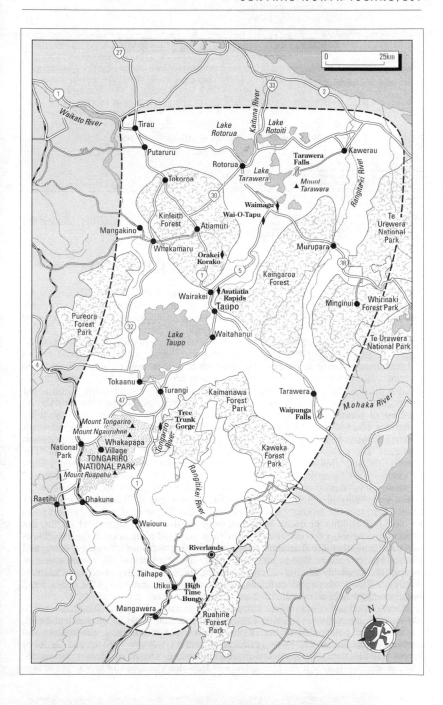

Rotorua area is more **balmy** on the whole, but can still be cool in winter, making the thermal areas steamier and the hot baths all the more appealing.

ROTORUA AND AROUND

There is little doubt that the "Sulphur City" of **Rotorua** is New Zealand's tourist destination par excellence. For this is one of the world's most concentrated and accessible geothermal areas, where twenty-metre geysers spout among kaleidoscopic mineral pools, steam wafts over cauldrons of boiling mud and terraces of encrusted silicates drip like stalactites. Everywhere you look there's evidence of **vulcanism**: birds on the lakeshore are relieved of the chore of nest-sitting by the warmth of the ground, graves in Ohinemutu and Whakarewarewa churchyards have to be built topside as digging the ground is likely to unearth a hot spring, and hotels are all equipped with geothermally-fed **hot tubs**, perfect for easing your bones after a hard day's sightseeing. Throughout the region, sulphur and heat combine to form **barren landscapes** where only the hardiest of plants brave the trickling hot streams, sputtering vents and seething fumaroles. Plant life may be absent, but there is no shortage of **colour** from iridescent mineral deposits lining the pools: bright oranges juxtaposed with emerald greens and rust reds. The underworld looms large in Rotorua's lexicon: there is no end of "The Devil's this" and "Hell's that" – a state of affairs that prompted George Bernard Shaw to ruminate on his colourful past while visiting the Hell's Gate thermal area and famously quip, "It reminds me too vividly of the fate theologians have promised me".

But hydrothermal activity is only part of Rotorua's appeal. The naturally hot water lured Maori to settle around Lake Rotorua and Lake Tarawera, using the hottest pools for cooking, bathing in cooler ones and building their *whare* (houses) on the hot ground to drive away the winter chill. Here they managed to hang on to their traditions and tribal integrity more than almost anywhere else in the country, forging a strong and vibrant **Maori culture** that is part of the daily life of a third of the region's people. Despite the inevitably diluting effects of tourism, there is no better place to get an introduction to Maori values and traditions, dance and song than at one of the concert and hangi evenings held all over Rotorua and on nearby marae.

Maori-owned and operated tour companies often make the most educational, not to say entertaining, ways of exploring Rotorua's surrounding area. To the south and east, the forests are punctuated by over a dozen **lakes** tucked into bush-girt hollows and overlooked by the mountainous products of ancient volcanic activity and its more recent manifestation, the shattered five-kilometre-long chasm of **Mount Tarawera**. During one cataclysmic night of eruptions in 1886 this chain of volcanoes split in two, destroying the region's first tourist attraction, the Pink and White Terraces, entombing the nearest settlement, the so-called **Buried Village**, and creating the **Waimangu Thermal Valley**. Waimangu is just one of four magnificent thermal areas open to the public; the Pohutu Geyser at **Whakarewarewa**, on the outskirts of Rotorua, and the Lady Knox Geyser at **Wai-O-Tapu**, to the south, demand particular attention.

Some history

The Rotorua region is home to the Arawa people, who trace their ancestry back to the **Arawa canoe** which struck land at Maketu, at the mouth of the Kaituna River on the Bay of Plenty, after its long journey from the Polynesian homelands of Hawaiki sometime in the fourteenth century. The leader of one of the first parties to explore the interior was the *tohunga* (priest), **Ngatoroirangi**, who made it as far as the freezing summit of Mount Tongariro, where he feared he might die from cold. His prayers to the gods of Hawaiki were answered with fire, which journeyed underground, first surfacing at the volcanic White Island in the Bay of Plenty, then at several more points in a line between there and the three central North Island volcanoes. Ngatoroirangi was saved, and he and his followers established themselves around Lake Rotorua, where they lived contentedly until another Arawa sailor, the wily **Ihenga**, duped Ngatoroirangi out of his title to the land. The victor named the lakes as he reached them along the Kaituna River: Lake Rotoiti ("small lake") and Lake Rotorua ("second lake").

In revenge for an earlier raid on an island in nearby Green Lake, the Northland Ngapuhi chief, **Hongi Hika**, led a war party here in 1823. The Arawa got wind of the attack and retreated to the sanctuary of Mokoia Island, in the middle of Lake Rotorua; undaunted, Hongi Hika and his warriors carried their canoes overland between lakes (the track between Lake Rotoiti and Lake Rotoehu still bears the name Hongi's Track). The Ngapuhi, equipped with muskets traded with Europeans in the Bay of Islands, defeated the traditionally armed Arawa then withdrew, leaving the Arawa to regroup in time for the New Zealand Wars of the 1860s, in which the Arawa supported the government. This worked in their favour when, in 1870, **Te Kooti** (see box on p.401) attacked from the east coast, and the colonial troops helped turn them back.

By this time a few **Europeans** – notably a Danish trader Philip Hans Tapsell and the missionary Thomas Chapman – had already lived for some years in the Maori villages of Ohinemutu and Whakarewarewa, but it wasn't until Te Kooti had been dispatched that Rotorua came into existence. **Tourists** began to arrive in the district to view the **Pink and White Terraces** using Ohinemutu, Whakarewarewa and Te Wairoa as staging posts. The Arawa, who up to this point had been relatively isolated from European influence, were quick to grasp the possibilities of tourism and helped turn Rotorua into what it is today.

Rotorua

You smell **ROTORUA** long before you see it. Hydrogen sulphide drifting up from natural vents in the region's thin crust means that the whiff of rotten eggs lingers in the air, but after a few hours you barely notice the smell. No amount of bad odour, however, will keep visitors away from this small, ordered place clinging to the southern shores of the near-circular **Lake Rotorua**. Rotorua's northern and southern limits are defined by the two ancient villages of the Arawa sub-tribe, Ngati Whakaue. The lakeshore **Ohinemutu** and the thermal reserve of **Whakarewarewa** were the only settlements before the 1880s, when Rotorua became New Zealand's only city with its origins firmly rooted in tourism. Specifically, Rotorua was set up as a **spa town** on land leased from the Ngati Whakaue, under the auspices of the 1881 Thermal Springs Districts Act. By 1885, the fledgling Rotorua boasted the Government Sanatorium

Complex, a spa designed to administer the rigorous treatments deemed beneficial to the "invalids" who came to take the waters. The original **Bath House** and recreational **Blue Baths**, both set amid the oh-so-English **Government Gardens**, are now part of the **Rotorua Museum** which successfully puts these early enterprises into context.

Arrival and information

InterCity and Newmans **buses** pull up outside the Tourism Rotorua complex (see below), as does the budget Little Kiwi Bus Co (☎0800/759 999), who run here from Auckland via Hamilton. The once-daily Geyserland Express **train** from Auckland and Hamilton arrives on Railway Road, 1km northwest of the centre, and is met by the Sightseeing Shuttle, which runs into town for $2. Air New Zealand and Ansett **flights** from Auckland, Wellington and Christchurch land 8km northeast of town at the lakeside airport (☎07/345 6175). The door-to-door Super Shuttle (☎07/349 3444) charges $8 for the first passenger and $2 for each extra to the same place, and **taxis** (see p.284) run into town for around $15.

The Tourism Rotorua complex, at 1167 Fenton St, contains a foreign exchange counter and two efficient but often busy **visitor centres** (both daily: Nov–Easter 8am–6pm, Easter–Oct 8.30am–5.30pm; ☎07/348 5179, fax 348 6044, *www.rotoruanz.co.nz*, *grant.delamore@rdc.govt.nz*). The Rotorua office deals with local tourism, while the New Zealand office covers the rest of the country and onward travel ticketing. The latter also handles DOC bookings and track hut tickets, as does the Map And Track Shop, 1225 Fenton St (daily 9am–6pm; ☎ & fax 07/349 1845, *map-track@clear.net.nz*), where you'll probably get a more detailed picture, along with information on just about anything outdoorsy hereabouts. If you have a specific interest in **Maori-owned and operated tours**, hangi and concerts, bustle along the street from the visitor centre to the Best of Maori Tourism, 1189 Fenton St (☎07/347 4226), a souvenir and crafts shop which promotes Maori businesses.

For a general advert-oriented round up of what's happening around town, pick up the free weekly *Thermal Air Visitor's Guide*, and if there are two of you spending a few days sightseeing around Rotorua, you can make good **savings** by buying the "Rotorua Good Time Card" ($25 per couple), which gives two-for-the-price-of-one deals on many of the sights and activities around town, plus discounts on movie tickets and even meals.

Central Rotorua has recently instituted a new block-based **numbering system** that increases south and west from the corner of Whakaue and Hinemaru streets near the lake, starting with the 1000 block. Confusingly, outlying areas haven't been renumbered so some streets – such as Fenton Street – increase from 1000 to aroound 1600 then start again at about 200.

City transport

Richies Coachlines (timetable hotline ☎07/349 2994 ext 2902) provide the most basic level of urban **bus** transport, centred on Pukuatua Street between Tutanekai and Fenton streets. Buses leave weekdays for Ngongotaha, passing Rainbow Springs (#2 roughly hourly) and Whakarewarewa (#3 every 2hr), and costing $2.20 each way. Saturday service is very limited, and on Sunday it is non-existent.

In the main, the "Magic of the Maori" **sightseeing shuttle** (☎0508/300 333, *www.magicmaori.com*, *magicnz@wave.co.nz*; daily 9am–5pm) is much more convenient, completing a circuit of Whakarewarewa, the Polynesian Pools, Rainbow Springs, Skyline Skyrides, the Agrodome and the visitor centre every hour and a half or so. Day **passes** ($12) are available, as well as section fares ($4 to Whakarewarewa, $5 to the Agrodome). There are also any number of **tours**, most geared towards the more distant sights (see "Around Rotorua", p.284).

The points visited by the sightseeing shuttle are mostly within 7km of central Rotorua and there are no substantial hills, so **cycling** is a viable way to go; **car-rental** rates are also fairly competitive here (see "Listings", p.283, for details of bike- and car-rental outlets).

Accommodation

Rotorua's accommodation has one big advantage: no matter how low your budget, you can stay somewhere with a **hot pool**, and for a little more you might even get a private tub in your room. In fact there is barely a place in town without a hot pool – the best of them directly fed with mineral water, others artificially heated.

The range is wide, including a clutch of quality **hostels**, all close to the city centre, all eager to advise on local activities and many offering small discounts on trips and tours. There must be more **motels** in Rotorua than just about anywhere else in the

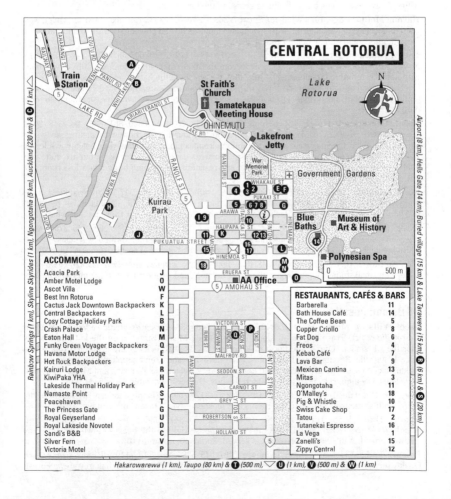

CENTRAL ROTORUA

ACCOMMODATION

Acacia Park	J
Amber Motel Lodge	O
Ascot Villa	W
Best Inn Rotorua	F
Cactus Jack Downtown Backpackers	K
Central Backpackers	L
Cosy Cottage Holiday Park	B
Crash Palace	N
Eaton Hall	M
Funky Green Voyager Backpackers	Q
Havana Motor Lodge	E
Hot Rock Backpackers	I
Kairuri Lodge	R
KiwiPaka YHA	H
Lakeside Thermal Holiday Park	A
Namaste Point	S
Peacehaven	T
The Princess Gate	G
Royal Geyserland	U
Royal Lakeside Novotel	D
Sandi's B&B	C
Silver Fern	V
Victoria Motel	P

RESTAURANTS, CAFÉS & BARS

Barbarella	11
Bath House Café	14
The Coffee Bean	5
Copper Criollo	8
Fat Dog	6
Freos	4
Kebab Café	7
Lava Bar	9
Mexican Cantina	13
Mitas	3
Ngongotaha	11
O'Malley's	18
Pig & Whistle	10
Swiss Cake Shop	17
Tatou	2
Tutanekai Espresso	16
La Vega	1
Zanelli's	15
Zippy Central	12

Rainbow Springs (1 km), Skyline Skyrides (1 km), Ngongotaha (5 km), Auckland (230 km) & (1 km)

Airport (8 km), Hells Gate (14 km), Buried village (15 km) & Lake Tarawera (15 km), (6 km) & (20 km)

Hakarewarewa (1 km), Taupo (80 km) & (500 m), (1 km), (500 m) & (1 km)

country, most of them lining Fenton Street, which runs south towards Whakarewarewa. Competition is fierce and at off-peak times you may well get rock bottom prices, but it is a busy road and you might find it quieter in motels tucked away down side roads. **B&Bs and guesthouses** come liberally scattered around Rotorua and maintain a typically high standard, while **hotels** mostly cater to bus-tour groups and charge prohibitive prices if you just walk in off the street; though again, surprisingly good deals can be struck in the off season. We've mainly recommended **campsites** right in town, but there are dozens of others scattered around the region; most are listed with the visitor centre, who can advise on availability.

Between Christmas and March is the busy season, when you would do well to **book** a few days **in advance**.

Hotels and motels

Amber Motor Lodge, 1296 Hinemaru St (☎07/348 0595, fax 348 0795). Middle-of-the-road motel with only average rooms but well situated close to the town centre. ⑤.

Havana Motor Lodge, 1078 Whakaue St (☎07/348 8134 & 0800/333 799, fax 348 8132). Quiet, well-sited motel close to the lakefront with spacious grounds, a heated pool and two small mineral pools. Decent units are gradually being renovated. ④.

The Princess Gate, 1057 Arawa St (☎07/348 1179 & 0800/500 705, fax 348 6215, *princes.gate@clear.net.nz*). The sole survivor from the days when all of Hinemaru Street was lined with hotels catering to the ailing while they took the waters at the bathhouse across the road. This lovely old wooden hotel is now restored with en-suite rooms fronting onto lovely wide verandas, a tennis court and in-house video. Off-peak B&B specials are sometimes available ⑥; otherwise room only ⑦.

Regal Geyserland Hotel, 424 Fenton St (☎07/348 2039 & 0800/881 882, fax 348 2033, *geyserland@silveroaks.co.nz*). Book early to get a third- or fourth-floor room with unsurpassed views over the "Whaka" thermal area; watch the mud volcanoes plopping below your balcony while you wait for Pohutu to perform. The rooms and public areas have seen better days, but are quite adequate and there's an outdoor pool, small gym and restaurant/bar. Some budget viewless rooms ⑤, but what's the point? ⑥.

Royal Lakeside Novotel, Lake end Tutanekai St (☎07/346 3888, fax 347 1888). Swankiest of the big hotels, with elegant modern rooms, some with lake views, and all the usual facilities, plus thermal pool and massage facilities. Rack-rate ⑨; though for most of the year there are specials ⑦–⑧.

Silver Fern Motor Inn, 326 Fenton St (☎07/346 3849 & 0800/118 808, fax 346 2765, *www. silverfernmotorinn.co.nz, silverfernmotorinn@xtra.co.nz*). Top-of-the-line motel with new studios and one-bedroom units, all with spa baths, Sky TV, sunny balconies and oodles of space. Studios ⑥, units ⑦.

Victoria Motel, 10 Victoria St (☎07/348 4039, fax 348 8298, *victoria.motel@xtra.co.nz*). Good-value motel with small studio rooms, each with private hot pool, and larger self-catering units which share a pool. ④.

B&Bs and guesthouses

Ascot Villa, 7 Meade St (☎07/348 4895, fax 348 8384, *www.ascotvilla.co.nz, reservations @ascotvilla.co.nz*). Travelling south along Fenton Street, Meade Street is on the left immediately after the BP station. One of the finest of Rotorua's B&Bs, with eclectically decorated rooms in a large 1940s villa. Rooms share bathrooms, don't have TVs and aren't supplied with tea and coffee making facilities, so you are encouraged to join the very welcoming Warwick and Michael for afternoon tea, a pre-dinner drink or just to watch the box. Dinner is available for $35. ⑥.

Best Inn Rotorua, 1068 Whakaue St (☎ & fax 07/347 9769). Pristine, modern B&B right in the centre with attractively simple, clean rooms and Japanese-style "Onsen" mineral baths. ⑤.

Eaton Hall, 1255 Hinemaru St (☎ & fax 07/347 0366, *www.eatonhallbnb.cjb.net, eatonhallbnb@xtra.co.nz*). Floral, olde worlde guesthouse right in the heart of town that's friendly and well-priced. A full cooked breakfast is served. Rooms ④, en suites ⑤.

Kairuri Lodge, 24 Mark Place, Lynmore (☎07/345 5385, fax 345 7119, *dspeedy@clear.net.nz*). Quality homestay 6km northeast of the centre, and right on the edge of the Whakarewarewa Forest.

Rooms all have en-suite or private bathrooms, and guests have the run of their own lounge where tea, coffee and port are available. Dinner by arrangement $30–40. ⑤.

Namaste Point, 187 Te Akau Rd, Lake Rotoiti (☎07/362 4804, fax 362 4060, *mysite.xtra.co.nz/~namastepoint, namaste.point@xtra.co.nz*). A kind of homestay/apartment beautifully sited beside Lake Rotoiti some 20km north of Rotorua near Okere Falls. Perfect as a rural retreat, you get a beautifully decorated self-contained suite with, TV, stereo, fresh flowers and gourmet breakfast supplied. Guests have free use of the spa pool, canoe, dinghy and a jetty for swimming or fishing. ⑦.

Peacehaven, 10 Peace St (☎ & fax 07/348 3759, *peacehaven@clear.net.nz*). Suburban homestay close to Whakarewarewa with friendly hosts, comfortable rooms, a large thermally-heated pool in the back yard and a lovely little mineral pool. ④.

Sandi's B&B, 103 Fairy Springs Rd (☎07/347 0034, *sandi.mark@xtra.co.nz*). Just one good-value, comfortable and nicely decorated en-suite room close to Rainbow Springs, with continental breakfast. ④.

Hostels

Cactus Jack Downtown Backpackers, 1210 Haupapa St (☎ & fax 348 3121). A snazzy paint job and enthusiastic staff add character to this ageing warren of rooms and cabins with reasonably spacious dorms, twins and doubles, and bike rental for $20 a day. A large spa pool and pool table ensures it is always pretty lively. Dorms ①, rooms ②.

Central Backpackers, 10 Pukuatua St (☎ & fax 07/349 3285). Small but spacious, homely and easygoing hostel in an immaculately kept, large house, with beds rather than bunks in the four- and six-bed dorm rooms. Bikes are rented at $10 a day and there's a spa pool out back. Dorms ①, rooms ②.

Crash Palace, 1271 Hinemaru St (☎07/348 8842, fax 348 8862, *crashpalace@clear.net.nz*). Recently revamped former YHA with spacious and airy public areas, a spa pool and rooms, four-shares and doubles all made up with sheets. Internet access, and mountain bikes available for $25 a day. Dorms ①, rooms ③.

Funky Green Voyager, 4 Union St (☎07/346 1754, fax 350 1100). Very relaxed hostel in a suburban house ten minutes' walk from downtown with an easy-going communal atmosphere fostered by the idiosyncratic owner, Gerard. Cooking facilities in particular are excellent and there's a hot tub and a cosy, TV-less lounge. Dorms ①, rooms ②, en-suite room ③.

Hot Rock, 1286 Arawa St (☎07/347 9469, fax 347 8099, *www.acb.co.nz/hotrock, hotrock@acb.co.nz*). Large, lively and, at weekends, noisy hostel, a perennial favourite with patrons of the backpacker tour buses, kept entertained in the two mineral pools, a heated outdoor swimming pool and the *Lava Bar* next door. Accommodation is in four-shares or larger dorms, each with private bathroom, and there are backpacker doubles, and nicer en-suite rooms with kitchens. Internet access. Dorms ①, rooms ③.

KiwiPaka YHA, 60 Tarewa Rd (☎07/347 0931, fax 346 3167, *www.kiwipaka-yha.co.nz, stay @kiwipaka-yha.co.nz*). Huge and well-organized modern complex on the far side of Kuirau Park, with camping space and a series of accommodation blocks ranged around a pool and a low-cost café and bar. Six- and four-bunk dorms are good value, and the doubles and modern chalets are a bargain too. Tent sites $7, dorms ①, rooms ②, chalets ③.

Campsites and motor parks

Acacia Park, 137 Pukuatua St (☎07/348 1886, fax 348 1867, *www.acaciapark.co.nz, stay @acaciapark.co.nz*). Very well appointed holiday park that's the closest to the city centre, and has an outdoor pool and spa. A spacious camping area has tent and powered sites, basic but serviceable cabins, and more luxurious tourist flats and motel units. Tents $10, powered sites $11, cabins ②, flats ③, units ④.

Blue Lake Holiday Park, Tarawera Road, Blue Lake (☎07/362 8120, fax 362 8600, *www.topparks.co.nz, bluelake@xtra.co.nz*). Large and well organized site 9km from Rotorua on the way to the Buried Village and just across the road from Blue Lake. Extensive facilities include games room, spa pool, and aquatic paraphernalia for rent. Tents $10, powered sites $11, cabins ②–③, flats ④, motels ⑤.

Cosy Cottage Holiday Park, 67 Whittaker Rd (☎07/348 3793, fax 347 9634, *cosycottage @xtra.co.nz*). Excellent holiday park a couple of kilometres from town with an extensive range of comfortable cabins and tourist flats, powered and tent sites, some of which are on geothermally-heated ground – great in winter but less appealing in summer. Along with all the usual facilities, there's a swimming pool, a couple of pleasant mineral pools, naturally-fed steam boxes for hangi-style cooking, and bikes for rent ($16 a day). Tents $10, powered sites $12, cabins ③, flats ④.

KiwiPaka YHA (see "Hostels" on previous page). Huge and well-organized modern complex with camping space and hostel-style accommodation. Tents $8.50, powered sites $10.

Lakeside Thermal Holiday Park, 54 Whittaker Rd (☎ & fax 07/348 1693, *relax@lakesidethermal .co.nz*). Small and compact lakefront motor camp 2km from the city, with kayaks for guests' use, a barbecue overlooking the lake, a genuine mineral-water pool and mineral water baths where you can adjust the temperature to suit. Tent and powered sites $10, cabins ②, tourist flats ③, lakeside flats ④.

The Town, Lake Rotorua and Whakarewarewa

Rotorua's sights are scattered: even those around the centre of town require some form of transport, though half a day can be spent on foot visiting the fine collection of Maori artefacts and bath-house relics in the **Rotorua Museum**, located in the former bath-house in the formal **Government Gardens**, then strolling around the shores of **Lake Rotorua** to Ohinemutu, the city's original Maori village with its neatly carved church. For a soak in a hot pool in the slightly surreal setting of a native bird sanctuary, catch a boat out to **Mokoia Island**, the romantic setting for the tale of two lovers, Hinemoa and Tutanekai.

The majority of sights require a little more effort, though a shuttle bus (see p.270) does the rounds. Top of most sightseeing lists is **Whakarewarewa**, a large thermal reserve now divided into two sections: **The Thermal Village**, where folk still go about their daily lives amid the steam and boiling pools; and **Maori Arts and Crafts Institute**, with its two large geysers and a fascinating carving and weaving school. Where Rotorua's northwestern suburbs peter out, Mount Ngongotaha rises up, providing the necessary slope for a number of gravity-driven activities at the **Skyline Skyrides**. In its shadow, **Rainbow Springs** provides a window into the life cycle of trout, with some fine specimens swimming in pools richly draped in ferns, while Rainbow Farm offers a slightly different twist on the sort of sheep-centred farmshow pioneered by the **Agrodome**, nearby.

Government Gardens and around

In the early years of the twentieth century, Rotorua was already New Zealand's premiere tourist town, a fact it celebrated in confident civic style by laying out the **Government Gardens** (unrestricted entry) on a small peninsula jutting into the lake east of the town centre. A rather bizarre vision of an antipodean little England as interpreted by the colonial administrators, the gardens delight with their juxtaposition of the staid and the exotic: white-suited bowls players mill around sulphurous steaming vents; palm trees loom over rose gardens; and, commanding the centre, there's the neo-Tudor **bathhouse**, built in 1908 in a style commensurate with the expectations of patrons familiar with European spas. Heralded as the greatest spa in the South Seas, "antagonistic" waters were supplied from the nearby Rachel and Priest springs to 84 baths, all fitted with the latest balneological equipment. But this was no pleasure palace, more a state-of-the-art non-residential hospital where patients suffering from arthritis, alcoholism, nervous disorders, in fact just about anything, underwent ghoulish treatments involving electrical currents and colonic irrigation as well as the more traditional pampering. Sadly, the bathhouse opened as the era of the grand spas was coming to a close; it limped along until 1963, when a combination of low patronage and maintenance costs hiked up by corrosive hydrogen sulphide in the waters hastened its demise.

The building has gone through a number of incarnations and now houses the **Rotorua Museum of Art and History** (daily: Nov to mid-March 9.30am–6pm, mid-March to Oct 9.30am–5pm; $7.50, combo with Blue Baths $10), where one of the principal attractions is the old baths themselves, complete with gloomy green and white tiling and exposed pipes. Several rooms from the spa's sixty-year existence have been preserved in a state of arrested decay and filled with photos of the glory days. The rest of the building is devoted to two main exhibitions. The small but exquisite and internationally significant **Te Arawa** exhibition showcases the long-respected talents of Arawa carvers who made this area a bastion of pre-European carving traditions. This collection contains some lovely pieces, several returned from European collections, and all powerfully presented. Among the magnificent figures, dog-skin cloaks, *pounamu* (greenstone) weapons and intricate barge-boards, prized pieces include the flute played by the legendary lover Tutanekai (see below), an unusually fine pumice goddess, and rare eighteenth-century carvings executed with stone tools. The photos around the walls depict faces tattooed with detailed *moko* (traditional tattoos), and a portrait of the Tarawera guide Sophia (see p.288) standing outside the Whakarewarewa meeting house. The remainder of the museum covers the dramatic events surrounding the **Tarawera eruption**. The extensive displays include an informative relief map of the region, eye-witness accounts and reminiscences, and photos of the ash-covered Temperance Hotel at Te Wairoa and of the similarly smothered Rotomahana Hotel, both now demolished.

The main bathhouse promoted health: when the adjacent **Blue Baths** (daily 9.30am–5pm; $7.50, combo with museum $10) opened in 1933 it promised only pleasure. Designed in the Californian Spanish Mission style so popular at the time, this was one of the first public swimming pools in the world to allow mixed bathing. Like its neighbour, the Blue Baths hit hard times and closed in 1982, only to reopen in 1999. You can still swim in an ancillary outdoor pool ($7), though the bulk of the building is now a museum charting its decades at the centre of Rotorua's social whirl. People's recollections are posted on panels amid the old changing cubicles, and serve to reinforce the sense of loss you get strolling around the main pool, now filled in and grassed over.

Immediately to the south lies the **Polynesian Spa**, Hinemoa Street (daily 6.30am–11pm; Polynesian Pools $10, Lake Spa $25) a mostly open-air complex landscaped for lake views and comprising three separate areas. The main **Polynesian Pools** section comprises thirty-odd hot mineral pools claimed to treat all manner of ailments, principally arthritis and rheumatism. The vast majority of visitors bathe in either the slightly alkaline main pool or the small and turbid Radium and Priest pools, where the acidic waters bubbling up through the bottom of the tub vary from 33°C to 43°C. Private pools (an additional $10 per person for 30min), where you can adjust the temperature yourself, are ranged around the Radium and Priest pools, but for real exclusivity, opt for the adjacent **Lake Spa** section, with nicely designed shallow rock pools, private relaxation lounge and bar and access to a water-jet massage (an additional $25 for half an hour). Families are catered for in the new **Family Spa** ($24 for up to two adults and four kids), with one chlorinated 33°C pool, a couple of small mineral pools, and a water slide.

Lake Rotorua

From the Government Gardens it is a short walk along the waterfront to the Lakefront Jetty, the starting point for trips onto **Lake Rotorua** and out to **Mokoia Island**, 7km to the north of the jetty. New Zealand's only inland, predator-free bird sanctuary, Mokoia is the scene of a successful and longstanding breeding programme for saddlebacks and North Island robins – often spotted at the feeder stations – and a fledgling one for the little spotted kiwi. The island is better known, however, for the story of **Hinemoa and Tutanekai**, the greatest of all Maori love stories and widely considered to be more truth than legend. It tells of two lovers, the young chief Tutanekai of Mokoia Island, and his high-born paramour, Hinemoa, whose people lived along the western shores of the lake. Hinemoa's family forbade her from marrying the illegitimate Tutanekai and prevented her from meeting him by beaching their heavy *waka* (canoe), but the strains of Tutanekai's lamenting flute still wafted across the lake nightly and the smitten Hinemoa resolved to swim to him. One night, buoyed by gourds, she set off towards Mokoia, but by the time she got there Tutanekai had returned to his *whare* (house) to sleep. Hinemoa arrived at the island but, without clothes, was unable to enter the village, so she immersed herself in a hot pool. Presently Tutanekai's slave came by to collect water, and Hinemoa lured him over, smashed his gourd and sent him back to his master. An enraged Tutanekai came to investigate, only to fall into Hinemoa's embrace. The site of Tutanekai's *whare* and **Hinemoa's Pool** can still be seen, along with the grave of the first *pakeha* born in the Rotorua district. A **landing fee** of $15 per adult is charged.

There are a couple of ways to get out on the lake and to Mokoia Island. The unfortunately named Scatcat tour (☎07/347 9852; 4 daily; $25) takes a speedy **catamaran** around the island on their hour-long trip, and if you catch one of the early boats you can be put ashore on Mokoia Island ($15 additional landing fee) and picked up by a later boat, leaving time for an extended soak or to wander the trails with an eagle eye out for native birdlife. Clearwater Charters (☎07/348 4186) offer comfortable self-drive **pontoon boats** carrying up to eight people (1hr $75, 3hr or more for $55 an hour) which can be taken to Mokoia Island or used for lake fishing; and rent an assortment of kayaks and peddle boats.

If it is just a cruise you are after, consider the leisurely *Lakeland Queen* (☎0800/862 784), a replica **paddle steamer** which runs a series of trips: the Morning Tea Cruise (10am; 1hr; $18), Lunch Cruise (12.30pm; 1hr; $28), Afternoon Tea Cruise (2.30pm; 1hr; $18) and occasional dinner cruises.

Ohinemutu

Before the town of Rotorua grew up around its government buildings, the principal settlement in the area was at **OHINEMUTU**, 500m northwest of the centre, on the lakeshore. It occupies a perfect site chosen for its proximity to fishing and transport on the lake, and to hot springs along its shore perfect for washing and cooking. Ohinemutu remains an overwhelmingly Maori village centred on the springs and the small wooden **St Faith's Anglican Church**, built in 1914 to replace its 1885 predecessor. The church's simple half-timbered neo-Tudor exterior gives no hint of the gloriously rich interior where there is barely a patch of wall that hasn't been carved or covered with *tukutuku* (ornamental latticework) panels. Everything has been intricately worked, from pew ends and support beams to the entrance to the chancel, which has been made to look like the barge boards (*maihi*) of a meeting house. Even the pulpit has been inlaid with geometrically patterned cloth. Wonderful though all this is, it is treated as a sideshow to the main attraction, a window with the figure of Christ, swathed in a Maori cloak and feathers, etched into it and positioned so that he appears to be walking on the lake. Outside is the grave of Gilbert Mair, a captain in the colonial army who twice saved Ohinemutu from attacks by rival Maori and became the only *pakeha* to earn full Arawa chieftainship.

At the opposite end of the small square in front of the church stands the **Tamatekapua Meeting House**, again beautifully carved, though the best and most ancient of the work, some dating back almost two hundred years, is inside and is most easily viewed during the "Magic of the Maori" concert held nightly (see p.283)

Immediately south of Ohinemutu, on Ranolf Street, lies **Kuirau Park**, its northern end pockmarked by fairly modest steaming hot pools, while the southern end has some minor thrills for kids: crazy-golf, a miniature railway, play areas and the like.

Whakarewarewa thermal reserve and forest park

To New Zealanders, mention of Rotorua immediately conjures up images of the **Whakarewarewa Thermal Reserve** – or "Whaka", as it is more commonly known – the closest thermal area to the city. Until 1998 this was a single entity, but local infighting has now thrown up a barrier through the middle leaving two entirely separate complexes. Around two-thirds of the active thermal zone and the lion's share of the infrastructure have been inherited by the **NZ Maori Arts & Crafts Institute**, Hemo Road, 3km south of central Rotorua (*www.nzmaori.co.nz*; daily: Nov–March 8am–6pm, April–Oct 8am–5pm; $18), which is the start of a series of walkways past glooping pools of boiling mud, sulphurous springs and agglomerations of silica stalactites. The main attractions are New Zealand's most spectacular geysers, the ten-metre **Prince of Wales' Feathers** and the granddaddy of them all, the twenty-metre **Pohutu** ("big splash"), which generally performs several times a day, always preceded by its neighbour. Occasionally it puts on even more dramatic performances, and as we go to press, Pohutu has been spouting continuously for over 40 days. Ambling around is undoubtedly more appealing when the weather is good, but don't be too dismayed if the weather is poor: low barometric pressures often bring out the best in the geysers, while cool winter conditions condense the steam into thick clouds, making the place even more ethereal.

The area would be worth visiting if that was all there was, but it also contains a replica of a traditional Maori **village**, its entrance marked by a carving of lovers Tutanekai and Hinemoa embracing, and the **Arts and Crafts Institute** itself (same hours; included with entry). The institute serves both to teach young Maori the traditional carving and weaving techniques and to demonstrate those same skills to visitors. Half an hour spent here can be wonderfully inspirational and informative, as skilled artisans produce flax skirts and carvings, which can be bought in the classy but expensive shop. The institute also hosts **Mia Ora** (6pm, in winter 5pm; $65) comprising a Maori welcome, concert and steam-cooked feast.

The remainder of the Whakarewarewa Thermal Area falls under the auspices of **The Thermal Village**, Tryon St, 3km south of central Rotorua (daily 8.30am-5pm; $15), which unlike the other thermal areas, is a living village founded in pre-European times and enlarged by an influx of displaced people in the aftermath of the Tarawera eruption. With the division of the thermal area, you can't get really close to the geysers and the more dramatic geothermal manifestations from here, but there is considerable compensation in being able to wander around the houses, many of them fairly new constructions as the hydrogen sulphide issuing from the ground tends to rot concrete. You might even see people using steam boxes for cooking, though the most common experience of geothermally cooked food is the sweetcorn stand near the entrance. You are free to wander at leisure past assorted souvenir shops demonstrating carving and weaving skills, but entry also includes a full guided tour by one of the residents. Time it right and you can even take in a **hangi** (served at 12.30; $15), which is bookended by two **cultural performances** (11.15am & 2pm; $30 including hangi).

The western fringe of the Whakarewarewa thermal area borders the **Whakarewarewa Forest**, experimentally planted a century back to see which exotic species would grow well under New Zealand conditions. Redwoods were found to grow three times faster than in their native California, creating the awe-inspiring **Redwood Grove**, which is threaded by a number of short paths. The **Fletcher Challenge Forests' Visitor Centre**, Long Mile Road (Oct-March Mon-Fri 8.30am-6pm, Sat & Sun 10am–4pm; April-Sept Mon–Fri 8.30am–5pm, Sat & Sun 10am–4pm; ☎07/346 2082, fax 347 3372, *redwoods@fcf.co.nz*) has details of these and the numerous **mountain-biking trails** (see p.280).

West of the Lake: Around Ngongotaha

Aside from visits to the thermal areas, much of Rotorua's daytime activity takes place between five and ten kilometres northwest of central Rotorua around the flanks of Mount Ngongotaha which is increasingly being surrounded by the city's suburbs. Closest to downtown, there's all manner of gravity-driven activities at the Skyline Skyrides site, and gentler pursuits at either Rainbow Springs, or around the mountain at Paradise Valley Springs. Sheep take centre stage (literally) a little further out at the Agrodome, centrepiece of an adventure park which is rapidly wrestling the adrenaline torch from the Skyline Skyrides.

Skyline Skyrides, Rainbow Springs and Paradise Valley Springs

First stop, around 4km from town, is the **Skyline Skyrides** (daily 9am–11pm; $12), an aerial gondola that whisks you 200m up to the top station for superb views across the lake and town, scenic but uninspired dining in the restaurant and café, and a bevy of adventure activities. Among these, the most fun is the **luge**, a kind of plastic tray on wheels on which you hurtle down banked concrete tracks at speeds of up to 60km per hour. A chair lift carries you back up to the top either for another run or a ride on the **Skyline**, a five-stage flying fox (zipwire), which is exciting enough to require a body harness and fully enclosed footwear, or an easier descent on the **Sidewinder**, where you sit on a little buggy as it is guided down a gently shelving track. Tickets ($4.50 for 1 descent, $10 for 3 and $15 for 5) are interchangeable between the three rides, or you can buy a combined gondola-and-five-rides ticket for $22. Backpackers are offered a gondola-and-two-rides ticket for $12, and on Friday and Saturday mornings (7–10am) early-rising **mountain bikers** can use a series of tracks and have unlimited gondola rides back up for $10. Bikes can be rented in town (see p.283). Air guns, a flight simulator and helicopter flights complete the summit set-up.

At the foot of the gondola hill lies **Rainbow Springs** (daily 8am–5pm; $18), an all-too-neat series of trout pools linked by nature trails which, along with the adjacent and now integrated Fairy Springs, has been admitting visitors since 1898 when a *tapu* on the springs was lifted. Fresh water flows through the crystal-clear pools, some with glass sides for superb viewing of some of the largest rainbow, brown and North American brook trout you will ever see. Adult fish all have free access to the lake, but know when they're on to a good thing and return for the near-constant supply of food tossed in by visitors. Other marginal attractions include animal pens, an aviary, a freshwater aquarium, a kiwi house and an extensive collection of ferns, but it all feels far too regimented and unless you're here early in the day it can be very crowded. You can usually escape the crush at the quieter Fairy Springs section, which has more of the same stuff. Across the road is the **Rainbow Farm** section (included in ticket price; shows at 10.30am, 11.45am, 1pm, 2.30pm & 4pm), with a huge fluffy shop and a covered area from where you can watch sheepdogs rounding up a flock, followed by a fake auction and a display of shearing prowess.

If you want to see trout, but prefer lions to sheep, eschew Rainbow Springs in favour of **Paradise Valley Springs**, 13km west of Rotorua on Paradise Valley Road (daily 8am–5pm; $13; *www.paradisev@xtra.co.nz*). It is an altogether more peaceful setting with boardwalks guiding you past pools of trout, native birds and an attractive wetland area. Their biggest draw is the breeding pride of lions, and if you catch it lucky there may be **lion cubs** on hand, which can be petted (under guidance) until they are six months old.

The Agrodome and Agrodome Adventure Park

Just about every bus touring the North Island stops 10km north of Rotorua at the **Agrodome**, Western Road, Ngongotaha (☎07/357 4350; shows at 9.30am, 11am &

2.30pm; show $10, farm tour $13, show & farm tour $20), where the star attraction is a slick 45-minute **sheep show**, a legacy of the 1970 Osaka World's Fair. Though undoubtedly corny, the spectacle is engaging: rams representing the nineteen major breeds farmed in New Zealand are enticed onto the podium; a sheep is shorn; lambs are bottle-fed; and there's an impressive sheepdog display. Shows are followed by a 45-minute farm tour, complete with honey tasting, deer viewing and, between April and June, kiwifruit picking.

A totally different market is catered for at the adjacent **Agrodome Adventure Park** (daily 9am-5pm or later), where they've gone all out to lure adrenaline junkies. Rotorua now has a **bungy jump** ($80) from a huge metal arm which is hoisted into the air to create a platform for a 43m plummet. The same arm, along with a couple of stayed towers, creates **Swoop** ($40 for one, $35 each for two, $30 each for three), in which up to three of you are lashed into a hang-gliding harness, winched up to 40m and released for a giant swing at speeds of up to 130km per hour: a larger number produces greater momentum. All this overlooks the **Agrojet** ($30) where tiny racing jetboats, de-tuned but still pumping out 450 horsepower, hurtle around a short artificial course. You get less than five minutes, but are left breathless.

Nearby at the **Zorb** (one go $40, two goes $60) you can dive into the centre of a three-metre diameter clear plastic ball and roll down a 200-metre hill. Currently you can either do it "dry", harnessed in for a head-over-heels roll; or "wet", with no harness but a couple of buckets of water inside so you slosh around madly. It is a fair bit of cash for a small thrill, but it's quite a laugh all the same, and even kids can have a go in a smaller, more sedate version. Lastly, there is the novel **DirtThingz** (*www.dirtthingz.com*; $35), basically motorized skateboarding on a dirt track attaining speeds of up to 55km per hour.

Combo packages will suit just about anyone's desires, and a **free shuttle bus** runs out to the Agrodome and Adventure Park (4 daily) from the visitor centre and some of the backpackers.

Activities

As you might expect in a place which attracts visitors in such numbers, numerous companies have sprung up in Rotorua to offer all manner of adventure activities – rafting, kayaking, mountain biking or even fishing. The **adventure tourism** scene hasn't quite snowballed to the degree it has in Queenstown, but there is still loads to keep you occupied. In addition to the activities detailed below, brochures everywhere advertise water-skiing on Blue Lake, horse riding, quad biking, hot-air ballooning and much more (see "Listings", p.283).

Rafting, whitewater sledging and kayaking

Rotorua has developed a considerable reputation for its rafting trips; in fact, there's a better range of trips available here than anywhere else in New Zealand. Much of the hype is reserved for the Grade III–IV **Kaituna River**, or at least the 2km section of it after it leaves Lake Rotoiti, 20km north of Rotorua, and enters a narrow, verdant gorge. As the river twists around rocky bluffs, it periodically plummets over vertical drops, including the spectacular **Tutea's Falls**, where the river tumbles almost seven metres. The trip is a short one, only spending around forty minutes on the water, and everyone comes out wanting more. In the summer, the half-dozen or so companies operating out of Rotorua take several trips a day, charging around $60–65, and even in the depths of winter someone's bound to be running the river.

While the Kaituna is a great trip, the river to go for, if you can get the timing right, is the Grade IV+ **Wairoa River**, 80km by road from Rotorua, on the outskirts of Tauranga, which relies on dam-releases for raftable quantities of white water

(Dec–March every Sun; Sept–Nov & April–May every second Sun). This is on-the-edge rafting and one of the finest short trips in the world, negotiating a dangerous and immensely satisfying stretch of water, and shooting rapids such as Mother's Nightmare, Devil's Hole and the Toaster, which has a nasty habit of tipping rafts over immediately above the toughest rapid on the river, the Roller Coaster. This is essentially a trip for those with some rafting experience and a good appreciation of the hazards of white water; several companies do the run, charging around $70–75 for the six-hour trip from Rotorua (90min actually on the water), often including a post-deluge barbecue. Some companies offer a double run for just a few dollars more.

If your tastes lean more towards appreciation of the natural surroundings with a bit of a bumpy ride thrown in, opt for the Grade III **Rangitaiki River**, which also shoots Jeff's Joy, a Grade III–IV drop that's the highlight of the trip. Trips from Rotorua cost around $85. With more time, and money on your hands, it is well worth considering a **multi-day wilderness rafting trip** on Eastland's **Motu River** (see box, p.375).

Currently over half a dozen **companies** run trips from Rotorua, all rafting the same stretches of water at pretty much the same **prices**, though it pays to ask around for special offers and backpacker discounts. There's little to choose between them, but Kaituna Cascades (☎0800/524 886, *kaituna.cascades@clear.net.nz*) have a good reputation, and White Water Excitement (☎07/345 7182) link up with a jetboat ride and helicopter flight for the "Kaituna Triple Tremble" ($235).

To up the ante a few notches, consider **whitewater sledging** with Kaitiaki Adventures (☎0800/326 376, *www.kaitiaki.co.nz*), who equip you with a wetsuit, helmet and a buoyant plastic sledge before guiding you down one of the rivers described above. Extra vulnerability and eye-level intimacy with the water makes this a good deal more exciting and potentially more risky than rafting. The most sensible trips are those on the Rangitaiki River where you can opt for the thrilling Jeff's Joy Run (Grade II–IV; $98), though first timers might prefer the more modest lower section (Grade II; $90). Risks go up appreciably when running either the Kaituna or the Wairoa ($110 plus), and some sceptical folk around Rotorua are wondering just how long it will be before there's a serious accident.

Excitement and risk come together in similar proportions with **tandem kayaking**, undertaken by Kaituna Cascades on the Kaituna River and including the 7m Tutea's Falls. If you are under 85kg, are physically fit and have a spare $95 you'll be stuck in the front of a double kayak, given basic instruction then steered down the river by an experienced paddler in the driving seat behind you.

If any of this inspires you to **rent kayaks** or undertake **kayaking courses**, get in touch with the Sun Spots Kayak Shop, SH33, Okawa Bay (☎07/362 4222, fax 362 4324, *www.sunspots.co.nz*, *sunspots@iconz.co.nz*), 14km north of Rotorua. They rent recreational kayaks ($20 per half-day), sea kayaks ($30 per day), and full whitewater set-ups ($30 per day) and run all manner of courses including the half-day introduction to kayaking ($90).

Mountain biking

This is one of the finest **mountain biking** areas in the country with large areas of the redwoods, firs and pines threaded by single-track biking trails especially constructed with banked turns and jumps under a sub-canopy of tree ferns. Better still, it is only fifteen minutes' ride from town. Altogether there's over 20km of track divided into circuits of different standards, the easiest climbing up to a fabulous viewpoint overlooking the Blue and Green lakes (see p.289). Moving up in difficulty there's the appropriately named Challenge circuit, then a specialist jumps loop. You can just head out there and hope that the meagre signposting is enough to help you back to the start, though a waterproof **trail map** ($2.50) is available in town from the Map and Track Shop (see p.270), or out at the forest from the Fletcher Challenge Forests' Visitor Centre (see p.277).

There is **no charge** to enter the forest or use the trails, which are most easily accessed from the obvious car park on Waipa Mill Road, 5km south of town off SH38. On summer weekends you'll find folk renting bikes here, or sturdy front- and full-suspension machines are available from one of the bike rental places in town (see p.283); most models available at hostels aren't up to the task. If you prefer **guided mountain biking**, call Planet Bike (☎07/348 9971, *www.planetbike.co.nz, ride@planetbike.co.nz*) who run trips through the forest at all experience levels ($49–59 for 2hr) as well as night rides ($69), half-day scenic rides ($79); they even offer "women guides for women's rides".

Fishing

The Rotorua Lakes District has a reputation for trout fishing only matched in the North Island by the rivers and streams flowing into Lake Taupo. With eleven gorgeous lakes, the angling could hardly be more scenic and all the lakes are stocked with strong-fighting rainbow trout; a typical summer catch is around 1.5kg, though in winter this can creep up towards 3kg. The proximity of **Lake Rotorua** makes it a perennial favourite, reached by charter boats from the Lakefront Jetty (2hr minimum; $80–90 an hour, including tackle but not licences – see below).

If you are going it alone, consult the visitor centre for a set of Byzantine rules, and obtain the latest on lake and river conditions, weather reports and regulations from the free helpline (☎0800/TROUTLINE), which also gives credit-card holders the opportunity to buy the necessary **licence** (24hr, $13; 7 days, $25; year, $65). These are available from the visitor centre and larger sports shops, and cover the whole country except for the Taupo fishery region. In broad terms, the fishery is open year round, though restrictions apply. For further guidance, pick up the free *Lake Rotorua & Tributaries* leaflet published by Fish & Game NZ from sports shops such as Hamill's Hunting & Fishing, 1271 Fenton St (☎07/348 3147, fax 348 3146). Fly-fishing guides will generally set you back around $500 a day.

Eating, drinking and nightlife

In recent years Rotorua has made great culinary strides and there are now quite a few quality **restaurants**, most congregated along a short strip at the lake end of Tutanekai Street – known locally as "The Streat". Nowhere is outrageously expensive, but the assiduously budget-conscious will fare better at less flashy places further from the main drag. Unlike the shops, which close up for much of the weekend, the restaurants and bars are generally open all week, most staying open as long as custom demands; unless you're part of a large group, there's little need to reserve a table.

Despite its exalted status as New Zealand's tourist mecca, Rotorua remains a small city and the nightlife is correspondingly limited. There are a few lively **bars** to keep you entertained, but almost everyone spends one evening of their stay attending one of the **hangi and Maori concerts** in one of the tourist hotels or, preferably, at one of the outlying marae.

Restaurants and café/bars

Barbarella, 1263 Pukuatua St. The hippest of Rotorua's cafés, dark and definitely the place to be seen, particularly at night when the pool table comes alive and the music (occasionally live) gets cranked up.

Bath House Café, Blue Baths. Gracious tea-rooms recently recreated in the renovated Blue Baths complex complete with potted palms, linen napkins, cakes off an Art Deco trolley and a couple of huge portraits of the Queen and Duke of Edinburgh in their younger years. Pick a window seat and watch the bowls outside in Government Gardens while you indulge in tiffin ($13), Devonshire tea ($9), or lunches such as shepherds pie or calzone. Licensed.

The Coffee Bean, 189 Tutanekai St. Better-than-average café that opens early for those pre-bus breakfasts and serves bargain snacks all day.

Copper Criollo, 1151 Arawa St (☎07/348 1333). One of Rotorua's more distinctive restaurants, serving robust portions of classy Creole cooking in a cosy room arranged around a copper still. Cajun music accompanies wonderful breads, blackened chicken livers, gumbo and jambalaya. The Creole versions of traditional breakfasts are particularly good. Licensed & BYO.

Fat Dog, 1161 Arawa St. Rotorua's funkiest café and bar, with mismatched furniture, eclectic wall hangings and good food with vegetarian leanings. Background music can be anything from jazz to drum 'n' bass. Licensed.

Freos, 1103 Tutanekai St. Quality modern Kiwi café dining at reasonable prices both inside and out. Good for burgers, focaccia sandwiches, pasta dishes and chargrilled meats. Licensed & BYO.

Kebab Café, 1159 Arawa St. Plain and simple café serving lamb, beef and chicken kebabs and felafel, either in a roll for $8 or as a main meal for $15. Licensed.

Mitas, 1114 Tutanekai St (☎07/349 6482, *www.mitas.co.nz*). Beautifully prepared and presented predominantly Balinese food offered in traditional and adapted modern forms. Prices are modest and it can all be washed down with java roasted on the premises. Licensed.

Swiss Cake and Confectionery Shop, 1230 Tutanekai St. Excellent pastries and handmade chocolates to take away.

Tastebuds Mexican Cantina, 1213 Fenton St. Ever-popular Mexican eat-in and takeaway, serving hefty helpings of Tex-Mex staples at low prices.

Tatou, 1142 Tutanekai St (☎07/349 4483). Fashionable joint serving modern variations on Pacific and Maori cuisine such as tuatua chowder ($7), steamed green-lip mussels ($9), and lambs fry bruchetta with puha (a kind of watercress; $15). Licensed and BYO.

Tutanekai Espresso, 1226 Tutanekai St. Daytime café with a good line in panini, crepes and BLTs, plus good coffee. Closed Sun.

La Vega, 1158 Whakaue St. Bustling restaurant and bar concentrating on gourmet wood-fired pizzas, pasta and steaks.

Zanelli's, cnr Amohia St & Hinemoa St (☎07/348 4908). Always lively northern Italian restaurant with a good range of starters, pasta dishes also available as mains and *segundi piatti* such as chicken thigh with eggplant, zucchini, mushroom salsa and mozzarella. Booking recommended; closed Sun & Mon.

Zippy Central, 1153 Pukuatua St. Rotorua's grooviest restaurant, with haphazard retro Fifties and Sixties Pop décor. Purple and green walls, and Formica tables only temporarily distract you from the great coffee and small selection of imaginative and well-prepared food, from bagels and smoothies to marinated lamb and tabouleh salad or pumpkin gnocchi ($12–15). Licensed and BYO.

Bars and clubs

Lava Bar, 1286 Arawa St. A house converted into a bar that's found favour with backpackers, rafting guides and local youth. Basic meals are available and there's an early-evening happy hour, pinball machines and a pool table – if you can get to them.

O'Malley's, 1287 Eruera St. Ersatz Irish bar with a strong line in draught Irish beers and bargain meals. Live entertainment every Friday with happy hour.

Pig & Whistle, cnr Haupapa St & Tutanekai St. Lively bar in a former police station with good locally brewed beers on tap, excellent-value tasty bar meals and a garden bar. Rock and pop covers bands at weekends, when tidy dress is required and a small cover charge applies.

Hangi and Maori concerts

Rotorua is far and away the best place to sample food steamed to perfection in the Maori earth oven or **hangi** and watch a **Maori concert**, typically an hour-long performance of traditional dance, song and chants. Although not entirely satisfactory introductions to Maori culture, these are at least accessible and good value. Approaching a dozen groups vie for your custom, with offerings that fall into two distinct camps: hangi-and-concert extravaganzas laid on by Rotorua's major hotels (typically $45–50); and packages operated and organized by Maori groups ($55–60) that involve a trip to an out-of-town marae, and exhibit a degree of authenticity with a strong sense of *Maoritanga* as a living culture. All trips run for three or four hours from 6 or 7pm, with buses picking up and dropping off at hotels and hostels around town; some of the hotels offer hangi-only or concert-only deals for about half the cost.

The two groups running **out-of-town packages** are distinctly different, though they follow largely the same format, giving instruction on marae customs and protocol (see "Maoritanga" in Contexts, p.859) as you are driven out to a Maori village, followed by a formal welcome. By far the most popular is Tamaki Tours (☎07/346 2823, *tamaki@wave.co.nz*; $58), where you, and several more busloads, are driven out to a specially built "Maori village" south of town (see p.289) for a spine-chilling welcome. Everything is so professionally done that it is hard to quibble, though its popularity has become its biggest downfall and sightlines can be restricted at the busier times of year. In contrast, Rotoiti Tours (☎07/348 8969, *rotoiti@voyager.co.nz*; $55) lacks some of the panache, but is a much more engaging (and in some ways more authentic) affair, with almost the whole *whanau* (extended family group) contributing to the proceedings, which take place in the beautifully decorated meeting house on the Rakeiao Marae at Tapuaekura Bay on the shores of Lake Rotoiti some 20km north of Rotorua.

The big **hotels** take a more cabaret approach to the whole affair, usually eating first and relegating the concert to a form of after-dinner entertainment. The food is four-star-hotel standard, though in a misguided desire to present imaginative salads and precisely carved slices of meat they veer away from the more robust hangi style, usually resorting to steam boxes rather than traditional earth ovens. The content of the concert is almost identical to the marae-based shows but the tone is quite different, less intimate and more consciously choreographed, with sophisticated lighting and a disembodied voice commentating. There's little to choose between the hotels though the *Sheraton*, Fenton Street, near Whakarewarewa (☎07/348 7139; $49) and the Novotel's *Matakiki* show, Tutanekai Street (☎07/346 3888; *rotorua@novotel.co.nz*; $52), both have good reputations.

If none of these suit, the Ohinemutu Cultural Group conduct Rotorua's original **concert-only** Magic of the Maori (☎07/349 3949 & 0508/300 333, *www.magicmaori.com*, *magicnz@wave.co.nz*; 8pm; $15) each evening inside the Tamatekapua Meeting House at Ohinemutu (see p.276), and there are concerts held at Whakarewarewa (see p.277) at both the NZ Maori Arts & Crafts Institute, and The Thermal Village.

Listings

Airlines Air New Zealand Travelcentre, 1103 Hinemoa St (domestic ☎07/348 7159, international ☎07/347 9564, arrival and departure info ☎07/345 6299); Ansett NZ (☎0800/267 388).

American Express Galaxy United Travel, 1315 Tutanekai St (☎07/347 9444).

Automobile Association 1191 Amohau St (☎07/348 3069).

Banks and exchange ANZ, cnr Hinemoa St & Amohia St (☎07/348 2169); BNZ, cnr Haupapa St & Tutanekai St (☎07/348 1099); National, cnr Fenton St & Hinemoa St (☎07/349 5300); Westpac, cnr Hinemoa St & Tutanekai St. See also American Express and Thomas Cook.

Bike rental Runaround bikes are available from many of the hostels, plus Lady Jane's Ice Cream Parlour, 1092 Tutanekai St (☎07/347 9340; $15 per day). Front suspension machines perfect for Whakarewarewa Forest trails are available from Rotorua Cycle Centre, 1120 Hinemoa St (☎07/348 6588), and Pins Cycles, 1275 Fenton St (☎07/347 1151), both charging around $15 for the first hour and $10 thereafter (slightly more for full-spec bikes).

Bookshops Idle Hour Book Inn, 1186 Eruera St (☎07/347 6806) for secondhand books; Whitcoulls, 1238 Tutanekai St (☎07/348 3699) for new.

Car rental Link, 1222 Fenton St (☎07/349 1629 & 0800/652 565, *www.autohire.co.nz, info@ autohire.co.nz*), offers a fully insured unlimited mileage runabout for $55 a day (3-day minimum); Budget, 1230 Fenton St (☎07/348 8127, fax 346 1078, *rotbb@budget.co.nz*), matches these rates most of the time.

Cinema Hoyts Movieland 5, 1263 Eruera St.

Climbing wall The Wall, 1140 Hinemoa St (☎07/350 1400) is open daily 10am–10pm. Entry $12, gear rental $8.

Horse riding The Whakarewarewa Forest is the venue for rides with Foxwood Park, Long Mile Rd (☎07/345 7003); Mountain Action, 525 Ngongotaha Rd (☎07/348 8400, *mountain.action @xtra.co.nz*); and the Maori-run Peka Horse Trekking (☎07/346 1755). All offer one-hour, two-hour and longer treks at competitive prices.

Internet access Fast access and all the expected capabilities at *Contact Cyber Café*, 1217 Fenton St (*cyberz@ihug.co.nz*); *Cybershed*, 1176 Pukuatua St; and *Nomads Cyber Café*, 1195 Fenton St. All are open from around 9am until around 9pm or later.

Left luggage In the Tourism Rotorua complex ($2 for 3hr, $4 per day).

Library The public library is on Haupapa St (☎07/348 4177).

Medical treatment Lakes Primecare, cnr Arawa St & Tutanekai St (☎07/348 1000), offer accident and urgent healthcare (daily 8am–11pm).

Pharmacy Lakes Care Pharmacy, cnr Arawa St & Tutanekai St (☎07/48 4385), is open daily 9am–9.30pm.

Police 64–98 Fenton St (☎07/348 0099).

Post office The main post office, 79–85 Hinemoa St (☎07/349 2397), has poste restante facilities.

Showers In the Tourism Rotorua complex ($5, towel and soap extra).

Skydiving Taupo has the reputation, but you get a more personal experience and equally spectacular scenery for much the same money (around $180) with Tandem Skydiving Rotorua (☎07/345 7520).

Taxi Fast Taxis ☎07/348 2444; Rotorua Taxis ☎07/348 1111.

Thomas Cook, Air New Zealand Travelcentre, 1103 Hinemoa St (☎07/343 1103, fax 343 1101).

Tours See box on p.286.

Travel agents Budget Travel, cnr Fenton St & Eruera St (☎07/348 4152); Flight Centre, 1228 Tutanekai St (☎07/346 3145); Galaxy United Travel, 1315 Tutanekai St (☎07/347 9444).

Around Rotorua

Much of the best Rotorua has to offer lies outside the city among the lakes to the north and east and around the most dramatic of the volcanic zones half an hour's drive south towards Taupo. Without your own transport, you are pretty much reliant on the huge variety of **shuttles** and **tours** run by numerous companies (see p.286), and just about any combination of sights can be packed into a full-day tour.

Travelling independently, minor sights along the eastern shore of Lake Rotorua can be quickly dispatched, leaving time for the seldom-crowded **Hell's Gate** thermal area, and the opportunity to watch terrified rafters plunging over **Tutea's Falls**. Having your own boat opens up the best of lakes Rotoiti, Rotoehu and Rotama, though they're pleasing enough just to drive past on the way to Whakatane and the East Cape. Rewards are more plentiful to the east and south especially around Mount Tarawera which, in 1886, showered tonnes of ash on the **Buried Village**, where partly-interred Maori dwellings graphically illustrate the volcano's immense power. As the village and the Pink and White Terraces were being destroyed, the **Waimangu Thermal Valley** was created and now ranks as one of the finest collections of geothermal features in the region alongside kaleidoscopic **Wai-O-Tapu**, with its daily-triggered **Lady Knox Geyser** and multicoloured pools.

Northeast of Lake Rotorua: Hell's Gate and the northern lakes

SH30 hugs the eastern shores of Lake Rotorua, bound for Whakatane (see p.371) and passing through the region's greatest concentration of lakes and plenty of twisting hill country. Scenery aside, there isn't a great deal to stop for along the way apart from the **Te Ngae 3D Maze**, Te Ngae Park, 10km north of Rotorua (daily 9am–5pm; $5), a wooden affair with bridges linking separate sections and complicating things immeasurably.

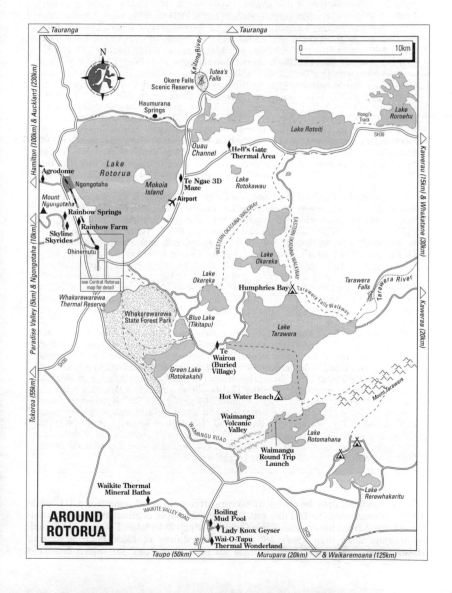

SIGHTSEEING TOURS FROM ROTORUA

To get out to the sights around Rotorua without your own transport, you've got a choice of shuttles, which just do the running around, and a bewildering array of minibus tours, ranging from a couple of hours to a full day. The latter all include admission to sights, have a commentary of some description and the itineraries can be quite flexible, particularly when numbers are small.

Most comprehensive is the **shuttle** operators is Thermal & Cultural Shuttle (☎0800/287 296) who make six daily circuits of Wai-O-Tapu, Waimangu, Tamaki Maori Village and the Waikite hot pools, picking up at hostels around Rotorua. A $15 all-day pass lets you get on and off as you please. Santa Fe Shuttle (☎07/345 7997) will run you out to Hell's Gate or the Buried Village for $10 return; and Wai-O-Tapu for $12 return.

Of the **minibus tours**, Carey's Tours, 1148 Haupapa St (☎07/347 1197) run a vast array of trips, including the excellent-value Geothermal Wonderland (4hr; $65) out to Wai-O-Tapu and Waimangu. Full-day trips add the Redwood Grove and the Buried Village (8hr; $100), while the scenic Waimangu Round Trip (9hr; $140) visits the Waimangu Thermal Valley, cruising across Lake Rotomahana, bushwalking to a second cruise on Lake Tarawera, ambling around the Buried Village and finishing with a soak in the Polynesian Spa. Their backpacker-oriented trips – known as Carey's Capers – include lunch and a dip in natural hot pools in the bush but are otherwise almost identical. One particularly good combination is Get Volcanic (9hr; $140), which takes in Wai-O-Tapu, Waimangu and a trip up Mount Tarawera. Another low-cost favourite is The Pink Bus (☎0800/222 231), which runs straightforward trips out to Wai-O-Tapu (3hr; $35) and Waimangu (3hr; $40).

One destination that isn't accessible with your own vehicle is the shattered line of craters atop **Mount Tarawera**, which can be reached on foot (see box opposite) and on tours with 4WD companies such as Tarawera Mountain Sightseeing Tours (☎07/348 5179; half-day $70) and Mount Tarawera 4WD Tours (☎07/348 2814, *mttarawera@xtra.co.nz*; half-day $70), who link up with rafting and helicopter companies for a range of combo deals. Most trips give the option of a 200-metre run down a scree slope into the crater. A good choice is to combine the geothermal areas, Mount Tarawera, a dip in a natural pool and a good dose of local lore and humour on the superb, full-day TeKiri Trek (☎07/345 5967; $120), a Maori-run venture which kicks off with a visit to Wai-O-Tapu and a hot dip, followed by a 4WD trip up Mount Tarawera, barbecue lunch and more off-roading to Tarawera Falls (see p.288), where you can take a much cooler swim.

The majesty of Mount Tarawera is best appreciated from the air, on **fixed-wing planes** or by helicopter. Flights start from as little as $40 for a quick spin over the lake, $140 for Tarawera flights and something closer to $400 for an overflight of White Island out in the Bay of Plenty; Volcanic Wunderflites (☎0800/777 359, *wunderflites@xtra.co.nz*), Volcanic Air Safaris (☎0800/800 848, *volcanicair@xtra.co.nz*), and Lakeside Aviation (☎0800/535 363) all run competitive trips. **Chopper flights** will set you back a little more, and you won't get to Mount Tarawera for much under $190; more like $250 if you want a short landing, though it is worth noting that it is hardly a peaceful experience with the rotors kept running. Try Volcanic Air Safaris, NZ Helicopters Rotorua (☎07/348 1223, *collinsj@new-zealand-heli.nzl.com*) or the Wai-O-Tapu-based Heli-Kiwi (☎07/366 6611, *www.helikiwi.co.nz*, *info@helikiwi.co.nz*), which also organize several combination trips, linking up with 4WD operators, rafting companies and lake cruises.

Immediately north of the maze, SH30 veers off right to Whakatane (see p.371) while SH33 continues north to Te Puke and Tauranga. A couple of kilometres along the latter and you'll cross the riverine Ohau Channel, which links lakes Rotorua and Rotoiti. Haumurana Road then spurs left around the shores of Lake Rotorua passing **Haumurana Gardens**, 773 Haumurana Rd (daily 9am–5pm; $5), which boast the largest natural spring in the North Island – though in a land where crystal clear waters are commonplace it seems strange to pay to see a spring.

Sticking with SH33, you soon come upon signs to the **Okere Falls Scenic Reserve**, which surrounds the rafting mecca of the Kaituna River - follow signs up Trout Pool Road, 4km north of the Haumurana Road junction. From the first car park, 400m along Trout Pool Road, a broad track follows the river to a second car park (2.5km return; 40min–1hr) passing glimpses of the churning river below, and a viewing platform that's perfect for observing rafters plummet over the seven-metre **Tutea's Falls**. From here, steps descend through short tunnels in the steep rock walls beside the waterfall to **Tutea's Caves**, thought to have been used as a safe haven by Maori women and children during attacks by rival groups.

Most of the traffic out this way sticks to SH30, the route to **Hell's Gate** (*Tikitere*; ☎07/345 3151; daily 9am–5pm, and often later; $10), 14km northeast of Rotorua. The least-visited and smallest of the major thermal areas, this is also one of the fiercest and most active, with an abundance of bubbling mud and seething gunmetal-grey waters. Its fury camouflages a lack of notable features, however, and the only real highlights are the bubbling mud of the Devil's Cauldron and the hot **Kakahi Falls**, whose soothing 38°C waters once made this a popular bathing spot (though now off-limits to bathers).

Beyond Hell's Gate lies **Lake Rotoiti**, which translates as "little lake", though it is in fact the second-largest in the region and is linked to Lake Rotorua by the narrow Ohau Channel. This passage, along with the neighbouring **Lake Rotoehu** and **Lake**

ROTORUA AREA WALKS

Although Rotorua isn't especially well endowed with serious tramps, it does work well as a staging post for forays into the Whirinaki Forest (see p.291) and further afield to Waikaremoana (see p.401). If you're keen to stretch your legs around these parts, you are best off with there-and-back day walks. Trying to link up multi-day hikes is all but impossible without a compliant driver to pick you up at the other end. The best map is the 1:60,000 Holidaymaker *Rotorua Lakes* map ($13.50).

Mount Tarawera (14km return; 4–5hr; 400m ascent). If you've got a car and don't want to pay for a 4WD ascent of Mount Tarawera, the alternative is to drive as far as you can then get out and walk. Everyone decides to abandon their car at different spots as the road gets worse, then has to walk with 4WD vehicles and mountain bikes periodically clattering by. The reward is a 15km-long gash of craters that can be explored for as long as you wish, always keeping an eye out for cloud which can quickly disorientate in this trackless domain. The hike starts on Bob Annett Road, off SH38 around 35km by road southeast of Rotorua. If road conditions are good and you have reasonable clearance on your rig, you should make it to the car park where a fee of $2 is charged to cross Ngati Rangitihi land, or for road maintenance depending on who you believe.

Okere Falls Scenic Reserve (2.5km return; 40min–1hr; see above). An easy stroll with river views and spectacular angles on rafters shooting Tutea's Falls. Starts 18km north of Rotorua.

Tarawera Falls Walk (1–8km return; 30min–4hr; 100m ascent; see overleaf). Gorgeous bush walk to a great view of Tarawera Falls, and on past swimming holes to the outlet of Lake Tarawera. Starts 80km by road from Rotorua and 24km south of Kawerau.

Tikitapu (Blue Lake; 5.5km loop; 2hr; 500m ascent). A pleasant and non-too-arduous loop around the Blue Lake through regenerating bush then Douglas firs and past some sandy beaches perfect for a dip. The single major climb takes you away from the lake to a viewpoint over the Blue and Green lakes. Starts at the eastern end of the beach opposite the Blue Lake Holiday Park, 9km southeast of Rotorua.

Rotama, traditionally formed a part of the canoe route from the coast. A section of this route, apparently used on a raid by the Ngapuhi warrior chief Hongi Hika, is traced by **Hongi's Track** (3km; 1hr return; negligible ascent), a beautiful bushwalk which runs through to Lake Rotoehu passing the Wishing Tree, which is often surrounded by plant offerings.

Kawerau and Tarawera Falls

Around 6km beyond Lake Rotama, a good sideroad leads to the planned timber-mill town of **KAWERAU**, which sits on a flood plain of the Tarawera River at the foot of the . distinctive hump of Mount Edgecumbe (*Putauaki*). You are unlikely to want to stay longer than it takes to visit the **visitor centre**, Plunket St (Mon–Fri 8.30am–4.30pm, Sat & Sun 10am–3pm; ☎07/323 7550) for the **compulsory permit** ($2 here, or free from the Fletcher Challenge Forests' Visitor Centre in Rotorua) and directions to the region's main attraction, **Tarawera Falls**, 24km to the south. It is at its most impressive when the underground Tarawera River appears to burst in a solid stream out of the cliff face. It is less impressive after a dry spell, but still worth the 15min walk (mostly flat) along the Tarawera Falls/Tarawera Outlet walkway to the falls viewpoint. You can see where the Tarawera River dives underground a further 10–20min walk upstream (and uphill), and by pressing on a further 5min you come across a wonderful safe swimming hole with natural diving spots and a rope swing. The track continues a further hour to the DOC's popular lakeside Tarawera Outlet **campsite** ($5; toilets and water only), also accessible by forest road. Note that **driving can be hazardous** on metalled forest roads – keep your headlights on at all times and steer well clear of the billowing clouds of dust thrown up by huge logging trucks.

Southeast of Rotorua

Volcanic activity again provides the main theme for attractions southeast of Rotorua, most having some association with **Lake Tarawera** and the jagged line of volcanic peaks and craters along the southeastern shore, collectively known as **Mount Tarawera**, which erupted in 1886.

Before this, Tarawera was New Zealand's premier tourist destination, with thousands of visitors every year crossing lakes Tarawera and Rotomahana in whale boats and *waka*, frequently guided by the renowned Maori guide Sophia, to the **Pink and White Terraces**, two separate fans of silica which cascaded down the hillside to the edge of Lake Rotomahana. Boiling cauldrons bubbled away at the top of each formation, spilling mineral-rich water down the hillside where, over several centuries it formed a series of staggered cup-shaped pools, the outflow of one filling the one below. The White Terraces (*Te Tarata* or "Tattooed Rock"), were the larger, but most visitors favoured the Pink Terraces (*Otukapuarangi* or "Cloudy Atmosphere"), which were prettier and better suited to sitting and soaking. The chemical reaction which gave them the pink tint was discovered in the 1980s, since when there has been much idle talk of trying to recreate the terraces.

All this steamy bliss came to an abrupt end on the night of June 10, 1886, when the long-dormant Mount Tarawera ripped itself asunder, creating 22 craters along a 17km rift, and covering over 15,000 square kilometres in mud and scoria to a depth of 22 metres. The Pink and White Terraces were shattered by the buckling of the earth, covered by ash and lava, then submerged deep under the waters of Lake Rotomahana which, dammed by earth upheavals, grew to twenty times its previous size.

The cataclysm had been foreshadowed eleven days earlier, when two separate canoe loads of *pakeha* tourists and their Maori guides saw an ancient *waka* glide silently out of the mist, with a dozen warriors paddling furiously, then vanish just as suddenly; this was interpreted by the ancient *tohunga* (priest) Tuhoto Ariki as a sign of imminent disaster. The fallout from the eruption buried five villages, including the staging post for the Pink and White Terrace trips, **Te Wairoa**, where the *tohunga* lived. In a classic case of blaming the messenger, the inhabitants refused to rescue the *tohunga* and it wasn't until four days later that they allowed a group of *pakeha* to dig him out. Miraculously, he was still alive, though he died a week later.

The chain of eruptions which racked the fault line during that fateful night in 1886 created an entirely new thermal valley, **Waimangu**, running southwest from the shores of the newly enlarged Lake Rotomahana. Still geothermally active, Waimangu struggles to outdo the supremely colourful thermal area of **Wai-O-Tapu**, a few kilometres further south.

Beyond the volcanic zone, the Kaingaroa Forest stretches away east to the little-visited tramping territory of the **Whirinaki Forest Park**, and the Kinleith Forest straggles west to **Tirau**, **Putaruru** and **Tokoroa**, minor way stations on the route from Auckland to Taupo and the Tongariro National Park.

The Blue and Green lakes, the Buried Village and Lake Tarawera

To nineteenth-century tourists Rotorua was merely a staging post before they continued their journey to the shores of Lake Tarawera, 15km southeast, where canoes would take them across to view the Pink and White Terraces. Latter-day sightseers still follow the same route, passing a ridge-top viewpoint that overlooks the iridescent waters of **Blue Lake** (*Tikitapu*) and **Green Lake** (*Rotokakahi*), which get their hues from subterranean mineral activity.

The road reaches the shores of Lake Tarawera just past the Te Wairoa **Buried Village** (☎07/362 8287, *www.buriedvillage.co.nz*; daily: Nov–April 8.30am–5.30pm; May–Oct 9am–5pm; $12), the partly excavated and heavily reconstructed remains of a settlement that, at the time of the Tarawera eruption, was larger than contemporary Rotorua. Numerous houses collapsed under the weight of the two or three metres of ash that settled on Te Wairoa on June 10, 1886; others were saved by virtue of their inhabitants hefting ash off the roof to lighten the load. Much of the village was excavated in the 1930s and 1940s, though work continues slowly today. **Free guided tours** take place on the hour (11am–3pm), or you can make your own way through the grounds where there is less of a sense of an archeological dig than of a manicured orchard: half-buried *whare* and the foundations for the Rotomahana Hotel sit primly on mown lawns among European fruit trees gone to seed, marauding hawthorn and a perfect row of full-grown poplars fostered by a line of fenceposts. Many of the *whare* contain small collections of implements and ash-encrusted household goods, contrasting with the stark simplicity of other dwellings such as **Tohunga's Whare**, where the ill-fated priest lay buried alive for four days before being released from his ashen tomb. Look out too for the extremely rare, carved-stone *pataka* (storehouse), and the bow section of a *waka* once used to ferry tourists on the lake and allegedly brought to the district by Hongi Hika when he invaded in 1823.

Beyond the formal grounds, a sequence of steep steps and slippery boardwalks dives down the hill alongside **Te Wairoa Falls**, then climbs up through dripping, fern-draped bush on the far side. By the entrance to the Buried Village complex is a new **museum** which does a great job of capturing the spirit of the village in its heyday and the aftermath of its destruction, through numerous photos, some fine aquatints of the Pink and White Terraces and more ash-encrusted knick-knacks. Tarawera Landing, 2km east of the Buried Village, is the jetty for summer-only cruises across **Lake Tarawera** aboard the restored coal-burning *Torrey* (bookings recommended ☎07/362 8698). Forty-five-minute cruises (daily 1pm & 2pm; $16) just putter around the lake, but the morning three-hour cruise (10am; $28) calls at the naturally warm waters of Hot Water Beach where you can spend an hour soaking.

Tamaki Maori Village

Heading south from Rotorua, bound for Waimangu and Wai-O-Tapu, you'll pass the palisades and red-painted warrior statues of **Tamaki Maori Village** (daily 9am–4pm), a modern creation built as a base for the Tamaki Tours concert and hangi (see p.283). It is an attractive site, nestled beside a patch of native bush, with *whare* (houses) ranged around a central area where the hangi is cooked. The place really comes alive at night and can be a little lacklustre during the day, but you can pop in and poke around the shops selling quality Maori crafts and clothing. Free guided tours take place on the hour except at noon when buses roll in for a daytime concert.

Waimangu

At the southern limit of the volcanic rift blown out by Mount Tarawera lies **Waimangu Volcanic Valley** (*www.waimangu.co.nz*; daily 8.30am–5pm; $16), 19km south of Rotorua on Waimangu Road, via SH5, and 5km off the highway. Among the world's youngest thermal areas, this is also New Zealand's largest and most lushly vegetated.

A visitor centre by the entrance hints at the sights lining the streamside path, which cuts through a valley choked with scrub and native bush that has re-established itself since 1886. The regeneration process is periodically interrupted by smaller eruptions, including one in 1917 which created the 100m-diameter **Frying Pan Lake**, the world's largest hot spring. Impressive quantities of hot water welling up from the depths is the attraction of the **Inferno Crater**, an inverted cone where mesmerizing steam patterns partly obscure the powder-blue water. The water level rises and falls according to a rigid 38-day cycle – filling to the rim for 21 days, overflowing for 2 days then gradually falling to 8m below the rim over the next 15 days. More run-of-the-mill steaming pools and hissing vents line the stream, which also passes the muddy depression where, from 1900 to 1904, the **Waimangu Geyser** regularly spouted water to an astonishing height of 400m, carting rocks and black mud with it.

The path through the valley ends at the wharf on the shores of Lake Rotomahana, where the rust-red sides of Mount Tarawera dominate the far horizon. From here, frequent free shuttle buses run back up the road to the visitor centre and gentle, commentated, 45-minute **cruises** (6 daily; $20) chug around the lake past steaming cliffs, fumaroles and over the site of the Pink and White Terraces.

Wai-O-Tapu

The tussle for Rotorua's geothermal crown is principally fought between Waimangu and the **Wai-O-Tapu Thermal Wonderland** (daily 8.30am–5pm; $13), 10km south of Waimangu (and 30km from Rotorua), just off SH5. This combines a vast expanse of multi-hued rocks and pools, New Zealand's largest and most impressive lake of boiling mud and the **Lady Knox Geyser**, which is ignominiously induced to perform on schedule, at 10.15am daily. Buy your entrance ticket at the main entrance then double back 1km along the road to the geyser where, as the crowds fill the serried ranks of benches, a staff member pours a packet of soap flakes into the vent. Within a few minutes, the soap reduces the water's surface tension, and superheated steam and water is released in a jet which plays initially to around 10m and continues at half that height for anything up to an hour. Everyone then bundles into their vehicles and drives back to the main site for the crawl around the hour-long walking loop track as it wends its way through a series of small lakes which have taken on the tints of the minerals dissolved in them – yellow from sulphur, purple from manganese, green from arsenic and so on. The gurgling and growling black mud of the **Devil's Ink-Pots** and a series of hissing and rumbling craters pale beside the ever-changing rainbow colours of the **Artist's Palette** pools and the gorgeous, effervescent **Champagne Pool**, a circular bottle-green cauldron wreathed in swirling steam and fringed by a burnt-orange shelf. The waters of the Champagne Pool froth over **The Terraces**, a rippled accretion of lime silicate that glistens in the sunlight.

As you drive back to the main road, follow a short detour to a huge and active **boiling mud pool** which plops away merrily, forming lovely concentric patterns. On the opposite side of SH5, Waikite Valley Road runs 6km to **Waikite Valley Thermal Pool** (daily 10am–9.30pm; $4), a naturally fed geothermal pool that's a good deal more low-key than the pools in Rotorua, but hardly justifies a special journey; guests at the adjacent motor camp (tent sites $8.50) get in free.

Whirinaki Forest Park and the road to Lake Waikaremoana

Midway between Waimangu and Wai-O-Tapu, some 25km south of Rotorua, SH38 spurs southeast, running arrow-straight through the regimented pines of the Kaingaroa Forest towards the jagged peaks of Te Urewera National Park, a vast tract of untouched wilderness which separates the Rotorua lakes from Poverty Bay and the East Cape. The Kaingaroa Forest finally relents 40km on, as the road crosses the Rangitaiki River by the predominantly Maori timber town of **MURUPARA**. Apart from a couple of shops and takeaways, the only reason to pull over is the DOC's **Rangitaiki Area Visitor Centre**, 1km southeast of town on SH38 (Dec–March daily 8am–5pm; April–Nov Mon–Fri 8am–5pm; ☎07/366 1080, fax 366 1082), with diverting displays and a stack of information on Te Urewera National Park and the Lake Waikaremoana region (see p.401).

Particular emphasis is given to the easily accessible **Whirinaki Forest Park**, a wild and wonderful slice of country which harbours some of the densest and most impressive stands of bush on the North Island: podocarps on the river flats, and native beech on the steep volcanic uplands between them, support a wonderfully rich birdlife with tui, bellbirds, parakeets and even the rare brownish-red kaka. The forest is now protected from the loggers' chainsaw, after a close shave in the late 1970s and early 1980s, when it saw one of the country's fiercest and most celebrated **environmental battles**. In early 1978, protesters had succeeded in preventing logging by occupying trees in the Pureora State Forest to the west of Lake Taupo. Anticipating similar action at Whirinaki and fearing for their livelihood, the local Ngati Whare people blockaded the road into the forest in June 1978; conflict was only avoided through intense negotiation. By 1987 logging of all native timber had ceased (except for totara cut for ceremonial-carving purposes), the mill had closed and the entire logging village of **MINGINUI**, 25km south of Murupara, was unemployed. Today, this moribund village ticks by on a trickle of tourism: even the sole community shop is only open sporadically.

River Road runs 8km south from Minginui to the Whirinaki car park, from where, in four hours or so, you can sample some of the best of the Whirinaki Forest Park – the Whirinaki Falls, where the Whirinaki River cascades over an old lava flow, and the churning Te Whaiti-nui-a-tio Canyon – on the first stretch of the **Whirinaki Track** (27km; 2 days). To penetrate deeper into the forest, you can follow the rest of this gentle track, though you'll need to carry your own cooking stove, food and sleeping bag. By linking several tracks and staying in some of the nine Category 3 **huts** ($5) that pepper the park, more robust walkers can tramp for four or five days and, if you aren't constrained by having to return to your vehicle, it is even possible to walk through to the Napier-Taupo Road (SH5), emerging close to the tiny village of Te Haroto, through which buses pass three times daily. The DOC's *Whirinaki Forest Park* leaflet ($1) covers the main routes, with expanded coverage on their *Whirinaki Short Walks and Tracks* leaflet ($1.50) and on the NZMS 260 series V18 *Whirinaki* map. It is also possible to explore the area on **guided treks** with Rotorua-based Whirinaki Trax (☎07/366 4756; 1 day; $70), which uses Maori guides and visits a local vineyard; they also do a Rotorua-based drop-off and pick-up service for the Whirinaki Track ($48). The only alternative is the Pink Bus (☎0800/222 231) which runs full-day tours from Rotorua to Wai-O-Tapu and Whirinaki ($99) giving a brief taster.

PRACTICALITIES
With the exception of the Pink Bus and Whirinaki Trax, there is **no public transport** out this way, making it difficult to get to Whirinaki or through to Lake Waikaremoana without a car. Even a car can be a liability as vehicles left at the Whirinaki car park aren't safe, so the best bet is to enlist the assistance of *Whirinaki Forest Lodge*, on Minginui Road, 1km south of its junction with SH38 (☎ & fax 07/366 3235). As well as running a trampers' shuttle service for the Whirinaki Track (price dependent on numbers), the lodge also offers **accommodation** in comfortable dorms and motel units, or in the lodge with all meals included (dorms ①, units ②, lodge ⑥), and organizes horse treks ($15 per hour). *Jail House*, 2km south along Minginui Road (☎07/366 3234; ④), also operates track transport from their self-contained jail-turned-chalet, which sleeps up to seven. Minginui itself has the informal riverside *Mangamate Waterfall campsite* ($6 per tent).

West of Rotorua: Tirau, Putaruru and Tokoroa

Fifty-odd kilometres northwest of Rotorua, SH5 and SH1 meet at the small farming centre of **TIRAU**, a highwayside strip adorned with a wonderfully kitsch corrugated-iron sheep housing a wool shop. It has become something of a town icon and has spawned a similarly constructed sheepdog containing the **visitor centre** (☎ & fax 07/883 1202, *thedogtirau@xtra.co.nz*; daily 9am–5pm). There is a handful of **places to eat** along SH1, notably the *Alley Cats Espresso Café*, opposite the dog, which serves good quiches, pizza slices and cakes. If you need to break your journey, **stay** at the well-priced *OK Tirau Motor Inn*, SH1 (☎07/883 1111, fax 883 1999; rooms ④, unit ⑤), which has modern rooms and large self-contained units. There is usually someone in town offering beds at backpacker prices though this changes frequently so call the visitor centre in advance; or treat yourself to the hotel at Okoroire Hot Springs (see below).

There is little to do actually in town but Okoroire Street, beside the sheep, runs 8km to the lovely **Okoroire Hot Springs**, a series of private open-air, sandy-bottomed concrete pools located in a glade by a cascading stream, each accommodating up to twelve sybaritic souls. The pools cost $10 an hour, and can be booked at the adjacent *Okoroire Hot Springs Hotel* (☎ & fax 07/883 4876, *oko.hotel@xtra.co.nz*), which has regular rooms (⑤) and allows camping ($10 per tent) among the mature poplars and conifers; the hotel also has a bar, serves meals, and lets you onto their nine-hole golf course for $10 a day.

East of Tirau the roads split again, with SH5 forging on to Rotorua, while SH1 turns southeast towards Taupo, passing through **PUTARURU**, 8km further on, and the **Putaruru Timber Museum** (☎07/883 7621; daily 9am–4pm; $5), a further 2km south, where the region's timber-milling heritage is pulled together in a well laid-out collection of minor historic buildings relocated from around the district. If you do nothing else, climb the totara-built 1930s fire lookout to get an inkling of just how extensive the Kaingaroa Forest really is.

SH1 continues through rolling farmland to pungent **TOKOROA**, 25km southeast, a modern place downwind of the nearby Kinleith pulp mill, the principal reason for the town's existence. There's little to stop for, but it is almost 70km to Taupo, the next place of any consequence, so **cyclists** might need to overnight at the barely acceptable *Tokoroa Motorcamp*, 22 Sloss Rd (☎ & fax 07/886 6642; tent & power sites $8, cabins & flats ②–③), at the northern entrance to town, or one of the motels dotted among the fast-food joints beside the highway. Newmans and InterCity buses stop outside the visitor centre, on SH1 (Nov–March Mon–Fri 8.30am–5.30pm, Sat & Sun 9am–3pm; shorter weekend hours in winter; ☎07/886 8872, *tokoroa.info@xtra.co.nz*). If KFC isn't to your taste, try *Scoffers Café* on Rosebery Street, which runs parallel to the main highway.

The Western Bays Highway

Most likely you'll want to stick on SH1 to Taupo, but if the Tongariro National Park (see p.305) beckons, follow SH32 30km south from Tokoroa to Whakamaru and turn left for the **Western Bays Highway** (still SH32) direct to Turangi. There are very few facilities down this way, but one lovely place to break your journey is *South Claragh B&B*, 12km south of Whakamaru, (☎07/372 8848, fax 372 8047; *paul.hill@xtra.co.nz*; room ④, self-catering cottage ⑤), situated on a small working farm – lambs, donkeys etc – where you are encouraged to join the family for an excellent three-course dinner with wine ($30).

TAUPO AND AROUND

TAUPO, 80km south of Rotorua and slap in the centre of the North Island, is very much a Kiwi holiday resort slung around the northern shores of Lake Taupo, New Zealand's largest lake, which stretches 30km southwest towards three snow-capped volcanoes. In this magical setting, with the altitude (360m above sea level) and the reflected light from the lake's glassy surface creating an almost alpine radiance, this small town has grown up at the point where the impossibly deep-blue waters of the Waikato River ("flowing water" in Maori) start their long journey to the Tasman Sea. Both lake and river frontages are lined with parks, the pace is slow and there is an undeniably appealing tenor to the place.

For decades, Kiwi families have been descending en masse for a couple of weeks' holiday, bathing in the crisp cool waters of the lake, fishing its depths and lounging around their holiday homes that fringe the lakeshore. Although you could easily follow their lead and spend a relaxing few days here, there is no shortage of stuff to see and do, most notably around the spectacular rapids and geothermal badlands of **Wairakei Park**, immediately north of town. Thousands more come specifically for the **fishing**: the Taupo area is perhaps the most fecund trout fishery in the world, extending south to Turangi and along the Tongariro River and with an enviable reputation for the quality and fighting-spirit of its fish. Year-round, you'll see boats drifting across the lake with lines trailing and, particularly in the evenings, rivermouths choked with fly casters in chest-high waders.

Lake Taupo itself is a geological infant, born a mere two thousand years ago when a massive volcano erupted, spewing out 24 cubic kilometres of rock, debris and ash – ten times more than was produced by the eruptions of Krakatoa and Mount St Helens combined – and covering much of the North Island in a thick layer of pumice. Ash was ejected so high into the atmosphere that it was carried around the world, enabling historians to pinpoint the date of the **eruption** as 186 AD – when the Chinese noted a blackening of the sky and Romans recorded that the heavens turned blood-red. As the underground magma chamber emptied, the roof slumped, leaving a huge steep-sided **crater**, since filled by Lake Taupo. It is hard to reconcile this placid and beautiful lake with such colossal violence, though the evidence is all around: entire beaches are composed of feather-light pumice which, when caught by the wind, floats off across the lake. **Geologists** continue to study the causes and effects of the eruption and treat the lake as a kind of giant spirit-level, in which any tilting could indicate a build-up of magma below the surface that might trigger an eruption.

The local Tuwharetoa people ascribe the lake's formation to their ancestor, **Ngatoroirangi**, who cast a tree from the summit of Mount Tauhara, on the edge of Taupo, and where it struck the ground water welled up and formed the lake.

Taupo

Nowhere in Taupo's compact low-rise core is more than five minutes' walk from the waters of the Waikato River or Lake Taupo, which jointly hem in three sides. The fourth side rises up through the gentle slopes of Taupo's suburbs. Most of the commercial activity happens on, or just off, SH1, which passes through the middle of town as the main Tongariro Street and the aptly named Lake Terrace. Room for expansion is limited to the southeastern quarter, where ever more motels and timeshares are springing up along the lakeshore.

Although Taupo bears little trace of the vigorous Tuwharetoa settlement that existed into the middle of the nineteenth century, there was scant European interest in the area until the New Zealand Wars of the 1860s, when the Armed Constabulary were try-

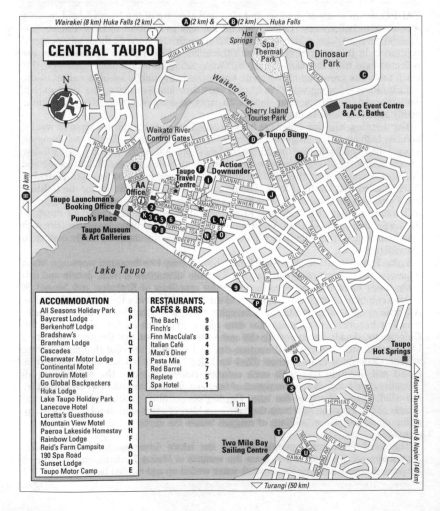

CENTRAL TAUPO

Wairakei (8 km) Huka Falls (2 km) △   Ⓐ(2 km) & △Ⓑ(2 km) △ Huka Falls

Hot Springs
Spa Thermal Park
Dinosaur Park ❶
Ⓒ

Waikato River

Taupo Event Centre & A. C. Baths
Cherry Island Tourist Park
Waikato River Control Gates
● Taupo Bungy
Ⓓ

Taupo Travel Centre Ⓕ
Action Downunder
Ⓔ
Ⓖ
AA Office
Ⓗ (3 km)
Taupo Launchman's Booking Office
Punch's Place
Ⓙ
Taupo Museum & Art Galleries
Ⓚ 3 4 5 6
7 8
Ⓛ Ⓜ
Ⓝ Ⓞ
2

Lake Taupo
9
Ⓟ

Taupo Hot Springs
Ⓠ

Mount Tauhara (5 km) & Napier (140 km) ▷

Ⓡ
Ⓢ

Two Mile Bay Sailing Centre
Ⓣ
Ⓤ

▽ Turangi (50 km)

ACCOMMODATION		RESTAURANTS, CAFES & BARS	
All Seasons Holiday Park	G	The Bach	9
Baycrest Lodge	P	Finch's	6
Berkenhoff Lodge	J	Finn MacCulal's	3
Bradshaw's	L	Italian Café	4
Bramham Lodge	Q	Maxi's Diner	8
Cascades	T	Pasta Mia	2
Clearwater Motor Lodge	S	Red Barrel	7
Continental Motel	I	Replete	5
Dunrovin Motel	M	Spa Hotel	1
Go Global Backpackers	K		
Huka Lodge	B		
Lake Taupo Holiday Park	C		
Lanecove Hotel	R		
Loretta's Guesthouse	O		
Mountain View Motel	N		
Paeroa Lakeside Homestay	H		
Rainbow Lodge	F		
Reid's Farm Campsite	A		
190 Spa Road	D		
Sunset Lodge	U		
Taupo Motor Camp	E		

0   1 km

ing to track down **Te Kooti** (see box on p.401). They set up camp one night in June 1869 at Opepe, 17km southeast of Taupo (beside what is now SH5), and were ambushed by Te Kooti's men, who killed nine soldiers. Garrisons were subsequently established at Opepe and Taupo, but it was Taupo that flourished, enjoying a more strategic situation and being blessed with hot springs for washing and bathing. By 1877, Te Kooti had been contained, but the Armed Constabulary wasn't finally disbanded until 1886, after which several soldiers and their families stayed on, forming the nexus of European settlement.

Taupo didn't really flourish as a resort until the prosperous 1950s, when the North Island's roads had improved to the point where Kiwi families – equipped with caravans, boats and all manner of playthings – could easily drive here from Auckland, Wellington or Hawke's Bay. For the most part, the town just languishes by the lake, with what diversions there are limited to tacky tourist fodder, but Taupo makes a great base for exploring the natural wonders of the surrounding area.

Arrival, information and transport

InterCity and Newmans **buses** stop at the Taupo Travel Centre bus station, 16 Gascoigne St, around two hundred metres from Taupo's **visitor centre**, Tongariro Street (daily 8.30am–5pm; ☎07/378 9000, fax 378 9003, *www.thinkfresh.co.nz*, *taupo@thinkfresh.co.nz*), right in the heart of town. Taupo's **airport**, 10km south of the centre, is served by Air New Zealand flights; shuttle buses to and from town are run by Taupo Taxis (☎07/378 5100; $10).

Taupo has no scheduled bus service, but almost everything you'll want to visit in the centre can be reached on foot, with Stop Cabs (☎07/378 9250) and Taupo Taxis (☎07/378 5100) filling the gaps. To visit the surrounding sights without your own vehicle, you'll be reliant on **tours** (see p.301). **Renting a bike** gives greater freedom: the most sophisticated machines will set you back roughly $25 a half-day and $35 a day (see p.300, for details of outlets – and for **car-rental**).

Accommodation

Taupo manages to maintain a very high standard of accommodation for all budgets. Finding somewhere to stay is unlikely to be a problem except when the crush is on (Christmas to end-Feb), when you should **book** several days in advance, especially at weekends. As befits a Kiwi holiday resort, there is no end of places catering to families, with much of the lakefront taken up by **motels**, and grassy spots on the fringes of town given over to **campsites**. Hostels are abundant too and uniformly good, though differing in style.

Hotels and motels

Baycrest Lodge, 79 Mere Rd (☎07/373 3838 & 0800/229 273, fax 378 4007, *baycrest@reap.org.nz*). Luxuriously appointed top-of-the-range motel with spacious multi-room units, a heated pool, poolside bar and Sky TV. ⑤–⑧.

Cascades, SH1, Two Mile Bay (☎0800/996 997, fax 07/378 0372, *cascades@clear.net.nz*). Classy motel with units either on the waterfront or with access to an attractive pool. Studio and family units are all spacious with deluxe fittings, a full kitchen, mezzanine sleeping area, a patio and a spa baths. ⑤.

Clearwater Motor Lodge, 229 Lake Terrace (☎07/377 2071 & 0800/639639, fax 377 0020). Beautiful lakeside accommodation with great views, in-room spas and some rooms with small balconies. ⑥.

Continental Motel, 9 Scannell St (☎ & fax 07/378 5836). Comfortable, low-cost, central motel with small but well-maintained units. ④.

Dunrovin Motel, 140 Heu Heu St (☎07/378 7384). Older, budget units that are well-kept and characterful, being built of wood rather than the ubiquitous concrete blocks. ④.

Lanecove Hotel, 213 Lake Terrace (☎07/378 7599 & 0800/880055, fax 378 7393; *www.lanecove .co.nz*). Modern, top-of-the-line luxury hotel fronting the lake with elegant rooms. The more swanky rooms carry stratospheric price tags, but there are some at more reasonable rates. ⑥–⑨.

Huka Lodge, Huka Falls Rd, 4km north of Taupo (☎07/378 5791, fax 378 0427, *www.hukalodge.com, reservations@hukalodge.co.nz*). One of the first and still the best-known of New Zealand's exclusive lodges, located just upstream from Huka Falls. It costs a cool $800 per person a night, including cocktails, dinner and breakfast. ⑨.

Mountain View Motel, 12 Fletcher St (☎07/378 9366 & 0800/800128, fax 377 3076, *mt-view@xtra.co.nz*). Budget, central motel with spa pool, Sky TV, games room and kids' play area. The family units are huge, and the studios are at the bottom end of this price code. Studios ④, family units ⑤.

B&Bs and guesthouses

190 Spa Rd (☎07/377 0665, *orbiii@reap.org.nz*). Plain, simple and friendly non-smoking homestay made special by its sunny garden on the cliffs high above the Waikato River and the views of Cherry Island and the Taupo Bungy. ④.

Bradshaw's, 130 Heu Heu St (☎ & fax 07/378 8288). Good-value guesthouse with pleasant floral decorated rooms with showers, let at very reasonable rates, with breakfast an optional extra. There are also new and very well appointed three-bedroom units which can work out good value for groups. Rooms ③–④, units ⑧.

Bramham Lodge, 7 Waipahihi Ave (☎07/378 0064, fax 378 0065, *bramham@reap.org.nz*). Spacious homestay with expansive lake and mountain views, a couple of comfortable rooms with private facilities, and delicious breakfasts. ⑤.

Loretta's Guesthouse, 135 Heu Heu St (☎07/378 4927). Pleasant rooms in the main house and out back, all come with cooked or continental breakfast, and some have their own bathroom. ④.

Paeroa Lakeside Homestay, 21 Te Kopua St (☎ & fax 07/378 8449). Luxurious homestay in a lush garden setting with great lake views five minutes' drive southwest of Taupo, with en-suite double and bathless twins, all with balconies. ⑥.

Hostels

Action Downunder, 56 Kaimanawa St (☎07/378 3311, fax 378 9612). Modern associate YHA hostel close to town and with good lake and mountain views from the kitchen and barbecue balcony, and a spa pool. Dorms sleep three to five, there are doubles, and bikes can be rented for $20 a day. Dorms ①, rooms ②.

Berkenhoff Lodge, 75 Scannell St (☎ & fax 07/378 4909). Bustling and slightly cramped hostel fifteen minutes' walk from the centre but with free use of bikes. The games room and on-site bar are perennially popular and they run a $6 barbecue every evening by the pool and spa. Each dorm has a bathroom, doubles and twins come with linen, and everyone gets free continental breakfast. Coin-op Internet access. Dorms ①, rooms ②.

Go Global Central Backpackers, cnr Tongariro St & Tuwharetoa St (☎07/377 0044, fax 377 0059, *goglobal@reap.org.nz*). Large and central hostel in a former hotel, above an Irish bar and popular with the backpacker buses. Dorms and a multitude of rooms, all are clean and comfortable and there's bike rental for $28 per day as well as Internet access, though self-catering facilities are a bit cramped. Dorms ①, rooms ③.

Rainbow Lodge, 99 Titiraupenga St (☎07/378 5754, fax 377 1568, *rainbowlodge@clear.net.nz*). Spacious, relaxed and spotless purpose-built backpackers with a comfortable lounge, coin-op sauna, bikes for rent at $15 a day, fishing gear for $11 a day, a stack of local information and little touches that create a homely atmosphere. Dorms have between six and nine beds and there are spacious triples and doubles, many of them en suite. Dorms ①, rooms ②.

Sunset Lodge, 5 Tremaine Ave (☎07/378 5962, *sunset@reap.org.nz*). Small, low-key and friendly hostel at Two Mile Bay some 3km from town but with courtesy pick-ups, free use of bikes, and daily drop-offs at the Craters of the Moon. The more capacious three-bed rooms are worth the extra dollar over the larger dorms. Dorms ①, rooms ②.

Campsites and motor parks

All Seasons Holiday Park, 16 Rangatira St (☎07/378 4272 & 0800/777 272, fax 378 1272, *ithp @voyager.co.nz*). Compact site just over 1km from town, with tent sites scattered among nice new cabins and a range of good tourist flats. Tent sites $10, cabins ①, flats ③.

Lake Taupo Holiday Park, 28 Centennial Drive (☎ & fax 07/378 6860). Wonderfully spacious site 2km from town with good communal facilities and excellent range of clean and new tourist cabins, tourist flats and fully self-contained cottages, and easy access to the A.C. Baths. Tent sites $10, cabins, flats & cottages ③–④.

Reids Farm, 3km north of Taupo on Huka Falls Rd. Spacious free campsite right by the Waikato River just upstream of Huka Lodge. The makeshift slalom course makes it a popular spot with kayakers.

Taupo Motor Camp, 15 Redoubt Rd (☎ & fax 07/377 3080). Very handy site on the banks of the Waikato River right in town. Tent sites $10, cabins & on-site vans ②–③.

The Town

True to its family-resort status, Taupo specializes in entertainment for the kids and adventure activities for adults. Perhaps the best all-round crowd-pleasers are the **hot pools**; the pick of the two being **Taupo Hot Springs**, 3km southeast of the centre on SH5 (*www.taupohotsprings.com*, daily 7.30am–9.30pm; $7), a couple of large outdoor pools filled with natural mineral water that's oddly slippery on the skin. For an extra dollar you can also soak in one of the private mineral pools, which come in a range of temperatures, while $4 gets you as many descents as you like on the hot-water hydroslide. Without your own vehicle, you'll find it more convenient to head for the **Taupo Events Centre**, A.C. Baths Avenue (daily 8am–9pm), a sparkling new sports hall and twelve-metre climbing wall which incorporates the long-standing **A.C. Baths** ($4), where the entry fee includes use of the large freshwater hot pool and private mineral pools, but not the sauna (an extra $4 all day) or the water slides ($3). From the junction opposite the baths, Spa Road forges north to the **Spa Hotel**, site of the first hot spring used by the Armed Constabulary and now ignominiously overlooked by the thirty life-size ferro-concrete dinosaurs of the **Spa Dinosaur Valley** (daily 10am–4pm; $5). Jurassic Park it ain't, but the "realistic" dinosaur noises will probably still scare young kids witless. Just west, Spa Avenue runs down to the green swathe of **Spa Thermal Park**, where a path leads to the Waikato River past some naturally hot bathing pools (unrestricted entry) and, in an hour or so, downstream to Huka Falls (see box below).

WALKS AROUND TAUPO

For those who just fancy a bit of a stroll, there are a few relatively easy **walks** near town. By far the most popular is the **Great Lake Walk**, which is more modest than it sounds: just follow the lakeshore east from town, covering as much of its 7km extent as you like, passing hot springs right at the water's edge.

On the northern edge of town, County Avenue leads to the **Spa Thermal Park**, where there's a pleasant thirty-minute bushwalk, which can be combined with a riverbank walk to **Huka Falls** (4km; 1hr one-way), and further extended to the Aratiatia Rapids (8km; 2hr one-way), though you've then got to get back – if you set off early, you could conceivably walk back via the Wairakei visitor centre and the Craters of the Moon (12km; 3hr).

Finally, if you have your own transport and a taste for magnificent lake and town views, try the track to the summit of **Mount Tauhara** (6km; 2–3hr return), the hill behind Taupo, which is approached on Mountain Road, which turns off SH5 to Napier after 6km.

A few hundred metres upstream, the river swirls through the narrows of Hell's Gate, the 45m white cliffs providing the launch pad for **Taupo Bungy**, 202 Spa Rd (☎0800/888 408; *www.taupobungy.co.nz*; daily 9am–5pm, until 7pm in high season; $89, repeat jumps $39), one of New Zealand's finest bungy sites cantilevered 20m out from the bank, and with optional dunking. Perhaps the best spot for viewing your mates' bungy antics is the outdoor café adjacent to Cherry Island Tourist Park, Motutahae Road (daily 9am–5pm; $9.50), a feeble and overpriced display of trout, deer and exotic birds which occupies most of a tiny islet beautifully set in the clear river waters.

Few are going to want to spend long summer days indoors, but a dose of wet weather, or an abiding interest in local history, could send you scurrying back to the centre of town and the Taupo District Museum of Art and History, Tongariro Park (daily 10.30am–4.30pm; free), with its varied exhibits covering pioneering days and fishing in some depth, before moving on to a curious collection of scale models of every plane which took part in World War II. On better days, there's more pleasure in lolling about outside on the pleasant grassy expanse of Tongariro Park, which sweeps down to the lakeshore and the Taupo Boat Harbour, departure-point for cruises, fishing trips and a multitude of aquatic pursuits.

Lake cruises and activities

As you would expect of Taupo, there's plenty of activities to relieve you of your holiday money. Some of the best are water-based, either cruising gently across Lake Taupo, rafting down the raging waters of the Tongariro or Rangitaiki rivers or fly-fishing the rivers and streams for trout. Taupo's magnificent scenery has also given it something of a name for tandem skydiving.

Cruises and water-borne activities

One of the most satisfying ways to relax in Taupo is to take one of the **lake cruises**, run from the Taupo Boat Harbour and setting course for some striking modern **Maori rock carvings**, which can only be seen from the water at Mine Bay, 8km southwest of town. The carvings, dating from the late 1970s, depict a stylized image of a man's face heavy with *moko*, together with tuatara (lizard-like reptiles) and female forms draped over nearby rocks. The most characterful of the trips – as much for the sea-dog skipper as the boat – is aboard *The Barbary* (☎07/378 3444; 10am & 2pm; 2hr; $25), a 1926 ketch once owned by Eroll Flynn (who, it is colourfully claimed, won it in a card game) and subsequently co-opted into the 1973 Greenpeace anti-nuclear-testing flotilla that sailed to Mururoa Atoll. If you're not too bothered about seeing the carvings, take the summer-time-only **sunset trip** which is a little shorter and only costs $20.

For a touch of gin-palace style, opt for the *Cruise Cat* (☎07/378 0623 & 0800/252 628; 11.30am; 1hr 30min; $24), which motors past the carvings. Different atmospherics are offered by the *Ernest Kemp* (☎07/378 3444; daily: Dec–Feb 10am, 2pm & 4.15pm; Oct–Nov & March–April 10am & 2pm; May–Sept 2pm; $22), a replica 1920s steamboat that chugs to the carvings and back in a couple of hours. Finally, you can compress the carvings trip into one eye-streaming hour ($39) on the *Superjet* (☎0800/278 737, *www.superjet.co.nz*), a powerful catamaran that also does a two-hour circuit around most of the lake for $59.

Trips can be **booked** either direct with operators or through the visitor centre. Bookings can be made at Punch's Place, Lakefront Terrace (☎378 5596, fax 378 1747; daily 8am–6pm; 24hr), or along the river at the Taupo Launchman's Booking Office, Redoubt Street (☎07/378 3444; 8am–5pm; 24hr). Punch's Place is also the place to go for other lake-based watersports, such as **parasailing** (10min; $50), **waterskiing** ($50 per half-hour for up to three skiers), and **jet biking** ($50 per half hour).

If you'd rather be self propelled, head around the lake to Two Mile Bay, where Two Mile Bay Sailing Centre (☎07/378 3299; daily 9am–6pm in summer, otherwise sporadically) rents rowboats ($20 per hr), kayaks and canoes ($20 per hr), **windsurfers** ($25) and **catamarans** ($40).

Fishing

New Zealand's arcane fishing rules dictate that trout can't be sold, so if you've got a taste for their succulent flesh you'll have to catch it yourself. No one is going to guarantee you'll land a fighting rainbow or brown but the chances are better here than most places. If dinner is more of an incentive than sport, then your best approach is to **fish the lake** on a boat chartered through the visitor centre or directly from either the Taupo Launchman's Booking Office or Punch's Place (see opposite). Smaller **boats** go out for a minimum of two hours, but more usually three or four, and cost $65 an hour, taking up to six people with four fishing at a time. **Book in advance** from mid-December to February – and at any other time of year if you want the booking offices to help reduce your costs by matching you up with other interested parties. Boat operators have all the tackle you need and will organize a Taupo fishing licence ($12 per day, $26 per week, $36 per month and $55 for the full July-to-June year) for you.

The rivers flowing into Lake Taupo are the preserve of **fly-fishers**, particularly from March to September when mature rainbow trout enter the mouths of the streams and rivers and make their way upstream to shallow gravel hollows where they spawn. Brown trout are also in these waters, but they tend to be more wily. You can **rent tackle** from Sullivan's Taupo Sports Depot, Tongariro Street (☎07/378 5337) and the Fly & Gun Shop, Heu Heu Street (☎07/378 4449) and pick your own spot, but average catches are much larger if you engage the services of a **fishing guide**, which will set you back close to $200 for a full day with gear and licence: the tourist office has a list of guides.

Rafting, scuba diving, jumping and flying

There are no whitewater rivers right on Taupo's doorstep, but the town makes a viable base for **rafting**. The main rivers run from Taupo are the Tongariro (covered under Turangi – see p.307), the Rangitaiki and the Wairoa (both detailed on pp.279–80), and a two-day trip on the relatively gentle upper section of the Mohaka, camping on the riverbank overnight. Rapid Sensations (☎07/378 7902 & 0800/227 238, *www.rapids.co.nz*) run the Tongariro for $80, and Kiwi River Safaris (07/377 6597 & 0800/723 857, *www.krs.co.nz*) organize trips to the Wairoa ($85), the Rangitaiki ($85) and the overnight Mohaka trip ($260, including meals). Closer to town, Bruce Webber Adventures (☎07/377 1236 & 0800/529 256) offer guided **kayaking** trips on the Waikato (2hr, $40), with a welcome emphasis on scenic appreciation.

Sticking with the water, qualified **scuba diving** enthusiasts can experience the crystal clear waters of the Waikato river with Rapid River Dive (☎07/378 1926, *diveinn@reap.org.nz*), spending up to an hour making a fast drift dive with a guide ($55 with your own gear, otherwise $75) downstream from Cherry Island: a car and shopping trolley mix it with wonderful rock formations and aquatic life.

Taupo has rapidly gained a reputation as one of the cheapest places to go **tandem skydiving** – and one of the best, with magnificent scenery all around, if you dare to look. At times it can feel like a production line, but two companies, Great Lake Skydive (☎0800/373 335 & 0800/FREEFLY) and Taupo Tandem Skydiving (☎07/377 0428 & 0800/2SKYDIVE), currently vie for your business, both offering jumps for $165 from 9000 feet, adding roughly $10 for each additional thousand feet. This is currently the only place in New Zealand where you can do oxygen-assisted jumps from 15,000 feet ($295). If you'd prefer to stay in the plane, there are fixed-wing **scenic flights** over Wairakei Thermal Area and the Huka Falls on a float plane from the Taupo Boat

Harbour with ARK Aviation (☎07/378 7500; 10min; $45). An extensive range of longer flights down to the volcanoes are operated by Air Charter Taupo (☎07/378 5467; 15min–1hr; $30–130). Helistar Helicopters (☎0508/554 422, *www.helistar.co.nz*) offer **helicopter flights** over the Huka Falls and Craters of the Moon (10min; $75), and will combine them with a ride on the Huka Jet (see p.303) for $120.

Eating, drinking and nightlife

Taupo is a town of a hundred **tearooms** and coffee lounges, but come five o'clock eating well becomes more problematic, though new places are springing up all the time, some making use of their waterfront setting. The better lakefront motor lodges all have pricey **restaurants**, some of them very good, and **bars** around town serve decent budget meals, leaving the middle ground somewhat rocky. However, for a small provincial town, there's a reasonable nightlife, with holidaymakers converging on several pubs and **clubs**.

Restaurants and cafés

The Bach, 2 Pataka Rd (☎07/378 7856). Modern dining in an easy-going atmosphere. Choose from wood-fired crispy pizza, a select range of $25 mains such as seared venison tenderloin with roast garlic potatoes, and an extensive selection of New Zealand wines by the bottle and glass. Dinner daily; lunch Sat & Sun, also Mon–Fri in high season; licensed.

Finch's, 64 Tuwharetoa St (☎07/377 2425). Glass-top tables and concrete-block walls should spell disaster, but somehow it works in this least formal of Taupo's top restaurants, where you can feast on beautifully composed and presented international dishes such as grilled feta, fried artichokes and roasted garlic on naan bread with tapenade. Daily noon–midnight; licensed.

Holy Cow!, 11 Tongariro St. A bar noted for its $5 and $9 backpackers' specials – reliable favourites, including burgers, toasties, potato wedges, chicken curry and caesar salad.

Italian Café, 28 Tuwharetoa St. Reliable, if unexceptional, Italian trattoria of the gingham-table-cloth-and-Chianti-bottle ilk, with a range of traditional pizza and pasta ($13–16) and meat and fish dishes (around $20). Takeaways also available. Licensed & BYO.

Maxi's Diner, 38 Roberts St. A good standard of burgers, toasties and steak 'n' chips meals 24 hours a day, and lake views to boot.

Pasta Mia, 7 Horomatangi St. Relaxed daytime café with a small but immaculate line in simple pasta dishes ($13) and the best coffee in town.

Replete, 45 Heu Heu St. Despite inconsistent service, this remains Taupo's finest deli and daytime café, run by a former chef from the esteemed Huka Lodge and serving excellent quiches, pizza slices, cakes and coffee until 5pm Mon–Fri, 3pm Sat & Sun.

Bars and clubs

Finn MacCuhal's, cnr Tongariro St & Tuwharetoa St. Ersatz Irish bar very popular with the locals as well as the backpackers staying upstairs at *Go Global*. You come here for the Guinness, but they also do good-value steaks, pasta dishes and salads.

Holy Cow!, 11 Tongariro St. The liveliest late-night bar in town, spinning an eclectic selection of rock and dance tunes and turning clubby late on. Very popular with backpackers.

Red Barrel, 4 Roberts St. Traditional beer-and-darts pub with decent bar meals and seats outside with lake views.

Spa Hotel, Spa Rd (☎07/378 4120). Cavernous beer barn with live music several nights a week, mostly at weekends.

Listings

Automobile Association 93 Tongariro St (☎07/378 6000).

Bike rental Most of the hostels have basic bikes for guests' use: *Rainbow Lodge* and *Go Global* backpackers also rent to non-guests. You can rent scooters from Zip Zap Scooter Hire, cnr Roberts St & Titiraupenga St (☎07/378 9198) for $40 a half day: you only need a car driver's licence.

Buses The joint InterCity and Newmans network (both booked through the Taupo Travel Centre, 16 Gascoigne St; ☎07/378 9032), serves Rotorua, Tauranga, Hamilton, Auckland, Napier, Palmerston North and Wellington.

Car rental A1 Car Rentals, cnr Tamamutu St & Gascoigne St (☎06/378 3670), and Rental Car Centre, 7 Nukuhau St (☎06/378 2740), undercut the big guys.

Horse riding Taupo Horse Treks, Karapiti Rd (☎07/378 0356) do one-hour ($25) and two-hour ($40) treks through the pine forests around the Craters of the Moon (see p.303), and will do courtesy pick-up for booked two-hour jaunts.

Internet access Cheapest rates are at *Central Plateau Reap*, cnr Heu Heu St & Kaimanawa St (☎07/378 8109) though there are longer opening hours at *Contact Cyber Café*, 10 Roberts St (☎07/378 3697) where you get 15 minutes free with a coffee purchase.

Left-luggage Lockers are available at the Superloo, Tongariro St (daily: Dec–Jan 7.30am–9pm; Feb–Nov 7.30am–5.30pm; $1 a day).

Medical treatment Taupo Health Centre, 115 Heu Heu St (☎07/378 7060).

Pharmacy Main Street Pharmacy, cnr Heu Heu St & Tongariro St (☎07/378 2636), is open daily until 8.30pm.

Police Story Place (☎07/378 6060).

Post office cnr Horomatangi St & Ruapehu St (☎07/378 9090) has poste restante facilities.

Tours The best local sightseeing tours are Walter's Tours (☎07/378 5924), run by characterful guy with a many an anecdotal story to tell; options include the Craters of the Moon and Huka Falls (2hr; $15 for one, $10 each for two or more), while longer trips add Aratiatia Rapids (3hr; $20/$15), and Orakei Korako to the itinerary (5hr; $30/$25). Paradise Tours (☎07/378 9955) visit most of the same places, plus the Wairakei geothermal field (2hr 30min; $25), while Rapid Sensations (☎07/378 7902) run guided bike tours around Wairakei (2–3hr; $50). Finally, Discover Taupo (☎07/377 0774) do a town tour in a 1951 London double-decker bus (Sat, Sun & school holidays; every 30min; 15min; $5), starting from the cnr Tongariro St & Lake Terrace. (See also "Lake cruises and activities", on p.298.)

Travel Agents Budget Travel, 37 Horomatangi St (☎07/378 9799); Grace United Travel, Taupo Travel Centre, 16 Gascoigne St (☎07/378 9005); James Travel Holiday Shoppe, 28 Horomatangi St (☎07/378 7065).

Around Taupo

Taupo's town attractions are limited in their appeal, but the same can't be said for region immediately to the **north**, a fabulously concentrated collection of natural wonders. Within a few minutes of each other you can find boiling mud, hissing steam harnessed by the Wairakei power station and the clear, blue Waikato River, which cuts a deep and swirling course northwards, occasionally turning wild as it squeezes through some of the country's most powerful rapids. The highlights – **Huka Falls**, **Aratiatia Rapids**, and the **Craters of the Moon** geothermal area – are all within 10km of Taupo, but you'll have to venture further to reach a second thermal park, **Orakei Korako**, 40km north. To get out this way, you'll need your own vehicle, or the services of one of Taupo's tour companies (see "Listings" above).

Moving **south** from Taupo, SH1 follows the lakeshore to Turangi (see p.307), while heading east along SH5 towards Napier (see p.405), there are a couple of things to detain you along the way.

Along Huka Falls Road

The bulk of the sights and activities around Taupo flank the Waikato River as it wends its way north, and lumped together under the collective title of **Wairakei Park**. The park is reached via Huka Falls Road, which loops off SH1 a couple of kilometres north of Taupo and passes the Reids Farm free campsite and the exclusive *Huka Lodge* (see

TAUPO AND AROUND

Orakei Korako (20km) & Auckland (260km)△

Rotorura (70km)△

Wairakei Natural
Thermal Valley

Wairakei
Village

Geothermal
Borehole
Lookout

Wairakei Geothermal
Visitor Centre

Geothermal
Power Station

NZ Woodcraft

Prawn Park & Huka Jet
Jetty for Otunui

Volcanic Activity
Centre

Wairakei
International
Golf Course

Honey Hive

Helistar Helecopters
& Café

Craters of
the Moon

KARAPITI RD

Huka Falls
Lookount

Huka Falls

KARAPITI RD

Waikato River

Taupo Walkway

Huka
Lodge

HUKA FALLS RD

Reid's Farm

Taupo Walkway

Aratiatia Rapids (1km) & Rapid Jets (4km)

Nukuhau

ACACIA BAY ROAD

RIFLE RANGE ROAD

Taupo

Tapuaeharuru Bay

Acacia
Bay

Waipahihi

see Central Taupo
map for detail

Lake
Taupo

Rainbow
Point

SH5

Napier (140km)△

Wharewake

SH1

N

Taupo
Airport

0   2km

△ Turansi (50km), The Volcanos (90km) & Wellington (380km)

p.296) en route to the first point-of-call, the impressive and justly popular **Huka Falls** (*hukanui*, or "great body of spray"). Here the full flow of the Waikato River, one of New Zealand's most voluminous rivers, funnels into a narrow chasm then plunges over an eleven-metre shelf into a seething maelstrom of eddies and whirlpools; the sheer power of some four hundred tonnes of water per second make it a far more awesome sight than its relatively short drop would suggest. A footbridge spans the channel, providing a perfect vantage point for watching the occasional mad kayaker making the descent, usually on weekend evenings.

A large Russian helicopter marks the launch pad for Helistar flights (see p.300) en route to the cutaway hives and educational video at the **Honey Hive** (☎07/374 8553; daily 9am–5pm; free), 1km further north along Huka Falls, which shouldn't divert you long, though they do have an excellent range of honey varieties, including the wonderful manuka. Press on to the **Volcanic Activity Centre** (Mon–Fri 9am–5pm & Sat–Sun 10am–4pm; $5), a highly instructional museum where the dense text is alleviated by striking photos and interactive computer displays on all things tectonic. Watch one of several films run continuously then check out the seismograph linked to sensors on Mount Ruapehu, an earthquake simulator and a large relief map of Taupo Volcanic Zone, which extends from Mount Ruapehu to White Island.

Moving swiftly past **NZ Woodcraft** (☎ & fax 07/374 8555), essentially a shop selling turned native woods, you'll come to the Wairakei geothermal power station. Most of the excess heat generated by the station is discharged into the river, though a portion is channelled into large open ponds, where tropical Malaysian prawns are raised in an enterprise known as the **Prawn Park** (daily 11am–4pm, tours hourly; $6). Even if the "Day in the life of a Prawn" tour of the complex doesn't stir your imagination, you can at least indulge in the scrumptious platters dished up by the *Prawn Works Bar & Grill* while seated by the deep-blue water of the Waikato.

The peace is periodically shattered by the **Huka Jet** (☎07/374 8572 & 0800/485 2538, *www.hukajet.co.nz*; 30min; $55) as it roars along the river between Huka Falls and the Aratiatia Dam. The boats leave from a **jetty** by the Prawn Park (courtesy bus from Taupo), and play all the usual tricks – close encounters with rock faces and 360-degree spins – but if you are heading to the jetboating heartland around Queenstown, save your money until then. A more amiable way of appreciating the scenic pleasures of the river is to board the paddle-wheeler **Otunui** (☎07/374 8338; roughly hourly in summer; 1hr; $20), a 1907 Whanganui riverboat which has been shifted here for cruises up to Huka Falls from a jetty 500m upstream from the Prawn Park. Pleasant though these daytime cruises are, the one to go for is the Moonlight Glow Worm Cruise (daily: Nov–March 9pm; April–Oct 7.30pm; 1hr–1hr 30min; $25), which drifts along while spotlights pick out aquatic life and glow-worms illuminate the gorge walls. Small discounts are available if you book the Otunui and Rapids Jet (see overleaf) at the same time.

Craters of the Moon and the Wairakei Valley

The Huka Falls loop road rejoins SH1 opposite the **Wairakei International Golf Course** (☎07/374 8152), one of the country's finest. Just south of the intersection, Karapiti Road runs west to the **Craters of the Moon** (unrestricted entry; donation appreciated), an other-worldly geothermal area which sprang to life in the 1950s, after the construction of the Wairakei geothermal power station had drastically altered the underground hydrodynamics. What it lacks in geysers and colourful lakes, it more than makes up for in hyperactivity: the belching steam is so vigorous that the custodian on duty (8am–7pm) will insist you wear closed footwear to walk the 2km of trails that wind among roaring fumaroles and huge rumbling pits belching out pungent bad-egg smells. The culprit can only be visited vicariously through the self-promotional **Wairakei Geothermal Visitor Centre** (daily 9am–4.30pm; free), 3km north on SH1, with its relief map of the whole Tongariro and Waikato power schemes, an explanatory video shown on demand, and plenty of stuff on the intricacies of harnessing the earth's bounty. Outside, shiny high-pressure-steam pipes twist and bend the 2km to the power station from the borefield, which can be viewed from the **Geothermal Borefield Lookout** just down the road.

The same forces that created the Craters of the Moon stole the thunder of the **Wairakei Natural Thermal Valley** (daily 9am–5pm; $6), Taupo's original thermal area but now a mere shadow of its former self.

Aratiatia Rapids, Rapids Jet and Crazy Catz Adventure Park

Around 2km downstream from the Wairakei power station lies the first of the Waikato River's eight hydroelectric dams, the Aratiatia Dam, which holds back the Waikato immediately above the **Aratiatia Rapids**, a long series of cataracts that were one of Taupo's earliest attractions. In the 1950s, when plans to divert the waters around the rapids were revealed, public pressure succeeded in preserving the rapids. Though it's something of a hollow victory, since the rapids are left empty most of the time and only seen in their full glory during three or four thirty-minute periods each day (Oct–March 10am, noon, 2pm & 4pm; April–Sept 10am, noon & 2pm). Stand on the dam itself or at one of two viewpoints downstream and wait for the siren that heralds the bizarre spectacle of a parched watercourse being transformed into a foaming torrent of waterfalls and surging pressure waves, then easing back to a tame trickle.

Whatever the state of the Aratiatia Rapids, you can still ride the river downstream with **Rapids Jet** (☎07/378 5828 & 0800/RAPIDS; $55), located on Rapids Road 3km beyond the Aratiatia Dam. This is no slick bus-them-in operation, but New Zealand's only true commercial whitewater jetboating run, taking you down and up Fuljames rapid. The entire boat gets airborne and the company makes no secret of having sunk three boats on the rapid, but no one has been injured: just listen closely to the safety spiel, hang on and prepare to get very wet.

If this is your kind of thing, you might also want to trip along to **Crazy Catz Adventure Park**, on SH5 16km north of Taupo (☎07/374 8111; daily 8.30am–5.30pm), where the deer petting, farm tour, mini golf and maze are no match for riding a quad bike around a dirt track ($10 for 10min), upgrading to a low-slung and very quick Maxcar ($20 for 10min), or aping around the ropes course. The biggest single kick is the giant fifteen-metre swing ($15) that's as heart-stopping as many a bungy and a lot cheaper; but there's also a Triple Challenge ($35) which adds in a giant trapeze and flying fox (zip wire), and a maze of high ropes and wires ($59 per half-day) requiring nerves of steel. They do free courtesy transport from Taupo for two or more.

Orakei Korako

There's yet more geothermal activity 40km north of Taupo at **Orakei Korako: The Hidden Valley** (daily: 8am–4.30pm in summer, 4pm in winter; $17), which is reached by travelling 14km east off SH1 or 23km west off SH5. The site's main distinguishing feature is its means of access, via a short shuttle-boat journey across a dammed section of the Waikato River, which drops you at the foot of a large silica terrace tinged orange, pink and green by heat-loving algae. From here, an hour-long self-guided walking trail loops past bubbling mud pools, through an active geyser field, and down into the mouth of Ruatapu Cave, a sacred site once used by Maori women to prepare themselves for ceremonies – hence *Orakei Korako*, "a place of adorning".

You can **stay** on the opposite side of the river at *Orakei Korako Lodge* (☎07/378 3131, fax 378 0371, *ok@reap.org.nz*; dorms ①) in self-catering bunk-style budget accommodation, with a big lounge, a pool table, hot tubs, and canoes for rent at $7 an hour.

The Taupo–Napier Road

Travelling beyond the immediate vicinity of Taupo, SH1 hugs the lake as it heads southwest to Turangi (see p.307), while SH5 veers southeast along the **Napier–Taupo Road**, a twisting but increasingly speedy ninety-minute run through some of the North Island's remotest country. Much of the early part of the journey crosses the Kaingaroa Plains, impoverished land cloaked in pumice and ash from the 186 AD Taupo volcanic eruption and of little use save for the pine plantations which stretch 100km north. The history of this route to Napier is traced by the **Napier–Taupo Heritage Trail**; pick up a free booklet from Taupo or Napier visitor centres. Many of the 35 stops are of limited interest, but be sure to call in at **Opepe Historic Reserve**, 17km from Taupo, where, on the north side of the road, a cemetery contains white wooden slabs marking the graves of nine soldiers of the Bay of Plenty cavalry, killed by followers of maverick Maori leader Te Kooti in 1869. A half-hour bush walk winds through a fine stand of totara, rimu and kahikatea alive with birdsong. Across the road, a couple of trails lead to a well, water trough and a sawpit used by the Armed Constabulary during the construction of the Taupo–Napier telegraph line.

After another 11km, Clements Mill Road leads 30km south into the northern reaches of the **Kaimanawa Forest Park**, a remote rugged mountain wilderness, almost untouched, and little-visited by recreational trampers, but a perennial favourite with deer hunters and anglers. There is no public transport out this way and tracks are not well marked, but if you are experienced and determined, get hold of the detailed *Guide to Kaimanawa State Forest Park* map and set off on the remote **Te Iringa–Oamaru Circuit** (60km; 4–5 days), staying in a series of Category 3 huts ($5 per night). Some 25km southeast of the Clements Mill Road turn-off, the Waipunga River, a tributary of the Mohaka, plummets 30m over the **Waipunga Falls**, and continues beside SH5 through the lovely Waipunga Gorge, packed with tall native trees and dotted with picnic sites which double as overnight "freedom" **campsites** with no facilities but river water. Soon, the highway descends to the Mohaka River and the appealing riverside accommodation at the *Riverlands Outback Adventures*, 5km south of SH5 (☎06/834 9756, fax 834 9724, *riverlnds@xtra.co.nz*; camping $8, dorms ①, rooms ②, self-contained units ③), a residential multi-activity centre where the prime attractions are **horse trekking** (2hr, $30; 4hr, $40) along farm trails and down to the river; and **whitewater rafting** on Grade I–II stretches of the Mohaka (2hr, $55), or the more exciting and wonderfully scenic Grade III section (full day; $80), which runs through a narrow gorge that's just great for jumping off the cliffs either side. Beyond the Mohaka River, the highway climbs the Titiokura Saddle before the final descent through the grape country of the **Esk Valley** into Napier (see p.405).

TONGARIRO NATIONAL PARK
AND AROUND

New Zealand's highly developed network of national parks owes much to Te Heu Heu Tukino IV, the Tuwharetoa chief who, in the *pakeha* land-grabbing climate of the late nineteenth century, recognized that the only chance his people had of keeping their sacred lands intact was to donate them to the nation – on condition that they could not be settled nor spoiled. His 1887 gift formed the core of country's first major public reserve, the **Tongariro National Park**. In the north a small, outlying section of the park centres on **Mount Pihanga** and the tiny **Lake Rotopounamu,** but most visitors head straight for the main body of the park, dominated by three great volcanoes, which rise starkly from the desolate plateau to pierce the hard blue sky: the broad-shouldered

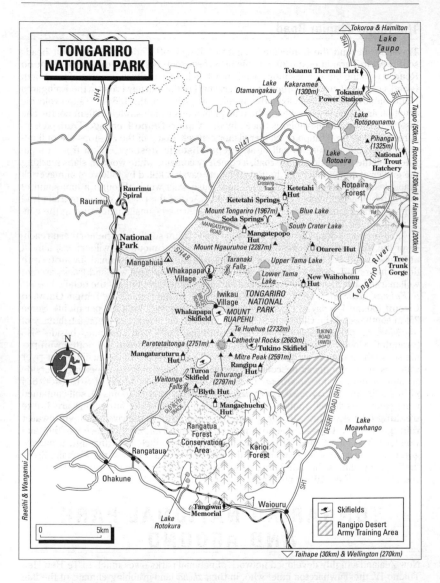

ski mountain, **Ruapehu** (2797m), its squatter sibling, **Tongariro** (1968m), and, wedged between them, the conical **Ngauruhoe** (2287m).

According to the **Maori**, there used to be a lot more mountains hereabouts. All were male but for the beautiful Pihanga in the northern section of the park, whose favours were widely sought. Pihanga loved only Tongariro, the victor of numerous battles with her other suitors, and the vanquished mountains fled: Taranaki carved out the Whanganui River as he made for the west coast of the North Island; Putauaki got as far north as Kawerau; but Tauhara was reluctant to leave and continually glanced back, so that by dawn, when the mountains could no longer move, he had only reached the northern shores of Lake Taupo, where he remains to this day, "the lonely mountain".

To the local Tuwharetoa people these mountains were so **sacred** that they averted their eyes while passing and wouldn't eat or build fires in the vicinity. The *tapu* stretches back to legendary times when their ancestor **Ngatoroirangi** came to claim the centre of the island. After declaring Tongariro *tapu* he set off up the mountain, but his followers broke their vow to fast while he was away and the angry gods sent a snow storm in which Ngatoroirangi almost perished before more benevolent gods in Hawaiki saved him by sending **fire** to revive his frozen limbs.

Within the boundaries of the park is some of the North Island's most striking scenery – semi-arid plains, crystal-clear lakes and streams, steaming fumaroles, virgin rainforest, an abundance of ice and snow – and two supremely rewarding tramps, the one-day **Tongariro Crossing** and the three-to-four-day **Tongariro Northern Circuit**, one of New Zealand's Great Walks. The undulating plateau to the west of the volcanoes is vegetated by bushland and golden tussock, while on the eastern side the rain shadow of the mountains produces the **Rangipo Desert**. Although this is not a true desert, it is still an impressively bleak and barren landscape, smothered by a thick layer of volcanic ash from the 186 AD Taupo eruption. These features combine to create a unique landscape, which was designated a **World Heritage Site** in 1991.

The park captured world headlines in 1995 and again in 1996 when **Mount Ruapehu**, the highest and most massive of the three volcanoes, burst into life, blasting a plume of ash and dust 12km into the atmosphere and emptying the crater lake down the side of the mountain in great muddy deluges known as lahars. Although the **eruptions** drastically curtailed the ski season, they have had little lasting damage; what made them newsworthy was the dramatic contrast between the black spume of ash and the pristine snowy peak, all offset by a cloudless sky – images now endlessly recycled on the walls of local cafés and visitor centres.

The northern approach to the region is through **Turangi**, not much in itself but a reasonable base both for the Tongariro tramps and for rafting and fishing the Tongariro River. What it lacks is a sense of proximity to the mountains – something much more tangible in the service town of **National Park**, and more so again in **Whakapapa Village**, 1200m up on the flanks of Ruapehu. The southern gateway is **Ohakune**, a more appealing place than National Park but distinctly dead outside the ski season. Heading south, the Army Museum at Waiouru marks the southern limit of the Volcanic Plateau, which tails off into the pastoral southern half of the island around the agricultural town of **Taihape** and the bungy centre at **Mangaweka**.

Pretty much everyone comes to the park either to **ski** or to **tramp**, staying in one of the small towns dotted around the base of the mountains. While a **car** makes life easier, there is a reasonable network of **minibuses** plying the more useful routes and providing trailhead transport for trampers (see box on p.313). Note that this whole region is over 600m above sea level, so even in the height of summer you'll need some **warm clothing**.

Turangi

TURANGI, 50km south of Taupo, is a small, flat and seemingly characterless place planned in the mid-1960s and built almost overnight for workers toiling away at the tunnels and concrete channels of the ambitious Tongariro Power Scheme (see box overleaf). It doesn't even make the best of its location – Lake Taupo is 4km to the north and the town centre is separated by SH1 from its trump card, the **fishing** and **rafting** waters of the Tongariro River. Nonetheless, it is very popular with trout fishers, and works well enough as a base for a smattering of sights and activities in the immediate vicinity and

THE TONGARIRO POWER SCHEME

The **Tongariro Power Scheme** provides an object lesson in harnessing the power of water with minimal impact on the environment. Its two powerhouses produce around 7 percent of the country's electricity, while the outflows that feed into Lake Taupo add flexibility to the much older chain of eight hydroelectric dams along the Waikato River. Certainly there are those who argue it is unacceptable to tamper with such a fine piece of wilderness, and it has caused fluctuations in the levels of nutrients in the Tongariro River and erosion along some of the service tracks, but the scheme has many admirers.

In fact, if it weren't for the scale models in visitor centres and the ugly bulk of the Tokaanu power station, only astute observers would be aware of the complex system of tunnels, aqueducts, canals and weirs unobtrusively going about their business of diverting the waters of the Tongariro River and myriad streams running off the mountain slopes, back and forth around the perimeter of the national park, using modified natural lakes for storage. Mount Ruapehu poses its own unique problems: the threat of lahars is ever-present and, after the 1995 eruption, tephra (a highly abrasive volcanic ash) found its way into the turbines of the Rangipo underground powerhouse, causing an unscheduled seven-month shutdown.

for the Tongariro National Park (see p.312), just beyond the steep volcanic range to the south. It has also become a major jumping-off point for the Tongariro Crossing (see p.314) with a selection of hostels offering transport to and from the trailheads.

European settlement began early this century soon after trout were released into the Taupo fishery, but although the collection of fishing lodges warranted a shop and post office, no town existed until 1964 when well-paid work on the power scheme lured workers to the area, notably Italian tunnellers, many of whom subsequently settled here.

The massive amount of trout fishing in this area makes it essential that rivers are continually restocked with fingerlings raised at fish-breeding facilities such as the **Tongariro National Trout Hatchery**, on SH1, 5km south of Turangi (daily 10am–3pm; free), set among native bush between the Tongariro River and one of its tributaries, the Waihukahuka Stream. Ever since its inception in 1927 the centre has used wild rainbow trout collected from the stream – as opposed to the more common practice of using hatchery-raised fish – and stripped them of their eggs and milt to produce fry that are genetically more varied and disease resistant. The fish are then left to grow for around a year until they reach 150mm before being released into streams all over the country. There isn't a lot to see, but you are free to wander through buildings where tanks hold the tiniest fish, among the rearing ponds outside and into an underground viewing chamber where you can view wild trout in the Waihukahuka Stream.

Fauna in its natural state is best seen on the educational two-hour-plus **Tongariro River Delta Wetland Tour** run by Tongariro Eco Tours (☎07/386 6409 & 0800/101 024, *rafting@xtra.co.nz*; around dawn & dusk; $40). Aboard a specially-designed shallow-draught boat you putter around the fringes of the lake while guides well-versed in local ecosystems explain the dynamics of one of the country's largest delta wetlands, which is home to black swans, dabchicks, four species of cormorant, white-faced heron and Canada geese.

Heading away from the delta region, the **Tongariro River Walk** (10km; 3hr return) is a pleasant trail which starts from the Major Jones footbridge at the end of Koura Street on the edge of town and follows the river south to the Red Hut footbridge. Ten kilometres south of Turangi, off SH47, the **Lake Rotopounamu Circuit** (5km; 1hr 30min) encircles a pristine lake surrounded by bush alive with native birds.

Activities

Three companies offer **rafting** year round on the lower reaches of the Tongariro River, which runs through one of the most scenic and accessible river gorges in the country. The river's natural flow patterns have been modulated by the Tongariro Power Scheme, limiting the possibilities of a really wild time on the Grade II and Grade III rapids, but what sets the Tongariro apart is the **range of trips** you can do on one piece of water – some involving a two-hour run in traditional river rafts, some employing inflatable kayaks and some combining fishing with the rafting.

The two cheapest **operators** (both $75) are Tokaanu-based Rock 'n' River Rafting (☎07/386 0352, *www.laketaupo.co.nz/rafting, rock.n.river@xtra.co.nz*) and Turangi-based Tongariro River Rafting, Atirau Road (☎07/386 6409 & 0800/101 024). Taupo's Rapid Sensations (☎0800/227 238 & 07/378 7902, *www.rapids.co.nz, info@rapids.co.nz*) are also very competitive at $79. All three offer straightforward whitewater-rafting trips, though Tongariro River Rafting also allow you to paddle yourselves with a guide in hailing distance, and offer the Tongariro Duo ($120), which spends the best part of a day careering along mountain-biking trails and then rafting the river.

Big rafts make the modest scale of the lower Tongariro seem a little tame, and more fun can be had on **inflatable kayak** trips run by Eddyline Adventures (☎07/386 5081 & 0800/852 925, *edline@reap.co.nz*): first trips must be on the Grade II section (1hr 30min on the water; $58), after which they'll let you loose on Grade III rapids (3hr on the water; $120).

If you're keen to try hauling a trout from Lake Taupo or one of the local rivers, the visitor centre will help pair you with a **fishing** guide to match your experience and aspirations; expect to pay around $100 for a couple of hours with gear and guiding. You can rent a boat and tackle at moderate prices from Braxmere Lodge, Little Waihi (☎07/386 7513), on the lakeshore just northwest of Turangi. River fishing takes place pretty much year-round, but the most productive months for are the spawning season from April to October.

To combine the last two activities, Tongariro River Rafting will take you for a full day **raft fishing** (Dec–May only) which involves rafting the Grade III section of the Tongariro, stopping off at otherwise inaccessible pools along the way to cast a fly. Rates are $450 a day for two people – roughly the same as you'd pay for a guide alone.

If you'd prefer to just take off on a **mountain bike**, either in the forests hereabouts or over the 42 Traverse (see box on p.313), call Tongariro River Rafting who rent bikes at $20 for two hours ($40 per day) and can provide transport and guides – though you'll need a group of three or four to bring prices down to manageable levels.

Practicalities

Alpine Scenic Tours and Bellbird Connections (see box on p.313) both run low cost daily **bus** services from Taupo dropping off pretty much where you want. The majors – InterCity and Newmans – both pull in at the Turangi Bus & Travel Centre, Ohunga Road (Mon–Fri 9am–5pm; ☎07/386 8918, fax 386 8397), which sells tickets when open. Otherwise buy them from the **visitor centre**, Ngawaka Place (daily 8.30am–5pm; ☎07/386 8999 & 0800/288 726, fax 386 0074, *www.thinkfresh.co.nz, turangi @thinkfresh.co.nz*), which is packed with local information, including informative panels on trout fishing and a relief model of the Tongariro Power Scheme. They also sell Taupo fishing licences, topo maps, DOC tramping brochures and hut tickets, though if you have detailed tramping enquiries you can trot down the street to the small **DOC office**, Turanga Place (Mon–Fri 8am–5pm; ☎07/386 8607, fax 386 7086).

Turangi's need to cater to anglers, skiers and trampers bound for the Tongariro National Park has left it with a decent range of **accommodation**; the budget places congregate in the town centre, while the plusher lodges and B&Bs line the Tongariro River to the east, though nowhere backs right onto the river. At the cheaper end it is a toss-up between three **hostels**: *Bellbird Lodge*, on the corner of Tautahanga Road and Rangipoia Place (☎07/386 8281, fax 386 0723, *bellbird@reap.org.nz*; dorms ①, rooms ②), a popular and homely backpackers occupying several suburban houses with home-made cakes each evening; *Club Habitat*, Ohuanga Road (☎07/386 7492, fax 386 0106, *habitat@voyager.co.nz*; tent sites $7, dorms ①, rooms ③, cabins & units ④), an activity-oriented associate YHA that comes with a spacious games, bar and dining complex, a spa and sauna, and is a favourite with the backpacker tour buses; and *Extreme Backpackers*, 26 Ngawaka Place (☎07/386 8949, fax 386 8946, *ebpcltd@xtra.co.nz*; tents $10, dorms ①, rooms ②, en suites ③), which charges a dollar or two more for superior spartan rooms built around a central courtyard, spacious common areas and Internet access.

The best of the **motels** are the simple and low-cost *Creel Lodge*, 183 Taupahi Rd (☎ & fax 07/386 8081; ④), a fishing-oriented cluster of self-contained one- and two-bedroom units in grounds running down to the river edge with communal fish smoker and barbecue; and *Parklands*, on the corner of SH1 and Arahori Street (☎07/386 7515, fax 386 7509, *www.prklands.co.nz*, *info@prklands.co.nz*; tents $15, campers $10, studios ④, units ⑤), an extensive motel with an outdoor pool, private hot tubs, games room and a small restaurant serving home-style dinners.

For more style and comfort, try *Ika Lodge*, 155 Taupahi Rd (☎ & fax 07/386 5538, *ikalodge@xtra.co.nz*; ⑥), a superior **homestay**-cum-fishing lodge by the Tongariro River, with three en-suite rooms and succulent game and fish dinners for $40; or *River Birches*, 21a Koura St (☎ & fax 07/386 5348, *gillo@voyager.co.nz*; ⑦), a lovely two-bedroom **self-contained house** in the woods a stone's throw from the river and right by the start of the Tongariro River Walk. Everything is laid on with full cooking facilities, a range of teas and coffees, extensive library, complimentary pre-dinner drinks in the main house and breakfast included.

Eating is more limited; the *Grand Central* on Tautahanga Street does great take-aways, and *Valentino's*, Ohuanga Road (☎07/386 8812; closed Tues), serves reasonable Italian and Kiwi mains ($18–22) in drab surroundings. The rest of the places are restaurants associated with lodges, the best of which are the *Kaimanawa Bistro*, 258 Tauhapi Rd (☎07/386 8709; closed Sun) where mains cost $20–25, and the more basic but hearty restaurant at *Club Habitat*, which is also the best place to **drink**, with an on-site microbrewery and early evening happy hours.

Tokaanu

Turangi's smaller neighbour, **TOKAANU**, 5km west, was the main settlement in the area in pre-European times. Maori were drawn by the geothermal benefits of what is now the **Tokaanu Thermal Park** (unrestricted entry; free), a compact patch of low scrub, beautifully clear hot pools and plopping mud threaded by a fifteen-minute trail. The adjacent **Tokaanu Thermal Pools**, Mangaroa Road (daily 10am–10pm; $3), are just great for soaking your bones after a day's tramping in the national park, with an open-air public pool and hotter, partly enclosed private pools ($5 per hour). Nearby you can spend a very pleasurable hour or two gently **paddling** along a narrow, lush, bush-fringed channel, past the hot tubs and back gardens of the locals in boats rented from Tokaanu Canal Kayaks (☎07/386 7558; daily 10am–5pm). They charge $20 for an hour, $40 for three and will even provide transport if you don't fancy paddling back upstream. Take the Tokaanu road out of Turangi and look for the sign on the left, just over the bridge.

To **stay** in Tokaanu, try the *Oasis Motel and Tourist Park*, SH41 (☎07/386 8569, fax 386 0694; tents $8.50, cabins ②, studios ③, units ④), an extensive campsite with mineral hot pools, spa pools and simple but well priced on-site accommodation.

Whakapapa and around

Tiny **WHAKAPAPA**, the only settlement set firmly within the boundaries of the Tongariro National Park, hugs the lower slopes of Mount Ruapehu some 45km south of Turangi on SH48, which spurs off SH47. Approaching from the north, an open expanse of tussock gives distant views of the imposing form of the *Grand Chateau* hotel, framed by the snowy slopes of the volcano behind and overlooked by the arterial network of tows of the Whakapapa skifield.

From Whakapapa, SH48 continues as Bruce Road 6km to **IWIKAU VILLAGE** (known locally as the "Top o' the Bruce"), an ugly jumble of ski-club chalets which, from late June through to mid-November, and in exceptional circumstances as late as Christmas, becomes a seething mass of wrap-around shades and baggy snowboarders' pants. Outside the ski season, the village dies, leaving only a couple of chair lifts ($15 return) to trundle up to the *Knoll Ridge Café*, New Zealand's highest at 2020m above sea level.

Arrival and information

The only **bus services** to Whakapapa are the shuttle buses from Turangi and National Park (see box on p.313), which drop off close to the DOC's helpful **visitor centre** (daily: Nov–March 8am–6pm, April–Oct 8am–5pm; ☎07/892 3729, fax 892 3814, *whakapapavc@doc.govt.nz*). The centre is stocked with all the maps and leaflets you could need and is equipped with extensive displays on the park, including the tiny *Skiing on the Volcano* museum and a couple of videos that are shown on demand. *Ring of Fire* (15min; $2) is a fairly simplistic discussion of vulcanism in general and its manifestations here, while *The Sacred Gift of Tongariro* (25min; $2) combines Maori legends surrounding Tongariro with impressive footage of the landscape through the seasons and the activities that take place in it.

Accommodation

There's not much to Whakapapa beside a café and four **places to stay**, all within a couple of minutes' walk of each other and all often booked up in advance. You'll do well to reserve as far ahead as possible through the ski season and over the Christmas and January school holidays. The most prominent is the *Grand Chateau* (☎07/892 380 & 0800/242 832, fax 892 3704, *www.chateau.co.nz*, *reservations @chateau.co.nz*; ⑥), a vast brick edifice built in 1929 with gracious public areas including a huge lounge with full-size snooker table and great mountain views. Guests have use of the highest nine-hole golf course in New Zealand, tennis courts, gym and a small indoor pool, and stay in rooms modernized to international hotel standard; you'll need a premium room (⑧) to get plenty of space and good views, and can save money in spring and autumn when there are often discounts of around thirty percent. The Chateau also manages *Fergussons Family Chalets* (⑦), self-contained units, some sleeping up to six; and organizes the Tongariro Trek (see p.313). The only other hotel is *Skotel* (☎07/892 3719 & 0800/756 835, fax 892 3777; backpacker rooms ②, standard rooms ⑤, chalets ⑥), a rambling place with a sauna and a range of rooms from self-catering hostel-style affairs (though with very limited kitchen facilities) to relatively luxurious rooms, some with views of Ngauruhoe and Tongariro. Note that rates are hiked up considerably in the ski season (cheapest room ④) and they have **Internet access**. The best budget option is the *Whakapapa Holiday Park* (☎ & fax 07/892 3897; camping $8, dorms ①, cabins ②, flat ③), nicely set in a patch of bushland with spacious tent and powered sites, simple cabins that are let as backpacker dorms in summer, and a more luxurious en-suite tourist flat. There is also the

DOC's toilets-and-water *Mangahuia campsite* ($4), on SH47 close to the foot of the Whakapapa access road.

Iwikau Village has no public accommodation, only ski-club lodges and a café (daytime in summer, evenings also during the ski season).

Around Whakapapa

Outside the **skiing** season (see box on p.316), Whakapapa is a lot less frenetic but is still alive with trampers, since it makes a fine base for both **short walks** and long tramps. The Tongariro Northern Circuit and the Round the Mountain Track (see p.315) can both be tackled from here, but there are also easier strolls covered by the DOC's *Whakapapa Walks* leaflet ($1). Three of the best of these are the **Whakapapa Nature Walk** (1km; 20–30min), highlighting the unique flora of the park; the **Taranaki Falls Walk** (6km; 2hr return), which heads through open tussock and bushland to where the Wairere Stream plunges 20m over the end of an old lava flow; and the **Silica Rapids Walk** (7km; 2hr 30min return), which follows a stream through beech forests to some creamy-coloured geothermal terraces.

Eating and drinking

You can **eat** lunches and snacks cheaply at *Fergussons Café*, opposite the visitor centre, though you might prefer the better quality across the road at the Chateau's *Pihanga Café*, which serves the likes of Cajun beef on jambalaya rice ($14) and seafood pasta ($10) from 11am to 11pm. Alternatives are *Skotel*, which serves breakfast (continental $12, cooked $18) and good-value bistro meals, or pizza at *Trails Bar*, which also boasts the cheapest **drinks** in the village. If you want to reward yourself for the successful completion of a major tramp, the place to do it is the Chateau's *Ruapehu Room*, with very good à la carte meals which might include dill and vodka cured salmon on green salad ($13) followed by roasted venison on kumara rosti ($30).

Tramping in Tongariro National Park

The Tongariro National Park contains some of the North Island's finest walks. The **Tongariro Crossing** alone is rated as the best one-day tramp in the country, and it would be hard to dismiss the claim, but there are many longer possibilities, notably the three- to four-day **Tongariro Northern Circuit**, which rates as one of the New Zealand Great Walks; both pass through spectacular and varied volcanic terrain. Mount Ruapehu has the arduous but rewarding **Crater Rim Walk** and a circuit, the **Round the Mountain Track**, which offers a narrower variety of terrain and sights than the Tongariro tramps, but is consequently less used.

Preliminaries

The 1:80,000 *Tongariro Park map* ($13.50) is ideal for these tramps, but the **DOC leaflets** ($1 each) covering the tramps separately are informative and perfectly adequate. The main points of **access** to the walks are Mangatepopo Road and Ketetahi Road for the Tongariro Crossing and Tongariro Northern Circuit; and Whakapapa for the Tongariro Northern Circuit, the Ruapehu Crater Rim and the Round the Mountain Track. **Shuttle buses** serve the trailheads from Turangi, National Park and Whakapapa (see box opposite); with the exception of the unmarked Crater Rim walk, the tracks are all well maintained and sporadically signposted, so you can judge your progress if you've a bus to catch.

Other than **accommodation** in Whakapapa Village (see previous page), the only places to stay are the **trampers huts** and adjacent **campsites**. In summer (roughly late Oct–May, but check current dates), huts on the Tongariro Northern Circuit –

GETTING TO AND AROUND TONGARIRO NATIONAL PARK

The major bus companies don't run through the Tongariro National Park, leaving several smaller companies, many associated with backpacker hostels, to fill the void.

From Taupo, Taupo Fun (☎07/377 0435, *www.hotyellow98.com/taupofun*) pick up and drop off Tongariro Crossing-bound trampers (6.45am departure; $30 return) and will provide wet weather gear and walking poles. Alpine Scenic Tours (☎07/378 7412, *alpine.scenic@xtra.co.nz*; 6.30am departure; $25 return) undercut the opposition by providing fewer frills, and in winter they run the hour and a half down to the Whakapapa skifield in the morning and back again each evening.

From Turangi, Alpine Scenic Tours (☎07/386 8918, *alpine.scenic@xtra.co.nz*) do a particularly useful run three times a day, calling at Whakapapa and the start and end of the Tongariro Crossing with one run (11am from Turangi) going right through to National Park. Bellbird Connection, based at the *Bellbird Lodge* (☎07/386 8281), *Club Habitat* (☎07/386 7492), and *Extreme Backpackers* (☎07/386 8949) all run a similar service open to everyone, with *Bellbird* dropping off at the trailhead half an hour earlier than the others (7am departure from Turangi), giving you a head start on the pack. **Fares** are very competitive – each charges $20 for the Tongariro Crossing drop-off and pick up and $15–20 one-way to either Whakapapa or National Park. All services become skifield shuttles in winter.

From Whakapapa, Tongariro Track Transport (☎07/892 3716) runs a daily shuttle leaving the visitor centre at 8am for the start of the Tongariro Crossing ($15 return), and meeting you at Ketetahi at 4.30pm.

From National Park, shuttle buses serve the trailheads in summer and skifields in winter. All the hostels will arrange transport, but the biggest operator is *Howard's Lodge* (☎07/892 2827) which runs its own all-comer buses, charging $15 for drop-off and pick-up at either end of the Tongariro Crossing or from Whakapapa, and $25 for Turoa. Tongariro Track Transport (see above) picks up in National Park at 7.45am then continues to Whakapapa and Mangatepopo.

From Ohakune, Tongariro National Park Shuttle Transport (☎0800/825 825) do door-to-door Tongariro Crossing shuttles ($25 return) and include a free DOC brochure. They're also helpful for linking Ohakune with National Park and Whakapapa.

Mangatepopo, Ketetahi, Waihohonu and Oturere – are classed as Great Walk huts ($12); in winter they lose their cooking facilities and revert to Category 2 ($10). **Hut tickets** do not guarantee a bunk, so at busy times you could still find yourself on the floor. Campers (summer $6, winter $5) stay close to the huts and use the same facilities. Huts on the Round the Mountain Track – Whakapapaiti, Mangaturuturu, Blyth, Mangaehuehu and Rangipo – are Category 2 huts all year ($10, camping $5). Hut tickets can be bought in advance from the DOC in Whakapapa and Ohakune, or the DOC and the visitor centre in Turangi; if bought from a hut warden you pay an extra 25 percent.

There are several **organized treks**, too: the *Grand Chateau* hotel in Whakapapa Village runs the **Tongariro Trek** (mid-Dec to mid-April; $995; ☎07/892 3809 & 0800/242 832, fax 892 3704, *www.trek.co.nz*, *reservations@chateau.co.nz*), which combines the Ruapehu Crater Rim walk, the Tongariro Crossing and four nights to recover from it all at the Chateau. The **Whakapapa Skifield Guided Walk** (☎07/892 3738; Christmas to mid-April daily 9.30am; $55, including chair-lift ride) ascends to the Ruapehu Crater Rim, providing interesting commentary on the geology and flora en route.

The **weather** in the mountains is extremely changeable, and the usual provisos apply. Even on apparently scorching summer days, the increased altitude and exposed windy ridges produce a wind-chill factor to be reckoned with, and storms roll in with frightening rapidity. Any time from the end of March through to late November there can be snow on the tracks, so if you are planning a tramp during this period, enquire locally about current conditions. Always take warm **clothing** and rain gear – and if you plan to scramble up and down the volcanic cone of Mount Ngauruhoe, take gloves and long trousers for protection from the sharp scoria rock.

Tongariro Crossing

The **Tongariro Crossing** (16km; 6–8hr; 750m ascent) is by far the most popular of the major tramps in the region and for good reason. Within a few hours you climb over lava flows, cross a crater floor, skirt active geothermal areas, pass beautiful and serene emerald and blue lakes and have the opportunity to ascend the cinder cone of Mount Ngauruhoe. Even without this wealth of highlights it would still be a fine tramp, traversing a mountain massif through scrub and tussock, before descending into virgin bush for the final half-hour. It can be a long day out if you're not particularly fit, but it's not excessively arduous. Note too that this isn't a wilderness experience – on weekends and through the height of summer well over a thousand people complete the Crossing, so it pays to aim for another season or stick to weekdays.

Car parks at both ends of the track have a reputation for break-ins and it is a good idea to leave your vehicle in Turangi, National Park or Whakapapa and make use instead of the many shuttle buses (see box on previous page). The track can be walked in either direction but by going from west to east you save 400m of ascent: all shuttle buses are conveniently scheduled around a west to east traverse, usually depositing their charges at Mangatepopo Road End, six gravel kilometres east of SH47, at about 8.30am and picking up at Ketetahi Road around 4.30pm. Some shuttle operators do a 6pm pick-up allowing you to tack on an ascent of Ngauruhoe; ask when you book. To avoid the worst of the crush, steal a march on the others by choosing a shuttle operator prepared to drop-off at Mangatepopo Road a little earlier; or dawdle behind the mob and plan to stay the night at Mangatepopo Hut; or get dropped off at Ketetahi Road late in the day and sleep at Ketetahi Hut ready for a crack-of-dawn start next day.

From Mangatepopo Road End the first hour is fairly gentle, following the Mangatepopo Stream through a barren landscape and passing the Mangatepopo Hut. The track gradually steepens as you scale the fractured black lava flows towards the **Mangatepopo Saddle**, passing a short side-track to the **Soda Springs**, a small wildflower oasis in this blasted landscape. The Saddle marks the start of the high ground between the bulky and ancient Mount Tongariro and its youthful acolyte, **Mount Ngauruhoe**, which fit walkers can climb (2km return; 2hr return; 600m ascent) from here and still make the shuttle bus at the end of the day. The two-steps-forward-one-step-back ascent of this thirty-five-degree cone of red and black scoria must be one of the most exhausting and dispiriting walks in the country, but it is always popular – both for the superb views from the toothy crater rim and the thrilling headlong descent among a cascade of tumbling rocks and volcanic dust.

From the Mangatepopo Saddle, the main track crosses the flat pan of the South Crater and climbs to the rim of **Red Crater**, with fumaroles belching out steam, which obscures the banded crimson and black of the crater walls. Colours get more vibrant still as you begin the descent to the Emerald Lakes, opaque pools shading from jade to palest duck-egg, and beyond to the crystal-clear Blue Lake. Sidling around Tongariro's **North Crater**, you begin to descend steeply on golden tussock slopes to **Ketetahi Hut**, a major rest stop with views of Lake Rotoaira and Lake Taupo. From here you pass close to the steaming Ketetahi Springs, then begin the final descent through cool streamside bush to the car park on Ketetahi road.

Tongariro Northern Circuit – and the Round the Mountain track

If the Tongariro Crossing appeals, but you are looking for something a little more challenging, the answer is the **Tongariro Northern Circuit** (41km; 3–4 days), one of New Zealand's Great Walks. The section from **Whakapapa to Mangatepopo Hut** (9km; 2–3hr; 50m ascent) is now so eroded and prone to flooding that the DOC recommend taking the shuttle bus to Mangatepopo car park and starting from there. If you decide to walk you'll find the track undulating through tussock and crossing numerous streams before meeting the Tongariro Crossing track close to Mangatepopo Hut. From **Mangatepopo Hut to Emerald Lakes** (6km; 3–4hr; 660m ascent), you follow the Tongariro Crossing (described above), then have the choice of continuing on the Crossing **to Ketetahi Hut** (4km; 2–3hr; 400m descent) and returning to this point the next day, or branching right **to Outere Hut** (5km; 1–2hr; 500m descent), descending steeply through fabulously contorted lava formations towards the Rangipo Desert. The initial section from **Outere Hut to Waihohonu Hut** (7km; 2–3hr; 250m descent) crosses open, undulating country, then descends into the beech forests before a final climb over a ridge brings you to the hut, where you can drop your pack and press on for twenty minutes to the cool and clear Ohinepango Springs. The final day's walk, from **Waihohonu Hut to Whakapapa** (14km; 5–6hr; 200m ascent), cuts between Ngauruhoe and Ruapehu, passing the Old Waihohonu Hut (no accommodation) that was built for stage coaches on the old road in 1901. The path then continues alongside Waihohonu Stream to the exposed **Tama Saddle** and, just over a kilometre beyond, a junction where side tracks lead to Lower Tama Lake (20min return) and Upper Tama Lake (1hr return), both in-filled explosion craters. It is only around two hours' walk from the saddle back to Whakapapa, so you should have time to explore the **Taranaki Falls** before ambling back through tussock to the village.

If you'd prefer to steer clear of the popular Northern Circuit but still circle around a mountain, try the **Round the Mountain Track** (65km; 4–5 days) which loops around Mount Ruapehu, most easily tackled from Whakapapa. This track can also be combined with the Northern Circuit to make a mighty five- or six-day **circumnavigation** of all three mountains. For these two you need backcountry hut tickets or an annual hut pass. Huts are Cat 2 ($10) and camping is $5. A Great Walks pass is necessary for Waihohonu hut which is also part of the Northern Circuit Great Walk.

Ruapehu Crater Rim

The ascent to the **Ruapehu Crater Rim** takes around eight hours return from the Top o' the Bruce (15km), and a much more appealing five hours from the top of the **Waterfall Express chair lift** (9km), avoiding a long slog through a barren, rocky landscape. Even from the top of the chair lift, this is one of New Zealand's more gruelling short hikes, but the destination makes it all worthwhile. Volcanic instability makes it dangerous to go beyond the **Dome Shelter** (no accommodation), at 2672m the highest structure in the country and typically surrounded in snow. It perches on the rim of the crater, with great views across the upper reaches of a small glacier to the dramatic silhouettes of Cathedral Rocks, west to Mount Taranaki and down into the crater lake, currently in the process of refilling after thousands of tonnes of water were ejected during the 1995 and 1996 eruptions. The route is not waymarked, but from Christmas until the first snows arrive, the ascent can usually be made in ordinary walking boots without crampons or an ice axe. If you are in any doubt or would appreciate some commentary, join an organized trek (see p.313).

National Park

The evocative moniker attached to **NATIONAL PARK**, 15km west of Whakapapa Village, belies the overwhelming drabness of this tiny settlement – a dispiriting

MOUNT RUAPEHU SKIFIELDS

When the snows come, around two-thirds of New Zealand's skiers generally turn their attention to Mount Ruapehu, home to the North Island's only substantial skifields. Every weekend from around late June to early November, cars pile out of Auckland and Wellington (and pretty much everywhere in between) for the four-hour drive to either **Whakapapa**, the more extensive skifield on the northwestern slopes of Mount Ruapehu, or **Turoa**, easily beaten into second place on the south side. Both fields have excellent reputations for pretty much all levels of skier and the orientation of volcanic ridges lends itself to an abundance of dreamy, natural half-pipes for snowboarding. Only club members with 4WDs battle their way to the tiny **Tukino** field on the eastern flank of the mountain.

The two main fields have had poor attendance of late and both offered significant reductions in season ticket prices for the 2000 season, though day prices are unaffected. Neither has public **accommodation** on site. Ski clubs maintain dozens of chalets at the foot of the main tows in Whakapapa's Iwikau Village, but casual visitors (unless they can get invited to a lodge as a guest) have to stay 6km downhill at Whakapapa Village (see p.311) or 22km away at National Park (see opposite). Almost everyone skiing Turoa stays in Ohakune (see p.318).

WHAKAPAPA

With over thirty groomed runs, a dozen major chair lifts and T-bars and the dedicated learners' area of Happy Valley, **Whakapapa** is New Zealand's largest and busiest **ski area** (information ☎07/892 3738, up-to-the-minute details on premium-rated Snowphone ☎0900/99833; *www.whakapapa.co.nz*). It offers the longest North Island **season** (usually late June to early Nov and sometimes through to Christmas), 675 vertical metres of snow, plus snow-making equipment, ski schools, a huge gear-rental operation, crèche and a couple of cafés. **Access** is along the toll-free, sealed Bruce Road. Chains are sometimes required, in which case a fitting service miraculously appears beside the road. Car parking is free and there is a free courtesy bus from the lower car parks. Shuttle buses run from Whakapapa Village, National Park, Turangi and Taupo.

Lift passes cost $49 a day, $221 for five days, and there is a Learn to Ski Pack ($48) that includes gear rental, an hour-and-a-half lesson and a learners' area lift pass. On-site **ski rental** for one day costs $26–36, $40 for snowboard and boots, and there are discounts for rentals of five or more days. Several places in National Park also offer competitive rates and a wide selection of equipment.

TUROA

Turoa (information ☎06/385 8456; premium-rated Snowphone, ☎0900/99444) has developed in a much more controlled fashion than Whakapapa, and offers the country's greatest vertical drop – 720m – a skiable area almost as extensive as Whakapapa's with wide groomed trails particularly aimed at intermediate skiers and, at Ohakune, the region's best après ski. The **season** usually runs from mid- to late June through to mid-October, though poor snowfall in recent winters has limited the season and forced the skifield into receivership: new owners aren't likely to change operations greatly. It is usually possible to drive straight up the sealed, toll-free, 17km **access** road from Ohakune without chains, and park for nothing. Again, the skifield operators will fit chains ($20) when needed, or you can rent from shops in Ohakune for a little less and fit them yourself. Several shuttle buses run up from Ohakune, charging $10–15 return. **Lift tickets** go for $52 a day or $234 for a five-day pass. Ski **gear** can be **rented** for $25 a day, $39 for snowboard and boots, and there is a Learn to Ski package ($49) that includes gear, an introductory lesson and learner tows.

collection of A-frame chalets sprouting from a scrubby plain of pines, eucalyptuses and flax, with only the superb views of Ruapehu and Ngauruhoe to lend it any grace.

Arrival and information
National Park comprises a grid of half a dozen streets wedged between SH4 and the parallel rail line. **Trains** stop at the deserted platform on Station Road, while InterCity **buses** pull up outside what used to be the National Park Store, now just a telephone box 100m north on Carroll Street. Bus tickets can be bought a further 100m up the road at *Howard's Lodge* (see below). There are no banks or cash machines in National Park so unless you have an EFTPOS card, bring plenty of cash.

Accommodation
Accommodation is in great demand during the **ski season** – when prices will be at least one price code higher than those given here – and can fill up from Christmas to the end of January, but is otherwise plentiful. *Howard's Lodge*, on Carroll Street (☎ & fax 07/892 2827, *howards.nat.park@xtra.co.nz*; dorms ①, rooms ②–③) is the most organized and well-equipped of the **lodges**, with a spa pool, track transport and two accommodation sections – one catering to backpackers and the other offering plusher kitchen and lounge for the better-heeled guests. Rooms range from basic dorms (separate for men and women) and doubles, to appreciably more modern and comfortable en-suite rooms; mountain bikes are available to rent ($20 for 2hr), as is tramping and climbing gear, and there's Internet access. Alternatives include *Pukenui Lodge & Backpackers*, SH4 (☎0800/785 368, fax 07/892 2900, *www.tongariro.cc*, *pukenuilodge@xtra.co.nz*; dorms ①, rooms ③, en suites ④, motels ⑤), with a spacious lounge, great mountain views, plain and comfortable dorms and doubles, some en suite; the *National Park Lodge and Motel*, back on Carroll Street (☎07/892 2993 & 0800/861 861, fax 892 2846, *natparklodge@xtra.co.nz*; dorms ①, units ③), offering marginally the cheapest dorms and some ageing but perfectly functional motel units; and *National Park Backpackers*, Finlay Street (☎ & fax 07/892 2870, *nat.park.backpackers@xtra.co.nz*; tents $10, dorms ①, rooms ②, made-up doubles ③), with good facilities, but chiefly notable for being built around an indoor **climbing wall** ($8, plus $2 for boots and harness). Guests only pay once for climbing during their visit.

Almost all the accommodation places organize transport for the Tongariro Crossing, some offering fare discounts if you stay two nights.

The Town
Though initially founded as a way station on the main Auckland–Wellington train line, it owes its continued existence to skiers and trampers bound for the adjacent Tongariro National Park, and paddlers heading for the **Whanganui River Journey** (see p.253). With the limited accommodation at Whakapapa Village, visitors to Tongariro, Ngauruhoe and the northern side of Ruapehu are all but forced to stay in National Park, using shuttle buses (see box on p.313) to get to Whakapapa and the Tongariro tramps.

In National Park itself, there is precious little to do except for a few adventure activities. To go **mountain biking**, sign up with Freedom Rentals, Carroll Street (☎07/892 2773), who rent bikes for $30 a half day and offer guides for $25 an hour; or Go For It Tours, based in the train station (☎07/892 2705), who rent out mountain bikes for $10 an hour and also operate guided trips through rivers and along muddy tracks on motorbikes or two-rider **quad bikes** (2hr–full day; $50–60).

Eating and drinking
All lodges do **breakfast**, but for main meals you're better off at the licensed *Eivins Off Piste Café and Bar*, a wayside diner in a former petrol station on the corner of Carroll

Street and SH4. In fact it is worth going out of your way for a coffee and muffin or such delicacies as pumpkin and Galliano soup ($8) or chilli prawn hot pot with sun-dried tomato and couscous ($18) served inside or out, both with superb mountain views. Steaks, pub grub and dedicated drinking and pool-playing are to be had at the typically rowdy *Schnapps Bar*, on SH4, next to Pukenui Lodge, or you can get **fish 'n' chips** and a jug of beer at the *National Park Hotel* on Carroll Street.

Ohakune

OHAKUNE, 35km south of National Park, welcomes you with a huge carrot, celebrating its position at the heart of one of the nation's prime market-gardening regions. This is easily forgotten once you are in town among the chalet-style lodges and ski-rental shops geared to cope with the massive influx of winter-sports enthusiasts who descend from mid-June to early November for the **skiing** at Turoa (see box on p.316), 20km north up Ohakune Mountain Road.

Arrival and information

Ohakune is strung between two centres. The main trunk line passes through Ohakune Junction where there's the **train station** and a cluster of hotels and restaurants mostly serving the skiing fraternity. The commercial heart lies 2km to the southwest, where InterCity **buses** on the Hamilton–Taumarunui–Wanganui run (daily except Sat) stop outside the **visitor centre**, 54 Clyde St (Mon–Fri 9am–5pm, Sat & Sun 9am–3.30pm; ☎06/385 8427, fax 385 8527), which has all the general information you'll need and sells both bus and train tickets. For more specific tramping information, the mountain weather forecast, and a detailed low-down on local flora and fauna, make for the **DOC field centre** at the foot of Ohakune Mountain Road (school and public holidays daily 8am–noon & 1–5pm; all other times Mon–Fri 8am–noon & 1–3pm; ☎06/385 0010, fax 385 0011, *ohakunevc@doc.govt.nz*); weather and tramping information is available in the foyer which stays open 24hr. **Internet access** is available at The Video Shop, 53 Clyde St.

There are no regular buses around Ohakune, so you might want to **rent a car** from Rimu Park Lodge, 27 Rimu St, for around $45 a day, or a **mountain bike** from either the Powderhorn Chateau, 194 Mangawhero Terrace ($25 per half-day, $35 full-day), or from Turoa Sports Ski Shed, 71 Clyde St (☎06/385 8887) where the machines range in quality and start from $15 for 2hr (tandems $25).

Accommodation

Ohakune has stacks of **places to stay**, though several of them close outside the ski season and are packed once the snows arrive – when prices get hiked up by around thirty percent more than those quoted here. Enough places are open in summer to satisfy almost all budgets, the most comprehensive and appealing being *Rimu Park Lodge*, 27 Rimu St, Ohakune Junction (☎ & fax 06/385 9023, *http://homepages.ihug.co.nz /~rimulodg, rimulodg@ihug.co.nz*; dorms ①, rooms ②, cabins ③, units ④, carriages ④, chalets ⑤), a 1914 villa containing spacious six-bunk dorms and comfortable doubles. The grounds are dotted with simple cabins, en-suite units with TV and fridge but no kitchen, fully self-contained chalets sleeping between four and ten, and several railway carriages fitted out as self-contained units with separate lounge and sleeping quarters. In Ohakune junction you'll also find the top-of-the-range *Powderhorn Chateau*, 194 Mangawhero Terrace at the base of Ohakune Mountain Road (☎06/385 8888, fax 385 8925; ⑥), an immense log-cabin style edifice with a lovely indoor swimming pool, sun beds, and en-suite rooms, the best with balconies and mountain views; and cheap beds at the excellent *Station Lodge*, 60 Thames St (ski season only; ☎ & fax 06/385 8797; ①), in the former stationmaster's house right by the train station.

Folk arriving on InterCity buses will find it more convenient to stay in the main town. Here there's budget accommodation at the clean, spartan and recently renovated *Matai Lodge*, 17 Clyde St (☎06/385 9169, fax 385 9196, *matai.lodge@xtra.co.nz*; dorms ①, rooms ②), with free laundry and cheap Internet access; and next door at the small, well maintained and delightfully old-fashioned *YHA*, 15 Clyde St (☎ & fax 06/385 8724; dorms ①, rooms ②, en suite ③), which has a nice little garden. Good budget beds can also be found at the *Alpine Motel Lodge*, 7 Miro St (☎ & fax 06/385 8758, *alpine.motel@xtra.co.nz*; lodge ②, units ④, chalets ⑤), with two-, three- and four-berth lodge rooms, studio units and fully self-contained chalets sleeping up to eight, all with access to Sky TV, a spa and drying room. For homestay you can't beat the very cosy and welcoming *Villa Mangawhero*, 60b Burns St (☎06/385 8076; ④); or for B&B, the very tasteful and amiable *Whare Ora*, 14 Kaha St, (☎ 06/385 9385, fax 385 9385, *whareora@xtra.co.nz*; ⑥–⑦), 6km east in the village of Rangataua, with two rooms (one with spa bath and both with diverting modern art works), a lounge with unsurpassed mountain views, and delicious dinners available on request ($45 per person with wine).

Campers have a choice of the *Ohakune Holiday Park*, 5 Moore St (☎ & fax 06/385 8561, *ohakune_holiday_park@xtra.co.nz*; tents $9, on-site vans & cabins ②, en suite cabins & tourist flats ③), right on the edge of the bush but still central, and the DOC's toilets-and-water *Mangawhero Campsite* ($4), 1.5km up Ohakune Mountain Road from the field centre.

The Town and around

For four short months Ohakune comes alive, bars and restaurants swing into action, everyone makes their money for the year and then shuts up until next season. Consequently it is pretty quiet in summer, but once the snows have melted, the trails are open for tramping, mountain biking and horse trekking.

Unlike at Whakapapa, the Turoa chairlifts rarely run outside the ski season, but the 17km Ohakune Mountain Road makes an impressive drive through stands of ancient rimu and provides access to a number of fine **walks**, including the Round the Mountain Track (see p.315). The pick of the shorter trails are: the **Mangawhero Forest Walk** (3km return; 1hr), a short and well marked loop track from opposite the DOC field centre; the **Waitonga Falls Walk** (4km return; 1hr 10min) to a spectacular waterfall, starting 11km up the Mountain Road; and the hike to **Lake Surprise** (12km return; 5hr), an undulating route along the Round the Mountain track to a shallow lake which starts from the 15km mark on Ohakune Mountain Road and passes evidence of volcanic debris which swept down the mountain during the 1975 and 1995 eruptions.

Most of the walking tracks, and any inside the bounds of the national park are off-limits for **mountain biking**, but you can coast 17km down Ohakune Mountain Road on The Ohakune Mountain Ride, 16 Miro St (☎06/385 8257; Nov–June; $28), or rent a bike (see above) and head 12km east to the forest roads around Rangataua; consult the DOC or the visitor centre for more details.

A less arduous approach is to let **horses** take the strain at *Ruapehu Homestead*, 4km east on SH49 (☎06/385 8799), which runs back-country trail rides through bush and rivers (2hr; $35), as well as easier trips for the less experienced.

Eating, drinking and nightlife

During the ski season, Ohakune Junction is very much the happening place to spend your evenings. In summer though, when hardly any of the half-dozen restaurants, bars and clubs bother to open, you're better off in **central Ohakune**, where the tastiest meals are served at *Utopia*, 47 Clyde St (closed Sunday in summer), an ideal spot for idling away an hour or two over great coffee and sumptuous all-day brunches; you might even catch them open in the evening, but don't bank on it. Other good bets are succulent gourmet kebabs from *Mountain Kebabs*, 29 Clyde St (generally winter only), where chicken, lamb, seafood and vegetarian fillings are doused with a stack of tasty sauces; and *Sassi's*, at the *Alpine Motel Lodge*, which reliably dishes up tasty and nicely presented bistro mains for $15–20 and has a broad wine list with most available by the glass.

At the **Junction**, the *Powderhorn Chateau* harbours two restaurants: the fine-dining *Matterhorn* (✆06/385 8888; licensed), serving the likes of venison with a juniper and port glaze, and Italian-style lamb shanks; and the more modest *Powderkeg* brasserie/bar, where you can fight for a prized place on the balcony with mountain views. Next door, the *Fat Pigeon Garden Café*, Mangawhero Terrace, serves excellent café-style meals and coffee, but in summer is often only open weekends. In winter, *Margarita's*, 5 Rimu St, do warming and tasty enchiladas, tostadas and other faux-Mexican favourites, and *Hot Lava*, 30 Thames St, kicks up a storm until the early hours.

Dine early, and you'll have time to catch Kiwi Encounters (✆06/385 9505) who take highly informative three-hour **kiwi-spotting** trips into the Waimarino Forest ($25; minimum two people) leaving around 7.45pm, and with a fair chance of an encounter.

The Desert Road and Waiouru

South of Turangi, and past the trout hatchery, SH1 sticks to the east of the Tongariro National Park running roughly parallel to the Tongariro River. This is the **Desert Road**, which climbs up over an exposed and barren plateau. This isn't a true desert (the rainfall is too high), but it's about as near as you'll get anywhere in New Zealand. Road cuttings reveal the cause as they slice through several metres of volcanic ash – a timeline of past eruptions – that's so free-draining any vegetation struggles to take hold.

Initially you're deep in pine forest with side roads periodically ducking off to the east and the assortment of hydro-electric tunnels, intakes and tailraces of the Tongariro River. Some 9km south of Turangi, Kaimanawa Road runs 2km down to the river and beyond to a good **free camping** area by a stream (best found in daylight). After crossing the river, keep left on a tarmac road following signs to Waihaha Valley. The site is 500m back from the substation at the end of the road, and a narrow track through the bush leads to some toilets. A further 5km south along SH1, Tree Trunk Gorge Road leads again to the Tongariro River at a spot where it squeezes through a narrow fissure known as **Tree Trunk Gorge** – one for river devotees mainly.

Back on the highway you soon climb out of the forest for great views of the three volcanoes off to the east and the blasted territory ahead. It is a dramatic scene, somehow made even more elemental by the three lines of electricity pylons striding off across the bleak tussock towards Waiouru.

Waiouru and the Army Museum

The **Desert Road** (SH1) and the roads flanking the western side of Ruapehu, Ngauruhoe and Tongariro meet at **WAIOURU**, an uninspiring row of service stations and tearooms perched 800m above sea level on the bleak tussock plain beside New Zealand's major army base. The serene view of the mountains from here can be fabulous but the peace is often disturbed by troop movements and even target practice.

The place to take cover is in the three concrete bunkers of the **QEII Army Memorial Museum** (daily 9am–4.30pm; $8), a showcase of national military heritage from the New Zealand Wars through the Anglo-Boer and two World Wars to New Zealand's involvement in Vietnam. Mannequins in regimental regalia set in lifeless dioramas do little to prepare you for the impact of the *Roimata Pounamu* ("Tears on Greenstone") **wall of remembrance**, where a veil of tears symbolizes mourning and cleansing as it streams down a curving bank of heavily veined greenstone tiles while

Harbour Bridge, Auckland

Sheep-shearer statue, Te Kuiti,
Western North Island

Treaty House, Waitangi, Northland

Maori war canoe, Matauri Bay

Marae Hako Bay, Eastland

"Lost World" abseil, Waitomo Caves

Waiotapu Thermal Area, Rotorua

Commercial Hotel, Whakatane, Bay of Plenty

Lake Taupo

Whanarua Bay, Eastland

Tree ferns, Northland

the name, rank and place of death of each of the 33,000 New Zealanders who have died in the various wars is recited. A twenty-minute audio-visual presentation sets the scene for the rest of the chronologically arranged exhibits, which are brought to life by oral histories, including some heart-rending ones that recount the bungled Gallipoli campaign of World War I. The emphasis is small-scale and personal: one particularly affecting case contains artefacts made by soldiers in the trenches – cribbage boards, chess sets and a cigarette holder that completely encased the cigarette so it could be smoked without risk of the enemy seeing the telltale glow.

The *Rations Café*, inside the Army Museum, is as good as any hereabouts. Should you need to stay, try the budget *Oasis Hotel and Motel*, SH1 (✆ & fax 06/387 6779; ④), with mostly twin rooms and some motel units.

Northern Rangitikei: Taihape and Mangaweka

Continuing south along SH1, you descend from the volcanic plateau into the **Rangitikei District**, with the Rangitikei River never far away, though seldom seen as its waters have carved down through some of the youngest and softest rock in New Zealand to leave off-white cliffs as the only evidence of the river's course. This is prime **farming country**, pretty much the Kiwi archetype of sheep farms stretching to the horizon over angular green hills characterized by "terracettes" – a kind of corrugated effect caused by minor slumping on land too steep to support grass. The pastoral nature of the region is reflected in the character of the region's largest town, **Taihape**, an agricultural service centre of only passing interest, though it works well enough as a base for some superb whitewater rafting, a bungy jump and some fine gardens.

Taihape

For want of any more interesting features, the small town of **TAIHAPE**, 30km south of Waiouru, pronounces itself "New Zealand's one and only Gumboot City", something it showcases each November (first weekend) with the World Annual Gumboot Throwing Festival, a tongue-in-cheek celebration of this archetypal Kiwi footwear. Said boots are increasingly hard to find in the hardware stores and farm-supply shops that line the main street, though gumboot-shaped postcards and souvenirs seem all the rage. The horticultural theme continues in several showpiece **gardens** all listed and pinpointed in the *Garden Tour of The Rangitikei* leaflet available free from the Taihape **visitor centre**, in the Town Hall, Hautapu Street (daily: Nov–March 9am–5.30pm, April–Oct 9am–5pm; ✆06/388 0350, fax 388 1090, *www.rangitikei.com*, *info@rangitikei.com*). The best of the gardens are around twenty minutes' drive northwest of Taihape. They're unexpectedly sited amid farmland and relish the cool inland high-country climate. Outside the peak summer season it pays to call before heading out to either the hillside **Rongoiti** (✆06/388 7866; Sept–April daily 10am–5pm; $5), noted for its giant Himalayan lilies and woodland setting, or the hilltop **Waitoka** (Oct–May daily 10am–5pm; $7), a more formal affair with broad lawns, formal vegetable garden and mature exotic trees.

For most it is enough to stop for a **bite to eat**, and Taihape has easily the best eating on SH1 between Taupo and Wellington. The main contenders here are: *The Venison Kitchen*, 65b Hautapu St, which claims to be the only farmed venison café in the world, and serves it in burgers, souvlaki and pies for under $9; the cottagey *Brown Sugar Café*, Huia Street (✆06/388 1880; closed Tues), which serves excellent light meals, cakes and coffee during the day, as well as dinner on Friday and Saturday evenings (booking advisable); and the more modern *Café Exchange*, Huia St (✆06/388 0599), which has a good deli selection, breakfast and snacks throughout the day and a few more substantial dishes in the evening. *Brown Sugar* and *Exchange* both have garden seating.

If you need to **stay**, there are rock-bottom rooms at the *Gretna Hotel*, corner of SH1 and Hautapu Street (☎06/388 0638; dorms ①, rooms ②); units at the *Safari Motel*, SH1, 1km north (☎0800/200 046, fax 06/388 1116; ④); and hilltop homestay at *Korirata*, 25 Pukeko St (☎ & fax 06/388 0315; ④), which has great views over Taihape and Mount Ruapehu and offers dinner for $22. There's camping at the *Abba Motor Camp* (☎06/388 0718; tents $15, cabins ②, motels ③), 3km north of town on the Old Abattoir Road.

Around Taihape: rafting and bungy jumping

Driving through Taihape, there is little to suggest that the hilly country to the east hides one of New Zealand's most thrilling whitewater-rafting trips and the North Island's highest bungy jump.

The Grade V gorge section of the Rangitikei River is one of the toughest regularly used sections of **whitewater-rafting** river in the country. Ten major rapids are packed into the 2–3hr run. Operators will take first-timers, but newbies can make it safer for everyone if they choose to raft elsewhere first. Trips on the Rangitikei are run from Mangaweka (see below), or more directly from *River Valley*, Pukoekahu (☎06/388 1444, fax 388 1859, *www.rivervalley.co.nz*, *rivervalley@xtra.co.nz*; ①–③), a mostly back-packer-oriented complex well-sited right by the Rangitikei at the pull-out point for the rafting trips some 30km east of Taihape (see map p.267). Morning, and occasionally afternoon, trips ($95) are run throughout the year, though when water levels are low, rafts are replaced by paddle-yourself one-person inflatable kayaks (also $95) launched in convoy with guides helping out the more tentative paddlers. River Valley also offer **scenic rafting** ($95; 5hr) down the quieter Grade II section immediately downstream of the lodge, **kayaking** ($40 per half day), horse trekking ($45 for 2hr), mountain biking ($30–35 per day), abseiling down a 30m cliff ($10) and 9-hole pitch-and-putt ($10). Customers, many of them from the Kiwi Experience buses which call nightly, typically **stay** in 16-bunk or slightly pricier six-berth dorms (①), pleasant double or twin rooms (③), tents ($10), or ten-minutes up the road in shearers' quarters nicely converted into a self-contained house (①). Straightforward low-cost meals are served and there's a bar on site.

With a detailed map you can follow the backroads from River Valley to the eighty-metre High Time **bungy** (☎0800/802 864; daily 9am–5pm; $99), though it is simpler to turn off SH1 at Utiku, 7km south of Taihape, and follow the signs 15km east. You jump from a bridge over Rangitikei River far below, get lowered onto a raft, then get spirited back to the bridge on a water-balanced chair lift, a ride available separately for non-jumpers ($25 for two people).

Mangaweka

The brightly-painted form of a DC3 beside SH1, 24km south of Taihape, is about the only indication that there might be a reason to stop in the dilapidated hamlet of MAN-GAWEKA, scattered across a plain high above the Rangitikei River. The *Aeroplane Café* is cheap, basic and an obvious lure, but there is more of interest at the adjacent service station, from where Rangitikei Whitewater (☎ & fax 06/382 5747) operate **whitewater rafting** on the Grade V Rangitikei Gorge (see above; $119 including trans-port to the river), along with more family-oriented **fun rafting** down a gentle stretch of the river (1hr $25, half-day $49).

Unless you are planning to stay – and good reasons to do that are listed opposite – continue 6km south to *Flat Hills Park*, a café complex that's a popular refreshment stop for InterCity and tourist buses. A better reason to pause is Flat Hills **Jet Sprint** (daily 8.30am–5pm; $20), a short, sharp burst of adrenaline delivered by having 450 horses right behind your head as you hurtle around an artificial course in a de-tuned three-seater racing jetboat. It might not be scenic and you only get five minutes, but you'll remember the G-forces and the engine heat on the back of your neck.

From here it is 60km to Bulls (see p.255) with little to see in between. You may, however, want to **stay**, either at the bargain *Mangaweka Motor Camp*, Ruahine Road, by the river 1.5km north of town (☎07/382 5730; $6 per tent, $8 per van); or 11km further along Ruahine Road at the excellent *Mairenui Rural Retreat*, (☎06/382 5564, fax 382 5885, *www.mairenui.co.nz, mairenui@xtra.co.nz*; villa ④, retreat ⑤, homestead ⑥), on a working farm in typical Rangitikei sheep country. Here you have a choice of simple rooms with self-catering facilities in a colonial villa ($30 a head), self-contained accommodation in a modernist secluded retreat, or lovely en-suite B&B rooms in the homestead. Tasty evening meals start at $25 (including a pre-dinner drink), and self-catering guests can get breakfast from $10.

travel details

Trains

From National Park to: Auckland (2 daily; 5hr 30min); Ohakune (2 daily; 30min); Palmerston North (2 daily; 3hr 30min); Waiouru (2 daily; 1hr); Wellington (2 daily; 5hr 30min).

From Ohakune to: Auckland (2 daily; 6hr); Wellington (2 daily; 5hr).

From Rotorua to: Auckland (1 daily; 4hr 15min); Hamilton (1 daily; 2hr 15min).

Buses

From Kawerau to: Rotorua (2 daily; 45min); Whakatane (2 daily; 45 min).

From National Park to: Auckland (1 daily; 5–6hr); Ohakune (1 daily; 30min); Wellington (1 daily; 5–6hr).

From Ohakune to: Auckland (1 daily; 5–6hr); Wellington (1 daily; 5–6hr).

From Rotorua to: Auckland (7 daily; 4hr); Gisborne (1 daily; 4hr 45min); Hamilton (7 daily; 1hr 30min); Kawerau (2 daily; 45min); Taupo (4 daily; 1hr); Tauranga (4 daily; 1hr 30min); Whakatane (2 daily; 1hr 30min).

From Taihape to: Auckland (5 daily; 7hr); Taupo (5 daily; 2hr); Turangi (5 daily; 1hr 10min); Wellington (3 daily; 5–6hr).

From Taupo to: Auckland (8 daily; 4–5hr); Palmerston North (5 daily; 4hr); Rotorua (4 daily; 1hr); Turangi (5 daily; 45min); Wellington (5 daily; 6hr).

From Tokoroa to: Hamilton (4 daily; 1hr 40min); Taupo (4 daily; 40min).

From Turangi to: The Chateau (4 daily; 1hr).

Flights

From Rotorua to: Auckland (4–6 daily; 45min); Christchurch (2 daily; 1hr 15min); Wellington (2-3 daily; 1hr 10min).

From Taupo to: Auckland (2–3 daily; 50min); Wellington (1 daily; 1hr).

CHAPTER FIVE

THE COROMANDEL, BAY OF PLENTY AND EASTLAND

T he long coastal sweep to the east of Auckland is split into three distinct areas, among them two of the most popular summer-holiday destinations on the North Island; the other is one of the least-visited parts of the country, whatever the time of year. Heading east from Auckland by road you'll first cut across at least

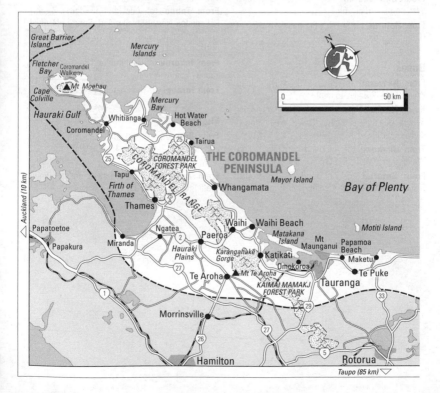

a portion of the **Hauraki Plains**, a wedge of dairying land at the foot of the Coromandel Peninsula, its two main towns serviced by buses. Principally a transit point to more exciting places, the area nonetheless holds a few pleasant surprises for anyone willing to dawdle for an extra day or so. In the town of **Te Aroha**, you can languish in a private **spa bath** that's fed by natural soda water in a laid-back thermal reserve at the foot of a mountain before taking in the astounding **views** from the summit; near **Paeroa** there are pleasant **walks** in the lush **Karangahake Gorge**, once the scene of intensive gold mining.

Directly across the Hauraki Gulf from Auckland (and accessible by road or by ferry from the city), the long and jagged **Coromandel Peninsula** is blessed with some of the country's best sandy beaches and a gorgeous climate. But if this conjures up images of overcrowding and overdevelopment, then think again. This is an outdoors kind of place, offering great coastal scenery, solitude, walks to pristine beaches, and tramps in luxuriant mountainous rainforest. The two coasts are markedly different, the **east** supplying the softer, more idyllic tourist beaches and short coastal walks, while the **west** has a far more rugged and atmospheric coastline, plus easier access to the volcanic hills and ancient kauri trees of the **Coromandel Forest Park**. The scattered towns are generally less interesting than the scenery, working best as bases from which to explore the landscape. The chief access point to the peninsula from the west and south is **Thames**, a small town rich in gold-mining history, while the northernmost town of any significance is the tiny **Coromandel**, set in rolling hills beside an attractive harbour. The principal towns of the east are **Whitianga**, in the north, and

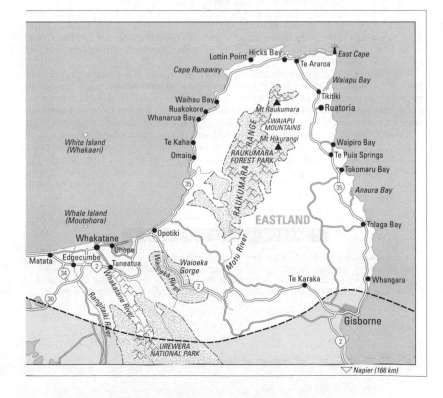

Whangamata in the south, both of which are blessed with long, luxurious, sandy beaches. Near Whitianga attractive coastal walks lead to a series of isolated beaches, among them the unusual **Hot Water Beach**, where natural thermal springs bubble up through the sand and you can create your own open-air spa pool right on the edge of the Pacific Ocean. Nearby, **Cathedral Cove Marine Reserve** acts as a playground for dolphin-spotters and snorkellers, and access point to some magnificent geological formations.

From the open-cast gold-mining town of **Waihi** at the base of the Coromandel Peninsula, the **Bay of Plenty** sweeps down and east to Opotiki, punctuated by an outstanding sequence of golden beaches and great surf, and traced along its length by the Pacific Coast Highway (SH2), which links Auckland with Gisborne. The bay earned its name from **Captain Cook**, who sailed in on the *Endeavour* in 1769 and was struck by the number of thriving Maori settlements living off the abundant resources, as well as by the generous supplies they gave him. This era of peace and plenty was shattered by the **New Zealand Wars** of the 1860s, as fierce fighting led to the establishment of garrisons at both Tauranga and Whakatane, and the easternmost town of Opotiki gained notoriety as the scene of the death of a European missionary – allegedly murdered by a Maori prophet.

This area has the best climate on the North Island, making it a fertile fruit-growing region – particularly citrus and kiwifruit – and another much-visited resort area. The **coast**, though popular with Kiwi holidaymakers, has remained relatively unspoiled, offering great surf beaches, a good variety of offshore activities and walks in the forest-clad hills of the inland **Kaimai-Mamaku Forest Park**. On top of that it's home to the country's fastest-growing city, **Tauranga**, in the western Bay of Plenty, and the contiguous beach town of **Mount Maunganui**, the region's most popular resort. Of the three, Tauranga is the more modern and vigorous, with a thriving café and bar scene, while Mount Maunganui has suffered from too much attention, becoming decidedly over-commercialized.

The **eastern** Bay of Plenty centres on historic and sunny **Whakatane**, primarily of interest for boat excursions to the fuming, volcanic **White Island**, opportunities to swim with dolphins, and as a base for wilderness rafting on the remote Motu River.

Contrasting with these two regions is the splendid, rugged and isolated **Eastland**, once a wealthy part of New Zealand but today run-down and sparsely populated. With a dramatic coastline, and a rich and varied Maori history, this region provides a taste of a secluded way of life long gone in the rest of the country. At its easternmost point – the **East Cape** – is a lighthouse that overlooks East Island, the first place in the country to see the sunrise. All of the region's small communities, each with its own distinctive personality, are dotted along the coastline, against the dramatic backdrop of the **Waiapu Mountains**.

ACCOMMODATION PRICES

Accommodation listed in this guide has been categorized into one of nine price bands, as set out below. The rates quoted represent the **cheapest available** double or twin **room** – except for category ①, which are per-person rates for a dorm bed. Note that fees for **tent sites** and **DOC huts** (quoted in dollars) are also per-person, unless otherwise stated.

① under $20 per person	④ $60–80	⑦ $140–180
② under $40 per room	⑤ $80–100	⑧ $180–240
③ $40–60	⑥ $100–140	⑨ over $240

For more on accommodation, see p.34.

The Hauraki Plains

Approach the Coromandel Peninsula from the west and you can't help but pass through at least a part of the fertile **Hauraki Plains**, a wedge of former swamp at the peninsula's southern end. It's bordered to the north by the Firth of Thames, final destination for a number of meandering rivers which drain this sweep of rich pastoral farmland. Attractions are admittedly limited, and most people rush through on their way to the scenic splendour to the north and further east, missing out on at least a couple of sights worth a minor detour.

Journeying east from Auckland along the scenic route of "The Seabird Coast" you meet the plains at **Miranda** (see p.123), whereas approaching from the west along the more direct SH2, you'll first strike the tiny settlement of **Ngatea**, worth a fleeting visit for the curiosity value of a warehouse crammed with rock crystals. The hub of the plains, though, is **Paeroa**, at the meeting-point of routes north, south, east and west, but the town pales in comparison to the scenic river valley of **Karangahake Gorge**, which runs from Paeroa to Waihi (see overleaf). This leafy landscape contains a few good walks along the banks of the rushing Ohinemuri River and past the skeletal remains of old gold workings, plus a short scenic train journey to Waihi.

However the real jewel in the crown is the small and often-ignored Edwardian town of **Te Aroha**, tucked away at the southern extremity of the plains. A detour here allows for a relaxing soak in natural hot springs of soda water at the foot of Mount Te Aroha after returning from a half-day walk to the mountain's summit for breathtaking views. There's also access to tramps in the **Kaimai–Mamaku Forest Park**, which covers the rugged Kaimai Range, stretching from the Karangahake Gorge in the north almost as far as Rotorua in the south.

Getting around the Plains by public transport isn't too difficult with InterCity running two or three services a day from Auckland through Ngatea, Paeroa and the Karangahake Gorge to Waihi and Tauranga. Te Aroha is out on a limb though Turley-Murphy run a service (Mon–Fri one daily) between Hamilton and Thames via Te Aroha.

Ngatea

The first settlement you'll reach heading east on SH2 is tiny **NGATEA**, set amid green rolling hills 70km from Auckland. The only reason to stop is to visit **Wilderness Gems**, 13 River Rd (*www.wildernessgems.co.nz*; daily 9am–5pm; free), signposted just before the river bridge, 200m off the main road. It is essentially a warehouse stuffed with rock crystals from the nearby Coromandel Peninsula, around New Zealand and from as far away as Australia, Mexico, USA and India. The main room contains a wealth of polished stone and marble ornaments – candlesticks, napkin rings, vases, carved animals, chess sets and so on – many of them fairly ghastly but with choice pieces among the dross. Elsewhere petrified wood, agates and rose quartz compete for bench space with jewellery crafted from carved jade and bone, and geodes sliced to reveal the hollow crystalline interior. The best examples of these are just for display but some pretty snazzy specimens are available for $300 down to as little as $2. You can catch a glimpse of the cutting and polishing operation through a window, or press on to the dark and pokey Fluorescent Room, where a five-minute programme illustrates how a range of minerals react to UV light, vibrantly glowing bright yellow, green, purple and red.

From here the highway continues to Paeroa, where you can branch off on SH26 northwards to the Coromandel Peninsula or southwards to Te Aroha.

Paeroa

Continuing 25km southeast from Ngatea on SH2 you reach the small and rather drea-ry **PAEROA**, which briefly became a significant port during the early gold-mining days when boats from Auckland could go no further up the Ohinemuri River. This facet of the town's past is poorly illustrated at the well-publicized **Maritime Museum** (Mon–Fri 10.30am–3pm; $4), which includes a desultory collection near the site of the original jetty and the rotting remains of an old paddle steamer, inexplicably marooned on a riverbank within the grounds.

To Kiwis, Paeroa is simply the birthplace of **Lemon and Paeroa** (L & P), a home-grown soft-drink which still holds its own against international competition, despite substituting the original natural mineral water, discovered here in the nineteenth cen-tury, with water from an Auckland bottling plant. Undaunted by this harsh reality, a giant brown L & P bottle stands at the junction of SH2 and SH26, greeting those enter-ing town from the south, and Paeroa gets as much mileage as it can from the drink's promotional catchphrase "World Famous in New Zealand".

On the main road, opposite the junction with Hall Street is the pleasant but limited **Paeroa Museum** (Mon–Fri 10.30am–3pm; $2), run by the local historical society. Avoiding the usual mind-boggling clutter, its neatly displayed exhibits cover the town's history, early shipping and gold mining in the Karangahake Gorge. Of particular inter-est is a huge collection of Royal Albert bone china, while among the few Maori artefacts is a stack of collection drawers containing tools and ornaments: stone adzes, cutting tools, bone fish-hooks and carved *tiki* (pendants).

Practicalities

Paeroa's **main street** is Belmont Road (SH2) and the town centre is concentrated into a small area wedged between the Domain and the junction with SH26. InterCity **buses** between Auckland and Tauranga drop off near the **visitor centre**, at 1 Belmont Rd (Oct–April Mon–Fri 9am–5pm, Sat & Sun 10am–3pm; May–Sept Mon–Fri 9am–5pm; ☎ & fax 07/862 8636), which is well stocked with bumph on the Coromandel Peninsula, takes bus bookings, and makes a point of selling cans of L & P.

There are a couple of reasonable **places to stay**. The *Paeroa Hotel*, on Belmont Road, opposite the visitor centre (☎07/862 7099; ③), is a big nineteenth-century wood-en building with twenty clean and simple rooms, each with a washbasin. There's little to choose between the motels, but try the pleasant *Casa Mexicana Motel*, two minutes' drive away on the western fringes of town, at 71 Puke Rd (☎ 0800/654040, fax 07/862 8216; ④), which has six spacious units and a spa bath. An appealing rural alternative lies 8km east in the Karangahape Gorge (see below)

Café culture has come to Paeroa in the form of the BYO and licensed *Lazy Fish*, 56 Belmont St, so you can **eat** well on Mediterranean-inspired mains, or just grab a coffee and muffin. Otherwise, you're limited to fairly standard, inexpensive cafés such as the licensed *Tui Coffee Lounge*, 18 Belmont Rd, which dishes up hearty **breakfasts** and lunches (Mon–Sat) and dinners (Fri only), including delicious country-fried chicken.

The Karangahake Gorge

Paeroa visitors bound for the Coromandel Peninsula to the north (see p.332) or Te Aroha to the south (see opposite) should still take time to explore the leafy tranquillity of the magnificent **Karangahake Gorge**, scene of the Coromandel's first gold rush in 1875. Independent miners, armed only with picks and sluice pans, were quickly super-seded by large companies that could afford the powerful equipment needed to extract the metal. Today it's hard to envisage such frenetic activity in this scenic spot. The steep-sided gorge begins 8km east of Paeroa along the narrow, snaking continuation of SH2 as it traces the Ohinemuri River to Waihi. The **Karangahake Gorge Historic Walkway** (fully described in a $1 leaflet available from the Paeroa visitor centre) covers 7km of a former rail line and is accessed from three entry points along the gorge (each with a car park), allowing for shorter excursions. Much the best of these is a **loop walk** (3km; 1hr) which starts at Crown Hill Road, 8km east of Paeroa, where a double-decker bridge crosses the river. The trail heads upstream alongside the Ohinemuri River past remnants of the gold workings and into the Karangahake Gorge hugging the cliffs and winding through regenerating native bush. The loop is completed by crossing the river and walking right through a 1km-long tunnel (usually lit). This walk encircles the site of the Karangahake township, now reduced to the reliable *Talisman Café*, and the *Ohinemuri Estate Winery and Café*, Moresby St (☎07/862 8874, fax 862 8847, *ohinemuri-wines@clear.net.nz*; ⑤), which has a delightful courtyard where you can sample the wines and tuck into well-prepared examples of the usual Kiwi café fare (daily in summer; Fri–Sun in winter). On summer Sunday afternoons there's a classical guitarist on duty, and you can even **stay** in a smart, self-contained apartment built into the hay loft.

At the eastern end of the gorge is the tiny village of **WAIKINO**, where an information centre (daily 10am–4.30pm), next door to the old train station, has displays on local history and walks in the area. From here you can also take a short scenic train trip to Waihi and back through the upper reaches of the Karangahake Gorge, on the Goldfields Vintage Railway (see p.355 for details).

Eight kilometres south of the Karangahake Gorge lies another entry point to the scenic **Kaimai-Mamaku Forest Park**, this time through the rugged **Waitawheta Valley**, whose own dramatic gorge was extensively logged for majestic kauri around the turn of the century. Access to the valley is along the Waitawheta Camp Road, which branches off from the Owharoa Falls midway along the Karangahake Gorge. At the end of the road turn into Franklin Road, which culminates in a car park, from where tracks follow old logging routes and rivers through a diverse mix of regenerating bush and podocarp forest, all described in the DOC's *Guide to the Waitawheta Valley* leaflet. The moderately easy **Kauri Loop Track** (8km; 2hr 30min) climbs through forest to two giant kauri trees that somehow escaped the axe, before descending steeply past dramatic bluffs to the car park.

Te Aroha

On the fringes of the Hauraki Plain, 21km south of Paeroa on SH26, the dairy-country settlement of **TE AROHA** is not really on the way to anywhere; something of an outlier despite its status as New Zealand's only intact **Edwardian spa**. It benefits from relative obscurity, and those prepared to make the journey are rewarded with a neat little town hunkered below the imposing bush-clad slopes of the **Kaimai-Mamaku Forest Park**. The 954-metre **Mount Te Aroha** rears up immediately behind the town centre providing a reasonably challenging goal for determined hikers, while gentler pleasures are pursued in hot **soda baths**.

The town itself was founded in 1880 at the furthest navigable extent of the Waihou River and the following year rich deposits of gold were found on Mount Te Aroha, sparking a full-scale **gold rush**, with the reefs of gold-bearing quartz producing handsome yields until 1921. Within a few months of settlement, the new townsfolk set out the attractive hilly Hot Springs Domain around a cluster of soda springs which, by the 1890s, was New Zealand's most popular mineral spa complex, frequently compared with those of Vichy or Baden. People flocked to enjoy the therapeutic benefits of its waters – the hottest soda springs in the country at 38–41°C – and enclosures were erected for privacy, most rebuilt in grand style during the Edwardian years early in the twentieth century. Spas went out of favour in the 1950s, but today the fine suite of original buildings has been beautifully restored and integrated with more modern pools fed by the hot soda springs. Perhaps the only drawback to a peaceful half-day spent here are the strong and biting winds that assault the town from time to time.

The Town

Te Aroha's centrepiece is the **Hot Springs Domain**, a 44-acre **thermal reserve** of formal gardens, rose beds and a bandstand only brought into this century by the skate park adjacent to the croquet lawns. To find the baths, just follow your nose; a slightly smoky yet not unpleasant smell emanates from the modern **Spa Baths** complex (daily 11am–11pm), which comprises five private, enclosed pools each with hydro-therapeutic water jets. Choose a stainless steel one if you fancy adding aromatherapy oils (not supplied); otherwise the wooden tubs are more comfy and spacious. A ten-minute soak followed by a prolonged spa bath is said to extract polluting heavy metals from your system – shower first to open up your pores and be sure to drink plenty of water afterwards, to help counteract the dehydrating effects of the mineral-rich water. You could also call in at the Te Aroha Domain Therapy Clinic (☎07/884 8022), on Whitaker Street by the tourist office, and indulge in Swedish massage, aromatherapy, acupressure and all manner of holistic jiggery pokery ($20 for 30min).

Nearby, a brand-new outdoor **Wyborn Leisure Pool** complex ($4) contains one of the original communal bath houses, the 1878 **No. 2 Bathhouse** (daily: Nov–March 11am–9pm, April-Oct 11am–7pm; $7 per person per half-hour), best suited to larger groups of up to fifteen, with one large pool which, at 32°C, is slightly cooler than the Spa Baths.

Just uphill from the baths is the erratic **Mokena Geyser**, which spurts to impressive heights on good days, going off roughly every half-hour. From here, a **trail** (see box, below) leads to the top of **Mount Te Aroha** which, legend has it, was named by a young Arawa chief, Kahumatamomoe, who climbed it after losing his way in the

---

WALKS IN AND AROUND TE AROHA

The most rewarding of Te Aroha's walks is undoubtedly the ascent of **Mount Te Aroha**, which tops out on the crest of the Kaimai Range from where there are sweeping views down to the Bay of Plenty and, on exceptionally clear days, across to mounts Ruapehu and Taranaki. The **Te Aroha Mountain Track** (950m ascent; 8km return; 3hr 30min), starts from just behind the Mokena Geyser in the Domain and climbs steeply through native bush, zigzagging up a well-defined path to a viewing platform at **Whakapipi** (or Bald Spur), before dipping to a small saddle. From here, the final climb (which can be muddy and slippery after rain) becomes increasingly arduous, and you'll need to use your hands to pull yourself up in places, but the stunning views make it all worthwhile. To return, follow the **Tui Mine Track**, which drops through a stark, heavily mined landscape to link with the Tui Road back to town in one direction, and with the **Tui–Domain Track** in the other, a pleasant bushwalk past a waterfall back to the Domain. If the thought of an uphill slog right to the top is too much, the **sector** as far as the **Whakapipi Lookout** (2km; 50min) gives good views over the town and its surroundings.

Other walks of varied grades and duration lie south of Te Aroha in the **Waiorongomai Valley**, part of the **Kaimai-Mamaku Forest Park**. Formerly the scene of intense mining activity, several tracks following historic miners' trails are described in the leaflet *Guide to the Waiorongomai Valley* ($3), available from Te Aroha visitor centre (see opposite). Access is from a car park on the Waiorongomai Loop Road, which is signposted 4km south of town off the Shaftesbury Road – but note that this is an extremely rugged area punctuated by old mines and shafts that are dangerous to enter. **Overnight hikes** should only be attempted by experienced, fit and well equipped trampers; hut tickets can be bought from the visitor centre in Te Aroha.

region's vast swamp while on his way home to Maketu in the Bay of Plenty. Delighted to see the familiar shoreline of his homeland, he called the mountain *Te Aroha*, meaning "love", in honour of his father and kinsmen.

An old sanatorium, just below the spa baths and in front of the croquet lawn, houses the town **museum** (Oct–April Sat & Sun 1–4pm; May–Sept Sat & Sun 1–3pm; other times by arrangement with visitor centre; donation). There are three exhibit-packed rooms and two finely decorated Royal Doulton Victorian lavatories. A large part of one room is given over to a selection of wind-up gramophones, another to a collection of black-and-white photos of the town and its people, plus a chemical analysis of the local soda water. There is also memorabilia of an old silent movie called *Tilly of Te Aroha*, made when the film industry was in its infancy, and a racy picture for its time.

By the Boundary Street exit from the Domain you'll find the 1926 **St Mark's Anglican Church**, on the corner of Church Street and Kenrick Street, insignificant but for the incongruously sited 1712 organ, said to be the oldest in the southern hemisphere. Built in England by Renatus Harris, it is the sole survivor of ten built after Queen Anne petitioned Parliament to raise taxes so that the finest pipe organs of the day could be put into ten London churches. This particular organ has led something of a charmed life: brought to New Zealand in 1926, it was restored to its original specification in 1985 by an Auckland firm who found that part of the finely carved English heart oak casework predates the organ and probably came from the famed Grinling Gibbons's workshop. If you can get a group together and are prepared to make a small donation, an organ recital can be arranged through the visitor centre.

Practicalities

The town's main street is Whitaker Street and everything of interest – banks, post office, library with Internet access – is along it or close by: the **visitor centre** (Nov–April Mon–Fri 9am–5pm, Sat & Sun 10am–3pm; May–Oct closed at weekends; ☎07/884 8052, fax 884 8259, *www.tearoha-info.co.nz, infotearoha@xtra.co.nz*) is at 152 Whitaker St by the entrance to the Domain, and has DOC information for the local area.

For a small place, Te Aroha has a reasonable choice of **accommodation**. The *YHA* on Miro Street, off Burgess Street (☎07/884 8739; office open 5–8.30pm; dorms ①, room ②), is one of the simplest in New Zealand, about ten minutes' walk from the visitor centre in an attractive cottage on the lower slopes of Mount Te Aroha, with great views and a pretty garden. The hostel has just two bunkrooms and one twin room, and a charming kitchen stocked with plenty of basic cooking ingredients. Beside the Domain is the *Te Aroha Motel*, at 108 Whitaker St (☎07/884 9417; ④) with functional, well-kept units. Campers should head 4km out on the road to Hamilton (SH26) to the delightful *Te Aroha Holiday Park*, 217 Stanley Rd (☎07/884 9567, fax 889 7910; tent sites $8, on-site vans ②, cabins & flats ③), set among well-established oak trees with a few free-range chickens strutting around and free use of bikes.

The best **restaurant** in town is the cosmopolitan *Café Banco*, 174 Whitaker St (no credit cards), which occupies a magenta-coloured former bank building and dishes up daytime meals mainly based on **Italian flatbreads** dressed with a range of ingredients and rounded off with good, strong coffee. In the evening these are supplemented by mains ($20–25) such as Cajun chicken with roasted vegetables and salad. If you'd rather dine within the sylvan confines of the Domain, try the *Domain House Restaurant*, where lunch and dinner is served in a lovely 1906 colonial building with broad verandas; dishes such as chicken breast filled with camembert on fettuccine and pork fillets on wild rice with prune and red wine sauce go for $20–25. The low-key *Mokena Restaurant*, in a rambling old wooden hotel at 6 Church St (☎07/884 8038; licensed), is a big hit with locals, offering evening **smorgasbords** (Fri–Sun from 6pm; $22; book ahead) of fresh, home-cooked fare.

The Coromandel Peninsula

A long, broad thumb jutting out between Auckland and the Pacific Ocean, the **Coromandel Peninsula** is a rugged region of scenic splendour, fringed with beautiful surf and swimming beaches that bask in a balmy climate. The forested mountainous interior is sparsely populated and a haven for tramping and horse trekking, while the northern section of the peninsula is a world apart – a virtually uninhabited, craggy landscape of long-deserted dairy farms reverting to bush, traced by a three-hour **coastal track**. The two coasts are starkly different: on the **west** coast, cliffs drop sharply to the sea; while the gentler **east** coast harbours sweeping white-sand beaches and sheltered coves ripe for exploration. The wild character of the west has protected it, leaving it relatively untouched, but the east is marred by pockets of over-development. The whole region is distinguished by the **pohutukawa** trees that line the west coast, erupting in a blaze of rich red from mid-November to December, and a **rock** of a gorgeous deep-rose colour, commonly known as **Coromandel Pink** and most noticeable on exposed bluffs.

Over the last few decades, the wonderful juxtaposition of bush, hills and beaches, along with low property prices as gold towns have declined, has exerted a powerful effect on hippies, **artists** and New Agers. Keep your eyes peeled and you'll spot folk eking out a living from the land, running holistic healing centres and holding quasi-religious retreats. Less vigilance is required to find painters, potters and craftspeople, many of them very good, often hawking the fruit of their labours from their homes and studios. The free and widely available *Coromandel Craft Trail* leaflet details thirty-odd mostly rural craft outlets all over the peninsula, selling items ranging from silk flowers to bronze and concrete sculpture. Unsurprisingly, the evil weed is also prevalent, and it won't be long before you'll meet someone passing around a jazz cigarette. This all adds up to large scale support of the Green Party, and sure enough, at the end of 1999, the Coromandel's Jeanette Fitzsimmons became New Zealand's first elected **Green MP**.

Notwithstanding the bohemian flavour and a stack of scenic splendour, there's not a hell of a lot to do here, though it's easy to spend a few days exploring. Prime areas include the forested **Kauaeranga Valley** behind Thames; the east coast's **Mercury Bay**, which bags some of the best coves and sandy beaches, including Hot Water Beach, the **Cathedral Cove Marine Reserve**, and the **Mercury Islands**, where you can snorkel, dive or swim with dolphins in crystal-clear water; and the **Coromandel Walkway** at the northernmost point. For a change of pace, take a ride on the narrow-gauge **Driving Creek Railway**, near Coromandel township. Cultural pursuits are limited to an excellent **bone-carving** course in Whitianga and historical displays of the region's **gold-mining history** in museums on the west coast. The peninsula's thin spread of people only sporadically coalesces into the peninsula's few small towns scattered along each coast, chiefly **Thames**, the southern gateway from Auckland and rich in gold-mining history, and the smaller **Coromandel township** on the west coast; **Whitianga**, on Mercury Bay, and the surfie hangout of **Whangamata** on the east. The southern limit of the peninsula is **Waihi**, site of a massive opencast gold mine, where huge quantities of gold-bearing quartz are still extracted. Just a few kilometres further east are the Pacific Ocean surf and golden sands of the popular **Waihi Beach**.

Along the peninsula's spine runs the craggy **Coromandel Range**, sculpted millions of years ago by volcanic activity into a jagged and contorted skyline, since clothed in dense rainforest. To Maori, the range represents a canoe, with **Mount Moehau**, at the peninsula's northern tip, as its prow, and Mount Te Aroha (see p.330) in the south, bordering the Hauraki Plains, as its sternpost. The **summit** area of Mount Moehau is

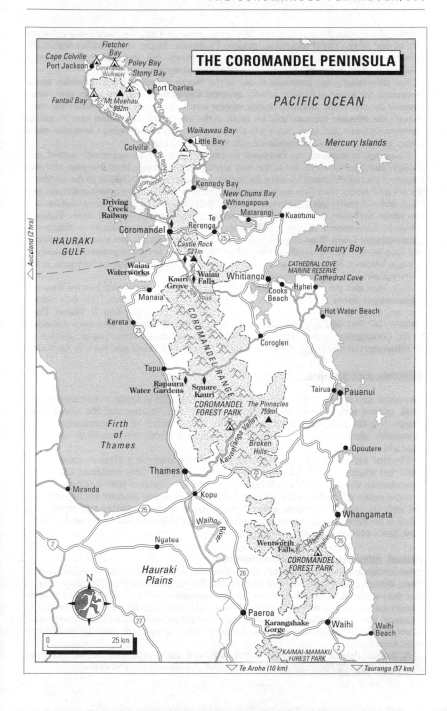

THE COROMANDEL PENINSULA

PACIFIC OCEAN

Cape Colville
Port Jackson
Fletcher Bay
Coromandel Walkway
Poley Bay
Stony Bay
Port Charles
Fantail Bay
Mt Moehau 892m
Port Jackson Rd

Waikawau Bay
Little Bay
Colville
Mercury Islands

Kennedy Bay
New Chums Bay
Whangapoua
Matarangi
Kuaotunu

Driving Creek Railway
Te Rerenga

Coromandel

HAURAKI GULF

Castle Rock 521m

Mercury Bay

Waiau Waterworks
Kauri Grove
Waiau Falls
Whitianga
CATHEDRAL COVE MARINE RESERVE
Cathedral Cove

Manaia
Cooks Beach
Hahei

Kereta
Hot Water Beach

COROMANDEL RANGE

Coroglen

Tapu

Rapaura Water Gardens
Square Kauri
COROMANDEL FOREST PARK
The Pinnacles 759m

Tairua
Pauanui

Firth of Thames

Kauaeranga Valley
Broken Hills

Opoutere

Thames

Miranda

Kopu

Whangamata

Waihou River

Ngatea

Hauraki Plains

Wentworth Falls
COROMANDEL FOREST PARK

N

Paeroa
Karangahake Gorge
Waihi
Waihi Beach

KAIMAI-MAMAKU FOREST PARK

0   25 km

Auckland (2 hrs)

Te Aroha (10 km)   Tauranga (57 km)

sacred Maori-owned land, the legendary burial place of Tama Te Kapua, the commander of one of the Great Migration canoes, *Te Arawa*. Many of the **walks** within the
mountain range are badly maintained and overgrown, but there are excellent ones
nearer the coast, a mix of bush and coastal tracks of varying length.

Not surprisingly, the peninsula is one of the North Island's principal holiday spots,
becoming the scene of frenetic activity **around Christmas**, but thankfully more manageable the rest of the summer. During **winter** much of the peninsula is deserted, even
though the **climate** remains mild for most of the year. The pleasantest time to visit is
between October and April, but try to avoid the two weeks following Christmas when
it can be hard to find accommodation – or book well ahead.

It's easiest to negotiate the Peninsula by **car**. The main roads are mostly sealed, and
though many to the more out of the way stretches are gravel, very few pose any real
danger if you take it steadily – even the infamous roads beyond Colville to the northern
tip are a lot better than they once were. **Bus** travel is a little more problematic and limiting, but still pretty good. Timetables all but dictate that you cover the peninsula in a
clockwise direction, with InterCity providing a regular loop service from Thames,
north to Coromandel, across to Whitianga and back down and across to Thames: a
Coromandel Loop Pass costs $47; the fare from Auckland to Rotorua, incorporating
the loop service is $89. Go Kiwi (☎07/866 0336) offer a very competitive door-to-door
service between Whitianga, Tairua, Thames and Auckland running to Auckland in the
morning and back in the afternoon.

You could also get to the Coromandel from Auckland using Pakatoa Ferries, who run
a **passenger ferry** from downtown Auckland to Coromandel town. The only reason
you are likely to want to fly to the peninsula is as part of the **Top 3 Travel Pass**
(☎0800/767 786; $235), which allows you to make a cost effective loop from Auckland
to the Coromandel by bus, a flight from Whitianga to Great Barrier Island, another on
to Whangarei in Northland, then a bus up to the Bay of Islands and back to Auckland.

Thames and around

The small and rather dull former gold town of **THAMES** is home to just seven thousand, packed into a coastal strip between the Firth of Thames and the Coromandel
Range. It is the peninsula's main service town with a variety of accommodation, a few
reasonable places to eat and transport connections for both the immediate surroundings and the rest of the peninsula.

The first big discovery of gold-bearing quartz was made in a Thames creek bed in
1867, but mining activity tailed off during the 1880s, and little remained after 1913.
Nonetheless, the legacy of the **mining** heyday forms the basis of town's attractions, and
you can easily spend half a day visiting them and wandering backstreets liberally dotted with the erstwhile owners' grand homes. Even more interesting and within easy
reach is the **Kauaeranga Valley**, a popular centre for visitors to the Coromandel Forest
Park that's often busy at weekends.

Arrival, information and accommodation

InterCity **buses**, and associate services to Coromandel and Whitianga, drop off all over
town, including outside the **visitor centre**, 206 Pollen St (Mon–Fri 8.30am–5pm, Sat &
Sun 9am–4pm; ☎07/868 7284, fax 868 7584, *thames@ihug.co.nz*), which has stacks of literature on the town and the Coromandel Peninsula, and deals with accommodation and
transport bookings. Pollen Street is the main shopping thoroughfare and home to what
is left of Thames' traditional gold-era hotels: few places are more than fifteen minutes'
walk from here.

Accommodation in Thames is rather scattered, most of it lying outside the town
centre, though it's generally of a good standard and there's plenty of choice.

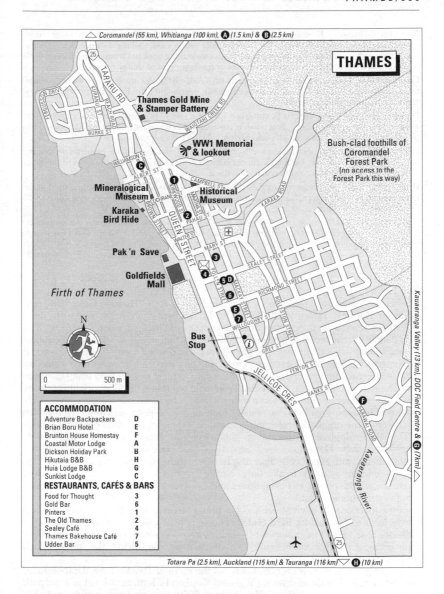

Coromandel (55 km), Whitianga (100 km), **Ⓐ** (1.5 km) & **Ⓑ** (2.5 km)

THAMES

Thames Gold Mine
& Stamper Battery

WW1 Memorial
& lookout

Bush-clad foothills of
Coromandel
Forest Park
(no access to the
Forest Park this way)

Mineralogical
Museum

Historical
Museum

Karaka
Bird Hide

Pak 'n Save

Goldfields
Mall

Firth of Thames

Bus
Stop

N

0   500 m

Kauaeranga Valley (13 km), DOC Field Centre & **Ⓖ** (7km)

ACCOMMODATION

Adventure Backpackers	D
Brian Boru Hotel	E
Brunton House Homestay	F
Coastal Motor Lodge	A
Dickson Holiday Park	B
Hikutaia B&B	H
Huia Lodge B&B	G
Sunkist Lodge	C

RESTAURANTS, CAFÉS & BARS

Food for Thought	3
Gold Bar	6
Pinters	1
The Old Thames	2
Sealey Café	4
Thames Bakehouse Café	7
Udder Bar	5

Totara Pa (2.5 km), Auckland (115 km) & Tauranga (116 km) **Ⓗ** (10 km)

Adventure Backpackers Coromandel (ABC), 476 Pollen St (☎ & fax 07/868 6200). Good clean low-cost hostel in the centre of town with 4–8 bed dorms and TV-equipped en-suite doubles all above the *Udder Bar* and *Krazy Cow* nightclub. Dorms ①, rooms ②.

Brian Boru Hotel, cnr Pollen St & Richmond St (☎07/868 6523, fax 868 9760, *brian.boru@xtra.co.nz*). Impressive 1868 building with cheap and tolerable rooms, some done in Victorian decor and most sharing facilities. A modern building alongside has motel-style units and there are murder-mystery weekends held half a dozen times through the year. Rooms ③, units ⑤.

Brunton House Homestay, 210 Parawai Rd (☎07/868 5160, fax 868 5160, *bruntonhouse@xtra.co.nz*). A fine, large Victorian villa within easy walking distance of the centre. Three rooms share one guest bathroom and there's a swimming pool and tennis court. Dinner ($25) is also available by arrangement; room rates are at the lower end of this price code. ⑤.

Coastal Motor Lodge, on SH25, 2.5km north (☎07/868 6843). A complex of pleasant "cottage" units and modern A-frame chalets (all self-contained), overlooking the Firth. Predictably, the best views are from the pricier chalets. ⑥.

Dickson Holiday Park, Victoria St (☎07/868 7308, fax 868 7319). Large, well-run campsite and associate YHA in a pretty valley 3.5km north of the centre. Excellent facilities include a pool and bus pick-up from Thames. Tent sites $10, backpacker cabins ①, flats & units ②–③.

Hikutaia B&B, on SH26, about 10km south (☎07/862 4710). Excellent-value, grand yet welcoming old country house with four big double rooms (shared facilities) near the bottom end of this price code. Full cooked breakfast; swimming pool in the grounds. ④.

Huia Lodge B&B, 589 Kauaeranga Valley Rd (☎ & fax 07/868 6557). Peaceful setting right in the valley, amid bush and pasture, 8km from town. Two modern en-suite units, dinner available for $20. Free transport from Thames. ④.

Sunkist Lodge, 506 Brown St (☎07/868 8808 & 0800/767 786, *sunkist@xtra.co.nz*). An atmospheric backpacker hostel in a historic building; dorms hold 4–10 bunks, and there are also a few double rooms. Facilities include a well-equipped kitchen, sun deck and garden, and baggage storage; and the InterCity bus stops outside. The owner is a mine of information on both the Coromandel Peninsula and Great Barrier Island. Dorms ①, rooms ②.

The Town

The best introduction to the town's gold-mining past is at the **Thames Gold Mine and Stamper Battery**, Tararu Road (daily: Oct–March 8am–6pm; April–Sept 10am–4pm; $6), where you join an informative tour through the old battery: machines are fired up for a couple of minutes, which is ample considering that deafness was an occupational hazard among battery workers. The place is noisy and smelly, with the diesel-powered machinery crushing the quartz and transferring tiny particles by water onto a shaking table, where the minerals are separated according to their weight, gold being the heaviest. The tour continues through a claustrophobic old mine, the shaft originally cut by hand and just high enough to clear a miner's head. Life down the mine is convincingly portrayed through sound effects, realistic-looking mannequins, anecdotes from guides all related to the original Cornish miners, and an extensive historical photo museum.

The **Mineralogical Museum**, on the corner of Brown and Cochrane streets (Oct–March daily 11am–4pm; April–Sept Tues–Sun 11am–3pm; $2.50), continues the mining theme with a vast collection of quartz, crystals, rocks and fossils displayed in cases – one for geology freaks only. Neither is the Victoriana-stuffed **Historical Museum**, on the corner of Pollen Street and Cochrane Street (daily 1–4pm; $2), anything to write home about.

At the junction of Brown Street and Cochrane Street, a boardwalk across the mangroves leads to the **Karaka Bird Hide**: a couple of hours either side of high tide is the optimum time to spot migratory birds such as knots, godwits, shags and terns, especially between October and February. An information board details the species which frequent the mangroves.

You can get a good view over the town and the Firth of Thames from the **lookout** at the war memorial; walk or drive up Waiotahi Road and Monument Road to a car park just below the monument, then follow a short flight of stone steps leading up to the viewpoint.

Kauaeranga Valley

The steep-sided **Kauaeranga Valley**, to the east of town, stretches towards the spine of the Coromandel Peninsula, a jagged landscape of bluffs and gorges topped by **The Pinnacles** (759m), with stupendous views to both coasts across native forest studded

KAUAERANGA WALKS

The Kauaeranga Valley is blessed with a wonderful range of easily accessible tramps ranging from a twenty-minute stroll to a satisfying two-day circuit with a night spent at the large and relatively plush **Pinnacles Hut** (Category 1; 80 bunks; $15; advance booking essential ☎07/867 9080). There are also a couple of remote and very basic DOC **campsites**: one near the Pinnacles Hut and another at Billygoat Basin (both $7.50). The *Kauaeranga Kauri Trail* DOC leaflet ($1) covers the basics, though you might prefer the detail provided by the 1:50,000 Thames topo map ($12): both are available from the DOC office and the Thames visitor centre.

Billygoat Landing (1.5km return; 20–30min). The shortest walk in the valley, giving excellent views of the 180-metre Billygoat Falls.

Edwards Lookout (1km loop; 40min–1hr). A fine viewpoint over manuka-towai forest from a rocky saddle reached by a track starting 5km beyond the DOC office.

Pinnacles Circuit (14km loop; 2 days). This is the way to really get to grips with the region, following the **Kauaeranga Kauri Trail** and overnighting in the *Pinnacles Hut* (see above) about a third of the way along. It is really just a day and a half, starting at the road end and spending the first 2–3hr following Webb Creek up to *Pinnacles Hut* and the well-restored Dancing Camp kauri dam. From the hut there is a steep 50min climb to The Pinnacles themselves. The second day is longer (7–8hr) and passes the sad remnants of a couple of kauri dams, an old logging camp and some more fine viewpoints. A there-and-back trip to the Pinnacles can be done in 6–7hr.

Short Trestles Walk (5km return; 2hr). The most satisfying walk if you've only got a couple of hours, climbing up above the Atuatumoe (Billygoat) Stream to the Short Trestles, one of the last remnants of an old logging tramway. Return the same way, and see if you can find a path down to the stream and a good swimming hole a couple of hundred metres down from the lowermost trestle.

Wainora Track (6km return; 2–3hr). Moderate, well formed track to a couple of large kauri – pretty much the only ones left standing hereabouts – that starts from the Wainora campground, 6km beyond the DOC office.

with original giants such as rata, rimu and the occasional kauri. All this is reached along a scenic and mostly-tarmacked road snaking beside the river, providing access to some of the finest walks in the Coromandel Range, and the only backcountry DOC hut on the entire peninsula. The Backcountry Trekking **shuttle bus** (☎07/868 7597; $20 return) runs on demand from Thames; or you can **drive** by heading out of the southern end of Thames, along Parawai Road, which becomes Kauaeranga Road. Thirteen kilometres along you reach the **DOC office** (☎07/867 9080, fax 867 9095; daily 8am–4pm), where you can stock up on maps, buy hut tickets and examine displays on early kauri logging in the valley. From here a loop track (500m; 10min) leads to a working **scale model** of a kauri driving dam, the type once used extensively in this forest. Along the eight unsealed kilometres beyond the DOC office to the road-end, an assortment of tracks (see box above) lead off into the bush that's full of "pole stands" of young kauri that have grown since the area was logged a century back: only a handful in each stand will reach maturity. Most of the hikes head into the bush near one of the half-dozen simple roadside **campsites** ($5; toilets and water) dotted the length of the stretch.

Eating and entertainment

Central Thames is packed with inexpensive but pleasant places to **eat** (most of them open daily), while a couple of friendly **bars** provide musical entertainment over the weekends, but that's as far as the nightlife goes.

Food for Thought, 574 Pollen St. Serving the tastiest lunches in town at modest prices, this small café specializes in pastries, lasagne, cakes and *pastizzi* (Lebanese pies), much of it vegetarian; and good coffee too. Mon–Fri 7.30am–5pm.

Gold Bar Ale House & Eatery, 404 Pollen St. The place in town for a night out. There's a good selection of wine, plus an all-day menu of snacks, salads and pasta for under $10, and straightforward steak and chicken dinners for about $20. Occasional live jazz, blues or rock on Fri & Sat evenings.

The Old Thames, cnr Pollen St & Pahau St. Licensed restaurant popular among families for its broad range of moderately priced seafood, steaks, pizzas and generous desserts. Daily from 5pm.

Pinters, 719 Pollen St (☎07/868 9178). Popular, friendly and airy, with eclectic food and a garden bar. The menu ranges from light snacks to reasonably priced dinners. Lunch & dinner daily; book ahead for Sun brunch; DJ or live music Fri & Sat nights.

Sealey Café, 109 Sealey St. Laid-back place in an attractive, high-ceilinged house with a pleasant courtyard. Light lunches of burgers and big sandwiches go for under $10, and dinner mains ($20–25) revolve around generous helpings of steak, meat and fish. Daily from 11am; licensed & BYO.

Thames Bakehouse Café, 326 Pollen St. Very traditional daytime tearooms serving pies, toasted sandwiches, burgers and cakes at low prices. Mon–Fri 7am–4.30pm, Sat & Sun 7am–3.30pm.

Udder Bar, 476 Pollen St. Sparsely furnished bar with a value-for-money line in bar meals and a lively clientele who dutifully troop through to the *Krazy Cow* nightclub (in the same building) on Fri & Sat nights.

Listings

Airlines Air Coromandel (☎07/866 4016) fly twice daily between Auckland and Whitianga, calling at Thames, Coromandel town, Pauanui and Matarangi, plus Great Barrier Island and Tauranga.

Automobile Association Inside the tourist office, 206 Pollen St (☎07/868 9375).

Banks All major banks have branches along Pollen St, with ATMs.

Bike rental and repairs Paki Paki Bike Shop, in the Goldfields Mall (☎07/868 8311), will supply plenty of advice about cycling on the peninsula and sometimes have bikes for rent at reasonable rates.

Buses InterCity (☎09/913 6100) and various local partner companies (reached through the same number) link Thames with Auckland, Tauranga, Hamilton, Coromandel town, Whangamata and Whitianga.

Car rental The Rental Car Centre, 503 Queen St (☎07/868 8838 & 0800/736 822, *thames @therentalcarcentre.co.nz*) allow their budget cars onto the peninsula's roughest roads.

Medical treatment Thames Hospital, Mackay St (☎07/868 6550); Thames Medical Centre, 817 Rolleston St (☎07/868 9444).

Police 730 Queen St (☎07/868 6040).

Post office The post office at 545 Pollen St, between Sealey St & Mary St (☎07/868 7850) has poste restante facilities.

Swimming Thames Pool, cnr Pollen St & Grey St (☎07/868 8441).

Taxis Thames Gold Cabs (☎07/868 6037).

North to Coromandel

From Thames, SH25 snakes 58km north to Coromandel Town tracing the grey rocky shoreline of the **"Pohutukawa Coast"** past a series of tiny, sandy bays, most with little more than a few houses and maybe a campsite. Hills and sand-coloured cliffs rise dramatically from the roadside for the first 19km to **TAPU**, where the **Tapu–Coroglen Road** peels off to the Coromandel's east coast. It is a wonderfully scenic 28km run of narrow, unsealed but manageable driving leaving behind the marginal farmland on the coast and climbing over the peninsula's mountainous spine. Even if you aren't tackling the traverse, it is worth making a detour 6.5km along the road (and just beyond the end of the tarmac), to **Rapaura Water Gardens** (daily 10am–5pm; $7), a cleverly landscaped "wilderness" of bush and blooms, punctuated by lily ponds and a trickling stream. Hidden away against a backdrop of bush and threaded by numerous paths, the gardens fully tap into the Coromandel ethos by posting philosophical messages urging you to stop and think awhile, and it's easy enough to spend half a day doing just that – though you could get around most of the gardens in an hour. One of the highlights is a lovely three-tiered waterfall, reached by a well-kept track from the car park at the entrance (15min); picnicking is confined to the car parking area (which has plenty of trees, grass and space away from the cars), and a broad grassland area around a large pond, on the way to the waterfall. The road continues 3km on to the (easily missed) "square kauri" signpost near the road's summit, opposite a rough lay-by and just before a small bridge. Steep steps through bush (175m; 10min) lead to this giant of a tree (1200 years old, just over 41m high and 9m wide), whose unusual, angular shape saved it from loggers. From here it's another rough and windy 19km **across the peninsula** to Coroglen, linking with the main road between Whitianga and Whangamata, or 9.5km back to Tapu and the continuation of SH25 north.

Back on SH25 the road lurches inland soon after Kereta (about 12km north of Tapu), snaking over hills to the roadside **Manaia-Kereta Lookout** (206m), which has great views of the northern peninsula, the majestic Moehau Range and Coromandel Harbour. Beyond, Great Barrier Island may be visible on a clear day – a giant block of rock with vertical cliffs rising from the sea. Ducking and diving in and out from the rocky shoreline and the blue-green vistas of the Firth of Thames, SH25 continues for 20km to the turn-off to **309 Road**, 3km south of Coromandel, which cuts **across to Whitianga** by way of a few roadside attractions, all within 8km of Coromandel (see "East to Whitianga", p.343).

Coromandel Town

The northernmost town of any substance is the pretty, spruce little **COROMANDEL**, 58km north of Thames, huddling beneath high, craggy hills at the head of Coromandel Harbour, and known to many visitors simply as the jumping-off point for the **Coromandel Walkway** (see box on p.342), 57km away at the peninsula's northern tip. It's worth taking time, though, to soak up the atmosphere of this old gold town and ride its **scenic railway** into the local hills; or use it as a base from which to explore the jagged landscape of the **northern peninsula**, either on your own or as part of a guided trip.

The town (and peninsula) took its name from the geographically dissimilar Coromandel Coast, south of Madras in India; an anomaly which stems from the visit here of a British Admiralty supply ship of that name which called into the harbour in 1820 to obtain kauri spars and masts and to extend Captain Cook's brief survey of the Hauraki Gulf.

A more mercenary European invasion was precipitated by the 1852 discovery of **gold**, near Driving Creek, in the northern part of town, but modern visitors will be more interested in the discovery of a couple of **supermarkets** and petrol stations, a BNZ bank, a cluster of **cafés** and a broad range of **accommodation**.

Moving on you've a choice of striking **east to Whitianga**, via the continuation of SH25 (see p.344) past the deserted beaches of Whangapoua and Kuaotunu, or taking the more rugged 309 Road (see p.343).

Arrival, information and transport

The combined **visitor centre** and **DOC office**, 355 Kapanga Rd (Nov–March daily 9am–5pm; April–Oct Mon–Fri 9am–5pm, Sat & Sun 11am–3pm; ☎07/866 8598, fax 866 7285, *coroinfo@ihug.co.nz*), is at the northern end of town, just over the bridge. Daily InterCity **buses** pull into the car park opposite, which is used by Turley Murphy

(☎07/884 8208) running daily direct to Thames. There's also a service to Whitianga from Coromandel Bus Services (☎ & fax 07/866 8045), who also offer reasonably priced **guided trips** to local points of interest, or will drop you at your chosen destination; see box on p.342 for details of transport to the start of the Coromandel Walkway at Fletcher Bay. Pakatoa Ferries (☎09/379 0066; $32 one way, bikes $10) run a **passenger ferry** from downtown Auckland to Hannaford's Point Wharf, 10km south of Coromandel, from where a bus brings you into town. The only **car rental** firm in town is Rent-a-Dent, 5 Kapanga Rd (☎07/866 8626; around $36 a day, plus 20¢ per km), which also allows its cars onto the unsealed roads north of Colville; if the office is closed, enquire at the *Pepper Tree Restaurant* next door.

Accommodation

For a small place, Coromandel offers a good range of **places to stay**, from a campsite in the town centre through to a luxurious lodge in an idyllic setting a few kilometres north. Most are within easy walking distance of the town centre.

Buffalo Lodge, Buffalo Rd, signposted north of town past the Gold Stamper Battery (☎ & fax 07/866 8960, *www.buffalolodge.co.nz*). Luxurious, award-winning accommodation in an architect-designed house set high up in the bush, with superb views across the Hauraki Gulf. Run by two Swiss artists, the decor in the three en-suite double rooms is modern and elegant; two of them have private decks. Superb dinners are offered to guests for $85 a head. Reserve well in advance; closed May–Sept. ⑨.

Celadon House Motel & B&B, Alfred St, about 1km north of town (☎ & fax 07/866 8058, *wilsonmc@wave.co.nz*). This charming self-contained A-frame on a bush-clad hillside, with town and harbour views, operates as a motel. There are two double rooms and a couple of two-bed bunkrooms plus a separate B&B section that has two en-suite rooms with sun decks. Motel ⑤, B&B ⑤.

Coromandel Colonial Cottages, 1737 Rings Rd, 1.5km north of town (☎ & fax 07/866 8857, *coromandel_colonial_cottages@xtra.co.nz*). Tranquil, luxury cottages sleeping 2–6. Excellent facilities include a swimming pool and BBQ area. Good value for money. ⑤.

Coromandel Town Backpackers, 732 Rings Rd (☎07/866 8327). Modern, spic and span hostel close to the centre of town with budget bunks and some clean and attractive rooms. Bikes can be rented for $10 a day. Dorms ①, rooms ②.

Jacaranda Lodge, 3km south on SH25 (☎ & fax 07/866 8002, *jacarandacoromandel@xtra.co.nz*). A modern house in farmland offering B&B in extremely comfortable and spacious rooms. Breakfasts are made from organic ingredients, dinner is available on request ($30), and the single room rate makes it good value for lone travellers. ⑤.

Long Bay Motor Camp, 3200 Long Bay Rd, 3km west of town (☎07/866 8720). Attractive beach-front campground with safe swimming and good facilities including kayak, dinghy and fishing tackle rental plus some basic new units, and some fridge- and microwave-equipped cabins which sleep up to six. Additional tent sites ($8) are located at the secluded Tucks Bay, a 1.5km drive through the bush or a five-minute walk around the headland. Tent sites $9, units ②, cabins ③.

Rose Cottage B&B, Pagitt St (☎07/866 7047). Good value and fairly central place opposite the Historical Museum. Stay in the attractive, old kauri homestead (shared bathroom facilities) or in an en-suite double in a pleasant separate building. ③.

Tidewater Tourist Park, 270 Tiki Rd (☎07/866 8888, fax 866 7231). The most central campsite in town with barbecue, sauna and $10 a day bike rental, all set in large, leafy grounds by the harbour. Also operates as an associate YHA. Tent sites $9, backpacker dorms ①, cabins, flats & units ②–⑤.

Tui Lodge, 600 Whangapoua Rd, just off SH25 (☎07/866 8237). A ten-minute walk south of town (and right on the InterCity bus route), this is the best-value backpackers in town. Set in a relaxed, rambling house by an orchard, perks include free linen, laundry, tea and coffee, fruit (in season), and use of bikes. Tent sites $8, dorms ①, chalet & rooms ②.

The Whitehouse Backpackers, cnr Rings Rd & Frederick St, 1km north of visitor centre (☎07/866 8468, *whitehos@wave.co.nz*). Small and relaxed hostel in an attractive white house in bushland on the edge of town. Internet access available. Tent sites $7, dorms ①, rooms ②.

The Town and around

The town centre, such as it is, spreads along the main road, with a few old buildings left from gold-mining days. From the south, SH25 becomes Tiki Road and then splits into two: to the left is Wharf Road, which skirts the harbour; to the right you immediately enter the heart of the town, on Kapanga Road, lined with shops and cafés. A couple of blocks further on, it becomes Rings Road, before heading northwards out of town as Colville Road.

About 300m north of the visitor centre is the small **Coromandel Historical Museum**, at 841 Rings Rd (Oct–March daily 10am–4pm; April–Sept Sat & Sun only 1–4pm; $2). Based in the old School of Mines (1898), this is a mishmash of domestic items and mining memorabilia, including a number of evocative black-and-white photographs from early mining days.

The main attraction in the immediate vicinity is **Driving Creek Railway**, Driving Creek Road, 3.5km north of town (book ahead on ☎07/866 8703; daily 10am & 2pm, extra trains at noon & 4pm during holidays; 1hr return; $12). Built mostly by hand over twenty years, this is the country's only narrow-gauge hill railway, the brainchild of Barry Brickell, an eccentric local potter and rail enthusiast who wanted access into the clay-bearing hills. Wood is still brought down to fire the kilns, though the railway is now mainly used to carry visitors on a delightfully shambolic trip through bush where 13,000 native saplings have been planted over the last 25 years. The track is only 381mm wide and carries specially designed, articulated diesel trains, which climb 120m over a distance of about 3km. The rewards of this leisurely, commentated trip are spectacular views and extraordinary feats of engineering, including a series of viaducts, spirals and tunnels, a zigzag section, and a unique steel "double-decker" viaduct straddling a deep ravine, as well as increasingly elaborate embankments and cuttings, initially built of wine and beer bottles and later lined with inventive murals. At the end of the line is a lookout point with panoramic views of Coromandel town, over the Hauraki Gulf and Waiheke Island, and across the Firth of Thames to the Hunua Ranges. The journey starts and ends at the **workshops**, kilns and sheds, where you can see various types of pottery: stoneware and earthenware items for the home and garden, and sculptures made from terracotta that has been wood-fired to produce a variety of subtle colours.

Around 1.5km north is the turn-off to the **Gold Stamper Battery**, another 300m or so along Buffalo Road (Oct–Dec Thurs–Mon 10am–4pm; Jan–March daily 10am–5pm; guided tour $5), where the 100-year-old machinery is operated briefly to demonstrate the processing of gold. Outside is a pleasant garden scattered with old bits of machinery and picnic tables by a stream where, for an extra $5, you can try your hand at gold panning.

Eating and entertainment

For a small town, Coromandel is surprisingly well endowed with decent places to eat, with several good **cafés** touting for your business and a couple of fancier restaurants. Evening **entertainment** is restricted to live bands (summer weekends only) at the *Pepper Tree* bar.

Castle Rock Eatery, 22a Wharf Rd, near cnr Tiki Rd. Eat-in or take-out pizzeria with a fair selection of tasty gourmet pizzas as well as meat and veggie kebabs. Licensed and BYO.

Coromandel Café, 36 Kapanga Rd, opposite the *Pepper Tree*. Cheap snacky place, pretty standard but pleasant enough. Dec–March daily 8am–8pm, rest of year closed weekends.

Craft Café, cnr Tiki Rd & Kapanga Rd. Cheerful, daytime, bare-boards café usually hung with local artworks and serving panini, lasagne, salads, cakes and good coffee either inside or in the courtyard. Internet access too.

Pepper Tree, 31 Kapanga Rd. A very popular bar and restaurant, with main courses for $20–25 and an all-day snack menu ($10 or less); eat indoors or on the veranda. Open daily; live bands on weekend nights in summer.

The Success Café, 102 Kapanga Rd. An intimate place with smart white tablecloths and covered outdoor dining at the back. Plenty of seafood and steak, mostly around the $22 mark. Open all day; licensed & BYO.

Top Pub, *Coromandel Hotel*, 611 Kapanga Rd, cnr Te Tiki St. An evening bistro, known for its seafood, but also serving steaks and other meat dishes as a set three-course meal for under $20. Closed Sun in winter (May–Sept).

North to Fletcher Bay and Port Charles

The landscape **north of Coromandel** is even more rugged than the rest of the peninsula, its green hills dropping down to seemingly endless beaches, clean blue sea and white surf. The tourist authorities have dubbed the area the **Pohutukawa Cape**, and this title is justified – the dirt roads are lined with ancient pohutukawa trees, creating a blaze of red blooms from early November until just after Christmas. There are **few facilities** up here: one café and a couple of places to stay pretty much wraps it up – so replenish your supplies in Coromandel town. As elsewhere on the peninsula, signs have sprung up to deter freelance **camping** outside the few commercial sites between Coromandel and Colville. The Department of Conservation have responded by opening five waterside campsites around the northern peninsula, all marked on the Coromandel map (see p.333). For the two weeks after Christmas the campsites will be full, but for most of the rest of the year you'll have this unspoilt area to yourself.

From Coromandel, the road snakes for some 20km along the coast, then cuts inland to the tiny settlement of **COLVILLE**, little more than a post office, a petrol pump and a general store set in a quiet green valley that greatly appealed to counter-culture aspirants in the 1970s. The spirit of those times lives on in the distinctly bohemian BYO *Coromandel Caff*, that's great for breakfast, lunch or just to stock up on food for the Coromandel Walkway (see box below) and to check on the state of the road north of Port Jackson. On summer weekends they also do evening meals; currently burgers on Friday, pizza on Saturday and seafood on Sunday. If you fancy **staying** up this way, you can't go far wrong with *Colville Farm*, Main Road, 1.5km south of Colville (☎ & fax 07/866 6820; tents $5–9, dorms ①, rooms ②, bush lodge ③, house ④), a very relaxing

---

THE COROMANDEL WALKWAY AND CYCLE ROUTE

Other than a bit of swimming, fishing or lolling around on the beaches, the only activity in the far north of the peninsula is to hike from Fletcher Bay to Stony Bay along the **Coromandel Walkway** (7km; 3hr one way), a gentle and clearly route-marked path with lovely sea views. The walk starts at the far end of the beach in Fletcher Bay and heads off into a no-man's-land, first following gentle coastal hills that alternate between pasture and bush, then giving way to wilder terrain as you head further south past a series of tiny bays. Several hilltop **vantage points** punctuate the walk, yielding spectacular vistas of the coast and Pacific Ocean beyond, before the track dips once more into pockets of dense bush. From the pretty, rocky inlet of **Poley Bay** a steep, short climb out cuts through regenerating bush to **Stony Bay**, a sweep of pebbles with a bridge across an estuary and safe swimming.

Mountain bikers can make a complete circuit of the northern peninsula by going off-road from Fletcher Bay to Stony Bay using a longer route further inland which starts and finishes at the same points as the walkway.

Coromandel Bus Services (☎07/866 8045) operate daily minibus **coastal walkway tours** ($60) from Coromandel town to Fletcher Bay. Here you can either stay on the bus for the ride or hike the Coromandel Walkway to Stony Bay where they meet you with a cup of tea and drive you back to town.

backpackers on a sheep and cattle farm with the opportunity to go hiking, horse trekking or hand-milk a cow. Accommodation ranges from bush and pasture campsites, to backpacker dorms in a piano-equipped cottage, a bush lodge, and a self-contained house with TV and fabulous views. To be closer to the beach, try *Colville Bay Lodge Motel*, Wharf Road (☎ & fax 07/866 6814; tents $8, units ④), the Coromandel's northernmost motel with units and campsites all overlooking Colville Bay.

Beyond **Colville** the road is unsealed, and becomes narrower, rougher and dustier the further north you go, though there's really nothing difficult about driving up here. Most of all, it is best taken at a steady pace, all the better to fully appreciate the tiny bays flanked by shelves of volcanic grey rock. Three kilometres north of Colville the road splits, with the right fork heading east over the hills to Stony Bay and the southern end of the Coromandel Walkway (see box opposite). The left fork runs 35km north to Port Jackson and Fletcher Bay at the very tip of the peninsula, following the coast all the way. The scenery becomes even more dramatic as you go, particularly at the abandoned **granite wharf**, halfway along, where a small harbour was fashioned for loading rock from a nearby quarry. A couple of kilometres beyond, you'll find the diminutive and lovely *Fantail Bay Recreation Reserve* ($7), the first of the DOC **campsites** which come equipped with toilets and a water supply. The road then cuts briefly inland, over hills rising straight from the shore, to reach **PORT JACKSON**, just two houses and a one-kilometre sandy crescent of beach. It's safe for swimming and backed by a grassy DOC reserve, where you can **camp** ($7) with views across to Great Barrier and Little Barrier islands. From here the road deteriorates further for the final 7km to **FLETCHER BAY**, probably the best beach of all, its eastern end marking the start of the **Coromandel Walkway** (see box opposite). The beach is backed by yet another DOC **campsite** ($7), with flush toilets and cold showers; and there's also accommodation at the small and comfortable *Fletcher Bay Backpackers* (☎ & fax 07/866 6712, *js.lourie@xtra.co.nz*; ①) set 400m back from the beach up on a hill overlooking the bay.

Stony Bay, at the southern end of the Coromandel Walkway, is reached by two perilously twisty gravel roads – one across the Coromandel Range from Coromandel, the other traversing the Moehau Range from just beyond Colville. The latter runs 14km from Colville to the small holiday settlement of **Port Charles**, and a further 6km to Stony Bay, where there's another DOC campsite ($7), also with flush toilets and cold showers.

East to Whitianga

The drive east from Coromandel to Whitianga can be done in under an hour, but you could easily spend much of a day on either of two highly **scenic roads** which cross the mountains: the more direct, snaking, gravel **309 Road** (33km; no public transport) spends much of its time in the bush, while the main (and mostly sealed) **SH25** climbs through forested hills before switchbacking down to the coast, 46km away.

Coromandel to Whitianga: the 309 Road

From the junction with SH25, 3km south of Coromandel, the 309 Road twists 5km east to **Waiau Waterworks** (daily 9am–5pm; $6), a garden carved from the bush and liberally dotted with whimsical water-powered contraptions and contrivances. It is the product of ten years' work (so far) by one Chris Ogilvie, who is realising his lifelong passion to do "fun stuff with water". And it is a great success; quirky at every turn yet explained in enough detail to satisfy the more engineering minded. You are greeted with a waterwheel built from construction helmets, teapots and gumboots and continue through the gardens, occasionally coming across a static bicycle shooting a jet of water when you peddle or a raised waterway where you can play an elaborate form of pooh sticks. Perhaps the highlight is a huge clock powered by jets playing against a row of empty pop bottles arranged on a pendulum: apparently it keeps remarkably good time unless the wind blows the pendulum off kilter. Allow a couple of hours and bring a picnic, especially if you've got kids who'll appreciate the swimming hole and flying fox.

One hundred metres past the waterworks, an access road on the left climbs steeply for 3km to the trailhead for the track to **Castle Rock** (2km return; 40min–1hr 30min), the most easily accessible peak on the Coromandel Peninsula. It is a climb that gets progressively steeper towards the final tree-root claw onto the 521-metre summit of this old volcanic core, but your efforts are well rewarded by fantastic views to both coasts: the Whangapoua peninsula and the Mercury Islands on the east coast, and Coromandel and the Firth of Thames to the west.

A further 2.5km along the 309 Road, the **Waiau Falls** crash over a rockface into a pool below. They're not that impressive, but they are right next to the road and offer a gorgeous spot to cool off on a hot day. About a kilometre further on, a car park heralds the easy bush track to the magnificent **Kauri Grove** (1km return; 30min). Fortuitous gaps in the bush make this one of the best places in the country to really get a sense of the size of the kauri, and appreciate just how they stand head and shoulders above the rest of the forest trees: a boardwalk allows you to get face-to-bark with these delicate-rooted giants.

The road then tops out at the 306m saddle and descends towards Whitianga, passing the relaxing riverside **accommodation** at *Honey Cottage*, 9km beyond the Kauri Grove and 12km short of Whitianga (☎07/866 5151; tent sites $5, dorms ①).

Coromandel to Whitianga: SH25

From Coromandel town, **SH25** follows an attractive route through lush native forest, also plied by **buses** and passing a couple of isolated but pretty beachside settlements with campsites. About 14km from Coromandel is the 5-kilometre turn-off (where buses also stop) to the secluded village and beach of **WHANGAPOUA**, whose long stretch of white sand is lined by *baches* and a single general store/petrol station. At the end of the road is a pleasant walk to the idyllic sandy beach of **New Chums Bay** (4km return; 1hr): from the beach, cross the estuary and follow the bushline around the headland to a saddle; on the other side is New Chums Bay (accessible at low tide only). A basic but scenic **campsite**, *Whangapoua Beach Camping Ground* (tent sites $8), lies 300m along the left fork as you enter town. Continuing along SH25, about 34km from Coromandel, you drop down to the attractive seaside village of **KUAO-TUNU**, with a shady and well-equipped **campsite**, on Bluff Road (☎07/866 5172, fax 866 5163; tent sites $9, on-site vans & cabins ②–③, cottage ④). About 4km past Kuaotunu, on SH25, is Twin Oaks Riding Ranch, the base for extremely **scenic horse treks** (book ahead on ☎07/866 5388; daily 10am & 2pm, plus twilight trek at 6pm Nov–March; 2hr; $30), offering breathtaking views of Mercury Bay and the northern Coromandel; transport from Whitianga can also be arranged. From here, SH25 continues through farmland to Whitianga and the stunning expanse of Mercury Bay.

Whitianga and around

The attractive town of **WHITIANGA** clusters where the estuarine Whitianga Harbour meets the broad sweep of **Mercury Bay**. This huge bite out of the Coromandel coast was named by Captain Cook who stopped here in 1769 so that his party of scientists could observe Mercury pass across the face of the sun; the ostensible justification for his South Pacific peregrinations. Now a popular Kiwi summer-holiday destination, the population of about 3000 swells dramatically during January as vacationers flock to the town's **Buffalo Beach**, a long sweep of surf-pounded white sand.

Whitianga makes a good base from which to make a series of half-day and **day trips** to some wonderfully secluded spots, so allow a couple of days here. Just across the narrow harbour mouth and strung along Mercury Bay's eastern shore are several unusual beaches, reached by passenger ferry to **Ferry Landing,** from where you can catch a **bus** or strike out along scenic coastal tracks. The area is also served by roads branching off the southbound SH25, which loops around the deeply indented harbour. Two gems here are **Cathedral Cove**, a stunning geological formation, and **Hot Water Beach**, renowned for its natural hot-water springs bubbling beneath the sand. Bordering part of the eastern shore is **Cathedral Cove Marine Reserve**, whose protected waters are a great spot for snorkelling and scuba diving. In addition, **boat trips** to the outer reaches of Mercury Bay and the volcanically formed **Mercury Islands**, 25km offshore, explore pristine waters and shoreline – and search for bottlenose **dolphins** and **whales**. Whitianga is also one of the best places in New Zealand to try your hand at **bone carving**, creating your very own *tiki* in as little as half a day, while 10km north of town you can enjoy astounding views of the whole region on a **scenic horse trek** (see opposite).

Arrival, information and transport

InterCity and Go Kiwi **buses** drop off at accommodation around town and outside the **visitor centre** at the corner of Albert Street and Blacksmith Lane (Christmas–Jan daily 8am–6pm; Sept–Christmas & Feb–June daily 9am–5pm; July & Aug Mon–Fri 9am–5pm, Sat 9am–1pm; ☎07/866 5555), which has **Internet access**. Air Coromandel (see "Listings", p.350) lands at the **airport**, 3km south of the town centre and reached by a $5 taxi ride.

The surrounding **beaches** are served by ferry and buses. The **passenger ferry** to Ferry Landing (daily 7.30am–noon & 1–6.30pm, until midnight in summer; $1 one way) takes a mere three minutes and leaves from the end of the marina, past the harbour master's office. Hot Water Beach Conxtions (☎07/866 2478; book a day ahead if possible) run hop-on, hop-off **excursion buses** from Ferry Landing to Cooks Beach, the Purangi Winery, Hahei and Hot Water Beach (3–5 daily; $20 all-day pass), with some services continuing to Dalmeny Corner on SH25 for connection with buses to Auckland and Whitianga.

Accommodation

As one of the Coromandel's main tourist centres, Whitianga itself has plenty of **accommodation** to suit all tastes. Further out, beside the secluded **beaches** of Mercury Bay, is a small selection of perfect places to unwind, mostly at Hot Water Beach and Hahei. During January, places get booked up about two months beforehand, so **book as far ahead** as possible if your visit coincides with this peak period, and be prepared for **higher prices** than on the rest of the peninsula.

CENTRAL WHITIANGA

Buffalo Beach Resort, Eyre St (☎ & fax 07/866 5854, *buffalo@xtra.co.nz*). Extremely well-equipped campsite adjacent to the beach, in shaded parkland a three-minute walk from the town centre. Tent sites $8, chalets & units ③.

Camellia Lodge B&B, cnr Golf Rd & SH25, near the airport (☎ & fax 07/866 2253). An attractive modern house in extensive well kept gardens, run by extremely friendly and helpful hosts, with four comfortable guest rooms; regular barbecues on summer evenings; swimming pool and spa. Dinner on request ($25). ⑤.

Cat's Pyjamas Backpackers, 4 Monk St (☎ & fax 07/866 4663, *catspyjamas@xtra.co.nz*). Small, friendly and clean place with two dorms and two doubles, just a couple of minutes' walk from the wharf. Perks include free linen, tea and coffee, occasional fresh fruit and seafood – and sometimes home brew. The owner will proudly show you the plane he's building and maybe take you up for a scenic flight (in a different completed plane of course). Dorms ①, rooms ②.

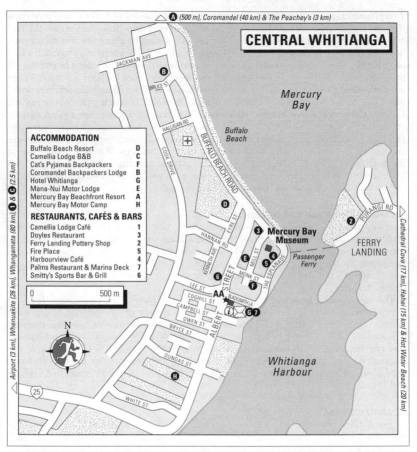

Central Whitianga

ACCOMMODATION
Buffalo Beach Resort	D
Camellia Lodge B&B	C
Cat's Pyjamas Backpackers	F
Coromandel Backpackers Lodge	B
Hotel Whitianga	G
Mana-Nui Motor Lodge	A
Mercury Bay Beachfront Resort	E
Mercury Bay Motor Camp	H

RESTAURANTS, CAFÉS & BARS
Camellia Lodge Café	1
Doyles Restaurant	3
Ferry Landing Pottery Shop	2
Fire Place	5
Harbourview Café	4
Palms Restaurant & Marina Deck	7
Smitty's Sports Bar & Grill	6

Coromandel Backpackers Lodge, 46 Buffalo Beach Rd (☎ & fax 07/866 5380, *corobkpk@wave.co.nz*). Ten minutes' walk from town, overlooking the bay, this is a particularly welcoming and well-equipped hostel, with free use of kayaks, fishing lines, spades for hot water beach and courtesy transport. They also rent bikes for $20 a day, and have Internet access. Dorms ①, rooms ②.

Mana-Nui Motor Lodge, 20 Albert St (☎ & fax 07/866 5599). Centrally located, comfortable and well-kept motel with seven fully self-contained units. ⑤.

Mercury Bay Beachfront Resort, 111–113 Buffalo Beach Rd (☎07/866 5637, fax 866 4524, *mbbf@mercurybay.co.nz*). Luxurious motel with eight excellent spacious units, half with great sea views and half having direct access to a garden with spa pool and barbecue area. There are kayaks, a dinghy, fishing rods, boogie boards and bikes for guests' use and courtesy transport from the airport and bus depot avoids the 25-minute walk from the centre. ⑥.

Mercury Bay Motor Camp, 121 Albert St (☎07/866 5579, fax 866 4891). Large, sheltered and well-equipped site about 400m from the town centre with kayak and bike rental ($10 a day), a pool and spa. Tent sites $10, cabins & flats ②–④.

The Peachey's, Centennial Drive (☎ & fax 07/866 5290, *dypeachey@xtra.co.nz*). Attractive and welcoming B&B overlooking Mercury Bay, 4km north of Whitianga. Afternoon tea on arrival, and dinner available on request ($25). ⑤.

Hotel Whitianga, The Esplanade (☎ & fax 07/866 5818). Pleasant, refurbished harbourside hotel with nine well-tended rooms, most of them en-suite and all with TV and washbasin. Can get noisy on Fri or Sat nights, with live music in bar. ④, en-suite ⑤.

AROUND WHITANGA

Auntie Dawn's Place, Radar Rd, Hot Water Beach (☎07/866 3707, fax 866 3701, *auntiedawn @mercurybay.co.nz*). Tranquil modern hillside house overlooking the beach with comfortable, fully self-contained apartments, plus backpacker beds in summer only (Oct–April). Backpacker beds ①, apartments ④.

Hahei Holiday Resort, Harsant Ave, Hahei (☎ & fax 07/866 3889, fax 866 3098, *info@ haheiholidays.co.nz*). Located on half a kilometre of beachfront and within an easy walk of Cathedral Cove, this spacious site is close to a shop and restaurants. Tent sites $10, dorms ①, flats & units ②–④.

Hot Water Beach Holiday Park, adjacent to the general store, Hot Water Beach (☎07/866 3735). Well-kept site right by the beach. Tent sites $10, plus $2 for a power hook-up.

Tatahi Lodge, Grange Rd, Hahei (☎07/866 3992, fax 866 3993). Several luxurious self-contained wooden units set in bush and gardens plus backpacker accommodation in dorms and doubles, with free linen; courtesy van. Backpacker dorms ①, rooms ②, units ⑤.

The Town

The town's **main street** is Buffalo Beach Road (SH25), becoming Albert Street as it forks south through the town centre and heads on out of town. The Esplanade branches off from Buffalo Beach Road and leads to the wharf. Much of the pleasure in hang-

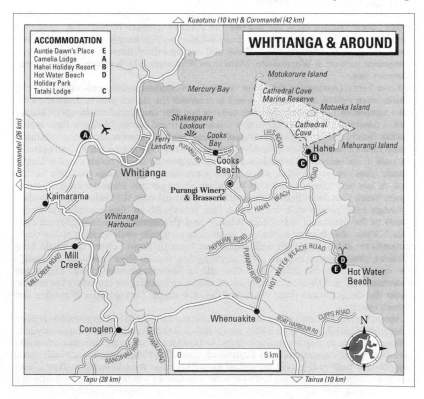

△ Kuaotunu (10 km) & Coromandel (42 km)

ACCOMMODATION

Auntie Dawn's Place	E
Camelia Lodge	A
Hahei Holiday Resort	B
Hot Water Beach Holiday Park	D
Tatahi Lodge	C

WHITIANGA & AROUND

Motukorure Island

Mercury Bay

Cathedral Cove Marine Reserve

Motueka Island

Shakespeare Lookout

Cathedral Cove

LEES ROAD

Ferry Landing

PURANGI RD

Cooks Bay

Hahei

Mahurangi Island

Cooks Beach

Whitianga

Purangi Winery & Brasserie

HAHEI BEACH

Kaimarama

Whitianga Harbour

HEPBURN ROAD

PURANGI ROAD

HOT WATER BEACH ROAD

Mill Creek

MILL CREEK ROAD

Hot Water Beach

Whenuakite

BOAT HARBOUR RD

CUPPS ROAD

Coroglen

KAPOWAI ROAD

RANGIHAU ROAD

◁ Coromandel (26 km)

0   5 km

N

▽ Tapu (28 km)

▽ Tairua (10 km)

ing around Whitianga for a day or two is in getting out of town, easily done with time spent at Cathedral Cove or Hot Water Beach, or by taking boat trips on Mercury Bay (see below). If inclement weather or a surfeit of beaches drives you indoors, about the best thing you can do is to try your hand at **bone-carving course**, an increasingly popular pursuit where, with guidance, you can produce a *tiki*, in half a day or so. Two places currently offer very similar carving classes, the most convenient and reliable being Bay Carving, The Esplanade (phone the day before ☎07/866 4021; daily 8am–10pm; $25–40, dependent on size of carving); the cost is the same no matter how long you take to complete your masterpiece, and there's free tea and coffee (plus soup in winter). Choose your design from over a hundred (either traditional Maori or contemporary) and set to work on a specially prepared hunk of cow bone. Dentists' drills and plenty of sanding by hand transform the bone into a glossy, white pendant. If you lack patience, you might do better to check out the ready-carved pieces for sale at the workshop at very reasonable prices ($30–40 for a small piece).

Next door, in an old butter factory, is the big **Mercury Bay Museum** (Jan daily 10am–4pm; Oct–Dec & Feb–April daily 11am–3pm; May–Sept Tues–Thurs & Sun 11am–2pm; $2), which won't detain you for long. It focuses mainly on colonial history with the usual slight nod to Maori artefacts. Points of interest are an extensive exhibition on Captain Cook and his discovery of the peninsula; also informative displays on kauri-gum digging (including carved blackjack gum), minerals and local shipwrecks.

Ferry Landing and the beaches

The beaches across the estuary are accessible by passenger ferry to **Ferry Landing**, where buses continue on to the beaches (see p.345 for details); by boat (see "Exploring Mercury Bay", opposite); or by car from Whitianga. The longer **road route** travels south along SH25, skirting the harbour and cutting inland through hill country to a signposted turn-off at Whenuakite, 26km from Whitianga, which strikes north towards Mercury Bay.

From Ferry Landing the first point of interest is **Shakespeare Lookout**, atop a cliff which, when viewed from the sea is said to resemble the Bard's profile. From the lookout – signposted 1.5km along the road, and reached after another kilometre uphill to a car park – panoramic views stretch east to Cooks Beach and across Mercury Bay, west to Buffalo Beach, and north towards Mount Maungatawhiri. A memorial plaque commemorates James Cook's anchorage in Mercury Bay in 1769. Signposted tracks lead from the car park to the secluded Lonely Bay and on to the popular family holiday spot of **Cooks Beach** (2km one way; 20min), which is also accessible from the main road 2km further east. At low tide (check times with Whitianga visitor centre) from the eastern end of Cooks Beach you can **walk to Cathedral Cove** (5km one way; 1hr) following a rock shelf – though most people walk from Hahei (see below). About 3km southeast of Cooks Beach on the main road is **Purangi Winery and Brasserie** (*www.purangi.co.nz*; daily 9am–5.30pm, often later in summer), a great place to dawdle while soaking up the rustic atmosphere and tasting their fruit wines and liqueurs (free). These are made from kiwifruit, plums, apples and just about anything they can lay their hands on; the results are variable to say the least. They also offer a blackboard menu (see "Eating and Entertainment", p.350) of reasonably priced snacks and meals, served indoors or outside under the vines; choose from steak, seafood or a simple cheeseboard with salad and French bread.

About 3km further east along the main road is the turn-off to the tiny beachside community of **HAHEI**, a further 6.5km along Hahei Beach Road, which makes a viable alternative place to stay if you don't fancy the bustle of Whitianga. The main attraction here is the hilly coastal **track to Cathedral Cove** (30–40min one way), which starts from the car park at the western end of the village. The walk is steep in places, with patches of pine-dominated bush, and affords great views out to sea. Tracks lead down to a couple of rocky coves along the way, but most people continue to Cathedral Cove itself; striking white cliffs hugging a long, sheltered, sandy beach and bisected by an impressive rock arch which vaults out over the beach like the nave of some great cathedral. A walk through the arch reveals another delightful beach on the other side, while offshore the remains of several arches are stranded at sea. Bring a towel and a picnic, sink into the sand and relax to the deceptively gentle sound of the waves. This is also a great place to **snorkel**, because the rich waters here are protected as part of the **Cathedral Cove Marine Reserve**.

If there is one place hereabouts that trumps Cathedral Cove, it is **Hot Water Beach**, 5km along Hot Water Beach Road, the last place you'll come to from Ferry Landing and the first you'll reach arriving by road from Whitianga via SH25. The beach itself is split in two by a rocky outcrop which creates dangerous tidal rips (read our surf warning, see box p.117), but also provide the setting for the hot springs which give the beach its name. Be sure to visit an hour and a half either side of **low tide** (check tide times at the visitor centre or in the local paper), then dig a hole and you can sit in the hot water while being refreshed by waves of incoming sea water. In summer, the springs area will be pockmarked by other visitors' diggings, but if no one has been here before you, you'll need to **rent a spade** from the **general store** (daily 9am–5pm; $2 for 2 hours, plus $20 deposit); the store also sells burgers, toasted sandwiches, hot dogs, tea and coffee, ice cream and milk shakes.

Exploring Mercury Bay

You can combine exploring Mercury Bay and **swimming with dolphins** through Mercury Bay Seafaris (book through visitor centre; enquiries only on ☎025/398 826), who run three highly informative boat trips **from Whitianga** wharf. You need to bring warm clothes and swimming gear; they supply wetsuits, snorkelling gear and hot drinks; you should also contact them the night before to check on sea conditions. Their Dolphin Quest (Oct–April daily 8am; 3–4hr; $90) takes you to Mercury Bay's outer reaches in a high-speed vessel, aiming to spot dolphins, orca and other whales. The Seven-Island Seafari (daily: Oct–April 3pm; May–Sept 9am; 3–4hr; $75) is a **scenic cruise** around the Mercury Islands, visiting caves, pristine beaches, island sanctuaries and bush-clad bays; there's great snorkelling among these volcanic islands, and you may also have the chance to swim with bottlenose dolphins. If you'd rather not get wet, join their glass-bottom boat trip (year-round, times according to demand; 1hr 30min; $40), which follows the coast to Cathedral Cove and the marine reserve. Good **boat trips** also run **out of Hahei**: the Hahei Explorer (☎07/866 3910; book previous evening or before 9am on the day) is the only set-up with a DOC licence to land at Cathedral Cove; they specialize in cave trips, visiting a blowhole between Cathedral Cove and Hot Water Beach in their rigid-hull inflatable (year-round; 1hr; $35), and guided snorkelling trips (gear rental $25 a day).

The fastest way to see the bay is by **jetboat** with Mercury Bay Scenic Jet (Dec–April; 1hr; $30; book at visitor centre; after hours ☎07/866 4125), which leaves from Whitianga wharf for an adrenalin-pumping spin to Cathedral Cove. More leisurely exploration is afforded by **guided sea kayak tours**, equally enjoyable in summer or winter. Based in Whitianga, Mercury Bay Sea Kayaks (☎07/866 5879) offer a range of trips, from half-day to multi-day adventures (half-day trips start at $42), taking in Cathedral Cove, the caves of offshore islands and snorkelling. Coromandel Safaris (☎025/394 597) run kayaking trips for similar prices, but also organize dive trips and door-to-door transport from Auckland, Hamilton, Tauranga and Rotorua. **Scuba diving** in Cathedral Cove Marine Reserve can be arranged through Hahei-based Cathedral Cove Dive (☎07/866 3955): a one-dive trip costs $75, two-dives $130, less if you have your own gear. **Non-divers** can learn basic scuba skills ($95), and they also run other PADI courses, from beginners to advanced.

Eating and entertainment

As you'd expect from such a happening spot, Whitianga and its surrounds have a good choice of places to **eat**, many of the better places clustered along The Esplanade close to the marina, just as they should be. Entertainment options are sadly limited to the *Hotel Whitianga*, with live **bands** once a week (Fri or Sat) in summer.

Breakers, Beach Rd, Hahei. A highly recommended, relaxing daytime café and evening restaurant and bar in a peaceful spot, with an attractive enclosed veranda, large windows, and jasmine growing overhead. Scallops collected from a local bay are a speciality along with $20–25 mains based on duck, ostrich and salmon. Licensed and BYO.

Camellia Lodge Café, cnr Golf Road & SH25, Whitianga (near the airport). Inexpensive daytime snacks and light meals are served in this small café in beautiful tree-shaded gardens. Terrific Greek salad and ploughman's lunch (with salami and fresh fruit).

Doyles Restaurant, 21 The Esplanade. Fairly upmarket à la carte dining from a pleasant first-floor vantage point overlooking the beach. The menu extends from simple fish and chips ($18) to pan roasted pork fillet on a pumpkin and spinach frittata ($24), and there's a lighter brunch menu. Breakfast, lunch & dinner Oct–April; dinner only May–Sept.

Ferry Landing Pottery Shop, Purangi Rd, Ferry Landing. About 100m up the hill from the wharf, this attractive garden café is perfect for light meals, coffee, and a rest among flowers and greenery. Daily from 10am until late afternoon.

The Fire Place, 8 The Esplanade. Smart but casual restaurant that brings big city style to Whitianga with a lovely deck overlooking the water. Wonderful gourmet pizzas ($14–19) are helped down with the likes of haloumi, asparagus and prosciutto salad ($9) and followed by desserts such as vanilla bean crème brûlée ($9).

Harbourview Café, 10 The Esplanade (☎07/866 4263). A good lunch and dinner spot that's popular with locals – not least for its generous portions; an all-day breakfast is also on offer, with yummy pancakes. Lunches cost around $12, dinners (book ahead) $20. Licensed & BYO ($5 corkage).

Palms Restaurant & Marina Deck, in the *Hotel Whitianga*, The Esplanade. An airy, comfortable restaurant overlooking the marina that's especially good for dinner, with main courses costing $18–25. There are also a couple of bars serving snacks all day. Daily Oct–April, closed Sun May–Sept. Licensed.

Purangi Winery Brasserie, 450 Purangi Rd, near Hahei (☎07/866 3724). Rustic, secluded restaurant in a picturesque setting proffering high-quality snacks, barbecued steak, seafood and yummy sausages, all for $20 and under. Lunch year round, dinner in Jan & Feb and by arrangement. Licensed.

Smitty's Sports Bar & Grill, 37 Albert St. A hacienda-style bar, serving well-priced snacks, lunches and dinners daily from 11am. Grilled meats are the speciality here and the burgers are excellent, though they make a few concessions to vegetarians. Dine in the barn-like interior, or out on the deck.

Listings

Airlines Air Coromandel (☎0800/900 600) flies twice daily to and from Auckland (around $100) and three times weekly to Great Barrier Island ($90 one way).

Banks all found along Albert Street and all with ATMs.

Buses InterCity (☎09/913 6100) serves Thames, Coromandel town, Opoutere, Whangamata, Tauranga, Rotorua and Auckland; Go Kiwi (☎07/866 0336) run daily to Tairua, Thames, Auckland, Whangamata and Tauranga.

Horse Trekking Ace Hi Ranch (☎07/866 48797, *acehitreks@xtra.co.nz*) offer 2hr trekking trips ($30) along with their "Pub Crawl on Horseback" (price dependent on numbers) which involves a day-long ride to the Coroglen pub, where you overnight before returning the next day. The ranch is on SH25 8km south of Whitianga, and they offer courtesy transport for two or more.

Medical treatment Mercury Bay Medical Centre, 87 Albert St (☎07/866 5911).

Pharmacy Emergency after-hours service ☎07/866 4146.

Scenic flights Air Coromandel (☎0800/900 600) offer flightseeing, with prices in the range of $35–99.

Taxis Mercury Bay Taxis (☎07/866 5643).

Water taxis Hahei Explorer (☎07/866 3910) operates a water-taxi service between Hahei and Cathedral Cove (on demand; 10min; $30 return).

South to Whangamata

The run along SH25 from Whitianga **south to Whangamata** is a pleasant enough journey, though you seldom get a good eyeful of coastal scenery, and when you do it has often been spoiled by over-development. To some degree this is true of **Tairua**, the midway point, and especially so of its neighbour across the harbour, the luxury retirement and holiday resort of **Pauanui**; reminiscent of the worst excesses of Florida, and best avoided altogether. All is not lost though; there is great bush country just inland, with the **Broken Hills** area particularly rich in gold-mining relics. Unspoilt beaches can also be found, particularly the delightful **Opoutere**, a tiny harbourside retreat at the foot of a mountain, with a wild sweep of beach and a beautifully situated hostel. From there, you're best off making a beeline for Whangamata.

Tairua

The small but overdeveloped beachside town of **TAIRUA** lies on SH25, 16km south of the turn-off to Hot Water Beach and 42km from Whitianga. It huddles between pine-forested hills and the calm estuary of the Tairua River, separated from the crashing Pacific breakers by two opposing and almost touching peninsulas. One is crowned by the imposing volcanic Mount Paku and the other is entirely covered by the ghastly suburban sprawl of exclusive **Pauanui**, accessible (if you must) by a five-minute passenger ferry ride from Tairua, or a 25km drive. The combination of surf and sheltered waters makes Tairua popular in summer with holidaying Kiwis, who also find it a good base for Hot Water Beach, more easily reached by car from here than from Whitianga.

With time on your hands, you could stop briefly for a dip, or to climb **Mount Paku** (15min up) for spectacular views over the town, its estuary and beaches: the track starts at the end of Paku Drive, reached by following the estuary around to the north. You could also hook up with Kiwi Dundee Adventures (see p.354), for one of their extremely informative and light-hearted **eco-tours**, or try your hand at windsurfing (see p.354).

InterCity **buses** from Whitianga and Thames drop off a couple of times a day at Tairua post office, a few steps from the **tourist office**, Main Road (☎07/864 7575; Mon–Sat 9am–4pm). Go Kiwi buses pass through once a day in each direction dropping off at the numerous motels and at *Tairua Backpackers*, 200 Main Rd (☎ & fax 07/864 8345; dorms ①, rooms ②), the best of several hostels in town, located south of the centre across the river bridge. It is set among trees near the water's edge, with free use of canoes, shonky bikes (better models are $5 a day), windsurfers (tuition available at $10 a session), and you can help yourself to the garden's fruit, vegetables and eggs when available. The best-value **eating** option is *Gazebo*, Main Road just where the bus stops, which offers hearty servings of Kiwi café favourites.

Broken Hills

Upstream from Tairua, the Tairua River emerges from the peninsula's mountainous spine at **Broken Hills**, an unsung but attractive swathe of bush reached along a 7km spur off SH25 17km south of Tairua, immediately opposite the road to Pauanui. Several tracks (listed in the DOC's *Broken Hills* leaflet; $1) disappear into the bush, mostly in pursuit of relics from the early years of the twentieth century when the small town of Puketui (now gone) was the focus of fevered gold mining and kauri logging. Most are short, and you can knock off a few in a day, or base yourself at the DOC's *Broken Hills Campground* ($7; toilets and water) for more extensive explorations. The easiest trail is the **Gem of the Boom Creek Walk** (500m loop, 15min) which visits the site of the former town jail, essentially an abandonned mining tunnel. For something more strenuous, try the **Golden Hills Mine Track** (7km loop; 3hr) which climbs steeply before plunging into a 500m-long tunnel, emerging near the remains of a stamper battery and finishing through mature podocarp forest.

Opoutere

Around ten kilometres south of the Broken Hills junction is the turn-off to **Opoutere**, the road hugging the shoreline of Wharekawa Harbour, fringed by pohutukawa trees and overlooked by pine-covered hills towering above. This tiny settlement comprises only a handful of houses, a campsite and a hostel, all strung along the single road. People come here to enjoy the tranquillity, birdlife, plentiful shellfish – and a four-kilometre expanse of **wild** white-sand **beach** protected from development by the forest reserve that backs it. It's the sort of place you plan to visit for a day and wind up staying a week. Swimming on the beach is reasonably safe but there can be a strong undertow, making the calmer waters of the estuary better for swimming. The wetlands flanking the estuary yield delicious shellfish – so long as you don't mind getting your feet wet – and provide good bird-watching spots.

There are also a couple of good **walks**. Just outside the hostel gate is the start of a summit track up **Mount Maungaruawahine** (1km one way; 20min). The track goes through tall coastal bush and the climb to the summit is quite steep, passing elderly, gnarled pohutukawa and other native trees. The **summit** gives excellent views on the seaward side across the Mayor and Aldermen islands, the estuary-harbour mouth, the length of the beach and the green flats just inland.

Further down the road are two tracks to **Ocean Beach**, starting at a small arched bridge over the Wahitapu Stream. Beyond the bridge the track forks: the **right-hand track** (1.2km one way; 15min) emerges from pine forest to follow the estuary before venturing out on to a sandspit (a bird sanctuary and breeding ground for New Zealand dotterels, oystercatchers and various species of tern; roped off during the Nov–March breeding season); crossing the spit brings you to the white sand and roaring surf of Ocean Beach, from where you can loop back through bush and back over the bridge to the car park. The **left-hand fork** is a more direct track (800m one way; 10min) that passes through pines, lupin and mingimingi, before reaching the beach.

PRACTICALITIES

InterCity services around the Coromandel link up with Whangamata Tours (☎07/865 8613) who run an on-demand service to Opoutere, and Go Kiwi call off on their Whitianga to Rotorua run. Both stop outside the **YHA** (☎07/865 9072, fax 865 6172; tent sites $10, dorms ①, rooms ②), which is by far the best place to stay. It is set back from the main road at the harbour mouth end and enjoys one of the finest sites of any hostel in New Zealand. Overlooking the river estuary, the hostel sits in a dip at the foot of the mountain, wallowing in its own mild micro-climate. As if this idyllic situation wasn't enough, there's also the chance of seeing glow-worms on your nocturnal wanderings, and canoes are available for guests' use (on the estuary only). The small **campsite**, *Opoutere Park Beach Resort* (☎ & fax 07/865 9152; tent sites $10, flats & chalet ②–④), is about 700m up the road towards the beach.

There's no general store in Opoutere, but the campsite and hostel both have basic **provisions** for sale.

Whangamata and the Wentworth Valley

The long, straggling resort of **WHANGAMATA**, on SH25 towards the southern end of the Coromandel Peninsula, is bounded on three sides by estuaries and the ocean, and on the fourth by bush-clad hills: nowhere else on the Coromandel do bush and beach sit so closely together. This single-storey town of 4000 grows tenfold in January, when holiday-makers flock to its four-kilometre **Ocean Beach**, a crescent of white sand that curves from the harbour entrance to the mouth of the **Otahu River**. The bar at the harbour end has an excellent break making this one of New Zealand's true **surfie** meccas.

Arrival, information and accommodation

Whangamata Buses (☎07/865 7088) run a service (not Sun) to Whitianga from Waihi in the south and from Hikowai in the north, which is accessible on InterCity's Whitianga–Thames run. **Buses** drop off daily outside the centrally located **visitor centre** on Port Road, beside the BNZ (Mon–Sat 9am–5pm, Sun 10am–4pm; ☎ & fax 07/865 8340, *info-whangamata@xtra.co.nz*), and most places are within easy walking distance of here.

As a tourist centre, Whangamata has plenty of **accommodation**, most of it pricier than elsewhere on the peninsula, especially over the two weeks following Christmas, when rates can shoot up by as much as fifty percent. Wherever you stay, you won't be far from the town centre.

Brenton Lodge, 1 Brenton Place (☎ & fax 07/865 8400, *www.brentonlodge.co.nz*). Very attractive retreat right on the edge of Whangamata with sea views from the two cottages and one suite. Lovely understated décor, fresh flowers and delicious breakfasts. ⑧.

Bushland Park Lodge, in the Wentworth Valley, 7km southwest of town (☎ & fax 07/865 7468, *www.wellness.co.nz*). A very appealing hideaway and classy restaurant (see "Eating and drinking", overleaf) in private grounds close to the start of the track to Wentworth Falls. There are four immaculate and cheerfully decorated en-suite doubles with free use of the sauna and hydrotheraputic spa; and there's on-site yoga, t'ai chi and massage to help you completely unwind. Breakfast is in the Black Forest-style with bread, cheese and ham, most ingredients of German origin. ⑦.

Cedarwood Motor Hotel, 413–419 Port Rd (☎ & fax 07/865 9211). The biggest motel in town, offering fairly modern, spacious units sleeping up to eight. Facilities include a BBQ, several bars, a bistro and tennis courts. ⑤.

Garden Tourist Lodge, cnr Port Rd & Mayfair Ave (☎ & fax 07/865 9580, ☎0800/659 580, *gardenlodge@xtra.co.nz*). An immaculate backpackers and motel. The well equipped hostel section has small dorms, double rooms, free use of surfboards and transport to walks; while the motel has well-appointed, smart and spacious motel units. Backpacker dorms ①, rooms ③, motel ⑤.

Pinefield Holiday Park, at the southern end of Port Rd (☎ & fax 07/865 8791, *pinefield@xtra.co.nz*). An excellent, shady site that gets very busy over summer weekends. On-site accommodation comes well-equipped; there's a barbecue and a large swimming pool. Tent sites $11; cabins, flats & units ②–⑤.

Wentworth Valley Campground, end of Wentworth Valley Road. Lovely campsite with streamside pitches, barbecues and cold showers right by the start of the track to Wentworth Falls, 7km southwest of Whangamata. $7.

The Town and around

Kiwis flock to this small town during their summer holidays, booking it out during the first two weeks after Christmas, but it's pretty quiet for the rest of the year. The **main street** is Port Road, which runs straight through the small town centre, linking it with the highway.

Surfies should make straight for the well-stocked Whangamata Surf Shop, 634 Port Rd (daily 9am–5pm), owned by surfing legend Bob Davie and heaped with designer gear to keep the coolest of customers happy. It is the only place in town where you can **rent a surfboard** ($10 per hr, $18 half-day, $25 full-day) or a **boogie board** ($5 per hr, $12 half-day, $16 full-day); they also rent out wetsuits and fins for $5 per day. The Windsurfing School, up the harbour past the boat ramp (☎07/865 8186), operates daily during summer holidays for up to three hours either side of high tide (and throughout the year on bookings); **sailboard** rental costs $20 per hour, a group lesson $25, and a private lesson $30.

Aside from enjoying the surf, there are only a couple of other diversions in the foothills of the Coromandel Range, right on the edge of town. One is a pleasant **walk to Wentworth Falls** (10km return; 2hr) in the nearby Wentworth Valley. Take SH25 south for 2km to the signposted turn-off to Wentworth Valley Road; at its end (4km) is a campsite (see previous page) and the start of the track through regenerating bush past numerous small swimming holes ideal for wallowing away a couple of hours in the heat of the day. The track continues into the heart of the mountains, but most turn around at the two-leap Wentworth Falls, best viewed from a small deck from where it is possible to scramble steeply down to the pool at the bottom of the falls. The other reason to come here is to join one of the extremely popular **eco-tours** run by Kiwi Dundee Adventures (☎ & fax 07/865 8809, *www.kiwidundee.co.nz*; book as far ahead as possible). For twenty years, the passionate conservationist Doug Johansen (popularly known as "Kiwi Dundee") has been getting his message across in his own distinctive way, generally accompanied by a good deal of showmanship. Operating year-round, the company offers a variety of tours (a basic one-day "Nature and Coast" trip is $140), taking small groups off the beaten track for a day or more to explain history, geology, Maori medicines and natural history, with departures from Tairua, Pauanui and Whangamata.

Eating and drinking

Port Road is lined with several **tearooms**, takeaways and **restaurants**, but few stand out, so you might want to venture further afield for more inspiring fare.

Café Rossini, Port Rd. Modern café serving the town's best range of panini, cakes, good coffee and pizzas, either inside or on tables on the street.

Cedarwood Motor Hotel, Port Rd. Popular bistro-style restaurant that serves lunches for under $15 and dinner for under $20. The *Beach Bar* also has light meals of trendy, snacky food for under $10, and also a sports bar and garden bar.

Ginger's Health Food Café, 601 Port Rd. Reasonably priced veggie place, open daily from morning until mid-afternoon. Great muffins. BYO.

Nero's, Port Rd. The best pizzas in town, mostly gourmet style with combinations like salmon and shrimp ($18), chicken and mango ($16) and plain vegetarian ($16).

Nickel Strausse, 7km southwest of town on the Wentworth Valley Road, off SH25 (☎07/865 7468). Excellent and good-value dining in an intimate restaurant set in rural surroundings. A charming German couple serve typical Black Forest lunches ($8–25) and dinners (around $50), including exquisite Black Forest gateau made fresh daily. Licensed, with an international wine list. Booking required for dinner.

Waihi and Waihi Beach

SH25 continues 30km south from Whangamata to the town of **WAIHI**, where it meets SH2 at the entrance to the Karangahake Gorge (see p.328). Gold was first discovered at Waihi in a reef of quartz in 1878, but it was not until 1894 that a boom began with the first successful trials in extracting gold using cyanide solution at Karangahake. By 1908 Waihi was the fastest-growing town in the Auckland Province, and today it remains a mining district some five thousand strong. Although underground mining came to a halt in 1952, extraction was cranked up again in 1987 when the focus of activity moved to the opencast but well hidden Martha Mine. You can visit the mine, learn about its past in a good **museum**, or hop on a steam train for a scenic ride into the nearby **Karangahake Gorge**.

And, if you're in need of some light relief, the popular surf beach of **WAIHI BEACH** lies 12km east of town, off SH2: its long, thin strip of golden sand stretches for 8km and is one of the safest ocean beaches in the country.

The Town

At the eastern end of town, **Martha Mine** still produces gold (and silver) to the value of about one million dollars a week, and is one of the few working mines in New Zealand that you can visit. **Guided tours** (book a couple of days ahead ☎07/863 9880; Mon–Fri, according to demand; 75–90min; donation) take visitors around the opencast gold mine and processing areas, providing background history and details of the environmental work the company is supposedly doing.

Even if you decide against the gold-mine tour, it's worth taking a couple of minutes to follow the short **Goldmine Walkway**, signposted beside the visitor centre, which goes to the imposing 1901 concrete pump house which once housed the steam engines and machinery needed to continuously pump water away from the workings as they sunk to a depth of nearly 600m. From here you can peer down into the vast red-earth pit where the laden trucks are dwarfed by the sheer scale of the earthworks, and the noise of the mechanical diggers labouring at the bottom are strangely muffled by the distance. Meanwhile, out of sight, a two-kilometre-long conveyor belt transports about 30,000 tonnes of ore a day through a tunnel to the treatment plant just outside town.

Heading back along the main road towards Paeroa, you'll come across the **Goldmining Museum & Art Gallery** (Mon–Fri 10am–4pm, Sat & Sun 1.30–4pm; $3) just off the roundabout at 54 Kenny St. More than anything else, this is a showcase for the fine and intricately detailed models on mining themes that were made between 1976 and 1986 by ship's engineer, Tom Morgan, in his spare time. You can't help but admire the effort that went into the working model of a miniature stamp battery, which makes almost as much racket as the original, or the delightful working model of Waihi's pump house. There are also some evocative dioramas depicting miners at work, interesting ephemera about their lives, and historical accounts of the violent Waihi Strike of 1912 which helped galvanise the labour movement and eventually led to the creation of the Labour Party. The small art gallery in the same building exhibits the work of local and invited artists.

At the western end of town, the ramshackle wooden station at the end of Wrigley Street is home to the **Goldfields Vintage Railway**, which operates scenic 6km rail trips in summer to Waikino in the Karangahake Gorge (☎07/863 8251; daily 11am, 12.30pm & 2pm, with extra services on Sun, returning from Waikino 45min later; 20min each way; $7 one way, $10 return). An old steam engine pulls 1930s carriages over a stretch of track built between 1900 and 1905 by gold-mining companies; travelling alongside SH2, you get spectacular views of the Ohinemuri River.

Practicalities

Both InterCity **buses** and Whangamata Tours (☎07/865 7088) shuttle services pull up at Rosemont Road Service Station, just a couple of hundred yards from the mine and **visitor centre**, Seddon Street (daily: Oct–April 9am–5pm; May–Sept 9am–4.30pm; ☎07/863 6715): follow Rosemont Road to the town's central crossroads and turn right. There are several **places to stay** in Waihi itself and a few others at the beach (see overleaf). A ten-minute walk from town, the *Waihi Motor Camp*, 6 Waitete Rd, off Seddon Rd (☎07/863 7654; tent sites $8.50, dorm bunks ①, cabins & flats ②–③), enjoys a quiet creekside setting, while the *Waihi Motel*, on Tauranga Road/SH2 (☎07/863 8095; ④), two minutes' walk south of the centre, has good-sized units and a spa pool; and the central *Chez Nous B&B*, 41 Seddon Ave (☎07/863 7538; ③), offers quiet rooms in a pleasant modern house, and dinner by arrangement.

At the western end of town, on Waitete Road, the pleasant *Waitete Orchard* **winery** and **café** (daily 8.30am–5.30pm, later in summer) serves great-value, freshly cooked snacks, light meals, fresh fruit juices and naturally brewed beer; they use organic produce wherever possible and sell organic fruit and vegetables, too. A favourite is their authentic Indian samosas, served with salad ($4). Just up the road is an excellent licensed and BYO **restaurant**, *Grandpa Thorn's*, 4 Waitete Rd (☎07/863 8708; Tues–Sun evenings only; book ahead); diners travel from as far afield as Tauranga and Hamilton to eat high-quality country-style Kiwi cuisine (around $20 a main course), such as rack of lamb with leek and mint compôte, in this log-cabin setting.

At **Waihi Beach** a few **accommodation** places are strung along the waterfront Seaforth Road. Try the small *Shalmar Motel*, 40 Seaforth Rd (☎07/863 5439; ⑤), near the shops, or the secluded *Bowentown Holiday Park* (☎07/863 5381; tent sites $10, cabins & flats ②–③), which sits right at the southern end of the beach. Good beachside fodder can be found at *Cactus Jack's*, 31 Wilson Rd, a BYO sit-in and takeout burger bar perfect for a chilli burger and shake.

Into the Bay of Plenty: Katikati and around

Waihi and the Karangahake Gorge mark the southern limit of the Coromandel Peninsula. From here on the coast begins to curl eastwards into the **Bay of Plenty** leaving behind the bush-clad mountains and taking on a gentler, more open aspect of rolling hills carved up by tall evergreen shelter belts which provide protection for valuable hectares of kiwifruit vines. In summer, numerous roadside stalls spring up selling ripe fruit straight from the orchards, often at knockdown prices. It takes less then an hour to drive from Waihi to Tauranga, but you may be induced to pause a while over the **murals** of Katikati or press on to the swimming beach at Omokoroa and the hot pools at Plummers Point.

> Although, strictly speaking, **Rotorua** lies in the Bay of Plenty, it is covered along with the rest of the volcanic plateau region in Chapter Four, starting on p.269.

Katikati

Some twenty kilometres south of Waihi you arrive in **KATIKATI**, an ordinary little town which was dealt a devastating economic blow when the price of kiwifruit collapsed in the late 1980s. The town reacted by fashioning itself as "Mural Town", a fairly desperate but reasonably successful attempt to catch passing tourist traffic. Colourful and well-painted murals have since sprung up on buildings all over town, many reflecting the heritage of the original settlers from Ulster and the growth of the town: a couple of the best are "Waitekohe No. 3", on a block wall on the right as you enter the main street from the north, and the photo-realist "Central Motors", a little further along on the left. More information on the town and its murals is available in the volunteer-staffed **visitor centre** (Mon–Fri 10am–4pm & Sat–Sun 10am–2pm; ☎07/549 1658) in the library building at 36 Main Rd/SH2.

For something to **eat** try *The Landing*, a café/bar on Main Road that does a good Mediterranean salad for $6 and wood-fired pizzas from $10. If you fancy **staying overnight** in these parts, head 6km south and turn up Thompson's Track to *Jacaranda Cottage*, 2.3km along at #230 (☎ & fax 07/549 0616, *jacaranda.cottage@clear.net.nz*;

backpacker beds ①, cottage ④, B&B ④), a homestay with individual beds let to back-packers (bring a sleeping bag), and a self-catering cottage with extensive Kaimai Range views. The genial host also takes folk horse riding in the woods nearby ($20 first hour, $10 thereafter).

Around 8km south of Katikati on SH2 the South African **Cape Dutch-style** archi-tecture of the *Morton Estate* winery (sales and tastings daily 10.30am–5pm) hoves into view. It is a charming place ringed by mountains and standing at the foot of a sloping vineyard with roses planted at the end of each row, in classic French tradition. Much of the grape juice is tankered here from their more extensive plantings in Hawke's Bay but it is here they produce an extensive range of quality wines, and offer **tastings**, free except for a few of their finer drops which cost $2 a sample, refunded if you make a pur-chase. You can also **eat** at *The Vineyard* (reservations advised ☎07/552 0620; closed Sun evening & Mon), where the likes of chicken and pear salad and garlic rack of lamb are served in an airy conservatory or outside by the vines.

Omokoroa Beach
A further 11km on, and still 15km short of Tauranga, a dead-end road spurs 5km to pretty **OMOKOROA BEACH** (no bus service), a safe swimming beach backed by a grassy reserve. From the point are excellent views across the water to Matakana Island, accessible from here by ferry (see p.365). You can stay at the quiet beachside *Omokoroa Tourist Park*, 165 Omokoroa Rd (☎07/548 0857; tent sites $10, cabins & chalets ②–③, motel units ④), but it is more enjoyable to stay a few kilometres away at the *Plummers Point Caravan Park* (☎ & fax 07/548 0669; tent sites $10, on-site vans and tourist cabins ②), where they've got well tended **hot mineral pools** (free to guests, otherwise $2.50). They're 3km along Station Road, which runs off SH2 2km south of the Omokoroa turn-off. From here it is a fifteen-minute drive into Tauranga, reached through Te Puna (home of the Paparoa Marae; see p.369), and the satellite community of **Bethlehem** (see p.368).

The western Bay of Plenty: Tauranga and Mount Maunganui

The western end of the **BAY OF PLENTY** centres on the prosperous, port city of **TAURANGA** ("safe anchorage"), and its beachside acolyte, **MOUNT MAUNGANUI**, effectively a suburb of Tauranga. This amorphous settlement, sprawled around the numerous glittering tentacles of Tauranga Harbour, is New Zealand's sixth largest, and is currently the **fastest-growing city** in the land. A combination of warm dry summers and mild winters initially attracted retirees, followed in recent years by telecommuters and folk who have worked out how to run their profitable small businesses from home. The result is a wealthy community that has fuelled increasing expansion – driving into the area you see new, often spacious, housing developments everywhere – and helped create a vibrant café society.

Once through the protecting ring of suburbs, it's apparent that rampant development hasn't spoilt central Tauranga, which occupies a narrow peninsula with several city parks and gardens backing a lively waterfront area. Progress has been less kind to the over-commercialized beach resort of Mount Maunganui, which huddles under the extinct volcanic cone of the same name – a landmark visible throughout the whole west-ern Bay of Plenty. "The Mount", as hill and town are often known, was once an island but is now connected to the mainland by a narrow neck of dune sand (a tombolo) cov-ered with high-rise apartments, shops, restaurants and houses. The Mount's saving grace is a 20km-long golden strand of Ocean Beach that's wonderful for swimming and surfing. No surprise, then, that the area's a big draw for Kiwi **holiday-makers** throughout January and on summer weekends, when Tauranga and Mount Maunganui can be rather overwhelming and accommodation hard to come by.

Visit outside the three peak weeks of summer madness and the region's charms quickly become apparent – though you'll do best if you have access to the surrounding area. Beyond the beach and a couple of walks around the volcano, Mount Maunganui's appeal runs only to a flourishing **restaurant** and **bar scene**. This it shares with Tauranga, which is best used to get out on the water: trips primarily head to **Matakana Island**, which acts as a barrier to Tauranga Harbour, and **Mayor Island**, a bush-clad retreat out in the Bay of Plenty. Boats also take clients out to **swim with dolphins**, cruise the harbour, or on excellent full-day **sailing trips**.

Beyond the city limits, there are opportunities to go **kayaking**, scale an outdoor climbing wall, ride horses, and wrangle quad bikes at a couple of adventure parks, or engage in more peaceful pursuits like **wine tasting** or picnicking beside some delightful swimming holes at **McLaren Falls**.

Finally, Tauranga is in a major **kiwifruit picking region**, but be warned, it's tough and prickly work and you must commit yourself to a minimum of three weeks (if this doesn't put you off, check out "Listings" on p.368).

Arrival, information and transport

InterCity and Newmans **buses** generally stop at both the Tauranga and Mount Maunganui visitor centres (see below), while the Call-a-bus (☎0800/100 550, *www.callabus.co.nz*) service from Auckland drops off at accommodation around both towns. The daily *Kaimai Express* from Auckland and Hamilton pulls into the **train station** on The Strand in central Tauranga at around 9.30pm leaving for Auckland the following morning at 8am. The **airport** receives daily Air New Zealand flights from Auckland and Wellington, and lies midway between Tauranga and Mount Maunganui, roughly 3km from each: a taxi (see "Listings", p.368) to either costs about $8.

The Tauranga **visitor centre** at 95 Willow St (Mon–Fri 7am–5.30pm, Sat & Sun 8am–4pm; ☎07/578 8103, fax 578 7020, *www.visitplenty.co.nz*, trgvin @tauranga-dc.govt.nz) handles transport and accommodation bookings, as well as selling town plans (50¢) and more substantial maps ($3.75). There is a **DOC office** (Mon–Fri 8am–4.40pm) but it is inconveniently sited in Chadwick Road, Greerton, some 3km south of central Tauranga; for maps try Absolute Adventure, 94 Willow St, by the visitor centre. The Mount Maunganui **visitor centre** is on Salisbury Avenue (Mon–Fri 9am–5pm, Sat & Sun 9am–3pm; ☎07/575 5099).

Two **local bus** services (City Travel ☎07/544 5494, Newloves ☎07/578 6453; pick up timetables at the visitor centres) run weekday services that cover most places in the immediate vicinity. Newloves provide an hourly Tauranga–Mount Maunganui service (Mon–Fri; $3 one way), but these dry up around 5pm. After that you'll have to shell out for a taxi ($15–20), either from the **taxi** stand in The Strand in Tauranga or by calling one of the radio-cab companies (see "Listings", p.368). During summer, there's also a daytime **ferry** (Christmas–Feb; $5 one way) to Salisbury Wharf in Mount Maunganui from Coronation Wharf on The Strand in Tauranga. **Drivers** crossing the Harbour Bridge will be charged a $1 **toll** in each direction. For **bike and car rental** see "Listings" on p.368.

Accommodation

On arrival, your first move is to decide which side of the water you want to stay. If you've got a car you might prefer to stop in **Tauranga**, where the choice is wider and prices tend to be a little lower, though you're further from the beach. Without your own

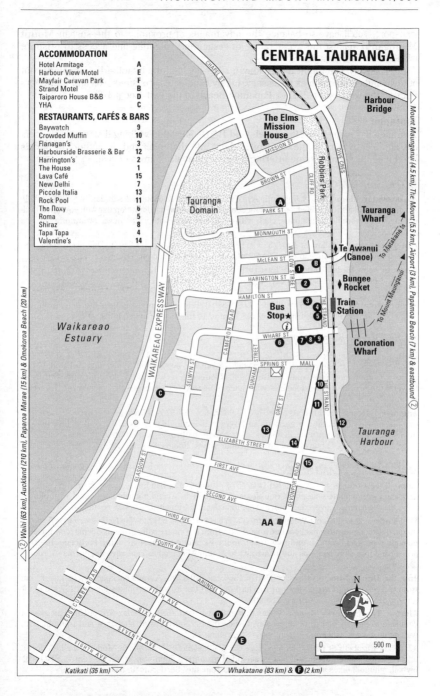

CENTRAL TAURANGA

ACCOMMODATION

Hotel Armitage	A
Harbour View Motel	E
Mayfair Caravan Park	F
Strand Motel	B
Taiparoro House B&B	D
YHA	C

RESTAURANTS, CAFÉS & BARS

Baywatch	9
Crowded Muffin	10
Flanagan's	3
Harbourside Brasserie & Bar	12
Harrington's	2
The House	1
Lava Café	15
New Delhi	7
Piccola Italia	13
Rock Pool	11
The Roxy	6
Roma	5
Shiraz	8
Tapa Tapa	4
Valentine's	14

Harbour Bridge

The Elms Mission House

Tauranga Domain

Waikareao Estuary

Robbins Park

Tauranga Wharf

Te Awanui (Canoe)

Bungee Rocket

Train Station

Bus Stop ★

Coronation Wharf

Tauranga Harbour

WAIKAREAO EXPRESSWAY

AA

N

0   500 m

Mount Maunganui (4.5 km), The Mount (5.5 km), Airport (3 km), Papamoa Beach (7 km) & eastbound (2)

To Matakana's

To Mount Maunganui

(2) Waihi (63 km), Auckland (210 km), Papamoa Marae (15 km) & Omokoroa Beach (20 km)

Katikati (35 km) ▽   ▽ Whakatane (83 km) & F (2 km) transport, you'll have to balance the advantages of proximity to the surf in **Mount Maunganui** against the wider range of restaurants, nightlife and access to offshore islands that Tauranga offers.

Alternatively, you might like to stay further afield at the **beachside campsites** out of town and commute in as necessary. Likely candidates are Omokoroa and Plummers Point to the west (see p.357) or Papamoa Beach to the east (see p.370).

Tauranga

Tauranga has many **hostels**, **motels** and **B&Bs** all within walking distance of the centre, and plenty more in the suburbs and out into the hinterland. A plethora of motels line Fifteenth Avenue, some offering good deals at slack times of year.

HOTELS AND MOTELS

Ambassador Motor Inn, 9 Fifteenth Ave (☎07/578 5665 & 0800/782 922, fax 578 5226). Well-appointed motel a short drive from the city centre and near the harbour. Popular well equipped budget units and more luxurious ones, each with a spa and some with water views; swimming and spa pools. ⑤–⑥.

Hotel Armitage, 9 Willow St (☎07/578 9119 & 0800/276 482, fax 577 9198). This place is big and central, with Sky TV, pool and other perks of international chain-dom. ⑥.

Harbour View Motel, 7 Fifth Ave East (☎07/578 8621, fax 578 7123, *harbview@wave.co.nz*). Small, quiet and fairly simple place a stone's throw from the bay. Rates are at the lower end of this price code. ⑤.

Strand Motel, 27 The Strand (☎ & fax 07/578 5807). Budget, central and near the waterfront, but on a noisy corner. Sea views from the decks of most of the fully equipped units. ④.

B&BS AND GUESTHOUSES

Hollies, Westridge Drive, Bethlehem (☎07/577 9678, fax 579 1678, *www.hollies.co.nz*, *stay @hollies.co.nz*). Extremely spacious homestay surrounded by well-tended grounds and a pool in an exclusive subdivision 8km south of Tauranga. Rooms are very comfortable and come with fresh flowers; the breakfasts are delicious with juice squeezed from oranges just picked off the trees. Rooms ⑥, suite ⑧.

Taiparoro House, 11 Fifth Ave (☎07/577 9607, fax 577 9264, *kl.Kelly@clear.net.nz*). Beautiful colonial house surrounded by gardens and trees, a five-minute walk from the centre. Five period-furnished rooms have private facilities, plus phone, bathrobes and sumptuous breakfasts. The suite comes with a CD player and good harbour views. Rooms ⑦, suite ⑧.

HOSTELS AND CAMPSITES

Apple Tree Cottage, 47 Maxwell Rd (☎07/576 7404). A suburban house 1.5km from the centre of Tauranga with a limited supply of doubles and dorm beds around a garden equipped with plunge pool, barbecue and a covered cooking area. Relaxed and friendly. Dorms ①, rooms ②.

Bell Lodge, 39 Bell St, off Waihi Rd (☎07/578 6344, fax 578 6342, *bell.lodge@host.co.nz*). A clean, modern and comfortable backpacker hostel 3km from the centre with spacious dorms, comfortable en-suite rooms and some brand new motel units. Excellent facilities including barbecue, Internet access and free daily pick-ups and transport to Mount Maunganui. Tent sites $8, dorms ①, rooms ②, units ③.

Just the Ducks Nuts, 6 Vale St (☎07/576 1366, fax 549 0336). A small backpackers just over 2km from the centre, with great views of the harbour and the Mount, and bikes for rent ($7 a day for guests, $15 non-guests). Dorms ①, rooms ②.

Mayfair Tourist Park, Mayfair St, off Fifteenth Ave (☎07/578 3323, fax 578 5910). The closest campsite to the city centre (2.5km away, beside the harbour). Large, sheltered and tranquil, with well equipped cabins; linen $5. Tent sites $10, cabins ②.

YHA, 171 Elizabeth St (☎07/578 5064, fax 578 5040, *yhataur@yha.org.nz*). Modern, well equipped and very hospitable, this hostel lies in secluded grounds a 5min walk from the centre. BBQ, volleyball, minigolf; bikes and bodyboards for rent. Tent sites $8, dorms ①, rooms ②.

Mount Maunganui

Mount Maunganui is close to the surf and though much of the accommodation is geared towards **long-staying** Kiwi holidaymakers you'll also find several motels and a couple of hostels.

Blue Haven Motel, 10 Tweed St (☎07/575 6508, fax 575 4817, *bluehaven@xtra.co.nz*). Popular budget motel close to a fairly quiet section of beach with ground-floor units fully equipped for cooking, and with Sky TV and videos. ④.

Fitzgerald's Irish Inn, 463 Maunganui Rd (☎ & fax 07/575 4013, *fitzgeraldsinn @hotmail.com*). A friendly Irish-themed guesthouse with a homey atmosphere that extends to a pool table and a guitar and piano to hone your skills. Rooms are small and share a bathroom but come with TV and free tea, coffee and cake. ④.

Mount Backpackers, 87 Maunganui Rd (☎ & fax 07/575 0860). Small, clean and newly renovated though slightly cramped hostel right in the thick of things – close to restaurants, bars and the beach. There's bike rental ($15 a day) and Internet access. Dorms ①, rooms ③.

Mount Maunganui Domain Motor Camp, 1 Adams Ave (☎07/575 4471, fax 575 4476). A sizeable, terraced **campsite** very close to the beach in a pleasant spot beside the hot saltwater pools and right at the foot of the Mount. Tent sites $20, on-site vans and cabins ③.

Ocean Waves Motel, 74 Marine Parade (☎ & fax 07/575 4594). Nicely located motel as close as you'll get to the popular end of the beach with ocean views from many units. ⑤.

Pacific Coast Backpackers, 432 Maunganui Rd (☎07/574 9601, fax 574 9622, *www.actionstations.co.nz, bookings @actionstations.co.nz*). Vast, rambling hostel with good facilities (spacious dorms, comfortable rooms with sheets, large kitchen, games room, barbecue area) and a strong eco/recycling ethic, but a little soulless and well away from the restaurants and the fashionable end of the beach. Dorms ①, rooms ③.

The city of Tauranga

Tauranga's flat **city centre** is concentrated between Tauranga Harbour and Waikareao Estuary. It's a dense kernel of shops, restaurants and bars where

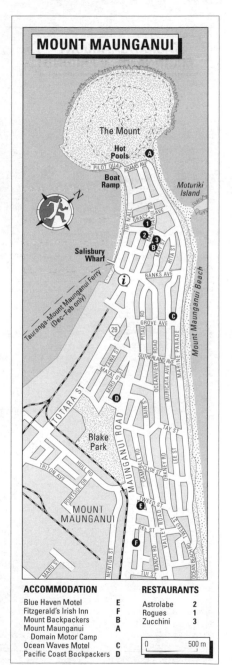

ACCOMMODATION		RESTAURANTS	
Blue Haven Motel	E	Astrolabe	2
Fitzgerald's Irish Inn	F	Rogues	1
Mount Backpackers	B	Zucchini	3
Mount Maunganui	A		
Domain Motor Camp			
Ocean Waves Motel	C		
Pacific Coast Backpackers	D		

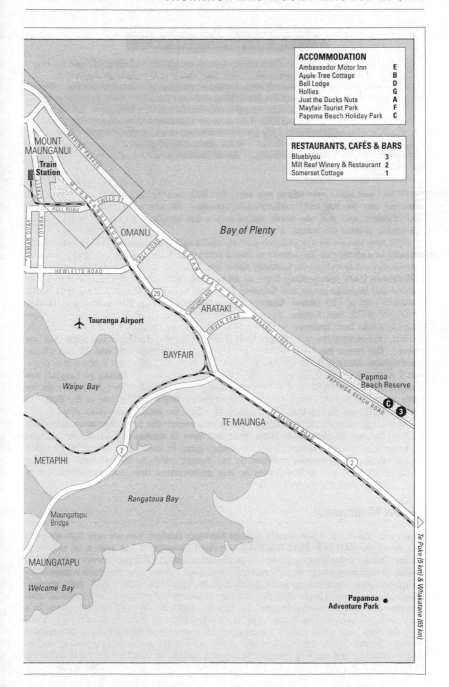

ACCOMMODATION

Ambassador Motor Inn	E
Apple Tree Cottage	B
Bell Lodge	D
Hollies	G
Just the Ducks Nuts	A
Mayfair Tourist Park	F
Papoma Beach Holiday Park	C

RESTAURANTS, CAFÉS & BARS

Bluebiyou	3
Mill Reef Winery & Restaurant	2
Somerset Cottage	1

MOUNT MAUNGANUI

Train Station

MARINE PARADE

TOTARA STREET

MAUNGANUI ROAD

TWEED ST

HULL ROAD

ASMAN QUAY

HEWLETTS ROAD

OMANU

OCEAN BEACH ROAD

Bay of Plenty

29

CONCORD AVE

ARATAKI

GIRVEN ROAD

MARANUI STREET

Tauranga Airport

BAYFAIR

Waipu Bay

PAPAMOA BEACH ROAD

Papmoa Beach Reserve

C 3

TE MAUNGA

TE MAUNGA ROAD

2

METAPIHI

2

Rangataua Bay

Maungatapu Bridge

MAUNGATAPU

Welcome Bay

Papamoa Adventure Park

Te Puke (5 km) & Whakatane (65 km)

THE BATTLE OF GATE PA

In 1864 the tiny community of Tauranga became the scene of the **Battle of Gate Pa**, one of the most decisive engagements of the **New Zealand Wars**. In January the government sent troops here to build two redoubts, hoping to prevent supplies and reinforcements from reaching the followers of the Maori King (see box on p.214), who were fighting in the Waikato. Most of the local Ngaiterangi hurried back from the Waikato and challenged the soldiers from a pa they quickly built near an entrance to the mission land, which became known as Gate Pa. In April, government troops surrounded the pa and pounded it with artillery. Nonetheless, the British lost about a third of their assault force and at nightfall the Ngaiterangi slipped through the British lines to fight again in the Waikato.

---

you'll find just about everything you need, but little of abiding interest other than boat trips out onto the bay and its islands (see opposite). Downtown Tauranga is a pleasant spot though, and you can easily spend half a day strolling along the waterfront or mooching around the couple of minor sights.

First stop should be the ornately carved traditional **war canoe** – *Te Awanui* stands proudly in a shelter on the corner of Dive Crescent and McLean Street, and is used on ceremonial occasions on the harbour. About one block up and entered from Cliff Street, is **Robbins Park** (dawn–dusk; free), an attractive swathe of green equipped with a rose garden and begonia house, and boasting fine views across to Mount Maunganui. At the northern end of The Strand, Mission Street is home to **The Elms Mission House** (☎07/577 9772; Sun 2–4pm, and by appointment; $5). One of the country's oldest homes, it was built between 1835 and 1847 by an early missionary, Archdeacon A.N. Brown, who tended the wounded of both sides during the **Battle of Gate Pa** (see box above). The house has been restored to its original form complete with Brown's thousand-volume library. However, unless you strike it lucky and catch it when it is open, you'll only get to see the pretty **garden** (dawn–dusk; free), including an English oak planted by Brown in 1838 and a reconstruction of the original chapel. Inside is a dining table at which Brown entertained several British officers on the eve of the Battle of Gate Pa, little suspecting that over the next few days he would bury most of them.

Back on the waterfront, you might want to experience the 5g acceleration meted out by the **Bungee Rocket** (daily 10am–5pm, and later in summer; $35), a kind of cross between a fairground ride and a reverse bungy jump in which two people sit strapped into a tubular metal cocoon attached by two bungy cords to 30m towers. When the catch is released you rocket skywards: less intimidating than and traditional bungy jump, but as much fun for less money.

Mount Maunganui

From the end of the 3.5km-long Tauranga Harbour Bridge, you are still 3km short of the heart of **MOUNT MAUNGANUI**, reached through a big industrial estate of cement works and a bitumen plant: not an auspicious start. Things improve as you head to the northern tip where the 232-metre Mount itself rises above the golden **beach**, an unbroken sweep stretching over 20km east to Papamoa (see p.370) and beyond. Habitually sun-kissed in the summer. It is consequently very popular, and high-rise condos and apartments have colonized the beach's fashionable northern kilometre in a very un-Kiwi fashion. The Mount also has a reputation as something of a party town with the New Year revelry often featuring on TV coverage of bad behaviour around the country. Nevertheless the beach is still great, perfect for a day or two playing volley-ball, swimming and **surfing** (premium-rate surf hotline ☎0900/90098), while still within easy reach of good restaurants and bars where everyone gravitates for sundowners.

The big draw is the mountain itself, which has a fine **walking track** around the base (3km loop; 45min), mostly level and offering a great sea and harbour outlook from under the shade of ancient pohutukawas. You can also **hike to the summit** (2km one way; 1hr), which is tough going towards the top but well worth the effort for views of Matakana Island and along the coast. Both tracks start from the northern end of the beach, right by the outdoor **hot saltwater pools**, Adams Way (daily 6am–10pm; public pool $2.50, private $3.50 per half hour; use of towel $2, togs $2), which form Mount Maunganui's other main attraction.

Activities and day-trips

It would be a shame to come to the western Bay of Plenty and not get out **on the water**, something easily done from the Tauranga Wharf, with many trips also picking up at Salisbury Wharf in Mount Maunganui. A full range of boats is ready to take you cruising, fishing, sailing, parasailing and **swimming with dolphins**.

The island retreats of Matakana and Mayor are both prime Bay of Plenty boat-trip destinations. Strictly speaking the former is, in fact, two islands: the tiny **Rangiwea** and the long sheltering sweep of **Matakana**, nestled close to Tauranga Harbour and used primarily for farming and forestry. **Mayor Island** is the cone-shaped dormant volcano, protruding from the Bay of Plenty 40km off the coast of Tauranga and increasingly geared towards eco-tourism.

Boat trips on the bay

About the cheapest way to get on the water is on a historic six-hour **harbour cruise** aboard the 1938 line-fishing boat *Ratahi* (☎07/578 9685; $25) as it chugs across the bay to Omokoroa and back with afternoon tea on the way. If you'd prefer to go under **sail**, try the *Slipstream* catamaran (☎07/576 1841; half day $50, full day $80), a sleek and highly advanced 8.5-metre sailing craft that can drop anchor almost anywhere and is a great thrill to sail. An equally leisurely day out at sea, but with the option of **swimming with dolphins**, is run by Gemini Galaxsea (book a day ahead ☎07/578 3197; full day; $85, take your own lunch). The skipper, Butler, is a real character, a good-natured sea dog and militant greenie who has a high success rate of finding dolphins. His secret is to allow plenty of time, so don't be surprised if you're out well into the evening; if there's time you also get to snorkel around a reef. Trips run most of the year, but only in good weather conditions. If you are pressed for time and still want to swim with dolphins, try Dolphin Safaris (☎0800/326 8747; 3–4hr; $85) who run trips in the morning and afternoon.

Scores of boats are available for **fishing charters**, many through Blue Ocean Charters, Tauranga Wharf (☎07/578 9685): game fishing for marlin tuna and kingfish (Dec–April) is likely to cost about $250 a day per person, but if you go out for the bottom fish (snapper and tarakihi) it's cheaper at around $40 per half day.

Matakana Island

MATAKANA ISLAND has 24km of beach and great surfing on its eastern side, not to mention a general store and pub for more mundane requirements. However, it's worth knowing that much of the island is Maori land with limited access, so even if you take your own wheels you will be fairly restricted. Perhaps the best way to experience the island is to join the tribal owners on Matakana Island Tours' day-long trip (☎07/548 1919, fax 548 1917; Nov–March; $75) from Tauranga by boat to Matakana and then in a restored 1914 covered wagon hauled by Clydesdale horses to a barbecue in the shade of walnut trees.

Otherwise two regular **barges** head out on 15min crossings to the island: *Forest Lady* departs from Sulphur Point, along The Strand in Tauranga (☎025/937 426; Mon–Fri

6.45am & 3.45pm; passengers $2.50 one way); and the *Matakana Ferry* (☎025/927 251; daily 7.45am & 4pm; passengers $2 one way) leaves from Omokoroa (see p.357), 20km west of Tauranga.

Mayor Island (Tuhua)

Dormant volcano, **MAYOR ISLAND**, has a crater now virtually overgrown and a third of its coast designated a **marine reserve** in readiness for low-key eco-tourism. There are some great **walking tracks** around the island's base and through its centre, and boats coming out here will rent snorkelling gear ($10 per day) so you can explore the aquatic world. The area, however, is particularly well endowed with **wasps** and anyone allergic to stings should pack medication or just not risk it.

As the island is privately owned by the Tuhua Trust Board, all visitors are charged a **landing fee** (day-visit $10) but this is included in commercial boat fares. Blue Ocean Charters (☎07/578 9685) organize **boats** to the island leaving Tauranga for Mount Maunganui then on to the island's only landing site, Opo Bay, at the south end – though sailings are often cancelled in rough weather. Regular services operate in summer (Nov to mid-April), but the rest of the year you may need to charter a boat; contact Tauranga visitor centre for details and the going rates. The **crossing** usually takes two to three hours depending on boat and conditions, and will cost you $60, though there are sometimes trips including lunch and off-shore fishing for $75. It is also possible to get to Mayor Island **from Whangamata** on MV *Te RA* (☎07/865 8681) or MV *Tawa* (☎07/865 6651).

Your only **accommodation** option on the island is the *Tuhua Campsite* at Opo Bay (☎07/577 0531; tent sites $9, bunks ①, cabins ②) which sits beneath tall pohutukawa trees behind an idyllic bay. It has showers and toilets, but you'll need to bring a cooking stove, all utensils and food.

Eating

Tauranga and Mount Maunganui have both fully embraced modern café/bar culture, Tauranga in particular rating as something of a regional culinary hotspot. As elsewhere, distinctions between eating and drinking places are becoming ever more blurred and you may well find yourself enjoying a drink at one of the places listed below.

In **Tauranga**, most of the cafés and restaurants are right in the centre – a slew of them strung along Devonport Road with a bunch more lining The Strand and the streets running back from it. There is also a restaurant at the *Mills Reef* winery (see p.368) in the suburbs, and additional fine dining in Bethlehem nearby. **Mount Maunganui** doesn't have Tauranga's selection, but you'd have to be finicky not to be able to find something appealing on the half-dozen blocks of Maunganui Road that make up the centre.

Tauranga and Bethlehem

Baywatch, cnr Wharf St & The Strand (☎07/578 8322). Award-winning brasserie and bar decorated in French blue, with great first-floor views over the harbour. Food with flair might include calamari and vegetable stack with Thai dressing ($15) followed by chargrilled cervena with mushroom ravioli ($28). Early evening three-course dinner (5.30–7pm) for $30. Licensed.

Crowded Muffins, 22 Devonport Rd. Great, cheap muffins to take away or munch here over a coffee. Daily 7am–5pm.

Harbourside Brasserie & Bar, under the railway bridge at the southern end of The Strand. A big, airy building right on the harbour, with great views and a sizeable deck built over the water where you can feed the fish below; in summer, boats moor alongside. Lively cosmopolitan ambience and food, with mains for $20–25 and cheaper light meals. Licensed.

The House, 15 Harington St (☎07/578 6828). Breezy, modern café, restaurant and bar with plenty of outdoor seating for those sunny days and balmy evenings. Full breakfast or eggs Florentine goes for $9, lunch might be a stuffed sandwich or gourmet pizza ($12–14), and there are mains such as lamb shanks with garlic mashed potato. Licensed.

Lava Café, 130 Devonport Rd. Laid-back, groovy little café ideal for reading the paper over a coffee and a muffin.

New Delhi, 20 Wharf St (☎07/578 5533). Recently opened and unpretentious Indian restaurant with a good range of north Indian mains including vegetarian dishes. The chicken tikka masala ($13) goes nicely with a mint paratha. Delivery available. Licensed and BYO.

Piccola Italia, 107 Grey St (☎07/578 8363). Admirable northern Italian café and restaurant with wonderfully prepared authentic dishes served with aplomb. Closed Mon & Tues lunch and all day Sun. Licensed.

The Rock Pool, 64 Devonport Rd. A cheerful, inexpensive BYO café and wine bar, serving great Mediterranean-style food along with some of the best cakes in town. Breakfast and lunch daily, dinner Fri & Sat.

Shiraz, 12 Wharf St (☎07/577 0059). Tasty Middle Eastern and Mediterranean food, excellent service and reasonable prices for lunch (under $15) and dinner (under $20) make this a popular and often packed place; reservations recommended. Leisurely eating in a small café and covered courtyard. Closed Sun.

Valentine's, cnr Devonport Rd & Elizabeth St. The local manifestation of a nationwide chain noted for its bargain all-you-can-eat buffets. Lunch ($18) runs noon–2.30pm, there are several sittings for dinner ($26) from 5.30pm, and on Sunday they are open all day from 9am ($18 all day). Licensed.

Mount Maunganui

Astrolabe, 82 Maunganui Rd. A large and popular diner-cum-drinking hole, with a beachy and slightly upmarket tenor and some late-night boogie. They serve lunch and dinner, salads and pasta, as well as char-grilled steak and fish along with a large range of beers.

Rogues, cnr Pacific Ave & Maunganui Rd. Very popular restaurant and bar serving breakfast in high season, focaccia and burritos for lunch, and main meals which might extend to kumara, cranberry and camembert strudel ($12) or tempura prawns ($20). Licensed.

Zucchini, 70 Maunganui Rd. A seriously good espresso bar with imaginative vegetarian meals that justify a look even for the staunchest of carnivores. The soups are superb, and they do pizza, panini and felafel all for around $10.

Drinking, nightlife and entertainment

In both Tauranga and Maunganui the restaurants double as **bars**: neither town is especially jumping in the off season, but come summer the evenings hot up with Mount Maunganui earning a reputation for boisterous behaviour. Of the two only Tauranga boasts a couple of dedicated watering holes and a **nightclub** or two, all in the same downtown area. **Films** are shown at the Cinema 6 Complex on Elizabeth Street; screening times are listed in the *Bay of Plenty Times* (every Fri; 70¢), which is the best general source of entertainment **listings**.

Tauranga clubs and bars

Flanagan's Irish Pub, Hamilton St. A big and friendly Irish pub with a energetic late-night vibe and live bands on Fri & Sat nights.

Harington's, 10 Harington St. A bar-cum-nightclub, usually packed by midnight and open until 5am. Mostly dance music (every night Oct–April; rest of the year Thurs–Sat 9pm–5am). During the summer holidays they often hold theme evenings and beach parties.

Roma, 65 The Strand. One of the more upmarket bars, open from 4pm, serving gourmet pizzas until 2am or so, and often with live jazz, plus dancing on Fri & Sat nights. Closed Mon.

Tapa Tapa, 67 The Strand. Café-style Pacific Rim dining throughout the day but best treated as a café and a great place to gaze across the top of your glass at the boats catching the setting sun.
The Roxy, 40 Wharf St. The grooviest bar in town; small but perfectly formed and with animal print sofas. A crowd of regulars indulge in bar snacks, dancing and general mischief.

Listings

Automobile Association cnr First Ave & Devonport Rd (☎07/578 2222).

Bike rental Around $20 a day from Bike and Pack Warehouse, 1 Dee St, Mount Maunganui (☎07/575 2189) or Gravity's Edge Cycles, 229 Maunganui Rd, Mount Maunganui (☎07/575 8997), though several of the hostels have cheaper machines – some available to non-guests.

Buses InterCity and Newmans (☎07/578 2825) run several daily services to Mount Maunganui, Auckland, Hamilton, Rotorua, and Thames (via Katikati, Waihi and Paeroa).

Car rental Budget deals from Johnny's Rentals, 111 Hewletts Rd, Mount Maunganui (☎07/575 9204) as well as international companies in Tauranga such as: Avis, cnr First Ave & Cameron Rd (☎07/578 4204); Hertz, 150 Elizabeth St West (☎07/578 9143); and Rent-a-Dent, 19 Fifteenth Ave (☎07/578 1772).

Internet Tauranga Library, in the Civic Shopping Centre behind the visitor centre (Mon–Thurs 9.30am–5.30pm, Fri 9.30am–7pm, Sat 9.30am–12.30pm) has Internet access at reasonable rates.

Kiwifruit picking The best time for picking is late April to mid-June, but pruning is also necessary from mid-June to early Sept and again from end-Oct to Jan. For picking, you're paid by the bin, so speed is of the essence; an average rate is $70 a day, but quick workers can earn $100. The best sources of up-to-date information are the backpacker hostels which will often help you to find work.

Medical treatment After-hours medical care and an emergency pharmacy is available at the Baycare Medical Service Centre (☎07/578 8111; Mon–Fri 5pm–8am, Sat & Sun 24hr), cnr Edgecumbe Rd & Tenth Ave.

Post office The post office, 17 Grey St, at Spring St (☎07/577 9911; Mon–Fri 9am–5pm, Sat 9am–12.30pm) has poste restante facilities.

Taxis Citicabs (☎07/577 0999); Coast Line (☎07/571 8333); Tauranga Taxis (☎07/578 6086). Thomas Cook 63 Devonport Rd (☎07/578 3119).

Trains The *Kaimai Express* (☎0800/802 802) runs once daily to Auckland; information and bookings at the visitor centre.

Whitewater rafting Locally-based Woodrow Rafting (☎07/576 2628) run Wairoa River trips for $55. All other rafting companies running the Wairoa operate out of Rotorua (see p.279), though many will pick up in Tauranga; call around.

Around Tauranga and Mount Maunganui

Unless you are happy spending days on the beach, or are keen to explore the Bay of Plenty and its islands, you'll soon exhaust the temptations of Tauranga and Mount Maunganui. Help is at hand in the hinterland, where **Mills Reef winery** drapes across fertile countryside backed by the angular peaks of the **Kaimai-Mamaku Forest Park**. Rivers cascading down the slopes and across the coastal plain supply water for assorted activities at **Waimarino Adventure Park**, and periodically fire up **McLaren Falls**, where shallow rock pools make great swimming holes. At the coast, the great sweep of Mount Maunganui's Ocean Beach extends to **Papamoa Beach**, great for surfing and swimming away from the glitz of The Mount.

Bethlehem: Mills Reef winery and Waimarino Adventure Park

The suburb of Bethlehem justifies a little of your time, particularly if you fancy a visit to the Art Deco-style **tasting rooms** (daily 10am–5pm; free) at *Mills Reef* on Moffat Road. The place markets wine under three different ranges, Mere Road Selection, Reserve and Elspeth; their most popular wines are the Reserve Chardonnay and Elspeth Chardonnay, though they also produce Rieslings, Sauvignons, some sparkling wines and Cabernet Sauvignons. The adjoining **restaurant** (☎07/576 8844) enjoys an elevated position overlooking the vines, perfect when tucking into light meals such as vodka salmon with dill hollandaise and a Caesar salad ($18) or mains like lamb with a warm artichoke salad ($26); and you can test your skills in a post-prandial game of petanque in the grounds. It this doesn't suit, drive a couple of kilometres back towards Tauranga to *Somerset Cottage*, 30 Bethlehem Rd (☎07/576 6889; licensed), an extremely popular and traditional restaurant that oozes charm and attracts a dedicated band of regulars for their excellent value mains (around $25).

All this eating and wine tasting could work as a perfect finale to a half a day spent at the riverside **Waimarino Adventure Park**, Taniwha Place (☎07/576 4233, fax 576 1203, *www.kayaks.co.nz*, *waimarino@xtra.co.nz*; daily 10am–6pm) which conducts a huge range of mainly water-based courses and activities. The most accessible are the **activity sessions** around the centre ($12–25 per person depending on what you opt for) which all include rope swings, a hydro-slide, spa pool, ropes course and trampolines ($12 per person) and can include water-bikes and kayaks ($18) and the climbing wall ($25). **Kayaking** trips start with the Wairoa River Trip (3hr; $25), a tide assisted and unguided flatwater paddle down a lower stretch of the Wairoa River to the adventure park; a moonlit version costs $35 and booking is essential. If whitewater rafting isn't thrilling enough for you, try the Extreme Boating (3hr; $120–140), where you are stuck at the sharp end of a double kayak and guided down either the Wairoa (certain Sundays only; Grade IV+) or the Kaituna (Grade III–IV): for descriptions of both rivers see p.279.

Paparoa Marae

The community of **Te Puna**, 15km west of Tauranga, is chiefly notable for the **Paparoa Marae**, Paparoa Road (☎ & fax 07/552 5796), which welcomes cultural exchange, is well-organized and mercifully free of rampant commercialism The marae regularly runs organized afternoon and evening events for groups (around $40). These involve a traditional *wero* (challenge) at the gate, a visit to the simple meeting-house, where the carvings are explained, and a display of Maori crafts. On an evening visit you can partake in a hangi followed by a haka and other entertainment, involving some audience participation. As long as you phone ahead, you can visit independently, or join an event or a cultural-exchange group – where you learn how to make something Maori in return for teaching a craft. To get there, follow SH2 westwards to Te Puna, where you branch off on to Te Puna Road, turning onto Borell Road and finally onto Paparoa Road.

McLaren Falls

Most summer Sundays, **McLaren Falls**, signposted 11km south of Tauranga off SH29, becomes the scene of frenetic activity as hundreds of rafters and kayakers congregate to run the Grade IV+ rapids of the Wairoa River (for rafting trips see our account on p.279). The ten-metre cataract itself is only worth viewing on the Sundays when the upstream dam releases its charge (Dec–March every Sun; Sept–Nov & April–May every second Sun) but pretty much every day of the summer locals flock here to wallow in a lovely series of shallow pools hewn out of the bedrock. It can get crowded in the height of summer, but a few minutes rock-hopping should secure you a pool to yourselves: bring a picnic and some sun screen.

The dam that holds back the Wairoa River forms Lake McLaren, centrepiece for **McLaren Falls Park**, 1km upstream from McLaren Falls (daily: Nov–March 8am–7.30pm, April–Oct 8am–5.30pm; free), a large area of parkland, native bush and exotic trees, with barbecue areas and the freedom to **camp** anywhere ($4). To use the shower and cooking facilities, campers will need to make arrangements with the two basic on-site **hostels** (☎07/577 7000; ①), which are open to backpackers.

Kaimai–Mamaku Forest Park

Tauranga and Mount Maunganui have a deserved reputation for balmy weather, a result of the rain shadow cast by the broad, forested spine of the **Kaimai Range** which rises up south of the Karangahake Gorge (see p.328) and extends 70km south. This rugged landscape was created about five million years ago when vast quantities of lava, scoria and ash were spewed across the region, forming a chain of large **volcanic cones**. The entire range falls within the **Kaimai-Mamaku Forest Park**, not the most hospitable nor accessible of the tramping regions, though it contains some **tracks** worthy of exploration, scenic lookouts and a network of back-country **huts**, which can be reached either from Te Aroha in the west (see p.329), the Karangahake Gorge in the north (see p.328) and from Tauranga. The northern sector of the park is an extension of the Coromandel Range and has been intensively mined for gold and logged for its kauri, while the southern sector is largely plateau country, much of it dissected by deep streams. The DOC produce a useful leaflet on the area ($1), as well as several booklets detailing walks in the park. If you'd prefer a **guided tramp** with an experience bushman (though you'll still need most of your own gear), contact Kaimai Bush Adventures (☎ & fax 07/552 5454) who run custom designed tramps from half a day up for as little as $35.

Papamoa Beach

Mount Maunganui's stunning Ocean Beach stretches 20km east to **Papamoa Beach**, a burgeoning community accessed off the Pacific Highway (SH2). Backed by the dramatic Papamoa Hills, it makes a pleasant spot for a beach break away from the city, facilitated by the extensive *Papamoa Beach Holiday Park*, 535 Papamoa Beach Rd (☎ & fax 07/572 0816, *www.papamoabeach.co.nz*; tent sites $11, cabins & flats ②–④, motel units ⑤, villas ⑥), with a broad selection of accommodation including beachfront campsites and some gorgeous new villas with wonderful sea views. The licensed, nautically themed *Bluebiyou* café/restaurant next door has a covered deck that leads right on to sand and surf, and a kitchen that serves light meals all day, lunch, dinner and Sunday brunch.

In the hills a couple of kilometres back from the beach, there's fun to be had at **Papamoa Adventure Park**, 1162 Welcome Bay Rd (☎ & fax 07/542 0972, *papamoa.adventure.park@xtra.co.nz*), where they'll take you **horse trekking** ($25 per hour) over open hill country and through forest tracks. For something more energetic you can career down a steep dirt track at frighteningly high speed in a wheeled buggy known as the **luge** (1 ride $10, 3 for $25), join a **quad bike** tour ($25 per 25min trial, $50 per 1hr tour, or head into the forest for a **paintball** game (from $23). It is a great spot to spend a few hours, and there's farm animal feeding to entertain the younger members.

Eastern Bay of Plenty

Moving away from Tauranga toward the **Eastern Bay of Plenty**, the urban influence wanes noticeably; the pace slows and everything seems that much more rural, with orchards and kiwifruit vines gradually giving way to sheep country. You'll also find a gradual change in the racial mix, for the Eastern Bay of Plenty is increasingly Maori country; appropriate since some of the first **Maori** to reach New Zealand arrived here in their great *waka* (war canoes). In fact Whakatane is sometimes known as the birthplace of *Aotearoa*, for it was here that the Polynesian navigator **Toi te Huatahi** first landed.

The westernmost town, **Te Puke**, is very much New Zealand's kiwifruit capital, and is well inland, but the sea is still the focus of the region. The heyday of its major port has long passed, but **Whakatane** remains the largest town, prettily set between cliffs and a river estuary, and currently improving its image with new street paving and feature lighting on the town waterfall. It makes a great base for forays out to volcanic **White Island**, the bird reserve of **Whale Island**, or inland to **Taneatua**, home of an incongruous art gallery and the embassy of the Tuhoe people. Further east, **Opotiki** is the gateway to Eastland in one direction and to Gisborne in the other, as well as providing access to some interesting walks in the hills to the south and to trips on the mighty **Motu River**.

Te Puke

Te Puke, 31km southeast of Tauranga on SH2, comes justifiably billed as the "kiwifruit capital of the world". Not surprisingly, this is home to **Kiwifruit Country**, a further 6km past Te Puke (daily 9am–5pm; 30–40min guided tours $10), a massive orchard and processing plant that also operates as a horticultural theme park, its gateway surreally decorated with a giant slice of kiwifruit. The complex is as tacky and commercialized as you would expect, but it's the only place to be if you're curious about how these little green, furry fruits grow and are harvested. The "Kiwi Kart" guided tours tell you everything you ever wanted to know about them (and much more besides). Watch out for the busloads of tourists and avoid the overpriced souvenirs and café.

Next door to Kiwifruit Country is the **Vintage Auto Barn** (daily 9am–5pm; $6), literally a big barn of some ninety-odd vintage and classic cars from 1906 to 1970, all kept in exceptional condition. One of the more touching exhibits is The Beast, a racing car hand-built in the late 1950s by a young man dying of cancer. For his "final fling" he sped around the streets of Pirionga (near Te Awamutu) in this jalopy. Among the older models is a 1912 Model C Renault in pristine condition, complete with wooden-spoked wheels, and assorted models up for sale at prices that are astonishingly low given the amount of work that's gone into them: on last visit an immaculately restored Model A Ford was under $20,000. Car fanatics might easily lose a few hours in the extensive motoring library.

From Te Puke it's 66km along SH2 to Whakatane, the road hugging the coast for much of the way, but with little worth breaking your journey for. The one possible exception is **Longridge Park**, SH33, 3km south of its junction with SH2 (☎07/533 1515; daily 9am–5pm), where kids can feed farm animals and see captive eels ($1.50), while the adults take a highly scenic **jetboat** ride up the Kaituna River ($55), spend 45 minutes driving an **off-road 4WD** through all manner of devious mud traps and bogs ($55), or take a more sedate tour of the kiwifruit vines and working farm ($12).

Whakatane

The main settlement of the Eastern Bay of Plenty is **WHAKATANE**, a 17,000-strong town sprawled across flat farmland around the last convulsions of the Whakatane River, before it spills into the sea. It is all pretty dull except for a genuinely attractive centre wedged between the river and bush-clad hills which rise steeply from the town. There's an excellent **museum and gallery**, while the only other notable feature in the town is the **Pohaturoa** rock outcrop. The real attractions lie outside, in the shape of lovely beaches and bays like **Ohope Beach**, which is one of the most popular in the district. The main spine of the hills that overshadow the town runs out to **Kohi Point**, where there is an excellent lookout over the entire region.

The Whakatane area seems to have had more than its fair share of dramatic events. The **Maori** word Whakatane means "to act as a man" and comes from a legendary incident when the women of the *Mataatua* canoe were left aboard while the men went ashore; the canoe began to drift out to sea, but touching the paddles was *tapu* for women. Undeterred, the high-spirited Wairaka took matters into her own hands and paddled back to the safety of the shore, shouting *Ka Whakatane Au i Ah au* ("I will act as a man"), and a statue at Whakatane Heads commemorates her heroic act. The first **Europeans** to set foot in the area, apart from a brief sortie by Cook, were flax traders in the early 1800s and a trader called Philip Tapsell, who established a store in 1830. The next turning point in Whakatane's history came when, in March 1865, missionary **Carl Volkner** was killed at Opotiki, and a government agent, **James Falloon**, arrived to investigate. At this unwelcome intrusion, supporters of a fanatical Maori sect, the Hau Hau, attacked Falloon's vessel, killing him and his crew. In response, the government declared **martial law**, and by the end of the year a large part of the Bay of Plenty had been confiscated and Whakatane was being peopled by military settlers. The mem-

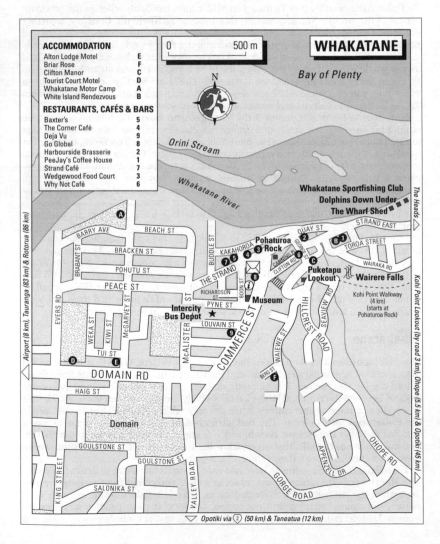

ory of this led **Te Kooti** (see box on p.401) to choose Whakatane as his target for a full-scale attack by his Maori force in 1869, burning and looting buildings before being driven back into the hills of Urewera. In more **recent times**, the Whakatane has led a relatively quiet life as a trading area and service town for the surrounding regions, and as a tourist attraction with access to many areas of natural beauty.

Unsurprisingly, most activities in Whakatane revolve around the sea, with the most exciting trips being to **White Island**, a live volcanic outcrop billowing white plumes of smoke far from the shore, though you can opt for the more soothing charms of **Whale Island**, a DOC-controlled wildlife reserve teeming with birds, or the more intimate pleasures of **swimming with dolphins**. Inland, **jetboating** and **whitewater-rafting** trips take on the Motu River or venture into Te Urewera National Park, while on the riverbanks anglers cast for the massive **trout** and salmon for which the area is renowned.

Arrival, information and accommodation

InterCity and Newmans **buses** run a service from Rotorua to Whakatane and on to Opotiki and Gisborne along SH2. They stop once a day in each direction at the Travel Centre, Pine Street, from where it is a five-minute walk to the small and helpful **visitor centre**, Boon Street (Mon–Fri 9am–5pm, Sat 9am–1pm, Sun 10am–2pm; ☎07/308 6058, fax ☎308 6020, *whakataneinfo@xtra.co.nz*), which is well-stocked with DOC leaflets for the local area. There's **Internet access** across from the visitor centre at Artex, 34 Boon St, and the **post office**, corner of Commerce Street and The Strand (☎07/307 1155) has poste restante facilities.

There's a reasonable selection of **accommodation** in Whakatane, much of it firmly mid-range with a preference for motels and campsites. Luxurious places are fairly thin on the ground and there is currently no hostel, though some entrepreneur is bound to open one in the near future. It is also worth considering staying 7km west at Ohope (see p.376).

Alton Lodge Motel, 76 Domain Rd (☎07/307 1003 & 0800/500 468, fax 308 5438). A comfortable modern motel with eleven luxury units with full kitchens and an indoor pool; good value for money. ④.

Briar Rose, 54 Waiewe St (☎07/308 0314, fax 308 0317). Very welcoming homestay B&B 1.5km uphill from the centre of Whakatane and surrounded by bird-filled bush. There's one room in the house and one self-contained cottage but you are encouraged to socialise in the house, and even stay for dinner ($25 by arrangement) which may well be wild pork or venison. ④.

Clifton Manor, 5 Clifton Rd (☎ & fax 07/307 2145, ☎0800/307 214, *cliftonmanor@xtra.co.nz*). Lovely, friendly old home with a large swimming pool, three well-kept guest rooms (some with private bath) let on a B&B basis, and two self-contained motel units. ⑤.

Tourist Court Motel, 50 Landing Rd (☎07/308 7099, fax 307 0821). A very friendly establishment with eight fully self-contained, clean and comfortable units and a retro 1970s feel. ③–④.

Whakatane Motor Camp, at the end of McGarvey Rd (☎07/308 8694, fax 308 2070). A well-equipped, sheltered campsite ten minutes' walk from The Strand. Tent sites $10, cabins ②.

White Island Rendezvous, 15 The Strand (☎07/308 9500 & 0800/242 299, fax 308 0303, *whiteisland@ellconweb.net.nz*). Smart, modern motel with clean rooms attractively decorated in blues and greens, and equipped with Sky TV and microwave. Downstairs units have polished wooden floors, though you'll need an upstairs unit for sea views. Units ⑤, spa unit ⑥.

The Town

Driving into Whakatane, Commerce Street hugs cliffs which were once lapped by the sea. The junction with The Strand is effectively the town centre, marked by Whakatane's defining feature, a large rock outcrop called **Pohaturoa** ("long rock"). The place is sacred to Maori and the small park surrounding the rock contains a canoe, carved benches and a black marble monument to Te Hurinui Apanui, a great chief who propounded the virtues of peace and is mourned by *pakeha* and Maori alike. This site was once a shrine where rites were performed by Maori priests, and the seed that grew into the karaka trees at its base are said to have arrived on the *Mataatua* canoe. From here, it is a short walk along Canning Street to the base of **Wairere Falls** (see box below) from where you can rejoin The Strand and stroll out along the river to the heads (1km each way), a lovely late afternoon walk rewarded by the sight of the bronze statue of Wairaka on top of the rock, often behatted by local wags after a good night out.

About the only unmissable sight in town is the **Whakatane & Districts Museum and Gallery** on Boon Street (Tues–Fri 10am–4.30pm, Sat 11am–1.30pm, Sun 2–4pm; $2 donation); it's the modern building with a steam engine from Tunnicliffe's Sawmill outside. The gallery is a small area that caters for travelling exhibitions, but the museum is more interesting with its own archives, research library and well-conceived displays on geological, Maori and European history – particularly as they relate to the Eastern Bay of Plenty. The collection is rich and varied with over 25,000 photographs and an important collection of Maori *taonga* (records) from the local *iwi*, tracing their descent from the *Mataatua* canoe.

Activities

To go **swimming with dolphins**, contact Dolphins Down Under, 2 The Strand (☎0800/354 7737, fax 07/308 4636, *www.dolphinswim.co.nz*, *flipper@dophinswim.co.nz*; 3–4hr; $85; book at least 2 days ahead between Dec & Feb), but you should avoid April when dolphins make themselves scarce – and note that in winter (April–Oct), trips run according to demand. If you can face an early start, you're likely to be rewarded by calm seas and light winds. All gear is supplied and the company has a high success rate of finding dolphins; there is a resident pod of common dolphins in the area and other types occasionally visit. If you see nothing at all, you receive a twenty percent refund. They also run excellent **snorkelling trips** around Whale Island (2–3hr; $35) and **dive trips** ($45 plus $35 for gear).

If rivers are more your thing, it is well worth considering a multi-day **wilderness rafting trip** on the nearby Motu River (see box opposite). Whakatane Raft Tours (☎ & fax 07/308 7760, *moturaft@wave.co.nz*) also offer cheaper trips on the local Waimana River ($50), and trips to the more distant Wairoa and Rangitaiki rivers ($68 & $88 respectively; for accounts of both see pp.279–280). A swifter, though noisier, way of

---

KOHI POINT LOOKOUT WALK

One of the most interesting walks in the area is to **Kohi Point Lookout** (8km loop; 3hr 30min), combining part of the Whakatane Town Centre Walk with the Nga Tapuwae o Toi ("Sacred Footsteps of Toi") Walkway, which traverses the domain of the great chieftain Toi, and ends at Kohi Point with panoramic views of Whakatane, Whale and White islands and Te Urewera National Park.

The walk starts in Commerce Street, from where you turn right between the escarpment and Pohaturoa, climb the steps to Hillcrest Road, then cross over to Seaview Road, where you will find the track leading to **Ka-pu-Terangi**, which passes the head of the **Wairere Falls**, a cool and peaceful spot. From here you walk through regenerating bush to the **Toi pa**, reputedly the oldest in New Zealand. The track continues along the cliff top past a number of other pa sites and food pits through more bushland, including honeysuckle and pohutukawa, before emerging onto flax and scrub towards the Kohi Point. If you wish, you can continue from here along the headlands to **Otarawairere Bay**, an excellent swimming and picnic spot; the steep walk down to the bay is quite beautiful, as is the bay itself. From here you can press **on to Ohope**, but the scenery doesn't get any better and the return journey makes for a long and tiring day.

There are a number of other walks in the area, all detailed in the *Walks Around Whakatane* booklet from the visitor centre ($1).

WILDERNESS RAFTING ON THE MOTU RIVER

Some of the best **wilderness rafting** trips in New Zealand are on the Grade III–IV **Motu River**, which is hidden deep in the mountain terrain of the remote Raukumara Ranges, with long stretches of white water plunging through gorges and valleys to the Bay of Plenty coast. In 1981, after a protracted campaign against hydro dam builders, the Motu became New Zealand's first designated "wild and scenic" river. Access by 4WD, helicopter and jetboat makes one- and two-day trips possible, but to capture the essence of this remote region you should consider one of the longer trips when you'll see no sign of civilization for three days; a magical and eerie experience. In all cases transport, camping equipment and food are provided, though you may need to supply your own sleeping bag. On all except the dedicated wilderness trips, the final flat drift to the coast is skipped in favour of a jetboat ride.

Whakatane Raft Tours (☎ & fax 07/308 7760, *moturaft@wave.co.nz*) run a number of trips. The one-day lower gorge trip can be done with access either by 4WD ($295) or helicopter ($395). Two- and three-day trips ($350–585) also take in the upper gorge and can be 4WD or helicopter access. For the full wilderness experience (and the best value for money), go for the four-day option ($480) where you drive into the highest raftable section.

Rotorua-based Wet'nWild Adventures (☎07/348 3191 & 0800/462 7238, fax 349 6567, *wetnwild@wave.co.nz*) start their trips from Opotiki and offer a similar range of trips, though they don't bother with helicopter access, using 4WD vehicles to get you in there. Some trips are consequently cheaper, though on the whole you pay more for identical trips.

enjoying the rivers is by **jetboat**. Kiwi Jet Boat Tours (☎07/307 0663 & 0800/800538, *kiwijet@xtra.co.nz*; 1hr 15min; $60) is run by an ex-world champion jetboat racer, who takes you onto the Rangitaiki River, from the Matahina Dam to the beautiful Aniwhenua Falls, over a number of modest whitewater sections. There are also innumerable **fishing** guides, mostly working on a charter basis from the local marina; check at Whakatane visitor centre for the best deals.

Eating, drinking and entertainment

Whakatane isn't quite up to speed with café culture, but it is getting there with decent espressos available and a couple of appealing waterside **restaurants** doubling as good spots for an evening tipple. There's virtually no entertainment, except for the **Cinema 5**, a multiplex on The Strand; check the local paper for screening times.

Baxter's, 208–210 The Strand. A simple, daytime chips-with-everything cafe. Mon–Fri 7.30am–5pm, Sat 9.30am–2.30pm.

Go Global, cnr The Strand & Commercial St. A pleasant first-floor bistro-style place with balcony views. The menu plunders the world with the likes of Pad Thai, Madras curry, kangaroo loin fillet and vegetarian ravioli, plus a good range of fresh seafood, all around the $20 mark. Open Mon–Sat for lunch, daily for dinner from 6pm; licensed and BYO.

Harbourside Brasserie, 62 The Strand (☎07/308 6721, reservations recommended). A light and airy, popular family restaurant, serving the biggest and meanest steaks in town at reasonable prices. Also a selection of lamb and poultry dishes of equally large proportions. Daily 11.30am–2.30pm & 5.30–10pm; licensed.

Reef, The Heads, Muriwai Drive, overlooking Whakatane Harbour entrance. A good licensed restaurant in an excellent location, about ten-minutes' walk from the centre. Open daily for à la carte lunches and dinners, with a good-value and impressive smorgasbord on Sundays.

PeeJay's Coffee House, 15 The Strand. The best espressos in town help wash down mostly vegetarian quiches, salads, muffins and cakes. Located in the *Rendezvous Motel* building where you meet for PeeJay Charters White Island trips.

Strand Café, 214 The Strand. The best place to eat in town at any time of the day. A relaxed licensed BYO café with simple, colourful decor and reasonable prices. A variety of excellent breakfasts, snacks and main courses such as lamb kebabs, seafood and steaks, as well as mouth-watering desserts.

Wedgewood Food Court, The Strand, opposite junction with Commercial St. Without doubt the cheapest place in town, with breakfasts, lunches and snacks for practically no money at all. Daily 8am–midnight.

Why Not Café, in the *Whakatane Hotel*, cnr The Strand & George St. A friendly and welcoming little eatery and bar, serving lunches and dinners ($15–23), including steaks and delicious seafood fettucine. Daily 11am–midnight.

Whakatane Sportfishing Club, The Strand. Spacious public bar with huge windows overlooking the boats and river, great for cheap drinks, good-value bar meals at lunch and dinner, and a Friday and Saturday evening smorgasbord ($17). It is a private club, but visitors can just stroll up to the bar and ask to be signed in.

The Wharf Shed, The Strand. Smart, modern café that's great for watching the sun set over the river while tucking into the like of Creole prawns on rice ($11), Moroccan spiced venison ($24), and spiced fish of the day ($22). Licensed.

Around Whakatane

One of New Zealand's premier beach resorts, **Ohope**, lies just to the east of Whakatane, while just off the coast are the twin pearls of White and Whale islands. The active volcanic **White Island**, stranded way out to sea in the Bay of Plenty, is the more spectacular, and a cruise here is one of the region's principal excursions. **Whale Island**, much nearer the shore, is the remainder of a volcanic cone which has eroded, leaving two peaks and hydrothermal activity, in the form of hot springs; it is also a wildlife sanctuary and the site of a pa. A more esoteric diversion heads inland to tiny **Taneatua**, the unlikely site of a notable art gallery that doubles as a tribal embassy for the Tuhoe people.

Ohope

Seven kilometres east of Whakatane, the tiny settlement of **OHOPE** extends along the beach in a thin ribbon to the entrance of **Ohiwa Harbour**. Ohiwa ("a place of watchfulness"), is the site of a natural shellfishery for pipi and cockles, and a place of numerous pa sites, signifying the importance of a convenient and renewable food source to the Maori way of life. This is very much a beach resort, and when you've had enough of the surf and sand you'll want to press on, though Ohope makes a pleasant enough base from which to explore Whakatane and its surroundings.

Ohope's **accommodation** is crammed to bursting between December and the end of January – when you'll be lucky to find anything and will probably have to retreat to Whakatane – but is quiet the rest of the year. *Ohope Beach Resort*, 5 West End (✆ & fax 07/312 4692, *flange@voyager.co.nz*; Dec–Feb ⑤, rest of the year ④) is a complex containing spacious motel units, restaurant, bar and nightclub, all just a stone's throw from the beach and sea. For a self-catering apartment, try *Henton's*, 295 Pohutukawa Ave, 3km east (✆ & fax 07/312 5095, *hentons@xtra.co.nz*; ④), or continue a further 5km east to *Ohope Beach Holiday Park*, Harbour Road (✆ & fax 07/312 4460; tent sites $10, cabins & motel units ②–④), a popular site overlooking the beach.

Casual resort-style bars and diners are the focus of Ohope's **eating and drinking** scene, and most of them are to be found at the northwestern end of the community where the road from Whakatane enters it. The most appealing is *Julie's*, 19 Pohutukawa Ave, a stylish café and bar with eclectic cuisine (mains $8–24). The liveliest place to while away an evening is at the *Ohope Beach Resort*, where the *Kauri Café* dishes up straightforward but generous food at reasonable prices, with a predominance of fresh seafood; the pub upstairs isn't bad either, but give the disco a miss. Finally, if you're after supplies of fresh seafood, stop off at the *Ohiwa Oyster Farm* (daily 10am–7pm), a shack beside Ohiwa Harbour, 1km south of the beach and the road to Opotiki.

Taneatua and the Tuhoe Embassy

The small rural village of **TANEATUA**, 12km south of Whakatane, could hardly be a less likely spot to find an **art gallery** of national importance, but its location is very significant. This is the northern edge of tribal lands held by the **Tuhoe iwi**, among the most resistant to *pakeha* intrusion of all Maori tribes. Their heartland stretches south through Te Urewera National Park to Lake Waikaremoana (see p.401) where the Aniwaniwa visitor centre was the scene of the June 1997 "liberation" of "Urewera Mural", an epic canvas by renowned New Zealand painter, Colin McCahon. Tuhoe activist **Te Kaha** was eventually convicted of the theft, but not until after he and fellow activist **Tame Iti** – their faces both liberally covered in *moko* (traditional tattoos) – struck up a friendship with Auckland arts patron, Jenny Gibbs, and returned the damaged work. "Urewera Mural" was subsequently repaired and returned to the Aniwaniwa visitor centre.

Meanwhile Gibbs, Tame Iti and Te Kaha together promoted Maori art abroad and raised its profile in New Zealand. By late 1998, Tame Iti and Te Kaha working with the local Tuhoe community opened **Te Ao Kohatu Gallery**, 57 Tuhoe St (☎07/312 9568; daily 10am–6pm, closed Mon & Tues in winter), with the partial aim of doing something positive in an area with minimal economic activity and precious little hope. All the works displayed are by Maori artists, the majority by Tuhoe, who are only now beginning to exploit their rich vein of talent. There have certainly been some impressive works on show from fine oils on canvas to angry images executed in house paint on corrugated iron. In an interesting twist, Tame Iti has taken up the paint brush and dashed off his own pieces including an interpretation of the McCahon work; it was hung in his gallery and promptly sold to an American buyer. Traditional Maori artwork is also for sale, including *pounamu* carving by Te Kaha.

The gallery doubles as the **Tuhoe Embassy**, a vehicle for maintaining the high profile of Tuhoe issues, initially raised by the "Urewera Mural" disappearance.

Whale Island

Whale Island (*Motohora*), 10km offshore, is a DOC-controlled haven where, in the 1980s, considerable efforts were made to eradicate goats and rats. Native bush is now rapidly returning and the island has become a bird reserve and safe environment for saddlebacks, grey-faced petrels, sooty shearwaters, little blue penguins, dotterels, oystercatchers, as well as three species of lizard – geckos, and speckled and copper skinks – and the reptilian tuatara; there are also occasional visits made by the North Island kaka and falcon, as well as fur seals.

Once the site of a **pa**, the island's inhabitants sent out several canoes when Cook was tacking near its coastline and some **trading** took place. The history of the island is quiet from then until 1829, when a trading schooner, *Haweis*, was attacked by the Nga Tiwawa chief, who wanted to get hold of the muskets aboard the ship to defend himself against neighbouring *iwi*. The attack took place while some members of the crew were ashore on the island, salting pork. Noticing something was amiss, they rowed for their lives to Tauranga, where they met the schooner *New Zealander*, which duly sailed back and regained control of the *Haweis*.

Access to the island is on one of only half a dozen **guided tours** a year (between Dec and mid-Feb), which depart from Whakatane and can be arranged through the visitor centre for around $35 per person.

White Island

Many people ignore Whale Island in favour of the more obvious and spectacular attractions of **White Island** (*Whaakari*), so named by Cook, for its permanent shroud of mist and steam. Over twice the size of Whale Island, White Island lies a sometimes-rough 50km offshore. Neither this nor its seething vulcanism deters visitors, who flock to appreciate its desolate, other worldly landscape, with its billowing towers of gas, steam and ash, spewing from a crater lake sixty metres below sea level, and to marvel at the smaller fumaroles surrounded by garish yellow and white crystal deposits that re-form in new and bizarre shapes each day.

Whaakari is a living embodiment of the ongoing clash between the Indo-Australian Plate, and the Pacific Plate, which has been driven beneath it for the last two million years. This resulted in the upwards thrust of super-heated rock through the ocean floor creating a massive **volcanic** structure. **Sulphur**, for use in fertilizer manufacture, was sporadically mined on the island from the 1880s, but all enterprises were plagued by catastrophic eruptions, landslides and economic misfortune. The island was abandoned in 1934, and these days is home only to 60,000 grey-faced **petrels** and 10,000 **gannets**.

An excellent **guided trip** to White Island is run from Whakatane by PeeJay Charters (☎07/308 9588 & 0800/733529, fax 308 0303, *www.whiteisland.co.nz*; daily 8.30am; 5hr; $95, including lunch), weather permitting; allow at least a couple of days so as not to be disappointed. After a fairly precarious transfer to the shallow-water jetty, the two-hour tour of the island begins at the site of a 1924 sulphur processing factory, which is gradually being eaten away by the high sulphur content of the atmosphere, and progresses to the open-sided crater. Here, amid pools of bubbling mud and skyscraper pillars of smoke and steam, you get the chance to stand in the wind-driven clouds (with a gas mask on) and experience a spooky and disorienting white-out.

With plenty of cash and clement weather, you can also visit White Island by **helicopter** with Vulcan Helicopters (☎07/308 4188 & 0800/804 354, *www.vulcanheili.co.nz*; 3hr; $315, including a walking tour of the island). East Bay Flight Centre (☎07/308 7077 & 0800/550 880, *www.ebfc.co.nz*) operate a number of **scenic flights** over White Island (45min; $150; minimum 2 passengers).

Opotiki

The small settlement of **OPOTIKI**, 60km from Whakatane, is the easternmost town in the Bay of Plenty and, though it doesn't amount to much in itself, does act as an effective gateway to Eastland. Sitting at the junction of SH2 and SH35, the town is a useful stopping-off point from which to explore its beautiful surroundings and your last place to stock up on supplies and petrol before heading on.

From Opotiki, **SH2** strikes inland **to Gisborne**, while, **SH35** meanders along the more circumspect roads around the perimeter of **Eastland**, never straying far from its rugged and windswept coastline.

Arrival, information and accommodation

InterCity **buses** from Whakatane and Gisborne drop off at the Elliott Street bus station; Super Shuttles from Gisborne also stop off here en route to Rotorua. The combined Opotiki **visitor centre** and **DOC office**, on the corner of St Johns Street and Elliott Street (Mon–Fri 10.30am–5pm, plus mid-Dec to Jan Sat & Sun 10am–3pm) is a good place to pick up information and advice for Opotiki and the whole of the Eastland region.

For **accommodation** Opotiki has a couple of very good **hostels**: the small and friendly *Central Oasis Backpackers*, 30 King St (☎07/315 5165; dorms ①, rooms ②), in a hundred-year-old renovated kauri villa right in town; and the laid-back *Opotiki Backpackers Beach House*, 7 Appleton Rd, 5km west of Opotiki on SH2 (☎07/315 5117; tents $10, dorms ①, room ②), right by the beach and with free use of kayaks, body boards, fishing rods and so forth. The *Magnolia Court Motel*, on the corner of Bridge Street and Nelson Street (☎07/315 8490 & 0800/556 246, fax 315 5444; ⑤) has ten clean, comfortable and modern **motel** units, but for a more intimate place to stay, head for the *Fantail Cottage* **B&B**, 318 Ohiwa Harbour Rd, 9km west of Opotiki (☎07/315 4981; ④, dinner by arrangement $25), in a quiet location with panoramic views of the harbour, an outdoor spa, and one of the friendliest welcomes in New Zealand. Heading 15km south on SH2, you'll find *River View Cottage* (☎ & fax 07/315 5553, *riverview .cottage@xtra.co.nz*; ⑥), a modern and spacious two-bedroom cottage on a property that runs down to the Waioeka River where the hosts run kayak trips (see p.380).

Campers wanting to stay centrally should try the sheltered and well-kept *Opotiki Holiday Park* (☎ & fax 07/315 6050; tent sites $8.50, on-site vans & cabins ②–④), on the corner of Potts Avenue and Grey Street: follow Elliot Street west to the war memorial then 100m right along Potts Avenue. For a more rural setting, head 6km east along SH35 to *Tirohanga Beach Holiday Park* (☎ & fax 07/315 7942; tents $8, cabins ②), right by the beach.

The Town and around

The small settlement of Opotiki has few sights of interest to keep you before you head on around Eastland or cut across to the bright lights of Gisborne, but it does have some lush countryside and beaches around it. The main street is Church Street, which contains all the historic buildings of note and most of the eateries.

The **Opotiki Museum**, 123 Church St (Mon–Sat 10am–3.30pm, Sun 1.30–4pm; $2), is right in the historical centre of Opotiki on the site of the livery stables once used by the overland stagecoach to Whakatane. Its collection is garnered from the local area, resulting in the usual ill-assorted domestic, farming, and military bric-a-brac, here ameliorated by an extensive range of black and white photographs. Opposite, the innocent-looking white clapboard **St Stephen's Church**, set among trees and chirruping birds, was once the scene of a notorious murder, for it was here, in March 1865, that local missionary **Carl Volkner** was allegedly killed by a prophet, Kereopa Te Rau, from the militant Hau Hau sect (see box below). The case is far from clear-cut, however: at the time,

---

THE HAU HAU

Missionaries encouraged many Maori to abandon their belief structure in favour of a zealous **Christianity**, but as land disputes with settlers escalated the Maori increasingly perceived the missionaries as agents for land-hungry Europeans.

When **war** broke out and the recently converted Maori suffered defeats, they felt betrayed not only by the Crown but also by their newly acquired god, and some formed the revivalist **Hau Hau** movement, based on the Old Testament. Dedicated to routing the interlopers, disciples danced around *nui* poles, chanting for the *pakeha* to leave the country. The name is derived from the **battle cry** of the warriors, who flung themselves at their enemies with their right arms raised to protect them from bullets, believing that true faith prevented them from being shot. The movement began in 1862 and by 1865, having capitalized on widespread Maori unrest at the land situation, there was a *nui* pole in most villages of any size from Wellington to the Waikato. The Hau Hau were some of the most feared **warriors** and involved in the bloodiest and bitterest battles, but the movement began to fade after their **leader** and founder, Te Ua Haumene, was captured in 1866. Some of the sect's ideas were **revitalized** when the infamous rebel **Te Kooti** (see box on p.401) based parts of his **Ringatu** movement on Hau Hau doctrine.

many Maori believed that missionaries doubled as spies, duly reporting their findings to the settlers and military, and it appears that Volkner had indeed written many letters to Governor Grey espousing settlers' land-grabbing ambitions. Local Maori claim Volkner was justly executed after being confronted with the evidence and denounced as a traitor. Whatever the truth, the settlers used the story as propaganda, fuelling intermittent skirmishes over the next three years. The museum will usually let you have a key so that you can nip in and see the gorgeous *tukutuku* panels around the altar.

The small and unspoiled **Opotiki (Hukutaia) Domain** (dawn–dusk; free), is full of native palms, lianas and trees, including an ancient puriri tree once used as a burial tree by local Maori. There is also a good lookout over the Waioeka Valley and a series of short but interesting rainforest tracks. To get to the domain, head south from the centre of town on Church Street as far as the Waioweka River Bridge, cross it and then bear left along Woodlands Road for 7km.

Getting a little more active, there's **horse trekking** 6km east of Opotiki on SH35 with Tirohanga Beach Treks (☎07/315 7490; 2hr for $40), and water-based activities either on the **Waioeka River** south of town, or on the **Motu River** which surges through the hills to the east of Opotiki and meets the sea 45km to the northeast. On the former, Waioeka River Kayak Trips (☎ & fax 07/315 5553, *riverview.cottage @xtra.co.nz*) run gentle three-hour paddles down a beautiful stretch of river for $48. Multi-day wilderness **rafting trips** on the Motu River (see box, p.375) are some of the best in the country, and two **jetboat** operators offer scenic, flat-water trips from $30 for half an hour to around $80 for the full two and a half hours on the lower 50km: call Motu River Jet Boat Tours (☎07/315 8107), or Motu Adventure Tours (☎07/315 7996).

Eating

There are a number of small daytime **cafés** in town, the best of which is the *Flying Pig*, 97 Church St. Once this closes, things get pretty sketchy with only a handful of burger bars, some doing sit-in steak and egg dinners until around 7.30pm. For **meals** you are better heading to *The Fejean*, at the corner of Bridge Street and Church Street on SH2, which does good breakfasts and dishes that seem very fancy for these parts: scallops in bacon and white wine sauce, or pan fried tarakihi. The *Masonic Hotel*, a large colonial-style building on Church Street, is also passable, but in fine weather you could do a lot worse than a newspaper full of **fish and chips** from the *Ocean Seafoods Fish and Chips* at 88 Church St.

The Inland Route to Gisborne

From Opotiki, **SH2** strikes out south to **Gisborne** (137km away), dotted with tiny settlements as it twists its way through the scenic and bush-clad **Waioeka Gorge**. Following the river for 30km, the route becomes increasingly narrow and steep before emerging onto rolling pastureland on the Gisborne side and dropping to plains. From there it runs straight as an arrow through orchards, vineyards and sheep farms to Gisborne (covered in Chapter Six; see p.391). The only part of the route worth breaking your journey for, or exploring from Opotiki, is the first 72-kilometre stretch to Matawai, along which a number of interesting **walks** branch off either side of the road. Ten scenic tracks through forest, ranging from fifteen minutes to ten hours one way, are described in the DOC leaflet *Walks in Waioeka and Urutawa* ($1), available at Opotiki visitor centre. This is also where you'll find River View Cottage and Waioeka River Kayak Trips (see both above).

Eastland

The corner of land jutting out into the South Pacific, to the east of Opotiki and Gisborne, **Eastland**, is one of the most sparsely populated areas in New Zealand, rarely visited and something of a backwater lost in time. From Opotiki and Gisborne, the 330km scenic main road (SH35) curves around the peninsula hugging the **rugged coastline** most of the way, twisting in and out of small bays and providing spectacular views out to sea on a fine day. As soon as you enter the region you'll notice a **change of pace**, epitomized from time to time by the sight of a lone horseback rider clopping along the road. This is one of the most unspoiled parts of the North Island, steeped in **Maori** history (see box below) and not to be rushed. Contemporary Maori, who make up a significant percentage of Eastland's population, draw on their strong culture to cope with the hardships of this untamed landscape and uncertain economic prospects. Over eighty percent of land tenure here is in Maori hands, something which sits well with the people: most feel in greater control of their destiny than Maori do elsewhere.

Eastland is a reminder of how New Zealand once was, and the response to strangers splits into two camps: downright hostile, and while this may be intimidating at first, a little openness and acceptance on your part may turn things around, or more often

LEGENDS OF THE EASTLAND MAORI

According to legend, a great *ariki* (leader) from Eastland was drowned by rival tribesmen and his youngest daughter swore vengeance: when she gave birth to a son called **Tuwhakairiora**, she hoped he would make good her promise. As a young man, Tuwhakairiora travelled and encountered a young woman named **Ruataupare**; she took him to her father, who happened to be the local chief. A thunderstorm broke, signalling to the people that they had an important visitor among them, and Tuwhakairiora was allowed to marry Ruataupare and live in Te Araroa. When he called upon all the *hapu* of the area to gather and avenge the death of his grandfather, many warriors travelled to Whareponga and sacked the pa there. Tuwhakairiora became renowned as a famous warrior, dominating the area from **Tolaga Bay** to Cape Runaway, and all Maori families in the region today trace their descent from him.

Ruataupare, meanwhile, grew jealous of her husband's influence. While their children were growing up, she constantly heard them referred to as the offspring of the great Tuwhakairiora, yet her name was barely mentioned. She returned to her own *iwi* in **Tokomaru Bay**, where she summoned all the warriors together and started a war against rival *iwi*; victorious, Ruataupare became chieftainess of Tokomaru Bay.

The other legend that has shaped this wild land is one of **rivalry** between two students – **Paoa**, who excelled at navigation, and **Rongokaka**, who was renowned for travelling at great speed by means of giant strides. At the time, a beautiful maiden, Muriwhenua, lived in Hauraki and many set off to claim her for their bride. Paoa set off early but his rival took only one step and was ahead of him; this continued up the coast, with Rongokaka leaving huge footprints as he went – his imprint in the rock at Matakaoa Point, at the northern end of Hicks Bay, is the most clearly distinguishable. En route, they created the **Waiapu Mountains**: Paoa, flummoxed by Rongokaka's pace, set a snare for his rival at Tokomaru Bay, lashing the crown of a giant totara tree to a hill; recognizing the trap, Rongokaka cut it loose. The force with which the tree sprang upright caused such vibration that Mount Hikurangi partly disintegrated, forming the other mountain peaks. Finally, Rongokaka stepped across the Bay of Plenty and up to Hauraki, where he claimed his maiden.

you'll find folk warm and friendly. As for the **climate**, it tends towards extremes – hot in summer, wet in winter, and extremely changeable at any time of year.

The **coast** is very much the focus here, and whatever time isn't spent gazing out of the car or bus window is likely to be consumed on the beach or in the water. That said, there are limited hiking opportunities, and just about everywhere you go there will be someone happy to take you **horse trekking**, either along the beach or into the bush. In general, the **towns**, such as they are, don't have much to recommend them and you're better off planning to stay between towns, though at weekends you might like to find a pub if you fancy a country music jukebox singalong. **Campgrounds** are the staple along much of the route, though free beachside camping (once the norm) is now outlawed just about everywhere.

Inland, a central core of mountains runs through Eastland: the inhospitable **Waiapu Mountains**, encompassing the northeastern Raukumara Range and the typical native flora of the Raukumara Forest Park. The isolated and rugged peaks of Hikurangi, Whanokao, Aroangi, Wharekia and Tatai provide a spectacular backdrop to the coastal scenery, but are only accessible through **Maori land** and **permission** must be sought (further information is available at the DOC offices in Gisborne and Opotiki). **Raukumara Forest Park** was gazetted in 1979 and covers just over 1150 square kilometres, including the upper catchments of several rivers that drain into the Bay of Plenty. The desolate terrain and limited access discourage most visitors from exploring the park, but the tough, full-day trek up **Mount Hikurangi** (the highest peak is 1752m) is quite popular, offering the early riser the opportunity of being among the first in New Zealand to see the sunrise.

The road is sealed all the way around the coast and takes around six hours to drive, though three or four days is better. The further around you go, the fewer the **services**, including food stores and petrol pumps. Notwithstanding a couple of steak and chips places attached to pubs and motels, there isn't anywhere in Eastland that you'd describe as a real restaurant. Unless you've arranged to stay in B&Bs which serve meals you really need to be prepared for self-catering, or accept a diet of toasted sandwiches and fish'n'chips.

Driving can be particularly hazardous on dole days, which are associated with a good deal of drunken driving and abandoned vehicles; note, too, that **theft** from parked cars is also a big problem in Eastland, both within communities and in car parks at the start of walks. **Campervans** are particularly vulnerable because thieves know they contain everything their occupants have taken on holiday with them; try to lock valuables out of sight, or else take them with you.

Public transport in Eastland is limited, though a few **shuttle bus** services exist. The best daily service is with Matakaoa-Coastline (☎06/864 4627), leaving Opotiki at 2pm and arriving at Hicks Bay at 4.45pm. The company runs a similar daily service leaving Hicks Bay at 6.30am and arriving in Gisborne at 9.20am. Almost the same thing works in reverse with Gisborne departures at 12.30pm and Hicks Bay departures at 6.45am. Various other companies fill in the gaps, so with detailed planning you could manage half a dozen stops in three or four days. Contact the Gisborne or Opotiki visitor centres for full details.

Opotiki to Waihau Bay

The road from Opotiki to **Waihau Bay** covers 103km, generally sticking close to the sea, but frequently twisting up over steep bluffs only to drop back down to desolate beaches heavy with driftwood logs. These have been washed down from the Raukumara Range by the numerous rivers which reach the sea here, typically forming delightful fresh-water swimming holes. This is probably the section of East Cape where you'll want to spend most of your time. You'll find family campsites every few kilometres along, never far from the beach but never right beside it either. Nonetheless, most make the best of their proximity to the sea with a wealth of aquatic activities offered to guests – from boogie boards and canoes to half-day fishing and dive trips – along with horse riding and bikes to search out your own secluded cove.

Omaio and Te Kaha

Leaving Opotiki you soon hit a section of the coast which sets the scene for the next couple of hours of driving. Swimming beaches are scarce initially and, once past Tirohanga, the only place you are likely to want to stop is *Oariki Farm House*, 40km from Opotiki (☎ & fax 07/325 2578; ⑤), a gorgeous B&B and separate self-catering cottage completely surrounded by gardens and native bush and overlooking the sea. Call for directions, and either cook your own meals or eat three-course dinners ($25) made largely from organically grown produce. Some rooms have a balcony with views of White Island, and there are opportunities to go fishing and diving.

Continuing, you soon cross the Motu River and after 6km reach **OMAIO** where there is a store and one of the very few places in these parts that you can free **camp**: turn sharp left onto Old Coast Road by the store. A further 12km on, the *Te Kaha Hotel and Motel* (☎ & fax 07/325 2830; ④) marks the beginning of **TE KAHA**, a region which spreads 7km along the highway in a beautiful crescent shape, with spectacular headlands and a deserted beach strewn with driftwood. You can swim safely here and nearby there's the *Te Kaha Holiday Park* (☎07/325 2894; tent sites $9, dorms ①, cabins, flats and motels ④–⑤), a **campsite** with a store and petrol pump as well as access to the shoreline.

Whanarua Bay

Te Kaha is about the closest land to White Island, 50km offshore, which continues in view as you proceed 5km to the hospitable *Waikawa B&B* (☎ & fax 07/325 2070; ④), a nice little spot above a rocky cove with a couple of en-suite **rooms** and cooked breakfast. **WHANARUA BAY**, ten minutes' drive further on, is another ideal opportunity to stop and enjoy the beaches and rugged countryside. What's more you can stay comfortably either at *Robyn's Place* (☎07/325 2904; bunks ①, room ②), a small **hostel** with a personal touch and sea views from the veranda; or next door at *Rendezvous on the Coast Holiday Park* (☎ & fax 07/325 2899; tents $8, dorms ①, on-site vans ②, cabins and flats ②–④), a large **campsite** with opportunities for mountain biking, kayaking and fishing. If this is all too much, continue 1km along SH35 to the simple, beachfront *Maraehako Camping Ground* (☎07/325 2047; tents and campers $5).

Waihau Bay

Still hugging the coast, SH35 winds 10km to **Ruakokore**, where a picture perfect, white clapboard Anglican church stands on a promontory overshadowed by a couple of Norfolk pines. From here it is five minutes' drive to **WAIHAU BAY**, another sweeping crescent of sand and grass that's ideal for swimming, surfing and kayaking. The abundance of shellfish and flat fish here might encourage you to forage or sling a line in to land a tasty supper. If you choose to break your journey here, the best place to **stay** is the very hospitable *Waihau Bay Homestays B&B* (☎07/325 3674, fax 325 3679, *n.topia@clear.net.nz*; ④), at the far end of the bay. They offer self-contained accommodation in a house overlooking the beach, with a very friendly and welcoming atmosphere, and a superb seafood dinner by arrangement ($25). Campers should head for *Waihau Bay Holiday Park* (☎07/325 3844, fax 325 3980; tents $9, dorm & on-site vans ①, cabins ③) which has a store and the closest thing to a modern café – there's an espresso machine – between Opotiki and Gisborne.

Lottin Point to Te Puia Springs

Beyond Waihau Bay the highway continues close to the water for a few more kilometres before veering inland at Cape Runaway, Eastland's northernmost point. For the next 125km you hardly see the coast again, with the significant exception of the area around Hicks Bay, Te Araroa and East Cape, the only real points of interest along this stretch. Further on, the church at Tikitiki and the East Cape's largest community, Ruatoria will only briefly distract you, though the hot springs at Te Puia may have more abiding appeal.

Keen anglers might want to make a 6km detour from the small community of Potaka, 25km east of Waihau Bay, north to **Lottin Point**, said to offer the best **snapper fishing** in New Zealand. **Accommodation** needs are catered for at the *Lottin Point Motel* (☎ & fax 06/864 4455; ④) which has simple rooms, a restaurant, gear rental and bait.

Hicks Bay

The small coastal township of **HICKS BAY** (*Wharekahika*), 44km from Waihau Bay, shelters between headlands and rock bluffs about halfway along SH35. It was named after Lieutenant Zachariah Hicks of Cook's *Endeavour* expedition, who was the first to sight its black volcanic beach which gives way to a sandy bay that's safe for swimming and consequently popular in summer with campers. If you take time to explore the Hicks Bay region you'll find numerous pa sites in varying states of repair, some of which were modified for musket fighting during the 1860 Hau Hau uprising.

Beachside **accommodation** in the area is provided by *Hicks Bay Backpackers Lodge*, Onepoto Beach Road (☎ & fax 06/864 4731, *hicksbaybackpackers@xtra.co.nz*; tents $7, dorms ①, rooms ③), a pleasant little **hostel** with comfortable rooms, meals ($8–10), and a variety of canoes, bikes, fishing lines and wave skis to keep you amused. They also run special sunrise trips to the East Cape Lighthouse (departing 4 or 5am; $15). For something a little more upmarket, head back 4km towards Opotiki to *Te Puna Frontier* (☎ & fax 06/864 4862; ⑥), a very attractive **B&B** with en-suite cottages each set in their own little garden: a three-course dinner is $30 each. In addition they do a range of guided **horse treks** – from twilight rides to Tahuroa Plateau overlooking the bay, followed by mugs of manuka tea (2hr; $30) to all-day rides along the Wharekahia River with a campfire lunch ($65). Alternatively continue 2km east of Hicks Bay along SH35 to the sizeable *Hicks Bay Motel Lodge*, on the main road at Hicks Bay (☎06/864 4880 & fax 864 4708; ⑤), with scenic views over the bay. There are 27 units without cooking facilities but otherwise well-equipped, and 12 fully self-contained ones; the motel also has a licensed **restaurant** (meals $15–20) and house **bar** (daily 4pm–1am). Behind it, overlooking Horseshoe Bay, is a glow-worm grotto, which you're welcome to visit in the evenings.

Te Araroa

From Hicks Bay SH35 climbs over a hill and drops back to the coast (still only 6km from Hicks Bay) at the excellent *Te Araroa Holiday Park* (☎06/864 4873, fax 864 4473; tent sites $8.50, dorm bunks $12, cabins & flats ②–③), which has loads of facilities including a shop (7am–7pm), runs early-morning trips to the lighthouse (5am; $50 for two), and best of all, a small indoor **cinema** (the most easterly in the land); ask at the shop for programme details and tickets. It's also worth taking a sunset walk through the field behind the holiday park and out onto the beach for an unforgettable display of colours on a clear night.

From here it is 6km to the drab village of **TE ARAROA** ("long pathway"), virtually midway between Opotiki and Gisborne. It is set on the foreshore of the long and magnificent Kawakawa Bay, a broad beach with good surfing at either end. Te Araroa was once the domain of the famous Maori warrior Tuwhakairiora and of the legendary figure of Paikea, who is said to have arrived here on the back of a whale. Ironically, the first Europeans in the area occupied a **whaling station** not far from the present township. These days the settlement contains little more than a pub, garage, store and a takeaway, on the right-hand side of the main street as it runs towards the beach, which sells spanking fresh **fish and chips**. In the grounds of the local school stands a giant pohutukawa tree, reputedly the largest in New Zealand.

East Cape

The New Zealand mainland's easternmost point is marked by the **East Cape Lighthouse**, reached by a 21km rough, dirt road from Te Araroa: follow the sign east along the foreshore. It is a dramatic coastal run which ends in a car park from where you clamber up five-hundred-odd steps to the lighthouse which looks out over East Island, just offshore, and the grey-shelved promontory (140m) provides great views of the inland mountain ranges. All in all, it is an atmospheric spot that's well worth the bumpy trip out here, particularly if you also pay a visit to **Coastal Arts** (☎06/864 4890), a couple of kilometres along the road from Te Araroa. It is run by painter and ceramic artist, Pru Davis, who produces robust, expressive works that reflect the landscape in flowing shapes and bright colours; painted plates (around $40) and tiles ($25) make good buys.

Tikitiki, Ruatoria and Te Puia Springs

From Te Araroa SH35 cuts inland through 24km of sheep-farming country, before reaching **TIKITIKI**, a village which will only delay you long enough to peek inside the modest wooden Anglican **church**, on a rise as you enter the town. The plain exterior hides a treasure trove of elaborate and fine Maori design, *tukutuku* and carving; unusually, the stained glass is also in Maori designs, and the rafters painted in the colours of a Maori meeting-house.

Inland **RUATORIA**, 19km south of Tikitiki, is the largest town since Opotiki some two hundred kilometres back, though that's not saying much. The main highway skirts the town and with only a petrol station, a pub, a couple of grocery shops and the *Kai Kart* takeaway (all on the main street) as temptation. Alternatively you can stay on SH35 for meals at the *Mountain View* café, two kilometres south of town: they serve lunch, afternoon teas and well-prepared hearty dinners extending from steak, fish and mixed grills $11–17, to crumbed oysters at $22.

At Kopuaroa, around 15km south of Ruatoria, a rough and unsealed loop road heads 6km to **Waipiro Bay**, a busy port in its heyday, but now a beautiful and secluded inlet. Phone ahead for instruction if you want to **stay** at the welcoming *Waikawa Lodge Backpackers* (☎06/864 6719; ③), which has just two double rooms with stupendous views in a unique bush setting where you can muck in, or cater for yourself.

The loop road to Waipiro Bay rejoins SH35 at the small settlement of **TE PUIA SPRINGS**, where a small lake picturesquely surrounded by deciduous trees comes as something of a surprise after the green paddocks and cabbage trees. The eponymous **hot springs** (roughly daily 6am–midnight; private pools $2 per 30min) lie a kilometre further on behind the *Te Puia Hot Springs Hotel* (☎06/864 6755; ③), which has been here since the sulphur-rich waters first gained popularity during the early 1900s as a way of easing aching bones. They also have rooms, a campsite with pitches at $8 per person, and reasonable meals.

Tokomaru Bay to Gisborne

At **Tokomaru Bay** the road emerges from the inland bush and pastoral country to reveal the North Island's east coast in all its glory. For the remaining 80km to

Gisborne you stay mostly inland but catch frequent glimpses of yawning bays and crashing surf, accessed either on SH35 itself, or by taking short side roads to little-visited coves. In the days before a decent road was put in, this was a thriving area with coastal traders calling to drop off supplies and pick up sheep (or their dressed carcasses). The subsequent decline is most evident at Tokomaru Bay, though things pick up progressively as you approach Gisborne.

Tokomaru Bay

TOKOMARU BAY (known affectionately as "Toko"), 11km south of Te Puia Springs, sits at the base of steep green hills with rocky headlands sheltering a broad expanse of **beach**, dotted with driftwood and pounded by surf. With good accommodation, excellent seaside and hill walks, and plenty of small-scale social history in the form of ruined and abandoned buildings, Toko makes a pretty decent place to idle away a couple of relaxed days.

The Maori that settled here trace their descent to Toi te Huatahi, the great navigator and the first to arrive from the ancestral home of Hawaiki. In 1865 the Mawhai Pa was the scene of several attacks by a party of Hau Hau, but they were repulsed by a small garrison of old men and women. About the biggest thing since was the 1988 cyclone which flattened many of Tokomaru Bay's historic buildings, including the turn-of-the-century *Te Puka Hotel*, now replaced by a modern **tavern**.

At the northern end of town, a long wooden wharf and ruined buildings of a freezing works (abattoir) testify to the former prosperity of this once-busy port, which thrived until improved road transport forced the factory's closure in 1953. The town now gets by on the merest hint of a craft industry, with locals making possum-fur hats and slippers, painting pictures and shaping pottery. To see (and buy) what's being made, call at the **craft shop**, Waitangi Street by the supermarket (irregular hours) which has some particularly fine Maori craftwork: woven flax goods such as *kete* (baskets), hats and sometimes *pupu* (skirts).

There isn't a great deal to do here except take long walks on the beach or the short **waterfall walk** (3.5km; 45min) through regenerating bush – take the road along the beach towards the wharf, cross the concrete bridge and go through the gate on the other side, then follow the river round to the start of the track. If you tire of surfing and swimming, you can **explore on horseback** with a series of bush and beach treks (from $30 for 2–3hr) available at *Brian's Place* (see below), where the owner knows the country like the back of his hand.

Budget **accommodation** starts with the *Mayfair Camping Ground*, Waitangi Street (☎06/864 5843; tent sites $8.50, cabins ②), conveniently located beside the general store (which also contains the campsite office) and petrol station, and opposite the supermarket which is open daily. **Backpackers** should head to either the *House of the Rising Sun*, Potae Street (☎06/864 5858; tents $10, dorms ①, rooms ②), which has good facilities and a great sunny veranda with sea views, or up the hill to *Brian's Place*, Potae Street (☎06/864 5870; dorms ①, rooms ②), a very small and welcoming place on the hill with two doubles (one with sunny balcony) and a loft dorm: horse riding and hunting trips optional. For a complete change of pace, try *Tironui* **farmstay** (☎06/864 5619, fax 864 5620, *d.jefferd@xtra.co.nz*; ④), where the pleasant and practical hosts will show you around the farm and let you use the pool and grass tennis court: take SH35 5km south from Toko, then Mata Road for 7km to the easy-to-miss sign.

As elsewhere in Eastland, self-catering is the way to go, though the *Te Puka Tavern* on Beach Road, serves inexpensive **meals** consisting largely of steak, pork or seafood, served in hefty portions. It is the liveliest (in fact only) place in town for a drink and can be quite boisterous at the weekend.

Anaura Bay

Continuing 20km south from Tokomaru, you'll pass the turning to rugged **ANAURA BAY**, 6km off SH35 along a sealed road. This is one for surfies, with a broad sweep of sand and jagged headlands. At the north end of the bay is the **Anaura Scenic Reserve**, a large area of bush that has mixed broadleaf trees and is famous for its large puri trees and a wealth of native birds. Starting near the end of the road, and signposted to the west by the reserve is the **Anaura Bay Walkway** (3.5km loop; 2hr), which follows the course of the Waipare Stream into thick green bush, up a gently climbing valley and then out into scrubland before turning back towards the bay and a lookout point with magnificent views.

Just beyond the start of this walk (about 100m) is a very basic DOC **campsite** (free), beside the beach. At the opposite end of the bay, the simple *Anaura Bay Motorcamp* (✆06/862 6380; tent sites $9) is superbly sited just back from the beach and always has a relaxed feel. Facilities are in the former schoolhouse and there's a store selling essentials and frozen food, and dispensing heaps of local information. If they're not too busy the owners might arrange a visit to the local marae.

Tolaga Bay to Gisborne

TOLAGA BAY (*Uawa*), 36km from Tokomaru, is the first place since Opotiki with the tenor of a thriving, viable town; six hundred strong and one of the better-serviced communities in Eastland. Once again, rugged headlands enclose the bay which was the scene of a 1769 visit by Captain Cook and his crew. They are commemorated in the town's street names: Banks, Solander, Forester and, of course, Cook.

Cook, anchoring to replenish his stocks of food and water, named the bay "Tolaga", owing to a misinterpretation of the Maori name for the prevailing wind (correctly called *teraki*). One character who stayed a little longer – and may well have provided the historical basis for the character played by Harvey Keitel in the film *The Piano* – was an early flax trader called Barnet Burns. He wore full *moko*, and stayed in the bay for three years, marrying a Maori woman and fathering three sons, before decamping; his wife, Amotawa, went on to marry the great Maori chief Te Kani-a-Takirau.

Heading south on the main road through town (SH35) and over the Uawa River bridge you will come to a signposted turn-off to the wharf (after about 1.5km). About 1.5km down this sealed road is the start of the **Cooks Cove Walkway** (2.6km; 45min), which involves a steep and often muddy climb through bush and birdlife, rewarding the effort with good views across the bay. About another kilometre along the sealed road is the 660m-long concrete **wharf** itself, the longest concrete jetty in the southern hemisphere. It is in a sorry, near-ruinous state, jutting out past steep sandstone cliffs. Built in the late 1920s to service coastal shipping, it soon became redundant after an improved road was put through to Gisborne. It hasn't been used commercially since 1963, and is no longer strong enough for vehicles, though you can wander to the end which makes a picturesque spot for a picnic: be warned there are no safety rails. A determined bunch of local residents are now trying to raise $3 million to preserve the structure and a collection vault is located by the entrance to the wharf.

Accommodation hereabouts is limited: the incongruous mock-Tudor facade of the *Tolaga Bay Inn*, at the corner of Solander and Cook streets (✆06/862 6856; ③), hides bright and cheerful rooms with access to a balcony overlooking town, while the public areas have a very relaxed and friendly atmosphere. Bar and restaurant **meals** are served, with prices in the region of $15 for generous and filling steaks, seasonal fresh fish and stodgy puddings; there's also a bottle shop – and occasional live music (Fri & Sat night). Comfortable **B&B** is found at *Puketea*, 34 Bank St (✆ & fax 06/862 6772; ④), and beachfront accommodation at *Tolaga Bay Motor Camp*, Wharf Road (☎06/862 6716; tent sites $8, cabins & cottages ②), which has a store and great views.

The 47-kilometre stretch from Tolaga Bay to Gisborne, via the small settlement of **Whangara**, becomes both tamer and bleaker the further south you travel, the land despoiled by clearance for farming. The road climbs in and out of more small bays, occasionally providing panoramic vistas of sea and close-ups of the slate-grey rock shelves that characterize this coast. Eventually, the comparatively enormous town of **Gisborne** (see p.391) looms into view.

travel details

Trains

From Tauranga to: Auckland (1 daily; 3hr 30min); Hamilton (1 daily; 1hr 30min).

Buses

From Coromandel to: Thames (1 daily; 1hr 15min).

From Opotiki to: Gisborne, via SH2 (1 daily; 2hr), via SH35 (1 daily; 5hr).

From Tauranga to: Hamilton (2 daily; 2hr); Rotorua (4 daily; 1hr 30min).

From Thames to: Auckland (4 daily; 2hr); Coromandel (2-3 daily; 1hr 15min); Hamilton (2 daily; 1hr 30min); Mount Maunganui (3 daily, 2hr); Tauranga (3 daily; 1hr 45min).

From Whakatane to: Gisborne (1 daily; 3hr); Opotiki (2 daily; 1hr); Rotorua (2 daily; 1hr 30min).

From Whitianga to: Thames (5 daily; 1hr 30min).

Ferries

From Coromandel to: Auckland (1 daily; 2hr 15min).

Flights

From Tauranga to: Auckland (7 daily; 40min); Wellington (1 daily; 1hr 20min).

From Whakatane to: Auckland (3-5 daily; 50min); Wellington (1 daily; 1hr 15min).

From Whitianga to: Auckland (2 daily; 30min).

CHAPTER SIX

POVERTY BAY, HAWKE'S BAY AND THE WAIRARAPA

From the tip of Eastland, the North Island's mountainous backbone runs 650km southwest to the outskirts of Wellington, defining and isolating the **East Coast**. A region comprising the characteristically dry and sunny provinces of Poverty Bay, Hawke's Bay and the Wairarapa, this is sheep country, with large stations commanding the rich pastures of the expansive Heretaunga Plains around central Hawke's Bay and the sharp-ridged hill country to the north, frequently contoured into small terraces, hallmarks of a young land eroded by overgrazing. But the region isn't all pastoral: the contiguous Raukumara, Kaweka, Ruahine, Tararua and Rimutaka mountain ranges protect much of the coast from the prevailing westerlies and cast a long rain shadow, the bane of farmers who watched their land become parched dirt, the grass leached to a dusty brown. Increasingly, these rain-shadow pastures are being given over to viticulture, and all three provinces are now noted **wine regions**. Any tour of the wineries would have to take in **Poverty Bay**, a major grape-growing region, where the main centre of **Gisborne** is both the first city in the world to see the light of the new day and was the first part of New Zealand sighted by Cook's expedition in 1769. Finding little but apparently hostile natives, he named it Poverty Bay and sailed off south across Hawke Bay – named after Admiral Sir Edward Hawke, a boyhood hero of Cook's – to a second disastrous encounter with Maori at **Cape Kidnappers**, now the location of an impressive gannet colony.

ACCOMMODATION PRICES

Accommodation listed in this guide has been categorized into one of nine price bands, as set out below. The rates quoted represent the **cheapest available** double or twin **room** – except for category ①, which are per-person rates for a dorm bed. Note that fees for **tent sites** and **DOC huts** (quoted in dollars) are also per-person, unless otherwise stated.

① under $20 per person	④ $60–80	⑦ $140–180
② under $40 per room	⑤ $80–100	⑧ $180–240
③ $40–60	⑥ $100–140	⑨ over $240

For more on accommodation, see p.34.

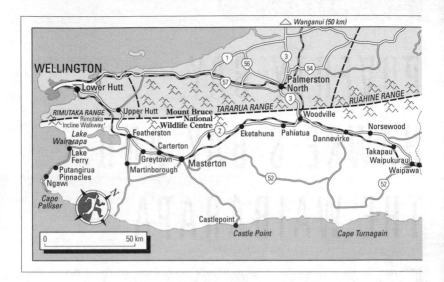

The surrounding region of **Hawke's Bay** has long been dubbed "the fruit bowl of New Zealand", famed for orchard boughs sagging under the weight of prime apples, pears and peaches. In recent years the torch has passed to grapes, which have been producing the sort of fine vintages that enhance the Hawke's Bay wine country's reputation as one of the foremost in the country. The district is best visited from **Napier**, the single most appealing city on the East Coast, as much for its seafront location and range of minor attractions as for the wealth of Art Deco buildings constructed after the city was flattened by a massive earthquake in 1931. Nearby **Hastings** suffered much the same fate and wove Spanish Mission-style buildings into the Art Deco fabric, though this won't delay you long from pressing on south through the uninspiring "Scandinavian" towns of southern Hawke's Bay. These run almost seamlessly into the similarly lacklustre settlements in the sheep lands of the **Wairarapa**, which takes its name from Lake Wairarapa ("glistening waters"), the eye in the fish that is the North Island, according to Maori legend. Unless you've a taste for the competitive sheepmanship of the Golden Shears competition in **Masterton**, the main goal in this region is **Martinborough**, surrounded by another collection of fine vineyards, most of which can be visited on foot.

Access to the mountainous **interior** of this region is limited, with only six roads winding over or cutting through the full length of the ranges. The most tortuous and one of the most scenic of these is SH38, which forges northwest from the small town of **Wairoa**, midway between Gisborne and Napier, to Rotorua. En route it wends its way through the remote wooded mountains of **Te Urewera National Park**, past beautiful Lake Waikaremoana, which is encircled by the four-day **Lake Waikaremoana Circuit** tramping route, as well as many appealing shorter lakeside strolls.

The East Coast is privileged to have the North Island's most appealing summertime **climate**: the grape-ripening heatwaves come with just enough sea breeze to make vigorous activity tolerable. The slight chill of spring and autumn mornings has its advocates, but winter can be cold and damp. As elsewhere, the **Christmas** and January

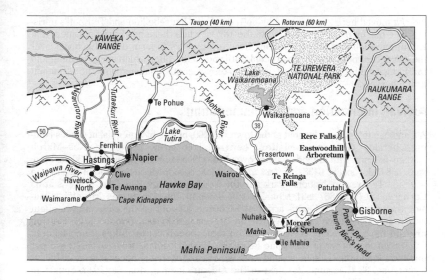

madness packs out the motor camps and motels, but even Napier, the most visited destination, is manageable at this time.

Getting around is pretty straightforward since the East Coast is serviced by InterCity **buses** (combined with Newmans); a main **train** line running from Wellington and Palmerston North to Napier and Hastings; and **flights** into Gisborne and Napier airports from Wellington and Auckland (Gisborne also receives flights from the smaller North Island centres of Hamilton and Palmerston North).

Gisborne and around

The small city of **GISBORNE**, near the junction of the inland SH2 (which straddles the Raukumara Range) and SH35 or the Pacific Coast Highway (which skirts the rugged coast of Eastland), is New Zealand's easternmost city – and the first in the world to see the light of the new day. It is also one of New Zealand's more relaxing and gently appealing places, not overly endowed with brash entertainments, but easy-going enough for a peaceful day or so. Broad streets come lined with squat weatherboard houses, which are warmed by long hours of sunshine, and are interspersed with parkland hugging the flanks of the Pacific, the harbour and three rivers – the Taruheru, Turanganui and Waimata.

Gisborne holds a special place in the European history of New Zealand, for it was here in October 1769 that **James Cook** first set foot on the soil of *Aotearoa* – and immediately ran into conflict with local Maori, killing several before sailing away empty-handed. He named the landing site **Poverty Bay**, since "it did not afford a single item we wanted, except a little firewood". The fertility of the surrounding lands belies the appellation, but the name stuck and looks set to prevail, despite the wishes of some **Maori** who would rename it *Turanganui a Kiwa* – in honour of a Polynesian navigator, rather than continually harking back to that unfortunate first Maori–*pakeha* encounter. Early-nineteenth-century Poverty Bay remained staunchly Maori and few

pakeha moved here, discouraged by both the Hau Hau rebellion and Te Kooti's uprising (see box on p.401). It wasn't until the 1870s, when these had been contained, that
Europeans felt safe enough to flock here in numbers to farm the rich alluvial river
flats. A decent port wasn't constructed until the 1920s, after which sheep farming and
market gardening really took off, activities only recently challenged by the ascendant
grape harvest.

Arrival, information and accommodation

A Canadian totem pole donated to the town in 1969, on the bicentennial of Cook's landing, heralds Gisborne's **visitor centre**, 209 Grey St (daily: Nov–March
7.30am–5.30pm, with extended hours over Xmas & New Year; April–Oct 7.30am–5pm;
☎06/868 6139, fax 868 6138, *info@eastland.tourism.co.nz*), which has helpful displays on
walks in Te Urewera National Park and the Waioeka Gorge. The DOC office is at 63
Carnarvon St (☎06/867 8531; Mon–Fri 8am–4.30pm). InterCity **buses** drop off just outside the visitor centre. Flights arrive at Gisborne **airport** on the edge of town about
2km west of the town centre, which can be reached by taxi (around $10). **Getting
around** most of the city is easily done on foot, though **rental bikes** from Maintrax
Cycles, on the corner of Gladstone Road and Roebuck Road (☎06/867 4571; $15 per
day) are good for a spin around the wineries. **Internet access** is available at
Cyberzone, 83 Gladstone Rd (next to the Odeon cinema; Mon–Sat 10am–8pm, Sun
noon–6pm; *info@cyberzone.co.nz*), which is not a café.

Despite the huge number of motels, chiefly along the main Gladstone Road and the
waterfront Salisbury Road, **accommodation** can sometimes be hard to come by, particularly during the month or so after Christmas when booking is advisable and prices
rise a little from their normally modest levels. Campsites also tend to be full of holidaying families at this time, but you should be able to get into one of the hostels. B&Bs
are relatively rare, with a few small-scale homestays scattered around the city and a real
gem further afield.

Motels

Blue Pacific, 90 Salisbury Rd (☎06/868 6099, fax 867 0481, *reservations@seafront.co.nz*).
Presentable beachfront motel with fully-equipped units, a sauna and spa pool. ⑤–⑥.
Endeavour Lodge Motel, 525 Gladstone Rd (☎06/868 6075, fax 868 6074). One of Gisborne's
cheapest motels, but maintained to a high standard and equipped with an attractive pool. ④.
Whispering Sands, 22 Salisbury Rd (☎06/867 1319, fax 867 6747). Beachfront motel with large
modern units, all with great sea views. ⑦.

B&Bs and homestays

Fawnridge, 29 Richardson Ave (☎06/868 8823, fax 867 6902). Very comfortable, hillside homestay
2km from the town centre with just one double room, great views over the city and a spa pool. ⑤.
Repongaere, 339 Lavenham Rd, Patutahi (☎ & fax 06/862 7717). This peaceful, large kauri homestead 18km west of Gisborne is one of the region's most appealing B&Bs, and comes complete with
tennis court, swimming pool and lovely rooms. Breakfasts are delicious and 4-course evening meals
for around $45 are served. ⑨.
Sea View, 68 Salisbury Rd (☎06/867 3879, fax 867 5879, *raewyn@regaleggs.co.nz*). Attractive, modern beachfront B&B, a 10min walk into town. Both double rooms have their own bathrooms. ⑤.
Thomson Homestay, 16 Rowiri St (☎ & fax 06/868 9675). Modest homestay with pleasant rooms,
all sharing bathrooms; substantial breakfasts feature home-preserved fruit. Canoe available for
guests' use. ④.
Tudor Lodge, 573 Aberdeen Rd (☎06/867 7577 & 0800/621 234). Bargain self-contained apartments in an attractive house with a garden running down to the Taruheru River. The units aren't
flash but they're comfortable nonetheless and there are kayaks for guests' use. ④–⑤.

Hostels

Flying Nun, 147 Roebuck Rd (☎06/868 0461, fax 867 7067, *eastbroke@clear.net.nz*). Fifteen minutes' walk from town, this vast and well-kept former convent boasts a pool table in the chapel, where sofas take the place of the altar and the confessionals have become phone booths. Some of the spacious dorms front onto verandas, and singles cost little more than dorm beds; doubles tend to be a bit cramped. Campsites are available in the extensive grounds and there's Sky TV. Tent sites $10, dorms ①, rooms ②.

Gisborne Backpackers/Sycamore Park, 690 Gladstone Rd (☎06/868 1000, fax 868 4000). Somewhat sterile former orphanage with good, clean facilities 15min walk from the centre. Doubles are especially capacious, dorms less so, and there's plenty of camping space in the grounds. Tent sites $8, dorms ①, rooms ②.

YHA, 32 Harris St (☎06/868 3269). Well-run associate hostel in a large house with big grounds, conveniently close to town. Tent sites $9, dorms ①, twins and doubles ②.

Campsites

Showgrounds Park Motor Camp, Main Rd (☎06/867 5299). The more distant of the two campsites, but with perfectly reasonable facilities and rock-bottom prices. Tent sites $11 for two, cabins ②.

Waikanae Beach Holiday Park, Grey St (☎06/867 5634, fax 867 9765). Wonderfully-sited motor park right by Gisborne's main beach and five minutes' walk from town, with tennis courts and comfortable cabins and flats. Tent sites $9, cabins ②, flats ③.

The Town

Perhaps more than any other East Coast town, Gisborne makes the best of its location, with almost everywhere in this compact city an easy stroll from the excellent and popular swimming and sunbathing strand of **Midway Beach**. Elsewhere, pleasant parks and green spaces run along the three rivers which converge at the largely disused harbour, below the steep hummock of Kaiti Hill.

Most of Gisborne's sights are connected in some way to the historical accident of Cook's landing and the dynamic between Maori and *pakeha* cultures it engendered. The first of James Cook's crew to spy the mountains of *Aotearoa*, a couple of days before the first landing, was the twelve-year-old surgeon's boy, Nick Young, who thereby claimed the gallon of rum Cook had offered as a reward. Honouring a second pledge, Cook recorded this white-cliffed promontory, 10km south of Gisborne across Poverty Bay, on his chart as Young Nick's Head. Young's keen eyes are commemorated with a pained-looking statue on the western side of the rivermouth in Gisborne, and on the opposite bank, an obelisk marks **Cook's landing site**, now a couple of hundred metres inland following reclamation for the harbour facilities. By contrast, early Maori explorers are commemorated with **Te Tauihu Turanga Whakamana** – a striking symbolic sculpture in the small Heipipi Park, beside the river-bridge where Gladstone Road meets Customhouse Street. Created by a local artist the piece resembles a Maori *tauihu* (canoe prow) with several figures carved into it: the top one represents Tangaroa (god of the sea); directly below him is Maui (half god, half man), and a third is Toi Kai Rakau (one of the earliest Maori to settle in New Zealand). On the splash covers facing the river are the first two Maori who came into contact with Cook; they face the nearby site of that meeting. The overall design is based on the interlocking spiral, a powerful Maori spiritual motif and meaning, among other things, the separation of the earth goddess from the sky god. Meanwhile Cook's botanist gets recognition near the obelisk at the waterfront in **Banks' Garden**: a locale full of species – especially low-growing varieties such as ngaio, tutu, karo and puriri – that he and his accomplice Solander collected here and at Anaura Bay and Tolaga Bay as they sailed north. Behind, Titirangi Domain climbs the side of **Titirangi** (Kaiti Hill) to the Cook Bicentenary Plaza, designed around a satisfied-looking Cook, with his back turned on

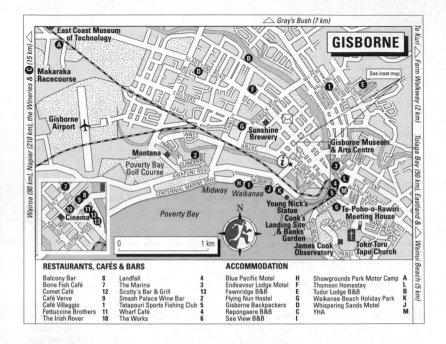

RESTAURANTS, CAFÉS & BARS

Balcony Bar	8	Landfall	4
Bone Fish Café	7	The Marina	3
Comet Café	12	Scotty's Bar & Grill	13
Café Verve	9	Smash Palace Wine Bar	2
Café Villaggio	1	Tatapouri Sports Fishing Club	5
Fettuccine Brothers	11	Wharf Café	4
The Irish Rover	10	The Works	6

ACCOMMODATION

Blue Pacific Motel	H	Showgrounds Park Motor Camp	A
Endeavour Lodge Motel	F	Thomson Homestay	L
Fawnridge B&B	E	Tudor Lodge B&B	B
Flying Nun Hostel	G	Waikanae Beach Holiday Park	K
Gisborne Backpackers	D	Whispering Sands Motel	J
Repongaere B&B	C	YHA	M
Sea View B&B	I		

the spot where he first set foot on New Zealand, now a log storage area. The highest point of the hill is occupied by the James Cook Observatory, which runs public stargazing nights on Tuesdays (Nov–March 8.30pm; April–Oct 7.30pm; $2).

Behind Titirangi lies the **Te Poho-o-Rawiri Meeting House**, which is among the largest in the country. The interior is superb, being almost completely covered in fine ancestor carvings, interspersed with wonderfully varied geometric *tukutuku* (woven panels). At the foot of the two support poles, ancient and intricately carved warrior statues provide a fine counterpoint to the bolder work on the walls. This is one of the most easily accessible working **marae**, but it is still necessary to arrange permission to enter the site (☎06/868 5364 or 868 0458), preferably a day or two beforehand, and a *koha* (donation) is appreciated. Adjacent is the small and decorative **Toko Toru Tapu Church**, though this is seldom open (entry can be arranged by phoning the marae number, above).

Ten minutes' walk north of here, across the Waimata River, is the **Gisborne Museum and Arts Centre** (*Te Whare Taonga o Tairawhiti*) on Kelvin Rise, Stout St (Mon–Fri 10am–4pm & Sat–Sun 1.30–4pm; free). Frequently changing shows augment extensive displays on East Coast Maori and a strong line in contemporary Maori arts: here you'll find beautiful *kete* (flax baskets), greenstone and *tiki* (pendants). Several disused buildings from around the region are clustered outside, notably the six-room, 1872 **Wyllie Cottage** (same hours; donation appreciated), the oldest extant house in town, and the **Sled House**, built on runners at the time of the Hau Hau uprising (see box on p.379), so that it could be hauled away by a team of bullocks at the first sign of unrest. The museum site incorporates the riverside **Star of Canada Maritime Museum** (same hours), originally the wheelhouse and captain's quarters of the 12,000-tonne *Star of Canada*, which ran aground on the reef off Gisborne's Kaiti Beach in 1912.

Most of the ship was scuttled but the bridge was turned into Gisborne's most distinctive house, a role it fulfilled for seventy years before being bequeathed to the city and moved to its present site. At the time of writing plans are afoot to also exhibit changing exhibitions in a new maritime gallery here.

A spot of less historically-minded sightseeing might take you on a tour of the small but excellent boutique **Sunshine Brewery**, near the town centre at 109 Disraeli St (Mon–Sat 9am–6pm). It has won armfuls of awards for its natural brews – such as Gisborne Gold (pilsener lager) and Black Magic (all-malt stout) among others – which have taken off in a big way in Wellington. Although several bars in town keep Sunshine beers on tap (notably *Smash Palace* and the *Irish Rover* see p.398), the small shop here has better prices than elsewhere. A winery worth a visit within Gisborne itself is **Parker MC**, behind the DC3 at Smash Palace Village, Banks Street off Awapuni Road (☎06/867 6967; daily: Oct–mid-March 10am–6pm; rest of year 10am–4pm; tastings $5, discounted from bottles purchased), which uses hand-harvested grapes from the Gisborne district for their bubblies (a classical Chardonnay Brut and a red Merlot Brut version), a Beaujolais-style light red that is the first wine released in the world each year (Firstlight Red), and a "crackling" Gewürztraminer semi-sweet dessert wine. Run by the owner of the whackiest bar in town (*Smash Palace* around the corner; see p.398) it's imaginatively designed with recycled materials putting all the empties to good use.

A more active alternative is beginner's surfing at **Waikanae Beach**: it has the smallest surf of the local beaches; there's easy access from the end of Grey Street; and **surf lessons** are available from Sue McGregor (☎06/867 2970; $20 per hr, including all gear) one-to-one or for small groups. To go it alone, **rent gear** from Blitz, 34–36 Wainui Rd (☎06/868 4428; daily: mid-Dec to mid-Jan 8am–8pm; rest of year: Mon–Fri 9am–5.30pm, Sat 9am–4pm, Sun 10am–3pm; wetsuits $10 per day; surf boards $20 half day, $30 full day); they also give daily surf reports on 89.3FM at 7am, noon and 4pm.

Around Gisborne

Winery visits with free tasting, easy walks and a smattering of specific attractions make a day or so spent around Gisborne an agreeable prospect. One tour company is geared to this kind of thing, offering informative trips of varying price and duration (Trev's Tours ☎06/863 9815, fax 863 9515; around $80 for a full day); otherwise public transport is of little use and you're pretty much on your own. If you don't have a car, your best bet is to rent a bike and head out on the flat roads to the wineries before retiring to one of the short walks just north of the city. Should, however, you be reluctant to settle into some serious tippling or gentle walking, the brave among you could always clamber into a shark cage and be lowered into the Pacific Ocean for a much more pulse-raising experience.

Before setting off for the wineries, walks or water, pay a visit to the **East Coast Museum of Technology**, Main Road, Makaraka, 5km northwest of the city (daily 9.30am–4.30pm; $2), where a former dairy factory has been used to hoard just about every imaginable piece of discarded household, industrial or agricultural junk. Little is labelled, let alone interpreted, but the enthusiasm of the staff is infectious and everyone should find something of interest among the ancient petrol pumps, early photocopiers and VCRs and Coke cans through the years. A couple of kilometres further northwest along SH2 lies the diminutive wooden **Matawhero Presbyterian Church**, the only building left standing by Te Kooti's raids in 1868.

Wineries
Further west along SH2 you are well into highly fertile wine country, where roadside windbreaks of poplars are a common sight, protecting the vines beyond. Most of the

wineries you can visit are **small concerns** that open according to demand; hours given below are a guideline only, and you'd do well to **call in advance**.

Occupying a free-draining alluvial plain, in the lee of the Raukumara Range and blessed with long hours of strong sun with warm summer nights, these wineries have made Gisborne the country's self-professed Chardonnay capital. The region has earned itself a reputation as a viticultural workhorse, churning out vast quantities of Chardonnay, Riesling, Müller-Thurgau and Gewürtztraminer grapes to be blended into cheerful wines for everyday glugging, and the reds are putting in a good show, too. The national giants of Corban's and **Montana** account for over eighty percent of the regional production, and anyone seriously interested in modern winemaking methods can take a tour around the factory-style operations of the latter at Lytton Road in Gisborne's suburbs (☎06/867 9819; mid-Dec to mid-Jan 2–4 tours daily; rest of year by appointment only; 45min–1hr; around $5). Here the whole process is explained in simple practical terms, while you take in the sheer size of their shiny 225,000-litre silos and taste wine straight from the barrel (take a jumper to keep out the chill). They produce several award-winning varietals, particularly Chardonnay and Gewürztraminer, under the labels of Ormond Estate, Patutahi Estate, Saints and Montana.

However visits to the more interesting **boutique wineries** tend to be more popular. Many of these are striving to break the Hawke's Bay and Marlborough stranglehold on international sales, which has led some commentators to predict that Gisborne will be the Next Big Thing. One of the closest and longest-established wineries is **Matawhero**, Riverpoint Road, 8km west of Gisborne (☎06/868 8366; Oct–April Mon–Sat 11am–4pm; rest of year times vary), renowned for its Gewürztraminer and beginning to produce some fine reds, but there is more interest at **Millton Vineyard**, Papatu Road, Manutuke, 2km west (☎06/862 8680; by appointment only). This is one of New Zealand's few fully certified **organic** wineries, and possibly the only one to apply the **bio-dynamic** principles espoused by Rudolf Steiner to all aspects of wine production. The timing of planting, harvesting and bottling are dictated by the phases of the moon, which cooperates to produce some delicious wines (especially Riesling, Chenin Blanc and late-harvest dessert wines) that can apparently be enjoyed even by those who experience adverse reactions to other wines. Considering the intricacy of such wine making, prices are surprisingly reasonable, so grab a bottle, indulge in a picnic among the vines and a leisurely game of petanque.

One of the few wineries that is open daily all year is **Pouparae Park** at Bushmere, 10km west of central Gisborne on Bushmere Road, 4km off the southbound SH2 (☎06/867 7931; daily except Xmas Day & Good Friday 10am–6pm; free tastings), where you are free to explore a park-like country garden boasting ancient native trees. Of special note is their Chardonnay, but the Merlot and Riesling are popular, as are the prices – around $10 less per bottle than at the majority of other wineries. While most wineries concentrate on whites, reds are beginning to make inroads, notably at the youthful **Shalimar Estate Winery**, Ngatapa Road, Patutahi, 15km west of Gisborne on the way to Ngatapa, off SH2 southbound and 6km from the roundabout where Ngatapa Rd meets SH2 (☎06/862 7776; daily 10am–5pm), which is gradually building a reputation for **quality reds**, and has already won medals for its Merlot (as well as its white, a Semillon), both of which can be sampled for free, their wines selling at reasonable prices ($8–15 a bottle).

Trees and walks

A bottle of wine tucked under your arm and a groaning picnic hamper is the most conducive way to enjoy New Zealand's largest collection of northern-hemisphere vegetation at **Eastwoodhill Arboretum**, Ngatapa–Rere Road, 35km northwest of Gisborne (daily 9am–4pm; $8). The parched hills surrounding the Poverty Bay plains stand in stark contrast to the arboretum's lush glens and formal lawns. Planting began in 1910, inspired by William Douglas Cook, who had grown to love British gardens and parks. Numerous trails thread through a unique mixture of over 3500 species – magnolias, oaks, spruce, maples, cherries – brought together in an unusual microclimate in which both hot- and cold-climate trees flourish.

Walks are not Gisborne's strong suit, but there are a couple detailed in DOC leaflets available from the visitor centre. The closest is **Te Kuri Farm Walkway** (5km; 2hr; closed during lambing season mid-July to Oct), off Shelley Road, 4km north of the centre of Gisborne. Apart from a lovely panorama over the city from a ridge-top section of pastoral land, this isn't a particularly exciting route – though you do get to walk the land owned by cartoonist Murray Ball, who immortalized this terrain in his archetypal Kiwi cartoon, *Footrot Flats*, which features "the Dog", or Te Kuri. On a hot day, a better bet is the short walk through the cool kahikatea, puriri and nikau woodlands of **Gray's Bush** (30min return), 9km northeast of the city, and the largest remnant of the tall forests that once covered the Poverty Bay flats.

Shark seeing

Adrenalin junkies can take a boat-trip out from Gisborne into the Pacific Ocean, to **view sharks from a shark cage** with Surfit Shark Cage Experience (☎06/867 2970, fax 867 2703, *Surfit.Enterprises@xtra.co.nz*; 4–5hr; from $150 per person including gear). Apart from Kaikoura this is currently the only place in New Zealand where you can try this. Small groups are taken about 15km offshore to find **mako sharks**, and two people at a time share the specially designed aluminium cage, in which the water only ever reaches as far as your chest. You duck-dive with a mask and snorkel or regulator, spending about half an hour in the water (which is plenty, given the excitement) during heart-pounding encounters. Mako sharks are curious rather than aggressive, usually 3–3.5m long, and broad, weighing in at 40–90kg. The boat can go out in virtually any weather, there's a fifty percent refund in the unlikely event of not seeing any sharks, and your whole experience is shot on video, which you can keep for an extra $25.

Eating, drinking and nightlife

For its size, Gisborne is surprisingly well supplied with decent **cafés** and **restaurants** to suit all budgets, many of them making good use of their locations on the city's beach, rivers or harbour by means of large glass doors thrown open at any hint of sun. Those same features make the restaurants the best bet for an evening **drink**, though there are several traditional pubs for straightforward beer consumption. A rough-and-ready **farmers market** is held each Saturday morning (6.30am to around 8.30am) in the park next to the visitor centre, where you can snap up some bargain ingredients in a bustling atmosphere – keep an eye out for some of the subtropical and citrus fruits that grow here all year for the export market. Unusually for New Zealand, where local catches of fish are often immediately exported or transported to other parts of the country, excellent prices for **fish** straight off Gisborne's boats can be had at the Moana Pacific Fisheries shop on The Esplanade and opposite the Tatapouri Sports Fishing Club (Nov–Feb: Mon–Fri 8.30am–5.30pm, Sat 9am–1pm; rest of year: Mon–Fri 8.30am–5.30pm), the simple reason being that the company owns most of these boats.

The town's excellent Odeon **cinema** is at 79 Gladstone Rd, near the junction with Peel St (☎06/867 3339), and two of the four screens are curved, which somehow enhances viewing; the complex also has its own convenient and inexpensive if somewhat uninspiring café-bar, the *Cinebar* (Mon–Sat all day and late into the night), where you can grab a drink, a bite or have a full meal.

Cafés and restaurants

Bone Fish Café, 57 Grey St. An uplifting all-day café concentrating on Mediterranean food at good prices. They make their own bread and excellent muffins (try the flaming variety with a coffee, or the spicy Morning Glory muffin that sells out by lunchtime). Licensed.

Comet Café, 2 Lowe St. Groovy welcoming café with sofas and magazines, Internet access, good coffee and mainly vegetarian food. Summer daily 8am till late; winter Sun–Tues 8am–6pm, Wed–Sat 8am–11pm.

Fettuccine Brothers, 12 Peel St. Relaxing pasta restaurant, the first and best one in Gisborne, which caters mainly to vegetarians for lunch and dinner (closed in between), with a bar in the next-door room. Closed Sun in winter; licensed.

Landfall, Shed 1, The Wharf on The Esplanade (☎06/867 2039). Fine dining by the water to a Mediterranean ambience, concentrating on seafood lunches and dinners in a restaurant owned by a local winemaker. Closed Mon & Sun in winter.

The Marina, Marina Park, Vogel St (☎06/868 5919). One of Gisborne's finest restaurants with a glass-sided dining room bedecked in crisp white linen and overlooking the confluence of the Taruheru and Waimata rivers. Food is of the modern Kiwi persuasion, along the lines of live crayfish followed by venison with roasted pepper sauce, at up to $25 for a main course. Dinner bookings essential & for lunches Dec–Jan; licensed.

Café Verve, 121 Gladstone St. Gisborne's grooviest all-day café and restaurant, with sofas and magazines at the back, Internet access, and gorgeous moderately priced food that extends to Moroccan vegetable tajine and a fabulous chicken curry. Closes 3pm Sun; BYO.

Café Villaggio, 57 Ballance St. Award-winning casual restaurant set in a suburban Art Deco house and spilling over into the courtyard. A great place for weekend brunch, lunches or simple yet delicious evening meals for around $20. Closed Sun & Mon nights; licensed.

Wharf Café, Shed 1, The Wharf on The Esplanade (☎06/868 4876). Light and airy harbourside café open daily from 9am till the early hours, serving good seafood lunches and dinners at reasonable prices. Licensed. Book ahead for weekend lunch or dinner.

The Works, cnr The Esplanade & Crawford Rd (☎06/863 1285). Airy Mediterranean-style café set back from the wharf offering snacks and well-priced light meals that feature seafood, salamis and locally made Waimata Cheese, including specialities such as Blue Brie, Farmhouse Blue, and Taepo (a creamy cheese rolled in grapevine ash and cured) – each the perfect accompaniment to the Chardonnay and Merlot of Longbush Winery (who own the café) and the wines of other local boutique wineries, available for tastings at a small charge.

Pubs and bars

Balcony Bar, 5th floor, Post Office Building, Grey St. Drab bar redeemed by a great view from its vantage point on the top floor of one of Gisborne's few tall buildings. This is the liveliest place mid-week and sometimes has live bands, but is often closed for functions on Sat nights – and, be warned, Thurs night is karaoke night.

The Irish Rover, 69 Peel St. A place of simple charms and warm atmosphere: Guinness, the natural Gisborne Gold, bar snacks and occasional live bands.

Scotty's Bar & Grill, 33 Gladstone Rd. Probably the best bar in town, certainly the classiest and longest established, occupying what was once a big ornate bank. This is a great all-rounder, open daily with good-value food, plenty of outdoor seating, and a DJ or live band on Fri & Sat nights.

Smash Palace Wine Bar, 24 Banks St. Wonderfully oddball bar where overalls from the surrounding industrial area rub shoulders with suits in a corrugated-iron barn adorned with all manner of junk heralded by a bright yellow Morris Minor at the entrance. The bar occasionally hosts theme evenings in summer, and is also an outlet for some fine local plonk made by Parker MC (see p.395). Food is basically snacks, favourites being flaming pizzas and the nachos flame-toasted with a blow torch. Mon–Fri & Sun open from 3pm; Sat from noon.

Tatapouri Sports Fishing Club, The Esplanade, opposite the *Wharf Café*. From Oct to April visitors are welcome to this barn-like pub/club right on the wharf (the rest of the year you must be signed in by a member), with veranda seating for the consumption of generous portions of satay, a "wharfie's plate" of seafood, or gourmet burgers, all under $15, while watching the sun set behind the hills beyond the dock.

Gisborne to Wairoa

All roads south of Gisborne involve lengthy travel through vast swathes of farmland, which are sparsely scattered with nowhere villages that offer little incentive to linger. There are **two routes**: the faster SH2, which sticks close to the coast before veering around Hawke Bay; and the inland SH36, which sees very little traffic – and no public transport.

From Gisborne, SH36 winds 70km through the interior over the steep slopes of the 360m Gentle Annie hill to **Te Reinga Falls**, where the Hangaroa and Raikituri rivers join forces to plunge into a river-sculpted ravine. A loop track (4km; 1hr 30min) follows a dry riverbed past towering limestone bluffs to an excellent viewpoint, though you should ask permission at the nearby marae for access – instructions are posted in the car park. If you're short of time, a ten-minute-return path leads to a less spectacular viewpoint. Continuing 25km south, SH36 joins SH38 at **FRASERTOWN**, where you can turn coastwards for Wairoa or turn inland to Lake Waikaremoana (see p.401).

Following the alternative **coastal route** of SH2 from Gisborne along the southern continuation of the Pacific Coast Highway, the Poverty Bay vineyards soon give way to the hill country of the Wharerata State Forest, where the first real diversion is provided by **Morere Hot Springs** (Dec–April daily 10am–5pm, except statutory and school holidays when it's 10am–8pm; $6, private pools an extra $2 for 30min), 60km south of Gisborne. Ancient sea water has been heated and concentrated along the fault line deep underground to form highly saline, iron-rich waters that well up along a small stream as it trickles down through one of the East Coast's last remaining tracts of native coastal forest. Grassy barbecue areas surround the pools and form the nucleus of numerous trails that radiate out through stands of tawa, rimu, totara and matai; a short streamside walk (10min) takes you to the Nikau Plunge Pools, where steel soaking tanks are surrounded by groves of nikau palms.

The adjacent settlement of **MORERE** has a shop and a couple of **places to stay**, both on SH2 as it passes through the village. The appealing *Peacock Lodge* (☎ & fax 06/837 8824; dorms ①, rooms ②) is a spacious and broad-verandaed house tucked away amid trees, which is well set up for families and small groups alike, with beds in small dorms and pleasant doubles; there's also accommodation at *Morere Springs Tearooms & Camping Ground* (☎06/837 8792, fax 837 8790; tent sites $9, dorms ①, cabins ②–④).

Mahia Peninsula

At **NUHAKA**, 8km south of Morere, the road flirts briefly with the sea before turning sharp right for Wairoa. A side road spurs east to the pendulous **Mahia Peninsula**, a distinctive high promontory that separates Hawke Bay from Poverty Bay. Linked to the mainland by a narrow sandy isthmus, surfers make good use of the rougher windward side, while the calmer beaches on the leeward side offer safe bathing and boating for the hundreds of families who descend each summer to swim, fish for snapper and hapuku, dive and generally chill out. Outside the mad month after Christmas it makes a relaxing place to break your journey, or to stretch your legs on the 4km loop track through the **Mahia Peninsula Scenic Reserve**.

At the northern end of the Hawke's Bay side of the isthmus is **OPUATAMA**, little more than a shop and the pine-surrounded *Blue Bay Holiday Resort* (☎06/837 5867, fax 837 5516; tent sites $8, cabins ②–③). The peninsula's main settlement of **MAHIA BEACH** lies at the southern end of the five-kilometre strand, where there are takeaways, a café and a pub, and the well-appointed *Mahia Beach Motel & Holiday Park*

(☎ & fax 06/837 5830, *mahia.beach.motels@xtra.co.nz*; tent sites $10, cabins ②, units
④–⑤) with spacious camping, simple tourist cabins and flashier motel units. You can
also stay just over the hill, closer to the surfie beaches, at tiny **TE MAHIA**, in the log-
built *Cappamore Lodge*, 435 Mahia East Coast Rd (☎06/837 5523, fax 837 5583,
oconnellcappamore@clear.net.nz; ⑤), a self-contained 2-storeyed house with a
bunkroom in the loft ($15 per each extra person in the bunkroom). Note that though
there are shops, there are no bottle shops or pubs on the peninsula, so come prepared
for those all-important sundowners.

Wairoa

Sleepy **WAIROA**, some 30km west of the Nuhaka junction, hugs the banks of the broad
willow-lined Wairoa River a couple of kilometres from its mouth, where ships once
entered to load the produce of the dairying and sheep-farming country all around.
Today the riverside wharves have all but disappeared, but the remnants make for a
pleasant enough stroll if you have a few hours to wait for bus connections inland to Lake
Waikaremoana and Te Urewera National Park.

The only real point of interest in town is the 1877 kauri lighthouse beside the bridge
at the town centre, which was relocated here in 1958 from Portland Island, off the
southern tip of the Mahia Peninsula. If you are staying a bit longer, try to visit the highly decorative **Takitimu Marae**: trips can be organized through the **visitor centre**, centrally located on the corner of SH2 and Queen Street (Nov–March daily 9am–5pm;
April–Sept Mon–Fri 9am–5pm; ☎ & fax 06/838 7440, *weavic@xtra.co.nz*).

Close by is the Wairoa Holiday Shop, on Marine Parade (☎ & fax 06/838 7574),
which sells tickets for InterCity and Newmans **bus** services to Gisborne and Napier. If
an early-morning bus necessitates an **overnight stay**, head for the *Riverside Motor
Camp* at 19 Marine Parade (☎06/838 6301, fax 838 6341; tent sites $8, cabins ②), the
Riverside Homestay, 48 Kopu Rd (☎06/838 7346; ④), the *Three Oaks Motel*, on the corner of Campbell Street and Clyde Road (☎ & fax 06/838 8204; ④), or *Vista Motor Lodge*,
on SH2 before the Wairoa bridge (☎ & fax 06/838 8279; ⑤), which has an on-site restaurant.

Te Urewera National Park

Te Urewera National Park, 65km northwest of Wairoa, straddles the North Island's
mountainous backbone and encompasses the largest untouched expanse of native bush
outside of Fiordland. Unusually for New Zealand, it is almost completely covered in
vegetation; even the highest peaks – some approaching 1500m – barely poke through
this dense cloak of primeval forests whose undergrowth is trampled by deer and wild
pigs, and whose cascading rivers are alive with trout. One road, SH38, penetrates the
interior, but the way to get a true sense of the place is to go tramping. For hardy types,
this means the **Lake Waikaremoana Circuit**, which is among the finest four-day
tramps in the country, encircling a steep-sided lake at the southern end of the park.
Created little more than two thousand years ago, **Lake Waikaremoana**, the "Sea of
Rippling Waters", is the undoubted jewel of the park, its deep clear waters fringed by
white sandy beaches and rocky bluffs making it ideal for swimming, diving, fishing and
kayaking.

Habitation is very sparse. The Tuhoe people, the "Children of the Mist", still live in
the interior of the park around the tramping base of **Ruatahuna**, but most visitors
make straight for **Waikaremoana**, which is barely a settlement at all, just a motor camp
and a visitor centre right on the lake shore. Immediately to the south, the quiet former
hydro-electrical development town of **Tuai** provides some additional basic services,

TE KOOTI

Te Kooti Rikirangi was one of the most celebrated of Maori "rebels", a thorn in the side of the colonial government throughout the New Zealand Wars of the late 1860s and early years of the 1870s. Depicted, at least in *pakeha*-biased school books, as a ruthless guerrilla leader and the wildest outlaw in Maori history, in truth he was a mild-mannered man with a neatly-trimmed beard and moustache rather than the more confrontational *moko* (traditional tattoos). An excellent fighter and brilliant **strategist**, Te Kooti kept the mountainous spine of the North Island on edge for the best part of a decade, eluding the biggest manhunt in New Zealand's history.

Though not of chiefly rank, Te Kooti could trace his ancestry back to the captains of several *waka* (canoes) and was born near Gisborne into a respected family around 1830, though little else is known of his early years. By the middle of the 1860s, he was fighting for the government against the **Hau Hau** (see box on p.379), a fanatical, pseudo-Christian cult which started in Taranaki in 1862. The cult spread to the East Coast where, in 1866, Te Kooti was unjustly accused of being in league with its devotees. Denied the trial he so often demanded, he was subsequently imprisoned on the Chatham Islands, along with 300 of his supposed allies. In 1867, he was brought close to death by a fever, but rose again, claiming a divine revelation and establishing a new religion, **Ringatu** ("the uplifted hand"), which still has some 6000 believers today. Ringatu took its cues from the Hau Hau, but developed into a uniquely Maori version of Christianity, drawing heavily on the Old Testament. Some say Te Kooti saw himself as a Moses figure, called to lead his people to freedom, and he was certainly charismatic in his approach – apparently given to dousing his uplifted hand in phosphorus so that it glowed in the dim meeting houses.

After two years on the Chathams, Te Kooti and his fellow prisoners commandeered a ship and engineered a dramatic escape, returning to Poverty Bay. Te Kooti sought the rugged safety of the **Urewera Range**, with the Armed Constabulary in hot pursuit, relentlessly tailing him through snow, mud and heat on horseback and on foot. Nonetheless, Te Kooti conducted successful campaigns, exacting revenge against government troops at Whakatane on the Bay of Plenty, Mohaka in Hawke's Bay and at Rotorua. The government posted a reward of £1000 on his head, but he was always able to stay ahead of the game and it was never claimed. With the end of the New Zealand Wars in 1872, Te Kooti took refuge in the Maori safe haven of the **King Country**. He was eventually pardoned in 1883, and in 1891 was granted a plot of land near Whakatane, where he lived out the last two years of his life.

including the closest pub and an attractive modern homestay at 9 The Esplanade (☎06/837 3701; ④), beside Lake Whakamarino and ten minutes' drive from Lake Waikaremoana, which has a twin and a double (queen); but otherwise you're on your own.

Lake Waikaremoana

The magnificent, bush-girt **Lake Waikaremoana** fills a huge scalloped bowl at an altitude of over 585m, precariously held back by the Panekiri and Ngamoko ranges which, at the slightest opportunity, seem ready to part and spill the contents down the pastoral valley towards Wairoa. The lake came into being around 2200 years ago when a huge bank of sandstone boulders was dislodged from the Ngamoko range, blocking the rivers that once drained the valleys and thereby forming the lake. Maori have a more poetic explanation of the lake's creation, pointing to the work of Hau-Mapuhia, the recalcitrant daughter of Mahu, who was drowned by her father and turned into a *taniwha*, or "water spirit". In a frenzied effort to get to the sea, she charged in every direction, thereby creating the various arms of the lake. As she frantically ran south towards

Onepoto, the dawn caught her, turning her to stone at a spot where the lake is said to ripple from time to time, in a watery memory of her titanic struggle.

Drivers can skirt the lake's eastern shores and get to the **Papakorito Falls**, a twenty-metre-wide curtain of water 2km east of the visitor centre, but to really see and get a feel for the place you'll need to **walk**. The DOC's *Waikaremoana Walks* leaflet ($1) details all the routes, including the Lake Waikaremoana Track (see below) – and a number of more manageable excursions, such as the stroll to the double-drop **Aniwaniwa Falls** (1km; 15min return), starting from beside the visitor centre, or the **Black Beech Track** (2km; 30min one way), which follows the old highway from the visitor centre to the motor camp. With the best part of a day to spare, take on the **Waipai–Ruapani–Waikareiti Round Trip** (15km; 6hr), which starts 200m north of the visitor centre and winds up through dense beech forest past the grassy-fringed Lake Ruapani to the beautiful and serene **Lake Waikareiti**, where you can rent row-boats ($10 per half day, $40 deposit), though you'll need to plan ahead, as the key is held at Aniwaniwa visitor centre. Return down the Waikareiti Track or head on around to the northern side of the lake (3hr one-way) and stay at **Sandy Bay Hut** (Category 3; ①; 18 bunks; you must pre-book through the DOC).

Another way to explore the lake area is by horse trekking through bush and private farms with Big Bush Holiday Park, at Kokako, 3km south of Onepoto (☎06/837 3777; $20 per hr; $60 per half day).

The Lake Waikaremoana Track

The **Lake Waikaremoana Track** (46km; 3–4 days; 900m ascent; book ahead through the Aniwaniwa visitor centre, see p.404) undoubtedly ranks among the finest multi-day tramps in New Zealand, and is often compared with the South Island's Routeburn and Milford tracks. But with the exception of an exhausting climb on the first day, this is a much gentler affair; well-paced and mostly hugging the lakeshore, the tramp offers plenty of opportunities to fish and swim, as well as to simply admire the majestic scenery and listen to the cacophonous birdlife. This is the most popular multi-day tramp in the North Island, so you'll need to choose your time to avoid the crowds: school holidays, especially the six weeks after Christmas, are always busy and the winter months (June–Sept) can be cold and wet, making spring and autumn the best times.

The DOC's *Lake Waikaremoana Track* leaflet ($1) provides all the information you need to walk the track, though **map** enthusiasts may fancy the 1:100,000 *Urewera Parkmap*. The walk is normally done in four days, spending nights in three of the four **huts** or five designated **campsites** scattered around the lakeshore. Huts and campsites must all be paid for in advance from the visitor centre or the DOC (huts $12, campsites $8). Each hut is supplied with drinking water, toilets and a heating stove, but a cooking stove and fuel must be carried. Most people prefer to walk clockwise around the lake, getting the challenging but panoramic ascent of Panekiri Bluff over with on the first day, though if the weather looks bad there's no reason why you shouldn't go anti-clockwise in the hope that it will improve on subsequent days.

TRAILHEAD TRANSPORT

Access to the start and finish of the Waikaremoana Circuit is by boat: whichever way you walk, you can be on the track by 9am, and you need to finish your last day's walk by 2pm. Vehicles and clobber are best left in the car park at Aniwaniwa Visitor Centre (free) or at the Waikaremoana Motor Camp ($3 per night, bags and bikes $4).

A **ferry service** (✆06/837 3729; 3 daily mid-Dec to Jan, rest of year on demand; $20 round-trip) runs from the Waikaremoana Motor Camp to Onepoto, Hopuruahine and anywhere else you might want to start or finish your walk (prices dependent on numbers but start at $10pp to Onepoto, $15pp to Hopuruahine); to reach the trailhead contact Noel Hinemoa (after hours only ✆07/837 3729), who also runs a **water-taxi** service – enabling you to walk shorter sections of the circuit by means of pre-arranged pick-ups from specified beaches. Costs are dependent on numbers, but are broadly comparable with the regular ferries.

THE ROUTE

When tackled clockwise, the first leg from **Onepoto to Panekiri Hut** (9km; 5hr; 600m ascent) is the toughest; carry plenty of drinking water and start at a shelter by the lakeshore close to SH38. The track climbs steeply past the site of a redoubt set up by soldiers of the Armed Constabulary in pursuit of Te Kooti (see box on p.401) to the Pukenui trig point, from where the track undulates along the ridge top. Steps up a rocky bluff bring you to the Panekiri Hut (36 bunks), magnificently set on the brink of the cliffs that fall away to the lake far below. Even if you've the energy to push on, it would be a shame not to stay here, though camping in this fragile environment is prohibited, so the hut is your only option. Committed campers must press on to Waiopaoa, a whopping nine hours' walk from the start.

From **Panekiri Hut to Waiopaoa Hut** (7.5km; 3–4hr; 600m descent) you lose the height gained the previous day, slowly at first along the descending ridge, then very rapidly through an often-muddy area where protruding tree roots provide welcome hand-holds. Occasional lake views and the transition from beech forests to rich podocarp woodlands make this an appealing, if tricky, section of track down to the hut (22 bunks) and campsite.

Pressing on beyond **Waiopaoa Hut to Marauiti Hut** (11km; 4–5hr; 100m ascent), you largely follow the lakeshore, initially across grassland and through kanuka scrub where a side track leads to the impressive 20m Korokoro Falls (25min return) and, just beyond the junction, the Korokoro campsite (1hr 30min from Waiopaoa Hut). Meanwhile, the main track climbs slightly above the lake past barely accessible bays, eventually reaching the Maraunui campsite and, after climbing the low Whakaneke

Spur, descends to the waterside Marauiti Hut (22 bunks). From **Marauiti Hut to Whanganui Hut** (12.5km; 4–5hr; 150m ascent) the track passes the lovely white-sand Te Kopua Bay and climbs an easy saddle, before dropping down to Te Totara Bay and following the lake to Waiharuru campsite; then on across a broad neck of land to the Tapuaenui campsite and beyond, following the shore to the pleasantly sited hut (20 bunks).

The last easy day covers the **Whanganui Hut to Hopuruahine** (5km; 2–3hr; 50m ascent), which skirts the lake and follows grassy flats beside the Hopuruahine River and across a suspension bridge to the access road.

Waikaremoana practicalities

SH38 from Wairoa runs around the eastern side of Lake Waikaremoana to the **Aniwaniwa visitor centre** (daily 8am–5pm; ☎06/837 3803, fax 837 3722, *urewerainfo @doc.nz*), the main source of information on Lake Waikaremoana and Te Urewera National Park, with excellent and extensive displays on the social history, geology and ecology of the region and a stack of brochures detailing the numerous walks in the area. There is no public transport between Wairoa and Rotorua.

At some point you'll need **accommodation**, which for most means the well-equipped *Waikaremoana Motor Camp*, on SH38, 1.5km south of the visitor centre (☎06/837 3826, fax 837 3825; tent sites $7.50, bunkhouse ①, cabins ②, chalets & units ③), with a compact but grassy camping area, a perfectly serviceable bunkhouse, cabins and more luxurious self-contained chalets and units; showers are available for non-guests at $2 a time. Other accommodation options are **in Tuai**, 3km south of Onepoto, where there's the *Big Bush Holiday Park* (☎ & fax 06/837 3777; tent sites $8, studio unit ③, motel units ④), with a daytime restaurant/bar (daily Labour Weekend to Easter, till the early hours; closed rest of year), which does good coffee. Tuai also has the pleasant *Lake Whakamarino Homestay* at 9 The Esplanade (☎06/837 3701; ④), a modern house right beside the lake and ten minutes' drive from Lake Waikaremoana, offering a twin and a double (queen); and the former construction workers' quarters of *Lake Whakamarino Lodge*, on The Esplanade (☎06/837 3876, fax 837 3872; dorms ①, rooms ③ & self-contained units ⑤), which is rather short on character, despite being wonderfully sited right on the shores of the trout-filled Lake Whakamarino; meals are available on request.

You'll largely have to fend for yourself when it comes to **eating**. Apart from the **restaurant/bar** at Tuai's *Big Bush Holiday Park*, the only food in the park is the limited range at the grocery shop in the *Waikaremoana Motor Camp*.

Beyond Lake Waikaremoana: the heart of the park

Beyond Lake Waikaremoana, SH38 twists and turns for two hours before regaining the tar seal at Murupara, almost 100km northwest of the lake and just an hour (62km) short of Rotorua. The road, which took 45 years to build and wasn't completed until 1930, makes a tortuous journey through the heart of Te Urewera National Park, the ancestral home of the Tuhoe people.

Historically, the Tuhoe had limited contact with Europeans; even today, they live in relative isolation in ramshackle roadside villages such as **RUATAHUNA**, 48km from Waikaremoana, which also serves as a base for a couple of little-used tracks into beau-

The **northward continuation** of SH38 beyond the border of the Te Urewera National Park is covered under "Whirinaki Forest Park and the road to Lake Waikaremoana" on p.291.

tiful and remote country north of SH38. These are most often used by anglers and hunters, but are excellent for tramping, too, with Category 3 huts ($5) at regular intervals. Two DOC leaflets ($1 each) cover these tramps, the easiest of which is the **Whakatane River Round Trip**, a three-to-five-day walk suitable for most levels of fitness through varied scenery encompassing river valleys, native forest, grassy flats and farmland. For tougher specimens, there's the **Upper Waikare River Guide**, an amalgam of several tracks, many of them following riverbeds (seek local advice on the likelihood of flooding) and enabling various route combinations (2–4 days). If you'd rather go on **horseback**, Te Urewera Adventures (☎07/366 3969; 1–5 days, $117–780) run **treks** from their Mataatua Marae in Ruatahuna, with overnight accommodation in permanently erected tents. They also run a **homestay** offering dinner, bed and breakfast (⑤).

In the village, the *Ruatahuna Motel* (☎07/366 3393; units ④) provides simple budget **motel** units, and breakfast and packed lunches on request; the motel also has a **takeaway** and sells the only **petrol** before Murupara. At Te Whaiti, 5km before Ruatahuna, there's a free **camping** area beside the highway.

Wairoa to Napier

Travelling by bus, or even by car, there is little to justify stopping in the inland farming country that lines the highway between Wairoa and Napier, though **cyclists** may want to break this 120km stretch. The most sensible place to do just that is three-quarters of the way at *Glenview Farm Hostel*, Aropaoanui Road, 2km east off SH2 (☎06/836 6232; tent sites $8, dorms ①, rooms ②), a small and well-organized backpackers with bargain dorm beds and self-contained rooms, plus a farm shop; a separate homestay section, 2km down the road, features an elaborate breakfast – and there's **riding** ($25 per half day, $40 a day) that includes swimming the horses in the river.

A few kilometres further south, the highway passes the small **Lake Tutira** and its diminutive neighbour, Lake Waikopiro, neither worthy of much attention though if you want a breath of air you could tackle one of three farmland loop walks (1km, 20min; 3.5km, 2hr; and 9km, 5hr; all closed Aug & Sept for lambing season), which start at the roadside car park, the shortest walk encircling Lake Waikopiro and the longest incorporating a lookout over both lakes (see DOC leaflet *Napier–Tutira Highway*, $1). On a hot day you might prefer the shade offered by **White Pine Bush Scenic Reserve**, 10km south, a dense clump of kahikatea, rimu and other podocarps, where loop tracks (650m, 30min; and 3km, 1hr) thread through the bush alongside the Kareaara Stream. From here it is just 25km to central Napier.

Napier and around

The port city of **NAPIER** is Hawke's Bay's largest, yet with its beautiful seafront position, a Mediterranean climate and a population barely touching 50,000, it is an easy place with which to come to terms. Add to that the world's finest collection of small-scale Art Deco buildings, heaps of amusements for kids and a burgeoning café society, and you have one of New Zealand's most likeable regional centres. There are even better reasons to stick around the Napier area, not least for the trip out to the gannet colony at Cape Kidnappers, and to tour the barrel-load of excellent **wineries** on the surrounding plains.

In 1769, James Cook sailed past **Ahuriri**, the current site of Napier, noting the sea-girt Bluff Hill linked to the mainland by two slender shingle banks and backed by a superb saltwater lagoon – the only substantial sheltered mooring between Gisborne and Wellington. Nonetheless, he anchored just to the south, off what came to be known as Cape Kidnappers, on account of a less-than-cordial encounter with the native Ngati Kahungunu people. Some thirty years later, when early whalers followed in Cook's tracks, Ahuriri was all but deserted, the Ngati Kahungunu having been driven out by rivals equipped with guns – the dubious contribution of European settlers in the Bay of Islands. During the uneasy peace of the early colonial years, Maori returned to the Napier area, which weathered the **New Zealand Wars** of the 1860s relatively unscathed and profited from the peace sustained by the guiding hands of men like the missionary printer William Colenso and Land Commissioner Donald McLean, both staunch supporters of sheep farming in Hawke's Bay. The port boomed, but by the early years of the twentieth century all the available land was used up and Napier had begun to stagnate.

Everything changed in two-and-a-half minutes on the morning of February 3, 1931, when the city was rocked by the biggest **earthquake** in New Zealand's recorded history, measuring a massive 7.9 on the Richter scale. More than six hundred aftershocks followed over the next two weeks, hampering efforts to rescue the 258 people who perished throughout Hawke's Bay, 162 of them in Napier alone. The centre of the city was completely devastated: almost all the brick-built shops and offices crumbled into a heap of smouldering rubble; the more flexible wooden buildings survived the initial tremor only to be consumed by the ensuing fire, which was fanned by a stiff sea breeze. The land twisted and buckled, finding a new equilibrium more than two metres higher; the sea drained out of the Ahuriri Lagoon, leaving trawlers high and dry and fish floundering on the mud flats. Three hundred square kilometres of new land were wrested from the grip of the ocean – enough room to site the Hawke's Bay airport, establish new farms and expand the city; cast your eye inland and you can still pick out a stranded line of sea cliffs a couple of kilometres away.

All this happened in the midst of the Great Depression, but Napier grasped the opportunity to start afresh: out went the trams; telephone wires were laid underground; the streets were widened; and buildings had to have cantilevered verandas, obviating the need for unsightly support poles. In the spirit of the times, almost everything was designed according to the precepts of the **Art Deco** movement, the simultaneous reconstruction giving Napier a stylistic uniformity rarely seen – and ranking it alongside Miami Beach as one of the largest collections of Art Deco buildings in the world.

Arrival, information and transport

Napier is the northern terminus of the *Bay Express* **train** from Wellington, which pulls in to the Napier Travel Centre, Munroe Street (☎06/834 2720), where InterCity and Newmans long-distance **buses** also drop off. **Flights** touch down at Hawke's Bay Airport, 5km north of town on SH2, where they are met by the Super Shuttle (☎06/879 9766), which charges $8 into town; taxis cost about the same.

The large and informative **visitor centre**, 100 Marine Parade (daily: Christmas–Jan 9am–7pm; Feb–Christmas 9am–5pm; ☎06/834 1911, fax 835 7219, *info@napiervic.co.nz*), is on the seafront, just along from Napier's former courthouse, which now houses the **DOC office**, 59 Marine Parade (☎06/834 3111, fax 834 4869; Mon–Fri 9am–4.15pm), where you can consult tide tables for the Cape Kidnappers walk (see p.414), pick up some free and mildly diverting heritage trail leaflets, and find out about walks into the remote Kaweka and Ruahine ranges to the west. For **Internet access** try *Cybers Internet Café*, 98 Dickens St (Mon–Fri 9am–8pm, Sat 10am–8pm, Sun 10am–7pm), which has a good selection of coffees. The **local paper** is *Hawke's Bay Today* (Mon–Fri; 75¢) with a Friday listings pull-out.

Getting around Napier's central sights is easily done on foot. Visiting the gannets and the wineries is a different matter: tours are an excellent way to go, but if you like a bit more freedom you'll need to rent a car (try Avis ☎06/835 1828; Hertz ☎06/835 6169; or Rent-a-Dent ☎06/834 1420) or a bike from one of the hostels (see below). The Nimbus local bus services (Mon–Fri only) to Napier's outlying districts leave from Dalton Street, between Dickens and Thackeray streets, but aren't a great deal of use except for getting to Hastings or Mission Winery (where they drop off within walking distance). The local taxi service is run by *Star Taxis* (☎0800/102 121).

Accommodation

Apart from the usual shortage of rooms during the month or so after Christmas, and to a lesser extent during February and March, you should have little trouble finding accommodation in Napier. In Kiwi-seaside fashion, there are dozens of motels around town, the greatest concentration being in Westshore, a beachfront suburb a few kilometres from the centre beside SH2 heading north. Right in the thick of things, Marine Parade has both low-cost backpacker hostels and classy B&Bs, but for homestays look no further than Middle and Bluff hills. Predictably, none of the campsites are especially central.

Hotels and motels

Albatross Motel, 56 Meeanee Quay, Westshore (☎06/835 5991, fax 835 5949). Large and good-value motel close to Westshore Beach, with a pool, spa, studio units and self-catering family rooms. Units from ③, rooms ④.

The County Hotel, 12 Browning St (☎06/835 7800, fax 835 7797, *countyhotel@xtra.co.nz*). Combined business and tourist hotel in the Edwardian former council offices building, one of the few to survive the earthquake. Rooms all come with en-suite facilities, Sky TV and writing desks. ⑧.

Gardner Court Motel, 16 Nelson Crescent (☎ & fax 06/835 5913). Quiet and reasonably central motel with a solar-heated outdoor pool and standard motel rooms at bargain prices. ④.

B&Bs and homestays

Madeira B&B, 6 Madeira Rd (☎06/835 5185). Wonderfully central homestay with just one double room and breakfast on the veranda overlooking the town. ④.

Mon Logis Guesthouse, 415 Marine Parade (☎ & fax 06/835 2125, *monlogis@xtra.co.nz*). Classy and sumptuously furnished boutique hotel with a French theme. Some rooms in this lovely two-storey wooden house overlook the sea. The tariff includes a delicious breakfast, but you'll have to stump up $55 for the superb five-course table d'hôte dinner. ⑦.

Parsons Garden Loft, 29 Cameron Rd (☎06/835 1527). Attractive and excellent-value homestay with just one en-suite double room set in the leafy grounds of a fine homestead on Middle Hill, five minutes' steep walk up steps from Dalton Street, beside the Municipal Theatre. Choice of breakfast. ④.

Sea Breeze B&B, 281 Marine Parade (☎06/835 8067, fax 835 0512). Low-cost B&B with smallish but pleasant rooms, some with sea views, and a self-service continental breakfast. ④.

Spences Homestay, 17 Cobden Rd, Bluff Hill (☎ & fax 06/835 9454). Sunny 1880 villa in a quiet area boasting a large attractive garden and grounds; the two queen bedrooms are spacious and en-suite. ⑤.

Treeways Homestay, 1 Lighthouse Rd, Bluff Hill (☎06/835 1527, *mckeeling@clear.net.nz*). Peaceful warm house amid garden and bush benefiting from good views over the sea, a sunny terrace with spa pool and home-grown fruit and vegetables; excellent parking. The rooms (double, and a twin converting to King size) share the guest bathroom. ⑤.

Hostels

Aqua Lodge Backpackers, 53 Nelson Crescent (☎06/835 4523, fax 835 4973, *aquabuck @inhb.co.nz*). Homely hostel with dorms and doubles shoehorned into a suburban house in a quiet area close to the train and bus station. There's a pool, good facilities and welcoming hosts. Dorms ①, rooms ②.

Criterion Backpackers Inn, 48 Emerson St (☎06/835 2059). Biggest hostel in town, converted from a hotel with large communal areas and a friendly atmosphere. Accommodation is in cramped 6–8 bed dorms at rock-bottom prices, more spacious triple and quad dorms, and double rooms (some en-suite). Facilities include a winter spa, free pick-up from bus and train, and guest phone (incoming and outgoing) in lounge. Dorms ①, rooms ②–③.

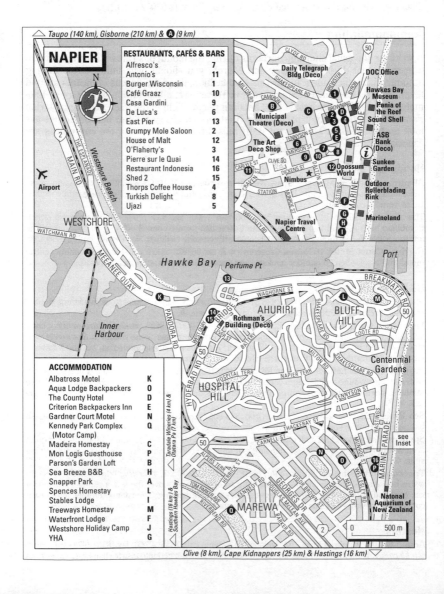

NAPIER

Taupo (140 km), Gisborne (210 km) & Ⓐ (9 km)

RESTAURANTS, CAFÉS & BARS

Alfresco's	7
Antonio's	11
Burger Wisconsin	1
Café Graaz	10
Casa Gardini	9
De Luca's	6
East Pier	13
Grumpy Mole Saloon	2
House of Malt	12
O'Flaherty's	3
Pierre sur le Quai	14
Restaurant Indonesia	16
Shed 2	15
Thorps Coffee House	4
Turkish Delight	8
Ujazi	5

ACCOMMODATION

Albatross Motel	K
Aqua Lodge Backpackers	O
The County Hotel	D
Criterion Backpackers Inn	E
Gardner Court Motel	N
Kennedy Park Complex (Motor Camp)	Q
Madeira Homestay	C
Mon Logis Guesthouse	P
Parson's Garden Loft	B
Sea Breeze B&B	H
Snapper Park	A
Spences Homestay	L
Stables Lodge	I
Treeways Homestay	M
Waterfront Lodge	F
Westshore Holiday Camp	J
YHA	G

Clive (8 km), Cape Kidnappers (25 km) & Hastings (16 km)

Stables Lodge, 321 Marine Parade (☎ & fax 06/835 6242, *stables@ihug.co.nz*). Attractive, small modern hostel tucked behind the Earthquake 31 building with good cooking facilities, a barbecue area in the central courtyard and free bike rental. Dorms ①, rooms ②.

Waterfront Lodge, 217 Marine Parade (☎06/835 3429, *waterfrontlodge@xtra.co.nz*). Converted B&B in a good location two-minute walk from the city centre, offering either backpacker or budget rooms, but the kitchen is small. There are 3- and 4-bed dorms, a few twins and doubles (better ones in the budget section), a few family rooms, and campsites in a small area; groups can go next door in a house. Free pick-up from bus or train. Tent sites $8, dorms ①, rooms ②–⑤.

YHA, 277 Marine Parade (☎06/835 7039, fax 835 4641, *yhanapr@yha.org.nz*). Well-run and recently revamped rambling hostel with a view of the sea and a good standard of facilities plus a suntrap of a courtyard at the back and big selection of videos for hire ($1). Bikes are rented out at $15 a day and there are small dorms, doubles, singles, twins and a 5-bed family room. Dorms ①, rooms ②.

Campsites

Kennedy Park Complex, Storkey St, off Kennedy Rd (☎06/843 9126, fax 843 6113, *info@kennedypark.co.nz*). The closest of Napier's campsites, 3km from the city centre, and with a pool and barbecue area. Tent sites $10–12, cabins ②–③, flats ④–⑤, units ④–⑥.

Snapper Park Motor Camp, Gill Rd, Bay View (☎06/836 7084). Beachfront yet sheltered campsite 9km north of Napier, beyond the airport and 200m to a market garden for fresh vegetables. Tent sites $8, power sites $8, on-site caravans $35.

Westshore Holiday Camp, 1 Main Rd, Westshore (☎06/835 9456). Located midway along Westshore Beach, 6km north of town, this site is a little less formal than the Kennedy Park Complex, but still has all the facilities you're likely to need. Tent sites $8, cabins ②, flats ③.

The Town

Napier is blessed with a fine location, neatly tucked under the skirts of **Bluff Hill** (*Mataruahou*), a 3km-long outcrop festooned with the twisting roads of the eponymous and highly desirable suburb. At its eastern summit is **Bluff Hill Domain Lookout** (daily 7am–dusk), offering views of Cape Kidnappers to the west, and right across to the distant Mahia Peninsula in the east.

On Bluff Hill's southern flank, steep roads and even steeper steps switchback down to the grid pattern of the **Art Deco commercial centre** where, at the whim of mid-nine-teenth-century Land Commissioner, Alfred Domett, streets were given the names of liter-ary luminaries – Tennyson, Thackeray, Byron, Dickens, Shakespeare, Milton and more. Bisecting it all is the partly-pedestrianized main thoroughfare of Emerson Street, whose terracotta paving and palm trees run from Clive Square, one-time site of a makeshift "Tin Town" while the city was being rebuilt after the earthquake, to the pine-fringed **Marine Parade**. The long strip of grey shingle flanking Marine Parade is Napier's main **beach**, where treacherous undertows and powerful surf make it unsafe for swimming.

Around the northeastern side of Bluff Hill lies the original settlement site of **Ahuriri**, long since abandoned to factories and car sales yards, but recently resurgent, with some of its warehouses being tarted up and a handful of trendy café/bars taking their chances.

Art Deco Napier

If the dark cloud of the 1931 earthquake had a silver lining, it was the chance it gave Napier to rebuild from scratch, not just with more quake-resistant materials but to com-pletely re-invent itself. Drawing on contemporary themes, Napier fell for **Art Deco** in a big way. A reaction against the organic and naturalistic themes of Art Nouveau, Deco embraced modernity, glorifying progress, the machine age and the Gatsby-style high-life, expressed by means of elaborate friezes featuring Adonis-like men, dancing women and springing gazelles. The onset of the **Great Depression** at the end of the 1920s pared down these excesses, not least because the key American exponents of the

ART DECO NAPIER TOURS AND TRAILS

Keen observers will find classic Art Deco everywhere, but for a systematic exploration of Napier's Art Deco revival, begin at **The Art Deco Shop**, in the Desco Centre, 163 Tennyson St (daily 9am–5pm), where you can watch a twenty-minute introductory video (shown on request, donations appreciated) and buy a leaflet for the **self-guided "Art Deco Walk"** (also available at the visitor centre; $2), outlining a 1.5km (1hr 30min to 2hr) stroll through the downtown area. Dedicated Deco buffs can also join the **Art Deco Afternoon Walking Tour** (Oct to end-May daily 2pm; rest of year Sat, Sun & Wed 2pm; 2hr; $10), which sets off from the Desco Centre and whose anecdote-laden patter brings Thirties Napier to life; the tour offers access to some of the finer buildings and gives you the chance to gaze around the interiors of shops and banks without feeling quite so self-conscious. The **Art Deco Morning Walking Tour** (Oct to end-May daily 10am; 1hr; $7) begins at the visitor centre and is a shorter version, while the **Quake Walk** (1 Jan to 26 Feb, Fri 9.30am; about 2hr; $15), again starting at the visitor centre, explores Marine Parade – the buildings that survived or were destroyed by the 1931 earthquake, and the fine gardens built on its rubble. The **Self-Drive Art Deco Tour** (leaflet $2.50) presents a broader sweep of the district's distinctive architecture, reverentially trawling through Napier's far-flung Deco buildings, Hastings' Spanish Mission structures, the totally non-Deco Havelock North and the former Taradale Hotel, now a McDonald's but tastefully remodelled after the multinational was successfully petitioned by the Art Deco Trust. Finally, for real Deco fanatics, there's also the self-guided **Marewa Meander** (leaflet $1.50), covering the less-sexy domestic architecture in Napier's principal Art Deco suburb.

style, Louis Sullivan and Frank Lloyd Wright, were restrained by Chicago and New York statutes which dictated that tall buildings had to be stepped back to let the sun penetrate the dark canyons below. Necessity became the mother of invention, and the recurring theme of ziggurats was introduced.

Napier's version of Art Deco was informed by the privations of this austere era. At the same time, the architects looked for inspiration to California's similarly sun-drenched and earthquake-prone **Santa Barbara** which, just six years earlier, had suffered the same fate as Napier, and had risen from the ashes. They adopted fountains (a symbol of renewal), sunbursts, chevrons, lightning flashes and stylized fluting, embedding them in highly formalized but asymmetric designs. What emerged was a palimpsest of early-twentieth-century design, combining elements of the Arts and Crafts movement, the Californian Spanish Mission style, Egyptian and Mayan motifs, the stylized floral designs of Art Nouveau, the blockish forms associated with Charles Rennie Mackintosh, and even **Maori imagery**. For the best part of half a century, Napier's residents went about their lives, unaware of the architectural harmony all around them and merrily daubing everything in grey or muted blue paint. Fortunately this meant that when a few visionaries recognized the city's potential in the mid-1980s and formed the **Art Deco Trust**, everything was still there. The trust continues to promote the preservation of buildings and provides funding for shopkeepers to pick out distinctive architectural detail in pastel colours.

Visitors with only a passing interest in architecture can get a sense of what the fuss is about by wandering along the half-dozen streets in the city centre, notably **Emerson Street**, with its particularly homogeneous run of upper-floor frontages. Worth special attention here is the **ASB Bank**, on the corner of Hastings Street, its exterior adorned with fern shoots and a mask form from the head of a *taiaha* (a long fighting club), while its interior has a fine Maori rafter design. On Tennyson Street, look for the flamboyant **Daily Telegraph** building with stylized fountains capping the pilasters; and the **Municipal Theatre**, built in the late 1930s and exhibiting a strikingly geometric and streamlined form.

The only building to merit a foray outside the centre is the **Rothman's Building** (interior Mon–Fri 9am–5pm only), on the corner of Bridge Street and Osian Street, in Ahuriri, whose entrance is probably the single most frequently-used image of Deco Napier and exhibits a decorative richness seldom seen on industrial buildings. The facade merges Deco asymmetry and the classic juxtaposition of cubic shapes and arches with the softening Art Nouveau motifs of roses and raupo (a kind of Kiwi bulrush).

Along Marine Parade

Napier's Art Deco finery may earn it a place on the world stage, but its defining feature is undoubtedly **Marine Parade**, a 2km-long boulevard lined with stately Norfolk pines and fashioned in the British seaside tradition. A restrained and faintly elegant promenade strung with attractions and entrance to two of the more major attractions – Marineland and the National Aquarium of New Zealand.

Marine Parade starts by Napier's port at the northern end of town and passes the foot of Bluff Hill, where native and exotic trees have been cultivated in **Centennial Gardens** (unrestricted entry), a former prison quarry backed by a picturesque waterfall cascading down the cliff face.

Pushing south you stroll past the outdoor swimming pool, floral clock and the ornamental Tom Parker Fountain, to the bronze cast of the curvaceous **Pania of the Reef**, a siren of Maori legend who lived on land with her lover until forcibly restrained in the briny depths by her kin when she paid them a final visit. Opposite, the **Hawke's Bay Museum**, 65 Marine Parade (daily 10am–4.30pm; $4), contains small but well chosen and competently presented exhibits, notably *taonga* (treasures) of the Ngati Kahungunu, including some exquisite clubs and fish-hooks. Downstairs there's detailed coverage of Hawke's Bay's colonial history; a photo display of the damage wrought by the 1931 earthquake, and a poignant 35-minute audiovisual of survivors' stories (on the half-hour 10.30am–3.30pm); and an excellent and manageable trawl through a century of design, from Art Nouveau and Art Deco through to the Philippe Starck-influenced Nineties. There's also a small yet intriguing display about paleontologist Joan Wiffen's 1979 discovery of a Megalosaur's tail bone in a creekbed northeast of Napier. Significantly, this proved dinosaurs had existed in New Zealand when it broke away from the supercontinent of Gondwana eighty-five million years ago, despite earlier scientific beliefs that they never lived here.

Assorted seafront constructions line the next piece of the promenade: the curving colonnade of the Veronica Sun Bay and the stage known as the Sound Shell give way to a putting course and some sunken gardens. Diagonally opposite the visitor centre is **Opossum World**, 157 Marine Parade (Mon–Fri: summer 9.30am–5pm; winter 9.30am–4pm; $3), a unique attraction where you can learn everything there is to know about New Zealand's greatest pest, the creature more commonly known as the possum. Well-considered witty displays recount the struggle against this voracious predator and destroyer of native bush, while a small shop sells all sorts of opossum products – including pelts, fur hats and garments knitted from opossum fur blended with merino wool – with the motto that every item bought saves a tree. For more on the possum, see box on p.873.

Continue beyond the sunken gardens and popular outdoor **rollerblading/skating** rink (Fri 7–10pm, Sat 1–4pm & 7–10pm, Sun 1–4pm; rollerblade hire and admission $5; becomes a skating rink in winter) you reach **Marineland** (daily 10am–4.30pm; dolphin & seal shows 10.30am & 2pm; $4 to visit between shows, $9 to include the shows, $15 for a behind-the-scenes tour), a small marine zoo that houses a leopard seal, sea lions and penguins – many of them recovering from injuries sustained in the wild. During the outdated shows performing dolphins and seals are put through their paces. In the summer months you should try to book a couple of days in advance (a couple of weeks immediately after Christmas) if you fancy **feeding the seals** or an hour-long **swim with the dolphins** in the pool (☎06/834 4027; $45, plus $10 for the near-essential wetsuit); they can usually be persuaded to play ball.

There's little need to cross the road to the **Stables Complex**, 321 Marine Parade (daily 9am–5pm; $6), a lifeless series of waxwork dioramas depicting trades from pioneering days, plus photos from the earthquake and an embarrassingly inept 'quake simulation. Instead stick with the seafront side, passing the go-karts and boating lake, to reach the **National Aquarium of New Zealand** (☎06/834 1404; daily: Christmas–Jan 9am–9pm; Feb–Christmas 9am–5pm; $7), one of the finest in the country, built around a central oceanarium teeming with Hawke's Bay aquatic life: rays, sharks, eels and fish of all sizes. At 3.15pm every day a diver jumps in to hand-feed them, and for $20 (and an additional $20 if you need to rent dive gear), certified divers can join them; book as far in advance as possible. Smaller tanks and reconstructions of inter-tidal zones and rock pools contain all manner of sea creatures and amphibians, including hawk-billed turtles, terrapins, rainbow-coloured tropical fish and the native tuatara. Again, you can feed these critters by booking a day or so in advance for the behind-the-scenes tour (daily 2.30–3.15pm; $12).

Eating and drinking

As elsewhere in New Zealand, Napier's dining scene has improved markedly over recent years and, while no match for larger centres, there are enough places to keep you well fed and watered for a few days. It is worth eating at least one lunch at one of the **wineries** around about (see p.416), getting there either under your own steam or on an organized tour, but there are plenty of **cafés** and **restaurants** scattered around the centre, and several more in the upper price bracket in waterside Ahuriri.

It is rare to find any really exciting entertainment, unless you hit town at **festival time** (see box on p.414), but a couple of the **bars** host live music at weekends and when touring bands pass through. Straightforward drinking happens along Hastings Street, mostly the short stretch between Browning and Emerson streets, where packs of revellers surge between any of half a dozen popular bars.

Alfresco's, 65 Emerson St. Big upper-level café/restaurant overlooking the steet, which is bright and airy during the day, romantic at night; serving mainly organic morsels, from pizza or pasta to chickpea and tahini rosti for lunch; lemon-scented fish or Scotch fillet for dinner. Summer daily 9am till late; closed Mon in winter; licensed.

Antonio's, cnr Carlyle St & Craven St. Unpretentious and good-value eat-in and takeaway pizzeria with some budget pasta dishes. Closed Mon. Licensed.

Burger Wisconsin, 10 Shakespeare Rd. One of a handful of these franchised eat-in and take-out burger joints, serving huge and well-built specimens stuffed with imaginative fillings – satay, avocado and bacon – and good coffee too.

Casa Gardini, Upper Level, 77 Dalton St (☎06/835 7788). Classy and relaxed upstairs bar and restaurant with a deck at the back for balmy evening supping and a spartan dining room serving the likes of asparagus and salmon terrine or wild mushroom ravioli. Licensed & BYO.

Café Graaz (and the Creative Cake Co.), 82 Dalton St. Great snack spot, from giant toasted sandwiches to their own specialized cakes, both sweet and savoury. Get stuck into their potato cakes with sour cream and relish or, on the sweeter side, their scroggan, chocolate sludge cake or fudge espresso cake. Closed Sun.

De Luca's, 180 Emerson St (☎06/834 1988). Excellent, elegant Italian café-style food and great coffee daytime during weekdays. Extends on Fri nights to unusual dips and antipasto platters, enjoyable with their small selection of local reasonably priced wines and boutique beers; while Sat nights see a set menu of tapas or antipasto for $22 a head. Weekend brunches are exotic affairs such as kumara hash browns with creme fraiche, or coconut and banana pancakes. They make all their own bread (except the sour dough). Tues–Thurs 9am–5pm, Fri & Sat 9am–9pm, Sun 10am–3pm; bookings recommended for Sat night; licensed.

East Pier, Hardinge Rd. Modern and breezy waterfront café/bar that's great for just relaxing by the water or dining on Nantucket pancakes ($14) and craggy range venison saltimbocca ($23), or cheaper bar snacks. Live music at weekends, pulling in crowds from all over New Zealand in high summer. Licensed

Grumpy Mole Saloon, cnr Hastings St & Tennyson St. Napier's most jumping party bar, styled in Wild West mode and offering nightly drinks specials, plus big-screen TV sport and pool tables. On Fri & Sat nights a DJ keeps the place pumping till the small hours. Closed Mon.

House of Malt, Hastings St. Lively town bar with a Kiwi-Irish feel, extensive range of beers, including Macs on tap and speciality bottled brews, and above-average pub food at prices to match.

Restaurant Indonesia, 409 Marine Parade (☎06/835 8303). Compact seafront restaurant dishing up Indonesian food at around $17 and a choice of rijsttafel spreads, including a vegetarian version ($25 to $32 a head). Licensed & BYO.

O'Flaherty's, 35 Hastings St. Lively Irish bar proffering simple bar food, big-screen TV sport when the rugby's on, and live music every Fri & Sat night.

Pierre sur le Quai, 62 West Quay, Ahuriri (☎06/834 0189). The place for that romantic dinner for two, exuding French provincial style and serving fabulous good-value seafood. Expect to pay around $40 a head, without wine. Closed Sun (except public holidays) & Mon; licensed.

Shed 2, cnr West Quay & Lever St, Ahuriri (☎06/835 2202). Currently the pick of Napier's trendy restaurant/bars, spreading in the spacious stripped-boards-and-corrugated-iron interior of a former woolshed overlooking the harbour. Saunter in for an afternoon coffee, beer or something from their huge selection of wines by the glass, then stick around for wood-fired pizza in the bar, or retreat next door for char-sealed salmon, or fish of the day for $20–25. DJs spin platters at weekends and there's occasional live jazz or stand-up comedy.

Thorps Coffee House, 40 Hastings St. Excellent eat-in and takeaway build-your-own sandwich place also serving good breakfasts, lunches, cakes, shakes and coffee; the interior features fine Art Deco details. Closed Sun.

Turkish Delight, 3 Market St. Excellent value authentic Turkish and Middle Eastern dishes, to eat in or take away. The boreks are to die for. Summer daily midday to midnight; winter Tues–Sat midday to 2pm, 6pm till late; licensed.

Ujazi Café, 28 Tennyson St. Small café with a vaguely alternative and somewhat erratic feel, serving largely vegetarian snacks for breakfast and lunch: quiches, pies, sandwiches and salads, plus scrumptious juices and good strong coffee. Best on Fri & Sat nights (rest of the week daytime only). This is the only place in town open all morning and afternoon on a Sunday.

Around Napier

Though appealing in itself, Napier's surroundings also reward exploration: the **gannet colony** at Cape Kidnappers and the forty or so **wineries** strung out between Eskdale, 12km north of Napier, and the banks of the Tukituki River, some twenty-odd kilometres to the south. Further afield and due west of Napier is the **Kaweka Forest Park**, which you can visit on a one- or two-day tour with First Light Adventures (see p.421), taking in bush tramps and soaks in thermal pools.

Heading towards Cape Kidnappers, Marine Parade (SH2) trawls through an industrial sprawl on the outskirts of Napier until 9km south it passes the windswept **Waitangi Mission site**, where a plaque records the establishment of Hawke's Bay's first mission station by William Colenso in 1844. A couple of kilometres beyond is the village of **CLIVE**, where the **Juke Box Museum**, 158 Main Rd (daily 9.30am–5pm; $3), holds a lovingly assembled hoard of radios, gramophones and over twenty working jukeboxes. Some are repro-classics, but most are originals, including one with a built-in slide projector and a mock-up milk-bar booth with an operational wall-box console. Each juke box plays records carefully matched to its era, and it's easy to get carried away by the owner's tremendous enthusiasm for his collection.

HAWKE'S BAY FESTIVALS

During January and February, Napier and nearby Hastings flip into festive mode. Small-time events take place in January, but the first of the major events is the **Harvest Hawke's Bay** (first weekend in February), when food and wine lovers from around the country flock to the Hawke's Bay Racing Centre, Prospect Rd, Hastings, for music, food and wine. Proceedings reach fever pitch for the Charity Wine auction, which is followed by a Sunday drive around the wineries. The **Mission Vineyard Concert** usually takes place in February (the precise dates are dependent on artists' bookings, and announced in November), when an internationally famous vocalist – Kiri Te Kanawa, Ray Charles and Dionne Warwick in recent years – performs outdoors at the Mission Estate Winery to an audience of around 20,000.

No sooner has the Hawke's Bay summer festival wound up, than Napier gears up for the **Art Deco Weekend** (☎06/835 1191; third weekend in February), five light-hearted days of merriment, extending to guided walks, open-house tours of domestic Art Deco, bicycle tours, Thirties-dress picnics, champagne breakfasts, dress balls, silent movies and the like.

Cape Kidnappers

After James Cook's ill-starred initial encounter with Maori at Gisborne, he sailed south to the southern limit of Hawke's Bay and anchored off the jagged peninsula known to the Ngati Kahungunu as *Te Matua-a-maui*, "the fishhook of Maui" – a reference to the origin of the North Island, which was dragged from the oceans by Maui. Here, Cook experienced a second unfortunate meeting. This time Maori traders noticed two young Tahitian interpreters aboard the *Endeavour*, believing them to be held against their will, the traders captured one of them and paddled away. The boy escaped back to the ship, but Cook subsequently marked the point on his chart as **Cape Kidnappers**.

Neither James Cook nor Joseph Banks, both meticulous in recording flora and fauna, mentioned any gannets on the peninsula's final shark-tooth flourish of pinnacles. However, a hundred years later, twenty or so pairs were recorded, and now there are four thousand pairs – making this the world's largest mainland **gannet colony**. Gannets are big birds, members of the booby family distinguished by their gold-and-black head markings and their apparent lack of fear of humans. The birds start arriving at Cape Kidnappers for nesting in June, laying their eggs from early July through to October, with the chicks hatching some six weeks later. Once fledged, at around fifteen weeks, the young gannets embark on their inaugural flight, a marathon and as-yet-unexplained 3000km journey to Australia, where they spend a couple of years before flying back to spend the rest of their life in New Zealand, returning to their place of birth to breed each year.

PRACTICALITIES

During the breeding season (July–Oct), the cape is closed to the public, and one colony, "the saddle", is always reserved for scientific study. At other times you can get within a metre or so of the remaining two sites: "the plateau", a few hundred metres back from the saddle, where 2000 chattering pairs nest beak-by-jowl; and the beachside "black reef", the largest colony, a couple of kilometres back from the tip of the peninsula, where there are a further 3500 pairs.

There are five ways to **visit the gannets**: three are tide-dependent, travelling to the colony along the beach below unstable hundred-metre cliffs; the fourth gains access overland through Summerlee Station. All start from well-signposted points in the adjacent settlements of **CLIFTON** and **TE AWANGA**, 20km southeast of Napier, both reached from the Napier or Hastings visitor centres with Kiwi Shuttle (☎025/593 669; booking essential; $15 return).

The least expensive way to get to the gannets is simply to **walk** the 8km along the beach from Clifton; no permits are needed, but you'll need to check tide tables with the DOC or the Hastings or Napier visitor centres and plan to leave between three and four hours after high tide; the useful DOC *Guide to Cape Kidnappers* ($1) contains a map and a few tips. The traditional way is aboard tractor-drawn **trailers** along the beach with Gannett Beach Adventures (☎06/875 0898; Oct to late-April daily; 4hr; $22), whose pace and approach

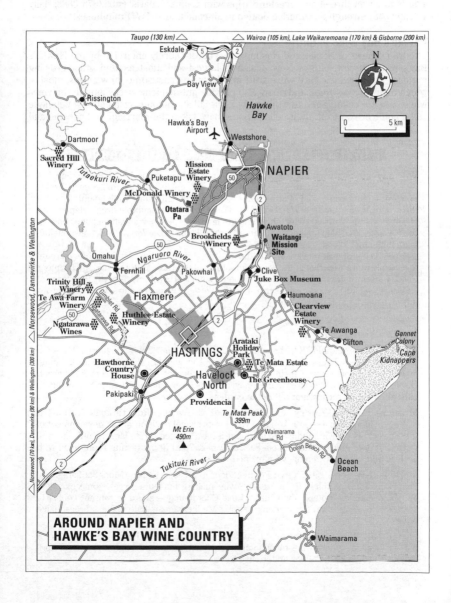

Taupo (130 km) △

△ Wairoa (105 km), Lake Waikaremoana (170 km) & Gisborne (200 km)

Norsewood, Dannevirke & Wellington

Norsewood (70 km), Dannevirke (90 km) & Wellington (300 km)

N

0   5 km

Eskdale

Bay View

Rissington

Hawke's Bay
Airport

Hawke's
Bay

Dartmoor

Westshore

Sacred Hill
Winery

Tutaekuri River

Mission
Estate
Winery

Puketapu

NAPIER

McDonald Winery

Otatara
Pa

Awatoto

Omahu

Ngaruoro River

Brookfields
Winery

Waitangi
Mission
Site

Fernhill

Pakowhai

Clive
Juke Box Museum

Trinity Hill
Winery

Haumoana

Te Awa Farm
Winery

Flaxmere

Huthlee Estate
Winery

Clearview
Estate
Winery

Ngatarawa
Wines

Gimblett Rd

Ngatarawa Rd

Te Awanga

Clifton

Gannet
Colony

Cape
Kidnappers

HASTINGS

Arataki
Holiday
Park

Hawthorne
Country
House

Te Mata Estate

Havelock
North

The Greenhouse

Pakipaki

Providencia

Te Mata Peak
399m

Mt Erin
490m

Waimarama
Rd

Ocean Beach Rd

Tukituki River

Ocean
Beach

**AROUND NAPIER AND
HAWKE'S BAY WINE COUNTRY**

Waimarama

give plenty of opportunities to appreciate the geology along the way and observe the birds at close quarters. Also jockeying for position on the beach are **quad bikes** from Quadventures (☎06/836 6652; Oct to late April daily; 3–4hr; $95 one rider, $140 for two riders on one bike), whose trips include complimentary wine to accompany a BYO picnic.

All these end at a DOC shelter, from where you face a twenty-minute uphill slog to "the plateau", where you'll have half an hour to admire the birds. One way to avoid this slog is to go on three-hour **overland** trips with Gannet Safaris (☎06/875 0888; daily 1.30pm; $38) through Summerlee Station in air-conditioned 4WD minibuses.

Hawke's Bay wine country

The twin centres of Napier and Hastings are almost entirely encircled by the Hawke's Bay's wine country, one of New Zealand's largest and most exalted grape-growing regions. The **Hawke's Bay wine trail** wends its way past some 30 wineries, most of which offer free **tastings**, and many also provide grassy picnic areas among the vines where you are encouraged to while away a blissful afternoon over a game of petanque and a bottle or two from their cellars. Some have taken the marriage of fine wine and

---

HAWKE'S BAY WINERIES - THE PICK OF THE BUNCH

With over 40 wineries in the region, we can't hope to give comprehensive coverage, but we've listed a few **favourites** below, concentrating on those that make good **lunch spots** or feature some sort of attraction other than the obligatory wine tasting. Most of them appear on the free *Hawke's Bay Wineries* leaflet (available from Napier and Hastings visitor centres), which has a handy map showing their locations; and those in the Hastings area also appear on the free *Western Plains Wine Route* leaflet, also including a mini-map.

Napier's closest wineries are 8km to the southwest in the suburb of **Taradale**, en route to a couple more wineries in the western foothills of the Kaweka Range along Dartmoor Road. Closer to Hastings, there are clusters outside **Havelock North**, 9km east of Hastings, and 10km west near **Fernhill**, in the Western Plains region – the fastest-growing wine district in Hawke's Bay.

NAPIER AND AROUND

Brookfields, Brookfields Rd, Meeanee (winery daily 11am–4.30pm; restaurant Dec–Feb daily; March–Nov Thurs–Sun & public holidays). Unusual for its 1930s winery building, in which you can sample their award-winning Cabernet Merlot, Reserve Cabernet, Gewürztraminer and Reserve Chardonnay; or enjoy an excellent authentic French lunch either in their barrel room or out in the gardens.

Mission Estate Winery, cnr Church Rd & Avenue Rd, Taradale (Mon–Sat 8.30am–5.30pm, Sun 1–4pm). Worth a visit for its pivotal position in the development of the Hawke's Bay's wine industry alone, but it hasn't rested on its laurels, offering well organized, free guided tours (Mon–Sat 10.30am & 2pm) and a tasting room lined with ancient wine casks brimming with fortified wines.

McDonald Winery, 150 Church Rd, next door to Mission Estate (Mon–Sat 9am–5pm, Sun 11am–4pm). A tolerably interesting wine-making museum (free), some excellent bottles to sample – notably the Church Road Chardonnay – and a restaurant (☎06/844 2053) that spills out into the gardens, serving Mediterranean-style dishes at reasonable prices.

Sacred Hill Winery, Dartmoor Rd, 20km west of Taradale. A lengthy excursion for a few sips of albeit superb wine, most notably Sauvignon Blanc and a light meal (Dec–April only), served on rustic tables under olive trees.

food one step further, and lunch at one of the **vineyard restaurants** is undoubtedly a Hawke's Bay highlight.

Hawke's Bay is largely the province of boutique producers, with an unshakeable domestic reputation and an international standing challenged only by the South Island's Marlborough region. One of New Zealand's most classically well suited areas for viticulture, with a climatic pattern similar to that of the great Bordeaux vineyards, Hawke's Bay produces fine Chardonnay and Cabernet Sauvignon. As scientific studies unravel the complexity of the local soils and microclimates, growers have begun to diversify into Merlot, which has gained a foothold north of Napier along the Esk Valley, while others predict that Hawke's Bay may one day topple Marlborough's Sauvignon Blanc primacy. Hawke's Bay is New Zealand's longest-established wine-growing region: vines were first planted in 1851 by French Marist missionaries, ostensibly to produce sacramental wine. The excess was sold, and the commercial aspect of the operation continues today as the Mission Estate Winery. Some fifty-odd years later, other wineries began to spring up, initially favouring the fertile plains, but as tastes became more sophisticated, such sites were forsaken for the open-textured gravel terraces alongside

AROUND HASTINGS

Clearview Estate Winery, Clifton Rd, Te Awanga (Nov–Easter Mon & Thurs–Sun 10am–5pm; Easter–Oct Fri–Sun 11am–4pm). Some of New Zealand's most highly rated wines are produced here, in tiny quantities and sold only from the vineyard. You do pay a premium for this sort of attention to detail, but the wines are superb, especially when enjoyed with the Clearview restaurant's equally classy southern Mediterranean lunches outside in the restaurant (☎06/875 0150). Can be combined with a visit to Cape Kidnappers (see p.414).

Huthlee Estate, 84 Montana Rd, near Bridge Pa (☎06/879 6234; summer Mon–Sat 10am–5pm, Sun 11am–5pm; winter Mon–Fri 1–5pm, Sat–Sun 10am–5pm). A smaller, extremely friendly winery west of Hastings and near the Gimblett Road area, renowned for its free-draining soil and unique microclimate. Here the emphasis is on reds, notably Merlot and Pinot Grigio, but their Sauvignon Blanc has done well, too. They will take you on a free vineyard walk and there's a picnic area, plus petanque.

Ngatarawa Wines, 305 Ngatarawa Rd, Bridge Pa, near Fernhill (daily 11am–5pm). An excellent first stop, a small winery with tastings of quality tipples (notably Chardonnay, Sauvignon Blanc and Cabernet Merlot, as well as highly acclaimed dessert wines from Riesling) in a century-old stable complex with attractive picnic areas and a petanque court.

Te Awa Farm, 2375 Roy's Hill Rd, off SH50, Hastings (summer Mon–Fri 9am–5pm, Sat & Sun 10am–6pm; winter Mon–Fri 9am–5pm, Sat & Sun 11am–4pm). Sited near Gimblett Road, with its own microclimate and mysterious subterranean streams, this winery produces exceptional reds (Merlot, Cabernet Merlot and Pinotage) that are more aromatic and livelier than many of their Hawke's Bay contenders; and their Chardonnays are pretty good too. An indoor and outdoor lunchtime café serves excellent platters and daily specials that are reasonably priced (summer Thurs–Mon; winter Fri–Sun).

Te Mata Estate, Te Mata Rd, Havelock North (Mon–Fri 9am–5pm, Sat 10am–5pm, Sun 11am–4pm). Produces some reputable wines but is on most people's itinerary for the highly distinctive house adjoining the winery, designed by controversial architect Ian Athfield (see box on p.442).

Trinity Hill, 2396 State Highway 50, near Fernhill (summer daily 10am–5pm; winter daily 10am–4pm). Another great vineyard in the Gimblett Road area 15min drive from Hastings, creating remarkable reds – chiefly Cabernet Sauvignon, Syrah, and Cabernet Sauvignon Merlot – as well as great Chardonnay. From the strikingly modern winery they also supply cheeseboards and picnic-style food (Nov–Feb) to enjoy in the park-like grounds, plus the use of BBQs by arrangement.

the Tutaekuri, Ngaruroro and Tukituki rivers, which retain the day's heat and are free from moist sea breezes.

If you have your own **transport**, head for the hills with a copy of the *Hawke's Bay Wineries* leaflet (free from Napier and Hastings visitor centres), which lists wineries open to the public, along with current opening hours and facilities – and see box on the previous page for the pick of the bunch. If you can't find an abstemious driver, take a **wine tour**, most of which visit four or five wineries over the course of an afternoon. Jenne's Wine Tours (☎06/843 6953) are very popular, offering a basic four-stop tour (daily 1pm; $30) and a five-stop lunch tour (daily 11.30am; $40, food not included), and will pick up from Hastings or Havelock North for an additional fee. For a more intimate experience, opt for Vicky's Wine Tours (☎06/877 5707), which offer a choice of a lunchtime tour visiting five wineries (11.30am; $45 excluding lunch) or another four tours, each making four stops and designed for different tastes (all 1pm; $35); or Vince's Wine Tour (☎06/836 6705; daily 1pm; $30), which benefits from chatty enthusiasm and a stack of local knowledge. An upmarket operator for fully customised personal tours based on your interests – be they vineyards, wine varieties, food or local places of interest – is Hawke's Bay in a Glass (☎06/843 2478, *noel@qualityhb.co.nz*; prices vary).

Hastings and around

As little as ten years ago, inland **HASTINGS**, 20km south of Napier, was a rival to its northern kin as Hawke's Bay's premiere city, buoyed by the wealth generated by the surrounding farmland and orchards. In recent years, shifting economic patterns, the closure of Hastings' two huge freezing works (abattoirs) and Napier's ascendancy as a tourist destination have put Hastings firmly in second place.

The city centre is all but moribund, with suburban malls usurping the functions of the far more handsome central buildings that were erected after the same 1931 earthquake that rocked Napier. Hastings was saved from the worst effects of the ensuing fires, which were quenched using the artesian water beneath the city before they could take hold. Nonetheless, the centre had to be rebuilt. As in Napier, **Art Deco** predominates and, though Hastings lacks the flamboyance and overall exuberance of its neighbour, there are some unusually harmonious townscapes along Russell, Eastbourne and Heretaunga streets. Hastings also enthusiastically embraced the **Spanish Mission** style, and two exemplary buildings warrant a brief visit.

Hastings is at the heart of the wonderful Hawke's Bay **wine country** (see p.416), though the proliferation of Napier-based tours and the easy charms of that city make it a better base. Long before grapes were big business, Hastings relied on apples, pears and peaches, all still grown in huge quantities. The harvest, which begins in February and lasts three or four months, provides casual **orchard work** for those willing to thin, pick or pack fruit; the hostels (see opposite) are the best sources of work and up-to-the-minute information. Other than that, Hastings is home to a fine **micro-brewery** and New Zealand's first fully themed **waterpark**.

As Hastings steadily declines, neighbouring upmarket **HAVELOCK NORTH**, 3km east at the foot of the striking ridge-line of **Te Mata Peak**, becomes increasingly appealing. There isn't a great deal to it and the only diversion is a drive up the peak, but the cobbled central streets give it a village atmosphere and the proliferation of tranquil **B&Bs** in the vicinity make good bases for exploring the central Hawke's Bay area.

Arrival and information

Trains startle shoppers as they rumble right through the centre of town, stopping at the Hastings Travel Centre, Caroline Road (☎06/878 0213), which is also used by both

Newmans and InterCity **buses**. Local bus operator Nimbus (☎06/877 8133) runs to Napier, Havelock North and Flaxmere (Mon–Fri only) from the corner of Eastbourne Street East and Russell Street. Also on Russell Street, near the K-Mart complex, is the Hastings **visitor centre** (Mon–Fri 8.30am–5pm, Sat & Sun 10am–3pm; ☎06/873 5526, fax 873 5529, *vic@hastingstourism.co.nz*); at the time of writing it was planning to move down the road. You'll find **Net access** at Internet World Cyber Café, 102 E Queen St (Oct–April Mon–Fri 8.30am–9pm, Sat & Sun 9am–5pm; May–Sept Mon–Fri 8.30am–7pm, Sat & Sun 10am–4pm).

Accommodation

Hastings' **accommodation** is greatly affected by the harvest: from mid-February to May, there is precious little chance of finding a bed at any of the cheaper places, which meet the demand for self-catering and longer stays. If you're hoping to secure a bed for the **fruit-picking season**, plan to arrive early in February and expect to pay around $80 a week for a bunk in a cramped room. Occupancy in the more expensive places is dictated by the normal summer-holiday pattern, and it's advisable to **book** a few days ahead if you'll be here between December and February. Some of the nicest places to stay are scattered through the countryside around Havelock North, where exclusive **B&Bs** and swanky self-catering houses are the mainstay.

Hastings

AJ's Backpackers Lodge, 405 Southland Rd (☎06/878 2302). The pick of the hostels, this pleasant Edwardian villa is popular with orchard workers but usually keeps a bed or two for overnighters, and has bikes for guests' use. Dorms ①, rooms ②.

Hastings Backpackers Hostel, 505 Lyndon Rd East (☎06/876 5888). Comfortable house near the centre, with good facilities, but full of pickers in the season. Dorms ①, rooms ②.

Hastings Holiday Park, Windsor Ave (☎06/878 6692, fax 878 6267, *vin_norm@clear.net.nz*). Appealing campsite on the edge of Windsor Park, with tent sites and a range of modern units, though it does get busy over the fruit-picking season. Tent sites $9, cabins ②, tourist flats ③.

Kelston Orchard B&B, Ormond Rd (☎06/879 7301, *kelston.orch@xtra.co.nz*). Attractive and extremely relaxing homestay in a big beautiful rose garden attached to an apple orchard about 2km from the town centre. In the house are two twin rooms, sharing a bathroom, and in the garden is a self-contained double en-suite. Dinners available for $20 by arrangement. ④.

Travellers Lodge, 606 St Aubyn St West (☎06/878 7108). Suburban house, with a sauna and garden, that's reasonably spacious and comfortable, but is effectively closed to overnighters during the Feb–May season. Tent sites $9, dorms ①, rooms ②.

Woodbine Cottage, 1279 Louie St (☎06/876 9388, *nshand@xtra.co.nz*). B&B in an attractive cottage on the outskirts of Hastings with a large garden, tennis court and pool, and pleasant sunny rooms. ④.

Havelock North and around

All the following places to stay are marked on the map on p.415.

Arataki Holiday Park, Arataki Rd (☎ & fax 06/877 7479, *arataki.motel.holiday.park@xtra.co.nz*). One of the few inexpensive places around here that doesn't take fruit pickers, so you should be able to find space even during the harvest. Tent sites $9, cabins ②, flats & motel units ④.

The Greenhouse, Te Mata Rd (☎06/877 4904, fax 877 4598, *The.Greenhouse@xtra.co.nz*). Superbly equipped self-catering cottage, surrounded by beautiful vineyards and sleeping up to four. ⑧.

Hawthorne Country House, 420 SH2, 7km west (☎ & fax 06/878 0035, *hawthorne@xtra.co.nz*). Beautiful and very welcoming B&B in an Edwardian villa surrounded by croquet lawns and farmland. Huge en-suite rooms are decorated with understated elegance and the breakfasts are delicious. ⑦.

Providencia, Middle Rd, 3km south (☎ & fax 06/877 2300, *provi@voyager.co.nz*). One of the region's finest B&Bs, this beautifully preserved homestead was built in 1903 and is set among orchards and vineyards. Everything is immaculate, including wonderful cooked or continental breakfasts and optional five-course dinners at $50 a head. ⑧.

△ Napier (18 km)

HASTINGS

RESTAURANTS, CAFÉS & BARS

Cat & Fiddle Ale House	5
Corn Exchange	2
Dominion Restaurant	7
Picollo's	4
Roosters Brewhouse	1
Rush Munro's	3
St Vinee's	6
Vidal's Winery Brasserie	8

ACCOMMODATION

AJ's Backpackers Lodge	C
Hastings Backpackers Hostel	D
Hastings Holiday Park	E
Kelston Orchard B&B	A
Travellers Bakpak Hostel	B
Woodbine Cottage	F

0   500 m

▽ Southern Hawke's Bay & Wellington (315 km)   ▽ Havelock North (2 km)

The Town

After the 1931 earthquake, Hastings looked to the Californian-inspired **Spanish Mission** style of architecture. The result lacks the homogeneity of Napier, but a couple of key buildings set the tone, with rough-cast stucco walls, arched windows, small balconies, barley-twist columns and heavily overhung roofs clad in terracotta tiles. All the finest examples can be seen in an hour or so, using the self-guided *Heritage of Hastings* walk leaflet (free from the visitor centre), but if time is short, limit your wanderings to Hereteunga Street East, where the **Westerman's Building**, on the corner of Russell Street, is adorned with gorgeous bronzework and sumptuous leadlighting. The **Municipal Theatre**, on the corner with Hastings Street, was actually built fifteen years before the earthquake, but was remodelled to create the region's finest Spanish Mission facade. Also worth a quick look is the **Hawke's Bay Exhibition Centre**, in the Hawke's Bay Civic Square opposite the junction of Eastbourne Street and Karamu Road (Mon–Fri 10am–4.30pm, Sat & Sun 11am–4pm; admission fees depend on exhibition), which hosts all manner of local, national and international art shows, and has a relaxing café with good coffee (see "Eating and drinking" opposite).

Beer (and wine) fans might fancy a trip to the small family-run **Roosters Brewhouse**, 1470 Omahu Rd (Mon–Sat 10am–7pm), 5km from central Hastings, whose traditional natural brews are made from hops from Motueka and malt from Inverness in Scotland. Take your pick and sip at your leisure in their pleasant café or outdoors at garden tables, tucking into straightforward hearty dishes; or take home beer in a 2-litre flagon ($6–8) or keg. These indefatigable people also produce wine under the Beach House label, which you can sample for free (daily 10am–5pm).

Families may well find themselves at **Splash Planet**, Grove Road (☎06/876 9856; daily 9am till late; $15 for the whole park or $38 for a family), the first fully themed waterpark in the country, centred on a replica Disney-like castle and offering a welter of amusements from a double-dipper dual-tube ride and a "Never Ending River Ride" to hot pools ($7.50 without a parkwide ticket) and boating lake. You can hire togs, towels and armbands, and in winter there's an ice-skating rink (closes early Oct; $9.50 rink only).

From Hastings and Napier informative guided **adventure tours** into the Kaweka Forest Park, 35km or so to the west, are run by First Light Adventure Tours (☎06/870 9901, *g.garland@xtra.co.nz*; Oct–April only; 1-day $40; 2-day $99), who take small groups tramping in the bush of the scenic Kaweka Ranges, passing on their knowledge of native plants and local history along the way. You'll enjoy some great scenery, a swim in the Mohaka River (or trout fishing) and a soak in hot pools.

Te Mata Peak

Driving from Hastings to Havelock North, the long ridge of limestone bluffs which make up the 399m **Te Mata Peak** looms into view. The ridge is held to be the supine form of a Maori chief, Rongokako, who choked on a rock as he tried to eat through the hill – just one of many Herculean feats with which he attempted to woo the beautiful daughter of a Heretaunga chief. The long and winding Te Mata Peak Road climbs the hill to a wonderful vantage point overlooking the fertile plains, north across Hawke's Bay and Cape Kidnappers, and east to the surf-pounded strands of Ocean Beach and Waimarama, the main swimming **beaches** for Hastings and Havelock North.

For the keen there are several walking tracks through the hill's patches of parkland at its base and on its flanks, which are steep in places. The best are the nature trail (2hr round trip), beginning at the car park at the main entrance at the bottom of the hill and passing through most of the planted areas; and the Te Mata walk starting on the summit road 200m above the *Peak House* restaurant, winding through groves of native trees, before crossing a wetland area and ending at the head of the main redwood grove.

Overcome with grief at her father's death, Rongokako's own daughter threw herself off the peak – something you can emulate by **tandem paragliding** (Tandem Paragliding ☎06/877 8804 & 025/223 6999; Oct–April only; from $120), an activity which uses the thermals and winds off the Pacific to carry you along the ridge and back for at least fifteen minutes.

Eating and drinking

As in most other things, Hastings **dining** and entertainment doesn't really rate alongside that of Napier, though keep an eye out for Hawke's Bay summer festival happenings (see box on p.414) and lunches at the wineries are a great option. You'll also find a few reasonable eateries both here, where they tend to be scattered, and in Havelock North, where they congregate conveniently near the centre.

Hastings

Cat & Fiddle Ale House, 502 Karamu Rd. A traditional English-style pub with a huge range of tap and bottled beers and bargain chips-with-everything meals.

The Centre Café, at the Hawke's Bay Exhibition Centre, 201 Eastbourne St. Bright and functional venue for snacks and light lunches under $10. Closed Sun; licensed.

Corn Exchange, Maraekakaho Rd, near cnr with Heretaunga St West. The trendiest of Hastings' restaurant/bars, converted from an attractive 1940s grain store on the western fringes of the city and serving $6–17 brasserie lunches and $18–25 dinners, or just drinks.

Dominion Restaurant, 229 Heretaunga St East. Very basic fish-and-grills daytime restaurant with a Deco exterior, a faded Sixties interior and a good feed for under $10.

Picollo's, cnr Lyndon Rd & Nelson St (☎06/878 1188). Modern Kiwi and Pacific Rim cuisine extending to Szechuan kangaroo, lamb sweetbreads and Cajun chicken, all served indoors or outside in the garden. Closed Sat lunch and all day Sun & Mon; licensed.

Roosters Brewhouse, 1470 Omahu Rd. Small welcoming brewery, offering traditional natural brews as well as wine, good home-roasted coffee and hearty food at reasonable prices. Closed Sun. (See also p.421.)

Rush Munro's, 704 Heretaunga St West. A small ice-cream garden and takeaway that's been packing in the locals for some seventy years. Its sumptuous and intensely fruity natural ice cream is fashioned into distinctive, peaked cones. New fangled concoctions of coffee, chocolate and nut are now available, but it is hard to beat the traditional fruit flavours – feijoa is particularly scrumptious, though something of an acquired taste. They also sell ice-cream sundaes and take-home packs. Daily Dec–Feb 10am–9pm; March–Nov 10am–6pm.

St Vinee's, 108 Market St South. Well-regarded wine bar and café in the centre of Hastings, serving an innovative selection of mid-range mains, plus potato wedges, nachos, venison sausages and light lunches. Licensed.

Vidal's Winery Brasserie, 913 Aubyn St East (☎06/876 8105). Popular café and restaurant attached to a winery; a big pleasant place to enjoy reasonably priced lunch or dinner Mon–Sat and brunch on Sun, amid huge wine barrels. Book ahead at weekends.

Havelock North

Diva Café & Bar, in the Village Court, Napier Rd (☎06/877 5149). Casual daytime café and evening restaurant with a blackboard menu of tasty mains from around $18; alfresco dining out the back. Licensed.

Rose & Shamrock, 15 Napier Rd. A fair attempt at an English/Irish pub with Guinness and a broad range of Irish beers, draught ales, guest beers from Kiwi micro-breweries, and occasional Irish folk bands.

Southern Hawke's Bay

South of Hastings, the main road (SH2) gives the coast a wide berth, taking you through the relentless sheep stations of **Southern Hawke's Bay**, a region uncluttered by places of genuine interest. Small farming towns stand as fitting memorials to the steadfast pioneers who tamed the region, spending the latter half of the nineteenth century clearing the huge totara trees of Seventy Mile Bush, pushing through communication links, and then establishing sheep runs on the rich plains.

None of the towns are especially interesting and if time is short you'd do as well to push straight on through, but with a little more leisure, the "Scandinavian" settlements of **Norsewood** and **Dannevirke** warrant a brief stop. The New Zealand Wars of the 1860s had discouraged British immigrants and, as new areas were opened up for colonization, the authorities took their search for settlers elsewhere, briefed to find rugged folk with strong ties to the land. In 1872, Danes, Norwegians and a few Swedes answered the call, arriving in Napier ill-prepared for the hardship ahead of them. Their promised plots of land turned out to be tracts of impenetrable bush; the wages paid to construction workers who toiled to build road and rail links barely covered exorbitant food costs; and when the government demanded that the settlers repay their passage, many promptly upped sticks for North America, leaving little trace of their brief sojourn.

Almost all traffic follows SH2, but visitors in search of the esoteric might want to stray along **SH52**, which loops east towards the rugged coastline from dull **Waipukurau**, 50km south of Hastings, re-emerging at Masterton in the Wairarapa (see p.425). Fifty kilometres south of Waipukurau, a sign marks the hill known as **Taumatawhakatangihangakoauauotamateaturipukakapikimaungahoronu-kapokaiwhenuakitanatahu**, which, unsurprisingly, rates as the world's longest place name; roughly, this mouthful translates as "the hill where Tamatea, circumnavigator of the lands, played the lute for his lover".

Whichever way you head south, the coastline is almost entirely inaccessible, apart from at Castlepoint (see p.427), reached by a 65-kilometre road from Masterton.

Norsewood

Some 85km south of Hastings, SH2 enters a cutting which bisects the hilltop village of **NORSEWOOD**, invisible from the highway and easily missed. Predominantly settled by Norwegians, it manages to retain a mildly Scandinavian tenor. Like most southern Hawke's Bay towns, it was carved out of the forest, but in 1888 the bush bit back, and a raging bushfire virtually razed the place. Some regarded the devastation as an act of God precipitated by a local plebiscite that ended temperance – but, as the local paper noted, "the church was burnt down and the pub was saved".

The village is in two parts. Upper Norsewood is basically just one short, quaint and deathly quiet main street (Coronation Street) that runs past a glassed-in boathouse containing the fishing boat *Bindalsfareing*, a gift from the Norwegian government on the occasion of Norsewood's centenary, and a small **visitor centre** staffed by volunteers in a gift shop called The Barn (☎06/374 0991; hours vary). Opposite is the **Pioneer Museum** (daily 8.30am–4.30pm; $2), a cottage museum full of reminders of pioneering days housed in an 1888 house. Kiwis are more familiar with Lower Norsewood, 1km to the south, which is mainly strung along Hovding Street and home to **Norsewear**, a company famed for its hard-wearing woollen garments in rustic Scandinavian designs; the socks in particular last for years. If a chill wind is swooping down from the Ruahine Range, check for bargains in the **factory shop** (Mon–Fri 8.30am–5pm, Sat & Sun 9am–5pm; end of season sale in Oct).

InterCity **buses** stop on SH2 at the turn-off for town. There are daytime **cafés** in both the upper and lower village, and you can stay at *The Beahive*, Arthur Rd, on the other side of the highway and 500m east of Upper Norsewood (☎06/374 0849; Nov–April only; ③), a well-kept self-contained 2-bed bunkhouse in a tranquil garden with reasonably priced meals available on request.

Dannevirke

There's no reason for more than the briefest of stops in **DANNEVIRKE**, a small farming town 20km south of Norsewood, that struggles to play up its heritage, with little more than a rather unpleasant modern windmill in Copenhagen Square on the main street to support its cause. Records and artefacts amassed in the **Gallery of History**, Gordon Street (Mon–Fri 9.30am–4pm, Sat & Sun 1.30–4pm; $2), provide comprehensive coverage of the founding of the town in 1872, when the forest was hacked away to create Dannevirke ("Dane's Work") – a name recalling both the ninth-century defensive earthwork constructed across the waist of the Jutland peninsula in their homeland and the task ahead, the forging of a road from Wellington to Napier. Early photos give a sense of the hard life that drove away many of the Danes, their place taken by British migrants lured by the opening of the Napier–Wellington railway in 1884. The few Danes who remained were soon outnumbered; only a flick through the telephone directory or a glance at some of the shops and street signs betray Dannevirke's Scandinavian heritage.

Napier–Wellington **trains** and **buses** all stop in town not far from the **visitor centre**, 156 High St (Mon–Fri 8.30am–4pm; ☎06/374 6167), and there's the usual selection of tearooms, plus *State of the Art*, 21 High St, a reputable café and **espresso bar**. Should you want to **stay** the night here, check out the *Dannevirke Holiday Park*, George Street (☎06/374 7625; tent sites $8, cabins ③), which has a heated indoor pool and is beautifully set in a dell surrounded by a few remnants of bush; or the *Viking Lodge Motel*, 180 High St (☎06/374 6669, fax 374 6686; ④), where the cheaper units have no cooking facilities.

South of Dannevirke, SH2 runs 25km to Woodville, the junction of SH3, which strikes west through the Manawatu Gorge to Palmerston North (see p.255), and SH2, which continues south into the Wairarapa.

The Wairarapa

The Wairarapa is self-effacing enough to promote itself as New Zealand's least-visited region, a claim that is both believable and justly earned. This is archetypal Kiwi sheep country, with white-flecked green hills etched sharply behind towns which share much in common with the workaday service centres of southern Hawke's Bay. But the Wairarapa is increasingly trying to align itself with Wellington, a source of free-spending day-trippers mostly bound for **Martinborough**, the region's wine capital and far-and-away its most appealing town.

The Wairarapa is separated from the capital by the Rimutaka Range, a persistent barrier to communication that kept the region relatively isolated for decades, until the spell was broken by the establishment of New Zealand's earliest sheep station close to present-day Martinborough. Soon the rich alluvial lands were selected for development by the **Small Farm Association** (SFA), a brainchild of Joseph Masters, a Derbyshire cooper and a long-time campaigner against the "Wakefield Scheme" of settlement, which promoted the separation of landowner and labourer. Aided and abetted by liberal governor George Grey, Masters founded the progressive association, which had the express aim of giving disenfranchised settlers the opportunity to become smallholders. At Grey's suggestion, SFA representatives sallied forth in 1853, persuading Maori to sell land for the establishment of two towns – Masterton and Greytown.

Initially **Greytown** prospered, and it retains an air of antiquity rare in New Zealand towns, but the routing of the rail line favoured **Masterton**, which soon became the main town, famed chiefly for the annual Golden Shears shearing competition. North of Masterton, the **Mount Bruce National Wildlife Centre** provides a superb opportunity to witness ongoing bird conservation work; to the south, **Featherston** is a base for walks up the bed of the Rimutaka Incline Railway. Back on the coast, **Castlepoint** is the place for swimming, **Cape Palliser** for blustery mind-clearing walks and dramatic coastal scenery.

Mount Bruce

The northern half of the Wairarapa is very much a continuation of southern Hawke's Bay, with rolling grasslands stretching away either side of SH2, which is strung with unexceptional service towns. Leave a couple of hours in your schedule, though, for the award-winning **Mount Bruce National Wildlife Centre**, in majestic forest 50km south of Woodville (daily 9.30am–4pm; $8), undoubtedly one of the best places in the country to view endangered native birds and a pioneer in the field of captive-breeding programmes (though much of this happens behind the scenes). Visitors have the chance to see some of the world's rarest birds – kokako, saddleback, kea, kakapo, kiwi and takahe – in spacious aviaries set along a 1km trail through part of the last remnant of the Forty Mile Bush, lowland primeval forest which once covered northern Wairarapa. Beyond the trail several thousand hectares of forest are used for reintroducing birds to the wild. The generous size of the cages on the trail and the thick foliage often make the birds hard to spot, so you'll need to be patient (Jan & Feb are the best times); more immediate gratification comes in the form of abundant aquatic life on the duck pond, a stand of Californian redwoods, a nocturnal kiwi house (take a sweater), tuatara (unique reptiles), and a closed-circuit camera trained on a kokako nest in the breeding season (Oct–March). A continuously running 20-minute audiovisual in the visitor centre gives a moving account of the decline of birdlife in New Zealand; while at 3pm each day a flock of kaka come to feed, causing quite a stir, and eels are fed at 1.30pm, ducks ten minutes later. Visitors can make use of a designated picnic area or relax in the café, which serves good coffee and snacks, indoors or out on the decking. The centre relics heavily on donations, so give if you can. Tranzit **buses** between Palmerston North and Masterton drop off and pick up outside the centre.

Masterton and around

As the Wairarapa's largest town, workaday **MASTERTON**, crouched at the foot of the Tararua Mountains some 30km south of Mount Bruce, makes a tolerable base for exploring a few minor sights. Despite boasting the only cinema in the Wairarapa, you'll find the town itself dull and lifeless – unless your visit coincides with the annual **Golden Shears** shearing competition, effectively the Olympiad of all things woolly, held on the three days leading up to the first Saturday in March. Contestants flock from many lands to demonstrate their prowess with the broad-blade handset; a top shearer can remove a fleece in under a minute, though for maximum points it must be done with skill as well as speed and leave a smooth and unblemished, if shivering, beast. Sideshows include wool-pressing and wool-handling competitions, and even a wool-inspired fashion parade. Proceedings are centred on the War Memorial Stadium, opposite the visitor centre; tickets go for $8–15 for the preliminary heats on Thursday and Friday, $20 for the Saturday finals, and $100 for the wind-up dinner and cabaret (bookings through the visitor centre).

If you front up the last Sunday in February, make for the large, formal Queen Elizabeth Park, immediately east of the centre, where local winemakers and restaurateurs ply their wares as part of the **Wairarapa Wine and Food Festival**. Across the road, the **Wairarapa Arts Centre**, Bruce Street, (Mon–Fri 10am–4.30pm, Sat & Sun 11am–4pm; free), presents temporary exhibitions that are usually worth a peek, and has a lovely café and wine bar. The local **micro-brewery**, Burridges, is in an upstairs café bar on Queen Street North, on the corner with Shoe Street (daily noon–2pm and 5–8.30pm), worth a visit for the elegant surroundings with a view into the gleaming brewery itself and a choice of three beers made on site, but service is erratic so skip the food.

Draped over the hills to the west of town, the **Tararua Forest Park**, while not among New Zealand's tramping hotspots, offers some excellent walking through beech and podocarp forests to the sub-alpine tops, where the weather is notoriously fickle, so it can be dangerous. Serious trampers should consider the **Holdsworth–Jumbo Tramp**, a twelve-hour circuit that can be broken down into two or more manageable days by staying at **huts** (two Category 2 at $10, & two Category 3 at $5; hut passes must be bought in advance from Masterton visitor centre or from the DOC) evenly spaced along the route. The track starts at the backcountry-hut style *Holdsworth Lodge* (tent sites $4, lodge $8), 25km west of Masterton at the end of Norfolk Road, off southbound SH2 (accessible only by taxi ☎06/378 2555; about $20), where day-trippers can undertake easy riverside walks (1–2hr) and bathe in the cool waters.

For details of all these tramps, pay a visit to the Masterton DOC field centre (see below).

A half-day **gastromic self-drive** tour of the area is another option: you could take in three next-door wineries and two unusual cheese outlets. All of these, among others, are marked on the *Wairarapa Wines, Cheeses and Places of Interest* map, free from the visitor centre. First off is Solstone Estate Winery, 119 Solway Crescent on the outskirts of Masterton (Mon–Fri 8am–5pm, Sat & Sun 10.30am–4.30pm), who turn out a fine Merlot. Next is the friendly Gladstone Vineyard in a beautiful sheltered spot on Gladstone Road, about 20km south of Masterton (Tues–Sun 11am–5pm), which is strong on whites, especially Sauvignon Blanc. Its tree-filled garden café offers lunches (☎06/379 8563, booking recommended; Oct–March Fri–Sun), and during the last week of February the vineyard is home to a summer Shakespeare season, run by Victoria University (tickets around $15; book through the vineyard). Next door is Fairmont Estate (daily 9am–5pm), best known for their Pinot Noir including an "old vines" version, with Chardonnay a close runner-up. For a different experience try the pasteurized and organically produced goat's cheese on offer at a farm called Saratoga, on Caveland Road off the Masterton–Martinborough road and about 10km southeast of Masterton (☎06/372 7730; daily 3.30–5pm or by arrangement; free), where you can watch the milking of the goats (4–5pm, except June and July) and sample cheeses which are low in salt, suitable for vegetarians and about $5 a go. Finally, 5 minutes' drive east of Masterton takes you to a farm creating soft French-style hand-crafted sheep's cheese such as Brie and Camembert. At Kingsmeade, Olivers Road off Te Ore Ore Road (☎06/377 5252; Mon–Fri 2–5.30pm, Sat & Sun 9am–5.30pm; appointments preferred but not essential; free), you can watch the cheese-making process at any time or sheep-milking from around 3.30pm (except March–May), and sample the product, for sale at reasonable prices along with cow's-milk cheese.

Practicalities

Masterton's commercial heart is strung along the parallel Chapel, Queen and Dixon streets. Tranzit **buses** (☎06/377 1227 in Masterton & 04/801 7000 in Wellington) pull up on Queen Street, between Russell and Smith streets, around 300m from the **visitor centre**, at 5 Dixon St (Mon–Fri 9am–5pm & Sat–Sun 10am–4pm; ☎06/378 7373, fax 378 7042, *tourwai@xtra.co.nz*), which backs on to Queen Elizabeth Park. Tranz Metro (☎04/498 3000 ext 44933) run commuter services from Wellington to the **train station**, at the end of Perry Street, a fifteen-minute walk from the centre, or call Masterton Radio Taxis (☎06/378 2555). For trampers, the DOC maintain a **field centre** (☎06/378 2061; Mon–Fri 8am–5pm), opposite the aerodrome at the western end of South Road, the continuation of Queen Street. Without your own transport, getting around the Wairarapa's sights can be frustrating and time-consuming, but Tranzit make it easier with their sightseeing **tours** to Mount Bruce ($34 from Wellington, $18 from Masterton, Featherston, Greytown or Carterton), Cape Palliser ($65/$50), and Martinborough ($30/$20); and a farm visits tour, which includes time in Masterton and at a vineyard ($58/$44).

Masterton is littered with motel **accommodation** and has numerous homestays around about. A relaxing motel is the well-appointed Cornwall Park, 119 Cornwall St (☎06/378 2939; ④) in a quiet suburb a 5-minute drive from central town, with a pool and spa. For a B&B try the excellent hospitality of *Fulton House*, 1 Homebush Rd (☎06/378 9252; ⑤), a pretty house in a beautiful English garden only 2km from the town centre, offering a double room with private bathroom next door; or the self-contained *Amaru Cottage*, a 10-minute drive south of Masterton on RD4 at Amaru (☎06/378 6256; ③

including breakfast), in a small peaceful garden and with room for three. In the absence of hostels, budget accommodation is limited to Kildare House, 31 Renall St (☎06/378 6606; single ②, double ③), a central homestay with two double rooms and four singles. Central, en-suite hotel rooms with breakfast thrown in can be had at the *Empire Lodge*, 94 Queen St (☎06/377 1902, fax 377 2298; ④), which also offers courtesy transport to the bus and train; while campers should make for the spacious and attractive *Mawley Park Motor Camp*, 15 Oxford St (☎ & fax 06/378 6454, *jclarke@contact.net.nz*; tent sites $10, cabins ②), ten minutes' walk north of the centre. If proximity to town is less of an issue, try the lovely *Lyndor Homestay*, Lees-Pakaraka Road (☎ & fax 06/378 8105; ⑤), which occupies a modern house by a small vineyard ten minutes' drive from Masterton.

Budget eating is best at the sedate *Slug and Lettuce*, on the first floor, 94 Queen St, an ersatz English pub with bargain steaks and lasagne-type meals from as little as $5 available daily all day from 11am, plus a good range of snacks such as curry samosas, wontons and chicken satay sticks; this is also a good spot for a coffee or pot of tea. For Masterton's best food, or just a good strong coffee, head upstairs to *Bloomfields*, first floor, Leecroft Chambers, on the corner of Chapel Street and Lincoln Road (☎06/377 4305; closed Sun; lunches Wed–Fri, dinners Mon–Sat; licensed), which turns out the likes of pork medallions with figs, mango and mint coulis for around $20.

Castlepoint

The 300km of coastline from Cape Kidnappers, near Napier, south to Cape Palliser is bleak, desolate and almost entirely inaccessible – except for **CASTLEPOINT**, 65km east of Masterton, where early explorers found a welcome break in the "perpendicular line of cliff". A commanding lighthouse presides over a rocky knoll which is linked to the mainland by a thin hourglass double **beach** that encloses a sheltered pool known as The Basin. Nearby is a small settlement where Wairarapa families retreat for summer fun in the calm **lagoon**, walking to the lighthouse or the cave at its foot, riding the breakers or surfcasting from a huge rock platform. Castlepoint is at its most frenetic around the third or fourth Saturday in March, when there's an informal **horse race** along the beach – a somewhat unorthodox betting set-up requires punters to bet "blind" on numbers before they are allocated to particular horses.

In the absence of a visitor centre, ask for **information** at the Castlepoint Store (☎06/372 6823). You can **stay** here at the *Castlepoint Holiday Park* (☎06/372 6705, fax 372 6717; tent sites $8, cabins ②) or the *Castlepoint Motel and Cabins* (☎ & fax 06/372 6637; units ⑤), which also has a "Cookhouse" with beds and bunkrooms (①), plus a garden cottage (④).

Carterton

Once you've shaken free of the outskirts of Masterton, a string of small towns guide you towards the Rimutaka Range and over into the Hutt Valley (see p.460). Staunchly conservative **CARTERTON**, 15km south of Masterton, hides a treat for lovers of kitsch souvenirs. The **Paua Shell Factory**, at 54 Kent St (Mon–Fri 8am–5pm, Sat & Sun 9am–5pm; free), is an Aladdin's Cave of tacky objects fashioned from this beautiful rainbow-swirled seashell. Superbly polished examples of the shells themselves retail for up to $50, but other extraordinary items can be yours to treasure for a much more modest sum. The factory supplies just about every tourist knick-knack shop in the country and, if you can't resist, you can even take a brief, free tour to see how the stuff is made.

Some 5km south of Carterton, a road runs 15km west into the foothills of the Tararua Range to **Waiohine Gorge**, a picturesque chasm that's ideal for picnics and safe swimming.

Greytown

There's a more traditional appeal to **GREYTOWN**, 9km south of Carterton. Laid out in 1853, the town still retains something of its Victorian feel, despite the traffic that now trundles between the rows of two-storey wooden buildings. Until the end of the nineteenth century, this was the Wairarapa's main settlement, but railway planners diverted the new line around the flood-prone environs and set the seal on a gradual decline that was only arrested by the development of profitable orchards and market gardens in the latter half of the twentieth century.

The real appeal here is the selection of **cafés** along Main Street, notably the excellent and moderately priced *Main Street Deli*, at no. 88 (✆06/304 9022; licensed & BYO), which provides reason enough to stop in Greytown to stock up on unusual breads, cheeses and the like; or pause at the cosy café attached, for breakfast, lunch, coffee and cakes (daily), or even for dinner (Fri & Sat only). If you feel you need to earn your lunch, spend an hour among the re-sited Victorian buildings and stagecoach paraphernalia at the **Cobblestones Museums**, 169 Main St (Mon–Sat 9am–4.30pm, Sun 10am–4.30pm; $2.50); or take a **historical walk** guided by the *Heritage Trails of Wairarapa* booklet ($2) from the volunteer-run **visitor centre** (hours vary) in the Public Services building on Main Street.

Featherston and the Rimutaka Incline

The last of the Wairarapa towns before SH2 climbs west over the Rimutakas is **FEATHERSTON**, 13km south of Greytown, where the **visitor centre**, in the Old Courthouse on Fitzherbert Street (daily 10am–3pm; ✆ & fax 06/308 8051), stands in front of the town's pride and joy. The **Fell Engine Museum**, Lyon Street (Oct–April Sat & Sun 10am–4pm; every weekend 10am–4pm and all through the school holidays same hours; other times ask at the visitor centre and for $5 they will open it for you; donations to museum appreciated) contains what, to the casual observer, appears to be an ordinary old railway engine. Nevertheless, steam buffs cross the country to this last surviving example of the locos which, for 77 years (until the boring of a new tunnel in 1955), climbed the 265m, one-in-fifteen slope of the Rimutaka Incline over the range into the Hutt Valley, gaining purchase by gripping a central rail.

The rails have long been pulled up, but you can follow the trackbed on the **Rimutaka Incline Walkway** (17km; 6hr; 300m ascent), which starts 10km south of Featherston at Cross Creek, passes old shunting yards and shuffles through the 576-metre summit tunnel, before descending to Kaitoke. A free leaflet from the visitor centre details the route, provides background information and pinpoints three basic, grassy campsites along the way. Many walk just an hour or two from either end and back, but if you fancy the full trek, contact South Wairarapa Tours (✆06/308 9352), who will organize pick-ups (cost depends on numbers). There's no public transport to Cross Creek, but Masterton–Wellington buses pass within 1km of the Kaitoke end of the walkway.

Buses also stop 3km north of the end of the walkway near *The Black Stump* YHA Hostel, Marchant Road (cnr with SH2), Kaitoke (✆04/526 4626; dorms ①, rooms ②), a basic 10-bunk place in the tradition of youth hostels of yore with a twin/double; bring most of the supplies you need, though there's a basic store and café/bar 200m away. Accommodation options in Featherston are pretty limited: there's a big homestead B&B and backpackers combo, *Fareham House*, Underhill Rd (✆06/308 9074; dorms ①, backpacker rooms ②, B&B rooms ③), in a peaceful rural setting with pool and tennis courts; or the more central *Empire Hotel* with budget rooms on Johnston St, opposite the train station (☎06/308 9540; ② including breakfast). The best spot for **eating** is *The Loft*, Tarureka Estate, 38 Donald St (☎06/308 8173), a café and wine bar in a converted 1869 Dutch barn, serving good coffee, fine wine and wholesome farmhouse dishes (lunch Tues–Sun, dinner Thurs–Sun).

Martinborough and its wineries

In the last ten years tiny **MARTINBOROUGH**, 18km southeast of Featherston, has been transformed from a small and obscure farming town into the centre of a compact wine region synonymous with some of New Zealand's finest red wines. Being within easy striking distance of Wellington, weekends see the arrival of the smart set, ready to lunch at the handful of appealing cafés and restaurants and load up their shiny landcruisers at the dozen-or-so wineries that surround the town. On Mondays much of the town simply shuts down to recover. Go midweek, though, and Martinborough is a beguiling place – so small that you immediately feel at ease and

---

MARTINBOROUGH WINERIES

For visitors, Martinborough has the edge over other wine regions in that ten of its wineries are accessible **on foot**, and half a dozen more are easily reached by car or a **bike** rented from Pedalpushers (☎06/306 9364; $10 a day). The best guide is the free Winemakers of Martinborough brochure (from the visitor centre on Kitchener St, see overleaf), which details the hours and facilities of the sixteen wineries that conduct **tastings**. Should you prefer a guided tour of several wineries, tailored to your needs and with someone else driving, try Laura's Wairarapa Tours (☎06/377 3534, fax 377 4834; prices vary), which are half-day or full-day trips taking in other local sights if you wish.

Here's our pick of the wineries to kick-start your explorations.

Ata Rangi, Puruatanga Rd (while stocks last: Oct–April Mon–Fri 11am–3pm, Sat & Sun 11am–5pm; Dec–Feb daily 11am–5pm; tastings $2, refundable on purchase). A great place to start as it's central and increasingly well known for its Pinot Noir and Chardonnay, as well as its Pinot Gris and Rosé. In 1999 this became one of the first wineries in the world to achieve ISO 14001 accreditation – an international environmental management system recognized in 54 countries.

Martinborough Vineyard, Princess St (daily 11am–5pm). A Martinborough original and still one of the largest, producing top-quality Pinot Noir and Chardonnay, with an ISO 14001 accreditation (see Ata Rangi above). Picnicking is encouraged.

Muirlea Rise, 50 Princess St, across the road from Martinborough Vineyard (Oct–April Fri–Mon 10am–6pm; May–Sept Fri–Mon 10am–4.30pm). Top-quality Pinot Noir to go with a ploughman's lunch and lovely coffee.

Nga Waka, Kitchener St (☎06/306 9832; from Nov while stocks last, Sat & Sun 1–5pm). One of the small, young boutique wineries known for their bone-dry whites with elegant fruit.

Palliser Estate, Kitchener St (daily 10.30am–4pm, and till 6pm at weekends Oct–April; free tastings). This pioneering Martinborough winery with an ISO 14001 (see Ata Rangi above) limits its impact on the environment while producing premium wines – Pinot Noir, Chardonnay, Sauvignon Blanc and Riesling; picnics are encouraged in the pleasant formal garden.

Te Kairanga, Martins Rd, 5km southeast (daily 10am—5pm). A consistent award-winner which produces some delicious small-volume reserve wines; tastings are held in a 130-year-old pit-sawn-plank cottage moved to the vineyard from Martinborough. Casual tours on Sat & Sun at 2pm.

with a number of excellent vineyards within easy strolling distance of the centre (see box on previous page).

The town was initially laid out in the 1870s by patriotic landowner John Martin, who named the streets after cities he had visited on his travels and arranged the core in the form of a Union Jack centred on a leafy square. Martinborough languished as a minor agricultural centre for over a century until the first four wineries – Ata Rangi, Dry River, Chifney and Martinborough (all of which produced their first vintages in 1984) – re-invented Martinborough as the coolest, driest and most wind-prone of the North Island's grape-growing regions. With the aid of shelter belts that slice the horizon, the wineries, which now number almost twenty, produce some outstanding Pinot Noir, very good Cabernet Sauvignon (though it is losing favour as the grapes fail to fully ripen in poor years), crisp and fruity Sauvignon Blanc and wonderfully aromatic Riesling.

Martinborough is no slouch at promoting its viticultural prowess, and the best time to visit is during one of its **festivals**. The first of the summer is **Toast Martinborough** (third Sun in Nov), a specifically wine-orientated affair with all the vineyards open, free buses doing the rounds, and top Wellington and local restaurants selling their produce; it is an exclusive event and tickets (sold from first Mon in Oct through Ticketek ☎04/384 3840 Wellington, ☎09/307 5000 Auckland, *www. ticketek.co.nz*; $45) are hard to obtain. There's a considerably more egalitarian feel to the two **Martinborough Fairs** (first Sat in Feb & March), a huge country fête, during which the streets radiating from the central square are lined with stalls selling all manner of arts and crafts.

Practicalities

Wairarapa Coachlines **buses** (☎06/378 2911 & 025/916 971), shuttling between Featherston, Masterton and Martinborough, meet the TranzMetro commuter **trains** from Wellington (☎0800/843 596; Mon–Fri, plus weekend day-trips in summer) from Wellington and drop off at the small but informative **visitor centre** on Kitchener Street (daily 10am–4pm; ☎06/306 9043, *tourwai@xtra.co.nz*). **Net access** is available at the library on Jellicoe Street (☎06/306 9758; daily, times vary so call or check at visitor centre).

The range of **accommodation** leans heavily towards mid- and upper-price B&Bs and homestays, most of them in rural surroundings out of town, or self-contained cottages starting at around $100 midweek, $120 at weekends (the visitor centre has an up-to-date list). There are no hostels. Of the B&Bs, try *Oak House Homestay*, 45 Kitchener St (☎06/306 9198, fax 306 8198, *chrispolly.oakhouse@xtra.co.nz*; ⑤), run by a local winemaker with attractive rooms in a Californian-style bungalow, substantial breakfasts and dinners from $35 with wine. *Olivo* (☎06/306 9074, fax 306 9089, *twhd@clear.net.nz*; ⑥–⑦), 3km from town on RD4/Hinakura Road and surrounded by olive groves, is another good bet, with continental breakfast brought to your room (king size or queen); though for real luxury, stay at the sumptuously refurbished two-storey colonial *Martinborough Hotel*, on the corner of Kitchener Street and Memorial Square (☎06/306 9350, fax 306 9345, *info@martinboroughhotel.co.nz*; ⑧). At the cheaper end, try the central *Martinborough Motel*, 43 Strassburg St (☎ & fax 06/306 9408; units ③–④); the *Martinborough Camping Ground*, Princess Street (☎06/306 9336; $10 per site); or *Mangapari*, 10 minutes drive from Martinborough on RD4 (☎ & fax 06/306 9440; ④), a big 1912 homestead on a sheep and cattle station, offering a queen, a double and a twin.

Martinborough caters to discerning diners, many of them weekending Wellingtonians, with half a dozen **restaurants** on, or close to, Memorial Square. Plenty charge city prices but others are more reasonable. Accolades are heaped on the *Martinborough Bistro*, at the Martinborough Hotel, with beautifully prepared and presented dishes drawing on traditional French and modern Mediterranean cuisines at around the $25 mark. Also popular for evening dining is *Zodiac* in the old post office building, corner of Kitchener Street and The Square (☎06/306 9661, essential to book ahead; dinner only; BYO; closed Sun & Mon). Simpler and cheaper fare can be had at *Huntaways Bar & Brasserie*, The Square; or *The Flying Fish Café*, corner of The Square and Jellicoe Street (Nov–April daily, rest of the year closed Mon–Wed; licensed & BYO), an intimate all-day café for great coffee, snacks, all-day brunches, light meals and takeaways in an attractive old building with a garden bar; while *The Grapevine*, 48 Kitchener St, is a small summertime café and garden bar offering lunchtime platters and local wine in a peaceful vineyard setting; and the local pub, the *Pukemanu Tavern*, The Square, near the corner of Kansas Street sells cheap lunches and dinners in its steakbar restaurant.

Cape Palliser

The low-key cosmopolitanism of Martinborough stands in dramatic contrast to the bleak and windswept coast around **Cape Palliser**, 60km south. The southernmost point on the North Island, the cape was named in honour of James Cook's mentor, Rear Admiral Sir Hugh Palliser. Apart from a few gentle walks and the opportunity to observe fur seals at close quarters, there's not a lot to do out here but kick back, especially since swimming is unsafe and the weather changeable owing to the proximity of the Tararua Range, but the breeze will soon blow away the cobwebs.

From Martinborough, a sealed road leads 25km south to **LAKE FERRY**, a tiny laid-back surfcasting settlement on the sandy shores of Lake Onoke, which once had a ferry service on the coastal route to Wellington before the Rimutaka Road was completed, and where there is a small basic **hotel**, the southernmost of the North Island. *Lake Ferry Hotel* (☎06/307 7831, fax 307 7868), has modest hotel rooms (③–④) and cheaper backpacker dorms (①) and rooms (② including breakfast) with no kitchen, but the in-house pub restaurant churns out big portions of simple food that won't break the bank. Bear in mind there is no store around here. Three kilometres before Lake Ferry is a well-kept **campground**, the *Gateway Holiday Park*, on the main road 3km before Lake Ferry (☎ & fax 06/307 7780; tent sites $8.50, on-site caravans $29, cabins ②–③, self-contained units ③–④), which has a pool. From a road junction just before Lake Ferry, the Cape Palliser road twists for 13km through the coastal hills until it meets the sea near the **Putangirua Pinnacles**, dozens of grey soft-rock spires and fluted cliffs up to 50m high, formed by wind and rain selectively eroding the surrounding silt and gravel. The pinnacles lie within the little-visited Aorangi (Haurangi) Forest Park, and can be reached along an easy streambed path (1hr return) from the roadside Putangirua Scenic Reserve, where there are barbecue areas and a primitive **campsite** ($5); longer walks of up to 5hr are outlined on a map in the car park.

From here, the partly metalled road hugs the rugged, exposed coastline for 15km to **NGAWI**, a small fishing village where all manner of bulldozers grind out their last days, hauling fishing boats up the steep gravel beach. It is five rough kilometres on to the Cape proper, where the only well-established **fur-seal colony** on the North Island lies right beside the road, overlooked by the century-old Cape Palliser **lighthouse**, standing on a knoll 60m above the sea at the top of a long flight of some 250 steps. It is easy enough to get within 20m of the seals, but you should keep your distance from any pups – and their protective parents – and don't get between any seal and the sea.

travel details

Trains

The main train line runs from Wellington and Palmerston North, through the Manawatu Gorge to Woodville and up through the southern Hawke's Bay towns to Hastings and Napier.

A separate passenger service to the Wairarapa also originates in Wellington, and terminates in Masterton; no trains link Masterton with Woodville.

From Hastings to: Dannevirke (1 daily; 1hr 50min); Napier (1 daily; 20min); Palmerston North (1 daily; 3hr); Wellington (1 daily; 5hr).

From Masterton to: Carterton (2–5 daily; 15min); Featherston (2–5 daily; 30min); Wellington (2–5 daily; 1hr 30min).

From Napier to: Dannevirke (1 daily; 2hr 10min); Hastings (1 daily; 20min); Palmerston North (1 daily; 3hr 20min); Wellington (1 daily; 5hr 30min).

Buses

InterCity combined with Newmans run most of the bus services through the region, with a service connecting Gisborne with all the Hawke's Bay towns, Palmerston North and Wellington; one linking Gisborne to Rotorua via Whakatane; one running from Napier and Hastings to Auckland via Taupo; and another joining Palmerston North, Masterton and Wellington. Tranzit connect Wellington with the main Wairarapa towns.

Local Gisborne buses ply SH35 around Eastland to Opotiki; see Chapter Five for full coverage of this area.

From Gisborne to: Auckland (1 daily; 9hr 15min); Hastings (3 daily; 4hr–4hr 30min); Napier (3 daily; 3hr 30min–4hr); Rotorua (2 daily; 4hr 30min); Wairoa (3 daily; 1hr 40min).

From Hastings to: Auckland (3 daily; 8hr); Dannevirke (4 daily; 1hr 30min); Gisborne (3 daily; 4hr–4hr 30min); Napier (Mon–Fri 16 daily & Sat–Sun 4–5 daily; 30–45min); Norsewood (4 daily; 1hr 10min); Taupo (3 daily; 2hr 30min–3hr); Wellington (4 daily; 5hr 20min).

From Masterton to: Carterton (2 daily; 25min); Greytown (2 daily; 40min); Featherston (2 daily; 1hr); Palmerston North (4 daily; 2hr 10min); Wellington (2 daily; 2hr).

From Napier to: Auckland (3 daily; 7hr 30min); Dannevirke (4 daily; 2hr); Gisborne (3 daily; 3hr 30min–4hr); Hastings (Mon–Fri 16 daily & Sat–Sun 4–5 daily; 30–45min); Norsewood (4 daily; 2hr); Taupo (3 daily; 2hr 30min); Wellington (4 daily; 5hr).

From Wairoa to: Gisborne (3 daily; 1hr 40min); Napier (3 daily; 2hr).

Flights

From Gisborne to: Auckland (5–7 daily; 1hr); Hamilton (1–2 daily; 55min); Napier (1 daily; 40min); Palmerston North (1 daily; 1hr 10min); Wellington (3–4 daily; 50min).

From Napier to: Auckland (5–7 daily; 1hr); Wellington (5–6 daily; 55min).

CHAPTER SEVEN

WELLINGTON AND AROUND

L ying at the southwestern tip of the North Island, at the junction of SH1 and SH2, **Wellington** is the capital city of New Zealand and the seat of government. With a population of 400,000, it is also the country's second-largest city and enjoys a scenic **setting**, wedged between steep hills and the broad harbour of **Port Nicholson**. An engaging and friendly place to explore, Wellington boasts plenty of outdoor activities, a decorative and bustling **waterfront**, a stimulating combination of historical and modern **architecture**, and an exuberant **café society** and nightlife, complemented by a buzzing entertainment and cultural scene. However, Wellington lives up to its nickname of **"the windy city"**, lashed most days by air funnelled through Cook Strait, an effect that's amplified by the city's high-rise buildings, which create wind tunnels. The **harbour**, on the other hand, remains relatively sheltered and is a perfect spot from which to appreciate the cityscape. With its **ferry** terminal and airport, Wellington is the principal departure point for the **South Island**, but the city warrants much more than just a fleeting glimpse. You're best off allowing three to four days to explore the sights concentrated within the central city and to make the most of the harbour, the beaches and bays, and Somes Island.

East of Wellington, where the **Rimutaka Range** separates the Hutt Valley from the Wairarapa (see p.424), a forest park offers several popular bushwalks that make for a pleasant day away from the city. The meagre attractions of the **commuter-belt communities** of the Hutt Valley and Porirua, on the other hand, don't really warrant a special trip. To the north, the **Kapiti Coast** is a pretty thirty-kilometre stretch of silvery beach scattered with tiny communities full of holiday and retirement homes, bowling greens and golf courses, with the region's most significant attraction just offshore: the long thin **Kapiti Island**, a bird sanctuary that you can visit on a day-trip from

---

ACCOMMODATION PRICES

Accommodation listed in this guide has been categorized into one of nine price bands, as set out below. The rates quoted represent the **cheapest available** double or twin **room** – except for category ①, which are per-person rates for a dorm bed. Note that fees for **tent sites** and **DOC huts** (quoted in dollars) are also per-person, unless otherwise stated.

① under $20 per person	④ $60–80	⑦ $140–180
② under $40 per room	⑤ $80–100	⑧ $180–240
③ $40–60	⑥ $100–140	⑨ over $240

For more on accommodation, see p.34.

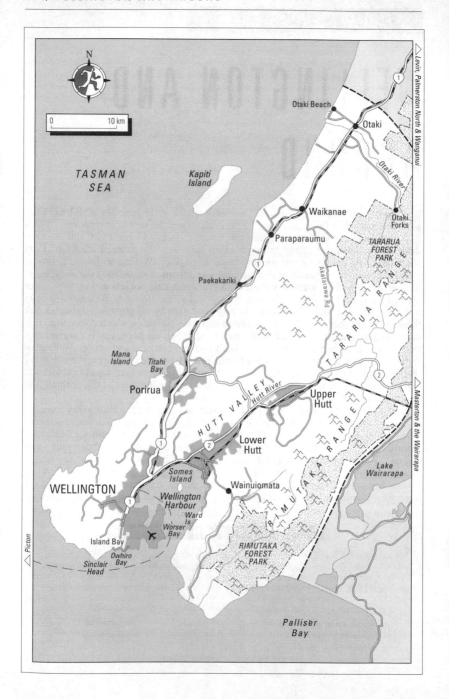

Paraparaumu Beach. Finally, Wellington is well placed for exploration of New Zealand's premier **wineries**, with Martinborough (see p.429) only a short scenic drive away through the Rimutaka Range to the Wairarapa, and the sunny Marlborough wineries (see p.520) accessible by boat across Cook Strait.

WELLINGTON

The vibrant city of **WELLINGTON** is the cultural, political and commercial capital of New Zealand, though this is not what most Aucklanders would have you believe. A healthy antipathy exists between the two cities, fuelled by Auckland's conviction that it should be capital. Wellington is by no means a pale shadow of Auckland, though, not least because of the high levels of investment in recent years, aimed at making the city worthy of its capital status and more attractive to visitors. Most of the city is built on precipitous hills overlooking a magnificent harbour, fringed by beaches, marinas and warehouses. The inner city is an energetic mix of historic stone buildings and modern structures, most notably the radical **contemporary architecture** of Ian Athfield, one of New Zealand's best-known architects, while the suburbs are a combination of grand residential villas and unspectacular commercial buildings. The surrounding hills have provided a natural barrier to the unbridled development typical of other New Zealand cities, helping to keep central Wellington an easily walkable area with a definite identity.

Wellington is truly **cosmopolitan**, offering a huge range of culinary experiences, alongside nightlife and artistic culture from all over the world. The most exciting months to visit are February and March, when the city hosts three separate **festivals**: the annual Wellington Fringe Festival, a carnival along the lines of the Edinburgh Festival; the biennial International Festival of the Arts, a month-long celebration that draws the best international acts in opera, theatre and music; and the annual Dragon Boat Festival (in late February), which attracts huge crowds to the inner harbour.

Some history

Maori believe that the first Polynesian navigator, Kupe, discovered Wellington Harbour (in 925 AD) and he is said to have camped here for some time on the Miramar Peninsula at the harbour mouth, naming the harbour's islands Matiu (Somes Island) and Makaro (Ward Island) after his daughters. Several *iwi* (tribes) settled around the harbour over the centuries, including the Ngati Tara people, who enjoyed the rich fishing areas and the protection that the bay offered. Both Abel Tasman (in 1642) and Captain Cook (in 1773) were prevented from entering Wellington Harbour by fierce winds and, apart from a few whalers, it was not until 1840 that the first wave of **European settlers** arrived, not long after the New Zealand Company had purchased a large tract of land around the harbour. The first settlement, named Britannia, was established on the northeastern beaches at **Petone**; shortly after, the Hutt River flooded, forcing the settlers to move around the harbour to a more sheltered site known as Lambton Harbour (where the central city has grown up) and the relatively level land at **Thorndon**, at that time just north of the shoreline. They renamed the settlement after the Iron Duke and, finding flat land scarce, began land **reclamations** into the harbour in the 1850s, a process that continued at intervals for more than a hundred years.

By the turn of the century the original shoreline of Lambton Harbour had all but disappeared, replaced largely by wharves and harbourside businesses. The growing city, at the hub of coastal shipping, became a thriving import and export centre, and in 1865 it superseded Auckland as the **capital** of New Zealand, largely because of its central location and fine harbour. Wellington has prospered ever since, and these days around seven million tonnes of cargo pass through the wharves each year. Parts of the waterfront no longer needed by the modernized shipping industry have been redeveloped for public use, while along the coast a number of **shipwrecks** are further testament to the city's maritime history, victims of the region's notorious high winds. Sailing ships of the 1800s were particularly susceptible, but even as late as 1968 a modern roll-on roll-off ferry, the *Wahine*, foundered at the harbour entrance in the worst storm of the century (see p.443).

Arrival and information

Wellington International Airport is about 5km from the city centre and has one terminal, shared by Qantas, Air New Zealand and Ansett flights, along with domestic airlines. Note that when leaving New Zealand from Wellington, a departure tax of $25 applies. Also operating from here is the smaller airline, Soundsair, that makes the short hop over Cook Strait to the South Island. There is a **visitor centre** in the terminal (daily 7am–8pm, also open for flight arrivals), as well as **left-luggage** lockers and a **bureau de change** (Mon–Fri 4–7am & 8.30am–5pm, Sat noon–5pm, Sun 8.30am–5pm, & open for all arrivals at night). Three **shuttle-bus** companies, ShuttleExpress (☎0800/579 957), Super Shuttle (☎04/387 8787) and A.P. Shuttles (☎0800/959 595), run a 24hr door-to-door service to central Wellington (daily; $8–10 first passenger, $2 per extra person), plus a direct service to Wellington train station (roughly every 30min at peak times, otherwise hourly Mon–Fri; $6–12). A **taxi** ride from the airport costs the same, or around $20 for ten passengers.

The main **train station** is in downtown Wellington on Bunny Street, just off Waterloo Quay, and is the last destination on the main north–south rail line from Auckland and the branch line from Napier. Newmans and InterCity **buses** also pull in here (at platform 9). Arriving **by road**, SH1 and SH2 merge just north of the city, continuing into the centre, after running briefly along the harbourside and giving excellent views of the city ahead. Most **ferries** from Picton on the South Island arrive at the Interislander ferry terminal just off SH1, 2km north of the train station, but the *Topcat* pulls in at Waterloo Quay, opposite the train station. A free shuttle service operates between the ferry terminal and train station; the Super Shuttle bus (see above) costs $3, and a taxi $5–6.

> For details of sea and air routes from Wellington **to the South Island**, see "Crossing Cook Strait", p.450.

The well-stocked and efficient **visitor centre** is on the corner of Wakefield Street and Victoria Street (Mon & Wed–Fri 8.30am–5.30pm, Tues 8.30am–5pm; Sat & Sun 9.30am–5.30pm, 4.30pm in winter; ☎04/802 4860, fax 802 4863, *wgtnvisitors @hotmail.com*). They sell city maps for $1 and provide a useful free booklet, *Wellington – What's On*, published by Jasons and including a central-city map. The **DOC office** is in the Old Government Buildings at the corner of Lambton Quay and Whitmore Street (☎04/472 7356; *phewson@doc.govt.nz*; Mon–Fri 9am–4.30pm, Sat & Sun 10am–3pm), with stacks of information on walks in the Wellington region, including tramps on Kapiti Island and the forest parks around the city; hut passes are also sold here, as are permits to visit Kapiti Island ($8).

City transport

Wellington has a comprehensive **local bus** service that links the inner city to most of the central suburbs (Mon–Sat 7am–11pm, Sun 8am–11pm, plus a limited hourly service

Sat & Sun 1–3am). Daytime services depart from the train station or the main city bus stop at Courtenay Place, at the intersection with Cambridge Terrace; the after-midnight service departs from Courtenay Place, then from Dixon Street (near Cuba Mall) three minutes later and picks up from all city stops; a free general bus and train guide, plus free route maps and timetables are available from the visitor centre and train station. Frequent **trolley buses** also trundle around the city, running on overhead cables between the eastern end of Courtenay Place and the train station, along Lambton Quay. Bus fares are $1 within the inner city, beyond which a zonal system comes into operation, with fares ranging from $1.10 to $3, and all journeys on the weekend after-midnight service at $3; buy tickets from the driver. "Daytripper" **passes** ($5) are also available from bus drivers, giving unlimited travel for a day (after 9am) and including the cable car to the Botanic Gardens (see p.443). For **information** on all trains and local buses in the Wellington region, call the Ridewell Service Centre (Mon–Sat 7.30am–8.30pm, Sun 9am–3pm; ☎04/801 7000).

    Driving around the inner city is simple once you get used to the extensive one-way system and remember to avoid the rush-hour traffic (7–9am & 4.30–6.30pm), but since it's so easy to get around on foot or by public transport you're best off ditching the rental car at your earliest opportunity and, if crossing to the South Island, picking up a new one there, thus reducing costs on the ferry. Finding a space to **park** in the inner city is a nightmare. Thankfully at weekends you can park at meters and in car parks for up to two hours for free, after which both cost $3 per hour (see "Listings" on p.458 for location of car parks). The hills around the city are a mecca for **mountain-bike** enthusiasts (pick up the $1 leaflet *Off-road Mountain Biking in Wellington City*, containing maps and full descriptions of tracks in the Town Belt), but cycling is also a great way to enjoy the scenic coastal route around the harbour and its bays; most **bike rental** companies (see p.458 for recommended outfits) charge $25 for half a day.

Accommodation

Your best bet is to plump for **accommodation** in the city centre, close to all the action. There are plenty of hostels, B&Bs (many in beautifully preserved Victorian villas) and hotels, but only a few centrally located motels and, curiously for New Zealand, the city has **no campsite**. Instead you have to head all the way out to the Hutt Valley on the harbour's northeastern shore for the *Hutt Park Holiday Park*, 95 Hutt Park Rd, Lower Hutt (☎04/568 5913, fax 568 5914, *info@huttpark.co.nz*; tent sites $9.50, cabins ②, tourist flats ④, motel units ⑤), about 14km from Wellington's train and bus station, but close to beaches, shops and bush walks.

    On the city centre's western fringes, but within easy walking distance of all the attractions, the leafy and characterful suburb of **Thorndon** contains a couple of delightful B&Bs and a pleasant historic hotel, while the inner-city's eastern border, the suburb of **Mount Victoria**, offers a range of accommodation within a stone's throw of the busiest part of town. Finally, if you're after bucolic surroundings within easy **driving distance** of the city, you could do a lot worse than *Braebyre B&B* near Porirua (see p.463).

    Availability anywhere in the inner city is limited during the busiest part of the summer (Xmas, Jan & Feb), so it pays to book as far ahead as possible: for the most popular hostels, you need to allow a week or more. **Prices** are a touch above average: in hostels, most dorms are four- to six-bed and rates hover around $19, while doubles and twins go for $42–46. At the other end of the scale, hotels are expensive during the week, but most offer special weekend deals, sometimes shaving off as much as fifty percent. For B&Bs you pay on average at least $20 more than you would elsewhere.

Hotels and motels

Abel Tasman, cnr Willis St & Dixon St (☎04/385 1304, fax 385 8416, *hotelnz@xtra.co.nz*). Extremely central hotel with good weekend discounts and regular rates towards the lower end of this price code. ⑤.

Apollo Lodge, 38–49 Majoribanks St (☎04/385 1849, fax 385 1846, *accommodation@apollolodge.co.nz*). Central, medium-sized motel, 400m from Courtenay Place. Most units have fully equipped kitchens. ⑥.

Carillon Motor Inn, 33 Thompson St (☎04/384 8795, fax 385 7036). Cheaper prices reflect an average location, about a kilometre south of Courtenay Place, and a communal kitchen simply equipped with a microwave and fridge. ④–⑤.

Majoribanks Apartments, 38 Majoribanks St (☎04/385 8879, fax 385 1846, *accommodation @apollolodge.co.nz*). Several big, fully self-contained apartments in a modern block close to the heart of the city; off-street parking. ⑥.

Parkroyal, cnr Grey St & Featherston St (☎0800/857 585, fax 495 7865, *reservations@wellington. parkroyal.co.nz*). The most expensive place in town, this luxurious international hotel in a tower block near Queens Wharf is geared chiefly to businesspeople, but has half-price weekend rates (around $175). Facilities include a gym and a pool, a classy restaurant and an airport limousine service. ⑨

Plaza International, 148 Wakefield St (☎0800/475 292, fax 473 3929, *ressies@plazainternational.co.nz*). A gleaming modern corporate hotel on the waterfront near Civic Square, with an a la carte restaurant and brasserie. Marginally cheaper than the *Parkroyal*, especially at weekends. ⑨.

Shepherd's Arms, 285 Tinakori Rd, Thorndon (☎0800/393 782, fax 472 0523, *shepherds@xtra.co.nz*). Near the Parliamentary District, this small 1870s hotel (reputedly New Zealand's oldest) with bar and restaurant is tastefully renovated in period style, but with all mod cons, ⑦. There's also a self-contained cottage, ⑧.

Trekkers, 213 Cuba St (☎0800/873 553, fax 382 8873, *info@trekkers.co.nz*). Central, basic hotel-cum-motel-cum-backpackers that's showing its age badly in places. Hotel and motel rooms (singles and doubles) are kitted out with private bathrooms, TV, radio and phone; off-street parking. ⑤.

Wellington Motels, 14 Hobson St (☎04/472 0334, fax 472 6825, *wellington.motels@clear.net.nz*). Small, quiet and well equipped, this is the closest motel to the Picton ferry terminal. ⑤–⑥.

B&Bs and guesthouses

Dunrobin House, 89 Austin St, cnr with Derby St, Mount Victoria (☎04/385 0335, fax 385 0336). An elegant turn-of-the-century villa about 1km from Courtenay Place, with three comfortable, big rooms and an abundance of fresh flowers. Mornings begin with a gourmet breakfast which, in fine weather, is served in the sheltered garden. ⑤–⑦.

Holdsworth, 292 Tinakori Rd, Thorndon (☎04/473 4986, fax 473 9566, *mkp@voyager.co.nz*). An attractive 1890s house in a cottage-garden setting, five minutes' walk from Parliament Buildings, with big, welcoming rooms. Excellent breakfasts; off-street parking. ⑦.

The Mermaid, 1 Epuni St, cnr with Aro St (☎ & fax 04/384 4511, *mermaid@paradise.net.nz*). A luxurious guesthouse for women only, set in a restored turn-of-the-century house among bush-covered hills, a ten-minute walk from downtown. Four tastefully furnished rooms (one with private bathroom), each with a view of the garden or hills. Kitchen and lounge. ④–⑥.

Talavera, 7 Talavera Terrace, Kelburn (☎04/471 0555). An 1897 villa on a quiet, leafy hill above the central business district, five minutes' walk from Lambton Quay and on the cable-car route. Sweeping views from a self-contained flat with a veranda. ⑦.

Tinakori Lodge, 182 Tinakori Rd, Thorndon (☎04/473 3478, fax 472 5554, *100035.3214 @compuserve.com*). A well-appointed, big Victorian villa, a short walk from the Parliamentary District, with several airy rooms and a conservatory that looks onto a bushland reserve. ⑤–⑥.

Hostels

Downtown Backpackers, 1 Bunny St (☎04/473 8482, fax 471 1073, *db@downtownbackpackers.co.nz*). Huge and rather impersonal hostel occupying a 1930s hotel, opposite the train station but a bit of a walk from the action on Courtenay Place. The doubles are en-suite, some even with TVs (a few with views of the Beehive) and dorms vary. Extra perks include a courtesy pick-up from the ferry, bargain bar (the cheapest beer in the city) and a café serving low-cost breakfasts and dinners. Dorms ①, rooms ③.

Lodge in the City, 152 Taranaki St (☎04/385 8560, fax 385 8531, *litcnz@voyager.co.nz*). This rambling but central 1950s building – a recent conversion from student lodgings – is gradually being revamped with enthusiasm. Cyber café, Sky TV, bar, free shuttle to the ferry, bus and train are all available, plus a roof garden with great views over the city and a glimpse of the harbour. Dorms ①, rooms ③, self-contained units ④–⑤.

Trekkers, 213 Cuba St (☎04/385 2153, fax 382 8873, *info@trekkers.co.nz*). Another central backpackers but warrenlike and getting rather run-down; also a hotel and budget motel. Backpacker rooms have thin mattresses (basic singles, 2-bed bunkrooms and slightly shabby doubles with handbasins) and share bathrooms; linen costs an extra $3. The complex has a grim kitchen, but free off-street parking, café, bar and a travel centre. 2-bed dorms ①, rooms ③.

Wellington City YHA, 292 Wakefield St, cnr Cambridge Terrace (☎04/801 7280, fax 801 7278, *yhawgtn@yha.org.nz*). The best hostel in town and hugely popular. It's big, modern and fairly luxurious, right in the heart of the city, with great harbour views from the top-floor rooms. Most rooms are en suite (singles, doubles, and 4- or 6-bed dorms). To get a dorm bed or double in summer, you'll need to book at least a week in advance. New World supermarket opposite; bike storage; car park nearby on Wakefield St; travel desk for all bookings. YHA members only on public holiday weekends. Dorms ①, rooms ③.

Wide World, 291 The Terrace (☎0508/888 555, fax 802 5590, *wide.world@paradise.net.nz*). Bright and cheerful hostel in an attractive house with singles, doubles and twins (and dorms planned at the time of writing), and a free public phone for local calls. Prices include breakfast and a complimentary glass of wine in the evening. Dorms ①, rooms ③.

The City

Wellington's **city centre** is compact and easy to cover on foot, with most of the major attractions within a two-kilometre radius. The heart of the city stretches from the train station in the north to Cambridge and Kent Terraces at the eastern end of Courtenay Place, taking in the waterfront along the way, while the central business district runs along The Terrace and Lambton Quay; the latter is also the principal shopping thoroughfare. The main districts for eating, drinking and **entertainment** are Courtenay Place, Cuba Street, Willis Street, and down to the waterfront at Queens Wharf. Cuba Street is also the "alternative" **shopping** district with secondhand bookshops, record stores, retro clothes retailers and quirky cafés.

Meanwhile, the main **sights** are concentrated in four distinct areas: around Civic Square and the waterfront, the Botanic Gardens, the Parliamentary District, and the historic suburb of Thorndon. The nearest **beach** to the city centre is Oriental Bay, skirted by an elegant **esplanade**, Oriental Parade, which is a favourite spot for jogging, walking, swimming, or simply admiring the view of the city and harbour, especially at night. On the hills enclosing the city centre is the **Town Belt** – originally set aside in 1839 by the New Zealand Company for aesthetic and recreational purposes, it contains several good walks and many of the city's best **lookout** points.

Civic Square and the waterfront

The thoroughly modern **Civic Square**, behind the visitor centre, is a good place to start your sightseeing before making the short walk to the waterfront and Wellington's star attraction, the Museum of New Zealand (*Te Papa Tongarewa*). A popular venue for outdoor events, Civic Square was revamped in the early 1990s by Wellington architect Ian Athfield (see p.442) and is full of interesting sculptures, with a couple of buildings worth a quick visit.

Just around the corner from the visitor centre and flanked by striking metal nikau palms is the big and refreshingly bold **Wellington Public Library** (Mon–Thurs

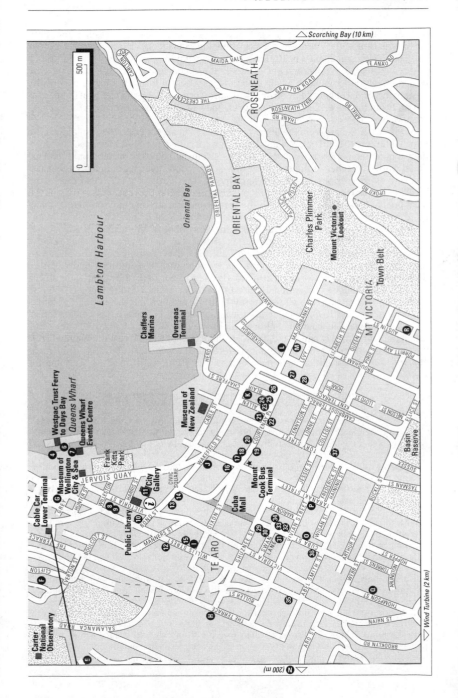

9.30am–8.30pm, Fri 9.30am–9pm, Sat 9.30am–5pm, Sun 1–4pm), accessible from both Civic Square and the main entrance around the corner on Victoria Street. Another Athfield design and opened in 1991, it's a far cry from the fustiness of most libraries – a spacious high-tech environment of steel, stone and timber. Instead of being concealed, inner workings such as air ducts are exposed to form an integral part of the design, the whole enhanced by strong sculptural forms, colour and plenty of light flooding in. From the upper floor, you get a great view of Civic Square through the curving glass wall.

Across Civic Square from the library and housed in an Art Deco 1939 building is the **City Gallery** (☎04/801 3952; daily 10am–5pm; free, except $8–15 for special exhibitions), a contemporary art gallery that hosts touring shows of national and international works. Attached is the stylish *Nikau Gallery Café*, opening onto an outdoor terrace and offering drinks, snacks and light meals (see "Eating", p.452). Also here is the small arthouse **City Cinema** (details of screenings from the visitor centre or in the local press). Linking the square with the waterfront is a striking modern **bridge** decorated with timber sculptures of birds, whales and celestial motifs. The work of Maori artist Para Matchitt, completed in 1993, these symbolize the arrival of Maori and European settlers and, by extension, that of present-day visitors from the sea to city.

About 500 metres east of the bridge, on Cable Street, is the monolith of the **Museum of New Zealand** or *Te Papa Tongarewa* (*www.tepapa.govt.nz*; daily 10am–6pm & Thurs till 9pm; free entry; map $1; rides $6–7.50; parking $2 per hr), Wellington's star attraction and the country's first national museum. A major project (to the tune of $350 million) occupying a purpose-built five-storey building right on the waterfront, the museum opened in early 1998. You'll need at least half a day to explore this celebration of New Zealand's people, land and cultures, all brought to life with ambitious state-of-the-art technology aimed at adults and children alike. You may find it easiest to spread your visit over two days to avoid information overload. It's well worth buying the *Te Papa Explorer* guide ($2), outlining routes such as "Te Papa in a Hurry" or "Te Papa for

---

THE ARCHITECTURE OF IAN ATHFIELD

The work of New Zealand's most influential and versatile living architect, **Ian Athfield**, generates the kind of love-hate reaction usually associated with the Lloyd's Building in London and the Pompidou Centre in Paris. His principal motif is the juxtaposition of old and new, regular and irregular, as seen in the facade of the **Palmerston North Public Library** (see p.258). However, many of the finest examples of Athfield's work are in his home town of Wellington, where the facade of the **Moore Wilson Building** from 1984 (a food warehouse at the corner of College and Tory streets), explores fractures, while the **Oriental Parade Apartments**, built in 1988 near the start of the Southern Walkway on Oriental Parade (see p.446), have an almost Egyptian facade. Athfield also likes artwork to appear as part of his buildings, as demonstrated by the sculptural forms of the **Wellington Public Library** (see p.439). Perhaps the best example of his work is **Logan House** at Windy Point in Eastbourne, across the bay from Wellington (see p.451), where he has cleverly combined an old structure with a new one, making full use of the natural surroundings and revitalizing a disused building. However, many people's favourite Athfield building is a house-cum-office on a hillside in the northern suburb of **Khandallah** (at 105 Amritsar St; closed to the public). Visible from the Wellington motorway and – at some distance – from the ferry to Days Bay, it seems to grow organically down the hill, showing a respect for the environment and a willingness to engage with it that's often lacking in New Zealand architecture. In contrast, the house adjoining the **Te Mata Winery** in Havelock North (see p.417) is a sly backhanded tribute to the modernists of the 1930s and an expression of the architect's humour, though it still manages to look perfectly placed in its surroundings.

Kids", and others that focus on nature, Maori culture, history or art. If time is limited gain an overview by joining the 45-minute guided tours (daily 10.15am, $9) or phone ahead to arrange one at a time to suit you. During school holidays you're wise to arrive early and buy tickets in advance for the main rides, which run every 15 minutes or so throughout the day. The best are based in the Time Warp zone on Level 2 where computer wizardry will jolt you forwards to Wellington 2055 ("Future Rush") or back to a prehistoric New Zealand to witness the extraordinary formation of the land ("Blastback"). Other Level 2 highlights are an interactive section on earthquakes and volcanoes, where you can experience a mild quake in a house, watch Mount Ruapehu erupt on screen and hear the Maori explanation of the causes of such activity; and an interesting "X-Ray Room" housing the skeletons of great sea creatures such as whales, dolphins and seals. Level 4 is home to an excellent Maori section including a thought-provoking display on the Treaty of Waitangi dominated by a giant replica of this significant document (see Contexts, p.848). On the same floor there's also an active marae with a modern meeting house painted in rainbow colours mirrored by a stunning stained-glass window and protected by a sacred boulder of *pounamu* (greenstone). Note that you cannot enter the meeting house unless invited. The rest of the museum contains extensive exhibitions on art, heritage, navigation and Maori history. This is also the home of one of New Zealand's top restaurants, the *Icon* (see p.454) and the museum also has two simpler cafés.

In the opposite direction and on the waterfront north of the visitor centre sits the **Museum of Wellington City and Sea** on Queens Wharf, beside Jervois Quay (daily: Nov–March 9.30am–6pm; rest of year 9.30am–5.30pm; $5), which unfolds the social and maritime history of Wellington. Occupying a former bond store (customs house), display highlights inside this fine stone building of 1892 include a unique tall cinema screen featuring one of four short films every 30 minutes. In addition are a 12-minute special effects show telling Maori creation legends and a gripping 12-minute film commemorating Wellington's worst disaster to date: the sinking of the inter-island ferry, *T.E. Wahine*, in April 1968, with the loss of 51 lives. Returning from Lyttelton with 734 people on board, the ferry entered the harbour just as one of the most violent storms ever recorded in New Zealand struck up. Rescue attempts were repeatedly thwarted until, finally, the weather calmed enough for passengers to start abandoning ship, only to find there were insufficient lifeboats; imagine the desperation that ensued.

While at **Queens Wharf**, take a few moments to soak up the atmosphere. Bustling and modernized, this T-shaped wharf dating from 1862 is a popular spot for a drink or a bite to eat (see "Eating", p.452) and has a large state-of-the-art Events Centre that functions as a sports stadium and a venue for bands. Past the Events Centre and on the left is **Shed 5**, the oldest building on the waterfront (1886) and, along with **Dockside** next door, one of the last two remaining timber warehouses. In the 1990s they were both sympathetically converted into trendy restaurant bars, quickly becoming two of the most popular watering holes in the city. Also at Queens Wharf is a hugely popular **climbing wall** at Ferg's Rock & Kayak opposite Shed 5 (Mon–Fri 10am–10pm, Sat & Sun 9am–10pm). It's worth popping in to watch the activity and if it inspires you to have a go you're best off either in a pair or group of three so you can relay ($7 per person for 1hr including introductory lesson; equipment and shoes $4). The centre also hires out **rollerblades** (from $7 per half day including pads) for use at nearby Kitts Park and all manner of **kayaks** (see p.451) for paddling on the harbour.

The Botanic Gardens, Cable Car and the Carter Observatory

Wellington's **Botanic Gardens** (daily dawn–dusk; free) form a huge swathe of green on peaceful rolling hills high above the city and make for a pleasant hour or two's distraction, containing an observatory, a gorgeous rose garden, a begonia house and an atmospheric Victorian cemetery (pick up the useful free leaflet and map of the gardens from Wellington visitor centre). There are main entrances on Glenmore Street and Upland Road, but the best way to get there is via the short yet scenic **cable-car** ride to Kelburn. The cable car departs every ten minutes from Cable Car Lane, just off Lambton Quay (Mon–Fri 7am–10pm, Sat & Sun 9am–10pm; $1.50 one way, $2.50 return), climbing an extremely steep incline, making four stops on the way and giving great views over the city and harbour. Operational since 1902, the cable cars were originally driven by steam but succumbed to electricity in 1933; in 1978 the current Swiss system was installed, whereby two shiny red, modern cars, each at either end of a single rope, are propelled by an electric motor at the top station. There's a **lookout** at the top, just inside the Botanic Gardens, offering spectacular views over the city, brought into focus by coin-operated binoculars. At the terminus itself is a small building that, at the time of writing, was to become a museum recording the cable car's history. On the other side of the track, the licensed **Skyline Café** (daily 10am–4pm; see "Eating", p.452) is a great spot to sit with a drink, enjoying views of the city through panoramic windows, or, when the wind abates, from an outside balcony.

Once inside the Botanic Gardens, several paths lead back down to the city, meandering through stands of pohutukawa, remnants of dense native forest and ornamental flower beds. It's a two-minute walk from the Kelburn terminus to the 1941 **Carter National Observatory**(Mon–Fri 10am–4pm, Sat & Sun noon–5pm; free) where during the day you can check out the astronomy displays, computers and telescope; and take in a planetarium show (Mon–Fri noon; Sat & Sun continuous; $7). Three nights a week you can also view the southern skies: the programme includes a thirty-minute planetarium show, audiovisual presentations, a short talk on astronomy, and, weather permitting, telescope viewing (phone ahead for details ☎04/472 8167; Tues, Thurs & Sat from 6.30pm; planetarium show at 6.40pm & second show later in evening; $10). Within sight of the Carter Observatory is the recently renovated 1912 **Thomas King Observatory**, which still contains its original instruments. One of the first observatories in the Wellington area, it played a vital role in navigation and time-keeping.

The *tour de force* of the gardens and their most visited section is the **Lady Norwood Rose Garden**, on flat ground at the city end, near the Centennial Entrance on Glenmore Street, and also accessible by car or buses #12, 13 or 21 (Mon–Fri only). The fragrant garden blooms throughout the summer, with 300 varieties of roses laid out in a formal wheel shape around a fountain and the whole enclosed by a colonnade of climbing roses. Adjacent is the large **Begonia House** (daily: Oct–March 10am–5pm; April–Sept 10am–4pm; free), which is divided into two areas: the tropical, with an attractive lily pond and a small cage containing carnivorous plants; and the temperate, which has seasonal displays of begonias and gloxinias in summer, changing to cyclamen, orchids and impatiens in winter. Further down from the rose garden, a striking memorial to New Zealand's most lauded politician, Richard Seddon, marks the entrance to **Bolton Street Memorial Park**, an attractive Victorian **cemetery** where many of the city's early pioneers are buried. Old-fashioned roses clamber over the ageing headstones and twist through ironwork in the shade of mature trees. Established in 1840 as three separate cemeteries (Anglican, Jewish and public), in 1892 the cemetery was closed to all except new burials in existing plots. In the 1960s, amid public outcry, it was abandoned altogether, and over 3500 bodies were exhumed and relocated to make way for the motorway that now bisects it.

From Robertson Way, the main pathway through the memorial park, a footbridge crosses the motorway. It leads to the smaller half of the cemetery, which contains a small chapel (daily 10am–4pm) with a few displays, and comes to an abrupt end where the high-rise buildings of The Terrace back onto it. It's a short walk from here to the Parliamentary District.

The Parliamentary District

On the way north to the Parliamentary District, you'll pass the imposing redbrick Art Deco edifice housing **Wellington Railway Station** (1937), worth a quick look for its sheer scale. Stepping through the unashamedly self-important entrance, framed by two towering stone pillars, you'll find a magnificent marble entry hall, its spectacularly vaulted ceiling decorated with ornate plasterwork.

Beyond, in the Parliamentary District proper, is Wellington's architectural masterpiece, the **Old Government Buildings** (Mon–Fri 9am–4.30pm, Sat & Sun 10am–3pm; free), at the corner of Lambton Quay and Whitmore Street. At first glance an opulent Italian Renaissance construction of cream stone, it is, in fact, built from wood, its entrances decorated with grand columns and porticoes. Designed by Colonial Architect William Clayton (1823–77) to mark the country's transition from provincial to centralized government, it was the largest building in New Zealand when completed in November 1876, and it remains the second-largest timber building in the world. Built on a small block of reclaimed land, it was physically isolated from the rest of the city and dominated Lambton Harbour. This grandiose building housed government ministers and most of the Wellington-based public service for many years, and Cabinet regularly met in the room immediately above the main entrance from 1876 to 1921. As departments grew, they moved to other buildings and by 1975 only the Education Department remained. Fully restored, it is now the home of Victoria University's Law Faculty. At the entrance is a visitor centre, managed by the DOC, which provides maps for a free self-guided tour through part of the building, including the Cabinet Room with its great view of the Beehive (see below). Compared to the exterior, you'll find the interior quite a restrained affair of honey-coloured kauri panelling, except for two carved rimu staircases that are among the finest in the country. Downstairs are photographic displays of the building's construction and mid-1990s restoration, while in the hallway you'll find commemorations for staff of note.

Visible across Lambton Quay are the **Parliament Buildings** in use today, a complex of three highly individual structures: the unmistakable **Beehive** (often confused with Parliament House itself, but in fact the executive wing, where ministers and civil servants huddle), the Edwardian Neoclassical **Parliament House**, and the Victorian Gothic **Parliamentary Library**. You can visit all three on a free **guided tour** (departing on the hour: Mon–Fri 10am–4pm, Sat 10am–3pm, Sun 1–3pm; 45min) from the visitor centre in the ground-floor foyer of Parliament House, parliamentary meetings and functions permitting (call ☎04/471 9999 to check). The highly informative and anecdotal tour begins with a short video on the extensive and detailed restoration work that was carried out after a fire in 1992, which began in the library and swept through parts of Parliament House. Incorporated into the restoration is some pretty impressive anti-earthquake work (Parliament House stands a mere 400m from a faultline), which puts it at the cutting edge of earthquake technology. The remainder of the tour highlights some exquisite architecture and a few surprisingly modern areas and artworks juxtaposed with the old, before you enter the library. The latter was built in 1899 by Thomas Turnbull, who was famous for designing churches and endowed the library with a strong Victorian Gothic, ecclesiastical feel. A striking contrast to such European style is found in the **Maori Affairs Select Committee Room** at the front of the building – included in the tour if a committee is not sitting. It's remarkably decorated with specially commissioned carvings and *tukutuku* (woven panels) in the different styles of all the *iwi* (tribes) of New Zealand.

When Parliament is not in session (☎04/471 9999, *www.parliament.govt.nz*), tours continue into the comfortable-looking Debating Chamber itself, where the first MPs elected by New Zealand's system of proportional representation took their seats on the inauspicious date of Friday, December 13, 1996. On the other side of Parliament House, you briefly enter the foyer of the modernist **Beehive**, designed by British architect Sir Basil Spence, which was started in 1969 and completed in 1982. The story goes that

Spence designed this curiosity on a napkin after dinner, having been inspired by the label on a box of matches. The building is apparently impractical and hell to work in. Opposite the Parliament Buildings, on Molesworth Street, is the 1893 **Backbencher Pub**, where MPs go to relax, and worth popping into to admire the decor, sporting satirical cartoons and puppets of various Kiwi politicians.

The National Library and Archives

In the next block north from the pub along Molesworth Street is the **National Library of New Zealand** (*Te Puna Matauranga o Aotearoa*), on the corner with Aitken Street (Mon–Fri 9am–5pm, Sat 9am–1pm; free), the most comprehensive research library in New Zealand and home of the **Alexander Turnbull Library**, a vast collection of volumes, documents, paintings and so on, mostly relating to New Zealand and the Pacific, which was assembled by a wealthy Wellington merchant and gifted to the Crown in

---

WALKS AROUND WELLINGTON

There are several worthwhile walks around Wellington, the most popular being the **Red Rocks Coastal Walk**, beginning about 7km south of the city centre and tracing a shoreline reserve to an unusual volcanic rock formation. Other, **longer tracks** pass through sections of the **Town Belt**. The best of these, and the easiest to reach from the city centre, are the **Southern and Northern Walkways**, which are described in leaflets from the visitor centre, each with a helpful map. The Town Belt also contains numerous **lesser tracks**, but their layout is confusing, so don't attempt them without a map.

Well worth a visit for its several short bush walks and variety of Kiwi plantlife is the **Otari Native Botanic Garden** (or "Otari-Wilton's Bush"), on steep slopes dissected by the deep Kaiwharawhara streambed. The reserve lies 6km northwest of the city centre, and is best visited on a calm day, since the prevailing northwesterlies can gust to over 96km per hour in exposed places.

RED ROCKS COASTAL WALK

The easy **Red Rocks Coastal Walk** (4km each way; 2–3hr return) follows a rough track along the coastline from Owhiro Bay to Sinclair Head, passing a quarry and the eponymous **Red Rocks** – well-preserved volcanic pillow lava, formed about 200 million years ago by underwater volcanic eruptions and coloured red by iron oxide. Maori variously attribute the colour to bloodstains from Maui's nose or blood dripping from a paua-shell cut on Kupe's hand, while another account tells how Kupe's daughters cut themselves in mourning, having given up their father for dead. From May to October Sinclair Head is visited by an established colony of New Zealand **fur seals**.

The track **starts** at the **quarry gates** at the western end of Ohiro Bay Parade, where there's a car park. To get there by **bus** you have several options: from the central city take the frequent #1 to Island Bay (daily), get off at The Parade at the corner of Reef Street and walk 2.5km to the start of the walk; at peak times, catch #4 instead, which continues to Happy Valley, only 1km from the track. Otherwise, take a #1 or #4 to Wellington Hospital, at the intersection of Adelaide Road and John Street, and change to the #29 (Mon–Sat), getting off at Happy Valley, again about 1km from the start of the track.

THE SOUTHERN WALKWAY

The **Southern Walkway** (11km; 4–5hr, or as shorter segments) cuts through the Town Belt to the south of the city centre, between Oriental and Island bays, and is fairly easy going overall, despite a few steep stretches. The walk offers plenty of **variety**, yielding excellent views of the harbour and central city, shade and tranquillity in the Town Belt forest, and exposed coastline between Houghton and Island bays. Much of the walkway is **shaded**, richly scented by exotic trees, and covered with pine needles; among the birds you might

1918. The ground-floor area has a range of reference books that you can take into a reading room, but the rest of the books are off-limits to the public. Also worth checking out is the library's large **gallery** (Mon–Fri 9am–5pm, Sat 9am–4.30pm, Sun 1–4pm), which regularly hosts free exhibitions, lectures and events (listed in Wednesday's *Evening Post* and Friday's *Dominion*).

Opposite the library is the pink concrete monstrosity of **St Paul's Cathedral**, a curious mix of Byzantine and Santa Fe styles, designed in the 1930s and 40s by Cecil Wood of Christchurch, a renowned ecclesiastical architect. Queen Elizabeth II laid the foundation stone in 1954 but the cathedral was not completed until 1998, replacing Old St Paul's, one street away. The interior is cavernous and you can't escape the powder pink or the concrete, but there are some interesting modern stained-glass windows, and a distinctive organ that was built in London and first installed in Old St Paul's.

encounter are fantails, grey warblers and wax-eyes. Highlights include the **sweeping views** from the lookout at the Mount Victoria summit (196m) and from Mount Albert (178m), the rugged coastline of Houghton Bay, and the safe and popular **beach** at Island Bay.

The walk can be undertaken in either direction and is clearly marked by posts bearing orange arrows. To **start** at the city end, take the #14 Kilbirnie (via Roseneath) **bus** to Oriental Parade (near Ian Athfield's Egyptian-style Oriental Apartments); the walkway entrance is signposted near the *Hotel Raffaele*, at no. 360. To begin at the other end, take the #1 bus to Island Bay and follow the signs from nearby Shorland Park.

THE NORTHERN WALKWAY

Extending through tranquil sections of the Town Belt to the north of the city centre, the **Northern Walkway** (16km; 4hr, or tackled in sections) offers spectacular views. Stretching from Kelburn to Johnsonville, it covers five distinct areas (Botanic Garden, Tinakori Hill, Trelissick Park, Khandallah Park and Johnsonville Park), which can be accessed from various suburban streets and are served by public transport. Highlights are the **birdlife** on Tinakori Hill (tui, fantails, kingfishers, grey warblers, silver-eyes); regenerating native forest in **Ngaio Gorge** in Trelissick Park; great views across the city and the harbour and over to the Rimutaka and Tararua ranges from a lookout on **Mount Kaukau** (430m); and, in Johnsonville Park, a disused tunnel hewn through solid rock.

From the city end, the track **starts** at the Botanic Garden lookout at the top of the **cable-car** terminus, or you can begin instead at the Tinakori Hill section by climbing St Mary Street, off Glenmore Street, and following the orange arrows through woodland. Starting at the far end means taking a **train** to Raroa station (Mon–Sat), or a #49 Johnsonville **bus** (Sun only)

OTARI NATIVE BOTANIC GARDEN

The **Otari Native Botanic Garden** (daily dawn till dusk; free) offers 80 hectares of mature and regenerating native bush. It's best approached via the main entrance, junction of Wilton Road and Gloucester Street, where you'll find a map of the walks and an unmanned visitor centre (daily 9am–5pm) with simple displays. From here a 100m "Canopy Walk" of sturdy decking high in the trees crosses the streambed far below. The **Nature Trail** (30min) is a good introduction to the New Zealand forest and its many plants; the track is steep in places and has many steps. The **Circular Walk** (30min) follows the Kaiwharawhara Stream through plant collections, native forest, lawn areas and a picnic site. Three other bush trails push further afield (2 at 40min; 1 at 1hr). The streamside picnic site (with coin-operated BBQs; $0.50) is ten-minutes' walk from the main entrance. To reach the reserve by bus take #14; by car follow Molesworth Street north from the centre, which becomes Wadestown Road and then Blackbridge. At the junction with Churchill Drive turn left and continue till it becomes Wilton Road, off which is the main entrance.

A stone's throw away, at the junction of Aitken Street and Mulgrave Street, are the **National Archives** (Mon–Fri 9am–5pm, Sat 9am–1pm; free), which exhibit a number of important documents relating to New Zealand's social and constitutional development. On permanent display and sealed into an environmentally controlled display case in the centre of the **Constitution Room** (really a vault) is the original **Treaty of Waitangi** (see Contexts, p.848), which barely survived a long spell lost in the bowels of the Old Government Buildings, suffering water damage and the gnawings of rodents before it was rescued in 1908. Other archives on display in the room highlight important milestones on the country's road to independent nationhood. There's a facsimile of an extensive petition for **women's suffrage**, a significant contribution on the way to New Zealand becoming the first country to enfranchise women (look for Kate Sheppard's signature), and **Maori petitions** dating back to 1909, which complain of broken treaty promises. Outside the Constitution Room is a small container of water, to help Maori neutralize *tapu* (ill-effects caused by a taboo action or object) after viewing the treaty. Mounted on a wall nearby is an enlarged copy of the treaty and a map, showing who signed where; the great Maori chief Te Rauparaha signed it twice, in two different locations, each time receiving muskets and blankets. Other galleries display some great Maori carvings and *tukutuku* (woven leather and flax panels), alongside rotating exhibitions of works by well-known Kiwi artists and of material relating to New Zealand history.

Thorndon

From 1866 to 1964, the modest-looking **Old St Paul's**, at the corner of Mulgrave Street and Pipitea Street (Mon–Sat 10am–5pm; free), was the parish church of **THORNDON**. The church's stunning wooden interior was crafted in early English Gothic style (more commonly seen in stone), the native timbers having since darkened with age to a rich mellow hue. The serried ranks of arches, the pews, pulpit and choral area are all highlighted by fabulous stained-glass windows and the sheen of polished brass plaques on the walls. Consecrated in 1866, the church was the major work of an English ecclesiastical architect, Reverend Frederick Thatcher, who designed it for Bishop Selwyn and was vicar here for a few years.

Head north for about ten minutes, crossing the bridge over the motorway into Thorndon, Wellington's oldest suburb, and you'll reach the **Katherine Mansfield Birthplace**, 25 Tinakori Rd (daily 10am–4pm; $4). A modest wooden house with a small garden, this was the first childhood home of New Zealand's most famous short-story writer and is described in some of her works, notably "Prelude" and "A Birthday". Stuffed with antiques and ornaments, the house has a cluttered Victorian charm and unusual decor, which was avant-garde for its time, inspired by Japonisme and the Aesthetic Movement. This has been beautifully restored and the walls are bright with colour and reprints of original wallpapers. In the kitchen is a doll's house, reproduced from the story of the same name, while an upstairs room is set aside to recount a history of the author's life and career, with some black-and-white photos of Wellington and the people that shaped her life, and an excellent 45-minute video, *A Woman and a Writer*. Born Kathleen Mansfield Beauchamp in 1888, the writer lived here for five years with her parents, three sisters and beloved grandmother before they moved to a much grander house in what is now the western suburb of Karori. At 19, Katherine left Wellington for Europe, where she spent the rest of her short life, before dying of tuberculosis in France in 1923.

Mount Victoria Lookout and southwest to Brooklyn Hill

To the east of the city centre, the **Mount Victoria Lookout** (196m) is one of the best of Wellington's lookout points, offering sweeping panoramic views, day or night. You can

Gannet colony, Cape Kidnappers

Vineyards, Marlborough

Beehive and Parliament House, Wellington

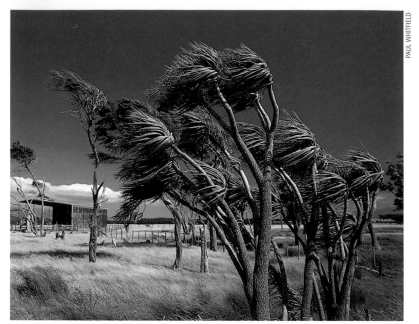

PAUL WHITFIELD

Cabbage trees, Wairarapa

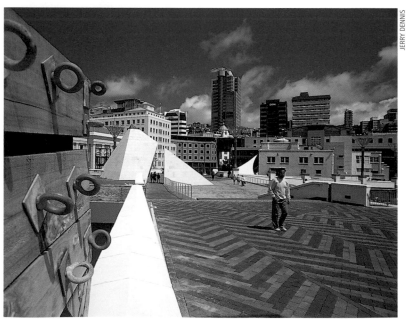

JERRY DENNIS

Civic Centre complex, Wellington

Rothmans Building, Napier

Lake Rotoiti

Yellow-eyed penguin

PAUL WHITFIELD

Moeraki Boulders, Oamaru

JERRY DENNIS

FOOTPRINTS

St Michael's Church, Christchurch

Canterbury Plains, seen from a balloon

get there by car, by bus (#20; Mon–Fri) or on foot as part of the Southern Walkway (see p.446). If you're driving, follow Hawker Street, off Majoribanks Street, then take Palliser Road, which twists uphill through Charles Plimmer Park; on the other side, turn into Thane Road, which snakes up to the lookout. Next to the car park at the top is the **Byrd Memorial**, a triangular construction faced with multicoloured tiles and intended to simulate an Antarctic expedition tent, with the Southern Lights playing across it. The memorial honours the American aviator and Antarctic explorer Richard E. Byrd (1888–1957), who mapped large areas of the Antarctic and was the first man to fly over the South Pole, using New Zealand as a base for his expeditions. From the memorial, there's an impressive view of the city waterfront, the docks and the airport. Up a short flight of steps is the lookout proper, giving magnificent 360-degree views of the surrounding hills, the city and its suburbs, the harbour, Hutt Valley and eastern harbour bays.

You can get another fantastic all-round view of the Wellington region from the further-flung **wind turbine** crowning **Brooklyn Hill** in the southwestern part of the city. The turbine, a sort of giant plane propeller loudly whirring atop a mighty tower (31.5m), has generated power for Wellington since 1993, at its maximum capacity supplying over a hundred homes. On a clear day you can see as far as the Kaikoura Ranges on the South Island. To reach the turbine by car, take Brooklyn Road from the end of Victoria Street, turn left at Ohiro Road, then right at the shopping centre up Todman Street and follow the signposts (the road up to the turbine closes at 8pm Oct–April and at 5pm May–Sept). Bus #7 (daily) drops you within walking distance.

Wellington Harbour

The sight of multicoloured sails scudding across the water should be enough to convince you that it's impossible to come to Wellington and ignore the lure of the water. On top of that, **Wellington Harbour** and its reliable winds offer excellent sailing experiences. Take your pick between a harbour cruise, a thrilling hands-on **sailing** trip, **kayaking**, and **windsurfing**.

If you prefer to have a destination in mind, you can take a ferry to **Somes Island**, a hilly little knoll stranded in the northeastern waters of the harbour. Steeped in history and abounding in wildlife, the island enjoys panoramic views across the harbour. You can combine a day-trip here with a stint at the city's favourite beach of **Days Bay**, one of several **beaches** around the harbour that Wellingtonians flock to in good weather. For visitors there's really more fun to be had out on the water or exploring the city, but if you must hit the beach try **Scorching Bay**, a crescent of white sand 13km east of the city centre on the main coastal road, which has safe swimming and a play area. At peak times you can take bus #30 all the way there; otherwise, catch bus #11 to Seatoun (daily) and change onto the #26 (Mon–Fri) or #30 (peak times).

Exploring the harbour

Aimed at novice and experienced sailors alike are the **harbour cruises** run by Mountain Marine (☎04/586 0699; Nov–April daily; rest of year by arrangement). Groups of five to eight are taken out on an 8.5-metre yacht for a short cruise (3hr; $35) or a day-trip (7hr; $70, including lunch); you can either lend a hand or just sit back, and wet-weather gear and lifejackets are supplied. An awe-inspiring way to cruise the harbour, but harder on the pocket, is on board the former Whitbread Round-the-World yacht, the 24-metre *Phantom of the Straits* (hotline tells you where it's sailing during your stay ☎04/477 3503; bookings ☎04/499 4410, fax 477 0242, *phantom@sailnz.co.nz*), better known for its adventure trips across Cook Strait to the Marlborough Sounds (see box overleaf), which casts off from Queens Wharf. Tamer options, for which you need

---

CROSSING COOK STRAIT

From Wellington, planes, ferries and the fast *Lynx* wave-piercer and *Topcat* catamarans cross **Cook Strait**, linking the **North and South islands**; the most exciting way to make the crossing, though, is on a sailing trip.

FERRIES

Ferry and catamaran services to Picton depart from Wellington's **Interisland Ferry Terminal** (☎0800/802 802), except for the *Topcat* fast ferry, which leaves from Waterloo Quay (☎0800/486 7228); a complimentary shuttle-bus service runs from the train station 45 minutes before each scheduled sailing. The standard **ferries** (daily year-round; 3hr) have a basic one-way fare of $46, but this can be reduced by as much as half if you book in advance or take a night or early morning crossing (but saver fares sell out fast so book as far ahead as possible) and there are special rates for day excursions; add $10 each way for a bike or surfboard, $46 for a motorbike, and $165 for a car or campervan. The *Lynx* **wave-piercer** (Dec–April only) costs $59 each way (plus $12 for bikes, $190 for cars and campervans), less in advance or in conjunction with special offers (the cheapest offer is $30 one way), but be warned that crossings tend to get cancelled in rough weather. The *Topcat* (3 daily mid-Nov to end May, 2 daily rest of year; 1hr 40min) is the latest addition to the fleet, a huge comfortable catamaran giving a smooth ride with great views from the Sky Lounge, charging $59 for a standard one-way ticket, plus $12 for a bike, $15 for surfboard or kayak, $59 for a motorbike, and $190 for a car or campervan.

FLIGHTS

Soundsair Shuttle (☎04/801 0111) **fly** daily to Picton (20min; $50 one way, $95 return), and twice daily between Paraparaumu on the Kapiti Coast (see p.463) and Picton ($59 one way, $110 return).

SAILING

If you can afford it, the most thrilling way to cross Cook Strait is aboard the majestic 24-metre *Phantom of the Straits* on the **Cook Strait Challenge** (mid-Nov to late April; book as far ahead as possible, ☎04/499 4410, fax 477 0242; a hotline tells you the boat's activities during your stay ☎04/477 3503; *phantom@sailnz.co.nz*), a full day of action, activity and fun on an ex-Whitbread round-the-world racing yacht. As well as a leisurely cruise through the gorgeous waterways of the Marlborough Sounds, chances are that you'll glimpse dolphins, seals, and maybe even whales. As a member of the "guest crew" (20 maximum), you get to participate in the actual sailing, under the expert guidance of the permanent crew. The **crossing** can be undertaken in either direction (7hr between Wellington and Picton, allowing for stopoffs; $195), or as a more energetic **round trip** (11hr, with stopoffs but venturing a shorter distance into the Sounds; $225); a sail-out, fly-back option is also available (6hr; $550). All gear, meals and drinks are included, luggage is carried for free and you can arrange to stay on board the night before a crossing.

---

no previous experience, include a jaunt around the inner harbour (7.45am & 5.45pm; 1hr 30min; $45 including breakfast or a lager and nibbles), a breakfast cruise (7.30am; 2hr; $65), a lunch cruise (noon; 2hr; $70), a twilight supper cruise (6.30pm; 3hr; $75) and a Harbour 'n' Heads cruise (5hr; $145). The food and drink are great, as are the views, and you'll feel spoilt rotten; you'll need to book ahead for any of these trips, even though they take up to forty people at a time.

Windsurfing is huge here and a popular spot is Kio Bay, to the east of Oriental Bay and around the point towards Evans Bay (bus #24, Mon–Fri). Near the bus stop is good wave-jumping water. For lessons, try Wildwinds Sail & Surf back at the overseas terminal, off Oriental Parade and beside Chaffers Marina (☎04/384 1010; 2hr; $60 including gear). You can also explore the harbour by **kayak** from Ferg's Rock 'n' Kayak, Shed 6, Queens Wharf (☎04/499 8898; sit-on-top kayaks $5 per 30min; single kayaks $7 per 30min, $40 per day; double kayaks $20 per hr, $80 per day; $50 bond per kayak), who let you loose without a guide as long as there are two or more people and also run guided trips in double kayaks on calm nights, for a minimum of four people (3hr 30min; $35).

Somes Island and Days Bay

Once a focal point for Maori canoes navigating their way out into the Pacific, **Somes Island** has long held spiritual significance to Maori. Kupe is said to have named it Matiu, meaning "peace", when he sailed into the harbour in the tenth century. The first **Maori** to arrive in the Wellington area settled the island and their descendants lived here until the 1830s. Later, European settlers renamed the island after **Joseph Somes**, then deputy governor of the New Zealand Company which "bought" it. For eighty years it was a **quarantine station** for animals, and until the 1920s travellers suspected of carrying diseases such as smallpox were also quarantined here; subsequently, German, Italian, Turkish, Mexican and Japanese **prisoners of war** were kept in camps on the island during both world wars.

Now managed by the DOC, the island is open to the public (daily 8.30am–5pm; free) and permanently staffed by a DOC officer, but your best bet for further information is the city's DOC office in Government Buildings (☎04/472 7356). Work has recently started in earnest to revitalize native vegetation and plans are afoot to restore several historic buildings. Currently, the island is home to sheep, three species of lizard, a breeding colony of about a thousand black-backed **gulls** and several hundred little blue **penguins**, and **seals** are gradually drifting back to its shores. In 1998 about fifty **tuatara** (New Zealand's small, unique reptile-like creatures with an ancient ancestry) were released, the majority hatched at Victoria University in Wellington.

A number of **Westpac Trust Ferry** sailings to Days Bay (see below) stop here (Mon–Fri 1 daily at noon; Sat & Sun 3 daily) enabling you to explore the island for a couple of hours or so before catching a later ferry on to Days Bay. A popular option is to take a picnic lunch onto the island. Note that this a protected reserve, so smoking is not allowed. From the wharf at the island's northeastern end, a 500-metre sealed road runs uphill to the **DOC field centre**, in an old hospital, which has maps of the island but you're better off picking one up in advance from the city DOC office.

Days Bay

There's not much at **Days Bay** except for the beach (at the foot of sheer bush-covered hills), a single main road lined with a few holiday homes, a park, and a popular café; and a remarkable house designed by Ian Athfield, visible from the harbour as you approach. The cliffside **Logan House** at Windy Point, 500m from the Days Bay wharf, is best viewed from the main road, which runs in front of it. It was built around and within two big old stone chimneys, whose thick walls were punctured by arrow-slit windows, like medieval towers. Athfield then designed the rest of the house to link with not only the chimneys but also the cliff-face directly behind them, so that the new structure fully interacts with its natural surroundings.

A stone's throw from the wharf, on the main road, is *Cobar*, a large glass-fronted bar, restaurant and **café** looking out onto the bay and serving international cuisine and weekend brunches (see "Eating", overleaf). From the Days Bay Boatshed beside the wharf (☎04/562 8150; Boxing Day to mid-Feb daily from 10am; Oct–Christmas Day & mid-Feb to April Sat & Sun from 10am), you can **rent** waveskis and canoes (both $8 an hour), rowing boats ($10 an hour), windsurfers ($20 an hour) and catamarans ($30 an hour) for use in and around the bay; prices include wetsuits if needed. The nearest shops are at **Eastbourne village**, a kilometre further south along the coast, which also has a few cafés and restaurants.

The **Westpac Trust Ferry**, a powerful catamaran (☎04/499 1282, timetable ☎04/499 1273), runs daily to Days Bay (Mon–Fri up to 8 daily 6am–6.30pm, Sat & Sun 5 daily 10.15am–5pm; 30min; $7 one way, $14 return or $16 if via Somes Island; bikes carried free), departing from the end of Queens Wharf, behind the *Shed 5* café/bar. You can also get there and back by **bus** (#81 or #83 daily until 6pm, #82 Mon–Fri), or by **bike**, taking the SH2 around the harbour.

Eating

The gastronomic centre of New Zealand, Wellington is reputed to have more restaurants and cafés per head of population than New York City. It's a **cosmopolitan** scene, with a plethora of ethnic restaurants catering to all tastes, and new places opening up all the time. Recent years have seen an explosion of Indian and kebab outlets, especially in Courtenay Place. There's also a thriving **coffee culture**, and Wellingtonians have a penchant for indulgent **weekend brunches**, especially on Sundays. As in many capital cities but somewhat jarring in New Zealand, be prepared for the "attitude" projected by staff in some of the busiest cafés.

During the **day**, Wellington's **food courts** offer bargain grazing from an array of international fast-food outlets: try the licensed *Gourmet Lane*, in the BNZ Shopping Centre on the corner of Willis Street and Willeston Street (Mon–Thurs 9am–5.30pm, Fri 7am–8pm, Sat 10am–4pm); *James Smith Markets Food Court*, 53 Cuba St (Mon–Thurs 10am–6.30pm, Fri–Sat 10am–late, Sun 6.30am–6.30pm), which also has a bar that's very popular on Fridays; or the *Asian Food Market*, Cable Street, where authentic Indian, Chinese, Malaysian, Middle Eastern and Bengali food is served at weekends (Fri–Sun 10.30am–6pm), albeit in rather dowdy surroundings. An excellent specialist **bakery** is *Pandoro*, on the corner of Wakefield and Allen streets (Mon–Fri 7am–6pm, Sat & Sun 7am–3pm), supplying all manner of loaves, as well as bap sandwiches for $5 or under, to eat at one of their two tables, washed down with a coffee. In the **evenings**, attention shifts to **Queens Wharf** and **Courtenay Place**, offering a choice between waterfront dining or the buzz of the city.

Cafés and takeaways

Axolotl Café, 34 Courtenay Place. Stylish, central and friendly spot for a snack such as seafood chowder with garlic focaccia or a main course for up to $20, and good weekend brunches (from 3am). Mon–Fri 5pm–3am, Sat & Sun 24 hr; licensed.

Café Brava, 2 Courtenay Place (☎04/384 1159). Next to the Downstage Theatre, this classical, modern and airy café/bar serves well-priced all-day breakfasts, lunches with Mediterranean flair, and scrumptious Sunday brunches. Daily from 7am, until 3am on weekends & show nights. Book for pre-theatre dining. Licensed.

The Catch, 48 Courtenay Place. Inexpensive sushi bar with dishes revolving on the counter (colour-coded according to price), to take away or eat in; also side orders and bigger meals ($10–20) from a set menu. Closed Sun; licensed.

City Limits, 122 Wakefield St. The unpretentious and friendly founding father of Wellington's café society, open from early morning until late (Sun till 5pm). Big breakfasts and snacky lunches are served, progressing to a broad dinner menu of well-presented food later in the day. Licensed & BYO.

De Luxe, 10 Kent Terrace, beside the Embassy Theatre. Cheap, snacky counter food, most of it vegetarian, served in a hip bar that's popular with the post-cinema and theatre crowd. Excellent sandwiches alongside sushi and samosas; and good coffee from their own roasted beans. Daily morning to midnight.

Expressoholic, 128 Courtenay Place. Seriously hip café, with great coffee, breakfast for $7–15, and big portions of soup, filled focaccia, salad and pasta the rest of the day for $10–15. Also plenty of newspapers and magazines for perusing. Daily 7.30am till late (Sun–Thurs midnight, Fri & Sat 3am); no alcohol.

Felix, cnr Cuba St & Wakefield St. A happening all-day café bar where you can enjoy pasta or udon noodles for under $18, or a brunch, while browsing their newspapers.

Fidel's, 234 Cuba St. Great value all-day breakfasts and snacks (check out the imaginative food stacks) in a fun and cosy den plastered with pics of Fidel Castro. There's a camouflaged open-air bar at the back. Licensed.

Fiebigs, 55 Mulgrave St, opposite Old St Paul's. Good coffee and fresh seasonal food for breakfast, lunch and dinner at moderate prices, all in a warm and clubby atmosphere or out in the courtyard. Mon–Fri 8am–11pm, Sat from 6pm only, closed Sun; licensed.

Kopi, 103 Willis St. Something of an antidote to Wellington coffee-houses. Good-value Malaysian dishes such as roti and chicken korma (from 10am till late) in a cosy café on two floors, with smoking allowed on a small balcony upstairs. Licensed & BYO.

Krazy Lounge, cnr Cuba St & Ghuznee St. This convivial, hip café/restaurant serves pasta and char-grilled mains for $10–20. Mon–Fri 7.30am till the early hours, Sat & Sun 9am–3pm; licensed.

Midnight Espresso, 178 Cuba St. A caffeine junkie's heaven, this mellow coffee-house peddles beans for all palates. Sip a cup on its own, with breakfast or alongside a cheap snack (good toasted sandwiches, focaccia and pizza, plus vegetarian and vegan food), while poring over their reading material. Mon–Fri 8.30am–3am, Sat & Sun 9.30am–3am.

Café Neo, 132 Willis St. Extra-quick service and big servings at great prices in a warm bustling atmosphere for breakfast and lunch. Delicious pancakes are filled with banana and covered in maple syrup, or choose from an array of salads, pasta, and focaccia sandwiches. Closed Sun; licensed & BYO.

Nikau Gallery Café, in the City Gallery, Civic Square. Well-priced café/bar with stylish contemporary fare in a setting to match, opening onto an outdoor terrace. Mon–Thurs 7am–5pm, Fri 7am–8pm, Sat & Sun 9am–4pm.

Café Paradiso, cnr Courtenay Place & Blair St (☎04/384 2675). An icon of Wellington café society, buzzing all day and packed till late (dinner bookings required), offering superb food plus a lounge bar at the back. Light meals cost under $14–22, mains set you back around $18–24. Lunch Mon–Fri, dinner daily; licensed.

Roti Chenai, 120 Victoria St. Tiny, simple South Indian and Malaysian café with an open kitchen in the middle where roti are prepared in front of your eyes, as well as delicious dosai, murtabak, curries and rendang. Lunch 11.30am–2pm, dinner 5pm onwards; BYO.

Sahara Café, 39 Courtenay Place (☎04/385 6362); not to be confused with the kebab takeaway next door). An intimate venue for quality Middle Eastern dinners at good prices. Book ahead at weekends. Licensed & BYO.

The Vegetarian Café, 179 Cuba St. Calming, mostly vegan spot with a broad-ranging menu that includes huge open sandwiches ($12) and meals in a bowl ($5–10). Mon–Sat 11am–9pm, Sun 11am–4pm; no alcohol.

Wholly Bagels, 39 Johnston St. The only place in New Zealand where you can get a decent bagel to take away, freshly made every day and sold on their own or as sandwiches, plus salads from the deli. Mon–Fri 7.30am–3.30pm, Sat 8.30am–3pm; closed Sun.

Zest, 146 Cuba St. Funky bistro bar serving well-priced weekday lunches and dinners, and weekend brunches (from 10am) and dinners. Licensed.

Restaurants

Cobar, 12 Main Rd, Days Bay. Virtually opposite the wharf, this stylish bar, restaurant and café specializes in seafood and international cuisine; they also do weekend brunches. Mon–Fri from 11am, Sat & Sun from 10.30am.

Dockside, Shed 3, Queens Wharf (☎04/499 9900). High-quality restaurant and bar in a vast converted wooden warehouse with a glass frontage overlooking the harbour, serving lunch and dinner, plus brunch at weekends (10.30am–3pm). Hot on seafood – try New Orleans blackened fish for around $20. Book if you want a window seat; licensed.

Great India, 141 Manners St (☎04/384 5755). The best dinner restaurant for tandoori, biryani or curry (all under $15). Licensed & BYO (corkage $1.50 per person); book for Fri & Sat nights.

Icon Restaurant, Level 2, Museum of New Zealand (☎04/801 5300). One of New Zealand's top restaurants, offering an inspired range of good-value dishes for lunch on weekdays (noon–3pm), brunch at weekends (11am–3pm) and dinner daily (6–10pm) in an elegant contemporary setting overlooking the harbour. Dinner mains cost around $23–28, plus side dishes of $4–5 each, and the in-house cellar boasts an excellent selection of wines. The pleasant bar is open all day every day and serves bar snacks from 11am.

The Opera, cnr Courtenay Place & Blair St. Swish theatrical restaurant above a large airy bar, spilling onto a wrap-around balcony. Pasta and salads cost less than $20, with more substantial and varied dishes available for under $25; a downstairs café serves snacks for around $10 and mains for under $20; licensed.

The Orange Dining Room, 3 Swan Lane, off Cuba St. Asian-Italian fusion in an attractive converted 1911 bakery open for lunch (Tues–Sat from midday) and dinner (Mon–Sat from 5.30pm), including an "Express" menu for $15, for lunch or pre-theatre dinner. Closed Sun; licensed.

Petit Lyon, 220 Willis St (☎04/384 9402). A big hit for its imaginative food and original decor, this bistro, salon and café straddles three storeys. Lunches cost around $20, while dinners start at $25, except in the café where prices are nearer $15. Book ahead for bistro and salon. Closed Sun; live jazz Thurs evenings; licensed.

Shed 5, Queens Wharf (☎04/499 9069). Thriving upmarket café, restaurant and bar, proffering great seafood in a stylishly converted 1888 woolshed. Lunch, dinner and weekend brunches are served, and prices start at $23 for char-grilled yellow-fin tuna, rising to $30 for West Coast whitebait. Book ahead for the restaurant Licensed.

The Skyline, 1 Upland Rd, Kelburn, near the Botanic Gardens (☎04/475 8727). Sweeping views over the city enhance this glass-fronted café, bar and split-level restaurant designed by Ian Athfield. The café (10am–4pm) has cheap snacks, while the restaurant lays on good-value lunchtime buffets, with a broad selection of seafood, hot and cold meat dishes, vegetarian alternatives, salads and desserts.

Strawberry Fare, 25 Kent Terrace. Open all day for luxurious desserts at just over $10, washed down by a glass or two of dessert wine. Also serves scrummy breakfasts ($10–13); and Mediterranean-style lunches and dinners ($12–20). Closed Mon–Fri 3–5pm; licensed & BYO.

Uncle Chang's, 72 Courtenay Place. The best Chinese in town, for lunch and dinner daily. Great rice noodle soups and combination menus for $22–38 per person. Licensed & BYO.

Drinking, nightlife and entertainment

The capital city has the best **nightlife** in the country, with a huge array of late-night cafés, restaurants, bars and clubs, all within walking distance of each other, and with new ones constantly joining their ranks. Wellington's playground is **Courtenay Place** and a few streets just off it (Blair, Allen and Dixon streets), extending to Willis Street and Lambton Quay. The scene spreads from there to **Queens Wharf**, ten minutes' walk away, where mostly upmarket **bars** overlook the harbour. The **partying** goes on late into the night, and pumps hardest from Thursday to Saturday. The distinction between pubs, bars and **clubs** is often blurred, since many of the bars have free live music and dancing in the evenings, especially at weekends.

Neither is Wellington short of **live arts performance**, for this is the home of not only four professional theatres but also the Royal New Zealand Ballet, the New Zealand Symphony Orchestra, the Wellington Sinfonia, the Wellington Opera Company and the New Zealand Schools of Dance and Drama. On top of that, there's the month-long **International Festival of the Arts** in March of even-numbered years, which draws the top performers from around the world to the country's biggest cultural event. Celebrating the huge diversity of the arts, performances include classical music, jazz and pop, tragic opera, puppet shows and the Grotesque, cabaret, poetry readings, traditional Maori dance, modern ballet and experimental works – and most of the venues

GAY AND LESBIAN WELLINGTON

The **scene** in Wellington is focused in the inner city (particularly around Courtenay Place), woven into the general café/bar mainstream and, though smaller than that of Auckland, it tends to be less cliquey and judgemental. In the centre, at least, gays openly express affection in public, and gays, lesbians, transgender and bi-folk mix freely together. Fairly low-key for most of the year, the scene takes off during the annual festival, **Deus**, which combines with the **Gay & Lesbian Fair**, a big traditional fair of stalls and live entertainment ending with a big all-night dance party. Anyone's invited as long as they get into the over-the-top spirit of things (one Saturday in Feb/March; around $20; info on Deus from *hindley@consumer.org.nz*). The annual finals of the national competition **Mr Gay New Zealand** are often held in Wellington in October: check out *www.mrgaynz.org.nz*, or email *info@mrgaynz.org.nz*.

For **information** on venues and events at other times, check out the national gay **magazine** *Express* ($2), available from the YHA and Unity Books (see "Bookshops", p.458); the free *City Voice* (which has a Queer City section every six weeks); or the national *OUT* magazine. Other contacts are the Gay Switchboard (☎04/385 0674), the Lesbian Line (☎04/389 8082) or Bisexual Women's Group (☎04/385 1162). The Lesbian & Gay Advisory Group also produces a free all-encompassing *Venue Guide* in an A4 folder, available from various venues.

The most established Wellington **venues and meeting places** include two saunas: Wakefield, 15 Tory St, behind OUT bookshop (☎04/385 4400) and Sanctuary, 39 Dixon St (☎04/384 1565), both among the best sources of information on what's happening. Other choices are *Flipp Brasserie*, RSA Building, 103 Ghuznee St (☎04/385 9493), a café/bar offering continental cuisine to a predominantly business crowd (daily for lunch and dinner, brunch on Sat & Sun; mixed); *Zest Café*, 146 Cuba St (☎04/801 8007); *Evergreen*, 141 Vivian St, an after-hours coffee lounge (from 10pm; mixed/trannies); a big dance venue, *Bojangles*, 60 Dixon St (Tues–Sat), which occasionally hosts special evenings, as advertised in *The Express* and around town, though entertainment sometimes carries a cover charge; *The Dome* piano and garden bar, middle of Kent & Cambridge Terraces (☎04/385 6566), which has long been run by Wellington's leading bar host (Mal Vaughan) who's a great contact; and *The Valve*, 154 Vivian St, a bar that turns gay on Wed nights only from 8pm, with Valve Night (☎0800/422 326; *boyznite @badboyz.co.nz*, $2–5 cover charge).

The non-profit New Zealand Gay and Lesbian Tourism Association, Private Bag MBE P255, Auckland (☎09/379 0776, fax 303 4262, *secretariat@nzglta.org.nz*), provides **travel information** aimed at gay, lesbian and bisexual visitors. Gaytravel Net in Wellington (☎04/384 1865 & 0800/429 872, fax 04/384 1835, *www.gaytravel.net.nz*, *reznz @gaytravel.net.nz*), can advise on gay, lesbian, trans and bi-friendly **accommodation** and offers a **reservations** service; likewise TWG Ltd (☎04/479 8224, *robert.twg@clear.net.nz*); and Gaylink International Ltd (☎04/384 1877, fax 384 5187, *www.gaytravel.net.nz/nz*, *operations@gaylink.co.nz*), which is an information/consultancy company for gay and lesbian tourism within New Zealand. A Web site devoted to women's travel and accommodation is at *www.womenstravel.co.nz*. For general gay/lesbian information on New Zealand, check out the Virtual Gay New Zealand Tour on the Internet at *http://nz.com/glb/tour*.

are within easy walking distance of one another. For more information and bookings, call ☎04/473 0149 or email *nzfestival@festival.co.nz*; for bookings only call ☎04/384 3840. Originally part of the Arts festival, the vibrant **Wellington Fringe Festival** (information and bookings ☎0800/226 6548) is now run as a separate event every March, filling the inner city with street and indoor theatre. October sees a two-week **Wellington International Jazz Festival**, bringing some of the world's best performers. As well as official mid-evening concerts there are free performances in restaurants and bars, and improvised sessions in Civic Square, on the waterfront and all over the city. For more information on the jazz festival, check out the visitor centre and free pamphlets and flyers around town.

The best introduction to **what's on** is the *Wellington – What's On* booklet, free from the visitor centre and from accommodation around the city. There are also weekend listings in *The Dominion* and *The Evening Post*, while bland reviews and more useful **listings** appear in both of the city's free ad-ridden weeklies, *City Voice* and *Capital Times*, which you can pick up at the visitor centre and from racks around town. The visitor centre also provides **CityLine** (☎04/494 3333, on reply punch in code 1325), which gives a brief rundown of events.

Pubs and bars

Most pubs and bars are **open** daily, from around eleven in the morning until around midnight or later. Those closest to Cuba Street are the most expensive.

The Backbencher, cnr Molesworth St & Kate Sheppard St, opposite Parliament House. Lively, comfortable pub, a bolt hole for MPs who quench their thirst amid satirical cartoons and *Spitting Image*-style puppets. Bar snacks all day and a well-priced café serving unpretentious fare. At its busiest Fri night, when there's free live music from 7.30pm.

Bar Bodega, 286 Willis St. Great atmosphere is the draw in this small bar aimed at a slightly older drinking crowd, offering an excellent range of boutique beers on tap and doubling as a venue for bands (see below).

Coyote, 63 Courtenay Place. Urban Mexican-style bar that pulls in the dance crowds on Fri & Sat nights.

The Grand, 69–71 Courtenay Place. Sophisticated nightspot on three levels in a big converted hotel of bare brick walls. Downstairs is an elegant restaurant bar with palm trees; upstairs are two main bars, the first incorporating a balcony over Courtenay Place, a covered garden bar and relaxing sofas (disco on this floor Fri & Sat nights); the top floor is a pool bar.

The Paradiso Bar, 20 Courtenay Place. An intimate bar at the back of the buzzy *Café Paradiso*.

Chicago, Queens Wharf, opposite the Events Centre. Huge, American-style sports bar with a dance floor, packed on Fri and Sat nights, when live bands are followed by a DJ. Reasonably priced snacks are available to soak up all that Bud.

Kitty O'Shea's, 28 Courtenay Place. Cosy Irish bar with a mix of live music Tues–Sun (traditional Irish on Thurs).

The Loaded Hog 12–14 Bond St, off Willis St. Big lively bar serving naturally brewed beer and reasonable food. Live music and dancing Wed–Sun nights.

The Malthouse, 47 Willis St. Airy, yuppie first-floor bar with table service and a pleasant balcony over the street where over thirty high-quality naturally brewed Kiwi beers are on tap at any one time, swilled by suits from the office, especially on Friday evenings. Closed Sun in winter.

Molly Malone's, cnr Taranaki St & Courtenay Place. Hugely atmospheric, loud and in-your-face Irish pub, with foot-tapping live Irish music every evening (jam sessions on Mon night). Upstairs is the quieter *Dubliner* restaurant and bar, serving snacks, $10 lunches, reasonable dinners and weekend brunches, though Sat nights a musician plays up here too.

The Opera, cnr Courtenay Place & Blair St. Spacious and slick bar with live bands on Thurs.

Tupelo, 6 Edward St. Intimate chic bar/club just off the beaten track with a European café feel, serving meals earlier in the day, becoming a bar at night. Excellent wine and beer list, including Emerson's real ale and Bookbinder beer. Mon–Tues from 5pm, Wed–Fri from noon, Sat from 6pm.

Clubs and gigs

Live **bands** (usually Kiwi but sometimes international) are a regular fixture, playing in bars or at bigger venues such as the Queens Wharf Events Centre (☎04/472 5021), and supplemented in summer by occasional **free concerts** in the waterfront Frank Kitts Park or in Civic Square.

Bar Bodega, 286 Willis St. Wellington's longest-running musical institution. Every Kiwi band worth its salt has played here; DJs also visit, and it sometimes hosts dance parties.

The Blue Note, cnr Cuba St & Vivian St. Intimate club open every night from 4pm (till 6am Sun–Fri, till 3am Sat) regularly hosting live jazz or acoustic bands; occasional cover charge of $5.

La Luna Club, Oaks Complex, Dickson St. Popular hideaway for a youngish crowd into pool, hip-hop and light dance music. Bands play regularly and there are two bars.

Matterhorn, 106 Cuba St. Smallish bohemian venue so typical of Cuba Street. A café during the day and a bar/club at night, specializing in cocktails, wines and European bar food. In a marquee at the back bands play one night a week, DJs four nights.

Studio Nine, upstairs at the *Edward Street Café*, 9 Edward St. Cool dance club that draws the young and hip with DJs playing house, techno and jungle (cover charge $15); also one-off raves at weekends.

Tatou, Ground floor, 22 Cambridge Terrace. Upmarket techno bar and dance club attracting smart young professionals to its two bars that stay open until 6am. Gets very busy later on; occasional visiting DJs.

Valve, 154 Vivian St. Small, studenty drinking den and club, open nightly till 3am, with all kinds of music (sometimes live), from jazz and reggae to jungle and techno. Beer for $2 on Tues night; pool and pinball.

Wellington Sports Café, cnr Courtenay Place & Tory St. Late-night, post-pub dancing in a sports bar. Live music every other Wed, DJs Thurs–Sat and dance shows every weekend, but watch out for the expensive drinks. Mon & Tues till 3am, Wed–Sat till 6am, Sun till 1am.

Classical music, theatre and cinema

The city regularly hosts **orchestral** and other performances, while four professional **theatres** stage Kiwi and international shows. Tickets normally cost $20 upwards (average price around $30), but the visitor centre sells theatre tickets for $16 depending on availability. In addition to its quota of multiplexes, Wellington also has a smattering of arthouse **cinemas**. The cheapest night to head for the movies is Tuesday, when tickets cost $8 all day, instead of the usual $11; in some cinemas tickets are also $8 for screenings before 5pm, Monday to Friday.

You can book **tickets** direct at venues or, for a small fee, through two **booking agencies**: Ticketek, State Opera House, 111–113 Manners St (☎04/384 3840; Mon–Fri 9am–5.30pm, Sat 9am–4pm), for events throughout the Wellington region; or MFC Ticketing, 111 Wakefield St (☎04/801 4263; Mon–Thurs 9am–5.30pm, Fri 9am–7pm, Sat 10am–1pm), for shows and events held in the city only.

Theatres and concert halls

Bats, 1 Kent Terrace (☎04/802 4175). Lively theatre concentrating on alternative works.

Circa, cnr Taranaki St & Cable St (☎04/801 7992). One of the country's liveliest and most innovative professional theatres, which has fostered the skills of some of the best-known Kiwi directors and actors. At either of the two spaces in this brand-new complex (the main house and a 100-seater studio) you can count on intimate, imaginative productions.

The Downstage, cnr Courtenay Place & Cambridge Terrace (☎04/801 6946). Stages both its own productions and the best touring shows: a mix of mainstream and new drama, dance and comedy, with the emphasis on quality Kiwi work. Cheaper gallery seats available.

Michael Fowler Centre, Town Hall, 111 Wakefield St (☎04/801 4325). Wellington's major venue for orchestral and other performances. More details at *www.wcc.govt.nz/wfcc*.

State Opera House, 111–113 Manners St (☎04/384 3840). Hosts opera, ballet and musicals.

Taki Rua Theatre, 85 Victoria St (☎04/472 7377). Original Kiwi works, mostly influenced by Pacific Island culture.

Westpac Trust St James, 77–83 Courtenay Place (☎04/802 4060). A newly refurbished theatre in a fine 1912 building, home to the Royal New Zealand Ballet and host to opera, dance, musicals and plays. It also has a licensed café for pre- and post-performance drinks.

Cinemas

Embassy, 10 Kent Terrace (☎04/384 7657, *www.deluxe.co.nz*). Mainstream and independent movies on a single giant screen in the city centre. You can take a glass of wine or beer in with you.

Hoyts Manners Mall (☎04/472 5182, *www.hoyts.co.nz*) & Hoyts Mid City, Manners St (☎04/384 3567). Central five-screen complex showing standard general releases.

Paramount, 25 Courtenay Place (☎04/384 4080, *info@deluxe.co.nz*). A central venue showing both arthouse and mainstream movies on three screens, which you can watch while sipping a glass of beer or wine.

Rialto Film Centre, cnr Cable St & Jervois Quay (☎04/385 1864, *www.rialto.co.nz*). Independent and avant-garde productions, plus special screenings of New Zealand films from their archives. The ground floor has regular exhibitions on movies, video and television (Mon–Thurs & Sun noon–5pm, Fri & Sat noon–8pm; $3).

Listings

Airlines National airlines: Air Nelson/Air NZ Link (☎04/472 6034); Air New Zealand (☎0800/737 000 & 04/474 8950); Ansett (☎0800 ANSETT & 04/471 1146); Mount Cook (☎04/388 5020); Soundsair (☎04/801 0111). International airlines: British Airways (☎04/472 7327); Malaysia (☎0800/657 472); Qantas (information and reservations ☎0800/808 767); Singapore (☎0800/808 909); United (☎04/472 0470).

Airport buses Shuttles between the central city and airport are operated by Super Shuttle (☎04/387 8787) and A.P. Shuttles (☎0800/959 595), who run a 24hr door-to-door service to central Wellington (daily; $8 first passenger, $2 per extra person), plus a direct service to Wellington train station (roughly every 30min at peak times, otherwise hourly Mon–Fri; $6).

American Express Sun Alliance Centre, 280–292 Lambton Quay (☎04/473 7766).

Automobile Association 342–352 Lambton Quay (☎04/470 9999).

Banks and foreign exchange ANZ at 215–229 Lambton Quay (☎0800/180 925); BNZ at 1 Willis St (☎04/474 6000); National Bank of NZ at 60–64 Courtenay Place (☎0800/741 100). There's a Thomas Cook bureau de change at 108 Lambton Quay (☎04/473 5167; Mon–Fri 8.30am–5pm).

Bike rental Pins Cycles Wellington, cnr Willis St & Boulcott St (☎04/472 4591; half day $15, full day $25); Penny Farthing Cycle Shop, 89 Courtenay Place (☎04/385 2279; full day $25, or $40 for a full suspension bike; $100 for a week for a mountain bike.

Bookshops There are loads in the city, and Cuba St is the place for secondhand. The biggest general bookshops are London Bookshops, 310 Lambton Quay (☎04/472 9694) and 89 Cuba Mall (☎04/384 8179); and Whitcoulls, 312 Lambton Quay (☎04/472 1921); other options include Dymocks, 366 Lambton Quay (☎04/472 2080), and Unity Books, 57 Willis St (☎04/499 4245), which has the best range of Kiwi literature. The following have good secondhand and book exchange sections: Arty Bee's Books, 17 Courtenay Place (☎04/385 1819); Bellamy's, 105 Cuba St (☎04/384 7770; open daily), which also stocks tapes and CDs; and Crossroads, 110 Featherston St (☎04/499 5212). There's a gay-interest section at Unity Books, 57 Willis St (☎04/499 4245). New Zealand's largest comics shop is Comics Compulsion, 105 Cuba Mall (☎04/384 2691).

Buses InterCity and Newmans (☎04/472 5111) head north to Auckland via the Kapiti Coast and Hamilton; and to Rotorua, Tauranga and the Coromandel. Heading northwest they link with New Plymouth via Palmerston North and Wanganui; and to the northeast they run to Gisborne via Hastings and Napier.

Camping and outdoor equipment Mainly Tramping, 39 Mercer St (☎04/473 5353); Kathmandu, 34 Manners St (☎04/801 8755); and Ski & Camping, 181 Wakefield St (☎04/801 8704), who also provide a repair service for tents, backpacks, stoves and lights.

Car parks Council car parks: Civic Centre (entry at Harris St; 7am–midnight); Clifton, Shell Lane (entry off The Terrace; 7am–6pm); Jacobs Place (entry off Tory St; 24hr); James Smith (entry on Wakefield St; 24hr); Michael Fowler Centre (entry on Wakefield St; 24hr; suitable for campervans); Lombard Parking Building (entry off Bond St; 24hr). Independent car parks: Capital Carpark, Boulcott St (Mon–Thurs till 9pm, Fri till midnight); Condrens, Wakefield St (secure; $4 overnight till 9am; $7 for 24hr); Midland Carpark, Waring Taylor Street (Mon–Thurs till 7pm, Fri till 10pm, Sat 10am–4pm). Charges are $10 per day Mon–Fri 6am–6pm, free Sat & Sun.

Car rental Multinationals: Avis, at the airport (☎04/802 1088), ferry terminal (☎04/801 8108 & 0800/655 111) and 25 Dixon St (☎04/801 8108, *avis.res@xtra.co.nz*); Budget, at the airport (☎04/388 9878) and 81 Ghuznce St (☎04/802 4548 & 0800/652 227, *reservations@budget.co.nz*); Hertz, at the airport (☎04/388 7070) and cnr Tory St & Buckle St (☎04/384 3809 & 0800/654 321). Mid-range firms: Ace, 150 Hutt Rd (☎04/586 2533 & 0800/535 500); NZ Rent-a-Car, 82 Tory St (☎04/384 2745); Nationwide, 147 Thorndon Quay (☎04/473 1165, *ppetersen@xtra.co.nz*). Budget rental firms: Rent-a-Dent, 50 Tacy St, Kilbirnie (☎04/387 9931, *wellington@therentalcarcentre.co.nz*); Shoestring Rentals, 138 Adelaide Rd, Newtown (☎04/389 2983, fax 389 2704, *shoestring@carhire.co.nz*); Thrifty at the airport (☎04/388 5841), in the city (☎04/499 5691 & NZ-wide 0800/737 070, fax 388 5862, *reservations@thrifty.co.nz*); and Welco (☎04/238 2326 & 0800/RENTWELCO).

Embassies and consulates Australia, 72 Hobson St, Thorndon (☎04/473 6411); Canada, 61 Molesworth St (☎04/473 9577); France, 34–42 Manners St (☎04/384 2555); Germany, 90–92 Hobson St, Thorndon (☎04/473 6063); Italy; 34 Grant Rd, Thorndon (☎04/473 5339); Netherlands, cnr Ballance St & Featherston St (☎04/473 8652); UK, 44 Hill St (☎04/472 6049); USA, 29 Fitzherbert Terrace, Thorndon (☎04/472 2068); see the Yellow Pages, under "Diplomatic representation".

Ferries Westpac Trust Ferry (☎04/499 1282, timetable ☎04/499 1273) runs daily between Wellington (Queens Wharf) and Days Bay (see p.452 for details); some scheduled sailings stop at Somes Island. Services across Cook Strait (see p.450) to the South Island are operated by the Interislander Ferry (☎0800/802 802), *Lynx* (same number) and *Topcat* fast ferry (☎0800 486 7228).

Gay and lesbian Wellington See box on p.455.

Internet Email services are readily available, but try the Wellington Public Library (see below); *Net Arena Cybercafé*, 175 Cuba St (Mon–Fri 9am–10pm, Sat & Sun 10am–10pm); or *Moving Planet*, 10 Majoribanks St, who also offer good rates on international phone calls and faxes, plus discounts for YHA members (Mon–Fri 10am–8pm, Sat & Sun noon–8pm, *mike@movingplanet.co.nz*).

Library Wellington Public Library is on Victoria Street, where it backs onto Civic Square (Mon–Thurs 9.30am–8.30pm, Fri 9.30am–9pm; Sat 9.30am–5pm, Sun 1–4pm).

Market James Smith's Market is a popular flea market on cnr Cuba St & Manners St, second floor (Mon–Thurs, Sat & Sun 10am–6pm, Fri 10am–9pm).

Medical treatment Call the Free Ambulance (☎04/472 2999) for the nearest on-duty doctor. For urgent night-time medical care, accident treatment and X-rays, contact the After-Hours Medical Centre, 17 Adelaide Rd, Newtown, near Basin Reserve (☎04/384 4944; 24hr). Wellington Hospital is on Riddiford St, Newton (☎04/385 5999). For dental care, try Central Dental Surgery, Harbour City Tower, 29 Brandon St (☎04/472 6306), or Symes deSilva & Associates, 2nd Floor, Olympic House, 97 Courtenay Place (☎04/801 5551; daily); for emergency dental services, call ☎04/472 1394.

Newspapers The main local daily is *The Dominion*, whose Friday edition has events and entertainment listings, as does *Contact*, a free local rag published every Thursday.

Pharmacy Unichem Eddie Fletcher Pharmacy, 204 Lambton Quay (☎04/472 0362); After-Hours Pharmacy, 17 Adelaide Rd, Newtown (☎04/385 8810; Mon–Fri 5–11pm, Sat, Sun & public holidays 9am–11pm).

Police Wellington Central Police Station, cnr Victoria St & Harris St (☎04/382 4000).

Post office The main post office is in the train station lobby (☎04/496 4951) and post restante mail can be collected here Mon–Fri 8.30am–5pm (addressed to Post Restante, Wellington Post Office, Wellington Railway Station, Bunny St, Wellington).

Swimming Freyberg Pool and Fitness Centre, 139 Oriental Parade (☎04/384 3107; daily 6am–9pm, except Fri till 5.30pm), has a 33-metre indoor pool (closes Fri 5.30pm during school terms), plus gym, spas, saunas, steamroom, fitness classes and massage therapy.

Taxis Wellington Combined Taxis (☎04/384 4444 & 0800/384 444) are the biggest company and offer YHA departure rate of $15 to the airport; try also Central City Taxis (☎04/499 4949) or Gold & Black Taxis (☎04/388 8888). Authorized stands are located at the train station; on Whitmore St (between Lambton Quay & Featherston St); outside the *James Smith Hotel* on Lambton Quay; off Willis St on the Bond St cnr; outside Woolworths on Dixon St; and at the junction of Willis St & Aro St.

Thomas Cook See Banks and foreign exchange.

Tours Wally Hammond's Wellington City Scenic Tours run a city bus tour, departing from the visitor centre and Travelworld Holidaymakers, cnr Mercer St & Victoria St (☎04/472 0869; daily 10am

& 2pm; 2hr 30min; $25), which shows you all the highlights in a relaxed manner; they also run tours to the Kapiti Coast (half-day from 9am or 1.30pm; $55) and the Wairarapa (full day; $110). Similar tours to the Wairarapa (daily from platform 9 at the train station; $30–65) are operated by Dynamic Tours (☎04/801 6900). More intimate trips are given by Laura's Wairarapa Tours (☎06/377 3534), and luxury excursions (to Martinborough wineries or to Mount Bruce National Wildlife Centre) are offered by Five Star Tours (☎04/479 1356; $130). Excellent quad bike expeditions on Wellington's northern hills are operated by All Track Adventures (☎0800/494 335, *alltrack@xtra.co.nz*; 1hr 30min–3hr; $99–149), who don't let you loose until you're fully confident and they can arrange pick-ups from the city.

Trains Tranz Metro (☎04/801 7000 & after hours ☎04/498 3013) operate regular electric trains from Wellington station daily to Johnsonville, Paraparaumu, the Hutt Valley and the Wairarapa. The national Tranz Scenic (☎04/498 3000 & 0800/802 802) provide a daily link with Auckland, via Palmerston North and Hamilton; and with Napier via Palmerston North and Hastings.

Travel agents Air New Zealand Travel Centre, cnr Lambton Quay & Panama St (☎04/474 8950), for all airlines; Budget Travel, Cable Car Complex, Lambton Quay (☎04/472 8342); for national train travel, Tranz Rail Travel Centre at the main train station, Bunny St (☎04/498 3000 & 0800/802 802; Budget agencies include the travel desk at the YHA, 292 Wakefield St (☎04/801 7280); STA, 130 Cuba St (☎04/385 0561); The Hub in *Trekkers Hotel/Motel*, 213 Cuba St (☎04/385 3580; Mon–Fri 9am–5.30pm); and Lambton Quay Flight Centre, 182 Lambton Quay (☎04/471 2995).

AROUND WELLINGTON

Only two major highways fork from Wellington: SH1, striking north through the satellite city of Porirua and then skirting the Kapiti Coast; and SH2, heading **east** to the Wairarapa, via the built-up commuter settlements of the **Hutt Valley**. To the north and east, the wild scenery of the Rimutaka and Tararua ranges has shrugged off Wellington's advances, leaving the **Rimutaka Forest Park** the sole preserve of weekend picnickers, while the more rugged **Tararua Forest Park**, accessible from Otaki at the northern end of the Kapiti Coast, is largely a place for serious trampers and adventurers.

On SH1 due north of Wellington, the satellite city of **Porirua** holds only a Police Museum and the Colonial Knob Walkway to detain you, and you'll do better to hotfoot it along SH1 to the **Kapiti Coast**. Focused on the wonderful bird sanctuary and marine reserve of **Kapiti Island**, after which this shoreline is named, the coast itself is little more than a string of greyish sand beaches serviced by small communities, which, though popular among Kiwi holidaymakers during the summer season, aren't high on the list of priorities for international visitors.

East of Wellington

Crouched on the northeastern shore of Wellington Harbour, 15km from the city centre, is the **Hutt Valley** and its satellite towns of Upper Hutt and Lower Hutt. Bisected by SH2, this is little more than a transit point to the Wairarapa and the Hawke's Bay region further up the east coast, and barely merits the trip – unless you happen to be staying at Wellington's closest campsite (see p.437), which languishes in Lower Hutt. Further around the harbour, some respite from suburbia is provided by the **Rimutaka Forest Park**, prime picnicking and tramping territory for weekending Wellingtonians.

The Hutt Valley

Built on the alluvial plains beside the meandering Hutt River are the twin towns of **LOWER HUTT** and **UPPER HUTT**, 15km apart and hemmed in by steep bush-covered hills. Accommodating the overspill from the capital, this urban sprawl stretches from the suburb of **Petone**, site of the first, short-lived European settlement in the Wellington region, up the Hutt Valley to the Tararua Range, 30km north. If you have time on your hands, you could do worse than visit the **Dowse Art Museum**, in the Civic Centre, 45 Laings Rd, Lower Hutt (Mon–Fri 10am–4pm, Sat & Sun 11am–5pm; free), a gallery showcasing high-calibre, contemporary New Zealand art, with a strong leaning towards jewellery, ceramics, textiles and glass, well displayed in changing exhibitions. The art theme continues 3km southeast at **Indigenous**, 58 Guthrie St in the suburb of Waiwhetu (☎04/560 4630; by appointment only), a good-quality Maori art studio, gallery and shop where you can feast your eyes on carvings (wood, greenstone and bone), paintings, basketry, fibre arts, clay works and stone sculpture. An informative 1hr guided tour for two people upwards (book ahead; $18) fills you in on Maori customs and tradition and offers a range of hands-on activities such as touching a kiwi-feather cloak and making a flax souvenir.

To get here **by car**, exit the motorway at the Petone off-ramp; **by train**, take one of the regular daily TranzMetro commuter services from Wellington train station to Waterloo, from where the Dowse Art Museum is a 1.5-kilometre walk northwest down Knights Road; Indigenous is ten-minutes' walk from the station in the opposite direction, along Guthrie Street off Cambridge Terrace. Eastbourne and Big Red **buses** depart hourly from Courtenay Place to Lower Hutt's Queensgate shopping centre on Knights Road, where there's a small **information** kiosk on the ground floor (Mon–Wed & Fri–Sun 9am–5.30pm, Thurs 9am–7pm), stocking local leaflets and public transport timetables. An official Hutt City visitor centre is at Andrews Avenue (☎04/560 4715, Mon-Fri 10am–5pm, Sat & Sun 10am–3pm), which covers the entire Wellington region, taking bookings for transport, accommodation and activities.

Should you want to **stay** cheaply and unwind between the Hutt Valley and the Wairarapa, there's the simple *Black Stump YHA*, Marchant Road (cnr with SH2), Kaitoke (☎04/526 4626 before 9pm; dorms & rooms ③), a small hostel near a river in an idyllic valley on the edge of the Tararua Forest Park 13km northeast of Upper Hutt and 39km from central Wellington. It is equipped with twins, doubles and family rooms, and basic food needs are catered to at a general store-cum-café bar and another café, all 200 metres away. It makes a good base from which to explore some of the ancient forest, the Rimutaka Incline (see p.428 or swimming holes in the secluded river. You can get here by **bus** with Tranzit Coachlines or InterCity (once daily) from downtown Wellington; or from Masterton (departing Tranzit Coachlines depot on Queen Street twice a day).

Three kilometres north of Upper Hutt, the scenic **Akatarawa Road** branches off SH2 and snakes 35km northwest through the Akatarawa Range and sumptuous bushland **to Waikanae** on the Kapiti Coast (see overleaf). Along the way are several roadside picnic and river-swimming spots, before the road climbs a 450-metre pass and descends to Waikanae.

Rimutaka Forest Park

Due south of Lower Hutt is the main entrance to the **Rimutaka Forest Park**, popular among jaded city-dwellers for its series of easy short and **day-walks** in the attractive Catchpool Valley; there's also a well-maintained **campsite**, and picnic and barbecue facilities. Some 20km from Wellington along the Coast Road, a signpost marks the **park entrance** (gates open 8am–dusk), from where Catchpool Road winds a further 2km up the valley to the car park, the starting point for most of the walks. Keen walkers/campers will want to get as far as the braided Orongorongo River, from where a startlingly grand landscape begins; you can camp for free along the riverbanks. A regular **bus** service (#80, Mon–Fri) runs between Wellington and **Wainuiomata**, where you can pick up a taxi at Queen Street for the last 12km to the park entrance. Two hundred metres beyond the park entrance is a well-equipped **DOC field centre** (daily Oct–April 9am–5.30pm; May–Sept Mon–Fri 8am–4.30pm, Sat & Sun 11.30am–4.30pm; ☎04/564 8551), which stocks the useful *Catchpool Valley/Rimutaka Forest Park* leaflet (50¢), detailing walks in the vicinity.

North of Wellington

Separating Wellington from the Kapiti Coast, the small, modern satellite city of **Porirua**, 21km north of the capital on SH1, has a couple of attractions, but little to delay your progress to the short sweep of the **Kapiti Coast**, 24km further north. A narrow coastal plain, bounded on the west by the Tasman Sea and rising steeply in the east to the rugged Tararua Range, its silver sandy beaches make this a summer playground for Kiwis. However, the ravages of overdevelopment have taken their toll, peppering the coast with retirement villages and golf courses. Only **Kapiti Island**, 5km offshore and the area's principal attraction, has escaped this fate. A bush-covered bird sanctuary and marine reserve, the island is open to the public by arrangement, so you'll need to plan ahead. Otherwise, your best option is to pass straight through the Kapiti Coast, using the few sights scattered along the main highway as minor diversions on your journey north or south. The highway, **SH1**, follows an inland route for 35km along the coast, passing through a series of uninspiring small towns that are split between the highway and their beachside communities a few kilometres to the west. The region extends from the seaside village of **Paekakariki**, in the south, to just beyond **Otaki** in the north, passing through **Paraparaumu** and **Waikanae**.

The coastal towns are served by the main north–south rail link between Auckland and Wellington, and by commuter **trains** between Palmerston North and the capital. The main **bus** companies also run to Paraparaumu and Otaki.

Porirua

Built on hills around the small, double-armed Porirua Harbour, the rapidly growing settlement of **PORIRUA** has a population of 46,000, but for the passing visitor holds only a handful of brief distractions, among them **Titahi Bay**, a great little surfing beach, 4km off SH1 along Titahi Bay Road.

In central Porirua itself the **Pataka Porirua Museum of Arts and Cultures**, on the corner of Norrie Street and Parumoana Street (Mon–Sat 10am–5pm, Sun 11am–4.30pm; free) shows local works, plus exhibitions by leading contemporary New Zealand artists, and hosts regular Maori and Pacific Island dance performances. You can watch them practice in the dance rehearsal rooms if you ask first.

More of a curiosity, on a hill just north of Porirua and near SH1, is the **New Zealand Police Museum**, in the grounds of the Royal New Zealand Police College, Papakowhai Road (Wed–Sun 10am–4pm or by appointment ☎04/238 3141; $5), detailing police history with carefully laid out displays. One particular strength is the attention paid to specific cases such as the sinking of the Greenpeace flagship *Rainbow Warrior* by two agents of the French Government's DGSE security force in Auckland Harbour in 1985; and the Springbok Tour of 1981, which sparked demonstrations of a size and intensity seldom previously seen in New Zealand, a strong anti-apartheid lobby clashing with more traditional sports fans. Both events are described in detail, alongside pertinent objects such as the engine-room clock of the *Rainbow Warrior*, which stopped at the exact moment the blast ripped through the hull; and a mounted Springbok head given by the rugby team to the New Zealand Police to thank them for their efforts in policing the tour. To get there **by car**, continue 2km north from the main roundabout on SH1 on the outskirts of the city centre. Turn right onto Whitford Brown Avenue, then onto Papakowhai Road. If you travel **by train** alight at Porirua station and take a #31 bus that leaves every hour on the half hour (Mon–Sat only, 8.30am–3.30pm, $1.40; ask for the police college), or a cab ($6–7) or walk the 1.75km (about 30min).

For a change of pace, tackle the moderately hard **Colonial Knob Walkway** (7.5km; 3–4hr return), a hill track across the forested hills to the west of Porirua and the highest point within the Wellington urban area. From the summit of Colonial Knob (468m) there are amazing **views** of Mana and Kapiti islands, Mount Taranaki to the north, Wellington and its harbour, and south as far as the Marlborough Sounds and the Kaikoura Ranges. The walk begins at Elsdon, in the western part of Porirua, from either the car park on Broken Hill Road, off Raiha Street, or from Camp Elsdon Camping Ground on Raiha Street. To get here from Porirua train station it's a 15-minute walk through the city centre to Camp Elsdon, a bus ($1.40) drops off within easy walking distance of Camp Elsdon, or a cab from the station costs around $6.

Practicalities

Porirua's small and helpful **visitor centre** is centrally located at 8 Cobham Court (Mon–Sat 9am–5pm, Sun 11–3pm; ☎04/237 8088, *poriruainfo@visitorshop.co.nz*) and acts as agent for bus, train and ferry bookings. If you're looking for somewhere to **stay** that's near the capital but out of the hubbub, the visitor centre can recommend B&Bs and homestays; or try the upmarket and relaxing *Braebyre B&B*, Flightys Road, Pauatahanui, north of Porirua (call for directions ☎04/235 9311, fax 235 9345; ⑤–⑦), some twenty minutes' drive from Wellington. Set amid rolling hills and incorporating a small mohair-goat farm, this big modern house has a private guest wing with three rooms (one en-suite) and the cooking is great (dinner on request, $30).

To get to Porirua by public transport, take one of several daily TranzMetro trains from Wellington train station to Porirua city centre (Mon–Fri every 30min, more frequently at peak times; ☎04/801 7000; $3.60 one way at peak, $2.70 off-peak). By bus to or from Wellington, the three times daily Intercity/Newmans and the twice daily White Star drop off at the combined bus and train station.

Paraparaumu and around

The coast's main tourist centre and the only jumping-off point to Kapiti Island (see overleaf), **PARAPARAUMU** lies 45km from Wellington. Paraparaumu's main shopping and business centre is on the highway, while its small beachside settlement, imaginatively named **Paraparaumu Beach**, is 3km west along Kapiti Road. The long sandy beach is safe for swimming and looks directly out onto Kapiti Island. The beach community is small, consisting of just a few holiday homes, cafés and bars, and a shopping centre straddling three main streets, Maclean Street (branching off Kapiti Road and leading to the beach), Marine Parade at the waterfront, and Seaview Road, one block back.

Anyone with a sweet tooth should stop off at **Nyco Chocolate Factory** (daily 9am–5pm), a kilometre or so south of Paraparaumu, on the corner of the main highway and Raumati Road, to visit their shop stuffed with goodies or join a guided tour (Mon–Fri 10.30am & 2.30pm except public holidays; $1). Up to 90,000 chocolates are made here every day, and the informative tour comprises twenty minutes in the factory itself, with plenty of background on the manufacturing process and a demonstration of melting and moulding, followed by a further fifteen minutes in Kapiti

Candies, an adjacent lollipop and fudge factory that makes the fillings. More savoury tastes are catered for at the touristy **Lindale Farm Complex**, about 2km north of Paraparaumu on SH1, where you can sample the myriad French-style **Kapiti Cheeses**, among New Zealand's finest, which are made in the complex and sold in a small shop (daily 9am–5pm; free); or take a break at the well-priced café *The Farm Kitchen*, (daily 7am–5pm), offering hearty snacks, light lunches and great cakes and coffee.

A couple of kilometres further north, signposted off SH1 at Otaihanga Road, is the **Southward Car Museum** (daily 9am–4.30pm; $5), a stunningly comprehensive collection of veteran and vintage cars, kept in mint condition and displayed in rotation in a specially built showroom, each accompanied by a detailed history. Gems include Marlene Dietrich's Rolls-Royce, a 1915 Stutz Racer, a gull-winged Mercedes Benz and a Chicago gangster's armour-plated Cadillac.

Practicalities

The volunteer-run **visitor centre** is in the car park of the Coastlands shopping centre, on SH1 (Mon–Sat 9am–4pm; ☎ & fax 04/298 8195, *kapiti.info@levin.pl.net*), and has local and DOC information. InterCity and Newmans' **buses** drop off at the train station opposite, as do local services from Wellington; the **train station** is directly opposite Coastlands and the visitor centre ($7.50 one way from Wellington, or $10 return after 10am). Places to **stay** are limited to a backpackers and a luxury motel at the beach; and a number of run-of-the-mill motels at the beach and in the main town, plus a campsite at the Lindale Farm Complex. Just across from the beach, *Barnacles Seaside Inn*, 3 Marine Parade (☎04/298 4856, singles ①, doubles ②–③), is a comfortable backpackers with rooms but no dorms. For luxury try the beachside motel *Wrights by the Sea*, 387–389 Kapiti Rd (☎04/902 7600, fax 902 7601, *wrights@paradise.net.nz*), while the newest of the motels in the main town is *Lindale Lodge*, on SH1 2km north of Coastlands (☎04/298 7933, fax 297 2544, *lindale_lodge@xtra.co.nz*; ⑤). Just north of town, off SH1, is the *Lindale Motor Park* (☎04/298 8046, fax 297 1910; powered sites $10, cabins ②, tourist flats ④).

Eating is best done at Paraparaumu Beach. Top choice is *Brier Patch*, 9 Maclean St (☎04/902 5586; book ahead Thurs–Sat evenings; BYO & licensed), an intimate restaurant specializing in superb, moderately priced Creole and Cajun food for lunch (Wed–Fri), dinner (daily from 6pm) and weekend brunch (10am–3pm); there's a separate bar for casual drinking, coffee and desserts. Otherwise settle for the cheap and cheerful *Fagins Eatery*, in the *Copperfield Motel* complex, 7–13 Seaview Rd, a cosy BYO restaurant that dishes up traditional roast beef and Yorkshire pudding. They also do an all-day breakfast for $10, and snacks along the lines of savoury pancakes with brie, avocado and bacon.

Kapiti Island

One of the few easily accessible island **nature reserves** in New Zealand, **Kapiti Island** is a magical spot, its regenerating bush home to birdlife that has become rare or extinct on the mainland. In 1822, infamous Maori chief **Te Rauparaha** captured the island from its first-known Maori inhabitants and, with his people the Ngati Toa, used it as a base until his death in 1849; it's thought that he may be buried somewhere on the island, but the site of his grave is kept secret. For this, and other reasons, the island is considered extremely spiritual to Maori.

Designated a reserve in 1897, the island is a mere 10km long and about 2km wide. Late January and February are the best months to visit, when the **birds** are at their most active, but any time of the year is good. Among those you're likely to see are kaka (bush parrots that are apt to land on your head or shoulder), weka, kakariki (parakeets), whiteheads (bush canaries), tui, bellbirds, fantails, wood pigeons and robins, though there are many others including a handful of the 200 takahe that exist in the world. The island can be explored on three **walking tracks**, two of them linking up to lead to the island's highest point (521m), which gives spectacular views, though the best variety of birdlife is found along the lower parts of the tracks – take your time, keep quiet and stop frequently (allow about 3hr for the round-trip). Most people only have time to go to the top and back. The easiest approach is to ascend **Trig Track** and descend the steeper, and sometimes slippery, **Wilkinson Track**. The third option (2–3hr), **North Track**, follows the coast to the island's northern end, climbing quite steeply in places to about fifty metres above sea level and leading to a lagoon thronged with waterfowl such as royal spoonbills.

The exceptionally clear waters of the marine reserve make for great **snorkelling** around the rocks close to the shore and **scuba diving** (see below for dive operators), particularly to the west and north of the island, where there are some interesting formations such as a rock archway known as the Hole-in-the-Wall. Three types of habitat – a boulder bottom, sheltered reef and sand bottom – are home to a rich variety of marine life, including orange and yellow sponges (some very rare), and luxuriant seaweed beds feeding kina and paua. Visiting ocean fish like moki and kingfish are common, and occasionally you'll see rare and subtropical fish.

Practicalities

The DOC manage the island but allow limited numbers of visitors on **day-trips** (daily except Christmas day & New Year's day) and a handful at a time on expensive overnight trips. A maximum of fifty are allowed onto Kapiti Island each day, having first arranged **landing permits** ($8 per person, valid for 6 months in case weather prevents a crossing) with the Department of Conservation in Wellington (see p.436). **Book** as far **ahead** as possible, allowing at least a day, but note that weekends from December to March are booked three months in advance. To arrange **transport** from Paraparaumu Beach, contact either of the two launch operators, both of whom depart from Paraparaumu at 9am and return around 3.30pm, charging $30 return per person for the ten- to fifteen-minute trip: Kapiti Marine Charter (☎04/297 2585 & 0800/433 779) or Kapiti Island Alive (☎04/237 7965 & 0800/527 484), the latter make another sailing at 9.30am and also run excellent tours (see below).

On **arrival**, you are greeted by the ranger, whose 30-minute talk explains what there is to do and see on the island; a copy of the informative DOC booklet, *Kapiti Island Nature Reserve* (usually $2), is included in the price of the landing permit. Perhaps the best way to get to grips with the island is by joining one of Kapiti Island Alive's enlightening guided tours (book ahead by phone as above, or on *Kapiti_Tours@clear.net.nz*; 1hr; $10–15), focusing on either cultural or natural history, or a mixture of the two. Alternatively PADI-qualified **divers** can arrange a full-day trip with New Zealand Sea Adventures, 65 Omapere St, Wellington (☎04/236 8787; full day $80), who are members of DINZ (Dive Industry New Zealand) and can supply gear and transport.

The island has a single lavatory at the landing point, and if you take a picnic lunch be sure to bring back all the rubbish. However, should you fancy **staying** for the astounding dawn chorus your options are limited: *Kapiti Nature Lodge* (☎06/364 8818, fax 364 5828; ⑨) offers a 4-bed bunkroom or 2-bed room for a whopping $130 per person and $140 per person respectively, including all meals.

Waikanae

WAIKANAE, 7km from Paraparaumu, is another small town divided between the highway and a beach community, 4km away along Te Moana Road. The broad, dune-backed sandy **beach** has no facilities but is safe for swimming.

The Kapiti Coast's main **DOC office** is here, at 10 Parata St, one street west of the main highway (☎04/296 1112, fax 296 1115, *kapiti.info@levin.pl.net*; Mon–Fri 8am–12.30pm & 1–4.30pm), and can advise on Kapiti Island permits but do not sell them (see previous page). The **train station** (limited commuter service) is centrally located on SH1 near the volunteer-run **visitor centre** (Mon–Fri 9.30am–3pm, Sat 9am–noon; ☎04/293 3278) in the library in Mahara Place shopping centre off Ngaio Road (in turn off SH1). InterCity and local (Mana Coach Services ☎04/235 8819) **buses** pull in at the corner of Ngaio Road and SH1.

The only real reason to stop is the **Nga Manu Sanctuary**, a large man-made bird sanctuary (daily 10am–5pm; $7.50), with easy walking tracks and some picnic spots. A 1.5-kilometre loop track cuts through a variety of habitats, from ponds and scrubland to swamp and coastal forest, which attract all manner of birds. There is also a nocturnal house containing kiwi, morepork and tuatara, plus eels are fed at 2pm daily. To get here, follow Te Moana Road off SH1 for just over a kilometre and turn right at Ngarara Road; the sanctuary is a further 3km.

Otaki and around

The northern gateway to the Kapiti Coast, **OTAKI** lies beside a broad, braided section of the Otaki River, in a rich fruit-growing area. For most of the year, this is a quiet place with a strong Maori heritage but, like other towns along this coast, it changes beyond recognition during the high-summer months of December to March, when its population of 4500 swells by a further 2000 or so.

Divided into three parts, the town is announced by a scattering of services on the main highway. Two kilometres towards the sea along Mill Road is the tiny main centre, consisting of little more than a few bars and shops, a post office and a couple of banks. **Otaki Beach**, 2.5km further on, is a long gentle curve of grey sand, backed by dunes and reasonably safe for swimming in summer, being well patrolled by the surf club. There's little here except holiday homes and a small general store.

On Te Rauparaha Street, off Mill Road and 2.5km from the main highway, is the barren site of what was once the finest **Maori church** in New Zealand. Rangiatea Church, begun in 1849, burned to the ground in 1995. All that's left is the graveyard, at the far end of which is a tombstone shaded by two Norfolk pines and bearing the name of Maori chief Te Rauparaha – though it's thought that his remains may have been exhumed by a group of his followers and re-interred on Kapiti Island.

Otaki Gorge and Otaki Forks

A kilometre south of the town, a scenic one-way detour, **Otaki Gorge Road**, branches off from the main highway (signposted just before the bridge). Striking deep into the hills of regenerating bush, the road twists for 19km through the dramatic gorge of the Otaki River to **Otaki Forks**, the main western entrance to the **Tararua Forest Park**, the last 7km being unsealed and narrow. A shuttle service (Silver Shuttle ☎06/364 5167) from Otaki runs to the park for around $20 per person.

Straddling the spine of the southernmost prong of the North Island, the wild terrain of the **Tararua Forest Park** can also be accessed from **Levin** in the west (see p.263) and from **Masterton** in the east (see p.425).

Along the road is the **Tararua Outdoor Recreation Centre** (☎06/364 3110, fax 364 2210, *TORC@xtra.co.nz*), specializing in adventure activities on the river (Grade II–III) and in the park. Based on the principle that not all whitewater rafting has to be white knuckle, the team offer **rafting** and other outdoor activities, including abseiling (prices on request), kayaking (from $45) and mountain biking ($25 per half day, $35 per day). A highlight is the night rafting (from $55), an exhilarating trip between riverbanks illuminated by flickering glow-worms, with the gorge eerily silent save for the roaring of the rapids. River-wise groups of two or more can also freedom rent rafts or kayaks ($20 or $30 per person per day; wetsuit $10). There's an affordable on-site licensed café here and you can arrange with the centre to be picked up from Otaki train station for free; if their driver is unavailable a shuttle from Otaki costs $10 per person.

Most of the forest park is accessible only to serious trampers, though there are a few shorter and less intimidating **walks** from **Boielle Flat** at the end of the main road, where a resident ranger provides assistance and information, and keeps an intentions book in his house opposite the picnic site; there's also a basic campsite at **Schoolhouse Flat**, partway along the road. The majority of walks in this area take in the remains of old boilers, stone walls, and remnants of abandoned logging and farming endeavours that are gradually being engulfed by regenerating bush. At the Waiotauru car park, at the road-end, is the start of the **Fenceline Walk** (about 3km; 2hr), offering excellent views of the river flowing down the valley to the coast.

Practicalities

Buses drop off outside the **visitor centre** at Centennial Park, on the corner of SH1 and Mill Road (Mon–Fri 8.30am–5pm, Sat & Sun 9am–3pm, with extended hours in summer; ☎06/364 7620, fax 364 7630, *kapiti.info@levin.pl.net*), and the **train station** is a two-minute walk away. The visitor centre has free town maps, sells **hut passes** for tracks in the Tararua Forest Park and acts as a booking agency for InterCity/Newmans, White Star, Tranz Rail, and for ferries to the South Island.

There's pleasant backpacker **accommodation** just outside town, on the southern side of the Otaki River, at *Toad Hall Backpackers*, off Addington Road (☎06/364 6906, *toad_hall@xtra.co.nz*; tent sites $8, dorms ①, rooms ②), a carefully renovated manor house set in farmland; they offer a free pick-up service from town. One block back from the beach, the large *Otaki Beach Motor Camp*, 40 Moana St (☎06/364 7107, fax 364 8123; tent sites $7, cabins & on-site vans ②), is well kept and simple. For more trappings, head for *Byron's Resort*, 20 Tasman Rd (☎06/364 8121 & 0800/800 122, fax 364 8123, *byrons.resort@xtra.co.nz*; tent sites $11, tourist flats ④, motel units ⑤), a multi-faceted complex at the beach with a restaurant and bar, spa and swimming pool; or their attractive beachside cottage (⑥), just around the corner at 44 Marine Parade.

Eating in Otaki is best done at *Brown Sugar*, on SH1 at the southern outskirts of town, just over the Otaki River bridge (daily 9am–5pm), probably the best little café on the Kapiti Coast, serving delicious cakes, snacks and light lunches either inside or in a leafy garden. Otherwise try *Byron Brown's* in *Byron's Resort* (see above), a licensed restaurant offering good-quality dinners at moderate prices, plus daytime snacks and light meals.

travel details

Buses

From Wellington to: Masterton via the Hutt Valley (4 daily; 2hr); New Plymouth (3 daily; 6hr 30min); Paraparaumu (9 daily; 50min); Porirua (9 daily; 25min).

From Paraparauma to: Levin (9 daily; 1hr 20min); Otaki (9 daily; 1hr 5min); Palmerston North (9 daily; 2hr 15min).

Trains

From Wellington to: Auckland (2 daily; 11hr); Hutt Central/Waterloo (daily every hour; 20 min); Johnsonville, a suburb of Wellington (daily every 15min 6am–11.30pm; 21min); Levin (3 daily; 1hr 34min); Napier (1 daily; 5hr 30min); Otaki (1 daily; 1hr 14min); Palmerston North (3 daily; 2hr 15min); Paraparaumu (every hour 7am–5.15pm; 1hr); Porirua (daily every hour; 18min); Upper Hutt (daily every hour; 50min).

Ferries

From Wellington to: Picton (8–12 daily; 3hr or 1hr 45min; see p.450).

Flights

From Wellington to: Auckland (14 daily; 1hr); Bay of Islands (9 daily; 2hr 45min); Blenheim (20 daily; 25min); Christchurch (29 daily; 45min); Dunedin (12 daily; 2hr); Gisborne (8 daily; 1hr 10min); Hamilton (10 daily; 1hr 10min); Hokitika (5 daily; 2hr 15min); Invercargill (7 daily; 2hr 20min); Kaitaia (4 daily; 3hr 25min); Milford Sound (6 daily; 4hr 20min); Motueka (2 daily; 1hr 15min); Mount Cook (7 daily; 2hr 25min); Napier/Hastings (15 daily; 1hr); Nelson (20 daily; 35min); New Plymouth (8 daily; 55min); Palmerston North (19 daily; 35min); Picton (12–15 daily; 25min); Queenstown (10 daily; 3hr 20min); Rotorua (7 daily; 1hr 15min); Taupo (4 daily; 1hr); Tauranga (11 daily; 2hr 20min); Te Anau (5 daily; 4hr 5min); Timaru (7 daily; 1hr 50min); Wanaka (4 daily; 3hr 5min); Wanganui (4 daily; 45min); Westport (2 daily; 55min); Whakatane (10 daily; 2hr 10min); Whangarei (15 daily; 2hr 30min).

CHAPTER EIGHT

MARLBOROUGH, NELSON AND KAIKOURA

M any people's first impression of the South Island is formed when they travel by boat or plane to its northern end, and is crystallized by the intricacy of The Marlborough Sounds, the sweep of the bays from Nelson as they curl towards Farewell Spit, the splendour of the national parks, mountain lakes and streams, the ease of the wine region and the natural wonders of Kaikoura. In fact, if you had to choose only one area of New Zealand to visit, this would be a strong contender.

Most visitors travel between the North Island and the South Island by ferry, striking land at the schizophrenic town of **Picton** – drab in the winter, lively in the summer and surrounded by the consistently rugged and beautiful **Marlborough Sounds** where bays full of unfathomably deep water lap at tiny beaches and rickety boat jetties and the land rises steeply to forest or stark pasture. From here you will be within easy reach, to the west, of some of the country's most spectacular walking tracks and dazzling golden beaches, heading out from the lively city of **Nelson**. Each of the national parks in the region has a distinct identity: the most famous is the **Abel Tasman National Park**, while the newest is **Kahurangi**, through which the rugged and spectacular **Heaphy Track** forges a route to the West Coast. Hemmed in by these two national parks, **Golden Bay** is an isolated oasis on the far side of a marble mountain with a strange grassy moonscape pockmarked by limestone grottoes. The curve of the bay culminates

---

ACCOMMODATION PRICES

Accommodation listed in this guide has been categorized into one of nine price bands, as set out below. The rates quoted represent the **cheapest available** double or twin **room** – except for category ①, which are per-person rates for a dorm bed. Note that fees for **tent sites** and **DOC huts** (quoted in dollars) are also per-person, unless otherwise stated.

① under $20 per person	④ $60–80	⑦ $140–180
② under $40 per room	⑤ $80–100	⑧ $180–240
③ $40–60	⑥ $100–140	⑨ over $240

For more on accommodation, see p.34.

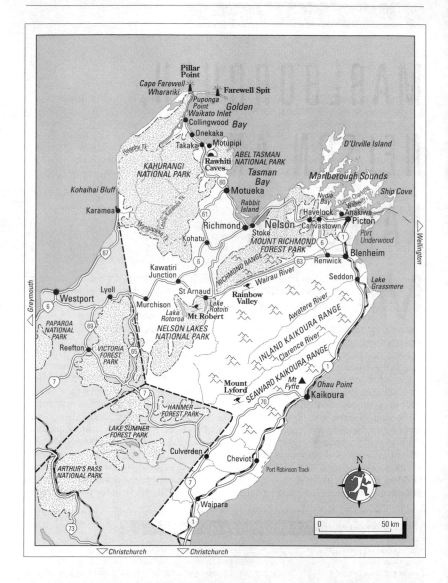

in a long sandy bar that juts into the ocean, **Farewell Spit**, an extraordinary and unique habitat. The most neglected of the region's national parks is the **Nelson Lakes**, a lively and exciting ski area in the winter and in the summer a sparsely populated, slumbering territory with access to Alpine lakes, flora and fauna, as well as providing a launch pad for rafting assaults on the Karamea and Buller rivers.

Heading in the opposite direction, east from Picton, you can slurp your merry way through **Marlborough**, the most famous wine-making region in New Zealand, with

Blenheim at its heart. The diversity of the region's communities makes for a certain individual outlook, while their rich farmland and coast inspires an easy-going **lifestyle** reminiscent of Mediterranean climes, attracting people from all over the world to settle and perfect their art, brewing techniques, wine, cooking and hospitality. Sated with good living, you can indulge the more spiritual side of your nature by watching **whales** and swimming with **dolphins** in **Kaikoura**. From here, you also have access to a number of challenging skifields – as yet blissfully uncrowded and inexpensive. The Kaikoura coast is a much more desolate-looking landscape which repays the observant traveller with the time to look beneath the surface. The **Kaikoura Ranges**, divided into the landward and seaward, provide a spectacular backdrop to travel along the coast, as well as evocative views from some of the highest peaks and most solitary tracks anywhere outside the Southern Alps.

Marlborough and Nelson enjoy more sunshine than most other parts of New Zealand in the spring and summer and a mild **climate** for most of the year; likewise, the Kaikoura region is generally mild, though often windy. Marlborough and Nelson are both extremely popular from Christmas to early February, with the Abel Tasman and Queen Charlotte **walkways** both attracting big **crowds**. This means solitude, beach space, bus seats and accommodation are difficult to find and it makes more sense to visit on either side of the most popular times, if you can. The tourist hot spot in Kaikoura is the town of Kaikoura itself, from where **whale-watching** excursions, and swimming with dolphins and seals run virtually year-round but it is important to **book** them **in advance** and to allow a day or two for cancellation and rescheduling, especially closer to winter.

Buses and **boats** provide access to the Nelson region and its coastal national parks, while **trains** and buses from Picton head east through Blenheim, Kaikoura and down the coast to Christchurch.

The Marlborough Sounds

The **Marlborough Sounds** are undeniably picturesque, whetting the appetite for the rest of the South Island and providing a lingering first impression for those travelling by ferry from the North Island. The Sounds' coastline is a stimulating filigree of bays, inlets, islands and peninsulas rising abruptly from the water to rugged, lush green wilderness and cleared farmland. Large parts are only accessible by sea, which also provides the ideal vantage point for witnessing its splendour. The area is part working farms, including salmon or mussel farms, and part given over to some fifty-nine reserve areas – a mixture of islands, sections of coast and land-bound tracts. The Sounds' nexus, **Picton**, is the jumping-off point for the rewarding **Queen Charlotte Walkway**, while close by is the small community of **Havelock**, which is well worth a stop to explore the delightful **Pelorus Sound** before pressing on to Nelson and the Abel Tasman National Park.

Picton and around

Sandwiched between the hills and the sea, **PICTON** is where the main **ferries** that ply the Cook Strait dock. Indeed, since the early 1960s, the town's fortunes have been largely determined by the machinations of ferry companies, never more so than in recent years when there has been talk of relocating the ferry terminal to the Blenheim or Nelson areas. The European settlement of Picton dates from 1827, when John Guard established a **whaling** station on its shores. Following the New Zealand Company's purchase of the town site for £300 in 1848, Picton flourished, acting as a port and **service town** for the Wairau Plains to the east.

These days Picton has a population of 4500 and acts as little more than a transit town but beneath its workaday surface it serves as a fascinating introduction to the delights of the South Island, with three **museums**, two focusing on New Zealand's **maritime heritage** and one concerned with Maori, and the whaling, gold, logging, fishing and farming interests that have dominated the lives of people who have settled here. As you would expect of a port, Picton also boasts an immense range of accommodation and a couple of fine eating houses, trading off the superb seafood found in the area.

Arrival and information

Ferries dock in Picton Harbour, 600m from the town centre, the **train station** is right by the ferry terminal, and **buses** drop off just outside. Koromiko **airport** is 9km from town – Soundsair Buses will run you into the centre for free if you're flying with them, or you can pick up a taxi for around $10 (see "Listings", p.476).

The combined **visitor centre** (daily: Oct–Dec 8.30am–6pm, Jan–Feb 8am–8.30pm, March–Sept 8.30am–5pm; ☎03/573 7477, fax 573 5021, *www.marlborough.co.nz*, *pcvin@nzhost.co.nz*) and **DOC office** (daily 8.30am–5pm; ☎03/520 3002, fax 520 3003) is on the foreshore, five minutes' walk from the ferry terminal. Here you can accumulate an enormous amount of bumph about the town and the South Island: take your pick from *Picton Walkways*, which details short walks around town; *Queen Charlotte Walking Track*; *Sidewalks and Byways*, which covers historic walks and drives en route to Blenheim and Havelock; *Art and Craft Trail*, which selects the best of the shops and galleries in the Marlborough region; and *Wines of Marlborough* for a rundown of all the wineries and their locations (all free); or the *Marlborough Sounds* leaflet ($1).

Almost directly opposite the official visitor centre and using a deceptively similar logo is The Station (9am–5pm; ☎03/573 8857) in the train station, which is actually a private **booking office** for trips, accommodation and onward travel – one of many in Picton.

Details of **transport** between the **North and South islands** are given in Chapter Seven; see "Crossing Cook Strait" on p.450.

Accommodation

As a major **transit centre**, Picton has a disproportionately large number of accommodation options for its size, ranging from backpacker hostels to swanky hotels, and you should have no difficulty finding somewhere to suit your needs within walking distance of the gangplank for most of the year, although **around Christmas** it makes sense to **book** in advance.

HOTELS AND MOTELS

Beachcomber Inn, 27 Waikawa Rd (☎03/573 8900, fax 573 8888). A large hotel complex overlooking the harbour with a swimming pool and spacious comfortable rooms; rates are higher for rooms on the upper floors with better views. ④–⑤.

Bellbird Motel, 96 Waikawa Rd (☎03/573 6912). Set back from the road, these 20-year-old units offer simple self-contained accommodation at a bargain price. ③.

Harbour View Motel, 30 Waikawa Rd (☎03/573 6259, fax 573 6982). Twelve modern, fully self-contained units with views over the harbour. ⑤.

Jasmine Court, 78 Wellington St (☎03/573 7110, fax 573 7211). Non-smoking throughout, these beautifully kept, luxury motel units are within walking distance of everything. ⑥.

Tourist Court, 45 High St (☎ & fax 03/573 6331). The best of both worlds – centrally located but quiet, these units (some with fridges and toasters, others with full kitchens), are roomy and comfortable. ③.

Queen
Charlotte
Sound

Havelock (scenic route)

△ Havelock (scenic route)

Queen Charlotte
Sound

PICTON

Fish & Chip Shop △ Blenheim (alternative route), Waikawa Bay, Te Awhina Kaha Marae & Port Underwood

Ferry
Terminal

Edwin Fox Museum
& Boat

Echo Gallery
& Museum

Dolphin
Watch
Community
Museum

Cougar Line &
Beachcomber
Cruises

Train
Station

Coat Hanger
Footbridge

ACCOMMODATION

Alexander's Holiday Camp	L
Atlantis Backpacker's	C
Beachcomber Inn	E
Bouganvillea Lodge	G
Echo Lodge	A
The Gables	I
Harbour View Motel	H
Jasmine Court	K
Picton Lodge	B
Tourist Court	D
The Villa	F
YHA Wedgewood House	J

RESTAURANTS, CAFÉS & BARS

Le Café	2
Expresso House	6
Holty's	5
Marlborough Terranean	3
Toot 'n' Whistle	1
The Settler's Arms	4

N

0   250 m

▽ ● (750 m) & Blenheim

B&BS AND HOMESTAYS

Echo Lodge, 5 Rutland St (☎03/573 6367). A pretty B&B with simple well-kept rooms, a friendly welcome and delicious home-made bread for breakfast, courtesy car available. ④.

The Gables, 20 Waikawa Rd (☎03/573 6772). An exceptional B&B run by considerate hosts who offer transport to ferries and planes, and cook up superb and filling breakfasts. Rooms are spacious and have private facilities. ⑤–⑥.

Lazy Fish Guest House, in the Sounds (☎03/579 9049). Accessible only by water taxi from Picton (20min; see "Listings" on p.476) or by seaplane from Wellington (Float Air ☎03/573 6433), this guesthouse offers beautiful views, seclusion and comfort at very reasonable prices. Dorms ①, rooms ③.

Ocean Ridge Homestay, on an unsealed road off the Port Underwood Rd, about 15km from Picton on the way to Blenheim (☎ & fax 03/579 9474). Overlooking Ocean Bay and Robinhood Bay, this homestay enjoys one of the most spectacular settings of any on the South Island. Perched high on a hill, with its own short walking tracks to the sea's edge, there are superb panoramic views from most rooms – which are large and have private bathrooms. There is also a squash court/half basketball court, stimulating company (the owners make and sell their own jewellery and pewter work) and superb food – dinners by arrangement, around $35. ⑤–⑥.

HOSTELS

Atlantis Backpackers in the dive school, Diver's World, cnr Auckland St & London Quay (☎03/573 7390). Central, purpose-built backpackers, this is small, comfortable and friendly with a free heated swimming pool and free breakfasts. Dorms ①, rooms ②.

Bouganvillea Lodge, 42 Auckland St (☎ & fax 03/573 6536). The smallest hostel in town, this is a friendly, comfortable place run by German speakers, who often turn their hand to home-made apple cake, pretzels and bread. Dorms ①, rooms ③.

Lochmara Lodge, Queen Charlotte Sound (☎ & fax 03/573 4554), accessible only by boat ($12–$15 each way). A mixture of backpacker and chalet (with kitchen) accommodation in this idyllic spot where you can just sit back and listen to the peace of the Sounds. Dorms ①, chalets ⑤.

The Picton Lodge, 3 Auckland St (☎03/573 7788, fax 573 8418). This purpose-built hostel is the closest to the ferry terminal and railway and noisier as a result, with a range of twins, doubles and dorms. Discounts for VIP and YHA members, $3 extra for linen and towel. Dorms ①, rooms ③.

The Villa, 34 Auckland St (☎ & fax 03/573 6598). One of the most-often-recommended hostels on the backpackers' grapevine, this 100-year-old house is close to the ferry terminal, offers free pick up, free breakfast, free soup in the winter, and a spa pool, as well as being friendly and a good place to pick up lots of information on things to see and do in the area (they produce their own seasonal newsletter). Dorms ①, rooms ③.

Wedgewood House (YHA Associate Hostel), 10 Dublin St (☎03/573 7797), restricted office hours (8–10am, 1–2pm, 5–6.30pm, 8–10pm). Central and cosy hostel in a small house but there are extra, larger rooms next door. Dorms ①, rooms ②.

CAMPSITES AND MOTOR PARKS

Alexander's Holiday Camp, southeastern end of Canterbury St (☎03/573 6378). This campsite by a creek is about 2km from the ferry terminal, with camping space, cabins and two converted railway carriages that ooze charm. Tent sites $16, cabins & carriages ②–③.

Blue Anchor, 70–78 Waikawa Rd (☎ & fax 03/573 7212). Centrally located campsite with a swimming pool, children's playground, cabins (bedding $1) and motel-style units, in a pleasant spot with trees providing shelter. Tent sites $18, cabins & motel units ②–④.

Waikawa Bay Holiday Park, 302 Waikawa Rd (☎ & fax 03/573 7434). Five minutes' drive from the ferry terminal, this large, sheltered site has views over the water. Tent sites $17, cabins & motel units ②–④.

The Town

The town heads back from the ferry terminal toward the surrounding hills where dense native and introduced forest and foliage provides a green backdrop. Most of Picton's most interesting sights are on or near the foreshore, a pretty area with palms, mini golf and picnic benches overlooking the harbour.

Between the ferry terminal and the town centre is the hulk of the **Edwin Fox** (daily 8.30am–5pm; $5), the sole survivor of the fleets that once brought migrants to New Zealand. You access the shell of the ship from the centre alongside, which contains fascinating displays on what remains of this 1853 ship, constructed from saul timber in India, and its colourful life, as well as the mammoth task of preservation that lies ahead. The *Edwin Fox* operated as a troop carrier in the Crimean War and transported convicts to Australia, before bringing free settlers to New Zealand. In later years, the ship was put to service as a merchant vessel, including a spell helping to establish the frozen meat trade in New Zealand. Towed into Shakespeare Bay (just west of Picton), in 1967, for twenty years the *Edwin Fox* received only the attentions of the weather and vandals until, in 1986, surprisingly still sound below the waterline, the vessel was floated back to Picton Harbour where she was finally dry-docked in a purpose–built berth.

Heading further around the bay, the foreshore area is home to the **Picton Community Museum**, on London Quay (daily 10am–4pm; $3). The main feature of the museum are displays devoted to the Perano Whaling Station, which operated in Queen Charlotte Sound until 1964. There are photographs of the station in its heyday, and a harpoon gun from one of the steamboat chasers as well as some excellent examples of scrimshaw (whale-bone carving). Smaller displays deal with Maori and *pakeha* local history, and there is a finely carved chair inlaid with *paua* (blue-green shell), as well as a large collection of brightly coloured shells from all over the world.

Continuing around the harbour and across the Coat Hanger footbridge, it is a short walk to the unique **Echo Gallery and Museum** (Sept–April daily 10am–6pm; $2.50), a tribute to the scows and scowmen of New Zealand that's well worth an hour or two of your time. Built in 1905, the *Echo* was a top-sail schooner, with a square bilge scow-type hull, developed to take cargo from the sea upriver to the remote communities of New Zealand. From 1920 she ran river services out of Blenheim, and was the last ship to trade commercially under sail in New Zealand waters, before entering the fray in World War II. Retrieved from a ships' graveyard, she was used by the US Navy as a supply ship for the New Hebrides, Solomon Islands and New Guinea area – a phase in her long history that inspired the 1961 Hollywood film *The Wackiest Ship in the Army*, a copy of which is shown on the shipboard video from time to time. There are also restored home movies of New Zealand scows at work, paintings and photographs around the hull walls and exhibits and explanations of the important role these ships played in the country's development.

The **Shelly Beach/Bob's Bay Track** starts just by the Marlborough Cruising Club, next to the Echo and extends for a kilometre along the shoreline, passing small, safe-swimming beaches and providing great views across the water to the ferry terminal and up the Queen Charlotte Sound before ending at Bob's Bay. From here the path heads away from the bay for about 500m to **Victoria Domain** for more superb views and meets the track on to **The Snout** (5km; 1hr 15min one way), whose evocative Maori name, *Te Ihumoeone-ihu*, translates as "the nose of the sand worm". At the tip of the promontory, you are rewarded with panoramic views of the Sounds and the ferries.

Just over three kilometres from Picton on the Waikawa Road is the **Te Awhina Kaha Marae**, 210 Waikawa Rd (☎03/573 7970), a superbly carved meeting house containing some excellent *tukutuku* (Maori panel work made of flax and wood); call ahead to see if there are any activities arranged – hangi are sometimes organized for groups, and you may be able to tag along but this can be expensive. If you continue along the Waikawa Road for about another kilometre, you will come to a turning for **Waikawa Bay** where, beside a picnic area, the impressive Maori ceremonial *waka* (canoe) *Te Awate Te Hou* is moored.

Eating and entertainment

Picton has a number of typical New Zealand **tearooms** offering cheap and cheerful fare near the foreshore and **cafés** serving snacks and coffee, with little to choose between them; the best of the rest are listed below.

The free weekly *Marlborough Express* newspaper contains **entertainment listings**, most of which is centred on several large, slightly tacky **pubs** along the waterfront that serve drink and cheap food all day.

Le Café 33 High St. Good quality, moderately priced European-influenced coffee house, plus veggie filo and salads adorned with a famous dressing, lamb and venison sausages and traditional home-made muffins. Daily 8am–10pm, BYO.

Expresso House, 58 Auckland St. Minimalist surroundings are relieved by rimu flooring, New Zealand oak tables and Native American photographs on the walls. Great food includes chicken satay, beef salads with yam cakes, salmon and brie melts, and crepes served with home-made maple yoghurt; day-time menu under $12, night-time under $18. Sept–March daily 11am–late, April–Aug closed Wed; BYO.

Holty's, cnr High St & Dublin St (☎03/573 8823). Quality, eat–in or takeaway emporium occupying a converted garage. Serves breakfast, pizzas, fish and charcoal-grilled chicken and is now opening another branch in Palmerston North. Daily 9am–9pm; licensed.

Marlborough Terranean, 31 High St (☎03/573 7122). Still the tastiest food in town and one of the best restaurants on the South Island. Fine dining in comfortable surroundings with a relaxed jazz-soaked atmosphere, and imaginative dishes such as Marlborough rack of lamb on garlic potato mash with tarragon jus, fresh fish in a choice of three delicious sauces – and frighteningly good desserts. They take food seriously, offer a very broad selection and then have fun. Evening meals only (main courses $20–30). Licensed.

The Settlers Arms, 33 Wellington St. This 1903 building was once a branch of the Bank of New Zealand, but has found a new lease of life as a cosy café-bar, quiet, of limited ambition and flair, offering good value for money. Daily 11am–late.

Toot'n Whistle, Auckland St, next to the *Picton Lodge Backpackers*. Friendly bar which serves massive portions of simple, cheap, typical pub food and offers the chance to meet most of the locals. Daily 9am–late.

Listings

Airlines Soundsair (☎0800/505 0005) operate services to Wellington (see box on p.451 for details).

Airport buses Soundsair Buses (☎0800/505 0005), Blenheim Taxis (☎03/578 0225).

Banks Picton has branches of a couple of the major banks (ANZ and Westpack Trust), on High Street.

Bookshops Paper World, 28 High St (Mon–Sat 9am–5pm).

Buses InterCity (☎09/357 8400) run to Nelson, Blenheim and Christchurch via Kaikoura; Deluxe Travel Line (☎03/578 5467) go to Blenheim; Nightline Buses (☎03/577 2024) serve Nelson and Blenheim. Sounds to Coast (☎03/578 0225) go to St Arnaud on Mon, Wed and Fri. Atomic Shuttles (☎0508/108 359) run to Christchurch. Fares are in the region of $10–$15 to Blenheim, $20–$30 to Nelson and $30–$40 to Christchurch.

Car rental Most of the major international and Kiwi companies have offices at the Ferry Terminal: Avis (☎03/573 6363), Avon (☎03/573 6009), Budget (☎03/573 6081), Hertz (☎03/573 7224), New Zealand Rent A Car (☎03/573 7282). Elsewhere, try Pegasus, 5 Auckland St (☎03/573 7733), or Rent-a-Dent, cnr London Quay & Auckland St (☎03/573 7787).

Diving Divers World, cnr London Quay & Auckland St (☎03/573 7323) offer gear rental, dive trips and SSI (from $390) or PADI courses (from $395). Wreck dives are especially popular, exploring the wreck of the Mikhail Lermontov, a Russian liner which sank in the Sounds in 1986.

Medical treatment Picton Medical Centre, 74 High St (☎03/573 6092).

Pharmacy Mc Guires, 3 High St (Mon–Sat 9am–5pm). The free *Marlborough Express* and the *Seaport News* contain lists of after-hours duty pharmacists and emergency services.

Post office The main post office is in the Mariners Mall on High Street (Mon–Fri 9am–5pm, Sat 9am–12.30pm).

Sailing Just Sailing, Waikawa Marina (☎03/573 4440, fax 573 4577) offer half- and full-day fun sails ($40–$80), or introductory sailing courses and skills development packages (from $300).

Taxis Blenheim Taxis (☎03/578 0225); see also "Water taxis" below.

Tours De Lux Wine Trail (☎03/578 5467 & 0800/500 511) run a day-trip, taking in a number of the better wineries, for around $40; The Sounds Connection (☎03/573 8843), offer a number of tours, buses to the skifields and Queen Charlotte Walkway.

Trains Tranz Scenic (☎0800/802 802) run to Christchurch once a day, with fares starting at $31 one way.

Water sports Sunnyvale Motel, 384 Waikawa Rd (☎03/573 6800) rents out windsurfers ($25 an hour), kayaks ($50 per half day), laser yachts ($40 per half day), and a catamaran ($50 per half day).

Water taxis Arrow Water Taxis (☎03/573 8229); Beachcomber Fun Cruises (☎03/573 6175); Cougar Line (☎03/573 7925, *westbay@xtra.co.nz*); Endeavour Express (☎03/579 8465); The Sounds Connection (☎03/573 8843) and West Bay Water Transport (☎03/573 5597).

Weaving The House of Glenora, at 22 Broadway (☎03/573 6966, fax 573 7735), is a weaving school set in a beautiful old house; tuition costs $50–80 a day, and a workshop to learn a certain technique will take 5–7 days.

Exploring the Sounds

The Marlborough Sounds enclose moody, picturesque **bays**, small deserted sandy beaches, peninsulas of grandeur and great variation, **headlands** with panoramic views and cloistered **islands**. The Sounds offer shelter from the winds and storms in Cook Strait and solitude for the contemplative fisherman, kayaker or tramper. For a taster of the labyrinthine waterways around Picton, by all means take one of the many **day-cruises** available, but to really appreciate their tranquil beauty, you're far better off **kayaking** round the bays or **tramping** the Queen Charlotte Walkway.

Cruises and tours

Several companies run cruises on the Sounds, or you can catch a **water taxi** to various points and explore on your own (see "Listings", opposite). The best of the **cruises** available are run by Beachcomber Fun Cruises (see "Listings", opposite) on their state-of-the-art ships: a twice-daily short cruise around the bays (2hr; $35), and a daily luncheon cruise with a stop at Torea Bay (5hr; $38); however the best trips are the **mailboat runs** (Mon, Tues, Thurs & Fri 11.15am; 5hr; $62), which alternate between two routes, either calling at bays in the Queen Charlotte Sound, as well as the Regal Salmon Farm and the Perano Whaling Station, or heading into Endeavour Inlet, Resolution Bay and Ship Cove. Another mailboat runs through Pelorus Sound from Havelock (see p.480); on all the mail trips, tea and coffee is provided, but you must bring your own lunch. The *Cougar Line* (☎03/573 7925 & 0800/504 090) offers a variety of one-day **walking trips** with drop off and pre-arranged pick up in the bays of the Queen Charlotte Sound ($43), as well as scenic cruises (8am, 10am & 1.30pm; 3hr; $43) to Ship Cove.

Excellent in their own right and a good compromise between the standard cruises and the close-up approach of kayaking are the **eco-tours** offered by Dolphin Watch (☎03/573 8040). From their office next door to the visitor centre in Picton, they drive you to Waikawa Bay, about 4km northeast, where you board their small boat at either 8.45am or 1.45pm (connecting with the ferry). The trip focuses on Queen Charlotte Sound (half day; $60 return, $45 one way to Ship Cove), offering the chance of seeing enormous numbers of sea birds (including penguins), before landing at the stunning **Motuara Island**. The island has a superb lookout over Cook Strait – and is home to the South Island bush robin, bellbird, pigeon, blue penguin and the rare saddleback. All the birds are quite fearless, since they live in a relatively predator-free environment, and will rest and fly startlingly close to you. The tour continues to Ship Cove, where you'll get a rundown on Cook's history and from where you can either return to Picton, or stay and tackle the Queen Charlotte Walkway (see overleaf).

Kayaking

Of the many companies offering kayaking, Marlborough Sounds Adventure Company (☎03/573 6078, fax 573 8827, *msac@msadventure.co.nz*) is the best organized and most professional, and their membership of the SKOANZ (Sea Kayaking Operators Association of New Zealand) indicates a high level of care. Their **guided kayak trips** range from one to four days (day-trip $85, including meals; 4 days, 2 days' kayaking and 2 days' walking, plus accommodation $750). Another popular jaunt is their twilight paddle, with a barbecue against a background of the sparkling lights of Picton ($60). Marlborough Sounds Adventure Company also offer guided and self-guided track walks (see overleaf). Sea Kayaking Adventure Tours, Anikawa (☎ & fax 03/574 2765, *skata@xtra.co.nz*), have one-day guided tours ($65) as well as walk and paddle options which involve walking the Queen Charlotte, or part of it, and then sea-kayaking back or vice versa. Both companies have **rental kayaks** (around $40 per day) for independent paddlers and Sea Kayaking Adventure Tours rent out mountain bikes ($30 per day).

The Queen Charlotte Walkway

The **Queen Charlotte Walkway** (67km; 3–5 days) is a spectacular walk through the Marlborough Sounds from Ship Cove to Anakiwa or vice versa. It boasts wonderful views of the Queen Charlotte and Kenepuru sounds and passes through dense coastal forest and golden sandy bays, and sometimes lords over it all on skyline ridges. A classified, DOC-administered track, it is broad and relatively easy going – it doubles as a **mountain-biking** track between March and November (allow 2–3 days), while Punga Cove to Anakiwa is open to bikes all year round. A leaflet outlining the walk and biking dos and don'ts is available from the visitor centre ($1).

Queen Charlotte Sound was an important trade route and provided good shelter and bountiful food for **Maori**, who carried canoes over the low saddles of the walkway to avoid long, unnecessary and hazardous sea journeys around the full length of the Sounds. **Captain Cook** stopped at Ship Cove on five occasions and made it his New Zealand base, spending over 100 days there between 1770 and 1777. The shelter and fresh water made it an ideal spot and its plentiful supplies of (what became known as) Cook's scurvy grass were particularly valued for its vitamin C content, which provided vital relief from scurvy.

The changing seasons are reflected by splashes of colour: karaka groves are laden with bright yellow berries in the summer; native clematis (puawanga) are festooned with creamy-white **flowers** in the spring; and supplejacks and kohia (Kiwi passion fruit) produce red and orange fruits in the autumn. As a result, there is no shortage of **birds**, with tui and bellbirds in profusion, as well as the ever-friendly fantails and little piebald robins. The forests also contain the owls known as moreporks (so named for their cry, which sounds like a request for "more pork"), while the beaches and crag faces boast an abundance of shags, gannets, terns and shearwaters, as well as the stooping oystercatchers patrolling in pairs. If you are lucky, you may even spot a little blue penguin making its way to the fishing grounds in the morning or on its way home in the evening.

ACCESS

Most people walk from Ship Cove to Anakiwa: **water taxis** (see also "Listings", p.476) link with Ship Cove and almost anywhere in between it and the tiny Torea Bay, close to Anikiwa, so you can pick and mix sections fairly easily.

Beachcomber Fun Cruises (☎03/573 6175) will run you anywhere in the Queen Charlotte Sound or Tory Channel and operate a Picton–Torea Bay **ferry** ($16) or Picton–Anakiwa ($19); they also cater for day walkers with several drop-off and pick-up itineraries. Cougar Line (☎03/573 7925 & 0800/504 090) will drop you at Ship Cove and then deliver your pack to each night's accommodation ($48), and also offer day-walk options. Endeavour Express, based in Endeavour Inlet (☎03/579 8465) have daily departures for Ship Cove (9.30am; $30, pack transfers free; round trip $45), and return trips to Bay of Many Coves and Torea Bay for **day-trippers** ($15–25 each way). One of the quickest water taxi services is West Bay Water Transport offering Torea Bay, Double Cove, Lochmara Bay, Onahau Bay, Waterfall and Mistletoe Bays all for $15 one way, and Tirimoana, The Grove and Momorangi for $19 one way. In addition, **shuttle bus** services between Picton and Anakiwa are offered by Sounds Connection (☎03/573 8843) and the Rural Mail Run, both bookable through the Picton visitor centre (☎03/574 2765); they charge around $10–$15 per person, although Sounds Connection impose a minimum of four or a charge of $45.

Marlborough Sounds Adventure Company (☎03/573 6078, fax 573 8827) offer a four-day **guided walk** along the Queen Charlotte Walkway ($845, fully inclusive); a cheaper option is to **self-guide** but have all your accommodation and transport needs taken care of ($410). Sea Kayaking Adventure Tours, Anikawa (☎03/574 2765) can arrange various trips that combine **biking** and walking the track.

ACCOMMODATION
Compared with some of the remoter tracks, the Queen Charlotte Walkway has plenty of **places to stay**. The DOC administer seven **campsites** (all $4), which have water and toilets. There are also several privately owned places to stay on or near the track, for which bookings are essential. Most have a range of accommodation, from camping space and **backpacker bunks** to self-contained **resort units** and luxurious rooms; those offering the better deals are listed below.

Anikawa Backpackers, near the trail finish or head at Anikawa (☎03/574 2174, *gemresort@xtra.co.nz*). A straightforward, clean and simple hostel. Dorms ①.

Endeavour Holiday Resort, Endeavour Inlet (☎03/579 8381). A quiet and idyllic place near the water, with a restaurant, shop and safe swimming area. Dorms $20 without linen, chalets & units ④–⑤.

Furneaux Lodge, Endeavour Inlet (☎03/579 9411). A swanky lodge with a bar and restaurant and some shared accommodation. Dorms ①, chalets ⑤.

Gem Resort, Arthur's Bay (☎03/579 9771). Cabins tucked away in a corner of the Bay of Many Coves. Dorms ①, cabins ④–⑥.

Portage Hotel, Kenepuru Sound, ten minutes' walk along the road from Torea Bay (☎03/573 4309). Resort hotel with a friendly lounge bar and restaurant. Dorms ①, rooms ⑥–⑧.

Resolution Bay Cabins, Resolution Bay (☎03/579 9411). The closest accommodation to Ship Cove (4.5km), in a pretty spot offering swimming and canoes. Dorms ① cabins ③, cottages ⑤.

Smiths Farm and Holiday Park, 4km from the end of the track (☎03/574 2806). Not too far to walk and they have camp sites for $9 as well as cabins ② and en-suite rooms ③.

Te Mahia Resort, Te Mahia Bay, Kenepuru Sound (☎03/573 4089). Close to the walkway with a store – and glow-worms – nearby. Dorms ①, self-contained units ⑤.

THE ROUTE
The track passes through some grassy **farmland** and bleak gorse-covered **hills**, but both ends of the track are **forest** reserves with lush greenery, including nikau palms and climbing keikie, right down to the shoreline. There are a number of **detours** off the main track to places of interest, including a short walk from Ship Cove to a pretty forest-shrouded waterfall, a scramble down to the Bay of Many Coves, or a foray to the Antimony Mines (where there are exposed shafts – stick to the marked tracks). The most spectacular **views** are to be had en route to the mines and at Torea Saddle and Kenepuru Saddle.

Beginning at **Ship Cove**, the track climbs steeply away from the shore through largely untouched forest to a lookout with great views of Motuara Island, before dropping down into **Resolution Bay** (4.5km; 2hr), where there's a DOC campsite and other accommodation, or you can press on along an old bridle path over the ridge into **Endeavour Inlet** (15km; 5hr). From here, you have an easy second day, rounding the inlet, climbing to the **Kenepuru Saddle** and returning to the shoreline; there's a campsite in **Camp Bay** (11.5km; 4hr), but you may decide to push on for another four hours to **Bay of Many Coves**, where there is another campsite and cabin accommodation. Otherwise, day three, the longest and most rewarding stretch, takes you from Camp Bay along the ridge that separates the Kenepuru Sound from the Queen Charlotte Sound to **Torea Saddle** (20.5km; 9hr), where you can follow the road to Cowshed Bay for the DOC campsite or stay at the plush *Portage Resort Hotel*. On day four, you can choose a short ridge walk through beech and manuka forest to **Mistletoe Bay** (7.5km; 4hr) or a long slog high above the water, before descending to the DOC campsite at **Davies Bay** and continuing to the road at **Anakiwa** (20km; 9hr), where you can crash at the *Anakiwa Backpackers*, before meeting a pre-arranged water taxi pick-up.

Havelock and around

The 28km trip between Picton and **HAVELOCK** is quite spectacular (as is the 75km on to Nelson). Nestled in the heart of the Pelorus Sound, the town itself is tiny and looks uninspiring – a shortcoming more than made up for by the stunning Pelorus Sound, an exciting maze of sunken seaways with high mountain peaks that can be explored by boat or on foot.

A hundred years ago Havelock was a **boom town**, revelling in the wealth created by an inland gold rush and rampant logging, but then reverted to a sleepy fishing village with a straggle of buildings spread out along the main road and down by the wharf. Today it has, at least partially, revived as a result of the travellers who explore the Sound, discovering the fun to be had in these quiet environs. Havelock is the greenshell mussel capital of the world, and you simply can't leave before you've purchased some choice morsels from the wharf or better still taken some on board at the excellent **Mussel Boys Restaurant**. Until recently its other claim to fame was as the erstwhile home of itinerant author **Barry Crump**. Crumpy, as he was affectionately known, began life as a hunter and bushman, culling deer and pigs in some of New Zealand's roughest country – a way of life he described in a series of humorous, poignant and superbly descriptive novels (see Contexts p.878). The larger-than-life Crump presented television and radio shows and "researched" his books (a euphemism for dedicated drinking) until his demise in 1996. The **Havelock Museum**, on Main Road, near the Shell Garage (daily 9am–5pm; if locked, ask Mr Skinner, 9 Cook St, at the corner with Peel Street, or call Mrs Jacobson ☎03/574 2176; donation), is housed in two small cream wooden buildings and is probably only worth the trouble if it's already open. Among the usual collection of bric-a-brac is a wood-milling display and the honour rolls from Havelock School, which feature Ernest Rutherford, who first split the atom – and went to school here, in the building now occupied by the YHA, from 1886 to 1894.

Practicalities

Buses between Picton and Nelson all stop at Havelock, while local bus and **water-taxi** operators offer services to Kenepuru and Pelorus sounds. Of the three rival **information** outlets here, the Outdoor Adventure Centre, 65a Main Rd (daily: May–Oct 8.30am–5pm; Nov–April 8am–8pm; ☎03/574 2114), is the best with access to all DOC information, facilities for kayak and boat trip booking, Internet access, and mountain bike rental ($30 per day); second choice is Pelorus Enterprises, 60 Main Rd (☎03/574 2633; Dec–March Mon–Fri 8.30am–5pm, Sat & Sun 9am–4pm; April–Nov Mon–Fri 8.30–5pm, Sat 9am–4pm), where they also book trips (not necessarily the same ones) and have a pretty good local knowledge; last of the trio is Marlborough Travel Centre, 73 Main Rd (☎03/574 2532), which is geared to booking excursions or onward travel.

Accommodation options include *Havelock Garden Motel*, at 71 Main Rd (☎03/574 2387; ③–④), with six fully self-contained units and helpful hosts. On the corner of Main Road and Lawrence Street, *Pelorus Motor Inn* (☎03/574 2412; ④–⑤), has a few simple units without cooking facilities, though you can get a cheap meal in the tavern attached. Centrally located in the characterful old schoolhouse is the much improved *Rutherford YHA Hostel*, 46 Main Rd (☎03/574 2104; tent sites $7, dorms ①, rooms ②). Surrounded by large, ancient trees this friendly hostel has bright rooms and the staff are a mine of information on the best trips and things to see. Next door is the Marlborough Sounds Wilderness Company (see opposite). Off the beaten track at **Canvastown**, 10km west of Havelock, *Pinedale Motor Camp* (☎03/574 2349; tent sites $8, cabins & units ②–④) is a delightful spot to relax for a few days, with bushwalks, glow-worms, gold-panning and 1km of river frontage with swimming holes.

Food in Havelock has changed drastically in recent times for where once it was difficult to get hold of the glorious green-lipped mussels native to the area, now it couldn't be easier. Without doubt the best place to eat in town is the *Mussel Boys Restaurant*, 73 Main Rd (daily: Nov–March 11am–9pm; April–Oct noon–7pm; licensed) where they dish up mussels in a myriad of different guises, excellent chowder and a farmer's platter for those who don't like shellfish. Around the restaurant are details about mussels and a step-by-step guide on the best way to eat them. Other recommendations in town are *Pelorus Jack's Café*, corner of Main Road and Inglis Street, for breakfast, lunch or dinner (daily 6am–9pm); and the massive portions at the *Pelorus Tavern*, the *Pelorus Motor Inn* (see opposite), where for under $20 Shirley makes sure you stock up on carbohydrate before attempting any of the local walks. Finally for those hankering after an even slower pace there's the *Clansman Bar and Café* at 72 Main Rd where you can have a beer and eye the goodies in the deli.

Exploring Pelorus Sound

One of the best ways to see the Sound is aboard the *Pelorus Mail Boat*, run by Beachcomber Fun Cruises (☎03/573 6175; Tues, Wed & Thurs 9.30am; 7hr; $75), which sets off from Havelock Marina on its leisurely **mail run**, calling at isolated homesteads, a mussel farm and passing countless unspoilt beaches. The same company operates the **French Pass** cruise (8hr; $69, on demand with a minimum of twenty) along Pelorus Sound past Maud Island, and around to French Pass, at the entrance to the seething channel where the ship of nineteenth-century French explorer D'Urville was spun by tumultuous whirlpools. On both these trips, you need to bring your own lunch and a couple of jumpers out of season.

Here too, a good way to get into the nooks and crannies of Pelorus Sound is by **kayak**. Marlborough Sounds Wilderness Company has excellent guided trips (☎03/574 2610, *soundswild@xtraco.nz*; full day $75, overnight $95, from two to five days $140 per day), run from beside the YHA hostel, and are members of SKOANZ (see Basics p.55); they also offer freedom rentals for $40 a day. The alternative is Havelock Sea Kayaking Company, bookable through the Outdoor Adventure Centre, who have an almost identical array of trips, rentals and prices, but are not members of SKOANZ.

Walks around Havelock

A good vista can be had, by car or on foot, by heading west out of Havelock for about 5km and then following the logging road on your left, up hill for about fifteen minutes where you will, on a clear day, see great views of the Sounds.

Eighteen kilometres west of Havelock on SH6 is the **Pelorus Bridge Scenic Reserve**, which contains superb examples of black beech trees and golden green rimu, as well as kahikatea, miro and the blue-green foliage of matai trees. There is also an abundance of tui, grey warblers and bellbirds – and many swimming holes along the trout- and salmon-rich, sandy-beached rivers. This fertile area saw a succession of Maori settlements, which prospered until Te Rauparaha conquered the north of the South Island in the 1820s. The misery caused by the casualties of war and the encroachment of European settlers drove most of the Maori away – the few that remained produced flax that Te Rauparaha could trade for rifles.

Facilities include a basic DOC **camping** area (☎03/571 6019; tent sites $7, cabins ②) and several walking tracks. The **café** (daily: Nov–March 8.30am–7pm; April–Oct 8.30am–4pm) at Pelorus Bridge incorporates a **DOC office** and a small **shop**, as well as purveying delicious home-made coconut muffins, pastries, quiche and a selection of light meals.

Most of the **walks** in the reserve are fairly flat, well maintained and well marked: the **Totara** (1.5km return; 30min) and **Circle** (1km return; 30min) routes pass through the low-lying woodland for which the area is famous, while the **Trig K** (2.5km one way; 2hr), after a steady climb to 417m, offers stunning views of the whole area. From the summit you can head straight down or follow the **Beech Ridge Track** (3km; 90min), via two waterfalls, which takes the scenic route back to the start of the Trig K track. Some sources of information mention a track known as the Takarika but ignore them, this track is poorly-marked and you are liable to get lost.

Another rewarding tramp near Havelock is the **Nydia Track** (20km; 2 days), which starts at **Kaiuma Bay**, passes Nydia Bay and finishes at **Duncan Bay**. Following a series of bridle paths, the route makes its way through pasture, shrubland and virgin forest, with great views from the Kaiuma Saddle (387m) and Nydia Saddle (347m), as well as along the head of the bay. Maori called Nydia Bay *Opouri*, which means "place of sadness", because when a *hapu* (one faction of a tribe) was preparing to migrate from the North Island to the Sounds, their leader sacrificed a young boy to Tangora the sea god to ensure a safe journey. When the boy's father found out, he sought *utu* (revenge), storming across to Pelorus Sound and slaughtering the disgraced *hapu*.

Kaiuma Bay is 32km from Havelock by road: turn off SH6 12km west of Havelock onto Daltons Road – a car park at the end marks the beginning of the track. **Accommodation** is available at the *Nydia Lodge* (①), halfway along the track – but you'll need to get the key at the Outdoor Adventure Centre in Havelock (see p.480) or from the caretaker, whose house is signposted from the lodge; or at *Driftwood Lodge* (✆03/579 8454; ①) just beyond *Nydia Lodge* and very cosy.

Nelson and around

In a broad basin between the Arthur and Richmond ranges lies the thriving city of **NELSON**, which provides easy access to three national parks and Golden Bay. Add to this the universal appeal of sandy beaches and abundant sunshine, and it will come as no surprise that the Nelson region is one of the most popular destinations in New Zealand, with a mass of great activities and opportunities to indulge in the bounty of the land. The small satellite town of **Richmond**, 14km to the west, holds some of the area's most salubrious guesthouses and serves as a suburban retreat for commuters. Located at the junction of SH6 and SH60, it also marks the parting of the ways: south via the market gardens on the flat land of Hope, Brightwater, Spring Grove, Wakefield and Belgrove towards Murchison (see p.515); or northwest via Motueka to the Abel Tasman National Park (see p.493).

Nelson has the air of a bustling go-ahead city, something which can detract from its **historical pedigree** as one of the oldest settlements in New Zealand – a place where many early European immigrants got their first taste of the South Island. By the middle of the sixteenth century, the Ngati Tumatakokiri occupied most of the Nelson area, providing a reception committee for **Abel Tasman**'s long boats at Murderer's Bay, where they killed four of his sailors. By the time Europeans arrived in earnest, Maori numbers had been decimated by internecine fighting and the nearest pa site to Nelson was at Motueka, although this did little to prevent land squabbles, culminating in the **Wairau Affray** in 1843. Despite assurances from Maori chiefs Te Rauparaha and Te Rangihaeata that they would abide by the decision of a land commissioner, the New Zealand Company went ahead regardless, sending surveyors south to the Wairau Plains. A skirmish ensued, during which Te Rangihaeata's wife was shot. The bereaved chief and his men slaughtered twenty-two people in retaliation. The settlers continued undeterred in their ways of land acquisition but due to illness and hardship the community was dying on its feet when the arrival of industrious German immigrants saved it from complete dissolution.

Today, basking in one of the sunniest and most scenic areas in the country, Nelson has found a new lease of life as a holiday centre, with its busy **fishing port** and a rich fruit- and vegetable-growing **hinterland** scattered with breweries and wineries. It is also a haven for **artists**, who are drawn by the sunlight, the landscape and the unique raw materials for pottery and ceramic art that lurk beneath the rich green grass.

Arrival, information and transport

Flights arrive at Nelson **airport**, 8km west of the centre, and are met by a daily **shuttle** and door-to-door service provided by Super Shuttle Nelson (☎03/547 5782; $6), or **City Taxis** (☎03/528 8225; around $15). All **buses** drop you near the centre of the city, within easy walking distance of most accommodation. InterCity pulls in at 27 Bridge St, while the other companies all stop outside the **visitor centre**, on the corner of Trafalgar Street and Halifax Street (daily 8.30am–5pm; ☎03/548 2304, fax 546 7393, *www.nelson.net.nz*, *vin@tourism-nelson.co.nz*). This large and welcoming centre has heaps of leaflets on Nelson and the surrounding region, including guides to the national parks, local studios and workshops; the centre also functions as a booking office for trips, accommodation and onward travel. Inside the visitor centre is the main **DOC office** (same hours) and an additional, less useful DOC Office is located at 186 Bridge St (☎03/546 9335; Mon–Fri 8am–4pm), in the Munro Building next to the Courthouse.

SBCL **buses** (☎03/548 0285; Mon–Fri 8am–6pm, Sat 8am–12.30pm) run between Nelson and its satellite communities from the terminal on Lower Bridge Street, while numerous smaller **shuttle buses** run further afield to Golden Bay, the Abel Tasman, Kahurangi and Nelson Lakes national parks. Otherwise, you can get around most of the sights in the immediate vicinity with the help of a **rental car** or **bike**, while plenty of **tours** take in the highlights of the city and its surroundings (see "Listings", p.493, for details of all these).

Accommodation

The best places to stay, with a few notable exceptions in the shape of some **outlying B&Bs**, are in Nelson itself, where you have a choice of relaxing **beachside** locations or the bustling **centre** within reach of cultural diversions and nightlife. **Camping**, on the other hand, is not such a good option here, and you'll do better to settle for a **hostel** in the city and save camping for the prettier areas around Motueka.

Hotels and motels

Carmel Court, 50 Waimea Rd (☎03/548 2234). This motel offers twelve fully self-contained units in a well-kept modern building with off-street parking. ④–⑤.

Kings Gate, 21 Trafalgar Street (☎03/546 9108, fax 546 6838). Central motel with comfortable well-kept rooms including full kitchens. ⑤.

Quality Hotel Rutherford, Trafalgar Square (☎03/548 2299, fax 546 3003, *escape@rutherfordhotel. co.nz*). An international-style hotel with a number of impressive facilities, including a café, bar and excellent Japanese Restaurant, as well as large, well appointed rooms, some with impressive views. It doesn't hurt to try negotiating during the slacker months of March and April. ⑦.

Riverlodge, 31 Collingwood St (☎ & fax 03/548 3094). One of the better motels, giving value for money in clean and comfortable rooms. ④–⑥.

B&Bs and guesthouses

Aloha Lodge, 19 Beach Rd (☎03/546 4000, fax 546 4420). Beachside accommodation in a hideous building with a tacky pseudo-Japanese gate; inside it's surprisingly comfortable, offering B&B or self-contained units. ⑤.

Althorpe, 13 Dorset St, Richmond (☎ & fax 03/544 8117, *rworley@voyager.co.nz*). A pretty B&B with just two neat bedrooms in an 1880s homestead in the tranquil neighbourhood of Richmond. ⑤–⑥.

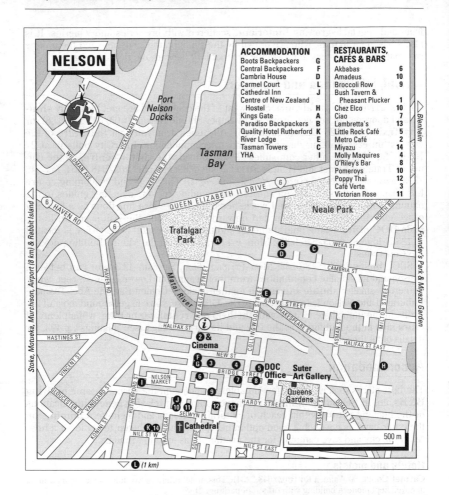

ACCOMMODATION
Boots Backpackers   G
Central Backpackers   F
Cambria House   D
Carmel Court   L
Cathedral Inn   J
Centre of New Zealand
  Hostel   H
Kings Gate   A
Paradiso Backpackers   B
Quality Hotel Rutherford   K
River Lodge   E
Tasman Towers   C
YHA   I

RESTAURANTS, CAFÉS & BARS
Akbabas   6
Amadeus   10
Broccoli Row   9
Bush Tavern &
  Pheasant Plucker   1
Chez Elco   10
Ciao   7
Lambretta's   13
Little Rock Café   5
Metro Café   2
Miyazu   14
Molly Maquires   4
O'Riley's Bar   8
Pomeroys   10
Poppy Thai   12
Café Verte   3
Victorian Rose   11

Cambria House, 7 Cambria St (☎03/548 4681, fax 546 6649). This 140-year-old weatherboard house boasts a lovely back deck and garden, beautiful fireplaces, and a wide choice of breakfasts – all just ten minutes' walk from town on a quiet road. ⑥–⑨.

Cathedral Inn, 369 Trafalgar St South (☎03/548 7369, fax 548 0369, *cathedral.inn@clear.net.nz*). In the centre of town, this newly restored manor offers elegantly styled, charming rooms and hearty breakfasts. ⑥–⑦.

The Honest Lawyer, 1 Point Road, Monaco (☎03/547 8850 & 0800/921 192, fax 547 8868, *thl@ts.co.nz*). A surprisingly accurate reconstruction of an English pub in all elements except that it has some luxuriously comfortable en-suite rooms for guests who can't drag themselves away. ⑦.

Kershaw House, 10 Wensley Rd, Richmond (☎03/544 0957, fax 544 0950). A large, welcoming B&B in a 1929 house in Richmond, which has been authentically restored – a highlight is the gorgeous dark-stained rimu staircase. All rooms are smartly decorated and have private facilities. ⑥–⑦.

Mapledurham, 8 Edward St, Richmond (☎ & fax 03/544 4210). A beautiful rimu villa encircled by a wide, grey-floored veranda and a well tended garden. The house is light and airy, dressing gowns are provided, and the breakfasts are superb; dinners are available by arrangement ($45, including wine). ⑥–⑧.

Hostels

Beach Hostel, 25 Muritai St (☎03/548 6817, *nelsonbeachhostel@xtra.co.nz*). An intimate hostel by the beach, with free bikes, a lounge with deck and good views, free pick-up from the city and a twice-daily shuttle service, as well as breakfast (free) and Internet access. Dorms ①, rooms ②.

Central Backpackers, 163 Trafalgar St, cnr Trafalgar St & Bridge St (☎ & fax 03/548 9001). Vibrant and colourful murals and cartoons adorn the walls of this busy hostel. The kitchen is very small and the place is only slowly getting the attention it needs, but Internet access is available. Key deposit for rooms $10. Dorms ①, rooms ②.

Centre of New Zealand Hostel, 193 Milton St (☎03/546 6667, fax 545 6667). Dorms, twin and double rooms cluster inside this lovely weatherboard house just 500m from the city centre. There's a large kitchen and dining area, plus a balcony with good views over Bridge Street. The entrance to the car park is next to 183 Milton St. Dorms ①, rooms ②–③.

Hecate House, 181 Nile St East (☎03/546 6890, fax 546 6895) is a pleasing, relaxed, tucked-away historic house for women only. ③.

Paradiso Backpackers, 42 Weka St (☎03/546 6703, fax 546 7533). Based in a large 97-year-old house, this hostel has a swimming pool, good facilities and a friendly atmosphere. Dorms ①, rooms ②.

Tasman Towers, 8–10 Weka St (☎03/548 7950, fax 548 7897). A purpose-built hostel three minutes' walk from town. Good-sized dining and kitchen areas, a large lounge, and clean spacious rooms make this a sound choice. Dorms ①, rooms ②.

YHA, 59 Rutherford St (☎03/545 9988, fax 545 9989, *yhanels@yha.org.nz*). This purpose-built hostel in a central location remains the best in town, with a wide range of accommodation, including connecting rooms for families and two disabled-accessible units. Big kitchens and a bike store add to its appeal, as does Internet access, very helpful staff and discounted rates in winter. Dorms ①, rooms ②–③.

The City

The city of Nelson is dominated by the glowering, greystone edifice of the cathedral, perched on a hill with fine views across the harbour and city below, where the streets are laid out in a grid pattern. The liveliest **thoroughfares** are Trafalgar Street and Bridge Street, while the **seafront** to the north is strewn with palm trees and parks where you can hear the thrum of cicadas in summer. And, for respite from the city, there are the long, golden-sand **beaches** and inland a green oasis of shady paths in the central public **gardens**. To get further away from it on a short day-trip, head for **Rabbit Island**, which is accessible at low tide.

Fortunately, the interior of the Anglican **Christ Church Cathedral** is nowhere near as grim as its exterior. Dazzling stained-glass windows illuminate the building, with ten particularly noteworthy examples tucked away in a small chapel to the right of the main altar. The cathedral has had a chequered history, which may account for its ugliness. English architect Frank Peck's original 1924 design was gradually modified over many years due to lack of money; World War II further intervened, and even now the cathedral tower looks as if it is still under construction.

The modern city architecture and well-disguised older buildings of Nelson are enlivened by the temporary presence of the **Nelson Market** (Sat 7am–1pm), which takes over the car park between Rutherford Street and Trafalgar Street at the back of the YHA, two minutes' walk from the cathedral. Multicoloured stalls are laden with clothes, jewellery, toys, locally made wood carvings, art and crafts. Food stalls totter under the weight of mounds of fruit, endless varieties of fresh bread and fish, Thai and vegetarian dishes, burgers and hot dogs, coffee and cakes, to sustain you while you browse.

The Suter Te Aratoi o Whakatu, a small public art museum, just off Trafalgar Street at 208 Bridge St (daily 10.30am–4.30pm; $2), was built in 1899 as memorial to

FESTIVAL MANIA

The **Wearable Arts Festival** has become an international event, staged every year around September 24 (check with visitor centre for exact dates). This unique fashion show combines elements of sculpture, performance art, theatre, choreography and dance to create an extraordinary spectacle. The bizarre circus lasts for two nights (tickets around $35) and is performed on a sparkling 100m catwalk, and afterwards, the best of the costumes go on display at the Suter. Indeed, many of them are more sculpture than haute couture, being fashioned from household junk, food, metal, stone, wood – and a surfeit of imagination. An arts festival has also sprung up around the show, spanning three weeks and including jazz sessions, alternative performances and exhibitions. Sadly the whole thing has grown into such a success that one of these days it may be moved to Wellington.

The **Taste Nelson Festival**, an annual day-long event held at the end of January or early February, espouses much more conservative ambitions. Essentially a celebration of the quality food, beers and wines that are produced in this area, as well as an excuse for local entertainers and bands to strut their funky stuff, the festival attracts over 10,000 gourmands. The **Nelson Jazz Festival**, held from around January 27, also livens up the town around this time of year.

Andrew Burn Suter, Bishop of Nelson from 1866 to 1891. One of the finest in the South Island, this wee gallery hosts visiting exhibitions and shows relating to the local area, as well as changing exhibitions from the gallery's own and Suter's collections. Watercolours predominate – especially those of John Gully, a friend of the bishop's whose works here largely depict scenes from the surrounding area – but there are also a number of oil paintings and over a hundred works by Sir M. Tosswill Woollaston, a founder of the modernist movement in New Zealand art. Woollaston was one of a group of artists and writers who, during the 1930s and 40s, began exploring notions of a New Zealand culture independent of colonial Britain. Particular significance in the gallery is given to a famous 1909 portrait by Gottfried Lindauer of Huria Matenga, a Maori women who, with her husband and friends, saved many lives from the wreck of the *Delaware* in 1863. Her status is indicated by *moko* (traditional tattoos), feathers, bone, greenstone jewellery and the ceremonial club she holds; in the background is the foundering American ship. The other significant part of the permanent collection is devoted to ceramics and the work of local potters; the Nelson area is rich in raw materials for potters and ceramic artists. The gallery also mounts temporary exhibitions of a range of Maori art, from early more traditional carvings to contemporary work, and also briefly showcases the winners of the various categories in the famous Wearable Arts Festival. If this were not enough there's a 159-seat arthouse cinema (see "Drinking, nightlife and entertainment", p.491).

The **South Pacific Distillery** and Bottle Store, 285 Wakefield Quay, run a ten-minute tour (Mon–Sat 2.30pm; free): all their spirit products have a "roaring forties" guarantee, and all have forty percent alcohol content. The main reason for visiting is to raid the bottle shop for something suitably potent and uplifting.

Gardens and beaches

Next to the Suter art museum is **Queens Gardens** (daily 8am–dusk; free), hemmed in on three sides by Bridge, Tasman and Hardy streets. This pretty Victorian garden, with its mature trees and a well populated duck pond, is a tranquil haven in an otherwise bustling city. Respite can also be found further out of the city in the delightful, Japanese-style **Miyazu Gardens** (daily 8am–dusk; free). To get here, walk east along Bridge Street to the junction with Milton Street, turn left and follow Atawhai Drive for about

300m. This quiet oasis has a traditional tea house, ponds, azaleas, Japanese irises and flowering cherries; the gardens are at their best during December and January. **Founders Park**, 87 Atawhai Drive (daily 10am–4.30pm; $5), 75m back from the gardens, is less impressive, with a collection of old buildings conspiring to produce a somewhat sanitized version of early colonial history.

For an excellent walk with fine views, head west on Haven Road, past the junction with Queen Elizabeth II Drive, and on to Wakefield Quay. Then walk along Rocks Road (SH6) until you reach the **Tahunanui Beach Reserve**, just past the sea wall, some 5km from the city centre. Grassland and drifting dunes back the long, golden beach, which has safe swimming, a fun park, zoo and children's playgrounds – the place swarms around Christmas time. If you don't feel like walking to the reserve, buses run regularly along SH6 from the city.

Some 18km from the reserve (along SH6 and then northwest on SH60), is Nelson's other beach area, **Rabbit Island**, with golden sands backed by trees. This is much less developed, and all the better for it: the views are stunning, and it is picture-book pretty. Access is by the Redwood Road (off SH60, just after the Waimea River Road Bridge), but note that the road is barred at dusk each day.

Stoke

The small satellite town of **STOKE** lying 8km southwest of Nelson on SH6, is linked to the city by suburban buses, and hides a couple of attractions.

One of the best diversions around Nelson is the **Mac's Brewery Tour**, 660 Main Rd (☎03/547 8097; Mon–Sat: Nov–April 11.15am & 2pm; May–Oct 11.15am; 1hr; $3 tasting), which takes you through the completely natural brewing process: the brewery sits on its own spring, and uses local Motueka Hops. The highlight is the tasting of superior brews – and, inevitably, there's a large shop selling brewery products and souvenirs.

Also in the suburb of Stoke, just off Marsden Road (entrance in Hilliard Street), is **Isel Park** (daily 8am–dusk; free) and **Nelson Provincial Museum** (Mon–Fri 10am–4pm, Sat & Sun noon–4pm; $2). The museum celebrates the local human and natural heritage, primarily through its photographic collection of over a million plates, some dating back to the 1870s. Meanwhile in the Maori Gallery you will learn, among other things, that, "By eating a worthy enemy you would increase your own strength and consign their souls to perpetual misery". Even more grisly is the exhibition dealing with the nineteenth-century **Maungatapu Murders**, so-named after the track between Nelson and Pelorus along which a notorious gang of four (Sullivan, Kelly, Burgess and Levy) perpetrated their crimes. One of their more harebrained schemes entailed the use of strychnine to murder the staff of the Nelson branch of the Bank of New South Wales, so that they could make off with the money. Quite how they intended to administer the poison is less clear, and their plot went badly wrong. Sullivan turned Queen's evidence before the raid even took place and Levy, Kelly and Burgess were all hanged; Levy's death mask is sometimes on display here as a gruesome reminder (the museum rotates its exhibits so you may have to ask to see it). Also in the museum are two elaborate *waka*, which were salvaged from the sands of Farewell Spit (see p.507).

The grounds also contain **Isel House** which dates from 1848 and is now owned by the council but not open to the public. Built as a farmhouse for the Marsden family, it still contains much of the original furniture, china and paintings, and is set in woodland of some grandeur.

Activities

A number of companies offer **rafting** trips starting from Nelson, most venturing onto the **Buller River** via Murchison and the Nelson Lakes National Park or onto the **Karamea River** in Kahurangi National Park. Along both rivers, the scenery is breathtaking, the water swift – and the sandflies omnipresent, so don't forget the insect repellent.

The pick of the operators are Ultimate Descents and The Rapid River Adventure Company. Both offer a variety of trips: with Ultimate Descents, based in Murchison (☎03/528 6363 & 0800/748 377, *ultimate@rivers.co.nz*), itineraries range from day-long excursions on the Buller (Grade III & IV; $105 including lunch) to amazing five-day safaris on the Buller and Karamea (including Grade V; $595 & $675 all inclusive). Their day-trips seem to spend slightly longer on the river than most others, leaving plenty of time for fun with inflatable kayaks and water sledges, as well as for getting your teeth into some serious rafting and a deceptively high cliff jump. A recent addition to the repertoire is "river bugging", the use of purpose-built individual rafts in which you sit and shoot rapids, although not terribly serious ones (3–4 hr; $89). Rapid River (☎03/545 7076, fax 545 7076) do a good-value day-trip from Nelson ($110, including BBQ lunch) that gets you on the river just after lunch for four hours' rafting on Grade III and IV stretches of the Buller and Gowan rivers, ending at the Owen River Tavern for a well-earned pint.

You won't escape the buffeting on land, either. Just off Cable Bay Road, about ten minutes' drive east of Nelson on SH6, Happy Valley 4x4 Motorbike Adventures (☎03/545 0304, fax 545 0347) have a number of **quadbikes** and all-terrain vehicles. With over 4000 square kilometres of forest and 40km of track at their disposal, there is an enormous variety to their **safaris**. Along the way you will see monstrous matai trees as you climb above the tree line for expansive views of Cable Bay and the ocean. Prices range from $25 to $100, and evening forays include glow-worm viewing. The most popular trips are the "Big View" (2hr; $75), and the BBQ trip (3hr; $95).

West of Nelson, about 17km along SH6, through Richmond, the Haycock Road turns off to the historic Clover Road stables, home to **Stonehurst Horse trekking** (☎03/542 4121, fax 542 3823). The majority of the shorter treks (1hr $30, 90min $65, 2hr $65) take place in the foothills of the Richmond ranges and offer great views of the coast and beyond; there are horses to suit all abilities, the routes are challenging but not frightening, there's a full safety briefing and protective head gear's available.

When you've had your fill of Nelson's earthly pleasures, spice things up with a spot of **parachuting**. Tandem Skydiving (☎03/546 4444 & 0800/422 899; $195) operate out of Nelson Airport – or, if the weather is unsuitable there, they adjourn to Motueka. You can even get some pictures of yourself trying to look happy before you plummet from an altitude of 3000m. Although you may have other things on your mind, the scenery is excellent and the expert parachuting "buddies" are helpful and friendly. Out in Richmond, Nelson Paragliding offer **tandem paragliding** (☎03/544 1182; from $110): a hair-raising drive up the hill to the launch site reveals a spectacular landscape, before you run like hell then glide off into the quiet up-drafts for 15–20 minutes of eerily silent flight, surrounded by stunning views. Airborn Paragliding (☎03/548 5520; from $150) is an alternative offering similar trips, as well as the less ethereal joys of **rock climbing** and **abseiling** (☎03/543 2669; half day $70, full day $110). Less exciting but useful if you're pushed for time are **flights** with Tasman Bay Aviation (☎ & fax 03/547 2378) who run trips over Abel Tasman National Park (including one-way trips to Awaroa; $68pp, three minimum), Kahurangi National Park, Marlborough Sounds and local Nelson scenic flights ($25–180).

Around Nelson

Most of Nelson's attractions, including the wineries, breweries and galleries for which it is renowned, lie beyond the city. The combination of the soil, natural spring water and climate make this area ideal for the production of **wines** or **beers**, and the attractiveness of the scenery will tempt you to linger and sample a glass of either. If the galleries in town whet your appetite for art, make time to investigate the studios of the enormous number of contemporary artists working in the Nelson region, many of whom exhibit in their own small **galleries**, showcasing ceramics, glass-blowing, woodturning, textiles, sculpture and painting. More details can be found in the *Nelson Potters, Winemakers* and *The Coastal Way* leaflets, all free from Nelson visitor centre.

Almost everything worth seeing outside the city of Nelson lies to the south and west: either just off SH6 before it reaches the junction with SH60 or in a slim corridor of land flanking either side of SH60. Nelson Suburban Buses run along SH6, through Richmond and as far as Wakefield, but do not go along SH60; however, **bus tours** run to the wineries and galleries (see "Listings" on p.492).

Heading west along SH6, you'll reach the **Craft Habitat Centre** (daily 10am–5pm, some craftspeople arrive late so to see everything visit around 2pm), 12km from Nelson on the southernmost edge of Waimea Inlet, opposite the junction with Champion Road. Set up by Jack Laird and his wife, stalwarts of the Nelson pottery scene, the centre was developed by their son Paul, a potter of unusual and engaging pieces inspired by the landscape and animal life. As well as pottery, the centre displays glass-blowing by Lynette Campbell (of Höglands fame – see below), jewellery, weaving, spinning and knitting, leadlighting and woodturning. To satisfy more mundane appetites, there's also a very good **café** called, unsurprisingly, *Habitat* (daily 10am–4pm); have the mussel chowder, if it's on. For something to wash down your chowder, press on through the fruit-growing country to another combined operation, the **Grape Escape**, at the corner of SH60 and Mc Shanes Road (Oct–April daily 10.30am–4.30pm; May–Sept Wed–Sun 10.30am–4.30pm), where you can sample the respective products of the Richmond Plains Organic Winery and the Te Mania Winery, both of which produce good Sauvignon Blanc and Pinot Noir (free tastings). Also attached are a tacky gift shop and passable but expensive café. From here if you head off up SH6 for five minutes you'll come to the **Greenhough Winery**, on Patons Road near Richmond (Dec–Feb daily 1am–5pm; Nov–March Sat & Sun 1am–5pm), where you can sample fine vintages, or just pick up an excellent Sav' Blanc for later.

Högland's Glass Blowing Studio, Korurangi Farm, Lansdowne Road (daily 9am–5.30pm), is signposted from SH60 just after it leaves SH6. In addition to glass-blowing demonstrations, there's a fine licensed café, live Irish folk music at weekends, a gallery and park-like gardens inhabited by farm animals. The glass-blowers slickly combine art and entertainment, and may even let you blow a glass bubble. The style of the glassware (mostly tableware) is Scandinavian-influenced, which works best in the bigger, bolder pieces with clean lines and bright, unusual colours. Sticking with the Scandinavian theme, the **café** serves excellent lunches and light snacks; try the open sandwiches or the platter of smoked delicacies which is usually enough for two.

The **Seifried Estate Winery**, at the corner of SH60 and Redwood Road, is a slick operation with an excellent if overly posh restaurant and shop; tastings take place further up SH60 at Appleby near the Rabbit Island turn-off (daily 9am–5pm; wine tasting $3, redeemable against purchase). The **Silkwood** gift shop (daily 10am–5pm), 4km along SH60 from the Seifried Estate Winery, is famed more for its method of construction than its touristy, high-quality but expensive wares. Made of bales of straw plastered over with concrete – a method originally used in the United States in timber-poor areas – the building is virtually fireproof, safe in earthquakes, cool in summer, and warm in the winter. Inside, among the usual tourist tat, is some beautifully designed knitwear made from the wool of the llama, angora and alpaca that graze the property. The **Bronte Gallery**, at the end of Bronte Road East, which veers east off SH60, is recommended for the diversity of its pottery and painting, and for its selection of tableware by internationally recognized practitioner, Darryl Robertson. The work here provides a useful benchmark for assessing the quality in other outlets; what's more, the gallery enjoys a fine location near the coast, where there are sweeping views across Waimea Inlet to Rabbit Island.

Mapua Wharf is at the end of the Arunui Road, which turns off SH60, 34km from Nelson. Overlooking the west end of Rabbit Island and the Waimea Estuary, the wharf was once legendary for producing smoked fish from a quirky jumble of old buildings. These days Mapua Nature Smoke is a considerably slicked up organization but thankfully still produces an excellent product to take away or eat at its specially created waterside licensed café (☎03/540 2280; $15–20 per head, considerably more if you have booze): there are mussels, a staggering variety of fish and a fish paté, widely acclaimed as the best in the country, all smoked over manuka wood after being cured in a salt and sugar solution. You're best to try lunch times as this spot is now so popular that it's booked up almost every evening. Heading back towards SH60, you'll pass Mapua Village and its **Village Rest**, a licensed café with excellent coffee in an impressive modern building with a large deck where you can also sup a pint of locally brewed beer (McCashins, Bays and Pink Elephant are all on tap).

On the opposite side of SH60, the Seaton Valley Road heads west and inland to the eccentric **Glover's Vineyard** (daily Oct–April 10am–5pm, closed May–Sept; tastings $2), a small concern that produces fine reds and whites and boasts especially good Cabernet Sauvignon and Pinot Noir (most costing $18 or more); you can draw your own conclusions from the fact that the owner, a serious wine nut, used to tuck a Wagner CD into every package destined for overseas. The **Nuerdorf Winery** (Mon–Sat Sept–May 10am–5pm, or by appointment ☎03/543 2643; free tastings), an altogether more down-to-earth prospect, is further inland. Once you hit the junction with Moutere Highway, join Nuerdorf Road by heading southeast on the highway for 100m and turning right. The winery is in a low-slung wooden building covered by vines with simple outdoor seating in the shade of some tall ancient trees, where a glass of Chardonnay is complimented perfectly by cheese, bread, olives and other simple fare that is served here ($8–12). From Nuerdorf head further inland by shooting south along the Moutere Highway as far as Sunrise Valley Road, and follow the signposts for 2km to **Moutere Hills Vineyard** (daily Oct–April 11am–6pm, or by appointment ☎03/543 2288) where there's a good café serving large platters and some lovely Sauvignon Blanc, Chardonnay with a bite and good Merlot-Cabernet Franc, all for around $17.

Returning to SH60 on the Seaton Valley Road, head 2km west to the junction with Korepo Road, along which you'll find the idyllic **Ruby Bay Winery** (Oct–April daily 11am–6pm; May–Sept Sat & Sun 11am–6pm), under very friendly management and set on a hill overlooking the tiny Ruby Bay. Here you can sit under a vine-covered trellis in a lovely garden, or inside the unusual and bright main building, and slurp your way through a wine-tasting tray ($3, redeemable against purchase), or try the antipasto, salads or bagels along with the crisp Chardonnay, pert Pinot or the smooth Rosé. About 2km from Ruby Bay, back on SH60, is **Steve Fullmer's Gallery** (daily 10am–5pm), near the Tasman Store on Baldwin Road. One of the best galleries in the region, this place is worth a browse even if you can't afford any of the remarkable ceramic art or solid tableware.

Eating

The enviable lifestyle of Nelson residents is reflected in the **vast choice** of decent places to eat within easy reach of the town centre. And when you tire of these, there's always fine food and wine in gorgeous settings at the **wineries**. If fast food beckons, try out the local **pie cart** that's parked near the central post office on Trafalgar Street every evening from 5.30pm–4am. Don't forget Nelson's pubs (see opposite) for a quick snack either.

Amadeus, 284 Trafalgar St. Posh-looking licensed coffee house cum restaurant where the coffee, cakes and handmade chocolates are to die for and don't cost as much as you might expect. In fact this relaxing Viennese style stop-off is well worth an hour of anyone's time.

Akbaba's Turkish Kebabs, 130 Bridge St. Plenty of cheap kebabs and salads ($4–11) to munch in the canopied area out back, or in booth seating on low floor cushions; Turkish decor and music create a lively and casual atmosphere for lunch and supper (closed Sunday).

Boat Shed, 350 Wakefield Quay (☎03/546 9783). Converted for its new role, this boat shed has large windows offering unimpeded and spectacular sunsets over Tasman Bay. Exceptional seafood and a bustling ambience mean that it suffers somewhat from its own popularity. It's definitely worth coming here, but try to avoid the insanely crowded and rushed Friday and Saturday nights. Mains cost $15–25. Licensed.

Broccoli Row, 5 Buxton Square (☎03/548 9621). Lunches, afternoon snacks and dinners are all served in generous portions at this vegetarian and seafood restaurant, with outdoor dining and blackboard specials ($6–19). Particular favourites are the $8.50 salad bowl with home-made focaccia and the Mediterranean tapas. Mon–Sat 9.30am–10pm; book for dinner at weekends; BYO.

Chez Eelco, 296 Trafalgar St. No visit to Nelson is complete without stopping here. This was the first café-bar in Nelson, and although Eelco has since decided to hang up his apron, the place is still going strong.

Ciao, 94 Collingwood St (☎03/548 9874). An exclusive fine dining experience in a lovely old wooden house. Excellent food with fresh local ingredients and Italian peasant flare and some sumptuous desserts. Dinners daily; BYO.

Lambretta's, 204 Hardy St. Open from 9am daily to serve good coffee in the shadow of the eponymous scooter mounted on the wall above the bar. Casual and serving reasonable snacks and main meals with an Italian bent, including the usual pizza and pasta. This place also gets quite lively in the evenings and is sometimes the venue for jazz and blues bands. Licensed.

Café Metro, above the cinema, 91 Trafalgar St. A popular stop-off for cool dudes hanging out, the waiting cinema crowd and shoppers who've walked far enough. It has a blackboard menu of simple veggie and vegan fare, balcony on which to see or be seen and occasionally some acoustic jazz or folk in the evenings. Daily; licensed.

Miyazu, Japanese Restaurant in the *Quality Rutherford Hotel*, Trafalgar Square (☎03/548 2299). Predictably expensive but excellent Japanese restaurant; authentic preparation and stylish surroundings make this worth a splurge when nothing but sashimi will do. Licensed.

Pigglettes, 7 Alma Lane, Buxton Square. Grim decor in an old bakery but serving the cheapest lunches and dinners around. Closed Monday.

Pomeroys, 276 Trafalgar St. A quiet and classy restaurant and wine bar (plus BYO), with the Vauxhall motor car crest as its logo (Pomeroy started the company). The food is fresh and attractive, starting with imaginative breakfasts, and moving on to filled focaccia for lunch. Blackboard specials for dinner might include Thai chicken curry, peppered lamb salad or local fish dishes. A full meal will set you back between $12 and $25. Daily 9am–10pm.

Poppy Thai, 142 Hardy St. Fully licensed very authentic Thai restaurant where the excellent food and good value make up for its palpable lack of charm. Mon–Sat for lunch and dinner.

Ribbetts, 20 Tahuanui Drive (☎03/548 6911). Despite the tacky frog theme that extends to two dining frogs in the front window, this restaurant serves excellent local produce, prepared with an international slant; main courses cost between $19 and $23. Escape the frogs in the covered, candle-lit courtyard with wooden tables and stone floors. Daily 10am–10pm; licensed.

Café Verté, 123 Bridge St. Coffee house open daily until the wee hours (except Sunday when it closes at 6pm) and rightly renowned for its kick-ass java, some iffy decor and good value grub. Licensed and BYO.

Walnut Café, 251 Queen St, Richmond (☎03/544 6187). A classy wine bar and bistro in a conservatory-like setting with modern decor, lots of greenery, glass and white trellising. Lunch and dinner are served (Tues–Sun), with main courses around the $20 mark; their pumpkin puree with fish, coriander and red onions comes highly recommended, as does the Vietnamese calamari; there's also plenty of choice for vegetarians. Service can be slow at busy times. Licensed and BYO.

Drinking, nightlife and entertainment

While most of its neighbours retire early to sip their cocoa, Nelson stays up all night and has a party – most noticeably at various venues on or near Bridge Street. Pubs and **bars** of all sorts dominate, many with **live music** at weekends – some absolutely dreadful; check out the Friday edition of the *Nelson Mail* (70¢) to find out **what's on**.

Attached to The Suter, at 208 Bridge St, is a 159-seat arthouse **cinema**, a comfortable venue for films you're unlikely to see in the mainstream multiplex down the road; screenings are generally on Thursday to Sunday evenings (check the local paper for details). The State Cinema Centre, opposite the central post office, shows the latest releases, and movie munchies and booze are available at the *Metro Café* upstairs.

Bush Tavern and Pheasant Plucker, 87 Grove St. More along the lines of an English pub, this place has some outdoor seating and good-value bar meals ($3–16) in huge portions. Sun–Thurs 11am–11pm, Fri & Sat 11am–1am.

The Honest Lawyer, 1 Point Rd. A comfortable, country pub with a tree going through the centre and a beer garden overlooking the beach. Pouring Nelson-brewed beers, including Pink Elephant, Bays Ales and Macs, and serving superb pork pies and fresh seafood from a blackboard menu (snacks from $2.50, main meals $10–21). Weekend-evening entertainment is provided by a piano player, Irish folk bands and cover bands. Daily 11am–11pm. Live music Fri, Sat & Sun.

Little Rock Cafe, 165 Bridge St. Very lively, with food ranging from burgers through pizzas to Tex-Mex but most popular as a dance venue on Fridays and Saturdays when they have a broad-ranging DJ-led party. Daily 4pm–2.30am.

Molly Maquires, Bridge St. Once a wild west bar it has transformed itself into a wild Irish pub with the usual Irish-sounding bands and a mixture of Irish brews. Daily 11am–1am.

O'Reilys Bar, in the *Royal Hotel*, 152 Bridge St. More in keeping with the usual spit-and-sawdust Kiwi hotel, complete with obligatory bottle shop. Food ranges from pies, quiche, lasagne, and fish to burgers, with lunch specials for $5. Sky TV entertains you while you eat and drink, augmented by live cover bands and (allegedly) Irish music on Thurs, Fri & Sat.

Victorian Rose, 281 Trafalgar St. Olde English pub opposite *Chez Eelco*, with a richly deserved good reputation and probably the best spot in town. An excellent atmosphere is enhanced by a wide variety of locally brewed beer, and food at bargain prices ($3.50–23). Jazz sessions on Tuesday evenings, Blues Thursday, and live music most evenings in the summer. Daily 11am–midnight.

Listings

Automobile Association 45 Halifax St (☎03/548 8339).

Bike rental Avanti Pro Cycle Centre (☎03/548 3877) and Natural High (☎03/546 6936) offer bikes at around $15 for half a day, $20 a day.

Buses Among hundreds of buses and routes, below are a few of the most useful services available from Nelson.

Abel Tasman National Park Travel (☎03/548 0285, atc@nelsoncoaches.co.nz) leave Nelson at 7.20am daily for Marahau or Totoranui, via Motueka, connecting with launch services deeper into the park and operate a service to the head of the Heaphy Track; InterCity (☎03/548 1539) offer daily services to Picton, Blenheim and Christchurch or to Richmond, Motueka, Takaka and Totaranui; Kahurangi Buses (☎0800/173 371) go to Abel Tasman, Golden Bay and the Heaphy; KiwiLink (☎03/577 8332) go to Blenheim, Golden Bay and the Heaphy, Picton, Totaranui and Havelock; Knightline (☎03/528 7798) run to Motueka, Blenheim and Picton; Lazerline (☎03/388 7652) run between Christchurch and Nelson via Maruia Springs and Hamner; Nelson Lakes Transport (☎03/547 5912) run to the lakes and offer ski transport; Nelson SBCL (☎03/548 3290) run buses to Stoke, Richmond and small communities in the circle as well as to the Abel Tasman National Park; the Rose Express (book through information centres) go to Picton and Blenheim; and White Star (☎03/758 3338) go to Westport, Christchurch, Hamner Corner, and Reefton. In addition, the Westcoast Express (☎03/546 6703) is a low-key backpacker bus service that runs to Queenstown and back a couple of times a week and Westcoast Tours (☎03/789 5544) run to Westport.

Campervan rental Kiwi Campervans (☎03/543 2022); Sunrise Holidays (☎03/543 2753 & 0800/668 837).

Camping and outdoor equipment Wet-weather clothing and camping gear can be bought from Rollo's BBQ and Camping Centre, 12 Bridge St, or Basecamp, 295 Trafalgar St.

Car rental Avis (☎03/547 2727), Budget (☎03/547 9586), Hardy Cars (☎03/546 6829), Hertz (☎03/547 2299), National (☎03/548 1618) and Rent-a-dent (☎03/546 9890); daily rates start at about $60.

Diving Scuba gear can be rented from Richmond Sportsworld, 213 Queens St, Nelson, Divers World, cnr of London Quay and Auckland St, Picton and Motueka Sportsworld, 201 High St, Motueka.

Internet Aurora Tech, 5 Montgomery Square (Mon–Fri 8am–7pm, Sat & Sun 8am–10pm).

Medical treatment Nelson Public Hospital, Waimea Road (☎03/546 1800; main entrance on Kawai Street).

Pharmacy Prices Pharmacy, cnr Hardy & Collingwood St, after-hours duty pharmacies are listed in the *Nelson Mail* on Friday.

Post office cnr Trafalgar St & Halifax St, opposite the visitor centre.

Rock climbing Courses at the Airborne Alpine Sports School (☎03/543 2669), range in price from $38 for a half-day to $125 for a full-day course, all amid spectacular scenery.

Scenic flights Both based at Nelson Airport, the following companies operate various airborne tours of the region: Tasman Bay Aviation (see p.488) and The Aero Club (book through the visitor centre).

Swimming Riverside public swimming pool (daily 6.30am–6.30pm; $2.80).

Taxis and shuttle services Bickley Motors (☎03/525 8352), Collingwood Bus Services (☎03/524 8188), Crown Bus and Shuttle Services (☎03/548 0600), Nelson Taxis (☎03/548 8225), Rural Services (☎03/548 6858), Sun City Taxis (☎0800/422 666), Super Shuttle Nelson (☎03/547 5782 & 0800/438 238) and Transport for Trampers (☎03/545 1055) all offer on-demand services.

Tours Bay Tours offer art and craft and wine tours (☎03/544 4494 & 0800/229 868); JJ's Wine Tours (☎03/544 7712) visit local wineries and provide ski transport; Nelson Day Tours (☎03/548 4224) do the lot – wine, crafts, city districts, Golden Bay and beaches; Nelson Explorer (☎0800/868 687) have bird watching, fishing, wineries, crafts and ski transport; and Wine Tours (☎0800/229 868) are as the name suggests.

Abel Tasman National Park and around

Abel Tasman National Park is a stunningly beautiful area with an international reputation – resulting in large crowds of trampers, kayakers and day-trippers all through the summer. Don't let this put you off though: within the park are beautiful golden sandy beaches lapped by crystal-clear waters and backed by lush green bushland and forest, all interspersed with granite outcrops and inhabited by a multitude of wildlife. The goal of most visitors is the **Abel Tasman Coastal Track**, combining as it does a picturesque mixture of dense coastal bushwalking with gentle climbs to lookouts and walks across idyllic beaches, but this is also a wonderful place to get into a **kayak** and explore the mercurial coastline and rivermouths.

The park's dearth of settlements means that often all you can hear is birdsong and the gently soporific lapping of the waves on the shore. **Motueka** acts as a gateway and service centre for hungry trampers and locals alike, while the peaceful communities at **Kaiteriteri** and **Marahau**, en route to the park entrance, each have a smattering of places to stay. Marahau, virtually at the park gate, is the base for many kayaking and tramping trips, as well as swimming with seals.

Motueka

Famous for plentiful sunshine, and surrounded by fertile plains, **MOTUEKA**, 47km from Nelson, is really just a jumping-off point for more interesting destinations – most notably the Abel Tasman National Park. The name Motueka means "land of the Weka", a reference by Maori, who lived in the area for over a thousand years growing kumera in the fertile soil and exploiting the plentiful marine life, to the abundance of these edible birds. However, the arrival of European settlers in 1842 heralded the demise of the community-based traditional Maori lifestyle in the region.

Arrival, information and accommodation

Most of the **bus** companies pick up and drop off on the corner of High Street and Parker Street. Regular **flights** from Wellington land at the grass airfield on College Street, about 3km south of the centre; Motueka Taxis (☎03/528 7900) will take you into town for around $7, and will ferry you to the more out-of-the-way places.

The **visitor centre**, Wallace St (daily: May–Nov 8am–5pm; Nov–Dec 8am–7pm; Jan–Oct 8am–5pm; ☎03/528 6543, fax 528 6563, *mzpvin@xtra.co.nz*), sells bus tickets, arranges tours and accommodation and will deal with all your Abel Tasman and Heaphy track needs and questions. Pick up a copy of *Welcome to Motueka* (free), which is well worth getting for the map and descriptions of points of interest. If you're in training for the Abel Tasman Coastal Track, there's also a *Motueka District Walks* leaflet ($1), describing many day walks in the surrounding area. The **DOC office**, on the corner of High Street and King Street (Mon–Fri 8am–4.30pm; ☎03/528 9117), also gives out information on the national park, and sells tickets for the track. **Camping** and tramping **gear** can be **rented** from Coppins, 255 High St, and Twin Oaks, 25 Parker St.

Accommodation options are limited. *Abel Tasman Motel and Lodge*, 45 High St (☎03/528 6688 & 0800/845 678; ④), offers six basic but clean units. Other central places are *Motueka Backpackers*, 200 High St (☎03/528 7581; dorms ①, rooms ②), which is in dire need of some sprucing up, and *Twin Oaks*, 25 Parker St (☎03/528 7882; dorms ①, rooms ③), which also rents out camping and tramping equipment for the Abel Tasman and Heaphy tracks. The nearest **campsite** is *Fearon's Bush Camp*, 10 Fearon St (☎ & fax 03/528 7189; tent sites $9.50, cabins & units ②–④), a verdant site with plenty of trees for shelter and clean, well kept facilities just six minutes' walk from the town centre.

The Town

Motueka is strung along SH60, with quieter streets fanning out from the main highway. The quay and seafront run parallel to SH60 about five minutes' walk down old Wharf Road or along Tudor and Harbour streets.

One of the most interesting diversions in town is provided by a short walk down to the **Motueka Quay**, where the ghost of this once-busy port lingers among the scant

---

WALKS AROUND MOTUEKA

A good spot to view Motueka and the surrounding country is **Mount Arthur and the Tablelands**, and the various walks that cross them, as detailed in the new $1 DOC leaflet, *The Cobb Valley, Mount Arthur and Tablelands*, which suggests a series of excellent tramps and is available from the visitor centre in Motueka. The tracks in these areas are always quiet, because most visitors are in a mad rush to join the crowds at Abel Tasman.

The starting point for many of the best walks is the Flora car park, on the Graham Valley Road, which leads off SH61 south of Motueka. From here there are commanding views of the lowlands, with Mount Arthur dominating the southern skyline. From the car park you can take a walk (1hr each way) to the **Mount Arthur Hut** (Category 2; $10), from where you can continue on to Mount Arthur in another 3 hours, or tackle the summit of Mount Lodestone (1448m; 2hr).

There are similar tracks up the **Cobb Valley** (see Takaka p.503) a little further northwest, or starting 28km along the Upper Takaka turn-off in Golden Bay; further leaflets are available from the Motueka visitor centre although most of what you'll need is in *The Cobb Valley, Mount Arthur and Tablelands* leaflet (see above). Here too, you can lose yourself in beautiful, forested high country, with panoramic views above the tree line.

remains of the old jetty and store houses. Here too the hulk of the *Janie Seddon* – named after the daughter of Richard Seddon, premier of New Zealand from 1893 until his death in 1906 – gracefully decays. Built in Scotland in 1901, then purchased by the New Zealand government and used as a pilot vessel in Wellington, the ship served in both world wars, patrolling the waters of Cook Strait and Wellington Harbour. In 1946 she was bought by the Motueka Trawling Company, but local regulations outlawing steam-powered craft made her redundant, and she was ignominiously beached near the old wharf in 1955.

The tiny **Motueka Museum** (daily 10am–4pm; $2), delves into the area's history through copious black-and-white photographs and a few Maori artefacts relating to the area, as well as the *94 Motueka Carvings*, four skilfully carved friezes depicting the livelihoods that have traditionally sustained Tasman Bay.

Eating and drinking

Despite its modest size, Motueka has a number of restaurants, cafés and bars, catering to the enthusiastic appetites of fresh-air freaks.

Annabelle's Café, in the Museum Building, High St. Strong coffee, light meals (bacon and eggs) and snacks – a simple formula, but it hits the spot. Mon–Fri 9am–4pm, Sat & Sun 10am–2pm.

The Grain and Grape, 218 High St. A pub/café serving brunch and light meals from 11am–2pm, and dinner from 5.30–10pm. This is the place to satisfy a craving for steak and chips.

Hot Mama's, 105 High St. A brightly hued interior, patio garden and simple furniture create an attractive and intimate ambience in which to enjoy a wide range of Italian, Spanish, French and Kiwi-influenced food ($6–22), great coffee – and occasional appearances by touring New Zealand folk, jazz, acoustic and rock acts. The coolest and probably best spot in town. Daily 8am–late; licensed & BYO.

The Hop Inn, part of *Gothic Gourmet*, High St. A café and Motueka's only nightclub cohabit in the neo-Gothic setting of a former church. Food is reasonable quality, with imaginative French and Italian touches at reasonable prices ($6–15). Lunch & dinner daily; licensed.

Jacaranda Park Café and Nursery, 3km southwest of town, just off College St (☎03/528 7777). Commanding views over the countryside and a lovely garden and nursery, provide a suitable back-drop for the exquisite food served at this café-restaurant. Specials might include home-baked flans or chicken apricot roulades ($8–25), there is an extensive wine list and surrounding views of the plains. Daily 10am–5pm.

Pizza Paradise, 94 High St. This takeaway pizza place was run by an eccentric Dutchman with an infinite variety of chat-up lines but sadly he's gone. The pizzas are still pretty good though ($15–28). Daily 4.30pm–late.

Kaiteriteri

Overlooking Tasman Bay on the beach road, 6km off SH60, as it heads towards the southern end of the Abel Tasman National Park is the tiny resort settlement of **KAI-TERITERI**, some 15km from Motueka. There are few **places to stay**, unless you bring a tent, and even fewer places to eat. One of the best for both is the *Kimi Ora Holiday and Health Resort*, a hillside complex on Martin Farm Road, signposted from the beach road (☎03/527/8027, fax 527 8134; ④–⑥, depending on season). Set in a pine forest with views of the bay, this is a comfortable place to stay, or to indulge in the various fit-ness or therapy sessions they run. The *Kimi Ora Café*, in the resort's comfortable, wood-lined dining room, serves healthy, vegetarian **lunches** and **dinners**. All starters are $6, mains $15, and desserts $6, or you can go the whole hog for $25, rounded off by a range of coffees, teas and juices. Next to the beach is the *Kaiteriteri Motor Camp* (☎03/527 8010, fax 527 8031; tent sites $9.50, cabins ②) with shop, a seasonal restau-rant and takeaway, safe bathing, water sports, walking and some good views of the quiet and beautiful bay.

Marahau

About 6km further long the beach road from Kaiteriteri, **MARAHAU** is poised right at the southern entrance to the Abel Tasman National Park and is more tourist-orientated, acting as the base for many operators of tours into the park.

The beach road runs through the settlement before petering out at the park entrance, where a dirt track, Harvey Road, swerves left to a couple of **places to stay**: the *Barn Backpackers and Campground* (☎03/527 8043; tent sites $8.50, dorms ①, rooms ②) offers camping and backpacker accommodation, plus secure parking ($2 a night), a mere minute's walk from the park entrance; just beyond, *Old MacDonald's Farm* (☎03/527 8288, fax 527 8289; tent sites $9, dorms ①, cottages ②, caravans ③, B&B ⑥; day visitors $2) is a large, tranquil, friendly, family-run campsite with cottages and a B&B for those not happy about being under canvas. You share the grounds with llamas, alpacas and a host of other animals, there's secure parking ($3 a night), a well–stocked shop and gear storage, and they're planning a fish and chip shop – open summer months only. Back down the beach road from the park entrance is the Marahau Valley Road, where about 200m along is *Abel Tasman B&B* (☎03/527 8181; ④) a comfortable spot close to the park and the kayaking and boating operators.

The **park entrance** is marked by an unmanned DOC office with an intentions book and search and rescue cards. Next to the centre is the only real **café** in the area, *Park Café* (Sept–May daily 8am–late; licensed), which is legendary among walkers coming out of the park at this point and serves fine, wholesome food and excellent coffee to an appreciative crowd; try the home-made cakes for a sugar boost, or check out the blackboard for specials. From here, a long boardwalk across marshland leads into the national park.

Abel Tasman National Park

The **Abel Tasman National Park** covers a relatively small area, its boundaries running along the coast from Marahau, about 60km from Nelson, north up to Wainui Bay at the eastern end of Golden Bay, and inland to cover parts of Takaka Hill. Road **access** extends only as far as the park entrances and to get into the park itself you must either walk, take a boat/kayak or a plane. The main **bases** for forays into the coastal areas of the park are **Motueka** and **Marahau** in the south, and **Golden Bay** in the north (from Takaka, see p.502). The **northern entrance** to the park is marked by **Totaranui** – little more than limited accommodation options and a lovely beach, from where water-taxi operators head back to their Marahau and Kaiteriteri bases stopping in the bays on the way home – or you can stay at *Awaroa Lodge and Café* in the heart of the park and explore either direction in comfort. If you're kayaking you'll probably start at Marahau and work your way north before either cruising or walking back; if you're tramping you'll find it doesn't make too much difference which way you go as long as you miss the tides – consult the tide tables or visitor/DOC centre staff to find out which direction gives you the most time to cross the inlets and bays.

With a range of habitats from sea level to 1000m, Abel Tasman is full of rich and varied **plant life**. In the damp and torpid gullies, shrubs dominate, but elsewhere several species of beech tree hold sway. Kanuka tolerates the wild and windy areas and manuka thrives on land that has been subject to repeated burnings – as this has, at the hands of both Maori and European settlers. At **higher altitudes**, there is a proliferation of silver and red beech mixed with rata, miro and totara. **Birds** you might encounter include tui, native pigeons, bellbirds (their presence betrayed by their distinctive call), fantails that flutter close by, feeding off the insects you disturb as you walk through the bush

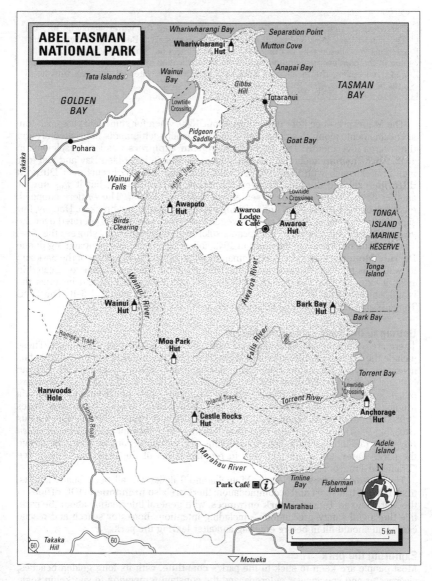

ABEL TASMAN
NATIONAL PARK

Whariwharangi Bay
Separation Point
Whariwharangi Hut
Mutton Cove

Tata Islands
Wainui Bay
Anapai Bay
TASMAN BAY

Gibbs Hill

GOLDEN BAY
Lowtide Crossing
Totaranui

Pidgeon Saddle
Goat Bay
Pohara

Wainui Falls
Lowtide Crossings

Awapoto Hut
Awaroa Lodge & Café
Awaroa Hut
TONGA ISLAND MARINE RESERVE

Birds Clearing
Tonga Island

Wainui River
Wainui Hut
Bark Bay Hut
Bark Bay

Rameka Track
Moa Park Hut

Harwoods Hole
Torrent Bay
Lowtide Crossing

Canaan Road
Inland Track
Torrent River
Anchorage Hut

Castle Rocks Hut
Adele Island

Marahau River
N

Park Café
Tinline Bay
Fisherman Island

Marahau

Takaka Hill
0   5 km
60
60

▽ Motueka

and if you're lucky the bobbing, ground–dwelling weka. There are also a large variety of seabirds around the headlands and on the beaches, ranging from the distinctive orange-beaked oystercatchers to shags who dive to great depths in search of fish. The fresh waterways burbling through the park are invariably the colour of tea (but not drinkable – see box overleaf), due to tannin leached from the soil.

> The organism that causes **giardia** is present **in much of the water** supply of the Abel Tasman National Park and many other streams in this area. Basics, p.17, outlines precautions you should take to minimize the risk of infection. Some huts and accommodation in the park are now equipped with water purification systems but it pays to check, and don't believe the locals who tell you they drink the water all the time with no ill effects.

The **Maori** presence here dates from about 1500, when for some 500 years, seasonal encampments along this coast and some permanent settlements flourished around the Awaroa Rivermouth. The arrival of **European explorers** was less auspicious: in 1642, **Abel Tasman** anchored his two ships near Wainui in Golden Bay and lost four men in a skirmish with the Ngati Tumatakokiri; and in 1827, Frenchman **Dumont d'Urville** explored the area between Marahau and Torrent Bay, but it was not for another 23 years that European settlement began in earnest. The settlers chopped, quarried, burned and cleared until nothing was left but gorse and bracken. Happily, few signs of their invasion remain and the vegetation has vigorously regenerated over the years. Named after the first European explorer to experience its shores, the Abel Tasman National Park was **gazetted** in 1942, following the tireless campaigning of one **Perrine Moncrieff**, a determined woman by all accounts. The sanctity of the park and its wildlife is preserved offshore by the **Tonga Island Marine Reserve**, created in 1993; it extends from Awaroa Head to just beyond Mosquito Bay and includes the island which is famous for its fur seal colony, seabirds and plentiful fish. The DOC Tonga Island Marine Reserve leaflet is well worth the investment of $1.

Getting to the park – and information

There are a number of **buses** that run **from Nelson** and **Picton** to the park. These include the big names, InterCity and White Star, plus any number of other shuttle bus operators plying the same route (see "Listings" for Nelson, p.492). Abel Tasman National Park Travel (Nelson ☎03/548 0285, Motueka 03/528 8850, *atc@nelsoncoaches. co.nz*) leaves Nelson at 7.20am daily for Marahau ($20) or Totoranui ($26), via Motueka, and connects with launch services deeper into the park; Kahurangi Buses (☎0800/173 371) go to Marahau $12, Totoranui $26, and Takaka $20; and Book-a-Bus (☎03/525 9864) run daily **from Takaka** to Pohara, where they meet the *Spirit of Golden Bay* water taxi into the park, before continuing to Totoranui. From harbours that fringe the park, **water taxis** can take you to remoter areas of the park (for details, see "Trailhead Transport" on p.500).

The **visitor centres** at Nelson, Motueka and Takaka will all book boats, kayaks, track tickets, transport and accommodation; there are also **unmanned** DOC **offices** at the Marahau and Totaranui **park entrances**, with general information about the park, tide times and safety precautions – including intentions books or search and rescue cards you should fill in before entering and after leaving the park.

Exploring the park

Most people are keen to stick to the park's **coastline**, with its long golden beaches, clear water and spectacular outcrops, and the constant temptation to snorkel in some of the idyllic bays. **Tramping** is one of the most popular ways of getting to grips with the park, and the Coastal Track, in particular, provides easy access to a wilderness area of great beauty and variety (see "The Abel Tasman Track" on p.500 for details). For those who don't wish to walk independently there are now **guided walks** through the park, stopping at comfortable accommodation along the way with all food and transport needs taken care of, at a price (see opposite).

If you have a few days to spare, a **stay** at the *Awaroa Lodge and Café* (☎03/528 8758; dorms ③, units ⑥) is one of the most relaxing ways of experiencing the splendours of the park. Nestled in Awaroa Bay are a number of well-designed comfortable units, as well as backpacker accommodation (bedding $4 extra) with an outdoor kitchen. The Lodge **café** (daily 7.30am–8pm) serves all meals in a stylish and relaxed atmosphere, enhanced by an enormous fireplace and unusual wooden furniture. The lodge is accessible from Takaka by car/bus or boat and short walk (see p.503), by plane from Motueka and Nelson, by boat from Marahau, Kaiteriteri and Tarakohe Harbour – and, of course, on foot via the Coastal Track. The surroundings are beautiful and peaceful and the owner occasionally lays on barge trips ($5) up the river for guests.

The perfect way to explore the park's remoter shores is by **sea kayak**. In spite of the increasing number of operators plying their trade (during the height of the summer two hundred kayaks may be on the water at any one time) the incredibly clear waters and possibility of being accompanied by seals or, more rarely, dolphins ensure this is still a unique experience. Two of the most reliable and longstanding operators from the southern end of the park are in Marahua, situated next door to one another. Abel Tasman Kayaks (☎03/527 8022 & 0800/527 8022, *atk@kayaktours.co.nz*) run a series of guided trips ranging from a $90 one dayer with beach buffet, informative guide and kayak sail back, to a fully-catered four dayer at $630. They also offer various kayak and walk options, and rent out kayaks for freedom paddling (to experienced, water-confident kayakers) with all the equipment you'll need as well as a rigorous safety check and compulsory instruction ($60 a day, with a sliding rate getting cheaper the more days you opt for). Ocean River Adventure Company (☎03/527 8266 & 0800/732 529) run similar guided trips for between one and five days, the most popular being the day-trip ($92, including barbecue). They also do some enticing trips which involve paddling and walking over a couple of days and staying at the *Awaroa Lodge and Café* from around $240. One final recommended kayak operator, Planet Earth Adventures (☎03/525 9095), runs from the northern end of the national park, Tenyson St, Pohara Beach, near Takaka. Also a SKOANZ operator this small outfit offer intimate half- and full-day trips ($45 & $75), taking a look at the Tata Islands shag colonies and the spectacular Taupo Point. They also provide freedom rentals starting in Wainui Bay and windsurf rentals in an encouraging area for beginners.

Abel Tasman Experiences (☎03/528 7801, fax 528 6087, *info@abeltasman.co.nz*), part of Abel Tasman National Park Travel (see "Getting to the Park", opposite), offer **sightseeing** trips, scenic **cruises**, a **water taxi** service, and three- and five-day **guided walks** including stopovers at the comfortable *Awaroa Lodge*, where the excellent food re-energizes you for the next day's exertions. A five day guided walk is $1200, three day $800, while cruises and taxis beginning from Kaiteriteri to Tinline Bay are $5, Torrent Bay $16, Bark Bay $19, Awaroa $26 and Totaranui $27. They can also arrange multi–day kayak and walk trips.

This is also one of the best places in New Zealand to **swim with seals** and Abel Tasman Seal Swim, Marahau Valley Road, Marahau (☎ & fax 03/527 8136, ☎0800/527 8136, *sealswim@ihug.co.nz*; Oct–April, 8.45am & 12.30pm; 3–4hr; book at least 5 days ahead; $65) can provide all the gear as well as a safe, professional and unforgettable excursion. Swimming with seals can be a lot more fun than swimming with dolphins simply because seals are often more curious and, having greater manoeuvrability, are capable of tying a mere human in knots in no time. Underwater visibility in the area is usually crystal, and the operators try to minimize the impact on the seals by insisting that you wait for the seals to come and swim with you rather than just leaping in and splashing about among them. The company also offer a full water taxi and scenic trip service with a scenic tour the full length of the park costing $40.

The last of the scenic cruise/water taxi operators of note is Aqua Taxi (☎03/527 8083 & 0800/278 282, *aquataxi@xtra.co.nz*) who run their trips from Marahau to coincide with incoming buses. They are fast and efficient using a powerful naiad that can get into the shore a lot closer than most boats and provide an amusingly commentated scenic cruise that takes in the split apple rock ($40).

The Abel Tasman Track

Although, strictly speaking, the Abel Tasman Track encompasses both the tremendously popular **Coastal Track** and the much less crowded and more arduous **Inland Track**, the Coastal Track is almost universally known simply as the **Abel Tasman Track**. Part of the attraction of this coastal route is that it is, along with the Queen Charlotte Track (see p.478), the **easiest** of New Zealand's Great Walks, and lack of fitness is no impediment: the track is clear and easy to follow, entry and exit to the beach sections clearly marked and you are never more than four hours from a hut or campsite. All of this has made the Abel Tasman Track one of the most popular in the country and from December to the end of February there is an endless stream of hikers heading along the route.

The **route** traverses broad golden beaches lapped by emerald waters, punctuated by granite pillars silhouetted against the horizon and zigzagging gentle climbs through tiny stream valleys. As well as the two major tracks, there are a number of shorter **day walks** with access by road or from the major tracks; leaflets (50¢–$1) on all of these are available at local visitor centres.

ACCOMMODATION

The best way to do either the coastal or the inland track is to walk independently and stay in the DOC huts or at the campsites, including the *Totaranui Campground*. Owing to the track's enormous popularity, the DOC recently imposed a **booking system** with the intention of controlling numbers and stopping the trampers' race that used to occur as people shot along the track in an effort to make sure of a bunk. There's now a two night limit on each hut and campsite throughout the year, and from October 1 to April 30 you have to pre-book by buying a Summer Season Pass (hut $14 per night, $7 rest of the year; campsite $7 per night). You can do this by post from the Motueka Visitor Centre, Wallace St, Motueka, by phone or fax (☎03/528 0005, fax 03/528 6563), or by visiting one of the local visitor or DOC centres. Even with this system the large number of park campgrounds mean the track still gets pretty busy at the height of the summer, and it's better to walk it in early spring, mid-autumn, or perhaps even the beginning of winter, when you'll appreciate it more.

Along the **Coastal Track**, the four **DOC huts** (all Category 2) are spaced around four hours' walk apart, and have heating, showers and toilets, but no cooking facilities so you have to carry a stove; bunks are basic but comfortable, and you need a sleeping bag. The other option is camping: there are 21 designated **campsites** along the coastal route either on or near the beaches or the DOC huts (whose facilities you can use); all sites have a water supply and toilets, but you will be carrying more gear and you'll need an ocean of sandfly repellent. Finally, for a treat midway along the track, book ahead at the *Awaroa Lodge and Café* (see previous page) or just drop in for a well-deserved beer and feed when you're staying at the Awaroa Hut.

Camping is not permitted on the **Inland Track**, but there are four backcountry huts ($7) spaced no more than five hours' walk apart, and there is rarely competition for beds. Water supplies and toilets are provided, but you'll need take a cooking stove.

TRAILHEAD TRANSPORT

The Coastal and Inland tracks share the same starting and finishing points, running between **Marahau** in the south and **Totaranui** or Wainui in the north, all of which are well served by transport.

Buses run to the Marahau or Totaranui entrances to the park from Nelson, Motueka and Takaka (see "Getting to the park" on p.498 for details). Several **water taxis** offer drop-off and pick-up services to and from Totaranui for trampers and casual walkers, calling at the bays en route to cater for those who don't want to walk the whole track. They all charge roughly the same (for details of operators see "Exploring the park" on p.498) as competition is stiff. **From Kaiteriteri,** Abel Tasman National Park Transport run motorized catamarans, and Abel Tasman Water Taxis (☎03/528 7497 & 0800/423 397) operate smaller, quicker naiads. **From Marahau** to Totaranui, choose between the zippy Abel Tasman Seafaris Aqua Taxi and Abel Tasman Seal Swim, who both offer an excellent and speedy service.

THE COASTAL TRACK
Consult the visitor/DOC centre or a local tide table when planning your trip along the **Coastal Track** (51km; 2–5 days) because crossing the Awaroa Inlet, Torrent Bay and Wainui Bay is **tide-dependent**; there is no alternative at Awaroa and the inland diversion at Torrent Bay adds at least one hour to the walk. Tide times will help you decide which way you're going to do the track – if there are low tides in the afternoon you'll probably want to head south, if they're in the morning north. Before setting off you should also arrange your transport drop-offs and pick-ups (see "Exploring the park" on p.498).

From **Marahau to Anchorage Hut** (11.5km; 4hr), the track follows a wooden causeway and crosses the Marahau estuary to the open country around Tinline Bay before rounding a point overlooking Fisherman and Adele islands just off the coast. As the track winds in and out of gullies, the surroundings are obscured by beech forest and tall kanuka trees until you emerge into Anchorage Bay, with its hut and campsite. On the second day, **Anchorage Bay to Bark Bay Hut** (9.5km; 3hr), you have to cross Torrent Bay at low tide, before climbing out of the bay through pine trees and meandering through valleys and a gorgeous inlet before reaching the Falls Rivermouth and the Bark Bay hut, beside the Bark Bay estuary. Day three is a gentle stroll from **Bark Bay Hut to Awaroa Hut** (11.5km; 4hr), overlooking the Tonga Marine Reserve and Tonga Island. The track climbs to the Tonga Saddle before descending to the Awaroa Inlet and the hut, with a campsite alongside; *Awaroa Lodge and Café* is also within easy walking distance.

From **Awaroa Hut,** you must cross the Awaroa estuary (2hr either side of low tide) and head along Goat Bay and up to a lookout above Skinner Point before reaching **Totaranui** (5.5km; 1hr 30min), where there is an extensive campsite, or you can press on over and around rocky headlands as far as Mutton Cove, where the track leaves the coast and climbs to another saddle before descending to **Whariwharangi Hut** (7.5km; 2hr) and campsite. From here it's possible to take a short hike to **Separation Point,** where there is a fur seal colony and a good lookout, or to tackle the strenuous climb up **Gibbs Hill** for even better views. The last day, **from Whariwharangi Hut to Wainui** (5.5km; 1hr 30min), involves crossing Wainui Bay (2hr either side of low tide) or following the road around the bay. If you follow the road, you can also take in the short climb up to the Wainui Falls which heads off the road at the base of Wainui Bay.

THE INLAND TRACK
The considerably less popular **Inland Track** (42km; 3–5 days), is a more strenuous walk, and should only be attempted by well-equipped and moderately fit trampers. The route climbs from sea level to **Evans Ridge** past many granite outcrops and views of the coast: highlights include the Pigeon Saddle, the moorlands of Moa Park and the moon-like Canaan landscape; you can also link up with the Rameka Track on Takaka Hill and the Harwood's Hole Track (see overleaf) along the way.

Starting the walk **from Marahau** in the south, the Inland Track splits away from the Coastal Track at Tinline Bay, following a steady climb through regenerating forest to the **Castle Rocks Hut** (11.5km; 4hr 30min), which is perched near rocky outcrops and has great views of the Marahau Valley and Tasman Bay. From **Castle Rocks to Moa Park Hut** (3.5km; 2hr), is a steeper climb, followed by an undulating section over tussock. The walk from **Moa Park to the Pigeon Saddle** (14.5km; 6–7hr) involves walking along Evans Ridge and descending to the **Awapoto Hut**, while the last day is an easy stroll to **Wainui** (6km; 2hr 15min), with only a short climb to the summit of Gibbs Hill, from where you get some of the most expansive views across the park and meet up with people who took the Coastal Track.

Takaka Hill

From Motueka, SH60 climbs **Takaka Hill**, providing the only **road access to Golden Bay** – and glorious views of the seascape from Nelson north to D'Urville Island. Skirting the inland border of the Abel Tasman National Park, it is possible to explore the hill's fascinating geology from either the Inland Track (see previous page) or from the highway.

The first diversion off SH60, 20km out of Motueka, are the **Ngarua Caves** (Sept–June daily 10am–4pm, guided tours only; 35min; $10), reached along a short bumpy track. A celebration of tackiness, the caves contain numerous examples of stalactites and stalagmites, including some with musical accompaniments and grand illuminated formations such as the Wedding Cathedral. Tour guides also point out bones from moas and regale you with an informative commentary on the caves' history and geology.

A kilometre or so further along SH60 from the caves turn-off is the entrance to the unsealed 12-kilometre Canaan Road, at the end of which is the starting point of the forty-minute walk to **Harwoods Hole**, a huge vertical shaft 183m deep (don't get too close to the edge), and a fantastic place to explore and survey the surroundings. The walk begins in an enchanted forest landscape, then follows a dry rock-strewn riverbed through eerie country before reaching a viewpoint atop the cliff walls of Gorge Creek, where forests, coastline and sea are all laid out before you. Back on the Canaan Road, you can join the clearly signposted **Rameka Track** (5km; 3hr one way) for more punishment. This follows one of the earliest surveyed routes into the Takaka Valley, from Canaan to central Takaka, with superb views of the granite outcrops and the surrounding country. From here, SH60 twists its way across the mountain before descending in a series of steep, tight, eye-opening switchbacks that eventually straighten out as you roll down into Golden Bay.

If you get **hungry** when you go over the hill or fancy a break before attempting the switch-back descent into Golden Bay then try *Jade Café*, well-signposted beside the road and offering home-made cakes plus more substantial meals. From here either admire the views to the west or the excellent bird paintings of Janet Marshal that grace the café walls.

Golden Bay

Occupying the northwestern tip of the South Island, **GOLDEN BAY** curves gracefully from the northern fringes of the Abel Tasman National Park to the encircling arm of **Farewell Spit**, all backed by the magnificence of the Kahurangi National Park. A relatively flat area hemmed in by towering mountains on three sides and with waves lapping at its exposed fourth side, its inaccessibility has kept it almost pristine. The coastline is washed by clear, sparkling water, creating excellent conditions for windsurfing, while its hinterland is home to the country's largest freshwater springs, **Pupu Springs**, as well as a number of other curious geological phenomena.

Historically, the bay was also the point where Abel Tasman struck land, guaranteeing his place in history as the first European to encounter New Zealand and the local Maori. Today's bayside communities are small, their growth still hindered by **isolation** – the road over Takaka Hill is twisting and treacherous and there is no access from the West Coast, save for a long footslog on the Heaphy Track. This perhaps explains the air of **independence**, self-reliance and stoic forbearance and also why the bay has become so attractive to alternative lifestylers and artists producing work of real merit. Sunny, beautiful and full of fascinating sights, Golden Bay is well worth a few days of your time.

Takaka and around

The small town of **TAKAKA** is situated on SH60, cradled by the sweep of the bay. East of the town and linked to it by road are **Pohara Beach**, where there's safe swimming, and Tarakohe Harbour and Wainui Bay, both providing access to the northern end of the Abel Tasman National Park (see p.501). South of Takaka, **Pupu Springs** emerge from their underground lair, while to the north yawns a considerable stretch of beautiful bay, running parallel to SH60 as it rolls into Collingwood.

Arrival and information

The airline you fly with from Nelson or Wellington should run you the 5km from the **airport** into town. Most **bus** companies drop off outside the information centre on Willow Street (see below). Local shuttle buses will get you to most of the major destinations in Golden Bay, but you can also rent cars or bikes (see "Listings", p.506).

On Willow Street, just south of the main part of town, the **visitor centre** (daily 9am–5pm; ☎03/525 9136, *gb.vin@tourism-nelson.co.nz*) acts as a booking centre for the national parks and tracks, and stocks a number of leaflets detailing local attractions, including a useful one on the Pupu Springs, and local walks. The **DOC office** on Commercial Street shuns public attention for the most part, but if you are going backcountry tramping seek them out for advice (☎03/525 9061; Mon–Fri 9am–noon & 1–4pm, closed for two weeks over Christmas). Another useful source of information relating to the whole bay is *The G.B. Weekly*, a free newspaper containing events, places to visit, entertainment listings and general tittle-tattle.

Accommodation

Golden Bay is a popular holiday spot with both Kiwis and foreign visitors; as a result there is a lot of good quality accommodation in and around Takaka.

Anatoki Lodge Motels, 87 Commercial St (☎03/525 8047, fax 525 8433, *anatoki@xtra.co.nz*). Modern, fully self-contained units close to the centre of town, with great service and helpful staff. ④–⑥.

Autumn Farm Lodge, a turn off 3km before Takaka on the eastern side of the road, the lodge is 200m up on the left (☎03/525 9013). Very comfortable, charming gay (male) friendly accommodation in a six hectare plot with a laidback atmosphere. Camping $10, rooms ①–③.

Golden Bay Lodge and Garden, Tukurua, signposted off SH60 17km north of Takaka (☎03/525 9275). Two fully self-contained units plus two B&B rooms overlooking a lovely garden and the sea, with easy beach access. ⑥.

Golden Bay Motel, 132 Commercial St (☎03/525 9428, fax 525 8362). A pretty, well kept little motel with off-street parking and spacious rooms. ④–⑤.

Marina Motel, Pohara Beach, 10km east (☎03/525 9620, fax 525 8636). Motel units with full cooking facilities, near a safe swimming beach, with an on-site bar and restaurant. ③–④.

The Nook, between Takaka (9km) & Pohara (1km) on the way to the Abel Tasman Park (☎03/525 8501, *nook@clear.net.nz*), with a pick–up service from Takaka by arrangement. Backpackers run by a friendly couple but too far from town for people without their own transport. The bonus is a lovely straw extension building, either used as two doubles or rented as a self-contained unit. Dorms ①, double ②, straw doubles ③, whole unit ⑤ for two.

Rose Cottage Motel and B&B, on SH60, 5km from Takaka heading towards Takaka Hill (☎03/525 9048). Three beautifully maintained motel units set in a large, lovingly tended garden, plus a homestay option, all with friendly and helpful hosts. ④.

Sans Souci Inn, Richmond Rd, Pohara Beach, 10km east (☎ & fax 03/525 8663, *reto@sanssouciinn. co.nz*). A most unusual and endearing B&B in an architecturally unique building, whose charm has grown since our last visit. Reflecting the Mediterranean atmosphere of the bay, the inn has been constructed using mudbricks, with sods as the roofing material and distinctive floor tiles. In keeping with the owners' environmental ethos, the toilets are self-composting and occupy a stunning block that effortlessly combines sanitation and horticulture. These days they have an excellent restaurant attached (see opposite). Breakfast costs $7–12, dinner $19–22 remember to book. ④.

Shambhala, Onekaka,16km north on SH60 (☎03/525 8463, fax 525 9734). Near the infamous *Mussel Inn* (pick-up can arranged), is this quirky lifestyle accommodation. Dorms are in the main house, or there are spacious twin and double rooms with good views in a separate block, complete with a solar-heated shower and a self-composting toilet. There is easy beach access so you can go out and gather your own mussels, or stay home and munch on a lentil pie or muffin. The only drawbacks are small kitchens and despite the laidback feel almost everything costs, including a $5 charge for bed linen. Dorms ①, rooms ②.

The Town and around

Despite being the bay's largest settlement, the town itself is a low and architecturally barren affair where three roads, SH60 (Commercial Street as it passes through town), Motupipi Road and Meihana Street, form a triangle.

Close to the centre of town on Commercial Street, the restored old post office (1899) now houses the **Golden Bay Gallery** (daily 10am–4pm; free) which balances art and crafts. In amongst the usual detritus are wonderful silk paintings by Sage Cox, striking oil paintings by Peter Green and some unusual, but over-priced sculptures and clocks. The adjacent **Golden Bay Museum** (entry through the Gallery; $1) is well worth a look even if it's only for the breathtakingly detailed diorama depicting Abel Tasman's ill-fated trip to Wainui Bay in 1642. The rest of the museum houses Maori artefacts, some fascinating geological and natural history material, as well as the usual mishmash of bits and bobs rooted out of attics or accumulated during travels abroad (usually to wars).

Of all the cave trips in the area, the most charming and relaxed is to be had at the **Rawhiti Caves** (☎03/525 9061; tours on demand; 3hr; $14), reached via a ten-minute drive along Motupipi Road and over the Motupipi Bridge towards Pohara Beach and then a fifty-minute walk from the car park. The pendulous stalactites that hang from the caves' wide mouth are stained by the earth and rain to hues of dirty brown, brightened by the rich green of the moss that covers some of them. Fortified by a cup of tea, you descend into the caves to see the fascinating formations, including transparent stone straws full of water, a discarded billy can now encased in rock deposited from the dripping ceiling and rock pools containing perfectly round stone "marbles".

Where Motupipi Road meets the Clifton Crossroads, turn right to reach the wonderful **Grove Scenic Reserve** (unrestricted access; free), a mystical place in greygreen that could have been transplanted straight from the *Lord of the Rings* novels or Arthurian legend, where massive rata trees sprout from odd and deformed limestone outcrops. A ten-minute walk from the car park takes you to a narrow slot between two enormous vertical cliffs where a lookout reveals the flat expanse leading to the beaches of Pohara – and the real world. On the opposite side of the Abel Tasman Drive near Three Oaks, Scott Road leads to Labyrinth Lane and after a short well-signposted jaunt heads on to **Labyrinth Rocks Park** (daily 1–5pm; $5). This is a maze-like commercial concern with a variety of limestone features and impressive mosses and trees, and a large number of plastic spiders, gnomes and dinosaurs left in curious places. The spot is well worth the entry fee, containing as it does 2km of easy tracks; a useful map is provided.

Back on the Pohara Road, heading west towards the scattered houses of Pohara Beach and Wainui Bay, about 9km from the Clifton Crossroads, you'll see signs for the unsealed 500-metre road to **Wainui Falls**. The falls themselves are a forty-minute return walk from the road, heading up through dense bush and criss-crossing the river on several bridges, with the roar of the falls growing ever louder. Nikau palms shade the banks of the river, and a curtain of spray swathes the rather lovely falls – a great place to just sit and dream.

About five minutes' drive (5km) out of Takaka on SH60 towards Collingwood is **Pupu Springs Scenic Reserve** (unrestricted access; free), New Zealand's largest freshwater springs set in a reserve of old gold workings, regenerating forest and a vestige of mature forest. There are at least sixteen springs in Pupu, with two major vents in the main springs, one major and several minor vents at Dancing Sands (where the sands, pushed by the surging water, literally dance), and about twelve springs in the Fish Creek. The water that emerges from the main springs is cold and the visibility excellent, making for superb viewing of the rich variety of brightly coloured plants beneath the surface – which can be seen by means of a reverse periscope on one of the boardwalks.

Eating and entertainment

There's a surprising number of good places to **eat** in Takaka, most clustered on Commercial Street. If you're self-catering though, don't miss the Golden Salami, which has replaced the Motupipi Butcher Shop as a place of legend. Golden Salami are a right turn at the Clifton Crossroads, off the Abel Tasman Drive 7km from Takaka and signposted from there about 1km; they produce a variety of delicious, totally natural salami from their own aggressively healthy animals and some other secret ingredients. **Drinking** and music tends to be confined to the big old hotels/pubs, the *Whole Meal Café* or *Mussel Inn* some way out of town. If you are in Takaka and stuck for something to do try the atmospheric local **cinema**, Commercial St (☎03/525 8453 or *The G.B. Weekly* for programme details).

The Dangerous Kitchen, 48 Commercial St (☎03/525 8686 for takeaway orders). Peculiarly named though perfectly serviceable little café that specializes in excellent pizzas and has Internet access. Daily 8am–midnight in the summer, 8am–7pm otherwise.

Milliways, 90 Commercial St. A café/wine bar that serves fantastic brunches, lunches and dinners at realistic prices in charming surroundings. Leave room for the desserts, which are a knock out. Daily 9am–late.

Mussel Inn, just off SH60, 16km north of Takaka. Do not miss this place – whether you want to eat, enjoy wine or ale (they brew their own), sit and read, play chess or soak up the lively atmosphere of a live band. The purpose-built wooden building is adorned with bits of local art and some clumpy but comfortable wooden furniture. You can always get a simple, fresh and wholesome meal; try a plate of the local mussels for around $10. Sept–March daily 11am till the last one leaves, April–Aug 5pm till the last one leaves.

Sans Souci Inn, see opposite. This simple restaurant has a daily set menu: hot smoked fish on Saturdays, beef fillet with spätzle (traditional Swiss pasta) on Sunday and so on, although veggie options are available each night. There's also a choice of sumptuous freshly made desserts. Licensed with meals ranging from $19–$29; bookings essential and dinner starts at 7pm.

Whole Meal Café, in the arcade on Commercial St, opposite the supermarket. Good bread, pizzas and pastries, all served with a variety of colourful and healthy salads, delicious cakes and excellent coffee. Well worth stopping in though currently the regular evening menu is always variations on the curry theme, from $10 small to $15 large. In the evenings there is sometimes live music. Daily 8am–9pm; licensed.

Listings

Airlines Takaka Valley Air Services, 38 Motupipi St (☎03/525 8613 & 0800/501 901) fly direct to Golden Bay from Motueka ($40 one way) and Wellington ($135).

Bike rental Quiet Revolution, 7 Commercial St (☎03/525 9555) rent out mountain bikes for $30 a day. Not open weekends.

Buses Bickleys and Collingwood Services Buses, 98 Commercial St (☎03/524 8188) serve Collingwood. Both also offer a Heaphy Track service, as do Kahurangi Buses and Abel Tasman Transport (see "Listings" for Nelson, p.492).

Car rental Golden Bay Rentals, the garage on the cnr Buxton Lane & Motupipi St (☎03/525 9392).

Internet Access The Gazebo, 7 Hiawatha Lane, 5min walk from the town centre; Mon–Fri 6–10pm, Sat & Sun 2–10pm.

Paragliding Takaka Tandems, operates out of the town (☎03/528 9283) and offers fun flights for $110.

Tours Quiet Revolution, 7 Commercial St (☎03/525 9555) are mountain-biking experts who recommend the best tours and day-trips.

Collingwood and around

As you might expect from somewhere that marks the end of the road for SH60, **COLLINGWOOD** is a quiet kind of a town, with one store, a couple of cafés, a friendly pub, a petrol station and a tiny museum. However, its proximity to the Heaphy Track, which traverses Kahurangi National Park (see p.509), and to the wilderness of Farewell Spit, places it firmly on the tourist circuit.

TOURS ON AND NEAR THE SPIT

Collingwood is the only place where you can take a tour to **Farewell Spit**. The most famous and longest-running of the two operations is The Original Farewell Spit Safari, Tasman St (☎ & fax 03/524 8257, *enquiries@farewellspit.co.nz*), which bounces around in characterful ex-army trucks adapted to this unique environment. The pick of their trips is the **Lighthouse Safari to the Gannet Colony** (daily, departure times dependent on tides; 6hr 30min; $66, including lunch). Starting in Collingwood, a bright commentary, peppered with local lore, enlivens the ride to Puponga and across the sands of the spit to the historic lighthouse at Bush End Point. During the day, you'll see vast numbers of birds, seals, fossils and the skeletons of wrecked ships, climb an enormous sand dune and visit a massive gannet colony towards the end of the spit.

Collingwood Bus Services/Farewell Spit Nature Tours, The Old Post Office, Tasman St (☎03/524 8188, fax 524 8091), operate two tours. Their **Nature Tour** (Oct–June; 7hr; $65, including lunch), uses a modern air-conditioned bus; they don't venture as far as the gannet colony, but do go to Pillar Point Light House, where you are treated to a panoramic view of Golden Bay and Cape Farewell. The scenic **Mail Run** (Mon–Fri, 10.30am; 5hr 30min; $45), passes beautiful bush and seascapes in remote rural areas, visits a cray-fishing base and the foot of Farewell Spit and has an entertaining historical commentary.

Two kilometres along the road to Whariariki Beach from Puponga, you'll find excellent Cape Farewell Horse Treks (☎ & fax 03/524 8031), where a relaxed philosophy and horses combine to offer some of the most visually spectacular **horse riding** in the South Island – with Mount Beale on one side, views of Farewell Spit, and the Burnett Range forging away down the West Coast. Although they don't actually go onto the spit this is a good way of becoming familiar with the area. There are a broad range of well-organized trips: Pillar Point (90 min; $30); Triangle Valley (2hr; $35), Whariariki Beach (3hr; $50); overnight to Pakawau, along beaches and to Kahurangi and the lighthouse ($140); and any number of other trips from one to seven days. The company provides everything you need, including a horse suited to your temperament and abilities; these days they also offer some pretty special, out-of-the-way accommodation (see "Practicalities", p.508).

The Town

Over the years, many of the town's older wooden edifices have been burned down, leaving only a few buildings of note on Tasman Street, where the small **Collingwood Museum** (daily 9am–6pm; gold coin donation) is devoted to the history of the early settlers and the impact of gold mining on the area. The museum also contains exhibits relating to Collingwood's ambitions to be the capital of New Zealand, with plans of the proposed streets and submissions as to why this tiny community, literally at the end of the line, should be the country's principal city.

Collingwood's surroundings, however, offer endless opportunities for meandering around country galleries situated on its winding roads. About halfway between Takaka and Collingwood on SH60 is **Onekaka Arts**, a gallery containing hand-crafted jewellery and scrimshaw (whale bone carving), created by Peter Meares (☎03/525 7366 for opening times). Eight kilometres southeast of Collingwood on SH60, winding behind Para Para Beach, is Lookout Road, where you'll find **Decorator Pots** (Dec–April daily 10am–5pm), a gallery and potters' studio situated in manicured gardens with great views. The gallery section displays conservative but high-quality stoneware, porcelain and burnished carved blackware. About 2km north on SH60, just after the Para Para Estuary before you enter Collingwood, are signs to **Estuary Arts** (Dec–April daily 10am–5pm). Run by Rosie Little and Bruce Hamlin, this is one of the best pottery galleries in the bay, with brightly coloured tableware of striking and bold design, and a gallery of some of Rosie's evocative paintings as well as a great panoramic view across the bay.

Southwest of Collingwood, on the road to Rockville and toward the Heaphy Track, is a striking natural sculpture: two plinths of limestone on either side of the road support bulbous overhangs – dubbed the **Devils Boots** for their resemblance to two feet protruding from the ground.

North to Wharariki Beach

Travelling the 29km to Farewell Spit on SH60, take a detour west to the distinctive **Wharariki Beach**. A twenty-minute walk from the car park at the road end, the beach provides a startling introduction to the rigours of the West Coast: exposed to the harsh winds and waves, Wharariki is backed by striking cliffs gouged with caves. Rock bridges and towering arches are stranded just offshore, while deep dunes have blocked rivermouths, forming briny lakes and islands where fur seals and birds have made a home. The beach is a superb place to swim, explore, watch seals in the rock pools at half-tide and lounge around. Head back towards the car park and join the northeasterly cliff path, which leads after 3km to the **Pillar Point Lighthouse**, perched on the shoulder of the spit, with far-reaching views down the West Coast and over the bay.

Farewell Spit

Farewell Spit stretches out to the very tip of the South Island, with access through Puponga Farm Park, 29km from Collingwood – although the only way you can explore the spit up close and personal is with one of the two licensed tour operators (see box opposite). The 25km-long spit is a **nature reserve** of international importance, providing a variety of habitats for birds: saltmarsh, open mudflat, freshwater and brackish lakes and bare dunes. Formed by debris sluiced out of West Coast rivers in flood and then carried by coastal currents, an uninterrupted desert of sand inches its way into the ocean and curls back towards Golden Bay, whose shores capture much of the wind-blown sand from the spit's exposed side.

The Farewell Spit **visitor centre and café**, 26km north of Collingwood (Nov–April daily 9am–6pm; May–Aug closed; Sept–Nov Mon–Sat 9am–6pm; ☎03/524 8454, fax 524

8259), is in the Puponga Farm Park, on a hill overlooking the spit. The centre has displays and some evocative photographs that recount the history of the area and the sad story of a mass whale-stranding in 1991, and has leaflets on walking tracks. You can also enjoy the spit from a distance in the viewing room (with binoculars), or the **café**, which offers giant muffins, cakes, good coffee and quality main meals, including hearty platters – and more views of the spit.

Clustered around the base of the spit is a complex of middens over 50m wide and running for almost 1km, composed mostly of burned shell and evidencing **Maori settlement** over a period of at least 700 years. Puponga Point was the site of a defended pa, with the ditches and house terraces clearly visible, and at Whau Creek there are deep pits and extensive midden spilling down to the stream, indicating a *kainga*, or undefended living area. In 1846 explorer Charles Heaphy reported seeing *waka* (Maori canoes) heading to the ocean beach and down the West Coast, and in 1867 Edmund Davidson collected two *waka*, adorned with elaborate artistic designs, now in the Nelson Provincial Museum in Stoke (see p.487). The spit was named by Captain Cook in 1770. The original **Farewell Spit Lighthouse** was erected in 1870, from materials carried along the spit, and trees were transplanted to the area to provide shelter for the keepers' dwellings.

The most important feature of the spit these days is the **wildlife** it supports. It's a twitcher's paradise, with over ninety **bird species** recorded, ranging from keas to spoonbills; each year thousands of waders, including the bartailed godwit, wrybill, long-billed curlew and mongolian dotteral, fly the 12,000km from Siberia to escape the fearsome Arctic winter. The spit harbours breeding colonies of Caspian terns and gannets, but you might also spot hawks, wekas and skuas, as well as large numbers of black swans. However, the spit also seems to exert a negative influence on some wildlife, as shown by the frequency with which whales beach themselves here: it appears that their navigational system is confused by the unusual shape of the coastline. If you follow one of the tracks on the spit, you might well come across the wasting carcass of a stranded pilot whale – a sobering sight amid such wild beauty.

There are some interesting **walks** on the spit, restricted to the landward end away from the vehicle tracks and the far end of the sand spit. Starting from the visitor centre, the outer beach track is 2.5km and the inner beach track about 4km; both provide good views of the spit and its wading bird population and offer an undiluted experience of this rather odd landscape.

Practicalities

Buses from Nelson, Motueka and Takaka drop-off in the centre of Collingwood, near the **general store** on Tasman Street (Mon–Sat 9am–6pm), while the **petrol station** (Mon–Fri 7.20am–6pm) is on Haven Road (SH60) as you enter or leave town.

There are a few **places to stay** in town and others en route to Farewell Spit and the Kahurangi National Park. *Beachcomber Motel*, Elizabeth Street (☎03/524 8499, fax 524 8599; ③–④), backs onto the river estuary with lovely views and clean, self-contained units. Also near the estuary is *Collingwood Motor Camp*, William Street, at the junction with Tasman Street (☎03/524 8149; tent sites $9, cabins ③–⑤), a pretty, sheltered site just two minutes' walk from the shops and pub. One of the best homestays in Golden Bay is the *Collingwood Homestead*, just off Elizabeth Street (☎03/524 8079, fax 524 8979; ⑥–⑦), a beautiful, 1904 colonial-style homestead with spacious comfortable rooms, excellent breakfasts and dinner by arrangement ($35, including wine). There's the chance to sit on the balcony or in the gazebo, and watch the birds in the exemplary garden, but to stay you'll need to book at least a couple of weeks in advance at the height of the season. Halfway between Collingwood and Pakawau, at a stop on the Kahurangi bus route, is *The Inlet* (☎03/524 8040, *jhearn@xtra.co.nz*; dorms ①, rooms & self-contained cottages ③–⑥), on Waikato Inlet, which now offers a wide variety of accommodation and a series of worthwhile inexpensive guided trips to underground rivers or kayaking to nearby lakes. Walking and caving trips are $55, while river kayaking trips start at $65 and involve exploring the tidal rainforest. A little further along the same road, at a bus stop on the beach side is *Pakawau Beach Park* (☎03/524 8327, fax 524 8509; camping $10, cabins ③, motel unit ④) under improved management and with excellent value cabins by the beach, opposite the *Old School House Café*, a shop and some sit-on kayaks for rent (1hr; $10). Still further away but well worth the effort is the romantic hideaway of *Cape Farewell Horse Treks* (see box on p.506), who have designed and built a self-contained cabin that sleeps two (④) in regenerating bush near a babbling brook. There's no electricity, gaslight, cooking facilities or shower, just solitude and the sound of birds and running water.

The only place worth getting a **drink** in town is the *Collingwood Tavern and Bistro* (closed Sun), opposite the Old Post Office on Tasman Street, which is also a reasonable place to fill up on steak and chips ($16). Close to the pub, *Collingwood Café* serves straightforward **food** every day at no-nonsense prices but undoubtedly the best place to eat is the licensed *Courthouse Café*, based in the atmospheric, 1901 courthouse at the corner of Gibbs Road and Elizabeth Street (☎03/524 8572 for bookings; Oct–Feb daily 8am–late; March–Sept 11am–late). They serve excellent coffee, good cakes and have a reasonably priced but imaginative menu on the blackboard, including pan-fried monk fish and lots of veggie options. At Pakawau Bay, on the way to Farewell Spit, *The Old School House Café Restaurant* (daily 11am–11pm; licensed) dishes up simple food in a quiet and relaxed atmosphere, concentrating on locally grown veggies, fish and lamb.

Kahurangi National Park

The huge expanse of **Kahurangi National Park**, only designated in 1996, covers 40,000 square kilometres of the northwestern South Island; appropriately enough, its name means "treasured possession". The park enfolds the exposed western side of the Wakamarama Range, which are among the wettest mountains in the country and include the peaks of Mount Owen and Mount Arthur. A remote and beautiful place (presently with relatively few other visitors to detract from your enjoyment), the best way to appreciate its extraordinary landscape is on foot. In fact, this is the only way to get to much of the park and most people come here to walk the **tracks** – primarily the **Heaphy Track**, though its lesser-tramped cousins offer equal rewards and more solitude. The best bases for visiting the Kahurangi National Park are **Collingwood** or **Takaka**, from where buses run to the head of the Heaphy Track. **Motueka** also provides access to the Tablelands, Mount Arthur and the Leslie–Karamea Track from the Flora Saddle car park, while the Anatoki River Valley can be reached from **Takaka**.

Geologically it is an incredibly diverse area, comprised of sedimentary rocks faulted and uplifted from an ancient sea, as well as limestone and marble riddled with deep caves, bluffs, natural bridges and arches, sink holes and strange outcrops. Over half of New Zealand's native **plant species** are represented in the park, as are most of its alpine species, while the remote interior is a haven for birds and **animals**, including rare carnivorous snails and giant cave spiders.

Around 800 years ago, the area was well travelled by **Maori**, as they made their way to central westland in search of *pounamu* (greenstone) for weapons, ornaments and tools. From Aorere, they traversed the Gouland Downs, crossed the Heaphy rivermouth and headed down the coast, constantly at risk of being swept away. The first **Europeans** to arrive were the Australian sealing gangs in the 1820s, who within twenty years had almost wiped out the entire seal population. In 1856 the first **gold rush** ignited interest in the area and although it had petered out three years later, prospectors tarried on at the Aorere Gold Fields (now a reserve) and deeper into the interior.

Ironically, now the area is protected it faces its greatest test as millions of **possums**, which invaded the area in the late 1960s, obliviously munch their way through the native plants and devastate the snail population.

Exploring the park

There are a number of **walking** tracks in the park, the most famous being the **Heaphy Track**, all of which offer a taste of this unusual and still relatively unknown area. **Information** on the park and all the walks and activities are available at visitor centres and DOC offices in Takaka, Motueka and Nelson. Local shuttle buses provide **trail-head transport**, and Abel Tasman Coachlines (Nelson SBCL), Abel Tasman National Parks Transport, Kahurangi Buses and Bickley Motors Ltd run regular services to the park (see "Listings" for Takaka, p.506).

Two quite arduous but rewarding and uncrowded tracks are the **Wangapeka Track** (60km; 4–5 days), usually walked from Little Wanganui, just south of Karamea on the West Coast (see p.510 for details), and the **Leslie-Karamea Track** (90km; 5–7 days; 1795m ascent), which links the Wangapeka Track with Mount Arthur and the Tablelands above Motueka. The Leslie-Karamea Track starts at the Flora Saddle car park near Motueka (see p.493) and heads south along the Leslie and Karamea rivers and through beech forest before joining the Wangapeka Track near the Luna Hut. There are seven main huts (all Category 3; $5) along the track, which is quite rough in places and should only be attempted by reasonably fit and well equipped trampers. A map of the track ($1) is available from DOC offices and visitor centres.

If you're not inclined to tramp the park on your own, then check out the guided walks organized by **Kahurangi Guided Walks** (☎ & fax 03/525 7177; $30–720) on the Heaphy, Mount Arthur, Wangapeka Track or in Golden Bay.

The Heaphy Track

Crossing the Kahurangi National Park from Golden Bay to Kohaihai Bluff on the West Coast (or vice versa), the **Heaphy Track** (77km; 4–6 days) is one of New Zealand's Great Walks, renowned for the beauty and diversity of landscapes it covers, taking in the confluence of the boiling Brown and Aorere rivers, broad tussock downs and forests, and emerging on the rugged West Coast. The track is named after Charles Heaphy who, with Thomas Brunner, became the first Europeans to walk the route in 1846, accompanied by their Maori guide Kehu.

ACCESS AND ACCOMMODATION
A **map** of the track ($1) is available from visitor centres and DOC offices, whom you should advise of your intentions – and of your safe return. Along the route, there are seven **huts** (Great Walk huts; $15), with heating, water and toilets, and ten designated **campsites** ($8). Before setting off, you must purchase a hut or camp **pass** from DOC offices, visitor centres, some hostels and travel agents in Nelson, Motueka, Karamea and Westport, though this does not guarantee a bunk and there is a two-night limit in each hut. It's a tough track so go well-equipped and be prepared for sudden changes of weather and a hail of sandflies. There is nowhere along the track to pick up **supplies** so you must take all provisions with you – and carry out all your rubbish.

TRAILHEAD TRANSPORT
The Heaphy Track is particularly awkward in one respect: if you leave your gear or vehicle at one end, you'll have to re-walk the track or undertake a long journey by road to the place you started. Abel Tasman National Parks Transport (☎03/528 8850, fax 548

0285, *atc@nelsoncoaches.co.nz*; $40) operate a service from Nelson and Motueka, stopping at most points along the way; Kahurangi Buses (☎0800/173 371) leave Nelson and go to Motueka, Golden Bay and the Heaphy ($38); while Bickley Motors Ltd run from Takaka to the Heaphy at 10.15am daily for $20.

THE ROUTE
The Golden Bay entrance to the **eastern end** of the Heaphy Track is near **Browns Hut**, at the end of the road that runs (28km) from Collingwood past Bainham; the **West Coast entrance** is at Kohaihai Bluff, 10km north of Karamea.

If you are walking the track from east to west, the hardest day is the first, from **Browns Hut to Perry Saddle Hut** (16km; 5hr), by way of the Flanagans Corner viewpoint – at 915m, the highest point on the track. The second day can either be a very easy walk across the Perry Saddle through tussock clearings to the valley before crossing limestone arches to **Goulands Hut** (7.5km; 2hr), or a more strenuous tramp to **Saxon Hut** (12.5km; 3hr 30min). From Saxon Hut **to Mackay Hut** (11km; 3hr) involves crossing grassy flatlands, winding in and out of small streams as they tip over into the Heaphy River below. If you have the energy, it is worth pressing on to **Lewis Hut** (12km; 3–4hr), a haven for nikau palms – and less welcome sandflies. Next day can either be a long slog to the **Kohaihai Rivermouth** (24km; 8hr), but it's more enjoyable to take your time and stop at the **Heaphy Hut** (8km; 2–3hr), near where you can explore the exciting Heaphy rivermouth: its narrow outlet funnels river water into a torrid sea, resulting in a maelstrom of sea and fresh water. The **final day** (16km; 5hr) is a gentle walk through forest down the coast until you reach Crayfish Point, where you can cross the beach if you are within two hours of low tide; otherwise, take the high-tide track. Once you reach Scott's Beach, you have only to climb over **Kohaihai Bluff** to find the car park on the other side – and hopefully your pre-arranged pick-up from Karamea (see p.707).

Nelson Lakes National Park and around

Around 118km southwest of Nelson, the **Nelson Lakes National Park** encompasses tranquil mountains, beech forest and mirror-like lakes, with spectacular tramping in summer and skiing in winter. The park is best known, though, for its two glacial lakes, **Rotoroa** ("long lake"), and **Rotoiti** ("little lake"). Lake Rotoiti is very popular among anglers, kayakers and yachties, and is surrounded by mountains, stands of beech forest and flax, all criss-crossed with fine walks. The vast expanse of deep blue water that is Lake Rotoroa is rather more rarefied, its enclosing mountains becoming barren and grey at its southern extremity. The park's sub-alpine rivers, lakes, forests and hills are full of bird life, but it has offered little solace to man: Maori passed through the area and caught eels in the lakes, but the best efforts of European settlers and gold prospectors yielded meagre returns.

The main bases for forays into the park are **St Arnaud**, a tiny community on SH63, just over 100km southwest of Blenheim and 25km from Kawatiri Junction on the road between Nelson and Murchison (SH6); or **Murchison** itself, 35km further southwest and a little larger.

Once clear of Murchison, SH6 romps alongside the Buller River through the Buller Gorge to the **West Coast** town of Westport, a route covered in Chapter Twelve (see p.700). If you're heading for the **east**, you can retrace your route along SH6, then cut across to Blenheim (see p.516), 162km away on SH63.

St Arnaud

ST ARNAUD is a spec of a place poised on the north shore of Lake Rotoiti, which provides accommodation and food for visitors to the Nelson Lakes National Park, its population of around a hundred swelling with trampers and skiers in season. Little more than a jumble of two-storey buildings on either side of the road, the settlement has little to detain you, but if you're after some background on the region, the visitor centre (see below) shows a fifteen-minute video on the Buller River and its unique ecosystem, which supports giant eels, a variety of bird life (including the endangered blue duck), and abundant brown trout. Displays in the centre also provide information on the Nelson Lakes National Park and its vegetation, including manuka and kanuka trees – the leaves of the latter were used by Cook and other early visitors to supplement their dwindling stocks of tea, giving them their common name of tea trees.

Practicalities

Most **shuttle buses** (Atomic, Kahurangi, Nelson Lakes Shuttles and West Coast) drop you right in St Arnaud, but InterCity and White Star **coaches** between Nelson and Murchison drop you at Kawatiri Junction, from where you'll need to pick up a Blenheim-bound bus along SH63, or call Nelson Lakes Shuttles (☎03/521 1887; $17).

The commercial hub of St Arnaud is the **service station and store** (daily 7.30am–6.30pm), which also acts as a post office and cafeteria (closes at 6pm). The **DOC office**, on View Road overlooking Kerr Bay (☎03/521 1806, fax 521 1896; Mon–Sun 8am–4.30pm, until the last visitor is ejected during summer holidays), is guarded by a red Maori statue depicting Rakaihautu, creator of the lakes. The centre has copious information on the region, including walks and mountaineering around Nelson Lakes – and the exceptional caves to be explored around Mount Owen; they also book hut tickets and trips, offer advice and provide intentions or search and rescue cards as necessary. There are two websites relating to the the the area: *www.webnz.com/nelson/lakes* and *www.destination.co.nz/Marlborough*, the latter concentrates on the Rainbow ski field

A range of **accommodation** is available in two modern wooden buildings just off the main road (SH60) at *Alpine Chalet and Lodge* (☎ & fax 03/521 1869, *enquiries@alpinelodge.co.nz*; dorms ①, rooms ③–⑥); facilities include a licensed restaurant, bar, café and spa pool. *The Yellow House* and *St Arnaud Log Chalets*, 150m from the service station (☎ & fax 03/521 1887; dorms ①, rooms ③, chalets ⑤), is a small hostel with doubles, twins and shared rooms, kitchen, TV and a wealth of information, plus a few delightful, fully self-contained chalets next door. Around 30km out of town on SH6, near Kawatiri Junction, and signposted from the road, is *Hu ha Backpackers* (☎03/546 9413; dorms ①, rooms ②), an old cottage on a farm which makes a good spot for cyclists, trampers or those who just want to get away from it all; inexpensive breakfasts and dinner can be ordered. Finally, there are two DOC **campsites** (☎03/521 1806; $8), both overlooking the lake, at Kerr Bay and West Bay, with kitchens, toilets and pay showers.

Aside from the homely **snacks** and meals to be had at the service station café (daily 8am–6pm), the only other place to eat in St Arnaud is at the *Alpine Chalet and Lodge* (see above), whose licensed **restaurant** offers breakfast and dinner (daily 8–9.30am & 6.30–9pm), or you can opt for bar meals (daily 5.30–9pm) of burgers, soups, salads and grills.

Getting to – and exploring – the lakes

Lake Rotoiti is the more accessible of the two lakes, easily reached on foot along a short road very close to the settlement of St Arnaud. The Gowan Valley Road to Lake

SKIING IN MOUNT ROBERT AND RAINBOW VALLEY

The two skifields close to St Arnaud are very different in character. At both, the **season** usually runs from June to October, and Nelson Lakes Shuttles (☎03/521 1887), Nelson Lakes Transport (☎03/547 5912) and JJ's Ski Transport (☎03/544 7081) operate **shuttle services** out to both fields ($20 minimum, $10pp) for the duration.

The **Mount Robert Skifield** (☎03/548 8336), 15km from St Arnaud, is a small ski area that remains quiet due to the ninety-minute walk to the field from the car park and the variable snow fall, though a helicopter provides lifts at weekends (on demand; $40, minimum 4; $15 for packs and skis). Downhill and cross-country skiers enjoy good powdery snow – and two lodges, which provide refreshment. Gear rental is available in St Arnaud village (☎03/521 1850), and lift passes cost $20 per day.

The much more commercial **Rainbow Valley Ski Area** (☎03/521 1861 & 0800/754 724, *info@skirainbow.co.nz* web *snow.co.nz/rainbow*), 32km from St Arnaud, has an enormous variety of runs catering for a wide variety of skiing and snowboarding abilities, with lessons and equipment rental if needed. Access is via a toll road ($10), and the car park is very close to the lifts ($44 daily).

Rotoroa, which veers off SH6 between Nelson and Murchison just after the St Arnaud turn-off, is unsealed; near the end of this road, the **Lake Rotoroa Ranger Station** (☎ 03/523 9369; Mon–Fri 8am–noon & 1–5pm, Sat & Sun 9am–noon & 1–5pm) offers good advice and literature on the area. Nelson Lakes Shuttles (☎03/521 1887) run on demand to Mount Robert car park, Lake Rotoroa, Kawatiri Junction, Howard Valley and Wairau Valley ($60 minimum, $20pp). St Arnaud Guiding Services (☎03/521 1028), offer **guided** walks and 4WD **safaris** in the park (from $55 a half day).

There are **water taxi** services on both lakes; minimum charges roughly equivalent to four one-way fares apply to all their services. Lake Rotoroa Water Taxis (☎03/523 9199) ply the length of the lake ($60 minimum, $20pp), giving you a chance for a good look around. Lake Rotoiti Water Taxis (☎03/521 1894) run to the head of Lake Rotoiti ($40 minimum, $10pp), and between Kerr Bay and West Bay ($32 minimum, $8pp). Alternatively, you can take a scenic cruise around Lake Rotoiti in one of the taxi vessels (1hr 30min; $60 minimum, $15pp); the company also rents out **kayaks**, canoes, row boats ($20 half day, $40 per day).

There are a few short walks by **Lake Rotoroa**, but although the lake is pretty, there is not much here apart from a few wily fish and some ridiculously expensive accommodation – the exclusive preserve of dedicated anglers and stressed-out executives. The *Lake Rotoroa Lodge*, at the northern lakeside (☎03/523 9121, fax 523 9028; ⑨) and based in a 1920s building garlanded with US and New Zealand flags, is typical.

Mountain biking

There are a number of mountain-biking possibilities around the national park, including the spectacular **Rainbow Road** (1–2 days; impassable in winter) that connects St Arnaud to Hanmer Springs, 112km to the southeast. The road crosses some private land, for which keys and permission must be arranged at the DOC offices at either end. The highest point on the route is **Island Saddle** (1347m), with panoramic views of the Tarndale Lakes, Lake Tennyson and the surrounding countryside. For **accommodation** en route, there are two Category 3 backcountry huts at Connors Creek and Island Gully ($5) and campsites at Tarndale Lakes and Lake Tennyson, both with a cold water supply and toilets ($4); be sure to boil or filter the water before use. Less energetic is the old 4WD track between Lakes Rotoiti and Rotoroa (3.5hr) with some steep climbs and great views.

Walking

There are many walking options in the area, with 270km of track wending its way across the park, served by twenty huts. If you feel the need of a well informed, friendly **guide** to accompany you on your tramps, St Arnaud Guiding Services (☎03/521 1028) are your best bet. The lakes area also provides access to a number of **longer tracks**, two of which – the tramp to the Angelus Hut and the Travers–Sabine Circuit – are particularly recommended. These are alpine tracks so you must be equipped with good boots, and warm and waterproof clothing, as well as the relevant DOC maps and leaflets, and hut tickets from the DOC office in St Arnaud. Both tracks **start** from the **upper Mount Robert car park**, which can be reached by **bus**, Nelson Lakes Transport (☎03/548 6858) and Nelson Lakes Shuttles (☎03/521 1887).

AROUND LAKE ROTOROA

Just before the Rotoroa Bridge on Braeburn Road, close to the **Lake Rotoroa Ranger Station**, is the start of a short section of the **Braeburn Track** (8km; 2hr), which heads along the western shore of the lake, passing through the dense green podocarp forest that surrounds it. The lake's eastern shore is traced by the rather overgrown **Lakeside Track** (28km; 2 days), which heads through the forest to the Sabine Rivermouth at the southern end of the lake and then scrambles up to the Sabine Hut (Category 2; $10), where you'll have to stay overnight before heading back down.

AROUND LAKE ROTOITI

Better walking can be had on the network of tracks that explore the edge of **Lake Rotoiti**, and then head into forests and up the surrounding hills. There are a number of **leaflets** detailing the various tracks in the area as well as the geology and wildlife, available from the DOC office in St Arnaud (50¢–$1).

Four of the best **shorter walks** are the Peninsula Nature Walk, St Arnaud Range Track, Bellbird Track and Whiskey Falls Track; you can even avoid backtracking by taking a water taxi across the lake and then walking back. The **Peninsula Walk** (2km; 1hr 30min) is a nature trail around the peninsula that divides Kerr Bay from West Bay, and makes an easy and rewarding introduction to the area. Slightly more strenuous is the **St Arnaud Range Track** (18km return; 6hr; 1650m ascent), also beginning at Kerr Bay, before climbing through beech forest, with spectacular views of the lake and mountain once you emerge from the bushline. At the car park by Kerr Bay are signs to indicate the Lakehead Track and a variety of others cut fairly recently, the best and least strenuous of which is the **Bellbird Track** (a twenty-minutes' stroll). This forms a short circle briefly joining the Honey Dew Walk (1hr) – so named because it contains a large number of beech, the hairy bark of which is coated with a clear, sweet honey – and passing the entrance to The Loop Track, that slips up and down through the regenerating bush and forest for about ten minutes. The Bellbird Track is best appreciated in the early evening when the large numbers of bellbirds and tui are particularly noisy and frisky. For more walking you can begin on the Mount Robert Road on the western shore of the lake, a 5-kilometre lakeside track leads to the **Whiskey Falls Track** (4hr return, including lakeside section). Almost always shrouded in mist and fringed by moss and hanging ferns the falls are forty metres high and particularly grand after heavy rain.

TO THE ANGELUS HUT

The best route to the recently upgraded **Angelus Hut** (14km; 7–8hr), if the weather is fine, is by way of **Robert Ridge**, which involves walking up the face of Mount Robert to 1411m, then tracing the broad ridge, overlooking the whole area. Head southwest across the Julius Saddle, sticking to the ridge until the beautiful Angelus basin with its welcoming hut unfolds before you. The Angelus Lake is really an alpine tarn, a legacy of glaciers that retreated over 10,000 years ago, leaving the characteristic steep-sided valley walls, bluff-ringed creeks, sharp ridges and water-filled basins. From the Angelus Hut, the easiest route is southeast along the **Cascade Track** (14km; 5hr), which descends beside a stream before heading back to Lake Rotoiti, via either the Lakehead Hut on the eastern shore or the Coldwater Hut on the western shore. The longer and tougher option is to head southwest toward Mount Cedric and the Sabine Hut and then follow the **Speargrass Track** (22km; 9hr) back to the Mount Robert car park. From the Mount Robert car park, you can either walk back to St Arnaud (5km) or pre-arrange a pick-up with one of the shuttle bus services.

THE TRAVERS-SABINE CIRCUIT
Not mentioned in the same breath as New Zealand's Great Walks (and, as a consequence, delightfully uncrowded), the **Travers-Sabine Circuit** (80km; 4–7 days) is none the less spectacular for its lowly status.

The track probes deep into remote areas of lakes, fields of tussock and 2000-metre mountains, of which the highlight is the Travers Saddle (1780m) and a deep bowl fed by a 20-metre cascade and subject to freezing conditions at any time of year. At the height of summer, the track verges are briefly emblazoned with yellow buttercups, white daisies, sundew and harebells. According to Maori legend, the area's fecundity and peppering of lakes is due to Rakaihautu, a famous chief who travelled the great mountains with his *ko* (digging stick), digging enormous holes that he filled with water and food for those that followed. The circuit requires a good level of **fitness**, though it is fairly easy to follow, with bridges over most streams. You must obtain **hut tickets** at the DOC office in St Arnaud (all the huts have been recently upgraded) before commencing the walk, as well as stocking up on food, water and the requisite **maps** – the DOC's *Sabine-Travers Circuit* ($1) leaflet is quite adequate, but the more detailed and expensive TopoMaps are also available. There are nine huts along the track and **camping** is allowed – but fires aren't, so carry a stove and fuel.

Murchison and around

MURCHISON, 35km further along SH6 from Kawatiri Junction, is a service centre for local farmers and beloved of shooting, hunting and fishing types due to its proximity to the Matakitaki and Buller rivers. It also makes a feasible base from which to explore some of the old gold workings and the Nelson Lakes, raft the Buller River (see below), or just tramp some of the impressive walks in the area.

Only a few colonial hotels stand as testimony to Murchison's glory days. **Gold** was found in the Murchison district in 1862, though the workings were in remote and rugged areas and difficult to reach. Prospectors flocked to Murchison from Nelson and Collingwood, paddling up the Buller River in Maori canoes to reach the goldfields; the last gold rush was in 1915.

The town itself has little to offer the passing visitor but it is home of the fun loving **Ultimate Descents**, 51 Fairfax St (☎03/523 9899 & 0800 RIVERS, *ultimate@rivers.co.nz*), who run excellent rafting, river bugging and inflatable kayaking trips on the Buller, Wairoa and Karamea, from one day to five ($489–$750; see p.488). Less arduous is a brief peek at the **Murchison Museum**, on Fairfax Street (daily 10am–4pm; donation requested); if the museum is locked, get the key from the petrol station opposite the café. This wooden, barn-like building houses the obligatory ancient telephone exchange and, from the gold-rush era, a collection of Chinese pottery, plus opium bottles that once granted temporary oblivion to Chinese gold diggers. There are also newspaper clippings, photographs and various oddities, such as an antique flint-lock musket from Afghanistan – and Bob Bunn's bike. A formidable pioneer, who for many years was a forward in the Murchison rugby team alongside his similarly broad-shouldered brother, Bob sold his last timber mill when he was 82 and died eight years later. He is remembered as "a rugged individualist and colourful personality, known for his down-to-earth philosophy of life, his strong political views, and love of cycling" (hence the bike).

Around Murchison

Murchison is surrounded by mountains and river valleys, in a district dominated by rugged escarpments, bush-clad ranges, lakes and many rivers. A good way to explore the area is by **bike**, which can be rented from Pedal Power and Auto Engineers, 27 Grey St, just off SH6 (☎03/523 9425; $25 a day). A leaflet (50¢) detailing several mountain-bike trails (16–85km) is available at the visitor centre; all routes begin and end in Murchison. If you want to try your hand at **gold-panning**, pick up the *Recreational Gold Panning* leaflet (50¢ from the visitor centre): this lists the likely places to strike it rich – Lyell Creek, Ariki Falls and the Howard Valley – and advises on technique.

The **Skyline Walk** (6km return; 2hr; leaflet from visitor centre, 50¢) makes a pleasant diversion. The route starts from the car park 500m past the bridge crossing the Matakitaki River, at the junction of SH6 and Matakitaki West Bank Road. Climbing up through the native forest to the skyline ridge above Murchison, the walk yields views of the township and the confluence of the Buller, Matakitaki, Maruia and Matiri rivers.

Practicalities

Bisected by SH6 (Waller Street or Main Road, as it passes through), everything of note in the town hugs either this main thoroughfare or Fairfax Street which meets it at a right-angle in town. **Buses** drop off close to the blue-roofed *Collin's Tearooms* on Fairfax Street (see below), or outside the summer-only visitor centre on Main Road, putting you within an easy walk of anywhere in the town. The summer-only, volunteer-run, **visitor centre**, Main Road (Oct–April daily 10am–4pm; ☎03/523 9350), has a number of leaflets on walks and other activities in the Murchison area; they can also book bus tickets to other destinations. Like many small towns Murchison has lost its bank but managed to hang on to a **post office**, on the opposite corner of Main Road (SH60) and Fairfax Street.

The *Commercial Hotel*, on the corner of Main Road and Fairfax (☎03/523 9696, fax 523 9848; ③), is a classic Kiwi **hotel**: the rooms have linen and towels supplied and all guest accommodation is away from the pub, so there's no noise problem. On Hotham Street, clearly signposted about 1km from town, *Mataki Motel* (☎03/523 9088; ③–④) is old but clean and quiet; some units have full kitchen, others make do with a kettle and toaster. A kilometre east of town on SH6, the *Riverview Holiday Park* (☎03/523 9315; tent sites $12, cabins ②, tourist flats ③, motel units ④) is a delightful, bird–filled, shady **campsite** by the gurgling Buller River.

Eating in Murchison is not up to much but the modern, green-roofed timber construction, the *Beechwoods Restaurant* (daily 6.30–9.30pm; licensed), on SH6 near the bridge over the Maitakitaki River, serves good salads, burgers, snacks, fish and steaks. *Collin's Tearooms* (daily 7am–8.30pm) on Fairfax Street – look for the blue roof – is a large store/cafeteria-style eatery serving up snacks and full meals in no-fuss surroundings and also doing bookings for InterCity and Whitestar **buses**. For a quiet pint and a **pie**, head for the *Commercial* (see above) where pub grub, including fish, burgers and a monstrous mixed grill, is served from 8am–late.

Blenheim and around

There are two ways to travel the 27km from Picton to **BLENHEIM**: either the scenic **coastal route**, which takes in the sights of old whaling stations via Port

Underwood, as the road winds tightly up and down the bluffs; or the more **direct route** along SH1, which passes one or two wineries and other sights, including the small community of **Korimiko**, where a garage beside the road sells ridiculously cheap, locally smoked salmon. Just up the road and by its side, in the same town, is one of New Zealand's premier cheese factories, with a wide variety available for tasting and purchase. If you are travelling from the **Nelson Lakes** there is only one road to follow, the long scenic SH63 which accompanies the Wairau River as far as **Renwick** and then darts right through the centre of the wine region before penetrating Blenheim.

Blenheim, with a population of 24,000, is a rural **service town** for all the farming and wine-growing activity on the **Wairua Plains**, where the river valleys of Awatere and Wairau rivers create rich land in the shelter of the **Richmond Range**. Like the plains it stands on, Blenheim is a well manicured, slightly sterile town, which makes a passable base for visiting the internationally renowned **wineries** of the **Marlborough** region.

Arrival, information and accommodation

The **train station** is on Sinclair Street, about five minutes' stroll from Seymour Square and the centre of town; **buses** also drop off just outside the station. The **airport** is 7km south of town, and flights are met by Airport Super Shuttle (☎03/572 9910; about $10). The **visitor centre**, 2 High St is an unmissable converted petrol station (Nov–April daily 8.30am–6.30pm; May–Oct Mon–Fri 8.30am–5.30pm, Sat & Sun 9am–2pm; ☎03/578 9904, fax 578 6084, *blm_info@clear.net.nz*). It provides a large number of useful leaflets, including maps and details of the wineries and art and craft galleries in the area, and has well-informed and helpful staff.

Accommodation

Blenheim and the wine region surrounding it attract gourmet travellers, and they are catered for by **luxury** homestays and **B&Bs** (out of town near the wineries), as well as a stunning **hotel** in town. There are, however, a handful of backpackers in Blenheim and Renwick.

BLENHEIM

Blenheim Backpackers, 29 Park Terrace (☎03/578 6062). In the rather unusual setting of an old maternity home on the banks of the Opawa River, 500m from the centre of town, this hostel is cosy with a friendly welcome. Dorms ①, rooms ②.

Hotel d'Urville, 52 Queen St (☎03/577 9945, fax 577 9946, *hoteldurville@clear.net.nz*). This former bank right in the centre of town has been turned into a world-class, highly individual hotel and restaurant, with each room thematically and colourfully decorated. The best, and some say the only, place to stay in town. ⑧–⑨.

Koanui Backpackers, 33 Main St (☎ & fax 03/578 7487). A short walk from the visitor centre, this small but cheery hostel has recently been much improved. Dorms ①, rooms ②.

The Marlborough Hotel, 20 Nelson St (☎03/577 7333, fax 577 7337). Modern, luxury accommodation with Mediterranean decor that somehow fails to capture the spirit, two restaurants, a bar and large airy rooms. ⑦.

THE WINE REGION

Charmwood Farmstay, cnr Murrays Rd & Rapaura Rd (☎03/570 5409, fax 574 5110). This beef farm is a homely, welcoming place to stay, with large rooms and hearty breakfasts of home-grown produce. ⑤–⑥.

Cranbrook Cottage, at the bottom of Giffords Rd, off Rapaura Rd, about 9km from town (☎03/572 8606, fax 572 8707). Handy for the wineries, this superb self-contained picture-book cottage has the added bonus of breakfast delivered to your door from the main house. Romantic and quiet it's almost too good. ⑦.

Old Saint Mary's Convent, Rapaura Rd, close to the junction with Hammerich's Rd (☎ & fax 03/570 5700, *old.st/marys@convent.co.nz*). A delightful and stylish, wood-dominated historic house with individually decorated rooms, a billard room, library and charming dutch hosts. ⑧.

Uno Piu, 75 Murphys Rd (☎ & fax 03/578 2235, *unopiu@iname.com*). Run by Gino, an ultra friendly, former Italian-restaurant owner, who makes this homestay magical. It is hard to imagine being better looked after anywhere else in the country: the food is gorgeous and the accommodation reassuring. You'll have to book in advance. ⑥.

Watson's Way Backpackers, 56 High St, Renwick (☎ & fax 03/572 8228). A very comfortable spot in the shade of large trees with a tennis court out back, snug rooms, easy access to the wineries and very helpful owners who can't do enough for you. Dorms ①, rooms ②.

The Town

Blenheim is pretty much devoid of either tourist attractions or charm and most people pass through quickly or use it as a base from which to visit the wineries. The town retains few of its early buildings, but a stroll following the route in the *Sideways and Byways* leaflet from the visitor centre unearths some vestiges. In the centre of the town is the pretty **Seymour Square** with its flowerbeds and distinctive stone clock tower, a popular lunch spot in fine weather and a useful landmark. About ten minutes' walk north from Seymour Square across Nelson Street (SH6) is **Pollard Park** (7am–dusk, main entrance on Parker St), a charming park area with rose gardens, rhododendrons, native rock garden and ponds – as well as a number of tennis courts, a nine-hole golf course and croquet green catering to more active pursuits.

Some 2.5km south of the town centre, off New Renwick Road is **Brayshaw Park** (Sat 10am–4pm, Sun 10am–1pm; $2 for museum) a lack-lustre reconstruction of an early settlers' community, with many of the historic buildings moved brick by brick from their original sites. The open-air museum also has a formidable collection of vintage farm machinery and vehicles, plus various accoutrements of pioneering life, including an array of textiles. At the opposite end of town (north), on SH1, is a small 1860s **Cobb Cottage** (Sat 10am–4pm, Sun 1–4pm; donation requested), which has been restored to house yet more displays on the lives of early settlers.

The wineries

Most of the wineries of note are at the other end of SH6 from Blenheim, dotted around **Renwick** – a small, unremarkable town 10km west which has a decent brewery – or strung along the highway heading to Nelson. A couple more vineyards are out on a limb on SH1 between Blenheim and Picton and the remainder tend to be on or adjacent to the southwestern end of Rapaura Road. The region, sheltered by the protective hills of the Richmond Range, records approximately 2400 hours of grape-ripening sunshine a year and is famous for its Sauvignon Blanc, but also produces good Chardonnay, a high-quality Methode Champenoise and some good reds. All the vineyards are set up for visitors with **tastings** (either free or for a small charge, which is often deducted from any subsequent purchases), cellar-door sales, gardens and **restaurants** where you can relax and enjoy some excellent food. All will ship cases overseas – a popular practice is to accumulate bottles from various wineries, filling a case and then arranging shipment at the last winery you visit, but it's not cheap. In recent years the area has been the centre of attention for wine writers, TV programmes and all manner of hype and as a result it's less friendly than it once was and a good deal more expensive.

Maps and descriptions of the wineries are available at the visitor centre in Blenheim (including the snazzy *Wines of Marlborough Map*; $2), but don't be tempted to cram too many into a day; most are more suited to leisurely vineyard lunches than whistle-stop tours. The main transport to the wineries is with **organized tours**, which may also appeal

---

MARLBOROUGH WINE AND FOOD FESTIVAL

If Blenheim ever really springs into life it is on the back of the wine region upon which it relies so heavily. The second Saturday in February can usually be counted on as an upbeat time, when 10,000 people flock into town for the annual **Marlborough Wine and Food Festival** ($30, includes a glass for slurping). The festival takes the form of a vast field full of tents offering local wines and food for purchase, with live music and general revelry; in the week leading up to the festival, Blenheim is thronged with people meandering between arts and crafts demonstrations, exhibitions, markets and special events.

Deluxe Travel Line run **buses** ($6) to the festival site from the town and the airport, as well as from Picton ($14), while The Suburban Bus Company run day-tours from Nelson ($40). There are also shuttle services from Renwick and Spring Creek. The Interislander and Topcat ferry companies also offer good excursion rates at festival time.

to drivers keen to avoid the pitfalls of too many tastings. **Rental bikes** are also a possibility (see "Listings", p.522, for details of both), though the wineries are fairly spread out; so the people renting out bikes have got used to picking them up when the original rider's been too appreciative to cycle home. If wine's not your bag try the **Art and Craft Trail** leaflet from the visitor centre (free) – it's not on a par with Nelson but will kill an afternoon.

Cellier Le Brun, Terrace Road, on the outskirts of Renwick (daily 9am–5pm). Producer of extremely high-quality Daniel Le Brun Methode Champenoise offers free non-vintage tastings, reasonably priced bottles and a small café full of simple but wholesome food.

Cloudy Bay, Jacksons Rd (daily 10am–4.30pm). An internationally famous winery offering free tastings and tours around the vineyard.

Domaine Georges Michel, Vintage Lane, off Rapaura Rd (daily: Oct–March 9.30am–5pm, April–Sept 10am–4pm). A heavy French influence ensuring lime crisp Sav' Blanc and some sharp Chardonnay.

Fromm, Godfrey Rd, SH6 nr Renwick (Mid-Dec to Feb Tues–Sat 11am–5pm, otherwise Sat only 11am–5pm). A vineyard that is turning winemakers heads with a very hands-on approach and producing about ninety percent red: excellent Pinot Noir, and peppery Syrah as well as a Riesling with echoes of the best German efforts. Visit if you're serious about the subject and you'll taste some live-wire product that's a match for anywhere in the world, at a price.

Highfield Estate, Brookby Rd, between Blenheim and Renwick (daily 10am–5pm). Easily recognizable by its Tuscan-inspired tower, which you can climb for excellent views. It also provides some of the best food in the region, with tapas and antipasto platters for $25 that will easily feed two, plus free tastings.

Hunter's, Rapaura Rd (Mon–Sat 9.30am–4.30pm, Sun 11.30am–3.30pm, restaurant daily noon–2.30pm & 6–9pm). One of the bigger players, *Hunters* offers a broad range of wines (tastings $2) and a fine restaurant specializing in traditional haute cuisine, leavened by Italian snacks such as antipasto and focaccia.

Johannesdorf Cellars, in Koromiko, 20km north of Blenheim on SH1 (Tues–Fri 10am–4.30pm, Sat & Sun 11am–4.30pm). Famous for its historic underground cellars carved out of the face of the hill (30min tours) and its good-quality cellar door tastings (free) and sales.

Lawson's Dry Hills, Alabama Rd, northeast of Blenheim on the way to SH1 (daily 10am–5pm). A relaxed vineyard offering free tastings all year round and provider of the wine for Kaikoura Winery (see p.527). They specialize in Gwertztraminer and Sav' Blanc and have a very good restaurant.

Montana Marlborough Winery, 5km south of Blenheim on SH1 (Mon–Sat 9am–5pm, Sun 11am–4pm). One of the oldest and largest in the area, now operating a highly commercial operation, which takes away some of the charm, though they do have some excellent vintages not readily available in the shops.

Ponder Estate, New Renwick Rd, parallel to SH6 (Oct–May only, Mon–Sat 11am–5pm). A comparatively small operation that concentrates its efforts on pressing superb olive oil and producing two very good wines (free tastings). It also showcases the oil paintings of Mike Ponder, which depict typical New Zealand scenes – with his trademark splash of red somewhere in the picture.

Seresin, Bedford Road, nr Renwick (Oct–March daily 10am–4.30pm; April–Sept Mon–Fri 10am–4.30pm). The passion of an NZ-born photographer based in the UK who wants to make the vineyard organic. Despite the emphasis on "design" they make some gentle Pinot Gris and some lovely Reserve Chardonnay.

Stoneleigh, Jacksons Rd (daily 10am–4.30pm). A winery with stony, well-drained soil producing highly individual wines, including Chardonnay vinted in the traditional Burgundy style.

Wairau River Wines, Rapaura Rd (daily 10am–5pm). At the foot of the Richmond Range, this splendid rammed earth and rimu timber construction by the river deals with the wine from three wineries, *Wairau River*, *Shingle Peak* and *Foxes Island*. They offer free tastings and very good quality lunches and snacks, including spicy Thai-style mussels and Manuka smoked salmon salad.

The breweries

If at any point you get turned-off by the wineries and all the hot air that circulates about them then a truly refreshing alternative can be found in either of the two quite wonderful breweries in the area: both offer tastings and brewery door sales.

Cork and Keg Inkerman St, Renwick (daily 11am–11pm). Comfortable English-style pub that brews its own beer and cider and serves inexpensive bar meals, including proper pork pies. The beer has got better over the years and they now make some excellent natural draught wheat beer and some powerhouse cider. Run by an ex-London cabbie, the bar has a warming stone hearth and darts, dominoes and bar skittles are all played with abandon.

Pink Elephant, opposite Vintage Lane on Rapaura Rd (Wed–Sun 11am–5pm). This inelegant brewery is where another ex-Englander really does the business with malt, sugars and hops. Using traditional brewing techniques and a lively sense of humour that extends to the names of the beers, Roger Pink makes some of the best beer in New Zealand. Well worth a visit.

The Richmond Range

Twenty-six kilometres southwest of Blenheim, the **Richmond Range** of mountains is well supplied with **walks** and Scenic Recreation Areas. The DOC leaflets *Central Marlborough Recreation Areas* (50¢ from the visitor centre) and *Mount Richmond Route Guide* ($1) are useful guides to the facilities and trails.

Mount Richmond itself is 1760m high, with expansive views from its summit, taking in the entire Wairau Valley, the Kaikoura and St Arnaud ranges. Easily accessible from the Top Valley and Timms Creek routes, it is possible to tackle the summit on a day-trip from the wineries. The **Top Valley route** (7.5km; 3.5hr one way) is ideal for a single-minded assault on the **summit**, whereas **Timms Creek** (10km; 4hr 30min) provides access to the **Mount Richmond Hut** (Category 3; $4) and longer, more ambitious tramps into the park. Both routes **start** from the **Northbank Road** (16km from Blenheim on SH6) and, if you don't have your own car, you'll need to arrange **drop-off** and **pick-up** with a local shuttle company, such as Deluxe Travel Line (☎03/578 5467), or talk to the visitor centre in Blenheim.

Of numerous other walks in the area, the **Wakamarina Track** (details in the DOC's *Wakamarina Track* leaflet, 50¢) is a useful short cut for trampers and mountain bikers, crossing the Richmond Range from the Wairau Valley to the Wakamarina Valley near Havelock. There are three backcountry **huts** along the track (Category 3; $5), which is best walked or ridden from south to north: trampers should allow two days to cover the 12-kilometre track; bikers should be able to manage it in a day.

Eating, drinking and entertainment

A lot of eating and drinking can be done quite painlessly at the **wineries** (see p.519), but Blenheim itself also has a few restaurants worth exploring, although they tend to overcharge due to the proximity of the grape growers. **Entertainment listings** can be found in the Friday edition of the daily *Marlborough Express* (70¢).

China Café, 70 High St. Excellent teas and coffees from all over the world. Mon–Sat 10am–5pm.

Bacchus, 3 Main St. Long gone are the cowboy boots and chilli burgers to be replaced by some stylish kiwi favourites with a European touch. Dinner only from 6pm, daily and licensed.

First Lane Café Deli, 1 Main St. Simple, wholesome and home-made food with good coffee and lots of veggie options. Cheap, BYO and open Mon–Sat for brunch, lunch and afternoon snacks, with a good choice of deli food if you haven't time to stop.

Henry Dodson's Restaurant and Wine Bar, 1 Dodson St (☎03/577 6634). Stylish mid-range restaurant specializing in fresh, high-quality New Zealand produce – simple lamb, steak and fish dishes, rounded off with rich desserts and excellent wines – served in a comfortable and atmospheric building. Daily, evenings only.

Hotel d'Urville, 52 Queen St. Classy and lively restaurant and wine bar with a Cajun and Mediterranean bent. Try Marlborough mussels steamed in white wine, black bean, tomato and garlic broth ($13.50), d'Urville Chowder ($13) or gravalax of salmon ($12). Lunch & dinner.

Paddy Barry's Irish Pub, 51 Scott St. An unassuming log-cabin-style exterior hides the dark wood and lively atmosphere of a popular local boozer, with a Guinness pump to justify the name and reasonably priced bar snacks of pies, hotpots, salads, platters and burgers ($5–12). Occasional live music and regular dedicated drinking at weekends.

Paysanne, 1st floor, The Forum, High St. A stylish café/wine bar with views of the shopping locals. Serves good cakes and coffee during the day and some excellent main meals from $15, including very passable pizza. Occasional live music in the evening but essentially a place to chill.

Redwood Bakkeris, 75 Cleghorn St & 69 Queen St. Odd name, great bread and pastries and their own very distinctive and reasonably priced ice cream. Mon–Fri 8.30am–4.30pm, Sat 9am–1pm.

Rocco's, 5 Dodson St (☎03/578 6940). The undoubted pick of the bunch. An authentic and enjoyable Italian restaurant, which makes its own fresh pasta daily. For a blow-out, order the awesome chicken Kiev alla Rocco – chicken breast filled with ham, garlic butter and cheese, all wrapped in a veal schnitzel. Daily, evenings only. Licensed.

Listings

Airlines Soundsair (☎04/388 2594) operate daily scheduled flights to Wellington.

Airport bus Airport Super Shuttle (☎03/578 9910).

AA (Automobile Association) 23 Maxwell Rd (☎03/578 3399).

Bike rental Blenheim Hire Centre, Redwood St (☎03/578 1111), and Spokemans Cycles, Queen St (☎03/578 0433), both charge around $30 a day.

Car rental Hertz (☎03/578 0402); Rent-a-dent (☎03/577 8347).

Cinema Marlborough Movies, 15 Maxwell St (☎03/577 5333), plus the Cinema 3, Kinross St (☎03/577 5559).

Local produce Taste of Marlborough, cnr Queen St & George St, stocks a large range of regional wines and food and offers tastings; Marlborough Fruit Distillers, Riverland Estate and Gallery, 6km from Blenheim off SH1, offer a variety of fruit liqueurs and preserves, as does the Prenzel Pacific Distilling Company, also in the Riverland Estate. Prices Traditional Preserves, Selmes Rd, off Rapaura Rd, 5km north of Blenheim, have a small shop peddling multifarious pickles and jams.

Medical treatment Medical Centre, George St, about 100m from junction with Queen St.

Post office Central post office, cnr Scott St & Main St (Mon–Fri 9am–5pm, Sat 9am–1pm).

Rafting Action in Marlborough (☎03/578 4531) offer a number of whitewater-rafting trips on the Karamea and Buller rivers (Grade III–V; 1–5 days; $60–695).

Taxis Blenheim Taxis (☎03/578 0225); Red Band Taxis (☎03/577 2072).

Tours and travel De Luxe Travel Line (☎03/578 5467) do wine tours for around $40; Highlight Tours (☎03/578 9904) ply the wine and beer trails, and will arrange gardens, arts and crafts itineraries on demand; Marlborough Travel Centre (☎03/577 9997) offer a number of day-trips and cruises ($30–68) in the Sounds, the surrounding hills or just to the wineries, as well as taking onward travel bookings; and Molesworth Back country Tours (☎03/575 7525 & 0800/104 532), do wine trails and nature trips, including a trek up to Molesworth and multi–day trips on to Hanmer (from $45–$375).

Trains The travel centre (☎03/577 8811) in the station has a booking office for onward travel or excursions.

Kaikoura and around

State Highway 1 ploughs south from Blenheim to Kaikoura, with the coast on one side and the Seaward Kaikoura Range on the other. Not long after you pass through the small community of **Clarence**, about 25km from Kaikoura, is the **Ohau Point Seal Colony**, the largest on the South Island and a popular stopping point. Although you can see the seals from the road, a signposted lay by and designated lookout points beside the road and down the steps provide safer viewing. The Mangmanu Beach on the way into Kaikoura offers excellent **surfing** for advanced and experienced boarders only, while the beach opposite *the Peketa Camp Ground*, 7km south of town, has good surfing for those not quite so adept.

KAIKOURA, perched on the east coast almost midway between Blenheim (129km away) and Christchurch (180km south), is famous for its whalewatch and swimming with dolphins, but it is also a good spot for sea kayaking, bird-watching, shark experiences and tramping on the peninsula and in the **Kaikoura Ranges**, as well as the underrated pleasures of swimming with seals. If you happen to be in the area in the **winter**, the newest and one of the most diverse of New Zealand's skiing areas at **Mount Lyford** is worth investigating.

Kaikoura was named by an ancient **Maori** explorer who stopped to eat crayfish and found it so good he called the place *kai* (food) *koura* (crayfish). Maori legend also accounts for the extraordinary coastline around Kaikoura. A young deity, Marokura, was given the job of finishing the region: first he built the Kaikoura peninsula and a second smaller peninsula (Haumuri Bluff), then he set about creating the huge troughs in the sea between the two peninsulas, where the cold waters of the south would mix with the warm waters of the north and east. Tuterakiwhanoa (the god), realizing the depth of Marokura's accomplishment, said that the place would be a gift (*koha*) to all those who see its hidden beauty – and it is still known to local Maori as Te Koha O Marokura.

The first **Europeans** to settle in the area where whalers, followed relatively quickly by farmers. The trials and tribulations of their existence are recorded in the Kaikoura Museum and the more evocative Fyffe House. Recent history has been kind to the town, the Maori-owned whalewatch and various tourist spin-offs having brought relative prosperity which continues to grow.

Arrival and information

All the **buses** and shuttle services drop off on Westend Parade, in the town car park near the visitor centre. The *Southerner* **train** between Picton and Christchurch arrives at the station on Whaleway [sic] Station Road, while flights land at the grass Peketa

airfield, about 8km from the centre of town and served by Kaikoura Taxis (☎03/319 6214; $6). Most places in town are within walking distance but if you feel like supporting local trade in an environmentally friendly and entertaining way let Darren of **Kaikoura Pedal Cabs** (☎03/319 7333; Nov–May; town to seal colony $8 for one, $15 for two) take the strain. He also offers an all night pub and café tour ($50 for three).

The large **visitor centre**, a log cabin–like construction on Westend Parade (daily: Dec–Jan 8am–6pm; Feb–April 8.30am–5.30pm; May–Aug 9am–5pm; Sept–Nov 8.30am–5.30pm; ☎03/319 5641, fax 319 6819, *www.kaikoura.co.nz, info@kaikoura.co.nz*) is full of helpful information and competent staff. Various activities can be booked here, and there are sometimes video and audio visual/multi-media displays about the area ($3). The **DOC office** (☎ & fax 03/319 5714; Mon–Fri 8am–4.30pm, Sat 8am–1pm) is on Ludstone Road, about 500m from the town centre but for information on walks and huts stick to the more conveniently located visitor centre.

Accommodation

The success of Kaikoura as a tourist destination means that there is a disproportionate amount of accommodation for a settlement of its size. Most of the places to stay are strung out along SH1, just before it veers away from the centre of town, along Westend and The Esplanade which head out onto the peninsula itself, or at the top of the hill on the seaward side overlooking the town and bisected by SH1.

Hotels and motels

Admiral Court, 16 Avoca St (☎ & fax 03/319 5525, ☎0800/555 525). Spacious and well kept motel units a little way out of the town on the peninsula. ④–⑤.

Beachcomber Motel, 169 Beach Rd, at the junction with Gillings Lane, 1.5km north of town (☎ & fax 03/319 5623). A charming small motel with well kept studio units, free use of mountain bikes, and warm and welcoming hosts. ④.

Panorama Motel, 266 Esplanade (☎ 03/319 5053, fax 319 6605). There are superb views from these stripped-pine, clean units with a chalet feel; you'll pay $10 extra for the better view from the first floor. ④–⑤.

B&Bs and homestays

Beachfront B&B, 78 Esplanade (☎03/319 5890, fax 319 5895, *beachfront@xtra.co.nz*). Simple, comfortable rooms, quiet and very friendly with a balcony looking out over the bay and the offer of an excellent crayfish meal in the evening. ④–⑤.

Dillondale Farmstay, Stag'n'Spey Rd (☎ & fax 03/319 5205). Forty minutes' drive inland from Kaikoura is this very professionally run farmstay far away from all the world's worries. Rates are for dinner, bed and breakfast. ⑥.

Donegall's B&B, about 15 minutes' drive from town, north on SH1 and then 2km up School House Rd (☎03/319 5083). Comfortable B&B accommodation adjacent to the Irish bar in the middle of a farm. Sounds odd but the owner's friendly and the bar is welcoming. ⑤.

Nikau Guesthouse, 53 Deal St (☎ & fax 03/319 6973, closed June–Aug). Based in a lovely, predominantly wooden, 1925 house with lively front garden and a great view. The most relaxing accommodation in Kaikoura with airy reassuring rooms. ⑤.

Old Convent B&B, cnr Mount Fyffe Rd & Mill Rd, 4km from town (☎03/319 6603). A characterful, high-ceilinged, 1912 ex-convent building in spacious grounds with a quiet rural atmosphere and engaging, individually decorated, colourful rooms. ⑥.

Hostels, campsites and motor parks

A1 Kaikoura Holiday Park, 11 Beach Rd (☎ & fax 03/319 5999, *kaimotel@voyager.nz*). Close to the bridge and the train station, this motor park offers a variety of accommodation from motel units through five different types of cabin, to backpacker bunks and campsites, all on a smart site that backs onto the river. Tent sites $9, dorms ①, cabins & units ②–⑤.

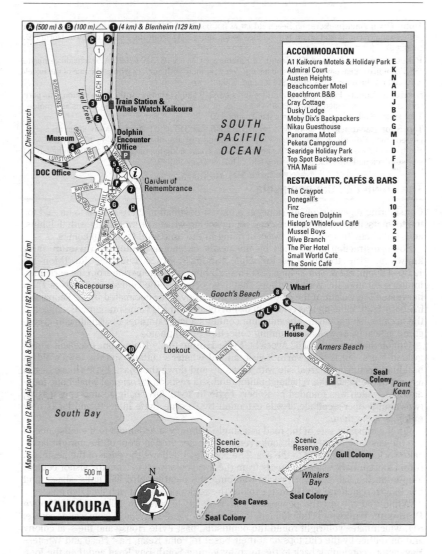

ACCOMMODATION

A1 Kaikoura Motels & Holiday Park	E
Admiral Court	K
Austen Heights	N
Beachcomber Motel	A
Beachfront B&B	H
Cray Cottage	J
Dusky Lodge	B
Moby Dix's Backpackers	C
Nikau Guesthouse	G
Panorama Motel	M
Peketa Campground	I
Searidge Holiday Park	D
Top Spot Backpackers	F
YHA Maui	I

RESTAURANTS, CAFÉS & BARS

The Craypot	6
Donegall's	1
Finz	10
The Green Dolphin	9
Hislop's Wholefood Café	3
Mussel Boys	2
Olive Branch	5
The Pier Hotel	8
Small World Café	4
The Sonic Café	7

KAIKOURA

Cray Cottage, 190 Esplanade (☎03/319 5152). Cosy and comfortable backpacker-style accommodation with a down-home feel, where they offer free bikes and home-smoked fish. As a result they are always full and you'll need to book in advance, although they are opening a new purpose-built hostel, *Sunrise Lodge*, 74 Beach Rd (☎03/319 7444). Dorms ①, rooms ②–③.

Dusky Lodge, 67 Beach Rd (☎03/319 5959). A decent size, modern hostel with Internet access, free bikes for scooting into town, and communal spit-roasts every second night in the summer. On the downside it's popular with the rowdy Kiwi Experience. Dorms ①, rooms ②.

Maui YHA, 270 Esplanade (☎03/319 5931). Much improved by a recent refurbishment, this is the best hostel in the town: spacious with excellent facilities, a great view over the beach and up the coast and Internet access. Dorms ①, rooms ②.

Moby Dix's Backpackers, 65 Beach Rd (☎ & fax 03/319 6699). A large, brightly decorated and professionally run hostel about ten minutes' walk along SH1 from the centre of town. Dorms ①, rooms ②.

Peketa Camping Ground, 7km south of Kaikoura (☎ & fax 03/319 6299). A beachside campsite ($8.50) of great peace with cabins and a shop. Very popular with surfers who make use of the excellent surf on the doorstep. Cabins $16 for one, $30 for two.

Searidge Holiday Park, 34 Beach Rd (☎ & fax 03/319 5362). Handy for the train station, this park with trees and upgraded amenities offers a range of accommodation, including cabins and motels. Tent sites $8.50, cabins ②–③, tourist flat ③, motel ④.

Top Spot Backpackers, 22 Deal St (☎03/319 5540, fax 319 6587). Tucked away 200m up a signposted track (the Lydia Washington Walkway) starting by the library, this very friendly and well-run hostel boasts good views over Kaikoura and the coast, a log-burning fire, mountain bikes, BBQ and sundeck and offers seal swimming trips. Dorms ①, rooms ③.

The Town and the peninsula

Considering its ever-growing status as a tourist destination there is little to be said for the town itself; most visitors are dead-set on seeing whales or swimming with dolphins, and other activities are simply ways of filling in the time until their turn comes.

Some distraction is provided by the newly extended **Kaikoura Museum** (also known as "the treasures of the Nga Taonga"), at 14 Ludstone Rd (Mon–Fri 12.30–4.30pm, Sat & Sun 2–4pm; $2). The exhibits cover the period from the early moa hunters, through the various groups that have occupied the land since. The Nga Tahu harvested the wealth of the land and seas until they were decimated by Te Rauparaha in about 1830. Whaling was established shortly after, in 1843, and immigrants came into the area to fish and farm. The museum contains a large number of argillite and greenstone artefacts, as well as a daunting collection of old photos.

Out on the peninsula, at 62 Avoca St, **Fyffe House** (daily 10am–6pm, excellent 30min guided tours; $6) is well worth a visit, an old whaler's cottage and the town's oldest building, occupying a great site with views up and down the coast. Fyffe House began as part of the Waiopuka Whaling Station (and still rests on its original whalebone foundations), which was founded by Robert Fyffe in 1842. Originally an unprepossessing two-room cooper's cottage, it was extended by George Fyffe in 1860, and looks now much as it did then.

On the opposite side of the road is a single chimney, a testament to the existence of the old customs house, which looks remarkable perched in front of the upright layercake rock strata that lead to the sea. The road itself follows the edge of the peninsula round to a car park where fur **seals** from the local colony (4km from the visitor centre) lounge on the flat, sea-worn rocks watching the plentiful bird life, gulls, shags, and black oystercatchers, who in turn explore the rock pools full of rich tidal detritus.

While you are on the peninsula, you may be tempted to follow the **Kaikoura Peninsula Walkway** (11km full length; 4hr 30min; leaflet available from visitor centre, $1), which takes you right round the peninsula, past Fyffe House and the seal colony and on (either by the cliff tops or at their base) to Point Kean, East Head and Whalers Bay, before continuing back to the town by joining South Bay Road and then the footpath over the hill, before the road reaches SH1. Kaikoura Peninsula is made of limestone and siltstone laid beneath the sea sixty million years ago, with a backdrop of rugged mountains and abundant wildlife. The shoreline section of the walkway from Point Kean, just beyond Fyffe House, to South Bay is particularly fine, revealing gaping sea caves, folded limestone rocks in thin layers and stacks at Atia Point. The walk from the peninsula carpark to Whalers Bay Lookout should take no more than half an hour one way. This stretch is also a favoured haunt of red-billed and black-backed gulls, oystercatchers, herons and shags, as well as a number of fur seals, rejoicing in being away from the crowds back at the car park.

Out of town is **Maori Leap Cave**, 2km south of Kaikoura on SH1 (☎03/319 5023; 35min tours daily at 10.30am, 11.30am, 12.30pm, 1.45pm, 2.30pm & 3.30pm; $8.50), which contains some remarkable limestone formations. Stalagmites and stalactites sprout from the floor and ceiling of the cave, and translucent stone straws seem to defy gravity by maintaining their internal water level. There are also examples of cave coral and algae that survive in the dank cave by turning darkness into energy – a kind of skewed photosynthesis. There are two rival explanations for the cave's name: one has it that a Maori warrior jumped to his death from the hills above the cave after he was captured by another tribe; the other has two thwarted lovers from different tribes plunging to their deaths.

Just 100m or so further south is the turning for the steep climb to **Kaikoura Wine Company** (daily 10am–5.30pm; tastings $3, redeemable against purchase), perched on the steep sided hill that overlooks SH1 and South Bay. At first it looks an unlikely place for a winery but with specially designed cellars beneath the local rock and fantastic scenic views, spice is added to the tour (on the hour; $7.50, including tasting), complemented by winery tastings of good unoaked Chardonnay and floral Gewurtztraminer. Currently wines are imported from the likes of *Lawson's* in Marlborough, but the intention is to make organic home-grown soon.

Whales, dolphins, seals, sharks and sea kayaking

Off the Kaikoura Peninsula is a complex network of trenches and troughs, forming an underwater canyon system, with unusually deep water very close to the coastline. This provides a rich habitat, constantly replenished from the Antarctic, which supports an enormous amount and variety of marine life.

One of the main reasons people come to Kaikoura is for a chance to see gigantic sperm **whales** (all year), migratory humpback whales (Jun–July) and Orca (Dec–Feb) at relatively close quarters. The Maori-owned and operated Whale Watch Kaikoura (☎03/319 6767 & 0800/655 121, fax 319 6564, *res@whalewatch.co.nz*) runs up to five sailings daily (Dec–Feb 5am, 7.30am, 10am, 12.30pm & 3pm; March, April, Sept & Oct 5.30am, 7.30am, 10am & 12.30pm; May–Aug 7.30am, 10am & 12.30pm; 2hr 30min; $95), using four different sized rigid-hulled inflatable and more conventional boats. Be warned, though, that trips are cancelled if **bad weather** threatens, so if you don't want to miss out, give yourself a couple of days in Kaikoura. And don't forget your camera.

The other way of seeing whales at Kaikoura is from the air, but you'll need a good pair of binoculars. Wings Over Whales (☎03/319 6580 & 0800/226 629) and Kaikoura Helicopters (☎03/319 6609) offer a number of scenic and whale-spotting flights lasting from twenty to forty-five minutes with prices dependent upon whether you go fixedwing, usually cheaper, or in the whirlybird. Thirty minutes in a plane is $95, while twenty in a helicopter is $150. Slightly better value for money, although it doesn't involve spotting whales, is **Pilot a Plane** (☎ & fax 03/319 6579), a chance to take the controls and pilot the plane for yourself for thirty minutes. Even without the scenery this would be an adrenaline buzz but in Kaikoura it's a special experience (from $69).

The other main reason people visit Kaikoura is to frolic with **dolphins**. Dolphin Encounter (☎03/319 6777, fax 319 6534, *info@dolphin.co.nz*) do three trips a day (6am, 9am & 1pm; $85 to swim, $65 to watch; book at least two weeks in advance). Many people find being in the water with the dolphins a vaguely spiritual experience. You'll get most out of the experience if you're a reasonably confident swimmer; the more you duck-dive and generally splash around, the more eager the dolphins'll be to investigate. One thing they find attractive is listening to you humming through your snorkel, any tune will do; they also love pregnant women. Whatever you do, don't get too carried away: dolphins have a penchant for swimming in ever-decreasing circles until lesser beings are quite dizzy and disorientated, so keep an eye on the boat. These days

Dolphin Encounter also offer bird watching (3 trips daily; 2hr; $60) – on a good trip you'll see shags, mollymawks, gannets, petrels and a couple of varieties of albatross but be warned the sharks' livers used to attract the birds have an evil stench and if you get downwind of it you may lose your breakfast to the sea.

Swimming with seals can be a lot of fun: seals tend to be more curious than dolphins, often coming closer to check you out. New seal-swim operators are constantly entering the fray, so check out the latest deals when you arrive. Among the most reputable outfits are Graeme's Seal Swim (☎03/319 6182) and Top Spot Kaikoura (☎03/319 5540). Run by two brothers who are very professional, friendly and knowledgeable, Graeme's offers two-hour trips between November and April ($40, underwater cameras provided on request), as do Top Spot Kaikoura (also $40). Both trips involve a beach entry and a fair bit of swimming so it helps if you've snorkelled before.

Another way to see the wildlife is **sea kayaking** with Matt Foy, a member of SKOANZ (☎03/319 5641, *kaikourapedalcab@hotmail.com*; half-day trips $55; twilight excursions $55). He offers evocative trips from South Bay or the town end and spends time appreciating the scenic beauty of the peninsula as well as enjoying the bays, birds and occasionally seals that can otherwise only be seen from the peninsula walkway.

The most recent addition to the plethora of water-based activities in Kaikoura is the **Kaikoura Shark Dive** (☎03/319 6777; Nov–May; 2 trips a day; 3hr; about 10min in the cage; $110), a novel experience that will certainly get the blood pumping. A lot is made of the danger but you'll be in a shark cage so unless you use your limbs to attract the sharks you'll be OK and you should see either or both of the Blue or Mako sharks.

Eating and drinking

The least expensive way to sample the local **crayfish** is to buy them ready-boiled from one of the shacks and caravans advertising their wares alongside SH1 north of town. You can buy good quality **fresh fish** from the Pacifica Seafoods (Kaikoura) Ltd, near the *Pier Hotel* (see opposite). There are also a number of chip shops in town producing excellent fried-fish **takeaways**; try the *Continental* on Beach Road or *Food Wonderful Food* on Westend Parade. Another good place to stop off is the *Coastline Dairy and Bakery*, 38 Westend (daily 6am–6pm) where they make gorgeous-smelling fresh bread. The **restaurants** in town are all a bit pricey, safe in the knowledge that you're not exactly spoilt for choice.

Caves Restaurant, 2km south of town on SH1, next to the Maori Leap Cave. Simple and generous meals that concentrate on local sea and farm produce; try the scallops or the massive seafood platter. Licensed. Mon–Fri, Sat 7am–6pm, Sun 7am–8pm.

Craypot, 70 Westend Parade. A café/wine bar with polished wooden floors and glass doors, offering breakfast, light meals and dinners with Mediterranean and Cajun influences, including some good seafood (around $22) and salads for $15. Daily 9am–11pm.

Donegall's, about 15 minutes' drive from town, north on SH1 and then 2km up School House Rd. If somebody said a farmer was suddenly going to build an Irish bar on his farm, that he'd make a good job of it, that the food would be tasty, the setting pretty and that people would enjoy visiting so much they'd send him CDs of truly dreadful Irish music from all over the world, would you have believed them? Here's your chance to visit a legend. Daily 11am–whenever.

Finz, South Bay Parade (☎03/319 6688). An excellent fine-dining restaurant and bar offering a broad range of well-prepared and wonderfully presented evening dishes made from local ingredients with New World panache.

Green Dolphin, 12 Avoca St (☎03/319 6669 in the summer). A lovely little café on the peninsula, serving good seafood and grills in a formal atmosphere (mains $20–24), with fine views out the front. Licensed & BYO. Daily 6–10pm.

Hislop's Wholefood Café, 33 Beach Rd. Excellent, healthful café serving teas and coffees, and all-organic meals including excellent daily fresh-baked bread to eat in with their lovely chowder or to take away. Daily 10am–6pm, evening dining at weekends.

Mussel Boys, 80 Beach Rd, cnr Beach Rd (SH1) & Edmund Ave. The delightful cousin of the Havelock restaurant (see p.481) where you can get wonderful shellfish and thick tasty chowder, washed down with wines from the Kaikoura vineyard at reasonable prices.

Pier Hotel, 1 Avoca St. A large colonial pub/hotel that was moved here from the original wharf opposite Fyffe House. With a wrap-around balcony and two atmospheric bars, they serve large portions of steak, scallops and fish of the day, all with either baked potato or chips, and side salad ($13–18). Daily 12–2pm & 6–8pm.

Small World Café, cnr Westend & SH1. Atmospheric and relaxing coffee house, serving the best java in town and some juicy Souvlaki, chicken and falafel, as well as having a pouch of tobacco on the premises for smokers who given up but can't take the strain any longer, or anyone just desperate for a fag.

Sonic Café, at the confluence of Westend & The Esplanade, directly opposite the visitor centre. Lively modern café-bar which offers simple, budget food including some very tasty pizzas and more substantial meals of steak, fish and chips or lamb. Most evenings it turns into Kaikoura's premier nightspot using its funky design to attract revellers for drinking and occasional live or DJ-manicured music. Summer 11am–late, off-season 5pm–late.

The Olive Branch, 54 Westend. A comfortable upmarket eatery and wine bar offering panini, platters, oysters, mussels and fish all prepared imaginatively with either an Asian influence or a soupçon of French style. Daily 10am–late.

Listings

Airlines Air Direct (☎0800/808 151) fly to Wellington ($120); Whale Watch Air (☎03/319 6580) fly to Christchurch ($95 one way, $165 return).

Bike rental Westend Motors, 48–52 Westend Parade (☎03/319 5065).

Buses In addition to the services of the major companies, Atomic Shuttles (☎03/322 8883) run to Christchurch and Picton via Blenheim; Compass Coachlines (☎03/578 7102) run to Blenheim, Picton and Christchurch; Kaikoura Shuttles (☎03/319 5846) operate a door-to-door service to Christchurch; and Southern Link Shuttles (☎03/358 8355) run to Picton and Christchurch.

Car rental Eades Garage, Westend Parade (☎03/319 5036).

Cinema The Esplanade, next to the *Beach Front B&B*.

Gallery Gold and Art Design, 129 Scarborough St, on the hill overlooking the town and accessed from SH1 (Mon–Sat 10am–5pm). The home of Swiss guilders who use gold leaf and produce some highly individual, off-the-wall mirrors and ornaments plus some entertaining expressionist cartoons (available in postcard format).

Jewellery/Paua, Southern Paua and Pacific Jewels, cnr SH1 & Whaleway Station Rd (Mon–Sat 9am–5pm) where you can pick up the beautiful paua shells and more expensive jewellery.

Medical Treatment Kaikoura Hospital and Doctors Surgery, Deal St, 50m from cnr Churchill St (☎03/319 5040).

Pharmacy Kaikoura Pharmacy, 37 Westend Parade (Mon–Sat 9am–1pm).

Post office Next door to the pharmacy (Mon–Fri 9am–5pm, Sat 9am–1pm).

Taxis Kaikoura Taxis (☎03/319 6214) operates taxi services, sightseeing and trailhead transport.

Tours/local shuttles Aitkens Picnic Tours (☎03/319 5091) cater to your preferences; Kaikoura Nature Walks (☎03/319 6622) will walk you round at a more leisurely pace while Lance "Krusty" Bowring tells you about the history and wildlife; Kaikoura Scenic Tours (☎03/319 5687) offer a 90min land tour of points of interest around town, including the seal colony ($12.50); while TJ's Tours (☎03/319 6803) run day-trips and shuttle services.

Around Kaikoura

The Seaward **Kaikoura Ranges** and Mount Fyffe completely dominate the town, creating a bleak and broody atmosphere. Leaflets (50¢–$1, from visitor centre in Kaikoura) outline some of the **walks** in the ranges.

MOUNT LYFORD SKIFIELDS

The **Mount Lyford Skifields** (Jun to mid-Oct, 9am–4pm; general information ☎03/315 6178, premium-rated snowphone 0900/34 444) are 60km from Kaikoura on the road to Waiau (SH70). The newest and smallest of New Zealand's ski areas, Mount Lyford caters for a broad range of abilities and is rarely crowded. There are two separate fields: **Stella** is ideal for advanced skiers and snowboarders, and **Terako** has a variety of intermediate and beginner runs, as well as some more ambitious routes in the Terako Basin. **Access** is along 4km of unsealed road (toll $5–10) off SH70, or by Mount Lyford Transport ski bus from Kaikoura (about $30 return; ☎03/319 6182). **Lift facilities** are limited to one fixed grip and two rope tows; heli-skiing is also an option, as is cross-country. Field charges are $35 per day, there's a learners' package for $55, and ski rental is available ($10–25 per day).

   Mount Lyford Village, 3.5km from the field, has comfortable **accommodation** at the *Mount Terako Lodge* (☎03/315 6677; B&B ⑤) and *Graeme Chambers Mount Lyford Lodge* (☎03/319 6182; dorms ①, rooms ③), while the *Chamois Café* serves snacks and meals at high-altitude prices.

Mount Fyffe is 1602m high and rewards the climber with views across the Seaward Kaikoura Ranges, Banks Peninsula to the south and up to the North Island. The path to the summit (18km return; 8hr) starts about 8km from Kaikoura: head along Postmans Road to the head of the Hinau Track, where there is parking and information. It is also possible to access the Inland Kaikoura Range and the huts of the **Clarence River Conservation Area** from Kaikoura, a journey of about 25km. Head south out of Kaikoura on SH1, then turn inland on the Kaikoura–Waiau Road to the reserve car park at the Kahutara Bridge. The Clarence River Conservation Area offers the opportunity to explore some uncrowded walking tracks in an area with some of the highest mountains outside the Southern Alps and some stunning geological formations. Should you decide to explore go well-equipped as the weather in this area can change in an instant.

   If this sounds too rugged, the privately owned **Kaikoura Coastal Track** (43km; 3 days) offers an excellent way to explore the area. The track begins 50km south of Kaikoura on SH1, where there's secure parking; Kaikoura Taxis (☎03/319 6214) and TJ's Tours (☎03/319 6803) will also run you out to the **trailhead**. The trail climbs through farmland and native bush across the Hawkeswood Range and along beaches, with spectacular views of the Seaward Kaikoura mountains and the Southern Alps, ending at *The Staging Post* (see below), where transport can be arranged to your next destination. **Accommodation** is in warm, clean cottages with fully equipped kitchens, baths and showers as well as fresh farm produce, milk, bread and home-cooked meals by arrangement. You must **book in advance** (☎03/319 2715; $110, including 3 nights' accommodation), and only a limited number are allowed to walk the track at any one time, although these days it's also open to mountain bikers ($50). If you want a gentle transition back to civilization after your walk, hole up for a day or two at *The Staging Post*, 2111 Parnassus Rd, Hawkeswood (☎03/319 2898; tent sites $7, dorms ①, cabins ②–③). This idiosyncratic place right at the end of the coastal track on a large sheep station reflects the personality of its ancient, flirty and amusing owner, and is well worth a look even if you don't intend to stay.

South from Kaikoura

Continuing south on SH1, the coastal landscape eventually dissolves into a relatively flat extension of the Canterbury Plains, with little to delay you before you hit the eastern suburbs of Christchurch that face out on to **Pegasus Bay** – a bite out of the coast-

line bounded by the **Hurunui River** and Banks Peninsula, more than a hundred kilometres further south. The main community along the way is the small town of **Cheviot**,
70km from Kaikoura and 115km from Christchurch, but there's little reason to linger
unless you're an angler keen to test your mettle on the cunning trout and salmon in the
nearby Hurunui and Waiau rivers or an ardent tramper bound for the Port Robinson
Track.

Cheviot and around

Like the other towns between Kaikoura and Christchurch, **CHEVIOT** suffers by comparison with those two destinations and has little to delay the discerning visitor for
more than an hour or two. SH1 becomes Main Street as it makes its way through the
town.

If you're here at a weekend, look in on the **Cheviot Museum**, Main Street (Sat
10am–noon, Sun 2–4pm, or by arrangement with Mr Cropp ☎03/319 8536; donation
requested), which provides some interesting insights into the origins of the town and
its surroundings. The three dominant collections consist of a large number of moa
bones; a display devoted to George Forbes, local lad made good, who rose to become
prime minister between 1930 and 1935; and a daunting collection of documents relating
to land redistribution. Forged in the hills around Cheviot, this policy marked a turning
point for land tenure in New Zealand. In 1893 Sir John McKenzie bought, on behalf of
the government, the Cheviot Estate (about 34,000 hectares of good land), following a
dispute about the valuation of the land and the tax that the Robinson family would have
to pay on it. McKenzie then parcelled the land into small farms and holdings, so the
same land could support 650 people, rather than just 80 – a process that was to be repli-
cated across New Zealand, breaking up the enormous landholdings of a few rich and
powerful men (as recounted in John Wilson's book, *Cheviot: Kingdom to Country*).

Gore Bay

To dispel driving fatigue or museum ennui, take a walk by the sea at **Gore Bay**, about
8km from Cheviot and well signposted. There's a lovely beach with safe swimming and,
at the east end of the bay, adjoining the road, a scenic reserve that shelters dramatic
examples of badland erosion. At the southern end of the reserve, siltstone cliffs called
The Cathedrals have been eroded into huge stalagmite-like fingers that resemble the
pipes of a cathedral organ. Also within the reserve is a 2.5km loop track between
Cathedral Gully and Tweedie Gully, with a few steep sections that make it ill-advised
outside the summer months.

A more rewarding track is the coastal trail from Gore Bay to Port Robinson and then
on to the mouth of the Hurunui River, **The Port Robinson Track**. The whole route
takes seven hours return, but most of the highlights – the "cathedrals", spectacular
bluffs, Port Robinson, Gibson's Point and the lighthouse – are encountered during the
Gore Bay to Manuka Bay sector, a three-hour round-trip. Beginning at the southern
end of the Gore Bay Scenic Reserve, the sector ends on the south side of Gibson's
Point, where the track passes the dead end of the road that leads back to Port Robinson
and then Gore Bay. The first part of the walkway is along the beach beneath the bluffs,
which must be accomplished at low tide; if you miss the tide, the walk can be joined
from the Gore Bay Road, turning down to the Port Robinson boat ramps and then
round the point and lighthouse. Self-sufficient trampers might want to take advantage
of the extremely basic DOC **campsites** ($5) at Gore Bay and the mouth of the
Hurunui River, though most will be content to explore briefly and then press on to
the more tangible rewards of Christchurch or Hanmer. Note that the track is closed in
October due to lambing and may be closed by the DOC between December and March
if they feel there is a fire hazard.

The road to Waipara

The road veers away from the coast until it reaches **Waipara**, weaving among gently rolling hills that alternate between green and golden brown depending upon the time of the year, and obscure the Pacific Ocean from view. At the tiny hamlet of Waipara, SH1 divides into two, climbing inland towards **Hanmer Springs** as the Lewis Pass Road/SH7 (see p.599), or continuing as SH1 down the coast to **Christchurch** (see p.535).

travel details

Buses

From Blenheim to: Christchurch (5–6 daily; 4hr 55min); Nelson (6 daily; 1hr 50min); Picton (10–11 daily; 30min); St Arnaud (1–2 daily; 1hr).

From Murchison to: Blenheim (1 daily; 4hr 40min); Nelson (2 daily; 2hr 25min); Westport (2 daily; 1hr 30min).

From Nelson to: Greymouth (2–3 daily; 6hr); Kawatiri Junction, for Nelson Lakes (1 daily; 1hr 5min); Motueka (5–6 daily; 1hr 10min); Murchison (2 daily; 2hr 25min); Picton (5–6 daily; 2hr 10min); Takaka (2–3 daily; 4hr).

From Picton to: Blenheim (10–11 daily; 30min); Christchurch (3–4 daily; 5hr 25min); Kaikoura (3–4 daily; 2hr 15min); Nelson (5–6 daily; 2hr 10min).

Trains

From Picton to: Blenheim (1 daily; 35min); Christchurch (1 daily; 5hr 25min); Kaikoura (1 daily; 2hr 20min).

Ferries

From Picton to: Wellington (8 daily; 2hr 15 min–3hr 15min).

Flights

From Blenheim to: Auckland (17 daily; 1hr 55min); Christchurch (31 daily; 1hr 40min); Wellington (35 daily; 25min); Westport (2 daily; 2hr 5min).

From Kaikoura to: Christchurch (1–2 daily; 1hr 20min); Wellington (1–2 daily; 1hr).

From Motueka to: Takaka (2 daily; 30min); Wellington (2 daily; 45min).

From Nelson to: Auckland (33 daily; 2hr); Blenheim (9–10 daily; 55min); Christchurch (18 daily; 1hr); Queenstown (6 daily; 3hr 20min); Wellington (21 daily; 25min); Westport (2 daily; 2hr 20min).

From Picton to: Wellington (7–9 daily; 25min).

CHAPTER NINE

CHRISTCHURCH AND SOUTH TO OTAGO

E ncompassing some stunning and varied scenery, the South Island's east coast perhaps comes closer to most visitors' expectations of New Zealand than any other part of the country. The main hub of the region is New Zealand's third city, **Christchurch**, stretched out between the Pacific Ocean and the agriculturally rich flatlands of the Canterbury Plains, and with the Southern Alps acting as a distant backdrop to the west. A relaxed, green city where parks and gardens rub shoulders with some fine Victorian architecture, it boasts its fair share of urban thrills, provided largely by the cafés, bars and pubs which crowd a busy downtown area. It's also a seaside resort in its own right, with **beach suburbs** like New Brighton and Sumner within easy reach of the centre.

Immediately southeast of Christchurch rise the **Port Hills**, providing welcome relief from the Canterbury Plains. Beyond them, **Banks Peninsula** is a popular escape for city residents, its coastline indented by numerous bays and harbours. Perched above these harbours are the two main communities of the peninsula, the brusque port of **Lyttelton** and the attractive, if slightly twee, town of **Akaroa**.

South of Banks Peninsula the main road and rail lines forge across the Canterbury Plains, a patchwork of rich fields and vineyards bordered by long shingle beaches littered with driftwood. Further south the countryside again changes character, with undulating coastal hills and crumbling cliffs announcing the altogether more rugged terrain of **North Otago**. The historic settlements dotted along the coast are a testament to the wealth that farming and mineral extraction brought to the region. The main centres here are the lively port of **Timaru**, close to a series of **Maori rock paintings** that indicate the region has a longer history than the imposed European feel would have you believe; and the quieter **Oamaru**, with an engaging nineteenth-century centre and

---

ACCOMMODATION PRICES

Accommodation listed in this guide has been categorized into one of nine price bands, as set out below. The rates quoted represent the **cheapest available** double or twin **room** – except for category ①, which are per-person rates for a dorm bed. Note that fees for **tent sites** and **DOC huts** (quoted in dollars) are also per-person, unless otherwise stated.

① under $20 per person	④ $60–80	⑦ $140–180
② under $40 per room	⑤ $80–100	⑧ $180–240
③ $40–60	⑥ $100–140	⑨ over $240

For more on accommodation, see p.34.

some captivating **penguin colonies** just outside town. Beyond here routes lead on towards Dunedin and the south, passing the unearthly **Moeraki boulders**, perfect spherical rocks formed by a combination of subterranean pressure and erosion.

Trains trundle up and down the east coast as rarely as once a day, but otherwise **transport** in the region is pretty straightforward, with numerous buses and shuttle buses plying the main routes out of Christchurch.

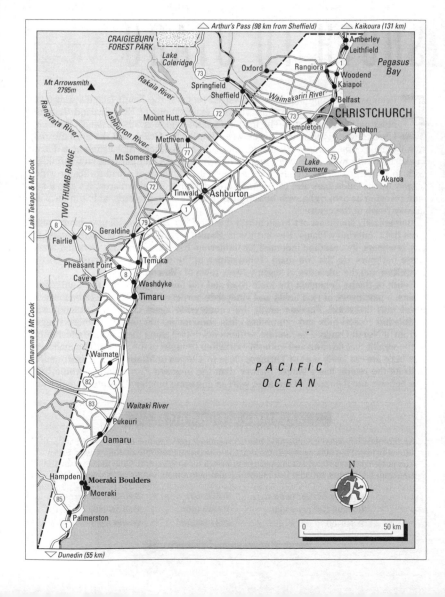

CHRISTCHURCH

Capital of the Canterbury region and the largest city on the South Island, **CHRISTCHURCH** (population 300,000) exudes a palpable air of gentility and a connectedness with the mother country. After all, it was perceived as an outpost of Anglicanism by its first settlers, was named after an Oxford college, and has some of the feel of a traditional English university town, with its neo-Gothic architecture and gently winding river. To some degree it pursues an archetype – the boys at Christ's College still wear striped blazers, and punts course along the Avon – but the Englishness is largely skin deep. Modern Christchurch is a lively melting pot of cultures, with a continental café scene and a distinct, ever-changing Kiwi identity of its own. Indeed, those who regard Christchurch as a quiet place in which to sleep off jet lag or take a break from the long journey across the South Island will be pleasantly surprised by the city's contemporary face. In recent years its traditional conservatism has gained a more youthful, bohemian edge, with an explosion of lively **bars and restaurants**, the emergence of underground **nightlife**, and a burgeoning of the visual arts, theatre, music and street entertainment. Such urban pursuits are nicely balanced by the Pacific Ocean suburbs of New Brighton and Sumner, both of which boast excellent **beaches**.

Straddling the main road and rail routes running down the east coast, Christchurch is used by many tourists as a base from which to explore the South Island, with the steep, angular terrain of **Banks Peninsula** and the **vineyards** of the Canterbury Plains proving the most popular out-of-town destinations. Many of the **outdoor activities** for which New Zealand is famous are accessible from here, with a plethora of city-based companies offering trips involving rafting, paragliding, ballooning and mountain biking in the surrounding countryside (see "Listings", p.560). The city is also within a two-hour drive of several good **skifields** to the west (again, see "Listings" on p.561 for a full rundown), making it possible to combine a day on the pistes with an evening in Christchurch's numerous nocturnal watering holes. Indeed the place's only real drawback is its cost: compared with the rest of the South Island, Christchurch is an expensive place to spend any length of time.

Some history

Located in what was historically a dry and windswept area populated only sparsely by Maori, Christchurch came into being as the result of a programmatic policy of colonization by the **Canterbury Association**. Formed in 1849 by members of Christ Church College Oxford, and with the Archbishop of Canterbury at its head, the association had the utopian aim of creating a new Jerusalem in New Zealand; a middle class, Anglican community in which the moralizing culture of Victorian England could prosper. The site of the city was chosen by the association's surveyor Captain Joseph Thomas, who was quick to recognize the agricultural potential of the surrounding plain. A few Europeans were already farming the area (notably the Scottish Deans brothers, who had arrived here in 1843, see p.550), although the main centre of white settlement at the time was the port of Lyttelton to the southeast, a base for whalers since the 1830s. It was at Lyttelton that four ships containing nearly 800 settlers arrived in 1850, bound for the new city of Christchurch – by this stage little more than an agglomeration of wooden shacks. Descent from those who came on the "four ships" still carries enormous social cachet among members of the Christchurch elite. The earliest settlers weren't all Anglicans by any means, and the millenarian aspirations upon which the city was founded soon faded as people got on with the exhausting business of carving out a new life in unfamiliar terrain. However, the association's ideals had a profound effect on the cultural identity of the city. The elegant neo-Gothic architecture which still characterizes Christchurch's public buildings oozes with the self-confidence of these nineteenth-century pioneers, while the symmetry of the city's grid-iron street plan hints at the order the planners hoped to impose upon the community.

Arrival and information

Christchurch Airport, 10km northwest of the city centre, stays open day and night so you may well find yourself arriving at the international terminal at some ungodly hour. Fortunately there's an ATM, plus a foreign exchange booth and a **visitor centre** (☎03/353 7774, fax 353 7754) which both stay open for all flights. In addition, there's a freephone board in the arrivals hall for accommodation and car rental bookings, and many Christchurch hotels will provide a free pick-up service from here if you've already booked a room. Failing that, there is one airport hotel (see box on p.538). The domestic terminal is next door and also has a visitor centre (Mon–Sat 6.30am–8pm, Sun 7.30am–8pm; same phone), beside which is a **left luggage** office (daily 6am–11pm; $1 per hour or $8 per day). Checked items can be retrieved out of hours by contacting security.

City buses (see "City transport" opposite) connect the airport with the central Cathedral Square every 30–60min (Mon–Fri 6.45am–9.15pm, Sat 8am–9pm, Sun 8am–7pm; $2.70); while various **shuttle** buses (see "Listings" for numbers) operate a door-to-door service (roughly every 20–30 minutes, although departures depend on demand; $6–10) linking the airport with the Christchurch destination of your choice. There are **taxi ranks** in front of the airport terminal building (otherwise ring Blue Star on ☎03/379 9799 or Gold Band on ☎03/379 5795), with the ride into town costing around $20.

Trains arrive at Addington Street Station at the southwestern tip of Hagley Park, just over 2km from Cathedral Square. You can pick up a **shuttle bus** ($3–5) or **taxi** ($8–10) from the station into the centre, although **city buses** don't serve the train station directly – you have to walk 400m down the station access road to the nearby thoroughfare of Blenheim Road to pick up bus #25 into town.

Most of the long-distance **bus** companies conveniently drop off at the major hostels and some hotels around town as well as near the visitor centre (see below) usually for no extra charge provided you are staying in the central area bounded by the so-called "Four Avenues" – Moorhouse, Fitzgerald, Bealey and Deans. Cathedral Square itself is within easy walking distance of most of the hostels, major hotels and some of the B&Bs and motels.

Information

The principal visitor centre for Christchurch and the surrounding area is the **Christchurch & Canterbury Visitor Centre**, in the former Post Office on the south side of Cathedral Square (Nov–March Mon–Fri 8.30am–6pm, Sat & Sun 8.30am–5pm; April–Oct Mon–Fri 8.30am–5pm, Sat & Sun 8.30am–4pm; ☎03/379 9629, fax 377 2424, *www.christchurchnz.net, info@christchurchnz.net*). You can book all forms of transport as well as trips and activities here; be sure to pick up the free *Christchurch City Centre Walks* leaflet, which provides a good introduction to local history, as well as the *Tramway* map, which details the main stops on this popular sightseers' route (see "City transport" opposite). The visitor centre is also the place to find out which of the city's many excellent **festivals** (see "Listings" on p.561) is currently in progress. As with visitor centres all over the country, they only promote places who pay to join the organization. If you'd prefer to broaden your options to include smaller companies, pop down the street to Trailblazers, 86 Worcester St (☎03/366

6033, fax 03/366 6173, *trailblazer@caverock.co.nz*), an **independent information and booking service** with stacks of helpful advice and bike rental (see "Listings", p.560)

The **DOC** (Department of Conservation) **office** is 1km northwest of Cathedral Square at 133 Victoria St (Mon–Fri 8.30am–4.30pm; ☎03/379 9758), and stocks specific information on wildlife and walking routes, as well as booking Great Walks throughout the South Island.

City transport

You can easily see most of what Christchurch has to offer **on foot**, resorting to public transport for the odd trip out to the suburbs or to get from one side of the centre to another.

Bus services are operated by several companies all co-ordinated by Canride who operate a **bus information centre** where Worcester Street meets Cathedral Square (Mon–Fri 7.30am–5.30pm, Sat & Sun 9am–3.30pm) and an **infoline** (Mon–Sat 6.30am–10.30pm, Sun 9am–9pm; ☎03/366 8855, *www.crc.govt.nz*). Most services currently fan out from Cathedral Square or nearby; though a new transport interchange at the junction of Lichfield and Colombo streets is due for completion in 2001. Tickets for short rides cost 90¢, most journeys (even to New Brighton and Sumner) are $1.80, while Lyttelton and the airport cost $2.70; multi-trip tickets give twelve rides for the price of ten. All routes run from 6am in the morning until about midnight (slightly longer in the case of more popular routes). In addition there's the free **Shuttle**, a distinctive yellow bus which runs from the Town Hall, through the Square, down Colombo Street to Moorhouse Avenue and back on a 10–15min cycle (Mon–Thurs 8am–10.30pm, Fri 8am–midnight, Sat 9am–midnight, Sun 10am–8pm)

Perhaps the best way of familiarizing yourself with the central city area is to hop on the **Tramway** (daily: Nov–March 9am–9pm; April–Oct 9am–6pm), which weaves a 2.5km circuit past many of the central sights, including the Arts Centre and Cathedral Square. The tramway was only installed a few years back, but the rolling stock is largely made up of lovingly restored 1905 originals. You can get on or off at any stop, depending upon the time limit of your ticket: a one-hour ticket costs $6 and an all-day ticket $7. Thrown in with the price is a rudimentary commentary that will at least identify landmarks and help you get your bearings.

Driving in Christchurch is pretty straightforward providing you avoid morning and evening rush hours. Most central parking spaces are metered from Monday to Saturday between 7am and 6pm (otherwise free). If you have to drive into town, there's free parking in the centre of Hagley Park (Armagh Street entrance).

Given the city's relatively quiet roads, **cycling** is an ideal way of appreciating some of the more out-of-the-way suburbs. Expect to pay around $20–25 a day for **bike rental** (see "Listings", p.560, for details of outlets). Finally, a sedate way of seeing some of the prettier parts of the city is by **punt** up and down the River Avon (daily 9am–dusk; $12–15 per person; book through the visitor centre); the water-level perspective is a refreshing one.

Accommodation

As the largest city in the South Island and a major port of entry, Christchurch has one of New Zealand's broadest ranges of accommodation, and although prices are by no means extortionate, they're understandably higher than in the South Island's smaller towns and cities.

AIRPORT ACCOMMODATION

With efficient shuttle services into the city, and establishments geared towards late arrivals and early departures, you are unlikely to need airport accommodation. If pushed you can stay five minutes' walk from the terminal at the *Airport Plaza*, corner Memorial Avenue and Orchard Road (☎0800/100 876, fax 358 3029, *www.airportplazahotel.co.nz*; ⑥), a modern business hotel with assorted restaurants and bars. It's quite pleasant if you can land a poolside room.

Most of the business hotels and backpacker hostels are situated within the **city centre**, as are a number of the better B&Bs, though there are also several fine B&Bs out in the leafier suburbs. The majority of hotels are close to Victoria Square, with motels strung out along Papanui Road to the northwest, and on Riccarton Road which runs west from Hagley Park. Predictably, campsites are scattered outside the city centre, mostly within walking distance of a bus stop. For those who want to wake up **close to the sea**, there's a variety of accommodation in the suburbs facing the Pacific Ocean: New Brighton and Sumner are the best places to aim for – they're about 8km east of the centre and reached by buses #5, #6 and #29 (for New Brighton); and #30 and #31 (for Sumner).

With Christchurch operating a 24-hour airport, most places are well used to accommodating **late arrivals** and early departures: when making a reservation it pays to double check the dates, especially if you're arriving around midnight.

Hotels and motels

Central Christchurch has plenty of large, flashy **hotels** often with rooms overlooking Hagley Park or Victoria Square. On the whole, these represent the most expensive option, and there are cheaper **motel** rooms not far away. The best hunting ground is around fifteen minutes' walk northwest of the Square: upwards of a dozen highly competitive places line **Papanui Road** which leads to the classy suburb of Merivale. Alternatively, try **Riccarton Road**, again just outside the Four Avenues and only twenty minutes' walk from the city through Hagley Park; or head out to beachside New Brighton (see box, p.552). Rates are pretty competitive, so you shouldn't have any trouble finding a studio for around $80, and many establishments offer **special deals** for weekend and long-term stays.

City centre

All the following hotels and motels are marked on the map on p.544.

Akron Motel, 87 Bealey Ave (☎03/366 1633, fax 379 1332, *akron.motel@xtra.co.nz*). A small motel in a quiet area set back off the road with plain but functional units, some of which open out onto a small garden, about ten minutes' walk from Cathedral Square. ④.

Avon River Centra, 356 Oxford Terrace (☎03/379 1180 & 0800/801 111, fax 366 7590, *www.centra.com.au*). Lovely business hotel on the edge of the CBD but beside the Avon River and with relaxing courtyard gardens. High-standard rooms and all the expected facilities including indoor pool, restaurant and bar. ⑧.

Cashel Court Motel, 457 Cashel St (☎ & fax 03/389 2768). Very reasonably priced motel, fifteen minutes' walk from the city centre and with an outdoor pool. Small but comfortable. ④.

Chateau on the Park, 189 Deans Ave (☎0800/808 999, fax 03/348 8990, *www.chateau-park.co.nz*, *gm@chateau-park.co.nz*). Two-hundred-room hotel, memorable for its lovely surroundings on the edge of Hagley Park, with an outdoor pool, restaurants and cocktail bar. Fifteen minutes' walk from the Square. ⑨.

Parkroyal, cnr Kilmore St & Durham St (☎03/365 7799 & 0800/801 111, fax 365 0082, *reservations@christchurch.parkroyal.co.nz*). This spectacular hotel is an outstanding modern architectural feature of the city – a sort of Mayan temple with a glass atrium. Overlooking Victoria Square, it has a magnificent lobby and foyer, but disappointing rooms. There are three bars and three restaurants, and it's well worth dropping in for a drink or afternoon tea, even if you're not staying here. ⑨.

Tudor Court Motel, 57 Bealey Ave (☎0800/488 367 & 03/379 1465, fax 379 1490, *tudor@xtra.co.nz*). Very small motel in a peaceful environment with simple units. Fifteen minutes' walk to Cathedral Square. ⑤.

Papanui Road
All the following hotels and motels are marked on the map on p.548.

Adelphi, 49 Papanui Rd, Merivale (☎03/355 6037 & 0800/335 560, fax 355 6036, *adelphi@xtra.co.nz*). Good-value motel a kilometre from the city centre, with spacious units, spa and playground around a courtyard car park. The rooms are a bit frumpy, but are clean, functional and have cooking facilities. ④.

Colonial Inn Motel, 43 Papanui Rd, Merivale (☎03/355 9139 & 0800/111 232, fax 355 5457, *colonialinn@xtra.co.nz*). A modern well-appointed motel about fifteen minutes' walk from Cathedral Square. Clean and comfortable units. ⑤.

Diplomat Motel, 127 Papanui Rd, Merivale (☎03/355 6009, fax 355 6007). Situated in the heart of Merivale, 2km from Cathedral Square and 8km from the airport, this smart motel has large self-contained units with separate kitchens, where the extra few dollars is justified by a nice outdoor pool and spa. ⑥.

Strathern Motor Lodge, 54 Papanui Rd, Merivale (☎ & fax 03/355 4411, freephone 0800/766 624, *www.strathern.com, strathern.motor.lodge@xta.co.nz*). Spacious and well-presented modern units all with a full kitchen, and one with its own spabath, located fifteen minutes' walk from Cathedral Square with its own spa pool. Excellent value. ⑤.

Riccarton Road
All the following hotels and motels are marked on the map on p.544.

Aalton Motel, 19 Riccarton Rd (☎0800/422 586, fax 03/348 0185, *www.aalton.co.nz, welcome @aalton.co.nz*). Very spacious, slightly ageing rooms represent good value and there's an indoor spa and poorly sited outdoor pool that's just about OK for a cooling dip. Close to Hagley Park and with Sky TV. ⑤.

Annabelle Court Motel, 42 Riccarton Rd (☎0800/808 707, fax 03/341 3030). Attractive modern motel with spacious and well appointed units, some with spa baths. Studios ⑤, spa units ⑥.

B&Bs and guesthouses

As elsewhere in New Zealand, the standard of **bed and breakfast** accommodation in Christchurch is very high. There's a sprinkling of excellent B&Bs in the centre and in the nearby, easily reached suburbs, and another concentration of places in the seaside communities of New Brighton and Sumner. All represent good value for money, and are invariably comfortable and friendly.

City centre
All the following guesthouses are marked on the map on p.544.

Ambassador's B&B, 19 Manchester St (☎ & fax 03/366 7808). A budget guesthouse ten minutes' walk from the Square with unspectacular but clean rooms, plus free pickup from bus, train and plane. ④.

Croydon Lodge, 63 Armagh St (☎0800/276 936, fax 03/377 6110, *www.croydon.co.nz, welcome@croydon.co.nz*). Very pleasant and well-run B&B with smallish modernized rooms in the main house and a couple of lovely cottages in the compact but appealing garden. There's a guest lounge with TV and chess, 24hr tea and coffee, and a cooked breakfast is served. Rooms ⑤, en suites and cottages ⑥.

Dorothy's, 2 Latimer Square (☎03/365 6034, fax 365 6035, *www.dorothys.co.nz, dorothys@xtra.co.nz*). Boutique hotel with five lovingly restored en-suite rooms and an appreciable gay following. There's continental breakfast plus a fine on-site restaurant serving á la carte inside or alfresco; the *Rainbow Bar* follows a Wizard of Oz theme. ⑥.

Hambledon, 103 Bealey Ave (☎03/379 0723, fax 379 0758, *hambledon@clear.net.nz, www. hambledon.co.nz*). Luxurious B&B with a rich Victorian theme in one of the city's oldest and grandest houses, built in 1856 for one of the early city fathers. Choose from an array of spacious suites inside the house, or a delightful Victorian cottage in the grounds. Complimentary port and sherry, and delicious breakfasts. Suites ⑦–⑧, cottage ⑨.

Home-Lea, 195 Bealey Ave (☎0800/355 321, fax 03/379 4099, *homelea@xtra.co.nz*). Comfortable and recently refurbished B&B in a two-storeyed wooden house, built in the 1900s and ten minutes' walk from the city centre. There's a quiet family atmosphere, the cosy bedrooms mostly have TVs, and continental breakfast is served. Rooms ⑤, en suites ⑥.

Orari, 42 Gloucester St (☎03/365 6569, fax 365 2525, *www.orari.net.nz, jenny@orari.net.nz*). Sumptuous and elegantly styled B&B just steps from the Arts Centre. The bright sunny rooms all have TVs, phones and either en suites or private bathrooms. Delicious breakfasts. ⑥.

Windsor, 52 Armagh St (☎03/366 1503, fax 366 9796, *www.windsorhotel.co.nz, reservations @windsorhotel.co.nz*). A traditional guesthouse with upwards of fifty rooms in a century-old former student hall of residence. Nothing flash, but the rooms are comfortable and mostly quiet, the staff friendly and the cooked breakfast keeps you going all day. ⑤.

Outside the Four Avenues

All the following guesthouses are marked on the map on p.548.

Elm Tree House, 236 Papanui Rd, Merivale (☎03/355 9731, fax 355 9753, *www.elmtreehouse.co.nz, elmtreeb.b@clear.net.nz*). A very appealing and welcoming B&B fashioned out of a listed historic building in the suburb of Merivale. Largely built from dark native timbers with fussy decor eschewed in favour of clean lines and plain colours. All rooms are en suite, there is a bath and outdoor pool, and a hearty breakfast is served communally. Evening meals by arrangement ($35). ⑥.

Fendalton House, 50 Clifford Ave, Fendalton (☎0800/374 298, fax 03/355 0959, *webnz.co.nz/bbnz/fendalt.htm, fendaltonhouse@xtra.co.nz*). Lovely upmarket homestay located in leafy Fendalton – a pleasant 25min walk from the city through Mona Vale and Hagley Park. There's three spacious en-suites, a spa and an outdoor swimming pool. ⑦.

Highway Lodge, 121 Papanui Rd, Merivale (☎ & fax 03/355 5418). Beautiful Tudor-style home about ten minutes' walk from the city centre, close to restaurants, shops and Hagley Park, with clean, well equipped en-suite rooms. ⑤.

Hostels

At last count there were around twenty **backpacker** hostels in Christchurch, most within the Four Avenues, or just beyond. We've picked the best ranging from fun downtown places where a solid night on the tiles is pretty much the norm, to those a few blocks out with gardens and a homely atmosphere (something Christchurch specializes in). Prices don't vary a great deal, generally just over $15 for dorm beds and around $40 for doubles and twins, a little more for doubles with sheets and towels. None of the hostels listed here have tent sites.

If you are arriving during the peak summer season, try to book accommodation a few days in advance to be sure of getting a bed; most hostels are prepared for late plane arrivals, and many have long-term storage for bike boxes and gear you won't need while in the South Island.

All the following hostels are marked on the map on p.544.

Chester Street, 148 Chester St East (☎03/377 1897). The city's smallest hostel (12 beds); very homely and more like a shared house with a few backpacker beds, and provision for longer-term stays for workers. Rooms are three-share (①) or made-up doubles (②).

Christchurch City Central YHA, 273 Manchester St (☎03/379 9535, fax 379 9537, *yhachch@yha.org.nz*). New, purpose-built and well equipped hostel with a TV room and common room, only three minutes' walk from Cathedral Square. Go for one of the exterior doubles as some in the centre of the building are cramped and airless. Good discounts on various trips and transport. Dorms ①, rooms ③.

Dorset House, 1 Dorset St (☎ & fax 03/366 8268, *www.dorsethouse.co.nz, dorsethouse@cyberxpress. co.nz*). New, small and spacious hostel in an 1871 house located in a quiet area and firmly pitched at the upper end of the backpacker market, with firm beds (no bunks) and sheets and duvets. There's Sky TV in a huge lounge fitted with stained glass windows, off-street parking and free tea and coffee. Dorms ①, rooms ③.

Dreamland, 21 Packe St (☎03/366 3519). Peaceful homely hostel in two suburban houses just outside the Four Avenues, but still only fifteen minutes' walk from the Square. Each house is self-contained so there's plenty of lounge and cooking space. All beds come with sheets and duvets, there's free bikes, free pick-up within the Four Avenues and Internet access. Dorms ①, rooms ②.

Foley Towers, 208 Kilmore St (☎03/366 9720, *foley.towers@backpack.co.nz*). Fairly big hostel in an old house with cosy rooms and a lovely garden. Despite its size, *Foley* manages to maintain an intimate B&B feel. Dorms ①, rooms ②.

Frauenreisehaus Women's Hostel, 272 Barbadoes St (☎03/366 2585, fax 366 2589). Wonderfully relaxed and superbly well-equipped women-only hostel in an old and fairly central wooden house. Much loved by those looking for scented candles, mood music, fresh herbs, spring water direct from the garden and non-violent videos. Spacious rooms have beds rather than bunks, there's also a games room, free local calls, free laundry and Internet access. Dorms ①, twins ②.

New Excelsior, cnr Manchester St & High St (☎0800/666 237, fax 03/366 7629, *homepages.ihug.co.nz/~newexcel, newexcel@ihug.co.nz*). Very central, large and fairly boisterous hostel in a former hotel with on-site café and bar, outdoor deck, reasonable kitchen and lounge areas and Internet access. Dorms ①, rooms ③.

The Old Countryhouse, 437 Gloucester St (☎03/381 5504). If you are prepared to be fifteen minutes' walk from the Square (bus #30) then this lovingly restored suburban house has to be one of Christchurch's finest small hostels. It's all polished wood and bold décor, the dorms are spacious, the kitchen well equipped and there's bike rental ($10 per day). Dorms ①, rooms ②.

Rolleston House YHA, 5 Worcester Boulevard (☎03/366 6564, fax 365 5589, *yhachrl@yha.org.nz*). The best-located accommodation in Christchurch: opposite the Arts Centre and full of character. Plenty of dorms but a limited number of doubles, so book ahead for a room. Dorms ①, rooms ②.

Vagabond Backpackers, 232 Worcester St (☎03/379 9677). Run by the very friendly Jan and Les, this place has only 25 beds, some in a wooden building at the back of the house; all are well kept, quiet, clean and recently redecorated – the kitchen even has a dishwasher. There's off-street parking, barbecue and a lovely garden area. Dorms ①, rooms ②.

YMCA, 12 Hereford St (☎0508/962 224, fax 03/365 1386, *chchymca@ymca.org.nz*). This is state-of-the-art as far as YMCA accommodation goes. Singles, doubles and apartments, many en suite, and equipped with telephone, tea and coffee facilities, and TV. Near the Arts Centre and five minutes' walk from Cathedral Square. Fitness centre, gym, squash courts, climbing wall, sauna and canteen. Dorms ①, rooms & apartments ③–⑤.

Campsites

Given the low cost of hostel accommodation in Christchurch, **camping** saves little money, and most of the sites are in any case some distance away from the city centre. There are some well-equipped motor camps within the city limits which are fine for campervans, offer tent sites and have good deals on cabins, but they tend to have a holiday-camp atmosphere.

All Seasons Holiday Park, 5 Kidbrooke St, off Linwood Ave, Linwood (☎03/384 9490, fax 384 9843). This modern park has a swimming pool, spa pool and large children's playground. Easy access to the beach (good for windsurfing), Linwood shopping centre and Sumner, and only ten minutes' drive from the city centre. Tents $9; cabins, on-site vans & tourist flats ②–③.

Amber Park, 308 Blenheim Rd, Upper Riccarton (☎ & fax 03/348 3327, *www.holidayparks.co.nz/amber*). Spacious grassy site with all the expected features just 4km south of the city (bus #21 stops right outside), and handy for the train station, Addington Raceway and Canterbury University. Tent sites $9, on-site vans & cabins ②–③.

Meadow Park, 39 Meadow St, St Albans (☎03/352 9176, fax 352 1272, *www.meadowpark.co.nz, meadowpark@xtra.co.nz*). Situated 4km north of Cathedral Square on SH74 (and reached by bus route #1/4) this campsite, close to supermarkets and restaurants, covers a large area and has a full range of facilities. Tent sites $10, on-site vans & cabins ②–③.

The City

The city centre, together with many of its more compelling sights, is encased within the **Four Avenues** of Moorhouse, Fitzgerald, Bealey and Deans. They define a useful border round the downtown area, in the very centre of which is **Cathedral Square**. Scattered in the streets around the square are the city's most attractive buildings, while over on the western edge of the four avenues lies **Hagley Park**, a focal point for leisure activities at weekends. Laid out in a grid pattern, Christchurch is very much a low-rise city, with the cathedral spire serving as a useful landmark. The architecture is predominantly nineteenth-century Gothic, a style which still informs many of the more modern buildings. Beyond the Four Avenues you pass into suburban districts like Riccarton, Fendalton, Merivale and St Albans, each characterized by one- and two-storey residential housing and beautifully kept gardens. Further west lie the coastal suburbs of New Brighton and Sumner, which provide access to the beaches of the Pacific Ocean.

Though very much an urban environment, Christchurch can also make a good base for outdoor activities. Ballooning, mountain biking, paragliding, tandem parachuting, skiing, and whitewater rafting are all covered in "Listings" on pp.560–62.

Within the Four Avenues

Christchurch is dominated by its **Cathedral** (Nov–March Mon–Fri 8.30am–7pm, Sat & Sun 9am–5pm; April–Oct Mon–Fri 8.30am–5pm; free: $3 guided tours Mon–Fri 11am & 2pm, Sat 11am, Sun 11.30am) and the square that surrounds it. You can climb the 134-step claustrophobic staircase of the 63-metre spire ($4) for the best panoramic views of the city. Designed by George Gilbert Scott, the cathedral was begun in the 1860s and completed in 1904 – a Gothic revival Anglican church with a cool and spacious interior. On the left-hand side from the main entrance, look out for the Maori contribution of *tukutuku* panels made of leather and rimu wood, celebrating the Maori proverb: "What is the most important thing in life? It is people, people, people". Visitors and worshippers contributed many of the stitches. To sample the marvellous acoustics of the building, drop by for choral evensong (Tues & Wed 5.15pm for the full choir, Fri 4pm for the boys only); note that this doesn't take place during school holidays, principally Christmas to early February.

Christchurch's grid of streets spreads out from **Cathedral Square** (or just "the Square") – a large, open, paved area typically abuzz with lunching office workers, skateboarders and tourists. You'll find yourself passing through several times a day if only to catch a bus or taxi. After a period of absence, the visitor centre has returned to Cathedral Square and is now resident in the **Old Post Office**, an Italianate building constructed in 1879 which, together with the Palladian-style former **Government Building** (1901), provides a pleasing contrast to the predominantly Gothic architecture on show elsewhere. The **Statue of Robert Godley**, the founding father of Christchurch and agent of the Canterbury Association, stands opposite the **Memorial of the Four Ships** outside the old post office, which shows the vessels sent by the Canterbury Association in 1850 to create a model Anglican community here.

Adjacent you'll find the **Southern Encounter Aquarium** (daily 9am–7pm; $12.50), which mimics a walk through the damper habitats of the South Island. It's on a small scale, but well presented with tanks full of crayfish, hands-in touch tanks fashioned after rock pools, a mock-up of a fly fishing lodge and tanks full of whitebait. Your visit is rounded off by three short films – all with dramatic commentaries and swelling music – and if you time it right you can watch **feeding** (eels 11am, marine species 3pm).

Another less permanent occupant of the square is the **Wizard** (*www.wizard.gen.nz*, usually Mon–Fri 1–1.45pm in summer), a local eccentric and former English lecturer who has been lambasting bemused audiences with muddle-brained but occasionally interesting rantings for over a quarter of a century. After arriving via red VW Beetle (made from two front ends welded together), he pontificates on the nature of the world, god and women.

The area south of Cathedral Square has the greatest concentration of shops, restaurants and bars, and you'll continually find yourself back here in the evening. There are no sights to speak of as such, but one area to make for is High Street, lined with the more off-beat music and clothes shops as well as the cooler end of the café scene. Parts of this area (particularly along Lichfield Street) can be pretty seedy at night, but it is seldom intimidating.

North of Cathedral Square

A grid of shopping streets and precincts spreads north from the Square, the most interesting section being around **New Regent Street** two minutes' walk east along Gloucester Street. Built in 1932, and home to some of the city's more interesting upmarket cafés and stores, it's one of Christchurch's most attractive streets, with pastel-coloured buildings and trellised balconies recalling the Spanish Mission style of architecture which flourished in eighteenth-century California and New Mexico.

One block west, the well-manicured Victoria Square is bounded to the north by the languid Avon River and Christchurch's starkly modern **Town Hall** (daily 9am–5pm), an angular piece of minimalist design linked by footbridge to the equally radical, glass-fronted Convention Centre on the opposite side of Kilmore Street. As Christchurch's premiere entertainment venue, the town hall harbours a magnificent 2300-seat auditorium – an impressive sight even when empty. It also contains the Women's Suffrage Commemorative Wall Hanging, commissioned in 1992 to commemorate Women's Suffrage Year and depicting aspects of women's lives over the last hundred years. You can enjoy views of Victoria Square from the *Town Hall Restaurant*, a good place to stop for coffee. Epicureans should nip around the corner to the venerable **Johnson's Grocers**, 787 Colombo St, a treasure trove stacked to the rafters with just about every packaged gourmet product imaginable.

Following the river a few steps to the southwest you find the **Provincial Government Buildings**, corner of Durham Street and Armagh Street (Mon–Sat 10.30am–3pm, also Oct–May Sun 2–4pm; donation requested), built between 1858 and 1865. These are the only provincial government buildings left in New Zealand and are widely regarded as the masterpiece of Christchurch's most renowned early architect, **Benjamin W. Mountfort**. Built in Gothic style with medieval-influenced ornamentation, the older wooden portion of the chambers has a fine flagstone-paved corridor. The stone council chamber, the high-Victorian Great Hall (1869), is magnificently decorated with an intricate ceiling and elaborate stonework. Masks of the two craftsmen responsible for all this finery appear in the stonework: on the east wall near the fireplace on the ground floor and on the east wall of the public gallery.

Heading northwest from here along Victoria Street, the Victorian **clock tower** houses a clock originally imported from England in 1860 to adorn the government buildings. Also on Victoria Street, at no. 30, Christchurch's **Casino** is open 24 hours all year round and contains the usual array of bars, table games and a flood of one-armed bandits. You have to be smartly dressed and aged over 18 to get in.

The Arts Centre

Ten minutes' walk west from Cathedral Square along Worcester Street brings you to the Gothic revivalist **Arts Centre**, built in 1874 as the University of Canterbury and

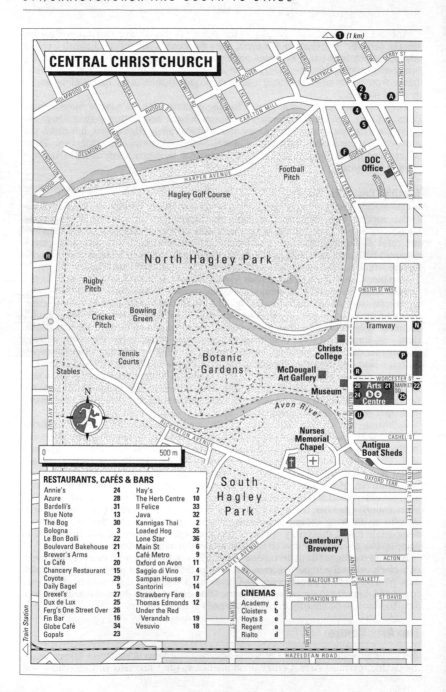

CENTRAL CHRISTCHURCH

(1 km)

WINCHESTER ST
ANDOVER
STEVESBURY
TONBRIDGE
BASTRICK
PAPANUI RD
CRANSTON
DERBY ST
STONEHURST

HOLMWOOD RD
ROSSALL ST
HEWITTS RD
CHELTENHAM
EXETER
DUBLIN ST
KNOX
VICTORIA ST
MONTREAL ST
WESTHOLD

RHODES ST
CARLTON MILL
PARK TERRACE
DORSET

DESMOND
HARPER AVENUE

FENDALTON RD
WOOD

DOC Office

Football Pitch

Hagley Golf Course

North Hagley Park

CHESTER ST WEST

Rugby Pitch

Cricket Pitch

Bowling Green

Tramway

Stables

Tennis Courts

Botanic Gardens

Christs College

McDougall Art Gallery

Museum

Arts Centre
MARKET SQ

WORCESTER ST

DEANS AVENUE

N

RICCARTON AVENUE

Avon River

ROLLESTON AVENUE

0   500 m

CASHEL ST

Nurses Memorial Chapel

Antigua Boat Sheds

MONTREAL STREET

OXFORD TERR

RESTAURANTS, CAFÉS & BARS

Annie's	24	Hay's	7
Azure	28	The Herb Centre	10
Bardelli's	31	Il Felice	33
Blue Note	13	Java	32
The Bog	30	Kannigas Thai	2
Bologna	3	Loaded Hog	35
Le Bon Bolli	22	Lone Star	36
Boulevard Bakehouse	21	Main St	6
Brewer's Arms	1	Café Metro	9
Le Café	20	Oxford on Avon	11
Chancery Restaurant	15	Saggio di Vino	4
Coyote	29	Sampan House	17
Daily Bagel	5	Santorini	14
Drexel's	27	Strawberry Fare	8
Dux de Lux	25	Thomas Edmonds	12
Ferg's One Street Over	26	Under the Red	
Fin Bar	16	Verandah	19
Globe Café	34	Vesuvio	18
Gopals	23		

South Hagley Park

HAGLEY AVENUE
WALLER
SELWYN ST
STEWART

Canterbury Brewery

ANTIGUA ST
ACTON
HALKETT

BALFOUR ST

CINEMAS

Academy	c
Cloisters	b
Hoyts 8	e
Regent	a
Rialto	d

HORATION ST
ST DAVID

STUART MILL

Train Station

HAZELDEAN ROAD

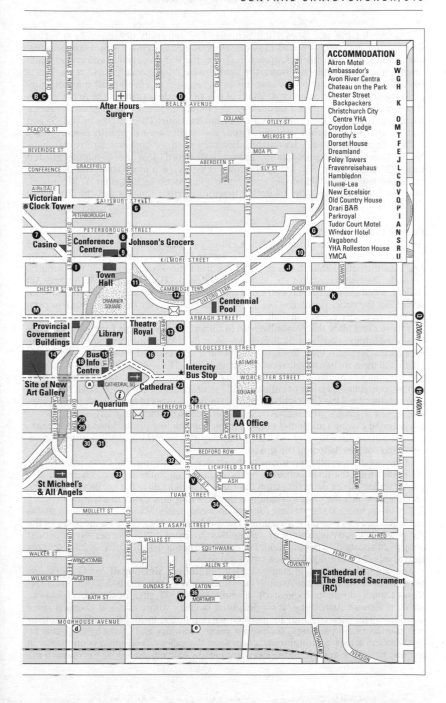

ACCOMMODATION

Akron Motel	B
Ambassador's	W
Avon River Centra	G
Chateau on the Park	H
Chester Street Backpackers	K
Christchurch City Centre YHA	O
Croydon Lodge	M
Dorothy's	T
Dorset House	F
Dreamland	E
Foley Towers	J
Fravenreisehaus	L
Hambledon	C
Home-Lea	D
New Excelsior	V
Old Country House	Q
Orari B&B	P
Parkroyal	I
Tudor Court Motel	A
Windsor Hotel	N
Vagabond	S
YHA Rolleston House	R
YMCA	U

Christchurch Girls' and Boys' High Schools. The university decamped to suburban Ilam in 1975 and, after a period of uncertainty, the Arts Centre, with its restaurants, food stalls, shops and galleries, moved in. Today the leafy courtyards and grassy quadrangles make a great place to watch the world go by: it is especially active at weekends when the Market Square on the east side is turned over to a lively **craft market**, complete with buskers and musicians. Much of what's on sale is made in the Arts Centre's stores and workshops dotted throughout the building. The arts centre also houses a number of restaurants, a couple of cinemas and the Court Theatre (see pp.554–55 and p.558); the **information centre** (☎03/366 0989, *www.artscentre.org.nz*; daily 8.30am–5pm) contains the basement laboratory used for post-graduate research by Noble Prize winning atom-splitter, Ernest Rutherford. Join the 45-minute **guided tours** (Mon–Fri 11am; $5), led by the town crier, to learn more about the buildings, fashioned in volcanic "bluestone" and Oamaru limestone by Benjamin W. Mountfort, who also designed the Christchurch Museum, Christ's College and the Provincial Chambers.

Hagley Park and around

Across Rolleston Avenue from the Arts Centre lies **Hagley Park** which, it is whispered by the mischievous priest of St Michael's, was put here in order to protect the solidly Anglican districts within the Four Avenues from the Presbyterians in the suburbs beyond. The park contains the spectacular Botanic Gardens, the McDougall Art Gallery, a golf course, sports centre and playing fields. At weekends you can find what seems like the entire population of Christchurch here, merely strolling around or playing hockey, tennis, cricket, netball, rugby or golf.

If there's one place that totally lives up to Christchurch's Garden City moniker it has to be the **Botanic Gardens** (Rolleston Ave gate; daily 7am until 1hr before sunset; conservatories 10.15am–4pm; free), an astonishing collection of indigenous and exotic plants and trees that's unrivalled on the South Island. Throughout summer and autumn the perennials here give a constant and dazzling display of colour. There is also a herb garden, containing a variety of culinary and medical plants; a rose garden with over 250 types of roses; and the Cockayne Memorial Garden, an area of native bush named after one of New Zealand's greatest botanists. Several conservatories, the largest of which is the galleried Cuningham House, contain tropical and indoor plants. Most of all, though, it is just a great place to hang out on a sunny day with picnicking families, studying students and couples flattening the grass.

In fine weather, conducted **tours** of the gardens in tractor-pulled carts (11am–4pm; $6) depart from the main entrance by the museum on Rolleston Ave. There are also guided walking tours departing from the *Gardens Restaurant* at the northern end of the gardens, of which the most intriguing is the **Te Puna Ora** (book in advance ☎03/377 2025; $6), an unusual storytelling tour which incorporates Maori and European myths and legends, as well as pure invention. The gardens are enclosed by a meander of the River Avon and you can explore by water either in a **punt** ($12.50 per person for 30min) or by paddleboats ($12 per half hour) or canoe ($6 per hour); all available from Antigua Boat Sheds, 2 Cambridge Terrace (☎03/366 5885).

Also within the grounds of Hagley Park is the **Robert McDougall Art Gallery**, just to the right of the Rolleston Avenue gate (daily: Nov–March 10am–5.30pm; April–Oct 10am–4.30pm; donation requested). Completed in 1932 after designs by Gisborne architect Edward Armstrong, it's a delightful building whose classical Oamaru stone exteriors blend perfectly into their green surroundings. Inside, the gallery contains over four thousand paintings, sculptures, prints, drawings and craft objects, many by New Zealand artists, although only a sample of the gallery's collection is on display at any one time. The gradual move away from art heavily influenced by European tradition, and the resulting emergence of an individual New Zealand style, is well reflected in the permanent displays. The gallery is expected to close during 2002, and the collection will be relocated to the new Christchurch Art Gallery, due to open a couple of blocks east (see map, p.544) in March 2003.

Immediately north of the Rolleston Avenue entrance to Hagley Park you'll find the **Canterbury Museum** (daily: Oct to mid-March 9am–5.30pm; mid-March to Sept 9am–5pm; $5 donation appreciated), a neo-Gothic structure founded in 1870 and initially directed by archeologist Julius Haast (who gave his name to the Haast Pass, see p.735). Its best exhibition is the "Exploration of Antarctica", covering the many expeditions that have used New Zealand as their jumping-off point. Otherwise, this museum has the traditional exhibits on moa hunters, Maori, European settlers, native birds and mammals, fossils and geology.

Adjacent, **Christ's College** is the city's most elite private school, a physical embodiment of the English tradition. You can visit the hallowed halls on ninety-minute **guided tours** (Oct to mid-March Mon–Fri 10.30am, 2.30pm & 7pm; $10) which include the college's oldest building, Big School (1863), and the Memorial Dining Hall designed by Cecil Wood in 1925.

On the southern borders of Hagley Park stands the Christchurch Hospital and, a little further on, the **Nurses' Memorial Chapel** (Mon–Sat 1–4pm, Sun 10am–4pm; free). Designed by J.G. Collins (who also worked with his father on the Arts Centre), it was constructed after the death of three Christchurch-trained nurses aboard the troopship *Marquette*, torpedoed in 1915. The walls are Oamaru stone with terracotta bricks and the roof is tiled in green slate, but the best feature is the extensively timbered interior. Windows and doors are framed with matai, and the simply patterned floors made of blackwood and oak, with redwood sarking and an elaborate oak panel behind the altar. There are nine stained-glass windows, including four by the English glass artist Veronica Whall, all with an uneven texture and a variety of colours set off by the otherwise dark, low-ceilinged interior.

Heading east back into town, along Oxford Terrace, you'll pass the lovely **St Michael and All Angels Church**, overlooking the river (Oct–April Mon–Fri 10am–5pm, Sat & Sun 2–5pm; guided tours on demand; April–Oct open for regular church services only). The church was designed by William F. Crisp and completed in 1875, combining elements of both the French and English medieval Gothic styles. Much of the architectural ingenuity that went into the building can be glimpsed in the impressive, dark-wood interior: the structure is made of matai timber (native black pine) on stone foundations, and supported by monumental pillars carved from single trees. The pine darkens as it grows older, so it is possible to spot new additions by gauging the blackness of the surrounding wood. The stained-glass windows covering both east and west wings are particularly beautiful, their bright colours contrasting with the dark hues of the surrounding timber. Look out also for the **Te Tapenakara o te Ariki** ("The Tabernacle of the Lord") hung from the ceiling over the central aisle, traditionally a container used by Maori chiefs to store *taonga* (treasure such as ceremonial feathers). This one was dedicated by the Bishop of *Aotearoa* for use as a Christian vessel to contain consecrated bread, and depicts symbols from both Maori and Christian tradition. The rather dainty belfry standing outside the church was designed by Mountfort in 1861, and houses a bell from one of the first four migrant ships. Historically it served as a timepiece for the settlers and was rung on the hour.

Two blocks south of St Michael's, St Asaph Street leads back towards Hagley Park, passing the **Canterbury Brewery Heritage Centre** at no. 30 – a welcome breather from the highbrow culture on display elsewhere. Fifty-minute guided tours (reservations advised ☎03/379 4940; Mon–Thurs 10am; $8) give you a brief history of brewing in the region, a glimpse of the working brewery itself, and the usual reward at the end.

Beyond the four avenues

Inspired by a couple of hours spent in the Botanical Gardens, you might fancy a stroll across North Hagley Park to their logical extension, the beautiful precincts of **Mona Vale** at 63 Fendalton Rd (grounds open daily Oct–March 8am–7.30pm; April–Sept 8.30am–5.30pm; free: guided tours Nov–March daily 9.30am & 1.30pm; $35). Originally part of the Deans' estate (see overleaf), the site became the property of the city in 1969 and is now tended by the Canterbury Horticultural Society. The gardens have majestic displays of roses, dahlias, fuchsias and irises, as well as magnolias, rhododendrons and herbaceous perennials. The Bath House has been converted for use as a greenhouse and the old homestead is open for lunch daily. You can rent a punt at the old homestead and enjoy the gardens from the river ($15 per person for 30min).

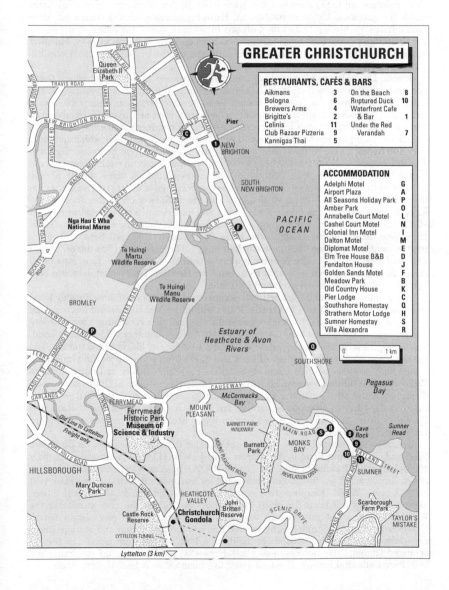

GREATER CHRISTCHURCH

RESTAURANTS, CAFÉS & BARS

Aikmans	3	On the Beach	8
Bologna	6	Ruptured Duck	10
Brewers Arms	4	Waterfront Cafe	
Brigitte's	2	& Bar	1
Celinis	11	Under the Red	
Club Bazaar Pizzeria	9	Verandah	7
Kannigas Thai	5		

ACCOMMODATION

Adelphi Motel	G
Airport Plaza	A
All Seasons Holiday Park	P
Amber Park	O
Annabelle Court Motel	L
Cashel Court Motel	N
Colonial Inn Motel	I
Dalton Motel	M
Diplomat Motel	E
Elm Tree House B&B	D
Fendalton House	J
Golden Sands Motel	F
Meadow Park	B
Old Country House	K
Pier Lodge	C
Southshore Homestay	Q
Strathern Motor Lodge	H
Sumner Homestay	S
Villa Alexandra	R

You could hardly make a greater botanical leap than to wander ten minutes to the southwest to the suburb of Riccarton and **Deans Bush** (daily dawn–dusk; free), an area of native forest containing several 500-year-old kahikatea trees. The survival of this valuable area of forest is largely due to Scottish brothers William and John Deans, who came to farm the area in 1843 and somehow resisted the temptation to put all their property to immediate agricultural use. Today a concrete path navigates the bush, with signs pointing out the species that still grow here. By the northern entrance off Kahu Road, the gracious, Victorian **Riccarton House** (generally closed except for functions), hides the black pine **Deans Cottage** (daily 9am–5pm), the oldest structure on the Canterbury plain, built by the Deans brothers upon their arrival in 1843. This tiny affair is furnished as it would have been until the deaths of William (1851) and his brother (1854).

Beyond Deans Bush, Memorial Avenue runs northwest to the airport where there are one or two attractions worth seeing. Much the most interesting is the **International Antarctic Centre**, Orchard Road (*www.iceberg.co.nz*; daily: Oct–March 9am–8pm; April–Sept 9am–5.30pm; $16), a well-presented and dynamic exhibit concentrating on New Zealand's involvement on the cold continent. Since the mid-1950s, Christchurch airport has been the base of the US Antarctic programme which sponsors over 140 flights a year to their base at McMurdo Sound, and the neighbouring New Zealand outpost at Scott Base. There's stacks here on Antarctic exploration and the fragile polar ecosystem with continuous video presentations, daily digital photos emailed from the ice depicting life at Scott Base, recordings of the current weather conditions, traditional and interactive displays and innovations such as the Snow & Ice Experience where you can don a down jacket and experience a snowy environment at –5°C, cooled further by a fan giving a wind chill of –25°C. Antarctic enthusiasts should leave time for the hourly **Hägglunds Ride** (Oct–March $20; April–Sept $15), a 45-minute jaunt in a genuine five-tonne tracked buggy. The centre also has the *60° South Cafe and Bar* and one of the country's more imaginative gift shops. True fans of all things Antarctic can even pick up a free *Antarctic Heritage Trail* leaflet detailing connected sites around Christchurch and Lyttelton.

Drivers can skirt around the northern perimeter of the airport – follow Russley Road then McLeans Island Road – to **Orana Park**, within the McLeans Island Recreational Area (daily 10am–5pm; $12), a well-organized zoological park containing a wide variety of native and imported animals, particularly from Africa. Volunteer guides are on hand, and highlights include endangered New Zealand bird species like kiwi and tuatara, and the chance to observe the feeding of lions and tigers from a treetop viewing balcony.

Although nowhere near as exciting as Orana Park, the smaller and more intimate **Willowbank Wildlife Reserve**, 60 Hussey Rd (daily 10am–10pm; $12), has some good displays of native birds including a glass-free kiwi house (11.30am–10pm). To get there, ride bus #1/4 from Cathedral Square as far as the junction of Harewood Road and Gardiners Road, then walk northeast up Gardiners Road for five minutes or so before turning right into Hussey Road.

Around twenty minutes' drive southwest of Hagley Park and accessible via Blenheim Road and Great South Road is **Air Force World** (☎03/343 9532, *www.afw.co.nz*; daily 10am–5pm; $10), located beside the former RNZAF base at Wigram. Among the two dozen aircraft you'll see the Dakota converted for use on the British Queen's state visit in 1953, and a WWII Dauntless that crashed in the Pacific islands of Vanuatu. Three flight simulators will keep the (big) kids happy, particularly the one simulating the WWII Mosquito as it engages in very realistic combat in the Norwegian fjords. Enthusiastic volunteer guides conduct free tours of the restoration and storage hangers (daily 11am, 1pm & 3pm); short flights in a Pitts Special stunt plane can also be arranged (20min; $195; booking essential). Buses #81 to Lincoln or #25 to Templeton, both from Cathedral Square, drop off about five minutes' walk from the entrance.

Anyone desperate to see a shed full of nicely restored old cars – Jaguar, Mercedes, Lancia and so forth – should continue a couple of kilometres further out to **Dr Heins Classic Car Collection**, 376 Great South Rd, Hornby (*www.classics.co.nz*; daily 10am–5pm; $5), where most specimens are only kept on display until sold.

The Christchurch Gondola and Ferrymead

The **Christchurch Gondola**, 10 Bridle Path Rd (daily 10am–10pm or later; $8 one way, $12 return) is a scenic and gentle way of seeing the surrounding countryside from the top of the Port Hills. The Gondola terminal is located in the Heathcote Valley about 25 minutes' drive from Cathedral Square, and is serviced by a free Gondola Shuttle operating from the visitor centre, as well as the Lyttelton bus (#28). The Gondola cable cars climb to the 945m summit of Mount Cavendish, providing views of Christchurch, the Canterbury Plains, the volcanic outcrops of the Banks Peninsula and the Southern Alps. The station at the top contains a "time tunnel" museum (same hours; free), which covers the geology and geography of the area as well as Maori legends, life aboard early migrant ships and a video about modern-day Canterbury. Also in the station are a viewing deck, souvenir shop, café, an indifferent restaurant, where you can eat while enjoying fantastic views of the city below – especially at night.

From the summit, you can take one of the footpaths that explore the hills or head straight back down – either by cable car, or the more intrepid methods of paragliding or **mountain biking**. The Mountain Bike Adventure Company (bookings essential ☎0800/424 534; free pick-ups from the visitor centre) offers a number of guided or self-guided descents: the "Mount Cavendish Experience" ($45), for example, allows two hours to explore the station and tackle one of three routes down the surrounding Summit Road system with bird's-eye views of Sumner's beaches, Lyttelton and the Banks Peninsula. If you're after more thrills, Nimbus (☎03/326 7922) or Phoenix (☎03/326 7634) will **paraglide** you down from near the summit of the gondola, in tandem with an instructor, for about $100.

If you cycle back down to the Gondola terminal in Heathcote, you'll pass through the neighbouring suburb of Ferrymead (also served by bus #30, #31 or #32 from the centre of town), home to the **Ferrymead Historic Park**, 269 Bridle Path Rd, Heathcote (daily 10am–4.30pm; $8), a large area with a reconstruction of a small Edwardian township, reached by restored engines and tram cars from bygone eras ($2 return). After a walk around the township, mingling with appropriately costumed locals, drop in at the *Kennaway Brothers Tearooms* for a doorstep sandwich or the old bakery for home-made pies and bread. Also within the complex are a mock-up of an airport terminal from the 1960s, indicative of the importance of air travel to New Zealand; a settlers' Cob Cottage, made of mud; and the Hall of Flame, a collection of antique fire engines.

Christchurch's beaches

As the summer sun bakes the city streets it's very tempting to head for the beach, and Christchurch has plenty on offer; all accessed by frequent buses, and with a choice of places to stay and eat if you fancy spending some time out there.

Around eight kilometres east of the centre a long swathe of sand runs from Waimari Beach south along a spit to the mouth of the Avon estuary – the whole area is a great place to swim or simply lounge on a towel. The centre of activity is **New Brighton** (bus #5, #6 or #29 from the city), locally famed in the 1970s and early 1980s for its Saturday shopping in the days when nowhere else was open at weekends. Its tenor has slipped a good deal since then, but New Brighton is resplendent with its long concrete **pier**, built seemingly just for the scores of anglers hanging over the sides. Cafés around the base of the pier, plus a good stretch of sand make this the place to hang out.

ACCOMMODATION AT THE BEACHES

Christchurch is a very manageable city and staying in the centre is by no means unpleasant, but there is something about waking up close to the beach. Staying in the city's waterside suburbs of New Brighton and Sumner is an appealing prospect particularly if you've got your own vehicle, though city buses are frequent.

All the following establishments are marked on the map on p.548.

Golden Sands Motel, 121 Estuary Rd, South New Brighton (☎03/388 7996, fax 388 2221). A small, clean and tidy motel with six units containing kitchens and TVs. There's a pool, kids' playground and you're only 500m from the beach. ④.

Pier Lodge, 97 Lonsdale St, New Brighton (☎ & fax 03/388 3388). A large friendly low-cost guesthouse with eight plain bedrooms, three shared bathrooms and a separate kitchen and dining room for guests. There's a big garden, petanque court and tea and coffee available all day. ④.

Southshore Homestay, 71a Rockinghorse Rd, Southshore (☎03/388 4067). Pleasant homestay with two clean and cosy bedrooms, located just south of New Brighton on a spit between estuary and sea. Twenty minutes' drive from Cathedral Square. Dinner on request ($25). ⑤.

Sumner Homestay, Panorama Rd, Clifton Hill, Sumner (☎03/326 5755, fax 326 5701, *panoramahomestay@xtra.co.nz*). Comfortable accommodation in one double room, with use of a separate guest lounge and a stunning terraced garden. Dinner by arrangement ($25). Three minutes' drive from the beach. ⑤.

Villa Alexandra, 1 Kinsey Terrace, Clifton Hill, Sumner (☎03/326 6291, fax 326 6069). A spacious villa overlooking Sumner Bay with a sunny veranda and turret, offering a couple of bedrooms and one loft apartment all en suite or with private bathroom. Welcoming hosts prepare meals using garden vegetables and their own free-range eggs (dinner $25). Rooms ④, loft ⑤.

Marine Parade runs north from here, close to **Queen Elizabeth II Park**, an impressive stadium built for the 1974 Commonwealth Games sited at the corner of Travis Road and Bower Avenue, about 500m inland. The complex contains an Olympic-sized swimming pool (Mon–Fri 6am–9pm, Sat & Sun 7am–6pm; $3), and a children-oriented fun park (same times; expect to pay about $4 per activity), which offers distractions such as mini-golf, mini-racing cars and mini-bikes.

South of New Brighton, a spit of land provides shelter for the waters of the Avon and Heathcote river estuary, which is backed by the quiet suburb of **Bromley** and the Te Huingi Manu and Te Huingi Martu **wildlife reserves** (daily dawn-dusk; free), a great place for bird watchers. The estuary basin provides an excellent spot for windsurfing and dinghy sailing.

Redcliffs and Sumner

On the whole, you are better off on the southern side of the river estuary where Redcliffs, and particularly Sumner (both accessed by bus #30 or #31 from Cathedral Square), have developed into tight beachside communities with plenty going on and a number of good places to stay and eat.

Redcliffs is significant mainly as the starting point for the 5km-long **Barnett Park Walkway** (1hr 45min round-trip), which begins at a car park just off Main Road. A well-formed track climbs through grassland onto rock outcrops, with steps giving access to a large rock shelter and several caves. The walkway then bisects a copse of native bush and passes a seasonal waterfall, before crossing a creek and descending via bluffs past **Paradise Cave**, home of a Maori family in the 1890s.

As you follow the coast around from Redcliffs you pass the river mouth, and estuary beaches become sea beaches, the best being at **Sumner**, a Norfolk Pine-backed strip

---

WALKS AROUND SUMNER

The *Christchurch Scenic Walk, Nicholson Park and Scarborough* leaflet (free from Christchurch visitor centre) describes a series of **short walks** (each around 15min) that can also be combined to form a **longer route** (2.5km; 1hr 30min).

Mouldeys Track starts just inland from the beach at the junction of Nayland Street and Herberden Avenue. After a short, sharp climb with the sea to the northwest and the head rising to the southeast, the path continues for about fifteen minutes before being crossed by a track to the Boat Shed. Head down this for a great view of Pegasus Bay, stretching away to the northwest (the bay is named after the *Pegasus*, in which Captain Chase sailed the coast looking for sealing grounds), and then join the **Boat Shed to Sumner Head Track**. This ploughs uphill again for about fifteen minutes, skirting the cliff edge and giving increasingly spectacular views.

From **Sumner Head** you can see the Kaikoura Peninsula in the west, and Godley Head and Banks Peninsula to the east. At this point you have two alternatives for reaching the botanical reserve of **Nicholson Park**: either head straight inland along a clay track to the park ten minutes away; or, more interestingly, continue around the cliffs, climbing quite steeply, for views down the eastern side of the head (20min). On entering Nicholson park the latter track leads onto a small point, from which you can see **Whitewash Head** (so named because of the large number of seabirds that nest on its cliffs), and the **Giants Nose**, a small finger of land behind which is the bay named **Taylor's Mistake**, where according to local lore, a captain named Taylor ran aground after mistaking the bay for the entrance to Lyttelton Harbour.

---

of craft shops, restaurants, cafés, wine bars, surf shacks and a cinema, all fronting a broad patch of golden sand. Named after Dr J.B. Sumner, Archbishop of Canterbury and president of the Canterbury Association in the 1850s, it's now one of Christchurch's more desirable suburbs and a popular destination on summer weekends. The highlight of the beach is **Cave Rock**, a geological anomaly of honeycombed rock – its underside is peppered with little caves like an enormous Swiss cheese – which you can walk through at low tide. You can also clamber up the rock to reach the lifeguard's lookout point on top. More or less opposite Cave Rock on the other side of Main Road, is a small, untidy and much-graffitied **moa cave**, where bones from these now-extinct flightless birds were discovered. Most interesting of all, though, are a series of short walks to and around Sumner Head (see box above) – a must if you lack the time to explore the Banks Peninsula further south.

Eating

Christchurch has the largest number and widest range of **restaurants** in the South Island. It has long discarded most of the dowdier establishments of old and has wholeheartedly adopted the national penchant for Pacific Rim cuisine with an admixture of influences from just about everywhere else. To whet your appetite, buy a copy of the comprehensive *Classic Canterbury Dining Out Guide* from the visitor centre ($4.95). Top-quality gourmet cuisine is increasingly well represented, and now nicely balances the selection of ethnic restaurants on offer. There's also a growing number of fun, themed establishments featuring live music, and for a more down-to-earth atmosphere, many of the city's **pubs** serve hearty food to soak up their brews.

With more and more **cafés** and **bars** offering substantial food, distinctions between eating and drinking venues are increasingly blurred, and many of the establishments listed under "Drinking" (p.557) are perfectly good places in which to enjoy a main meal. All the places listed below are open daily, unless otherwise stated.

Central Christchurch

For eating there is little reason to venture beyond the Four Avenues, in fact you'll find most of what you need in the grid of downtown streets close to Cathedral Square, notably along Colombo Street, Cashel Street, Manchester Street and High Street. One area which deserves special mention is Oxford Terrace between Cashel and Gloucester streets. This is what's recently become known as "The Strip", a run of restaurant/bars that all spill out onto pavement seating with views across the street to the River Avon. There's plenty of good dining, and as the evening wears on the lights go down, the music gets cranked up and booze flows freely. The clubbing set usually pops in for a couple of hours around 10.30pm before drifting off to livelier dancefloors.

Cafés and takeaways

Bardelli's Deli Café, 98 Cashel Mall. A popular spot for Italian-influenced brunches, such as focaccia sandwiches, as well as lunch and dinner at moderate prices. Becomes a lively bar late in the evening. Licensed.

Boulevard Bakehouse, in the Arts Centre, Worcester St. A delightfully simple place where you can get a good bagel, sit outside and watch the world go by; also serves breakfast, lunch and snacks ($5–15).

Le Café, in the Arts Centre, Worcester St (☎03/366 7722). This very popular café is open from 7am to midnight daily – except Friday and Saturday, when its stays open round the clock. Pop in anytime for breakfast specials, club sandwiches ($11), fruit crumble ($7) and coffee. BYO & Licensed.

Café Metro, cnr Colombo St & Kilmore St. One of the best cafés in this part of town, right by the town hall with great coffee, a good range of quiches, pies, muffins and cakes, and a varied stack of up-to-date mags to read.

The Daily Bagel, 179a Victoria St. Tiny shop with three tables and a few seats outside that serves authentic bagels with New York-inspired fillings, and superb coffee. Mon–Sat 7am–4pm.

Drexel's, 106 Hereford St (reservations advisable for Saturday and Sunday brunch ☎03/379 8089). Surprisingly comfortable American-style breakfast and lunch diner serving the likes of three-egg omelettes ($13), chicken fajitas ($14) and a full stack of pancakes ($8). Mon–Fri 6.30am–2pm, Sat & Sun 7am–2pm.

The Globe Café, 171 High St. Popular coffee spot and lunchtime hangout for students from the Jazz school across the road. The spacious interior and pavement seating are both great for watching the world go by over something from their huge selection of teas, or tucking into all manner of panini, salads and quiches. Try the pumpkin and kumara burger($12) or the lamb pesto salad ($15). Open daytime and Fri evenings.

Gopals, cnr Manchester St & Worcester St. An alcohol-free, strictly vegetarian café run by Hare Krishnas and serving good-quality food at rock-bottom prices ($3–7). Open for lunch Mon–Fri, and Fri for dinner.

The Herb Centre, 225 Kilmore St. Daytime eat-in and take-out café specializing in vegetarian and vegan cuisine served up with a range of caffeine-free drinks and organic coffee. For the dedicated, there's Piko Healthfoods, two doors up at no. 229, which sells great bread and self-catering supplies and has a good earthy noticeboard. Closed Sun.

Java, cnr High St & Lichfield St. Young and very groovy coffee bar with options on the strongest coffee in town and music at the more challenging end of the spectrum. Low-cost meals start with breakfast and continue with hot snacks, salads, sandwiches and cakes until the small hours. Open 24hr at weekends.

Sampan House, 168 Gloucester St (☎03/372 3388). Cheap and filling Khmer satay and noodle place to eat in or take out. Dishes include wonton noodle soup, sweet and sour satay, and Cambodian style fried rice ($5–6 each). BYO only.

Under the Red Verandah, 502 Worcester St. Delightful suburban, daytime café fifteen minutes' walk east of the centre, but worth the effort for its predominantly vegetarian fare – pumpkin and corn cakes, bacon and kumara frittata – organic breads and good coffee served in the bare-boards interior or out in the sunny courtyard. Closed Sun & Mon.

Restaurants

Annie's, The Arts Centre (☎03/365 0566). Superb wine bar and restaurant within the polished wood-floor confines of the Arts Centre and spilling outside into the courtyard. Lunches ($9–13) might include a summer frittata or Cajun baked chicken, though if there are a few of you order the antipasto plate ($18), groaning with mussels, squid, smoked salmon and salami. Dinner mains stretch from aubergine tofu ratatouille ($22) to baked Canterbury ostrich ($26). Licensed.

Azure, 128 Oxford Terrace. Bustling moderate to expensive restaurant and bar that is very much part of "The Strip", serving Mediterranean-inspired dishes on Oxford Terrace or inside. Occasional live jazz or solo piano, plus a DJ at weekends.

Blue Note, 22 New Regent St (☎03/379 9674). Restaurant and piano bar where diners spill out onto the pedestrianized street as they tuck into $20 mains such as fish of the day in sweet chilli and caper lemon sauce or chicken and mango salad. Live jazz from Thurs to Sun. Licensed.

Chancery, 98 Gloucester Rd (☎03/379 4317). Traditional, no-nonsense New Zealand restaurant – and that really does mean roast lamb, fried fish or steaks served with potatoes or chips, roast kumara (sweet potato) and possibly another vegetable, all at good-value prices and in tacky surroundings. Licensed.

Coyote, 126 Oxford Terrace. Full-on restaurant/bar that really started "The Strip", an American Southwest influenced place also serving a good range of pizzas either out on the pavement or in the cactus-ridden interior. Bustling at lunch, full of eager diners in the early evening tucking into Tijuana pizza ($14), huge burgers ($15) and Caesar salad ($14); then rowdy late on (see "Drinking" p.557). Licensed.

Dux de Lux, cnr Hereford St & Montreal St. Excellent restaurant and microbrewery (see p.557) that's one of the most popular places in town, with outdoor and indoor seating and a longstanding reputation for superb seafood and vegetarian meals at moderate prices. Licensed.

Hay's Café, 63 Victoria St (☎03/379 7501). A must for lamb aficionados, thought the fairly spartan interior gives little indication of the exceptional quality and presentation of the succulent lamb dishes prepared using animals reared on the owners' Banks Peninsula property. Mains around $25; closed Mon lunch and Sunday. Licensed.

Il Felice, 56 Lichfield St (☎03/366 7535). Excellent Italian restaurant, serving Tuscan-influenced cuisine and fresh, home-made pasta at moderate prices (with main courses around $26). Evenings only; licensed & BYO.

Le Bon Bolli, cnr Worcester St & Montreal St (☎03/374 9444). Don't let the modern brick exterior fool you, inside you could imagine you're in France. Lunch time attracts the business crowd to dine in the café downstairs. Upstairs is more formal with beautifully presented French cuisine such as duck in orange sauce ($18) and wild venison pie ($20).

Main Street Café & Bar, 840 Colombo St (☎03/365 0421). Very good vegetarian restaurant with a wide selection of dishes (some vegan) served in huge portions at low prices. Come with a big appetite and the capacity for $2 bottomless coffee. Licensed.

Oxford on Avon, 794 Colombo St (☎03/379 7148). Pub on the banks of the Avon, famed for the enormity of the portions as well as the great value. The winning formula is a hearty carvery roast in the English tradition for $11. The bar serves the usual stock of native beers. Evenings only.

Saggio di Vino, 185 Victoria St (☎03/379 4006). Classy tile-floored Italian restaurant where dishes such as chicken and artichoke salad ($24), or fresh grouper fillet ($25) can be accompanied by something from an extensive award-winning wine cellar; all available by the glass. Servings are small but everything's beautifully done. Dinner nightly; lunch Thurs & Fri. Licensed.

Santorini Greek Ouzeri, cnr Gloucester St & Cambridge Terrace (☎03/379 6975). A taste of the Greek islands with live Bouzouki Tues–Sat evenings only; licensed.

Strawberry Fare Dessert Restaurant, 114 Peterborough St. Classy and very correct establishment that's every sweet lover's dream, with over two-thirds of the menu given over to luscious desserts that will harden even the most obstinate arteries, and prices that will hasten a heart attack. Naughty but nice. Licensed & BYO.

Thomas Edmonds Restaurant, cnr Cambridge Terrace & Manchester St (☎03/365 2888). Beautifully located restaurant in a glass-sided bandstand on the banks of the Avon serving premium New Zealand cuisine such as Canterbury lamb cutlets and kumara or orange roughy with capsicums and shrimps for around $25. Closed Sat lunch & Sun dinner; licensed & BYO.

556/CHRISTCHURCH AND SOUTH TO OTAGO

Vesuvio, 182 Oxford Terrace (☎03/365 4183). East and west come together at this European-style café with plenty of teppanyaki cuisine all using fresh local ingredients. Open for lunch and dinner daily; positively riotous at weekends. Licensed.

Papanui Road and Merivale

There's little culinary reason to leave the city centre and head out to the suburbs, but if you are staying along Papanui Road or in the northern reaches of the city, then there are some handy and reputable places to dine nearby.

All the following places are marked on the map on p.548.

Aikmans, 154 Aikmans Rd, Merivale. A moderately priced café/bar with a laid-back atmosphere, and serving all-day breakfast, and a broad range of salads, pasta dishes and curries for lunch and dinner. More of a bar as the evening wears on. Licensed.

Bologna, 6 Papanui Rd (☎03/379 7497). Tiny country Italian restaurant with a short menu of traditional and gourmet pizzas plus pasta dishes and Italian desserts, all served without fuss at modest prices. There's a bottle store across the road; handy since it is BYO only.

Brigitte's Espresso/Wine Bar, Hawkesbury Building, Aikmans Rd, Merivale. Conveniently located opposite *Aikmans*, this is a another relaxed place with an open courtyard at the back, and good-quality Mediterranean and Kiwi-style food as well as some wonderful New Zealand-Thai combinations, all at moderate prices. Licensed.

Kannigas Thai, 18a Papanui Rd (☎03/355 6228). Great Thai food served in fairly soulless surroundings at low prices – try the chicken pad Thai ($12) or ginger prawn and rice ($15). BYO.

New Brighton and Sumner

You are not going to starve during your day at the beach. With one notable exception, New Brighton makes do with cheap-and-cheerful beachfront cafés and takeaways, but Sumner is well endowed with notable places to dine and drink. You might even want to come out here for the evening, especially considering the #31 bus back to the city runs until gone 11pm.

All the following places are marked on the map on p.548.

Celini's, 32 Nyland Rd, Sumner. Bright, bustling and modestly priced café serving a wide range of dishes from Indonesian sweet beef curry and Akaroa smoked salmon salad to Mediterranean vegetable stuffed pita, smoothies and coffee. Licensed and BYO.

Club Bazaar Pizzeria, 15 Wakefield Avenue, Sumner. Bar and elaborate balcony where you can sample cheap pasta dishes and pretty acceptable pizzas in a distinctive atmosphere of Kiwi nostalgia. Licensed.

On the Beach, 25 The Esplanade, Sumner. Excellent seafood dinners served up on the veranda or inside this light and spacious restaurant built out over the sand beside Cave Rock. Prices reflect the location, with mains starting around the $20 mark. Licensed.

Ruptured Duck, 4 Wakefield Ave, Sumner. Pizza palace where a large polystyrene duck watches your every mouthful of such popular favourites as Moroccan lamb and capsicums or pork with kumara – toppings that are an acquired taste but have a cult following. Licensed & BYO.

Waterfront Café & Bar, Marine Parade at the foot of the pier, New Brighton. New café that's become *the* place for coffee, lunches and dinners such as salmon ravioli ($13) or tempura seafood ($20). Sit inside or out, sheltered from the onshore breeze by glass panels. Licensed.

Drinking, nightlife and entertainment

Gone are the days when evenings in Christchurch revolved around decaying, male-dominated Edwardian pubs. The modern city harbours enough traditional hostelries, late-night cafés and throbbing music bars to suit most tastes, and many of these offer more than just booze: live music, resident DJs and good food are increasingly taken for granted. After about 10pm the restaurants of "The Strip" (see pp.554–5) metamorphose into rowdy bars and clubs: just follow the crowds.

Serious music and drama are centred on venues like the Town Hall and the Arts Centre, while less cerebral entertainment is offered by a concentration of downtown clubs and a clutch of city-centre cinemas. Entertainment **listings** are published in Christchurch's daily newspaper *The Press* (the "What's On" section on Fridays is best for live music and clubbing), and in the free monthly magazines *Volume* and *Presto*.

Drinking

Most drinking venues are to be found within the Four Avenues, with Colombo and Cashel streets harbouring a particularly dense concentration of watering holes. This is probably the best place to stroll at weekends, when a variety of establishments use loud music and late licences to pull in the crowds.

Pubs and bars

Azure, 128 Oxford Terrace. Live music bar with jazz or a solo pianist on selected evenings, and a DJ and lively atmosphere at weekends.

The Bog, 82 Cashel Mall. Rowdy Irish bar with draught stouts and bitters plus live music Wed–Sat evenings.

Brewers Arms, 177 Papanui Rd, Merivale. Northwest of the centre, this is a suburban pub with horse brasses, a range of beers, and English-style pub food in large portions at moderate prices. Open from 11am until late.

Coyote, 126 Oxford Terrace. The heart of "The Strip" (see p.554) which, around 10pm, becomes one of the main gathering places before a night's clubbing.

Dux de Lux, cnr Hereford St & Montreal St. Ever popular restaurant (see p.555) that doubles as a great bar with several award-winning beers bred on the premises. Live music Thurs–Sun and no cover charge.

Ferg's One Street Over, 165 Hereford St. A barn-like sports bar in the American tradition with big-screen TV, snacks, and a wide range of domestic and imported beers.

Fin Bar, Gloucester St. Traditional Irish pub with occasional live music.

Loaded Hog, cnr Manchester St & Cashel St. Comfortable but ever-busy city-centre boozer with ales brewed on the premises, and good bar meals in the $10—15 range served all day. DJs on hand Thurs–Sat.

Main Street Café & Bar, 840 Colombo St (☎03/365 0421). Ever popular bar attached to the vegetarian café of the same name (see p.555) with a huge range of imported an local beers, and the most avant-garde (and least comfortable) bar stools in town.

Clubs and gigs

Christchurch may not be the clubbing capital of the southern hemisphere, but there's a sprinkling of places within the Four Avenues offering a range of dance-music styles. Some of these are full-on **club venues**, although there's a growing number of bars which transform themselves into dancing venues at weekends by drafting in a DJ or two. There's a surfeit of bars offering **live music**, although most places content themselves with a meagre diet of cover bands or minor local rock acts. If you want to just stroll around and see where the crowds are going, make for Lichfield Street, a heady mix of cutting-edge dance clubs and seedy massage parlours.

There's a club info line (☎03/363 5000) giving a rundown of what's on from night to night.

BASE, 674 Colombo St (☎03/377 7149). Dark and sweaty high energy club with guest DJs mainly spinning platters from the UK dance scene. Open until late Thurs–Sat. Cover charge $3–10.

Civic, 186 Manchester St. Popular clubbing venue offering a range of themed nights (eg funk, hip-hop, rare groove, house, techno); check listings in *The Press* to see what's on. 10pm–6am.

The Edge, 85 Hereford St. Open-fronted bar that becomes more clubby as the evening wears on, purveying mainstream techno to a youthful clientele. Occasional spoken word and poetry performances too.

Illusions, cnr Chancery Lane & Gloucester St. Longstanding disco with conservative reputation, playing anything from the 1960s to the current crop of chart toppers, and hosting live dance music from time to time. Strict dress code (no trainers, sandals, jeans or T-shirts). Daily 9pm–late. Regular clubnights such as *Club Lovely*.

Lone Star, 26 Manchester St. A jumping bar and nightspot that also serves an eclectic mix of Southwestern and Cajun food.

Ministry, 88–90 Lichfield St (✆03/379 2910). About the biggest and liveliest of the clubs; deep, dark and with a thumping base 'till very late.

Occidental Pub and Chats Club, Hereford St, opposite Latimer Square. Buzzing spot with live bands on Fridays & Saturdays and dance music.

Platinum, 76 Lichfield St (✆03/377 7891). Dark cellar bar with thumping dance music In the main room and a quieter cocktail bar out the back.

Tuskers Bar and Bistro, 3km south of the centre at 155 Colombo St, Beckenham. Live music bar with local bands playing mostly mainstream rock covers.

A Maori concert, theatre, classical music, cinema and spectator sports

Apart from in Rotorua, the best chance you'll get to sample a Maori concert (and savour a hangi) is here in Christchurch at the **Nga Hau E Wha National Marae**, 250 Pages Rd ("Marae of the Four Winds"; ✆0800/456 898, fax 03/388 7692, *www. nationalmarae.co.nz*), which was set up in 1990 to symbolize the meeting of people from all points of the compass. The meeting house, one of the largest in New Zealand, is named Aoraki after Mount Cook (see box on p.622), and the carved posts (*poupou*) depict ancient and contemporary ancestors, acting as memory aids encouraging the continuation of oral tradition. A unique feature is the appearance of two European ancestors (one of which is Captain Cook), intended to symbolize the coming together of the two peoples (for more on *Maoritanga*, see "Contexts" on p.859). Provided they get enough advance bookings, there's a choice of two events: the "Night of Maori Magic" (daily 6.45pm; $60) follows pretty much along the lines of the Rotorua-style concert and hangi (see p.277) but includes a detailed look around the marae with a full explanation of the protocol and tribal history; the "Maori Tour and Concert" (daily 7.55pm; $27.50), is the same except that there's no hangi. Free transport is laid on for those with reservations.

The shining star in Christchurch's **drama** firmament is the Arts Centre's Court Theatre, 20 Worcester Boulevard (bookings ✆0800/333100 & 03/366 6992, *www.courttheatre. org.nz*), home to one of New Zealand's longest-standing and most highly reputed professional theatre companies. Their current and upcoming performances are well advertised around town and in *The Press*. Touring shows frequently play in the James Hay Theatre at the Town Hall on Victoria Square (box office ✆03/366 8899), which also has a programme of **classical music** and ballet in the main auditorium.

Concerts by touring **jazz** and **rock** acts take place either at the Arts Centre, or at the Theatre Royal on Gloucester Street (✆03/366 6326), a fine old Edwardian venue which attracts the glitzier, more mainstream acts. You can catch a host of local jazz and rock performers playing in some of the bars and clubs listed under "Drinking" and "Clubs and gigs", on p.557. There is also a varied programme of music events in Hagley Park throughout the summer (✆03/371 1495, *www.summertimes.org.nz*).

MOVING ON FROM CHRISTCHURCH

Straddling the main road and rail routes down the east coast, Christchurch provides easy air, road and rail access to most parts of the South Island.

The quickest way of getting around the South Island is **by air**, with Air New Zealand and Ansett New Zealand (for contact numbers see "Listings", overleaf) operating direct daily flights to Dunedin, Hokitika, Invercargill, Mount Cook, Nelson, Queenstown and Timaru, with other destinations reached via Wellington.

By comparison, **trains** (☎0800/692 378) represent a much cheaper but relatively time-consuming way of getting around, with only one passenger train daily heading south from Christchurch towards Dunedin and Invercargill, calling in at Ashburton, Timaru and Oamaru on the way. Services are equally sparse to Picton at the northern end of the South Island. By far the most popular train journey from Christchurch is the **TranzAlpine to Greymouth**, a Kiwi classic which crosses the Canterbury Plains then climbs the Southern Alps to Arthur's Pass before descending to the West Coast. So spectacular is this journey that many people treat it as a day out from Christchurch: for more details see box p.606.

Most inter-city journeys are best attempted by **bus** or **shuttle bus** which are reasonably frequent to major destinations, though it is worth bearing in mind that journeys from, say, Christchurch to Nelson or Queenstown are likely to take up most of the day. Almost all companies now operate a door-to-door policy picking up and dropping off at the visitor centres, main hostels, some hotels and airports where applicable. Usually there's no additional cost, though there is sometimes a charge if you are being picked up outside Christchurch's central Four Avenues area. The main exception to this rule is the nationwide InterCity/Newmans, whose services currently depart from the junction of Gloucester and Manchester streets. These companies run the following services:

Akaroa Shuttles (☎0800/500 929): to Akaroa.

Alpine Coaches (☎0800/274 888): to Greymouth and Hokitika via Arthur's Pass.

Atomic Shuttles (☎03/322 8883): north to Kaikoura, Blenheim, and Picton; south to Ashburton, Timaru, Oamaru and Dunedin; west to Greymouth, then down the West Coast to Queenstown; and inland through Geraldine and Twizel to Wanaka and Queenstown.

Catch-a-bus (☎03/471 4103): south to Ashburton, Timaru, Oamaru and Dunedin then inland to Wanaka and Te Anau.

Coast to Coast (☎0800/800 847): to Greymouth and Hokitika via Arthur's Pass.

EastWest (☎0800/500 251): to Westport via Hanmer Springs and Reefton.

InterCity/Newmans (☎03/379 9020): north to Kaikoura, Blenheim, Picton and Nelson; south to Ashburton, Timaru, Oamaru, Dunedin and Invercargill; west to Arthur's Pass and Greymouth with connections to Westport, Hokitika and the Glaciers; and inland to Methven, Mount Cook, Wanaka and Queenstown.

Lazerline (☎0800/220 001): to Nelson via Hanmer Springs and Murchison.

Methven Travel (☎03/302 8106): to Methven.

South Island Connections (☎03/366 6633): south to Ashburton, Timaru, Oamaru and Dunedin; and north to Kaikoura, Blenheim, and Picton.

Southern Link Shuttles (☎03/358 8355): north to Kaikoura, Blenheim and Picton; and inland to Wanaka and Queenstown via Geraldine and Twizel.

Supa Kut Price Shuttles (☎0800/662 722): to Dunedin via Ashburton, Timaru and Oamaru.

White Star (☎ 03/323 6156): to Nelson via Hanmer Springs and Murchison.

If it is first-run international **movies** you are after, head for the city-centre multiplexes: the Regent, 94 Worcester St (☎03/366 0140), right by Cathedral Square; Hoyts 8, Moorhouse Ave (5503/366 6367), at the southern end of Manchester Street; and the Rialto, 250 Moorhouse Ave (☎03/374 9404) on the corner of Durham Street. **Arthouse** movies are shown at the Academy and Cloisters cinemas (☎ 03/366 0167, *www. artfilms.co.nz*) in the Arts Centre.

Jade Stadium, southeast of the centre near the junction of Moorhouse Avenue and Ferry Road, is the main venue for the big spectator **sports**, hosting **cricket** in the summer and **rugby** on weekends throughout the autumn and winter. **Information** and **tickets** can be obtained from the stadium itself (☎03/366 2961) or from Canterbury All Sports (☎03/366 9688).

Listings

Airlines Air New Zealand, 702 Colombo St, Triangle Centre (☎03/353 2800, national reservations ☎0800/737 000, flight arrivals and departures ☎03/374 7100); Ansett New Zealand, Clarendon Towers, 78 Worcester St (☎0800/267 388 & 03/371 1185); British Airways (see Qantas); Japan Air Lines, Level 11 (☎03/365 5879); Korean Airlines, Christchurch International Airport (☎03/365 5147); Mount Cook Airlines, 91 Worcester St (☎0800/737 000); Qantas, Level 18, Price Waterhouse Building, 119 Armagh St (☎0800/808 767 & 03/379 6504); Singapore Airlines, Level 3, Forsyth Barr Building, cnr Armagh St & Colombo St (☎03/366 8003).

American Express 773 Colombo St (Mon–Fri 9am–5pm, plus Dec–Feb Sat 9am–noon; ☎03/365 7366).

Automobile Association 210 Hereford St (☎03/379 1280).

Ballooning Up Up And Away (☎03/358 9859) offers peaceful and eye-bulging hour-long balloon flights over Christchurch for around $200.

Banks and exchange Most banks have branches and ATMs on or near Colombo St and Hereford St. Foreign exchange is best conducted at American Express (see above); Thomas Cook (see p.562); Asia Pacific World Travel, cnr Hereford St & Manchester St (☎03/377 7703); and Travelex, 730a Colombo St (☎03/365 4194).

Bike rental The most convenient bike rental is from Trailblazers, 86 Worcester St by the Square (☎03/366 6033; $5 per hr, $20 per day), though you can also call City Cycle Hire (☎0800/343 848) who deliver machines to you accommodation or to the visitor centre. Note that Trailblazers also do long-term rentals with touring bikes equipped with panniers going for around $250 for 4wks.

Bookshops The majors, Whitcoulls and Dymock's are both in Cashel Street Mall. Other good highstreet bookshops are Editions Book Shop, 16 Colombo St; Kate Shepherd Women's Bookshop, 145 Manchester St; and Scorpio Books, 79 Hereford St; Liberty Books, 151 High St, are good for secondhand paperbacks; while Map World, 173 Gloucester St, have the best range of walking maps and street plans. Bookshops are generally open Mon–Thur 9am–5pm, Fri–Sat 10am–6pm.

Buying a vehicle Your best bet is to head along to the Canterbury Car Fair, Addington Raceway, Wrights Road (Sun 9am–noon; infoline ☎03/338 5525). There's usually a huge selection of used cars, vans, 4WDs and motorbikes and there are no fees for buyers (sellers pay $20). Hostel noticeboards are another good hunting ground with other hostellers often advertising their vehicle along with all sorts of accumulated paraphernalia – tents, sleeping mats, coolers, cooking equipment, deck chairs, you name it.

Car rental There are dozens of car rental places in Christchurch and yet from January to March you may have trouble landing anything if you don't book ahead. Deals come and go, so the best policy is to ring around either before you arrive, or plan to manage without a car for the first few days (you don't really need one in Christchurch) and call around once you arrive. Many companies have flyers all over town offering astonishingly cheap deals. Almost invariably they are less appealing on closer inspection with all manner of limitations and extra charges (mileage charges, long rental periods only, insurance etc). Of the majors, Avis, Budget, Hertz and Thrifty (see Basics p.30) all have offices at the airport; smaller agencies often deliver. The following are the majors plus some reputable local agencies: Ace, 237 Lichfield St (☎0800/202 029 & 03/366 3222, fax 377 4610); Avis, 26 Lichfield St (☎03/379 6133); Avon, 166 St Asaph St (☎03/379 3822); Better, 236 St Asaph St

(☎0800/269 696 & 03/365 2979, fax 365 6725); Budget, cnr Oxford Terrace & Lichfield St (☎03/366 0072, fax 365 7194); Hertz, 46 Lichfield St (☎03/366 0549, airport ☎03/358 6730); McDonalds, 156 Tuam St (☎0800/164 165 & 03/366 0929, fax 366 0927); National, 134 Victoria St (☎03/366 5574, fax 366 5027); Nationwide, 524 Wairakei Rd (☎03/359 2013, fax 359 2085); Pegasus, 127 Peterborough St (☎03/365 1100, fax 365 1104); Scotties, 288 Lincoln Rd (☎0800/736 825 & 03/338 0997, fax 338 0992); Thrifty, at the airport (☎03/358 7533); U–Save, 70 Moorhouse Ave (03/379 3492); Welco, 248 St Asaph St (☎03/366 2294).

Cruises see Lyttelton account on p.565.

Emergency services ☎111.

Festivals For the last few years the local city council has been enthusiastically backing a number of summer festivals, most of them much better than you'd expect to find elsewhere. Look out particularly for the Jazz Festival (mid-Oct); the World Buskers Festival (late Jan), which is lots of fun and free and mostly takes place around the Arts Centre and in front of the Dux De Lux; and the Festival of Romance (early to mid-Feb,) on the lead up to Valentine's Day.

Horse riding Heathcote Valley Riding School, 131 Bridle Path Rd, 500m from the Gondola terminal (☎03/384 1971), offers evening rides (Thurs & Sun 6pm; $30, including BBQ) and other horse treks in the Port Hills.

Internet access and email services Christchurch is littered with places offering Internet access, but none are bigger and more centrally sited than Vadal (daily 8am–10.30pm, *vadal@hotmail.com* on the north side of Cathedral Square, with fast connections, low prices and cheap international phone calls. Other places to try are: Cyber Café, 127 Gloucester St (Mon–Fri 8am–10pm, Sat & Sun 9am–8pm); Cyber Pass Internet Café, 27 Chancery Lane, near the Square (Mon–Fri 9am–9pm, Sat & Sun 11am–4pm); and E-Caf, 28 Worcester St above the Boulevard Bakehouse (daily 8am–midnight).

Left Luggage Vadal (see "Internet access" above) store luggage from $3 a day per item.

Library Christchurch Central Library, Gloucester St (Mon–Fri 10am–9pm, Sat 10am–4pm, Sun 1–4pm).

Medical treatment In emergencies call ☎111. Biggest of the hospitals is Christchurch Hospital, cnr Oxford Terrace & Riccarton Ave (☎03/364 0640; emergency dept ☎03/364 0270). For a doctor at any time call The 24 Hour Surgery, cnr Bealey Ave & Colombo St (☎03/365 7777, no appointment necessary). To obtain the number of the rostered after-hours **dentist** call the NZ Dental Association on ☎03/366 6644 ext 3002.

Mountain biking The Mountain Bike Adventure Company (☎0800/424 534) offers a range of trips, from just over an hour to a full day rattling around the hills ($45–70). For renting mountain bikes, see under "bike rental" opposite.

Paragliding Nimbus Paragliding (☎03/328 8383) and Phoenix Paragliding (☎ and fax 03/326 7634, *www.paragliding.co.nz*) both offer 20-minute tandem flights from around $80 per person; pick-ups available.

Pharmacies Urgent Pharmacy, 931 Colombo St, cnr Bealey Ave (☎03/366 4439) stays open daily until 11pm.

Police Central Police Station ☎03/379 3999.

Post office The main post office on Cathedral Square (☎03/353 1814) has post restante facilities.

Shuttle buses For airport and train station transfers shuttle buses offer a cheaper alternative to taxis. Try Carrington Services (☎03/352 6369), Just Shuttles (☎0800/742 000); PBS Shuttles (☎03/551 1111) and Super Shuttle (☎03/365 5655), who all run from Cathedral Square to the airport ($10 for one, $6 each for three). They'll also pick you up from your accommodation, although if you're catching a morning flight you should book your transfer the evening before.

Skiing Christchurch is within a couple of hours' drive of over ten skifields, all of which are covered elsewhere in the guide. They are Broken River (see p.610), Cragieburn (see p.610), Fox Peak (see p.621), Methven (see p.612), Mount Cheeseman (see p.610), Mount Cook (see p.630), Mount Dobson (see p.621), Mount Hutt (see p.615), Mount Olympus (see p.610), Porter Heights (see p.610) and Temple Basin (see p.610). For information on conditions dial the free Infophone number and enter the additional four-digit code for the service required (☎03/363 5000, plus 1101 for weather, 1102 for ski hire, 1103 for transport).

Swimming The handiest of the indoor pools is the Centennial Leisure Centre, Armagh St (Mon–Thurs 6am–9pm, Fri 6am–7pm, Sat & Sun 7am–7pm; ☎03/366 8917). There's also indoor swimming at the Queen Elizabeth II centre in New Brighton (see p.552); and an open-air pool at

Jellie Park Aqualand 4km northwest of the centre at Ilam Rd (Airport bus from Cathedral Square). Expect to pay $2–3 entry; waterslides may cost extra.

Taxis Blue Star (☎03/379 9799); Gold Band (☎03/379 5795).

Thomas Cook cnr Armagh St & Colombo St (☎03/379 6600; Mon–Thurs 8.30am–6pm, Fri 8.30am–8pm, Sat & Sun 10am–4pm).

Tours Guided walking tours (☎03/342 7634; daily: Oct–April 10am & 1pm; May–Sept 1pm; 2hr; $8), led by local volunteers who really know their stuff, start from a kiosk in Cathedral Square near the cathedral entrance. Christchurch Sightseeing Tours (☎0508/669 660, *www.christchurchtours.co.nz*) offer three tours and combinations which save $5–10): City Gardens (mid-Sept to early Dec & mid-Jan to March Tues–Sat 9.30am–12.30pm; $25) visits four or their roster of 20 gardens each day; Heritage Homes (Wed & Sat 1.30–4.30pm; $25) calls at three homes not normally open to the public; and Sightseeing (mid-Sept to mid-April daily 9am & 1.30pm, mid-April to mid-Sept 1.30pm) spends 3–4hr touring the vicinity including Mona Vale, Sumner, Lyttelton and the Summit Road. Christchurch Wildlife Cruises (☎0800/436 574; *www.blackcat.co.nz*) runs two-hour Hector's dolphin spotting cruises on Lyttelton Harbour (Nov–March 10am & 2.30pm; April–Oct 2.30pm only; $39). They depart from Lyttelton Marina at Magazine Bay, but there's a free shuttle running from the Christchurch visitor centre half an hour before the boat departure. For tours of the wineries, see box below.

Train information ☎0800/802 802.

Travel agencies Your best bets are Destinations Travel, 485 Papanui Rd (☎03/352 2612); Flight Centre, 761 Colombo St (☎03/377 1441); Guthrey United Travel, 126 Cashel St (☎03/379 3560); STA, 90 Cashel St (☎03/379 9098) or Student University Building, Canterbury University (☎03/348 6372); and Usit Travel Centre, 158 Cashel St (☎03/379 8046, fax 374 6519, *www.usitbeyond.co.nz*, *enquiries@usitbeyond.co.nz*).

Whitewater rafting Easily the best trip in these parts is with Rangitata Rafts (☎0800/251 251, *www.rangitata.rafts.co.nz*, *mail@rangitata.rafts.co.nz*) who run the Grade IV+ gorge section of the Rangitata River between September and May ($115). It is a full day out from Christchurch with around 3hr on the water.

AROUND CHRISTCHURCH

Far too many travellers head straight from Christchurch towards the mountains to the west or Otago to the south, thereby missing out on the many attractions on the city's own doorstep. North of Christchurch are the rich agricultural flatlands of the northern Canterbury Plains, a pleasantly rural area which harbours the sleepy town of **Kaiapoi**, and the vineyards and wineries included in the **Canterbury Wine Trail**, a popular tourist itinerary among more bibulous visitors. However, the city's main vacation area

---

THE CANTERBURY WINE TRAIL

Canterbury is now the country's fourth largest wine producing region with the cool, temperate climate lending itself to Chardonnay, Riesling and especially Pinot Noir. There are two main areas: the immediate vicinity of Christchurch has upwards of a dozen wineries within twenty minutes' drive of the city; while the go-ahead Waipara area, an hour's drive to the north, has another large and rapidly increasing concentration. Many are beautifully situated and there are plenty of opportunities to sample **fine wines** and **gourmet food**. For well written descriptions of the wineries and their historical context, pick up a copy of the *Canterbury Wine Trail* leaflet (free from Christchurch visitor centre), by A.K. Grant, one of New Zealand's leading wine writers.

To avoid the need for a designated driver, join either the afternoon-only Vin de Pays **wine tour** (☎03/357 8262, fax 358 2539, *www.canterburyvindepays.co.nz*; $49), which visits four wineries either around Christchurch or around Waipara; or the full-day trip with Canterbury Wine Trails (☎03/381 5320, fax 381 5020; $85) which tours up to six wineries around Waipara.

is **Banks Peninsula**, southeast of Christchurch, an imposing lump of largely volcanic rock penetrated by fiord-like fingers of deep water. At the peninsula's northern end, **Lyttelton** is a hard-edged international cargo port which controls access to the bays and coves of a large inlet known as **Lyttelton Harbour**. Further south, chintzy, French-influenced **Akaroa** is a classic seaside resort, enduringly popular with week-ending city folk. There are some excellent **walking** opportunities in the **Port Hills** between Lyttelton and Christchurch, and around **Mount Bradley** and **Mount Herbert** south of Lyttelton Harbour.

Kaiapoi, Lyttelton and Akaroa are all served **by bus** from Christchurch, although once you stray beyond these centres you'll be largely on your own.

North of Christchurch

North of Christchurch, SH1 heads straight and true along the coast. As you leave the city suburbs, you pass one or two vineyards (see "Canterbury Wine Trail" box opposite) and a lot of the patchwork-quilt fields so typical of the Canterbury Plains. With flat farm country to its west and Pegasus Bay to its east, the road bisects a series of tiny communities such as **Kaiapoi**, many containing camping facilities for holidaymakers wishing to gaze at the bay or fish the waters.

Kaiapoi and beyond
Nineteen kilometres north of Christchurch, SH1 crosses the braided Waimakariri River, and rolls into the small town of **KAIAPOI**. Once a flourishing port with a reputation for producing high-quality woollen goods, Kaiapoi faded into insignificance after it had been bypassed by the railway. It's now a satellite town for Christchurch commuters, who constitute about sixty percent of the town's population, and has little of note – unless you are an angler keen to flick the rivers for trout or salmon. The best thing to do in Kaiapoi is take a trip on the 80-year-old **MV Tuhoe**, a twin-masted, steam-powered schooner which is moored in the Kaiapoi River near the William Street Bridge. Most weekends, weather and tides permitting, the *Tuhoe* still chugs, albeit slowly, down the Kaiapoi until it merges with the Waimakariri River and the sea (1hr 20min; $10; buy tickets an hour before sailings at Williams Street Bridge kiosk; ☎03/327 8721). Tide and sailing times are published in Saturday's edition of *The Press*.

About 32km further north at the junction of SH1 and SH7 is **Waipara**, a town with six **wineries** within a 3km radius, each producing excellent, inexpensive white wines (tastings available on request 11am–5pm; expect to pay $3–5). From Waipara you can either head along SH1, a pretty unexciting haul towards Cheviot (see p.531) on the way to Kaikoura, or turn inland along the SH7 Lewis Pass Road towards Hanmer Springs (see p.599).

Banks Peninsula

Flying into Christchurch only the least observant could fail to be struck by the dramatic contrast between the flat plains of Canterbury and the rugged, fissured topography of **Banks Peninsula**, a volcanic thumb sticking out into the Canterbury Bight. When James Cook sailed by in 1769 he erroneously charted it as an island and named it after his botanist Joseph Banks. His error was only one of time, as this basalt lump initially formed as an island, one only joined to the land as silt sluiced down the rivers of the eastern flanks of the Southern Alps has accumulated to form the plains.

The fertile **volcanic** soil of the peninsula's valleys sprouted totara, matai and kahikatea trees which, along with the abundant shellfish in the bays, attracted early

BANKS PENINSULA

CHRISTCHURCH

N

ACCOMMODATION
Kaihope Cottage	A
Kawatea Farmstay	B
Le Bons Bay Backpackers	D
Le Bons Bay Motor Camp	E
Rosslyn Estate	C

Sumner
Lyttelton Tunnel
Taylor's Mistake
GODLEY HEAD RESERVE
Sign of the Takahe
Summit Road
Sign of the Kiwi
Governors Bay
Lyttelton
Lyttelton Harbour
Ripapa Island
Diamond Harbour
Quail Island
Parau
Sign of the Bellbird
Mt Bradley & Mt Herbert Walkways
Mt Bradley 855m
Port Levy
Port Levy Road
Pigeon Bay
Little Akaloa Bay
Little Akaloa
Okains Bay
Mt Herbert 920m
Sign of the Packhorse
Remarkable Dykes
Pigeon Bay
Summit Road
Maori & Colonial Museum
Le Bons Bay
75
Hilltop
Barrys Bay
Duvauchelle
Cooptown
Little River
Birdland Sanctuary
French Farm
ONAWE SCENIC RESERVE
Robinsons Bay
French Farm Winery
Takamatua
Lake Ellesmere
Kaitorete Spit
Kaituna Lagoon
75
Lake Forsyth
Tikao
Wainui
Akaroa
Long Bay Rd
Banks Peninsula Track
Birdings Flat
Southern Bays Track
Onuku
Akaroa Harbour
Long Bay Stony Bay
Te Oka Bay
Peraki Bay
Flea Bay
Christchurch (82 km)
0   5 km

A
B
D
E

Maori around a thousand years ago. The trees soon succumbed to the fire stick, a process accelerated with the arrival of European timber milling interests. The lumber yards ground to a halt when the trees ran out in the late 1880s and the peninsula is now largely bald, with large areas of tussock grass on the rolling hills, and tiny pockets of regenerating native bush.

Today, the two massive drowned craters which form Banks Peninsula are key to the commerce of the region. Lyttelton Harbour protects and nurtures the port town of **Lyttelton**, disembarkation point for many of the fledgling provinces migrants and now the South Island's major port. It is a workaday town, but interesting for its historic time-ball station, harbour cruises and a couple of entertaining places to eat and drink. It maintains a healthy disrespect for the more visitor-oriented activities out east where Akaroa Harbour has no commercial traffic at all, except for a few pleasure trips taking visitors **swimming with dolphins**. There's also an altogether more refined and pres-tigious tone to the town of **Akaroa**; picturesque and French-influenced on account of its first of batch settlers who arrived from France at the same time as northern Maori and the British were signing the Treaty of Waitangi. Elsewhere on the peninsula, a net-work of narrow, twisting roads – not least the ridge-crest-hugging Summit Road – wind along the crater rims and dive down to gorgeous, quiet bays once alive with whalers, sealers and shipbuilders, but now seldom visited except during the peak of summer.

Despite the denuded and parched nature of much of the landscape, Banks Peninsula is very popular for relatively easy **scenic walks**, with panoramic views, geological features (such as ancient lava flows, or the dykes caused when fissures filled up with molten rock), relics from the earliest Maori and European settlers, and great beaches. A number of tracks cross private land and there are folk offering their services to deliver your pack to your destination. As befits a city playground, the peninsula is also well endowed with **country-style accommodation**, especially B&Bs and farmstays, and, particularly in Akaroa, **fine restaurants**.

The peninsula merits at least a day-trip from Christchurch. With more time on your hands, you could enjoyably spend two to three days exploring the quieter nooks and crannies. From Christchurch, the **main route** to Akaroa is the **SH75**, via Lake Ellesmere and Little River, but a more picturesque route follows the **Summit Road** from Sumner via Lyttelton, along the Port Hills and ridges of the peninsula. **Buses** from Christchurch serve only the main towns of Lyttelton and Akaroa, and to reach the smaller communities tucked into the bays you'll need your own transport, whether motorized or pedal-powered (see Christchurch listings, p.560, for car and bike rental details). If you're planning on cycling, bear in mind that the peninsula is extremely hilly, and the routes linking the summit road with the various bays below can be very steep. A good alternative is to join the Akaroa mail run (see p.579), as the long-suffering mail van winds in and out of the tiny bays.

Although the peninsula is prone to **sea mists** and storms, both the Port Hills and the peaks across the neck of the peninsula shelter it from the winds that blaze across the Canterbury Plains. The climate tends to be very warm in the summer and extremely cold in the winter but the **weather** is noted for its unpredictability, so it's worth carrying rain gear at any time of year.

Lyttelton

Just 12km from Christchurch city centre, **LYTTELTON** is a world apart, hemmed in by the rocky walls of the drowned **volcanic crater** that forms **Lyttelton Harbour**. Attractive though its setting is, Lyttelton is foremost a port, one where countless European migrants disembarked to start their new lives. It still retains a raffish air: rowdy clanking from the docks, rumbustious waterfront bars, and plenty of overheard snippets of Polish, Russian and Filipino. Boats servicing the New Zealand and US bases in Antarctica leave from here, and there are even a few dozen cruise ships calling each year, though the passengers are bussed off to Christchurch as soon as they arrive.

The town itself overlooks the docks and quays, climbing up the Port Hills behind and spreading southwest along the coast toward Governors Bay. Running parallel to the waterfront, the main road of Norwich Quay is fringed by a series of down-at-heel pubs designed to attract dockers, ships' crews and lorry drivers. The web of streets behind are primarily residential, although it's here that the best bars, restaurants, shops and accommodation possibilities are to be found.

Arrival, information and accommodation

The quickest way **from Christchurch** to Lyttelton is through the 4km Lyttelton Tunnel which ejects you right in the heart of town, just twenty minutes after leaving Christchurch. The #28 **bus** from Cathedral Square leaves about every half hour (35min; $3.60 return) and can drop you right by the **visitor centre**, 20 Oxford St (daily 9am–5pm; ☎03/328 9093, fax 328 9094, *lyttinfo@ihug.co.nz*). The staff will hand out a leaflet describing a **self-guided walk** around Lyttelton's many historic sites and help you learn what lurks behind Lyttelton's workaday facade, pointing you to ninety-minute **guided historic walks** (Nov–March Tues & Thurs 11am, Sun 1.30pm; $5), which start by the Signal Box (see p.567).

Accommodation right in Lyttelton is somewhat limited, though there is an excellent backpackers and a couple of B&Bs. Most of the best places are some way out of town around Lyttelton harbour, along with the only campsite that is remotely close.

Dockside, 22 Sumner Rd (☎03/328 7344). Central, self-catering B&B apartment with a sunny ensuite room and a deck with panoramic harbour views. Continental breakfast included. ④.

Harbour View Homestay, 3 Harbour View Terrace, Cass Bay (☎03/328 7250, fax 328 7251, *harbourview.homestay@clear.net.nz*). Three kilometres west of Lyttelton on the way to Governors Bay, this relaxed house has one double and two single rooms with shared facilities, a sun deck around a solar-heated pool and sauna. ⑤.

Orchard House, Governors Bay (☎03/329 9622). Pleasant accommodation 8km from Lyttelton in a small, address-free settlement (phone ahead if you need directions). The house offers views of the harbour and surrounding farmland; the double room has French doors that open onto a deck where breakfast is served, weather permitting. ④.

Parau Motor Camp, Diamond Harbour (☎03/329 4702, fax 329 4212). Pleasant campsite situated among tall sheltering trees and across the road from the bay, 2km from Diamond Harbour and half an hour's drive from Lyttelton. There's cabins, a bunkhouse, a shop, pool and a kitchen. Tent sites $10 per pitch, dorms ①, cabins ③.

Randolph House B&B, 49 Summer Rd (☎03/328 8877, fax 328 8779, *randolph@netaccess.co.nz*). Set in a nineteenth-century wooden villa, this guesthouse has a double attic bedroom, comfortable rooms with shared facilities, grand views over the harbour and tasty breakfasts ⑥.

Tunnel Vision Backpackers, 44 London St (☎ & fax 03/328 7576). Without doubt the best place to stay in Lyttelton, this is a brightly decorated, well-maintained, first-class backpackers, occupying a renovated old hotel in a central location, right by the town's more interesting bars, cafés and restaurants. Added bonuses are an outside deck, free tea and coffee and a good selection of double and twin rooms some with harbour views. Dorms ①, rooms ②.

The Town

There is one attraction above all others for which Lyttelton is famous – the **Timeball Station,** Reserve Terrace (daily 10am–5pm; $2.50), a steep 1km climb up Sumner Road from the centre. Built by prisoners in 1876 it looks for all the world like a Gothic tower that has carelessly lost its castle. It is clearly visible from all over town and harbour, and for over fifty years mariners recalibrated their on-board chronometers – critical for accurate navigation – on the descent of a large black ball down the pole on the roof. Radio signals replaced the timeball in 1934 and the station fell into disrepair, but progressive restoration since the 1970s has left it in immaculate condition. Once again, the ball is hoisted up its pole every day at precisely 12.57pm, then on the stroke of 1pm (to the nearest half-second) it begins its descent. Inside the station are a number of exhibits explaining the importance of the timeball to navigational techniques, plus the oily mechanism itself. The view from the roof is superb, and you can see the battered zinc ball close up.

Another intriguing attraction is **Lyttelton Museum,** Norwich Quay (Tues, Thurs, Sat & Sun 2–4pm; donations appreciated), a former Seaman's Institute where you are greeted by a penguin. The nautical flavour lingers in a display of ancient telescopes, which straightfacedly informs visitors that the size and elaborateness of a sailor's telescope denoted his rank. Other exhibits reflect the town's history, while the Antarctic display spotlights Scott and Shackleton, both of whose expeditions set out from Lyttelton. Other curious artefacts have been salvaged from the small shelters built during the nineteenth century on various islands off the New Zealand shore, which were supplied with provisions to cater for unfortunate shipwrecked souls. Overall, the museum has the air of a long-neglected attic filled with a mishmash of collectibles, among which are occasional jewels such as a fossilized crab and watercolours of early Lyttelton personalities.

Opposite the museum is the wooden **Lyttelton Signal Box,** relocated here from the mouth of the Moorhouse Rail Tunnel through to Christchurch, and tagged by a 1902 halfpenny (above the entrance) marking the date of the box's construction.

Docked at the wharf opposite Norwich Quay, over the Overhead Bridge, is the black **Steam Tug Lyttelton** (Mon–Sat 10am–4pm; donations requested), the older of only two steam tugs still operating in the country. Built in Glasgow by the Ferguson brothers in 1907, this beautiful antique boat is maintained in full working order by an impassioned bunch of volunteers. If you climb aboard, one of the volunteers will escort you on an unofficial and extremely informative tour, which includes a museum occupying the captain's cabin, officers' quarters, saloon and other cabins. The boiler room is particularly impressive: all sparkling brass and oily pistons, it was at the cutting edge of technology in its heyday, with steam-power-assisted steering. On Sundays, throughout most of the year, the tug also fires up for some thrilling round-trip **cruises** (book ahead on ☎03/322 8911; 2pm; 1hr 30min; $12), steaming all the way to the head of the harbour.

Prettiest of the town's churches is the 1860 **Holy Trinity Anglican Church,** on the corner of Winchester Street and Canterbury Street, which was originally earmarked as the Cathedral of the Diocese, a status never afforded it once building started in

Christchurch. Diagonally opposite stands **Dr Upham's** 1907 house: for over fifty years the two-storey house served as the home for this saintly doctor. He is remembered for his devotion to the lepers of Quail Island, his refusal to accept money from patients who could not afford to pay, and his penchant for walking the town accompanied by his faithful hound. The good doctor is also commemorated at the end of Winchester Street by the **Upham Memorial Clock**, which stands in the Rose Garden on the site of the old jail – the remains of a couple of the cells can be seen on the northern side of the gardens. Built in 1851, the jail became the South Island's major penal institution, even accommodating sheep rustler James McKenzie (see box p.620) for a time. Above the jail site is the Old Cemetery, full of gravestones dating back to the earliest settlers, except for the seven who were hanged at the jail between 1868 and 1918 – they did not merit a stone.

Eating and drinking

Lyttelton has a well-founded reputation for quality food and a nightlife that's way livelier than you'd expect for such a small town. In fact, a trip to Lyttelton is justified solely on the intention to dine at the *Volcano Café* and then troop over to the road to sample the pleasures of the *Wunderbar*.

The Deluxe Café & Bar, 18 London St. Polished wooden furnishings and floors provide a relaxing setting for high-quality moderately priced lunches and dinners.

Dockside, 39 Norwich Quay. Small hexagonal building good for gourmet pizza ($18), mains based on organic beef and ostrich ($20), and good coffee and cake. From Friday to Sunday you can sit on the deck and watch the timeball do its thing over lunch, and every evening there are sunsets over the railway lines and port: a lot nicer than it sounds. Licensed.

Satchmo, 8 London St. Casual restaurant and bar with a good line in salads, gourmet pizzas (from $12) and pasta dishes ($14) served in a peaceful garden or inside with background jazz. Licensed.

The Ship Shape Café, 91 Norwich Quay. Breakfast is served from 7.45am ($7.50 and up), followed by lunch and Devonshire teas ($4); closes at 4pm. Closed Sat & Sun.

Volcano, 42 London St (☎03/328 7077). A Lyttelton institution fashioned out of a former fish and chip shop with bright, eclectic decor and meals served on Formica tables all with fresh flowers. Cuisine draws on Cajun, Mexican, Spanish and Italian influences, with all sorts of home-made treats in substantial portions (mains $20–25). Licensed and BYO.

Wunderbar, London St. An idiosyncratic late-night drinking-hole and club with decor ranging from crushed velour to a gruesome doll's-head lightshade. There's pool, table football and a wonderful deck overlooking the harbour that's great for a peaceful drink if you can't take the clamour within. Entertainment ranges from 1940s and 50s cabaret nights, through poetry, live bands, stand-up comics, club and disco music, to film noir evenings. Mon–Fri 5pm–late, Sat & Sun 3pm–even later. Entry is down steps beside the supermarket, and up an iron fire escape.

Around Lyttelton Harbour

Lyttelton would be nothing without its harbour, and it would be a shame to spend time here without venturing onto it to gain a sense of its maritime importance. Boats reached Lyttelton through "the heads", best seen from Godley Head – a moody, grass- and rock-covered promontory with steep sea cliffs offering excellent views. On the water, the main destinations are the small community of **Diamond Harbour**, and two islands: **Quail Island** in the centre of Lyttelton Harbour and the tiny **Ripapa Island** just east of Diamond Harbour. Both are havens for birds, as well as offering solitude and superb views; for access to the islands, see box opposite.

Godley Head

At the northernmost tip of the harbour, **Godley Head** stands guard – a spectacular piece of land with high cliffs and excellent views, administered by the DOC. Follow the signs east out of Lyttelton to the Summit Road, which takes you out onto Godley Head (about 10km) and the **Godley Head Reserve**, a delightfully scenic spot for walks and

---

LYTTELTON HARBOUR CRUISES AND KAYAKING

A variety of **cruises** depart from Lyttelton offering a splendid sea-level perspective on the harbour. If you can do without a commentary or simply want more time to explore, check out the regular ferry services to Diamond Harbour and Quail Island (see below) run by Lyttelton Harbour Cruises (☎03/328 8368) who depart from Jetty B opposite Norwich Quay: most sailings link with the #28 bus from Christchurch.

If you have more money to spare, Coastline Adventures will take you out from Jetty A on their wonderfully atmospheric *Fox II* (☎03/384 9238; daily 9.30am & 12.30pm; $50), a wooden boat built in 1922 and still powered by its original engine. The cruise takes a good look round Lyttelton Harbour, stopping in Governors Bay for lunch before leaving the Harbour to explore Pigeon Bay and Port Levy.

Another peaceful, though rather more energetic way to explore the harbour is with Quail Island Adventure Company who run guided four-hour **kayak trips** (☎03/328 7648; $56). With average fitness and some experience you can check out volcanic rock formations, beaches, islands, shipwrecks, bird colonies and caves, with the prospect of seeing Hector's dolphins and other wildlife up close.

Hector's dolphins are also the target of The Dolphin Adventure run by Canterbury Sea Tours (☎03/326 5607) who offer informative morning (2hr; $40) and afternoon (3hr 30min; $70) trips, the latter with Devonshire tea at Godley House in Diamond Harbour.

---

picnics. The walkway network is extensive, in places stumbling across installations left behind after World War II, including dark warren-like tunnels and searchlight emplacements perched like birds' nests on the cliffs. From here, you can also walk down to the tiny coastal settlements of Boulder Bay and Taylors Mistake (see box on p.553).

Diamond Harbour

In bright sunlight the harbour sparkles like a million gems at **Diamond Harbour**, directly across the water from Lyttelton. Harbour Cruises (see box above) operate passenger **ferries** (sailings every 1–2hr: Mon–Fri 6.15am–6.20pm, Sat & Sun 6.30am–5.30pm; $3.60 each way) across the harbour making a handy shortcut to Camp Bay, the Mount Herbert Walkway and the rest of Banks Peninsula. Arriving at the Diamond Harbour wharf you can generate a thirst with a 500-metre walk uphill, then slake it at either the *Country Store*, which does coffee, muffins and toasted sandwiches, or at **Godley House**, a popular vantage point with gardens and lawns overlooking Diamond Harbour which have attracted visitors from Christchurch and beyond for over a hundred years. The house has been co-opted by the conference market in recent years, but on summer weekends you can still buy a beer or lunch and sprawl out on the grass. If you want to stay over this way there's the *Parau Motor Camp* (see p.566) at Parau 2km east.

Quail and Ripapa islands

Set in mid-harbour, **Quail Island** was known by the local Maori as *Otamahau* because it was the place where children collected seabirds' eggs. It was used as a leper colony between 1907 and 1925 (when the afflicted were transported to Fiji), Shackleton and Scott quarantined their dogs here before his expedition to the South Pole, and the wrecks of several ships can sometimes be spied at low tide. These days it's a venue for day-trips, swimming and walking; it makes a relaxing and fascinating place to spend a day: pack provisions, plenty of drinking water (there's none on the island) and rain gear. Travel with Harbour Cruises (3–4 daily; $9 return), and pick up the *Quail Island Walkway* leaflet (50¢) from the Christchurch DOC office or the Lyttelton visitor centre, which details two circular **walking tracks** (1hr & 2hr 30min), both starting from the island's wharf.

Historically the defensibility of **Ripapa Island**, just off the southern shore of the Harbour near Diamond Harbour, has been its key feature. Successively a Maori pa, then the site of an 1880s fort built as a measure against a feared Russian invasion that never materialized, it later became a prison camp for Count Felix Von Luckner, a German "sea raider". The island now enjoys some peace as a historic reserve administered by the DOC, which can only be visited on **guided tours** run by Harbour Cruises (Christmas to mid-Jan daily 1.20pm; Nov–Christmas & mid-Jan to March Sun 1.20pm; $15).

Christchurch to Akaroa: SH75

With ample time on your hands and a taste for exploration consider approaching Banks Peninsula on the Summit Road (see box on p.572), which winds around the crater rim of Lyttelton Harbour then around the northern bays before finally dropping you down to Akaroa. A much faster and most convenient way of covering the 85km run **from Christchurch to Akaroa** is on SH75 which heads south from the city before curling southeast along the southern shore of the peninsula, then over the hills to Akaroa: it takes around an hour and a half, though there are reasons to pause along the way.

Lake Ellesmere and Little River
Around 30km from Christchurch SH75 tracks the water's edge of **Lake Ellesmere** (*Waihora*), a vast expanse of fresh water separated from the Pacific Ocean by the 30km-long Kaitorete spit, which juts southeastwards from Banks Peninsula to re-join the mainland. It's a picturesque area popular with fishermen, although other visitors will probably content themselves with the fine views of the lake to be had from the road. At the base of the spit is **Birdlings Flat**, a narrow shingle bank that has traditionally been a rich source of food for local Maori, who were granted protected fishing rights here in 1896; the accumulated shingle of the sheltering bank also provides a fossicking ground for greenstone and gems. Birdlings Flat separates the sea from **Lake Forsyth** (*Wairewa*), a long finger of water skirted by SH75 on the way to the tiny community of **LITTLE RIVER**, 53km from Christchurch, primarily of interest for the excellent café, bar and bakery of the *Little River Store*, and the **Old Railway and Craft Station** on Main Road, which houses a small **visitor centre** (Oct–April daily 9am–5pm; May–Sept daily 10am–4pm; ☎03/325 1255). There's also a reminder of the area's Maori heritage – a statue of Tangatahara, the famous chief of the ultimately unsuccessful defence of the Onawe Peninsula (see p.573), which stands in the town, alongside a lengthy Maori inscription describing many of his battles. Just before you enter town a sign on the right guides you to the **Birdlands Sanctuary,** Okuti Valley Road, 6km from Little River (*www.birdlands-sanctuary.co.nz*; Oct–April daily 9am–5pm; May–Sept Mon–Sat 9am–4pm; $8), a private venture dedicated to the preservation of New Zealand bird life, with a variety of paths running through different habitats. The kids will be happy hand-feeding the peacocks, ducks and pigeons; others may prefer a stroll through the bush along boardwalks to viewing platforms where bellbirds come to feed off the nectar supplied.

Little River is also the base for the circular **Southern Bays Track** (see box opposite). If you need somewhere to gather your strength for the Southern Bays Walkway or a place to rest up afterwards, try the *Birdland Sanctuary Holiday Park* right by the sanctuary (☎03/325 1141; tents $10.50, cabins ③). It's one of the prettiest **campsites** on the peninsula, with cooking facilities and a small shop.

Barry's Bay
From Little River, SH75 starts climbing the hills which separate Akaroa Harbour from the rest of Banks Peninsula. The road tops out at the *Hilltop Tavern* from where there

---

THE SOUTHERN BAYS TRACK

The spectacular **Southern Bays Track** (mid-Oct to May only), in the southwestern corner of Banks Peninsula, is a three-day (two-night) outing across private land, similar in character to the Banks Peninsula Track, but much more physically demanding, with many climbs and one **gruelling** ascent from sea level to 800m. The track crosses beaches, native bush, cliff tops and tussock, with the possibility of sighting shag colonies, seals and dolphins in between long vistas across to the Canterbury Plains and the Southern Alps.

There are three options, but all walkers spend both nights in comfortable road-accessible cottages equipped with hot showers, flush toilets, mattresses and cooking equipment. Those with confidence and strong legs can take the cheapest option – the so-called **Freedom Walk** ($98), where you carry your own food, sleeping bag and personal effects, and have to prepare your own meals. Less rugged individuals might prefer the **Freedom Walk – Packs Carried** ($98 per person plus a flat $110 for up to four people's packs), where your overnight gear is delivered to each cottage and the end of the walk. The most leisurely option is the **Guided Walk** ($680) where you just walk: everything is done for you, including making up the beds and cooking the meals.

Numbers are strictly limited, so advance bookings are pretty much essential; and there is a $10 fee to have your car delivered to the end of the track and safely stored: a wise course of action. Everyone needs good boots and wet-weather gear; Freedom walkers will also want a sleeping bag and enough food for three days.

---

is a great view of what is still to come, including the steep descent to **BARRY'S BAY**, right at the head of Akaroa Harbour. This is home to the settlers' original dairy factory, **Barry's Bay Cheese**, SH75 (☎03/304 5809; Mon–Fri 8am–5pm, Sat & Sun 9.30am–5pm), a bit of a tourist trap visited by all the coaches; though it is worth nipping in for free samples of their produce, much of which is pretty decent. Accounts of early cheese-making go back as far as 1844, when chessets (the traditional cheese moulds still in use today) were brought from Europe. Ironically, Banks Peninsula was one of the first areas in New Zealand to start producing and exporting cheese to Europe because the clean pastures produced such pure milk. All their cheeses are sold on the premises: try the cheddar, Barry's Bay Sharp, Havarti, Akaroa Mellow or Port Cooper, with one of the locally made chutneys or mustards on a piece of fresh bread for lunch.

In *Rosslyn Estate*, just off SH75 (☎ & fax 03/304 5804, *rosslyn@xtra.co.nz*; ⑥), Barry's Bay has one of the best **B&Bs** in the vicinity. It occupies a large 1860s country house with two luxurious en-suite rooms that contain queen-sized beds. There are extensive grounds for exploring, as well as home-baking on arrival and evening meals on request ($25).

French Farm

If you are interested in more formally presented cuisine, turn down the south fork off SH75 at Barry's Bay and head for **FRENCH FARM**. According to Maori tradition, the heights of French Farm were home to the *patupaiarehe* ("children of the mist"), whose chants can be heard on misty days or in the evenings. Of a more practical nature, the settlers in Akaroa used this fertile and sheltered area to establish orchards and vegetable plots to grow produce that would not otherwise have been available to them.

Some of the latter-day products of these plots can be sampled at the excellent **French Farm Winery and Restaurant**, French Farm Valley Road (☎03/304 5784, *www.frenchfarm.co.nz*; tasting daily 10am–5pm), a French-style villa set among native trees. They've only been producing wines for five years or so, but have already gained

THE SUMMIT ROAD AND BUSH WALKS FROM IT

Drivers – and particularly **cyclists** – should consider passing up the fast and relatively straight SH75 from Christchurch to Akaroa, in favour of the **Summit Road**, actually a sequence of connecting backroads which forms a giant S-shaped circuit around the peninsula's two crater harbours. Designed with pedestrians and wagons in mind, it keeps as close as possible to the ridge tops marking an undulating course – with few sustained ascents – and offering stupendous views all around. For cyclists, **traffic** is fairly sparse, but what there is tends to hare around blind corners, so keep your wits about you. Armed with the *Summit Road Map* ($6 from the Christchurch visitor centre) you can pinpoint the sights and identify trailheads for some of the fine short walks listed; nearly forty in all.

The Summit Road was the consuming passion of the public-spirited **Harry Ell**. He dreamed of building a highway with **walking tracks** and fourteen rest stations along the summit of the Port Hills and right around the peninsula. The project got under way at the turn of the twentieth century, and when Ell died in 1934 only four rest stations (mostly named after native birds) had been built. The first, sited at what was the southern limit of Christchurch trams (now bus #2), the junction of Dyers Pass Road and Takahe Drive, was the **Sign of the Takahe** – a Gothic-style house distinguished by enormous kauri beams, salvaged from a bridge that once spanned the Hurunui River. This house is now a café and evening restaurant, so for the price of a coffee you can still take a look at some unique friezes fashioned from old packing cases and stone quarried from the peninsula, which are kept in a memorial room. Look out for the heraldic embellishments relating to early governors of New Zealand, coats of arms of local families and shields portraying significant events in British history. From the Sign of the Takahe, Dyer's Pass Road runs 4km uphill to the Summit Road and the second rest station, the **Sign of the Kiwi**, now a reasonable café. This is perhaps the best place to start following the Summit Road. However, enthusiasts needing a sense of completeness should start at the true beginning by Godley head, near the Lyttelton Harbour entrance.

From the *Sign of the Kiwi* the Summit Road follows the ridgetops 9km southwest to the single remaining room of the third of Ell's structures, the **Sign of the Bellbird**, a stone picnic shelter with exceptional views. The last of the rest stations, the **Sign of the Packhorse**, is a trampers' hut off the Summit Road which can also be accessed on the **Mount Bradley Walkway** (13km return; 6hr). This starts from the Summit Road near Gebbie's Pass and heads through open country past the **Remarkable Dykes** – fissures created by the heat of volcanic activity, forming a receptacle for molten rock. As the molten rock cooled and solidified, it proved more resistant to erosion than the surrounding material, thereby creating the protruding ridges which were subsequently dubbed "dykes". The Walkway then skirts Mount Bradley through very old native bush and heads down to Diamond Harbour.

All Harry Ell's rest stations can also be reached as part of the worthwhile **Crater Rim Walkway** (18.5km; 4hr), a magical path along a part of the crater of the extinct Lyttelton volcano; the DOC's *Crater Rim Walkway* leaflet ($1) has a detailed map and further information

The Summit Road completes its circuit of Lyttelton Harbour by dropping down to Diamond Harbour and over to Port Levy, a tiny valley with a beach that once supported the largest Maori population in Canterbury. The Summit Road returns to follow the ridgetops, occasionally throwing spurs down the valleys to secluded coves such as **Pigeon Bay**, the lovely **Okains Bay** (see p.580) and **Le Bons Bay** (see p.579) before descending to Akaroa.

something of a reputation for their chardonnay and pinot noir ($1 per tasting, refunded with purchase). But the place is best known for its **food** and a better approach is to come for lunch or dinner and sample a glass with a meal at one of the two restaurants: the main restaurant garners the greatest acclaim with Pacific Rim cuisine served under an arbour (mains $25–30); *La Pizza* is less formal and serves excellent and large wood-fired examples ($19) along with grills and great gelato, again served outside.

Back on SH75 at Barry's Bay, it is only 12km to Akaroa, first passing a turn-off for the **Onawe Peninsula Scenic Reserve** (daily dawn–dusk), a peninsula that juts out into Akaroa Harbour, and once offered a highly defensible sanctuary for local Maori. Remains of the pa fortifications, deep ditches and ramparts are still distinguishable, despite years of farming. From there you pass through the tiny but pretty settlements of Duvauchelle, Robinson's Bay and Takamatua – originally known as German Bay after the first settlers who arrived with Akaroa's French.

Akaroa

The small waterside town of **AKAROA** ("long bay"), 82km from Christchurch on the eastern shores of Akaroa Harbour, comes billed as New Zealand's **French settlement**. Certainly the initial settlers came from France, some of their architecture survives and the street names they chose have stuck, but that's about as French as it gets. Nonetheless, the town milks the connection with a number of French-ish restaurants, some French sounding boutique B&Bs and a tricolour fluttering over the spot where the first settlers landed.

Still, it is a pretty place with attractive scenery all around, a smattering of low key activities to keep you occupied – including the **Banks Peninsula Track**, which starts and finishes nearby (see box on p.577) – and, most of all, a very relaxed air well suited to gentle strolls followed by quality cuisine and a comfy bed. These factors combine to make Akaroa a popular Kiwi holiday destination; a full two-thirds of its houses are *baches*, leaving only around 750 permanent residents.

Once the domain of the Ngai Tahu paramount chief, Temaiharanui, the site of Akaroa attracted the attention of some of Canterbury's earliest migrants. In 1838 a French Commander, Jean Langlois, purchased what he believed to be the entire peninsula for goods to the value of 1000 French francs, and returned to France to encourage settlers to sail with Captain Lavaud and populate a new French colony. However, while the French were making their way to New Zealand, the British sent Captain William Hobson to assume the role of lieutenant-governor over all the land that could be purchased; and just six days before Lavaud sailed into the harbour, the British flag was raised in Akaroa. Lavaud's passengers decided to stay, which meant that the first formal settlement under **British sovereignty** was comprised of sixty-three French – and six Germans who had come along for the ride.

You can treat Akaroa as a day-trip from Christchurch, although you'll only have time to scratch the surface of this beguiling spot; far better to spend a night or two in order to appreciate the town and its surrounds.

Arrival and information

Buses run by Akaroa Shuttle (book 24hr ahead ☎0800/500 929; Dec–March 3 daily; April–Nov 7–10 weekly; $15 one way, $25 day return) and French Connection (☎03/366 4556; Mon–Sat 1 daily; $10 each way) leave the Christchurch visitor centre (currently at 9am) for the 1hr 30min run to Akaroa. They drop off outside the **visitor centre** 80 rue Lavaud (☎ & fax 03/304 8600, daily 10am–5pm), which shares a building with the **post office**. There's a stack of free brochures, but you may also want to obtain various walks leaflets (50¢ each) and the *Akaroa Historic Village Walk* booklet ($3.50). The *Turenne* café across the street (see "Eating and drinking" p.578) has limited **Internet access**, as does the library on rue Jolie. Note that Akaroa has **no ATM**, though there is a BNZ bank (Mon–Fri 9.30am–4.30pm).

Accommodation

There is a wide choice of **accommodation** in and around Akaroa: although much of it caters to the weekend getaway set and is relatively expensive, there are some lovely B&Bs which have the edge over the motels in terms of home comforts and atmosphere. The cheapest option is offered by backpacker hostels – two in town, one in Onuku (see all below) and a fourth at Le Bons Bay (see p.579).

Akaroa Holiday Park, Morgan's Rd, off the Old Coach Rd (☎ & fax 03/304 7471). Sprawling across a terraced hillside overlooking the harbour and the main street running through town, this site has modern facilities, including a swimming pool. Tents $9; powered sites $10; cabins, on-site vans and tourist flats ②–③.

Akaroa Village Inn, 81 Beach Rd (☎03/304 7421 & 0800/695 2000, fax 304 7423. *www.akaroa.co.nz*). One of the prettiest hotels in Akaroa, situated in the heart of town opposite the main wharf and built on the site of the first residential hotel, which dated from 1842. The current incarnation is French-inspired, with iron lacework on the first-floor balconies, and has a swimming pool and a spa. There are attractive motel-style studio rooms as well as luxurious two-bedroom apartments ideal for two couples. Studios ⑤, apartments ⑧.

Bella-Vista, 21b Watson St (☎ & fax 03/304 7137). Comfortable family home containing two double rooms and a single, all with shared facilities. Continental breakfast is served, and there are great views from the veranda. ④.

La Belle Villa, 113 rue Jolie (☎ & fax 03/304 7084). B&B in a lovely wooden house with spacious light rooms, a large swimming pool and alfresco breakfasts in summer. ⑤.

Blythcliffe, 37 rue Balguerie (☎ & fax 03/304 7003, ☎0800/393 877, *www.nz-holiday.co.nz/blythcliffe*, *blythcliffe@xtra.co.nz*). One of Akaroa's finest bed and breakfasts in a grand old house – equipped with a full-size billiard table – surrounded by semi-formal gardens and bush. There are a couple of lovely rooms with private bathrooms and a delightful garden cottage. Rooms ⑥, cottage ⑦.

Bon Accord Backpackers, 57 rue Lavaud (☎03/304 7782). Small hostel fashioned from two tiny houses knocked into one. There's just eight bunks (in three rooms) and one double. Off street parking. Dorms ①, room ②.

Chez La Mer Backpackers, rue Lavaud (☎ & fax 03/304 7024, *chez_la_mer@ckear.net.nz*). Historic building dating back to 1871, and offering high-quality budget accommodation in a homely environment with a nice garden out the back. The staff are helpful, offer free use of bikes and some useful hand-drawn maps of local walks and points of interest. Dorms ①, en-suite doubles ③.

Grand Hotel, 6 rue Lavaud (☎03/304 7011, fax 304 7304). Basic singles and doubles, with shared facilities, above a refurbished 1860 pub with bottle shop, restaurant and beer garden. ③.

Lavaud House B&B, 83 rue Lavaud (☎ & fax 03/304 7121). Historic home overlooking the main swimming beach, with fresh flowers and antique furniture in every room. A comfortable and friendly place, with four bedrooms and a choice of cooked or continental breakfast. Rooms ⑤, harbour-view en suites ⑥.

Maison des Fleurs, 6 Church St (☎ & fax 03/304 7804). Boutique accommodation in a two-storey cottage (you get all of it), recently built from peninsula milled timbers. It's superbly appointed along allergy-free lines – no polyurethane varnishes, natural fibre beds etc – plus there's a sunny balcony, wood stove for winter, and always a heap of fresh flowers, complimentary port and current magazines. ⑧.

Mount Vernon Lodge and Stables, 500m uphill from the waterfront on rue Balguerie (☎03/304 7180). A bit of a climb, but well worth the effort for excellent accommodation in purpose-built wooden self-contained chalets, motel units, and budget beds in a dorm hut, all built on a hillside overlooking Akaroa and the bay. Other perks are a swimming pool, nature walks and a courtesy bus to and from the town centre. Dorms ①, chalets & motel units ③–④.

Onuku Farm Hostel, 6km south of town on the Onuku road (☎03/304 7612). Beside the bay, this secluded and quiet spot on a sheep farm has accommodation in the main house or in very cheap summer-only huts. Closed June–Aug. Tents $8, dorms ①, rooms ②.

La Rive Motel, 1 rue Lavaud (☎ & fax 03/304 7651, ☎0800/247 651). Large, curiously shaped motel (its open-sided, two-storey conical tower is an allusion to French chateau architecture) in a tranquil garden setting, with a white picket fence at the front and eight units, all containing full kitchens and TVs. ⑤.

Tree Crop Farm, 2km up rue Grehan (☎03/304 7158). Romantic retreat in one of three rustic huts (two without electricity) set on a private farm/gardens (see p.576), where they believe in "candles, flowers, herbs, hot bush baths under the stars and late, late breakfasts on the veranda". Bath robes are provided so you can stroll to your outdoor bath (heated for you after dark), and there is afternoon tea and brunch provided; though you pay a high price for simple comforts. ⑨.

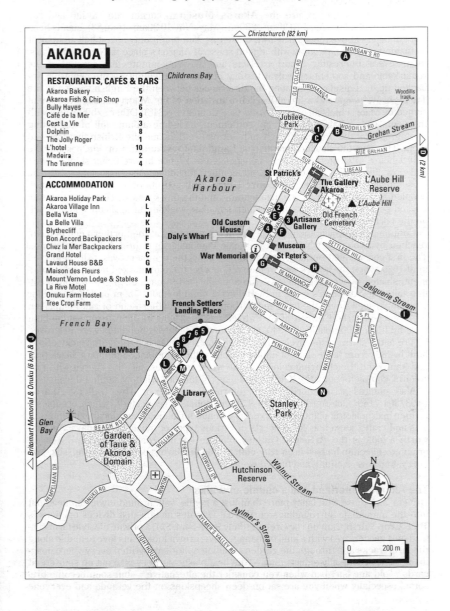

The Town

Akaroa is strung along the shore in a long, easily walkable ribbon. In fact the best way to get acquainted with the place is by following the **Akaroa Historic Village Walk** (booklet available from the visitor centre; $3.50), which pinpoints buildings of interest and architectural note.

Opposite the visitor centre, the **Akaroa Museum**, corner rue Lavaud and rue Balguerie (daily: Oct–April 10.30am–4.30pm; May–Nov 10.30am–4pm; $3), stands head and shoulders above most small-town museums. You might only spend half an hour or so inside but will come away with a good sense of Akaroa's place in New Zealand history. Several interesting Maori artefacts and a twenty-minute film account of the remarkable and sometimes violent history of Maori settlement on the peninsula are backed up by a display illustrating the differences between the English version of the Treaty of Waitangi, and a literal English translation of the Maori-language document signed by Maori chiefs all over *Aotearoa* (see Contexts, p.848). Other exhibits deal with the peninsula's whaling history and settlement, including albums full of fascinating photographs of the original French and German settlers and the British that followed them. The museum also incorporates the **Langlois–Eteveneaux Cottage**, possibly the oldest house in Canterbury, partly constructed in France before being shipped over, and now filled with French nineteenth-century furniture. Also associated with the museum are the town's former **Court House**, still with its original dock and bench peopled by some unconvincing mannequins, and the tiny **Custom House**, across rue Lavaud next to Daly's Wharf, from which spy glass-wielding officials once kept watch on the port below.

Continuing the Gallic theme is the **French Cemetery** at the northern end of town, reached by a footpath which leads from rue Pompallier into the L'Aube Hill Reserve. The first consecrated burial ground in Canterbury, the cemetery was sadly neglected until 1925, when the bodies were reinterred in a central plot marked by a single monument, shaded by weeping willows – romantically said to have been grown from a cutting taken at Napoleon's grave in St Helena. Continue about 150m up L'Aube hill for even better views over the town and harbour. At the northern end of rue Pompallier, the French-inspired **Church of St Patrick** has its origins in the mission station built here by Bishop Pompallier in 1840, but the first two church buildings were destroyed by fire and a storm respectively. The church you see today is a third-time-lucky effort, built in 1864 from large slabs of unplaned totara; the combination of totara, black pine and kauri, and the changing colours of the wood as it ages, fills the church with rich colours, complementing the bold stained-glass in the east window, behind the altar.

Also situated at the northern end of rue Pompallier is **The Gallery Akaroa** (☎03/304 7140; Oct–April daily 1.30–4.30pm; donation requested), which occupies a former hydroelectric plant, and serves as a venue for national and local exhibitions of arts and crafts, as well as for concerts of various types of music on Sundays. Another worth a look is the **Artisans Gallery**, 45 rue Lavaud (daily 10am–5pm), a sales-oriented collection housed in an 1877 cottage and displaying pottery, weaving, silk, jewellery, knitwear, clothing and turned wood.

The Akaroa hinterland and a couple of walks

Drivers, and those who fancy more than just a gentle walk around town, can head out into the immediate surroundings of Akaroa. One destination that divides opinions is **Tree Crop Farm**, 2km up rue Grehan (daily 9am–5pm; $2), a private lifestyle farm centred on a garden area with a kind of managed overgrown look. Fans love to amble along the farm tracks and through the gardens reading aphorisms written everywhere imaginable. They're initially entertaining – "the best plastic surgery is to cut up your credit cards", "old age isn't bad when you consider the alternative" – but soon become tiresome, especially when you are sat on deep sheepskins on the veranda and everyone

THE BANKS PENINSULA TRACK

One of the most popular tracks in the area is the **Banks Peninsula Track**, a 35km private track which traverses spectacular volcanic coastline, verdant farmland, exposed headlands and sandy beaches, as well as the Hinewai Nature Reserve (a marine reserve around the southeastern bays of the peninsula), before reaching the end of the track at Mount Vernon Lodge just east of Akaroa. The track is open from Oct 1 to April 30 and typically takes four days to walk (though there is a two-day option for robust hikers). Either way, a reasonable level of **fitness** is required, but because you're guaranteed a bunk at each hut you can walk at your own pace. The **fee** (before Christmas $120; after Christmas $140; 2-day option $75) includes transport to the start from Akaroa and accommodation along the way; though you'll need to bring a good pair of boots, sleeping bag and all-weather gear. You should also carry provisions for at least the first two days, although it is possible to augment your **supplies** with fresh farm produce at Stony Bay and snacks at Otanerito Beach.

Only twelve people are allowed to start the track each day, so **bookings** should be made well in advance through Banks Peninsula Track, PO Box 50, Akaroa (☎03/304 7612, fax 304 7738, *www.bankstrack.co.nz, bankstrack@xtra.co.nz*). For the less organized a standby (anything from a day to two weeks) rate saves you $20.

THE ROUTE

The trail starts at Onuku, 5km south of Akaroa, and the first night is spent in **Onuku hut** at the start of the track. There's usually enough time on the following day to explore neighbouring trails before embarking on the first stage of the walk proper from **Onuku to Flea Bay** (11km, 3hr 30min), passing three small waterfalls and providing views of the peninsula's east coast. Accommodation at Flea Bay is in a charming 130-year-old cottage with a veranda overlooking the beach, and comes complete with electric stove, lights and hot showers. The second day, **Flea Bay to Stony Bay** (8km; 2hr 30min) is an exposed hike along coastal cliffs, with a seal colony providing lunchtime distraction around the halfway point. The night is spent in one of the huts-cum-cottages in Stony Bay, where there's also a modest family museum, a bath under the stars, a small shop selling bread, tinned food and beer, and a few short tracks exploring the bay. The walk from **Stony Bay to Otanerita Bay** (6km; 2hr) takes care of the third day, with overnight accommodation provided in a farmhouse just 50m from a great swimming beach, run by New Zealand author Fiona Farrell and her partner. The fourth and final day's walk heads inland, from **Otanerita Bay to Mount Vernon Lodge** (10km; 3hr; 600m ascent), passing two waterfalls and providing a last glimpse of the ocean before descending to the calmer waters of Akaroa Harbour.

around you is quoting them to each other. A small café serves berry juices and exotic coffee drinks at relatively high prices, and there is accommodation (see p.575) in simple but nicely furnished huts.

Sticking to the waterside, there is an interesting walk (or drive) along **Beach Road to Onuku** (5km one way; 1hr 15min), taking in some of the historical sights. You first head towards Glen Bay and the nineteenth-century red-and-white wooden **lighthouse**, which used to stand at Akaroa Head to guide ships into the harbour before being moved to its current location in 1980. Continuing towards Akaroa Head for about fifteen minutes, you'll come to **Red House Bay**, the scene of a bloody massacre in 1830, when the great northern chief Te Rauparaha bribed (with flax) the captain of the British brig *Elizabeth* to conceal Maori warriors about the vessel and invite Te Rauparaha's unsuspecting enemies (led by Temaiharanui) on board, where they were slaughtered. Te Rauparaha and his men then feasted on the victims on the beach. The final part of the walk takes you to **ONUKU**, 5km from Akaroa, where you'll find the **Onuku Marae** and

---

DOLPHIN SWIMMING AND AKAROA HARBOUR CRUISES

Two main companies are eager to take you out **swimming with dolphins**: both also offering spectator-only rates effectively turning the trip into a **harbour cruise**. The big deal here is that you get to swim with **Hector's dolphins**, the world's smallest breed of dolphins, usually 1.2–1.4 metres in length.

The biggest operation is Akaroa Harbour Cruises, Main Wharf, Beach Rd (☎0800/436 574, *www.canterburycat.co.nz, ccat@voyager.co.nz*; ticket office daily 10am–4pm) who run a large modern catamaran (Nov–March 11am & 1.30pm; April–Oct 1.30pm; $65, spectators $29) which cruises to the mouth of the harbour and back via a rookery, a beautiful high-walled volcanic sea cave, colonies of spotted shags and cormorants, Penguin Caves (where blue penguins can sometimes be spotted) and a fish-feeding stop in Lucas Bay. Trips take around two hours and if you don't see any dolphins you can go again free of charge until you do, though this requires some flexibility in your schedule.

The alternative is Dolphin Experience, 61 Beach Rd (☎0508/365 744, fax 03/304 7726), a more personal and intimate experience (daily: Nov–April 6am, 9am & noon; May–Oct 9am & noon; $75) taking up to three hours. If you don't get to swim with the dolphins you can return at any time for a second try at $39. Dolphin Experience also run a fully commentated three-hour **Out of the Harbour Cruise** (daily: Nov–April 8.30am, 11.30am & 2.30pm; May–Oct 11am & 2pm; $35).

---

a tiny church, established in 1876–78. Onuku is even quieter than Akaroa: roughly translated, the name means "coming and going though never staying long" – and, sure enough, there's little to keep you here, except maybe more walks and the prospect of a bed for the night at the *Onuku Farm Hostel* (see p.574).

If you lack the time or inclination to tackle the **Banks Peninsula Track** (see box on previous page), there are some equally rewarding shorter walks. The best is the **Round the Mountain Walk** (10km; 4hr return) which circumnavigates the hills above Akaroa via the Purple Peak Road – the route is shown on a hand-drawn photocopied map, available for 50¢ from the visitor centre. For something a little longer, try the **Akaroa–Le Bons Bay** walking track (booking essential ☎03/304 8533; 16km; 5hr each way) which heads east over the hills to the Le Bons Bay Motor Camp (see opposite) where you spend the night, ready to return the next day (or later). It crosses private land, but no fees are charged if you stay at the motorcamp; pack transport can also be arranged.

Eating and drinking

With an eager tourist market and its **French heritage**, Akaroa is a very good place to eat, making it popular with people from Christchurch, who think nothing of driving 85km for their evening meal. This does tend to push up prices a little and means that more **expensive** establishments predominate, although there are the usual takeaways and cheaper cafés to fall back on. The reliance on the summer **tourist trade** also means that many places cut back their hours, or even close completely, during winter.

Akaroa Bakery, 51 Beach Rd. Excellent fresh-baked bread, plus a small café, serving sandwiches, pies, cakes, pizza and bottomless cups of coffee. Daily all year, from early morning to 5pm.

Akaroa Fish and Chip Shop, Beach Road, near the harbour. Takeaway "Fush 'n' Chups" with a New Zealand flavour. Daily lunch & dinner.

Bully Hayes, 57 Beach Rd (☎03/304 7533). Named after a famous local con-man, this place serves reliable, moderately priced dishes alongside great home-made breads – try chicken, leek and kumara soup, Peninsula Pork Fillet, Magnet Bay Crayfish or Lucas Bay Salmon Fillet. Open for lunch and dinner. Licensed.

Café de la Mer, 71 Beach Rd. Moderately priced lunches and dinners, including some impressive focaccia sandwiches, as well as mussels steamed in white wine and tomato sauce. Licensed.

C'est La Vie, 33 rue Lavaud (☎03/304 7314). Probably Akaroa's best restaurant: an exceptional, intimate dinner-only restaurant with relaxing live music. The fine French cuisine uses organically grown ingredients and fresh seafood, all rounded off with delicate pastries. Main courses such as canard á l'orange and escargots in herb butter are about $25 and it is BYO only.

Dolphin, 6 rue Balguerie (☎03/304 7658). Fresh and well-presented lunches and dinners, with mains from about $17, served in comfortable nautical surroundings. Open for lunch and dinner. Licensed.

L'Hotel, 75 Beach Rd. Airy café and wine bar with outdoor seating and harbour views, serving modern Mediterranean cuisine that won't break the bank, augmented by a broad selection of beers and spirits. Open for lunch and dinner.

The Jolly Roger, *Grand Hotel*, 6 rue Lavaud. Pleasant and reasonably priced lunch and dinner venue, with particularly tasty fish dishes and a few bar snacks. Mains $15–20. Licensed.

Madeira, rue Lavaud. Spirited Kiwi pub always jumping at weekends.

The Turenne, 74 rue Lavaud. Great daytime café with seats outside and Internet access within. There's a range of breakfasts, superb muffins and savouries such as gado-gado flan and pumpkin and mushroom pie, and bottomless coffee.

Listings

Fishing Bluefin Charters (☎03/304 7866) run three-hour harbour fishing trips ($45) and specialize in small-boat sea fishing charters ($80 per half day, $130 full day).

Horse riding Horse Trekking Akaroa, Mount Vernon Lodge and Stables, rue Balguerie (☎03/304 7180), offer various guided treks depending on the amount of time you want to be in the saddle over hilly country ($25 per hour).

Newspaper The *Akaroa Mail and Banks Peninsula Advertiser* carries events listings and advertisements for activities.

Off-road riding 4 Wheel Bike Safaris (☎03/304 7866) run two hour cross country trips on 4X4 bikes ($79) leaving from the Akaroa Heritage Park on Long Bay Road, 3km from town: sturdy shoes required.

Parasailing Cloud Nine (☎03/385 4739) will take you parasailing, towed behind a boat on the harbour for around $80; though they only operate during the school holidays.

Rural mail run The Akaroa mail run (booking essential ☎03/304 7207; Mon–Sat 8.20am; 4hr 30min; $20) follows a 110km rural delivery run, serving the eastern bays of the peninsula, including Okains and Le Bons Bays.

Seal Viewing Akaroa Seal Colony Safari (☎ & fax 03/304 7255, *double.l@xtra.co.nz*) run air-conditioned 4WD coaches to view New Zealand fur seals from Goat Point on the eastern tip of the peninsula. Tours (daily 9.30am & 1pm; $50) last over two hours and are limited to six people.

Around Akaroa

Unless you have reached Akaroa by means of the Summit Road, you'll have missed some of the best Banks Peninsula has to offer. Fortunately it is easy enough to drive over the hills to gems such as **Le Bons Bay** and **Okains Bay**, though getting around the twisty roads will take you longer than you'd expect.

Le Bons Bay

As SH75 enters Akaroa from the north, Long Bay Road rises off into the hills giving access to the Summit Road and the verdant **LE BONS BAY**, 20km from Akaroa. It is a small peaceful community with a number of holiday homes ranged behind a gorgeous sandy **beach**, framed on two sides by cliffs, that provides safe swimming. One satisfying way to get here is via the Akaroa–Le Bons Bay **walking track** (see p.572) which winds up at the *Le Bons Bay Motor Camp*, 15 Valley Rd (☎ & fax 03/304 8533, *lebonsholiday@xtra.co.nz*; tents $9.50, powered sites $10, dorms ①, on-site vans & cabins ②), a well kept and picturesque **campsite** by a stream, with a store, swimming pool, organized horse trekking, and mountain-bike rental.

The only other accommodation in the area is the wonderful family-run *Le Bons Bay* **backpackers** (☎03/304 8582; closed June–Sept; dorms ①, rooms ②), a cosy 120-year-old house situated 5km back from the beach, far enough up the bay to provide spectacular views. It is a great place to relax for a few days, lounging on the veranda or in the garden hammock, popping down to the beach to fish or gather shellfish which might be used in the communal evening dinner ($9, and well worth it), or taking long walks down the valley or across the hilltops. The owners run daily low-key **boat trips** (1hr 30min; $17) to see penguins, dolphins, shags and seals. Breakfast is free, and you should call to arrange pick-up from Akaroa.

Okains Bay

The next bay north from Le Bons Bay is **OKAINS BAY**, some 30km from Akaroa, a popular holiday and picnic area with a tiny permanent population. No public buses come this far, so those without their own transport will have to use one of the Akaroa mail runs (see p.579). The beach and the placid lagoon formed by the **Opara Stream** are excellent for swimming and boating, but the real reason to visit is a remarkable museum containing one of the best collections of Maori artefacts in the South Island. The **Okains Bay Maori and Colonial Museum** (daily 10am–5pm; $5), on the only road going into the bay, was originally the private collection of a Maori-obsessed local man, and is housed in the old cheese factory. Within the same compound, several out-buildings contain the more traditional exhibitions relating to European settlement, including a "slab" stable and cottage – simply constructed from large slabs of totara wood. Among the thought-provoking Maori exhibits are a god stick dating back to 1400, a war canoe from 1867 and various weapons, as well as a valuable *hei tiki* (a pendant with a design based on the human form) recovered in England and brought back to Okains Bay. Beside the Maori exhibition building, there is also a beautiful meeting house (it's *tapu* or sacred, although visitors are allowed to look around it), with fine symbolic figures carved by master craftsman John Rua.

Also on the only road descending to Okains Bay, the very welcoming *Kawatea Farmstay* (☎ & fax 03/304 8621; ⑥; dinner on request, $25), is a 90-year-old **homestead** set in lush gardens bordered by 5km of scenic coastline and offering three rooms decorated with native timbers and stained glass. At the end of this road is the *Okains Bay Domain* **campsite**, just behind the beach (office 200m back up the road; tents $6, dorms ①), which offers a choice of sites or bargain beds in the pavilion which has a fridge and stove. Be sure to bring supplies with you as there is nowhere to eat in the bay.

Pigeon Bay and Port Levy

The two largest bays on the northern side of Banks Peninsula are further west, closer to Lyttelton Harbour and reached by yet more narrow and steep lanes. Neither warrant a special visit though both are of some historical interest: Pigeon Bay was an important timber milling and shipbuilding settlement in the nineteenth century when the peninsula had trees; and Port Levy once held the largest Maori community in Canterbury. The main reason to come now is to rest up for a couple of days at Port Levy's lovely and historic *Kaihope Cottage* (☎03/329 4690, *rbarnett@clear.net.nz*; ③), situated on part of a deer and sheep farm, but right by the sea. The two-bedroom cottage sleeps six and is fully self-contained: bring bedding and food.

SOUTH TO OTAGO

Heading south from Christchurch both the principal road, SH1, and the rail line forge across the **Canterbury Plains** in an unrelenting straight line, bisecting small service towns catering for the farms on the rich flat land. The **Southern Alps** flank the route to the west and in clear weather provide awesome views. In the main though, it is a monotonous landscape broken only by the broad gravel beds of braided rivers, usually little more than a trickle spanned by kilometre-long bridges, though they can overspill their broad gravelly banks after heavy rain. The first of the bridges, the 1.8km-long structure spanning the Rakaia River 58km from Christchurch, was the longest in the southern hemisphere at the time of its construction in 1939. It leads into the tiny salmon-fishing and sheep-shearing settlement of **Rakaia**, where a minor road called Thompson's Track heads inland to link with SH77, which in turn grants access to Methven, Mount Hutt and Mount Somers, on the western fringes of the Canterbury Plains (see p.612). A further 27km south is the larger though equally quiet settlement of **Ashburton**, where SH77 joins SH1.

As the road (and the parallel rail line) passes the pottery town of **Temuka** and reaches the southern end of the Canterbury Plains, looming hills force it back to the shoreline at **Timaru**, a small city with a busy port and a fading holiday resort. Timaru is also the point where SH8 strikes inland towards Fairlie, Lake Tekapo and Mount Cook (see p.619). From here on, the trip south is a visual treat, with rolling hills inland and spectacular sea views, and yet another opportunity to cut inland. This time it is SH82 and SH83, which head along opposite banks of the Waitaki River – noted for its excellent whitebait, sea-run trout and quinnat salmon fishing – en route to Omarama, Mount Cook and Wanaka.

The coastal highway and railway continue south to the architecturally harmonious city of **Oamaru**, and the unique and fascinating **Moeraki Boulders**. You are also heading into **penguin** country with several opportunities to stop off and spy blue and yellow-eyed penguins. From Moeraki there is little to delay you on your progress toward Dunedin, except maybe the small crossroads town of **Palmerston**, where SH85, "The Pigroot" to **Central Otago**, leaves SH1, providing another opportunity to forsake the coast and follow a historical pathway to the goldfields inland (see p.595).

Ashburton

The long, thin and stubbornly suburban town of **ASHBURTON** lies 87km southeast of Christchurch, perched on the north bank of the Ashburton River, with an extension, **Tinwald**, across the bridge on the opposite bank. Built on a long defunct ceramics industry and maintained as a service town for the local farms, Ashburton is off the itinerary for most visitors, but if you are heading along SH1 you'll be passing through and may care to stop and examine the smattering of minor sights.

Breaking up the dreary huddle of the town centre the **Ashburton Domain** (daily 8am–dusk), facing West Street, is fringed by stately hundred-year-old European trees and contains expertly manicured gardens and an artificial lake, created from the water race of an old mill. Just north of the Domain is the **Ashford Craft Village**, at 429 West St (daily 9am–5pm), which comprises a café, antique shop, the Eastside Gallery, and a massive collection of spinning wheels, looms and accessories, all of which are for sale – though bargains are few and far between.

The **Historic Museum and Art Gallery**, 248 Cameron St (Tues–Fri 10am–4pm, Sat & Sun 1–4pm; donation requested), is a cool and airy place with temporary art exhibitions upstairs. The neat museum has an informative display on braided rivers and the bird life they support, such as the endangered black-fronted tern and the wrybill plover, which breeds only in this region. The most interesting of the town's other four small museums is the **Museum of Woodworking and Ornamental Woodturning**, tucked away at 103 Alford Forest Rd (open by arrangement ☎03/308 6611; $2). Housed in a woodturner's workshop, it contains a substantial collection of antique ornamental lathes, with plenty of intricately turned pieces on display. Ashburton's other museums – the

Plains Vintage Railway Museum (☎03/308 9621), the Ashburton Aviation Museum (☎03/308 3262) and the Vintage Car Museum (☎03/308 6070) – are primarily for enthusiasts and are only open limited hours or by arrangement.

Practicalities

Trains (booking information ☎0800/802 802) between Christchurch and Dunedin stop once daily in each direction at the station on East Street (SH1). InterCity and assorted shuttle **buses** pause outside the **visitor centre**, corner of East Street and Burnett Street (☎ & fax 03/308 1064, *infocentre@ashburton.co.nz*; Mon–Fri 8.30am–5pm, Sat 10am–3pm, Sun 10am–1pm), which stocks a free local map, timetable information for local buses and shuttles, and has **Internet access**. The **post office**, 390–408 East St (☎03/308 3184) has poste restante facilities.

Ashburton has an adequate range of **accommodation**, many places are either clustered at the south end of East Street, or across the river in Tinwald. In winter many cater to skiers from the Mount Somers and Mount Hutt fields just a short drive away. **Campers** and budget travellers should head for *Coronation Park*, 778 East St, adjacent to the Domain (☎03/308 6603; tents $9, dorms ①, on-site vans & units ②–④), though couples may prefer the relative comforts of the nearby *Academy Lodge Motel*, 782 East St (☎03/308 5503; ④), or the more homely environment at *Renfrew Country Homestay*, Mitcham Rd, on the edge of town (☎03/308 5559, fax 308 0148, *renfrew1@xtra.co.nz*; ⑤) where evening meals ($20) are served by arrangement. A little further out, try the pretty and secluded *Carradale Farmstay*, Ferriman's Rd, Lagmhor, 8km west of Tinwald (☎03/308 6577, fax 308 6548; ⑤) which presents the opportunity to join in farm activities and offers dinner by arrangement ($25).

Ashburton has a few decent **places to eat**. For good coffee, lunches and light evening meals, the place to go is *Kelly's Café and Bar* on East Street, though later on you might be tempted by *Cactus Jacks*, 209 Wills St, off East Street, one of the liveliest places in town, serving a New Zealand version of Tex-Mex at moderate prices. The finest dining in town goes on at *Jester's*, 9 Mona Square (☎03/308 9983; closed Sun; licensed), a very pretty two-storey wooden house, offering upmarket evening dining and more modest daytime fare.

Temuka

The small town of **TEMUKA**, 60km south of Ashburton on SH1, takes its name from the Maori for "fierce oven", and a large number of Maori earth ovens have been found in the area. It continues to live up to its reputation today with the presence of kilns for the ceramic factories built by immigrants from the "Potteries" area around Stoke-on-Trent in England. Within New Zealand, Temuka has become synonymous with **pottery**, and you can visit the Temuka Pottery shop (Mon–Fri 9am–5.30pm, Sat 10am–4pm) on SH1 at the junction of Dominion Avenue. Once a byword for dowdy patterns and colours, they've smartened their image in recent years, and if you are inspired enough to want to look around the factory, make sure you are here for the hour-long **factory tour** (Wed 1pm; free).

Across Dominion Avenue you'll find the old court house containing the **Temuka Museum** (Dec–June Mon–Fri 1–4pm, Sun 2–4pm; July–Nov Fri & Sat 2–4pm; donation requested) which has a fair bit on the pottery industry but, oddly, nothing on Temuka's favourite son, aviator **Richard Pearse** – locally held to be the first man to achieve powered flight in 1902, some months in advance of the Wright brothers. Pearse's plane was technically far ahead of that of his rivals, but Pearse himself did not believe his first powered flight was sufficiently controlled or sustained to justify his townsfolk's claim. He managed a rather desperate 100m, followed by an ignominious landing in gorse bushes. He was a lifelong tinkerer and inventor, although the true gauge of Pearse's genius was his idea for an aircraft that could fly and hover like a modern Harrier jump jet. There's a memorial to Pearse at the site of the legendary flight, about 13km from Temuka on the way to Waitohi; and further reminders of his achievements in the South Canterbury Museum at Timaru (see p.585).

Practicalities

Most buses will drop off and pick up in Temuka, and onward travel can be arranged at the **visitor centre**, which is situated in the library, 72 King St (Mon–Thurs 9am–5.30pm, Fri 9am–8pm; ☎03/615 9537, fax 615 9538). There is really little reason not to continue on to Timaru or beyond, but you'll find **accommodation** at the clean and comfortable *Highway One Motel*, 272 King St (☎03/615 7886, fax 615 7936; ④), or the *Temuka Holiday Park*, 1 Ferguson Drive (☎03/615 7241; tents $9, cabins ②), a spacious, well-looked-after site in the Domain, five minutes' walk from King Street.

You'll find a number of **pubs** and bars along King Street and one or two **restaurants**, but none of them beats the ultra-friendly *Benny's* **café/bar** at no. 134 (daily 11.45am–2pm & 5.30pm–late), which has good coffee, cheap and imaginative food including vegetarian options, plus wine and a tempting dessert menu.

Timaru

The small port city of **TIMARU**, 18km south of Temuka, is one of the South Island's larger provincial centres, weighing in with 28,000 residents. At the end of a straight and flat two-hour drive from Christchurch, the city's gently rolling hills mark a subtle change and provide the setting for an austere streetscape partly built of volcanic "bluestone" – the local council insisted on stone and brick constructions after a devastating fire in 1868. With the possible exceptions of the **Aigantighe Art Gallery** and the **South Canterbury Museum**, there is no vastly compelling reason to stop here; though if you are looking to rest up somewhere pleasant that doesn't have much in the way of tempting demands on your cash supply, then you may just have found your spot.

The name Timaru comes from *Te Maru*, **Maori** for "place of shelter", as it provided the only haven for *waka* paddling between Banks Peninsula and Oamaru. In 1837 European settlement was initiated by Joseph Price, who set up a **whaling** station south of the present city at Patiti Point. A large part of today's commercial and pastoral development was initiated by Yorkshiremen **George and Robert Rhodes**, who established the first cattle station on the South Island in 1839 and founded Rhodes Town not long after, just north of the existing settlement of Government Town – the towns gradually grew together and merged to form Timaru. Despite an influx of European migrants aboard the *Strathallan* in 1859, it was some years before a safe harbour was established on the rocky coast. A welcome by-product of the land reclamation that created the harbour in 1877 was the fine sandy beach of Caroline Bay. For a time, Timaru became a popular seaside resort, and its annual **summer carnival**, starting at Christmas and running for three weeks, is still well worth dropping in on.

Arrival and information

The **train station** on Station Street in the centre of the city is the principal drop-off and pick-up point for all trains and most buses; the Reservation Centre inside the station (☎03/688 3594) sells bus and train tickets for onward travel. Many buses drop you at your chosen accommodation, and a few stop outside the **visitor centre**, 14 Lower George St (Mon–Fri 8.30am–5pm, Sat & Sun 10am–3pm; ☎03/688 6163, fax 688 6162, *www.southisland.co.nz*, *info@timaru.co.nz*), which provides free maps of South Canterbury and Timaru, and leaflets for several historic walks about town. You probably won't need Timaru's **local bus service**, which is run by CRC, with a flat rate of $1

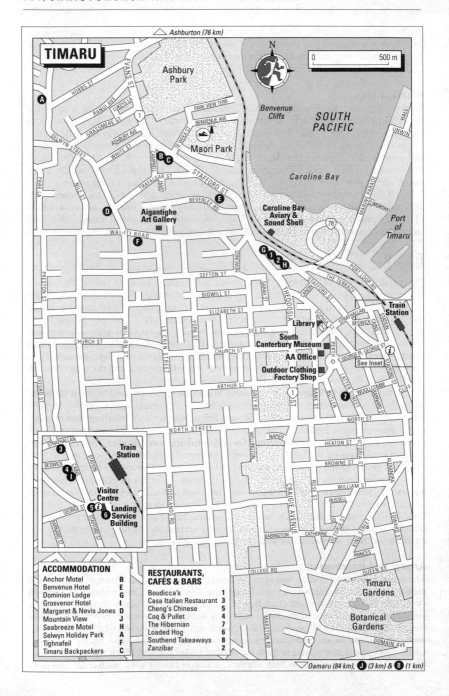

TIMARU

△ *Ashburton (76 km)*

Ashbury Park

Maori Park

Benvenue Cliffs

SOUTH PACIFIC

Caroline Bay

Aigantighe Art Gallery

Caroline Bay Aviary & Sound Shell

Port of Timaru

Library

South Canterbury Museum

AA Office

Outdoor Clothing Factory Shop

Train Station

Train Station

Visitor Centre

Landing Service Building

ACCOMMODATION

Anchor Motel	**B**
Benvenue Hotel	**E**
Dominion Lodge	**G**
Grosvenor Hotel	**I**
Margaret & Nevis Jones	**D**
Mountain View	**J**
Seabreeze Motel	**H**
Selwyn Holiday Park	**A**
Tighnafeil	**F**
Timaru Backpackers	**C**

RESTAURANTS, CAFÉS & BARS

Boudicca's	**1**
Casa Italian Restaurant	**3**
Cheng's Chinese	**5**
Coq & Pullet	**4**
The Hibernian	**7**
Loaded Hog	**6**
Southend Takeaways	**8**
Zanzibar	**2**

▽ *Oamaru (84 km),* **J** *(3 km) &* **8** *(1 km)*

for all journeys around the city and suburbs, including unlimited transfers within a four-hour period.

Accommodation

There's is a wide range of **accommodation**, generally in good supply except for the Christmas to mid-January period when you should book well in advance. Most places are fairly central, with motels lining Stafford Street to the north and B&Bs more widely distributed.

Anchor Motel, 42 Evans St (☎03/684 5067, fax 684 5706). A central, slightly run-down, 1960s two-storey building with off-street parking and eight comfortable units, some of which get put to use as part of *Timaru Backpackers* (see below). ④.

Benvenue Hotel, 16–22 Evans St (☎0800/104 049, fax 03/688 4049, *benvenue@voyager.co.nz*). Set on a hill with a good view of the bay and the town, this hotel has recently refurbished rooms, a bar, restaurant and heated indoor pool and spa. ⑤.

Dominion Lodge, 334 Stafford St (☎ & fax 03/684 4729). Vast, rambling former hotel run as a backpackers with cavernous lounges stacked with videos, spacious kitchens and a range of rooms (and prices) from 12-bed dorms down to en-suite doubles with made up beds and views of Caroline Bay. Some cheap single rooms too. Dorms ①, rooms b–③.

Grosvenor Hotel, 26 Cains Terrace (☎03/688 3129 & 0800/106 102, fax 684 8381). The most lavish centrally located accommodation, this imposing white-stone and red-roofed 1875 building was once known as the "Grand Old Lady of the South". It has fifty comfortable rooms, and even if you're not staying here, it's worth a look and a drink in one of the bars. ⑥.

Margaret & Nevis Jones, 16 Selwyn St (☎ & fax 03/688 1400). A lovely late 1920s house with lush gardens and its own grass tennis court. Rooms are either en suite or have private facilities, it is only fifteen minutes' walk from town and they pick up and drop off. ⑤.

Mountain View, 200m along Talbots Rd off SH1, 3km from Timaru (☎03/688 1070, fax 688 1069, *mvhomestay@xtra.co.nz*). Small farm B&B offering homely rooms with private bathrooms and a cooked breakfast. Dinner by arrangement ($20); venison a speciality. ④.

Seabreeze, 28 The Bay Hill (☎0800/443 443, fax 684 3118). Comfortable, well appointed and quiet motel close to town, Caroline Bay and a couple of good restaurants. ⑤.

Selwyn Holiday Park, 8 Glen St (☎03/684 7690 & 0800/242 121, fax 688 1004). Slightly pricey but high-standard holiday park close to the golf links and within walking distance of Maori Park. Tent sites $18, cabins ②–③, tourist flats ③, motel units ④.

Tighnafeile House, 62 Wai-iti Road (☎03/684 3333, fax 684 3328, *taighnafeile-house@timaru.co.nz*). Timaru's premiere boutique lodge in a grand 1911 house close to the art gallery. Rooms are all sumptuously decorated and every need is catered for. ⑦.

Timaru Backpackers, 44 Evans St (☎ & fax 03/684 5076, fax 684 5706). Associate YHA run jointly with the *Anchor Motel* (see above) to provide highly flexible accommodation – dorms, motel units, homestays and a variety of double and single rooms – along with a nice veranda that catches the afternoon sun. Free tea and coffee. Dorms ①, rooms ②–④.

The City

Timaru undulates over low hills, all roads eventually bringing you down to the reclaimed land of the harbour and the park-backed golden sweep of **Caroline Bay**, a good spot for the kids even if the beach is overlooked by the port. Nearby, at the southern end of Stafford Street, is the central business district. Here you'll find the train station and visitor centre separated by the 1870 **Landing Service Building**, built of volcanic "bluestone" and originally used to store goods unloaded from the small boats that were winched up onto a shingle beach in front – roughly where the railway lines are now. It now contains a restaurant and bar (see p.587).

A couple of hundred metres uphill, the **South Canterbury Museum**, Perth St (Tues–Fri 10am–4.30pm, Sat & Sun 1.30–4.30pm; donation appreciated) has recently expanded into new premises allowing more scope to display well labelled local Maori artefacts, some good examples of **scrimshaw** (intricate etchings on whale teeth and bone) and other memorabilia from the whaling station that occupied Patiti Point in the late 1830s and early 1840s. Look out, too, for the wonderful **E.P. Seally collection** – drawers crammed full of butterflies, moths, eggs, minerals, and rare colourful shells. A nineteenth-century naturalist, Seally collected hundreds of butterflies and moths from all over the world, each one conscientiously labelled, including the *Morpho Cypris*, a beautiful blue from Brazil; the smaller electric-aquamarine *Morpho Adonis*; and the (now sadly silent) yodelling cicada. Hanging over the main hall of the museum, and best viewed from the first-floor balcony, is a reconstruction of the 1902 **aircraft** used by Richard Pearse in his attempt to notch up the first powered flight in the world (see p.582).

Probably the best way to pass an hour or two is to visit the **Aigantighe Art Gallery**, 49 Wai-iti Rd (☎03/688 4424; Tues–Fri 11am–4pm, Sat & Sun noon–4pm; donation appreciated), constructed around a venerable Timaru house known as *Aigantighe* (Gaelic for "at home") in the days before it became a gallery. Original features of the house have been preserved and provide a suitable setting for a rotating permanent collection founded on donations and bequests from Timaru's wealthier families – some works date back to the seventeenth century. A vigorous purchasing policy has produced an enviable collection of works by South Canterbury artists including relatively minor, but often intimate and personal, works by native son Colin McCahon. Other artists to look out for are Frances Hodgkins, and the prolific Austen Deans whose luminous landscapes interpret the local countryside as well as any.

In 1990 Kiwi, Japanese and Zimbabwean sculptors came here as part of a symposium and carved thirteen works from soft Mount Somers Stone (see p.616). These have weathered nicely and now sit harmoniously in the gallery's small but impressive **sculpture garden**, a great place for a picnic (bring your own). Look particularly for *Baboon*, nearest the house, carved with power tools by a Zimbabwean who had only ever hand carved. The nodules in the animal's hand represent the seeds of knowledge gained by the experience. Call the gallery for details of temporary exhibitions.

Hector's dolphins have always swum around off the coast at Timaru, but Timaru Marine Cruises (☎0800/661 278) have only just got permission to run **dolphin watching** trips (daily 10.30am; $25) from the corner of Port Loop Road and Ritchie Street. On a fine day, you could also spend a quiet hour ambling around the **Botanical Gardens**, Queen Street (daily 8am–dusk; free), or strolling along the low cliffs north of Caroline Bay past the wooden 1878 **Blackett's Lighthouse** to Dashing Rocks. Wet days are better spent on the ninety-minute tour and sampling at the **DB Brewery**, Sheffield Street,

---

ROCK ART

Around five hundred years ago, Maori moa hunters visited the South Canterbury and North Otago coastal plain, leaving a record of their sojourn on the walls and ceilings of open-sided limestone rock shelters. There are over three hundred **rock drawings** around Timaru, Geraldine and Fairlie: the faded charcoal and red ochre drawings depict a variety of stylized human, bird and mythological figures and patterns. Some of the best cave drawings can be seen in the region's museums (notably the North Otago Museum in Oamaru, see p.591). Those remaining in situ are often hard to make out, but the best examples are at Risk Shelter, Acacia Downs, Blackler's Cave and Hazelburn Shelter, all on Three Mile Bush Road, which can be reached by driving northwest from Timaru along SH8 to Pleasant Point (15km distant), then continuing west along the Ohipi River.

Even equipped with your own wheels, and the free *Pleasant Point Ward Map* from the Timaru visitor centre, the paintings can be hard to find, and access is often across **private land**. The best bet is to call ahead for permission before you set out: the visitor centre will help you plan a route and provide any telephone numbers needed.

Washdyke, 2km north of town on SH1 (☎03/688 2059; Mon–Thurs 10.30am; free; no sandals).

Eating, drinking and entertainment

Timaru's **restaurants**, though numerous, don't offer great variety in terms of decor or ambitious cuisine, but you'll find the usual cache of fish and chip shops, as well as a couple of Italian and Asian eateries: the best of the bunch are listed below.

Things hot up in Timaru for the three post-Christmas weeks of the **summer carnival**, when there's a circus, a fair, and free concerts in Caroline Bay. Otherwise, Timaru is a pretty quiet place; if there is anything going on in town, then the **entertainment** listings in the daily *Timaru Herald* (particularly the Friday and Saturday editions) will provide details. You can catch first-run Hollywood **movies** at Movie Max 3, corner of Canon and Sophia streets (☎03/684 6987).

Boudicca's, 64 The Bay Hill. Good-quality café specializing in Middle Eastern and Kiwi cuisine. A kebab, salad and a variety of sauces, including delicious sweet chilli, will set you back $7.95, and there's felafel and other meat-free options, as well as mouth-watering, home-made desserts. Tues–Sun 11am till late; licensed.

Casa Italia Ristorante, 2 Strathallan St (☎03/684 5528). Located in the atmospheric Victorian Customs House, this is probably Timaru's finest restaurant. The Italian chef reliably turns out authentic cuisine with pasta made on the premises ($17), superb risotto ($17) and *segundi piatti* around the $25–30 mark. Leave room for the torta cioccolato ($8). Evenings daily; licensed.

Cheng's Chinese Restaurant, 12 George St. Excellent set menus, good fish dishes, and great chow mien, with main meals hovering in the $12–18 range. Open daily for lunch and dinner; licensed.

Coq and Pullet, 209 Stafford St. Daytime café and deli opening early for breakfast, and offering panini, gourmet pies and reasonable coffee.

The Hibernian, 4 Latter St. Pub serving enormous portions of Kiwi fare, including generous breakfasts. Carvery buffet Fri 5–10pm, smorgasbord Sun noon–2pm. Live local rock music in the bar on Fri & Sat.

Loaded Hog, Landing Service Building on George St. Former brewpub that now gets its supply from a sister operation in Christchurch, this cavernous establishment occupies a wonderful stone grain store. The blackboard menu features $5 lunch specials and mains such as Cajun chicken burger ($11), fish battered in the Hog's weiss beer ($14) and fettuccini ($10). Touring bands tend to play here (usually Thurs–Sun till 3am).

Southend Takeaways, 39 King St. One of the best fish and chip and burger bars for miles around.

Zanzibar, 56 The Bay Hill. Bustling, modern bar and restaurant with good views over the port and Caroline Bay, serving hearty helpings ranging from Thai chicken and noodle salad ($10) and Italian vegetable risotto ($17) to beer battered blue cod ($19). Licensed.

Listings

Automobile Association 26 Church St (☎03/688 4189).

Bike rental The Cyclery, 98 Stafford St (☎03/688 8892), rents bikes from $20 a day.

Car rental Rental Vehicles Ltd, 6 Barnard St (☎03/684 7179).

Internet access Bay City Internet, 47a Stafford St (☎03/688 6554; Mon–Fri 9am–6pm, Sat 10am–1pm) and Computer Shop Timaru 2000, 329 Stafford St (☎03/684 9333; Mon–Fri 9am–5.30pm, Sat 9am–noon).

Library Timaru District Library, Sophia St (Mon, Wed & Fri 9.30am–8pm, Tues & Thurs 9.30am–6pm, Sat 10am–noon, Sun 1–4pm).

Medical treatment Call ☎03/684 8209 for a duty doctor. Timaru Hospital is on Queen St (☎03/684 3089). Women's Refuge ☎03/684 8280.

Outdoor clothing Swanndri, 24 Church St (Mon–Sat 10am–3pm). A great place to pick up factory seconds from the manufacturer of the jackets favoured by New Zealand bushmen; also rugs, trusty oilskins, knitwear and country attire.

Post office the post office on Sophia St (☎03/688 5518) has poste restante facilities.

Pharmacies Faulks & Jordan, 234 Stratford St; Central Pharmacy, 266 Stratford St. Details of duty pharmacies are listed in the *Timaru Herald*.

Shuttle buses Shuttle bus companies operating Timaru–Christchurch, Timaru–Dunedin and Timaru–Twizel routes include Atomic Shuttles (☎03/322 8883); Catch-a-bus (☎03/471 4103); and Supa Kut Price Shuttles (☎0800/662 722).

Swimming There's an excellent summer pool at the Maori Park Aqua Land, Tewaka St (Nov–March; ☎03/688 4504); otherwise try the Century Pool, Craigie Ave (☎03/684 5379), which is open year-round. Precise opening times vary; ask at the visitor centre or consult the *Timaru Herald*.

Taxis Budget (☎03/688 8799) and Timaru Taxis (☎03/688 8899) both offer a 24hr service.

Oamaru

The former port town of **OAMARU**, 85km south of Timaru on SH1, is one of the New Zealand's more alluring (and undersold) provincial cities, making it a relaxed place to spend a day or two. Perhaps its most immediate appeal is the presence of two **penguin colonies** on the outskirts of town, which provide an unmissable opportunity to observe both the diminutive blue penguins and their larger yellow-eyed cousins. The town itself has attractions too, not least the well-preserved core of nineteenth-century buildings of its central **historic district**, built of the distinctive cream-coloured local limestone, which earned Oamaru the title "The Whitestone City". At the turn of the twentieth century it had a reputation as being the most attractive city in the South Island, and with the ongoing restoration it may well regain that status. For the moment, several grand edifices have yet to be restored, but it only seems a matter of time before the buildings will be taken over by cafés and chi-chi galleries.

The limestone outcrops throughout the area once provided shelter for Maori and later the raw material for ambitious European builders. As a commercial centre for gold-rush prospectors, and shored up by quarrying, timber and farming industries, Oamaru grew in wealth, giving shape to its prosperity in the elegant stone buildings that today grace the town centre. The port opened for **migration** in 1874, with three hundred ships arriving that year and a further four hundred between 1876 and 1878, although many foundered on the hostile coastline and wrecks littered the late nineteenth-century shore. After this boom period the fortunes of the town declined, and it's only in recent years that the town has begun to come alive again.

The writer Janet Frame (see Contexts, p.878) spent some of her childhood in Oamaru and lived here on and off in later years. Fans of her work may want to follow the **Janet Frame Trail** (a leaflet is available from the visitor centre, see below) which concentrates on locations used in varying degrees of disguise in her books – the former subscription library in the Athenaeum that featured in *Faces In The Water*, or the rubbish dump that formed the symbolic centre of *Owls Do Cry* – although such sights are hardly essential for the uncommitted.

Arrival and information

Buses drop off at the corner of Eden and Thames streets, while the dilapidated **train station** is just northeast of the centre on Humber Street. You can walk just about everywhere from here, but if you have heavy bags you can always call for a **taxi** (☎03/434 1234).

The **visitor centre**, 1 Thames St (Nov–Easter Mon–Fri 9am–6pm, Sat & Sun 10am–5pm; Easter–Oct Mon–Fri 9am–5pm, Sat & Sun 10am–4pm; ☎03/434 1656, fax 434 1657, *info@waitaki-dc.govt.nz*), is less than ten minutes' walk from the train station and bus stop. Enthusiastic staff dish out some useful leaflets, including *Historic Oamaru*, which focuses on the historic district, and *Heritage Trails of North Otago* ($1), which includes details of the Janet Frame Trail.

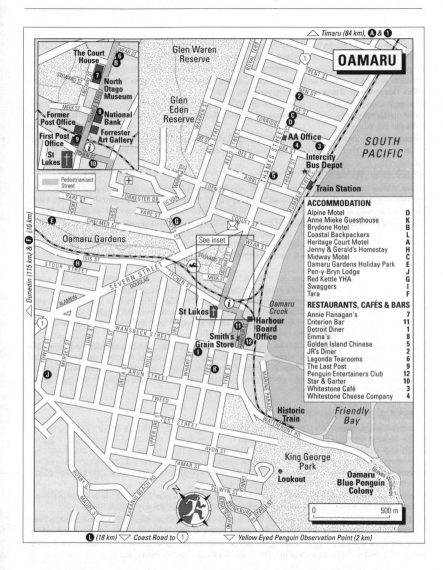

△ *Timaru (84 km),* Ⓐ & ❶

OAMARU

SOUTH PACIFIC

The Court House

North Otago Museum

Former Post Office

National Bank

Forrester Art Gallery

First Post Office

St Lukes ✝

Glen Waren Reserve

Glen Eden Reserve

AA Office

Intercity Bus Depot

★ Train Station

Pedestrianised Street

Oamaru Gardens

See inset

St Lukes ✝

Oamaru Creek

Harbour Board Office

Smith's Grain Store

◁ *Dunedin (115 km)* & Ⓕ *(16 km)*

Historic Train

Friendly Bay

King George Park

Lookout

Oamaru Blue Penguin Colony

N

0   500 m

ACCOMMODATION

Alpine Motel	D
Anne Mieke Guesthouse	K
Brydone Hotel	B
Coastal Backpackers	L
Heritage Court Motel	A
Jenny & Gerald's Homestay	H
Midway Motel	C
Oamaru Gardens Holiday Park	E
Pen-y-Bryn Lodge	J
Red Kettle YHA	G
Swaggers	I
Tara	F

RESTAURANTS, CAFÉS & BARS

Annie Flanagan's	7
Criterion Bar	11
Detroit Diner	1
Emma's	8
Golden Island Chinese	5
JR's Diner	2
Lagonda Tearooms	6
The Last Post	9
Penguin Entertainers Club	12
Star & Garter	10
Whitestone Café	3
Whitestone Cheese Company	4

Ⓛ *(18 km)* ▽ *Coast Road to* ①   ▽ *Yellow Eyed Penguin Observation Point (2 km)*

If you can manage it, the times to be here are from November to January when penguins are in greatest numbers, or over the third weekend in November when the streets of the historic district become a race track for penny-farthings, cheered on by local residents in Victorian attire and accompanied by a fair.

Accommodation

Most of the accommodation is on, or near, Thames Street. If your budget will stretch to it, try one of the homestays, which reflect Oamaru's charm.

HOTELS AND MOTELS

Alpine Motel, 285 Thames St (☎03/434 5038 & 0800/272 710, fax 434 6301). Modern building close to the town centre, with ten spacious studio units, some with full kitchens. ④.

Brydone Hotel, 115 Thames St (☎0800/279 3663, fax 03/434 5719). Magnificent old building of Oamaru stone with an ornate Italian facade, dating from 1880. Extensively renovated and redecorated, this is one of the smarter places in town. ⑤.

Heritage Court Motel, 346 Thames St (☎0800/732 200, fax 03/437 2600). One of the newer and more upmarket motels: modern, clean, spacious and comfortable units, with cooking facilities and in-house video. ④.

Midway Motel, 289 Thames St (☎ & fax 03/434 5388, ☎0800/447 744). Opposite the fire station and close to the centre of town, this budget establishment has units with full cooking facilities. ④.

B&BS AND HOMESTAYS

Anne Mieke Guesthouse, 47 Tees St (☎03/434 8051, fax 434 8050). A large suburban house offering B&B close to the town centre and the blue penguin viewing area. Each room has its own washbasin, bathrooms are shared and the rooms at the back of the house have views of the bay. ④.

Jenny and Gerald's Homestay, 11 Stour St (☎03/434 9628). About twenty minutes' walk from the bus stop, this attractive 1920s house contains an ornate staircase, a pleasant double with private facilities and two singles with shared facilities. Jenny and Gerald are very friendly and share an interest in local history, as well as running Slightly Foxed, a secondhand bookshop. Dinner by arrangement ($25). ⑤.

Pen-y-Bryn Lodge, 41 Towey St (☎03/434 7939, fax 434 9063, *www.penybryn.co.nz, admin @penybryn.co.nz*). One of the finer lodges in these parts; a splendid restored Victorian home on a hill overlooking the town, graced with hand-crafted floor-to-ceiling fireplaces, a billiard room, richly carved bookcases and a Florentine-style dining room of rimu timber and English oak. The large and luxurious rooms all have private facilities. Rates are $250 per person (May–Sept $175) and include a sumptuous four-course meal and breakfast. ⑨.

Tara, Springhill Rd (☎ & fax 03/434 8187, *smith.tara@xtra.co.nz*). Worth considering if you have your own transport, this rural homestay is set among rose gardens, native trees and farmland around 10km west of town off Weston Ngapara Road. They have just one twin room with a private bathroom. Good food, including free-range eggs, home-made bread and home-grown veg. Dinner by arrangement ($25). ⑤.

HOSTELS AND CAMPSITES

Coastal Backpackers, All Day Bay, 18km south of Oamaru near Kakanui (☎03/439 5411, fax 439 5242). Hugely relaxing rural backpackers well off the beaten track but within easy walk of a good beach and some coastal wetlands. Doubles and dorms are in a couple of separate buildings each with lounge and log burning stove; they've got free laundry and free use of bike, boogie boards and canoes; and there are $9 evening meals available. Oamaru pick-ups for booked guests, and Magic and Atomic both pass the gate. Dorms ①, rooms ②.

Oamaru Gardens Holiday Park, Chelmer St (☎0800/280 202, fax 434 7662). In a lovely sheltered setting, this site offers pitches, tourist flats and cabins. Tents $9, cabins & flats ②–③.

Red Kettle YHA, cnr Reed St & Cross St (☎ & fax 03/434 5008). Small, pleasant and well-managed hostel close to the town centre with small dorms and a couple of twin-bunked rooms. Dorms ①, rooms ②.

Swaggers, 25 Wansbeck St (03/434 9999, *swaggers@es.co.nz*). Small, homely hostel in a suburban house with twins, four-shares and one five bunk dorm. Dorms ①, twins ②.

The Historic District

Thames Street and the knot of streets around Tyne, Itchen and Harbour streets define Oamaru's Historic District, a dense cluster of grand civic and mercantile buildings that sets the town centre apart from any other in the land. The key is Oamaru stone, which hardens with exposure to the elements but, when freshly quarried, is what is known in the trade as a "free stone", easily cut and worked with conventional metal hand tools. While keeping the prevailing Neo-Classical fashion firmly in mind, the architects' imaginations ran riot, and the craftsmen were given free rein to produce deeply fluted pilasters, finely detailed pediments and elegant Corinthian pillars topped with veritable forests of acanthus leaves. Oamaru was given much of its character by architect R.A. Lawson and by the firm Forrester and Lemon who together produced most of the more accomplished buildings between 1871 and 1883. Incidentally, the local Parkside Quarry still produces Oamaru stone for use in modern buildings; witness the new Waitaki Aquatic Centre in Takaro Park

The majority of civic buildings are along Thames Street. The first of the nineteenth-century edifices to command attention is the Courthouse, an elegant, classically proportioned Palladian building showing the same Forrester and Lemon hand as the adjacent Athenaeum building, that served as a subscription library before providing a home for the **North Otago Museum** (Mon–Fri 1–4.30pm; plus Sun in Jan only 1.30–4pm; free). This absorbing collection documents all aspects of North Otago life focusing on the origin of Oamaru stone and its use in the town, along with its life as a thriving port. The Former Post Office, a few steps further along Thames Street, originally came without the tower, which was added by the architect's son, Thomas Forrester, in 1903. This building replaced the adjacent 1864 First Post Office, which predates all the other Whitestone work and is the town's only remaining example of the work of W.H. Clayton, whose simple Italianate design houses a very good restaurant and bar (see p.593). Directly opposite the one-time post offices are two of Lawson's buildings: the imposing National Bank has perhaps the purest Neo-Classical facade in town; while its grander neighbour now operates as the **Forrester Gallery** (Mon–Fri 10.30am–4.30pm, Sat 10.30am–1pm, Sun 1–4.30pm; donations welcome), which features touring exhibitions of contemporary and traditional art, alongside an extensive permanent collection of works by New Zealand artists.

Continuing along Thames Street, its junction with Itchen Street is dominated by **St Luke's Anglican Church**, topped by its looming 39m spire. The beautiful dark-wood interior boasts an 1876 Conacher pipe organ and three locally made stained-glass windows (on the left as you face the altar), depicting Christ flanked by saints Luke and Paul. Follow Itchen Street east and you'll come up to the against the infinitely more profane Criterion Hotel, with Italianate styling and a quaint bar serving fine ale (see p.593). Continuing towards the waterfront you enter Oamaru's original commercial quarter, again built of Whitestone and often flamboyant considering the mercantile purpose of the buildings.

The elegant **Smiths Grain Store** on Tyne Street, built in 1881 by stonemason James Johnson, now houses the equally elegant efforts of a tailor, who makes Victorian-style shirts, blouses and petticoats, ably assisted by a collection of old Singer sewing machines. Next door, in the old **Union Offices**, 7 Tyne St, is a traditional bookbinder's workshop (Mon–Fri 2–6pm; free), where you can watch fine bookmaking, binding and repair work; and see examples of old printing and letterpress machines. A block east of here on the waterfront, Harbour Street boasts the sadly neglected Venetian Renaissance-style Harbour Board Office, built in 1876 and one of the first public buildings designed by the prolific Forrester and Lemon. At the opposite end of Harbour Street is the striking Loan and Mercantile Warehouse which, when it was built in 1882, was the largest grain store in New Zealand. Look out for the ornamental rope design garlanding the second storey.

On weekends and public holidays you can gaze at the backs of some of these buildings from the **Oamaru Historic Steam Train** (03/434 1656; every 30min 11am–4pm; $5 return), which runs from a platform beside the visitor centre on Itchen Street a few hundred metres along the waterfront. The engines and carriages have been lovingly restored by a friendly bunch of fanatics, who also care for the blue penguins that nest in the engine shed at the end of the line.

The Oamaru Gardens

Five minutes' walk west of Thames Street along either Severn Street or Itchen Street lies the manicured natural beauty of the Oamaru Gardens (daily dawn–dusk, glasshouses 9am–4pm; free). These are among the most stunning gardens in New Zealand, dating back to 1876 and indicative of the wealth the town once enjoyed. The main Severn Street entrance leads to the spectacular Craig Fountain, built from Italian marble and surrounded by packed flowerbeds. Further on is the hundred-year-old Victorian summerhouse, full of bright blooms from around the world, with an extensive collection of cacti in a nearby purpose-built glasshouse. Flanking Oamaru Creek as it flows through the gardens are a rhododendron dell and two large ponds, while a splendid red Japanese bridge spans the creek to reach the Chinese and Fragrant Gardens. Most popular with younger visitors, though, is an enclosure at the far end of the gardens, full of wallabies and alpacas (daily dawn–dusk; free).

Penguin viewing

Oamaru is unique in having both yellow-eyed and blue **penguin colonies** within walking distance of the town centre. It is usually possible to see both colonies in one evening, since the yellow-eyes tend to come ashore earlier than the blues, but check at the visitor centre for expected arrival times. There are some important **guidelines** you must observe when viewing penguins, since these are timid creatures and are easily distressed. Flash photography is banned; you should keep quiet and still; and do not encroach within ten metres of the birds. Once disturbed, the penguins may not return to their nests for several hours, even if they have chicks to feed.

First up, about fifteen minutes' walk southeast of the town centre along Waterfront Road, is the **Blue Penguin Colony** (best visited just before dusk but check for exact times at the visitor centre; $8). At the viewing platforms, you'll be given a short talk on the history of the colony and information about the penguins. If you come during the breeding season (June–Dec), you'll see chicks – and hear them calling to their parents out at sea, hunting for food. When the parents return around dusk, travelling in groups (known as rafts), they climb the steep harbour banks and cross in front of the viewing area to their nests. Outside the breeding season the penguins indulge in much less to-ing and fro-ing, but provide an engaging spectacle nevertheless. In the peak season (Nov–Jan) you might hope to see a hundred penguins in a night, though this might drop to a dozen or so in March, June and August.

This stretch of coast is also home to the much larger **yellow-eyed penguins**, which nest in smaller numbers but keep more sociable hours, usually coming ashore in late

---

BLUE PENGUINS

Blue Penguins, the smallest of their kind, are found around the coasts of New Zealand, and along the shores of southern Australia, where they are known as fairy penguins. White on their chests and bellies, they have a thick head-to-tail streak along their back in iridescent indigo-blue. Breeding takes place from May to January, and the parents take it in turns to stay with the egg during the 36-day incubation period. The newly hatched chick is protected for the first two or three weeks before both parents go out to sea to meet the increasing demand for food, returning full of krill, squid and crustaceans, which they regurgitate into the chick's mouth. At eight weeks the chicks begin to fledge, but 70 per cent will die in the first year; the juveniles that do survive usually return to their birthplace. At the end of the breeding season the birds fatten up before coming ashore to moult: over the next three weeks their feathers are not waterproof enough for them to take to the sea and they lose up to half their bodyweight.

afternoon or early evening (best Oct–Feb). They mainly arrive on **Bushy Beach**, reached by road 2km along Bushy Beach Road, or on foot via the **Graves Walkway** (1.25km; 30min each way) which starts just past the blue penguin colony. The path curves round a headland at the end of Oamaru Harbour and continues to a point overlooking the small cove of Boatman's Harbour. This is worth exploring at low tide when **lava pillows** about 50cm in diameter are exposed in the cliff wall. These were formed millions of years ago when molten lava encased hard fossil-bearing limestone, producing a honeycomb effect with each cell defined by a rim of black lava. The walkway ends overlooking Bushy Beach, where a hide enables you to see the yellow-eyed penguins making their way across the beach.

Eating, drinking and entertainment

Oamaru isn't over endowed with good places to eat and drink, though you'll do well enough for a night or two, and a range of pockets are catered for. You shouldn't have to stray too far from the central Thames Street to find what you want.

Annie Flanagan's, 84 Thames St. An Irish bar Oamaru style with the usual range of draught Guinness and Kilkenny plus live music on Friday and Saturday nights and a pretty decent selection of stews, curries, soups, steaks and sandwiches mostly around the $10–15 mark.

Criterion Bar, *Criterion Hotel*, Tyne St. The strong Victorian feeling of the wooden bar and stone floors is carried over into an ancient till and barrels of really good beer, including London Porter and Emersons traditional ale, both of which are brewed on the premises.

Detroit Diner, on SH1, next to the Waitaki Truck Stop 4.5km north of the centre. Retro American-style diner serving breakfasts, snacks, grills and excellent clam chowder. Scallops are only $13 for a plate. Solid and cheap, this place is much favoured by truckies. Daily 5.30am–11.30pm.

Emma's Café, 15 Thames St. Hip café serving great coffee, bagels and wholemeal croissants. Exotic muffins pepped up with avocado and feta, olives and sun-dried tomatoes. Work by local artists decorates the walls. Mon–Sat 10am–6pm.

Golden Island Chinese Restaurant, 243 Thames St. Dependable and inexpensive Chinese with a good range of set menus for couples or groups, and some generous vegetarian dishes. Daily 5–9pm or later; licensed & BYO.

JR's Diner, 301 Thames St. A 24hr eat-in and takeaway snack shack, serving burgers, fish and chips, steak and superior Chinese food at reasonable prices ($8–12). BYO & licensed.

Lagonda Tearooms, 193 Thames St, cnr Eden St. One of the better greasy spoons in town, open for breakfast, lunch and early dinner. Also operates as the InterCity booking office and has Internet access.

Penguin Entertainers Club, off Harbour St. Oamaru's premier back-alley fun house and perhaps the coolest place in town; though events are irregular and not well publicized. Don't hold your breath, but it might be worth popping down to see if there is anything on: poetry, music, theatre, whatever. It is next to Willets Furniture Company; an unprepossessing alley with the sign "WFC In", leads to a stone building near the waterfront.

The Last Post, in the First Post Office building, Thames St. Upmarket bar/restaurant with a beer garden. Snacks and cocktails, as well as good lunch and dinner menus. Mon–Thurs 11am–10pm, Fri & Sat 11am–midnight, Sun 11am–10pm.

Star and Garter, 9 Itchen St (☎03/434 5246). Oamaru's premier restaurant, with a seventy-year history and vaudeville atmosphere, enhanced by a pianola and the exploits of the Foxy Club, the lively local amateur dramatic group. Great lunch and dinner menus, including fish dishes and huge desserts. This is a great place to stop off for a steamed pudding or Irish coffee on your way back from penguin viewing. Daily 10.30am–2am.

Whitestone Café, 3 Torridge St. Small café associated with the Whitestone Cheese Company, great simply for a coffee and cake, chicken panini or fettucini, but mainly the place for sampling their excellent cheeses with some of the local wine. Particularly good are the Farmhouse, a semi-soft cheese with a lemongrass aroma and nutty taste, the Brie, which has a hint of mushroom, the strong Airedale and the Windsor Blue, a creamy soft cheese – all made on the premises. Mon–Fri 8am–5pm, Sat & Sun 10am–4pm.

Listings

Bookshops Slightly Foxed, 11 Tyne St (Mon–Sat 1–5pm) sells secondhand books.

Car rental Smash Palace Rentals, 1 Meek St (☎03/434 9699), rents cars for $55 per day.

Cinema The Old Oamaru Opera House, cnr Medway St & Thames St, shows movies; screenings are advertised in the visitor centre, on a noticeboard outside the library, and in the newspapers.

Library Oamaru Public Library, next door to the North Otago Museum on Thames St (Mon–Thurs 9.30am–5.30pm, Fri 9.30am–8pm, Sat 10am–12.30pm).

Medical treatment Oamaru Hospital, Forrester Drive, cnr Devon Terrace & Warren St. In emergencies call ☎111.

Newspaper The Mon–Fri only *Oamaru Mail* has entertainment listings and emergency numbers.

Post office The post office, 2 Severn St (☎03/434 78840) has poste restante facilities.

Swimming The Queen Elizabeth II Outdoor Pool is opposite the Oamaru Gardens (Mon, Wed & Fri 6.30am–4.30pm & 5–6pm, Tues–Thurs 10am–8.30pm, Sat 10am–2pm, Sun 1.30–5pm; $1).

Tours Mrs Helen Stead (☎03/434 1173, or book through the visitor centre) takes guided walking tours of the town (1hr; $7.50).

South to Moeraki – and the Moeraki Boulders

SH1 heads south from Oamaru and constitutes the quickest way to the Moeraki boulders and Dunedin, though a more appealing alternative is to take the quieter backroads for the first 20km – follow Kakanui Beach Road (see map p.589). This route reaches the coast at Kakanui and continues 3km to All Day Bay, the peaceful location of *Coastal Backpackers* (see p.590), then winds back to the main highway.

Forty kilometres south of Oamaru on SH1, a car park and restaurant-cum-**visitor centre** (daily: Oct–April 8am–6pm; May–Nov 9am–5pm; ☎03/439 4827) overlooks the beach occupied by the strangely compelling **Moeraki Boulders**, visited on a short private trail ($2 in the honesty box at any hour). Large, grey and almost perfectly spherical, the boulders (some of which reach 2m in diameter) lie partially submerged in the sandy beach and by the wash of high tide. Their smooth skins hide honeycomb centres, which are revealed in some of the broken specimens. Despite appearances, the boulders did not fall from the sky, nor were they washed up by the sea, but rather lay deep in the mudstone cliffs behind the beach. As the sea eroded the cliffs, out fell the smooth boulders, and their distinctive surface pattern was formed as further erosion exposed a network of veins. The boulders were originally formed around a central core of carbonate of lime crystals which attracted minerals from their surroundings – a process that started sixty million years ago, when muddy sediment containing shell and plant fragments accumulated on the sea floor. The masses formed range in size from small pellets to large round rocks, some with a small void in the middle. There were a large number of these boulders in the area, but the smaller ones have all been souvenired over the years leaving only those too heavy to shift.

Maori named the boulders *Te Kai-hinaki* (food baskets), believing them to have been washed ashore from the wreck of a canoe whose occupants were seeking *pounamu*. The seaward reef near Shag Point (see below) was the hull of the canoe, and just beyond it stands a prominent rock, the vessel's petrified navigator. Some of the Moeraki Boulders were *hinaki* (baskets), the more spherical were water-carrying gourds and the irregular-shaped rocks farther down the beach were *kumara* (sweet potatoes) from the canoe's food store. The survivors among the crew, Nga Tamariki, Pukeṭapu and Pakihiwi Tahi, were transformed at daybreak into hills overlooking the beach.

Once you've had a good look at the boulders it's worth walking along the beach to the Moeraki Point whalers' lookout, where there's a view south down the coast to the lighthouse, and the likelihood of seeing Hector's dolphins, which often surf in the breakers off the beach. If you're in the area in the winter (June–Aug), you might chance upon some of the thin, silvery frost fish which beach themselves along the shoreline on frosty nights for no apparent reason.

Moeraki village

You can eat tolerably well in the restaurant/bar at the boulders' visitor centre which has great views of the ocean and boulders, but if you want to stay hereabouts your only options are in the sleepy fishing village of **MOERAKI**, 1km to the south along SH1 then 1.5km down a side road, which makes a tranquil place to break your journey.

On the right-hand side of the road just before you enter the village is the **Kotahitanga** ("One People") **Church**, built in 1862 and containing beautiful stained-glass windows, crafted in Birmingham in 1891. Considered unusual for its (at the time rather daring) portrayal of Maori alongside Jesus and Mary, the left light of the window is a portrait based on a photograph of Te Matiaha Tiramoreh of Moeraki, a respected leader of the Ngai Tahu who died in 1881. Sadly the church is only open for services (third Sunday of the month at 2pm), though you might get a glimpse of the stained glass through cracks in the church's frosted windows.

Of the **accommodation** available in the village, the *Moeraki Motel* (☎ & fax 03/439 4862; cottages ③, units ④), on the only road entering the village, is a friendly place located close to a beach with six cottages and four new two-storey units facing the bay, all with fully equipped kitchens. There's also the *Moeraki Motor Camp* (☎ & fax 03/439 4759; tent sites $8.50, cabins ②–③), situated on a hill further into the village, with cooking facilities (camp kitchens and outdoor barbecues) and a store.

Smaller shuttle bus companies will drop you in the village, although services run by the major companies merely drop off at the point where the side road into the village leaves SH1.

Shag Point

A number of smaller, odd-shaped boulders can be found at **Shag Point**, 10km south along SH1 (or an 11km walk along Katiki beach if you're feeling energetic). The beach near the point is sometimes visited by fur seals (Oct–March) and yellow-eyed penguins, which usually come ashore between 3.30pm and nightfall – there's a small hide where you can keep watch.

Palmerston

The lumber town of **PALMERSTON**, 22km south of Moeraki, marks the junction of two routes: SH1 running 55km south to Dunedin; and the "Pigroot" (SH85) inland to the Maniototo and the historic goldfield heartland of Central Otago (see p.742). There's little reason to stop long in Palmerston, though on even the briefest visit you'll notice the **monument** atop Puketapu Hill. It was erected in recognition of John McKenzie, a Scottish shepherd who, in the 1870s, rose to high office and pushed through the Land Settlement Act which effectively laid the groundwork for modern farming by breaking up the vast holdings of absentee landlords and making them available to new immigrants. To take in the extensive view from the monument, follow signs to Goodwood Road from the central junction.

Palmerston's culinary offerings are hardly an enticement to stop, though the *Postmark Café*, on the main street, is OK for a cuppa and something basic to eat. Simple **accommodation** is covered by *Pioneer Motels*, 56 Tiverton St (☎03/465 1234; ④), with self-contained units, and *Paradise Holiday Park*, 3km south of town on SH1 (☎03/465 1370; tent sites $10, dorms ①, cabins ②), which has been converted from an old sanatorium. For something considerably more luxurious, call for directions to *Centrewood*, Bobby's Head Road (☎ & fax 03/465 1977, *www.friars.co.nz/hosts/centrewood,* *centrewod@xtra.co.nz*; ⑥–⑧), a high-ceilinged 1904 homestead set amid English rose gardens well away from the road in the coastal hills and close to beaches frequented by seals and yellow-eyed penguins. The approach is low-key, but there is an effortless grace to the single suite of rooms let either as one room (⑥), a room and exclusive use of the vast lounge with polished rimu floors and a small billiard table (⑦), or the lounge and both bedrooms (sleeping up to four; ⑧). Evening meals ($30 and up) include wine and can be taken with the family who are descended from physicist Ernest Rutherford (see p.546), and keep a small collection of mementoes.

travel details

The main South Island **train** route runs from Picton through Blenheim and Kaikoura to Christchurch, then south through Ashburton, Timaru, Oamaru and Dunedin to Invercargill: there's just one train a day in each direction. The coastal **bus** route from Christchurch to Dunedin is the most hotly contested in the South Island with over half a dozen companies offering a range of schedules and very competitive prices. The inland run from Christchurch to Queenstown is another hot ticket, but services running inland from the coast are sporadic to say the least: InterCity (☎03/379 9020), Atomic Shuttle (☎03/322 8883), and Southern Link Shuttles (☎03/358 8355) have the broadest networks.

Trains

Ashburton to: Timaru (1 daily; 1hr).

Christchurch to: Arthur's Pass (1 daily; 2hr 30min); Ashburton (1 daily; 1hr); Dunedin (1 daily; 5hr 45min); Greymouth (1 daily; 4 hour 30min); Invercargill (1 daily; 9hr); Kaikoura (1 daily; 3hr); Oamaru (1 daily; 3hr 15min); Timaru (1 daily; 2hr); Picton (1 daily; 5hr 20min).

Oamaru to: Dunedin (1 daily; 2hr 30min).

Timaru to: Dunedin (1 daily; 3hr 40min); Oamaru (1 daily; 1hr).

Buses

Ashburton to Geraldine (2 daily; 40min); Timaru (9–11 daily; 1hr); Twizel (2 daily; 3hr 40min).

Christchurch to: Akaroa (1–2 daily; 2hr 50min); Arthur's Pass (3 daily; 2hr 10min); Ashburton (10–12 daily; 1hr–1hr 20min); Blenheim (7 daily; 4hr 30min–5hr); Dunedin (9–11 daily; 5–6hr); Geraldine (3–4 daily; 1hr 30–2hr); Greymouth (3 daily; 5hr); Hanmer Springs (1–2 daily; 2hr 30min); Kaikoura (7–8 daily; 2hr 45min); Lyttelton (every 30min 8.10am–11.25pm; 35min); Methven (3 daily; 1hr 15min); Mount Cook (1 daily; 5hr 20min); Nelson (3 daily; 7–8hr); Oamaru (9–11 daily; 3hr 30min–4hr 30min); Picton (7 daily; 5hr–5hr 30min); Timaru (9–11 daily; 2hr 30min); Twizel (5–6 daily; 3hr 30min–7hr); Queenstown (6–7 daily; 7–9hr); Wanaka (3–4 daily; 6hr 20min–9hr 20min).

Oamaru to: Dunedin (9–11 daily; 2hr 15min); Mount Cook (3 weekly; 2hr 30min); Twizel (1 daily; 2hr 15min).

Timaru to: Oamaru (9–11 daily; 1hr 20min); Mount Cook (3 weekly; 3hr 30min); Twizel (1 daily; 2hr 15min).

Flights

Christchurch to: Auckland (14 daily; 1hr 20min); Blenheim (1–2 daily; 50min); Dunedin (4–5 daily; 1hr); Invercargill (4 daily; 1hr 15min); Mount Cook (1–2 daily, 45min); Napier (2–3 daily; 1hr 30–2hr); Nelson (2–6 daily; 50min); Queenstown (3–5 daily; 50min); Rotorua (2 daily, 1hr 15min); Wellington (10–13 daily; 45min).

CHAPTER TEN

THE CENTRAL SOUTH ISLAND

T he **Central South Island** is one of the most varied and intriguing areas in New Zealand, with extensive pasturelands, dense native forests, and a history rich in tales of human endeavour. The defining feature of the region is however the rugged mountain ridge of the **Southern Alps**, which runs from north to south forming the South Island's central spine. The middle portion of this ridge, which culminates in New Zealand's highest peak, **Mount Cook**, presents an almost insurmountable barrier to travel between east and west coasts. The foothills of the Alps harbour rare and sometimes unique alpine plants and wildlife, including the famous Mount Cook Lilies, the largest white mountain daisies in the world; and the most mischievous of mountain parrots, the kea. A logistical nightmare to Maori and European settlers alike, the region is typical pioneer country, and the communities themselves (often named after the explorers and surveyors that opened the region up; Arthur's Pass and Lewis Pass being two prominent examples) are simple places, tinged with the toughness and idiosyncrasies of the early settlers.

The rugged nature of the terrain ensures that it's impossible to traverse the region on a north–south axis, and access to the area is determined by routes approaching the mountains from the east and west coasts. The most northerly of these routes is the **Lewis Pass Road**, which conveys traffic from the Canterbury Plains north of Christchurch to Westport on the west coast, passing the spa resort of **Hanmer Springs** on the way. Hanmer is a tranquil place surrounded by striking forested hill and mountain scenery, and a good base from which to visit the neighbouring Hanmer Springs Ski Area, as well as **Hanmer Forest** and **Maruia Springs** further west. South of here, another major cross-mountain route served by both road and rail links Christchurch with the western seaboard town of Greymouth via **Arthur's Pass**, historically an

ACCOMMODATION PRICES

Accommodation listed in this guide has been categorized into one of nine price bands, as set out below. The rates quoted represent the **cheapest available** double or twin **room** – except for category ①, which are per-person rates for a dorm bed. Note that fees for **tent sites** and **DOC huts** (quoted in dollars) are also per-person, unless otherwise stated.

① under $20 per person	④ $60–80	⑦ $140–180
② under $40 per room	⑤ $80–100	⑧ $180–240
③ $40–60	⑥ $100–140	⑨ over $240

For more on accommodation, see p.34.

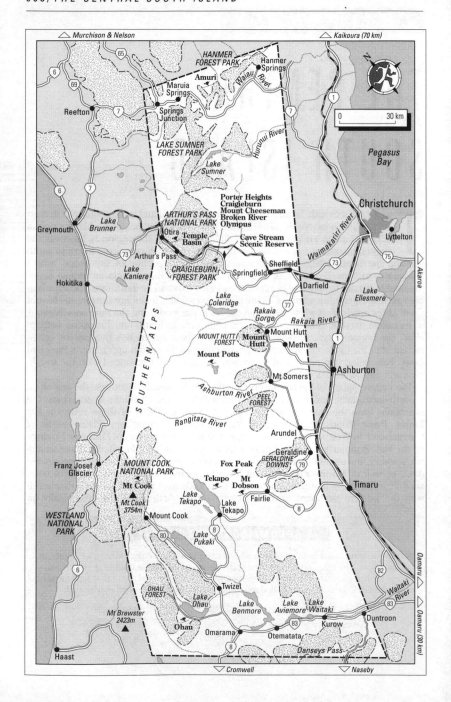

△ Murchison & Nelson
△ Kaikoura (70 km)

HANMER
FOREST PARK

Hanmer
Springs

Amuri

Maruia
Springs

Waiau River

Reefton

Springs
Junction

Hurunui River

LAKE SUMNER
FOREST PARK

Lake
Sumner

Pegasus
Bay

0   30 km

Christchurch

Greymouth

Lake
Brunner

ARTHUR'S PASS
NATIONAL PARK

Otira

Porter Heights
Craigieburn
Mount Cheeseman
Broken River
Olympus

Temple
Basin

Cave Stream
Scenic Reserve

Waimakariri River

Lyttelton

Arthur's Pass

CRAIGIEBURN
FOREST PARK

Springfield

Sheffield

Darfield

Akaroa ▷

Hokitika

Lake
Kaniere

SOUTHERN ALPS

Lake
Coleridge

Rakaia
Gorge

Rakaia River

Lake
Ellesmere

MOUNT HUTT
FOREST

Mount
Hutt

Mount Hutt

Methven

Mount Potts

Mt Somers

Ashburton River

PEEL
FOREST

Ashburton

Rangitata River

Arundel

Franz Josef
Glacier

MOUNT COOK
NATIONAL PARK

Mt Cook

Mt Cook
3754m

Mount Cook

Fox Peak

Tekapo

Mt
Dobson

Lake
Tekapo

Lake Tekapo

Fairlie

GERALDINE
DOWNS

Geraldine

Timaru

WESTLAND
NATIONAL
PARK

Lake
Pukaki

OHAU
FOREST

Lake
Ohau

Twizel

Lake
Benmore

Lake
Aviemore

Lake
Waitaki

Oamaru ▷

Waitaki River

Oamaru (30 km) ▷

Mt Brewster
2423m

Ohau

Omarama

Otematata

Kurow

Duntroon

Haast

Danseys Pass

▽ Cromwell
▽ Naseby

important trade route connecting the coalfields of the west coast with the port of Lyttelton. It's now much travelled by tourists, with the Christchurch–Greymouth **TranzAlpine Express** providing one of New Zealand's most spectacular rail journeys. It's also one of the best places to go tramping with hundreds of miles of walks available in the **Pass National Park**.

South of Christchurch, roads lead up from the southern Canterbury Plains towards the small but lively foothill settlements of **Methven**, **Mount Hutt** and **Mount Somers**, which together make up one of the most exciting ski areas on the South Island. It's a popular destination for adventure seekers in summer too, with whitewater rafting, kayaking, paragliding, climbing and ballooning proving the main attractions. South of here, the attractive town of **Geraldine** provides access to the Geraldine Downs, for many the most England-like landscape on the South Island; while **Farlie** stands at the borders of the **McKenzie Country**, an area renowned for massive sheep runs and the beautiful blues of its glacier-fed lakes, **Tekapo** and **Pukaki** – both of which shimmer beneath the Southern Alps' most imperious peak, Mount Cook. **Mount Cook Village**, nestling at the foot of the mountains and the starting point of numerous walks, is the best base from which to explore. Routes south from Mount Cook towards Otago pass through **Twizel**, a strange fledgling settlement of only thirty years; and the rural backwater of **Omarama**, which commands access to the scenic **Waitaki Valley** route east to Oamaru and the coast.

Upland areas of the South Island typically have a wide-ranging and very variable **climate**, with long hot summers, cold crisp winters, and over a metre of rainfall annually.

Hanmer Springs and Lewis Pass

Most northerly of the cross-mountain routes, the **Lewis Pass Road** (SH7) follows the course of a track that provided both Maori and early *pakeha* (European settlers) with a necessary link between the east and west coasts. For those travelling from the east coast the route starts at the town of Waipara, 80km north of Canterbury, where the SH7 leaves the coastal plain and begins its gradual climb between foothills of the Southern Alps. Lying just off this route in a side valley, the spa resort of **Hanmer Springs** acts as a base for summer walks and adventure activities, and as a convenient resting place for winter sports enthusiasts who enjoy the nearby **Hanmer Springs Ski Area**. It also offers the best range of accommodation hereabouts, a wooded mountain hinterland, and one of the top ten golf courses in the country. Some 60km further west, the **Lewis Pass** itself is set amidst some exhilarating subalpine terrain and deep forest; while **Maruia Springs**, just beyond the summit of the pass, is another elegant though smaller resort in which to soak in the soothing thermal waters. There is a variety of public **transport** into the region, with several daily buses making the trip from Christchurch direct to Hanmer Springs, and other services heading from Christchurch over the pass to Westport on the west coast.

Hanmer Springs

About 140km north of Christchurch, a side road leaves SH7 to head north towards the quaint spa resort of **HANMER SPRINGS**, some 10km distant. Just after the turn-off from SH7, you'll cross the spectacular **Waiau Ferry Bridge**, designed by John Blackett. This was considered a major feat of engineering at the time of its opening in 1887, and the locals threw such a party that the site of the hospitality tent became known as Champagne Flat. The bridge now witnesses the tortured expressions of bungy jumpers as they hurl themselves from its parapet. Hanmer Springs itself is pleasantly situated at the edge of a broad, fertile agricultural plain, with steep, forested hills

ACCOMMODATION
C Alpine Garden Motel
E Alpine Lodge Motel
F Cheltenham House
B Forest Peak Motel
A Hanmer Backpackers
H Hanmer Springs Forest Camp
G Mountain View Holiday Park
D Glenalvon Lodge B&B

RESTAURANTS AND CAFÉS
1 Alpine Village Inn
5 Garden House Café
3 Jaywalk Café
2 Keith's Café
4 The Old Post Office

above. Sadly apart from the highly-developed thermal pools, the motel-riddled, mall-infested town centre has little to offer. However, it does give access to some entertaining river trips and the **Hanmer Forest Park**, where the walks are particularly attractive in autumn when the birch, poplar, sycamore and rowan trees are rich in golden hues.

Arrival and information

There are a number of buses to Hanmer, including the Hanmer Connection (☎03/315 7575), which operate a daily service from Christchurch, either as a day-trip (90min each way; $40 return) or a one-way shuttle ($22). These and InterCity buses run direct to Hanmer from Christchurch and Kaikoura, and drop off near the visitor centre.

The **visitor centre** on Amuri Avenue, next to the Thermal Reserve baths (daily 10am–5pm; ☎03/315 7128, *www.hurunui.govt.nz*, *hanvin@nzhost.co.nz*), has helpful staff, handles all DOC enquiries and upstairs contains illuminating displays relating to the natural assets of the Hurunui region and journeys through the area by Maori, cattle drovers and the remarkable Park brothers who canoed across the main divide via Harper's Pass. Despite an excessive amount of accommodation development Hanmer has only two small supermarkets, no ATM and one bank (Mon, Wed & Fri 10am–2pm), so bring cash and supplies.

Accommodation

Hanmer's reputation amongst Kiwis as an elegant little resort has attracted a disproportionate amount of motel and mall development meaning that accommodation tends to be on the expensive side, although there's a modest sprinkling of backpacker-style dorms and inexpensive cabins. The town is busiest at the height of summer and during school holidays, when it's wise to book ahead.

Alpine Garden Motel, 3 Leamington St (☎03/315 7332, fax 315 7334, *alpinegarden@xtra.co.nz*). Clean, comfortable, self-contained units, in a quiet setting three minutes' walk from the thermal pools. ⑤–⑥.

Alpine Lodge Motel, 1 Harrogate St at the corner with Amuri Ave (☎03/315 7311, fax 315 7312, *reservations@alpinelodgemotel.co.nz*). Opposite the thermal pools these chalet units are comfortable and well equipped. ⑤.

Cheltenham House, 13 Cheltenham St (☎03/315 7545, fax 315 7645, *cheltenham@xtra.co.nz*). Just two minutes from the visitor centre this is the best B&B accommodation in the town at any price. There are four large, light-filled rooms set in a lovingly and tastefully renovated 1930s house and two cottages in the well-tended, three-quarter-acre garden. ⑥.

Glenalvon Lodge B&B, 29 Amuri Ave, diagonally opposite the visitor centre (☎03/315 7475, *glenalvon@xtra.co.nz*). Luxury accommodation in two B&B rooms in the main house or nine well-kept, motel-like units out the back. ④–⑥.

Forest Peak Motel, 4 Torquay Terrace (☎ & fax 03/315 7132). Ten minutes' walk from the visitor centre, this motel has ten clean comfortable units and three attractive pine cabins. Some of the units have open fires. ④–⑤.

Hanmer Backpackers, 41 Conical Hill Rd (☎03/315 7196). Previously the *Amuri Backpackers* this is one of the few budget options close to the village centre, offering mostly shared rooms, with one double. Not for the claustrophobic. Dorms ①, room ②.

Hanmer Springs Forest Camp, Jollies Pass Rd (☎03/315 7202, *hanmer.forest.camp@xtra.co.nz*). This YHA affiliate is a large holiday camp, clearly signposted 2km east of town, surrounded by trees from all over the world, with 150 or so beds, mostly in diminutive old wooden cabins. Wood-burning stoves provide hot water and drying areas; there's also an excellent accommodation block modified for people with disabilities (book ahead for this). A camp track links to several DOC walks. Tent sites $16 for two, dorms ①, cabins ②.

Mountain View Holiday Park, cnr Amuri Ave & Bath St (☎03/315 7113, fax 315 7188, *mtviews.hanmer@clear.net.nz*). A variety of tourist flats and cabin accommodation, in a large well-kept area. Tent sites $9, cabins & units ②–④.

The Village

The main street is Amuri Avenue, which forks into Conical Hill Road heading north and Jollies Pass Road heading northeast. Amuri Avenue is divided into two carriageways by a central, tree-shaded reservation that gives this small town a quiet, sheltered feel.

The **Thermal Springs**, Amuri Avenue (daily 10am–9pm; $8, $15 private pools), were discovered in 1859 by William Jones while he searched for stray cattle. The springs are fed by rainwater that seeps down through fractures in the rocks of the Hanmer Mountains, accumulating in an underground reservoir some 2km beneath the Hanmer Plain. After absorbing some minerals and being warmed up by heat radiated from the earth's core, the water rises to the surface via fissures in the greywacke rock. Hanmer became famous in the 1870s for the relaxing and curative powers attributed to its waters; and since then the springs have undergone massive development, thereby losing their Victorian charm. The modern pool complex contains various sized, artificially landscaped thermal pools full of light-blue springwater, as well as a standard chlorinated 25m swimming pool. There's also a toddlers' pool, a series of play pools including a large water slide, volcano lava pools, a gym, health and beauty centre and the *Garden House Café* (daily 10am–9pm; licensed), which provides snacks and light meals at extravagant prices.

The only other attraction in Hanmer Springs is the small, privately owned **Karter Kollection Museum** (Mon–Sat 8.30am–5.30pm, opening hours sometimes vary; $2), on Conical Hill about two minutes' walk from the Thermal Reserve, which contains a mish-mash of odds and ends that barely justifies the price of admission, unless the weather is awful and you are desperate.

Hanmer Forest Park

By far the best and least expensive entertainment to be had around Hanmer is exploring the forest. Ranged around the village to the north and east, the **Hanmer Forest
Park** can be reached by walking along Jacks Pass Road, Conical Hill Road, Jollies Pass
Road or by following McIntyre Road out to Mullens Road and the Mount Isobel Stream.
The park was created in 1901 using convict labour to plant a wide variety of exotic trees,
which are now protected from logging. An easy **Forest Walk** (2.5km; 1hr), accessible
from Jollies Pass Road leads through some of the oldest of the sycamore, oak, and silver birch, while another comfortable and rewarding trail is the **Woodland Walk** (2km;
45min), accessible from Jollies Pass Road, featuring a stream, flax wetland and ponds
teeming with birds. For the more adventurous there are moderately strenuous treks to
Conical Hill (1.5km; 150m ascent; 1hr), accessible from the Conical Hill Road (or as
an extension to the Woodland Walk), which offers a panoramic view; and the **Waterfall
Track** (2.5km; 400m ascent; 3hr), leading to the 41m-high Dog Stream Waterfall, connected to town by the **Upper Dog Stream Track** (3km; 2hr), accessible from Pawson
Road off Jollies Pass Road. These walks are detailed in the excellent DOC leaflet,
Hanmer Forest Recreation ($1), which highlights eighteen different trails in the forest,
ranging in timescale from an hour to a full day. The leaflet also contains an information
sheet on Moleworth Station (see below).

Hanmer forest is also renowned for **mountain biking** and hosts trail-bike races
twice a year (Sept–Oct & April–May). **Bike rental** ($25 per day) and **organized trips**
(2hr–full day; $19–75) are available at Dust 'n' Dirt, 20 Conical Hill Rd (☎03/315 7233),
and you can pick up a bike-track map from the visitor centre (10¢). One of the most popular routes follows an old Maori and then European packhorse route to Blenheim
(191km), via **Molesworth Station**, one of New Zealand's largest farms: a DOC leaflet,
Molesworth ($1), sets out information about the **scenic drive/bike ride**, and the cat-
tle station's history. The section through the station is 56km (2hr by car, cycling times
vary from 3hr 30min to 6hr), and is only open from 30th December to 13th February
because it is still a working farm. You must register at either the *Molesworth Cob
Cottage* at the northern end of the trail or the *Archeron Guesthouse* at the southern end,
both of which offer camping facilities. There is no camping elsewhere on the station.
The quiet and atmospheric station road traverses rugged terrain prone to landslips,
washouts and snow; note that caravans, campervans and buses are banned.

Activities

Scenic **rafting** trips on the Clarence, Hurunui and Waiau rivers are offered by Rainbow
Adventures on Amuri Avenue (☎ & fax 03/315 7401; half day on the Waiau River $60,
full day on the Hurunui River $98, 3–5 days Wilderness Trip on the Clarence River

---

THE HANMER SPRINGS SKI AREA

Hanmer Springs is a good place from which to enjoy the **Hanmer Springs Ski area**
(☎03/315 7233, fax 315 7201, *hbc@clear.net.nz*, formerly the Amuri Skifield), 40min drive
from Hanmer up the Clarence Valley Road on the slopes of Mount St Patrick and the St
James Ranges. **Transport** from Hanmer can be arranged with Rainbow Adventures (on
request; $15–20 return; ☎03/315 7401). All the field tows cost $28 per day, and conditions
tend to favour snowboarding and intermediate skiers; **equipment** can be rented from
Hanmer Springs Adventure Centre, 20 Conical Hill Rd, Hanmer (☎03/315 7233). At the
field there is also a centrally heated day lodge, with stoves, toasted sandwiches and tea
and coffee.

The Mount Lyford Skifield, 60km to the northeast, is also accessible from Hanmer via
SH1

$450). The same company also offers **fun-yakking** (half-day $65), in which you flop downriver in inflatable two-person kayaks, which are also rather ominously known as "divorce boats"; **canyoning** (half day $42), which involves walking, jumping and sliding your way through the eddies, falls and cascades of a mountain stream; and tandem **paragliding** (25min; $135, $80 with own transport). **Horse riding** in the area is run by the unconnected Rainbow Horse Trekking, Jacks Pass Road (☎03/315 7444; 1hr $25, half day $50, full day $110, Twilight Trail $40) who cater for people of all abilities and experience. Serious riders should contact Alpine Horse Safaris, based on Waitohi Downs near Hawarden, off SH7 about 60km south of Hanmer, who organize some of the best **horse safaris** in the region (☎03/314 4293; 2hr–10days; $25–$1200). Longer trips include all food and accommodation, but must be booked at least a month in advance.

For more thrills, go for a **jetboat** ride through the steep-sided gorges of the Waiau River with Amuri Jet/Thrillseekers (☎03/315 7046; a 20km, 1hr ride costs $60–65); or **bungy**, again with Thrillseekers ($89 per jump), based at the Waiau Ferry Bridge. The same company also offer half- and full-day rafting trips at similar prices to those of Rainbow Adventures.

Eating and drinking

Considering Hanmer is a highly regarded Kiwi holiday resort which has recently seen an epidemic of motel building it offers few options in terms of value for money **eating**. The friendliest place to dine is *Keith's Café*, on Amuri Avenue (daily 9am–8.30pm), a rustic-looking spot offering a wide range of mountainous, inexpensive snacks and meals including full cooked breakfasts and excellent fish and chips for under $15. The best food in town is served in *The Old Post Office*, Jacks Pass Road (☎03/315 7461; daily 6.30–11pm; licensed), a stylish, imaginative restaurant with $20-plus main courses and a surprisingly reasonable wine list. You can find good-value quality food at the *Jaywalk Café and Wine Bar*, Amuri Avenue (daily 11am–10pm, closed Mondays Dec–April; licensed), offering casual dining from a regularly changing menu and splendid mixed platters. Those in need of a **drink** should make for the bar of the *Alpine Village Inn*, behind the new shopping mall and beside the public car park, where they also serve basic bar food at economy rates.

West to Lewis Pass

West of the Hanmer Springs turn-off, SH7 continues on its climb towards the **Lewis Pass** 65km away. The high country around the pass was never actually settled by Maori, although it lay on a trail they tramped in search of *pounamu* (greenstone). Later, European pastoralists sought an easier route between east and west coasts, and in 1860, the surveyors Christopher Maling and Henry Lewis stumbled upon the pass. In 1866 a bridle track linking Hanmer Plain with Murchison was finished, and by 1936 a spectacular highway suitable for motor vehicles was finally opened.

The land between Hanmer and the squat hills of the **Boyle Bluffs**, which herald the **Doubtful River Valley** (a one-time gold diggers' route), is a rugged area of low-yielding grassland, with broom (a blazing yellow in the summer), spiky matagouri, manuka and kanuka taking hold where the farms have failed. As you approach the pass, red and silver beech forest begins to predominate. Shortly after the tiny cluster of houses that is the settlement of **BOYLE**, 50km out from Hanmer, you will come across **Sylvia Flat**, part of the Lewis Pass National Reserve, where it is possible to park and follow a track beside the Lewis River for about 50m to pools where warm water bubbles up through the rocks, mixing with the cold river water to create refreshing thermal pools. Be warned this area is difficult to find when the water levels of the river are high. The 907-metre-high **Lewis Pass** itself is just 15km further

---

ST JAMES WALKWAY

You can either start the **St James Walkway Subalpine Track** (66km; 5 days; 271m ascent; outlined in a DOC leaflet of the same name 50¢, the *Lewis Pass* leaflet 50¢, or the travel map of the area $13.50; all available from Hanmer Springs and Reefton visitor centres), 4km along SH7 from the Hanmer Springs turn-off, just south of the confluence of the Boyle and Lewis rivers at the Boyle Shelter car park, or at the Lewis Pass picnic area and car park, about 16km further up SH7. The better way is north to south, Lewis Pass to the Boyle and Lewis rivers, beginning with the descent to the **Cannibal Gorge Bridge**, an excellent short walk for the less adventurous (2km, 80min).

There are a number of **bus services** between Lewis Pass and Boyle, so you can get back to your car from either end of the track. This is a subalpine region, so go well-equipped with **all-weather gear** and a plentiful supply of **food**. Accommodation is provided by five DOC **huts** (category 2, 20 bunks; $10), all with wood stoves, firewood, intentions book and walkway map. A mixture of riverside walk, forest, farmland, descents, climbs, and tussock, this is a strenuous tramp: the hardest day involves an ascent to the highest point, Anne Saddle (1136m above sea level), with spectacular views to the Rokeby and Boyle Flat huts to the south and the Anne Hut to the north.

---

on, and offers views along the high-sided Cannibal Gorge (see above) towards the Spenser Mountains.

Maruia Springs and Springs Junction

Eight kilometres beyond Lewis Pass, **MARUIA SPRINGS** is another thermal spa resort, grouped around a swanky bath complex with **hot pools** (daily 9am–9pm; $6.50 communal pool areas; $20 private baths) that overlooks the Maruia River. The outside pools contain waters whose colours range from black to milky white, depending on the level of minerals they contain. The steaming waters are allegedly good for arthritis – but not so good for jewellery, which gets badly tarnished by the sulphurous fumes. **Accommodation** at the *Maruia Springs Resort* (☎03/523 8840; tent sites $18, dorms $26.50, units ⑤) ranges from camping to simple en-suite units; if you stay here, you're entitled to free and unlimited use of the springs. Within the complex there's a **café-bar** and two **restaurants**, one Kiwi-style and one Japanese.

Twenty kilometres west of Maruia Springs, there's a parting of the ways at **SPRINGS JUNCTION**, with the SH7 continuing west towards Reefton and the SH65 forging northwards to Murchison. Springs Junction itself has little to recommend it except an unmanned **DOC Information Centre** and walks; and essential services such as a petrol station and village shop.

Arthur's Pass and around

Another classic east–west route across the Southern Alps is the one linking Christchurch with Greymouth via **Arthur's Pass**. Traversed by both a highly scenic rail line and the equally breathtaking SH73, the route is easily accessible from Christchurch, making it a popular excursion for city-based travellers eager for a quick taste of the high country and winter sports enthusiasts who wish to take advantage of the many and varied ski fields.

The pass gets its name from civil engineer **Arthur Dobson**, who "discovered" it after hearing about it from local Maori, who had been using it for hundreds of years to bring *pounamu* from the west coast to the Canterbury Plains. Dobson surveyed the pass in 1864, and by 1866 horse-drawn coaches were using it to serve the Westland goldfields. The railway was built in 1923, coinciding with the booming interest in alpine tourism worldwide.

From Christchurch to Arthur's Pass

Whether travelling by road or rail, the trip from Christchurch to the pass is an adventure encompassing great geographical contrasts, beginning in the agriculturally rich Canterbury Plains and ending in an earthquake-shaken village 737m above sea level. The actual **summit** of the pass is at 912m, 4km to the west of Arthur's Pass village, marked by a large obelisk inscribed with the name Arthur Dudley Dobson, and is the start of many rewarding walks.

Initially both road and rail follow the course of the shingle-lined Waimakariri River, passing though a series of low-lying farm communities before beginning the gradual climb away from the neatly organized fields of the plains. The route ascends gently to **Springfield**, 70km out of Christchurch, at which point the river and the rail line veer away to the northwest, while the road continues climbing steadily past the sources of several rivers and streams to the 923m **Porter's Pass**, at the northern end of Lake Lyndon. As the route winds through increasingly dramatic gorges it passes the **Porter Heights Skifield** (see p.610), and then lakes Pearson, Grasmere and Sarah to the north, which are directly opposite **Craigieburn Forest Park**, and the **Craigieburn**, **Mount Cheeseman**, **Broken River**, and **Mount Olympus** skifields (see p.610). About 6km beyond Lake Grasmere is the small settlement of **Cass**, where the tarmac and track routes rejoin and once again accompany the Waimakariri River along its winding progress through the Southern Alps. On reaching **Bealey**, at the northern foot of the mountain of the same name (1823m), the river once again bids farewell before heading south to its source on the mountain, while the road and railway line push on to Arthur's Pass, in the centre of the national park, with 2271m **Mount Rolleston** to its southern side, and both 1705m **Mount Pfeifer** and the **Temple Basin Skifield** (see p.610) to its northwest. Just after Arthur's Pass the railway dives through the long glum **Otira Gorge Tunnel** while the road climbs beyond the settlement and then descends through the recently constructed **Otira Viaduct**, a spectacular engineering marvel that greatly improves the road's safety. After that both road and rail slip quickly down toward the pounding seas of the West Coast.

Springfield

Although it doesn't look much, **SPRINGFIELD**, 70km from Christchurch, is the first place worth stopping, especially if you fancy a high-speed boat trip down the **Waimakariri Gorge** to blow away the cobwebs. Waimak Alpine Jet, on Rubicon Road, off the Kowahi Bush Road (☎03/318 4881; 20min for $35, 1hr for $75), operate fourteen-seater jetboats on demand all year round. The gorge is narrow, and the river water as clear as gin, with many waterfalls making for a safe, spectacular and beautiful ride.

In town on the northwest side of SH73 (Main Road), just past the junction with SH72, is the local domain where you can easily spend a relaxing twenty minutes exploring the pleasing **monument** to Springfield's best-loved son, Rewi Alley. Named after Rewi Maniapoto, the Maori leader who shouted at the battle of Orakau, *Kaore e manu te tongo. Ake! Ake!* ("We will never make peace. Never! Never!"), Alley displayed similar resilience throughout his fascinating life. After World War I he worked as a missionary in China, setting up small manufacturing co-operatives during the hazardous Japanese occupation. He went on to found schools, help with oil development, translate Chinese poetry, write poetry and prose of his own and act as an unofficial ambassador for China, despite his misgivings about the direction of the post-war communist regime and his increasing isolation within the country. The peaceful, Chinese-style garden memorial includes rock and water features, Rewi's abridged biography

---

THE TRANZALPINE EXPRESS

The **TranzAlpine Express** (4hr 10min; $81 one way, $109 day return) from Christchurch **to Greymouth** leaves Christchurch train station at 9am every morning. The **train** has large viewing windows and comfortable seats, with an open-sided observation car to aid photographers. Complimentary morning or afternoon tea is served, and snacks are available at only slightly inflated prices.

The scenic, 231km, coast-to-coast journey rises from an altitude of three metres above sea level at Christchurch to 737m at Arthur's Pass (the railway tunnels beneath the 920m summit of the pass), passing through nineteen **tunnels** and crossing numerous **viaducts** spanning picturesque braided rivers. This area is noted for its relatively high rainfall of 1.2m a year, and purple **lupins** festoon the railway embankments, interspersed with yellow broom and beech forest beyond the crest of the pass. If you travel in December you will also see red and white rata in bloom, but the trip is at its romantic, snow-cloaked best in the **winter** months (June–Aug).

The **route** traverses the Canterbury Plain as far as Springfield, after which you start to see the mountains, and reaches the halfway point around Craigieburn, where the piped commentary used to give way to a TranzAlpine Rail pop song of Lloyd-Webber-like horror. There's a pause at Arthur's Pass itself to allow for a change of locomotive, after which the train dives through the 8.5km-long Otira Tunnel. Descending to the west coast, you'll be treated to impressive views of Lake Brunner before trundling into Greymouth (see p.714), having covered in less than five hours a journey that took the horse-drawn coaches of Cobb and Company two days – and shortened the average life expectancy of the draught horses to a mere eighteen months.

---

and a memorial to his remarkable mother, Clara, a leader in the New Zealand women's suffrage movement.

If you feel like breaking your journey, Springfield offers one of the friendliest and most comfortable affiliate YHA **hostels** on the South Island – *Smylie's* opposite the domain (☎03/318 4740, fax 318 4780, dorms ①, rooms ③). Busiest in the winter when it operates as a ski lodge *Smylie's* has great facilities, a refreshing Japanese influence (Japanese baths, winter only) and cosy rooms. If you feel the need of sustenance or a refreshing pint try the **Old Springfield Pub** on Main Street, offering a selection of ales, reasonably priced rustic snacks and substantial main courses.

Kura Tawhiti (Castle Hill Reserve)

About 30km west of Springfield, SH73 passes through the well-signposted **Kura Tawhiti** (Castle Hill Reserve), where there are a number of walks among the rising tussock-covered hills and rock outcrops. One of the most interesting is a twenty-minute stroll that starts from the old cattle station/main entrance (2km south of Castle Hill Village) and heads among large, grey, Stonehenge-like rocky outcrops protruding from mounds of grass and gorse. This rather surreal landscape also offers excellent rock-climbing and good photo opportunities. The lumpy tussock is brightened by mountain daisies (whose leaves are used for weaving by Maori) and Castle Hill buttercups in the summer.

Cave Stream Scenic Reserve

A bare wild area in the same vein as Kura Tawhiti, **Cave Stream Scenic Reserve** nestles among limestone outcrops with views of the Craigieburn and Torlesse ranges. Access is from SH73 6km west of Kura Tawhiti where a dirt, oval car park and a number of DOC information boards announce this rare opportunity to explore a limestone cave by blackwater hiking (362m; 1hr, mostly wading with a 3m ladder climb). Cave art, artefacts, signs of seasonal camps and the discovery of a wooden framed flax backpack, over 500 years old (now in the Canterbury Museum, see p.547), indicate that Maori once visited the area extensively. The cave itself contains bones, suggesting it was a burial site; it also provides a home for large harvestman spider-like insects and young eels who wriggle along the walls. This is an exciting, if wet, underground adventure (though the cave often hosts school outings so don't get too worried). If you venture ahead then dress warmly, take torches with spare batteries (there's no light in the cave) and make sure you have something dry to change into afterwards. The **walk/wade** itself involves entering at the downstream end where you'll cross a deep pool (waist high; if the water is higher, fast flowing, foaming and discoloured do not attempt the walk) before gradually climbing upstream. There are only two obstacles: a 1.5m rock-fall about half way and a 3m waterfall at the very end. The latter you'll negotiate by crawling along a short, narrow ledge and up a ladder of iron rungs embedded in the rock.

Craigieburn Forest Park – and Bealey

The **Craigieburn Forest Park** lies on the eastern ranges of the Southern Alps, about 15km beyond Kura Tawhiti, on the opposite side of SH73 from the Cave Stream Reserve and 42km before Arthur's Pass. It is chock-a-block with good walking tracks, longer tramps and climbing opportunities in the more rugged country further west. The park is dominated by dense, moss-covered mountain beech forest, alpine scrub and tussock grasslands, which are peppered with scarlet native mistletoe flowers from December to February. A variety of native birds streak and squawk through the forest, including bellbird, rifleman, silver eye and kea (alpine parrot), and between October and February, long-tailed and shining cuckoos join the throng. The nearby **Craigieburn skifield**, within the boundaries of the forest park, is one of the most exciting in the vicinity of Arthur's Pass – see box on p.610 for details.

In a signposted car park just off SH73 by Cave Stream, is the **Craigieburn Picnic Area** and a walkers' **shelter** with fixed maps of the local tramps. The *Craigieburn Forest Park Day Walks* leaflet (from local visitor centres; $1) details eleven of the best short and day walks in the park. From the picnic area the path up to and around the **Lyndon Saddle** (4km; 3–4hr) is worthwhile, but if you do nothing else take the **Hut Creek Walk** (2km; 1hr) beginning outside the Environmental and Education Centre (not open to the public) at the top of the winding, dirt road 3km further on from the picnic site and SH73, or accessible from the Broken River Skifield Road which jags away from SH73 1km south of the picnic area turn-off. The track itself winds down to the creek and continues through mountain beeches, emerging onto a slope of native hebe, dracophyllum (whose leaves shade from green to a reddish-brown in spring and autumn), cassinis and matagouri and allows great views from the lookout. The whole walk boasts an abundance of very watchable kea – but beware of the kleptomanic tendencies of these highly intelligent birds. To tack on a pleasant extra twenty minutes try the nature trail that also begins at the centre.

If you want to break your journey before the final assault on the pass, the solitary **Historic Bealey Hotel** (☎03/318 9277, fax 318 9014, *bealeyhotel@xtra.co.nz*; dorms ①, motel units ⑤) is around 40km further along SH73, just 10km short of Arthur's Pass Village. Easily spotted because of a large concrete replica Moa perched on top of the knoll out front, the hotel hunkers between gnarled escarpment faces by a flat broad riverbed. The reason for the Moa is that a previous owner claimed to have seen one long after they were extinct, massively boosting trade and then decamping with the proceeds. Once a stop off point for the Cobb Coaches that travelled to and from the west coast, the hotel now provides clean and simple backpacker and motel-style accommodation, beer and reasonable food in the *Klondyke Bar*, a bistro and a restaurant.

Arthur's Pass Village

ARTHUR'S PASS VILLAGE nestles in one of many steep-sided, forest-covered U-shaped valleys and forms a thin low-rise straggle along the main road (SH73), with power and telecommunication pylons as a fringe. The area receives over a metre of rainfall a year, and the village invariably hunches beneath mist or clouds: there's often a moody contrast between the white clouds that hover halfway up the valley wall, and the rich green trees and vegetation of the valley floor and slopes. Another common sight in and around the village in the early evening are the kea. whose lolloping sideways gate, scavenging tendencies and inexhaustible curiosity give much entertainment. If you're enjoying a sandwich you'll hear the ruffle of swift passing feathers and see the flash of red beneath their wings as they join you, but although they are mischievous and adorable you must never feed them.

The Arthur's Pass settlement came about in the early 1900s to provide shelter for tunnel diggers and rail workers, and nowadays ekes a living from the tourists visiting the surrounding **national park**. It's a superb base for walking and climbing, with the nearby **Temple Basin skifield** (see box on p.610) providing good skiing and snowboarding opportunities in the winter.

Practicalities

Regular coast-to-coast buses (Coast to Coast ☎0800/800 847, Alpine Coach and Courier ☎025/342 460) stop in the centre of the settlement on the main street. The TranzAlpine train also stops close to the centre of the village. Tickets for both are available at the Arthur's Pass Store, and bookings can be made through the visitor centre. The village is best explored on foot, but Arthur's Pass Taxis (☎03/318 9266) can take you to the start of out-of-the-way tracks, or run you up to look at the actual pass itself.

There is an excellent **DOC office** and **visitor centre**, on the main street, diagonally opposite the fire tender (daily: June–Oct 9am–4pm; Nov–May 8am–5pm; 24hr unmanned information area with search and rescue cards; ☎03/318 9211, fax 318 9210, *www.canterburypages.co.nz* or *www.softrock.co.nz*), with numerous walks leaflets and background information on the whole of New Zealand. The visitor centre also has extensive displays on wildlife, plants, geology and local history; and a video about the trail blazed by the stage coaches and the railway is played on request ($1). The only public phones are just outside the YHA. There's a rarely open **post office** (in a shed), a **petrol station** and a couple of stores in the village, but **no banks** although the bottleshop/store does take EFTPOS.

ACCOMMODATION

There's a reasonable choice of good-value accommodation in the village, although places fill up quickly during the high season (early Dec to late Feb), when it's a good idea to book in advance. If there's no room at the inn, you could always try the *Historic Bealey Hotel*, 10km to the east (see p.607).

Alpine Motel, on SH73 as you enter the village across Rough Creek, almost immediately on your left (☎03/318 9233). Basic motel units with private facilities, and simpler rooms at slightly cheaper rates. ④.

Sir Arthur Dudley Dodson YHA, on the main street, next to the phone box (☎03/318 9230). The country's first purpose-built hostel and the premier spot in the village, with friendly helpful and informed staff, large firewood-warmed common room, bike shed and gear storage. As the best-value central accommodation, this tends to get full, so book ahead. Tent sites $10, dorms ①, rooms ③.

The Chalet, west end of the village on the main road (☎ & fax 03/318 9236, *bohny@voyager.co.nz*). This excellent large alpine chalet offers B&B in eleven comfortable, individually decorated rooms with central heating and TVs. The guesthouse contains lots of woodwork courtesy of the owner's father, and displays paintings by the owner's mother. There's also a restaurant and bar. ⑥.

DOC Campsite, next to Arthur's Pass Public Shelter and backing on to the railway. Basic site with cold water and toilets. Tent sites $3.

Mountain House Backpackers, on the main road through the village, opposite the YHA and next door to the outdoor education centre (☎03/318 9258). Clean bunkroom accommodation, and some doubles and twins in separate units, plus a large common room and kitchen. Used in tandem with the Outdoor Education Centre to house school groups, so booking is important. Tent sites $9, dorms ①, rooms ②.

Outdoor Education Centre, next to the chapel on the main street (book through the visitor centre or the DOC office). Simple bunkroom accommodation available when not fully booked, as above, by school groups. ①.

EATING AND DRINKING

The village is small so **eating and drinking** options are limited and there are only two shops selling basic supplies and one bottle store/off-licence with prices reflecting the captive nature of the market. In the centre, on the main street near the public phones, is *Oscar's Haus* a licensed café (daily: June–Oct 10am–4pm; Nov–May 10am–10pm, kitchen closes 8.45pm), offering a different flavour of home-made muffins every day, a full bar, main meals (including some good veggie dishes) costing $12.50–20 and a selection of local art and gifts. Directly opposite is the *Arthur's Pass Store and Tearooms*, which is cheaper but less salubrious (daily 8am–7.30pm) with limited supplies, a bottleshop and local bits and bobs. The best place to eat or drink is *The Chalet*, also on the main street, which has a gift shop, bistro and bar (favoured by locals and open late) with a friendly atmosphere (occasional impromptu piano sing-alongs), where you can get snacks, lunch and dinner, plus a restaurant offering large portions of rustic New Zealand food with a hint of a Mediterranean influence (mains $10–22), and the ubiquitous nachos.

Arthur's Pass National Park

Despite the spectacular views you get from the pass itself, you really need to take one of the many day (or longer) walks to get a feel for this remarkable alpine landscape. The 720 square kilometres surrounding the pass was designated the **Arthur's Pass National Park** in 1929, and has exerted a powerful attraction over walkers and climbers ever since. The park encompasses much of the alpine flora unique to New

SKIFIELDS AROUND ARTHUR'S PASS

There are five skifields in the area around Arthur's Pass, each offering accommodation and equipment rental unless otherwise stated. Although there is not an enormous variety of runs they are unusual and challenging with some spectacular views, as well as reliable snow and relatively deserted slopes. To find out more about skiing here and in the rest of New Zealand visit *www.snow.co.nz* which also has information on snow conditions. The fields are described from east to west, heading along SH73 from Christchurch. Many people choose to access the skifields from Christchurch, but if you want to cut down on travelling stay at *Smylie's* in Springfield (see p.606) or in Arthur's Pass.

Only 96km west of Christchurch is **Porter Heights**, just off SH73 via a 6km unsealed road (☎03/379 7087, *ski@porterheights.co.nz*), which boasts the longest single run in the southern hemisphere. Lift passes cost $44 per day, learners' lift $30 per day, and learners' packages $48 per day.

Just over 100km out of Christchurch along SH73 another 6km-long side road leads to the **Craigieburn Valley skifield** (☎ & fax 03/365 2514), a challenging area whose extreme slopes (a 609m vertical drop) make it the best-kept secret in the southern hemisphere. It's only really suitable for intermediate and advanced skiers and boarders. Lift passes about $30 per day.

The **Mount Cheeseman skifield**, 112km from Christchurch along SH73, is an exceedingly well appointed club field (☎03/358 9249 or 379 5315, *cheeseman@ch.cyberxpress.co.nz*) with good facilities and a friendly atmosphere. There's a good variety of runs for intermediates, and a wilderness skiing option for those with experience. Lift passes are $41 per day.

The **Broken River skifield** (☎03/318 7270) lies 120km out from Christchurch, at the end of a 6km access road through native beech from SH73. It's a very well equipped field, offering night skiing and good snowboard terrain. Lift passes are $30 a day. Accommodation huts ②, instruction package $25 an hour. The ski area is only about 15min walk from the car park and there's a free goods lift.

Mount Olympus (☎ & fax 03/318 5840, *mtolympus@xtra.co.nz*), 128km from Christchurch, is in the Craigieburn range, set at the end of a road off SH73 only accessible by 4WD. This is a small field with deserted slopes suitable for all ability levels. Lift passes are $30 per day, learners tow $10 but there's no equipment rental on site (arrange this in Christchurch or at one of the other nearby fields).

Temple Basin (☎03/377 7788 or 318 9258, *ski@temple.org.nz*), is 4km west (45min walk) from Arthur's Pass Village and 300m on from the Dobson Memorial. It's a superb spot for snowboarding with a 430m drop, floodlit for night-skiing and has a variety of runs for all abilities. Lift passes cost $32 a day plus free goods lift.

Zealand, including the rich crimson of the southern rata trees; and also highlights the contrast between the tussock grasslands and scrub of the eastern South Island and the broad-leaved evergreen podocarp forest of the wetter west.

Although easily accessible, the park can still be a hazardous place: take simple precautions and use your common sense. The weather is highly changeable and often wet, so be sure to bring warm and waterproof clothing, sturdy footwear, a supply of drinking water and (even on the shortest walks) some energy-giving food. If you're embarking on tramps of a day or longer, inform the DOC office in Arthur's Pass Village, or fill in the relevant search and rescue action card (available at the DOC/visitor centre in Arthur's Pass), before setting out.

Suggested **short walks** are detailed in the *Walks in Arthur's Pass National Park* leaflet ($1), which is stocked by the DOC office in Arthur's Pass Village. Among the most popular short walks are the **Devil's Punch Bowl** (2km; 1hr return), an all-weather climb and descent to the base of a 131-metre waterfall, crossing two footbridges and zigzagging up steps, and the **Bridal Veil Nature Walk** (2.5km; 1hr 30min return), which ascends a gentle gradient through mountain beeches then crosses the Bridal Veil Creek before returning along the road.

Longer and more strenuous is the climb to **Avalanche Peak** (5km return; 6–7hr; 1000m ascent), which offers wonderful views of the surrounding mountains, but should only be attempted in reasonable weather. The best way is going up the Avalanche Peak track and then making a circuit of it by returning on the **Scotts Track** (total walking time 6–7hr).

For $5 you can obtain a set of leaflets listing eleven **longer tracks** (ranging from 2 to 5 days) from the DOC office in Arthur's Pass Village, which should be used in conjunction with the *Arthur's Pass National Park Map*. One of the most demanding is the **Harman Pass to Kelly Saddle** (55km; 4–5 days), a rewarding trip mostly along unmarked tracks and involving the crossing of unbridged rivers. Prospective trampers need to be fit and well-equipped; comfortable huts along the way are Category 2–3 ($5–10), and the best views are to be had from the ridges near Kelly Saddle. One of the slightly easier tracks that doesn't skimp on great views is **Casey Saddle to Binser Saddle** (40km; 2 days), a pleasant tramp crossing easy saddles on well-defined tracks through open beech forest, staying overnight in Casey Hut (Category 2; 16 bunks; $10). For those well-equipped and interested the **Mingha Deception** (25km; 2 days), is the route of the arduous Coast to Coast triathlon following marked and unmarked areas, and river crossings (there are no bridges so watch the water levels). If you're feeling particularly fit and travelling in the summer add on the 500m side trip to Lake Mavis, a high mountain tarn with some lovely views. You can use either the Goat Pass Hut (Category 2; 20 bunks; $10, with a radio link to Arthur's Pass Visitor Centre for emergencies) or the Upper Deception Hut (Category 3; 6 bunks; $5) and ponder how mad you'd have to be to run the route competitively.

For those feeling even more energetic, there is good **rock climbing** at Castle Hill (see p.606) and at the Temple and Speight buttresses on Mount Rolleston.

The South Canterbury foothills

Easily accessible from the east coast and its main artery, SH1, the **South Canterbury foothills** are often ignored by travellers hurrying westwards from Christchurch to Mount Cook (see p.621). Marking the transition from the flat Canterbury Plains to the more rugged and spectacular Southern Alps, the area is primarily known for the skifields grouped around the winter resort town of **Methven**, which serves the slopes of **Mount Hutt** and provides a jumping-off point for more distant pistes at Erewhon, now renamed **Mount Potts**. Things are relatively quiet here in summer, but there's a wealth of natural attractions in the region, with the **Mount Hutt Forest**, the **Rakaia Gorge**, and **walks** around **Mount Somers** rewarding travellers who make the effort to stop. Further south, inland from Timaru, the tiny communities of **Geraldine** and **Fairlie** link the east coast with the mountains and provide bases from which to enjoy either skifields or summer adventure activities. Fairlie is promoted as the "Gateway to the **McKenzie Country**", an area of farmland mixed with tussock and stands of forest, which gives hints of the high country to the west.

Main **routes** into the area from the east coast are the SH72 from near Sheffield on the Arthur's Pass Road, SH77 from Ashburton south of Christchurch, and SH8 from Timaru. **Buses** from Christchurch and Ashburton represent the main means of getting here by public transport, even though services may be limited to one or two per day.

Methven and around

Thirty-four kilometres northwest of Ashburton on SH77, **METHVEN** is the capital of a bustling winter sports area known as the "Snowfed Republic". Scotsman Robert Patton bought land in the area in 1869 and named Methven after his home town. The Scottish influence may also have had some bearing on the building of an outstanding 18-hole golf course, which keeps the thousand-strong population and many visitors entertained once the winter snows have receded.

Being close to Mount Hutt, Mount Potts (Erewhon) and Mount Somers, Methven makes a good base for some skiing or tramping amid spectacular scenery. Activity operators also offer ballooning, horse riding and jetboating, but the **ski season** (May–Oct) is essentially what everyone lives for. In summer the town is much quieter, so much so that many of the restaurants and hotels close down for several months.

Arrival and information

Buses stop on Main Road (SH77), outside the visitor centre which includes the Methven Travel Centre and Adventure Shop (☎03/302 8106), where you can buy tickets, arrange car hire (from around $50 per day) or local minibus tours. They also run a shuttle to Christchurch ($22 one way). The town itself is easily explored on foot, and a constantly changing array of companies offer minibus transport **to the skifields** (expect to pay around $18 return); the visitor centre has details of current operators.

The friendly and helpful staff at the **visitor centre**, on Main Road, opposite Bank Street and next to the BNZ Bank (daily: Nov–March 9am–5pm; May–Oct 7.30am–6pm;

☎ 03/302 8955, fax 302 9367, *nz-holiday.co.nz/methven*, *methven@clear.net.nz*), will do bookings, have lots of information about Methven, the skifields, and guided tramps in the vicinity. The town also has a small shopping centre, off Main Road, including banks, a post shop and several **ski shops** (specializing in gear rental and repairs), the best of which is Big Al's.

Accommodation

During the winter there is a wide variety of accommodation in Methven; in summer much of it disappears, but then so do most of the visitors. The advantage of being here in the summer is the scope it gives you for haggling.

Aorangi Lodge, 38 Spaxton St (☎03/302 8482). A single-storey simple wooden building with twin, double, triple and quad rooms, all with shared facilities. ②.

Bed Post, 177 Main Rd (☎ & fax 03/302 8508). Offers twenty beds in twins, doubles and shared rooms, plus cooking facilities and motel units. Dorms ③; rooms ②, motels ④.

Beluga Lodge and **Beluga House B&Bs**, 40 Allen St (☎03/302 8290, fax 302 9290). Luxurious accommodation, much loved by skiers, in two well-kept houses which have retained their original charm and are surrounded by tranquil gardens. Bathrooms are shared, robes are provided, and home-made bread accompanies a breakfast of your choice. ⑥–⑦.

Green Gables, 3km north of Methven on SH77 (☎03/302 8308). A peaceful rural B&B partly surrounded by a deer farm. Accommodation consists of one en-suite double, and one double and single with shared facilities. Breakfasts are generous, and dinner is available by arrangement ($30). ⑤–⑥.

Pudding Hill Chalets and Campground, SH72 (☎03/302 8416). Five kilometres northwest of town, this upmarket site offers spas and saunas, a drying room, on-site restaurant and well kept cabins. Very busy in winter, but prices are negotiable in summer. Tent sites $9, ski lodges ①–②, apartments ⑤–⑦.

Skiwi House, 30 Chapman St (☎03/302 8772). Cosy singles, doubles and bunk rooms, a TV lounge, kitchen and drying facilities in a white weatherboard house about five minutes' walk from the centre. Dorms ①, rooms ②.

Sovereign Resort Hotel, Rakaia Gorge Rd (☎03/302 8724, fax 302 8870). A modern hotel with good views from its 46 rooms. Set in extensive grounds, guest facilities include a spa, heated outdoor pool, 9-hole golf course, a plush restaurant, ski drying room and night-club with entertainment on Wed, Fri & Sat. ⑥–⑦.

The Town

A small and uninspiring place, widely scattered across the plain, Methven has two main streets: the Ashburton–Rakaia Gorge Road (aka Main Street; or SH77), which heads north to Mount Hutt and south to Ashburton; and the Forest Drive/Chertsey Road (SH72), which bisects SH77 in the centre of town. The shopping centre is on the southwestern corner of this intersection. The only outstanding building is the **Anglican Church**, on the corner of Chapman Street and Alington Street, and even that is an interloper. Built in 1880 in the tiny settlement of Sherwood 75km south, the church was transported to Methven by two traction engines in 1884. Turning right down McMillan Street and left on to Bank Street, you'll come to the **Methven Museum** (open by arrangement, ask at the visitor centre for the key; $1). This small redbrick building, with its displays on the Rakaia River and local history, makes a reasonable alternative to propping up a bar if it's raining.

Activities

Aside from skiing, the two most interesting things to do in Methven are horse trotting/racing and ballooning, but both come with a hefty price tag.

Horse trotting/racing happens at the intriguingly named Tondeleyo Bloodstock 20km north of Methven on Lauriston Barrhill Road, off SH77 (☎03/302 4800; daily 9.30am–1.30pm; $125 for a full day). Included are a tour and the opportunity to observe the usual preparations and participate in a race, riding tandem in one of the unstable-looking carts (a mess of poles, reins, rope and string) as it careers round the course behind a highly strung thoroughbred. The most spectacular activity in Methven, though, is **hot-air ballooning** with Aoraki Balloon Safaris (☎03/302 8172; sunrise trip 4hr; $255, including champagne breakfast): the fine views of the patchwork quilt of the Canterbury Plains and the magnificent Southern Alps make this one of the best balloon flights on the South Island and somewhat dulls the pain of the cost.

If you're an energetic (and very wealthy) skier or snowboarder, Methven Heli-ski (☎03/302 8108; $660 per person, 3–5 passengers) offers a rather drastic way of finding unsullied snow – by **helicopter**. The company usually operate five runs, with professional guides; and in summer, they switch to helicopter drop-offs for trampers and mountain bikers. Wetter, noisier but cheaper is a **jetboat ride** with Rakaia Gorge Scenic Jets (☎03/318 6515, fax 318 6512), whose tours range from 20 to 50min, with a standard trip weighing in at about $45. Slightly more edifying is to let them take you to end of the **Rakaia Gorge** ($10) and then walk back. The gorge offers a delightful and easy walk – take a picnic and it's a great way to spend an afternoon.

Eating and drinking

There are some snug little cafés and coffee houses serving thick, steaming soups to winter sportsmen or low-fat Italian salads and panini to the summer crowds, along with a smattering of pleasant if not overly lively bars. Some establishments open only in the winter but prices lean to the higher side no matter what the season. All of the places listed below are open year round except the *Eagle Rock Café*.

The Blue Pub, *Methven Hotel*, cnr Kilworth St & Barkers Rd. This 1918 hotel is more of a drinkers' den than somewhere for a civilized meal, though they do produce some cheap lunchtime and evening bar food, including grilled steaks or fish. It's crowded in winter, when entertainment is often laid on, although in summer things are fairly quiet.

Café 131, 131 Main Rd. A favourite local coffee hang-out with wooden floors and furniture creating a 1920s atmosphere. They serve light meals including delicious gourmet smoked-chicken open sandwiches and veggie samosas, plus full breakfasts for under $12. The coffee and brandy cake with cream is dreamy. Daily winter 7am–7pm, summer 9am–4pm; licensed.

Eagle Rock Café, Main Rd. Passable Italian specialities at pretty reasonable prices, alongside Asian influenced and more conventional Kiwi fare (mains $12–28). Dinner Thurs–Mon, 6.30pm–late; licensed.

Sovereign Resort, Rakaia Gorge Rd (☎03/302 8724) in the hotel (see "Accommodation" on previous page). Plush restaurant and carvery, serving high-quality food.

Uncle Dominics's Pizza and Kebabs, 253 Forest Drive, inside the main shopping centre. Surprisingly good pizzas and kebabs, at reasonable prices, to eat in or take away. Summer weekends only, winter daily; BYO.

Vee Tee's Family Bar and Bistro, Main St. Evening-only restaurant serving basic, snacky menu weighed down by the 500g Brontosaurus Steak. Lively après-ski venue. Summer Wed–Sun, winter daily; licensed & BYO.

Around Methven

Many winter sports enthusiasts choose to stay in Methven because of its easy access to the surrounding skifields. **Mount Hutt**, 26km to the northeast on SH72, is the nearest and most convenient, although **Mount Potts (Erewhon)**, 75km to the west and serviced by the nearby settlement of **Mount Somers**, is also within striking range (see p.616). The tiny settlements at both Mount Hutt and Mount Somers are little more than feeding stations for the skiers in the winter, and have a ghost-town feel for the rest of the year, although they border on regions of outstanding natural beauty. Around Mount Hutt to the north and west, the **Mount Hutt Forest** provides an opportunity to explore the native flora. Fourteen kilometres southeast of Methven is the **Rakaia Gorge** (see opposite), offering riverside walks and the chance to fish for salmon or trout.

MOUNT HUTT SKIFIELD

Twenty-six kilometres northeast of Methven, just off SH72, **Mount Hutt** is widely regarded as the best and most developed skifield in the southern hemisphere, with a vertical rise of 655m and a longest run of 2km. It also enjoys the longest season and offers a broad range of skiing and snowboarding conditions. A daily lift pass costs $55. Beginners can take advantage of a one-day starter pack, a five-day package, or the many learn-to-snowboard packages (around $40 per hour in a group session, including board rental). Leopard Coachlines run **buses** to and from Methven and Christchurch every day, dropping off in the morning and picking up in the afternoon (☎03/332 5000, $20 from Methven) and a variety of shuttle buses run between the skifield and Methven or Mount Hutt village. There's a Mount Hutt skifield information line (☎03/302 8811), or you can find out more at *www/nzski.com*, or email *admin@mthutt.co.nz*.

Mount Hutt Forest

Fourteen kilometres northwest of Methven and accessible via SH77 is the **Mount Hutt Forest**, which covers 444 square kilometres of tall trees on the eastern flanks of the Southern Alps, adjoining the **Awa Awa Rata Reserve** and **Pudding Hill Scenic Reserve**. Mountain beech is the dominant native species of tree, while snow tussock above the scrub line provides a home for a variety of native and introduced birds.

Free leaflets are available about the forest and reserves from local visitor centres, describing the flora and fauna as well as the many **walking tracks** you can explore – most of which can be accessed from the McLennans Bush Road entrance to all three reserves (reached by heading north from Methven on SH77 and turning left onto McLennans Bush Road after about 15km). It is worth taking a little extra time to examine the Mount Hutt flora during the spring and summer: of the **alpine plants** of New Zealand, 94 percent grow only in New Zealand, of which 130 species can only be found on Mount Hutt. One such is the unique vegetable *Sheep Raoulia eximia*, which forms huge grey mounds that look not unlike sheep lying down, from a distance. There's also the *Ranunculus haastii*, a beautiful species of buttercup with blue-grey leaves and luminous yellow flowers, and ten species of mountain daisies, *Celmisias*, which form huge cushions of flowers.

Rakaia Gorge

Along the northern stretches of the Rakaia River, 14km from Methven, is the **Rakaia Gorge**, a steep-sided defile created by an ancient lava flow and now lined in many places with regenerating forest. The **Maori** account of the gorge's formation tells how a *taniwha* (water spirit) lived nearby, hunting and eating moa and weka; his possessions, because of his status as a spirit, were *tapu*. One cold day he went to find a hot spring, and while he was away the northwest wind demon flattened his property. To prevent this happening again, the *taniwha* collected large boulders and stones from the mountains to block the course of the demon, and in so doing narrowed the Rakaia River so that it flowed between the rocky walls. The spirit became so warm because of his exertions that the heat from his body melted the snow and ice on the mountains, and his perspiration fell on the rocks and formed crystals in the riverbed.

Just off SH72, an information shelter has maps of the area and a list of activities, next to the head of the **Rakaia Gorge Walkway** (15km; 3–4hr return, one-way jetboat ride from Methven, see opposite). The path leads through several forest stands and spectacular geological areas, past hardened lava flows of rhyolite, pitchstone and andesite, to the upper gorge lookout. The Rakaia River is worth a look simply because it is a typical example of a braided river; a form found all down the east of the South Island.

Mount Somers and around

On SH72, 35km from Mount Hutt, at the junction of the road to Mt Potts/Erewhon Skifield (see box below) is the small settlement of **MOUNT SOMERS**. The town itself has little to offer, although those keen on geology and local history might want to look in on the **Foothills Museum** (open by arrangement, ☎03/303 9860; donation requested), in a shabby weatherboard shed on Hoods Road, next to the Anglican Church.

However the **Mount Somers Recreation and Conservation Area**, roughly 10km north of town on Flynn's Road, has some fine tramps (see the *Mount Somers Recreation and Conservation Area* leaflet in local visitor centres and DOC offices; $1); and along the road towards Mount Potts (Erewhon) a proliferation of lakes provide superb scenery, trout-fishing and, on **Lake Clearwater**, excellent windsurfing (details from the Methven visitor centre).

Walks around Mount Somers

The landscape around Mount Somers differs from its surroundings as it's formed from volcanic rhyolite rock, which is harder than greywacke and shows fault lines, exposing columns and fractures of darker andesitic material. As a result the terrain is generally more rugged, with outcrops of rock poking out from patches of regenerating beech forest and large areas of low-fertility soil subject to heavy rainfall turning to bog. Due to these conditions you'll find bog pine, snow totara, toatoa and mountain flax as well as the rare Whio (blue duck). The *Mount Somers Conservation Area* leaflet ($1, from visitor centres) describes in detail the geology and the history of the region, and also gives information on the 17km **Mount Somers Subalpine Walkway**, which passes abandoned coal mines, volcanic formations and a deep river canyon. The walk can be done in ten hours, although it's often treated as a leisurely two-day affair, with the *Mount Somers Hut* (see below) providing overnight accommodation. To get to the start of the walk, you'll have to drive (there's no public transport) west along the Ashburton Gorge for 11km, and turn right at the old trolley wheels, following the Jig Road to **Coalminers Flat picnic area** and the Woolshed Creek car park. From the picnic area, follow the Black Beech Walk to McClimonts Mine; from here, red markers lead to the 2188m summit of Mount Somers, with stunning high-country views. The track then goes down a stepladder to the Morgan Stream Junction, under the Spa Pool Waterfall and past the Emerald Pool to **Mount Somers Hut** (3hr; category 3; $5). On day two, take the steep steady climb to the 1170m Mount Somers Saddle (3–4hr), then follow the markers to the north face of the mountain and climb to Slaughter House Gulley (named in the days when red deer roamed the area – and were hunted in large numbers), near the Pinnacles Hut (category 3; $5) and One Tree Ridge, before descending swiftly to the bushline (2hr). The track then descends around the bluffs to a stream bed, before

---

MOUNT POTTS (EREWHON) SKIFIELD

The **Mount Potts** (previously Erewhon) **Skifield** (☎03/309 0960, *www.mtpotts.co.nz*, *mc@mtpotts.co.nz*), 40km west of Mount Somers, has the highest elevation on the South Island and remains a small-scale affair. Its change of name represents an attempt to market it as an exclusive, international-play-person field following lodge renovations and the introduction of a snowcat and heli-ski operation. The cat holds a maximum of 11 people and only 22 will be allowed on the field at any time; the helicopter element is not restricted to the field and can drop off in 60,000acres of virgin snow. A massive price hike has accompanied the new regime: cat passes cost $90 a day and a five-run heli day will set you back $549. Alternatively a week long "powder pig" deal on the cat costs $990 including accommodation.

climbing steeply up to Duke Knob (740m), then descending quickly to **Sharplins Fall car park** (3–4hr), where you can arrange to be picked up by local taxi.

There are also a number of **shorter walks**, taking from ten minutes to half a day, from either car park, all of which are well worth the effort.

Practicalities

InterCity **buses** drop off in the centre of the tiny Mount Somers community, where the best **accommodation** in the area is provided by the pleasant tree-filled campsite of *Mount Somers Holiday Park*, Hoods Road, 1km off SH72 (☎03/303 9719; tent sites $18, cabins ②–③).

The finest **food** in the region and in the top ten on the South Island is to be had at *Stronechrubie*, just south of Mount Somers on SH72 (bookings essential ☎03/303 9814; summer Wed–Sun 6.30–11pm, winter daily; licensed), where the Swiss chef uses fresh local ingredients and meat from a Swiss butcher in Auckland to produce mouth-watering dishes. Try the rack of lamb with Provençal herbs and mustard (under $25), or filleted grouper on a bed of marinated mushrooms (under $20), and for dessert don't miss the McRae's whisky cake and whisky sabayon. If you can't tear yourself away after dinner (or can't move), *Stronechrubie* also has five standard **rooms**, and three family rooms, all with kitchens, wicker furniture and views of the mountain (same phone number; ⑤).

Geraldine and around

The quiet, pretty town of **GERALDINE** lies 45km south of Mount Somers via SH72, and 15km west of the main coastal highway (SH1) along SH79. Set on the Geraldine Downs – gently rolling hills standing out in sharp relief against the craggy, snow-capped Southern Alps – the town is at the centre of a prosperous farming community. Geraldine has a surprising number of **craft shops** – some even interesting – and **galleries**; when you've exhausted the town's limited attractions, the walkways and brilliant rafting trips of **Peel Forest** beckon and are within easy reach.

Arrival and information

Buses drop off at *Oakes Restaurant* on the junction of Talbot Street with SH79, while InterCity services drop off at Orari, 15km away on SH1, where they're met by a shuttle bus into town (Geraldine Community Mini Buses ☎03/693 1007; $2.50). Direct bus services from Timaru to Geraldine and Geraldine to Fairlie (40km to the west, see p.619) also connect with shuttle services to Geraldine. Geraldine's **visitor centre**, 32 Talbot St (Mon–Fri 8.30am–5pm, Sat & Sun 10am–4pm; May–Sept 10am–2pm; ☎03/693 1006, *information@geraldine.co.nz*) is run by helpful staff who provide a full booking service, all the DOC leaflets for the area and have a broad range of local knowledge. They can also guide you to the nearest place to get any DOC passes.

Accommodation

There's a small concentration of accommodation in Geraldine, none of it too expensive, and it's rarely a problem getting a bed for the night.

The Crossing, Woodbury Rd (☎03/693 9689, fax 693 9789). This beautiful old English-style manor with a shady veranda houses a fully licensed restaurant and four en-suite guest rooms, each individually and lavishly decorated. Continental breakfast included. ⑥–⑦.

Crown Hotel, 31 Talbot St (☎03/693 8458, fax 693 9565). Upmarket pub with eight clean and airy rooms, all with en-suite bathrooms. ③–④.

Geraldine Backpackers, The Old Presbytery, 13 Jolie St (☎03/693 9644). Clean and well-kept dorm accommodation in a historic building opposite the Talbot Forest Reserve, with helpful hosts and a warm and friendly atmosphere. Dorms ①.

Geraldine Motel, 97 Talbot St (☎03/693 8501). Six pleasant fully equipped units close to the town centre. Complimentary newspaper in the morning. ④.

Geraldine Motor Camp, Hislop St (☎03/693 8147). Surrounded by sheltering trees, this spacious site is inside Geraldine Domain. Tent sites $8 per person, cabins ①.

Hislop House B&B, 20 Cox St (☎ & fax 03/693 8890). This single-storey wooden house built in the early 1900s offers two en-suite rooms and a warm welcome. ④.

The Town

In town, the tiny **Geraldine Historical Museum**, on Cox Street (Mon–Sat 9.30am–midday & 1.30–3.30pm, Sun 2–4pm; donation), has little of outstanding interest but is housed in a rather quaint blue-and-white stone building with an attractive garden. More extensive is the **Geraldine Vintage Car and Machinery Club**, 174 Talbot St (Nov–Feb daily 10am–4pm; March–Oct Sat & Sun only 10am–4pm; $4) which houses a surprising collection of old cars, tractors and planes, mostly well-kept but with a few not quite so well-loved.

To check out Geraldine's wealth of **artists, galleries and craft shops**, pick up the *Art Trail Map, Geraldine District Arts and Crafts Guide* or the *Geraldine* leaflet from the visitor centre. Stained Glass Windows, 177 Talbot St (Mon–Thurs 9.30am–4.30pm), where you can browse among the colourful lampshades and stained-glass work, is well worth visiting. Equally good to explore is The Giant Jersey, 10 Wilson St (Mon–Fri 9am–5pm, Sat & Sun 10am–5pm), where amongst the usual display of jumpers you'll find the Guinness Book of Records World's Largest Jersey (weighing 5.5kilos). There's also an array of heraldic mosaics and scenes of the Bayeux Tapestry (34m in length), made from tiny pieces of spring steel broken from knitting machines. These creations, of immense fiddliness, can never be repeated as the supply of machines is exhausted. Once you have inspected these and tried a few of the owner's homegrown, cypher-like alphametics and magic cubes you'll probably need some fresh air.

Just 1km from the town centre, at the end of Hislop Street, **Talbot Forest Scenic Reserve** is the last remnant of a once extensive native forest, with the largest radiata pine in the world and plenty of other mature native trees including matai, kahikatea and totara. It's a peaceful place to spend an hour or two with a picnic.

Eating and drinking

Given Geraldine's small size, you wouldn't expect to find a wide range of culinary choice in town, but there's something to satisfy most appetites nevertheless.

Berry Barn Bakery and Café, 66 Talbot St. The usual coach party stop-off where savouries, pies, chips and cakes are all served in cheap and cheerful surroundings. Next to *Barker's Winery*. Daily 6am–6pm.

The Oaks, 72 Talbot St, cnr Cox St. Bacon, eggs and chips for $9, great hash browns and the usual café fare. Daily 9am–5pm.

Papillon Chinese Restaurant, Tea Rooms and Takeaway, 40 Talbot St. A peculiar mix of East-meets-New-Zealand café: Chinese food, fish, burgers and chips. Closed Tues; licensed & BYO.

Plum's Café, 44 Talbot St (☎03/693 9770). Good-quality food, home baking and a wood-burning stove. Try the "Plum's Ultimate Snack", a combination of garlic bread, chicken, sour cream, salad and more for $7.50. Delicious lunches daily, dinner Fri & Sat; licensed & BYO.

Totara Bar and Restaurant, *Crown Hotel*, 31 Talbot St (☎03/693 8458). Large restaurant serving reasonably priced Kiwi nosh. The bar is one of two reasonable places in town for a drink (see *The Village Inn* below).

The Village Inn, 41 Talbot St. A broad selection of reasonably priced and fairly imaginative food for lunch or dinner in a comfortable bar setting, or on the outdoor terrace.

Around Geraldine: Peel Forest

One of the more beautiful places in the area is **Peel Forest Park**, enclosing a vast expanse of forest, scrub and alpine vegetation 19km northwest of Geraldine. To get there, head north on the SH72 as far as Arundel, before turning west onto the Cooper's Creek/Peel Forest Road. You'll pass through the hamlet of **PEEL FOREST** about 1.5km short of the reserve entrance, a useful spot for stocking up on supplies and picking up information from the **Peel Forest Store** (☎03/696 3567; Mon–Thurs 8am–7pm, Fri & Sat 8am–7.30pm, Sun 9am–7pm), which serves as a visitor centre, campsite booking office, bottle store, takeaway and tea rooms. It also displays various DOC leaflets on the area although the commercial operation tends to take precedence.

A free leaflet (available at the DOC office) describes the **Peel Forest Tracks**, twelve walking tracks ranging from forty-five minutes to six hours. Of these, the best are the **Acland Falls Walking Track** (1.5km; 45min one way), a steep climb followed by a short streamside walk to a fourteen-metre-high waterfall, and **Allan's Track** (4km; 2–3hr round-trip), a steady ascent past the head of Mils Stream and through podocarp forest which can be extended by joining the **Deer Spur Track** (5km; 2hr return), a steep but well-defined route which climbs above the bushline to a sparkling mountain tarn at an altitude of about 900m. Take time while you walk to admire the huge, ancient totara trees, rata and ferns, and to watch the antics of the fantails and tomtits – these little birds often hover around, feeding on the insects disturbed by trampers and picnickers.

The park is also the home of one of the best **whitewater-rafting** operators in New Zealand. Rangitata Rafts (☎0800/251 251, fax 696 3534, *mail@rangitata.rafts.co.nz*) at Peel Forest River Base, about 12km north of Peel Forest Store. The raft company offer **camping** ($10 per site), very basic bunk **accommodation** in their lodge (①, breakfast $5), and, of course, fantastic rafting **trips on the Rangitata River** (May–Sept daily at 11.30am; 3hr; $105 including lunch & dinner, or $115 as a trip from Christchurch). The whole operation is very professional and bucketloads of fun: a maximum of six rafts take to the river at once, with a full briefing beforehand and one guide for every nine passengers. The first part of the rafting is Grade I, which gives you a chance to get used to the self-baling boats before the thrilling trip through the high-sided Rangitata Gorge, where you traverse Grade I–V rapids; there's also an optional ten-metre cliff jump near the end. Afterwards, your ordeal by water is rounded off with welcome hot showers and a barbecue dinner.

There is also an Outdoor Pursuits Centre based 100m north of the Peel Forest Store (☎03/696 3800), which offers an introductory **rock-climbing** course (2 days; $140), introductory **kayaking** (3 days; $140), and a Clarence River rafting expedition (5 days; $270) – all including food and accommodation, although it tends to cater more for school groups.

Fairlie and around

Heading west from Geraldine towards the wilds of the McKenzie Country and the mountains around Mount Cook, you first pass through the small town of **FAIRLIE**. Defined by its position at the junction of the two main routes that strike inland from the east coast to Lake Tekapo – SH79 from Rangitata via Geraldine and SH8 from Timaru – Fairlie is a quintessential crossroads town, with a resident population of only 600. Originally called Fairlie Creek, the name was shortened after the telegraph office opened in 1892, the creek having long since dried up. The rail link with Timaru closed in 1960, and the town has pretty much remained in stasis ever since. Your best bet is to look around quickly and then move on.

Within reach of Fairlie are the **skifields** of Mount Dobson and Fox Peak (see box, p.621).

Arrival, information and accommodation

Daily InterCity **buses** stop near the centre of town on Main Street, from where everything's easily reached on foot. One ad hoc **visitor centre** is housed in The Sunflower

JAMES MCKENZIE

A Kiwi folk hero, James McKenzie lends his name to the crescent of flat land between Fairlie and Kurow (to the south on SH83) known as **McKenzie Country**. A Scottish immigrant of uncertain background, McKenzie was arrested in 1855 for being a sheep stealer on a grand scale. He stole over 1000 in all, most of them from the Rhodes brothers' Levels Run station near Timaru (see p.583), grazing them in the basin of rich high-country pastureland which now bears his name. McKenzie escaped from prison three times during the first year of his five-year sentence, and was finally released on condition that he leave the country never to return, which he subsequently did.

It's nowadays difficult to fathom why exactly McKenzie became such an important and popular figure in New Zealand lore. He was certainly a prodigious thief, somehow controlling a vast flock of rustled animals with the assistance of a single dog, Friday – a hound fondly remembered as the prototype for the many hard-working sheep dogs held in deep affection by South Islanders. McKenzie is also regarded as one of the great pioneers, opening up an area of hitherto undiscovered grazing land that contained some of the best sheep runs in the country. There is a poem in honour of the great man and his dog in the visitor shelter at Lake Pukaki near the turn off to Mount Cook.

Centre, just down the street at no. 31 (daily 8.30am–6pm; ☎03/685 8258), where there's a fair stock of leaflets but they're more interested in selling sesame seed buns than helping tourists so you're better off going to the *Resource Centre*, corner of Riddle and Talbot streets (Mon–Fri 10am–4pm). Should you be of a mind to stay the *Fairlie Districts Recreation Map* lists four walks in the settlement and three scenic drives. **Accommodation** options in Fairlie aren't particularly exciting or varied, but the town is rarely busy, so you shouldn't have too much trouble finding a bed.

Aorangi Motel, 26 Denmark St (☎ & fax 03/685 8340). This is the most central motel, with seven spacious self-contained units, plus a spa. ⑤.

Fairlie Lodge, 16 School Rd (☎ & fax 03/685 8452). Well cared for motel offering a very friendly welcome, clean, small units with their own facilities, microwaves, TVs and toasters. ③.

Fontmell Farmstay, 3km southwest of Fairlie on Nixons Rd (☎03/685 8379). Comfortable B&B accommodation in an English-style homestead, surrounded by pastureland and woods. There are two doubles and one single room with shared bathrooms. ④.

Pinewood Motel, 27 Mount Cook Rd (☎03/685 8599). Modern motel with airy, self-contained units close to the town centre. ④.

Mount Dobson Motel, 6km west of Fairlie on SH8 (☎03/685 8819). A quiet motel with large units next door to the *Silverstream Hotel* (which serves meals) and bottle shop, and 5km from the Toll Gate to Mount Dobson and Fox Peak skifields. Ski bus pick-ups arranged. ④.

The Town

The centre of the town is marked by the junction of Allandale Road (SH79) and Main Street (SH8), which becomes Mount Cook Road as it heads west out of town. The most interesting sight is the **Mabel Binney Cottage and Vintage Machinery Museum** (daily 10am–5pm; $2 turnstile), on Mount Cook Road, where three buildings are set back from the road with a Sampson wind pump (a tower surmounted by a wind-turned fan) out front. The display in the cottage remembers the first European settlers, and there's an extensive collection of early photographs. The museum is stuffed with farm machinery, wagons and traction engines. The third building on the site is the old railway station, which was moved here in 1968.

For a little exercise, wander along the **Fairlie Walkway** (3km; 40min one way). Beginning below the Allendale Road Bridge over the Opihi River, the walkway follows the willow-shaded riverbank past open pastureland and through trees to emerge near

MOUNT DOBSON AND FOX PEAK SKIFIELDS

Mount Dobson Skifield (☎03/685 8039, *mtdobson@xtra.co.nz*) is located in a 3km treeless basin 26km north of Fairlie, up a 15km unsealed road off SH8. The mountain is known for its powder snow, long hours of sunshine, uncrowded fields and suitability for all levels of skiing and snowboarding. Equipment rental is available, and there is a lodge serving hot pies and drinks. Lift passes cost $39 per day, beginners' packages $50 including lift passes (equipment rental is extra), and snowboard rental weighs in at around $30 per day; a full snowboard package is $58. The nearest accommodation is in Fairlie. There are shuttle buses from Fairlie in season; for details call ☎03/693 9656.

The **Fox Peak Skifield** (☎03/685 8539, snow phone 03/688 0044) is 30km northeast of Fairlie, with access from near the Mount Dobson access road, at the end of a 15km unsealed track. Although a small field it covers a good variety of terrain, catering for all abilities. Lift passes are $30 per day and there's a free learners' tow. There are no ski rental facilities and no accommodation, but refreshments are available. For information on Fairlie–Fox Peak shuttle buses contact ☎03/688 1870.

Talbot Road. **Guided walks** further afield are offered by Off the Beaten Track (☎03/685 8272; $15 per hour), run by local tramper Louise Wynn.

En route to Lake Tekapo or Mount Cook, you could also stop by the **Three Springs Historic Sheep Station** (☎03/685 8174; daily 10am–4pm, closed April–Nov) 5km west of Fairlie on SH8. Built from local limestone, the woolshed (where the shearing took place) is a magnificent example of early settler farm architecture, while the stable contains displays highlighting the station's history.

Eating and drinking

There's a good choice of eateries in Fairlie, offering a range of culinary styles and some very picturesque locations.

BB Stop, 81 Main St. Variations on a theme of meat, fish, chips and vegetables, followed by a touch of luxury in the form of Irish coffee. Burgers and light meals under $10, full meals $10–17. Daily 8.30am–10.30pm; licensed & BYO.

Old Library Café, 6 Allendale Rd. Originally built in 1914, this café is charming and very comfortable. The menu offers chef's specials, cheap breakfasts, light meals and snacks; there are always veggie choices, Thai curries and T-bone steaks. Prices are moderate, and there's occasional live music Fri & Sat evenings. Daily 8am–late; licensed.

Rimuwhare Country Retreat, 53 Mount Cook Rd (reservations advisable, ☎03/685 8058). A traditional English-style house in a lovely rustic setting. They do a cracking Spanish omelette for lunch, and a variety of Mediterranean-style dishes ($16–25) for dinner, plus some superb desserts. Daily lunch & dinner; licensed.

The Sunflower Centre, 31 Main St. A wholefood café and health-food shop, offering inexpensive meals and snacks, including soups and falafel but be warned – the veggie burgers are enormous ($5). Daily 8.30am–6pm; no licence or BYO.

Mount Cook and around

From Fairlie SH8 shoots, lupin- and broom-flanked in the summer, westward through the sheep-chomped grasslands of the McKenzie Country into the Mount Cook area, considered by many to be the most spectacular section of the Southern Alps. Dominating the region to the northwest, the 3764-metre **Mount Cook** is the highest point in New Zealand. Known as Ao-raki by Maori, who passed through the area on their way east or west in search of *pounamu*, it was named Mount Cook by Captain J.L. Stokes of HMS *Acheron* in 1851, although its summit wasn't conquered until 1894.

HOW MOUNT COOK (AO-RAKI) CAME TO BE

Both the **sky father** (Raki) and the **earth mother** (Papa-tua-nuku) already had children by previous unions. After their marriage, some of the sky father's children came to inspect their father's new wife. Four brothers, Ao-raki, Raki-roa, Raki-rua and Raraki-roa, circled around the earth mother in a **canoe** called Te Waka-a-Aoraki, but once they left her shores, disaster befell them. Running aground on a reef, the canoe was turned to stone. The four occupants climbed to the higher western side of the petrified canoe, where they too were turned to stone: **Ao-raki** became Mount Cook, and his three younger brothers formed flanking peaks. Ao-raki towers over his brother mountains in height, age and spiritual status, as an Atua (Maori god).

Mount Cook's permanent cover of snow and ice contrast vividly with the turquoise, glacier-fed **lakes Tekapo and Pukaki**, which stretch beneath its eastern flanks. Both lakes offer abundant fishing, water skiing and ice skating, although it's Lake Tekapo that has the bulk of the tourist facilities. Lake Pukaki is quiet in comparison, even though the view of Mount Cook across its still waters is one of the most memorable in New Zealand. Main access to the mountainous terrain around Mount Cook itself is provided by **Mount Cook Village**, which grew at the base of the mountain purely to cater for nineteenth-century tourists, who were brought here by horse-drawn coaches from Fairlie. You can walk from Mount Cook Village to the glaciers lurking beneath Mount Cook's flanks, most important of which is the 27km-long **Tasman Glacier**, running parallel to the Main Divide and fed by icefalls tumbling from the heavily glaciated peaks. Another good base from which to explore the area is **Twizel**, 70km south on the road to Cromwell and Queenstown, an unexciting modern town, which nevertheless rewards visitors with a glimpse of the extremely rare **Black Stilt**, wading birds that are protected in a reserve nearby. From **Omarama** 30km south of Twizel, SH83 runs eastwards down the **Waitaki Gorge** to Oamaru, providing a quick link between the Mount Cook area and the east coast. Public transport into the region is meagre but adequate, with Mount Cook Village served by daily **buses** from both Christchurch and Ashburton on the east coast, and three daily services from Queenstown to the south. In addition, Christchurch–Queenstown buses pass through Tekapo, Twizel and Omarama.

Lake Tekapo and around

About 42km from Fairlie on SH8, via Burke's Pass, is **Lake Tekapo** and **LAKE TEKAPO VILLAGE** – little more than a roadside ribbon of buildings, with a population of just 400. It's a popular tour-bus stop for obligatory photo-snapping, and shopping in the string of outlets whose stock leans towards high-priced tourist tat. To make the best of the place, stay overnight and enjoy the scenery and sunset free of the mob, then move on.

At an altitude of 707m, the area is reputed to have the clearest air in the southern hemisphere, and on a good day views really do have sharp edges and vibrant colours, making this is one of the best places from which to photograph the Southern Alps. The most striking thing about the **lake** itself is its colour: the light reflected from microscopic rock particles suspended in glacial meltwater lends its waters a vibrant turquoise hue. Fed by the **Godley** and **Cass** rivers, the lake covers 83 square kilometres and spills into the **Tekapo River**, which tumbles across the McKenzie Basin.

Arrival and information

Every other day **buses** complete the journey between Timaru and Twizel and drop off at Lake Tekapo Village, while each day at least one of the many bus and **shuttle bus** operators (InterCity, Atomic, Southern Link and so on) call in as part of the Christchurch–Queenstown route also plied by Kiwi Discovery Express and Magic. Timetables and fares for all these services are available from the visitor centre, where you can make bookings and buy tickets.

Buses pull into an area off SH8, opposite the main shops, and you can walk to all the accommodation and worthwhile sights from there. One of the **visitor centres** is in the Hide Shop, a retail outlet for souvenirs in the middle of the settlement (☎03/680 6721; daily: April–Oct 9am–5pm, Nov–March 8.30am–9pm), the other is at the far end of the *Godley Resort* hotel buildings, Lake Tekapo Visitor Centre (daily 9am–5.30pm; ☎03/680 6224). Both these places have an assortment of leaflets but are basically just trying to sell you something: in the case of the Hide Shop it's gifts; in the case of the other it's canoe hire on the lake, or one of the newly set up lake cruises.

Accommodation

Most accommodation in this tourist-oriented village is on the expensive side, and the few budget options tend to be oversubscribed – it's a good idea to book ahead. Meanwhile new investors are building more and more motels by the lake and gradually destroying what little character the village itself had.

The Chalets, 14 Pioneer Drive (☎03/680 6774). Six individually decorated, self-contained motel units overlooking the lake and well away from the highway, run by a friendly Swiss couple who also hire out holiday homes for four people and will do breakfasts. ⑤–⑥.

Godley Resort Alpine Inn, in the centre of the village by the Tekapo River Bridge (☎03/680 6848, *info@tekapo.co.nz*). The original inn building is 33 years old, though several new sections have been added since: old hotel rooms are cheaper than new ones, and motel units are cheaper still. The complex incorporates a variety of restaurants and shops, and various activities are arranged for guests. Lake views are costly so unless your legs are broken go for a room without. Prices might be worth negotiating if things seem quiet. ⑦–⑧.

Lake Tekapo Motel and Motor Camp, Lakeside Drive (☎03/680 6825, fax 680 6824). Situated among trees at the southern end of Tekapo, this is a large, well-equipped campsite. Tent sites $8, cabins ③, motel units ⑥.

Tailor-made-Tekapo Backpackers, 9–11 Aorangi Crescent (☎03/680 6700). Off SH8, five minutes' walk from the bus stop and shops, this friendly hostel has 30 bunks, plus an organic vegetable garden and a telescope – the clear mountain air makes for great stargazing. Dorm ①, rooms ②.

Tekapo YHA, Simpson Lane, just west of the village (☎03/680 6857, *info@yha.org.nz*). This improved lakeside hostel is now one of the best in New Zealand, offering doubles and twin rooms, as well as bunks; the common room has a floor-to-ceiling window so make the most of the magnificent view. Dorms ①, rooms ②.

The Village and around

The name Tekapo derives from the Maori *Taka* ("sleeping mat") and *Po* ("night"), suggesting that this place has long been used as a stopover between destinations. Although surrounded by heart-stopping scenery, there is little to the settlement itself – though you should pause long enough to look inside the tiny **Church of the Good Shepherd**, on Pioneer Drive. Overlooking the lake from a small raised platform, the stone church was built as a memorial to the pioneers of the McKenzie Country in 1935. Behind the rough-hewn Oamaru stone altar, a square window perfectly frames the lake and the surrounding hills and mountains; in the stillness of this simple church, the sunset can be quite a moving experience. About 50m east of the church is the perky-looking **Collie Dog Monument**, erected in 1966 by the sheep farmers of the McKenzie Country as a mark of their deep respect and affection for the dogs that make it possible to graze this harsh terrain.

Of a number of good **walks** in the area, the best is to **Mount John Lookout** (10km; ascent 300m; 3hr return), starting just past the motor camp on Lakeside Drive and climbing through a larch forest, full of birds, to a loop track which circles the summit of Mount John, with views of the McKenzie Basin, Lake Tekapo and the Southern Alps. You can either return the way you came or continue on the loop path and back along the lakeshore to your starting point, well worth the extra hour it adds. The *Lake Tekapo Walkway* leaflet gives a rundown of five alternative routes and is available from the local visitor centres ($1).

The air is so clear that organized **star gazing** (☎03/680 6565; starting between 7 & 9pm depending on season; $35) can be an educational and visually stimulating treat, but only when tour operator Hide (pronounced Ha–day) guides the trip himself. Other pursuits include skiing at the Tekapo Skifield, **ice skating** at the rink (May–Aug only) on Lakeside Drive, and guided **horse treks** through spectacular scenery with Tekapo Trekking (30min–2hr; $15–50; ☎03/680 6882).

Finally, determined sightseers short of time can join Air Safaris on SH8, about 6km west of Tekapo (free transfers arranged for customers), for a "Grand Traverse of Mount Cook". This **scenic flight** swoops across the Main Divide to the west coast, providing views of the Franz Josef and Fox glaciers, the Hooker and Muller glaciers, and, of course, Mount Cook (☎03/680 6880, bookable from their office in Tekapo ☎0800/806 880; hourly, weather permitting; 50min; $210).

Eating and drinking

Catering to a relatively captive market, most of the cafés and restaurants in Tekapo are quite pricey; if you're on a tight budget, your best bet is probably a picnic by the lake. Otherwise, the main street through the village has the *Reflections Restaurant* in the *Tekapo Tavern* (daily 9am–late) offering simple bar food and a good place for a beer with DJ orchestrated music on Friday and Saturday evenings, while best for filling cheap grub is the *Tekapo Bakery and Coffee Shop*, producing its own bread and pies and serving an economical all-day breakfast (daily 6am–8pm). *Jade Palace* (lunches 11.30am–2pm, dinner 5–9pm; licensed) is a modern, airy Chinese **restaurant** with very tasty set menus for under $25 a head. The pick of the restaurants in the *Godley Alpine Inn* complex, right in the centre of the village by the Tekapo River Bridge, is the highly expensive *Kohan* (evenings only; licensed), specializing in subtle Japanese cuisine, but there's also a Chinese dinner restaurant, and the all-day *Garden Buffet Bar* and European influenced *Garden Court Restaurant*, so you won't starve.

Towards Lake Pukaki

Southwest from Tekapo, SH8 heads towards **Lake Pukaki** some 47km distant, where SH80 branches off northwards towards Mount Cook Village. There's an **Information Shelter** made of local boulders at the road junction, housing several useful and interesting displays on Maori and *pakeha* history, a poem to McKenzie and his dog (see box on p.620) and a beautiful view of the lake – a massive blue-green expanse of water where winds sometimes whip up white-capped waves. It's also the starting point for a worthwhile **scenic drive**, which heads up the eastern side of the lake via Hangman Drive and Tasman Downs Road, offering over 40km of scenic lake and mountain views, before eventually petering out at the base of 2035m **Mount Burnett**.

Mount Cook Village

The road from the Lake Pukaki junction to Mount Cook heads north along the west bank of the lake for 55km, squeezed between the shore and an area of gorse- and tussock-covered hills. Thirty kilometres from the junction you'll pass **Peter's Lookout**, a popular viewing point on the lake side of the road and then the Glentanner Park campsite (see p.626).

Church of the Good Shepherd, Lake Tekapo

Foxgloves, Wanaka

Mackay Falls, Milford Track

FOOTPRINTS

CHRIS WHITEHEAD

Hooker sea lions, Catlins Coast

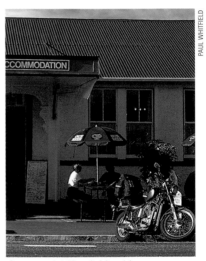

PAUL WHITFIELD

Ski plane, Tasman Glacier, Mount Cook National Park

JERRY DENNIS

Commercial Hotel, Murchison, West Coast

CHRIS WHITEHEAD

Fox Glacier

Kea

TranzAlpine train approaching Arthur's Pass

Town Hall, Dunedin

Mirror Lakes, Fiordland National Park

Bungy jumping off the Kawarau Bridge, Queenstown

POST
AND
TELEGRAPH

ARROWTOWN

SHOTOVER JET
NEW ZEALAND

Post Office, Arrowtown

Jetboat on the Shotover River

On hot days, an atmospheric white mist rises from the plain at the base of the mountain, as you approach the diffuse huddle of buildings that make up **MOUNT COOK VILLAGE**. At a height of 760m, this ugly, low-slung settlement is dominated by **The Hermitage**, an alpine-style hotel at the end of the valley that leads to the mountain; there's been a hostelry here since 1886 (though the current incarnation was built in 1958). Mount Cook is something of a company town, since the same people that own *The Hermitage* own just about everything else – and most of the summer population of 500 work for them. Rain frequently shrouds the village, but the scenery round about more than compensates (see p.627).

Practicalities

All the major operators run **buses** to Mount Cook from Christchurch via Tekapo, or from Queenstown to the southwest. There are additional services from Twizel and Tekapo, and most stop at Glentanner along the way. These days, as well as the usual suspects, you can get a Cook Connection (☎025/583 211; $45 one way) bus from either Timaru or Oamaru and a High Country Shuttle (☎0800/435 050; $35 & $40 respectively) from Queenstown or Wanaka. All the buses drop off in the car park near *The Hermitage*, from where everything is within walking distance, or at your accommodation. Mount Cook **airport**, 3km south of the village, is served by regular daily flights from Auckland, Christchurch, Queenstown, Rotorua, Taupo, Te Anau, Wanaka and Wellington.

The **DOC office and visitor centre** (daily: April–Sept 8.30am–5pm; Oct–March 8.30am–6pm; ☎03/435 1186, fax 435 1080, *www.mount-cook.com*), located among *The Hermitage*'s hotel buildings and chalets, is the best and friendliest place for information and advice on walks and activities. They stock everything from leaflets to detailed maps and a number of lavish gifts for the less discerning. There are also displays of Mount Cook memorabilia, and a **video** recounting Maori legends, the glacial history of the mountain, and a survey of the people who have, over the years, attempted to climb it (from 8.30am, English version on the hour; 20min; $2.50; the video may vary as a new version has been commissioned). Two hundred metres southeast of the centre is the **petrol station** while the post office is in The Hermitage gift shop. What meagre, overpriced supplies you can buy in Mount Cook Village are available at The Hermitage **Basement Coffee Shop** (daily: April–Sept 10am–5pm; Oct–March 7am–5.30pm) where any fresh produce is snapped up at dawn, while the more reasonably priced YHA shop offers tinned and frozen goods. Banking transactions can be completed at *The Hermitage*, and the Hermitage-owned bars take EFTPOS and credit cards. Alpine Guides, adjacent to the petrol pump (daily 8am–5.30pm; *www.alpineguides.co.nz*), offer experienced trekking and climbing guide and stock equipment, while *The Hermitage* rents out **mountain bikes** at an exorbitant $10 per hour. A better way to get around is the cheaper **Freedom Bus** (☎03/435 1077; operating a circuit throughout the day; $10) that will take you pretty much everywhere you'll want to go and drop you off, allowing you to explore on foot and then catch the same bus later to complete the circuit.

ACCOMMODATION

There is a lot of accommodation, nearly all owned by *The Hermitage*, but only a limited amount of budget rooms, which means booking early during the peak season (Oct–April & July–Sept) if you want to get into the last bastion of independence, the local YHA. Conversely, the village is deserted between April and June, a window between the summer tourist and winter skiing seasons, when it is generally possible to negotiate tariffs at the various forms of Hermitage accommodation.

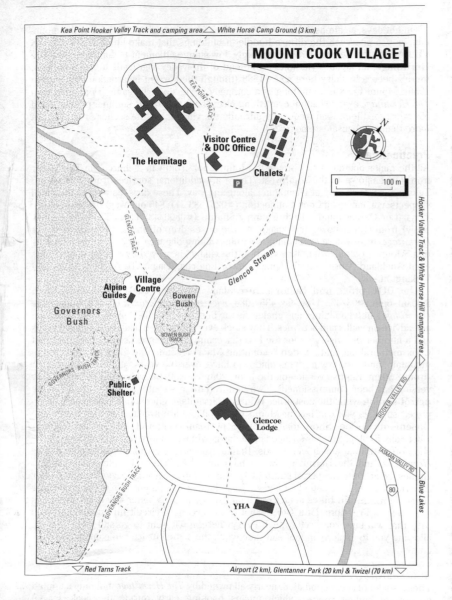

Kea Point Hooker Valley Track and camping area △ White Horse Camp Ground (3 km)

MOUNT COOK VILLAGE

KEA POINT TRACK

Visitor Centre
& DOC Office

The Hermitage

Chalets

N

0   100 m

Hooker Valley Track & White Horse Hill camping area ▷

GLENCOE TRACK

Glencoe Stream

Alpine
Guides

Village
Centre

Bowen
Bush

Governors
Bush

BOWEN BUSH TRACK

GOVERNORS BUSH TRACK

Public
Shelter

Glencoe
Lodge

HOOKER VALLEY RD

TASMAN VALLEY RD

▷ Blue Lakes

GOVERNORS BUSH TRACK

YHA

80

▽ Red Tarns Track   Airport (2 km), Glentanner Park (20 km) & Twizel (70 km) ▽

Glentanner Park, 20km south on SH8 (☎03/435 1855, fax 435 1854). Well-equipped site with shop, recently renovated restaurant, camping, new dorm-like accommodation and cabins in a wide open space, giving panoramic views of the mountains and the Tasman Valley. Tent sites $8, dorms $15, cabins $40–65.

The Hermitage, on the northwestern border of the village (☎03/435 1809, fax 435 1879, *hermitage.mtcook@xtra.co.nz*). This rambling wooden structure topped by a greeny-blue roof has several grades of room, all with a balcony, though not always a view. The complex also includes seven heated and fully self-contained A–frame chalets (often booked out by Kiwi Experience), 32 very popular motel units and the Glencoe Lodge. ⑥–⑨.

Mount Cook YHA Hostel, cnr Bowen Drive & Kitchener Drive (☎ & fax 03/435 1820, *yhamtck@yha.org.nz*). An excellent and friendly hostel with 66 beds in a wooden building and modern, well-kept facilities. Free videos are shown in the evenings, free saunas between 7 & 9.30pm and pizzas for the fixed price of $5.50. Office hours: 8–10.30am, 12–3pm & 5.30–9pm. Dorms ①, rooms ③.

White Horse Hill Camping Area, thirty minutes' walk north from the village at the start of the Hooker Track (no advance bookings). A serene and informal camping area with flush toilets and running water; camping spots are indicated by markers. Tent sites $5.

EATING AND DRINKING

The Hermitage will provide **picnics** for all-comers (ask in the lobby; under $25, given 24hr notice), with a free cooler bag thrown in, and within the hotel complex itself there are four eateries. The *Wakefield Restaurant* (Oct–April only; licensed) serves **buffet** meals (roughly $27 a plate, drinks extra), but the real attraction is the excellent view of Mount Cook. The *Alpine Room* opens all year for breakfast, lunch and dinner, with a full meal costing around $60 ($41 buffet-style; licensed), and the *Panorama Room* (Oct–March) specializes in **fine dining** and also has an excellent view (evenings only; $50–90; licensed). The lower echelons are catered for by the licensed **coffee shop** in the basement (all year round, see p.625 for times).

There are also two **bars** in the hotel, the best of which is the *Snowline Lounge*, with panoramic views of the mountain making this an excellent spot to sit and sup a couple of expensive beers as the sun goes down. If you manage to escape the clutches of *The Hermitage* the only other sanctuary is the *Chamois Bar* in the *Glencoe Lodge*, where bar food includes the usual pub fare to eat in or take away ($5–15) and a bottle shop operates from behind the bar.

Glentanner Park, on the shores of Lake Pukaki, 20km south on SH8, has the obligatory big-windowed restaurant, *The James McKenzie* (lunch & afternoon tea in winter, all day in summer), and the equally obligatory inflated prices.

Exploring the national park

The 700 square kilometres surrounding the peak and extending to the north and east forms the **Mount Cook National Park**, which was designated a **world heritage site** by UNESCO in 1986. With twenty-two peaks over 3000m, the park contains the lion's share of New Zealand's mountains, mostly made of greywacke laid in an ocean trench 250–300 million years ago. About 2 million years ago the Alpine Fault began to lift, progressively pushing the rock upwards and creating the Southern Alps. These days the process continues at about the same rate as erosion, ensuring that the mountains are at least holding their own, if not getting bigger. Mount Cook is at the heart of a unique mountain area, where the rock of the Alps is easily shattered in the cold, leaving huge amounts of gravel in the valley floors. The inhospitable ice fields of the upper slopes are contrasted by the tussock-cloaked foothills, where Mount Cook Lilies, summer daisies and snow gentians thrive. The weather here is changeable, often with a pall of low-lying cloud liable to turn to rain, and the mountain air is lung-searingly fresh. The valleys around the mountains tend to retain heat (unless the winds blow straight down them) and can feel airless and oppressive.

There are numerous **walking opportunities** catering for a wide range of abilities, with a variety of scenic trails beginning on the edges of Mount Cook Village itself. Main routes into the mountains from the village are the **Kea Point Track** northwest to the **Mueller Glacier**, the **Hooker Valley Track** northwards to the **Hooker Glacier** (although you can no longer climb to the Hooker Hut), and the **Tasman Valley Road** northeast to the **Tasman Glacier**. Walking as far as these glaciers is well within the capability of any moderately fit recreational walker, and longer walks for the more ambitious branch out from these basic routes. However you shouldn't actually walk on the surface of any of the glaciers unless you've already had experience of such walks and you've sought advice on conditions from the local DOC, or you're in the company of a qualified local guide. A *Walks in the Mount Cook National Park* **leaflet** ($1) is available from the visitor centre.

Although walking is an unbeatable way of exploring the park, the **scenic flights** on offer can provide you with glimpses of areas that you could never dream of reaching on foot. Such flights are extremely popular, and must be booked as far in advance as possible. Remember that flights are cancelled in high winds or if visibility is poor – and the weather can change by the hour, so if you get the chance to go, jump at it. The peak season for flights is from November to March, but in winter (June & July) the weather's often clearer, with better visibility. The Mount Cook region's **ski season** (see box, p.630) lasts from June to September, and the steep, inaccessible slopes (you're delivered to them by helicopter) present an exciting challenge to experienced skiers. Another alternative is **helihiking** which involves hopping on a helicopter and getting delivered three-quarters of the way along one of the walks, climbing to a summit and then walking back. If none of this appeals then one of the most entertaining experiences is a **boat ride** (see p.630) up the Tasman Lake, which gets you within touching distance of the terminal moraine and the honeycomb ice of the Tasman Glacier.

Walks

Walks range from gentle day-hikes to arduous and spectacular alpine treks that take several days. Tramping **information** is available from the DOC office in Mount Cook Village. Most of the trails are suitable for well-equipped independent walkers, but to help you on your way, Alpine Guides (☎03/435 1834) offer experienced **trekking** and climbing **guides**, although they concentrate on 7–10 day walking options (starting at $3450) and climbing instruction. Mount Cook Encounter (☎03/435 1809 ext 8410; based in *The Hermitage*) leads gentler **guided walks** (2–5hr; $20).

The DOC leaflet *Walks in Mount Cook National Park* ($1) describes the national park and lists twelve excellent **shorter walks** (10min–5hr), all of which can be extended by those with relevant experience. Each of the walks starts in Mount Cook Village and heads out along the banks of one of the two glacier-fed rivers, the Hooker River and the Tasman River. Of these, the most popular is the superb **Hooker Valley Track** (9km; 3hr 30min return). Crossing two swingbridges at the top and bottom of the Mueller Lake, the track climbs opposite the western side of Mount Cook, past the site of the original hermitage (a stone fireplace remains) and the viewpoint at the Alpine Memorial, ending at the Hooker Lake. If you want to continue and are fit and well-equipped: you can head back to the footbridge at the source of the Mueller Lake and make for the **Ball Shelter** (14km; ascent 300m; 6hr, category 3; $10), spend the night and walk down to the Blue Lakes (9km; 3hr) and then return on the Freedom Bus (check their timetable) or walk along the Tasman Valley Road back to the village (about 7km; 2.5hr).

The **Mueller Glacier**, nestling 5km northeast of Mount Cook Village beneath the hanging glaciers and icefalls of Mount Sefton, is reached by the **Kea Point Track** (3hr return), which starts just north of the DOC office and ends at a lookout over the Mueller Lake. Again, a more gruelling alternative is available to those who first check on weather conditions with the DOC, in the shape of the **Mueller Hut Track** (5km; 5hr one way), which requires moderate fitness. The route leaves the Kea Point Track just before its arrival at the glacier, climbing steeply westwards up the **Sealy Tarn Track** along a route marked by cairns. From the tarns the route to the hut is marked by the less romantic but more useful orange triangles (every 200m). The final assault is up a

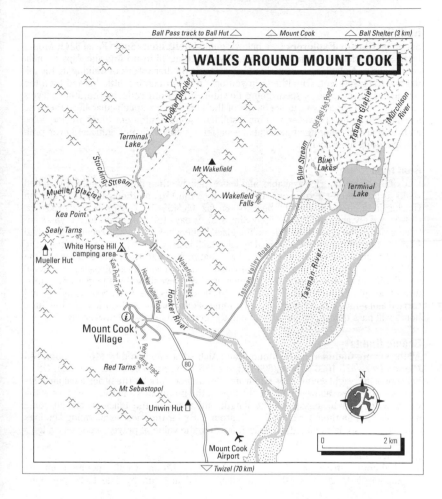

loose gravel slope to a skyline ridge, from which you head south towards the 1800m **Mueller Hut** (category 1; 12 bunks; $18). The views are quite startling and you are engulfed by almost perfect silence, interrupted only by the murmur of running water and the twittering of birds.

The trail to the **Tasman Glacier** starts from the Blue Lakes car park, 3km north of the village up the Tasman Valley Road, and leads to the **Glacier Lookout** (500m; 20min one way; 100m ascent). The glacier is 600m deep at its thickest, 3km across at its widest, and moves at a rate of 20cm a day. A gentleman called Sir Harry Wigley landed an Auster aircraft on the glacier in 1955, paving the way for today's squadrons of tourist flights. One last excellent walk which is achievable for the lazier traveller is the **Red Tarns Track** (2km; ascent 300m; 3hr return), a steep but short climb to two tarns named after the red pondweed that grows in them. From the tarns you have an uninterrupted panoramic view of Mount Cook, the village and along the Tasman Valley which is well worth the sweat.

Helihiking

Set up by **Glacier Explorers** (see below), guided **helihikes** (Snow Feast $241, Mount Dark $148) offer travellers the opportunity of getting high up into the Alps by helicopter, and completing tracks without having to do the hard work of walking up the initial few thousand feet. On either trip you only need to climb a little bit and then the remainder of the time is spent going downhill. This both reduces the fitness levels required and enables you to see some of the area's more spectacular but otherwise inaccessible sights. However, you must still have good equipment (they provide poles and food) and although going downhill is easier, it's still fairly energetic and even pretty knackering after a while.

Boat trips

One of the most fun trips available, and less expensive than flights or multi-day guided walks, is the **Glacier Explorer** – a short walk (25min) to and then ride up the Tasman Glacier in a moulded plastic boat (☎ & fax 03/435 1077, *glacier007@xtra.co.nz*; Oct–May daily at 10am, 2pm & 5pm; 3hr; $75). It pays to book in advance if you want to experience the eerie **boat ride** on the glacial lake where icebergs, recently detached from the glacier itself, drift around. The lake itself is grey in colour; a result of the large amount of ground-down rock, or rock flour, that mixes with the water and reflects the light. As you approach the glacier itself you'll be able to watch various-sized chunks of ice fall off and get the chance to examine it up close, revealing that the glacier is a mixture of beautiful honeycombed ice cells and the detritus that has been picked up and carried along its course. The guides are a mine of information and stories, and the three hours will pass quickly providing you had the good sense to wrap up warmly.

Scenic flights

All the **scenic flights** from the Mount Cook Airfield are operated by **Mount Cook Ski Planes** (☎03/435 1026 & 0800/800 702, fax 435 1886, *mtcook@skiplanes.co.nz*). Other helicopter and sightseeing trips run from Glentanner Park or the other local airfields (see below). These allow you to see the tops of the mountains and the steepness of the valley walls, and to appreciate the length and mass of the glaciers, and in some instances land on them for a quick walk around. By far the most exhilarating landings and take-offs are in the fixed wing aircraft, when the value of prayer becomes evident.

HELICOPTERS
The **helicopter** trips on offer in the vicinity of Mount Cook operate from the Glentanner Park, 20km south of the village, and are run by The Helicopter Line

MOUNT COOK SKI AREAS

The **skiing and snowboarding** around Mount Cook tend towards the exhilarating, although the experience doesn't come cheap. None of the steep runs is served by ski lift, so helicopters provide access during the season (June–Sept), thereby ensuring high prices and preserving the resort's status as a rather exclusive preserve. There are no runs suitable for beginners or intermediates. Access to the fields is generally provided by Alpine Guides (☎03/435 1834, fax 435 1898, *mtcook@alpineguides.co.nz*), who offer the chance to "Ski the Tasman", with two guided 10km runs on the Tasman glacier for enthusiastic and adept skiers and snowboarders ($595), while all-day skiing with helicopter transfers to a range of different runs starts at around $685 and advances swiftly to $895, with equipment rental extra.

(☎03/435 1801 & 0800/650 651, fax 435 1802), part of the same network that own the Mount Cook Ski Planes.

There are three fights on offer: the "Mountains High" flight over the village, circumnavigation of Mount Cook, traverse of the Southern Alps, snow landing, and views of the glaciers (45min; $300); "Alpine Explorer" cruise over the Ben Ohau Mountains, views of Mount Cook and the glaciers and a snow landing on the Richardson Glacier (30min; $225); and the "Alpine Vista" swoop over the Ben Ohua Range, snow landing and panoramic views (20min; $135). Each is an exciting and bumpy ride, hovering alongside the valley walls and peaks, or viewing the tumbling blocks of the Hochstetter Icefall and landing on the snow of the glacier when the weather allows, and when it's all over you'll get a commemorative glossy booklet.

Alternative helicopter trips run **from Twizel** with Glacier Southern Lakes Helicopters, opposite the *Mackenzie Country Inn* (☎03/435 0370, fax 435 0372, *gslhtwiz@es.co.nz*). They offer five trips ranging from $155 to $455 along similar lines to those from Glentanner but covering greater distances, with the longer you spend in the air adding to the amount you pay.

FIXED-WING PLANES
Mount Cook Ski Planes, based at the Mount Cook airfield offer the best four fixed-wing scenic adventures, the ultimate of which is the longest ("The Grand Circle"; 55min; $310), which circles Mount Cook, crosses (briefly) the Main Divide, then lands and takes off from the Tasman Glacier in a heart-stoppingly short distance. The glaciers are silent once the plane engine splutters off and wandering around on the footprint-free snow is almost as exhilarating as the landing and take-off. Of the three shorter flights on offer, one lands on a glacier and the others offer alternative routes around and between the Alps. They also (under the umbrella of Air Safaris) offer scenic flights from nearby Glentanner, Tekapo, Twizel or Omarama, with various flight plans including a whizz round the Mount Cook summit – although you'll be starting slightly further away from the mountains and consequently spending less time over them. It's best to go from Mount Cook airfield if you can, so only book one of the alternatives if it is impossible to do so there or you'd like a quick look at the mountains but have no intention of travelling to Mount Cook Village itself. There are also fly-overs and scenic flights available from the West Coast (see p.732).

Twizel and around

Seventy kilometres from Mount Cook, retracing your route on SH80 then veering south on SH8 at Lake Pukaki junction, you'll come upon **TWIZEL**, which sits on the west side of the main highway, a pretty tree-filled island surrounded by seas of pasture with a backdrop of alpine scenery.

This modest settlement began life in 1966 as a staff hostel for people working on the local hydroelectric scheme (see box on p.637), and was supposed to have been bulldozed flat after the project was finished. Some think this might have been a kinder fate: Twizel is a windy place, dry and cold in the winter, and dry and hot in summer. The two best reasons to come here are to take a trip out to the **Kaki (Black Stilt) Aviary**, 3km from town, which aims to save these rare wading birds from extinction and to indulge yourself in the **good food** and ale available in Twizel's premier bar, *Hunters*. Otherwise, you could try **helibiking**, a new addition to the long list of things you can do with a helicopter in this area, or content yourself with exploring the heavily forested banks, tall grassy hills and mountains surrounding **Lake Ohau**, where various tramps provide views over the broad turquoise lake.

Arrival and information

InterCity **buses** drop off in the car park of the DOC Office (closed to the public) on Wairepo Road, adjacent to SH8 and attached to one of the two **visitor centres** in this little town, WWW – short for Where, What, Why (Oct–April daily 8.30am–6.30am; May–Sept Mon–Fri 9am–4.30pm; ☎03/435 3118 & 0800/435 311, *wherewhatwhy @xtra.co.nz*). A variety of **shuttles** and coaches stop off in Twizel including Cook Connection (☎025 583 211), from either Mount Cook, Timaru or Oamaru, and High Country Shuttle (☎0800/435 050), from Queenstown and Wanaka. They tend to disgorge at the DOC car park (above) or the one outside the council buildings, just behind the town's central shopping mall. It is here that you'll also find the other visitor centre, Twizel Info (Oct–April daily 9am–7pm; May–Sept Tues–Sat 10am–4pm; ☎03/435 0066, *twizelnz@yahoo.com*), combining a gift shop and radio station. WWW is marginally more friendly, but both visitor centres offer booking services and keep a good stock of leaflets.

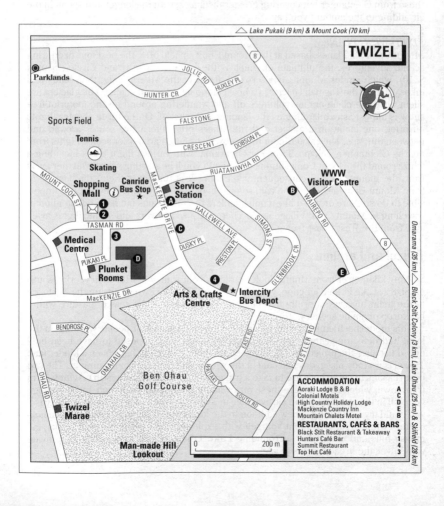

For further information try the monthly *Twizel Times* (free) an insight into the community's collective psyche. The town's accommodation is all within walking distance of either point of arrival; for exploring further afield, *Mackenzie Country Inn*, Warepo Road, offers **bike rental** ($10 a day). There is a **petrol station** on Mackenzie Drive, and a mall in the centre of town has a supermarket, restaurants and a **bank**.

Accommodation

Being only half an hour's drive from Mount Cook, Twizel's accommodation tends to be oversubscribed around Christmas, New Year and Easter, when the town is packed with holidaying New Zealanders. **Book ahead** if you plan to be here then.

Aoraki Lodge B&B, 32 Mackenzie Drive (☎03/435 0300, fax 435 0305, *aorakilodge@xtra.co.nz*). A luxurious spot with be-decked individual rooms, wheelchair access, en-suite bathrooms, the use of a large comfortable lounge and tastebud tingling breakfasts and dinners (3-course dinner $30; BYO). ⑥.

Colonial Motels, 36–38 McKenzie Drive (☎03/435 0100, fax 435 0499). Superior ground-floor units with full kitchens and facilities, and conveniently close to shops and restaurants. ⑤.

High Country Holiday Lodge, McKenzie Drive (☎03/435 0671, fax 435 0747). The former hydro-electric workers' camp, this has retained some of its institutional character, with barracks-like bunk rooms, and is part of a swiftly growing little empire offering budget accommodation. Hotel and motel rooms are a better bet, with a communal kitchen and there is also *The Summit* restaurant. Dorms ①, rooms ③.

Mackenzie Country Inn, Warepo Rd (☎03/435 0869, fax 435 0857, *bookings@mackenzie.co.nz*). A big brash modern hotel/motel with luxury accommodation, bar and restaurant, shuttle to Mount Cook and they can put together packages of activities for those too busy or lazy to do it themselves. ⑦.

Parklands, The Old Hospital, 122 MacKenzie Drive (☎03/435 0507, fax 435 0544, *parklands@xtra.co.nz*). A rejuvenated backpackers with spacious doubles, dorms and cosy cottages offering breakfasts ($8 continental, $10 cooked). Dorms ①, rooms ③, cottages ④.

Mountain Chalet Motels and Lodge, Wairepo Rd (☎03/435 0785, fax 435 0551). Ten spacious, light-filled, self-contained A-frame chalets. The adjacent lodge section offers simple clean and comfortable backpacker accommodation in dorms and rooms. Dorms ①, rooms ③, chalets ⑤.

The Town and Kaki Aviary

This two-storey town erupts into a brief summertime frenzy when tourists flock to visit Mount Cook and attend the various summertime boat races on the lakes, before lapsing back into its mundane existence as an administrative centre. Circular in design, the **Market Place Shopping Centre** provides the town's focal point. Opposite the DOC office and WWW visitor centre is a grey concrete statue, which was supposed to be Neptune, though sadly his fork has been removed. Nearby, a section of pipe partially buried to form an arch for the car park gives notice of the grassed area on the other side of the road where heavy earth-moving machinery used in the hydroelectric project acts as an attraction and children's play area.

You're best off heading straight out to the **Kaki (Black Stilt) Aviary**, which occupies a wetland area 3km south of Twizel on SH8. The colony is attempting to preserve the world's rarest wading bird from extinction – an urgent task as only 37 adults are left in the wild, nine or ten of them female, and 20 adults in captivity. Access is by guided tour only (you must book in advance ☎03/435 0802; Oct–March daily 10.30am & 2pm; April–Sept Mon–Fri 10.30am; 1hr; $12.50), but there is a hide where you can watch the birds without disturbing them; binoculars are provided. The long- red-legged kaki once thrived on the banks of braided rivers, feeding mainly on mayfly and exhibiting the endearing post-coital behaviour of walking cross-billed as if indulging in upright pillow talk. All this changed due to habitat loss as a result of introduced plant species, the Waitaki hydroelectric project and the introduction of mammalian predators such as cats, ferrets, rats and stoats.

The centre operates by incubating clutches from all the wild and captive kaki pairs, hatching the eggs in captivity and raising the chicks to three or nine months before releasing them into the wild. At present there's a relief-inducing eighty percent survival rate. Given that the majority of your $12.50 tour fee goes into the project you can both enjoy the education and get to feel good about it, unlike those individuals who have missed the point and with powerful binoculars look at the kaki from the road. If you want to know more about the kaki or other braided-river species and their habitat then get copies of the informative *Conservation of Braided River Birds, Braided River Care Code* and *Project River Recovery* leaflets, available in DOC offices and visitor centres.

Activities

What Twizel lacks, its surroundings make up for, and there are plenty of ways to get out there. If you're a fit and experienced **trail biker**, or just a willing one without a history of heart problems, then Heli Bike (☎03/435 0626 & 0800/435 424; *a.shearer@xtra.co.nz*) will drop you off somewhere and leave you to bike back (guided trips are also available). Routes take in such diverse places as the Benmore Range, beginning about 5km south of Twizel; Omahau Hill, 15km southwest of town; and the easier Pyramid Circuit (daily on demand, 2–4hr; from $65 to $120; bikes and other gear all available for hire). They also organize the annual Helibike Challenge (second Saturday in February) which is generally an excuse for groups to spend a day riding for fun, although there's always someone who takes it seriously. If you are intending to **climb** any of the peaks in the area, contact Shaun Norman (☎03/435 0622), a skilled and experienced guide who also offers introductory, intermediate and advanced mountaineering instruction. Finally, there are Mount Cook **scenic flights** operating from Twizel (see p.631 for details) – and there's always skiing at Mount Cook or Ohau (see opposite).

Eating and drinking

Unfortunately Twizel's contagious lack of charm extends to most of its **eating and drinking** options, which tend to be functional and uninspiring – with the notable exception of *Hunters Café Bar*.

Black Stilt Restaurant and Takeaway, 25 Market Place. A regular milk bar serving bacon and eggs ($10), light lunches and burgers ($5–15), and main meals (up to $16). Mon–Sat all day, Sun dinner only.

Summit Restaurant, McKenzie Drive. Restaurant serving typical Kiwi food in typically large portions (main dishes under $20). Licensed.

Hunters Café Bar, 2 Market Place. The best place to eat and party in town, run by a Scot with a weak spot for McKenzie Country-themed decoration, such as corrugated iron, a bit of barbed wire and wood. Generous well-prepared lunches and dinners ($6–20) include beer-battered fish, locally farmed salmon and merino lamb kebabs, rounded off with good coffee. The buzzy atmosphere is helped along by occasional live music and theme nights, not to mention cocktails such as McKenzie's Dog. Daily 11am–late.

The Top Hut Café and Bar, 13 Tasman Rd. Pub and glorified takeaway with chairs if you want to eat in, serving things with chips and now part of the High Country lodge empire. They've divided the building and added on a Chinese restaurant which is a touch more formal.

Lake Ohau

West of Twizel and around 25km along a narrow service road and over a few cattle stops, **Lake Ohau** is famed for its forest, river and **skifield** (see box opposite). Renowned for the purity of its water, the lake surrounds boast some distinctive natural features, such as kettles (small depressions left when blocks of glacial ice melt, causing sediment above to subside), and the terracing on its banks that reflects the light of summer sunsets. Although it lacks the colour of Lake Tekapo, it is popular for fishing and kayaking, as are the Dobson and Hopkins rivers that flow into the lake's northern

Ohau Skifield, about 42km southwest of Twizel, off SH8 (☎03/438 9885, *www.ohau.co.nz*; July–Oct), is a small high-country (1033m) field with powder snow and uncrowded slopes which, as a part of the Main Divide, has reliable snowfall. There are several slopes catering for all standards of skier and snowboarder, with the added bonus of spectacular views of Lake Ohau and the longest T-bar in New Zealand. The *Lake Ohau Lodge* (see below) provides **accommodation** near the field, while the **Ohau Ski Lodge** on the field has no accommodation but docs offer log burners, a sun deck with panoramic views, café and shop. **Equipment rental** is available at the field and lift passes cost $39 per day (or $33 if lodge guest), with access provided by **bus** from the Lake Ohau Lodge ($15 return); otherwise, transport can be arranged by phoning the skifield information number (see above). Learners' **packages**, with gear rental and passes thrown in, start at $25 for ninety minutes.

end (contact Twizel's visitor centres for details of boat rental). Ohau ("the place of the wind") was a seasonal food gathering stop-off for Maori making their way to and from the West Coast via Brodrick Pass and was the scene of many battles between rival *iwi*.

The **Ohau Forests** lie northwest from the lake, their stands of mountain beech and subalpine scrub criss-crossed by numerous tracks; the *Ohau Conservation Area* ($1), available from the visitor centres in Twizel, details various walks (30min–4hr). The forests flank wide valleys cut by once surging rivers (now a little more gentle unless in flood) and separated by narrow mountain ranges, with short tussock grasslands predominating around the lakes and lowlands. It's a pretty area but lacks any real points of interest so unless you're planning to head up to the backcountry huts to get away from it all you'll probably find more worthwhile entertainment and sights around Mount Cook or along the well-beaten roads running south.

As you enter the community near the lake you'll soon realize it is made up almost entirely of holiday homes, has no amenities and that the only **accommodation** is camping, the huts or at the lodge. If you become enamoured with the lake and forests, or simply want to stay and ski or tramp, *Lake Ohau Lodge*, on the southwestern shore of the lake, a 25km drive from SH8 along the Lake Ohau Road (☎ & fax 03/438 9885; dorms ①, rooms & chalets ③–⑥, camping $9), offers a wide variety of **accommodation**. Breakfast and dinner are available here, too. The huts on the tramps are all backcountry with a few bunks and nothing else ($5 a night).

Omarama and around

A crossroads town at the heart of the Waitaki Valley, on the edge of the McKenzie Basin, **OMARAMA** lies 30km south of Twizel. Sitting at the junction of SH8, which continues south to Cromwell, and SH83 to Oamaru, it is also on the main tourist route between Christchurch and Queenstown, via Mount Cook. The town itself has little to offer, with the nearby **Clay Cliffs Scenic Reserve** and the excursions offered by the local **gliding** club providing the main reasons to stop.

Arrival, information and accommodation

Regular **buses** plying the Timau–Twizel–Oamaru loop stop in Omarama, as do services from Queenstown and Wanaka and the major national bus companies, all dropping off at or near (InterCity drop off at the *Merino Café* opposite) the **visitor centre** on SH83, about 50m from the junction with SH8 in the Caltex Garage on the south side of the road (daily 7am–8pm; ☎03/438 9522), which provides leaflets and advice, accommodation reservations and bus or trip bookings.

As befits a passing-through kind of town, **accommodation** in Omarama is more geared to stopovers than to kicking back for a few days. The most conducive place is *Buscot Station*, about 8km north of Omarama on SH8 (they'll arrange pick-ups if you book ahead; ☎03/438 9646; dorms ①, rooms ②), a merino sheep farm where **backpacker** accommodation is provided in the old shearers' quarters, surrounded by a beautifully kept garden. Otherwise, you're faced with the usual choice of **campsite**, motel, or the local pub. *Omarama Holiday Park*, at the junction of SH8 and SH83 (☎03/438 9875; tent sites $18 for two, on-site vans & cabins ②) an expansive site with sheltering trees and modern well-kept facilities. A rambling low slung building on SH83, 50m away from the junction with SH8, the *Omarama Hotel* (☎03/438 9713; B&B ④) has clean basic **rooms** – a good bet so long as you don't mind some noise from the bar beside. The most expensive place in town is the *Ahuriri Motel*, on the corner of SH83 and Ahuriri Drive, 500m from the junction with SH8 (☎03/438 9451; ⑤), with comfortable and clean **motel** units in a rejuvenated building.

The Town and around

The name Omarama is Maori, and roughly translates as "place of light", but the town is short and squat with a population of just 300 – maybe it's the wrong kind of light. The settlement is mostly used as a way-station for picking up supplies, but there's one curiosity worth visiting if you're here in summer. Situated 4km back up SH8 towards Twizel then west for 15km up the Quailburn and then Henburn roads, the **Clay Cliffs Scenic Reserve** (☎03/438 9780; $5 per person) is a combination of bare pinnacles and angular ridges separated by narrow ravines and canyons. The braided Ahuriri River provides a picturesque backdrop to this eerie landscape of badland erosion – created when a 100m uplift caused by the Ostler Fault exposed gravels, which became differentially weathered.

The Maori name for the clay cliffs is *Paritea*, meaning white or light-coloured cliff, and they were so named by Araiteuru, who brought the *kumara* sweet potatoes from Hawaiki. The cliffs provided natural shelter for moa hunters, with several earth ovens indicative of early Maori settlement. If the weather is very wet don't risk going up to the reserve in your own vehicle – you may never get it back. If you're still keen then join a guided tour run by Omarama Safari Tours (☎03/438 9547; 1hr 30min; $25–35).

The northwesterly winds that blow across the basin make Omarama a fine spot for **gliding**, and Alpine Soaring (☎03/438 9600; 20–40min; $89–$175) takes advantage of the reliable wind and flat surrounds to provide spectacular flights in two-seater gliders. The land and rivers around Omarama are also prime territory for hunting chamois and red deer, and fly fishing for trout and salmon. The fish and the venison are delicious, but no one seems to know what to do with the chamois – except hang their heads on walls. Bookings for fly fishing can be made through Omarama visitor centre, licenses are $13 for 24hr.

Eating and drinking

A slightly unusual blackboard menu at the *Oasis Tearooms*, near the SH8–SH83 junction (daily: Oct–Feb 7am–9pm; March–Sept 8am–9pm; licensed) includes such exotica as satay and Asian-influenced soups, as well as pita and focaccia **sandwiches** and a great-value $9 cooked breakfast. Still in town, both the *Omarama Lodge* and the *Omarama Hotel* have capacious dining rooms that serve up large but uninspiring lunches and **dinners** at reasonable prices. Perhaps the best place to eat is the *Clay Cliffs Estate* (☎03/438 9654), 1km along SH8 from the junction with SH83, an eccentric spot where a hacienda-like building by a lake with weeping willows overlooks a 1960s

American police car in the yard. The stylish café-bar and vineyard have good-quality eclectic lunches and dinners ($5–$23) and produce some very drinkable wine (tastings $2, redeemable against any purchase).

The Lindis Pass and the Waitaki Valley

Travelling on from Omarama on SH8 towards Wanaka, Cromwell and Queenstown (see Chapter 13), you'll cross the **Lindis Pass**, a rewarding scenic drive on narrow roads through predominantly tussock and grassland, though in bad weather it can feel distinctly foreboding.

The **route to Oamaru** on the east coast is an easier drive, following SH83 as it passes through a string of small settlements, which are surprisingly evenly spaced along the **Waitaki Valley**. The valley itself has been irrevocably changed by a mammoth hydro-electric scheme and the lakes it **created** (see box below).

The first settlement you come to, 26km from Omamara, is **OTEMATATA**, with little to offer except the *Otematata Motor Hotel* (✆ & fax 03/438 7899; ⑤), which overlooks Lake Aviemore and provides accommodation, dining and a bar. **KUROW**, 30km further along SH83, is regarded as a fisherman's paradise. Twin wooden bridges (dating from 1880) span the salmon- and trout-filled Waitaki River, and there are a few limestone buildings of some grandeur in the settlement itself. Another 23km on, **DUNTROON** provides another chance to cut across to the goldfields area: a gentler route than the Lindis Pass, **Dansey's Pass Road** to Naseby dates from prospecting days. Just off this road, about 9km from Duntroon, are the weird limestone formations of **Elephant Rocks**, which are often used by rock-climbers and abseilers; the difficulty ranges from beginner to medium but it's advisable to have had some experience and be well-equipped.

Pressing on from Duntroon, the junction with the main east-coast highway (SH1) is just 35km away, and **Oamaru** (see p.588) is a further 8km south.

THE WAITAKI VALLEY HYDROELECTRIC SCHEME

The **Waitaki Hydroelectric Scheme** is made up of twelve power stations, built between 1925 and 1981, and currently provides nearly one-third of the nation's power. The scheme has its origins in the work of the engineer Peter Seton Hay, who in 1904 submitted a report to the New Zealand government indicating the extraordinary hydro-electric potential of the country, in particular the headwater lakes of the Waitaki river: Tekapo, Pukaki and Ohau. Construction of the Waitaki Power Station began some 24 years later. Most awesome of the stations are the Benmore, Aviemore and Waitaki, all ranged along the Waitaki River **east of Omarama**.

The nearest to Omarama, 15km away on SH83, is the earth-built **Benmore Dam** (✆03/3438 7848; daily 10.30am–4.30pm; tours Tues, Thurs, & Sun at 11am, 1pm & 3pm, or by request; closed May–Sept; 1hr 15min; $5). The tours take you around the control room and generators, past lots of gushing water and views from the top of the dam. The scale of the dam is quite breathtaking, and you can walk or drive to the top; there is also a loop track with distant views of Mount Cook. **Aviemore Dam**, between Otematata and Kurow, supports SH83, and lay-bys on either side enable you to admire its construction. Alongside the dam is a trout- and salmon-spawning canal, with the lake glinting aquamarine against the mountains. About 20km south of Aviemore Dam on SH83, **Waitaki Power Station** is the oldest station on the river, with good views from a platform just beyond the dam, near an immense grey 17-tonne turbine used in 1941 to drive the generators.

travel details

Trains

Arthur's Pass to: Christchurch (1 daily; 2hr 5min); Greymouth (1 daily; 2hr 5min).

Christchurch to: Arthur's Pass (1 daily; 2hr 5min).

Buses

Arthur's Pass to: Christchurch (2 daily; 2hr 10min); Greymouth (2 daily; 2hr).

Ashburton to: Fairlie (1 daily; 1hr); Geraldine (1 daily; 50min); Methven (1 daily; 45min); Mount Cook (1 daily; 3hr 10min).

Christchurch to: Arthur's Pass (2 daily; 2hr 10min); Fairlie (1 daily; 3hr 15min); Geraldine (1 daily; 2hr 5min); Hanmer Springs (2 daily; 2hr); Methven (2 daily; 1hr 30min); Mount Cook (1 daily; 5hr 30min); Tekapo (1 daily; 4hr 10min).

Fairlie to: Christchurch (1 daily; 3hr 15min); Tekapo (2 daily; 1hr); Timaru (1 daily; 50min).

Geraldine to: Christchurch (1 daily; 2hr 5min); Fairlie (2 daily; 35min).

Hanmer Springs to: Christchurch (2 daily; 2hr); Murchison (1 daily; 2hr 30min).

Methven to: Christchurch (2 daily; 1hr 30min); Geraldine (2 daily; 1hr 30min).

Mount Cook to: Ashburton (1 daily; 3hr 10min); Christchurch (1 daily; 5hr 30min); Queenstown (3 daily; 4hr); Tekapo (2 daily; 1hr 20min); Twizel (2 daily; 1hr).

Oamarama to: Oamaru (1 daily; 2hr); Queenstown (2 daily; 2hr 20min); Twizel (3 daily; 35min).

Tekapo to: Christchurch (1 daily; 4hr 10min); Fairlie (2 daily; 1hr); Mount Cook (2 daily; 1hr 20min); Twizel (2 daily; 3hr).

Twizel to: Mount Cook (2 daily; 1hr); Omarama (3 daily; 35 min).

Flights

Mount Cook to: Auckland (1 daily; 2hr 55min); Christchurch (1 daily; 45min); Queenstown (4 daily; 40min); Rotorua (1 daily; 3hr 25min); Taupo (1 daily; 5hr); Te Anau (1 daily; 1hr 25min); Wanaka (2 daily; 1hr 20min); Wellington (8 daily; 1hr).

CHAPTER ELEVEN

DUNEDIN TO STEWART ISLAND

The southeastern corner of the South Island contains some of the least-visited parts of New Zealand, yet, hidden away here are a couple of real gems. The first is the attractive city of **Dunedin**, lying 400km south of Christchurch on SH1. Once the commercial and cultural centre of the country, this harbourside city was made prosperous by the discovery of **gold** in the craggy mountains of Otago's hinterland in 1861. Today Dunedin is New Zealand's fourth-largest city, and still a seat of learning and culture, influenced by its university and strong Scottish tradition. From here down to Stewart Island, local accents are marked by a distinctive Scots "burr", the only true regional variation in the country. Within easy reach of the city is the inviting **Otago Peninsula**, an important wildlife haven where you can observe at close range a variety of marine life and seabirds, including **penguins** and even rarer **albatross**. South of Dunedin stretches the second highlight, the wild **Catlins Coast**, a large protected reserve reaching towards New Zealand's southernmost city of Invercargill. This is a magical, virtually forgotten region, home to several **rare species** and offering dramatically varied scenery, from hills covered with dense native forest to a shoreline vigorously indented with rocky bays, long sweeps of sand and unusual **geological formations**.

On the South Island's southern tip and bordered by rich pastureland, lies **Invercargill**. Servicing Southland's prosperous farming communities and New Zealand's export industry, it acts as the springboard to the country's third island, the comparatively small **Stewart Island**. Attracting as yet only limited numbers, the island is a growing tourist destination, its blanket of **virgin rainforest** offering a tramper's paradise. Others come for the abundant **birdlife**, to unwind in the restful setting, have a drink in New Zealand's southernmost pub, or to spot **kiwi in the wild**, on the only organized trip of its kind in the world.

ACCOMMODATION PRICES

Accommodation listed in this guide has been categorized into one of nine price bands, as set out below. The rates quoted represent the **cheapest available** double or twin **room** – except for category ①, which are per-person rates for a dorm bed. Note that fees for **tent sites** and **DOC huts** (quoted in dollars) are also per-person, unless otherwise stated.

① under $20 per person	④ $60–80	⑦ $140–180
② under $40 per room	⑤ $80–100	⑧ $180–240
③ $40–60	⑥ $100–140	⑨ over $240

For more on accommodation, see p.34.

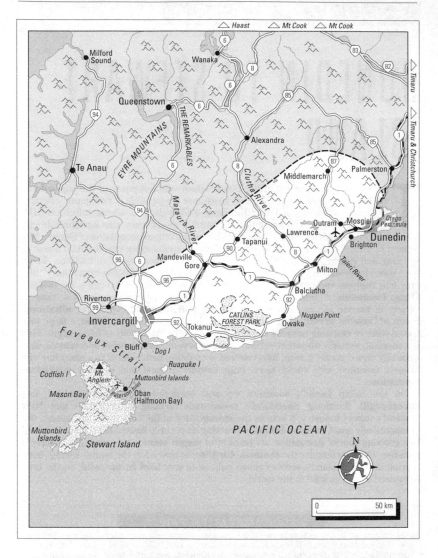

Generally, the **best time to visit** the region is during the summer months (Oct–April), when you're most likely to enjoy warm, though changeable, weather, with mid-summer temperatures averaging around 19°C in Dunedin. You'll also catch the best of the wildlife, coinciding with the breeding season of many species. Kiwis from more northern parts take great delight in condemning the **climate** of the southern South Island, describing a permanently harsh, cold and rain-lashed landscape – but this is an exaggeration. It's true, though, that the further south you go, the wetter it gets. The Catlins and Invercargill get their highest rainfall in the spring (Sept–Oct), while Stewart Island has showers most days in between bursts of sunshine.

Getting around is a straightforward business. The main east-coast train route connects Christchurch with Invercargill via Dunedin, and regular bus services link all the major towns as well as crossing the island to Queenstown and the West Coast. Stewart Island is served by ferries and planes from Invercargill.

To do the region justice you need to ease into the slower pace of life, allowing a minimum of three days for Dunedin and the Otago Peninsula, two or more days in the Catlins and at least a couple on Stewart Island.

Dunedin and around

A welcoming and pretty place, **DUNEDIN** is hilly but manageable in size, and blessed with numerous parks and gardens, a temperate, if changeable, climate, and pleasant beaches. Known as the "Edinburgh of the South", its name is a Gaelic translation of its Scottish counterpart, and it shares the same street and suburb names. Despite a compact city centre, Dunedin's official boundaries stretch far beyond its confining hills to accommodate a total population of around 120,000.

The city is home to **Otago University**, the first such institution in New Zealand, founded in 1871 and still occupying a substantial area near the city centre. The presence of eighteen thousand students contributes to a lively **arts scene**, helping to consolidate Dunedin's long-held reputation as a cultural and intellectual centre. To see the city at its busiest, visit during term time (mid-Feb to mid-June & July–Nov) when the **nightlife**, in particular, takes off, with students packing the bars, pubs and clubs, which foster Dunedin's thriving local music scene, known as the "Dunedin Sound". There are also a number of **festivals** during the year, including two internationally recognized film festivals (April & July); The Great New Zealand Craft Show (the country's largest professional show of its kind; late Sept to early Oct); the two-week-long Dunedin Festival, celebrating the region (February); and Scottish Week, commemorating the city's cultural roots (March). Springtime sees Dunedin ablaze with colour as the myriad **rhododendrons** for which it is famous burst into bloom, duly celebrated by Rhododendron Week (third week in October).

Dunedin's **architecture** is another defining characteristic, dating from the city's foundation in 1848 and, in particular, the boom years of the 1860s gold rush. Its streets brim with elegant and carefully preserved Victorian and Edwardian buildings: mansions and villas (many with whimsical towers and turrets), rows of terraced houses, churches with spires, an ornate cathedral and huge neo-Gothic piles. A variety of local stone was used in construction, ranging from bluestone (a hard, dark volcanic stone quarried near the city) to a pleasing creamy limestone originating in the coastal Oamaru to the north.

The jewel in Dunedin's crown, though, is its long sheltered **harbour**, site of two working ports and home to a rich variety of wildlife. Dunedin sits at the head of the bay, all but encircled by rugged hills, formed ten million years ago by a series of volcanic eruptions. Jutting out from the city to form one of the harbour's shores is the **Otago Peninsula** (see p.658), which most people visit on a day-trip from the city to view the rare and varied wildlife at its tip and take in a few sights along the way. Halfway along the bay's opposite shore lies the small and once-thriving **Port Chalmers** (see p.664), which still attracts a few container ships and supports a tiny community and is worth a quick look. Dunedin is also a major jumping-off point for the Otago Goldfields (see p.796) which lie on the way to Queenstown but also make a good day-trip out from the city.

Some history

By the time the first wave of Scottish immigrants arrived at the site of modern-day Dunedin, the area was rich in Maori history. Since about 1100 AD, **Maori** had fished the rich coastal waters of nearby bays, travelling inland to hunt moa, duck and fresh-water fish, and initiating trade in *pounamu* (greenstone) with other Maori based fur-ther north. Eventually they formed a settlement on both sides of the harbour, calling it *Otakou* (pronounced "O-tar-go") and naming the headland at the harbour's entrance after their great chieftain, Taiaroa. Today a well-developed marae occupies the Otakou site. Towards the end of the eighteenth century, the area became the scene of a pro-longed feud between three related chiefs of the Ngai Tahu tribe, and a general state of conflict lasted many years. The carnage caused by warfare, however, was nothing com-pared with the havoc wreaked by European diseases brought by the early nineteenth-century **whalers and sealers**, attracted to the only safe anchorage along this stretch of coast. By 1848 the depredations of measles and influenza had reduced the once-considerable Otakou population to a meagre 110. In the end, intermarriage between Maori and whalers bolstered numbers and formed a resilient cultural mix.

In 1840, the New Zealand Company (see Contexts, p.848) selected the Dunedin area as a suitable site for a planned **Scottish settlement**. Despite the Treaty of Waitangi (designed to preserve the Crown's right of pre-emption), the company was allowed to deal directly with Maori, who were finally persuaded to sell 1620 square kilometres for a meagre sum. On July 31, 1844, the deed was signed on the site of what later became Port Chalmers. In 1848, the migrant ships *John Wickliffe* and *Philip Laing* arrived, led by Captain William Cargill and the Reverend Thomas Burns, nephew of the Scottish poet, Robert Burns. Most of the 344 passengers were staunch Scots Presbyterians but they were soon in the minority, as the following year another seven hundred people joined them, among them English and Irish. However, Scottish fervour was sufficient to stamp a distinct character on the growing town, bequeathing not only fine churches, but also a passionate enthusiasm for education.

In 1861, a lone Australian prospector discovered **gold** at a creek near modern-day Lawrence, about 100km from Dunedin, in Central Otago. Within three months, gold fever struck and diggers poured in from Australia. As a port of entry, Dunedin suddenly found itself at the forefront of an international gold rush and, requiring a larger port area, it expanded onto land reclaimed from the tidal flats. In six months, its population doubled in size; within three years it trebled again, becoming New Zealand's most important city. This was Dunedin's period of unbridled construction, with the new-found wealth used to establish the university, Otago Boys' High School, and Otago Girls' High School. By the 1870s gold mania had largely subsided, but Otago sustained economic primacy through **shipping**, railway development and the efforts of thou-sands who stayed on to farm. Decline set in during the early years of the twentieth cen-tury, when the opening of the Panama Canal in 1914 re-routed British and European trans-Atlantic shipping away from the great colonial-era port of Otago Harbour to the country's northernmost city, Auckland. In the 1980s, however, the improvement in world gold prices and the development of equipment enabling large-scale recovery of gold from low-yielding soils, re-established **mining** in the hinterland. Today you can visit massive mining operations, including the one at Macraes, an hour's drive from Dunedin (see p.805).

Arrival, information and city transport

Dunedin **airport** is served by domestic flights from Auckland, Christchurch, Queenstown and Wellington, as well as international flights direct from Sydney and Brisbane. The airport is located 30km south of the city centre, just off SH1. Several shuttle bus companies operate from the airport to the city centre (from $10), meeting each flight and dropping off at accommodation along the way. A taxi ride to the city cen-tre will set you back about $30–40. You can change money at the airport **bureau de change** in the main terminal building (only open for international flights), which offers the same rate of exchange as the city's banks. Note that no bureaux de change are open in Dunedin at weekends, but the visitor centre can change money for you with a five percent commission.

The **train station** (☎03/477 4449) is centrally located in Anzac Square, off Stuart Street, a major stop on the Tranz Scenic Southerner Christchurch–Invercargill route. All long-distance bus and shuttle bookings are made here.

The long-distance InterCity **buses** drop off in the city centre at 205 St Andrew St. Two of the South Island's shuttle bus companies – Atomic and Southern Link – terminate at the train station; South Island Connections at the visitor centre (see below).

Information

You can't miss Dunedin's **visitor centre** (mid-Dec to mid-April Mon–Fri 8.30am–6pm, Sat & Sun 9am–6pm; mid-April to mid-Dec Mon–Fri 8.30am–5pm, Sat & Sun 9am–5pm; ☎03/474 3300, fax 474 3311, *www.CityofDunedin.com*, *visitor.centre@dcc.govt.nz*) in the grand stone Municipal Chambers that dominate the Octagon, an eight-sided grassland area at the centre of the city. The extremely helpful and well informed staff will book transport (InterCity, train and ferry; for long-distance shuttles book at the train station), accommodation and tours, and the centre is well stocked with leaflets and maps, including the excellent free *Focus on Dunedin* booklet and the *Art and Craft Guide* (also free), which lists the area's many artists and craftspeople. The **DOC** office is at 77 Lower Stuart St, first floor (Mon–Fri 8.30am–5pm; ☎03/477 0677) and has plenty of information on Otago, Fiordland and Mount Aspiring. They also sell hut tickets and passes for the Routeburn and Milford tracks. For free **Internet access** try the *Arc Cyber Café*, 135 High St (daily until late; see "Eating", p.654).

For entertainment and events **listings**, the most comprehensive source is the free weekly publication, *Fink*, a complete guide to music, exhibitions and movies in Dunedin (see also *www.fink.net.nz*). Chiefly aimed at students, it's available all over the city. The parochial *Otago Daily Times* (80¢) also has a listings section, best in the Friday and Saturday editions, and the visitor centre issues a free monthly paper, *Otago Happenings*, which is full of local attractions and events.

City transport

A number of different companies operate an efficient **bus** system throughout the city – you can pick up free timetables and route maps from the Dunedin City Council on the ground floor of the Civic Centre on the corner of the Octagon and George Street. Most services run Monday to Saturday and on public holidays (except Christmas Day, Good Friday and Easter Sunday), from around 7.30am to 11pm, and some services operate on Sunday from 1pm to 5pm. No public buses run to the Otago Peninsula or Port Chalmers on Sunday. Buses are identified by their route, for example, Octagon–Maori Hill, rather than by numbers. **Fares** are calculated according to the number of zones, with a single one-zone ticket costing $1.10, increasing by about 50¢ per extra zone; concessions are available at off-peak times on inner-city routes. If you're staying a couple of days or longer, it's a good idea to buy a **Multi-trip Ticket**, which gives ten or more journeys for a ten-percent discount. Most bus drivers sell these tickets direct or you can get them during business hours from the City Council in the Civic Centre.

There are several **taxi** ranks in the city centre (see p.658 for locations and details of taxi companies). If you're **driving**, note that strict parking restrictions are enforced in the city centre with meter parking operating Monday to Saturday (see p.657 for details of car parks). A one-way system operates through the inner city, connecting the northern and southern sections of SH1 and affecting Cumberland, Castle, Great King and Crawford streets.

Accommodation

There's a broad choice of accommodation in Dunedin, most of it in or near the city centre. The **hotels** are located in the heart of town, but with a couple of exceptions, are
bland affairs designed to attract businesspeople. Several **motels** line George Street,
with others dotted around the city, while the best **B&Bs and homestays** are in the hillside suburbs 2–5km from the centre. The three well equipped **campsites** are no more
than three kilometres out of town and two are on bus routes. As in all New Zealand's
major cities, **booking ahead** in summer is advisable, wherever you're staying. A small
but varied amount of accommodation is also available on the **Otago Peninsula** (see
pp.663–4), should you prefer to stay there and travel in to the city.

Hotels

Bentley's, 137 St Andrew St (☎03/477 0572, fax 477 0293, *bentleys.hotel@xtra.co.nz*). A fairly luxurious, modern place, right in the heart of the city, offering double rooms, a couple of studios and a
family unit, all with private facilities. There's an airy restaurant, a bar and café on the premises,
while next door is the lively *Rosie O'Grady's* bar (see p.655), owned by the hotel. ⑥.

Leviathan, 65 Lower High St, cnr Cumberland St (☎03/477 3160, fax 477 2385, *leviathan
@xtra.co.nz*). The most atmospheric hotel in Dunedin, and the best value. Built in 1884, it's grand
yet comfortable in the style of a classic railway hotel, and just a short stroll from both the Octagon
and the train station. Accommodation ranges from spacious suites and self-contained studios to
standard and budget en suites. There's also a bar and high-quality, moderately priced licensed
restaurant, plus a courtesy bus. Off-street parking. ④–⑥.

Manor Inn, 310 Princes St (☎03/477 1155, fax 477 7737, *manorinns@xtra.co.nz*). A corporate crowd
frequents this central but characterless hotel. Thoroughly modern rooms hide behind an ornate
nineteenth-century facade. On-site café, two restaurants and a fully-equipped gym. ④–⑥.

Southern Cross, cnr Princes St & High St (☎03/477 0752, fax 477 5776, *reservations
@southerncrosshotel.co.nz*). Huge hotel in the heart of the business district, five minutes' walk from
the Octagon. Three fully licensed restaurants and two bars, a fitness centre, Sky TV and off-street
parking. ⑦–⑧.

Motels

Allan Court, 590 George St, cnr Union St (☎03/477 7526, fax 477 4937, *allan.court
@earthlight.co.nz*). Central, modern, upmarket and comfortable, with cookers in all units and a
choice of breakfasts for an extra charge. In-house video and guest laundry. ⑤–⑥.

Cargills Motor Inn, 678 George St, near cnr St David St (☎03/477 7983, fax 477 8098, *cargills
@es.co.nz*). Adjacent to the business district and university, this stylish place offers a peaceful garden setting and a variety of well-appointed rooms equipped with minibars and fridges. The on-site
licensed *Garden Restaurant* serves Kiwi and international cuisine. ⑥–⑦.

Chequers, 119 Musselburgh Rise (☎ & fax 03/455 0778). Good-value motel in quiet surroundings,
five minutes' drive from the centre and close to the peninsula. Its large units are ideally suited to
families and there's a playground on the premises. ④.

858 George St Motel, 858 George St (☎ & fax 03/474 0047, *reservations@858georgestreetmotel.
co.nz*). Unusual, new and well-executed design by Dunedin architects, based on Victorian houses
divided into big luxurious units. ⑤–⑦.

Farrys, 575 George St (☎03/477 9333, fax 477 9038, *farrysmotel.co.nz*). An excellent family motel
next to the main shopping area offering one-, two- and three-bedroom units, all fully self-contained,
plus a free laundry and small playground. ⑤–⑥.

97 Motel, 97 Moray Place (☎03/477 2050, reservations only 0800/909 797, *bookings
@97motel.co.nz*). The best-located, friendliest motel in town with spacious, gleaming units, each
equipped with a microwave. ⑤–⑥.

Sahara, 619 George St (☎03/477 6662, fax 479 2551). A motel section round the back of the guesthouse of the same name (see below), with ten standard self-contained units. ④–⑤.

A (50m) , **B** (50m), **C** (2 km)△   △ *Christchurch (396 km)*

CENTRAL DUNEDIN

N

C (2 km)△

E (2 km)△

2.75 km & **I** (4 km) **J**

(200 m) **N**

(100 m) **T**

O Olveston House

Otago Museum

Otago University Campus

Botanic Gardens △

LYNWOOD AVE
PACIFIC ST
WALLACE ST
DUCHESS
QUEENS DRIVE
MELROSE ST
RD AL TERRACE
CORRIE
HERIOT ROW
PITT ST
COBDEN ST
ELDER
PARK ST
QUEEN ST
UNION ST
GREAT KING ST
CUMBERLAND ST
CASTLE ST
ST DAVID ST
CONSTITUTION
GEORGE STREET
MALCOLM ST
ALBANY ST
GOWLAND ST
TRENT ST
HYDE ST
CLYDE ST
FREDERICK ST
LEITH ST
HARROW ST
LONDON ST
SCOTLAND
FILLEUL ST
GREAT KING ST
HANOVER ST
ST ANDREW ST
CASTLE ST
ANZAC AVE
MORAY PLACE
STUART ST
BATH ST
BIRMINGHAM
PRINCES STREET
CUMBERLAND STREET
THOMAS BURNS ST
FISH ST
BOMBAY ST
CRESSWELL ST
WILLIS ST
FRYATT ST
CARGILL ST
YORK PLACE
TENNYSON ST
STUART ST
VIEW ST
RATTRAY ST
CANONGATE
MACLAGGAN ST
CLARK ST
HIGH ST
DOWLING ST
BROADWAY
MANSE ST
WATER ST
LIVERPOOL
JETTY ST
CRAWFORD ST
VOGEL ST
BURNS ST
POLICE ST
STAFFORD ST
HOPE ST
CARROLL ST
JERVOIS ST
MANOR PL
BIRCH ST
ROBERTS ST
BULLER ST
WHITE
KITCHENER ST
FRENCH ST
WHARF ST

St Paul's Cathedral
Municipal Chambers
Fortune Theatre
Dunedin Art Gallery
DOC Office
Regent Theatre
AA Office
First Church
Speights Brewery
Otago Settlers Museum
Mount Cook Landline
Train Station

Harbour Cruises
Harbour Cruises

Otago Harbour

InterCity

0 ——————— 500 m

Beaches (6 km), Airport (30 km) & Invercargill (217 km) ▽ **W** (4 km) & **X** (5 km) ▽ *Otago Peninsula (4 km)* & **Y** (4.5 km)

ACCOMMODATION

858 George Street Motel	A
97 Motel	L
Aaron Lodge Motel & Holiday Park	I
Adventurer Backpacker Lodge	O
Albatross Inn	B
Allan Court	G
Bentley's	K
Cargills Motor Inn	D
Chalet Backpackers	T
Chequers	Y
Dunedin Holiday Park	W
Elm Lodge	N
Farrys	H
Fletcher Lodge	R
Gowrie House	J
Hulmes Court	M
Leith Valley Touring Park	C
Leviathan Hotel	P
Lisburn House	X
Magnolia House	E
Manor House	V
Manor Inn	S
Sahara Guesthouse & Motel	F
Southern Cross Hotel	Q
Stafford Gables YHA	U

RESTAURANTS & CAFÉS

Abalone	8
Arc Café/Bar	24
Bacchus Wine Bar & Restaurant	15
Bath Street Bar	10
Bell Pepper Blues	25
Best Café	19
Café Cena	2
A Cow Called Berta	12
Etrusco	20
Everyday Gourmet	4
Fuel Café & Lounge Bar	5
Galata Kebab House	22
High Tide	26
Huntsman Steakhouse	7
Jizo Japanese Café & Bar	21
Joseph Mellor Restaurant	11
New Satay Noodle House	9
Old Spaghetti Factory & Bennu Bar	16
Ombrellos	6
Palms Café	23
Percolator Café	14
Potpourri Vegetarian & Natural Foods Café	18
Ra Bar	17
Tangente Café	13
Tukyo Garden	3
Thyme Out	1

B&Bs and homestays

Albatross Inn, 770 George St (☎ & fax 03/477 2727, *albatross.inn@xtra.co.nz*). Extremely hospitable Edwardian house of character close to the university and city centre, where rooms are en suite or have private bathrooms; some have their own kitchenette and dining facilities. ⑤–⑥.

Fletcher Lodge, 276 High St (☎0800/843 563, fax 03/474 5551, *lodge@es.co.nz*). Extremely luxurious and central B&B in a calm English baronial-style home built in 1924 for a leading Kiwi industrialist, Sir James Fletcher, with an established secluded garden. The living room is richly oak-panelled, everything is kept spotless and all rooms are en suite. There's also off-street parking and a laundry service. ⑦–⑧.

Gowrie House, 7 Gowry Place, Roslyn (☎03/477 2103, fax 477 9169). Excellent rural and city views from this small, cosy, turn-of-the-century house set on a hill five minutes' drive from the centre and on the Octagon to Maori Hill/Prospect Park bus route. Two double rooms, both light and airy with big windows and shared facilities. ③–④.

Hulmes Court, 52 Tennyson St (☎0800/448 563, fax 03/477 5310, *normwood@earthlight.co.nz*). One of the oldest homes in Dunedin, a big rambling affair built in the 1860s with plenty of character, just off the Octagon yet quiet. Rooms are big and individually themed, two of them en suite and two sharing bathrooms; off-street parking, free bus and rail pick-up, free mountain bikes, free email link. ⑤–⑥.

Lisburn House, 15 Lisburn Ave, Caversham (☎03/455 8888, fax 455 6788, *stay @lisburnhouse.co.nz*). Luxurious and beautifully preserved Victorian Gothic house in a suburb ten minutes' drive south of the city. Each of the three distinctly styled and spacious rooms has a four-poster bed, fine linen, fresh flowers and a private bathroom. Not suitable for children. ⑦.

Magnolia House, 18 Grendon St, Maori Hill (☎ & fax 03/467 5999). A spacious Victorian villa, set in a large garden in the leafy suburb of Maori Hill, 2km north of the Octagon (courtesy car available). Three well appointed doubles with shared facilities, and two house cats. ⑤.

Sahara Guesthouse & Motel, 619 George St (☎03/477 6662, fax 479 2551). Spacious central 1863 guesthouse where most rooms have shared facilities. TV lounge, off-street parking. ④–⑤.

Hostels

Adventurer Backpacker Lodge, 37 Dowling St (☎ & fax 03/477 7367, bookings 0800/422 257). A convivial newish hostel in the heart of the city, with dorms ranging from 2-bed to 9-bed and a few singles, doubles and twins; off-street parking. Dorms ①, rooms ②.

Chalet Backpackers, 296 High St (☎03/479 2075, bookings 0800/242 538, fax 479 2050). Central, comfortable hostel with a great atmosphere and excellent kitchen and dining facilities. Four-bed dorms, plus single and double rooms. Pool room, free bikes and free pick-up. Dorms ①, rooms ②.

Elm Lodge, 74 Elm Row (☎03/474 1872, bookings 0800/356 563, fax 477 8808, *ELM_WILDLIFE_TOUR@compuserve.com*). An airy, clean, 1930s house on a hill near the centre. The dorms are 4- or 6-bed. Free linen and pick-up service. Dorms ①, rooms ②.

Manor House, 28 Manor Place (☎03/477 0484, bookings 0800/477 0484, fax 477 8145, *mail @manorhousebackpackers.co.nz*). Well-equipped and beautifully kept colonial house on a hill fifteen minutes' walk south of the Octagon. Dorms are 4-bed to 8-bed; free pick-up service. Dorms ①, rooms ②.

Stafford Gables YHA, 71 Stafford St (☎ & fax 03/474 1919, *yhadndn@yha.org.nz*). One of the most characterful YHAs in New Zealand. A large, turn-of-the-century homestead ten minutes' walk from the Octagon. The dorms are 3- to 7-bed, double and twin rooms are generally large, some doubles come with balconies and there are also family rooms and a self-contained flat. Free linen. Dorms ①, rooms ②, flat ③.

Campsites and motorparks

Aaron Lodge Motel & Holiday Park, 162 Kaikorai Valley Rd (☎03/476 4725, fax 476 7925, *aaron.lodge@xtra.co.nz*). A sheltered, fairly spacious and well-tended site, in hills 2.5km west of the city centre. Facilities include a spa pool and playground. Tent sites $10, powered sites $11, cabins ②, flats ③ & motel units ④.

Dunedin Holiday Park, 41 Victoria Rd (☎ & fax 03/455 4690). Lying alongside St Kilda Beach, this well-appointed park is five minutes' drive from the city centre and served by the Octagon to St

Kilda bus. Standard and more comfortable en-suite cabins. There's a seven-day camp store. Tent sites $9, powered sites $12, cabins ②, en-suite units ③, tourist flats ④.

Leith Valley Touring Park, 103 Malvern St (☎03/467 9936, fax 467 9502). A small, pleasant campsite beside a creek at the foot of bush-clad hills, 3km north from the centre. The site is served by the Octagon to Garden Village bus on weekdays and there's a 24hr grocery within walking distance. Tent sites $9.50, on-site vans ② & flats ③.

The City

Day or night, the hub of Dunedin's activity is the **Octagon**, a green, tree-filled space in the heart of the city, bordered by historic buildings and circled by Moray Place. Restaurants, offices, banks, bars, clubs and most of the sights are concentrated around it, and the **shopping district** stretches immediately north and south along George Street and Princes Street. Further north lies the **university area** and the expanse of the **Botanic Garden**. To the east is the head of **Otago Harbour**, a sheltered inlet 22km long and no wider than a river in places. The waters are shared by windsurfers, yachts and sightseeing boats, and occasionally dolphins and whales. Two sandy **beaches** lie a short bus ride south from the city centre in the suburbs of St Clair and St Kilda. For an overview of the city, head for the **lookout points** on the hills around Dunedin (see box on pp.650–51) or take a double-decker **bus tour** with Citisights (☎03/477 5577; 1hr 30min; $15), which departs from the visitor centre at 10am and 3.30pm daily.

The Octagon

The **Octagon** was originally laid out in 1846 by Charles Kettle, the Chief Surveyor of the New Zealand Company, who subsequently died in a typhoid epidemic that swept the city during the 1862 gold rush. Today, following a substantial face-lift in the 1980s, it's a mixture of modern and beautifully preserved buildings overlooking grassland and trees, presided over by a statue of Robert Burns, a potent symbol of Dunedin's Scottish origins and literary associations. Every Friday (10am–4pm; also Sat Oct–Feb & daily in Dec; closed Dec 26–Jan10), the area spills over with **market** stalls selling locally made crafts, such as stained glass, pottery, woodwork and jewellery, while live bands provide free entertainment.

Dominating the Octagon is the **Municipal Chambers** building, a grand, classical structure with a clock tower, which originally opened in 1880. Constructed from limestone dramatically offset against volcanic bluestone, it's a fine example of a recurring combination of materials that's seen throughout the city and also of the handiwork of Scottish architect Robert A. Lawson, who designed many public buildings in Dunedin. Just behind the Municipal Chambers rise the twin white stone spires of **St Paul's Cathedral**, one of Dunedin's finest buildings and the seat of Anglican worship in the city. This impressive Gothic Revival edifice, entirely constructed from Oamaru stone, was designed by English architect Edmund Spedding and consecrated in 1919. Inside, the 65-metre-high stone-vaulted ceiling is the only one of its kind in New Zealand, and much of the stained glass in the impressive windows is original; the stark modern chancel and altar were added in 1971.

Across Upper Stuart Street from the Municipal Chambers and just off Princes Street, the spacious and gleaming **Dunedin Public Art Gallery** (Mon–Fri 10am–5pm, Sat & Sun 11am–5pm; $4 plus charges for special exhibitions) was completed in 1996, breathing new life into the Octagon. Designed by a Dunedin City Council architect, the gallery occupies six Victorian buildings, elegantly refurbished to create an airy, modern, split-level space of several exhibition areas – a contrast to the original public art gallery, founded in 1884 and the oldest in the country. The foyer of polished wooden floors, ironwork and a hundred-year-old spiral staircase is worth a look in itself. The gallery's main strength is a rotated collection of early and contemporary New Zealand works, including Van der Velden's powerful *Mountain Stream Otira Gorge* and William Goldie's well-known *All 'e same t'e Pakeha*, and many by Frances Hodgkins. There's also a small international assemblage spanning the Renaissance to the early twentieth century and boasting Old Masters such as Turner, Gainsborough, Salvator Rosa, and Machiavelli; and modern maestros such as Monet, Rousseau, Derain and Tissot. The space also regularly hosts temporary international shows.

South, across Princes Street from the art gallery, is the 1874 facade of the **Regent Theatre**, a one-time hotel that was transformed into a cinema in 1928 and, later, into a theatre. Today it's a venue for international shows and the Royal New Zealand Ballet, as well as live music (see p.655). Inside, elaborate nineteenth-century plasterwork and marble staircases juxtapose colourful 1920s stained-glass windows and geometric balustrades. During the one-day **Regent Theatre Book Sale** (around mid-May or June) the theatre is filled with all manner of books, from 50-cent copies to collector's items.

Behind the Regent Theatre, near the intersection with Burlington Street, soars the delicate, 54-metre stone spire of the **First Church of Otago**, a landmark easily spotted from many points around the city. The edifice, widely recognized as the most impressive of New Zealand's nineteenth-century churches, was designed in neo-Gothic style by Scottish architect Robert A. Lawson. Two other small, wooden churches had already occupied this site, and when Lawson's version was consecrated in 1873 it was the first Presbyterian church to open in Otago. Of particular interest inside are a wooden gabled ceiling and, above the pulpit, a brightly coloured rose window, while another large window commemorates those who fell in World War I.

South and east of the Octagon

Less than five minutes' walk southeast of the Octagon, a cluster of buildings at 220 Cumberland Street contains the **Otago Settlers Museum** (Mon–Fri 10am–5pm, Sat & Sun 1–5pm; $4), which catalogues two hundred years of social history in Dunedin and Otago, drawing from an exhaustive collection of artefacts, paintings and photographs. Highlights include the chance to sit on a penny-farthing; a restored double-ended Fairlie steam engine, one of the two locomotives that hauled the first Christchurch–Dunedin express train south from Oamaru in 1878; and the "Portrait Gallery", whose walls are plastered with black-and-white photographs of the region's early settler families. Also worth a look is "Window on a Chinese Past", providing an insight into the lives of the legions of Chinese who left their families behind to seek a fortune in the Otago Goldfields, many of them staying for years (see box on p.767 for more on the Chinese experience in New Zealand).

A stone's throw away from the museum, near the junction of Castle Street and Anzac Avenue, **Dunedin Railway Station** is an imposing building, faced with pale Oamaru stone. Opened in 1906, the station was designed by George A. Troup, and constructed on reclaimed swampland, which made it an extraordinary feat of engineering for its day. The exterior, complete with towers, turrets and minarets, is grand enough, but the real surprise lies inside. The main foyer, which has been preserved in its original state, gleams with majolica wall tiles made especially for New Zealand Rail by Royal Doulton, in gentle tones of green, yellow and cream. A fine, classical, china frieze of cherubs and foliage encircles the room, and elaborate tilework decorates the ticket booths. The mosaic floor celebrates the steam engine and consists of over 700,000 tiny squares of Royal Doulton porcelain. Upstairs on the balcony, a stained-glass window at each end depicts an approaching train, whose headlights gleam, no matter from which angle you look at them.

Further east beyond the train station is the **Hocken Library** at 90 Anzac Ave, near the junction with Parry Street (Mon–Fri 9.30am–5pm, Tues also 6–9pm, Sat 9am–noon; free), an extensive university research library that opened on campus in 1910, before moving here in the late 1990s. Its impressive collection of books, manuscripts, paintings and photographs relating to New Zealand and the Pacific was originally assembled by Dr Thomas

Morland Hocken, a Dunedin physician and one of the country's first historians. Details of exhibitions held in the library gallery (Mon–Fri 9.30am–5pm, Sat 9am–noon, Sun check on ☎03/479 1100 ext 8873; free) are regularly advertised in the *Otago Daily Times*.

Only those seriously interested in the brewing process should bother with a tour of **Speights Brewery**, one of New Zealand's oldest and smallest breweries, at 200 Rattray St (book on ☎03/477 7697; Mon–Thurs at 10am, 11.45am, 2pm & 7pm, Fri–Sun at 10am, 11.45am, & 2pm; 1hr 15min; $12), whose humorous tall chimney stack of a barrel crafted from stone is visible from around the city. The tour is loud and involves a good deal of walking up and down stairs while listening to dull hard-sell commentary about the company. The flipside is a chance to see traditional brewing techniques close-up, and your patience is rewarded with two glasses of lager, bitter or ale in the boardroom at the end of the tour. Back outside make a beeline for the drinking fountain near the front door, whose sweet-tasting water is pumped directly from the brewery bore, the same as that used to brew the beer; locals fill up their water bottles here.

North of the Octagon

A few minutes' walk north of the Octagon, at 419 Great King St, the **Otago Museum** (Mon–Fri 10am–5pm, Sat & Sun noon–5pm; donations requested) is a large and well-funded museum on three floors. You can easily spend half a day here, ambling through excellent and varied displays of Maori and Pacific Islands anthropology, New Zealand natural history, archeological finds and decorative arts from all over the world. Part of the ground floor contains a separate, hands-on interactive science centre called "Discovery World" ($6, children $3), which is primarily aimed at children. The most impressive exhibits are the huge collection of southern **Maori artefacts** and a group of **moa skeletons**.

OLVESTON

At 42 Royal Terrace, ten minutes' walk northwest of the Octagon, lies Dunedin's showpiece historic home of **Olveston** (booking essential ☎03/477 3320; guided tours only: daily 9.30am, 10.45am, noon, 1.30pm, 2.45pm & 4pm; 1hr; $11). Contained within the walls of this fine Edwardian house is a treasure trove of art and exquisite antiques collected from all over the world by one family and left just as they were when the last of the lineage passed away.

The collection was gradually assembled by a wealthy, Jewish mercantile family, the **Theomins**, who lived here from 1906 and were passionately interested in travel, art and music. The longest-surviving member of the family, Dorothy, outlived her parents and her brother, and on her death in 1966, bequeathed the house and its contents to the City of Dunedin.

Built in 1904–1906 for David Theomin and his wife, Marie, the Jacobean-style **house** is reminiscent of the English Arts and Crafts Movement. London architect Sir Ernest George filled the house with extraordinary decorative detail, incorporating such features as polished wooden floors, stained-glass windows, wood panelling, fine brass fittings and stairways leading to mezzanine galleries. A particularly striking piece of craftsmanship is the oak staircase in the Grand Hall, made in England and constructed without the use of nails. The house was also a masterpiece of modernity for its time, being among the first to be fitted with the conveniences of central heating, heated towel rails and an in-house telephone system.

THE UNIVERSITY

Less than ten minutes' walk north of the city centre lies New Zealand's oldest university, founded by Scottish settlers in 1869. Based on the design of Glasgow University, the **University of Otago** quickly expanded into a complex of imposing Gothic bluestone buildings, foremost among them the registry building on Leith Street with its

Gothic **clock tower**, an academic icon and one of the most-photographed landmarks in Dunedin. Today the campus covers several blocks between Albany and Dundas streets in one direction, and Cumberland and Clyde streets in the other, and is set in spacious grounds with the Water of Leith, a small river, winding through it. The **Student Enquiries Office** (Mon–Fri 9.30am–4.30pm) in the registry building has simple free campus maps for visitors and a stroll through the campus from Union Street to Leith Street will take you past the key buildings.

The **Hocken Building**, on the corner of Castle Street and Union Street, once housed the impressive Hocken Library, which opened here in 1910 before moving in the late 1990s to Anzac Avenue (see p.648).

THE BOTANIC GARDEN
Established in 1863 at the far northern end of the inner city, the well-tended **Dunedin Botanic Garden** (sunrise–sunset; free) lies at the foot of Signal Hill. The hilly Upper Garden contains an expansive Rhododendron Dell, where well-established specimens grow among native bush, flowering trees and plants. This is the star attraction during the city's annual **Rhododendron Week** in the third week of October. On the hills there's also an arboretum, a native plant collection and a modern aviary complex, home to native birds such as kea and kaka, as well as exotic birds from all over the world. The flat Lower Garden features exotic trees, Winter Garden conservatories (daily 10am–4pm), an Alpine House (daily 9am–4pm), a rose garden and a well-equipped playground. A volunteer-run information centre (daily 10am–4pm) lies between the tea

---

WALKS IN THE DUNEDIN AREA

From the city, a variety of walks (1–3hr) lead up to and along the skyline ridges surrounding the harbour, giving spectacular views of tussock-covered hilltops, fine bushland, river valleys and beaches. The DOC publishes factsheets describing each walk, $1 (or $5 for a folder on the Dunedin area) from the DOC office or visitor centre. Dunedin's weather is notoriously changeable, so equip yourself with warm clothing and wet-weather gear, just in case.

If these suggestions whet your appetite for tramping, see "Walks on Otago Peninsula" (p.663) for more routes in the vicinity.

SIGNAL HILL
A fairly gentle walk up **Signal Hill** (6km return; 1hr ascent, 30min descent), a scenic reserve just north of the Botanic Garden, culminates in a magnificent view over Dunedin, the upper harbour and the sea. At the top (393m), the Centennial Lookout sports two powerful bronze figures symbolizing the past and the future, a commemoration of one hundred years of British sovereignty (1840–1940) following the signing of the Treaty of Waitangi. Embedded in the podium is a tribute to Scotland: a chunk of the rock upon which Edinburgh Castle was built.

To reach the hill from the city centre, follow Great King Street to the northern edge of the Botanic Garden and turn right along Opoho Road for 1.25km. Signal Hill Road, which is the fourth on the left, leads to the top of the hill. The Opoho bus from outside the Savoy Building in Princes Street, will take you up and over Signal Hill and there's a stop at the top.

TUNNEL BEACH
One of the best walks – **Tunnel Beach** (1.5km return; 1hr) – is also the shortest and least strenuous, yet offers breathtaking coastal views of creamy sandstone cliffs and islets weathered into curious shapes. Untouched by lava flows, it gives a glimpse of Dunedin's geology before the volcanic eruptions that changed the landscape. A steep path drops through bush and pasture to impressive sandstone clifftops and a magnificent

kiosk and the Winter Garden, equipped with maps and displays on the Botanic Garden. The garden's tea kiosk (daily 9.30am–4.30pm) serves inexpensive snacks and meals. Access to the Lower Gardens car park is from Cumberland Street, while the Upper Gardens car park is on Lovelock Avenue.

BALDWIN STREET
Dunedin has the dubious honour of containing the steepest street in the world. In the northern part of town, off North Road, **Baldwin Street** has a maximum gradient of 1 in 2.9, an angle of over 38°. You can walk up to the top in about five minutes, but the views aren't anything special. During the annual "Gutbuster" event in mid-February (part of the Dunedin Festival) contestants run to the top and back down again – the current record is around two minutes.

Baldwin Street is a short **bus** ride from the city centre: take the Normanby bus from outside the Savoy Building in Princes Street to North Road, which drops you near the Gardens Shopping Centre. Head north along North Road for fifteen minutes; Baldwin Street is the tenth street past the shopping centre.

Dunedin's beaches
Four kilometres south of the city centre, the suburbs of St Kilda and St Clair culminate in a long wild sweep of creamy sand enclosed by two volcanic headlands (served by buses from the corner of the Octagon and Princes Street). **St Clair Beach** is excellent

sea-arch. Additionally, at low tide, you can walk down the steps of a short tunnel carved through the cliff in the 1870s, which leads to a pretty sandy beach on the other side with sandstone buttresses towering above – a pleasant spot for a picnic. The walk crosses private land and is closed during the lambing season (Sept & Oct).

The route starts from the car park at the end of Green Island Bush Road, some 16km from the centre on the city's southwestern outskirts. The Corstophine bus from the corner of the Octagon and Princes Street will drop you within a kilometre of the start of the walk – get off at Stanhope Crescent.

MOUNT CARGILL
Unrivalled panoramic views of the Dunedin area are the reward for making it to the windy summit of **Mount Cargill** on the city's northeastern outskirts. There are in fact three peaks – Cargill, Holmes and Zion – which to the Maori represent the petrified head and feet of an early Otakou princess. European settlers named the dominant peak after their lay leader, Captain William Cargill.

You can either drive to the summit car park – twenty-minutes from the city centre along Pine Hill Road – and just tackle the network of easy tracks around the summit area, or walk the whole track from Bethunes Gully picnic ground, about 7.5km northeast of the Botanic Gardens (8km return; 3hr). This skirts the mountain's northern flank and climbs steadily to 550m before sidling around to the saddle and onto the summit. To reach the picnic ground by bus catch the Normanby bus from outside the Savoy Building in Princes Street and get off at the junction of North Road and Norwood Street. From here it's about 2km northeast along Norwood Street to the picnic ground.

On the slopes of nearby Mount Holmes, an intriguing ancient rock formation called the **Organ Pipes** can be reached on foot, either from the Mount Cargill summit – following the peaks and saddles of Cargill, Buttar and Holmes (3km return; 90min) – or from a steep track starting at the car park on Old Mount Cargill Road (3km return; 1hr), on the mountain's eastern side (not accessible by public transport). Either way, the route passes through colourful remnant forest to a series of rock columns, formed about ten million years ago by molten lava that cracked as it cooled.

for surfing and is patrolled by lifeguards during the summer. For swimming in calmer waters, there's a large, outdoor, heated saltwater pool (Oct–March Mon–Sat 6am–7pm, Sun 8am–7pm; $2.50), beside the rocky point at the western end of the beach. About halfway along the strip, St Clair merges with **St Kilda Beach**, which is reasonably safe for swimming as long as you keep between the flags; it is also patrolled in summer. At the beach's eastern end, a headland separates St Kilda from the smaller **Tomahawk Beach** (not safe for swimming), often dotted with horses and buggies preparing for trotting races at low tide. The best swimming beach in Otago is only 15km south of Dunedin, at **Brighton Bay** (Brighton bus from New World supermarket in Cumberland Street), a combination of sand and rocky outcrops.

Taieri Gorge Railway
One of the world's most dramatic rail lines and a feat of Victorian engineering, the **Taieri Gorge Railway** stretches 77km from Dunedin inland to the high country of Otago, penetrating rugged mountain scenery that is only accessible by train. Once free of the city and its environs, the track follows the Taieri Gorge, deeply carved into the schist rock. Constructed between 1879 and 1921, the line extended 235km to the old gold town of Cromwell in its heyday, carrying supplies from Dunedin and transporting farm produce, fruit and livestock back to the port and points north. The journey is rewarding at any time of year, from the snow in winter to the searing heat of summer, and rainy days encourage the waterfalls.

Today, as well as offering **day-trips** from the city, the rail line is a good way of heading further inland to the Central Otago Goldfields, or even as far as Queenstown by linking with a bus. Bear in mind, though, that on day-trips the return journey can be rather dull. The train departs from Dunedin Railway Station and you need to book well ahead to be sure of a seat (☎03/477 4449, fax 477 4953, *reserve@taieri.co.nz*). The train itself is comfortable and air-conditioned, made up of a mix of modern steel carriages with large panoramic windows, and nostalgic, refurbished 1920s wooden cars. Storage space is available for backpacks and bicycles (bikes travel free) and there's a licensed snack bar on board. Ask ahead and you might even be able to ride with the driver for a spell.

The most frequent trip is to **Pukerangi** – a peaceful spot 58km from the city near the highest point of the track (250m), where you spend ten minutes – arriving back in Dunedin four hours later (April–Sept daily 12.30pm; Oct–March daily 2.30pm, plus end Dec–March extra morning service on selected days 9.30am, and Jan–March extra morning service on Sun 9.30am; $53 return). On Sundays in summer the train continues a further 19km to the old gold town of **Middlemarch** in the fertile Strath Taieri Plains, a five-hour round trip (Oct–Feb; $59 return). You can stay overnight around Pukerangi where there are various whitewater-rafting and horse-trekking activities (details from Dunedin Railway Station). In addition, the abandoned line between Middlemarch and Clyde, deep in the gold country, has been developed for walking and mountain biking. To get **to Queenstown**, you'll need an Otago Central Connection ticket (☎0800/244 844, fax 03/477 8147, *citibus.newton@xtra.co.nz*; $99), which links with a bus at Pukerangi or Middlemarch and follows a scenic route via the Maniototo Plain, a 6hr 30min journey from Dunedin. This journey can, of course, be done in reverse; or you can book a flight connection from Pukerangi (check details with Dunedin Railway Station).

Eating

In a city that's undeniably enthusiastic about food with cuisine from around the world, you'll never be at a loss for somewhere to satisfy your appetite, plus you'll seldom need to stray far from the **city centre**. Many eateries are strung along George Street, particularly from the junction with Hanover Street for two blocks, heading away from the Octagon; others are concentrated on or around the Octagon. You'll find there's an excellent range, across the board from classic espresso cafés to fine dining restaurants, but many places close on Sundays. Recent years have also seen an explosion in ethnic cafés and takeaways. In addition to the above, some of the city's **pubs** serve reasonably priced food (see p.655). Useful spots for **stocking up** are *Tangente Café and Bakery* for organic bread, the *Everyday Gourmet* deli (for both these venues see overleaf) and *Night 'n' Day*, a 24hr food store that's a Dunedin institution, located on the corner of George and Regent streets and handy after the pubs have closed for sandwiches, pies and snacks. Eating places on the **Otago Peninsula** are listed separately on p.664. Unless otherwise stated, those listed below are open daily and BYO relates to bottled wine only, usually carrying a small corkage charge.

Restaurants

Abalone, 1st Floor, 44 Hanover St, cnr George St, above the BNZ Bank (☎0800/222 2256). Slick, yuppie bar-cum-restaurant with modern metal furnishings, terracotta flooring and lots of glass. Moderately priced drinks, snacks and full meals. Seething with people at weekends; book ahead for dinner. Lunch Mon–Fri, dinner daily.

Bacchus Wine Bar & Restaurant, 1st floor, 12 The Octagon, cnr Lower Stuart St (☎03/474 0824). A great vantage point overlooking the Octagon from a prestigious historic building. Over fifty international wines, accompanied by moderately priced lunch and dinner. Popular office workers' lunch spot. Closed Sun.

Bell Pepper Blues, 474 Princes St (☎03/474 0973). Highly rated à la carte dinner venue, offering great value for money, with main-course prices averaging $25. The food is Pacific-rim, focusing on New Zealand ingredients, such as venison and salmon. Closed Sun; licensed & BYO. Book ahead at weekends.

A Cow Called Berta, 199 Stuart St (☎03/477 2993). Reasonably priced Swiss-style country dinners of simple strong flavours based on French cuisine, in the cosy yet classy ambience of a converted Victorian terraced house. Closed Sun; licensed.

Etrusco, 1st floor, Savoy Building, 8a Moray Place, cnr George St (☎03/477 3737). Authentic Italian fare presented in an airy and lovingly restored building. Moderate prices and friendly service. Dinner only. Good wine list, also BYO.

High Tide, 29 Kitchener St (☎03/477 9784). A quietly romantic and friendly waterside hideaway for evening meals, complemented by great views over the harbour and peninsula. The moderately priced menu consists of imaginative seafood, vegetarian and meat dishes, as well as home-made soups and desserts. Licensed & BYO.

The Huntsman Steakhouse, 311 George St. Great steaks for around $20 and including salad from a huge selection; dinner only and closed Sunday. Licensed & BYO.

Joseph Mellor Restaurant, 1st floor, Otago Polytechnic, cnr York Place & Tennyson St, entrance directly opposite Kavanagh College (☎03/477 3014). Unbelievably cheap, high-quality French/New Zealand cuisine prepared by world-class chefs and their students in a bustling restaurant with one of the best city views in Dunedin. Book a few days ahead. Open early Feb to early Dec Tues–Thurs only noon–1.30pm & 6–9pm; licensed and BYO.

Ombrellos, 10 Clarendon St, off Frederick St (☎03/477 8773). An attractive Mediterranean-style courtyard café/bar in the heart of the university area. Open all day, offering breakfast through to dinner and an affordable wine list. Closed Mon, plus Sun evening.

Palms Café, 18 Queens Gardens (☎03/477 6534). Something of an institution among locals, who enjoy its leisurely pace and genteel atmosphere; book ahead. From a turn-of the-century setting (complete with enormous windows and high ceiling), you can feast your eyes on the greenery of Queens Gardens, while tucking into hearty vegetarian, seafood and meat dishes. Two-course special for $15 (Mon–Fri 5–6.30pm) and a moderately priced, à la carte menu. Dinner only; licensed & BYO.

Thyme Out, 629 George St. A casual dinner venue for well-priced imaginative dishes from around the world. Closed Sun; licensed & BYO.

Tokyo Garden, 351 George St (☎03/474 5993; not to be confused with *Tokyo House* a few doors up). Easily affordable Japanese food in simple surroundings for lunch (except Sun; great specials for under $10) and dinner (except Tues & Wed) to eat in or take away, washed down with *sake* ($3–5). BYO.

Cafés and snack bars

Arc Café/Bar, 135 High St. Excellent big groovy cyber café/bar open all day for well-priced gourmet vegetarian and vegan snacks. In a separate clubby section at the back live bands or DJs play every night, and top Dunedin acts Fri & Sat (principal venue for the Dunedin Sound; see box on p.656). Free Internet access and a good range of herbal teas; licensed.

Best Café, 30 Stuart St. A local legend, despite the spartan decor, and the best spot for fish and chips, which have been served here for over fifty years. Closed Sat & Sun; no alcohol.

Café Cena, 466 George St. Another all-day student haunt and bigger than it looks, serving an imaginative blend of Mediterranean and Asian foods, and speciality coffees. Licensed & BYO.

Everyday Gourmet, 446 George St. A cosy deli-cum-café stuffed with specialist cheeses, salami, fine meat pies and other imported speciality foods. Also bagels, substantial sandwiches, take-home meals, great Anzac biscuits and excellent coffee. Closed Sun.

Fuel Café, 21 Frederick St. The closest café to the university and a big student zone, open till 3am and jam-packed from Feb to Oct. It's well known for all-day breakfasts and generous portions of great food – including vegetarian and vegan, but reverts to snacks late at night. There's also the *Lounge Bar* and *Fusion Niteclub* at the back (see opposite). Mon–Fri from 7.30am, Sat & Sun from 10am.

Galata Kebab House, 126 Princes St. Authentic, cheap Turkish food to eat in or take away, offering the usual mix of vegetarian dishes, falafels and kebabs, from 11am till late. Licensed & BYO.

Jizo Japanese Café and Bar, Savoy Building, 56 Princes St. Inexpensive sushi, miso soup, rice dishes and noodle soups to take away, or eat in at this small, split-level café. Lunch and dinner Mon–Sat; licensed & BYO.

New Satay Noodle House, 16 Hanover St. A cheep-and-cheerful all-day spot for noodle soups, satay, and Thai dishes from 11am. All the Asian students come here.

The Old Spaghetti Factory, Savoy Building, 68 Princes St (☎03/477 8001). Big, elegant and excellent pasta café/takeaway in a beautiful building, open for lunch (Mon–Sat) and dinner (Fri–Sun). At the back is the attractive *Bennu Bar* (see opposite).

Percolator Café, 142 Stuart St. A well-established inexpensive espresso bar just down from the Octagon, open from 9.30am till the early hours. Brunch served Sat & Sun morning, plus full lunch and dinner menu.

Potpourri Vegetarian and Natural Foods Café, 97 Lower Stuart St, near Moray Place. Established veggie venue got up to look like a church. Wholemeal baking, a big salad bar and great frozen yoghurt to eat in or take away. Closed Sun; no alcohol.

Tangente Café and Bakery, 111 Moray Place. Mellow spot next to the Fortune Theatre above the Octagon, using organic grains and flours, cold-pressed oils, free-range eggs, and filtered water to produce gourmet snacks and meals from breakfast onwards. Try a home-baked organic bread cup – a bowl made of bread filled with the concoction of your choice – while browsing their magazines. Dinner Thurs–Sun only, and a popular pre- or post-theatre stop; licensed & BYO.

Drinking, nightlife and entertainment

As the evening draws in, Dunedin shifts into a higher gear, especially during term time or one of its many festivals. Drinking is taken seriously here and there's no shortage of **pubs and bars**, many of them student hangouts where **local bands** play at weekends (see box on p.656), plus some of the **cafés** double up as bars or clubs (see above). You can also catch live bands at the Empire, 396 Princes St (☎03/477 8826), and the city is well served with **theatres**, **cinemas** (both arthouse and mainstream) and **concert halls**. For information on what's on, pick up a free copy of *Fink* or check the "Entertainments" section of the *Otago Daily Times*. The ornate **casino**, in a beautifully restored 1883 building, is worth a look even if you don't want to play. The local **micro-brewery** is Emerson's (not open to the public), which produces six beers – London Porter (a dark old English style), 1812 India Pale Ale, Organic Pilsner, Hefe Weissbier (Bavarian-style cloudy wheat beer), Bookbinder (a full, hop-flavoured English-style beer) and Dunkelweizen (dark wheat) – plus two or three seasonal brews a year. For a taste head for the *Arc Café/Bar* (see opposite), the *Inch Bar* or the *London Lounge* at the *Albert Arms*, as listed below. On Sunday many bars open at around 5pm, close early or don't open at all.

Pubs, bars and clubs

Albert Arms, cnr George St & London St. Sedate, tartan-decorated pub with live Irish music on Mon and anything from rock to blues on Tues and Wed. Bar snacks such as doorstep toasted sandwiches downstairs, while upstairs the *London Lounge* serves Emerson's beer on tap and good bistro fare (including steaks and roasts). Downstairs closes 7.30pm Sun.

Bath Street Bar, 1 Bath St (between the Octagon & Moray Place). Intimate and stylish studenty nightclub tucked away on a quiet road just below George St, where DJs play underground stuff. Cover charge $3 Thurs–Sat (and extra for special events); open from 10pm till around 5.30am; closed Mon.

Bennu Bar, at back of The Old Spaghetti Factory, Savoy Bldg, 68 Princes St. Young professionals are drawn to this elegant venue in one of Dunedin's finest buildings, decorated with a skylight right over the bar, and palm trees. (Mon–Sat from 11.30am; Sun from 5pm.)

Captain Cook, cnr Albany St & Great King St. A favourite student pub, reputed to have the highest turnover of beer in New Zealand and can be seedy. The downstairs bar has pool tables, cheap bar snacks, a pleasant garden bar and a happy half-hour every day 5.30–6pm. Upstairs has a DJ and disco (Thurs–Sat till 3am), with no cover charge. Open till 10pm Sun.

Champions Bar, 140 George St. Focuses on Kiwi sport, with local loyalties expressed through the blue-and-gold colours of Otago. Great atmosphere and toasted "doorstep" sandwiches. Closed Sun.

Dunedin Casino, cnr Princes St & High St. Men need to wear a collared shirt and no trainers or jeans are allowed in this ornate restoration of what was the *Grand Hotel* of 1883. You don't have to play the tables or slot machines to enjoy the gold-leaf plasterwork, a drink or a meal at their *Café Royale*. Sun–Thurs 11am–3am, Fri & Sat 11am–4am.

Fusion Niteclub & The Lounge Bar, at *Fuel Café*, 21 Frederick St. The university's closest club and bar, so they keep on pumping. The relaxed *Lounge Bar* has sofas and pool tables (open from 6pm) and *Fusion* has live bands and DJs (open from 8pm). Wed is $2-a-pint night and every second Sat from Feb to Oct is gay night ("Powder"). Closed Sun & Mon.

Inch Bar, 8 Bank St. Tiny hip watering hole with plenty of special beers on tap (including the locally brewed Emerson's) and a wide range of imported brands. Bar snacks available. Open daily from 5pm.

The Last Moa, 157 Frederick St. A student institution and pick-up joint, with dance floor (till 1am Fri & Sat) and occasional live acts.

Ra Bar, 21 The Octagon. An airy all-day street bar and café right in the thick of things, attracting the city's professionals who go for its palms and ironwork, as well as the light food and weekend all-day brunches. One of the few places open all Sun (from 9.30am).

Rosie O'Grady's, *Bentley's Hotel*, 137 Andrew St. Irish pub with a cosy, dark-wood interior. Varied live music Wed–Sat evenings. Bar meals available.

Statesman, 91 St Andrew St, opposite *Crossroads*. A big party pub where popular Kiwi rock bands play Thurs, Fri & Sat nights. Open till 3am Fri & Sat.

Theatre, cinema, classical music and sports

The Ticketek office in the Regent Theatre in The Octagon takes bookings for a selection of national and local events (☎03/477 8597, *www.ticketek.co.nz*; Mon–Fri 8.30am–5pm, Sat 10.30am–1pm) for a small handling fee on credit card bookings. Alternatively book through the venue.

The Fortune Theatre at 231 Stuart St (box office ☎03/477 8323; tickets around $22.50; closed Jan), in the Neo-Gothic converted Trinity Methodist Church, divides its programme between new works by Kiwi playwrights, fringe theatre, popular Broadway-style **plays** and occasional musicals. The Regent, 17 The Octagon (☎03/477 8597) is the city's largest and most ornate theatre, hosting musicals, ballets, touring plays and

---

THE DUNEDIN SOUND

In the late 1970s and early 1980s an idiosyncratic style of rock music began to emerge from Dunedin's local pub scene, and it was quickly tagged the "Dunedin Sound". Isolated from the commercial mainstream – the Kiwi music market constitutes a mere three million or so people – the bands indulged in songwriting for the sheer hell of it, which perhaps explains their originality and why so many of the early songs have stood the test of time. Spurred on by local record labels Flying Nun (now based in Auckland) and Xpressway, the bands developed over a number of albums and in relative obscurity until several – notably the Chills, The Clean, Straitjacket Fits and the Verlaines – started to find a receptive audience in Europe and the States.

The 1990s brought inventive new bands like Mink, Mestar, Cloudboy and HDU, while a strong body of singer-songwriters also proliferated at the city's premier music venue, *Arc Café/Bar* – among them Dunedin Sound pioneers David Kilgour and Martin Phillips. By this time the city enjoyed international status, prompting the *Chicago Tribune* in 1992 to call Dunedin the "Rock Capital of The World". At the end of 1999 it was announced that Otago University was introducing a degree in rock music under Verlaines singer-songwriter Graeme Downes. For the latest on the Dunedin Sound, check out *Fink*, the free entertainment pamphlet available all around town, including the visitor centre (or see *www.fink.net.nz*), which keeps track of Dunedin's bands, singers and songwriters.

---

performances by popular singers, comedians and groups. The small, intimate Globe, 104 London St (☎03/477 3274) features contemporary plays, classical drama and experimental works. You can catch more **fringe** on campus at Allen Hall on Clyde Street (☎03/479 8896), the showcase for the university's drama students.

Mainstream **films** are shown at Hoyts, a six-cinema multiplex at 33 The Octagon (☎03/477 7019), and at the Rialto, 11 Moray Place (☎03/474 2200), while there are international arthouse screenings at the delightful and tiny Metropolis, housed on the ground floor of the 1920s Town Hall on Moray Place (discounted tickets Mon–Fri before 6pm). This is the smallest public cinema in New Zealand, and it's essential to book ahead by leaving a message on their answer machine (☎03/474 3350); collect tickets ten minutes before screening time.

Regular **concerts** are given by the New Zealand Symphony Orchestra, the Dunedin Sinfonia (a semi-professional orchestra), and chamber music groups at the Town Hall or the Glenroy Auditorium at the Dunedin Centre (☎03/477 4477). The Dunedin Opera Company stages two or three productions a year at the Trust Bank Theatre, 100 King Edward St (☎03/455 4962) and regular public recitals are held by the music department of the University of Otago (see posters around town or ☎03/479 1100 during office hours).

Rugby matches are usually held every second weekend at the Carisbrook Stadium on Burns Street during the season (roughly the end of Feb to end of Oct; tickets can be booked through Otago Rugby Football Union ☎03/455 1191). A free schedule of games for the season is available from Otago Rugby Football Union, 28 Burns St, Caversham, Dunedin.

Listings

Airlines The offices of the domestic airlines are in the Octagon: Air New Zealand (☎03/479 6594), Ansett (☎0800/267 388). Freedom Air (☎0800/600 500, fax 0800/600 505) offers two international routes, to Sydney and Brisbane.

Airport transport Airport Express Shuttle Service (☎03/476 2519); Airport Shuttle City Taxis (☎03/477 1771); Airport Shuttle Bus & Taxi Service (☎03/477 9238); Airport Shuttle Service Ltd (☎03/477 6611); Call-a-Cab Shuttle (☎03/477 7800 & 0800/477 800); Dunedin Airport Shuttle (☎03/477 6611); Super Shuttle (☎03/456 0073).

Automobile Association Shopping Centre, Moray Place, near cnr Burlington St (☎03/477 5945, fax 477 9760). For road maps and travel and motoring products. Emergency breakdown service ☎0800/500 222. Road reports ☎0900/33222.

Banks and foreign exchange Branches of all major banks are clustered on George Street, most of them with ATMs, and some also line Princes Street. Thomas Cook is at cnr St Andrew St & George St (☎03/477 7204; Mon–Fri 8.30am–5pm, Sat 10am–12.30pm).

Bike rental R & R Sport, 70 Stuart St (☎03/474 1211) has mountain bikes for $20 a day; The Cycle Surgery, 67 Stuart St (☎03/477 7473) offers repairs, and rents bikes for $25 per day; Browns Avanti Pro Cycle Centre, Lower Stuart St (☎03/477 7259) has good-quality mountain bikes for short- and long-term rental ($25 per day), with helmets and locks, and does repairs.

Bookshops University Bookshop, 378 Great King St, opposite the Otago Museum (☎03/477 6976, *ubs@xtra.co.nz*; Mon–Fri 8.30am–5.30pm, Sat 9.30am–1.30pm), is a comprehensive independent bookshop on two floors, stocking a broad range of New Zealand and international fiction and non-fiction – bargains upstairs; Hyndman's, Civic Centre, 17 George St (just down from the visitor centre; ☎03/477 0174) stocks books on New Zealand, fiction, children's books and stationery. Scribes, cnr St David St & Great King St (☎03/477 6874; Mon–Fri 10am–5.30pm, Sat & Sun 11am–4pm) specializes in secondhand books on all subjects.

Buses National bus companies: InterCity Coachlines, 205 St Andrew St (coach terminal ☎03/477 8860, reservations ☎03/474 9600 or book through Dunedin visitor centre) links Dunedin with Christchurch, Queenstown, Te Anau, Wanaka and Invercargill. Local shuttle buses: Atomic Shuttles (to and from Christchurch and Queenstown; book through the train station ☎03/477 4449); and Southern Link Shuttles (☎03/474 3300; to and from Christchurch, Kaikoura, Invercargill and Queenstown) all run from train station.

Camping and outdoor equipment R & R Sport, 70 Stuart St, has the biggest range of camping, skiing, cycling and all sporting equipment; also mountain bike and pack rental. The Wilderness Shop, 101 Stuart St, has mountaineering, skiing and kayaking gear for rent and for sale; also tramping and alpine gear for sale.

Car parks City centre ($0.50 per 30min): off Upper Moray Place, opposite View St; Lower Moray Place, near Stuart St; Filleul St, between St Andrew & Hanover; Great King St, between St Andrew & Hanover; Anzac Ave, at junction with Castle St; Crawford St, at junction with Castle St, and another between Water & Liverpool; High St, near junction with Broadway.

Car rental Avis, 97 Moray Place (☎0800/655 111), also at Dunedin Airport (☎03/486 2780 & 0800/655 111); Budget, 330 Moray Place (☎03/474 0428) and Dunedin Airport (☎03/486 2660); Hertz, 121 Crawford St (☎03/477 7385 & 0800/654 321); Reliable Rentals, no office in Dunedin – they deliver to you (☎03/488 3975), for cars and minibuses; Rhodes, 124 St Andrew St (☎03/477 9950) for cars, vans, minibuses and 4WDs; Thrifty, 223 Hillside Rd (☎03/477 7087), also at the airport; and Welco, 8a Reid Rd, South Dunedin (☎03/455 5064). Cheapest of all are Rent-a-Dent, 212 Crawford St (☎03/477 7822) for cars, station wagons, vans and minibuses; and Jackies, 23 Cumberland St (☎03/477 7848).

CDs See Records.

Dentist Raymond J. George, 7th floor, National Mutual Building, cnr The Octagon & George St (☎03/477 7993, after hours 474 1277; 24hr).

Laundry The only one in Dunedin is Sudz Laundry, 4 Howe St, near the university.

Library Dunedin Public Library, cnr John St & Stewart St (☎03/474 3690; Mon–Fri 9.30am–8pm, Sat 10am–4pm), has excellent facilities, newspapers and Internet access.

Medical treatment Dunedin Hospital, 201 Great King St (☎03/474 0999). For general practice medical care, try Bell Hill Health Centre, 399 Moray Place (☎03/477 9183; Mon–Fri 8.30am–6pm).

Petrol stations Mobil Downtown 24hr Service Centre, 99 Crawford St.

Pharmacy After-hours service at Urgent Pharmacy, 95 Hanover St (☎03/477 6344; Mon–Fri 6–10pm, Sat, Sun & public holidays 10am–10pm).

Police Dunedin police station is at 25 Great King St (☎03/477 6011). In an emergency call ☎111.

Post office Dunedin Post Shop, John Wickliffe Plaza, 243 Princes St; Moray Place Post Shop, 233 Moray Place. Poste restante held at Dunedin Post Shop (Mon–Fri 8.30am–5.30pm, Sat 8.30am–noon).

Records, CDs & Tapes Records Records, 213 Stuart St (☎474 0789; Mon–Fri 10.30am–5pm, Sat 10.30–1pm), a new and secondhand music shop for local and international records, tapes and CDs; particularly strong on Kiwi music.

Swimming Moana Pool, cnr Stuart St & Littlebourne Rd (☎03/471 9780) is a leisure complex with a fifty-metre heated indoor pool, outdoor paddling pool, hydroslide, gym and sauna; St Clair Hot Saltwater Pool and Toddlers Pool (Nov–March Mon–Sat 6am–7pm, Sun 8am–7pm; ☎03/455 6352) is on the Esplanade and accessible from St Clair Beach (see p.651).

Taxis You'll find taxi ranks in the Octagon, between George St & Stuart St; on St Andrew St, between George St & Filleul St; and on Frederick St, between George St & Filleul St. Radio cabs include Call a Cab (☎03/477 7800), City Taxis (☎03/477 1771; 24hr service) and Dunedin Taxis (☎03/477 7777 & 0800/505 010).

Tours The visitor centre has information on the vast array of tours from Dunedin. Citibus Newton (☎03/477 5577) runs good city tours (daily 10am & 3.30pm; 1hr 30min, $15) and trips out to the Otago Peninsula (2hr 15min, $30); while the Otago Peninsula Express (book through the visitor centre) minibus runs to various points on the peninsula. Wings of Kotuku (☎03/473 0077) takes small groups to see the wildlife on Otago Peninsula, leaving first thing in the morning (Oct–March daily). Classic Jaguars (book through the visitor centre or ☎03/476 7261, *jaguars@ihug.co.nz*) run various classy tours to the Otago Peninsula; and to the largest open-cast gold mine in the southern hemisphere at Macraes Flat in the Otago hinterland ($149). Harbour and wildlife cruises on the *Monarch* leave from Dunedin Wharf, cnr Wharf & Fryatt Sts (☎03/477 4276, *monarch@wildlife.co.nz*; 5hr; from $59 or 1hr from Wellers Rock on the peninsula, $23), giving close-up views of royal albatross, seals, penguins, cormorants and waders on the peninsula. See box on p.669 for details of tours of the Catlins.

Trains The Tranz Scenic Southerner train between Christchurch and Invercargill stops at Dunedin train station, Anzac Square, off Stuart St (☎03/477 4449). The Taieri Gorge train to Pukerangi leaves from here, too (see p.652).

Travel agents Amo & Holmes Travel, 233 Stuart St (☎477 2233 & 0800/877 2233, fax 479 0678); STA, 32 Albany St (☎03/474 0146); Thomas Cook, cnr St Andrew St & George St (☎03/477 7204); Winston Darling, 138 Princes St (☎03/474 5483) for Ansett, Air New Zealand and other international flight bookings.

The Otago Peninsula

Jutting out to the east of Dunedin and dividing its harbour from the Pacific Ocean, the **OTAGO PENINSULA** is a lightly populated undulating area of natural beauty and exceptional wildlife. Its grass-covered hills afford excellent views of the harbour, the open sea and the spread of Dunedin against its dramatic backdrop of hills. Served by well-kept roads, the peninsula is easily accessible from the city, the trip from one end to the other taking an hour by car. You'll need to allow at least a day, though, to take in the sights and wildlife.

The chief reason for visiting the peninsula is to appreciate, at close range, the intriguing variety and abundance of **marine wildlife** that is drawn to its shores year round. At its tip is the small headland of **Taiaroa Head**, a protected area where several colonies of mammals and sea birds congregate. Unique among these is the majestic **royal albatross**, which breeds here in the only mainland colony of albatross in the world. Also concentrated on the headland's shores are **penguins** (little blue and the rare yellow-eyed) and **southern fur seals**, while the cliffs are home to other sea birds including three species of **shag**, **muttonbirds** (sooty shearwaters) and various species of gull. The peninsula's other beaches and inlets play host to a great variety of wading and waterfowl and, occasionally, New Zealand **sea lions** (see box on p.672; while offshore, orca and other **whales** can sometimes be spotted.

Although there's ample opportunity to see much of the wildlife without having to pay for the privilege, it's well worth forking out for one or more of the several official **wildlife tours** (see pp.660–63 for details), since they are informative and take you up close, yet cause minimal disturbance to the animals.

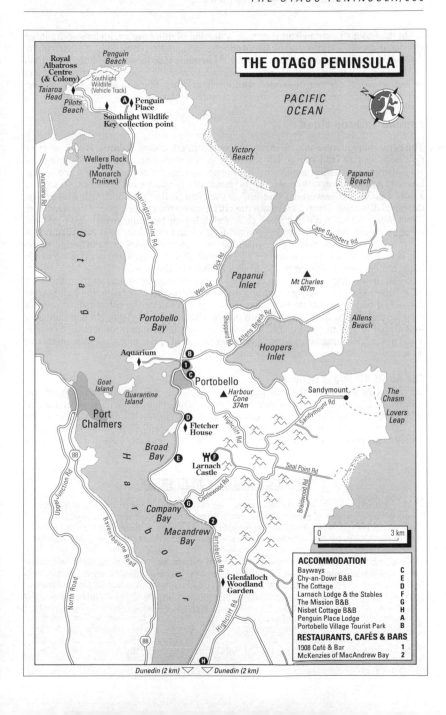

THE OTAGO PENINSULA

PACIFIC OCEAN

Royal Albatross Centre (& Colony)

Penguin Beach

Southlight Wildlife (Vehicle Track)

Taiaroa Head

Pilots Beach

A Penguin Place

Southlight Wildlife Key collection point

Wellers Rock Jetty (Monarch Cruises)

Aramoana Rd

Harington Point Rd

Victory Beach

Papanui Beach

Cape Saunders Rd

Dick Rd

Weir Rd

Papanui Inlet

Mt Charles 407m

Portobello Bay

Shepard Rd

Allens Beach Rd

Allens Beach

Aquarium **B**

1 C

Hoopers Inlet

● Portobello

Goat Island

Quarantine Island

Port Chalmers

Harbour Cone 374m

Sandymount

The Chasm

Lovers Leap

Sandymount Rd

88

Upper Junction Rd

D ♦ Fletcher House

Highcliff Rd

Broad Bay

E ♦♦ **F**

Larnach Castle

Seal Point Rd

Braidwood Rd

Ravensbourne Road

Castlewood Rd

G

Company Bay

2

Macandrew Bay

Portobello Rd

North Road

88

Glenfalloch Woodland Garden

Highcliff Rd

H

0   3 km

ACCOMMODATION

Bayways	C
Chy-an-Dowr B&B	E
The Cottage	D
Larnach Lodge & the Stables	F
The Mission B&B	G
Nisbet Cottage B&B	H
Penguin Place Lodge	A
Portobello Village Tourist Park	B

RESTAURANTS, CAFÉS & BARS

1908 Café & Bar	1
McKenzies of MacAndrew Bay	2

Dunedin (2 km) ▽   ▽ Dunedin (2 km)

On the way to Taiaroa Head there are a handful of other sights, including the large woodland gardens and walks of **Glenfalloch**, particularly renowned for their rhododendrons, azaleas and camellias; the bizarre **Larnach Castle**, which is little more than an overblown folly; **Fletcher House**, a delightfully restored small Edwardian villa; and an **aquarium**. A number of **scenic walks** cross both public and private land to spectacular views and unusual land formations created by lava flows.

Around Taiaroa Head

The peninsula's marine wildlife is mostly concentrated around **Taiaroa Head**, where a rich and constant food source is created by cold waters forced up by the continental shelf. Other than taking a tour, the best opportunities for seeing animals are on the beaches and inlets on either side of the headland. Southern fur seals can be seen at **Pilots Beach**, on the western side (follow the main road to the shore as it snakes past the Royal Albatross Centre) and from the **cliff tops** on the eastern side of the headland. Pilots Beach is also home to a small colony of little blue penguins, which are best visited around dusk but be sure to keep your distance and stay quiet or they'll turn tail. A short signposted walk from the Royal Albatross Centre car park to a **cliff-edge viewing area** unfolds spectacular scenes of a spotted shag colony, while royal albatross in flight can be spotted all year round from anywhere on the headland.

When **observing wildlife**, respect the animals by staying well away from them (at least 5 metres), and keeping quiet and still. **Penguins** are especially timid and easily frightened by people getting too close. They will be reluctant to come ashore (even if they have chicks to feed) if you are on or near the beach and visible. In summer, stay well away from them and keep to the track as they're extremely vulnerable to stress while nesting and moulting. Never get between a **seal** and the sea; these animals can be aggressive and move surprisingly quickly.

The Royal Albatross Centre

Serving as the gateway to the only mainland colony of albatross in the world, the **Royal Albatross Centre** (daily: Oct–April 9am–7pm; May–Sept 10am–5pm; free) at Taiaroa Head is 33km from Dunedin's city centre. Its galleries contain displays on local wildlife and history, and there's a comfortable café with panoramic windows. The centre's excellent **guided tours** (daily except Sept 17–Nov 23; booking essential on ☎03/478

THE ROYAL ALBATROSS

The majestic and mysterious **albatross**, one of the largest seabirds in the world, has long been the subject of reverence and superstition. A solitary creature that regularly circumnavigates the globe, the albatross spends most of its life in flight or at sea, and is traditionally held to be the embodiment of a dead sea captain's soul, condemned to wander the oceans for ever.

The largest of all the albatrosses is the **royal albatross** – a stunning sight, with an impressive **wing span** of up to 3.5 metres. They travel up to 190,000km a year, at speeds of 120kph and have a **life expectancy** of 45 years. The albatross mates for life, but male and female separate to fly in opposite directions around the world, returning to the same **breeding** grounds once every two years, and arriving within a couple of days of one another. The female lays one egg (weighing up to 500g) per breeding season, and the parents share incubation duty over a period of eleven weeks. Once the chick has hatched, the parents take turns at feeding it and guarding it against stoats, ferrets, wild cats and rats. Almost a year from the start of the breeding cycle, the fledgling takes flight and the parents leave the colony and return to sea.

0499 or through the Dunedin visitor centre; $23–27) include an introductory film and talk, plenty of time to view the birds from an enclosed area in the reserve (binoculars provided) and an optional but uninspiring visit to the labyrinthine tunnels of Fort Taiaroa beneath the nature reserve.

At Taiaroa Head, adult birds arrive for the new season in September. Courting and mating takes place in October and eggs are laid and incubated from November to December. The chicks hatch in January and February. The **best months** for viewing are between April and August, when parent birds leave the nests and return towards the end of the day to feed their chicks. By September the chicks and adults are ready to depart and new breeding pairs start to arrive.

Penguin-viewing

Two companies on the peninsula run markedly different yet equally appealing **yellow-eyed penguin** tours. The best months for viewing are mid-August to early March.

Southlight Wildlife, whose booking office is on Harington Point Road, 2.5km before the albatross colony (☎04/478 0287; daily dawn–dusk; $7.50), is the cheaper of the two tour operators, and allows repeated viewings on the same day at no extra cost, but you need your **own car** to reach the colony hidden away on the eastern shore. You'll be given a key to a signposted gate opposite the Royal Albatross Centre and after fifteen minutes' drive you reach a car park. The nearby cliffs overlook **Penguin Beach** with its colonies of yellow-eyeds (*hoiho*) and little blues. Viewing is unobstructed and aided by telescopes ($0.50–$1 to activate) and shelters. Penguins emerge and head across the

---

THE YELLOW-EYED PENGUIN (HOIHO)

Considered the most ancient of all living penguins, the **yellow-eyed penguin**, or *hoiho*, evolved in forests free of predators. Found only in southern New Zealand, it is an endangered species, numbering around four thousand birds, due to introduced predators (ferrets, stoats and cats), the loss of its forested habitat, disturbance by humans and livestock, and recurring food shortages. The small mainland population of just a few hundred occupies nesting areas dotted along the wild southeast coast of the South Island (from Oamaru to the Catlins); other smaller colonies inhabit the coastal forest margins of Stewart Island and offshore islets, and New Zealand's subantarctic islands of Auckland and Campbell.

Male and female adults are identical in colouring, with pink webbed feet and a bright yellow band that encircles the head, sweeping over their pale yellow eyes. Standing around 65cm high and weighing 5–8kg, they have a **life expectancy** of up to twenty years. Their **diet** consists of squid and small fish and hunting takes them up to 40km offshore and to depths of 100m.

Maori gave this rare penguin the name of **hoiho**, meaning "the noise shouter", because of the distinctive high-pitched calls (an exuberant trilling) it makes at night when greeting its mate at the nest. Unlike other penguins, the yellow-eyed does not migrate after its first year, but stays close to its home beach, making daily fishing trips and returning as daylight fails.

The **breeding season** lasts for 28 weeks, from mid-August to early March. Eggs are laid between mid-September and mid-October, and both parents share in the duties of incubation, a period of about 43 days. The eggs hatch in November and for the next six weeks the chicks are constantly guarded against predators. When the down-covered chicks are six or seven weeks old, their rapid growth gives them voracious appetites and both parents must fish daily to satisfy them. The fledglings enter the sea for the first time in late February or early March and journey up to 500km north to winter feeding grounds. Fewer than fifteen percent of fledged chicks reach breeding age, but those that do return to the colony of their birth.

swathe of sand to a high sandy bank, which they laboriously climb to reach their nests hidden in the grass above. There's also a large signposted seal colony further along the coast and a spotted shag colony five minutes' walk beyond the seals, in the cliff face. The best viewing spot is the hide directly above one of the nesting areas.

Employing a very different approach are the carefully controlled and extremely informative **guided tours** run by an award-winning penguin-conservation project. At **Penguin Place**, McGrouther's Farm, Harington Point Road, 3.5km before the albatross colony (book ahead on ☎03/478 0286 or through Dunedin visitor centre; daily; 90min; $25), you are given the rare privilege of entering a protected **nesting area** of around 200 birds through a unique system of hides and tunnels. The best months to visit here are between early November and May, but at any time of year, cold wet days make for especially good viewing. Tours begin with a talk about penguins and their conservation, before a guide takes you to the beachside colony, where well-camouflaged trenches and hides among the dunes allow an extraordinary proximity to the penguins and excellent photographic opportunities. Proceeds from the tours are used to fund the conservation work and a unit that looks after injured penguins. If you want **to stay** overnight, budget accommodation is available on the farm (see "Accommodation" opposite).

The rest of the peninsula

Lying between Dunedin and Taiaroa Head are four sights worthy of a brief diversion, most of them strung along the harbourside on Portobello Road. Eleven kilometres from Dunedin, the peaceful **Glenfalloch Woodland Garden**, at 430 Portobello Rd (daily dawn–dusk; donations requested), contains 120 square kilometres of rambling mature garden and bush, surrounding a homestead built in 1871. The garden is at its best between mid-September and mid-October, when it is resplendent with rhododendrons, azaleas and camellias and, to a lesser extent, magnolias, fuchsias and roses. Near the entrance, a licensed café (daily 10am–4.30pm) serves snacks and drinks, and also stocks leaflets on the peninsula.

Set high on a hill above the harbour, 16km from the centre of Dunedin and signposted off Castlewood Road, is a bizarre nineteenth-century Gothic Revival building. The so-called **Larnach Castle** (daily 9am–5pm; grounds only $5, grounds and castle $12) was the sumptuous residence of William Larnach, an Australian banker politician, who spent a fortune on its construction and decoration. Completed in 1871, it was designed by Scotsman R.A. Lawson, architect of the First Church and the Municipal Chambers in Dunedin. Most impressive is the sheer scale of the project. The very best local and overseas craftsmen were employed to build the family home entirely by hand, using materials shipped from all over the world: glass from Venice, marble from Italy and tiles from England. On arrival, these were punted across the harbour and then laboriously dragged up the hill by ox-drawn sleds. Today the castle is owned by a family who bought it in 1967 and renovated it, providing accommodation (see opposite) in two of the castle's buildings. Without your own transport, you'll have to take the Portobello **bus** either to Company Bay, from where it's a five-kilometre (signposted) walk, uphill all the way, or to Broad Bay from where you'll have an even steeper but shorter walk (2km).

Back on the coast, about halfway along the peninsula, **The Fletcher House**, 727 Portobello Rd, Broad Bay (daily 11am–4pm; April to mid-Oct Sat, Sun & public holidays only; $3) is an attractive small Edwardian villa, lovingly restored to its original state and furnished in period style. Built entirely of native wood in 1909, it was the family home of the Broad Bay storekeeper. Inside the house, the absence of restricting ropes allows you to appreciate fully the furniture and fine woodwork, including the tongue-and-groove panelling in the small kitchen and richly coloured rimu ceilings and floors.

Further east, at Portobello, Hatchery Road leads 2km along a headland to the **Aquarium** (daily noon–4.30pm; $5, or $10 per family), displaying marine life found in New Zealand's southern waters. The fun part is sticking your hands into the several shallow "touch tanks" to feel the small sea creatures. As part of a marine laboratory run by the University of Otago, this is an efficient venture, and staff are always available to answer questions. Visitors are also invited to participate in **fish feeding** (Sat 2–3pm; Dec–Feb also Wed 2–3pm).

Practicalities

With your own transport, access to the peninsula from Dunedin is easy, either via the snaky **Portobello Road**, which hugs the western shoreline overlooking the harbour or the inland **Highcliff Road**, which heads up and over the hills. Dunedin visitor centre supplies a handy free map of the peninsula. The public **bus** (Mon–Sat) from Cumberland Street in Dunedin runs halfway along the peninsula, as far as Portobello (35min), from where it's still another 14km to Taiaroa Head. Several **guided-tour buses** depart daily from Dunedin visitor centre ($25–49 return; all booked through the visitor centre or direct), the best being the guided Elm Wildlife Tours (☎03/474 1872, *tours@elmwildlifetours.co.nz*; up to 6hr, $43, plus optional extra $23 to visit the Albatross Colony). A couple of straightforward **shuttles** also operate: the Otago Peninsula Express (book through the visitor centre or ☎03/474 3300; $25 return, plus an optional Penguin Place or Royal Albatross Centre tour $23 & $22 respectively) runs to Taiaroa Head in the late afternoon; the Otago Explorer goes to Larnach Castle only (book through the visitor centre or ☎03/474 3300 or 0800/322 240; $30 return, including a guided tour of the castle). There are also daily harbour wildlife **cruises** on board the *Monarch*; see p.658 for details.

The Dunedin visitor centre can also help with tour bookings and accommodation, and stocks plenty of leaflets about the peninsula, including maps of various walking tracks.

Accommodation and eating

There's a limited amount of accommodation on the peninsula, and you'll find it pricier than in Dunedin. **Camping** is permitted only at the small *Portobello Village Tourist Park*, 27 Hereweka St, Portobello (☎ & fax 03/478 0359, *peninsula@es.co.nz*; ②–③), which has on-site caravans and cabins, as well as tent sites ($9) and powered sites ($10).

Budget accommodation is available at Taiaroa Head at the simple *Penguin Place Lodge*, McGrouther's Farm, Harington Point Rd (☎03/478 0286, fax 478 0257,

---

WALKS ON OTAGO PENINSULA

A free map from the Dunedin visitor centre or DOC office, *Otago Peninsula Tracks*, briefly describes several walks on the peninsula. Bear in mind that they cover hill country and that though most tracks are well defined, some are pretty steep. Also, the weather here can turn cold or wet very quickly, even on the sunniest days.

The most rewarding walks include the easy loop track to **Lovers Leap and the Chasm** (3km; 1hr; closed Aug–Oct) which crosses farmland to sheer cliffs dropping 200m to the sea, with collapsed sea caves and rock faces of layered volcanic lava flows visible. The track begins from the end of Sandymount Road, a 25-minute drive from the centre of Dunedin. Also good is the track along **Sandfly Bay** (3km; 80min) which leads to sweeping dunes visited by yellow-eyed penguins and, occasionally, New Zealand sea lions (see box on p.672). There's a penguin hide at the far end of beach. This walk begins at the end of Seal Point Road, a twenty-minute drive from the city.

penguin.place@clear.net.nz; single ①, double or twin ②, plus $5 linen hire), 3.5km before the albatross colony, with single, double and twin rooms, shared showers and kitchen; and at Company Bay at *The Mission B&B*, Mission Cove (☎03/476 1321, fax 476 1028, *cummings@deepsouth.co.nz*; ⑤), a former nurses' home with double and twin rooms, two guest bathrooms, a large garden and harbour views.

Mid-range options include three fully self-contained **motel** units with sundecks and harbour views at *Bayways Motel*, 697 Highcliff Rd, Portobello (☎03/478 0181, fax 478 0382; ④–⑤); a cosy, turn-of-the-century harbourside **cottage** aptly called *The Cottage*, 748 Portobello Rd, Broad Bay (☎03/478 0073, *thecottage@xtra.co.nz*; ⑤) with one double en-suite; and the *Chy-an-Dowr* **B&B**, 687 Portobello Rd, Broad Bay (☎ & fax 03/478 0306, *hermanvv@xtra.co.nz*; ⑤–⑥), a spacious harbourside house midway along the peninsula, with three double rooms (two en suite and one with a private bathroom) and a sunroom giving a panoramic view of the harbour. Further out there's also the tranquil 1930s *Nisbet Cottage B&B*, 6a Elliffe Place, Shiel Hill (☎03/454 5169, fax 454 5369, *wingsok@es.co.nz*; ⑥), ten minutes' drive from central Dunedin (also served by Shiel Hill bus), offering great hill views and en-suite double and twin rooms.

Alternatively you can choose to stay in greater **luxury** in a couple of buildings in the grounds of Larnach Castle (☎03/476 1616, fax 476 1574, *larnach@larnachcastle.co.nz*), but you pay a premium for the tranquil garden setting high above the harbour. The converted *Stables* (③) contains six basic rooms (sharing bathrooms), while the *Larnach Lodge* (⑦), refurbished to imitate a two-storey colonial farm building, has twelve en-suite rooms, each individually decorated in period style. All guests get a free tour of the castle during opening hours and you can also book for dinner in the castle's dining room (around $40pp plus wine).

Eating is limited to simple takeaway snacks at the MacAndrew Bay Store, 497 Portobello Rd (☎03/476 1107), a simple café/visitor centre at Portobello on Harington Point Rd and two reasonable waterfront venues, both cashing in on the harbour views and rustling up seafood, meat and vegetarian dishes. Closest to the city is the modern, glass-fronted *McKenzies of MacAndrew Bay*, 494 Portobello Rd, MacAndrew Bay (☎03/476 1081), which is open daily for dinner (plus lunch on Friday and Sunday) and combines a bar, expensive licensed restaurant and cheaper café. Further along, in Portobello, the elegant *1908 Café & Bar*, 7 Harington Point Rd (☎03/478 0801; licensed & BYO – bottled wine only), serves pricey lunches and dinners daily in summer (June–Aug lunches by prior arrangement only & dinner days vary; phone ahead) in a converted turn-of-the-century house, enhanced by excellent views of the harbour and city against a backdrop of hills. The varied menu includes enormous desserts.

Port Chalmers

If you have half a day left after exploring Dunedin and the Otago Peninsula, the small, attractive historic town and modern container port of **PORT CHALMERS**, on a tiny peninsula 12km along the western shore from Dunedin, is worth a trip. You'll be rewarded by magnificent harbour views offset by bush-covered hills, a short coastal walk, fine nineteenth-century buildings and a thriving artistic community.

The site was chosen in 1844 as the port to serve the proposed Scottish settlement of New Edinburgh, later called Dunedin. The first settlers arrived on the *John Wickliffe* in March 1848 and named the port after the Reverend Dr Thomas Chalmers, who had led the split between the Presbyterian and Free churches of Scotland. Development was slow until the Otago **gold rush** of the 1860s, which heralded a boom for Port Chalmers. Later, it served as the embarkation point for several **Antarctic expeditions**, including those of Captain Scott, who set out from here in 1901 and, ill-fatedly, in 1910. The first trial shipment of **frozen meat** to Britain was sent from Port Chalmers and today the export of wool, meat and timber is its chief business.

The Town

The main street, **George Street**, connects the docks with SH88 and is lined with several old stone buildings containing shops, galleries, a few cafés and a bank. Most of the town crawls up hills on either side, where two churches dominate. On Mount Street stands the tall stone spire and clock tower of **Iona Church**, completed in 1883 and once Presbyterian but now United (Presbyterian Methodist), and on the opposite side, on Grey Street, sits the squat Anglican **Holy Trinity** (1874), designed by Scottish architect R.A. Lawson and built from local bluestone (volcanic rock).

On the George Street waterfront, you'll find the small, rather atmospheric **Museum**, in the old post office building. Run by volunteers, its hours vary considerably (Oct–March daily; April–Sept by arrangement only; donations requested; ☎03/472 8233). Brimming with maritime artefacts and some local settler history, the highlights include a history of navigational equipment with splendid models and photographs. Downstairs is a large working electric model of a **gold dredge**, built in 1900 by a boilermaker apprentice. Staff can fill you in on local walking trails, and can also arrange escorted historical walks along the nearby beaches.

On the corner of Grey and George streets is the private studio (not open to the public) of artist **Ralph Hotere**, one of New Zealand's best-known abstract artists. The rest of George Street is lined with **art galleries** and **craft shops**. Port Chalmers Aero Club (Thurs–Sun; free), at no. 10, a delightful 1884 building, shows contemporary works by local artists displayed over several floors and has a **café** downstairs serving cheap lunches and snacks. Next door, occupying an old bank, The Crafty Banker (Thurs–Sun) is a pleasant gallery and craft shop, while further up the hill, Portfolio (Thurs–Sun or by appointment ☎03/472 7856) has a good selection of rugs, kilims and *objets d'art*.

For a spectacular panorama of the harbour and Otago Peninsula, a **coastal walk** (4km; 45min–1hr) starts from Wickliffe Terrace, at the junction with George Street. After crossing the rail line, the road takes you past Mussel Bay to the commanding headland. Continuing around the coast, home to a wide variety of sea birds including terns, oystercatchers, shags, gulls, herons and ducks, you reach Back Beach, and can return to George Street via a log-storage area or detour up to Flagstaff Lookout, above the headland.

Practicalities

By **car** from Dunedin, it's a ten-minute scenic harbourside drive along SH88, or you can take the longer scenic route, following Mount Cargill and Upper Junction roads. From the north on SH1, take the road to Port Chalmers from Waitati. **Buses** from Dunedin to Port Chalmers leave from Stand 4 opposite Countdown supermarket in Cumberland Street, dropping you off in George Street about 25 minutes later (Mon–Sat).

Eating options are limited to cafés and takeaways, the best being *Café Giardino* at the Aero Club, 10 George St, which serves cheap soups, sandwiches, bagels and quiches, and *Port Stables Bar & Café*, 56 George St, in tastefully converted stables with a pool table and a roaring fire in winter. You'll find scenic picnic spots along Peninsula Beach Road, just around from the harbour.

South from Dunedin: Balclutha and the Catlins Coast

The dramatic, rugged coastal route linking Dunedin and Invercargill, part of the **Southern Scenic Route** that continues on to Fiordland, is one of the least travelled highways in New Zealand, and traverses some of the country's wildest scenery along the **Catlins Coast**. Within this significant region is the largest area of native forest on the east coast of the South Island, most of it protected as the **Catlins Forest Park**, and consisting of rimu, rata, kamahi and silver beech. Roaring southeasterlies and the remorseless sea have shaped the coastline here into plunging cliffs, windswept headlands, white sand beaches, rocky bays and gaping caves, much of this accessible on a number of short bushwalks. Not surprisingly, this relatively untouched area abounds with **wildlife**, including several rare species of marine bird and mammal, and the whole region rings with birdsong most of the year, though the **birds** are at their most active during June to August when breeding. The Catlins have something to offer at any time of the year, but from mid-November to mid-December you benefit from spring/summer weather yet avoid the busy season during and after Christmas. The only major stop-off point between Dunedin and the Catlins Coast is **Balclutha**, which is a good place to stock up before entering the wilderness beyond. At Balclutha, SH1 turns inland, skirting the Catlins region before turning south to Invercargill at the town of **Gore**, a centre for brown-trout fishing.

Maori hunters once thrived in the Catlins region, one of the last refuges of the flightless moa, but by 1700 they had moved on, to be supplanted by European **whalers and sealers** in the 1830s. Two decades later, having decimated whale and seal stocks, they too moved on. Meanwhile, in 1840, Captain Edward Cattlin arrived to investigate the navigability of the river that bears his (misspelled) name. He purchased a tract of land from the chief of the Ngai Tahu and soon after, boatloads of **loggers** began to arrive, lured by the great podocarp forests. Cleared valleys were settled, bush millers supplied Dunedin with much of the wood needed for housing and, in 1872, more timber was exported from the Catlins than anywhere else in New Zealand. From 1879, the rail line from Balclutha began to extend into the region, bringing with it sawmills, schools and farms. Milling continued into the 1930s, but gradually dwindled and today's tiny settlements are shrunken remnants of the once-prosperous logging industry.

Although the 126-kilometre stretch of road through the Catlins should present no problems for vehicles, be aware that a twenty-kilometre section is **unsealed**, as are smaller roads edging out to the sea. For this reason, none of the major bus companies operates through the Catlins and there is no train either. Without your own transport, or if you just want to make a day-trip, you can take one of several **guided tours** (see box on p.669) which operate from Dunedin, Balclutha and Invercargill.

Balclutha

Located on SH1, 80km southwest of Dunedin and 185km from Invercargill, **BALCLUTHA** lies in the heart of South Otago, amid rich pastures. Nicknamed "Big River Town", Balclutha occupies both banks of the mighty **Clutha River**, with the town centre on the southern shore linked to SH1 by an unmissable, arched concrete bridge. The river was once a source of alluvial gold but today is used to generate hydroelectricity. Anglers are lured to Balclutha by the river's substantial stocks of brown trout and salmon; for non-fishing folk, there are few attractions in the small township apart from a laid-back **jetboat** trip on the river, and the main reason to stop is to pick up information and supplies for the trip south.

If you can't resist getting on the water, Blue Mountain Jet (☎03/415 9268) offer a range of **jetboat** tours (from 20min for $40 to 1hr at $65), filling you in on the local ecology and history. There's plenty of birdlife and they'll show you an 1896 paddle steamer that operates as a ferry, these days propelled by the current and a system of rudders and pulleys. The jetboat is also available for **fishing** charters (half day $350, full day $600) and the company runs a B&B.

All **buses** except InterCity stop outside the visitor centre (see opposite) – InterCity pull up outside the Café Italio on John Street – and the centrally located **train station** is at the junction of Scotland Street and Baxter Street. The Southerner passes through once a day, in each direction.

Balclutha's well-organized and helpful **Clutha visitor centre** is beside the bridge at 4 Clyde St (Mon–Fri 8.30am–5pm, Sat & Sun 9.30am–3pm; ☎03/418 0388, *clutha.vin@cluthadc.govt.nz*) and has plenty of information on the Catlins and Gore, including the excellent *Visitors Guide to the Catlins* ($2), a series of leaflets on walks in the Clutha district ($0.50 each), and the DOC pamphlet, *Southern Scenic Route* ($1). You'll find **Internet access** at Sound Trax record store, 36 Clyde St (Mon–Fri 9am–6pm, Sat 9am–4pm).

There's a small selection of **accommodation** in town. The best campsite is the small *Naish Park Motor Camp*, 56 Charlotte St (☎03/418 0088), five minutes' walk from the town centre and set in pleasant parkland with excellent modern facilities. There are plenty of tent sites ($8 per person), powered sites ($8 per person), one on-site caravan (②) and five cabins (②). The only hostel is the basic yet central *Balclutha Backpackers*, 20 Stewart St (mobile ☎025/291 7466; singles & dorms ①, rooms ②), a converted 1950s convent with tiny singles, small dorms and twins, and tent sites on the back lawn ($8). Among the motels, try the friendly *Helensborough Motor Inn*, 23 Essex St (☎ & fax 03/418 1948, reservations only 0800/113 355; ④), north of the bridge, with fully self-contained units, or *Rosebank Lodge*, 265 Clyde St (☎03/418 1490, fax 418 1493; ⑤), a quiet new complex with eighteen units, three bars, a restaurant, spa and sauna. Twelve kilometres north of Balclutha is the luxurious *Garvan Homestead B&B* (☎03/417 8407, fax 417 8429; ⑥), a large tudor-style retreat in rambling gardens with a good licensed restaurant.

Places to eat are strung along Clyde Street. *The Captain's*, a centrally located and pleasant **pub** at no. 13, serves reasonable and well-priced bar food, from snacks to steaks, and there's a good Chinese, *Gins*, at no. 27 (closed Tues; BYO). The moderately priced à la carte **restaurant** at *Rosebank Lodge* is the best place for something special.

The Catlins

The best way to enjoy the **CATLINS COAST** is to take it slowly, absorbing its unique atmosphere over at least a couple of days. There's plenty to see at any time of year, but if you visit during the week you'll avoid most of the summer day-trippers from Dunedin. From Nugget Point in South Otago (just southeast of Balclutha) to Waipapa Point in Southland (60km northeast of Invercargill), the wild scenery stretches unbroken, with dense rainforest succumbing to open scrub as you cut through deep valleys and past rocky bays, inlets and estuaries. The coast is home to **penguins** (both little blues and yellow-eyed), **dolphins**, several types of sea bird and, at certain times of year, migrating **whales**. Elephant **seals**, fur seals and increasingly, the rare New Zealand **sea lion**, are found on the sandy beaches and grassy areas, and within the mossy depths of the forest are abundant **birds**: tui, resonant bellbirds, fantails, grey warblers and colourful tree-top dwellers such as kakariki and mohau.

The most awe-inspiring natural features scattered along the way are **Nugget Point**, a rugged, windswept promontory favoured by fur seals and sea lions; the **Purakaunui Falls**, among the most photographed in New Zealand; the impressive **Cathedral Caves**, their high "ceilings" and deep chambers carved out of the cliffs by the sheer force of the sea; and **Curio Bay**, where an intriguing forest has been captured in stone.

The main settlement is **Owaka** (Place of the Canoe), a farming town 38km from Balclutha and inhabited by less than two hundred people. It has a small selection of accommodation, services and shops, including a pub, supermarket, store/diner/

The **western continuation** of the **Southern Scenic Route**, from Invercargill to Te Anau via Tuatapere, is covered in the *Fiordland* chapter, starting on p.809.

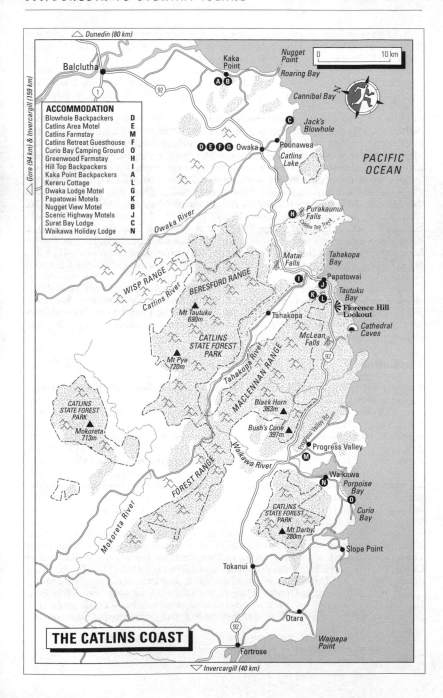

△ Dunedin (80 km)

Balclutha

Kaka
Point

Nugget
Point
Roaring Bay

Cannibal Bay

ACCOMMODATION
Blowhole Backpackers   D
Catlins Area Motel   E
Catlins Farmstay   M
Catlins Retreat Guesthouse   F
Curio Bay Camping Ground   O
Greenwood Farmstay   H
Hill Top Backpackers   I
Kaka Point Backpackers   A
Kereru Cottage   L
Owaka Lodge Motel   G
Papatowai Motels   K
Nugget View Motel   B
Scenic Highway Motels   J
Surat Bay Lodge   C
Waikawa Holiday Lodge   N

Jack's
Blowhole

Owaka   Pounawea

Catlins
Lake

PACIFIC
OCEAN

Owaka River

Purakaunui
Falls
Catlins Top Track

WISP RANGE

Catlins River

Matai
Falls

Tahakopa
Bay

BERESFORD RANGE

Papatowai

Tautuku
Bay
Florence Hill
Lookout

Mt Tautuku
690m

Tahakopa

CATLINS
STATE FOREST
PARK

McLean
Falls

Cathedral
Caves

Mt Pye
720m

MACLENNAN RANGE

Tahakopa River

CATLINS
STATE FOREST
PARK

Mokoreta
713m

Black Horn
363m

Bush's Cone
397m

Progress Valley Rd

Progress Valley

Waikawa River

Waikawa
Porpoise
Bay

FOREST RANGE

CATLINS
STATE FOREST
PARK

Curio
Bay

Mt Darby
280m

Slope Point

Mokoreta River

Tokanui

Otara

THE CATLINS COAST

Waipapa
Point

Fortrose

0   10 km

N

△ Gore (94 km) & Invercargill (159 km)

▽ Invercargill (40 km)

backpackers, pharmacy and a 24-hour medical centre. Elsewhere, there are general stores at **Kaka Point, Papatowai** and at **Curio Bay** Camping Ground. **Petrol** stations are few and far between, so fill up before you set off, then at Kaka Point, Owaka, Papatowai or Tokanui (pumps close at around 5pm). Note that there are **no banks** within the Catlins. Bear in mind, too, that **theft from cars** is on the increase in the region, especially in the remoter spots, so don't leave valuables in the car and be sure to lock it.

Kaka Point to Owaka

First stop inside the Catlins is **Kaka Point**, a tiny beachside community 22km from Balclutha (turn off SH92 at Romahapa). There's a general store here that doubles as café, petrol station and postshop, as well as a pleasant small **hostel**, *Kaka Point*

TOURS OF THE CATLINS

If you don't have your own transport, **guided tours** are really the only way of exploring the Catlins; trips start from Dunedin, Balclutha and Invercargill.

Highly recommended is an inspirational **eco-tour** run by **Catlins Wildlife Trackers**, sharing in-depth knowledge about the local ecology, history and geology. Fergus and Mary Sutherland are committed to conservation and offer an intimate two or four-day tour ($250 & $500 respectively) for groups of up to eight, which explores remote beaches and rich rainforest from their secluded coastal home deep in the Catlins at Papatowai. You can drive there or be picked up from Balclutha on Mon, Wed & Sat mornings. All meals, accommodation, transport and equipment are provided and a shuttle service to and from Dunedin can be arranged for an extra fee (advance bookings essential ☎03/415 8613, *catlinw@es.co.nz* or through Clutha visitor centre, see p.667). You stay in their tranquil house – overlooking native forest, an estuary, beach and ocean – in a separate section containing double and twin rooms sharing a bathroom.

A **no-frills** guided minibus tour, **Catlins Coastal Link**, shuttles from Dunedin to Invercargill along SH1 via Gore, returning the same or next day via the Catlins and allowing plenty of time off the bus for bush and beach walks, wildlife encounters and the major scenic sights. The tour is extremely friendly and relaxed and you can also get on or off where you like and pick up a later bus. Buses depart in both directions (daily mid-Nov to April only, book ahead through visitor centres; Dunedin one-day return $90, 2-day return $110, Invercargill–Dunedin one way via the Catlins $80; an optional popular extra on all trips is an overnight farmstay including a full day on a working sheep,beef and deer farm, $195 including the travel). The tour also links in with shuttles from Te Anau and Queenstown.

The Bottom Bus (☎03/442 9708), which supplements the Kiwi Experience bus trips in Southland, but in small personal buses without the reckless booze-bus approach, runs from Dunedin through the Catlins to Invercargill on its clockwise loop to Riverton, Te Anau and Queenstown, returning to Dunedin (3 days minimum; $160 for whole trip or other flexible options). You can travel sections of this journey if you don't want a ticket for the whole thing, and jump on along the way; departures from Dunedin are on Mon, Wed, Thurs, Sat & Sun mornings (Dunedin–Invercargill $75).

A more intimate **day-trip** from Balclutha, Kaka Point or Owaka, or **one-way overnight trip** from Invercargill to Dunedin can be had with **Catlins Natural Wonders** (☎0800 353 941, *cnw@ihug.co.nz*), who take groups of up to nine and allow plenty of time for walking. From 8 Nov to 10 April day-trips from Balclutha, Kaka Point and Owaka ($70, $65 & $55 respectively) run on Mon–Wed & Sat and offer an optional yellow-eyed penguin viewing in the evening for $20; tours from Invercargill to Dunedin leave Thurs ($85 plus accommodation of your choice; or an overnight package deal including supper, B&B and yellow-eyed penguin viewing for $295). During the rest of the year tours run on demand and during school termtime (check dates with visitor centres) the bus runs a shuttle service in both directions between Balclutha and Dunedin on Fri & Sun ($15).

Backpackers, 17 Rata St (☎03/412 8602, fax 412 8623, *nugview@catlins.co.nz*; dorm ①, room ②), with one 4-bed dorm and one double, plus mountain bikes, surf and body boards, sea kayaks and wetsuits for rent; and an extremely well-appointed hillside **motel**, *Nugget View & Kaka Point Motels* (☎03/412 8602, fax 412 8623, *nugview@catlins.co.nz*; ④–⑤), whose spacious units all have ocean views and decking. The motel also runs **boat trips** around Nugget Point (weather permitting) and fishing trips. The beach's golden sands are patrolled by lifeguards in summer, so it's a good spot for swimming as well as surfing. Just behind the township a fine scenic reserve of native forest is accessible on an easy loop track (2.5km; 30min; signposted from the top of Marine Terrace).

Nine kilometres further down the coast, accessed by road and a short track, is **Nugget Point**, a steep-sided, windswept promontory rising 133m above the sea. Just off-shore lie jagged stacks of rock (the nuggets), whose layers have been tilted over time. A lighthouse dating from 1870 still operates here and from the high-level track beside it you can see southern fur seals, elephant seals (on the only mainland breeding site in the world, Oct–March), penguins and a variety of seabirds, including gannets, spoonbills and three species of shag. Around the corner a track leads to a hide overlooking the sandy beach, **Roaring Bay**, from where you can watch yellow-eyed penguins (*hoiho*; see box on p.661) as they leave their nests at sunrise and descend the steep grassy cliffs to the sea or as they return two hours before dark. Their progress is slow, so you need plenty of patience, and binoculars are handy. To reach the next bay south, **Cannibal Bay**, you hit the road again, backtracking from Nugget Point a few kilometres to the turn-off to inland Otekura, before zipping back to the coast (about 20km in all). Rare New Zealand sea lions (see box on p.672) haul out onto the long crescent of sand – it's worth walking along the beach for a closer look (from a distance they look like logs) but keep at least five metres away from them and back off quickly if they rear up and roar.

As you approach the farming town of **OWAKA**, you'll see totara growing in abundance. On the main street is the tiny **Catlins Museum** (Dec–Feb daily 1–4pm; March–Nov Sun 1.30–4.30pm or by arrangement ☎03/415 8490; $1), focusing on local pioneer history, early settlement, sawmills, dairy factories and shipwrecks. Well-run **horse treks** in the unspoilt tussock hills are given by Valley View Horse Treks (☎03/415 8239, *lattajf@es.co.nz*; minimum of 2 people; 2hr, $85). The **Catlins visitor centre**, located in the diner on Main Road (daily 9am–5pm; ☎03/415 8371) has plenty of leaflets and tide tables to help you plan for a couple of the sights only accessible at low tide, and there's also an unmanned **DOC Field Centre** at 20 Ryley St (pick up the key from the visitor centre), with good displays of Catlins history, marine habitats, flora and fauna. The *Catlins Diner* (daily 9am–7pm) serves basic take away and eat-in food. Places to **stay** are limited to the functional *Blowhole Backpackers*, on Main Road (☎03/415 8830; dorm ①, room ③); the fresh and comfortable *Catlins Retreat Guesthouse*, 27 Main Rd (☎03/415 8830; ④); the pleasant *Catlins Area Motel*, corner Clark and Ryley streets (☎ & fax 03/415 8821, *catlinsareamotel@hotmail.com*; ⑤); and *Owaka Lodge Motel*, 12 Ryley St (☎03/415 8728; ③), which has four fully self-contained modern units. Tucked away in a peaceful spot at the coast five kilometres from Owaka is the well-kept *Surat Bay Lodge*, Surat Bay Road, Newhaven (☎ & fax 03/415 8099, *warren@voyager.co.nz*; dorm ①, rooms ③), overlooking the Catlins Estuary, with free pick-up from Owaka and kayaks for rent.

Owaka to Papatowai

This section contains an impressive **blowhole** and two sets of striking **waterfalls**, close to one another. **Jack's Blowhole** (closed Sept & Oct due to lambing), signposted 6km from Owaka, was created when the roof of a subterranean cave fell in and is pretty spectacular at high tide. It lies about 13km from the main road and you have to walk the last two kilometres along a track (30min). The renowned three-tiered **Purakaunui Falls**

THE CATLINS TOP TRACK

The longest and most varied walk in the region is **Catlins Top Track** (26km; 9–10hr $10; 2 days $25), which delivers the best views, true tranquillity, fascinating geology and a great variety of flora and fauna. It begins and ends at Papatowai, in the heart of the Catlins, crossing sweeping beaches and privately owned bush and farmland. You need to be moderately fit and most people walk it in two days rather than rushing.

The first day takes about six hours, starting with a walk along one of the finest open beaches in the Catlins, then following an old coach road and climbing to weathered sandstone cliffs and the night's accommodation beyond. The second day takes half the time and is very different: you pass through bush containing ancient trees and emerge at the walk's highest point (just over 300m) to spectacular views before following a former railway line to the McLennan River, and then either return by kayak (if arranged ahead) or continue on foot.

Numbers are limited to six overnight walkers, who stay in a converted 1960s trolley bus high up on a spectacular viewpoint, which has one double bed and four single bunks, electric lighting, a gas camping stove with cutlery and dishes, a wood-burning stove for heat in winter, and its own water supply. There's even a separate loo with a view. You need your own food, drinking water and sleeping bag, but the organizers, Catlins Wildlife Trackers (☎0800/228 5467, *catlinw@es.co.nz*) deliver your pack to the bus for $20 per group. All walkers are given an excellent booklet that details each section of the walk accompanied by a map. Catlins Wildlife Trackers can help with accommodation or take your pick from a range at Papatowai (see above); they also provide a pick-up service from Balclutha (Mon, Wed & Sat at 10am).

lie in a scenic reserve of silver beech and podocarp, signposted off the main road 17km from Owaka. There's a picnic area here and an easy track (10min) through the forest to a viewing platform. Just before the falls, *Greenwood Farmstay* (☎ & fax 03/415 8259; ⑤), a beautifully kept house on a sheep, cattle and deer farm offers accommodation and dinner on request. Two kilometres south of the Purakaunui turn-off, are the exquisite **Matai Falls**, best viewed late in the morning. The track to the falls (10min) cuts through regenerating podocarp forest, including fuchsia trees.

Across the estuary of the Maclennan River, the small settlement of **PAPATOWAI** offers a general store (Mon–Fri 9am–5pm, Sat 10am–1pm), several forest and beach walks, a craft gallery, and an excellent **eco-tour** with the Catlins Wildlife Trackers (book well ahead, see box on p.669) and the start of the **Catlins Top Track** (2 days; see box above). In a cheerful old bus beside the main road The Lost Gypsy Gallery (hours vary, closed June–Aug; cash only) sells reasonably priced Kiwi crafts such as jewellery, handmade flax paper and decorative tiles, mainly from the southern South Island. There are also a few good **places to stay**: *Hill Top Backpackers* (☎03/415 8028; ①), on a farm off the Tahakopa Road, just before the bridge near Papatowai is small and well kept, with astounding sea views; in town, *Papatowai Motels* (☎ & fax 03/415 8147; ④), next to the general store has three newish units with fully equipped kitchens; the modern self-contained *Kereru Cottage* (book through Catlins Wildlife Trackers (☎ & fax 03/415 8613, *catlinw@es.co.nz*; ⑥ for 2, $20 each extra person) can accommodate up to seven people, offers great ocean and estuary views and a queen-sized en-suite bedroom, plus bunks and a sofabed; the same people offer a homestay (⑤, dinner $20 each) with double and twin rooms; and at the beach, there's a self-contained cottage (☎03/415 8259; ④) which sleeps four.

Papatowai to Waipapa Point

From Papatowai the road seal runs out and stays that way for a further 20km or so to Waikawa, the road narrow and winding in places.

Just south of Papatowai is **Tautuku Bay**, a magnificent crescent beach of pale sand backed by extensive forest, with a great view point, Florence Hill Lookout, on the main road, offering a complete panorama of the bay, forest and coastline. The grandest and most accessible of about fifteen caves along this part of the coast are the **Cathedral Caves** ($2 per person or $5 per car), signposted 36km south of Owaka. Two connecting caverns with massively high walls have been created by furious sea action against the cliffs. They can only be entered one hour before or after low tide; times are published by the DOC at Owaka and are also posted at the turn-off from the highway. There's a picnic area and a pleasant, easy forty-minute walk to the caves. A kilometre or so further along the main road is the turn-off (along Rewcastle Road) to the spectacular **McLean Falls**, at the end of a 30-minute forest walk. At the fishing village of **WAIKAWA**, 40km from Papatowai, an old church houses a dolphin and penguin information centre and a coffee shop (Oct–April daily 9am–7pm). In summer and autumn (Nov–April), the world's rarest dolphins **Hector's dolphins** come close to the shore at nearby **POR-**

THE NEW ZEALAND SEA LION AND HECTOR'S DOLPHIN

Two extremely rare species – the **New Zealand or Hooker's sea lion** (*Phocarctos hookeri*) and **Hector's dolphin** (*Cephalarhynchus hectori*) – are found only in New Zealand waters. The former mostly live at the subantarctic Auckland Islands, 460km south of the South Island, but a small amount of breeding also occurs at the Otago Peninsula, the Catlins Coast and Stewart Island. The large, adult males are black to dark brown, have a mane over their shoulders, weigh up to 400kg and reach lengths of over 3m. Adult females are buff to silvery grey and much smaller – less than half the weight and just under 2m. Barracuda, red cod, octopus, skate and, in spring, paddle crabs together make up the diet, and although Hooker's sea lions usually dive less than 200m for four or five minutes, they're capable of achieving depths of up to 500m. Pups are born on the beach, then moved by the mother at about six weeks to grassy swards, shrubland or forest, and suckled for up to a year.

Sea lions prefer to haul out on sandy beaches and in summer spend much of the day flicking sand over themselves to keep cool. Unlike seals they don't fear people. If you encounter one on land, give it a wide berth of at least five metres (30m during breeding, Dec–Feb) and if it rears up and roars, back off quickly – they can move surprisingly swiftly. When swimming or diving near haul-out sites, be aware that the sea lions can be boisterous and don't antagonize or attempt to feed them.

The **Hector's dolphin**, with its distinctive black and white markings, is the smallest dolphin in the world and also one of the rarest (population 3000–4000). It's only found in New Zealand inshore waters – mostly around the coast of the South Island – with eastern concentrations around Banks Peninsula, Te Waewae Bay and Porpoise Bay, plus western communities between Farewell Spit and Haast. In summer they prefer shallow waters within 1km of the shore to catch mullet, arrowsquid, red cod, stargazers and crabs; they seldom venture beyond 8km in winter. Unusually perhaps, female dolphins are slightly larger than the males, growing to 1.2–1.4m and weighing 40–50kg. The main birthing season is from November to mid-February, and calves stay with their mothers for up to two years.

In Porpoise Bay – where the dolphin population is tiny (about twenty residents with occasional visits by others) and, in summer and autumn, regularly enters the surf zone or even comes within 10m of the beach – the following DOC **rules** apply: never approach a dolphin; always enter the water at least 50m away from any dolphin or pod, and always on the Curio Bay (southern) side; never surround, follow or pass through a pod; no boat or kayak should spend more than forty minutes within the 5 knot zone; don't touch a dolphin; don't feed the dolphins. In addition, under the Marine Mammals Protection Regulations of 1992 it is illegal to disturb or harass a marine mammal, or swim with juvenile dolphins or pods containing juvenile dolphins.

POISE BAY to rear their young. This is the only place in the world where dolphins live permanently so close to shore, and there are about twenty permanently resident, with others coming and going near the long arc of golden sands. Koramika Cruises operates sensitive, regular, one-hour **dolphin encounter trips** for small groups from Waikawa Jetty to the sheltered waters of Porpoise Bay (book ahead on ☎ & fax 03/246 8444; $45 per person); on their twilight cruise (2hr 30min, $65) you'll also see some spectacular geology and colonies of seals and yellow-eyed penguins. Since the dolphins are extremely shy and easily upset, swimming is not allowed on any of their trips. Whether on an organized trip or on your own it is important not to pester the dolphins in any way, either from the shore or in the water, as this has a significant impact on their feeding, which in turn affects their already threatened breeding rate (see box opposite). The dolphin information centre has a key to the nearby **Waikawa District Museum** (pick it up from the information centre), whose chief attraction in a higgledy-piggledy exhibition is a display on seafarers and logging. Opposite the information centre is a **place to stay**, *Waikawa Holiday Lodge* (☎03/246 8552; dorm ①, rooms ③), a clean friendly hostel in a renovated cottage with a four-bed dorm, a twin and a double.

CURIO BAY, next door to Porpoise Bay, is home to an international treasure, a fine example of a Jurassic **fossil forest** that's clearly visible at low tide. Over 180 million years ago, when most of New Zealand still lay beneath the sea, this would have been a broad, forested floodplain. Today, the seashore, composed of several layers of forest buried under blankets of volcanic mud and ash, is littered with fossilized tree stumps and fallen logs. **Hector's dolphins** often cavort in the surf here, but beach signs warn you to keep your distance (see box opposite). **Yellow-eyed penguins** can be viewed on the Porpoise Bay side, but again keep your distance (at least 10 metres) and stay hidden; most activity is at sunrise and towards the end of the day. The region's prime **campsite**, the *Curio Bay Camping Ground & Store* (☎03/246 8897; tent sites $4, powered sites $7.50, on-site vans ②), is located here, spread across a peninsula between Curio Bay and Porpoise Bay, with wonderful views on all sides, a store, and sites sheltered by long grass and shrubs; avoid the three-week Christmas and New Year period when the site is inundated. However, just fifteen-minutes' drive northeast of Curio Bay is the best place to stay in the Catlins – *Catlins Farmstay*, Progress Valley Road (☎03/246 8843, fax 246 8844, *catlinsfarmstay@xtra.co.nz*; ③). A comfortable **homestead** on a large, secluded sheep, deer and cattle farm, it has an en-suite queen room, a twin and a double, and also provides home-cooked meals ($30 per head for a three-course dinner). Two kilometres away, the farm also owns a four-bed **backpacker cabin** (①), hidden away in the bush and equipped with a pot-bellied stove and cooker, but no electricity. You need your own sleeping bag.

From Curio Bay your best bet is to press on along the unsealed road towards Otara, past the turn-off to **Slope Point**, the southernmost point in the South Island (accessed several kilometres off the main road and through private land) and aim instead for **Waipapa Point**, 22km beyond Curio Bay. In 1881 this was the site of New Zealand's worst civilian shipwreck (three years before the erection of a lighthouse) when 131 lives were lost on *SS Tararua*, nowadays it's the haunt of **fur seals and sea lions** that bask on the golden beach and rocky platform. Back on the main road, once past the windswept trees of Fortrose, it's a clear run of 60km along a bland inland stretch of SH92 to Invercargill.

Gore

Seventy-one kilometres west of Balclutha on SH1 is **GORE**, a pleasant enough transit point at the intersection of routes from Dunedin to Te Anau and Invercargill. Dominated by the Hokonui Hills, Gore spans the Mataura River ("reddish swirling water"), which is renowned for its plentiful brown trout. Apart from breaking your journey for a night or grabbing a bite to eat, there's little reason to linger unless you're heavily into fishing or country music. This is the **brown trout** capital of the world (celebrated by an enormous fish statue in the town centre), and New Zealand's centre of **country music**. For eight days during late May and early June, this normally quiet rural town is the scene of the **Gold Guitar Awards**, during which hundreds of would-be Country stars and a few established performers congregate to celebrate their art.

One attraction in town worth a brief visit is a combined museum and visitor centre, the **Hokonui Heritage Centre**, on the corner of Norfolk Street and Hokonui Drive (Mon–Fri 9am–5pm, Sat & Sun 1–4pm), where the **Historic Museum** (same times as visitor centre; donation requested) concentrates on local history through the usual kinds of memorabilia. More entertaining, however, is the **Hokonui Moonshine Museum** (Mon–Fri 9am–4.30pm, Sat & Sun 1–3.30pm; $5), detailing decades of illicit whisky distillation deep in the local bush-covered hills, which began in 1836 and reached a peak during Prohibition at the turn of the century. Among notable distillers were the Scottish McRae family, who settled in this area during the 1870s. Despite the best efforts of police and customs, the only people caught in the act were the Kirk brothers, whose cow shed and stills are on display. If you're here during the **fishing** season (Oct–April), and want to pit your wits against a wily brown trout you'll need a licence from the visitor centre (around $25 for a week). Tackle can be rented from B&B Sports, 65 Main St. Seventeen kilometres northwest of Gore on SH94 lies the Old Mandeville Airfield, home of **vintage aircraft** – a Tiger Moth, Fox Moth, Dominie and Dragonfly – which still take to the air in 20-minute **joyrides** including a few mind-blowing acrobatics, at probably the best prices in New Zealand (Croydon Air Services ☎03/208 9755, *croydon.aircraft@es.co.nz*; $45–70 depending on number of passengers). Twelve-minute taster flights minus the acrobatics are also available. You're welcome to have a look around the hangar, where renovation is constantly in progress on all sorts of aircraft, and there's a restaurant/bar here, too (see below). The eighth weekend of every year sees the **Mandeville Fly-in**, a two-day celebration of vintage and modern aircraft, classic cars, joyrides and so on (for more details contact the Gore visitor centre).

Practicalities

Gore is served by the Southerner **train** service between Dunedin and Invercargill and lies on the major **bus** route between the two cities. Buses drop off at the **visitor centre** on Hokonui Drive (Mon–Fri 9am–5pm, Sat & Sun 1–4pm; ☎ & fax 03/208 9908, *goreinfo@esi.co.nz*), opposite the giant trout, where you can book accommodation and transport and pick up information on the town and surrounding area.

ACCOMMODATION

Croydon Lodge Motor Inn, cnr SH94 & Waimea St (☎03/208 9029, fax 208 9252, *thelodge @esi.co.nz*). A modern hotel-cum-motel with two bars and restaurants, set in extensive grounds, including a golf course. ⑤–⑥.

Dellmount, Woolwich Street, East Gore (☎ & fax 03/208 1771). A super-friendly B&B-cum-farmstay on a small Arabian horse stud 2km from Gore town centre on the banks of the Mataura River. Dinner on request $20. ④.

Gore Motor Camp, 35 Broughton St (☎ & fax 03/208 4919). Well-run and fairly central campsite with tent sites for $9, powered sites $9, and cabins. ②.

Old Fire Station Backpackers, 19 Hokonui Drive (☎ & fax 03/208 1925, *siandvic@esi.co.nz*). Small clean hostel with dorms, doubles and twins. Dorms ①, rooms ③.

Riverlea Motel, 46–48 Hokonui Drive (☎ & fax 03/208 3130, *riverlea.shaw.com.nz*). About $15 more expensive than the town's other motels, but worth it for the well-equipped units and breakfast on request. ⑤.

EATING

Café 1901, cnr Main St & Ashton St. A fairly upmarket licensed café and wine bar, open daily for reasonably priced lunches and dinners. Pricey wine list.

Croydon Lodge Hotel, cnr SH94 & Waimea St. There are two licensed restaurants in this hotel on the outskirts of town, serving moderately priced lunchtime grills, à la carte dinners and a popular Sunday-night smorgasbord.

Da Vinci's, Medway St, next door to Howl at the Moon. Cheap and cheerful café for big portions to eat in or take away. Mon 4.30–8.30pm, Tues–Fri 11.30am–2pm & 4–11.30pm, Sat 11.30am–11.30pm, Sun 11.30am–10pm; closed Wed.

Howl at the Moon, 2 Main St. Airy all-day café/bar with a subdued cowboy feel, serving a good range of snacks and bigger meals for under $20. The bar hots up Thurs–Sat nights. Licensed.

The Moth, Old Mandeville Airfield, 17km northwest of Gore on SH94 (☎03/208 9662). Good-quality food and coffee at reasonable prices in a sumptuous, airy 1920s-style restaurant and bar kitted out with nostalgic aircraft mementos, open all day from 11am. Licensed. Closed Mon.

Table Talk, 70 Main St. Friendly café, offering a broad range of coffees, teas, big muffins and sumptuous cakes. Closed Sun.

Invercargill and around

For most visitors, the southern city of **INVERCARGILL** is little more than a transit point for some of New Zealand's most remote regions. Southland's thriving economic and cultural centre, with a population of around 50,000, it was settled in the mid-1850s, and has, like Dunedin, a predominantly Scottish character. Here the legacy is evident in streets named after Highland rivers, and a few fine old stone buildings in the city centre, ornately carved from white Oamaru stone transported from the east coast, beyond Dunedin.

Regularly lashed by harsh winds and rain yet occasionally blessed with bright days, Invercargill sprawls over an exposed, broad expanse of flat land at the head of an estuary, the monotony compounded by a low skyline, but much relieved by the city's huge parks and friendly people. Jutting out into the Foveaux Strait beyond, and partially enclosing the estuary, is a small peninsula, the departure point for ferries to Stewart Island and worth a half-day visit for a handful of sights and a couple of short coastal walks. At its tip sits the busy yet run-down island port of **Bluff**, linked to the city by a southbound finger of SH1. Across the choppy Foveaux Strait is the island retreat of **Stewart Island** (see p.682), twenty minutes away by plane and one hour by ferry.

Arrival, information and city transport

Invercargill's **airport** is 2.5km northeast from the city centre and receives domestic flights from New Zealand's main cities as well as Stewart Island. Spitfire Shuttles ($5.50) and taxis ($7–8) provide transport into town. The Southerner train service from Christchurch arrives every evening at the centrally located **train station** in Leven Street, on the corner of Esk Street. Arriving by **bus**, InterCity will drop you at the train station and most of the shuttles (Atomic, Walker Motors and Catch a Bus) stop at the visitor centre and train station, while Knightrider shuttles from Christchurch pull up at their depot on Tay Street. The city is laid out in a grid system of wide streets that is easy to negotiate by **car**. The main highways entering the city, SH1 from the east (Tay Street) and SH6 from the north (Dee Street), meet at right angles in the city centre. See "Listings", p.680, for locations of car parks.

The city's excellent **visitor centre** is in the foyer of the Southland Museum and Art Gallery, Victoria Avenue (Mon–Fri 9am–5pm, Sat & Sun 10am–5pm; ☎03/214 6243 or 214 9133, fax 218 4415, *www.invercargill.org.nz*, *tourismandtravel.invercargill*

@thenet.net.nz), and stocks free street maps and leaflets on Invercargill and Southland in general, plus Stewart Island and Fiordland. It is also a booking agency for travel, accommodation, activities and attractions all over the country. The **DOC office**, in the State Insurance Building on Don Street, near the junction with Dee Street (Mon–Fri 9am–4.30pm; ☎03/214 4589), is the best place to go for information on walks and wildlife in the Catlins, Stewart Island and Fiordland. For local events listings, check out *The Southland Times*. For **Internet access** try Gordon Data Services, 124 Dee St (Mon–Fri 10am–5.30pm, Sat 10am–noon).

There are ten **city bus routes**, most of them circular (Mon–Fri 7.10am–5.45pm, Sat 9.15am–1.45pm or earlier; timetables available from the visitor centre; information ☎03/218 7108). One-way fares to the inner suburbs cost 90¢; to the outer suburbs $1.20.

Accommodation

Accommodation prices this far south are very reasonable and there's a good choice in the centre close to the transport links, mostly on or near Tay Street. Motels are plentiful and good quality, starting at around $65. Bluff also has a couple of places to stay if you want to avoid Invercargill altogether on your way to or from Stewart Island.

Admiral Court Motel, 327 Tay St (☎ & fax 03/217 1117). Ten spotless, fully self-contained units with extras including breakfast delivered to your door and transport to and from the airport, train and bus stations. ⑤.

Awamoa Cottage B&B, 110 Leet St (☎ & fax 03/214 3164, *mgmiller@southnet.co.nz*). Extremely central B&B/homestay offering double rooms that share a guest bathroom. ⑤.

Balmoral Lodge, 265 Tay St (☎03/217 6109, fax 217 5755, *balmorallodge@xtra.co.nz*). Just outside the centre, this upmarket motel has 27 luxurious units with queen-sized beds. Breakfast available. ④–⑤.

Birchwood Manor, 189 Tay St (☎03/218 8881, fax 218 8880, *birch@birchwood.co.nz*). A well-run new complex with 35 spacious units just beyond the city centre. Spa baths; supermarket opposite; courtesy vehicle to and from public transport. ⑤–⑥.

Coachman's Inn, 705 Tay St, cnr Rockdale Rd (☎03/217 6046, fax 217 6045, *twilkes@southnet.co.nz*). Pleasant campsite beside a motel about 3km from the central city, with tent sites ($7.50), powered sites($7.50), and cabins & units. ②–③.

Gala Lodge, 177 Gala St (☎03/218 8884, fax 218 9148, *charlie.ireland@xtra.co.nz*). A welcoming, large and central homestay overlooking Queens Park, with extensive gardens and a double and a twin room sharing a bathroom; courtesy car. ④.

Gerrards, cnr Esk St & Leven St (☎03/218 3406, fax 218 3003). Nostalgic hotel right in the heart of the city, offering well-appointed budget rooms, B&B and suites; also a pleasant bar and licensed restaurant. B&B ⑤, rooms only ③–④.

Heritage Court Motel, 44 Thomson St (☎03/214 7911, *heritagemotels@clear.net.nz*). The most reasonably priced motel just outside the centre in a quiet sunny spot near Queens Park and the visitor centre. ④–⑤.

Lorneville Lodge, RD6, 8km east from Invercargill (☎03/235 8031, *lornepark@xtra.co.nz*). An attractive combined campsite and B&B on a 7-hectare farm, offering tent and powered sites ($8.50) and vans, cabins, flats and units (②–④). The B&B offers two doubles and a twin, sharing a guest bathroom. ⑤.

Montecillo Motel and B&B, 240 Spey St (☎03/218 2503, fax 218 2506). Central accommodation with good-value motel units and B&B in the airy en-suite rooms of a 100-year-old hotel. Motel ⑤, B&B ⑤.

The Oak Door, 22 Taiepa Rd, Otatara (☎ & fax 03/213 0633, *blstuart@xtra.co.nz*). A modern, airy B&B in a tranquil bush setting, three minutes' drive west of the centre, close to Oreti Beach. ⑤.

Riverside Guesthouse, 70 Filleul St (☎03/218 9207, *theriverside@xtra.co.nz*). Small hostel in a quiet setting 1.5km from the centre, with river views from the pretty garden. There are a 4-bed dorm, a single, a double with its own bathroom, and a simple cabin for two in the garden; free river kayaks. Dorm ①, cabin ②, room ②.

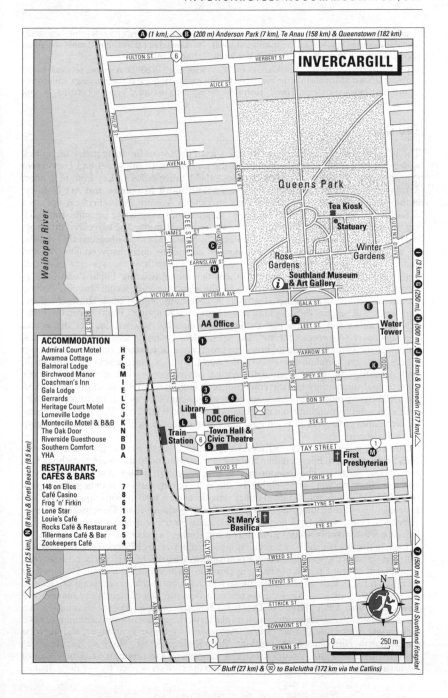

Ⓐ *(1 km)*, △Ⓑ *(200 m) Anderson Park (7 km), Te Anau (158 km) & Queenstown (182 km)*

INVERCARGILL

FULTON ST

HERBERT ST

ALICE ST

AVENAL ST

PHILIP ST

Waihopai River

Queens Park

Tea Kiosk

Statuary

DEE STREET

TIIAMES ST

LIFFEY ST

EARNSLAW ST

THOMSON ST

Ⓒ

Ⓓ

Winter Gardens

Rose Gardens

ⓘ Southland Museum & Art Gallery

QUEENS DRIVE

VICTORIA AVE

VICTORIA AVE

GALA ST

Ⓘ *(3 km)*

Ⓖ *(250 m)*

Ⓗ *(500 m)*

AA Office

LEET ST

Ⓕ

Ⓔ

Water Tower

BOND ST

Ⓛ *(8 km) & Dunedin (217 km)* ▷

YARROW ST

❶

❷

KELVIN ST

DEVERON ST

SPEY ST

JED ST

DOON ST

Ⓚ

LEVEN ST

❸

❺

❹

DON ST

Library

DOC Office

ESK ST

Ⓛ

Train Station

Town Hall & Civic Theatre

❻

TAY STREET

Ⓜ

① First Presbyterian

WOOD ST

FORTH ST

TYNE ST

Ⓩ *(500 m) & Ⓞ (1 km) Southland Hospital*

St Mary's Basilica

EYE ST

BOND ST

JERSEY ST

TODEL ST

ITH ST

CLYDE STREET

TWEED ST

CONON ST

JED ST

DOON ST

TEVIOT ST

ETTRICK ST

ANNAN ST

BOWMONT ST

CRINAN ST

①

N

0   250 m

Airport (2.5 km), ◁ Ⓝ *(8 km) & Oreti Beach (9.5 km)*

ACCOMMODATION
Admiral Court Motel	H
Awamoa Cottage	F
Balmoral Lodge	G
Birchwood Manor	M
Coachman's Inn	I
Gala Lodge	E
Gerrards	L
Heritage Court Motel	C
Lorneville Lodge	J
Montecillo Motel & B&B	K
The Oak Door	N
Riverside Guesthouse	B
Southern Comfort	D
YHA	A

RESTAURANTS, CAFÉS & BARS
148 on Elles	7
Café Casino	8
Frog 'n' Firkin	1
Lone Star	2
Louie's Café	2
Rocks Café & Restaurant	3
Tillermans Café & Bar	5
Zookeepers Café	4

▽ *Bluff (27 km) &* ⑨² *to Balclutha (172 km via the Catlins)*

Southern Comfort, 30 Thomson St (☎03/218 3838). The best of the city's hostels is this beautifully kept Art Nouveau villa set among manicured lawns. Pleasant, clean dorms and double rooms, an excellent kitchen, large dining room and free bikes. Dorms ①, rooms ②.

YHA, 122 North Rd, cnr Bullar St, Waikiwi (☎03/215 9344, fax 215 9382). A simple yet clean hostel in a quiet suburb 3.5km north of the centre, on the bus route (Mon–Fri & Sat morning), with dorms (2- to 8-bed), twins, doubles and family rooms. It's occasionally occupied by school groups, so book ahead. Dorms ①, rooms ②.

The City

The best place for an overview of the city is from the top of the forty-metre-high brick **water tower** (1889), centrally located at the junction of Doon Street and Leet Street (Sun & public holidays 1.30–4.30pm; outside these times collect a key from next door; $1). Invercargill's chief attraction is the large **Southland Museum and Art Gallery**, at the southern entrance to Queens Park on Victoria Avenue (Mon–Fri 9am–5pm, Sat & Sun 10am–5pm; $2 donation requested). Capped with a big white pyramid, the building houses a well laid out collection, over two storeys. Upstairs, the extensive and imaginative "Beyond the Roaring Forties" focuses on New Zealand's **subantarctic islands**, the tiny windswept clusters lying thousands of kilometres apart between New Zealand and the Antarctic. These are the only obstacles in the path of the westerly gales that rage through these latitudes, earning them the names Roaring Forties and Furious Fifties. In a region mostly made up of ocean, the islands provide a vital breeding ground for marine wildlife, including albatross. A 25-minute audio-visual show (Mon–Fri 11.30am & 3.30pm, Sat & Sun 11am, noon, 2pm, 3pm & 4pm; $2) introduces the history, flora, fauna and marine life of this extraordinarily exposed part of the world. Displays cover shipwrecks through the ages, wildlife, climate and so on. Downstairs, there's coverage of a successful breeding programme of **tuatara**, reptilian relics from the dinosaur age found nowhere else in the world. You can observe several of the small, well-camouflaged tuatara in simulated natural environments, but you'll need to peer hard to spot them (they usually come out of hiding on sunny days in the early afternoon). The remainder of the museum covers Southland's history, both human and natural, with exhibits ranging from moa bones to Maori artefacts and Victoriana. The simple **art gallery** displays international and national works, with exhibitions changing every few weeks.

The huge public gardens of **Queens Park** stretch north behind the museum from Gala Street and have been a public reserve since 1869. Today there are showhouses, a formal rose garden, a rhododendron dell, a walk-through aviary, a small animal park and a statuary, as well as an eighteen-hole golf course, various sports grounds and **Splash Palace** – a multi-million-dollar aquatic centre with a 50m sports pool and hydroslide (see p.681 for details). The park's main entrance is on Queens Drive; other entrances (with car parks) are located off Gala Street and Victoria Avenue, while there's pedestrian-only access from Kelvin and Herbert streets.

Back in the city centre, Tay Street has some distinctive **architecture**. At the junction with Jed Street is the so-called **First Presbyterian Church** of 1915 (in fact the second, built after the First Church of Otago, in Dunedin), which is kept locked. Designed by architect John T. Mair, in Romanesque style, it has impressive ornamental brickwork, fashioned into a mosaic. Near the corner with Deveron Street stands the magnificent **Town Hall and Civic Theatre**. The Town Hall was completed in 1906 and is a fine example of neo-Renaissance style with its plasterwork, pediments and ornamental parapets carved from white Oamaru stone. Two streets south, on Tyne Street and near the junction with Nith Street, the striking Roman Catholic **St Mary's Basilica** was designed by F.W. Petre, its brick exterior concealing a sumptuous interior lining of Oamaru stone, unfortunately only visible when the church is open for services. Its elegant copper dome can be spotted for miles around, but the best vantage point is from the gardens flanking the Otepuni Stream on the other side of the road.

Anderson Park and Oreti Beach

On the outskirts of Invercargill, 7km north of the city centre are the beautifully preserved grounds and stately home of **Anderson Park**. Donated to the city in 1951, the house contains an atmospheric **gallery** (daily 1.30–5pm; by donation except during special exhibitions) set amid extensive **grounds**, also open to the public (free). The Georgian-style mansion was built in 1925 as the family home of a local businessman. Designed by Christchurch architect Cecil Wood, it was constructed from reinforced concrete and set against a backdrop of forest. The delightful gallery displays a permanent collection of traditional and contemporary New Zealand art. During the month of October, a spring exhibition of recent Kiwi art replaces the permanent collection, and there are recitals each Sunday, when classical music drifts around the gardens. Behind the gallery, **The Maori House**, also built in the early 1920s, was used for dances, its doorway and porch decorated with carvings by Tene Waitere, a renowned Rotorua carver. Anderson Park is a three-kilometre drive along McIvor Road, via North Road/SH6, or during daylight hours through Donovan Park, off Bainfield Road. There is no bus service out to here; a taxi will cost you about $15 one way.

Oreti Beach, 9.5km west of the city centre, is a beautiful broad expanse of fine sand, sweeping 30km right around to the seaside resort of Riverton to the west (see p.840), and giving great views of Stewart Island and Bluff. In summer, it's popular for swimming (surf patrols operate), yachting and water-skiing, but there are sometimes shark alerts, and windy days cause violent sandstorms. Use the entrance off Dunns Road (the others are pretty rough going); there's no bus service to the beach.

Eating, drinking and entertainment

The culinary revolution well under way elsewhere in New Zealand has recently reached Invercargill, gradually gathering momentum and giving it several cosmopolitan cafés. Most of the eating places are concentrated on Dee Street, with a few on Tay Street. A strength is the local **seafood**, including excellent blue cod and Bluff oysters (in season, April–Nov). Another local delicacy is **muttonbird**, though the oily and rather fishy flavour is something of an acquired taste. Serious **drinking** doesn't generally start until Thursday night and there are three good **dance venues**.

148 on Elles, 148 Elles Rd (☎03/216 1000). An elegant and upmarket dinner restaurant, serving large portions of local seafood, steak, venison and ostrich in a restored 1912 building. Main courses will set you back $20–30. Closed Sun; licensed.

Café Casino, 200 Elles Rd, beside the *Strathern Inn*. Ludicrously inexpensive meals of huge portions at this intimate straightforward café/bar beside the casino, serving breakfast for $1, steak for $4 and roast lunch for $2. A reasonably priced à la carte restaurant is attached. Both Mon–Sat 8am–midnight, Sun noon–8pm; licensed.

Frog 'n' Firkin Café & Bar, Dee St, next door to the cinema. Good, economical pub food for lunch and dinner. A popular dance spot Thurs–Sat (with DJ and sometimes a live band beforehand on Thurs night); till 3am at weekends.

Lone Star, cnr Leet St & Dee St. Tex-Mex dinner venue in a big old building with a bar at one end and café at the other. One of *the* dance spots in town, with a DJ on Thurs–Sat nights.

Louie's Café & Tapas Bar, 142 Dee St (☎03/214 2913). A dinner café and popular bar run by the same owner as *Tillermans* (see overleaf), serving well-priced good-quality food, from pasta to Baba Louie's Beef. Closed Mon; licensed.

Rocks Café & Restaurant, Courtville Place, 101 Dee St (☎03/218 7597). A small and trendy, award-winning café-cum-wine bar where voices and background music reverberate off the brick walls. Food ranges from Pacific Rim to pasta and vegetarian, for economical lunches and dinners at $18.50–25 a main course. Licensed.

Tillermans Café & Bar (or **The Café**), 16 Don St (☎03/218 9240). This excellent-value local institution offers high-quality cosmopolitan food (lunch for under $10, dinner for under $20). The atmosphere is relaxed, and large vibrant paintings adorn the brick walls. Upstairs is a popular bar with pool tables, a focal point for live music on Sat nights. Closed Mon & Tues evenings, Sat lunch and all day Sun; licensed.

Zookeeper's Café, 50 Tay St. A zany, inexpensive, split-level café and bar easily identified by its ironwork giraffe in the window. From 10am (Sun 11am) till late they serve brunch, bar food, snacks (great seafood chowder) and meals from a wide-ranging menu with generous portions – nothing over $18. Best for brunch and lunch. Licensed.

Entertainment

Local bands play at several of the city's hotels on Friday and Saturday nights (check *The Southland Times* for details) and occasionally at local bars as already outlined. The only **nightclub** is *Saints & Sinners*, 34 Dee St (Thurs–Sat 9.30pm–3am; $3 cover charge).

For details of productions at the Civic Theatre in Tay Street, check *The Southland Times* **arts** page on Tuesday. Details on occasional shows at the Southland Museum can be gleaned from the visitor centre or reception at Invercargill City Council on Esk Street (☎03/218 1959). The four-screen Movieland **cinema** at 29 Dee St (☎03/214 1110) has reduced ticket prices ($7 instead of $10) on Monday and Tuesday and any weekday before 5pm.

Listings

Airlines Air New Zealand (☎03/215 0000 & 0800/737 000); Ansett ☎0800/267 388); Southern Air (for daily scheduled services to Stewart Island; ☎03/218 9129, *sthnair@xtra.co.nz*).

Automobile Association 47 Gala St (☎03/218 9033).

Bike rental Gladstone Cycles, 420 Dee St (☎ & fax 03/218 8822), $15 a day; Wensley's Cycles, cnr Tay St & Nith St (☎03/218 6206), $10 a half day, and bike repairs too.

Buses InterCity (☎03/214 0598) operate daily from the train station to Dunedin, Christchurch, Queenstown & Te Anau. Shuttle bus services include Atomic Shuttles (☎03/218 9000 or 24hr reservation line 216 0714) to Gore, Queenstown and Wanaka, and to Dunedin and Christchurch; Catch-a-Bus (☎03/218 9000) to Dunedin; Walker Motors (☎03/218 3308) to Gore, Balclutha and Dunedin; and Spitfire Shuttle Service (☎03/214 1851) to Te Anau, via the Southern Scenic Route. Campbelltown Passenger Service (☎03/212 7404) run regular buses to Bluff for the ferry to Stewart Island.

Car parks There's plenty of 1hr parking on the streets. Council car parks (24hr) are located in Don St, Deveron St & Esk St.

Car rental The multinational firms have branches in the city and Avis, Budget, Hertz & Thrifty have desks at the airport: Avis, 73 Airport Ave (☎03/218 7019); Budget, 157 Clyde St (☎03/218 7012); Hertz, 92 Airport Ave (☎03/218 2837). Cheaper alternatives include: Crawford Rentals, 166 Clyde St (☎03/218 3870); Inner City Rentals, cnr Clyde St & Tweed St (☎03/214 0457); Rent-a-Dent, Airport Ave (☎03/214 4820); Riverside Rentals, cnr Bay Rd & North Rd (☎03/215 9030); and Waikiwi Rentals, 376 North Rd (☎03/215 7328).

Ferry The Foveaux Express (☎03/212 7660; $74 return) departs Bluff for Stewart Island Sept–April Mon–Sun 9.30am & 5pm; May–Aug Mon–Fri 9.30am & 4pm, Sat 9.30am, Sun 4pm.

Laundry Glengarry Laundry Services, 77 Glengarry Crescent (☎03/217 2347). Open daily.

Library Invercargill Public Library is at 50 Dee St (Mon–Fri 9am–8.30pm, Sat 10am–1pm; ☎03/218 7025).

Medical treatment Southland Hospital, on Kew Rd (☎03/218 1949), has a 24hr accident and emergency department. For illness and minor accidents outside surgery hours, contact the Urgent Doctor Service in Don St (☎03/218 8821; Mon–Fri 5–10pm; Sat, Sun & public holidays 24hr).

Pharmacy Inside the Countdown supermarket (daily Mon–Fri 8.30am–10pm, Sat & Sun 9am–7pm); Ascot Pharmacy, 702 Tay St (☎03/217 7696; Mon–Sat 9am till late).

Police The central police station is at 117 Don St (☎03/214 4039).

Post office The main post office is at 51 Don St, near the junction with Kelvin St (Mon–Fri 8.30am–5pm, Sat 10am–1pm).

Swimming Splash Palace, Elles Rd (☎03/217 3838; Sat 6am–9pm, Sun 8am–8pm) is an impressive aquatic centre in Queens Park, with three pools, a hydroslide, spa and steam room.

Taxis Blue Star (☎03/218 6079); The Taxi Co (☎03/214 4478).

Tours Invercargill Passenger Transport (☎03/218 7108) run a two-hour city tour ($30 per person) taking in the Southland Museum, Queens Park, Anderson Park and a few historic landmarks. They also offer 3hr trips to Bluff ($40). Guided tours to the Catlins are operated by Catlins Natural Wonders (see box on p.669). Scenic flights to Stewart Island can be arranged with South East Air (☎03/214 5522) and Southland Air Charter (☎03/218 6171); see p.687 for more details.

Trains The Southerner departs for Christchurch every morning from the train station in Leven St (☎0800/692 378), returning in the evening.

Bluff

Twenty-seven kilometres south of Invercargill, perching at the tip of a peninsula, is the small run-down fishing town of **BLUFF** and its man-made port. Offering great views across Foveaux Strait, Bluff is the departure point of the **Stewart Island ferry**, and you may choose to avoid Invercargill altogether and stay here in the local B&B or hotel. You won't need more than half a day to get a good look at the place, but without a car this involves a good deal of walking as the town spreads along the shoreline for about 6km.

Bluff is the oldest European town in New Zealand, having been continuously settled since 1824. These days it's still struggling to recover from the 1980s recession, and has an increasingly tired feel about it. The **harbour**, however, flourishes, exporting Southland's meat, timber, aluminium, fish and wool, and importing a variety of goods from overseas. In addition the Foveaux Strait yields a highly sought-after delicacy – the **Bluff oyster**. This deepwater shellfish has a sweet and succulent taste, and is usually dredged from the end of March until November, depending on stocks, then processed in oyster sheds at Bluff before being sent all over the country. Between June and August you can watch them being processed at Johnson's Oyster Factory (daily 8am–5pm; free; bookings ☎03/212 8665) and buy them direct at factory prices. Across the harbour, at Tiwai Point, is the sprawl of a giant **aluminium smelter**, Southland's biggest employer. The smelter (☎03/218 5999; Mon–Fri 10am) is accessible by road from Invercargill, lying 25 kilometres south; phone ahead if you simply must have a free tour.

Bluff's small **Maritime Museum** (Mon–Fri 10am–4.30pm, Sat & Sun 1–5pm; $2), on Foreshore Road as you enter town from Invercargill, has historical displays focusing on whaling, the harbour development, oyster harvesting and shipwrecks. Pride of place is given to a vast triple-expansion steam engine, taken from a steam tug, *Monica*, which spent most of its life working the harbour. Back on the main road, you'll pass the ferry wharf and, three streets further, on the corner with Henderson Street, the kitsch **Paua Shell House** (daily 9am–5pm; free). This is the home of Fred and Myrtle, a couple who, until Myrtle's death in 2000, spent years amassing a collection of shells from all over the world – most noticeably iridescent paua shells gathered from local beaches, which are plastered all over their living-room walls, creating a wall-to-wall shimmer in blue and green.

From here it's another 1.5km to the end of the road, and **Stirling Point**, which feels rather like the end of the earth, with its jokey signpost marking the distance to major international cities. The views are impressive and, on a clear day, you can see as far as

Stewart Island, 35km away. From the car park at the end of the road you can set out on a couple of easy walks: the **Foveaux Walkway** (6.6km; 2hr one way) and, branching off it, the **Glory Track** (3.8km; 1hr return). The first is an exposed walk skirting Bluff Hill's rugged coastline, with some magnificent views, before cutting back across open farmland to the main road at the other end of town, near the old freezing works. The second is a loop track, mixing forest and coastal scenery. Short sections of the Glory Track are very steep, but the surface is sealed.

The turning to another good viewpoint, **Bluff Hill Lookout**, leaves the main road in town at Lee Street, opposite the ferry wharf. From here it's a three-kilometre drive, or a ninety-minute walk, to the car park and viewing platform beyond. From 267m up you get a 360-degree view of Stewart Island and the other, smaller islands in Foveaux Strait, Southland's estuaries and the harbour. The sunsets here are astonishing.

Practicalities

Bluff is a twenty-minute drive down SH1 from central Invercargill. Local **buses** run a regular daily service between the city and Bluff ($10, same-day return $20), to connect with the ferry. For details on sailings to Stewart Island, see opposite.

Good **accommodation** in Bluff is limited to the *Foveaux Hotel*, 40 Gore St (☎03/212 7196; ② breakfast included), which has four en-suite rooms and three sharing bathrooms, plus an in-house bar; and the four en-suite B&B rooms above the *Land's End Wine Bar and Café* at Stirling Point (☎ & fax 03/212 7575; ⑤). The *Land's End*, perched high on the hill, also serves **breakfast**, **lunch**, Devonshire teas and **dinner** daily, with specialities including pan-fried blue cod ($16.50) and oysters. Back in town, takeaway fish and chips can be had from the *Harbour Lights Café* at 158 Gore St.

Stewart Island

New Zealand's third main island is the small, rugged triangle of **STEWART ISLAND**, separated from the mainland by Foveaux Strait and largely ignored by tourists. Its lack of pulling power is understandable: it's fairly expensive to get to; most of the island is uninhabited and covered in dense native bush and coastal podocarp rainforest; the climate is temperate but unpredictable; and mainstream attractions are limited. Apart from some serious wilderness tramping and great sunsets (hence the island's Maori name of *Rakiura*, meaning "Land of the Glowing Skies"), the chief reason to come here is to visit **Ulva Island**, a protected predator-free haven for native New Zealand birds only eight minutes away by water taxi. The next best reason is to go **kiwi spotting** in the wild, either on your own at Mason Bay or on a guided trip that needs to be booked six months ahead in summer. Sea kayaking on the vast flooded valley of **Paterson Inlet** is proving another popular option. In addition, Stewart Island boasts one of New Zealand's Great Walks, **The Rakiura Track** (3 days), not to be confused with the island's mud-ridden North–West Circuit Track (10–12 days), only suited to the most experienced (and masochistic) tramper.

Inhabited by Maori from the thirteenth century and erroneously recorded as a peninsula by Captain Cook in 1770, the island was named after William Stewart, the first officer on a sealing vessel that visited in 1809. The island is characterized by bush-fringed bays, sandy coves, windswept beaches and a rugged interior of tall rimu forest and granite outcrops. The only settlement is tiny **Oban**, its bland buildings huddling around Halfmoon Bay and creeping up the hill towards the airfield, as if cut into the bird-filled bush.

The mainstay of the economy was once rimu milling, with three thousand people living on the island in the boomtime of the early 1930s, but the main industries today are **fishing** (crayfish, blue cod and paua) and **fish farming** (salmon and mussels) in Big

Glory Bay. Bear in mind that there are **no banks or bureaux de change** on Stewart Island, although most businesses take credit cards and visitors with New Zealand bank accounts can use EFTPOS at most businesses; some will also exchange foreign currency.

Island practicalities

The *Foveaux Express*, alternating between a sixty-five-seater and a hundred-seater catamaran **ferry**, leaves regularly from Bluff (☎03/212 7660; $37 one way, $74 return), usually taking one hour to cross the choppy Foveaux Strait (for more details see p.680). It docks at the wharf in Oban, a stone's throw from the town centre. A far easier journey is in the nine-seater Southern Air **plane**, which leaves three times daily from Invercargill Airport (☎03/218 9129; $65 one way, $120 return; student and YHA standby discounts of $45 one way, $80 return, bought on the day if available). Shuttle bus transfers between central Oban and the airfield are included in the price of your ticket. Note that a strict luggage allowance of 10kg per person applies and camping gas canisters are not allowed.

Since it's easy to walk around the inhabited part of the island, you're unlikely to need much **road transport** once you've arrived, although Oban Taxis & Tours (☎03/219 1456) operate a daily shuttle service and have two rental cars ($50 a half day, $70 full day). Alternatively, try Sam Sampson, based at Stewart Island Travel on Main Road in Oban (☎03/219 1269; after hours 219 1406). You can also rent single or double **motor scooters** from Oban Taxis & Tours (from $18/25 an hour, or $60/65 per day). **Mountain bikes** are rented out by Innes Backpackers on Argyle Street (☎03/219 1080; $10 per day including helmets). **Water taxis** operate between Stewart Island and Ulva Island, eight minutes away, departing from Golden Bay, a ten-minute walk from central Oban; both Seaview Tours (☎03/219 1014) and Stewart Island Water Taxi (☎03/219 1394) charge around $20 return per person or $16 per person for two or more. **Charter launches** are available for tailor-made diving, fishing or nature trips (Stewart Island visitor centre – see below – has a list); see box on p.687 for other Stewart Island **tours**.

Accommodation ranges from backpacker hostels and self-contained cabins or cottages to B&Bs, motels and hotels, some of them in Oban (see pp.685–6) and some in neighbouring bays. It's always advisable to book ahead, especially during summer; in general, accommodation here is more **expensive** than on the mainland, partly because sewerage charges are high, but check out reduced off-season prices. Several people on the island **rent** out spare **rooms** in their homes (different to the well-run B&Bs we have listed), but these can be cramped and claustrophobic, becoming especially difficult during prolonged bad weather. If you're staying for a week or more, and travelling as a couple or in a group, then consider renting a self-contained **holiday home** from Stewart Island Holiday Homes (see on p.686). A word of warning to women travellers: repeated reports on the grapevine suggest you should avoid the massage "therapy" advertised at *Andy & Jo's B&B*, and steer clear of *Innes Backpackers*.

Oban and around

It doesn't take long to get to grips with **OBAN**, which is enclosed by hills of dense bush and bisected by Main Road, linking the airfield with the other principal road on the island, the waterfront Elgin Terrace. This, in turn, extends in one direction to Horseshoe Bay and in the other to Leask Bay. The southeastern part of town is bounded by Golden Bay, the jumping-off point for boat trips to Ulva Island and Paterson Inlet. The township consists of little more than a few houses, a hotel with a pub (very much the social centre), the visitor centre, a tiny museum, a couple of stores and a couple of cafés.

Stewart Island's combined **visitor centre** (late Dec to end March Mon–Fri 8am–7pm, Sat & Sun 9am–7pm; rest of the year Mon–Fri 8am–5pm, Sat & Sun 10am–noon; ☎03/219 1218, fax 219 1555, *www.southland.org.nz*, *stewartislandfc @doc.govt.nz*) and **DOC office** (☎03/219 1130) is centrally located on Main Road and has excellent displays on the island's tracks and natural history. Staff are helpful and have free maps of Oban and neighbouring bays, and can advise on and book accommodation, activities, island flora and fauna, tracks and transport; they also sell hut passes for the two major Stewart Island tracks. There's a stock of free videos about Stewart Island, which you can watch at the visitor centre, the best being "Beyond the Mainland" (a general overview, 45min), "The Underworld of Paterson Inlet" (15min) and "The Other Side" (from the Heartland series, 45min). The other main **booking agencies** for activities are Oban Taxis & Tours on Main Road (☎03/219 1456), the Southern Air Depot on Elgin Terrace (☎03/219 1090), Stewart Island Travel on Main Road (☎03/219 1269) and the Adventure Centre in the ferry office on the wharf (☎03/219 1134), who all charge the same as booking direct. The **post office** is in the Southern Air depot, on the waterfront, near the junction with Ayr Street (daily: Oct–March 7.30am–6pm; April–Sept 7.30am–5pm), where stamps are still cancelled by hand. For **Internet access** try *Justcafé* on Main Road (see p.686).

Oban's sights are fairly limited: a compact museum, small craft shop, tiny theatre and a few short walks. The **Rakiura Museum** on Ayr Street (Mon–Sat 10am–noon, Sun noon–2pm; $1) is worth a few minutes, with its adequately displayed artefacts imparting some local history. The small Maori collection boasts a rare necklace of dolphin teeth, while the whaling display has two individual giant teeth from a sperm whale. Continuing less than 10 minutes' walk up the hill along Ayr Street until it becomes Golden Bay Road, you'll find **The Fernery** shop near the summit (☎03/219 1453; Oct–March daily 9am–5pm; winter by arrangement only), a cornucopia of souvenirs and gifts, all inspired by the island and handmade by New Zealand artists and craftspeople. Meanwhile the 20-seater **Gumboot Theatre** on Main Road opposite the hotel (daily shows, times displayed on blackboard outside; $5) plays short one-woman comedies about life on Stewart Island to a minimum of six people, usually in the late afternoon or early evening (with other times as advertised). Doors open ten minutes before the start.

Oban's short **walks** are listed in the $1 DOC pamphlet *Day Walks* and the main ones are also marked on the free street maps of Oban at the visitor centre. One takes you up to a lookout point and another through bird-filled bush. Definitely worthwhile is the stroll up to the hilltop vantage point of **Observation Rock** (15min). From here the panorama laid out below (best seen at sunset) includes Golden Bay and the island's highest point, Mount Anglem, on one side, and Horseshoe Bay on the other, as well as the expanse of Paterson Inlet, broken by the long strip of Ulva Island and the blobs of other islets. To reach the summit, follow Ayr Street and Golden Bay Road to just past The Fernery (see above), from where Observation Rock is signposted up Leonard Street and along a short forest track on the left to the lookout point. Return to town the same way or by entering Traill Park, opposite The Fernery, to follow the Fuchsia walk (see below). Or, instead of returning, you can continue away from town on the Raroa Walk from Traill Park (see below.)

For a taste of some stunning bush, first dominated by fuchsia, then by rimu, follow the signposted **Fuchsia Walk**, which begins at Dundee Street and emerges five minutes later up the hill at Traill Park. In summer the foliage rings with the birdsong of tui, bellbirds and pigeons. From the end of the Fuchsia Walk, you can return via Golden Bay Road or follow the **Raroa Walk** down through fine rimu forest to Watercress Bay (15min). Thule Road and Golden Bay Road lead back to town from the bay (1km; 30min). For details of the **Harrold Bay to Ackers Point Lighthouse** walk, see p.688.

Accommodation

Dave's Place, Horseshoe Bay Rd (☎03/219 1427, *chrisdillon@clear.net.nz*, no advance bookings taken). A small, friendly backpackers in relaxed surroundings 200m from the wharf, with TV, microwave and fridge. Dorms ①, rooms ②.

Ferndale Campsite, Horseshoe Bay Rd (☎03/219 1176). The only official campsite on the island and just 200m north of the wharf. Facilities include $2 coin-operated showers, a covered cooking area with hotplates and a washing machine. Tent sites $8.

The Cape, Ringaringa Beach (☎03/219 1036, *the_cape@xtra.co.nz*). Cheerful beachside B&B or room-only accommodation in a secluded house with magnificent views about a 20min walk from town, with a sunny en-suite double with its own entrance. The young lively owners also offer fishing trips, dinner by arrangement ($25 including wine), lunchboxes and free transfers. Room ④, B&B ⑤.

Deep Bay Cabin, Deep Bay (☎03/219 1219, *ewanjengell@xtra.co.nz*). Snug private self-contained wooden cabin hidden in the bush with four bunks, kitchen and shower. Roughly a 20min walk from

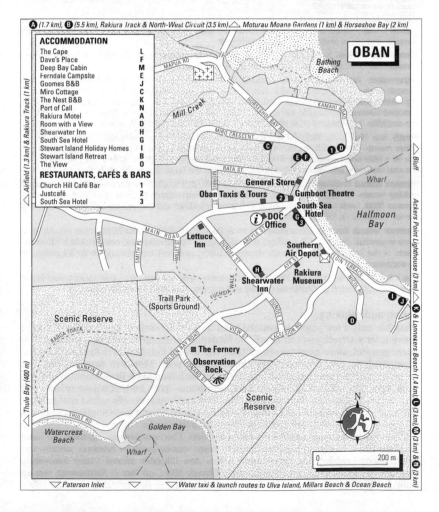

town and a great spot for resting after the longer tracks. There's a pot-bellied stove in winter. ②, $15 per extra person.

Goomes B&B, Elgin Terrace (☎03/219 1057). Five minutes' walk from the *South Sea Hotel*, this bright and comfy B&B offers two en-suite rooms with great sea views; free pick-up. ⑦.

Miro Cottage, 13 Miro Crescent (☎ & fax 03/219 1180, *janlance@xtra.co.nz*). New, airy and sunny self-contained cottage hidden in peaceful bush up a hill 3min walk from town, with a double room and a 4-bed bunkroom; free pick-ups. ⑨, $15 per extra person.

The Nest B&B, Lonnekers Beach (☎03/219 1310, *thenest@es.co.nz*). Two kilometres from the wharf (free pick-ups), this big, pretty house perched on a hill overlooking Halfmoon Bay and Lonnekers Beach has plenty of character. Two double rooms with shared facilities. ⑦.

Port of Call, Jensen Bay (☎ & fax 03/219 1394, *info@portofcall.co.nz*). Relaxing upmarket B&B in a big, secluded, beautifully designed sun-filled contemporary house overlooking the bay, 30min walk from Oban centre. The double/twin en-suite has sea views. Dinner by arrangement ($30 plus wine) and free pick-ups. ⑦.

Rakiura Motel, Horseshoe Bay Rd (☎03/219 1096). Great views over Halfmoon Bay from a hill just outside Oban, 2.5km from the wharf (a 25-minute walk, or $8 taxi ride). Five well-maintained units sleeping four to six people. Courtesy transfers. ⑨.

Room with a View, Kamahi Rd (☎03/219 1589, *soyabean@xtra.co.nz*). Comfortable self-contained en-suite unit on a hill near the wharf, with sea views. Courtesy transfers are available. ④.

Shearwater Inn, cnr Ayr St & Dundee St (☎03/219 1114, *shearwater@stewart-island.co.nz*). Central, large and basic, this hotel is divided into 20 rooms (mostly doubles and some 3-bed) sharing bathrooms, and a backpacker section of 4-bed dorms, twins and doubles. Everyone shares the cramped kitchen and sizeable lounge, but redesigning plans are afoot. A BBQ area and breakfast are available. 3-bed rooms ④, doubles & twins ④; backpacker dorms ①, rooms ②.

South Sea Hotel, cnr Main Rd & Elgin Terrace (☎03/219 1059, *southsea@stewart-island.co.nz*). Clean rooms – some with sea views – above the waterfront pub in a hundred-year-old building. It can be a little noisy, especially in Room 6 right above the bar. Facilities include a TV lounge; there are also nine new, spacious motel studio units behind the hotel. Rooms ⑤, units ⑥.

Stewart Island Holiday Homes, Elgin Terrace (☎03/219 1057). Two modern, fully self-contained holiday homes on a hill overlooking the harbour and surrounded by bush, run by the owners of *Goomes B&B*. Each has four bedrooms with good sea views and two private bathrooms; courtesy car for transfers. ⑥, $25 per extra person.

Stewart Island Retreat, Horseshoe Bay (☎ & fax 03/219 1071, *retreat@southnet.co.nz*). An ideal place to unwind, 6km from Oban wharf (free pick-up), is this spacious and comfortable B&B on the shore of the bay. Large rooms with shared facilities; excellent dinners and packed lunches by arrangement. ⑥.

The View, Nichol Rd (☎03/219 1328). Friendly, warm, spacious and clean, this backpackers is just 500m from the wharf, its double rooms just nudging into this code. Dorm ①, rooms ③.

Eating and drinking

Oban has only a few places to **eat** and even these close early in the evening. If you're cooking for yourself, you can buy basic foodstuffs, fruit and vegetables at the *Ship to Shore* **general store** near the wharf (end Oct to end Feb Mon–Fri 8am–6.30pm, Sat 10am–6.30pm, Sun 10am–4.30pm; rest of the year Mon–Fri 8am–5.30pm, Sat 10am–4pm, Sun 10am–3pm) and *Lettuce Inn* up the hill on Main Road (Mon, Wed & Fri noon–7pm, Tues–Thurs 9am–7pm, Sat & Sun 10am–7pm), both of whose prices compare well with those on the mainland. The *Ship to Shore* also sells salted muttonbirds ($5, an acquired tasted). Fresh fish and crayfish can be bought from Southern Seafoods at Horseshoe Bay (☎03/219 1389), or direct from the locals.

There are only a couple of decent **cafés** in Oban. The cosy *Justcafé*, up from the hotel on Main Road, has good fresh coffee and tasty snacks such as smoked salmon and cream-cheese sandwiches, plus lunch boxes and Internet access (daily 9am–5pm; closed May–Sept). Otherwise the licensed *Church Hill Café Bar & Restaurant*, just up Church Hill from the wharf with fine views of Halfmoon Bay from an airy late 1800s house, serves good-value brunch, lunch and dinner, specializing in local seafood (book for dinner ☎03/219 1323; Oct–April daily from 10am, rest of the year sometimes limited to Thurs–Sat), and runs a courtesy vehicle to get you home at night. The *South Sea Hotel* has a simple **restaurant** offering lunchtime snacks and unpretentious early-evening meals (closes 8pm). Just outside Oban, at Horseshoe Bay, the tiny café adjoining the *Stewart Island Retreat* serves coffee and cake, and with prior arrangement will provide lunchboxes ($10).

Drinking is confined to the two bars at the *South Sea Hotel*, the focus of most social activity in these parts. The local ale, once brewed on the island but now produced in Invercargill, is the powerful and aptly named "Roaring Forties".

Around Oban

North of Halfmoon Bay, twenty-minutes' walk along Horseshoe Bay Road, are the attractive and secluded **Moturau Moana public gardens**, which were donated to the island in 1940. Picnic tables, barbecues and a viewing platform looking out across the bay to Oban are set amid lawns, native plants and dense virgin forest.

One of the more interesting historical sites on the island is an abandoned Norwegian whaling base near **Millars Beach** at Prices Inlet, about 6.5km west of

---

STEWART ISLAND TOURS

Tours of **Ulva Island** and its plant and birdlife with a DOC ranger are arranged through the DOC (Jan & Feb; $27.50 half day; includes transport to the island). Thorfinn Charters (☎03/219 1210) include Ulva Island in their afternoon tour of Paterson Inlet ($50). To visit on your own, take a water taxi (see p.683) or go with Mareno Excursions (☎03/219 1023) who can drop you off after either a half- ($45) or full-day ($65) scenic or fishing trip in Paterson Inlet. Moana Charters (☎03/219 1202) offer a similar half-day scenic boat excursion ($50 per person), which includes stops for fishing and a visit to salmon farms on the way to the island, where you're dropped off and collected later. See p.688 for details of **kayaking** trips.

The next best tour on the island is the twilight **kiwi-spotting trip** which takes you to a remote area to see the Stewart Island brown kiwi (a sub-species of the mainland birds) in the wild. Bravo Adventure Cruises (book 6 months in advance in summer on ☎ & fax 03/219 1144, or email Stewart Island visitor centre *stewartislandfc@doc.govt.nz*; $60) run atmospheric four-hour trips every other night, leaving from the wharf in Halfmoon Bay around dusk. You'll need warm clothing, sturdy footwear and a flashlight. The adventure entails a short boat trip and a brief uphill bushwalk in the dark to a windswept beach, where the kiwi feast on tiny crustaceans. Great care is taken to avoid disturbing these timid birds.

General tours of the island are run by an irrepressible island character, Sam, who drives "Billy the Bus". A naturalist and historian, he humorously imparts his intimate knowledge of local history, flora and fauna and the islanders' way of life on a short tour leaving from Stewart Island Travel on Main Road (book ahead on ☎03/219 1269, fax 219 1355; most days at 11.30am & 2.30pm; 1hr 30min; $16). Also worthwhile are his longer afternoon excursions, which include guided walks (2hr 30min; $25). There are also more prosaic scenic bus tours with Oban Taxis & Tours (book ahead on ☎ & fax 03/219 1456; daily 11am & 1.30pm; 1hr 30min; $16), departing from their office on Main Road, opposite the visitor centre, who also run **sunset tours** (April–Oct, nightly at 7.30pm; 2hr; $20).

Tours to the old whaling base at **Millars Beach**, only accessible by boat, are given by Seabuzz Glass-Bottom Boat & Watertaxi (☎03/219 1282; $30).

Scenic flights can be arranged with Southern Air (☎03/219 1090, *sthnair@xtra.co.nz*), who will drop you off for sightseeing and tramping in inaccessible parts of the island, such as Mason Bay ($130 for two one way). Southland Air Charter in Invercargill (☎03/218 6171) also offer over-flights and operate as air taxis, dropping off trampers and day-trippers.

Oban. The only access is by boat, so you'll need to take the guided tour with Seabuzz Glass-Bottom Boat (see box on Stewart Island Tours, on previous page) or charter a water taxi or launch from Golden Bay to Millars Beach (15min; around $40 return), from where an easy twenty-minute coastal walk heads north from the beachside picnic shelter through native bush to the whaling base. Several eerie relics remain from 1923–33, when a fleet of Antarctic whaling ships was repaired here, and the beach is littered with objects left behind: old drums, cables, giant iron propellers, a boiler out in the water and, at the far end, a wrecked sailing ship deliberately sunk by the whaling company to create a wharf.

A good coastal walk, the **Harrold Bay to Ackers Point Lighthouse** track (1.25km; 20min), starts at the end of Leask Bay Road, 2.5km east of the post office along the waterfront, and gives you the chance to see **little blue penguins** and **muttonbirds** returning to their nests at dusk (Nov–Feb). Near the start of the track, you can follow a brief diversion to Harrold Bay, the site of a simple stone house built in 1835, making it one of the oldest European buildings in New Zealand. The main track continues through coastal forest to a lighthouse and lookout point from where you can watch the penguins arduously climbing to their nests hidden in the bush. You'll need a flashlight to find your way around after dusk, but it's important to keep the beam pointed to the ground to avoid disturbing the birds, which are easily distressed.

Ulva Island and Paterson Inlet

Well worth a visit for its astonishing bird life, pleasant walks, beaches and rich natural vegetation is the open sanctuary of **Ulva Island**, the largest of several islands in **Paterson Inlet**, a flooded valley cutting deep into Stewart Island. **Water taxis** ply out here regularly from the wharf at Golden Bay ($16–20 return) and you should allow a full day (bring a packed lunch) to explore the several gentle tracks around the island; see box on previous page for details of **guided tours**.

Clearly visible from Oban, the long, low island has largely escaped the effects of introduced predators and is full of birdsong. Thriving in its dense vegetation are weka, bellbirds, oystercatchers, kaka, yellow- and red-crowned parakeets, tui, fantails and pigeons, who fearlessly approach visitors out of curiosity. Plant life includes many species of fern and orchid, and the forest floor is covered in mosses and liverworts. Tracks begin from the wharf at Post Office Bay (where there's still a hundred-year-old post office, a remnant from the days when the island was the hub of the community) and there's a pleasant picnic shelter on the beach at Sydney Cove nearby. Note that camping overnight is not allowed.

The best way to explore the sheltered waters of Paterson Inlet without getting wet is on the **Seabuzz Glass-Bottom Boat** (☎03/219 1282; 1hr, daily at 11am depending on weather; $20), which allows underwater viewing. The adventurous will want a more thorough exploration by **sea kayak** or **diving**. Scattered around the inlet's margins are several navigable rivers and four DOC huts where you can stay overnight (arrange in advance with the DOC field centre in Oban). Frequent visitors to these waters are bottle-nosed dolphins and fur seals, while the tidal flats attract wading birds, including herons, oystercatchers, godwits and the New Zealand dotterel. Bear in mind that the waters around Stewart Island can be changeable and May to August brings the most settled weather; only extremely experienced kayakers should venture into these waters unaccompanied. Completely Southern Sea Kayaks (☎03/219 1275) based at Thule Bay rent kayaks ($40 per person per day), and their guided trips cost $40 for a half day, $60 full day. Qualified divers can go out with Stewart Island Seals (☎03/219 1180; $60 plus cost of tanks) for 2 dives.

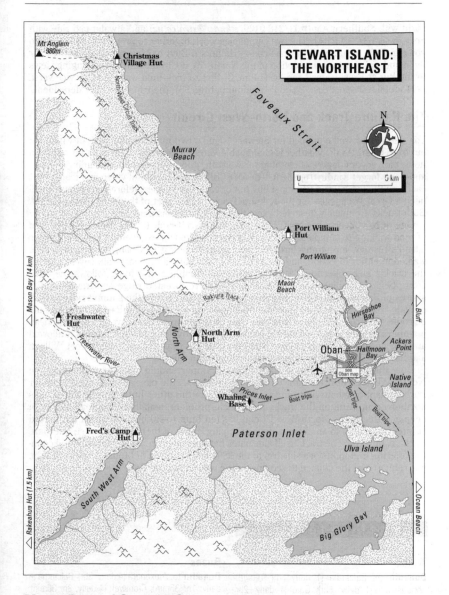

Mt Anglem
980m

Christmas
Village Hut

North West Circuit Track

Murray
Beach

**STEWART ISLAND:
THE NORTHEAST**

Foveaux Strait

N

0   5 km

Port William
Hut

Port William

Mason Bay (14 km)

Freshwater
Hut

Freshwater River

North Arm

Maori
Beach

Rakiura Track

North Arm
Hut

Horseshoe
Bay

Bluff

Ackers
Point

Oban   Halfmoon
Bay

see
Oban map

Native
Island

Whaling
Base

Prices Inlet

Boat trips

Boat trips

Boat trips

Fred's Camp
Hut

Paterson Inlet

Ulva Island

Rakeahua Hut (1.5 km)

South West Arm

Big Glory Bay

Ocean Beach

Mason Bay and Coast-to-Coast

If you want to visit Mason Bay and stay overnight in the trampers' hut to have a chance
of viewing kiwi in the wild, or see both the east and west coasts of Stewart Island without completing either of the major tracks, you can do all this by combining a scenic

flight with Southern Air (☎03/218 9129, *sthnair@xtra.co.nz*) and a water-taxi ride with Seaview (☎03/219 1014). The two companies work together to provide flexible trips so you can fly in or out from the east coast (Halfmoon Bay) to Mason Bay on the west, or fly in and walk an easy flat section of the North–West Circuit with ever-changing views to the hut at Freshwater Landing (14km, 3–4hr) to pick up a water taxi, or vice versa ($115 total transport cost, 2 people minimum, huts $5); the trip is weather dependent.

The Rakiura Track and North–West Circuit

You need to be well equipped for Stewart Island's two major walks, both of which fan out from Oban. As the weather is changeable, often mixing sunshine and rain within an hour, take several layers of clothing for warmth, good waterproofs (including gaiters) and don't forget sandfly repellent. The DOC office has a helpful video and leaflets ($1 each) on the tracks, and you must buy hut or campsite passes before you set out. You'll need a Great Walks pass for the Rakiura Track and for part of the North–West Circuit. Both tracks are usually deserted except for the Christmas period.

One of New Zealand's Great Walks, the **Rakiura Track** (29km, plus a further 7km of road walking to complete the circuit; 3 days) makes an excellent introduction to the island's history, forest and birdlife. Starting and ending in Oban, the circuit can be walked in either direction, and at any time of the year, since boardwalk covers most of the track's boggy sections. Staying within the bushline, the track follows the open coast, before climbing over a three-hundred-metre forested ridge and traversing the shores of Paterson Inlet. The highlight is a lookout tower on the summit ridge, which provides excellent views of Paterson Inlet and beyond to the Tin Range. The two huts en route (30 bunks; $8 per person) are equipped with mattresses, wood stoves for heating only, running water and toilets, but you'll need your own stove. Camping is allowed at three designated areas ($6 per person) along the way – Maori Beach, Port William and Sawdust Bay – and sites have water supply and toilets.

Only the hardiest and most experienced tramper should consider attempting the **North–West Circuit** (130km; 10–12 days; pass $38 – the pass allows a night in either Port William or North Arm, and up to 9 nights in the other huts) around the island's northern arm. Mud on the tracks is the main problem, usually widespread and often deep and thick. The North-West Circuit has ten huts (6–30 bunks), which are spaced at intervals suited to an average day's tramping, most of them on the coast, but there are no campsites. The track itself alternates between open coast and forested hill country, offering highlights of a side trip to the 980-metre summit of Mount Anglem (5.5km; 6hr return) and the chance to see kiwi in the wild at Mason Bay.

travel details

Trains

Dunedin to: Balclutha (1 daily; 1hr 10min); Christchurch (1 daily; 5hr); Gore (1 daily; 2hr 23min); Invercargill (1 daily; 3hr 18min); Oamaru (1 daily; 2hr 25min).

Invercargill to: Balclutha (1 daily; 2hr 8min); Christchurch (1 daily; 9hr); Dunedin (1 daily; 3hr 18min); Gore (1 daily; 55min).

Buses

Dunedin to: Alexandra (4 daily; 3hr); Balclutha (6 daily; 1hr 35min); Cromwell (4 daily; 3hr 30min); Gore (6 daily; 2hr 35min); Invercargill (6 daily; 3hr 10min); Lawrence (4 daily; 1hr 30min); Oamaru (5 daily; 1hr 30min); Queenstown (4 daily; 4hr 25min); Te Anau (4 daily; 4h 30min).

Invercargill to: Gore (2 daily; 55min); Queenstown (4 daily; 2hr 40min); Te Anau (2 daily; 2hr 25min).

Ferries

Invercargill to: Stewart Island (2 daily; 1hr).

Stewart Island to: Invercargill (2 daily; 1hr).

Planes

Dunedin to: Auckland (12 daily; 2hr 40min); Blenheim (9 daily; 3hr 5min); Christchurch (10 daily; 45 min); Gisborne (6 daily; 3hr 15min); Hamilton (7 daily; 2hr 30min); Hokitika (4 daily; 1hr 45min); Invercargill (2 daily; 30min); Kaitaia (3 daily, 4hr 20min); Napier/Hastings (6 daily; 3hr); Nelson (12 daily; 2hr); New Plymouth (5 daily; 4hr); Palmerston North (7 daily; 2hr 40min); Rotorua (7 daily; 3hr 50min); Taupo (4 daily; 3hr 50min); Iauranga (9 daily; 3hr); Wanganui (3 daily; 3hr); Wellington (12 daily; 1hr 10min); Westport (2 daily; 3hr); Whakatane (6 daily; 4hr 5min); Whangarei (8 daily; 3hr 45min).

Invercargill to: Auckland (8 daily; 3hr 30min); Blenheim (6 daily; 4hr); Christchurch (8 daily; 1hr 40min); Dunedin (3 daily; 30min); Gisborne (4 daily; 5hr); Hamilton (4 daily; 7hr); Hokitika (4 daily; 6hr); Kataia (2 daily; 4hr 40min); Napier/Hastings (4 daily; 4hr 30min); Nelson (7 daily; 4hr 30min); New Plymouth (4 daily; 4hr); Palmerston North (6 daily; 3hr 25min); Rotorua (4 daily; 4hr 25min); Stewart Island (3 daily; 20min); Taupo (6 daily; 3hr 45min); Tauranga (8 daily; 3hr 30min); Wanganui (3 daily; 4hr); Wellington (8 daily; 2hr); Westport (2 daily; 7hr); Whakatane (5 daily; 8hr); Whangarei (5 daily; 4hr 30min).

Stewart Island to: Invercargill (3 daily; 20min).

CHAPTER TWELVE

THE WEST COAST

T
he Southern Alps run down the backbone of the South Island, both defining and isolating **the West Coast**. A narrow, rugged and largely untamed coastal strip of turbulent rivers, lush bushland and crystal lakes that's seldom more than 30km wide, it comes fringed by astonishing surf-pounded beaches backed by the odd tiny shack or, more frequently, nothing at all. What really sets "the Coast" apart is the interaction of settlers with their environment. **Coasters**, many descended from early gold and coal miners, have long been proud of their ability to coexist with the wild primeval landscape – a trait mythologized in their reputation for **independent-mindedness** and intemperate beer-drinking, no doubt fuelled by a heavy admixture of Irish drawn to the 1860s gold rushes. Stories abound of late-night drinking sessions in pubs way past their closing times, and overall, your fondest memories of the West Coast might well be chance encounters one evening in the pub, rather than the sights.

Cook sailed up this way in 1770, when he described the Coast as "… an inhospitable shore, unworthy of observation, except for its ridge of naked and barren rocks covered with snow. As far as the eye could reach the prospect was wild, craggy and desolate". Little here then for early **European explorers** such as Thomas Brunner and Charles Heaphy, who made forays in 1846–47, led by Kehu, a Maori guide. They returned without finding the cultivable land they sought, and after a shorter trip in 1861 Henry Harper, the first Bishop of Christchurch, wrote, "I doubt if such a wilderness will ever be colonized except through the discovery of **gold**". Prophetic words: within two years reports were circulating of flecks of gold in West Coast rivers and a year later Greymouth and Hokitika were experiencing full-on gold rushes. The boom was soon over, but mining continued into the twentieth century, with huge dredges littering the landscape, looking like beached galleons as they worked their way up the gravel riverbeds, scuttling through spent tailings.

As gold was worked out, longer-lasting **coal** took its place (the West Coast still produces a third of the country's coal), laying the foundation for more permanent towns. Many of these have since foundered and a shrinking economy has tapped the resourcefulness of the people – you'll still find individual miners hacking away at a single coal seam or running a sawmill in the bush single-handed. Abundant open space and low land prices have also nurtured a thriving **alternative culture**, and you may well spot the smoke stack of some purple bus sticking out from behind the trees. In the last fifteen years or so, everything has been turned upside down by the challenge of increasing **tourism** and a greater awareness of the Coast's **fragile ecosystems**.

No discussion of the West Coast would be complete without mention of the torrential **rainfall**, which falls with tropical intensity for days at a time, every rock springs a waterfall and the bush becomes vibrant with colour. Such soakings have a detrimental effect on the soil, retarding decomposition and producing a peat-like top layer with all the minerals leached out. The result is **pakihi**, scrubby, impoverished and poor-looking paddocks that characterize much of the West Coast's cleared land. But the abundant sunshine that alternates with the downpours produces excellent conditions for **dope-growing**, a significant component of the local economy. Enthusiasm for marijuana growing is matched only by the springtime rush to catch **whitebait**, when fishers line the tidal riverbanks on rising tides trying to net this epicurean holy grail of Kiwi angling.

The boom-and-bust nature of the West Coast's gold- and coal-mining past produced scores of ghost towns, but also spawned its three largest towns – the harbour town of **Westport**, and the former ports of **Greymouth** and **Hokitika**. The real pleasure of the West Coast, though, lies in smaller places more closely tied to the countryside, where the Coasters' indomitable spirit shines through: places such as **Karamea**, on the southern limit of the Kahurangi National Park, the strike town of **Blackball** at the foot of the Croesus Track on the Paparoa Range, the gold town of **Ross** and windswept **Okarito**. With the exception of a couple of decent museums and a handful of sights, the West Coast's appeal is in its scenic beauty. The **Oparara Basin**, near Karamea, and the **Paparoa National Park**, south of Westport, exhibit some of the country's finest

---

ACCOMMODATION PRICES

Accommodation listed in this guide has been categorized into one of nine price bands, as set out below. The rates quoted represent the **cheapest available** double or twin **room** – except for category ①, which are per-person rates for a dorm bed. Note that fees for **tent sites** and **DOC huts** (quoted in dollars) are also per-person, unless otherwise stated.

① under $20 per person	④ $60–80	⑦ $140–180
② under $40 per room	⑤ $80–100	⑧ $180–240
③ $40–60	⑥ $100–140	⑨ over $240

For more on accommodation, see p.34.

---

limestone formations, including huge arched spans and the famous Pancake Rocks, while in the Westland National Park the frosty white tongues of the **Franz Josef and Fox glaciers** career down the flanks of the Southern Alps into dense emerald bush almost to sea level.

Most people visit from November to April, and you might expect that a place with such a damp reputation is a bad place to visit in **winter**, but temperatures are not as low as you might think and the greater number of clear days make for cloud-free viewing. Pesky sandflies are also less active in the winter. The West Coast never feels crowded but in the off-season you'll have even more room to move and accommodation will be cheaper; the downside is that **whitewater rafting, caving** and **scenic flights**, which require minimum numbers to operate, may be harder to arrange.

The simplest way to get around the West Coast is with your own **vehicle**. Likewise, **cycling** isn't such a chore: the coast road is undulating but the distances between towns aren't off-putting and you can always find somewhere to camp in between. Public transport, on the other hand, is fairly restrictive. **Trains** only penetrate as far as Greymouth; **bus services** are infrequent and, though they call at all the major towns, they won't get you to most of the walks. Having said that, with patience and a degree of forward planning it is possible to see much of interest, especially if you are prepared to walk a little. The major bus **route** along the coast is provided by InterCity (in Christchurch ☎03/379 9020), running once a day in each direction with an overnight stop in either Franz Josef or Fox Glacier. For service frequencies and journey times, consult "Travel Details" on p.740.

Some of the best deals are West Coast **travel passes** offered by several companies including the backpacker tour-bus operators, Kiwi Experience and Magic Bus, which both run southbound services several times a week (see Basics, p.29). The Westcoast Express (☎03/546 5007, fax 546 5300; $115) is designed along similar lines but with a more low-key approach, smaller numbers and a slower pace; they take six days to go from Nelson to Queenstown (or visa versa) stopping away from the main crowds at places like Punakaiki, Blackball, Fox Glacier and Lake Wanaka.

The northern approaches: along the Buller and Grey rivers

Stretching 169km from its source at Lake Rotoiti in the Nelson Lakes National Park to its mouth at Westport, the **Buller River**'s blue-green waters reflect sunlight dappled through riverside beech forests as they swirl and churn through one of the grandest of New Zealand's river gorges between the Lyell and Brunner ranges. The Maori name for the Buller is *Kawatiri*, meaning "deep and swift", a fitting description of its passage through a region which, in the national consciousness, is associated with two devastating **earthquakes**. The first, registering 7.8 on the Richter Scale, was centred on Murchison in 1929; the other had its epicentre near Inungahua and struck in 1968. Landslides associated with these catastrophic events have combined with the natural geology to soften the curves of rocky bluffs that shelter white-sand beaches inaccessible from the road but frequently used by rafting parties. Gold was discovered along the Buller in 1858, sparking a gold rush centred on Lyell, now a ghost town whose outlying remains can be visited on the Lyell Walkway.

The Buller is traced by SH6 from Kawatiri Junction to Westport through Inungahua Junction, where Greymouth-bound travellers turn south towards Reefton. From Reefton, SH7 hugs the **Grey River**, a far less dramatic watercourse than the Buller, as it flows through a wide valley to the east of the granite tops of the Paparoa Range past more evidence of long-dead gold and coal industries, principally at laidback Blackball and the Brunner Industrial Site.

The Buller Gorge

SH6 from Nelson passes through Murchison (see p.515) and follows the Buller River 11km to **O'Sullivan's Bridge** where you turn right to remain on SH6 as it enters the Upper Buller Scenic Reserve. After 6km, the road passes the **Buller Bridge** ($3 toll), the longest example of the swaying pedestrian footbridges known in New Zealand as swingbridges; crossing high above the Buller River, the 110m span has a hair-raising 145m-long flying fox alongside which you can ride for $15.

Fifteen kilometres on, a lay-by provides a **"View of Earthquake Slip"** which, thirty-odd years after the Inungahua earthquake, is gradually being recolonized but still bears the scars of the huge landslide that completely dammed the Buller River for several days. Following a 4km bend in the river, the road passes the grassy site of **Lyell**, a former gold-mining town named after the great geologist Charles Lyell. The town sat high above the Buller on flats beside Lyell Creek and, in its 1890s heyday, supported five hotels, two banks, two churches and even its own newspaper, all serving a population of three thousand spread between here, Gibbstown and Zalatown, further up the Lyell Creek. Fires and the gradual decline in gold mining saw off all three settlements, but a few mementoes remain, and can be visited via the short but fairly strenuous **Lyell Walkway**, which passes terraces where huts once stood, the sobering slabs that stand askew in the cemetery (15min return), and the ten-hammer Croesus quartz stamping battery (1hr 30min return). The roadside site of the former township itself is now a peaceful DOC **campsite** ($5).

The next town, 17km to the west, is **INUNGAHUA JUNCTION**, which is little more than a service station attached to a café and grocery shop, an excuse for a brief stop only, unless you want to stay at the very cheap *Inwoods Farm Backpackers* (☎03/789 0205; closed July & Aug; ①), a house with no more than three in a room, signposted 400m down Inwoods Road which spurs off beside the general store.

West of Inungahua Junction the river approaches Westport through the **Lower Buller Gorge**, the narrowest and most dramatic section. The road hugs the cliff-face in places, most notably at **Hawks Crag**, where the rock has been hewn to form a large overhang – the fact that the water level rose several metres above this carved-out section during a 1926 flood will give you some idea of the volume of water that can surge down the gorge.

Reefton and around

Located beside the Inungahua River at the intersection of roads from Westport, Greymouth and Christchurch, **REEFTON**, as its name suggests, owes its existence to rich gold-bearing quartz reefs. These were exploited so heavily in the 1870s that Reefton was considered by some "the most brisk and businesslike place in the colony". This frenzy of financial speculation put Reefton in the vanguard, and it became the first place in New Zealand, and one of the first in the world, to install electric street lighting powered by a hydroelectric generator. Such forward-looking activity soon abated and, despite decades as an important coal-mining town, Reefton weathered poorly. However, things are now looking up: a couple of interesting galleries and even a very good café opening in recent years, together with a couple of pleasant strolls on the outskirts of town mean you may want to tarry a while. After a couple of hours, though, you'll probably want to explore the Victoria Conservation Park to the north or press on down the Grey Valley.

Specific points of interest around town are linked by two walks, both the subject of brochures available from the visitor centre (see "Practicalities", opposite). The elegiac **Historic Walk** (40min) meanders around Reefton's grid of streets, bidding farewell to the dilapidated exteriors of once-grand buildings – the Masonic Lodge, the School of Mines and the Court House – all ripe for preservation. The pleasant **Powerhouse Walk** (40min) also recalls a more illustrious past but succeeds in being more uplifting, perhaps because of its course along the Inungahua River.

The water race for Reefton's original hydroelectric scheme was diverted 2km from Blacks Point, where the **Blacks Point Museum**, SH7 towards Springs Junction (☎03/732 8808; Oct–April Wed–Fri 9am–noon & 1–4pm, Sat & Sun 1–4pm; $2), occupies a former Wesleyan Chapel. The museum charts the district's cultural and mining history through engaging photos and a large collection of lamps, moustache cups, clunky old typewriters and the like. Outside, parts from two ancient stamper batteries

---

WESTLAND'S ENDANGERED FORESTS

If gold and coal built the West Coast's foundations, then the **timber industry** supports the structure. Ever since timber was felled for sluicing flumes and pit props, Coasters have relied on the seemingly limitless forests for their livelihood. As coal and gold were worked out, miners became loggers, felling trees which take from three hundred to six hundred years to mature and which, according to fossil records of pollen, have been around for 100 million years.

Few expressed any concern for the plight of Westland's magnificent stands of **beech** and **podocarp** until the 1970s, when the magnitude of the threat to the forests became clear. Environmental groups rallied around a campaign to save the Maruia Valley, east of Reefton, which became a touchstone for forest conservation, but it wasn't until the 1986 **West Coast Accord** between the government, local authorities, conservationists and the timber industry that some sort of truce prevailed. In recent years most of the forests have been selectively logged, often using helicopters to pluck out the mature trees without destroying those nearby. While it preserves the appearance of the forest, this is little comfort for New Zealand's endangered **birds** – particularly kaka, kakariki (yellow-crowned parakeet), morepork (native owl) and rifleman – and long-tailed **bats**, all of which nest in holes in older trees.

With the benefit of hindsight, many considered the accord far too weak: felling of the south Westland rimu forests stopped in 1994, but continued apace in Buller until the election of the left-leaning Labour–Alliance coalition government in 1999. Though torn between their commitment to jobs and to the environment, Labour leader Helen Clark honoured her election pledge and almost immediately banned the logging of beech forests by the State-owned Timberlands company. Precious West Coast jobs were immediately lost, the continued viability of several communities remains threatened, and thousands felt betrayed in this traditionally Labour-voting part of the world. The future may look brighter for the forests, but Coasters will probably become increasingly reliant on tourism for their survival.

have been knitted together to form one five-hammer battery hydro-driven by a Pelton wheel; the whole ensemble is cranked into action on Sunday afternoons and during school holidays. **Walks** along mining trails through the regenerating bush to the mine shafts and stamping batteries of the Murray Creek Goldfield start from behind the museum and range from half an hour to a day; pick up the informative *Walks in the Murray Creek Goldfield* leaflet from the visitor centre or museum.

Coal- and gold-mining heritage combines with a vast area of bushland in the **Victoria Conservation Park**, which cloaks the ranges right around the western side of Reefton. The park is well off the traditional tourist itinerary and is consequently little-visited, making it all the more appealing for wilderness freaks. Day-walks are possible, but most require overnight stays in DOC huts; the visitor centre in Reefton can fill you in on all the options.

Practicalities

Buses all stop on Broadway, Reefton's main street, within sight of the helpful combined **visitor centre** and **DOC office**, 67–69 Broadway (daily: Nov–Feb 8.30am–5.30pm; March–Oct 9am 4.30pm; ☎03/732 8391, fax 732 9661) which has **Internet access**, rents out gold pans for $2 a day and bikes for $25 a day.

Almost all Reefton's **accommodation** is on, or just off, Broadway, the cheapest place is *Reefton Backpackers*, 64 Shiel St (☎ & fax 03/732 8383; beds ①, rooms ②), a spacious house with just a few beds in each room and good self-catering facilities. It is managed from the neighbouring *Quartz Lodge B&B*, 78 Sheil St (☎0800/302 725, fax 03/732 8383; ④), which also serves $20 dinners. The best of the **motels** is the *Bellbird*, 93 Broadway (☎03/732 8444; ④); and **campers** should make for the *Reefton Domain Motor Camp*, 1 Ross St, at the top of Broadway (☎03/732 8477; tents $7, powered sites $18 for two, cabins ②), where there's good swimming in the Inungahua River, or head 10km south down the Grey Valley to the DOC's *Slab Creek* campsite ($5).

About the only culinary relief from rural tearoom hell is *The Emporium*, 10 Smith St, a wonderfully spacious and bright café and gallery serving muffins, sandwiches and good coffee. For something more substantial, try *Alfresco Outside Eatery* (closed Sun), on Upper Broadway, with light **meals** and decent pizza served at lunch and on summer evenings.

The Grey Valley

Southwest of Reefton, SH7 follows the Grey Valley, cut off from the Tasman Sea by the rugged Paparoa Range and hemmed in by the Southern Alps. From both sides, the bush is gradually reclaiming the mine workings that characterized the region for a century. Nothing has stepped in to replace them, and the small communities tick over, a few eking a living from inquisitive tourists keen to explore the former mining towns of **Waiuta** and **Blackball**, and to walk the **Croesus Track**.

Waiuta

The first diversion of any consequence lies 21km south of Reefton where **Hukarere** marks the junction for **WAIUTA**, a ghost town seventeen partly-sealed kilometres east. This was the last of the West Coast's great gold towns, attaining a population of 6000 in the 1930s.

The end came for Waiuta when a mine shaft collapsed in 1951, burying large deposits of gold-bearing reef-quartz 879m down, where it was uneconomic to extract them. Miners left for jobs on the coast, much of the equipment was bought by Australian mining companies and even many of the houses were carted off, but the town wasn't completely abandoned; four or the remaining five cottages are occupied and there are several more buildings scattered around, including the original post office. The rolling country pocked by waste heaps is slowly being colonized by pioneer species like gorse and bramble, but the cypresses and poplars that once delineated gardens and the fruit trees that filled them remain; the rugby field, whippet track, croquet lawns and swimming pool are faring less well.

The whole place is wonderfully atmospheric for just mooching around, guided by the invaluable *Waiuta* leaflet (available from Reefton visitor centre) and strategically placed interpretive panels. You can see the lot in a couple of hours, but Waiuta is an ideal place for well-equipped **campers**, who can pitch their tent just about anywhere. For the less hardy, there's the open-plan thirty-bunk *Waiuta Lodge* (book through the Reefton visitor centre; ①), with a fully equipped kitchen, TV and video and a public phone. There's no other accommodation, no public transport and nowhere to buy food, so come prepared.

Blackball

Both the Grey River and SH7 meander through inconsequential small towns until they reach **Stillwater**, 11km short of Greymouth, where side roads lead to Blackball and Lake Brunner.

Refugees from the blistering pace of Greymouth gravitate to languid **BLACKBALL**, a former gold- and coal-mining village spread across a plateau at the foot of the Paparoa Range, 11km northeast of Stillwater. Here, commuters, neo-hippies and gnarled folk still hunting and prospecting in the bush seem to coexist fairly harmoniously. Blackball owes its existence to alluvial gold discovered in Blackball Creek in 1864, but gold returns diminished by the early twentieth century and it was left to coal, also mined from 1893, to save the day. Coal supported Blackball until the mine's closure in 1964, along the way staking the town's place in New Zealand's history as the birthplace of the **labour movement**.

During the first three decades of the twentieth century, the whole of the Grey Valley was a hotbed of doctrinaire socialism, as organizers moved among the towns, pressing unbending mine managers to address the atrocious working conditions. Anger finally came to a head, resulting in the crippling 1908 "cribtime strike", when Pat Hickey, Bob Semple and Paddy Webb requested an extension of their "crib" (lunch) break from fifteen to thirty minutes. Management's refusal sparked an illegal ten-week strike – the longest in New Zealand's history – during which the workers' families (already suffering enormous sacrifice and deprivation) were fined £75 for their action. None had the money to pay and although the bailiffs tried to auction their possessions, the workers banded together, refusing to bid – one then bought all the goods for a fraction of their worth and redistributed them to their original owners. It is this spirit which eventually won the day: the workers returned to the mine and crib time was extended, but the £75 was extracted from subsequent wages.

The struggle led to the formation of the Miners' Federation, which later transformed itself into the Federation of Labour, the country's principal trade union organization. Eric Beardsley's historical novel *Blackball 08* (see "Books" in Contexts) gives an accurate and passionate portrayal of the 1908 strike, but the most powerful evocation of the labour spirit is in the TV room at *Formerly the Blackball Hilton* (see below), with its relics and press cuttings from the strike and red flags bearing rousing slogans.

Ironically, these days Blackball's tranquillity is the main draw, abetted by excellent walking through the gold workings of Blackball Creek and up onto the wind-blasted tops of the Paparoa Range along the **Croesus Track** (see box opposite).

Practicalities

Blackball's social life revolves around the welcoming and wonderfully low-key *Formerly The Blackball Hilton*, Hart Street (☎0800/425 225, fax 03/732 4708, *www. blackballhilton.co.nz*; tents $9, dorms ①, rooms ③, dinner B&B ⑤), the last of the mining-era hotels which opened as the Dominion in 1910 and subsequently operated as the Hilton – ostensibly named for the former mine manager remembered in Hilton Street nearby – until challenged by the international hotel chain of the same name. Apart from lively drinking with quirky local characters, the hotel offers **accommodation**, a hot tub for guests, gold panning in local rivers (2hr; $12), horse riding (half day; $45) and a hatful of suggestions for walks and exploration. Self-caterers should feast on venison sausages from the Blackball Salami Co. across the road; everyone else is limited to no-nonsense bar **meals** at the hotel and **takeaways** from the local dairy.

There is no public transport but the hotel can often organize a ride from Greymouth.

Lake Brunner

From Stillwater another sealed road runs 25km southeast to Lake Brunner (*Moana Kotuku*), a filled glacial hollow celebrated for its trout fishing and warm summer swimming (the lake is also accessible off SH73 between Greymouth and Arthur's Pass). Immediately before the lake, the **Moana Kiwi House and Zoological Garden**,

---

THE CROESUS TRACK

The DOC's informative *Croesus and Moonlight Walks* pamphlet shows adequate detail for walkers. The NZMS's 1:50,000 *Ahaura Topomap* is the one for map enthusiasts.

Prospectors seeking new claims gradually pushed their way up the Blackball Creek, cutting paths to get their reef-quartz rock down to stamping batteries and to get supplies back up to their shelters in the bush. The scant remains of decades of toil now provide the principal interest on the **Croesus Track**, the first half easily explored in a day from Blackball, the whole track over the 1200m Paparoa Range to Barrytown on the coast north of Greymouth taking two relatively gentle days or one eight-hour slog.

ACCESS AND ACCOMMODATION

The track **starts** at Smoke-Ho car park, at the end of a rough but passable road 5km north of Blackball and **finishes** opposite the Barrytown Tavern on SH6, where southbound and northbound buses pass twice daily. There are two **huts** along the track: the free Category 4 Garden Gully Hut, with two sack bunks and an open fire, and the Category 2 Cec Clarke Hut (24 bunks; $10), with panoramic views, pots and a good coal-burning stove; the adjacent Top Hut is now abandoned.

THE TRACK

Much of the track was designed to accommodate tramways and the requirements of a gentle, steady grade characterize today's track. The route wends through hardwood and native podocarps interspersed with ferns and mosses and vines, gradually giving way to hardier silver beech and eventually alpine tussock and herbfields above the tree line. Sea mist commonly cloaks the tops during the middle of the day.

The trail from **Smoke-Ho** begins along a well-graded track, gradually descending to cross Smoke-Ho Creek then rising gently to a clearing (reached in half an hour), from where a ten-minute return path leads to the former site of the **Minerva Battery**. Immediately after the clearing, the path crosses Clarke Creek on a new wire bridge above the remains of an old wooden bridge. Another half hour on, a side track leads to two more clearings that once contained **Perotti's Mill** (10min return) and the **Croesus Battery** (50min return), respectively. After almost an hour, another side path leads to the primitive **Garden Gully Hut** (5min return) and the **Garden Gully Battery** (40min return). The main track turns sharply west before reaching the **Cec Clarke Hut** on the tree line in around an hour: fill your water bottles here, there is no supply beyond. The top of the ridge near Mount Ryall (1220m) lies two undulating hours beyond, a little more if you run off to climb **Croesus Knob** (1204m) along the way. If it isn't cloaked in cloud, the broad ridge offers wonderful views down to the coast, which is reached in under three hours by a steep but well marked path that dives down into the bush.

An alternative for experienced and fit trampers is to follow a loop that joins the Croesus Track with **The Moonlight Track**, detailed in the DOC's *Croesus and Moonlight Walks* leaflet.

Stillwater–Jacksons Road (daily 9am–5pm; $10), boasts the country's largest kiwi house. The centre participates in the nationwide captive breeding programme and presents exotic and other native birds in something akin to their natural surroundings. The 2km **Velenski Walkway** meanders through unspoilt native bush beside the Arthur River nearby.

The only facilities are a couple of kilometres further on at the lakeside village of **MOANA**, where the TranzAlpine **train** makes a regular newspaper stop on Saturdays and will halt on request at other times. Accommodation extends to the drab but serviceable *Moana Hotel*, Ahau Street (☎ & fax 03/738 0083; cabins ①–②, rooms ③, units ④), and the neighbouring *Lake Brunner Motor Camp* (☎ & fax 03/738 0600; tents $8, powered sites $10, cabins ②). The *Stationhouse Café & Bar*, Koe Street (☎03/738 0158), has the best **eating** around about, with lunches from $10, dinners from $20 and excellent lake views.

Brunner Industrial Site

Back on SH7, a couple of kilometres past Stillwater, a tall brick Tyneside chimney marks the **Brunner Industrial Site** (unrestricted access). Roadside information panels mark the path to a fine old suspension bridge (now relegated to foot traffic only), which crosses the swirling river to the few remaining buildings and the largely intact ruins of distinctive beehive coking ovens.

On his explorations in the late 1840s, Thomas Brunner noted the seam of riverside coal. By 1885, the mine site was producing twice as much coal as any other mine in the country and exporting firebricks throughout Australasia, but in 1896 New Zealand's worst mining disaster (with 69 dead) heralded its decline. The site was finally abandoned in the 1940s, and only exhumed from dense bush in the early 1980s. Half an hour wandering around the foundations and the fifty-minute bushwalk to some of the old mine sites evoke a long-gone era.

Westport and around

WESTPORT runs Greymouth close for the dubious honour of being the West Coast's most dispiriting town, a drab low-slung place of wide streets and slim opportunities which nevertheless warrants a visit for the nearby sights, principally the seal colony of **Cape Foulwind** and the former coal towns of the **Rochford Plateau** to the north. Besides, as this is a principal transport interchange, you may well end up spending a couple of nights here, which is made tolerable by reasonable accommodation, some decent restaurants and pubs – and a few adventure activities to keep you entertained.

Westport was the first of the West Coast towns, established by one **Reuben Waite** in 1861 as a single store beside the mouth of the Buller River. He made his living provisioning the few Buller Gorge prospectors in return for gold, but when the miners moved on to richer pickings in Otago, Waite upped sticks and headed south to help found Greymouth. Westport turned to the more dependable coal and, while the mining towns to the north were becoming established, engineers channelled the river to scour out a **port**, which fast became the largest coal port in the country but now lies idle. Westport battles on, with a respectable-sized fishing fleet and the odd ship laden with the produce of New Zealand's largest cement works at Cape Foulwind, which is fuelled by coal from open-cast Stockton, the only large mine left.

Arrival, information and transport

Almost everything of consequence in Westport happens around Palmerston Street. The helpful **visitor centre**, 1 Brougham St (daily: Christmas–Jan 9am–7pm; rest of year

9am–5pm; ☎03/789 6658, fax 789 6668), is just off Palmerston Street, a few steps from the **DOC office**, at 72 Russell St (Mon–Fri 9am–noon & 1–5pm; ☎03/789 7742); both handle Heaphy Track **hut tickets**. There's **Internet Access** at the library opposite the visitor centre (Mon–Thurs 10am–5pm, Fri 10am–6.30pm, Sat 10am–1pm).

Bus stops are scattered around town. Atomic stops outside the visitor centre; Cunningham's Coaches from Karamea pull up at their depot at 179 Palmerston St; and InterCity stop outside the Caltex service station at 197 Palmerston St. The **airport**, with a direct daily flight to Wellington, is 8km south of the centre (Buller Taxis ☎03/789 6900; around $12). Westport is compact enough for you to **get around** on foot, though to reach the nearby attractions you'll need your own transport or the services of Karaka Tours, 50 Mill St (☎03/789 5080) who, in addition to a seal colony trip (see p.703), run

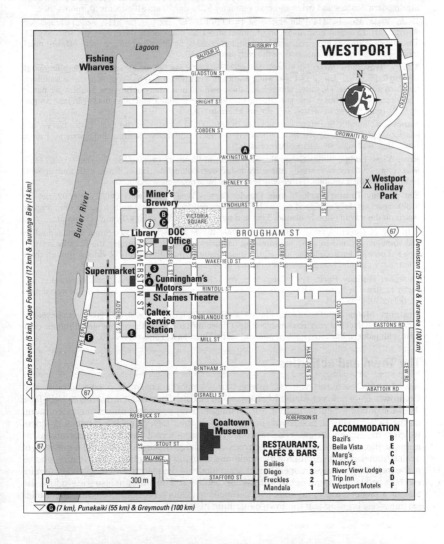

flexible **tours** to Denniston (4hr; $40), the Stockton Mine (4hr; $50) and the Charming Creek Walkway (4hr; $40). **Bike rental** is available from Becker's Sports World, 204 Palmerston St ($15 a day; ☎03/789 8787).

Accommodation

Accommodation is surprisingly abundant in Westport, so it isn't usually hard to find somewhere to stay. **Backpackers** are well catered for, and there's a cluster of decent **motels** along The Esplanade, though the choice of more luxurious places is limited.

Bazil's, 54 Russell St (☎0800/303 741, *bazils.backpackers@xtra.co.nz*). Attractive, airy house converted to backpacker accommodation, with a pleasant garden, a maximum of four in a room, some nice modern doubles and twins and bike rental for $20 a day. Tents $10, dorms ①, rooms ②.

Bella Vista Motels, 314 Palmerston St (☎0800/493 787, fax 03/789 8110, *bella.vista.westport @xtra.co.nz*). Excellent new motel on the main street, all units nicely decorated and with Sky TV. The cheapest studios are small and have limited cooking facilities, but larger units (⑤) are much more spacious and well equipped, some with spa baths. ④.

Marg's Travellers Rest, 56 Russell St (☎03/789 8627, fax 789 8396, *www.hotlink.co.nz/margs*, *margstr@xtra.co.nz*). Large and sprawling associate YHA hostel that has rooms in three buildings, the dorms all having TV, toilet, shower and their own kitchen. Many of the new doubles are particularly comfortable, cooked and continental breakfasts are available and non-guests can take a shower ($3). Tents $8, van hook-ups $16, dorms ①, rooms ③.

Nancy's, 42 Romilly St (☎03/789 6565, fax 789 8015). The quietest of the backpacker places, in a spacious old house that's a little run-down but has comfortable lounge and gardens. Closed June–Aug. Tent sites $8, dorms ①, rooms ②.

River View Lodge, Buller Gorge Rd, 7km south of Westport (☎0800/184 656, fax 03/789 6037, *friars.co.nz/host/riverview.html*). Attractive lodge overlooking the Buller River with four en-suite rooms each with a veranda. Three-course dinners by arrangement ($30). ⑥.

Seal Colony Tourist Park, Marine Parade, Carters Beach, 5km west (☎03/789 8002, fax 789 6732). Spacious, fully equipped site with some very comfortable motel units fronting onto a broad beach on the way to Cape Foulwind. Tent and powered sites $10, cabins ③, motel units ⑤.

Trip Inn, 72 Queen St (☎0800/874 746, fax 789 5401, *tripinn@clear.net.nz*). Small dorms, doubles and some family units in a big old rambling backpackers which discourages the backpacker tour buses. There's a barbecue area and all the usual features, including plenty of videos, though there is currently no quiet lounge. Tents $9, dorms ①, rooms ②.

Westport Holiday Park, 31–37 Domett St (☎03/789 7043, fax 789 7199). Smallish, low-key site partly hemmed in by native bush ten minutes' walk from the town centre. Tents $8, powered sites $9, dorms ①, chalets ②.

Westport Motels, 32 The Esplanade (☎ & fax 03/789 7575, ☎0800/805 909, *westport.motels @xtra.co.nz*). Older but very reasonable budget downtown motels, with well-appointed rooms, complete with modern kitchens; cooked and continental breakfast is also served. ④.

The Town and activities

Anyone with even the vaguest interest in Westport's coal-mining past should visit **Coaltown**, Queen Street (daily: Christmas–Jan 8.30am–5pm; Oct–Christmas & Feb–June 9am–4.30pm; July–Sept 9am–4pm; $6), an imaginatively presented museum concentrating on the Buller coalfield. Scenes of the workings in their heyday pack a fascinating video, which complements remnants salvaged from the site – a coal wagon on tracks angled, as it was in situ, at an unsettling forty degrees, and a huge braking drum – and a mock-up of a mine tunnel, complete with musty smells and clanking sound effects. Fascinating photos of the inclined tramways in operation, a scale model of the plateau and a collection of miners' hats and lamps round out this engaging exhibition. The museum also tries to fulfil the role of a pioneer museum, with less compelling exhibits on gold dredging, the Buller earthquakes, brewing and the town's maritime history.

Before leaving town, try the preservative- and chemical-free beers made by the co-operatively run **Miner's Brewery**, 10 Lyndhurst St (☎ & fax 03/789 6201; Mon–Fri 8.30am–5.30pm, Sat 10am–5.30pm), which distributes its beers throughout the West Coast and Marlborough. They'll give you a quick tour (Mon–Sat 11.30am & 1.30pm), let you sample their beers – a draught, a dark and the organic "Green Fern" lager – and sell you some to take away.

Once again we have Captain Cook, battling heavy weather in March 1770, to thank for the naming of Westport's most dramatic and evocatively titled stretch of coastline, **Cape Foulwind**, 12km west of town. Cook's name has stuck, and also lends itself to the undulating four-kilometre **Cape Foulwind Walkway**, which runs over exposed headlands, airing superb coastal views. It is perfect for sunset ambling between the old lighthouse, a replica of Abel Tasman's astrolabe and the **Tauranga Bay Seal Colony**, where platforms overlook New Zealand's most northerly breeding colony of fur seals. The seals are at their most active and numerous from October to January, often numbering three hundred or more, a sign of the welcome recovery from the decimation of 150 years of sealing.

The quickest access to the seals is from the sandy but treacherous beach of Tauranga Bay, accessible by road and at the southern end of the walkway, ten minutes along from the seals. To save retracing your steps all the way back, look for a marker around the halfway point, indicating an alternative route around the foot of the cliffs. Karaka Tours (☎03/789 5080) and Burning Mine Adventures (☎03/789 7277) both run two-hour **tours** to the seal colony for $20.

Wet and wild activities

As the largest town hereabouts, Westport has become the base for a couple of adventure companies, both operating trips some distance from town. The bread-and-butter trip for Norwest Adventures (☎0800/116 686, fax 03/789 7956, *norwest@xtra.co.nz*) is **Underworld Rafting** (4–5hr; $90), which starts with a minibus trip 28km south to the Charleston Tavern (where you can also join the trip; same price) and a bushwalk through a dramatic valley of rare limestone bluffs within the Paparoa National Park. The trip proper involves an informative guided walk through the Metro cave system; you'll be decked out in wetsuit and caver's helmet, and lugging a rubber inner tube, which comes into play for the final drift down a flooded glow-worm cave and out through a gorgeous ravine into the Nile River. None of it is tremendously arduous; if you like caves and water, you'll like this. For the more timid there's a scenic cave walk (3hr; $45); though adrenaline junkies should opt for **Adventure Caving** (4hr; $180), with a 35m abseil into a cave followed by a few tight squeezes.

Rafting and jetboating are run by Buller Adventure Tours (☎03/789 7286, fax 789 8104), located some 8km east of Westport on SH6. Throughout the year they run the six major rapids of the Grade IV "earthquake" section of the **Buller River**, 4km either side of Lyell, spending over two hours on the water for $75. Trips to more isolated rivers reached by helicopter are run less often and are dependent on numbers, so booking in advance is recommended. The most exciting is the stupendous Grade V **Karamea River** (Dec–March; 1 day; $195), while longer trips include the Grade IV+ **Mokihinui River** (Dec–March or April; 2 days; $325), which reaches the sea near Seddonville. Buller Adventure Tours also offer **jetboat rides** through the Lower Buller Gorge (1hr; $55), **horse trekking** through bush and along a river beach (from $40) and forty-minute rides in an eight-wheeled all-terrain vehicle ($20).

Eating, drinking and nightlife

Westport has fewer decent **places to eat** than the other towns on the West Coast, and if you want anything flasher than tearoom fare and pub meals you'll have to drive out to

The Bay House. **Pubs** are plentiful, most following the West Coast tradition, with those towards the northern end of Palmerston Street exhibiting a raw edge. **Nightlife** is limited to occasional bands at *Bailies* or *Diego* and second-run **movies** at the St James, 193 Palmerston St (☎03/789 8936).

Bailies, 187 Palmerston St. Westport's attempt at an Irish pub – only Guinness, pint glasses and the odd folk-music tape distinguishing it from the others. Pretty lively though, and with decent bar lunches, a cook-it-yourself barbecue and occasional live music.

The Bay House, Tauranga Bay (☎03/789 7133). Superb restaurant, café and gallery out towards the seal colony at the southern end of the Cape Foulwind Walkway. Coffee, lunch and Westport's best dinners (around $25) – along the lines of Malaysian seafood curry, roast lamb in tamarillo and port sauce and vegetarian cannelloni – are served in the cosy interior or on the terrace where you can watch the surfers on the bay. Lunch and dinner daily plus weekend brunch. Licensed.

Diego Restaurant & Bar, 18 Wakefield St (☎03/789 7640). Basically bar meals with a Tex-Mex flavour. Expect the likes of Mexican fish ($16) or enchiladas ($14). Occasional live music. Licensed.

Freckles, 216 Palmerston St. Probably the pick of the daytime cafés with simple breakfasts, hearty and straightforward sandwiches, quiches and cakes, and a few tasty treats such as Thai beef burgers ($8). Closed Saturday afternoon and Sunday.

Mandala, 110 Palmerston St (book for dinner ☎03/789 7931). Just a notch up from your average tearoom but a decent enough spot for burgers and toasted sandwiches.

Around Westport: coal country

Westport's role as a service town was entirely dependent on trade from the coal-mining towns to the north, towns often sited in such inhospitable spots that fresh vegetables were hard to grow and sheep were almost impossible to raise. Foremost among them was **Denniston**, for years New Zealand's most productive coalfield, located high on the Rochfort Plateau. Coal hasn't been mined here in any quantity for thirty years; houses have been carted away and the bush is rapidly engulfing what remains of the mining machinery. It makes an intriguing place to explore for half a day, or longer if you want to tackle the **Denniston Incline Walk**. All the other deep mines have gone the same way, leaving a legacy of inclines, tramways and rusting machinery that can be visited on a number of walks, the **Charming Creek Walk** being the best.

Denniston and its incline

The Karamea Road runs north from Westport 15km to Waimangaroa, the junction for a steep 9km road that wends its way 600m up to the lonely Rochford Plateau and the semi-ghost-town of **DENNISTON**, the finest and best-preserved example of once-numerous isolated mining communities. The old schoolhouse here has been turned into a small **museum** (Sun only 10am–3pm; free; check opening on ☎03/789 9755), containing historical photos and old mining machinery, which also acts as the local information centre. On a fine day the views across the coastal plain down to Westport and north towards Karamea are impressive, but even the vaguest suggestion of bad weather brings a blanket of cloud and damp fog down over the town, adding a suitably ethereal quality to this desolate landscape. At its peak, around 1910, the plateau supported three mining villages, Denniston, Coalbrookdale and Burnetts Face, which were home to over 2500 people, served by a post office, three hotels and numerous shops. After limping by on a skeleton staff for several years, the last coal was extracted in 1995, leaving the post office, a fire station, half a dozen scattered houses, twenty-two people and a treasure trove of industrial archeology centred on a gaunt winding derrick.

The Coalbrookdale Seam was first discovered by one John Rochford in 1859, and the plateau was soon humming with activity, though the difficult access slowed development until the construction of the **Denniston Self-acting Incline** in 1879. Regarded as something of an engineering marvel in its time, and still impressive today, this gravity-powered tramway was the steepest rail-wagon incline in the world, lowering coal-filled wagons 518m over 1.7km, while hauling up empty wagons. Throughout its 88-year lifespan, over a thousand tonnes of coal a day would rattle at a prodigious 70km an hour down to Conn's Creek, where they would be marshalled onto rail tracks for the trip into Westport. Initially everything destined for Denniston – goods, machinery and people – also came up the incline but after four people were flung to their death from careering wagons, a path was constructed in 1884 and sixteen years later the road was put in, finally easing some of the hardship of living up on the plateau. Considering how recently the mines were abandoned, there is surprisingly little left, save for foundations of mine workings and the remains of a few horse-drawn tramways – the greatest pleasure is in just rambling about (exercising some care not to disappear down mine shafts).

Fit and ambitious visitors to Denniston can approach on the **Denniston Walk** (2km; 2–3hr; 520m ascent), starting at Conn's Creek, 2km inland from Waimangaroa. The route follows the 1884 path roughly parallel to the incline, but the most interesting section is close to the top and can more easily be reached from Denniston. From Denniston to Middle Brake (1hr 30min return), the incline can still be seen among the bush, as can the midway point where wagons where disconnected from one hauling cable and connected to another for the lower half of the journey.

Minor roads continue beyond Denniston to the sites of Burnetts Face and Coalbrookdale, neither of which have much to detain you, but you can pass a day exploring the backroads and walkways then repair to *The Railway Tavern* in Waimangaroa to admire the photos of Denniston.

North to Seddonville

The road north of Waimangaroa passes a turn-off running 1km to the **Britannia Track** (3hr each way), which leads to the Britannia Battery and other remnants of the gold-mining era. **Granity**, 6km further on has the excellent *Drifters Café*, on SH67, decorated in a heady mix of modern murals and paintings along with relics of yesteryear. There's always a relaxed atmosphere, good coffee, all-day breakfasts, the likes of chick-pea curry and tempura fish fillets, and a lively bar. Granity also marks another junction, this time of a road that sweeps up the range to **MILLERTON**, an old coal town with a few houses still inhabited, and **Stockton**, the site of a vast open-cast mine, which is still worked and therefore inaccessible. It's worth going as far as the **Millerton Incline Railway Walk** (10min loop), a pleasant, gently graded stroll which starts 3km off the main highway and passes the 4.7km-long Millerton Incline; though less impressive than Denniston, this one is easier to visit.

At **Ngakawau**, 2km north of Granity, the coal depot signals the start of the lovely **Charming Creek Walk** (4km; 2hr one way; 100m ascent), which follows an old railway that was used for timber and coal extraction between 1914 and 1958. The first half hour is the least diverting, but things improve dramatically after the S-shaped Irishman's Tunnel, with great views of the boulder-strewn river below and, after a swingbridge river crossing, the Mangatini Falls. From here to the picnic stop by the remains of Watson's Mill is the most interesting section of the walk and is commonly the furthest people get (2–3hr return). The walk finishes among the manuka and gorse scrub and post-industrial wasteland of Charming Creek Mine, which is also accessible by 12km of mostly dirt road through the hamlet of Seddonville, just beside the Mokihinui River (see p.703).

Ngakawau merges imperceptibly with **Hector**, notably mainly for *The Old Slaughterhouse*, SH67 2km north of the village (☎03/782 8333; ③), a small **hostel** in a lovely wooden house perched on the hillside with wonderful views and access either on foot or by a 4WD buggy which meets you if arranged in advance.

There's a wider range of accommodation and meals some 15km further north at *The Cow Shed* (☎03/782 1826; dorms ①, cottages ③–④), a very relaxed place beautifully sited near the mouth of the Mokihinui River, 3km west of SH67. Fresh, wholesome and moderately priced meals – waffles, smoothies, stir fries, steak and fish mains – are served throughout the day in a much-converted cow shed or outside in the extensive grounds. **Accommodation** ranges from camping ($7; no kitchen privileges) and dorm beds (①), to three spacious and well-equipped self-catering cottages (③–④) all with either sea or river views: you'll want to stay longer than you planned.

Karamea and the Oparara Basin

The northwestern corner of the South Island competes with Fiordland as the least developed and most inaccessible region in the country, a fact sanctioned by the formation of the **Kahurangi National Park** in 1996. The second-largest park in the country, it embraces a vast wilderness of spectacular hill country supporting alpine meadows, the high Matiri ("Thousand Acre") Plateau, fifteen river catchment areas, New Zealand's finest karst landscape, dramatic windswept beaches and a coastal strip warm enough to support extensive stands of nikau palms. Charles Heaphy and Thomas Brunner surveyed the region in 1846, paving the way for European and Chinese gold-miners, who came a couple of decades later and sporadically took thin pickings as late as the Depression years of the 1930s. Pioneers followed, establishing themselves at **Karamea**, now the base for visiting the fine limestone country in the southern half of the park – and the first sign of civilization for walkers coming off the Heaphy Track (see p.510); other activities in the area are concentrated in the **Oparara Basin** and the final straight of the track.

The road north from Westport initially runs parallel to the coast, pinched between the pounding Tasman breakers and bush-clad hills as it passes through meagre hamlets with barely a shop or a pub. The journey takes roughly two hours if you don't stop, though there are plenty of opportunities to do so, not least at the coal towns around Westport (see p.704). North of the **Mokihinui River**, the road leaves the coastal strip, twisting and climbing over **Karamea Bluff** before descending again into a rich apron of dairying land. Rainfall begins to drop off and humidity picks up, promoting more subtropical vegetation, characterized by marauding cabbage trees and coastal nikau palms. At the foot of the bluff, **Little Wanganui** marks the turn-off for the start of the **Wangapeka Track** (60km; 4–5 days), which traverses the southern half of the Kahurangi National Park to Matariki, 50km west of Nelson. Though it lacks the coastal scenery of the more famous Heaphy Track, it easily compensates with dramatic mountain terrain. Trampers searching for something quieter than the Heaphy should pick up the DOC's *Wangapeka Track* leaflet (50¢), and be prepared for Category 2 and 3 huts; *The Last Resort* in Karamea (☎03/782 6617) and several companies in Nelson, Motueka and Takaka (see p.492) run transport to the trailheads.

> The **Heaphy Track**, which is generally walked from north to south, is covered in Chapter Eight; our account starts on p.510.

Karamea

Diminutive **KARAMEA**, 100km north of Westport, is one of those places where doing nothing seems just right. This peaceful and isolated spot is virtually at the end of the road; to continue any distance north, you'd have to go on foot along the Heaphy Track.

At the same time there is no shortage of things to do in the vicinity, the southern section of the Kahurangi National Park easily justifying a day or two of exploration.

Back in 1874, when land grants lured pioneers to a dense and isolated patch of bush at the mouth of the Karamea River, this was very much **frontier territory**, with the port providing the only link with the outside world. Settlers on the south shore of the Karamea River eked a living from **gold** and **flax**, but after a couple of fruitless years realized that the poorly drained pakihi wouldn't support them. Haunted by ill fortune, they moved upstream and north of the river to the current town site which, sure enough, soon after their move, was devastated by **floods**. Determinedly they pushed on, opening up the first road to Westport just in time for the upheavals of the 1929 Murchison **earthquake**, which altered the river flow and permanently ruined the harbour. Life hasn't been much better since: one sawmill remains, but **tourism** is increasingly the town's lifeblood.

Only devoted fans could spend more than ten minutes among the pioneering and sawmilling paraphernalia inside the **Karamea Centennial Museum**, SH67 (☎03/782 6652; Christmas–Feb Mon & Tues 11am–12.30pm, Thurs–Sat 1–5pm; other times by arrangement; $2). Otherwise there's **swimming** and **fishing** in the Karamea River, or **rafting** further upstream run by *The Last Resort* (☎03/782 6617); they negotiate the relatively gentle lower reaches (2hr; $30) and heliraft some magnificent Grade IV–V water far inland (1 day; $239). More modest waters can be tackled in canoes rented from the *Karamea Holiday Park* (see overleaf; $7 first hour, $16 half day)

Practicalities

Two scheduled **bus** services ply the Westport–Karamea route: Cunningham's Coaches (in Westport ☎03/789 7177) run to Westport in the morning (Mon–Fri only; $15 one way, bikes $5), returning in the afternoon; Karamea Express (Nov–Easter Mon–Sat; Easter–Oct Mon–Fri; $15 one way; call *The Last Resort*) also run to Westport in the morning and set off around 11.30am for the return journey. Minibus **charter services** at fairly competitive prices are run by Karamea Motors (☎03/782 6757). Karamea Express also serves the **Heaphy Track** end at Kohaihai with a daily run leaving Karamea at around 1.45pm and departing Kohaihai at 2pm (Nov–Easter daily; $5 one way; outside the season they run on demand charging $25 for up to five people.

The **visitor centre** at Market Cross, 2km east of the centre (Dec–March daily 9am–5pm; Feb–Nov Mon–Fri 9am–5pm & Sat 9am–1pm; ☎ & fax 03/782 6652, *karamea.info@xtra.co.nz*), has information about exploring the local area, **Internet access**, and issues **hut passes** for the Heaphy and Wangapeka tracks, as do *The Last Resort* and the *Karamea Tavern*.

In recent years Karamea has begun to gear itself towards tourism and there are now quite a few **places to stay**. The widest selection of rooms is at *The Last Resort*, unmissable on SH67 (☎0800/505 042, fax 782 6820, *last.resort@xtra.co.nz*; dorms ①, rooms ③, en-suite units ⑤, cottages ⑦), based around a lovely central complex consisting of turf-roofed buildings and low-profile salvaged-timber constructions containing backpacker dorms and doubles, comfortable en-suite hotel rooms, a small gym and spa ($5 per half-hour). They've lost the plot somewhat with the newer additions: plain and functional motel units and two-bedroom cottages. For **motels** you are much better off at the brand-new *Bridge Farm Motels*, SH67, 700m south of the visitor centre (☎0800/527 263, fax 03/782 6748, *brdgfarm@voyager.co.nz*; ⑤), with spacious units and a free continental breakfast; or the run-down but very cheap *Karamea Township Motel*, 17 Wharf Rd (☎03/782 6838; cabins ①–②, cottages ③), with a range of mis-matched but well appointed cabins and cottages. The only stand-alone **backpackers** in town is *Punga Lodge*, SH67 (☎03/782 6667; beds ①, rooms ②), which has a very ad hoc student flat kind of atmosphere and plenty of space out the back for barbecues and just kicking back. Whitebait fritters are sometimes produced for breakfast. There are $5 dorm beds at the *Karamea Domain* (no phone, enquire at adjacent caravan; tent sites $4, dorms ①); and a more organized **campsite** 3km south of town on the south side of the Karamea River at the *Karamea Holiday Park* (☎03/782 6758, fax 782 6738; tents $8, powered sites $18 per site, cabins ②, motels ③), a neat and well-kept site with ageing cabins and motel units. For farmstay, head 16km south to *Beachfront Farmstay*, SH67 (☎ & fax 03/782 6762, *bbnz.wcbnz.co.nz/karamea.htm*; ⑤), a relaxed spot where you can fish, gather mussels, go horse riding along the beach ($30 for 2hr), and eat dinner for $25.

The only **places to eat** are: the *Saracens Café*, opposite the visitor centre, which serves coffee, pies and sandwiches in a craft gallery; the *Karamea Tavern*, which dishes up straightforward bar meals and takeaways; and *The Last Resort*, with pub meals at the *LR Café & Bar*, and the main restaurant serving the only full meals in town.

The Oparara Basin and Kohaihai

Kahurangi's finest limestone formations lie east of the Karamea–Kohaihai Road in the **Oparara Basin**, a compact area of **karst** topography characterized by numerous sink-holes, underground streams, caves and bridges created over millennia by the action of slightly acidic streams on the heavily jointed rock. This is home to New Zealand's largest native **spider**, the gradungular spider (found only in caves in the Karamea and Collingwood area, where it feeds off blowflies and cave crickets), and to a rare species of ancient and primitive carnivorous **snail** that grows up to 70mm across and feeds on earthworms. Tannin-stained rivers course gently over bleached-white boulders and, in faster-flowing sections, the rare whio or blue duck swims for its supper. Even if your interest in geology is fleeting, the Oparara Basin makes a superb place for an afternoon **swim** or a **picnic** by one of the rivers.

Ten kilometres north of Karamea, North Beach marks the turn-off for the steep and narrow 16km dirt road to the **Honeycomb Caves**, only discovered in the 1970s and a valuable key to understanding New Zealand's fauna. The lime-rich sediment on the cave floor has helped preserve the ancient skeletons of birds, most of them killed when they fell through holes in the cave roof. Bones of over fifty species have been found here including those of the Haast Eagle, the largest eagle ever known with a wingspan of up to four metres. In total there are 15km of passages through the cave system, some of which are visited on the excellent and educational **Honeycomb Caves Tour** (☎03/782 6617; 5hr; $60 including lunch; run by *The Last Resort*). The tour is the only way you can get into the caves, but if you are exploring under your own steam you can join the tour group at the entrance (2hr; $30), so long as you book in advance. If you don't fancy the caves but want transport to the Oparara Basin area, they'll carry you for $30 return, provided they have space. As is common in limestone areas, the water-courses alter frequently, leaving behind dry caves, such as the adjacent **Crazy Paving and Box Canyon caves**, both accessible on a five-minute track from the road-end car park and good for spider-spotting.

The two most spectacular examples of limestone architecture lie at the end of beautiful, short bushwalks signposted from a car park 3km back down the road towards Karamea. The largest is the **Oparara Arch** (40min return), a vast two-tiered bridge 45m high, 40m wide and over 200m long, which appears magically out of the bush but defies any attempt at successful photography. The **Little Arch** (1hr return) is more easily captured on film but harder to reach, requiring a short fixed-rope descent and a good deal of mud, though the untouched, high-canopy native forest and a magnificent cavern make it all worthwhile. A short path to the deep black reflections in **Mirror Tarn** (20min return) spurs off the road nearby.

Kohaihai

Visitors with no aspirations to tramp the full length of Heaphy Track can sample the final few coastal kilometres from the mouth of the Kohaihai River, 17km north of Karamea, where there is good river (but not sea) swimming, a basic DOC **campsite** ($5) and an abundance of sandflies. In the heat of the day, you're much better off across the river in the cool of the **Nikau Walk** (40min loop), which winds through a wonderfully shaded grove dense with nikau palms, tree ferns and magnificent gnarled old rata dripping in epiphytes. When it cools off, either continue along the Heaphy to **Scott's Beach** (1hr 30min return), or stick to the southern side of the Kohaihai River and the **Zig-Zag Track** (35min return), which switchbacks up to an expansive lookout.

Paparoa National Park and around

South of Westport lies the Paparoa Range, a 1500m granite and gneiss ridge inlaid with limestone that separates the dramatic coastal strip from the valleys of the Grey and Inungahua rivers. In 1987, the limestone country of the South Island's western flank was designated the **Paparoa National Park**, still one of the country's smallest and least-known parks. The highlight is undoubtedly the **Pancake Rocks**, where crashing waves have forced spectacular blowholes through a stratified, pancake-like stack of weathered limestone. But to skip the rest would be to miss out on a mysterious world of disappearing rivers, sinkholes, caves and limestone bluffs best seen on the **Inland Pack Track**, but also accessible on shorter walks up river valleys close to Punakaiki.

Fertile limestone soils always support distinctive flora and fauna, a trait exaggerated here by the Tasman Convergence, a current warmed in the Coral Sea off Queensland, Australia. Striking this stretch of coast, the current creates a balmy microclimate favoured by the **Westland black petrel** and insects such as the **Captain Cook cicada**, the largest and noisiest of native cicadas.

The mild climate provided a sustaining bounty for **Maori**, who often stopped here while travelling the coast in search of *pounamu* (greenstone). Early **European explorers** followed suit seeking agricultural land. Charles Heaphy, Thomas Brunner and two Maori guides came through in 1846, finding little to detain them, but within twenty years this stretch of coast was alive with **gold** prospectors at work on the quartz veins at **Charleston** and **Brighton**, the former barely hanging on, the latter long gone.

Visitor interest is centred on **Punakaiki**, close by the Pancake Rocks where bus passengers get a quick glimpse and others pause for the obligatory photos. A couple of days spent here will be well rewarded with a stack of wonderful walks, horse riding, canoeing up delightful limestone gorges and just slobbing about.

Westport to Punakaiki

South of Westport, SH67 crosses the Buller River and picks up SH6, the main West Coast road. There's little reason to stop before you reach the **Little Totara River** and *Multi-Kulti* (☎03/789 6501, fax 789 6502, *jack.schubert@xtra.co.nz*; ②), 20km south of the junction. This small **café** and bar serves an array of meals and snacks – Thai curry, Greek salad, fruit shakes – and sandwiches on excellent sourdough rye bread, which is also sold by the loaf. Many of the ingredients are from the garden and are organic. The whole set-up is pretty laid-back, with a couple of colourful and very cheap **rooms** (②), free **camping** if you are eating here, a sauna, swimming in the creek and loads of great bush walking. A couple of kilometres further along SH6 is **Mitchells Gully Gold Mine** (usually open daily 9 or 10am–3 or 4pm; $5; call ☎03/789 6553 to check hours), a family-run mine working dating back to 1866, which has been reopened mainly to demonstrate the time-honoured methods used to extract fine gold held in a cement-like mass of oxidized ironsand. Along with a predictable collection of mining paraphernalia, you can see a restored overshot wheel driving a stamping battery, and water races and tunnels still in use.

The most intensive mining went on 3km to the south at **CHARLESTON**, then a rollicking boom town of around 18,000 people, but now with a mere thirty residents. The dozens of **hotels** that thrived on the gold spoils have collapsed or been burned down, leaving only the modern *Charleston Tavern*, which dishes up suitably modern fare of nachos and grills; Norwest Adventures convene here for their Underworld Rafting and abseiling trips (see p.703 for details). There really isn't much to be seen here, though there are a couple of short coastal walks and free primitive **camping** beside the lovely little Constant Bay. Other **accommodation** consists of the modest and very good value *Charleston Motel* (☎ & fax 03/789 7599; ④) and the *Charleston Motor Camp* (☎ & fax 03/789 6773; tents $9, powered sites $10, cabins ②).

Some 20km south of Charleston, the Fox River marks the site of the classic boom-and-bust town of **Brighton**, which experienced just four months of frantic activity in 1867, temporarily eclipsing Charleston for gold exports. Immediately to the south rise the 50m cliffs of Te Miko – tagged Perpendicular Point by Charles Heaphy, who in 1846 recorded climbing the cliff on two stages of ladders constructed of shaky and rotten rata vines while his dog was hoisted on a rope. The vines were later replaced by a chain ladder, but Te Miko remained an impenetrable barrier to pack animals until 1866, when the combined needs of traders and the new Westport–Greymouth telegraph line prompted the forging of the **Inland Pack Track**, a path now followed by the tramp of the same name (see box on p.712).

The coast road, finally completed in 1927, now climbs over Te Miko, passing the **Iraiahuwhero Point Lookout**, with stupendous coastal views extending to the Te Miko cliff and layered rocks similar to those at Punakaiki, 6km ahead.

Punakaiki and Pancake Rocks

The **Pancake Rocks** and blowholes at **PUNAKAIKI** are often all visitors see of the Paparoa National Park, as they tumble off the bus outside the visitor centre opposite the ten-minute paved track which leads from the road to Dolomite Point. Here layers of limestone have been weathered to resemble an immense stack of giant pancakes created by **stylobedding**, a chemical process in which the pressure of overlying sediments creates alternating durable and weaker bands. Subsequent uplift and weathering has accentuated this effect to create wonderfully photogenic formations. The edifice is undermined by huge sea caverns where the surf surges in, sending spumes of brine spouting up through vast **blowholes**. The rocks are magnificent even in calm conditions, but at high tide with a good swell from the south or southwest the performance is stunning.

More shapely examples of Paparoa's karst landscape are on show on a number of walks. The **Punakaiki Cavern Track** (5min return), 500m north, leads into a glowworm cave (torch essential), and 2km beyond that, the **Truman Track** (30min return) runs down from the highway to a small beach hemmed in by a wave-sculpted rock platforms.

No matter how slight your interest in birds, you could hardly fail to be impressed by the sight of **Westland black petrels** bundling through the trees at dusk to the world's only breeding colony of this, the largest of the burrow-nesting petrels. These relatives of the albatross glide effortlessly at sea, where they live most of their lives, but are less gainly when they leave their offshore rafts to crash land at their burrows. Birds arrive nightly from March to December, but activity reaches fever pitch from April to June, when the single egg is laid and hatched. Call Paparoa Nature Tours in advance for dawn and dusk **guided visits** (☎03/731 1826, or in Christchurch ☎03/322

7898; April–late Dec daily; 2hr; $25), using a viewing platform right in the middle of a sub-colony.

Kiwa Sea Adventures run excellent nature trips (☎03/731 1852, after hours ☎768 7765; Oct–March daily; 2–3hr; $85), taking to the ocean in search of Hector's, dusky and common dolphins with a maximum of five onboard. They make no promises, but usually find something and offer the opportunity to go **dolphin swimming**. More conventional **swimming spots** are rare along the West Coast but relatively abundant here, with good river swimming in the Pororari and Punakaiki rivers, and sea bathing at the southern end of Pororari Beach, a section also good for point-break surfing.

Keeping with aquatic pursuits, Punakaiki Canoe Hire (☎03/731 1870) rent out **kayaks** ($15 for the first hour, $40 per day) from their base beside the Pororari River. There's also excellent **horse riding** through bush and along the beach with Paparoa Horse Treks (☎03/731 1839), who charge $60 for a couple of hours; and a range of **caving and environmental trips** with Green Kiwi Tours (☎03/731 1141, fax 731 1142, *www.minidata.co.nz /therocks*), starting at around $25 for a two-hour trip.

Practicalities

North- and south-bound **buses** run by InterCity and Atomic stop for around half an hour outside the Punakaiki visitor centre, giving enough time for a quick look at the Pancake Rocks across the road. Both InterCity services pass in the middle of the day, but the northbound Atomic service arrives at 8.30am making it possible to treat Punakaiki as a day-trip from Greymouth with eight free hours before the south-bound Atomic comes through at 4.30pm.

Close by, the extensive DOC-run **Paparoa National Park visitor centre** (daily: Nov–Easter 9am–6pm; Easter–Oct 9am–4pm; ☎03/731 1895, fax 731 1896, *punakaikivc@doc. govt.nz*), and has excellent displays on all aspects of the park, information on activities and walking maps and leaflets.

Punakaiki's **accommodation** has formed two clusters: the first is by the Pororari Beach close to the rivermouth,

PUNAKAIKI AND THE INLAND PACK TRACK

△ Westport (50km)

0   2.5km

Ballroom Overhang

Fox River Cave

Fox River

Kaipakati Point

Waterfall Ck

Dilemma Ck

Fossil Ck

TASMAN SEA

PAPAROA NATIONAL PARK

INLAND PACK TRACK

Bullock Ck

BULLOCK CREEK ROAD

See Inset

PORORARI RIVER TRACK

CAVE CREEK KOTIHOTIHO WALK

TRUMAN TRACK

Punakaiki Cavern

Pororari River

Dolomite Point

Pancake Rocks and Blowholes

N

Punakaiki River

A

B C

TRUMAN TRACK

D
1
E

6

6

Dolomite Point

F

2
3

ℹ

ACCOMMODATION

Beach Hostel	E
Cottage motel	F
Punakaiki Motor Camp	D
The Rocks	A
Te Nikau Retreat	B
Te Puna Retreat	C

CAFES AND BARS

Punakaiki Crafts	3
Punakaiki Tavern	1
Wildcoast Café	2

Greymouth (40km) ▽

PAPAROA WALKS AND THE INLAND PACK TRACK

The 1:50,000 Paparoa National Park map covers the region in great detail, but the DOC's Inland Pack Track leaflet (50¢) provides enough information for that tramp.

The best way to truly appreciate the dramatic limestone scenery of the Paparoas is on the **Inland Pack Track** (27km; 1–3 days). Most of the terrain is easy going with only one pass to negotiate, but there are no bridges for river crossings, and while the water barely gets above your knees in dry periods, you need to be aware of the possibility of flash floods. With less time or greater demand for comfort, some of the best can be seen on two **day-walks**. The delightful **Punakaiki–Pororari Rivers Loop** (12km; 4–5hr; 100m ascent) follows the initial stretch of the Inland Pack Track as far as the Pororari River, which is then followed downstream between some magnificent limestone cliffs to return to Punakaiki. The **Fox River Caves Track** (12km; 4–5hr; 100m ascent) traces the last few kilometres of the Inland Pack Track from the Fox Rivermouth as far as the caves and returns the same way.

PRACTICALITIES

The Inland Pack Track can be walked in either direction, though by going from south to north (as described below) you eliminate the risk of missing the critical turn-off up Fossil Creek. There are **no huts** along the way and you're advised carry a tent. This isn't absolutely necessary, as trampers can shelter under the rock **bivvy** known as The Ballroom at the end of a long first day; by carrying full **camping gear**, though, you get protection from bugs, earn the freedom to break the walk into more manageable chunks and, perhaps most importantly, avoid a wet night in the open if the rivers flood. Choose a spot well away from flood risk areas and take care off the main track, as there are unmarked sinkholes. **Campfires** are permitted, but the DOC recommends carrying a stove, particularly for stays at The Ballroom, where most of the usable wood has already been burned. The latest **weather forecast** is available from the visitor centre in Punakaiki, where you should fill out an **intentions form**, remembering to check in on your return.

Drivers should leave their vehicle at the end of the walk and either hitch or catch one of the infrequent buses to get to the start. Alternatively, base yourself in Punakaiki and call *The Rocks* homestay (☎03/731 1141) who run a drop-off and pick-up service for $20 per run (maximum of four people.)

around 800m north of the visitor centre; the second is a further kilometre north, right by the Truman Track. There are two **hostels**, both are excellent. By the sea there's the relaxed and vibrantly painted *Punakaiki Beach Hostel*, Webb Street (☎0800/726 225, fax 731 1152, *punakaiki.beachhostel@xtra.co.nz*; dorms ①, rooms ②, motel unit ④), where guests can buy freshly baked wholemeal bread, surf the Net and use the outdoor spa pool. Up the road, *Te Nikau Retreat*, Hartmount Place (☎03/731 1111, fax 731 1154; dorms ①, rooms ②, en-suite doubles ③), must rank as one of the most relaxing backpackers in the country, carved out of bush that's peppered with nikau palms and occasionally reveals a building with small dorms, rooms and rustic huts for couples. Again, fresh bread and muffins are sold, and there's Internet access.

There are comfortable **units** at *Punakaiki Cottage Motels*, Mabel Street (☎03/731 1008, fax 731 1118; ⑤), with some overlooking the breakers; though you might prefer **homestay** at *The Rocks*, Hartmount Place (☎03/731 1141, fax 731 1142, *www.minidata. co.nz/therocks*; ⑥), a comfortable and welcoming spot with three rooms (all with private facilities and two with sea views), and meals available on request ($25–30). The same folk manage the **self-catering** *Te Puna Retreat*, Hartmount Place (⑥), a well-appointed and nicely designed modern home surrounded by bush and sleeping four. **Campers** should make for the spacious and grassy, DOC-run *Punakaiki Motor Camp*, SH6

THE INLAND PACK TRACK

The starting point of the Inland Pack Track is 1km south of the Punakaiki visitor centre at the end of a 1.5-kilometre track that follows the south bank of the Punakaiki River to a car park. From **Punakaiki River to Pororari River** (3.5km; 2hr 30min; 120m ascent, 100m descent), the track crosses to the right bank then cuts northeast, gradually rising to a low saddle then descending to the Pororari River, which is forded a couple of hundred metres upstream. From **Pororari River to Bullock Creek** (6km; 2hr; 100m ascent) it stays pretty level with views inland to the Paparoa Range before reaching Bullock Creek, which should be forded with some care – in flood conditions a wall of water courses down the creek's usually dry lower section. Camping is possible on the DOC-owned farm by the Bullock Creek crossing. From **Bullock Creek to Dilemma Creek** (8km; 2hr 30min; 100m ascent, 100m descent), the farm track soon becomes a path, skirting swampland then climbing to a ridge. Descend gradually to Fossil Creek, where you wade downstream from pool to pool, occasionally clambering over fallen tree trunks. After half an hour of this, Fossil Creek meets the main tributary of the Fox River, Dilemma Creek, by a small sign – keep your eyes peeled. Heading **downstream to Fox River** (2km; 1hr; gradual descent) is the most dramatic section of the trip but potentially the most dangerous, with 18 fords to cross between gravel banks in the bed of Dilemma Creek: if you have any doubts about the first crossing, turn back, as they only get worse. The lower river carves out a deep canyon between gleaming white vertical cliffs and, if you can find a patch of sun, this makes a great place to rest awhile. The track resumes by a sign on the left bank just above the confluence with the Fox River; a steep bluff on the right makes a useful landmark.

Even if you don't plan to stay, the vast limestone overhang of **The Ballroom** (1km; 30min each way; negligible ascent) is worth a look. A signposted track crosses to the right bank of the Fox River below the confluence, then crosses several more times higher up. There's no chance you'll miss the 100m-long lip, which could easily provide shelter for a hundred or more campers; a long-drop toilet has been installed and a huge fire pit has developed. Return the same way to **the confluence**, from where the track **to the Fox River mouth** (5km; 2hr; 100m descent) follows the left bank. A short distance along, a sign points across the river to the **Fox River Caves** (30min); the safest and most impressive of the caverns is the upper leftmost of the three. Meanwhile, the Inland Pack Track crosses to the car park by the Fox River mouth, some 12km by road from your starting point; the southbound InterCity **bus** currently passes around noon, or you can walk back along SH6.

(✆03/731 1894, fax 731 1897; tents $8.50, powered sites $10, dorms ①, cabins & units ②–④).

Daytime eating options are limited to the coffee shop at *Punakaiki Crafts*, by the visitor centre, where you can sit on the deck under nikau palms; and the appealing *Wild Coast Café* next door, which serves breakfasts, panini, lasagne and fish and chips until around 7pm. After that you've only got the good bar meals at the *Punakaiki Tavern & Bistro*, near the campsite, which can be eaten out in the garden. If you're **self-catering**, you'll do well to bring **supplies** from Westport or Greymouth.

Punakaiki to Greymouth

The road from Punakaiki to Greymouth is a spectacular drive, sometimes pushed onto the sea-cliffs by intrusive ramparts of the Paparoa Range, but there's little to stop for until you get close to Greymouth. The former gold town of **BARRYTOWN**, 16km south of Punakaiki, is no more than a scattered shock of houses and the *Barrytown Tavern* (✆03/731 1812; dorms ①, motel units ③), with a self-catering kitchen and good meals of locally caught fish; the tavern is principally used by those who stagger in from the **Croesus Track** (see p.699), though you might want to stop by for the occasional live music at weekends. A little further south, there's also the simple *Hexagon* **backpackers**, Golden Sands Road (☎03/731 1827; dorms ①, rooms ②–③), a nice little hostel with beds in a glassed-in hexagon, and a couple of lovely cabins, one featuring a sunhouse with cacti and a grapevine. Guests can help themselves to organic produce from the garden.

The next settlement of any consequence is **RAPAHOE**, which boasts about the safest bathing beach on the coast and has a reputation for gemstones among those in the know. Seven Mile Creek meets the sea here, by the beginning of the **Point Elizabeth Track** (5km; 3hr; 100m ascent), a lovely and little-used walk along former gold-miners' trails and through dense bush that ends 5km north of Greymouth at the end of Domett Esplanade, though you can go just as far as the excellent vantage of Point Elizabeth (2hr return). If you want to stay near here, try the *Rapahoe Beach Motor Camp*, 10 Hawken St (☎ & fax 03/762 7025; tents $8, on-site vans & cabins ②), which has a swimming pool and volleyball court, and is only a short stagger from the local pub.

Greymouth and around

The Grey River forces its way through a break in the coastal Rapahoe Range and over the treacherous sand bar to the sea at workaday **GREYMOUTH**, which ranks as the West Coast's largest town but still claims under ten thousand residents. Greymouth is hardly going to be a highlight on most visitors' itineraries, though there's a pleasant enough walk along the riverwall a couple of kilometres out to **Blaketown Beach** and a few worthwhile **adventure activities**. Best to do what you need to and move on, especially in winter when you might be plagued by **The Barber**, a razor-sharp cold wind that whistles down the Grey Valley and envelops the town in a thick icy fog.

The town began to take shape during the early years of the **gold rush** on land purchased in 1860 by James Mackay, who bought most of Westland from the Poutini Ngai Tahu people for 300 gold sovereigns. The deal was finalized on the site of their Mawhera pa, where the river bridge across to the suburb of Cobden now stands; a plaque beneath the bridge marks the spot. Several respectably **grand buildings** from the prosperous later decades of the nineteenth century pepper Greymouth's gridplan streets but there's nothing to give the place any defining character except for the river, which is deceptively calm and languid through most of the summer, but awesome after heavy rains. Devastating **floods** swept through Greymouth in 1887, 1905, 1936, 1977 and 1988; since the last great flood, the Greymouth Flood Protection Scheme, completed in 1990, has successfully held back most of the waters.

Arrival, information and transport

The stylish way to arrive in Greymouth is on the daily TranzAlpine **train** from Christchurch (see box on p.606), which pulls in at the station on Mackay Street and is met by InterCity **buses** (tickets from the visitor centre or the agency inside the station; ☎03/768 7080) running south to Hokitika and Franz Josef, and north to Westport and Nelson. Greymouth is also served by **shuttle buses** from Christchurch, Nelson, Picton, Hokitika and Queenstown. Greymouth's nearest **airport** is at Hokitika; Greymouth Taxis (☎03/768 7078) charge about $15 each way.

The **visitor centre**, inside the Regent Cinema, on the corner of Mackay Street and Herbert Street (daily: Nov–Easter 9am–7pm; Easter–Oct 9am–5pm; ☎03/768 5101, fax 768 0317, *www.westcoastbookings.co.nz, vingm@minidata.co.nz*), will provide a free street map, which is all you need for **getting around** the town on foot. Longer forays may demand a bike, rented from Scenicland Dolphin Adventure Tours (☎0800/929 991) for around $25 a day, or several other competitive outlets. You might also want to check out tours to the Pancake Rocks (9am & 2pm; 2hr 30min; $40) run by Kea Tours (☎0800/532 868, fax 768 0492, *www.minidata.co.nz/kea, kea-tours@minidata.co.nz*)

Folk planning to rent a car in Christchurch are increasingly riding the TranzAlpine then picking up a rental in Greymouth. In response, Avis and Budget both have **car rental** offices at the train station, though you may find it cheaper to go with one of several local outfits – starting from as little as $40 a day for long-term rentals, and often

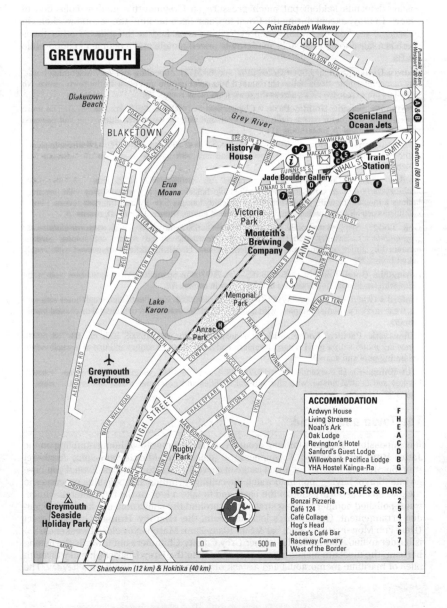

△ Point Elizabeth Walkway

GREYMOUTH

COBDEN

NELSON QUAY

Punakaiki (45 km) & Westport (100 km) △ A & B △ Reefton (80 km)

Blaketown Beach

COLLINS ST

COAKLEY ST

CROSBY ST

PACKERS QUAY

JOYCE ST

Grey River

GRESSON ST

JOHNSTON

MAWHERA QUAY

Scenicland Ocean Jets

BLAKETOWN

History House

ARNEY ST

MACKAY ST

C

1 2

3 4

6 5

i

GUINNESS ST

WHALL ST

Train Station

SMITH ST

MOUNT ST

RIGG ST

BLAKE STREET

Erua Moana

STEER AVE

RED STREET

PRESTON ROAD

Jade Boulder Gallery

LEONARD ST

HERBERT ST

7

D

CHAPEL ST

E

F

G

PUKETANI ST

LORD ST

Victoria Park

TAINUI ST

Monteith's Brewing Company

TURUMAHA ST

MURRAY ST

ALEXANDER

FREYBERG TERR

Lake Karoro

Memorial Park

FRANKLYN'S

6

RALEIGH ST

COWPER STREET

Anzac Park

H

WINNIE'S

AERODROME RD

✈ **Greymouth Aerodrome**

BUCKLEDGE ST

SHAKESPEARE STREET

PALMERSTON ST

LYDIA ST

MARSDEN RD

WATER WALK ROAD

HIGH STREET

MARLBOROUGH ST

Rugby Park

NELSON ST

BYRON ST

MILTON RD

JOYCE CR

CHESTERFIELD ST

△ **Greymouth Seaside Holiday Park**

TASMAN ST

MIRO

6

N

0   500 m

ACCOMMODATION

Ardwyn House	F
Living Streams	H
Noah's Ark	E
Oak Lodge	A
Revington's Hotel	C
Sanford's Guest Lodge	D
Willowbank Pacifica Lodge	B
YHA Hostel Kainga-Ra	G

RESTAURANTS, CAFÉS & BARS

Bonzai Pizzeria	2
Café 124	5
Café Collage	4
Hog's Head	3
Jones's Café Bar	6
Raceway Carvery	7
West of the Border	1

▽ Shantytown (12 km) & Hokitika (40 km)

charging little or no fee for cars dropped off in Queenstown or Christchurch. Try ring-
ing Value Rentals (☎03/762 7503, fax 762 7500), NZ Rent a Car (☎03/768 379, fax 768
0740, *greenfield@minidata.co.nz*) or Auto Rentals (☎03/768 4002, fax 768 9002).

Accommodation

Visitor demands seldom put much pressure on Greymouth's modest collection of
places to stay, except during the Coast to Coast Race (around the second weekend in
February; see box on p.718), when everything is packed to the gills. At other times
there is a fair choice of hostels, moderately priced motels and a couple of comfortable
B&Bs.

Ardwyn House, 48 Chapel St (☎03/768 6107, fax 768 5177). Appealing and very welcoming homestay in a comfortable 1920s house surrounded by a quiet garden and close to the town centre. No
en suites, but expansive views across the town from many rooms. ④.

Greymouth Seaside Holiday Park, 2 Chesterfield St (☎03/768 6618, fax 768 5873). The more
central of the two motor parks, right by the beach and with very good facilities. Tent and powered
sites $9–10, cabins ②, motel units ④.

Living Streams Parkside, 42–54 Cowper St (☎0508/542 636, fax 768 7276, *lsp@minidata.co.nz*).
Light and spacious hostel backing onto parkland and with kayaks to use on the adjacent tidal
stream. Dorms ①, rooms ②.

Noah's Ark Backpackers, 16 Chapel St (☎0800/662 472, fax 03/768 4868,
noahsark@minidata.co.nz). Large and comfortable hostel occupying a two-storey villa originally
built as a monastery, with great verandas, a spacious lounge, Sky TV and Internet access. Rooms
and dorms are all lavishly decorated with a different animal theme. Dorms ①, rooms ②.

Oak Lodge, SH6, 4km north of town (☎03/768 6832, fax 768 4362, *www.minidata.co.nz/
greymouthbnb/*). Swanky modern B&B with olde-worlde styled rooms set among gardens
enhanced by a nice outdoor pool, spa and tennis court. Lavish breakfasts are served with freshly
baked bread. ⑥.

Revingtons Hotel, Tainui St (☎03/768 7055, fax 768 7605). Spanish Revival-style hotel built in the
1930s with traditional hotel doubles and budget twin rooms. ④.

Sanford's Guest Lodge, 62 Albert St (☎ & fax 03/768 5605). Excellent-value small hotel with simple, fresh and airy rooms, complete with colour TV and the option of a continental or cooked breakfast. ③.

Willowbank Pacifica Lodge, SH6, 3km north of town (☎0800/668 355, fax 03/768 6022).
Sprawling motel with a good range of modern and older en-suite rooms and use of a small indoor
swimming pool and spa. ⑤.

YHA Kainga-ra, 15 Alexander St (☎03/768 4951, fax 768 4941, *yhagymth@yha.org.nz*). Relaxed,
low-key and central hostel, with all the usual facilities and good views over the town. Dorms ①,
rooms ②.

The Town and around

It is impossible to wander for long around central Greymouth without stumbling on the
Jade Boulder Gallery, 1 Guinness St (daily: Nov–March 9am–9pm; April–Oct
9am–5pm), a sales outlet for a vast range of carved greenstone pieces. Even if you have
no intention of buying, pop in to watch the cutting, grinding and polishing processes in
the glass-panelled workshop at the back, and to take a look at the raw material – huge,
water-polished boulders – lying strategically around the showroom in a kind of Zen garden arrangement. Greymouth's local museum, the **History House**, Gresson Street
(Dec–Feb Mon–Fri 9am–5pm, Sat & Sun 10am–2pm; March–Nov closed weekends; $3)
is harder to find. Hidden in the former Grey County Chambers out towards the fishing
harbour, the museum makes a good shot at relating the Grey District's history through
piles of maritime memorabilia and a stack of photos depicting the town's heyday. The

townspeople's long struggle to combat the floods is also given thorough and diverting treatment.

Rainy and sweltering days both provide equally good excuses to join the tastings and **brewery tours** at Monteith's Brewing Company, corner of Turumaha Street and Herbert Street (☎03/768 4149; Mon–Thurs 11.30am & 2pm; $5), where age-old recipes have recently been revived to produce some deep-brown, flavoursome brews popular all down the Coast. Sample them at the end of a brief tour.

Greymouth also makes a good base for the **Point Elizabeth Track** (see p.714), beginning over the river north of the suburb of Cobden and returning from Rapahoe by one of the twice-daily buses. If you're looking for a short walk and somewhere to watch the sun go down, try the ten-minute **Lions Walk**, starting up Weld Street in Cobden and meandering through the bush to a panoramic viewpoint over the city and the Southern Alps.

Activities

If you'd rather tackle something more thrilling, Wild West Adventures (☎0800/223 456, fax 03/768 9149) can oblige. Their **Dragons Cave Rafting** (5hr; $95) is a challenging caving trip into the Taniwha cave system; wetsuits and cavers' lamps are the order of the day for muddy scrambling down a fairly steep underground streambed, floating along deep sections on inner tubes and, for the adventurous, squeezing through some tight sections. The far more restrained **Chasms Underworld Whitewater Tunnel Rafting** ($125) has elements of its racier cousin, with a short spell underground in proper rafts, but more time spent above ground in a 4WD, learning about the gold-mining history of the region, European explorers and something of the local flora and fauna.

Few of the dramatically steep rivers spilling out of the alpine wilderness inland from Greymouth and Hokitika have any road access, and hardly any had been kayaked or rafted until recent years when helicopters were co-opted to reach them. Now, Hot Rock Rafting (☎0800/223 456, fax 03/768 9149) will take you **whitewater rafting** on one of the local rivers: the Grade III Taipo ($135), just south of Greymouth, requires 4WD access and gets you around an hour and a half on the water; the Grade IV Wanganui ($185), south of Hokitika, requires helicopter access and gives you four hours on the water, including time spent in some riverside hot pools; and the scary Grade V Perth ($265), inland from Whataroa, is another heli-raft trip with six hours of boating.

Equally pleasurable **whitewater-rafting** trips are run by Eco-Rafting (☎03/768 4005, *www.ecorafting.co.nz, info@ecorafting.co.nz*), such as half-day trips on the tame Arthur River ($70), or exciting heli-rafting day-trips on the Perth, Whitcombe and Hokitika rivers (from $210). **Dolphin- and seal-watching** trips (1hr 30min; $67) are run by Scenicland Dolphin Adventure Tours (☎0800/929 991, fax 768 7538, *www. dolphintours.co.nz, dolphintours@minidata.co.nz*), who use their nippy jetboat to chance the Grey Bar and head up the coast in search of Hector's dolphins. They'll also take you sea **kayaking** (4–6hr; $87) in areas often frequented by dolphins, or down-river kayaking (2hr; $67) on the relatively gentle Grey River.

Shantytown

The replica 1880s West Coast gold-mining settlement of **Shantytown** (daily 8.30am–5pm; entry and train ride $11.50, gold panning $3 extra), 8km south of Greymouth and 4km off the main highway, is unashamedly a tourist trap, frequented by a near-constant stream of visitors who pile off tour buses. Although mostly constructed since the early 1970s, the complex incorporates rescued older buildings: the 1902 Coronation Hall from Ross, an 1865 church originally from No Town in the Grey Valley, and a hotel cobbled together from parts. With the exception of the pristine

THE COAST TO COAST RACE

New Zealand is mad on multisport. Every weekend from early spring to late autumn you'll see scores of people toning their muscles and honing their skills on bikes, in kayaks, in the water or on foot. The ultimate goal of all true multisporters is the gruelling 239km **Coast-to-Coast Race** held annually between the West Coast and Christchurch in mid-February on the weekend after Waitangi Day.

The event is actually two races in one. Competitors in the two-day race make a predawn Saturday start from the beach near Kumara Junction, 15km south of Greymouth, aiming to finish at Sumner by the end of the following day. A 3km run leads to a 60km cycle uphill to Otira where jelly-kneed contenders tackle the most gruelling section, a run up and down the boulder-strewn creek beds of the Southern Alps before kayaking for several hours down Canterbury's braided Waimakariri River and then cycling the final stretch. A hundred elite tri-athletes compete in "The Longest Day", the same course in a time frame of less than 24 hours. Mere mortals – though admittedly extremely fit ones – can also compete by forming two-person teams sharing the disciplines.

From humble beginnings in 1983 the whole event has blossomed into a very professional affair with competitors training for months and serious contenders engaging the services of a highly organized support crew. The equipment too has become highly specialized; only the lightest and most high-tech of bikes will do and designers build racing kayaks especially for Waimakariri conditions.

Women compete in increasingly large numbers, but the event remains largely a macho spectacle that draws considerable press interest – with one journalist for every seven competitors – and correspondingly generous sponsorship. As an incentive to record-breaking a vehicle manufacturer is usually coaxed into offering a car or truck to the winner if they break a certain time. Several have gone to Kiwi super-athlete, Steve Gurney, who has won six of the last ten events and holds the astonishing course record, just over ten and a half hours.

church, though, even these have been insensitively restored, with scant regard for authenticity. The most interesting buildings to wander through are the printing shop, with its faded billboards advertising the latest films; the wonderful 1837 Colombian Press, which found its way here from Philadelphia via London, Auckland and Napier; the hospital, identical to one built in Greymouth; and the Gem Hall, with its collection of minerals. At the replica train station, your entry ticket entitles you to a 2-kilometre round-trip ride behind the 1887 steam engine *Kaitangata*, calling at a mine site and sawmill, where boards are cut on summer days and, of course, sage prospectors will help you pan for "colour" in salted tanks. As if that weren't more than enough schmalz, a mock hotel serves sandwiches, bar meals and beer in saloon surroundings.

No public transport runs to the site, but Kea Tours (see p.715) finish their **Goldstrike Tour** (2 daily; 2hr 30min; $32) around various gold rush sites at Shantytown.

Eating and drinking

You'll soon exhaust Greymouth's scope for eating and drinking, but there are enough places serving tasty and hearty dishes to last the night or two you're likely to stay.

Bonzai Pizzeria, 31 Mackay St. Cheerful licensed restaurant with tearoom staples through the day and a broad range of reasonably priced and tasty pizzas served daytime and evening.

Café 124 on Mackay. New café with a fine range of light meals, muffins and good coffee served inside or at outdoor seating suitably sheltered from the West Coast weather. Licensed.

Café Collage, 115 Mackay St (book in summer & at weekends, ☎03/768 5497). Greymouth's best, and priciest, food is served upstairs in this wooden-floored Art Deco room. The varied menu might include fish of the day, roast beef and butter chicken. BYO & licensed; closed Sun & Mon.

Hog's Head, 9 Tainui St. Lively downtown bar with occasional live music.

Jones's Café Bar, 37 Tainui St. Reliable spot for coffee and cake or filling and moderately priced full meals in the meat and boiled vegetables tradition.

Raceway Carvery, *Union Hotel*, 20 Herbert St. Huge plates of grilled and roast meat for under $10 and bargain all-you-can-eat barbecues nightly in summer.

West of the Border, 19 Mackay St. A Kiwi-style Tex-Mex restaurant serving groaning plates of barbecued chicken, buffalo wings, Cajun fish fillets and the like for $18–25.

Hokitika and around

South from Greymouth, SH6 hugs a desolate stretch of coast that's fine for long moody beachcombing walks, but there's little of abiding interest until **HOKITIKA**, 40km away. On initial acquaintance "Hoki", as it is known to its friends, appears only marginally more interesting than Greymouth – its jumble of mundane modern buildings interspersed with edifices from the town's golden days mouldering away, though some have recently been tidied up. Still, it is a long way to the next place of any size, and its proximity to the beach and good bushwalks, and a couple of quality restaurants give it the edge.

Like the other West Coast towns, Hokitika owes its existence to the **gold rushes** of the 1860s. Within months of the initial discoveries near Greymouth in 1864, fields had been opened up on the tributaries of the Hokitika River, and Australian diggers from Ballarat and Bendigo and Irish hopefuls all flogged over narrow passes from Canterbury to get their share. Hokitika boomed and within two years it had a population of 6000 (compared with today's 4000), streets packed with hotels, and a steady export of over a tonne of gold a month, mainly direct to Melbourne. Despite a treacherous bar at the Hokitika Rivermouth, the **port** briefly became the country's busiest, with ships tied up four deep along Gibson Wharf. As gold became harder to find and more sluicing water was needed, the enterprise eventually became uneconomic and was replaced by dairying and the timber industry. The **railway** started to transport the region's produce and the port closed in 1954, only to be smartened up in the 1990s as the focus for the town's Heritage Trail.

Arrival and information

Although a rail line comes as far as Hokitika, there are no passenger services. Coast to Coast run from Christchurch and terminate here, InterCity offer a southbound **bus** service in the afternoon as far as Fox Glacier, while Atomic come through in the morning making for Queenstown. All stop outside the Hokitika Travel Centre, 65 Tancred St (☎03/755 8134), and all except InterCity also stop at the visitor centre: both places sell tickets. Air New Zealand Link **fly** daily to Hokitika from Christchurch, arriving 2km east of the centre.

Hokitika's **visitor centre**, on the corner of Hamilton Street and Tancred Street (Dec–March daily 8.30am–6pm; April–Nov Mon–Fri 9am–5pm, Sat 10am–2pm; ☎03/755 6166, fax 755 5011, *www.westlanddc.govt.nz, hkkvin@xtra.co.nz*), is staffed by helpful folk. Just a few paces away, the **DOC office**, at the corner of Hamilton Street and Sewell Street (Mon–Fri 8am–4.30pm; ☎03/755 8301), is stocked with leaflets on local walks. **Internet access** is available at the Bookwise bookshop at 14 Weld St (Mon–Fri 9am–7pm, Sat 9am–noon).

While here, you may need to make some preparations for the long drive south. Though there are EFTPOS facilities in Franz Josef, Fox Glacier and elsewhere, the **banks** and ATMs here are the last before Wanaka, more than 400km away over the Haast Pass. **Cyclists** can obtain spares at the well-stocked Hokitika Cycles and Sports, 33 Tancred St (☎03/755 8662).

Accommodation

Apart from during the Wildfoods Festival (second weekend in March), **accommodation** is seldom hard to find.

Beach House Backpackers, 137 Revell St (☎03/755 6859, fax 755 6349, *beachhouse1999@hotmail.com*). A go-ahead backpacker empire, central and just across the road from the beach with a café/restaurant, a bar and campervan hook-ups. The hostel itself rates as a fun and friendly place with free use of dilapidated bikes, free email, fishing gear and gold pans. Tents $10, campervans $15, dorms ①, rooms ②.

Black Sands Motor Lodge, 252 Revell St (☎0800/755 222, fax 03/755 8772, *www.blacksands.co.nz*, *mail@blacksands.co.nz*). Spacious and recently renovated motel offering a range of comfortable units ten minutes' walk from the centre, plus swimming pool, spa, kids' playground and Internet access. ④.

Blue Spur Lodge, Cement Lead Rd (☎ & fax 03/755 8445, *bluespur@xtra.co.nz*). Spacious, modern and airy pine house, plus a new house with lovely en-suite doubles, all in a tranquil setting 5km from town but close to bushwalks, and with free pick-ups from town and free use of bikes. They'll also drop off and pick up at trailheads, and rent out kayaking and fly fishing gear at very reasonable rates. Dorms ①, rooms ②, en-suites ③.

Greymouth (40 km) & Christchurch (260 km)

HOKITIKA

ACCOMMODATION
Beach House Backpackers	C
Black Sands Motor Lodge	B
Blue Spur Lodge	G
Hokitika Holiday Park	F
Jade Court Motor Lodge	D
Shining Star	A
Teichelmann's B&B	E
Villa Polenza	H

RESTAURANTS, CAFÉS & BARS
Beach House Café Bar	1
Café Flix	5
Café de Paris	6
PR's Coffee Shop	4
Tasman View	2
Trapper's	3

TASMAN SEA

Cemetery

Hokitika Travel Centre
Westland's Water World
Seaside Jade
Hokitika Glass Studio
Clocktower
Westland Greenstone
Schroder's Handblown Glass
West Coast Historical Museum
Custom House
DOC Office
Mountain Jade
Signal Station Lookout

GIBSON QUAY

Hokitika River

0   500 m

Hokitika Gorge 35 km/ G (4 km) & H (3 km)
Lake Mahinapua (12 km), Lake Kaniere (18 km) F

(6), Lake Mahinapua (10 km), The Glaciers (135 km) & Haast (280 km)

Hokitika Holiday Park, 242 Stafford St (☎03/755 8172, fax 755 8127, *holidaypark@hokitika.com*). Hokitika's only campsite, neither spacious nor very appealing though it does have a good kids' playground. Tent & powered sites $8–9.50, cabins & motels ②–③.

Jade Court Motor Lodge, 85 Fitzherbert St (☎0800/755 885, fax 03/755 8133, *www.jadecourt.co.nz*, *jadecourt@minidata.co.nz*). Modern and very well-equipped motel five minutes' walk from town with in-house video and pleasant gardens. Some rooms have private spa baths and all come with coffee plungers. ⑤.

Shining Star, 11 Richards Drive (☎0800/744 6464, fax 03/755 8653, *www.nzcentre.co.nz/hokitika*, *shining@xtra.co.nz*). New establishment close to the beach with campervan hook-ups and eight attractive log cabins mostly with good self-catering facilities. Hook-ups $20, cabins ⑤.

Teichelmann's B&B, 20 Hamilton St (☎0800/743 742, fax 03/755 8239, *teichel@xtra.co.nz*). Comfortable, well-appointed and central B&B, with friendly hosts and a hearty continental breakfast. ⑤.

Villa Polenza, Brickfield Rd (☎0800/241 801, fax 03/755 79001, *www.friars.co.nz/hosts/polenza.htm*, *villapolenza@xtra.co.nz*). Luxurious bed and breakfast in a gorgeous Italianate mansion set on a plateau high above Hoki where you can watch the sun set amid lavender on Cape Cod chairs or bathe under the stars in a pair of tubs. Everything is very stylishly modern with swathes of bold colour and well chosen designer furniture. ⑧.

The Town

Hokitika's leading role in the West Coast gold rushes rightly occupies much of the **West Coast Historical Museum**, entered through the visitor centre (daily: Dec–Easter 9.30am–5pm; Easter–Nov 9.30am–4pm; $3, gold panning $5 extra) and, along with greenstone and pioneering life, forms the focus for an interesting audio-visual presentation every half hour. The photos of the submerged horrors of the Hokitika River bar and the pleasures of the hundred or so bars of another kind that once lined Tancred Street are highlights among a predictable collection of fire-fighting and shipping paraphernalia.

With interest suitably kindled, grab the free **Hokitika Heritage Trail** leaflet, which details the remaining landmarks from the town's past, including the centrepiece **clock tower** commemorating the Boer War, a statue of **Richard Seddon**, local boy made good to become prime minister from 1893 to 1906, and the Gibson Quay area. This former riverside dock has been tarted up in recent years and makes a pleasant place for an evening stroll from the 1897 **Custom House**, past an ugly concrete memorial to ships lost on the bar, to the spit-end **Signal Station Lookout**, where coloured flags and raised balls used to help guide ships into the rivermouth. The Heritage Trail also crosses the river to a plaque marking the site of the Southside Aerodrome where, in 1934, one Bert Mercer started New Zealand's first licensed air service to the glaciers, using a de Haviland Fox Moth, a replica of which stands outside Hokitika Airport.

Only those with kids to entertain and fans of immense fat eels will get much out of **Westland's Water World**, Sewell Street (daily: Nov–March 9am–8pm; April–Oct 9am–5pm; $10), which concentrates on Westland's river and sea fish and gives you a chance to catch your own salmon from indoor tanks. There's a lot more watery fun to be had going **whitewater rafting** with one of two Greymouth-based companies (see p.717), who both do pick-ups in Hoki.

Hokitika is crafts mad. Everywhere you look there is someone trying to sell you carved wood, blown glass, woven wool or a greenstone pendant, preferably with gold embellishments; and if you are in buying mode, there are quality pieces to be found. Greenstone (see box overleaf) is big business, and the shops with the best ranges are Mountain Jade, 41 Weld St, and Westland Greenstone Ltd, 22 Tancred St; both lay on stone-cutting and shaping demonstrations. Pacific Arts, 21 Tancred St, is one of the best of the smaller businesses with a limited range of attractive pendants at modest prices. Glass blowing is another longstanding Hoki tradition. There are currently two exponents, both with working artisans on show: the Hokitika Glass Studio, 25 Tancred

GREENSTONE

Maori revere **pounamu** (hard nephrite jade) and **tangiwai** (the softer, translucent bowenite), usually collectively known as **greenstone**. In *Aotearoa*'s pre-European culture, it took the place of durable metals for both practical, warfaring and decorative uses: adzes and chisels were used for carving, *mere* (clubs) were used for hand-to-hand combat, and pendants were fashioned for jewellery. Charles Heaphy observed a group of Maori producing a *mere* in 1846, and noted the process by which they "saw the slab with a piece of mica slate, wet, and afterwards polish it with a fine sandy limestone which they obtain in the vicinity. The hole is drilled with a pointed stick with a piece of Pahutanui flint. The process does not appear so tedious as has been supposed; a month sufficing, apparently, for the completion".

In Maori, the entire South Island is known as **Te Wahi Pounamu**, "the place of greenstone", reflecting the importance of its sole sources, the belt from Greymouth through the rich Arahura River area near Hokitika south to Anita Bay on Milford Sound – where the beautifully dappled tangiwai occurs – and the Wakatipu region behind Queenstown. When the Poutini Ngai Tahu arranged to sell most of Westland to James Mackay in 1860, the Arahura River, their main source of pounamu, was specifically excluded.

Its value has barely diminished. Mineral claims are jealously guarded, the export of raw greenstone is prohibited and no extraction is allowed from national parks; penalties include fines of up to $200,000 and two years in jail. **Price** is heavily dependent on quality, but rates of $50,000 a tonne are not unknown in the raw state – and the sky's the limit when the stone is fashioned into sculpture and jewellery. Many of the cheaper specimens are quite crude, but pricier pieces (and we're talking a minimum of $100 for something aesthetically pleasing, and closer to $1000 for anything really classy) exhibit accomplished Maori designs executed to perfection; at the other end of the scale, simple pendants can be picked up for as little as $10.

Hokitika is the main venue for greenstone shoppers: bear in mind that the larger **shops** and **galleries** are firmly locked into the tour-bus circuit so prices (and quality) are consequently high. They are fine for learning something about the quality of the stone and competence of the artwork, though it is worth checking out the smaller places which often have more competitive deals. Specific **recommendations** are given on p.721.

St, is the more venerable; Schroders Handblown Glass, 41 Weld St, goes for more contemporary designs.

The Hokitika year ticks by peacefully until the annual **Wildfoods Festival**, on the second Saturday in March (☎03/755 8322, fax 755 8026, *wildfoods@westlanddc.govt.nz*; $15 at the gate, $12.50 in advance). The town quadruples its population for this celebration of bush tucker, which takes place around Cass Square, where up to fifty stalls sell such delicacies as stir-fried possum, golden-fried huhu grubs, marinated goat kebabs and smoked eel wontons, all washed down with home-brewed beer and South Island wine. The gorging is followed by an evening hoe-down, the Wildfoods Barn Dance ($10).

Lastly, Wilderness Wings, out at the airport (☎03/755 8118) do a number of **scenic flights** (from $160), principally around Mount Cook and the glaciers.

Eating and drinking

In *Trapper's* and the *Café de Paris*, Hokitika is fortunate in having a couple of the best **restaurants** on the Coast – reason enough to make this an overnight stop before heading south. Neither are prohibitively expensive but if you are counting the pennies there are several cheaper cafés maintaining high standards. The most pleasant places to **drink** are the restaurants, though Hokitika has its share of beer barns. Evening entertainment is limited to a stroll to an attractive **glow-worm dell** about a kilometre north of the centre beside SH6; and the Regent cinema, 15 Weld St.

Beach House Café & Bar, 137 Revell St. Well reputed café below the backpackers of the same name serving daytime snacks and bistro-style meals in the evening – fish of the day ($19), sweet and sour chicken ($17). Licensed.

Café de Paris, 19 Tancred St (☎03/755 8933). This fine restaurant is tastefully decorated and has a relaxed atmosphere that doesn't rule out a daytime snack. An extensive selection of moderately priced breakfasts gives way to bistro lunches and more formal evening dining with a Mediterranean theme (from around $18 for a main course). Licensed & BYO.

Café Flix, 15 Weld St. Great lunch and coffee spot in the same building as the Regent cinema serving breakfast, muffins, cakes and coffee all day and imaginative pizzas on Friday, Saturday and Sunday evenings.

PR's Coffee Shop, 39 Tancred St. Popular and well-priced all-day café serving light lunches, dinners, cakes and coffees.

Tasman View, 111 Revell St (☎03/755 8344). Predominantly seafood restaurant with great sea views, mains from around $20 and a good-value smorgasbord on Friday evenings. Licensed.

Trapper's, 79 Revell St (☎03/755 5133). Try to block out the laboured theme and the heads of stuffed beasts around the walls and concentrate instead on the food: excellent chicken, salmon and vegetarian dishes are cooked in imaginative ways and prices around $20; trademark ostrich, kangaroo, wild boar and, in season, whitebait, cost a little more. Licensed.

Around Hokitika

Some of the best bush scenery and the finest **walks** hereabouts lie among the Taharoa Forest, where the dairying hinterland turns into the foothills of the Southern Alps some 30km inland along Stafford Street. Minor roads make a good 70km scenic drive (shown in detail on the DOC's *Central West Coast* leaflet available from the visitor centre; $1), passing the fishing, water skiing and tramping territory of **Lake Kaniere**, a glacial lake 18km from Hokitiki with several picnic sites and primitive camping ($5) along the eastern side. The most popular walk is the **Kaniere Water Race Walkway** (9km one way; 3hr; 100m ascent), which starts from the lake's northern end and follows a channel that used to supply water to the goldfields, through stands of regenerating rimu. Close by is the **Lake Kaniere Walkway** (13km one way; 3–4hr; flat), which traces the western lake margin by way of the basic Lawyer's Delight Hut – more of a lunch stop than a place to stay. The eastern-shore road passes the attractive **Dorothy Falls** and continues to a spur leading to the **Hokitika Gorge**, 35km from Hoki, where a short path leads to a swingbridge over the tranquil Hokitika River as it eases through a deep gorge.

Immediately south of Hokitika, SH6 runs inland for 15km before meeting the old coastal Rautapu Road near Lake Mahinapua. Take the old road to visit the **Lake Mahinapua Recreation Reserve**, from where there are a number of short walks plus the easy **Mahinapua Walkway** (16km return; 4hr; mainly flat), detailed in a free leaflet available from the Hokitika DOC office. There's a DOC **campsite** ($5) here, and the *Mahinapua Hotel* (☎03/755 8500; dorms ①, rooms ②), opposite the reserve, serves **meals**, good beer and has backpacker-style **accommodation**, though it is usually crowded with the backpacker tour-bus crowd. Gentle paddle-boat **cruises** along the Mahinapua Creek to the lake (☎03/755 7239; Dec–April 2pm; 1hr 30min; $20) start 5km south of Hokitika.

From Hokitika to the glaciers

The main highway leaves the coast **south of Hokitika** and snuggles in close to the Southern Alps for most of the 135km to the glacier at Franz Josef, the next town of any size. The journey through pakihi and stands of selectively logged native bush is broken by a series of **small settlements**, none of which warrant a long stay, though you may find yourself seduced by the sultry charms of **Okarito** and its lagoon.

Ross

The tiny village of **ROSS**, 30km south of Hokitika at the base of the bush-clad Mount Greenland, lies right on top of one of New Zealand's richest alluvial **goldfields**. The mining company is still chewing away at the large hole on the edge of town and would dearly love to get at the gold-bearing gravels underneath. The government have given consent provided all the townspeople agree to move off the land: around half are adamant they'll stay.

Once all the claims had been staked along the West Coast's original gold river, the Greenstone River near Hokitika, prospectors descended on the **Totara River** and soon there were over 3000 people here, digging down into the rich gravel layers of ancient riverbeds. By the early twentieth century, waterlogging and the lack of power for pumping put an end to a lengthy boom time, but just as things were winding up in 1909 a couple of diggers prospecting less than 500m from the current visitor centre turned up the largest gold nugget ever found in New Zealand, the 3.1kg "**Honourable Roddy**", named after the then Minister of Mines. The nugget was eventually bought by the government and given as a coronation gift in 1910 to Britain's George V, who melted it down to make royal tableware. A replica of the fist-sized lump of gold resides in the 1885 **Miner's Cottage**, Bold Street (daily 9am–4pm; free), surrounded by gold-rush photos.

DOC leaflets (from the visitor centre – see below) detail a couple of short strolls: the **Jones Flat Walk** past the source of the "Honourable Roddy"; and the more popular **Water Race Walk**, which passes the remains of fluming designed to supply water for gravel washing.

Practicalities

The **visitor centre**, 4 Aylmer St (daily 9am–4.30pm; ☎03/755 4077), presents an interesting show ($2) on the 1865 gold rush and subsequent sawmilling and farming history, and stocks DOC leaflets on local walks (50¢ each).

Accommodation is limited to the *Historic Empire Hotel*, 19 Aylmer St (☎03/755 4005, *raz-empross@paradise.net.nz*; tent sites $8, cabins ①–②, rooms ③), which has spacious verandaed doubles (some en suite), four-person cabins and tent and campervan sites, and the basic but functional *Ross Motel*, Gibson Street (☎ & fax 03/755 4022; ③). If there's nobody at the motel, ask at *Manera's General Store*. For sustenance, the *Empire Hotel* does good bar **snacks and meals**, and the *Roddy Nugget Café* does tearoom staples.

Pukekura

The roadside south of Ross is dotted with places that process sphagnum moss, which grows readily around here and is much appreciated by Japanese and Taiwanese orchid growers for its absorptive properties. The moss is also noted for being sterile and was used during the two world wars for swabs. The industry is covered in some detail at the **Bushman's Museum** (Dec–March 9am–6pm; April–Nov 9am–5pm; $2), inside the **Bushman's Centre** (free), which is marked by a giant sandfly at the hamlet of **PUKEKURA**, 25km south of Ross. The whole centre takes an entertaining and very light-hearted approach to showing how people make a living from the forest through timber milling and possum trapping, with opportunities to see several huge eels, and try your hand at knife- and axe-throwing. Once you've fed the captive possums, you can go next door to the *Wildfoods Restaurant* and eat their cousins (or a Bambi Burger), then buy a possum-fur trappers hat at the gift shop. Much the best way to experience the museum is on a guided tour ($3.50) only available for groups: tag along if one of the backpacker tour buses stops by. You can stay across the road at the *Kiwi Host Backpackers and Cabins* (☎03/755 4032; dorms ①, rooms ②), a converted house and a row of cosy cabins, all with self-catering facilities. Evenings are easily spent next door at the *Puke Tavern*.

Rest areas around beautiful **Lake Ianthe**, 4km south, make good picnic stops, but exploring the region in any more depth is for the committed only. An unsealed road winds 10km through the Lake Ianthe Forest to the exposed **Greens Beach**, from where it is an hour and a half's walk south to a seal colony.

Harihari

Lake Ianthe feeds a tributary of the Wanganui River, crossed just before the village of **HARIHARI**, 20km further south. Harihari's chief claim to fame is its proximity to the marshy landing site of **Guy Menzies'** aircraft when he flew from his home town of Sydney to New Zealand in 1931, becoming the first to do the trip solo, only three years after Charles Kingsford Smith and his team made the original crossing; he bettered Kingsford Smith's time by two and a half hours. Menzies' plane, the *Southern Cross Junior*, crash-landed in the La Fontaine swamp, leaving Menzies strapped in upside down in the mud. There's little reason to actually stop in Harihari but you might want to turn onto Wanganui Flat Road and drive 20km coastwards to the start of the **Harihari Coastal Walkway** (8km; 2–3hr; negligible ascent), which follows a track used by miners heading south in the 1870s. The route runs through kahikatea forest to a spectacular piece of coastline, a sandy beach and the Doughboy Lookout, with great views of the Southern Alps.

Harihari **accommodation** is limited to a couple of places on the main road (SH6): the old but pleasant and cycle-friendly *Tomasi Motel* (☎0800/753 3116; cabins ①–②, motel rooms ③) and the *Harihari Motor Inn* (☎0800/833 026, fax 03/753 3109, hhmi@xtra.co.nz; dorms ①, rooms ④), which also has a caravan site ($15 per site) and a spa; and the excellent *Wapiti Park Homestead* (☎ & fax 03/753 3074, whapitipark@countrylodge.co.nz; ⑤), a farmstay on the southern exit from town. Most **eating** happens at the *Harihari Motor Inn*, where there are good bar meals, or at the *Glenalmond* tearooms on SH6.

Whataroa and the herons

From November to February, New Zealand's entire population of the graceful white heron (*kotuku*) arrives to breed at the Waitangiroto Sanctuary, by the northern end of the Okarito Lagoon. The sanctuary is near **WHATAROA**, 35km south of Harihari, but access is strictly controlled and the only way to visit is on the DOC-sanctioned **White Heron Sanctuary Tours** (booking advised ☎0800/523 456, fax 03/753 4087, www.whiteherontours.co.nz; Nov–Feb 3–7 daily; 2.5hr; $89), which include a twenty-minute bus journey, a twenty-minute jetboat ride on the narrow Waitangitaona River, and half an hour observing the birds from a well-placed hide. Outside the heron season, there's still plenty to be seen on their Rainforest Nature and Jetboating Tours (all year; $89), essentially the same route but concentrating on what's appropriate to that season – tui and bellbirds feeding on flowering kowhai from August to October for example.

The White Heron Sanctuary Tours office on the main highway acts as the local **visitor centre** (no set hours; ☎03/753 4120) and also has **motel** units (④) and cabins (②). For **B&B** try *Sleepy Hollow*, SH6 (☎03/753 4139, fax 753 4079, hollow@xtra.co.nz; ⑤), which has comfortable rooms with a guest-share bathroom; or the *Whataroa Hotel* (☎03/753 4076; ④), which also has B&B, as well as a bit of wasteland out the back for campervans ($15). The *Whataroa Hotel* serves **dinners** and is the focal point of the town, while the *White Heron Tearooms* caters to daytime snackers.

Okarito

In 1642, Abel Tasman became the first European to set eyes on *Aotearoa* at **OKARITO**, a hamlet scattered around the southern side of its eponymous lagoon and reached by a 13-kilometre side-road, 15km south of Whataroa. Two centuries later, the discovery of gold sparked an eighteen-month boom that saw fifty stores and hotels spring up along the lagoon's shores. Timber milling and flax production stood in once the gold had gone but the community foundered, leaving a few holiday homes, around twenty permanent residents, and a lovely beach and lagoon used as the setting for much of Keri Hulme's Booker Prize-winning novel, *The Bone People*.

The best of the **Okarito Lagoon** is hard to fully appreciate from the shore, but Okarito Nature Tours (☎ & fax 03/753 4014, *okarito@minidata.co.nz*) run excellent-value and well-organized **kayaking trips**; generally self-guided using double sea kayaks and with emergency back-up in the unlikely event you strike difficulties. On the two-hour trip ($30), you get to paddle around the sheltered lagoon, and you'll venture further on the full-day trip ($50), but best of all is the overnight trip ($80), where you camp at a remote beach. Some experience is needed for the overnight trip, and all trips are tide-dependent: call ahead to check times. Guided trips are available, but for interpretation of the local ecology you're better off on one of their gentle two-hour **guided boat trips** (usually 9am; $45) around the lagoon.

Boating aside, Okarito seems to draw people in, mainly just to laze about and take long strolls along deserted beaches, the most popular being the **Okarito Trig Walk** (1hr 30min return; 200m ascent) at the southern end of town, which climbs to a headland with fabulous mountain and coastal views. An extension to the Trig Walk, the **Coastal Track Walk** (3hr return from Okarito; negligible ascent), should only be tackled on a receding tide.

Practicalities

There's no fancy **accommodation** here, but a good range of budget places. A memorial commemorating Tasman's sighting stands next to the associate YHA, The Strand (☎03/753 4124; ①), a simple two-room affair in the former schoolhouse, with twelve bunks (just $10) with bedding and a spacious and well appointed kitchen/living area. A little along the street is the quirky *Royal Motel & Hostel* (☎0800/398 080, fax 03/753 4180, *royalokarito@hotmail.com*; dorms ①, motel unit ②, hut ③), a hostel without dorms, comprising one motel unit, a house containing a double and a twin, and a nice self-contained hut; fishing gear is available and there are sometimes locally grown vegetables to be had. There's also a shady campsite ($5; no powered sites) with showers that take 50¢ coins; handy since the YHA has no showers. Note that Okarito has **no shop** or café, so bring everything with you. If you fancy staying for a few days, consider renting one of the houses along the main street (typically ④). Most of the owners live out of town, but someone local usually looks after the place: ask around when you arrive.

Back on SH6 just south of the Okarito junction, there's a fine DOC **campsite** ($5) at Lake Mapourika.

The glaciers

Around 150km south of Hokitika, two blinding white rivers of ice force their way down towards the thick rainforest of the coastal plain – ample justification for inclusion of this region in *Te Wahipounamu*, the South West New Zealand World Heritage Area. The glaciers are stunning viewed from a distance, but are even more impressive close up, generating a palpable connectedness between the coast and the highest peaks of the

To avoid confusion between the **villages** and the **glaciers** from which they derive their names, we've used a capital "G" for the Franz Josef Glacier (*Waiau*) **village**, and a lower-case "g" for the Franz Josef **glacier**; the same goes for the village of Fox Glacier (*Weheka*), which lies close to the foot of the Fox glacier.

Southern Alps, a sensation heightened by being able to walk on the glaciers on guided trips. Within a handful of kilometres the terrain drops from over 3000m to near sea level, bringing with it **Franz Josef glacier** and **Fox glacier**, the two largest and most impressive of the sixty-odd glaciers that creak off the South Island's icy backbone, together forming the centrepiece of the rugged **Westland National Park**. Legend tells of the beautiful Hinehukatere who so loved the mountains that she encouraged her lover, Tawe, to climb alongside her. He fell to his death and Hinehukatere cried so copiously that her tears formed the glaciers, known to Maori as *Ka Riomata o Hinehukatere* – "The Tears of the Avalanche Girl".

The park is equally characterized by the West Coast's prodigious **precipitation**, which here reaches its greatest expression, with five metres being the typical yearly dump. These conditions, combined with the rakish angle of the western slopes of the Southern Alps, produce some of the world's **fastest-moving** glaciers; stand at the foot for half an hour or so and you're bound to see a piece peel off. But these phenomenal speeds haven't been enough to completely counteract melting, and both glaciers have **receded** over 3km since Cook saw them at their greatest recent extent, soon after the Little Ice Age of 1750. In 1985 the process reversed, but after fifteen years of bucking the world trend by **advancing**, the glaciers look to be backtracking once again.

Art critic and arbiter of public taste in Victorian England, John Ruskin, once postulated that glaciers retreat "on account of the vulgarity of tourists", and Franz Josef and Fox had certainly turned their tail when contemporary **travellers** battled their way down the coast to observe these wonders of nature, initially named "Victoria" and "Albert" respectively. In 1865, geologist Julius von Haast renamed Franz Josef after the Austro-Hungarian Emperor, and following a visit by prime minister William Fox in 1872, the other glacier was bestowed with his name.

Activity in the glaciers focuses on two small **villages**, which survive almost entirely on tourist traffic. Both lie close to the base of their respective glacier and are near the start of numerous walks, and both offer a comparably wide variety of plane and helicopter **flights** and **guided glacier walks** (see box on p.732). Franz Josef has marginally better facilities, while Fox Glacier is the quieter, with a more rural aspect; with your own transport, it makes sense to base yourself in one of the two villages and explore both glaciers from there.

Franz Josef Glacier

Historically there has been little to choose between the two glacier villages, but in recent years **FRANZ JOSEF GLACIER** has edged ahead, with a wider range of places to stay and an improving culinary scene. The Franz Josef glacier almost licks the fringes of the village, the Southern Alps tower above and developers have done what they can with steeply pitched roofs and pine panelling, but the village somehow lacks alpine character, perhaps owing to the encircling rain-soaked bush. It is an appealing place though, and small enough to make you feel almost like a local if you stay for more than a night or two – something that's easily done, considering the number of fine walks hereabouts and the proximity of the glaciers.

GLACIERS FOR BEGINNERS

The existence of a glacier is always a balancing act between competing forces: snowfall at the **névé**, high in the mountains, battles with rapid melting at the **terminal** lower down the valley, the victor determining whether the glacier will **advance** or **retreat**. Snowfall metres thick gradually compacts to form clear **blue ice**, which accumulates to the point when it starts to flow downhill under its own weight. Friction against the valley walls slows the sides while ice in the centre charges headlong down the valley, giving the characteristic **scalloped effect** on the surface, which is especially pronounced on such vigorous glaciers as Franz Josef and Fox. Where a riverbed steepens, the river forms a rapid: under similar conditions, glaciers break up into an **ice fall**, full of towering blocks of ice known as **seracs**, separated by **crevasses**.

Visitors familiar with grubby glaciers in the European Alps or American Rockies will expect the surface to be mottled with **rock debris** which has fallen off the valley walls onto the surface; however, the glaciers here descend so steeply that the cover doesn't have time to build up and they remain pristine and white. Rock still gets carried down with the glacier though, and when the glacier retreats, this is deposited as **terminal moraine**. Occasionally retreating glaciers leave behind huge chunks of ice which, on melting, form **kettle lakes**.

The most telling evidence of past glacial movements is the location of the **trim line** on the valley wall, caused by the glacier stripping away all vegetation. At Fox and Franz Josef, the advance associated with the Little Ice Age around 1750 left a very visible trim line high up the valley wall, separating mature rata from scrub.

Arrival and information

Daily InterCity **buses** in both directions arrive in the evening and leave the following morning: the southbound bus drops off around Franz Josef then continues to Fox Glacier; in the morning it picks up in both villages and continues south. The northbound bus does the reverse, dropping off in Fox Glacier first. Atomic buses in both directions come through in the middle of the day on their Greymouth–Queenstown run.

First stop in Franz Josef should be the excellent combined **visitor centre** and **DOC office** on SH6 (daily: Nov–April 8.30am–6pm; May–Oct 9am–5pm; ☎03/752 0796, fax 752 0797), which has stacks of leaflets on walks in the area and first-class displays on every aspect of glaciation and the region's geology. Every half hour they show a documentary film ($3) discussing the whole South West New Zealand World Heritage Area with limited coverage of the glaciers.

Pretty much everything else you are likely to need is within a couple of hundred metres along, or just off, SH6. There are **no banks** or cash machines either here or in Fox Glacier, but several places have EFTPOS facilities and most places accept credit cards. There's fast and efficient **Internet access** in the building used by Franz Josef Glacier Guides and the Helicopter Line; and **bike rental** from Ice Flow Arts (☎03/752 0144; $4 per hr, $25 per day) right by the *Blue Ice Café*.

Accommodation

As a consequence of the bus schedules and the tendency for folk to spend at least two nights here, accommodation is very tight throughout the summer. Between December and March, you should aim to **book** at least a couple of days **in advance**. The better backpacker places are all clustered at one end of Cron Street, just along from a couple of good motels; guesthouses are a better bet than the large motor lodges.

A1 Rata Grove Motel, 25 Cron St (☎0800/101 933, fax 03/752 0741, *ratagrove@xtra.co.nz*). Central and fairly modern motel with kitchen-less studios and spacious fully equipped self-catering units. ⑤.

Chateau Franz, 8 Cron St (☎0800/472 8568, fax 752 0738). Well-organized and justifiably popular backpackers with an easy-going, if occasionally rowdy, atmosphere, a wide selection of videos, a pool table and Internet access. The caravans out back offer some of the cheapest doubles in town. Tents $10, dorms ①, rooms ②.

Franz Josef Holiday Park & Black Sheep Backpackers Lodge, 1km south on SH6 (☎03/752 0766, fax 752 0766, *fjhp@ihug.co.nz*). Big riverside complex just out of town with a large and well appointed backpackers that's tied into the Kiwi Experience backpacker tour buses, plenty of camping, and a wide selection of tourist cottages, fully self-contained tourist flats, and high-quality modern motel units. There's Internet access on site, an outdoor games area with petanque and a life-size chess set, and a café. Tents and powered sites $9–10, dorms ①, rooms ②, cottages ③, flats ④, motels ⑤.

Glow Worm Cottages, 27 Cron St (☎0800/151 027, fax 03/752 0173). Small and homely hostel with a spacious well-equipped kitchen, 6-bed dorms, four-shares with their own bathrooms and comfy doubles, some of them en suite. Dorms ①, rooms ②, en-suites ③.

Knightswood, SH2, 3km south of town (☎03/752 0059, fax 752 0061). Comfortable en-suite B&B rooms in a spacious modern native-timber house surrounded by bush and a deer farm. Hearty breakfasts put you in good stead for glacier hiking. ⑥.

Montrose, 9 Cron St (☎ & fax 03/752 0750, ☎0800/66 877). A well run and reasonably spacious backpackers in a re-sited house recently expanded with a large section containing good dorms and made-up doubles. Plenty of common space and a spa. Dorms ①, rooms ③.

Punga Grove, Cron St (☎0800/437 269, fax 752 0002, *www.pungagrove.co.nz*, *pungagrove @xtra.co.nz*). Very well kept combination motel and campervan park set on the edge of town but

FRANZ JOSEF GLACIER

Hokitika (135 km)

Fox Glacier (25 km) & Haast (165 km)

(2 km) Fox Glacier

Waiho River

Canavan Knob 251m

Docherty Creek

Lake Wombat

Alex Knob Track

Douglas Walk

Peters Pool

Alex Knob 1295m

Sentinel Rock

Information Boards

Tatare Stream

Callery River

Roberts Point

Franz Josef Glacier

0   2 km

Airstrip

Alpine Adventure Centre

Franz Josef Glacier Guides
The Helicopter Line &
Internet Access

COWAN ST

GRAHAM DR

CRON ST

CONDON ST

Visitor Centre & DOC Office

St James

0   100 m

the glacier

ACCOMMODATION

A1 Rata Grove Motel	E
Chateau Franz	F
Franz Josef Holiday Park	I
Glow Worm Cottages	D
Knightswood	J
Montrose	H
Punga Grove	B
Terrace Motel	C
Waiho Stables	K
Westwood Lodge	A
YHA	G

RESTAURANTS, CAFÉS & BARS

Batson's	2
Beeches	3
Blue Ice Café	5
Cheeky Kea Café	4
Way Out West Café	1

feeling more like it's in the bush. Those needing a roof have a choice of spacious motel units with kitchens, and appealing log cabins with en suites and kitchen. There's Internet access, a spa pool and you can have breakfast delivered to your room. Van sites $10, cabins ④, motels ⑤–⑥.

Terrace Motel, Cowan St (☎0800/837 7223, fax 03/752 0190, *terrace.motel@xtra.co.nz*). High-quality motel with all mod cons, close to the centre of town. ⑤.

Waiho Stables Country Stay, Docherty Creek, 6km south (☎03/752 0747, fax 752 0786, *www.waiho.co.nz, waiho@waiho.co.nz*). Boutique country stay with a strong environmental slant in very peaceful setting. Modern wood-panelled rooms come with bathroom and full continental breakfast, and a vegetarian BYO dinner is available for around $30. ⑧.

Westwood Lodge, 2km north on SH6 (☎ & fax 03/752 0111, *westwood@xtra.co.nz*). The best Franz Josef has to offer: a spacious, comfortable guesthouse with a cosy alpine lodge feel, well-appointed en-suite rooms, a full-size billiard room and a buffet continental or cooked breakfast. ⑦.

YHA, 2–4 Cron St (☎03/752 0754, fax 752 0080, *yhafzjo@yha.org.nz*). Modern, airy hostel with a spacious kitchen, clean comfortable rooms and a sunny lawn out the front. Dorms ①, rooms ②.

Walks – and more sedentary diversions

Top of everyone's list of **walks** is the one from the information kiosk and car park, 5km south of the village, **to the face of the Franz Josef glacier** (4km return; 1hr 20min; flat), a roped-off and ever-changing wall of ice beside an ice cave where the Waiho River issues from beneath the glacier. The rough track crosses gravel beds left behind by past glacial retreats, giving you plenty of opportunity to observe the glacier-scoured hump of Sentinel Rock just downstream, small kettle lakes, the trim line high up the valley walls and a fault line cutting right across the valley (marked by deep gullies opposite each other).

Worthwhile walks off this access road include one to **Sentinel Rock** (10min), the circular **Douglas Walk** (1hr) past Peter's Pool, a serene lake left by a retreat in the late eighteenth century, and the **Alex Knob Track** (12km; 6–8hr return; 1000m ascent), which climbs high above the glacier through several vegetation zones and offers fine views up the valley. The first few metres of the Douglas Walk are shared with the spectacular **Roberts Point Track** (9km; 5hr return; 600m ascent) which climbs up through dripping rainforest on the opposite (northern) side of the valley, high above the glacier. Slippery stream crossings and occasional rockface ladders make this an entertaining, though not especially strenuous walk. The only way to actually walk on the glacier surface is with a guide (see box on p.732).

The shortest walk from town follows SH6 for a couple of hundred metres south to **St James Church**, which once framed the glacier in the altar window. The ice retreated from view in 1953, and the church itself nearly did the same in 1995, when the flooded Waiho River scoured away the alluvial bank and left the church precariously poised on a cliff. The authorities have since constructed protective stop banks which also serve to ensure the town doesn't get flooded: the glacier's advance in recent years has pushed forward so much gravel that the riverbed is now higher than most of the town.

Glacier hikes tend to go in most weathers, but on misty and **wet days** you may well find that scenic flights and heli-hikes are called off and alternatives are limited. There's always the twenty-minute *Flowing West* wide-screen film (3–5 showings daily; $10) at the Alpine Adventure Centre, an over-produced journey around the region with all the spirit of a failed fizzy-drink commercial. A better bet might be to take a lowland interpretive **minibus tour** with Kamahi Tours (☎03/752 0793): they run to the glacier car park (1hr; $5); to the glacier terminal (2hr 30min; $25); to Lake Matheson (3hr; $45) and to Okarito (2–3hr; $40). **Off-road tours** in an eight-wheeled amphibious buggy are run by Wildtrax (☎03/752 0793; 2hr 30min; $50) who'll show you the bush and coastal wetlands. Alternatively, there may well be better weather up the coast, in which case you may consider a day-trip to Okarito (see p.726), the herons at Whataroa (see p.725), or even a heli-rafting trip on the nearby Perth River: call Hot Rock Rafting (see p.717).

Eating and drinking

With the opening of an innovative **restaurant** or two in recent years, a couple of days in Franz Josef doesn't mean culinary deprivation, and there's even a central **bar**. The relatively remote location keeps prices high though, and even if you are self-catering you can expect to pay over the odds for a limited stock of **groceries**.

Batson's, cnr Cowan St & Cron St. The best and most convenient of Franz Josef's two pubs – the other is out at the *Franz Josef Glacier Hotel*, 1km north of town – with a convivial atmosphere, pool table and a range of bistro meals for $12–15; a favourite with the locals.

Beeches, SH6. Easy-going café and restaurant with a good line in sandwiches, muffins and salads during the day and the likes of chicken filo parcel ($19), salmon fillet ($22) or even whitebait fritters ($25; seasonal) in the evening. Licensed.

Blue Ice Café, SH6. A modern and airy addition to the Franz Josef scene, with café-style all-day dining, and the best coffee in town. In the evening the restaurant serves imaginative and tasty mains for around $20 and a range of gourmet pizzas from $15, which can also be ordered to take away or eaten in the upstairs bar where the pool table and rowdy music draws in a lively backpacker-heavy crowd nightly.

Cheeky Kea Café, SH6. Cheerful and inexpensive BYO café serving a middle-of-the-road selection of grills, burgers, sandwiches and tearoom favourites.

Way Out West Café, *Franz Josef Glacier Hotel*, SH6 (☎03/752 0729). Formal dining in a cavernous restaurant that lacks atmosphere but serves good food – tuna fillets with charred pepper and lime or West Coast beef in thyme jus – for around $23.

Fox Glacier

FOX GLACIER, 25km south of Franz Josef, lies scattered over an outwash plain of the Fox and Cook rivers, and supports the local farming community, as well as sightseers. Everything of interest is near SH6 or Cook Flat Road, which passes the scenic Lake Matheson on the way to the former gold settlement and seal colony at Gillespies Beach. The foot of the Fox glacier lies around 8km away.

Arrival and information

The village of Fox Glacier experiences the same **bus** schedule as Franz Josef (see p.728) and consequently has similar problems with accommodation through the summer months. If you come unstuck, seek help at the combined **visitor centre** and **DOC office**, SH6 (May, June, Sept & Oct daily 8.30am–4.30pm; Nov–March daily 8.30am–6pm; July & Aug Mon–Fri 8.30am–4.30pm; ☎03/751 0807, fax 751 0858) which, besides providing information about the region, has displays concentrating on lowland forests.

Accommodation

Fox Glacier's range of places to stay is more limited than Franz Josef's but is generally pretty good and well priced; **booking** as far ahead as you can is a good idea if you are determined to stay in the village.

Fox Glacier Holiday Park, Cook Flat Rd (☎03/751 0821, fax 751 0813, *www.holidayparks. co.nz/fox*). Spacious campsite with standard facilities with tent sites, a bunkhouse and a range of cabins and flats. Camping $18, dorms ①, cabins & flats ②–③.

Fox Glacier Inn, Sullivan's Rd (☎03/751 0044, fax 751 0024). New backpackers that's somewhat cramped and unappealing at present, though this will probably improve as they get better organized. Tents $9, dorms ①, made-up rooms ②.

Fox Glacier Lodge and Campervan Park, SH6 (☎ & fax 03/751 0888, *www.holidayparks. co.nz/foxglacier*). The fanciest place right in town in a pine-lined alpine chalet with attractively furnished en-suite rooms (some with spa baths) all sharing communal cooking facilities and lounge area. A buffet breakfast is included, and there are campervan hook-ups outside but no tent sites. Bikes can be rented for $15 a day. Hook-ups $10, rooms ⑥.

GLACIER FLIGHTS AND GUIDED WALKS

The range of flights, glacier walks and activities available from Franz Josef Glacier and Fox Glacier are almost identical.

FLIGHTSEEING

On any fine day the skies above both villages are abuzz with choppers and light planes. Safety demands that specific **flight paths** must be followed, limiting what can be offered and forcing companies to compete on price; ask for youth, student, senior or just-for-the-sake-of-it **discounts**, most readily given if you can band together in a group of four to six and present yourselves as a ready-to-go plane or chopper load: YHA card holders are entitled to a 20 percent discount with the Helicopter Line. **Plane** flights tend to be longer for the same money, but apart from the Mount Cook Airline ski planes, only the **helicopters** land, usually on a snow saddle high above the glacier where the rotors are left running – hardly a serene setting. Of the **plane operators**, Air Safaris (☎0800/723 274, fax 03/752 0701) run overflights of both glaciers (30min; $150) and circuits of Mount Cook (50min; $215); Mount Cook Airline (☎03/752 0714 & 0800/800 702) do the same flights for similar prices and also do snow-landing flights (conditions permitting; 40–60min; $190–250). **Helicopter operators** Fox and Franz Josef Heliservices (☎0800/800 793, *fox_heli@xtra.co.nz*), Glacier Southern Lakes Helicopters (☎03/752 0755, fax 752 0778, *gslhfranz@es.co.nz*) and The Helicopter Line (☎03/ 752 0767 & 0800/807 767, *hinfo@helicopter.co.nz*) all charge similar prices for flights, including snow landings: one glacier (20min; $120–135), two glaciers (30min; $170–190), and two glaciers plus Mount Cook (40min; $250–260).

WALKING ON GLACIERS

Two companies are licensed to take visitors on **Franz Josef glacier walks**. The longest established are Franz Josef Glacier Guides, SH6 (☎0800/484 337, fax 03/752 0102, *www.franzjosefglacier.co.nz*, *walks@franzjosefglacier.co.nz*) who undertake a **half-day trip** (daily 9.15am & 2pm; $39) that involves a trudge across the braided riverbed below the glacier in hobnail boots then an hour or so on the ice, snaking up ample ice steps cut by your guide. Although you're steadied by a fixed rope, it can be unnerving balancing beside deep blue crevasses – vertigo sufferers beware. For a more tangible sense of adventure, fork out for the full-day **Icefall Climb** (daily 9.15am; $78) which gives around five hours on the ice, with an ice axe and specially designed flexible crampons that are easy to master for additional purchase on far smaller ice steps. Currently the fashion is for **Heli-hiking** (2hr 30min; $190), which combines a short helicopter flight with a couple of hours on a fascinating section of ice caves, pinnacles and seracs that you couldn't hope to reach on foot in a day: well worth saving up for. Try to be clear about your aspirations and abilities and you can be matched up with a party of like-minded folk. The Guiding Company (☎0800/800 102, *www.nzguides.com*, *glacier@voyager.co.nz*), offer an almost identical selection of trips, plus ice climbing ($150) – an instructional roped-up day in plastic boots with crampons and ice tools on steep ice.

Glacier walking is perhaps more rewarding on the **Fox glacier**, where entry is from the side, giving more immediate access to crevasses and seracs. Alpine Guides (☎0800/111 600, fax 751 0857, *www.foxguides.co.nz*, *foxguides@miniata.co.nz*) lead half-day walks (9.15am & 1.45pm; $39), with around an hour on the ice, and do **longer trips** (6hr total; $65), giving around three hours on the ice. For serious ice addicts, there are even **Ice Climbing Instruction Days** ($150).

Fox Glacier Resort Hotel, Cook Flat Rd (☎0800/369 800, fax 03/751 0868, *info@resorts.co.nz*). Ageing hotel with faded but still elegant public areas and widely varying rooms, ranging from economy twins to modern en-suites. Dorms ①, rooms ②–⑥.

The Homestead, Cook Flat Rd (☎03/751 0835, fax 751 0805). Friendly homestay in a lovely old house within walking distance of town, with views of Mount Cook and attractive en-suite rooms. A cooked breakfast is $5 extra. ⑤.

Ivory Towers, Sullivan's Rd (☎ & fax 03/751 0838, ☎0800/151 027, *ivorytowers@xtra.co.nz*). Friendly, clean and colourfully decorated hostel, most dorms having beds rather than bunks and some rooms (all with sheets) sharing a separate lounge area. The kitchen is spacious, there's a spa, and bikes can be rented for $15 a day. Dorms ①, rooms ③.

Mount Cook View Motel, Cook Flat Rd (☎ & fax 03/751 0814, ☎0800/828 814). High-standard motel with characterful older units and spacious, luxurious newer units, some with spa baths. ⑤–⑦.

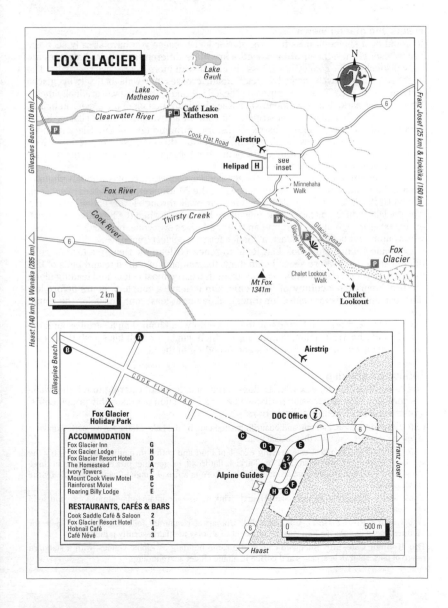

Rainforest Motel, Cook Flat Rd (☎0800/520 000, fax 03/751 0141, *rainforest@xtra.co.nz*). Log cabin exteriors belie the clean interior lines of smallish but attractive studio units and larger one-bedroom units. ⑤.

Roaring Billy Lodge, SH6 (☎ & fax 03/751 0815, ☎0800/352 121, *billy@xtra.co.nz*). Friendly homestay in the centre of Fox Glacier with simple rooms and a comfortable lounge area; venison sausages are occasionally on offer for breakfast. Billy also runs nature-guiding trips to order. ⑤.

Walks and glacier views

It would be a shame to miss the Fox glacier just because you have already seen the Franz Josef glacier: the **approach walks** are quite different and their characters are very distinct, the Fox valley being less sheer but with more impressive rock falls. The approach, imaginatively named Glacier Road, crosses the wide bed left by glacial retreats and is occasionally re-routed as "dead" ice under the roadway gradually melts. From the car park, 8km from the town, a track leads to the foot of the glacier in half an hour, crossing a couple of small streams en route. Part way back along Glacier Road, **River Walk** (2km; 30min) crosses a historic swingbridge to the Glacier Valley Viewpoint on Glacier View Road, which runs along the south side of the Fox River. From here, the **Chalet Lookout Walk** (4km; 1hr 15min return) climbs moderately for stupendous glacier and mountain views.

It's difficult to imagine a New Zealand calendar or picture book without a photo of Mount Cook and Mount Tasman mirrored in **Lake Matheson**, 6km west of town along Cook Flat Road. A well signposted lakeside boardwalk through lovely native bush encircles the lake, which was formed by an iceberg left behind when the Fox Glacier retreated 14,000 years ago. It takes around an hour and gives everyone, but particularly those who venture out before breakfast, a chance for that perfect image.

Continue 15km along Cook Flat Road to reach **Gillespies Beach**, a former gold-mining settlement where a small cemetery, the remains of a dredge and piles of tailings can be seen. Several **walks** fan out from there, the most celebrated leading along the beach north to a **colony of fur seals**; aim to leave a couple of hours before low tide (consult the visitor centre for times), allowing at least four hours for the round trip.

Back in Fox, there's no better way to fill an empty half hour than to stroll around the flat **Minnehaha Walk** (1km; 20min loop), which winds through lush bush that's cool and shady on a summer day, or dank and brooding in the rain.

Eating and drinking

For its diminutive size, Fox Glacier does a reasonable job of catering to hungry walkers coming off the glacier-side paths, with a small selection of reasonably priced **cafés**, a restaurant and a couple of lively **bars**.

Café Lake Matheson. Pleasant and beautifully sited café by the Lake Matheson car park 6km west of town; though it is not worth a special visit.

Café Névé, SH6. Fox's best café serving excellent food and coffee throughout the day – try the smoked chicken and brie salad, BLT on Turkish flatbread, or gourmet pizzas that come in three sizes ($8–15). Dinner mains cost around $25 and there is a broad range of wines available by the glass. Licensed.

Cook Saddle Café and Saloon, SH6. Hearty drinking in a mountain-lodge atmosphere and solid bar meals all day.

Fox Glacier Resort Hotel, Cook Flat Rd. Upmarket restaurant following the Kiwi taste for Mediterranean and Pacific Rim cuisine, adjacent to a noisy and fairly scruffy public bar.

The Hobnail Café, SH6. Adequate café in the same building as Alpine Guides, with a standard range of pies, sandwiches, cakes and coffee in alpine-chalet surroundings.

South Westland and Makarora

South from the glaciers, the West Coast feels remoter still. There wasn't even a road through here until 1965 and the final section of tarmac wasn't laid on the Haast Pass until 1995. SH6 mostly runs inland, passing the start of the ambitious **Copland Track** (see box below), through kahikatea and rimu forests as far as **Knight's Point**, where it returns to the coast along the edge of the Haast Coastal Plain, with its stunning **coastal dune systems** sheltering lakes and some fine stands of kahikatea. The plain continues south past the scattered township of **Haast** to the site of the short-lived colonial settlement of **Jackson Bay**. From Haast, SH6 veers inland over the Haast Pass to the former timber town of **Makarora**, not strictly part of the West Coast but moist enough to share some of the same characteristics and a base for the excellent **Gillespie Pass** Tramp.

South to Haast

Many visitors do the run from the glaciers to Wanaka or Queenstown in one day, missing out on some fine country that makes up for its relative lack of comforts with its sheer sense of remoteness. Facilities aren't completely absent: the majority of the accommodation and eating places are clustered around Haast, but there are a few pit-stops along the way. One place you might like to break your journey is **Bruce Bay**, 46km south of Fox Glacier, where the road briefly parallels a long driftwood-strewn beach perfect for an atmospheric stroll. Some 15km further south, the road crosses the **Paringa River**, where a plaque marks the southern limit of Thomas Brunner's 1846–48 explorations. He recorded in his diary the desire to "once more see the face of a white man, and hear my native tongue". Nearby, the *Salmon Farm* makes a good place to break for a snack or light lunch sat on a wooden deck overlooking salmon-rearing ponds. There's less appealing dining to be had 7km beyond at the *Lake Paringa Café* though you might wish to stay at the associated *Lake Paringa Motels* (☎03/751 0894, fax 751 0050; studios ④, units ⑤), located on the northern shores of **Lake Paringa** and equipped with a dinghy and fishing tackle for guests' use. They also sell fishing licences, handy if you are planning to fish for Quinnat salmon (Oct–March) and brown

---

WELCOME FLAT HOT SPRINGS AND THE COPLAND TRACK

The three-to-four-day **Copland Track** over the spectacular 2150m Copland Pass has long been regarded as the pinnacle of tramping achievement, on the cusp of real mountaineering. It requires competent use of an ice axe and crampons but is currently highly dangerous on account of unstable rock rubble beside the Hooker Glacier on the Mount Cook side. Guided crossings are currently suspended, though the DOC continues to issue an instruction leaflet and Alpine Guides in Fox Glacier and Mount Cook will rent out equipment. Conditions do change though, so ask locally; and note that the track is usually hiked from Mount Cook to the West Coast.

At present, the best compromise is to tackle just the sector from the foot of the **Copland Valley to the thermal pools** (17km; 6–7hr; 400m ascent), near **Welcome Flat Hut** (Category 2; $10; 30 bunks). It is pleasant bushwalking all the way and the open-air pools are a wonderful incentive. The track starts by a car park just off SH6, 26km south of Fox Glacier, and follows the right bank all the way to Welcome Flat, crossing numerous streams by hopping from rock to rock or wading. If the creeks are high, as they commonly are, you may have to use the flood bridges, which will add an hour or so; after really heavy rain, the track becomes impassable.

trout (all year) from the DOC's simple but beautifully sited Lake Paringa **campsite** ($5), a further kilometre to the south.

Around 18km south of Lake Paringa, the **Monro Beach Walk** (5km; 1hr 30min return) leads through lovely forest to one of the best places for spotting rare **Fiordland crested penguins** – mainly during the breeding season (July–Dec), but also occasionally in February, when they come ashore to moult. Nature lovers with ample wallets can gain a deeper appreciation of the fragile ecosystems of south Westland by staying nearby at the exclusive *Wilderness Lodge Lake Moeraki* (✆03/750 0881, fax 750 0882, *www.wildernesslodge.co.nz*, *lakemoeraki@wildernesslodge.co.nz*; ⑨) where, for around $200 per person per day, you get lodge **accommodation**, all meals, free canoe use and all manner of guided nature walks and safaris.

The highway finally returns to the coast 5km on at **Knight's Point**, where a roadside marker commemorates the linking of Westland and Otago by road in 1965; a dog belonging to one of the surveyors lends his name to this dramatic bluff fringed by magnificent seascapes where, with binoculars, seals can often be picked out on the rocks below. Ahead lies the **Haast Coastal Plain**, which kicks off at the tea-coloured **Ship Creek**, where a picnic area and information panels by a beautiful long surf-pounded beach mark the start of two lovely walks: the twenty-minute **Kahikatea Swamp Forest Walk** up the river through kahikatea forest to a lookout and the **Mataketake Dune Lake Walk** (2km; 30min return) along the coast to the dune-trapped Lake Mataketake.

From Ship Creek it is only another 15km to the 700m-long Haast River Bridge, the longest single-lane bridge in the country, immediately before Haast Junction.

Haast

HAAST is initially a confusing place, with three communities all taking the name: Haast Junction, at the intersection of SH6 and the minor road to Jackson Bay, Haast Beach, 4km along the Jackson Bay Road (see opposite) and Haast Township, the largest settlement 2km along SH6 towards the Haast Pass and Wanaka.

The first stop is Haast Junction, site of the distinctive **Haast World Heritage Centre** (daily: mid-Nov to mid-April 9am–6pm; rest of year 9am–4.30pm; ✆03/750 0809), which serves as the local visitor centre but is much more, with highly informative displays on all aspects of the local environment, and the short *Edge of Wilderness* film shown every half hour ($3). Time spent in here may well induce you to spend longer in what they are at pains to point out is part of the Southwest New Zealand World Heritage Area. To explore deeper into this region you should definitely consider joining a **jetboat safari** with Waiatoto River Safaris (✆0800/865382, fax 03/442 7146, *www.riversafaris.co.nz*, *info@riversafaris.co.nz*; daily at 9am, noon & 3pm; $99), a two-hour ride from the coast into the heart of the mountains with the emphasis firmly on appreciation of the area's history and scenery.

With the jetboat trip in mind, you may well want to stay over: you'll find everything you need on Pauareka Road, and remember that over the summer you should **book ahead** for a room. There's comfortable and welcoming **accommodation** at *Wilderness Backpackers* (✆ & fax 03/750 0029, ✆0800/750 029; dorms ①, rooms ②–③), with four-bed dorms, doubles and twins, some made-up and with en suites. Motel accommodation is best provided next door at *Heritage Park Lodge* (✆0800/526 252, fax 03/750 0869, *heritageparklodge@xtra.co.nz*; ④), which has modern, comfortable studios with TV and video, and some units (⑤) with self-catering facilities. You may need to fall back on the YHA associated *Haast Highway Accommodation* (✆03/750 0703, fax 750 0718; dorms ①, rooms ②), which has powered sites for vans ($10), and the linked *Aspiring Court Motel* (✆03/750 0777, fax 750 0718; studio ④, unit ⑥). The shabby *World Heritage Hotel* (✆0800/502 444; ⑤) is best avoided. **Campers** may be allowed to pitch a tent at the *Haast Highway Accommodation* ($10), but if it is raining or the manager decides the hostel facilities are already stretched you'll be forced to either travel 17km to the *Haast Beach Holiday Park* (see below), or use a little discrete imagination.

Visitors planning to self-cater should note that the supplies at the single small supermarket are limited and fairly expensive. Three places serve **meals**, but the only one worth recommending is *Smithy's Tavern* which offers standard fish and chips, steak and chips and perhaps a pasta dish in large portions for $15–18.

The road to Jackson Bay

A real sense of isolation soon sets in on the 50km **dead-end road** south to the fishing village of Jackson Bay. A modest number of inquisitive tourists make it down this way, to discover a place hanging on by its fingernails. Leaving Haast Junction, the canopies of windswept roadside trees are bunched together like cauliflower heads down to and beyond **Haast Beach**, 4km south, where there's a small shop, petrol and the decent *Erewhon Motel* (☎03/750 0803, fax 750 0817; studios ④, two-storey chalets ⑥). The one-time Maori fishing and greenstone-gathering settlement of **Okuru**, 10km further south, dates back to around 1300, and now comprises a strip of beach housing set back from a wild coastline. Just beyond, some 15km south of Haast Junction, the decent *Haast Beach Holiday Park* (☎ & fax 03/750 0860; tents $9, dorms ①, cabins ②–③) stands opposite the **Hapuku Estuary Walk** (20min loop), which follows a raised boardwalk over a brackish lagoon and through kowhai forest that gleams brilliant yellow in October and November. Old sand dunes support rimu and kahikatea forest, and there are occasional views out to the **Open Bay Islands**, noted by Cook in 1770 and later gainfully employed as a sealing base away from the sandflies of the coast. They are now a **wildlife sanctuary** and a major breeding colony for fur seals and Fiordland crested penguins.

The road continues 35km to **Jackson Bay** (Okahu), a former sealing station tucked in the curve of Jackson Head, which protects it from the worst of the westerlies. In 1875

GILLESPIE PASS: THE WILKIN AND YOUNG VALLEYS CIRCUIT

The DOC's Tramping Guide to the Makarora Region *($2) has all the detail you need for this walk, though the 1:150,000* Mount Aspiring National Park *and the 1:50,000* Wilkin *maps are useful.*

This tramp over the 1490m **Gillespie Pass** links the upper valley of the **Young River** with that of the **Siberia Stream** and the **Wilkin River**. The **scenery** is superb, the match of any of the more celebrated valleys further south, but is tramped by a fraction of the folk on the Routeburn or the Greenstone tracks; perhaps the biggest gripe for the tramping purist is the disturbance caused by **planes** flying into the Siberia Valley. The tramp can be divided up into smaller chunks, using the Siberia Experience's planes and jetboats (see p.740), but the full circuit (60km) takes **three days**.

ACCESS AND ACCOMMODATION

All the **huts** (Category 2; $10) in the Wilkin and Young valleys are equipped with mattresses and heating (but not cooking) stoves; hut **tickets** and annual hut **passes** are available from the DOC office in Makarora (see p.740). The walk is typically done up the Young Valley and down the Wilkin – the way we've described it here. **Access** at both ends of the walk is a question of **wading** the broad **Makarora River**. If it hasn't rained substantially in the last five days and you can pick your spot well (the river changes course frequently, so ask locally), you'll barely be in up to your knees but if you have any doubt, band together with other trampers and get a **jetboat** to drop you at the confluence of the Young and Makarora rivers (around $17 per person); it's also a good idea to arrange a **pick-up** by jetboat ($40) or plane ($70 for two) from Kerin Forks at the far end of the walk, unless you want to take your chances with river crossings or a stand-by flight out of Siberia Valley.

THE ROUTE

The walk proper starts on the northern bank of the confluence of the Young and Makarora rivers; from Makarora, walk 3km upstream, find a good crossing place upstream of the confluence then walk down the right bank of the Makarora to the bushside marker. From the **confluence to Young Hut** (15km; 7–9hr; 700m ascent), the easyto-follow track traces the left bank through beech forest then, after a fork, follows the left

it was chosen as the site for a "Special Settlement", a significant port and commercial centre to rival Greymouth and Hokitika. Assisted migrants – Scandinavians, Germans, Poles, Italians, English and Irish – were expected to carve a living from tiny land allocations, with limited and irregular supplies. Sodden by rain, crops rotted, and people were soon leaving in droves; a few stalwarts stayed, their descendants providing the core of today's residents, who eke out a meagre living from lobster and tuna fishing.

If you can bear the sandflies, try the **Wharekai Te Kau Walk** (40min return) across the low isthmus behind Jackson Head, the **Smoothwater Track** (3hr return), with great coastal views on the way to the Smoothwater River, or the longer **Stafford Bay Walk** (8–10hr return), with the possibility of a night at the Stafford Bay Hut (Category 3; $5). Details and tide tables are available from the Haast World Heritage Centre.

There are no facilities in Jackson Bay except for *The Cray Pot*, a kind of diner on wheels where you can get fish and chips away from the sandflies and gaze at the sea through fake leadlight windows.

Haast Pass and Makarora

From Haast it is nearly 150km over the **Haast Pass** (at 563m, the lowest road crossing of the Southern Alps) to Wanaka – a journey from the verdant rain-soaked forests of the bank of the South Branch, climbing steeply with some difficulty over a bad slip. It eases after a while and the track continues, sometimes indistinctly, through ever more stunted bush and occasional clearings to the tree line. Collect firewood here – you're now less than half an hour from the Young Hut (20 bunks), which is wonderfully sited on the right bank in a magnificent avalanche-scoured rock cirque crowned by 2202m Mount Awful, apparently named in wonder rather than horror.

Suitably rested, you've another fairly strenuous day ahead from **Young Hut to Siberia Hut** (9km; 6–7hr; 500m ascent, 800m descent) over the Gillespie Pass. Keep to the right bank until you reach a rock cairn, which marks the start of a steep and lengthy ascent, following snow poles to a saddle; it'll take two or three hours to reach this fabulous, barren spot with views across the snow-capped northern peaks of the Mount Aspiring National Park. Grassy slopes marked by more snow poles lead steeply down to Gillespie Stream, which is followed to its confluence with the Siberia Stream, from where it's a gentle, undulating hour downstream to Siberia Hut (20 bunks), though keen types might tag on a side-trip to **Lake Crucible** (4hr return) before cantering down to the hut. Those with more modest aspirations can spend two nights at Siberia Hut and do the **Lake Crucible side trip** (13km; 6–7hr return; 500m ascent) on the spare day. From the Siberia Hut, retrace your steps to the confluence of the Siberia and Gillespie streams, ford the Gillespie Stream and continue along the left bank of the Siberia Stream a short distance until you see Crucible Stream cascading in a deep gash on the far side. Ford Siberia Stream and ascend through the bush on the right bank of the stream. It is hard going, and route-finding among the alpine meadows higher up can be difficult but the deep, alpine lake tucked under the skirts of Mount Alba and choked with small icebergs is ample reward.

Planes fly in and out of the **Siberia Valley airstrip**, and you can take your chance on "backloading" **flights out** ($25). To continue tramping from **Siberia Hut to Kerin Forks** (6km; 2–3hr; 100m ascent, 300m descent), enter the bush at the southern end of Siberia Flats on the left bank of Siberia Stream and descend away from the stream then zigzag steeply down to the Wilkin River and the **Kerin Forks Hut** (10 bunks), where many trampers arrange to be met by a jetboat. If it has rained heavily, fording the Makarora lower down will be impossible, so don't forgo the jetboat lightly. The alternative is to walk from **Kerin Forks to Makarora** (17km; 6–7hr; 100m ascent, 200m descent), following the Wilkin River's left bank, then crossing the Makarora upstream of the confluence.

West Coast into the parched, rolling grasslands of Central Otago. Ngai Tahu used the route as a greenstone trading route and probably introduced it to gold prospector Charles Cameron, who became the first *pakeha* to cross in 1863; he was closely followed by the more influential **Julius Von Haast**, who immodestly named it after himself. The pass was finally opened as a vehicular road as far as Haast in 1960, linked through to Fox Glacier in 1965 and completely sealed in 1995.

The road starts beside the broad **Haast River** which, as the road climbs, narrows into a series of churning cascades. Numerous short and well signposted walks, mostly to waterfalls on tributaries, spur off at intervals. The most celebrated include the **Thunder Creek Falls** (10min), the roadside **Fantail Falls**, and the **Blue Pools Walk** (30min return), where a stream issues from a narrow gorge. Though there are few specific sights, it is a great area to linger a while, **camping** in one of the DOC's toilets-and-water sites (all $5 per person) along the way: first up is Pleasant Flat, 45km from Haast, followed by Davis Flat, 3km over the Pass, and Cameron Flat, just 3km beyond that and 14km short of Makarora.

Makarora

The hamlet of **MAKARORA** lies roughly midway between Haast and Wanaka, on the northern fringe of the Mount Aspiring National Park. If you're aching for the relative comforts of Wanaka and Queenstown there's little reason to stop, but keen trampers with a few days to spare should consider tackling Gillespie Pass.

In the nineteenth century the dense **forests** all about and the proximity of Lake Wanaka made Makarora the perfect spot for marshalling cut logs across the lake and coaxing them down the Clutha River southeast to the fledgling North Otago **gold towns** of Clyde and Cromwell. The creation of the national park in 1964 paved the way for Makarora's increasing importance as the main northern access point to a region of majestic beauty, alpine vegetation and dense beech-filled valleys.

About all you'll find here is a motor camp, a shop and a **DOC office** (Dec–March daily 8am–5pm; April–Nov Mon–Fri 8am–5pm; ☎03/443 8365, fax 443 8374), the place to go for information and hut tickets for tramps. The main justification for stopping here is to head out on the Gillespie Pass tramp (see box on pp.738–9) or to join Southern Alps Air's **Siberia Experience** (☎03/443 8372, fax 443 1082; mid-Oct to mid-April; 4hr; $150), an excellent combination of flying into the remote Siberia Valley, three hours of tramping to the Wilkin River and jetboating back to Makarora; the same operator also offers overflights of Mount Aspiring (around $120), and just about anywhere else if they can get the numbers. The **jetboating** can also be tackled separately with Wilkin River Jet (☎0800/538 945, fax 03/443 8351; 1hr; $45); as good value a jetboat ride as you'll find anywhere in New Zealand. Finally, if the Gillespie Pass seems a little daunting, there are a couple of **shorter walks** close to Makarora, the **Makarora Bush Nature Walk** (20min), which starts near the visitor centre and, branching off this, the **Mount Shrimpton Track** (5km return, 4–5hr, 900m ascent), which climbs very steeply up through silver beech to the bushline, then to a knob overlooking the Makarora Valley.

InterCity and Atomic buses pass through, and backpacker **buses** stop overnight at Makarora; everyone **stays** at the *Makarora Tourist Centre*, SH6 (☎03/443 8372, fax 443 1082; tent sites $9, chalets ②–④), a collection of self-catering and simpler A-frame chalets in a clearing. It is all very peaceful and there's a pool, making it a good place to hole up for a day or two, provided you are well supplied – the tearooms are only open until around 5pm and the shop has fairly limited supplies. The only alternative is *Larrivee Homestead*, SH6 (☎03/443 9177, *andrea_larrivee@hotmail.com*; ⑤–⑥), a lovely house hidden behind the visitor centre, with B&B in the main house and a cheaper cottage, plus dinners for $30.

Continuing towards Wanaka, the only place you are likely to want to break your journey is **Kidds Bush** ($5), a DOC campsite beside lake Hawea, 6km down a side road off SH6 at The Neck, where lakes Wanaka and Hawea almost meet.

travel details

The only passenger **train** services to the West Coast are from Christchurch over Arthur's Pass to Greymouth. An InterCity **bus** makes the journey from Christchurch over Arthur's pass, meets the train at Greymouth and continues north via Punakaiki and Westport, arriving in Nelson in the early evening. Another InterCity service also meets the train in Greymouth and heads south through Hokitika to Franz Josef Glacier and Fox Glacier. The following morning, this bus picks up in both glacier villages and continues south via the Haast Pass and Wanaka to Queenstown. Smaller **minibus** operators run **feeder services** to the main West Coast towns, running one or two services a day in each direction, and sometimes give a small fare saving over the InterCity. The most useful of these are Atomic Shuttles, who run a service from Picton to Greymouth via Blenheim, Nelson, Reefton, Westport and Punakaiki; another (summer only) from Picton to Greymouth via Reefton; and a particularly useful one south from Greymouth to Queenstown which leaves early and completes the journey in one day. All these feeder services run in both directions. The visitor centres have the latest details and handle bookings.

Trains

From Greymouth to: Arthur's Pass (1 daily; 2hr); Christchurch (1 daily; 4hr 30min).

Buses

From Fox Glacier to: Franz Josef (1 daily; 45min); Hokitika (1 daily; 2hr 45min); Makarora (2 daily; 4hr); Wanaka (2 daily; 5hr 15min).

From Franz Josef Glacier to: Fox Glacier (2 daily; 45min); Haast (2 daily; 3hr); Hokitika (1 daily; 2hr); Makarora (2 daily; 4hr 30min); Queenstown (2 daily; 8hr); Wanaka (2 daily; 6hr).

From Greymouth to: Arthur's Pass (3 daily; 1-2hr); Blenheim (1-2 daily; 4hr 45min-9hr); Christchurch (3 daily; 5hr); Fox Glacier (2 daily; 3hr 30min-4hr 30min); Franz Josef (2 daily; 3-4hr); Hokitika (2 daily; 30-45min); Murchison (mid-Nov to April 1-2 daily, May to mid-Nov 3 weekly; 3hr-3hr 30min); Punakaiki (2 daily; 40min); Reefton (mid-Nov to April 1-2 daily, May to mid-Nov 3 weekly; 1hr); St Arnaud (mid-Nov to April 1-2 daily, May to mid-Nov 3 weekly; 3hr 45min); Westport (2 daily; 1hr 40min-2hr).

From Hokitika to: Arthur's Pass (3 daily; 2hr); Christchurch (3 daily; 5-6hr); Franz Josef (2 daily; 2hr 30min-3hr); Greymouth (2 daily; 30-45min); Ross (2 daily; 25min); Whataroa (2 daily; 1hr 30min).

From Westport to: Christchurch (2 daily; 4hr 40min-7hr); Greymouth (2 daily; 1hr 40min-2hr); Karamea (2 daily; 1hr 30min); Murchison (3 daily; 1hr 15min-1hr 30min); Nelson (2 daily; 3hr 40min-4hr); Punakaiki (2 daily; 1hr); Reefton (2 daily; 1hr-1hr 15min).

Flights

From Hokitika to: Christchurch (2–3 daily; 35min).

From Westport to: Wellington (1 daily; 50min).

CHAPTER THIRTEEN

QUEENSTOWN, WANAKA AND THE GOLD COUNTRY

Wedged between the sodden beech forests of Fiordland, the fertile plains of south Canterbury, the city of Dunedin and the sheep country of Southland lies Central Otago, a region encompassing **Queenstown**, **Wanaka** and the surrounding **gold country**. Rolling, deserted hills to the east give way to the sharper profiles of the mountains around Queenstown and Wanaka, which rub shoulders with the final glaciated flourish of the Southern Alps. Meltwater and heavy rains course out of the mountains into the 70km lightning bolt of **Lake Wakatipu**, which in turn drains through the Kawarau River, carving a rapid-strewn path through the Kawarau Gorge. Along the way it picks up the waters of the Shotover River from the goldfields of Skippers and Arrowtown. To the north the pristine, glassy lakes of Wanaka and Hawea feed the **Clutha River**, which joins forces with the Kawarau at Cromwell and high-tails it to the coast through the heartland of the Otago gold country.

Queenstown is undoubtedly the region's jewel, with a legendary setting, looking across Lake Wakatipu to the craggy heights of the Remarkables range. New Zealand's self-professed adventure capital, it offers the chance to indulge in just about every adrenalin-fuelled activity imaginable: numerous competing operators have honed bungy jumping, jetboating, rafting and paragliding into well-packaged, forcefully marketed products – although they're no less exciting for all that. All this wonderful scenery and adventure has gained something of an international profile of late with a couple of major feature films – Peter Jackson's *Lord of the Rings* trilogy and Martin Campbell's *The Vertical Limit* – and the extreme adventure docusoap *Adventure Central* all being filmed, at least in part, in and around Queenstown.

No matter how abiding the appeal of Queenstown, you'll soon be looking for a break, something easily done in neighbouring **Arrowtown**, a popular day-trip destination from Queenstown which wears its gold heritage well. Visit the intriguing remains of a former Chinese settlement and take a day-long walk to the defunct gold mines around the nearby ghost town of **Macetown**.

Perhaps the perfect antidote to the rigours of Queenstown is the great outdoors, and some of the country's most exalted multi-day tramps start from the nearby town of **Glenorchy** at the head of Lake Wakatipu. Well organized track transport will drop you at the trailheads of the magnificent **Routeburn Track**, the match of any in the country; the less challenging **Caples** and **Greenstone** tracks, which can be combined with

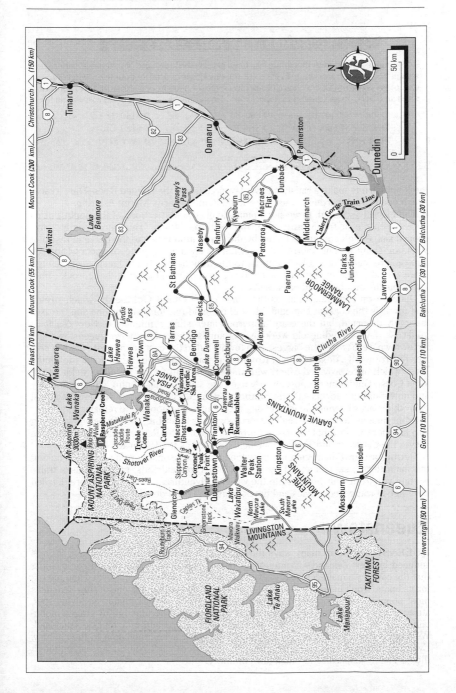

N

50 km

0   50 km

◁ Christchurch (150 km)
◁ Mount Cook (200 km)
◁ Mount Cook (55 km)
◁ Haast (70 km)

Balclutha (30 km) ▷
Balclutha (30 km) ▷
Gore (10 km) ▷
Gore (10 km) ▷
Invercargill (50 km) ▷

Timaru

Christchurch

Oamaru

Palmerston

Dunedin

Twizel

Lake Benmore

Dansey's Pass

Dunback

Kyeburn

Macraes Flat

Middlemarch

Taieri Gorge Train Line

Naseby

Ranfurly

Kyeburn

Patearoa

Clarks Junction

St Bathans

Lindis Pass

Becks

Paerau

LAMMERMOOR RANGE

Lawrence

Tarras

Bendigo

Lake Dunstan

Cromwell

Alexandra

Clutha River

Roxburgh

Raes Junction

Makarora

Lake Hawea

Hawea

Albert Town

Bannockburn

Clyde

GARVIE MOUNTAINS

Mt Aspiring
3030 m

Rob Roy Valley Walk

Raspberry Creek

PISA RANGE

Wanaka

Cardrona Road

Waiorau Nordic Ski Area

Matukituki R.

Cascade Saddle Route

MOUNT ASPIRING NATIONAL PARK

Treble Cone

Cardrona

Macetown (Ghost town)

Arrowtown

Kawerau River

Frankton

The Remarkables

Shotover River

Rees-Dart Tk

Skippers Canyon

Coronet Peak

Arthur's Point

Queenstown

Walter Peak Station

Kingston

EYRE MOUNTAINS

Lumsden

Glenorchy

Caples Tk

Greenstone Track

Lake Wakatipu

North Mavora Lake

South Mavora Lake

Mavora Walkway

LIVINGSTON MOUNTAINS

Mossburn

Routeburn Track

FIORDLAND NATIONAL PARK

Lake Te Anau

Lake Manapouri

TAKITIMU FOREST

ACCOMMODATION PRICE CODES

Accommodation listed in this guide has been categorized into one of nine price bands, as set out below. The rates quoted represent the **cheapest available** double or twin **room** – except for category ①, which are per-person rates for a dorm bed. Note that fees for **tent sites** and **DOC huts** (quoted in dollars) are also per-person, unless otherwise stated.

① under $20 per person	④ $60–80	⑦ $140–180
② under $40 per room	⑤ $80–100	⑧ $180–240
③ $40–60	⑥ $100–140	⑨ over $240

For more on accommodation, see p.34.

---

the Routeburn to make a satisfying five-day circuit; and the rugged **Rees–Dart Track**, which opens up the arduous Cascade Saddle Route towards Mount Aspiring.

The glacially scoured, three-sided pinnacle of "the Matterhorn of the South" forms the centrepiece of the **Mount Aspiring National Park**. This permanently snow-capped alpine high country is linked by the Matukituki valley to the peaceful resort of **Wanaka**, slung around the placid waters of its eponymous lake. Wanaka's laid-back atmosphere stands in marked contrast to the frenetic bustle of Queenstown, though there's no shortage of operators keen to take you canyoning, stunt flying, rock climbing or on any number of other pursuits.

Queenstown and Wanaka lie on the fringe of the **Otago Goldfields**, which stretch east towards the coast at Dunedin. Most of the gold has long since gone and the area is largely deserted, but there are numerous interesting reminders of New Zealand's gold-rush days, including old workings set amidst rugged scenery. Queenstown and Arrowtown were two of the biggest gold towns, but to the east lie the more modest centres of **Cromwell**, **Alexandra** and **Roxburgh**, scattered along the banks of the Clutha River which once provided Maori with the easiest path to the *pounamu* fields of the West Coast. Gold miners subsequently used the same paths, fanning out to found tiny and now moribund towns such as **Bannockburn**, **St Bathan's** and **Naseby**, the most enjoyable places in which to idle among the mouldering boomtime remains.

From June to October the region's focus switches to **skiing**, with Queenstown acting as a base for the downhill resorts of Coronet Peak and the Remarkables, while Wanaka serves the Cardrona and Treble Cone fields, as well as the **Waiorau** Nordic field.

Getting around the region is easily done on the reasonably frequent buses linking the main towns, supplemented by shuttle buses to trailheads, and minibuses transporting you from your hotel out to the various adventure activities. For more detailed coverage of route frequencies and times, consult "Travel details" on p.808.

Queenstown

QUEENSTOWN is in many ways the victim of it own popularity. Kiwis and visitors seduced by New Zealand's tranquil rural beauty can often be overheard complaining that the country's main centre for adventure sports is getting overcrowded and too big for its boots. Don't believe a word of it. There is no doubt that it is one of New Zealand's most popular and commercialized year-round resorts, but it remains an idyllic spot, attractively set beside the deep blue Lake Wakatipu and hemmed in by craggy mountains. Furthermore, it offers the best selection of restaurants outside Auckland, Wellington and Christchurch, and some of the finest accommodation in the country. Even the string of new hotels blighting the foreshore can't ruin its appeal, although they certainly jeopardize its small-town intimacy.

Queenstown is nevertheless best taken in small doses, either as a base from which to plan lengthy forays into the surrounding countryside, or as a venue for sampling one of the many outdoor activities on offer. The most prominent of these is undoubtedly **bungy jumping**. The town's environs now boast four of the world's most gloriously scenic bungy sites, visited either in isolation or as part of a multi-thrill package, perhaps including **whitewater rafting** and **jetboating** on the Shotover River, or a helicopter flight into the dilapidated former gold workings of **Skippers Canyon**.

Visitors after a more sedate time are equally spoilt for choice, with lake cruises on the elegant TSS *Earnslaw*, the last of the lake steamers; the **gondola ride** to Bob's Peak, which commands magnificent vistas over Queenstown and The Remarkables range; and a choice of **wine tours** around some of the world's most southerly wineries. Formal lakeshore gardens and hillside viewpoints provide the focus for easy local **walks**, with the heartier multi-day tramps all starting at Glenorchy (p.769) at the head of the lake.

Even the frantic summers are nothing in comparison to winter, when Kiwi and international skiers descend on **Coronet Peak** and **The Remarkables**, two fine ski fields within half an hour of Queenstown which are at their peak during the annual **Queenstown Winter Carnival** towards the end of July.

Arrival, information and city transport

Buses all arrive in the centre of Queenstown at The Top of the Mall, the intersection of the Mall and Camp Street, from where it's less than fifteen minutes' walk to most hotels and hostels; better still, most of the smaller bus companies will drop you off outside your chosen accommodation. Kiwi Discovery stop outside their office at 37 Camp St, but also do pick-ups and drop-offs around Queenstown – as do Atomic Shuttle, Southern Link Shuttles, Southern Explore, Magic Bus and Kiwi Experience.

Queenstown's **airport** is just outside Frankton, 7km northeast of central Queenstown; the Shopper Bus runs roughly hourly (9am–3.30pm; 15min; $3), and the Super Shuttle ($5) meets most flights. **Taxis** (☎03/442 6666 or 442 7788) charge around $15 for the ride into town. Most of the major car rental companies also have offices at the airport, and there's a small visitor centre that stays open for all incoming flights.

Information

Queenstown's main downtown area is concentrated around Rees Street, Shotover Street, Camp Street and the pedestrianized Mall, which runs from the Main Town Wharf eastwards to Ballarat Street. The main **visitor centre**, on the corner of Camp Street and Shotover Street (daily: Nov–April 7am–7pm; May–Oct 7am–6pm; ☎03/442 4100, fax 442 8907, *qvc@xtra.co.nz*, *www.newzealand-vacation.com*), is the place to go for all manner of impartial advice, something not offered by the dozen or so booking agents which masquerade as information centres in order to push their own tours and products. For more on booking adventure activities, see our comments on p.755.

The best unbiased information on walks in the area comes from the **DOC office** at 37 Shotover St (Dec–April daily 8am–7pm; May–Nov Mon–Sat 8am–5pm; ☎03/442 7933, fax 442 7932), which is stacked with leaflets on DOC activities, operates a **Great Walks Booking Desk** (July–April daily 9am–4.30pm) for aspiring Routeburn, Kepler and Milford track walkers.

City transport

Pretty much everywhere you are likely to want to go in central Queenstown can be reached **on foot**. Most of the activities – bungy jumping, whitewater rafting, mountain

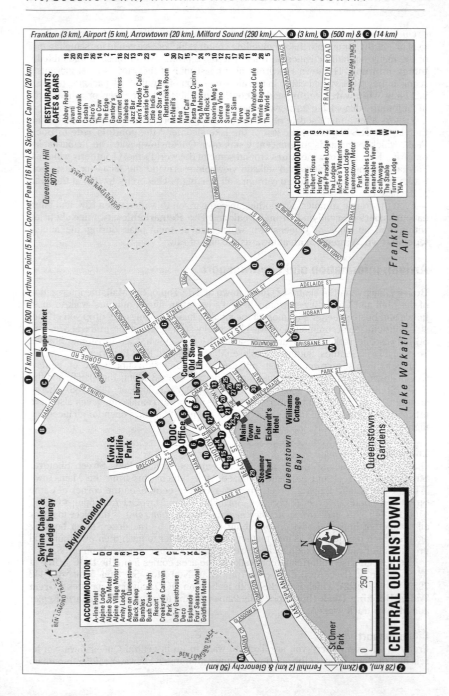

Frankton (3 km), Airport (5 km), Arrowtown (20 km), Milford Sound (290 km), △ ⓐ (3 km), ⓑ (500 m) & ⓒ (14 km)

RESTAURANTS, CAFÉS & BARS

Abbey Road	18
Avanti	20
Boardwalk	29
Casbah	19
Chico's	26
The Cow	14
The Edge	1
Gantley's	16
Gourmet Express	22
Habebes	13
Jazz Bar	9
Ken's Noodle Café	23
Lakeside Café	
Little India	
Lone Star & The	6
Rattlesnake Room	
McNeill's	30
Moa	27
Naff Caff	15
Pasta Pasta Cucina	7
Pog Mahone's	24
Red Rock	3
Roaring Meg's	10
Solera Vino	12
Surreal	21
Thai Siam	17
Verve	25
Vudu	11
The Wholefood Café	8
Winnie Bagoes	28
The World	5

ACCOMMODATION

Highview	b
Hulbert House	G
Hurley's	N
Little Paradise Lodge	Z
The Lodges	K
McFee's Waterfront	B
Pinewood Lodge	
Queenstown Motor	I
Park	
Remarkables Lodge	c
Remarkable View	H
Scallywags	M
The Stable	E
Turner Lodge	T
YHA	

ACCOMMODATION

A-line Hotel	L
Alpine Lodge	D
Alpine Sun Motel	Q
Alpine Village Motor Inn	a
Amity Lodge	R
Aspen on Queenstown	U
Black Sheep	O
Bumbles	A
Bush Creek Health	
Resort	C
Creeksyde Caravan	
Park	F
Dairy Guesthouse	J
Deco	X
Esplanade	P
Four Seasons Motel	S
Goldfields Motel	V

Skyline Chalet & The Ledge bungy

Queenstown Hill 907m

Skyline Gondola

Kiwi & Birdlife Park

Supermarket

Courthouse & Old Stone Library

Library

DOC

Office

Steamer Wharf

Main Town Pier

Eichardt's Hotel

Williams Cottage

Queenstown Bay

Queenstown Gardens

Lake Wakatipu

Frankton Arm

CENTRAL QUEENSTOWN

0   250 m

St Omer Park

N

ⓓ (7 km), △ ⓐ (500 m), Arthurs Point (5 km), Coronet Peak (16 km) & Skippers Canyon (20 km)

ⓔ (28 km), ⓥ Fernhill (2 km) & Glenorchy (50 km)

biking and the like – take place out of town, although all operators run courtesy buses from the centre of town to the site, usually picking up from accommodation en route. There's a **taxi rank** on Camp Street at The Top of the Mall, or call ☎03/442 6666 or 442 7788.

The only useful bus services are those to Arrowtown (see p.764) and the Shopper Bus, from The Top of the Mall (☎03/442 6647; daily departures every 1–2hr 8.15am–5.15pm), which runs out to Frankton and the airport.

More personalized transport comes in the form of **rental cars** and **bikes**, which are available from several outlets around town (see "Listings", p.763). It pays to shop around – especially for one-day or overnight rentals to Milford Sound, which can work out to be real bargains, with companies sometimes offering a group of four a car plus petrol and a Milford cruise for under $60 per person.

Drivers will have no problem negotiating Queenstown's relatively quiet streets, but may fall foul of stringent parking restrictions. Parking meters in the central streets (checked daily until 9pm) cover several spaces and it is easy to inadvertently pay for someone else's vehicle; there's usually some free parking to be found within a couple of hundred metres in any case.

Accommodation

Queenstown has the widest selection of **places to stay** in this corner of New Zealand, but such is the demand in the middle of summer and at the height of the ski season that rooms can be hard to come by and prices are correspondingly high.

With a few exceptions, all the accommodation is packed into a compact area less than fifteen minutes' walk from the centre of town. Good deals are sometimes offered by the big **hotels** in what passes for Queenstown's off season (essentially April, May & Nov) but in general you'll do better in smaller places, particularly the **B&Bs**, **homestays** and **lodges** of which there are some fine examples. Families, groups and keen self-caterers might consider **motels**, which match the Kiwi standard but tend to charge a little more than in less popular resorts. The best budget deals are to be found at the many **hostels** and backpackers, which compete fiercely for trade. Considering their number (over fifteen at last count), few of them are up to the standards found elsewhere: they generally offer a similar range of services – free activity booking, free luggage storage and the like – for much the same rates. The Queenstown district also has abundant **campsites** with attendant cabins, though only a couple of these are within walking distance of town.

If a less frantic atmosphere – and lower prices – appeal, it's also worth considering **Arrowtown** as a base for exploring the Queenstown area – see pp.765-6 for reviews of places to stay in the vicinity.

Hotels

A-Line Hotel, 27 Stanley St (☎0800/807 700, fax 442 4715, *aline@es.co.nz*). A cluster of nicely furnished rooms in A-frames with good lake views. This place is firmly on the tour bus circuit, but some discreet haggling when business is slow can bring rates down considerably. ⑥.

Aspen on Queenstown, 155 Fernhill Rd (☎03/442 7688 & 0800/427 688, fax 442 8906, *aspen@xtra.co.nz*). A sprawling hotel with a small indoor pool and great lake views. The abundantly equipped rooms and apartments are overpriced in high season but can be an off-peak bargain – especially the very comfortable two-bedroom apartments, whose rates drop by as much as a third. The hotel is 2km from the centre of Queenstown, so phone ahead to check discounted prices. ⑦.

Esplanade, 78 Park St (☎03/442 8611, fax 442 9635). Well-sited budget hotel and backpackers, right by the lake in a quiet part of town. Still undergoing renovation from years as a dowdy hotel but great value. Rooms are all en suite with TV and tea and coffee. Very cheap dorms are mostly in separate fully self-contained flats with no room having more that four bunks. There's also Internet access, breakfast available and an on-site bar. Dorms ①, rooms ④.

Hurley's, cnr Frankton Rd & Melbourne St (☎03/442 5999 & 0800/589 879, fax 442 5998, *www. hurleys.co.nz, hurleys@voyager.co.nz*). Tasteful, luxuriously appointed apartments and studios close to the centre of Queenstown, each equipped with a full kitchen, TV, CD and cassette player, spa baths and with free access to two saunas and a full gym. Studios ⑦, apartments ⑨.

Motels

Alpha Lodge, 62 Frankton Rd (☎03/442 6095, fax 442 8010). Good value, low-cost motel close to town with all basic amenities and a range of budget and studio units. ④.

Alpine Sun Motel, 18 Hallenstein St (☎03/442 8482, fax 442 6432, *alpine.sun@xtra.co.nz*). Good-value basic motel units with Sky TV, kitchenettes, spa and off-road parking. ⑤.

Alpine Village Motor Inn, 325 Frankton Rd (☎03/442 7795, fax 442 7738). Large place midway to Frankton (the Shopper Bus passes by) and frequented by tour groups. Most rooms and chalets come with views of the Remarkables, and all have the run of two restaurants, a tennis court and the jacuzzi. ⑥.

Amity Lodge, 7 Melbourne St (☎0800/556 000, fax 03/442 9433, *amity@queenstown.co.nz*). Modern and well maintained one-bedroom units, all fully self-contained and with microwaves. ⑥.

Four Seasons Motel, 12 Stanley St (☎03/442 8953, fax 442 7233). Reasonable downtown motel with off-street parking, good kitchens, mountain views, an outdoor swimming pool and a spa. ⑤.

Goldfields Motel, 57 Frankton Rd (☎0800/344 272, fax 442 6179, *nz.com/queenstown/goldfields, goldfieldsmotel@xtra.co.nz*). A range of decent chalets all equipped with TV and fridge. ⑤.

The Lodges, 8 Lake Esplanade (☎03/442 7552, fax 442 6493, *nz.com/queenstown/thelodges, the.lodges@xtra.co.nz*). Top-quality lakeside three-bedroom apartments with full kitchens, laundry and parking. Good value for groups of four or more. ⑧.

B&Bs and homestays

Bush Creek Health Retreat, 20 Bowen St (☎03/442 7260, fax 442 7250). This wonderfully secluded house 1km from central Queenstown is surrounded by beautiful organic gardens tended by Ileen Mutch, a renowned iridologist and holistic healer. A relaxing and rejuvenating place to stay. ⑤.

Dairy Guesthouse, 10 Isle St (☎0800/333 393, fax 03/442 5166, *www.thedairy.co.nz, thedairy@xtra.co.nz*). Very fine central B&B lodge tastefully decorated with historic Queenstown prints, ethnic rugs and kilims, and with very comfortable en-suite rooms. Complimentary wine on arrival sets the relaxed atmosphere; breakfast is served in the former dairy that gives the place its name. ⑧.

Highview, 17 Wakatipu Heights (☎ & fax 03/442 9414). Something between a homestay and a motel, *Highview* enjoys stunning lake views, and is just a $5 cab ride from town (20min walk). En-suite rooms are separate from the main house, but you are welcome to join the friendly hosts, who also deliver breakfast each morning. ⑥.

Hulbert House, 68 Ballarat St (☎ & fax 03/442 8767, *www.heritageinns.co.nz/hulbert.house*). In a rambling century-old Victorian villa built on the hill behind Queenstown Bay, this opulent but tasteful B&B has a large library, idyllic gardens and great breakfasts. ⑦.

Little Paradise Lodge, Meilejohn Bay, 28km along Glenorchy Rd (☎ & fax 03/442 6196). An idyllic homestay on a mostly self-sufficient lifestyle block close to the lake and with good walking and fishing nearby. Almost everything is made from logs cut or stone hewn by the Swiss owner and part-time forester, Thomas, including the non-chlorinated swimming pool fed by its own stream and complete with water lilies. Accommodation is in standard rooms and a charming en-suite chalet. You can cook for yourself and there is free use of kayaks, a dinghy and fishing gear. ⑤.

Remarkables Lodge, SH6, 14km from Queenstown (☎ & fax 03/442 2720, *nz.com/queenstown /remarkableslodge, remarkables@xtra.co.nz*). This is in the premier league of Kiwi boutique lodges and its exquisite meals are as much a part of the experience as the super-comfortable rooms, spacious and beautifully decorated lounge, outdoor pool, spa, tennis court and croquet lawn. Secluded at the foot of the Remarkables (exactly 3.4km south of the ski field approach road), there are walks into the foothills just beyond the helipad. Rates are around $300 per person including breakfast, pre-dinner drinks and dinner. ⑨.

Remarkable View, 22 Brecon St (☎03/442 9542). Friendly, traditional homestay with simple rooms. Guests share the family facilities, and are offered continental or cooked breakfast. ④.

Scallywags, 27 Lomond Crescent (☎03/442 7083, fax 442 5885). Pitched somewhere between an off-beat homestay and an upmarket backpackers' hostel, this suburban house is a ten-minute walk up from town (you can cut through the motor park). It has stupendous views and a very laid-back muck-in atmosphere, with use of a kitchen and free tea and coffee. Dorms ①, rooms ③, including towels & bedding.

The Stable, 17 Brisbane St (☎03/442 9251, fax 442 8293, *gimac@queenstown.co.nz*). Cosy and popular homestay stacked with books and housed in a former stable. Cooked or continental breakfasts are served, as are dinners ($35) if ordered in advance. ⑥.

Turner Lodge, 2 Turner St (☎03/442 9432, fax 442 9409, *nz-accommodation.co.nz/stay/turnerlodge, turnerlodge@xtra.co.nz*). Central, relaxed and modern place that operates as a comfortable homestay serving a cooked breakfast, and has three additional rooms which are let on a self-catering basis, sharing kitchen facilities, a lounge and a sun deck. Room only ④, B&B ⑤.

Hostels

Alpine Lodge, 13 Gorge Rd (☎03/442 7220, fax 442 7038). Small, welcoming and central hostel which can be a little cramped when full. Ask about the self-contained unit that's sometimes let separately to groups. Dorms ①, rooms ②.

Black Sheep, 13 Frankton Rd (☎03/442 7289, fax 442 7361). Converted motel that's spacious enough to cope with the backpacker tour-bus crowd who frequently pack out the four- to ten-bed dorms. Can be rowdy, but everything is very well organized, there's a barbecue out back near the spa pool and you can book just about everything at the 24hr reception; there's a $1 charge per night for storing luggage. Dorms ①, rooms ③.

Bumbles, 2 Brunswick St, cnr Lake Esplanade (☎0800/428 625). Among the best hostels in town and justly popular; well sited across the road from the lakefront and with recently renovated communal areas including a large kitchen, central lounge, barbecue area and plenty of washing facilities. Dorms ①, twins ②, made-up doubles ③.

Deco Backpackers, 52 Main St (☎03/442 7384, fax 442 6258). Small and peaceful hostel in an Art Deco-style house. It's a bit of an uphill trudge from town but worth the effort. Dorms ①, rooms ②.

Esplanade (see p.747). Well-sited budget hotel and cheap backpacker. Dorms ①, rooms ④.

McFee's Waterfront Hotel, 48a Shotover St (☎03/442 7400, fax 442 7403). Large hostel with good communal areas overlooking the lake; accommodation is in four-bed dorms, budget doubles with TV, and flashier en-suite rooms. Dorms ①, budget rooms ③, en suites ④.

Pinewood Lodge, 48 Hamilton Rd (☎03/442 8273, fax 442 9470). Scattered collection of new and older renovated buildings (all surrounded by lawns) jointly making up one of the Queenstown's nicer backpackers, located on the edge of town ten minutes' walk from the centre. Good facilities all round including a spa bath ($5 per half-hour) and bike rental ($25 per day). Tents $10, dorms ①, rooms ③.

Scallywags (see opposite). Off-beat homestay and upmarket backpackers. Dorms ①, rooms ③.

YHA, 88 Lake Esplanade (☎03/442 8413, fax 442 6561, *yhaqutn@yha.org.nz*). Always bustling, particularly in the ski season, this is one of New Zealand's flagship YHAs, ten minutes' walk along the waterfront from town. Accommodation is in spacious, mostly six-bed dorms and new doubles, many with good lake views. Dorms ①, rooms ③.

Campsites and motorparks

Arthur's Point Holiday Park, close to the Shotover Jet site at Arthur's Point (☎ & fax 03/442 9306, *top10.queenstown@xtra.co.nz*). Smallish, quiet and fully equipped site with a small pool. Tent and powered sites $9–9.50, standard cabins ②, tourist flats ③, motels ⑤.

Creeksyde Campervan Park, 54 Robins Rd (☎03/442 9447, fax 442 6621, *creekside@camp .co.nz*). This highly organized and spotlessly clean site ten minutes' walk from town is primarily aimed at campervanners, though there are tent sites. A central building houses a spa bathroom ($5 per half-hour for two), sauna ($10), ski store and drying rooms. Tents & powered sites $12.50, motels ④–⑤.

Kawarau Falls Lakeside Holiday Park, 7km north of Queenstown on SH6, near Frankton airport (☎03/442 3510, fax 442 3518, *www.campsite.co.nz, kawfalls@xtra.co.nz*). Very attractive lakeside campsite that's ideal for exploring the region. Excellent facilities extend to spacious tent sites, a backpacker-style lodge and three different grades of cabins, some with their own facilities. In peak season, the Shopper Bus comes to within 500m; within 1km out of season. Tents & powered sites $10, dorms ①, cabins ②–③.

Queenstown Motor Park, Man St (☎0800/482 735, fax 442 7253, *info@motorpark.co.nz*). Enormous site that sprawls over the base of Bob's Peak and seems to swallow just about all of Queenstown's campers. Facilities are extensive and accommodation runs the gamut from grassy tent sites ($11) to self-contained motel units, but it can hardly be considered peaceful. ②–⑤.

Twelve-Mile Creek Reserve, 5km south of Queenstown, off the Glenorchy road (no phone). DOC campsite with facilities limited to basic toilets and water. Tent sites $4.

The Town and around

The best all-round views of the Queenstown region and Lake Wakatipu are undoubtedly those from **Bob's Peak**, which rises up immediately behind the town and can be reached on one of Queenstown's gentler rides. The four-minute **Skyline Gondola**, Brecon Street (daily 9am–midnight; $13 return), deposits you at the Skyline Complex, where a fair proportion of passengers are herded into **Kiwi Magic** (daily 10am–8pm; 30min; $8), a well produced and engagingly corny promotional film that's beginning to show its age, not least because the lead, comedian Billy T. James, died a decade ago. Everyone else either peels off to The Ledge bungy (see p.756), the Luge (see below) or makes straight for the viewing balcony, getting their bearings off The Remarkables and Cecil and Walter peaks beyond Lake Wakatipu. The *Skyline Restaurant* (☎03/442 7860) serves good buffet lunches ($25) and dinners ($35), or there's outdoor seating at the reasonably priced *Skyline Café*, from where you can watch paragliders launch themselves from the conifer-clad slopes. If you're overcome by a sudden impulse to join their ranks, you can book an introductory paraglide ($130) at the booth just outside in the Skyline Complex.

A relatively recent addition to the attractions at Bob's Peak is The **Luge** (1 ride $4.50, 3 rides $10.50, 5 rides $16, 5 rides & Gondola $22), a twisting concrete track negotiated on a wheeled plastic buggy with a primitive braking system: take it easy on your first run. The complex can also be reached on foot in under an hour by following Kent Street up from town.

The base of the Gondola is reached along Brecon Street, which passes Queenstown's **cemetery** – the final resting place of Queenstown pioneer Nicholas von Tunzelmann, as well as Henry Homer, discoverer of the Homer Saddle on the Milford Road. Almost opposite, the **Kiwi and Birdlife Park**, on Bevan Street (daily: Nov–Feb 9am–7pm; March–Oct 9am–5pm; $10.50), an expanse of ponds, lawns, stands of bush and aviaries that are home to some of New Zealand's rarest birds. The effect is more zoo than wildlife park but does a good job of presenting morepork, kea, kereru (native pigeons), kakariki (native parakeets) and little owls, alongside the products of captive breeding programmes for the North Island brown kiwi, and the black stilt, one of the world's ten most endangered bird species.

Down in the town centre there's very little left of gold-rush Queenstown. At the Top of The Mall, Ballarat Street crosses a small stream spanned by an 1882 stone bridge to reach the **Courthouse** and **Old Stone Library** (now a Queenstown promotions office) both built in the mid 1870s and since dwarfed by century-old giant sequoias. At the opposite end of the Mall, the waterfront **Eichardt's Hotel** dates partly from 1871 when the Prussian Albert Eichardt replaced the Queen's Arms, a bar William Rees created from a woolshed in 1862. Around the corner on Marine Parade, **Williams Cottage**, dating from around 1866, has recently been restored and is open as a small historical museum (daily 10am–4.30pm; donations) fitted out with period furniture.

Marine Parade continues east past the cottages to **Queenstown Gardens** (unrestricted entry), an attractive parkland retreat which covers the peninsula separating Queenstown Bay from the rest of Lake Wakatipu. Two English oaks were planted when the land was first designated as a reserve in 1867; they're still going strong, as are sequoias and a stack of other exotics – ornamental cherry, maple, sweet chestnut and the like – lavished around the rose gardens and bowling lawns.

WALKS AROUND QUEENSTOWN

All the hard-sell on adventure activities in Queenstown can become a bit oppressive, and a few hours away from town can be wonderfully therapeutic. The majority of the walks outlined below – listed in ascending order of difficulty – are well covered by the DOC's *Queenstown Walks and Trails* leaflet ($1), which also includes a sketch map. Serious multi-day tramps in the region are centred on Wanaka and Glenorchy (see p.780 and p.769, respectively).

One Mile Creek Walkway (1hr 30min return; 6km; 50m ascent). Fairly easy walk through a gully filled with beech forest and following a 1924 pipeline from Queenstown's first hydroelectric scheme. The route starts on the lakefront by the Fernhill roundabout, and offers a good opportunity to acquaint yourself with fuschia, lancewood and native birds – principally fantails, bellbirds and tui.

Queenstown Hill Track (2–3hr return; 5km; 600m ascent). Starting from the top of York Street, this is a fairly steep climb up through mostly exotic trees to panoramic views from the 907m Queenstown Hill.

Frankton Arm Track (1hr–1hr 30min one way; 7km; flat). This easy path is ideal for an early-morning or sunset stroll. Start from Peninsula Street in Queenstown, follow the lakeside to Frankton, and continue a further 2km round to the Kawarau River outlet.

Ben Lomond Summit Track (6–8hr return; 11km; 1400m ascent). A full-day, there-and-back tramp scaling the 1748m Ben Lomond, one of the highest mountains in the region and consequently subject to inclement weather, especially in winter when the track can be snow-covered. Start by the One Mile Creek Walk or use the Skyline Gondola and walk up past the paragliding launch site to join the track, which climbs through alpine tussock to reveal expansive views. Gentler slopes approach Ben Lomond Saddle, from where it's a steep final haul to the summit.

Ben Lomond–Moonlight Track (8–10hr one way; 16km; 1400m ascent). A demanding and occasionally difficult-to-follow route which combines the ascent to Ben Lomond Saddle (see above) with a poled sub-alpine route to the site of the former gold town of Sefferstown and the eastern section of the Moonlight Track to Arthur's Point. Organize someone to pick you up at Arthur's Point or be prepared for a 5km slog back to Queenstown.

The Shotover River and Skippers Canyon

The churning **Shotover River** is inextricably linked with Queenstown. The majority of the town's adventure-based trips – bungy jumping, rafting, jetboating, mountain biking and more (see "Activities", p.755) – take place on, in or around the river and, if you are prepared to drive the treacherous road, there's also a stack of gold workings to explore.

The Shotover rises in the Richardson Mountains north of Queenstown and picks up speed to surge through its deepest and narrowest section, **Skippers Canyon**, and into the Kawarau River downstream from Lake Wakatipu. Tributaries run off Mount Aurum, beneath which is the mother lode of the Shotover goldfields – first discovered when a couple of pioneer shearers, Thomas Arthur and Harry Redfern, found gold in 1862 at what is now Arthur's Point, on the banks of the Shotover 5km north of Queenstown. Word spread that prospectors were extracting the equivalent of over ten kilos a day, and within months thousands were flocking from throughout New Zealand and Australia to work what was soon dubbed "The Richest River in the World". The river-edge gravels had been all but worked out by 1864, necessitating ever more sophisticated extraction techniques. With the introduction of gravity-fed water chutes, mechanical sieves and floating dredges, the construction of a decent road became crucial. From 1863, Chinese navvies spent over twenty years hacking away with pick and shovel at the Skippers Road; those who stuck out the harsh conditions began building quarters more substantial than the standard-issue canvas tents. Meanwhile, entrepreneurially minded pioneers began to exploit the boom, building 27 hotels along the 40km of road, and selling fresh fruit and vegetables at extortionate prices to miners as often as not suffering from scurvy. By the turn of the century the river was worked out, though a few stayed on; even today there are a couple of die-hards who make part of their living from gold panning and sluicing. Occasionally they get some extra company, and the heavy rains which caused substantial flooding in Queenstown in November 1999 sluiced down enough to tempt quite a few. As the townsfolk were mopping up and repairing their homes, and the turbid waters were clearing, happy hunters were out with their shovels. For a few days there it wasn't unusual to pan $600 worth in a couple of hours, hardly a fortune, but a good haul nonetheless.

The extremely narrow and winding **Skippers Road** is best left to experienced drivers. Locals who know the road like the back of their hand tend to hare around, leaving little space for oncoming traffic; besides, rental cars aren't insured for Skippers. Being driven into either the Pipeline bungy sites or the start points for the Skippers Canyon Jet and Shotover rafting trips (see p.755 for more on all of these) gives you a good chance to see the valley. By far the best way, though, is on a four-hour **tour** with Skippers Grand Canyon (☎03/442 5455, *www.grandcanyon.co.nz*, *admin @grandcanyon.co.nz*; $79), who take in most of the highlights, including the Skippers Canyon Jet, and also produce a useful, and widely available, free leaflet and map.

The Skippers Road, which follows the Shotover River only in its upper reaches, branches off Coronet Peak Road 12km north of Queenstown. It is approached along Malaghans Road through **Arthur's Point**, 5km north of Queenstown, marked by the historic *Arthur's Point Hotel*, the only one of the Skippers Road hotels still operating, adjacent to where Thomas Arthur first struck gold. Half a kilometre on, the Edith Cavell Bridge spans a gorge where the Shotover Jet performs its antics, its upstream progress limited by the Mother-in-Law rapid and the 1911 **Oxenbridge Tunnel**. After three years of drilling, this 200m-long bore – designed to absorb the flow of the Shotover while the gold-bearing riverbed was worked – reaped meagre rewards, returning only 2.5kg of gold.

Skippers Road soon begins to shadow the river, negotiating Pinchers Bluff, where Chinese and European navvies cut the road from a near-vertical cliff face. Upstream, the 1901 **Skippers Bridge** was the first high-level one built – and consequently survived the winter floods which had swept away all past efforts. For the first time, the township of Skippers had reliable access, though this did little to prevent the exodus that saw a population of 1500 dwindle to nothing once the gold ran out. The old schoolhouse has been restored and there are the ruins of a few more buildings scattered around, but otherwise it is a bleak, haunted place. You can **camp** here at a toilets-and-water site for a couple of dollars.

The wineries

Grapes have been grown commercially in the **Central Otago** district – essentially Wanaka, Queenstown and the Clutha Valley – only since the 1980s, but local winemakers have already garnered a shelf-full of awards. Widely billed as "the world's most southerly wine-growing region", the vineyards lie close to the 45th Parallel – in country which detractors pooh-poohed as too cold and generally unsuitable for wine production, despite the fact that the Rhône Valley lies on a similar latitude. A continental climate of hot dry summers and long cold winters prevails, which tends to result in low yields and high production costs, forcing wineries to go for quality boutique wines sold at prices which might seem high ($15–30) until you taste them.

The steep schist and gravel slopes on the southern banks of the **Kawarau River** were first recognized as potential vineyard sites as early as 1864, when French miner Jean Désiré Feraud, by now bored of his gold claim at Frenchman's Point near Clyde,

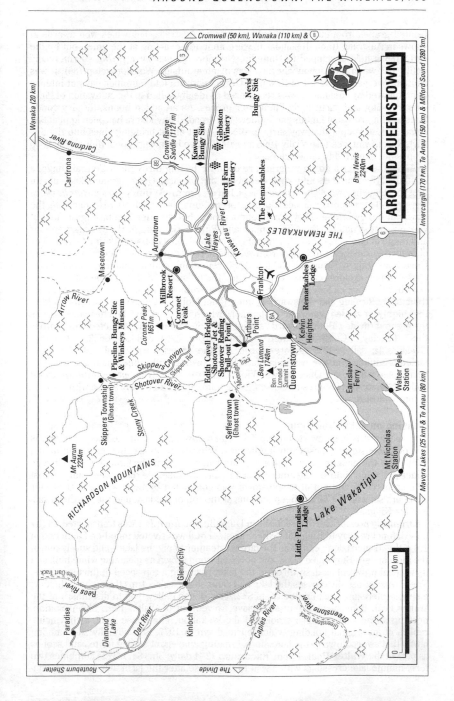

△ Cromwell (50 km), Wanaka (110 km) & Ⓢ

AROUND QUEENSTOWN

Crown Range Saddle (1121 m)

Kawarau Bungy Site

Gibbston Winery

Nevis Bungy Site

Chard Farm Winery

Ben Nevis 2240m

The Remarkables

THE REMARKABLES

Lake Hayes

Arrowtown

Frankton

Remarkables Lodge

Kelvin Heights

Macetown

Arrow River

Millbrook Resort

Coronet Peak 1651m

Coronet Peak

Arthurs Point

Ben Lomond 1748m

Queenstown

Earnslaw Ferry

Walter Peak Station

Pipeline Bungy Site & Winkeys Museum

Skippers Canyon

Skippers Rd

Edith Cavell Bridge, Shotover Jet & Shotover Rafting Pull-out Point

Moonlight Track

Ben Lomond Summit Tk

Shotover River

Skippers Township (Ghost town)

Stony Creek

Sefferstown (Ghost town)

Mt Nicholas Station

Mt Aurum 2234m

RICHARDSON MOUNTAINS

Lake Wakatipu

Little Paradise Lodge

10 km

Glenarchy

Rees River

Paradise

Diamond Lake

Dart River

Kinloch

Caples Track

Caples River

Greenstone River

Greenstone Track

Rees-Dart Track

0

◁ Wanaka (20 km)

△ Invercargill (170 km), Te Anau (150 km) & Milford Sound (280 km)

▽ Mavora Lakes (25 km) & Te Anau (80 km)

◁ Routeburn Shelter

▽ The Divide

Cardrona River

Cardrona

planted grapes from cuttings brought over from Australia. His wines won awards at shows in Australia (though standards were none too exacting at the time), but by the early 1880s he'd decamped to Dunedin. No more grapes were grown commercially until 1976, when the Rippon vineyard was planted outside Wanaka (see p.780). It was another five years before the Kawarau Gorge, with its long summer days of intense light followed by cool nights, was recognized as ideally suited to the cultivation of Pinot Gris, Riesling and particularly Pinot Noir grapes. As an added bonus, the dry conditions inhibit growth of fungus and mildew; the dreaded phylloxera has been kept at bay so far and, to keep it that way, strict protocols exist about bringing vines into the district. Recent vintages (especially 1998 and 1999) have been very good, though the 2000 crop is not expected to do wonders.

Altogether, over a dozen wineries are open for tasting throughout Central Otago, a handful of them on the southern slopes above the Kawarau Gorge, around 20km northeast of Queenstown. The closest is **Chard Farm Winery** (*www.chardfarm.co .nz*; daily 11am–5pm), reached down a precipitous dirt road off SH6 opposite the Kawarau bungy bridge. They don't conduct tours but do offer free tasting of current vintages, most notably the Chardonnay and Pinot Gris, though the Gewurztraminer and range of bubblies ($3 for 3 tastings) can be good too. **Gibbston Valley Winery** lies 5km further northeast towards Cromwell and is better geared to visitors, with a **Wine Cave Tour** (hourly 10am–4pm; 30min; $8.50, refundable with a minimum six-bottle purchase) which explores cellars burrowed into the hillside. This is not especially impressive, but the tour includes an informed and generous tasting session – highlights are the citrusy Riesling and the award-winning Pinot Noir. All these wines are also sold in the highly regarded vineyard restaurant, which is open for lunches and snacks throughout the day. Both vineyards are included on a couple of conducted **wine tours**: the full-day Central Otago Wine Tour (☎03/442 6622, *bookings @cowt.co.nz*; daily; $139) explores these and the wineries Cromwell and Clyde and includes sampling at five wineries plus cheese tasting and a fine lunch at *Oliver's* in Clyde (see p.800); the Queenstown Wine Trail (☎03/442 3799, *qwinetrail@xtra.co.nz*; daily 12.30pm; 4hr; $56) restricts itself to the immediate Queenstown area with tastings at four wineries.

Cruising on Lake Wakatipu

The coal-fired twin-screw steamship **TSS Earnslaw**, the last of the lake steamers, is one of Queenstown's most enduring images. Wherever you are, the encircling mountains echo the haunting sound of the steam whistle, as this beautifully restored relic glides gracefully out from Steamer Wharf. Before the lakeside roads were built, almost all commerce in and out of Queenstown was conducted by boat, with a fleet of four steamers serving the large sheep stations at the top of the lake and the southern railhead at Kingston.

Originally prefabricated in sections in Dunedin, the *Earnslaw* was transported on the now defunct railway to Kingston, where its steel hull was riveted together. Launched in 1912, the 51-metre-long craft was the largest steamer to ply the lake – and surely one of the most stately. Burnished brass and polished wood crown its gleaming white hull, and its vertical prow cuts a dash through the lake, reaching a top speed of thirteen knots. The *Earnslaw* usually crosses the lake and returns five or six trips throughout the day: a simple there-and-back **cruise** costs $32. This doesn't allow you to disembark at the Walter Peak homestead, a tourist enclave carved out of Walter Peak Sheep Station, nestling in the southwestern crook of Lake Wakatipu. The house itself, a convincing replica of an original building which burnt down in 1977, is beautifully sited among lawns that sweep down to the lakeshore, creating an elegant setting for tea and scones as part of the **Walter Peak Farm Excursion** (2–4 daily; 3hr; $47). This combines two forty-minute lake crossings with a visit to the house after the farm tour – an entertaining if sanitized vignette of farm life, with demonstrations of dog handling and shearing. The farm tour element can be substituted either with a forty-minute horse ride ($75 including the crossing), or with a wagon ride behind six Clydesdales in the Wagons to the Past package ($90). Mealtime options extend to the **Barbecue Excursion** ($75), which replaces scones with snags; or **Evening Dining** ($75), where you can tuck into a carvery buffet served up in the homestead ballroom.

Tickets for all these are available at the Steamer Wharf: up to eight hundred people can cram the decks of the *Earnslaw*, though there are usually far fewer, giving passengers the freedom to peer down at the gleaming steam engine or cluster around the piano at the back of the boat for a surprisingly popular music-hall sing-song. In June each year the *Earnslaw* is overhauled and replaced by a launch.

There are other ways to get a ride on the *Earnslaw*: if you have your own motorbike or bicycle, take a one-way trip to Walter Peak (adult $20, motorbike $10, bicycle free), where you'll have the freedom of the remote and unsealed 80km road up the Von River to SH94 at Burwood, 27km east of Te Anau. Alternatively, you could join the **Milford Backroad Adventure** (see p.821).

Activities

Queenstown has a vast array of operators running every conceivable type of **adventure** trip. Many essentially run their companies by mobile phone and don't operate an office as such, though most are directly associated with one of the **information** and **booking offices** that line Shotover Street. In practice, you can book just about any trip from any of these, or directly from your hotel or hostel. Prices don't usually vary, but it may be worth asking for discounts –YHA, backpacker and so forth – if you think you might be eligible. Almost all the booking offices are **open daily**, usually to around 9pm in summer, 8pm in winter. Two of the most useful are The Station, corner Camp Street and Shotover Street (☎03/442 5252 & 0800/367 874), A.J. Hackett's nerve centre and the main pick-up spot for Hackett bungy and the Shotover Jet; and the Information & Track Centre, 37 Shotover St (☎03/442 9708, fax 442 7038, *www.infotrack.co.nz, adventure@infotrack.co.nz*), a backpacker-oriented booking office and the main stopping point for Kiwi Experience.

Most activities in Queenstown are more **expensive** than elsewhere in the country, so to get the most action for the least money, check out one of the numerous **combination deals** knitting together two, three or four of the main activities – rafting, bungy jumping, jet-boating, helicopter rides, and maybe even river surfing or mountain biking – and tending to focus on either the Shotover or the Kawarau rivers. A basic triple combination such as the **Skippers Grand Slam** (5hr; $199) includes the Pipeline Bungy, Flying Fox and Skippers Canyon Jet. Alternatively, the **Awesome Foursome** (6hr) bundles all the top-money activities: a helicopter ride into Skippers Canyon, rafting the Shotover, joining the Shotover Jet, and tackling either the Pipeline Bungy ($339) or the Nevis Bungy ($378). Decide what you want to do and there'll probably be a combo to suit.

Photos of your jump, jetboat ride or rafting trip are pretty much de rigueur, so you'll frequently encounter photographers demanding a cheesy grin; the results are available for purchase within a couple of hours.

Bungy jumping
Even visitors who never had any intention of parting with a large wad of money to dangle on the end of a thick strand of latex rubber find themselves **bungy jumping** in Queenstown. A combination of peer-group pressure, magnificent scenery and hard-sell promotion eventually gets to most people and, let's face it, historic bridges high above remote rivers beats a crane over a supermarket car park any day.

The original, most famous and most frequently jumped of the bungy venues is A.J. Hackett's 43m **Kawarau Suspension Bridge** beside SH6, 23km northeast of Queenstown (☎03/442 4007 & 0800/286 495, *www.ajhackett.com, bungyjump @ajhackett.co.nz*; daily 9am–5pm; $125). The price includes a certificate, T-shirt and transport if required: $39 gets you a short video recording your fifteen seconds of fame. At busy times the whole scene resembles a rather ghoulish production line, as bungy initiates are trundled out, and tour buses disgorge spectators to fill several viewing platforms. This is the only Queenstown bungy site where you can get dunked in the river.

Some say that it is only the first metre that counts, but when it comes down to it, size matters. A.J. Hackett know this and have pulled out all the stops with the whopping 134m **Nevis Highwire Bungy** (same contact details as Kawarau Bungy above; $149, or $174 with exclusive T-shirt) – the highest in New Zealand – where jumpers launch from a partly glass-bottomed gondola strung way out over the Nevis River, a tributary of the Kawarau some 32km from Queenstown. Access is by 4WD through private property so spectators will have to fork out $35 to watch their buddies, though this does give you a ride out to the launch gondola and a wonderful view.

Same-day second jumpers often gravitate to the 47m **Ledge** (summer generally 3–7pm; winter 5–9pm; $99, including T-shirt and gondola ride), from the top of the Skyline Gondola, where it feels like you are diving out over Queenstown. Unlike the other sites, you can opt for a body harness allowing you to do running jumps, and if they aren't too busy you may be able to jump with all manner of "toys" (surf boards, bikes and the like) to add an extra dimension to your jump. Night jumps in winter make for yet another variation for the committed.

Jumping at any of these three sites gives you the option of a cheaper **second jump** ($42 at Kawarau or The Ledge; $95 at Nevis) if taken within 24 hours; and all three can be combined in the half-day "Thrillogy" ($229, no T-shirts included) with one jump from each site. Hackett's fourth site, the seldom-used 71m **Skippers Canyon Bridge**, 25km up Skippers Canyon, is occasionally pressed into service, particularly for the summer-only Full Moon Bungy ($159 including T-shirt), which only happens on full moons and involves a 4WD trip into Skippers Canyon, a barbecue, a night under canvas, and a moonlit jump.

Until late in 1999, the real knee-trembler had been the 102m **Pipeline Bungy** (☎03/442 5455; 9am–dusk; $135 including T-shirt, same-day repeat jumps $50, video $49), spanning the Shotover in Skippers Canyon, where the jumping platform is atop a reconstructed 1864 sluice-water pipeline. With the heat moving to the Nevis Highwire Bungy, the Pipeline has been somewhat sidelined, but it is still a fine jump and definitely worth considering as part of a combination deal.

Jetboating

Second in the adrenalin hierarchy of Queenstown activities is **jetboating**, and half a dozen operators would love to relieve you of seventy bucks or so for a quick spin. Aside from the excellent and scenic trips on the Dart River (based in Glenorchy, but also offering Queenstown pick-ups – see p.771), only two rivers are negotiated directly from Queenstown: the **Kawarau**, usually reached by a fifteen-minute buzz across the Frankton Arm of Lake Wakatipu; and the **Shotover**, accessed either at Arthur's Point, 5km north of Queenstown, or from the Skippers Canyon Road. Jetboat trips fall into two main categories – those dedicated solely to thrills, spills and close encounters with canyon walls; and those which take a more traditional approach, exploiting the boats' ability to negotiate shallow, braided rivers.

The most celebrated of all the jetboat trips is undoubtedly the **Shotover Jet** (☎03/442 8570; daily 9am–5pm; $75; 30min), a slick operation and the only company to run thrill-a-second trips down Shotover Canyon downstream from the Edith Cavell Bridge. Battered boats attest to a lifetime of close shaves with rocks and canyon walls.

Though more expensive than most other trips, this is undoubtedly the most thrilling, and half an hour of 360-degree turns and periodic dousings is quite enough. Courtesy minibuses run from The Station throughout the day.

The only other company with exclusive use of a section of the Shotover is the **Skippers Canyon Jet** (☎03/442 5455; $79) which runs a couple of trips every day in the upper section of Skippers Canyon. Small, nimble jetboats are used to negotiate the rapids and tight turns, offering occasional glimpses of the canyon's gold-mining heritage, such as the rusting hulk of an abandoned dredge, long-disused bridge supports and twisted metal sheets which once diverted the water around gold-bearing gravels.

The remainder of the trips work the braided sections of the Kawarau and lower Shotover from either Queenstown or Frankton. None is as thrilling as the Shotover Jet, as interesting as the Skippers Canyon Jet, or as scenic as the Dart River trips, and there's little to choose between them.

Rafting

The majority of jetboat operators stick to fairly flat water, leaving the rough stuff for **whitewater rafting**. The same two rivers – the Kawarau and the Shotover – are commercially rafted from Queenstown. The most reliable of the two is a 7km section of the large-volume **Kawarau River**, negotiating four Grade III–IV rapids (exciting but not truly frightening; see "Basics", p.56, for details of river grading) and culminating in the potentially nasty Chinese Dog Leg, said to be the longest commercially rafted rapid in New Zealand. Being lake-fed, its flow is relatively steady, though it peaks in spring and drops substantially towards the end of summer.

In contrast, the 14km rafted section of the Grade III–IV **Shotover River** flows straight out of the mountains and its level fluctuates considerably, thereby affecting its raftability. In winter the lack of sunlight reaching the depths of the canyon makes it too cold for most people (though some companies do run shorter and more expensive helicopter-access trips), while in late summer the flow can be too insubstantial to safely raft some rapids. If one operator deems the river to be unsafe for rafting, then no trips are run – the upshot of an agreement reached after seven deaths had occurred on the river since 1990. During subsequent investigations, the whole industry was condemned for its appalling standards of **safety** and training. Standards have undoubtedly improved – and, of course, thousands of people do these trips every year without incident – but you should bear in mind that rafting, in common with other adrenalin-charged sports, always entails a degree of risk. The Shotover in particular is a demanding river: revelling in names such as Mother Rapid and The Toilet, the rapids reach their apotheosis in the Mother-in-Law rapid, often bypassed at low water by diverting through the 170m Oxenbridge Tunnel (see p.752).

Trips on the Kawarau River take around four hours with a little over an hour on the water; those on the Shotover last an hour longer, with most of the extra time given over to more rafting. Rationalization during the late 1990s means there are essentially just two Queenstown rafting companies, both operating on both rivers and offering pretty much the same **package**, ferrying punters by bus to an out-of-town base where they kit you out in a wetsuit and provide showers afterwards. **Prices** vary considerably, but expect to pay around $90 for Kawarau trips and $110 to ride the Shotover. Note that rafting is usually limited to those **over 13** years of age. **Booking** tends to be done directly with the main operators: Queenstown Rafting Co. (☎03/442 9792), who also run trips booked through Challenge Rafting (☎03/442 7319); and Extreme Green Rafting (☎03/442 8517).

For those preferring a gentler rafting experience, Extreme Green run the Grade I–II Upper Shotover ($139) after flying in to a backcountry station; and Family Adventures (☎03/442 5112) drive into the Skippers Canyon then raft the same stretch of river with oar-rafts, so you don't even need to paddle ($150).

River surfing, whitewater sledging and canyoning

Through the summer months (roughly mid-Sept to mid-May) the rafted section of the Kawarau River has traditionally been a playground for the parallel sports of whitewater sledging and river surfing. Unfortunately, the floods of November 1999 have altered the riverbed and taken some of the edge off the experience by forcing operators to move to a less thrilling section of river lower downstream; though this may change in time. In both cases, small groups are equipped with a board or sledge, a padded wetsuit, a helmet and fins, then led downstream and encouraged to view their independence and freedom of movement as virtues rather than hazards.

River surfing involves floating downstream, grasping a foam boogie board and surfing as many as possible of the rapids' standing waves. While rafters bob around high up on their inflatable perches with little water contact, river surfers get right in the thick of it: what look like ripples to rafters become huge waves and the serious rapids can be thoroughly daunting, as froth engulfs you on all sides. Three- to four-hour trips are run by two companies (generally mid-Oct to April, both offering roughly the same with 1hr 30min in the water: Serious Fun (☎0800/737 468; $109 including T-shirt) who run the bouncy section twice, and Mad Dog River Boarding (☎03/442 9708; $99) who do a single longer run adding in rope swings and jet-skiing along the flat section.

Largely the same techniques are used in **whitewater sledging**. Suited primarily to shallow, rocky rivers, this involves grasping the handles of a foam or plastic "sledge" and snuggling arms and upper body down into a streamlined shape. The extra buoyancy gives a better roller-coaster ride over the waves and greater manoeuvrability for catching eddies, though surfing is more difficult. Trips are run by Wanaka-based Frogz Have More Fun (☎0800/338 737; $98 from Queenstown; 1hr on the water).

If either of these sports appeal then you'll probably also fancy **canyoning** with 12 Mile Delta (☎0800/22 696, fax 03/442 3315, *www.xiimile.co.nz*, *canyoning@xiimile.co .nz*) who take small groups down a verdant narrow canyon walking in the stream, swimming across pools, sliding down rocks and jumping off cliffs all suitably protected by wetsuit, helmet and climbing harness. For $95 you get three hours away from Queenstown, around half that time in the water. Trips run morning and afternoon.

Paragliding, hang-gliding, skydiving, fly-by-wire and scenic flights

A fine day with a little breeze is all it needs to fill the skies above Queenstown with people paragliding. Upwards of a dozen operators take folk **tandem paragliding** from the prime jump site, Bob's Peak, immediately above town and reached by the Skyline Gondola. In recent years they've all banded together and operate a system not unlike a taxi rank; so all you do is pay your way up the Skyline Gondola then stand in line until it is your turn. By handing over $130 you then get the next paraglider in the queue for your jump, which typically lasts ten to fifteen minutes. How many acrobatic manoeuvres are executed is largely down to you, your jump guide and the conditions. If you don't see anyone in the air during the main 9am–5pm operating times then the conditions aren't right and you don't need to trouble yourself with the Gondola ride.

There's more of a bird-like quality to **tandem hang-gliding**, where you and your instructor are harnessed in a prone position under the wing of a hang-glider and execute a number of progressively steep turns as you soar down from Coronet Peak to the Flight Park on Malaghans Road 700 metres below. Skytrek Hang Gliding (☎03/442 6311; $145 for 12–15min in the air) are the longest-standing operator running several flights a day throughout the year, sometimes launching from The Remarkables. They pick up from Queenstown and also offer a develop-yourself roll of shots taken from a wing-tip camera ($20).

Paragliding while being towed behind a boat goes by the name of **parasailing**, an activity offered by Parafly, Main Town Pier (☎03/442 8507; Aug–May daily 9am–5pm),

WINTER IN QUEENSTOWN

Two substantial ski fields – **Coronet Peak** and **the Remarkables** – within easy striking distance of numerous quality hotels, good restaurants and plenty of apres ski combine to make Queenstown New Zealand's **premier ski destination**. Both fields have interchangeable lift tickets, giving you the freedom to pick your mountain. The highlight of the season is the week-long **Queenstown Winter Carnival**, usually around the third week in July, which, as well as all the conventional ski events, has dog racing on snow and a great line-up of entertainment. Of the various other events, the Remarkables' family-oriented **Spring Ski Carnival**, in the first week of the September school holidays, is one of the best. The main fount of knowledge is *www.nzski.com* – the Web site for both of Queenstown's ski fields as well as Mount Hutt – which has contact details, sno-cams and all the latest pricing and rental availability info. Day passes are specific to each field, but there are **multi-day tickets** valid at all three (3-day $160, 5-day $265, 8-day $415).

Neither field has **accommodation** on site, but frequent shuttle buses run down to Queenstown, where the supply is plentiful – except during school holidays. See "Listings", p.763, for details of **ski rental**.

CORONET PEAK

Coronet Peak (☎03/442 4620, *service@coronetpeak.co.nz*), 18km north of Queenstown, opened in 1947, making it New Zealand's first real ski destination. The field boasts sophisticated snow-making equipment which extends its season into spring, when cobalt blue skies and stunning scenery earn it an enviable reputation. Its range of **runs** for skiers of all abilities, and over 400 vertical metres of skiing, only add to its popularity – get here early to avoid long waits for the tows. Throughout the season, which typically starts in early June and sometimes makes it into October, **buses** from Queenstown shuttle back and forth along the sealed access road (no toll). **Passes** for daytime skiing (9am–4pm) currently cost $60 a day; from mid-July to mid-September there's also floodlit night skiing (4–10pm) for $30 per session.

THE REMARKABLES

The Remarkables (☎03/442 4615, *service@theremarkables.co.nz*), 20km east of Queenstown, is one of the newer commercial fields, occupying three mountain basins tucked in behind the wrinkled face of the Remarkables. It is most renowned as learner and intermediate terrain but there are also good runs for advanced skiers, plus some excellent country for off-piste ski touring. Current **day pass** rates are $57. Though the bottom of the tows is 500m higher than at Coronet Peak, more snow is required to cover the tussock, giving a slightly shorter season (late June to early Oct). At 320m, the total vertical descent from the tows is also less than at Coronet, but you gain an extra 120m by taking the Homeward Run – a long stretch of powder with sparkling scenery – to the 14km unsealed **access road** (no toll), where frequent buses shuttle you back up to the chairlift.

who run a large motorboat saddled with a small helipad. For $65 each, you (and a buddy if you wish) are winched out on a rope until you reach a height of 100m above the lake surface and, after ten minutes admiring the scenery, winched back in again, theoretically still dry.

Queenstown is an expensive place to go **tandem skydiving** but the scenery does go some way in compensation. Ultimate JumpSkydive Tandem ($245; ☎021/325 961) take twenty minutes to reach an altitude of 2500m, from where you get around 25 seconds' freefall over Lake Wakatipu, landing by the foot of the Remarkables some five minutes later. Another airborne possibility includes a 25-minute spin in a Pitt Special **stunt plane** with Actionflite (☎03/442 9708; $195).

The majority of Queenstown visitors who take scenic **helicopter flights** do so as part of a combination deal alongside rafting or bungy jumping, though if you have the cash to spare you might want to try landing at the top of the Remarkables (20min; $125) with Southern Lakes Helicopters (☎03/442 3016), or a similar trip with the other main operator, The Helicopter Line (☎03/442 3034 & 0800/500 575).

There's yet one more way to get airborne, and a novel one currently only offered in New Zealand, the **Fly By Wire** adventure ride (☎025/300 474, *www.flybywire.co.nz*; $129). Boasting definite petrolhead appeal, this involves piloting a kind of miniature plane which is tethered by a hundred-metre leash to a fixed point on a wire strung between two hills. Loaded with a seven-minute charge of fuel, there's free rein to circle around, gaining height (up to almost 100m) and swooping down, potentially reaching 170km per hour. Once the fuel cuts out you drift back to earth. Trips from Queenstown out to the site (on private property) run 2–3 times daily, and videos of your flight are available ($30).

Horse riding and mountain biking

Superb scenery makes Queenstown a great place to go **horse riding**. Good-value trips are run from Shotover Stables on Malaghans Road, 7km north of town (☎03/442 7486); their treks ($50; 1hr 30min) emphasize local history, exploring gold-mining relics down by the Shotover riverbed and often visiting the old mining tunnel on St Kilda Hill.

If pedals appeal more than stirrups, Gravity Action (book through Backpacking Specialists ☎03/442 8178; mid-Nov to March) run exhilarating **mountain-biking** trips ($69, with over 2hr in the saddle), descending almost 600m down a narrow track which, until a better road was pushed through in 1888, was the only route into Skippers Canyon. For something less adrenalin-fuelled, consider Queenstown-based Adventure Biking (☎03/442 9708), who lead mountain-bike trips to the historic gold towns of Seferstown (3–4hr; $45) and Macetown (4–5hr; $59)

Eating

You can eat well in Queenstown. Some restaurants try, and usually fail, to be all things to all people, but those that concentrate on one cuisine shine, with **prices** to match. An increasing number of places are making the most of Queenstown's summer climate, spilling out onto the pedestrianized streets or stretching out along the waterfront, where you can sit and watch the *Earnslaw* glide in. **Breakfast** and **snack** places generally close by 6pm, though some serve early **dinners**, while restaurants often double up as bars as the evening wears on.

With the recent opening of Queenstown's first large **supermarket**, just five minutes' walk along Gorge Road from town, grocery prices have finally come more-or-less into line with city prices.

Breakfasts, cafés and snacks

Gourmet Express, Bay Centre, Shotover St. About the nearest you'll get in New Zealand to a genuine American diner, with pancakes, French toast, burgers and sandwiches at reasonable prices. BYO & licensed.

Habebes, Wakatipu Arcade, Beach St. Hole-in-the-wall vegetarian and Lebanese daytime café serving Queenstown's best felafel, tabouleh and Kiwi variations on Middle Eastern dishes, as well as juicy lamb and chicken kebabs and the thickest of smoothies.

Jazz Bar, 24 Camp St. Excellent dive of a place where you can (just about) eat inside or take away great plates of penne, fettuccine, slices of spanakopita and other filo pies, and a Thai green curry to remember. Real fruit smoothies come as thick as anything and there's (usually) jazz while you wait.

Ken's Noodle Café, 37 Camp St. Small and hectic east Asian joint serving an inexpensive menu of miso soup, tempura and a stack of noodle dishes daily until 9pm.

Lakeside Café, Wakatipu Arcade, Beach St. Lively breakfast and lunch spot with excellent muffins, sandwiches, soups and cakes served in bright folk-art surroundings or outdoors by the lake.

Naff Caff, 1/62 Shotover St. A relaxed daytime café that's great for hanging out over some of the best coffee in town, notably the *mega mucho* strong cappuccino. There's also a good range of muffins and Danishes for breakfast and, at lunch, they do pies, quiches and salmon and cream cheese bagels.

Vudu, 23 Beach St. One of Queenstown's groovier cafés with booths, comfy chairs and loads of recent magazines to while away half an hour. The place is strong on inexpensive breakfasts, quiches, panini, scrumptious muffins and good coffee, plus more substantial fare like chicken wraps, steak sandwiches and pasta.

The Wholefood Café, Plaza Arcade, between Beach St & Shotover St. An "almost vegetarian, almost healthy" place tucked away and serving wholesome salads, pies, quiches, soups, plus less healthy cakes and decent coffee.

Restaurants

Avanti, 20 The Mall. Cheery Italian place whose reasonable food at modest prices ($14–18 for main courses) guarantees popularity, especially on Wednesday seafood nights. Gourmet pizzas and bowls of pasta go for $12–18.

Boardwalk, Steamer Wharf (☎03/442 5630). Swanky, expensive restaurant that often caters to very distinguished guests. It serves the freshest seafood in town, imaginatively prepared and often with delicate Asian touches. Dress smartly and expect to pay $25–30 for mains.

The Cow, Cow Lane. Reasonably priced ($16 a head) and popular pizzeria that fails to live up to its exalted reputation. A small range of fairly mainstream dishes are served in a cosy stone house; be prepared to share a table. BYO & licensed.

Gantley's, Malaghans Rd, Arthur's Point (☎03/442 8999). Fancy restaurant serving beautifully cooked modern Kiwi food with French leanings in an 1863 former inn 7km north of Queenstown. Mains start at $25 and the wine list is extensive. Reservations are essential, and courtesy transport from Queenstown is laid on.

Little India Bistro & Tandoori, 11 Shotover St (☎03/442 5335). Tastefully decorated restaurant drawing influences from all over the sub-continent. Enormous banquets with spiciness adjusted to your taste are available ($20–32 per head), as are takeaways and home delivery. Licensed.

Lone Star Café and Bar, 14 Brecon St. Cajun, Southern and Mexican dishes of immense proportions ($20–27) are served in a rowdy "saloon"; see also "Drinking and nightlife" overleaf.

Moa Bar & Café, 5 The Mall (☎03/442 8372). Queenstown's most fashionable and cosmopolitan restaurant and bar, serving $5 tapas and an extensive blackboard menu of imaginative dishes. Eat early if you want to avoid the inevitable smoke and clamour as the place transforms itself into a lively wine bar (see "Drinking and nightlife" overleaf).

Pasta Pasta Cucina, 6 Brecon St (☎03/442 6762). Simply decorated Italian restaurant serving wonderful crisp pizza from the manuka-fired oven and great pasta dishes such as baby octopus in a sweet chilli sauce or vegetable ravioli with mushroom and sun-dried tomato for lunch and dinner. Desserts and coffee are equally superb. Takeaway service too. Licensed.

Roaring Meg's, 57 Shotover St (☎03/442 9676). Candlelit dining in an original Skippers goldminers' cottage reconstructed here in 1922. The lamb comes highly praised and alongside salmon en papillote or filet mignon. Mains $20–25. Licensed.

Solera Vino, 25 Beach St (☎03/442 6082). This small, informal and classy evening-only restaurant showcases western Mediterranean cuisine, served either in the smoke-free restaurant or upstairs in the bar. Main courses ($24) are modest in size but beautifully done, and you can always supplement your meal with $7 tapas from the blackboard selection. Closed Mon; licensed.

Thai Siam, 43 Beach St (☎03/442 4815). Straightforward Thai restaurant serving tasty food in simple surroundings at low prices. Try tom yum or tom kar soups ($11) or any of their fried rice, curry or noodle dishes ($11–13). Licensed and BYO.

Verve, 17 The Mall. Stylish restaurant serving the likes of jambalaya ($15), corn fritters in tomato coulis ($15) and cashew butter chicken with coriander and garlic naan ($15) with considerable panache. Licensed.

Winnie Bagoes, 7–9 The Mall. Boisterous bar (see "Drinking and nightlife" overleaf) noted for its excellent gourmet pizzas and pasta.

Drinking and nightlife

Despite its high profile and large number of visitors, Queenstown is still essentially a small town. Touring **bands** are relatively rare, there isn't much in the way of highbrow **culture** and even the **clubs**, though great fun, aren't exactly cutting-edge; some bordering on backpacker cattle markets, others just cheesy. That said, there is no shortage of lively places to drink (see below), many doubling as restaurants early in the evening, when there are often a couple of **happy hours** to help get things going. The free *Mountain Scene* newspaper, found all over town, gives up-to-date **listings**, including the **movies** shown at the Embassy Cinema, 11 The Mall (infoline ☎03/442 9990).

About the only regular entertainment is the **Maori Concert and Feast**, 1 Memorial St (reservations essential on ☎03/442 8878; Wed–Sat; $45, concert only $20), a five-course hangi buffet followed by an hour-long cabaret-style concert that takes a tongue-in-cheek romp through potted Maori mythology, the haka, poi dances and stick games. Yes, it is as corny as it sounds, but if you enter into the spirit of the thing, it can be fun.

Bars and clubs

Abbey Road, 66 Shotover St. Loosely Beatles-themed bar that is one of Queenstown's cheaper drinking haunts.

Casbah, 54 Shotover St. Late-night venue that plays crowd-pleasing dance favourites to locals and backpackers. Bargain drinks before 11.30pm, plus bungy and paragliding freebies.

Chico's, 15 The Mall (☎03/442 8439). The latest-closing of all Queenstown's late bars, this joint starts to jump when the others close around 2am. Some form of live music most nights.

The Edge, cnr Camp St & Robins Rd. A new club that's always jumping to top forty and mainstream dance tunes. Very cheesy but fun.

McNeill's Cottage Brewery Restaurant, 14 Church St. Micro-brewery built into an 1880s stone building and usually selling at least three beers – a lager, a malty bitter and a dark stout-like brew – in the cosy bar or outside. They also serve a good selection of wines by the glass and run a happy hour (5–7pm), featuring their own brews at $3 per pint.

Moa Bar & Café, 5 The Mall. This early-evening restaurant subsequently undergoes a transformation into a trendy bar with a grand selection of wines.

Pog Mahone's, 14 Rees St. Queenstown's Irish bar, typically crowded with folk clamouring for draught Guinness and loosely-Irish bar meals. It is even fuller for the live Irish music, usually Sunday and Wednesday evenings.

Red Rock, 48 Camp St (☎03/442 6850). Popular town bar with hints of a ski-lodge atmosphere and a good range of beers including Red Rock, which is usually discounted during happy hours (5–7pm & 9–11pm).

The Rattlesnake Room 14 Brecon St (☎03/442 9995). Part of the *Lone Star* complex (see "Eating", previous page), this upstairs bar is a rowdy spot for an early-evening drink with a happy hour (4–7pm), pool tables and DJs from Wed–Sun nights. Any touring bands in town are likely to be found here.

Surreal, 7 Rees St. Early evening restaurant which soon transforms into what is currently Queenstown's coolest bar/club with a harder edge to the dance beats and a less boozy tenor.

Winnie Bagoes, 7–9 The Mall. Italian eating joint (see "Restaurants", previous page) with occasional bands, happy hours (4.30–7.30pm & 10–11pm) featuring low-cost pints, and pool tables. The scene gets louder and distinctly less restaurant-like as the evening wears on; open until 3am most nights.

The World, 27 Shotover St. One of the livelier clubs with a dedicated budget clientele here for the happy hours and adventure give-aways.

Listings

Airlines Air New Zealand Travel Centre, 41 Shotover St (☎03/441 1900); Ansett New Zealand (☎0800/267 388).

Banks and foreign exchange All major banks are represented with a branch and ATM somewhere around the centre of Queenstown. Best bets for exchange services are Thomas Cook, cnr

Camp St & The Mall (☎03/442 8600; daily: Oct–May 8am–8pm; June–Sept 8am–7pm), and the ANZ Bank, 28–30 The Mall (☎03/442 8287; daily 9am–9pm), though Travelex, in the main visitor centre (same hours) also have reasonable rates.

Bike rental Outside Sports, cnr The Mall & Camp St (☎03/442 8883; 9am–9pm), rents out serious, suspension-equipped mountain bikes with local track information for $45–75 a day and $35–45 a half day – and also serves as a meeting place for keen off-roaders. More straightforward bikes go for $35 a day, or you can rent one-person **scooters** ($49 a day, $39 a half day), which require only a car licence and are fine for most purposes, but deemed unsuitable for Skippers Road. Bikes, tandems and scooters are also available from Queenstown Bike Hire, 25 Beach St (☎03/442 6039), at similar prices.

Buses Atomic Shuttles (☎03/442 8178) run to Christchurch, Dunedin and up the Coast to Greymouth; Catch-a-Bus (☎03/471 4103) operate a door-to-door service to Dunedin; InterCity (☎03/442 5628) operate the most extensive services to all major destinations; Kiwi Discovery (☎03/442 7340) run a fast service to Christchurch and minibuses to the major trailheads and Milford Sound; Kiwi Experience (☎03/442 9708) add a special Milford Sound run to their back-packer tour-bus setup; Magic Bus (☎03/442 8178) run through Queenstown en route from the West Coast to Dunedin; Southern Link Shuttles (☎03/442 8178) run to Dunedin, Christchurch and Picton; Super Shuttle (☎03/442 9803) meets planes from Queenstown's airport; and Wanaka Connexions (☎0800/879 926) run the most direct service to Wanaka.

Camping and outdoor equipment At the Small Planet Recycling Co, 17 Shotover St (☎03/442 6393; daily 10am–8pm), you can pick up used gear, including snowboards, ski gear, wetsuits, bikes, camping and tramping gear and books – all at good prices and with competitive buy-back deals. If you've got something to get rid of, they'll hawk it for 20 percent commission. See also "Ski rental", below.

Car rental Typical summer rates from the major firms start at $90 a day, rising to around $150 for 4WD vehicles. Smaller companies generally offer better deals, with rates for cars of $45–70 a day for week-long rentals, and around $80 per day for 4WD vehicles with snow chains included. Even in high summer you should be able to get something for $50 a day with unlimited kilometres, though for short rentals (for example a 2-day rental to go to Milford Sound) $70 a day is more likely. Apex, 18 Shotover St (☎0800/531 111); Budget, cnr Camp St & Shotover St (☎03/442 9274) and the airport (☎03/442 3450); NZ Rent a Car, cnr Camp St & Shotover St (☎03/442 7465); Queenstown Car Rental, 18 Shotover St (☎03/442 9220); Reg's Rentals, 23 Beach St (☎03/442 6039); Rent-a-Dent, 48 Shotover St (☎03/442 9922 & 0800/736 823).

Childminding Kids Klub (☎03/441 8539) and Safe & Sound (☎03/442 4608) both offer 24hr baby-sitting for all ages.

Dentist 24hr coverage on ☎03/442 8580 and ☎03/442 7274.

Guided walks Arrowtown Lodge and Hiking Co (☎03/442 1101, fax 442 1108, *www.arrowtownlodge.co.nz, hiking@queenstown.co.nz*) run a series of guided walks around the Queenstown, Glenorchy and Arrowtown areas, ranging from gentle scenic and historic walks (short half day; $40) to reasonably energetic alpine tramps (full day; $120).

Internet Fierce competition means good rates fast connections and long opening hours, often until 10pm or later. Places to look out for are *E Café*, 50 Shotover St; *Budget Communications*, 2nd floor, O'Connell's Mall (*budgetc@xtra.co.nz*); and *Internet Outpost*, 27 Shotover St (*outpost.queenstown@xtra.co.nz*).

Laundry Can usually be done where you're staying, but Alpine Coin Operated Laundrette, 10 Shotover St (daily 7.30am–9pm), do a $3 wash.

Library cnr Shotover St & Gorge Rd.

Medical treatment Queenstown Medical Centre, cnr Stanley St & Shotover St (☎03/442 7301, 442 3053 for after-hours doctor), and Lakes District Hospital, 20 Douglas St, Frankton (☎03/442 3053).

Pharmacy Wilkinsons Pharmacy, The Mall (☎03/442 7313), is open daily from 8.30am to 10pm.

Police 11 Camp St (☎03/442 7900).

Post office The main post office, cnr Camp St Ballarat St (Mon–Fri 9am–5pm) has poste restante facilities.

Scenic flights Air Fiordland (☎03/442 3404); Air Wakatipu (☎03/442 3148, *queenstown@flying.co.nz*); Milford Sound Scenic Flights (☎03/442 3065 & 0800/101 767).

Ski rental Outside Sports, cnr The Mall & Camp St (☎03/442 8883), rent skis, boots and poles from $28 per day for the basic kit to $45 for top-quality "executive" gear; snowboards go for $30 a day, as does telemark equipment. The excellent Brown's, 39 Shotover St (☎03/442 4003) offer similar rates on new gear, deliver to your hotel and also do overnight tuning.

Taxis Alpine Taxi (☎03/442 6666 & 0800/730 066); Queenstown Taxis (☎03/442 7788 & 0800/477 888).

Thomas Cook Inside The Station, cnr Camp St & Shotover St (daily: Oct–May 8am–8pm; June–Sept 8am–7pm; ☎03/442 6403).

Tours and booking agencies In Queenstown, the frenzied tour industry means that pretty much anywhere in the southern half of the South Island is fair game for a flight or a bus trip. Stewart Island and Mount Cook are both possibilities for visitors in a massive hurry, but those with a little more time on their hands will find trips to the Milford Sound area (see p.820) or a mosey around the old gold towns (see p.795) more rewarding.

Arrowtown and Macetown

The former gold-rush settlement of **ARROWTOWN** seems perched on the brink of tour-bus hell as day-trippers from Queenstown, 23km to the southeast, swarm around the sheepskin, greenstone and gold of its souvenir shops. But Arrowtown manages to retain the spirit of a living community, with the grocers' shops, pubs and post office fitfully coexisting alongside the gift-wrapped centre. The best way to appreciate Arrowtown is to linger on after the crowds have gone, leaving behind a peaceful farming town at the confluence of the Arrow River and Bush Creek. The sheltering hills give Arrowtown parched summers and snowy winters, thrown into sharp relief by autumn, when the deciduous trees planted by the mining community cast golden shadows on a central knot of picturesque miners' cottages.

Arrowtown's permanent population is only around 1200 but in summer, when holiday homes are full and tourists arrive in force, it comes close to regaining its 7000-strong peak attained during the **gold rush**. There is some debate as to whether American William Fox was actually the first to discover alluvial gold in the Arrow River in 1862, but there is no doubt that he dominated proceedings hereabouts, managing to keep the find secret while he recovered over 100kg of gold. Jealous prospectors tried to follow him to the lode, but he gave them the slip, on one occasion leaving his tent and provisions behind in the middle of the night. The town subsequently bore his name until Foxes gave way to Arrowtown. The eponymous river became known as the richest for its size in the world – a reputation which drew Chinese miners, who lived in the now partly restored **Arrowtown Chinese Settlement**, and enticed prospectors to the surrounding hills, where brothers Charley and John Mace set up **Macetown**, now an appealing ghost town.

As prospectors pushed further up the Arrow and Bush Creek, they began to populate **the valleys**; scattered communities sprang up along the banks, but were abandoned just as suddenly, leaving telltale poplar, rowan and willows to be reclaimed by nature. Where settlers' cottages once stood, **fruit** trees have colonized the riverbanks, and in autumn apples, pears and plums weigh down the branches, and bushes of blackberry, blackcurrant, gooseberry, raspberry and elderberry become rampant. There are few specific sights, but you can easily spend a lazy afternoon gorging on fruit and trying to identify the overgrown sites of houses. The surrounding hills are speckled with **rose bushes**: according to folklore, these were planted by miners seeking vitamin C (rosehips are one of the richest sources); others contend that they were planted primarily for their root systems, which could be fashioned into briar pipes.

Arrival and information

Two **buses** run from Queenstown to Arrowtown, both departing from The Top of the Mall on Camp Street in Queenstown and stopping outside the library on Buckingham

Street in Arrowtown. The **scheduled** Arrow Express (☎03/442 1900; 3–5 daily; 25min; $6 each way) runs mostly via Frankton and Queenstown airport, though some services go via the Shotover Jet and Millbrook Resort. The Double Decker Bus Tour uses a red London bus to operate Queenstown-based **tours** (☎03/442 6067; daily 10am & 2pm; 2hr 30min; $27), visiting the Kawarau bungy bridge en route and spending an hour in Arrowtown.

Arrowtown's **visitor centre** is inside the foyer of the Lakes District Museum at 49 Buckingham St (daily 9am–5pm; ☎03/442 1824, fax 442 0835, *museum@queenstown. co.nz*), where you can pick up the *Historic Arrowtown* leaflet ($1) and buy the informative *Arrowtown Chinese Settlement* booklet ($2.50). It also offers **Internet** access. Bike rental is available from Arrowtown Wines and Spirits on Ramshaw Lane ($25 per half day)

Accommodation

To see Arrowtown at its best, you really need to **stay** the night; happily, there's plenty of accommodation, much of it especially affordable for lone travellers, with single rooms just over half the price of doubles.

ARROWTOWN

RESTAURANTS, CAFÉS & BARS

Arrowtown Bakery	2
Coffee Rush	3
Saffron	4
The Stables	5
Wind in the Willows	1

ACCOMMODATION

Anne & Arthur Gormack	G
Arrowtown Caravan Park	J
Arrowtown Holiday Park	F
Arrowtown Lodge	B
Caernarvon Homestay	C
Golden View Motel	K
Millbrook Resort	H
Polly-Anna Cottage	E
Royal Oak Hotel	A
Settlers Motel	D
Speargrass Lodge	L
Viking Lodge Motel	I

Hotels and motels

Golden View Motel, 48 Adamson Drive (☎ & fax 03/442 1833, reservations ☎0800/246 538, *goldenview@southnet.co.nz*). Fairly standard motel with well-equipped rooms, an outdoor pool and mountain bikes to rent at modest rates. ④.

Millbrook Resort, Malaghans Rd, on the outskirts of town (☎03/441 7000 & 0800/800 604, fax 442 1145, *nz.com/queenstown/millbrook, mbmkting@millbrook.co.nz*). A highly-rated 18-hole golf course, several bars and restaurants, and luxury accommodation in suites and chalets make this one of New Zealand's more exclusive resort complexes – and account for its popularity with Queenstown tour groups. ⑨.

Settlers Motel, 22 Hertford St (☎03/442 1734 & 0800/803 801, fax 442 1936, *settlersmotel@clear.net.nz*). A lace-and-Laura Ashley place that has earned numerous plaudits. Studios and one- and two-bedroom units are all fitted out to a high standard, with decorations based on traditional pioneer motifs. ⑤.

Viking Lodge Motel, 21 Inverness Crescent (☎ & fax 03/442 1765, reservations 0800/181 900, *viking@inq.co.nz*). One of Arrowtown's best-value motels, featuring an outdoor pool and a cluster of one- and two-bedroom A-frame chalets with well-equipped kitchens and VCRs. ④.

B&Bs and homestays

Anne & Arthur Gormack, 18 Stafford St (☎03/442 1747). Comfortable, well-appointed rooms in a spacious modern homestay five minutes' walk from the town centre. Has a pool and badminton court, plus long views over the Arrow Basin. ⑤.

Arrowtown Lodge, 7 Anglesea St (☎03/442 1101, fax 442 1108, *www.arrowtownlodge.co.nz, hiking@queenstown.co.nz*). Four modern, comfortable and tastefully furnished cottages built from recycled nineteenth-century mud-bricks, each with en-suite bathroom and mountain views. Breakfast is served out on the sunny deck, and can be followed by guided walks (see Queenstown "Listings", p.763). There's also free Internet access and laundry. ⑥.

Caernarvon Homestay, 25 Caernarvon St (☎03/442 1227 & 0800/186 844, *daniels@es.co.nz*). The lowest-priced and one of the best of Arrowtown's homestays, in a large modern house with two attractive rooms – one en suite, the other with French windows opening onto the garden. ④.

Polly-Anna Cottage, 43 Bedford St (☎03/442 1347). Homestay in a tidily restored hundred-year-old miner's cottage with a sun deck and manicured lawns; close to the centre. ⑤.

Speargrass Lodge, Speargrass Flat Rd, 5km from Arrowtown (☎03/442 1417, fax 442 1497, *speargrass@xtra.co.nz*). One of the most attractive, spacious and luxurious country B&Bs around, surrounded by landscaped lawns and mature exotic trees. Simply decorated rooms are all en suite and there's free use of mountain bikes and a dinghy on nearby Lake Hayes. Breakfast is included ⑥.

Hostels and campsites

Arrowtown Caravan Park, 61 Devon St (☎03/442 1838). Smaller and more appealing of the two campsites, about ten minutes' walk from the centre. Tent & powered sites $10.

Arrowtown Holiday Park, 11 Suffolk St (☎ & fax 03/442 1876). Marginally the handiest and largest of the town's two campsites with showers and laundry available to non-guests ($3 each) and a tennis court. Tent/powered sites $9/10, standard cabins ②, tourist flats ④.

Royal Oak Hotel, 46 Buckingham St (☎03/442 1700). Old hotel in the centre of town with the cheapest beds in town in simple rooms sharing facilities. Singles go for $25. Rooms ②.

The Town

Twin rows of sycamores and oaks planted in 1867 have grown to overshadow the tiny miners' cottages along the photogenic **Avenue of Trees**, Arrowtown's most recognizable image. Most of the sixty or so cottages were built towards the end of the nineteenth century and they're unusually small and close together, the chronic lack of timber undoubtedly being a factor.

A visit to the informative nearby Lakes District Museum (see opposite) is probably the best preparation for a stroll around the **Arrowtown Chinese Settlement** (part of the Otago Goldfields Park; unrestricted entry). This string of heavily restored buildings

ARROWTOWN'S HIDDEN CHINESE HISTORY

The initial wave of miners who came to Arrowtown in the early 1860s were fortune-seekers intent on a fast buck. When gold was discovered on the West Coast, most of them hotfooted it to Greymouth or Hokitika, leaving a much-depleted community that lacked the economic wherewithal to support the businesses which had mushroomed around the mining communities.

The solution, as it had been ten years earlier on the Victorian goldfields of Bendigo and Ballarat in Australia, was to import **Chinese labour**. The first Chinese, who principally came from the Canton delta region of Kwangtung (now known as Guangdong), arrived in Otago in 1866, their number reaching 5000 by 1870. The community settled along Bush Creek, its **segregation** from the main settlement symptomatic of the inherent racism of the time – something which also manifested itself in working practices that forced the Chinese to pick over abandoned mining claims and work the tailings of European miners. Even Chinese employed on municipal projects such as the Presbyterian church were paid only half the wages paid to Europeans doing the same job.

A ray of light is cast amid the prevailing bigotry by contemporary newspaper reports, which suggest that many citizens found the Chinese conduct of their business "upright and straightforward" and their demeanour "orderly and sober" – perhaps surprisingly in what was an almost entirely male community. Most came with starry-eyed dreams of earning their fortune and returning home so, initially at least, few brought their **families**; a process of chain migration later brought wives, children and then members of the extended family. Few realized their dreams, but around ninety percent did return home, many in a box, driven into an early grave by overwork and poor living conditions. Many more were driven out in the early 1880s when recession brought racial jealousies to a head, resulting in the enactment of a punitive poll tax on foreign residents. There was little workable gold by this time and those Chinese who stayed mostly became market gardeners or merchants and drifted away, mainly to Auckland, though the Arrowtown community remained viable into the 1920s. Once the Chinese had left or died, the Bush Creek settlement was **abandoned** and largely destroyed by repeated flooding.

hugging a narrow willow-draped section of Bush Creek at the western end of Buckingham Street is easily the best-preserved of New Zealand's Chinese communities, and provides an insight into a fascinating, if shameful, episode in the country's history (see box above). Many of the buildings were originally built as temporary retreats from peripatetic prospecting and to provide shelter during the harsh winters, only becoming permanent homes as miners aged. With tin, sod and timber the principal building materials, little was left standing when an archeological dig was begun in 1983, and most of the dwellings languish in a state of graceful decay. Some schist, mortar and corrugated-iron buildings fared rather better and five of these have been restored. The best is **Ah-Lum's Store**, built in typical Canton delta style in 1883 for Wong Hop Lee and leased from 1909 to 1927 to Ah-Lum, one of the pillars of the Chinese community in its later years. By this time integration was making inroads: Ah-Lum sold European as well as Chinese goods, and operated an opium den and bank. Wood panelling divides the store into low-roofed rooms with mezzanine areas above, perhaps used for opium smoking. Beyond that it is mostly stone plinths and chimney breasts fleetingly brought back to life by interpretation panels.

Artefacts found during the 1983 Chinese Settlement dig are displayed inside the former BNZ building of 1875 that now operates as the **Lakes District Museum**, 49 Buckingham St (daily 9am–5pm; $4), a bits and bobs museum which nevertheless succeeds in bringing local history to life. Not surprisingly, it mainly covers the lives of the gold-miners and their families, with a particular emphasis on the Chinese community and the archeological excavations. There's also a feature on opium smoking, which remained legal in New Zealand until 1901, some twenty years after games of chance – fantan and pakapoo – were proscribed. Technophiles also get a look in, with displays on the quartz-reef mining used at Macetown and on the country's earliest hydro scheme, which once supplied mining communities in Skippers and Macetown with power.

Around Arrowtown: Macetown

As gold fever swept through Otago in the early 1860s, prospectors fanned out, clawing their way up every creek and gully in search of a flash in the pan. In 1862, alluvial gold was found at Twelve Mile, sparking the rush to what later became known as **Macetown** (part of the Otago Goldfields Park; unrestricted entry), now a ghost town of three buildings and a popular destination for mountain bikers, horse trekkers and trampers (see box below). On first acquaintance, it isn't a massively exciting place, but the grassy plateau makes a great free camping spot, sheltered by low stone walls and willow, sycamore and apple trees. The only facilities are long-drop toilets and river water, but walking in here with tent and provisions, and spending a day or two exploring the old mines and grubstake claims, is the best way to experience the place's unique atmosphere.

Macetown's story is one of boom and bust: at its peak, it boasted a couple of hotels, a post office and a school; but when the gold ran out, it couldn't fall back on farming in the way that Arrowtown and Queenstown did and, like Skippers, it died. All that remains of the town itself are a couple of stone buildings – the restored schoolmaster's house and the bakery – and a smattering of wooden shacks. The surrounding creeks and gullies are littered with the twisted and rusting remains of gold batteries, making

---

THE ARROWTOWN – MACETOWN CIRCUIT TRAMP

The 16km 4WD road up the Arrow Creek from Arrowtown to Macetown is the district's premier biking and trekking route, but walkers have the edge by being able to include the road as part of the fairly strenuous, full-day **Arrowtown–Macetown Circuit** (8hr; 32km).

The walk is best done in the months from **Christmas to Easter**, after the winter snows have melted and the swollen Arrow River has subsided a little, making the 22 river crossings on the Arrow Creek a little easier – though even in summer, access can be problematic after rain. The *Macetown and the Arrow Gorge* booklet makes a good companion for the route, interpreting sights along the way.

The walk starts by the confluence of the Arrow River and Bush Creek, following the northern bank of the latter westwards, then skirting the base of German Hill and branching up Sawtooth Gully. The gully emerges through open hill country to Eichardt's Flat, a terrace named after a local farmer and brother of the Queenstown hotelier. At this point, about an hour out of Arrowtown, you can pursue the **Sawpit Gully variation** east down Sawpit Gully to meet the Arrow River road and Arrowtown, thus making a two- to three-hour circuit.

From the Sawpit Gully junction, the Macetown path contours gradually around to the **Big Hill** saddle, with its expansive views back to Lake Hayes and the Remarkables. The route then drops steeply towards Eight Mile Creek, the path becoming indistinct – marked by infrequent poles – as it traverses soggy and potentially ankle-twisting country. After three or four hours, you stumble across the Arrow Creek road, just a couple of kilometres short of **Macetown**.

When you've had your fill of Macetown, follow the Arrow Creek road back to Arrowtown, occasionally diverting on to paths that run parallel to the road for respite from the dust.

a fruitful hunting ground for industrial archeology fans; the area is covered in some detail in the *Macetown and the Arrow Gorge* booklet ($4, available from the Lakes District Museum in Arrowtown).

Macetown is a full-day (or overnight, if you want to camp among the ruins) outing either on foot (see box, opposite), by **mountain bike** (you'll need to rent one from Queenstown unless you have your own), or on a **4WD** trip with Outback Tours (☎03/442 7386; 4–5hr; $75).

Eating and entertainment

In the last few years, Arrowtown's culinary scene has caught up with its accommodation choice, and there is now a good selection of quality places. Further afield there is also refined dining at the *Gibbston Valley Winery*, 14km away on SH6 (☎03/442 6910), whose fine restaurant is open for lunch and snacks throughout the day; or you could splash out at one of the **swanky restaurants** in the *Millbrook Resort* complex on Malaghans Road (☎03/441 7000), a few kilometres outside Arrowtown.

Finally, if your visit is during the week leading up to Easter, you can partake in the **Autumn Festival** (enquiries to the visitor centre), with all manner of historic walks, street theatre and hoe-downs, much of it free.

Arrowtown Bakery, in the Ballarat Arcade on Buckingham St. Reliable bakery which produces a prodigious range of tasty pies and wonderful breads – from Italian and sourdough to gluten-free and organic; try their "football", a kind of soft-bread calzone.

Coffee Rush, 4 Buckingham St. Little modern coffee place tucked back off the street and doing a nice line in muffins, sandwiches and, of course, good coffee.

Saffron, 18 Buckingham St. Smart polished wood and corrugated iron place equally suited to a coffee at the pavement tables, a lunchtime antipasto plate for two ($25), or classy meals which might start with lambs brains ($12) and follow with a red duck coconut curry. Licensed.

The Stables, 28 Buckingham St (☎03/442 1818; closed Mon). Beautiful old stone building with outdoor seating where you can feast on classy bistro-style dishes, such as Thai chicken or stuffed capsicum, or just nip along for a Devonshire tea.

Wind in the Willows, Ramshaw Lane. One of the best lunch spots in town, this combined bookshop and licensed café does pizza, quiche, soup, cakes and good coffee, all at decent prices.

Glenorchy and the major tramps

The tiny town of **GLENORCHY**, at the head of Lake Wakatipu 50km northwest of Queenstown, is quiet and supremely picturesque, making it a perfect retreat for a couple of days. For the majority of visitors, though, this still isn't remote enough, and for them Glenorchy is simply a staging post en route to some of the finest **tramping** New Zealand has to offer – a circuit of the Rees and Dart Rivers, the Routeburn Track and the Greenstone and Caples **tracks**.

Glenorchy and around

The Glenorchy region's fantastic scenery owes a debt to beds of ancient sea-floor sediments laid down some 220–270 million years ago and metamorphosed into the grey-green schists and *pounamu* (greenstone) of the Forbes and Humboldt mountains. The western and northern flanks of the Forbes Mountains were shaped by the Dart Glacier, now a relatively short tongue of ice which, at its peak 18,000 years ago, formed the root of the huge glacial system that gouged out the floor of Lake Wakatipu.

In pre-European times the plain beside the combined delta of the Rees (*Oware*) and Dart (*Oturu*) rivers was known as **Kotapahau**, "the place of revenge killing", a reference perhaps to fights between rival *hapu* over the esteemed *pounamu* littering an area centred on the bed of the Dart River. There's still greenstone up there, but most is protected within the bounds of the Mount Aspiring National Park, including a huge, 25-tonne boulder estimated to be worth some $15 million.

The first **Europeans** to penetrate the area were gold prospectors, government surveyors, and nearby runholders in search of fresh grazing. James McKerrow finished the first reconnaissance survey in 1863, about the same time as a party of five miners led by Patrick Caples made their way up the Dart River. The fledgling community of Glenorchy served these disparate groups, along with teams of sawmillers and workers from a mine extracting sheelite, a mineral used in the manufacture of armaments. Despite the lack of road access to Glenorchy, **tourists** began to arrive early this century, cruising across Lake Wakatipu on the TSS *Earnslaw*, before being decanted into charabancs for the 20km jolt north to the Arcadia homestead at **Paradise**. Disappointingly drawing its name from the locally abundant paradise ducks rather than its idyllic qualities, Paradise has nevertheless been deemed stunning enough to emulate the Rockies or the European Alps in numerous movies.

The **road from Queenstown** was eventually pushed through in 1962, opening up a fine lakeside drive that passes **Bob's Cove**, the best place to observe the lake's seiche, an ill-understood phenomenon which causes the lake level to cycle by around 150mm every five minutes. Glenorchy has remained defiantly rural, and while there has been a marked increase in tourist traffic since the road was finally sealed all the way through in 1997, the few tourist-oriented ventures barely disturb the bucolic atmosphere.

Arrival and information

Summer-only backpacker **buses** ply the Queenstown–Glenorchy route, charging around $10 for the one-hour run. Most frequent are those run by Backpacker Express (☎03/442 9939, fax 442 9940, *www.glenorchyinfocentre.co.nz*, *info@glenorchyinfocentre. co.nz*; 3–5 daily), though there are competing, and often cheaper, buses run by Upper Lake Wakatipu Tours (☎03/442 9986). A pricier but more scenic (and slightly quicker) alternative is the Glenorchy Scenic Express **hydrofoil** (☎03/442 8582; $20 each way) which leaves from the Main Town Pier in Queenstown three times a day and calls at Greenstone Wharf, handy if you want to get directly onto the Greenstone or Caples tracks.

The Backpacker Express is operated from the grounds of the *Glenorchy Holiday Park*, at 2 Oban St (☎03/442 7178), which is also the best source of **general information** and the place to go for post-tramp **transport bookings**. For the lowdown on tramping information, see p.774.

Accommodation

After the rigours of the tramp, Glenorchy is a welcome sight and, considering its size, there is a reasonable range of accommodation to suit most budgets.

Glenorchy Holiday Park & Backpackers, Oban St (☎03/442 7178, fax 442 7172, *glenpark@queenstown.co.nz*). This well-organized campsite is the cheapest place in town, with spacious tent ($8) and powered sites ($9), plus bunks, basic double or twin cabins. Non-residents can shower here for $3. Dorms ①, cabins ②.

Glenorchy Hotel, cnr Mull St & Argyll St (☎03/442 9902, fax 442 9912, *glenorchy.hotel@xtra.co.nz*). Good backpacker-style dorms, with communal kitchen and lounge, are hidden behind this hotel. From November to April, plain double rooms – but with great views up the Dart Valley – are also available. Dorms ①, rooms ④.

Glen Roydon Outdoor Lodge, cnr Mull St & Argyll St (☎ & fax 03/442 9968). Good modern rooms with a nod to ski-lodge style, all sharing the comfortable guest lounge with its open fire, TV and videos. ⑥.

Little Paradise Lodge, Meilejohn Bay, 16km along the Queenstown road (☎ & fax 03/442 6196; see p.748). ⑥.

Mount Earnslaw Motels, Oban St (☎03/442 6993, fax 442 7776, *thor.corrine@xtra.co.nz*). Glenorchy's only motel, right in the heart of town with seven new and nicely furnished self-contained studios plus barbecue and sauna. ⑤.

The Town and nearby activities

Glenorchy itself doesn't amount to much – a petrol station, a post office, a couple of pubs and cafés, some accommodation and a grocery shop. To get a feel for the area and its geography, follow the 2km loop of the **Glenorchy Walkway** from the wharf at the end of Islay Street along the edge of Lake Wakatipu and through the wetlands around the town's lagoon, a pleasant way to soak up the mountain scenery at either end of the day.

Almost all the non-tramping visitors are here for the excellent **jetboating** trips up the **Dart River**, a two-hour journey which fully utilizes the jetboat's shallow-water capabilities, picking routes through braided river beds and finally entering a short gorge before turning round at Sandy Bluff on the edge of the Mount Aspiring National Park. The usual jetboating antics are duly performed, but the real star is the magnificent scenery, featuring snowcapped mountains and dense bush, which is most easily appreciated from the middle of the river. The highlight is the brief stop to walk (or jetboat if conditions are right) in to **Rockburn Chasm**, where a small tributary of the Dart has carved out a narrow, twisting canyon filled with calm, clear water. Dart River Jetboat Safari (☎03/442 4933, fax 442 9075, *www.dartriverjet.co.nz, reservations@dartriverjet.co.nz*) runs two or three daily trips from Glenorchy (2hr; $125) and Queenstown (5–6hr; $140). Their Backroad Safari (same prices) involves a ride in a 4WD coach, a twenty-minute bushwalk then the downstream jetboat ride.

Better still, combine the upstream section of the Dart River Jetboat Safari with **canoeing** back downstream in Fun Yaks (☎0800/386 925, fax 03/442 6536, *www.funyaks.com, funyaks@inc.co.nz*), two- or three-person inflatable canoes carried upriver in the jetboats, then paddled down. Suitable even for absolute beginners, this is a gentle trip with no rapids and very little likelihood of an enforced swim. Trips run on demand, take eight hours return from Queenstown (6hr from Glenorchy) and cost $179 from either town, including lunch. A cheaper variation ($129 from either town) involves a 4WD ride upriver and the Fun Yak downstream. Trampers wanting to skip most of the last day's walking can pick up a jetboat at Sandy Bluff then switch to a Fun Yak for a couple of hours paddling and finally get dropped in Glenorchy ($99).

Dart River Jetboat Safari is part of the slick Shotover Jet operation, with all the production-line tourism and merchandising that that entails. If you'd prefer something a little more personal, go with Dart Wilderness Adventures (☎03/442 9939, fax 442 9940, *info@glenorchyinfocentre.co.nz*), who currently charge $109 from Glenorchy for a similar run up to Sandy Bluff and back.

If you're not here for the major tramps, and still fancy a hike, consider just walking the first couple of hours of the Routeburn from Routeburn Shelter, or tackle the **Lake Sylvan Walk** (5km; 1hr 30min; negligible ascent), which starts at a signposted car park 3km before Routeburn Shelter. It largely crosses gravel river terraces supporting beech and totara forest then loops around the Lake Sylvan, turned brown from its feeder streams leeching through the soil.

Eating

There's pretty decent **daytime** eating at *Ronda's Café* on Mull Street (closed Tues), which serves pies, light meals and coffee in a cosy wood-panelled café or outside, and sells good solid rye bread, which feels heavy in your pack but lasts the distance. Most **evenings** hungry and thirsty trampers gravitate towards the *Glenorchy Hotel*, which serves a good selection of Kiwi staples, with bar snacks from $8 and main dishes from

$15. Dinners are more formal across the road at the "Rod and Rucksack" in the *Glen Royden Lodge*, where substantial mains cost $18–22.

The widest selection of **tramping food** is to be found in Queenstown, where prices are also slightly lower, but you can always pick up some last-minute supplies from the store at the *Glenorchy Holiday Park*.

The major tramps: preliminaries

The fame of the **Routeburn Track** is eclipsed only by that of its westerly neighbour, the Milford Track (see p.824). Many justly claim that the Routeburn is superior, citing its more varied scenery, longer time spent above the bushline away from sandflies,

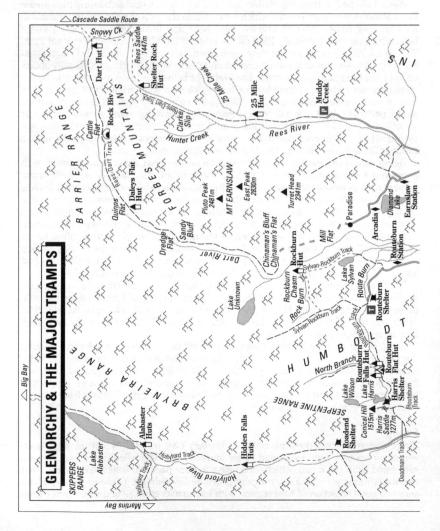

and better spacing of huts. It can't be denied that the Routeburn is one of New Zealand's finest walks, straddling the spine of the Humboldt Mountains and providing access to many of the southwestern wilderness's most archetypal features: forested valleys with rich bird life and plunging waterfalls are combined with river flats, lakes and spectacular mountain scenery. In the past the Routeburn was treated as a cheaper and less regimented alternative to the Milford Track, but overcrowding and the consequent introduction of a booking system have redressed the balance. The nature of the terrain means that the Routeburn is usually promoted as a moderate tramp, though the short distance between huts eases the strain considerably. Fit hikers might consider doing it in two reasonably long days, though that doesn't leave much time for soaking up the scenery and wallowing in the relative solitude. To return by road from the end of the Routeburn to the start is something approaching 300km, so to avoid a lot of backtracking, anyone with an extra day or two to spare should consider returning to Glenorchy by hiking either the Greenstone or Caples tracks.

Both the **Greenstone and Caples tracks** are easy tramps, following gently graded, parallel river valleys where the wilderness experience is moderated by grazing cattle from the high-country stations along the Lake Wakatipu shore. The Greenstone occupies the broader, U-shaped valley carved out by one arm of the huge Hollyford Glacier, but despite the grandeur of the surrounding mountain scenery, it is sometimes criticized for being dull. Its detractors prefer the track over the sub-alpine McKellar Saddle and down the Caples Valley, where the river is bigger and the narrow base of the valley forces the path closer to it.

As the Routeburn reaches maximum capacity, the **Rees–Dart Track** is now being primed for wider usage; in parts the path is being graded, the track is being re-routed to avoid a hairy stepladder and the huts are slowly being improved. Nonetheless, it remains the toughest of the major tramps in the area, covering some fairly rugged terrain and requiring six to eight hours of effort each day. It follows the standard Kiwi tramp formula of climbing one river valley, crossing the pass and descending into another, but adds an excellent side-trip to the Cascade Saddle and the choice of a jet-boat or inflatable kayak trip to complete the final day.

In **winter** the Routeburn takes on a different character and becomes a much more serious undertaking. The track is often snowbound and extremely slippery, the risk of avalanche is high and the huts are unheated. Return day-trips from Routeburn Shelter to Routeburn Falls Hut and from The Divide to the Lake Mackenzie Hut are much better bets. The lower-level Greenstone and Caples tracks also make a less daunting prospect – not least because the huts are heated by wood-burning stoves which can be used throughout the year – though the McKellar Saddle is often snow-covered. Only experienced, knowledgeable and well-equipped trampers should venture onto the Rees–Dart Track in the winter.

Information and maps

Tramping **information** is best sought at the **DOC office** on Glenorchy's Oban Street (Nov–April daily 8.30am–4.30pm; May–Oct Mon–Fri 8.30am–4.30pm; ☎03/442 9937, fax 442 9938; *greatwalksbooking@doc.govt.nz*), where you can fill in intentions forms (not required for the Routeburn), get the latest weather forecast, gen up on track conditions and either rent ($3, plus $10 deposit) or buy ($15) maps.

DOC's leaflets on *The Routeburn Track* ($1; free with hut booking – see opposite) and *The Greenstone and Caples Tracks* ($1), together with the 1:75,000 *Routeburn/Greenstone Trackmap* cover these three walks. For real route-finding, the detailed 1:50,000 *Eglinton Topomap* is better, though you can also make do (at least for the Routeburn) with the 1:150,000 *Mount Aspiring National Park* map. For the Rees–Dart Track, again the 1:150,000 *Mount Aspiring National Park* **map**, along with the DOC's *Rees–Dart* leaflet ($1), make good background material, but aren't really adequate for proper route-finding; the considerably more detailed 1:50,000 *Tutoko* and *Earnslaw* Topomaps are far better.

Remember that any mention of the **left or right bank** refers to their position when **facing downstream**.

Trailhead transport

During the summer **tramping season**, there is little difficulty with transport to or from either end of the tracks. Most walkers use Glenorchy as a base, where a couple of small **bus companies** (Backpacker Express ☎03/442 9939; Upper Lake Wakatipu Tours ☎03/442 9986) compete for trailhead business. Routes are divided into sectors –

Queenstown to Glenorchy; Glenorchy to the start of the Routeburn; Greenstone car park to Glenorchy; Glenorchy to the start of the Rees-Dart – and all cost $10. The only exceptions are the time-saving 4WD run to 25-mile Hut at the start of the Rees-Dart ($20) and the run from Chinaman's Bluff to Glenorchy ($20) at the end of the Rees-Dart.

Trampers wanting to be dropped off or picked up at The Divide (the western end of the Routeburn) can hop on buses plying between Te Anau and Milford Sound (ask visitor centres or the companies above for schedules); in addition, Fiordland Tracknet (☎03/249 7777, *tracknet@destinationnz.com*) operate a thrice daily loop service from mid-October to mid-May, leaving Te Anau (7.30am, 9.30am & 1pm) before calling at The Divide (8.30am, 11am & 2.15pm), Milford Sound (9.15am, 11.45am & 3pm), The Divide (10.15am, 3.45pm & 5.45pm), and returning to Te Anau (noon, 5pm & 7pm). From The Divide you can expect to pay $20 to Te Anau, $45 to Queenstown, and $15 to Milford Sound.

To save backtracking, trampers can also arrange to have their bags sent on to Te Anau for a small fee through the Backpacker Express people.

Hut and campsite bookings

The **Routeburn Track** has a compulsory system of booking **accommodation passes** for all four Great Walk huts and two campsites for the duration of the **tramping season** (Nov–April). It's a reasonably flexible system, allowing people to walk in either direction, retrace their steps and stay up to two nights in a particular hut. Numbers are limited, so you'll need to book as far ahead as possible – three weeks if you can be adaptable, three months if you need a specific departure date or are part of a large group. This does have the huge advantage of guaranteeing you a bed, so you don't have to get up at the crack of dawn and almost sprint to the next hut to be sure of a bunk. Huts are all equipped with flush toilets, running water (which must be treated, filtered or boiled), heaters and gas rings, but you'll need to carry your own pans and plates. The cost is $35 per person per night; everyone gets a twenty percent discount during the first ten days of the season, and families get that same discount throughout the season. A limited number of simple **campsites** (with long-drop toilets and water; $12) exist close to the Routeburn Flats and Mackenzie Huts; campers are not allowed to use hut facilities.

Credit-card phone or mail **bookings** are taken from July 1 for the following season: contact the Great Walks Booking Desk in Te Anau or, from November, the DOC visitor centres in Glenorchy or Queenstown. Accommodation passes can be collected from Te Anau or Glenorchy the day before you start and up to 2pm on your day of departure: those without accommodation passes will be charged $50 a night. If the track is closed due to bad weather or track conditions, full refunds are given – but new bookings can only be made if there is space. Changes can be made to existing bookings ($5 per alteration) either before you start or with the wardens at each hut, but again only if there is space. **Outside the season** the Mackenzie and Howden huts revert to backcountry Category 3 status and, like the campsites, cost $5 a night. Routeburn Falls and Flats huts become Category 2 ($10) as they have heating. Bookings are not required and annual hut passes are valid.

The **Greenstone and Caples tracks** are far less popular, and bookings are not necessary at any time of year. Each trail has two Category 2 huts ($10), but none of them have gas rings. One warden patrols each valley and may be inclined to sell you hut tickets, although you should really buy them in advance unless you have an annual hut pass (see "Basics", p.52). Free camping is allowed in both valleys along the fringes of the bush (but not on the open flats), but you are encouraged to camp close to (but at least 50m away from) the huts and use their outside facilities – long-drop toilets and water – for which you'll pay half the hut fee.

The three **Rees–Dart** huts (all Category 2; $10) currently cannot be booked in advance. Trampers should carry an annual hut pass or two hut tickets per night.

Guided walks

Routeburn aspirants who aren't confident about their level of fitness or who prefer not to lug heavy backpacks should consider joining a **guided walk**. The pace is fairly leisurely and walkers have to carry only their personal effects (no food or camping equipment); daily hikes are still typically 5–6 hours, occasionally on rough terrain, so anyone unused to hill walking should still do a good deal of preparatory hiking.

Accommodation is in clean, plain huts which are by no means luxurious, but do have hot showers, duvets on the bunks, and you'll be served cooked breakfasts and three-course dinners with wine. All you have to do is walk – but there's a **price** to pay for all this pampering: the **Routeburn Guided Walk**, PO Box 568, Queenstown (✆03/442 8200, fax 442 6072, *nz.com/southis/routeburn, routeburn@xtra.co.nz;* Nov–April), including return transport from Queenstown and three days' walking with two nights' accommodation in huts costs $950; while the **Grand Traverse**, a five-day, six-night walk combining the Routeburn and Greenstone tracks, will set you back $1250.

> Note that all **times** and **distances** given in the following accounts are **one way**, unless otherwise stated.

The Routeburn Track

Most people walk the **Routeburn Track** (33km; 2–3 days) westwards from Glenorchy towards The Divide; it can also be combined with the Greenstone and Caples tracks to make three- to five-day loops. The Routeburn isn't for everyone, though. The terrain is sometimes rough and the paths steep, but anyone of moderate fitness who can carry a backpack for five or six hours a day should have little trouble. That said, the track passes through sub-alpine country and snowfall and flooding can sometimes close it, even in summer.

The first day on the Routeburn is an easy one. Trailhead buses offer mid-morning and mid-afternoon start times, both leaving enough time to reach either Routeburn Flats or Routeburn Falls huts, and the earlier one giving ample opportunity to explore the North Branch of Route Burn. From **Routeburn Shelter to Routeburn Flats Hut** (7km; 2–3hr; 250m ascent) the route follows Route Burn steadily uphill on a metre-wide track, though it's never strenuous and has an even shingle surface. Because Route Burn is a tributary of the Dart River, you are following a side valley and will have experienced a wide variety of scenery – river flats, waterfalls and open beech forest – by the time you reach the Routeburn Flats Hut. The nearby Routeburn Flats campsite is superbly sited on the edge of wide alluvial flats at the end of a short path a couple of hundred metres beyond the hut. Only a few tents are permitted so there is plenty of space to spread out, and campers can make use of an open fireplace and a small shelter, the run-off from which provides water for cooking. Hut users are better off making the first day a little longer and tackling the next leg, **Routeburn Flats Hut to Routeburn Falls Hut** (2km; 1hr–1hr 30min; 300m ascent), which is considerably steeper and rougher, but the extra exertion is rewarded by a stay at the well-sited Routeburn Falls Hut, perched on the bushline above a precipice with eastward views looking back to Routeburn Flats and Sugar Loaf (1320m).

The second day is the longest, continuing from **Routeburn Falls Hut to McKenzie Hut** (11km; 4–7hr; 300m ascent, 250m descent) on the most exposed section of the track. Most of the day is spent above the bushline among the sub-alpine snow tussock of the Harris Saddle (1277m) and passing through bog country, where sundews, bladderworts and orchids thrive. You might even catch sight of chamois clambering on the rocks to either side of the saddle. The track climbs gradually enough to the Harris Saddle Shelter (2–3hr), which offers respite from the wind and has toilets; on a clear day, drop your pack here and climb up to the summit of **Conical Hill** (1515m; 2km return; at least 1hr; 240m ascent) for superb views down into the Hollyford Valley and along it to Martin's Bay and the Tasman Sea. Continuing from the Harris Saddle Shelter you cross from the Mount Aspiring National Park into the Fiordland National Park and skirt high along the edge of the Hollyford Valley, before switchbacking down through silver beech, fuchsia and ribbonwood to Mackenzie Hut. The bush beside the hut hides a campsite, a cramped affair that comes as a big disappointment after the Routeburn Flats site.

From **Lake McKenzie Hut to Howden Hut** (8km; 3–4hr; 400m descent), the track continues along the mountainside through a grassy patch of ribbonwood known as The Orchard and past the cascading Earland Falls to the Howden Hut at the junction of three tracks. The Greenstone and Caples tracks (handy for turning the tramp into a five-day Glenorchy-based circuit) head south, while the Routeburn continues from **Howden Hut to The Divide** (2.5km; 1hr–1hr 30min; 50m net descent), initially climbing for fifteen minutes to a point where you can make a half-hour excursion to Key Summit for views of three major river systems, the Hollyford, the Eglinton and the Greenstone. From the **Key Summit** (919m) turn-off, the track descends through silver beech to the car park and shelter at The Divide.

The Greenstone Track

Trampers starting on the **Greenstone Track** (35km; 2–3 days) at The Divide first cover the short section to Howden Hut (described in reverse, above), then walk south from **Howden Hut to McKellar Hut** (6km; 2hr–2hr 30min; 50m descent), passing (after 20min) a free primitive **campsite** where fires can be lit. The Greenstone continues beside Lake McKellar to McKellar Hut (Cat 3; $10; 20 bunks), just outside the Fiordland National Park.

The easy track from **McKellar Hut to Mid-Greenstone Hut** (12km; 4–6hr; 100m descent) starts by crossing the Greenstone River and follows the left bank down a broad, grazed valley mostly along river flats and through the lower slopes of the beech forests. A swingbridge then crosses Steele Creek, and the track continues for another half-hour to the Mid-Greenstone Hut (Cat 2; $10; 12 bunks), located on the edge of a grassy expanse.

It is eminently possible to finish the Greenstone in a day from here, though you might want to walk from **Mid-Greenstone Hut to Sly Burn Hut** (5km; 1hr–1hr 30min; 30m descent) and use the hut (Cat 3; $5; 8 bunks) as a base for exploring the gentle **Mavora Walkway** to the south, taking two to three days through open tussock country and beech forest to Mavora Lakes (see p.780); a couple of Category 3 huts provide accommodation en route.

From **Sly Burn Hut to Greenstone car park** (10km; 3–5hr; 100m descent), the track follows the left bank as the valley narrows and the river heads into a long gorge. The river soon meets the Caples River, an enticing series of deep pools that make great swimming holes. A swingbridge gives access to the left bank of the Caples River and the Caples Track; turn right to Greenstone Wharf (20–30min), or left to Mid Caples Hut (see overleaf).

778/QUEENSTOWN, WANAKA AND THE GOLD COUNTRY

The Caples Track

The **Caples Track** (27km; 2 days) follows the Greenstone Track from **The Divide to Howden Hut** and then the first half of the section from Howden Hut to McKellar Hut, turning off an hour south of Howden Hut and beginning the very steep bush-clad zig-zag up the **McKellar Saddle** (1005m). Try to asses your capabilities beforehand as many find the walk from The Divide to Upper Caples Hut (11km; 5–7hr; 550m ascent, 600m descent) too much for one day, but are obliged to push on, as camping is neither pleasant on the saddle's bogland nor permitted on what is very fragile open tussock. The descent mostly follows snow poles, crossing and recrossing the infant Caples River before regaining beech forest and the **Upper Caples Hut** (Cat 2; $10; 20 bunks).

Greenstone Wharf is within a day's walk of here, though you can break it up into two sections: from **Upper Caples Hut to Mid Caples Hut** (7km; 2hr–2hr 30min; 50m descent) you cross easy grassland, finishing up by a short but dramatic gorge right outside the Mid Caples Hut (Cat 2; $10; 12 bunks); then from **Mid Caples Hut to Greenstone Wharf** car park (9km; 2–3hr; 150m descent) the path crosses the gorge and follows the left bank, continuing alongside the bush edge and crossing grassy clearings before arriving at the junction with the Greenstone Track, from where it is only twenty minutes to Greenstone Wharf.

The Rees–Dart Track

The standard approach to the Rees–Dart Track is to walk up the Rees and down the Dart, an anticlockwise circuit which leaves open the option of finishing off with either a Fun Yak or a jetboat ride (see p.771). The track from **Muddy Creek car park to Shelter Rock Hut** (16km; 6–8hr; 450m ascent) follows a 4WD track across grass and gravel flats on the left bank of the braided lower Rees and requires a couple of foot-soaking stream crossings. You can save yourself the trouble (and a couple of hours hiking) by getting Backpacker Express (see p.774) to drop at the end of the 4WD track, 6km beyond the Muddy Creek car park, and close to the simple Twenty-five Mile Hut, which is owned by Otago Tramping Club but can be used (pay $3 to the DOC in Glenorchy). Press on across Twenty-five Mile Creek and over more river flats for another hour or so, with Hunter Creek and the peaks of the Forbes Mountains straight ahead. Just past the confluence of Hunter Creek, the Rees valley steepens appreciably and becomes cloaked in beech forests. Soon after, the track crosses a swingbridge to the right bank and climbs above river level, eventually coming out on the grassy flats of Clarke Slip. The track is bush-bound again up to just below the tree line, where it passes the site of the old Shelter Rock Hut then continues for a kilometre until you hit tussock country. One final crossing of the Rees River, now a large stream, takes you back to the left bank and the new Shelter Rock Hut (Cat 2; $10; 20 bunks).

The second day, from **Shelter Rock Hut to Dart Hut** (7km; 4–6hr; 500m ascent, 500m descent) is the shortest but one of the toughest, scaling the 1447m Rees Saddle. Stick to the left bank of the Rees over sub-alpine scrub and gravel banks for a couple of kilometres before crossing the river and gradually climbing up to a tussock basin and the saddle. Descend rapidly and then more steadily across snow grass following the left bank of Snowy Creek, which churns down a narrow gorge to your right. A kilometre or so later the track crosses a swingbridge to the right bank, commencing a loose and rocky descent past a long series of cascades to another crossing of Snowy Creek, just above its confluence with the Dart River. Grassy areas on the right bank provide camping spots and the Dart Hut (Cat 2; $10; 20 bunks) sits on the left bank;

this is the pinch point for Rees–Dart accommodation, with tramper numbers swelled by those staying two nights to explore the Cascade Saddle route (see "Walks in the Matukituki Valley" box on pp.792–3).

The track from **Dart Hut to Daleys Flat Hut** (16km; 6–8hr; 430m descent) initially climbs high above the river and stays there for 3km, passing through beech forest before dropping to Cattle Flat, 5km of grassed alluvial ridges traced by a winding and energy-sapping but easy-to-follow route. At the end of Cattle Flat the track returns to the bush and runs roughly parallel to the river until it reaches the beautiful grassy expanse of Quinns Flat (perfect in the late afternoon light), where the track turns inland. Within half an hour you reach the sandfly-ridden **Daleys Flat Hut** (Cat 2; $10; 20 bunks), redeemed by its pleasant location on the edge of a clearing.

Trampers planning to pick up a jetboat or Fun Yak to Glenorchy at 10.30am will need to leave around 8am for the **Daleys Flat Hut to Sandy Bluff** section (7km; 2hr–2hr 30min; 100m ascent, 110m descent). The walk skips through the bush for around 4km until Dredge Flat, where you make your own track, looking for markers on the left that indicate where you re-enter the bush. The track then climbs steeply up Sandy Bluff to reach a belvedere high above the river before dropping down to river level and the jetboat pick-up point.

If you are determined to walk all the way, you'll find the section from **Sandy Bluff to Chinaman's Bluff** (12km; 3hr; negligible descent) fairly easy, crossing the flats south of Sandy Bluff and following the river to Chinaman's Bluff. Pick-ups from here can be arranged, though you can continue on foot from **Chinaman's Bluff to Paradise car park** (6km; 2hr; negligible descent) through Dan's Paddock and along either the 4WD track or a more direct walking track.

Kingston and the road to Fiordland

Most people travel from Queenstown to Fiordland by road, making the 170km journey to Te Anau in under three hours. It is an attractive if unspectacular route that follows the lakeshore road, hugging the foot of the Remarkables then striking out across open Otago and Southland farming country.

As the Dart glacier retreated at the end of the last ice age, Lake Wakatipu formed behind the terminal moraine at what is now **KINGSTON**, a scattered community 46km south of Queenstown on SH6. The lake's waters formed the Mataura Valley to the south, but successive terminal moraines raised the lake level to the point at which it was able to carve out a new passage down the bed of the Kawarau, out of the Frankton Arm. In the 1860s the Mataura Valley provided a perfect route from the populated coast to new gold fields on the Shotover and Arrow rivers. Kingston became a major transit centre, accommodating up to five thousand people while they waited for boats across the lake or bullock carts to transport their spoils to Dunedin or Invercargill. By 1878, the railroad had reached Kingston, and the pre-fabricated parts for ever-larger steamers could be brought in and assembled on the lakeshore. The 1936 completion of the lakeside road to Queenstown drove the last nail into the coffin of the steamer freight trade, and goods trains went the same way, but the line has managed to struggle on thanks to the **Kingston Flyer** tourist train, Kent Street (☎03/248 8848, fax 248 8881, *dgarnett@tranzrail.co.nz*; daily Oct–April 10.15am & 3.45pm; $15 one way, $20 return). Initially it plied the 60km to Lumsden and was much eulogized in those halcyon days before Kiwi tourism went ballistic, but since 1982 the cut-down forty-minutes-each-way service only runs 15km to the nowhere town of Fairlight. Gleaming black steam engines haul creaky but sumptuous turn-of-the-century first-class carriages with embossed steel ceilings and brass gas lamps: arrive early to avoid being shunted down to the less exalted second-class seats, which are charged at the same rate.

The only **accommodation** in Kingston, and for some distance either side, is at the roadside *Kingston Stream Holiday Camp*, 10 Kent St (☎ & fax 03/248 8501; tent & powered sites $9, dorms ①, cabins & motel units ②–③).

Beyond Kingston there's little to delay your progress to Te Anau. Just short of the dull Southland farming town of **Lumsden**, a signposted short-cut diverts you to **Mossburn** and SH94. Some 14km west of Mossburn a narrow road cuts north towards **Mavora Lakes**, a very popular summertime retreat; the southern lake is reserved for quiet pursuits like fishing and canoeing while the larger North Mavora Lake hosts rowdy boats. Trails through the surrounding beech forests make great mountain-biking territory, and trampers can head north along the Mavora Walkway (see p.777) and link up with the Greenstone Track (see p.777).

Back on SH94 you soon enter the Red Tussock Conservation Area, named for a type of grass essential to the livelihood of the takahe (see Contexts, p.868), and before long you'll find yourself in Te Anau, perched on the brink of Fiordland (see p.811).

Wanaka

WANAKA, only 55 air kilometres northeast of Queenstown but an hour and a half by the main road, languishes in the shadow of its brasher southern sibling, though it offers a similar combination of beautiful surroundings and robust adventure activities. Situated at the point where the hummocky, poplar-studded hills of Central Otago rub up against the dramatic peaks of the Mount Aspiring National Park, it commands a wonderful spot on the shores of the willow-girt Lake Wanaka, with the jagged summits of the Southern Alps as often as not mirrored in its waters.

Founded in the 1860s as a service centre for the local run-holders and itinerant gold miners, the town didn't really take off until the prosperous middle years of the twentieth century, when camping and caravanning Kiwis discovered its warm, dry summer climate and easy-going pace. Today it is gradually picking up speed, but Wanaka remains a small and eminently manageable place, with the tenor of a village and an overwhelming feeling of light and spaciousness. It continues to promote itself as an adventure destination in its own right, and it's an excellent place in which to relax for a couple of days and eat well in some fine cafés and restaurants.

A half day spent exploring Wanaka's intriguing **maze** and absorbing **museums** will leave plenty of time to go kayaking, jetboating, rock climbing, horse riding or, best of all, canyoning. Wanaka is also the perfect base from which to explore the surrounding region, notably the Mount Aspiring National Park and the Cardrona Valley. During the winter months, Wanaka's relative calm is shattered by the arrival of **skiers and snowboarders** eager to explore the downhill ski fields of Treble Cone and Cardrona, and the Nordic terrain at Waiorau.

Arrival, information and transport

Daily direct **buses** from Christchurch, Dunedin, Queenstown and Franz Josef all arrive centrally: InterCity stop outside The Paper Place, 84 Ardmore St (☎03/443 7885), while Catch-a-Bus, Atomic and Southern Link Shuttles pull up in front of Wanaka Travel & Booking Agency, 99 Ardmore St (☎03/443 7414, fax 443 9434). You'll usually have to book in advance through these agencies or direct with the company, particularly for the Catch-a-Bus, Atomic and Southern Link services, which will generally drop off and pick up at your hotel if they're not too busy. Wanaka Connexions (☎0800/879 926) run a

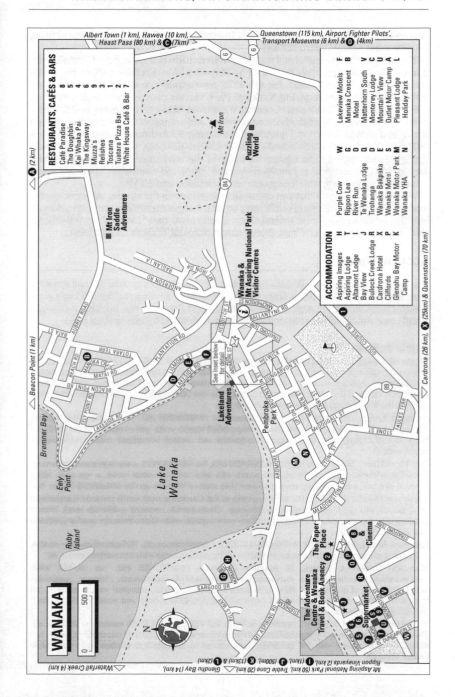

WANAKA

0 ————— 500 m

Lake Wanaka

Ruby Island

Eely Point

Bremner Bay

⟶ Beacon Point (1 km)

⟶ Waterfall Creek (4 km)

⟶ Mt Aspiring National Park (50 km), Treble Cone (20 km), Glendhu Bay (14 km), Rippon Vineyards (2 km), ⟶ (1km), ⟶ (500m), ⟶ (13km) & ⟶ (2km)

⟵ Albert Town (1 km), Hawea (10 km), Haast Pass (80 km) & ⟶ (7km) ⟶

⟶ ⟶ (2 km)

⟶ Queenstown (115 km), Airport, Fighter Pilots', Transport Museums (6 km) & ⟶ (4km)

⟶ Cardrona (26 km), ⟶ (25km) & Queenstown (70 km)

Mt Iron

Puzzling World

Mt Iron Saddle Adventures

Wanaka & Mt Aspiring National Park Visitor Centres

Lakeland Adventures

RESTAURANTS, CAFÉS & BARS

Café Paradise	8
The Doughbin	5
Kai Whaka Pai	4
The Kingsway	6
Muzza's	9
Relishes	3
Toscana	1
Tuatara Pizza Bar	2
White House Café & Bar	7

ACCOMMODATION

Aspiring Images	H	Purple Cow	W
Aspiring Lodge	T	Rippon Lea	G
Altamont Lodge	I	River Run	O
Bay View	J	Te Wanaka Lodge	D
Bullock Creek Lodge	R	Tirohanga	E
Cardrona Hotel	X	Wanaka Bakpaka	X
Cliffords	P	Wanaka Motel	S
Glenohu Bay Motor Camp		Wanaka Motor Park	M
	K	Wanaka YHA	N
Lakeview Motels	F		
Manuka Crescent Motel	B		
Matterhorn South	V		
Monterey Lodge	C		
Mountain View	U		
Outlet Motor Camp	A		
Pleasant Lodge			
Holiday Park	L		

The Adventure Centre & Wanaka Travel & Book Agency

The Paper Place

& Cinema

Supermarket

door-to-door service between Wanaka and Queenstown ($25 one way, $45 return) using the direct but windy Cardrona Road

The best source of general and tramping **information** is the combined **Wanaka visitor centre** (Nov–April daily 8am–4.45pm; May–Oct Mon–Fri 8am–4.45pm, Sat & Sun variable hours; ☎03/443 1233, fax 443 9238, *www.wanaka.co.nz*, *wpa@wanaka.co.nz*) and the DOC's **Mount Aspiring National Park visitor centre** (same hours; ☎03/443 7660, fax 443 8776), 500m east of central Wanaka on SH84 at the corner of Ballantyne Road. They'll give impartial advice on activities and transport in the region – though you're just as well served at The Adventure Centre, 99 Ardmore St (☎03/443 8174 & 0800/684 468, fax 443 8589; Nov–April daily 8.30am–6.30pm), which acts as the booking agent and central radio contact for many of the adventure travel companies both here and in Queenstown, and books flights to Milford and elsewhere. There are several **banks** around town, with foreign-exchange facilities and ATMs.

Wanaka is so compact that you can **walk** everywhere in the centre, and most accommodation is less than fifteen minutes' away on foot. Longer excursions are best made with **bicycles** or **cars** rented from several shops around town (see "Listings", pp.789–90); for short trips into the surroundings, there's always Wanaka Taxis (☎03/443 7999).

Accommodation

For such a diminutive town, Wanaka has a splendid range of accommodation, and **rates** are generally a fair bit lower than in Queenstown. You should have no problem finding a place to suit, except during the peak months of January and August, when **booking** is essential – and some establishments respond to the surge in demand by raising their rates.

Hotels and motels

Altamont Lodge, Mount Aspiring Rd, 2km west of Wanaka (☎ & fax 03/443 8864). The perfect ski lodge, with a pine-panelled alpine atmosphere, communal cooking and lounge areas, drying rooms, and ski-tuning facilities. Rooms are functional but attractive, with shared bathrooms and good rates for singles, reduced if you use your own bedding. The spa pool is open only during the winter season, but the tennis court is available year round. ④.

Aspiring Lodge, cnr Dungarvon St & Dunmore St (☎0800/269 367, fax 03/443 8914, *aspiring @voyager.co.nz*). Spacious and attractive wood-panelled studio units and executive suites, with full kitchens and drying room for ski gear. Continental and cooked breakfasts available. Studios ⑤, apartments ⑥.

Bay View Motel, Mount Aspiring Rd (☎0800/229 843, fax 03/443 9194, *www.bayviewwanaka.co.nz*, *bayviewmotel@xtra.co.nz*). Well-appointed motel with lake and mountain views, a spa pool, and a pleasant site well back from the road, just over 1km west of Wanaka up the Matukituki Valley. ⑤.

Cardrona Hotel, 26km along the sealed section of the Cardrona road south towards Queenstown (☎ & fax 03/443 8153, *info@cardrona-hotel.co.nz*). Characterful, restored gold-rush hotel. Decent bathless doubles are in a new extension and are very popular with skiers from the nearby Cardrona and Waiorau slopes. ④.

Lakeview Motel, 68 Lismore St (☎ & fax 03/443 7029, *bassgc@xtra.co.nz*). Well-placed en-suite studios, and slightly pricier but better-value larger units – all high above town with tremendous views. ④.

Manuka Crescent Motel, 51 Manuka Crescent (☎0800/626 852, fax 03/443 9066, *www.manukacrescentmotel.co.nz*, *manuka-crescent-motel-wanaka@xtra.co.nz*). Pleasant, good-value motel with a mix of modern and older units and a small pool. Twenty minutes' walk from town, but there's a courtesy minibus and guests can rent bicycles ($20 a day) and scooters ($35 a day). Breakfasts available. ④.

Matterhorn South Lodge, 56 Brownston St (☎03/443 1119, fax 443 8379, *matterhorn@xtra.co.nz*). This upmarket section adjoining the hostel of the same name (see opposite) has modern, nicely furnished en-suite rooms with TV and fridge, and access to an excellent kitchen and comfortable lounge area. ③.

Wanaka Motel, 73 Helwick St (☎ & fax 03/443 7545). Spacious two-bedroom units with huge lounges, a full-size kitchen and all mod cons. ⑤.

B&Bs and homestays

Aspiring Images, 26 Norman St (☎03/443 8358, fax 443 8327, *www.nzhomestay.co.nz/russell.html, grussell@xtra.co.nz*). Comfortable suburban homestay, with nice rooms, each with a terrace. Dinner by arrangement ($25). ⑤.

Monterey Lodge, Camphill Rd, Hawea Flat, 10km northeast of Wanaka (☎ & fax 03/443 1983, *nz.com/travel/monterey, john.bill@xtra.co.nz*). Comfortable modern house set on a hill in the middle of fifty hectares of open grassland with expansive views and not a house in sight. Paths to the river, a few farm animals and a pool inset with river boulders make it a great place for relaxing, and kids are welcome. There's even a child-minding service. The three en-suite rooms are spacious and evening meals are offered. ⑦.

Rippon Lea, 15 Norman Terrace (☎03/443 9333 & 0800/169 674, fax 443 9343, *williman @voyager.co.nz*). Longstanding and welcoming homestay comprising a two-bedroom apartment which is ideal for families. A generous continental breakfast is served, and they'll pick you up from central Wanaka, 2km away. ⑤.

River run, Halliday Rd, 7km east of Wanaka (☎03/443 9049, fax 443 8454, *riverrun@xtra.co.nz, nz.com/travel/riverrun*). Stylish lodge gloriously sited on ancient river flats with trails leading down to the Clutha River. The house, thoughtfully designed by the owners, contains five individually designed and beautifully appointed en-suite rooms as well as sunny verandas and a communal dining area where most guests stay for three-course meals of the highest quality ($75). Rates include breakfast and pre-dinner drinks, and the cheaper rooms only just nudge into this top price bracket. ⑨.

Te Wanaka Lodge, 23 Brownston St (☎0800/926 252, fax 443 9246, *www.tewanaka.co.nz, tewanakalodge@xtra.co.nz*). One of the finer B&B inns in central Wanaka, with twelve luxurious and quiet en-suite rooms, communal TV, and a cedar hot tub during winter. The sumptuous buffet breakfast is a mellow affair centred on a huge dining table, and there are also self-catering facilities. ⑥–⑦.

Tirohanga, 102 Lismore St (☎03/443 8302, fax 443 8702). Friendly homestay with stupendous views across the lake to Mount Roy. Sleep in either the modest twin room or the self-contained unit and eat a light breakfast with the family. Evening meals available. ⑤.

Hostels

Bullock Creek Lodge, 46 Brownston St (☎ & fax 443 1265, *bullockcreeklodge@clear.net.nz*). Former motel that's been turned into a first-rate hostel with en-suite and TV-equipped rooms pressed into service as four-shares, twins and doubles. There's a comfortable and spacious cooking and lounge area with a deck that catches the afternoon sun, and also a fully self-contained apartment. Beds ①, rooms ③, apartment ⑥.

Cliffords, 21 Brownston St (☎ & fax 3/443 6560, *peterwilliamson@bigfoot.com*). The place to go if you are looking for the cheapest beds in town. Fairly functional backpacker beds in single or double rooms with sheets provided, a communal lounge, kitchen and bathroom. Located at the back of a large town hotel of the same name. Dorms ①, rooms ②.

Matterhorn South (see opposite). Small but appealing hostel right in the centre of town with en-suite four-shares, cheaper 5- and 7-bed dorms, plus doubles, and a log fire surrounded by scatter cushions. Dorms ①, rooms ②.

Mountainview Backpackers, 71 Brownston St (☎ & fax 03/443 9010). New, small and fairly cosy hostel with cheery dorms and doubles that come with a free continental breakfast with home-made bread. There's also tent sites, free storage, barbecue and free use of basic bikes. Tents $9.50, dorms ①, rooms ②.

Purple Cow, 94 Brownston St (☎0800/772 277, *stay@purplecow.co.nz*). Large and spacious hostel in a former hotel with maximum 6-bed dorms, many in separate former motel rooms with their own lounge, bathroom and TV; and plenty of doubles (some with en suites). Sit and gaze at the fabulous lake view through the big picture windows or play pool and table tennis in the large lounge. Bike rental ($15 a day), frequent bargain barbecues in the evening and Internet access. Dorms ①, rooms ③.

Wanaka Bakpaka, 117 Lakeside Rd (☎03/443 7837, *wanakabakpaka@xtra.co.nz*). Low-key hostel five minutes' walk from town and with great lake and mountain views, a peaceful atmosphere, summer barbecues and rental of canoes ($24 a day), sea kayaks ($18 a day) and bikes ($20 a day). Cabins & dorms ③, rooms ②.

YHA, 181 Upton St (☎ & fax 03/443 7405, *yhawnka@yha.org.nz*). Decent all-day hostel ten minutes' walk from the centre with small dorms, cheap bike rental ($20 per day), and a good garden in which you can camp ($10). Dorms ①, rooms ②.

Campsites and motorparks

Albert Town Recreation Reserve, 6km northeast of Wanaka on SH6. Open, informal camping area with water and toilets on the banks of the swift-flowing Clutha River. $4.

Glendhu Bay Motor Camp, Mount Aspiring Rd, 15km west of Wanaka (☎03/443 7243, fax 443 7284, *glendhucamp@xtra.co.nz*). Popular lakeshore family campsite with fabulous views across to Mount Aspiring, boat-launching facilities, canoe and bike rental. Tents $7.50, powered sites $8.50, bunks ①, cabins ②.

Outlet Motor Camp, Lake Outlet Rd, 6km from Wanaka (☎03/442 7478, fax 443 7471). Beautifully sited campground at the point where Lake Wanaka becomes the Clutha River and in a great position for strolls along the lake or river frontage. Tent and powered sites $9, on-site vans ②.

Pleasant Lodge Holiday Park, 217 Mount Aspiring Rd, 3km west of Wanaka (☎ & fax 03/443 7360, *www.nzsouth.co.nz/pleasantlodge, plelow@xtra.co.nz*). Sprawling, family-oriented site with tent sites ($8.50), a range of cabins and heaps of amenities, including mountain-bike rental. Cabins ②, tourist apartments ③, motel units ④.

Wanaka Motor Park, 212 Brownston St (☎ & fax 03/443 7883). The most convenient of the campsites, ten minutes' walk from central Wanaka, with $10 tent sites and all the usual facilities including rooms in a new lodge which has bathrooms and kitchen under the same roof. Lodge and cabins ②–③, tourist flats ③.

The Town, its maze and museums

The solid lump of Mount Iron rises immediately east of town, pointing the way to **Stuart Landsborough's Puzzling World**, almost 2km away on SH84 (daily 8.30am–5.30pm; $7). Star attraction is "The Great Maze", a complex wooden structure comprising 1500m of dead-end passageways packed into a dense labyrinth, with overhead bridges linking the four sections. Should you choose to accept it, your mission is to reach all four corner towers, either in any order (30min–1hr) or in a specific sequence (at least 1hr), then to find your way out again; if it all goes horribly wrong, you can cheat by using escape doors. Put aside a couple of hours to appreciate this prototype for the Eighties maze-building boom that swept New Zealand and Japan – where Stuart Landsborough briefly enjoyed a fanatical following. The ticket price includes entry to the "Hologram Hall", full of the usual numbing circus of 3-D images, and the "Tilted House", which revels in tricks of perspective produced by the floor being fifteen degrees off the horizontal. Zip through these to get to the "Hall of Following Faces", a large octagonal room with seven of the sides made up by arrays of moulded images of famous people – Churchill, Einstein, Van Gogh, Lincoln, etc. As you walk around the faces appear to watch your every move in true Mona Lisa fashion. Leave half an hour aside for the café, where you can play with the puzzles scattered over the tables.

Wanaka's airport, 7km east of Puzzling World on SH6, is the base for a number of aerial activities (see "Activities", p.786) and the **New Zealand Fighter Pilots Museum** (daily: Christmas–Jan 9am–6pm; rest of year 9am–4pm; $7), which honours Kiwi pilots and ground crew who fought in the two world wars. This homage to the New Zealand contingent contains hagiographic profiles of the men and blow-by-blow descriptions of the major battles and campaigns, all accompanied by rousing war anthems. Star exhibits, all airworthy, are New Zealand's oldest Tiger Moth, Spitfire, a P-51D Mustang

WALKS AROUND WANAKA

Visitors shy of the beard-and-Gore-Tex walks in the Mount Aspiring National Park to the west might reap greater rewards from these more modest expeditions. No special gear is required, just robust shoes, wet-weather gear and sun protection.

MOUNT IRON

The most accessible of Wanaka's hilltop walks is up the 527m **Mount Iron** (2km; 1–2hr; 240m ascent), a glacially sculpted outcrop, its western and northern slopes ground smooth by the glacier that scoured its southern face. The path through farmland and the bird-filled kanuka woodland of the Mount Iron Scenic Reserve starts 1.5km east of Wanaka on SH84, climbing the steep southern face to the summit. Here you can enjoy magnificent panoramic views of Wanaka and the nearby lakes, before following the path down the east face of Mount Iron towards the entrance to Puzzling World (see oppoite).

MOUNT ROY

Mount Roy Walking Track (16km; 4–6hr; 1100m ascent) is a much more ambitious prospect, winding up to the 1581m summit of Roy's Peak for wonderful views over Lake Wanaka and surrounding glaciers and mountains. The path starts 7km west of Wanaka on the Mount Aspiring Road, but is closed during the lambing season (Oct to mid-Nov).

DIAMOND LAKE WALKING TRACK

The long vistas from Mount Iron and Mount Roy are only really challenged by those on the **Diamond Lake Walking Track** (7km; 2hr 30min), a community project which requests a $2 donation. From the car park 18km west of Wanaka on the Mount Aspiring Road there are a couple of short variations – but to get the views, you'll need to tackle the 775m summit of Rocky Hill.

BEACON POINT–CLUTHA OUTLET CIRCUIT

This is a long but undemanding riverbank and lakeside walk which starts from Wanaka and follows the shore to **Eely Point** (15min), a sheltered bay popular for boating and picnics. Beyond Eely Point is Bremner Bay and the continuation of the waterfront path to **Beacon Point** (a further 30min). Either return the same way or continue along Beacon Point Road to the Outlet Motor Camp and pick up the **Outlet Track**, which runs 4km to Alison Avenue, then down to SH6 not far from the Albert Town bridge. By following SH6 this can be turned into a loop back to Wanaka (16km in all), passing Puzzling World (see opposite) and the base of Mount Iron (see above). The map in the DOC's *Wanaka Walks and Trails* leaflet ($1) makes the route a little clearer.

WATERFALL CREEK TO DAMPER BAY

The westbound equivalent of the Beacon Point–Clutha Outlet Circuit leaves Roy's Bay along the **Waterfall Creek and Damper Bay Track** (5km one way; 1hr; negligible ascent), heading through Wanaka Station Park and past Rippon Vineyard to Waterfall Creek (35min). It continues along lakeside terraces to a high point on the Wanaka side of Damper Bay.

and several rare Soviet Polikarpovs – an equivalent of the Spitfire first used in the Spanish Civil War. Younger visitors may prefer the half-dozen linked PCs allowing you to engage in interactive combat. If any of this strikes a chord, then you might want to time your visit to coincide with the biennial, three-day **"Warbirds over Wanaka"** air show (☎03/356 0279 & 0800/496 920, fax 356 0298, *wow@skyshow.co.nz*). At Easter each even-numbered year up to 70,000 people descend to watch all manner of airborne craft – but predominantly small and vintage planes – take to the air; details and tickets ($15–25 per day; $55 for 3 days) are available from the Wanaka visitor centre.

A similar theme is explored in the adjacent **Wanaka Toy and Transport Museum** (daily: Nov–April 8.30am–6pm; May–Oct 9am–5pm; $5), an engaging hoard of cars, trucks and bikes preserved by Wanaka's dry climate. There should be something here to titillate anyone with even a passing interest in motor vehicles. Some machines are just well-kept examples of stuff still puttering around New Zealand roads, but there's also exotica such as a Centurian tank, a ten-seater Lockhead Lodestar used by the US Army in the 1950s, Velocette and BSA bikes, and the Solar Kiwi Racer, an aluminium and glass-fibre bullet-shaped car powered by solar panels on its roof. Many of the main exhibits are replicated along the walls with all manner of other toys. If some of your party are extra interested, others can pass the time in the adjacent **Wanaka Beerworks** (daily 9.30am–6pm; *wanaka.beerworks@xtra.co.nz*), an award-winning microbrewery where you can sample (free) products currently only sold through bars and restaurants in the immediate area.

The perfect antidote to the museums lies across the road at **Have A Shot** (daily 9am–6pm), where you can, well, have a shot with a golf club on the driving range ($5 for 40 balls), a gun at either the claybird range ($25 for 20 rounds) or the .22 smallbore range ($10 for 30 rounds), or a bow at the archery range ($10 for 20min). Groups of more active combatants can join battle with with spongy tennis balls in the battlefield ($5 for 20min).

Alternatively you might prefer the small but perfectly formed Rippon Vineyards, 3km west of Wanaka on the Mount Aspiring Road (Dec–April daily 11am–5pm). The dry, stony and sun-soaked slopes running down to Lake Wanaka were planted in 1974 and produced their first vintage in 1989. Five of their wines can be tasted for $3 – the typically excellent Pinot Noir and the Sauvignon Blanc come particularly recommended – while a bottle of the good stuff will set you back $20–35. The best approach to the vineyard from Wanaka is on foot, along the lakefront Waterfall Creek Walking Track (see box on p.785), though it is easy to go too far: turn up into the vines just before a brown cottage. In February 2002 (and hopefully subsequent even years), the one-day Rippon open-air music festival (*www.rippon.co.nz*; tickets around $50) takes place in the grounds.

Activities

Wanaka's relatively low profile and the absence of the hard sell and conveyor-belt style that characterizes some of Queenstown's slicker operations add up to a more relaxed approach – and frequently better value for money. Many, but not all, activities can be booked through The Adventure Centre, 99 Ardmore Street (☎03/443 8174 & 0800/684 468, fax 443 8589; Nov–April daily 8.30am–6.30pm), which acts as their booking agent and pick-up point.

On land

If abseiling down thirty-metre waterfalls and sliding down eighty-degree polished rock chutes into deep green pools appeals, then **canyoning** should fit the bill. You don't need any special experience, just a sense of adventure and water confidence – once you start into the canyon, there is only one way out. Deep Canyon (book through The Adventure Centre or on ☎03/443 8174; mid-Nov to April or May, *deepcanyon@xtra.co.nz*) take up to five canyoners with each guide, who secures all abseils with safety ropes and provides enough warm, protective clothing to ease the sense of vulnerability. First-timers usually tackle **Emerald Creek** ($165 for a full day), a narrow fissure where fern-draped verdure envelops you, in complete contrast to the parched landscape of the surrounding Matukituki valley. Half-time tea and biscuits are served on a huge slab wedged high above a cascade, and the day is rounded off with a fine picnic and strong camp-brewed coffee. Other canyons in the vicinity are roped into service for second trips including the 400m-high **Twin Falls**; prices depend on numbers and guide:client ratio.

Wanaka's dry, sunny climate is ideal for **rock climbing**. Tuition and guiding are offered by Wanaka Rock Climbing (contact The Adventure Centre), who run full-day top-roping, seconding and abseiling courses for two to four people ($130 each), inclusive of all transport and equipment. For the more experienced they offer one-on-one guided climbing ($195 a day); or you can get out onto the Matukituki valley schist and gneiss unsupervised with a copy of *Wanaka Rock* ($14, available from Good Sports – see p.790). On a wet day visit Wanaka Gym, 155 Tenby St, which houses a fairly basic bouldering wall; call ☎03/443 9418 for opening hours.

If the idea of performing gymnastics on roadside crags tends to pale beside the prospect of getting up into the ice and snow of the Southern Alps, then you can always try one of the expensive but professional all-inclusive **mountaineering** packages offered by Mount Aspiring Guides (☎03/443 9422, *aspguide@xtra.co.nz*). Their Summit Week ($2000 per person) sees two of you and one guide exploring the upper reaches of the Southern Alps (often around Fox glacier where ice climbing skills are honed) and bagging a number of peaks. Specific ascents include Mount Cook (Oct to mid-Jan; $2500), Mount Tasman (Oct–May; $2500), and Mount Aspiring (Oct–May) which has a four-day helicopter access option or a six-day walk in variation (both $1860). All these require a high degree of fitness and some mountain experience. Private mountain guiding will set you back around $225 per person per day, plus the cost of equipment rental, hut fees, transport and food.

Wanaka abounds with shops renting out all-terrain bikes, but for a day's guided **mountain biking**, join Alpine Biking (The Adventure Centre or ☎03/443 8943) who specialize in **heli-biking**, whisking you up to Treble Cone (Nov–April; 3–5hr; $185) or Mount Alpha (all year; 3–5hr; $165) for up to 1600 vertical metres of downhill track. They also run a 4WD-supported biking day-trip (Nov–May; 6hr; $100); and you can head to Cardrona ski field where, during January, they fire up a chairlift and turn some of the trails into a bike park (lifts $12 half day; bike rental $35).

Saddles of a different cut are employed by Mount Iron Saddle Adventures (☎03/443 7777), which runs **horse-riding** treks (2hr; $45) over farmland and through kanuka forest on the easy northern slopes of Mount Iron from their stables on Anderson Road, five minutes' drive northeast of Wanaka. More experienced riders can undertake a ride across open country ($50). A wider range of rides are offered by Backcountry Saddle Expeditions (☎03/443 8151; 2hr–2 days; $45–130) from their stables 25km south of Wanaka in the Cardrona Valley; they'll pick you up from Wanaka if you book in advance.

To explore some of the less accessible parts of Wanaka and its environs, try the **4WD tours** organized by Edgewater Adventures, 59a Brownston St (☎ & fax 03/443 8422, *ewa@clear.net.nz*; 2hr 30min; $85); or the **quad-bike tours** with Criffel Peak Safaris (☎03/443 1711, fax 443 1705, *criffelpeak.safaris@xtra.co.nz*) which start with a three-hour meander around a high-country deer farm ($85), and range up to a tour of nineteenth-century gold diggings (4hr 30min; $130). Budding photographers may fancy personalized **photographic tours** run by Aspiring Images (☎03/443 8358, *grussell@xtra.co.nz*; $70 per half day, maximum 4 people), who tour the prime viewpoints and provide professional cameras.

In the air

Magnificent scenery, clear skies and competitive prices make Wanaka an excellent place to get airborne. Bi-Plane Adventures (☎03/443 1000) will pick up in town and run you out to Wanaka airport for any of a number of one-pilot-one-passenger **scenic and stunt flights**. Cheapest (both $170) are the twenty-minute joyride in the open-cockpit 1920s Tiger Moth bi-plane and fifteen minutes in a closed-cockpit Pitts Special, which is designed specifically for aerobatics. For adrenalin junkies with money to burn there's also the 1940s-designed Mustang, which combines aerobatic agility with neck-snapping acceleration (20min; $2000). A twenty-minute scenic flight can be combined with a thirty-second freefall on a **tandem skydive** with Tandem Skydive Wanaka, Wanaka Airport (☎03/443 7207 & 025/796 877; $225; $195 with backpacker discount).

A less fraught approach to viewing the tremendous scenery is to go **tandem paragliding** with a difference, a kind of scenic flight and paraglide all in one with Lucky Montana's Flying Circus (0800/247 287; $130). You and your tandem guide are attached water-skiing-style to the back of a boat as you take off from the town beach and gradually gain around 600m over 15 minutes as the boat recedes to a dot below. You then detach from the tow line and begin the normal tandem paraglide turns and wing-overs back to the beach. If you'd rather take the controls you can learn **paragliding** with Wanaka Paragliding (☎03/443 9193), who offer various learn-to-fly courses from a basic introduction (1–3 days; $168), to the full solo rating ($600 plus equipment rental).

Flights to Milford (for a description of Milford Sound, see p.820) from Wanaka tend to be a few dollars more expensive than those from Queenstown, but you're in the air longer and fly over a wider range of scenery including Mount Aspiring, the Olivine Ice Plateau and the inaccessible lakes of Alabaster, McKerrow and Tutoko. Most local accommodation receives daily bulletins on Milford weather and flight conditions. Both Aspiring Air (☎03/443 7943 & 0800/100 943) and Alpine Scenic Flights (☎03/443 8787 & 0800/435 444) do an extensive range of flights, the most popular being a combination flight and Milford Sound cruise (4hr; $270).

On the water

With a beautiful lake, a number of decent rivers and a friendly, low-key approach, there's plenty of opportunity for getting wet in style. Lakeland Adventures, Main Wharf (☎03/443 7495), lay on all manner of waterborne activities, the most leisurely being the hour-long **lake cruise** ($30) around Ruby Island, Glendhu Bay, Pigeon Island and the lake outlet, and half-day trips landing on Pigeon Island and making the short walk to Arethusa Pool, a lake within a lake ($50). For thrills and spills, try the fifty-minute **jet-boat rides** onto the upper reaches of the Clutha with Clutha River Jet, Main Wharf (same phone; $60). Just along the beach Sail, Kayak Lake Wanaka (☎03/443 9180) rent yachts, catamarans, **windsurfers** and **sea kayaks** by the day or hour.

From October to April, Alpine River Guides (☎03/443 9023, fax 443 9553, *www.alpinekayaks.co.nz, paddle@alpinekayaks.co.nz*) will take you on a number of different full-day **kayaking** trips on the Matukituki, Clutha or Hawea rivers (all Grade II; $100). Independent paddlers may also be able to rent kayaks, depending on their abilities and intended river. A far cry from Queenstown's boisterous Kawarau and Shotover rivers, the **rafting trips** run by Pioneer Rafting (☎03/443 1246; Sept–April; half day $95, full day $145) are pitched at families, the emphasis being on appreciating the scenery, swimming and gold panning as you drift down the Upper Clutha or follow the historic timber-rafting route down the Makarora in oar-rigged rafts. No-holds-barred thrill-seekers need look no further than **whitewater sledging** with Frogz Have More Fun (☎0800/338 737), who mainly sledge the seven-kilometre stretch of the Kawarau River with its four major rapids (Grade II–IV; 1hr 30min on the water; $95). The season runs from November to April, though by late summer the low water levels mean that the rapids have lost much of their might.

Wanaka and Hawea lakes and the rivers flowing into them are popular territory for brown and rainbow **trout fishing**. There's a maximum bag of six fish per day and you'll require the sport fishing licence ($13 a day, $25 a week). Unless you really know your bait, you'll have a better chance of catching your supper with Lakeland Adventures;

charter rates start at $200 for two hours on a six-metre cabin cruiser (maximum 4 passengers), or they'll rent you a rod, reel and lures for $12 a day and a four-metre runabout carrying five adults for $50 an hour.

Eating and drinking

The sophisticated tastes and open wallets of Wanaka's skiers, combined with a healthy influx of summer tourists, have together fostered an abundance of very good places to eat. The town's drinking dens are less appealing, but you can always take refuge in the restaurant bars. Unless you strike lucky and catch a band passing through, the only entertainment is the wonderful Paradiso **cinema**, corner of Ardmore Street and Ballantyne Road (☎03/443 1505; closed Mon; $9), an off-beat place where you sit in beat up old sofas, armchairs, cushions and even a Morris Minor installed along one side. Unless there is a general consensus to press on through, there will be an interval when everyone tucks into cookies and ice-cream from the on-site café (see below). Films range from quality Hollywood to arthouse.

Café Paradiso, cnr Ardmore St & Ballantyne Rd. Groovy little café attached to its cinema namesake with Formica tables and piles of old *Empire* magazines to keep you occupied over muffins, sandwiches, coffee that's freshly roasted in the basement, cookies and home-made ice-cream that's free of additives and wondrously fruity.

The Doughbin, Pembroke Mall. Home-style bakery with good cakes and pies, including vegetarian versions.

Kai Whakapai, cnr Ardmore St & Helwick St. Undoubtedly Wanaka's essential daytime eating spot and a hot favourite with the locals, who come here for Danish pastries and croissants for breakfast, damn fine coffee and fabulous meals in gargantuan proportions through the day. Expect the likes of smoked chicken and avocado salad ($12), salmon ravioli ($20) and pizzas big enough for two ($22). Closed Sun evening; BYO & licensed.

The Kingsway, 21 Helwick St. The coolest bar in town, cavernous and airy with a pool table, the local Beerworks draught on tap, and music that gets cranked up as the evening wears on.

Muzza's, cnr Brownston & Helwick Sts. Restaurant and bar with unimaginative decor but good-value straightforward meals such as roast lamb ($13) and blue cod ($19). Licensed.

Relishes, 99 Ardmore St. Bustling, cheery restaurant with tables outside and indoors, by the fire. Popular for daytime sandwiches and light meals, before the chef moves on to eclectic dinners – from burritos to Cajun cod. Wines include some from the local Rippon winery. Closed 3–6.30pm; BYO and licensed.

Toscana, 76 Golf Course Rd (☎03/443 1255). Authentic and moderately priced Italian restaurant in a modern Tuscan cottage-style building with a wonderful view over the town and lake, and a terracotta patio flanked by fig trees. Expect antipasto ($15), and spinach and ricotta cannelloni ($19). Dinner nightly, lunch summer only. Licensed.

Tuatara Pizza Bar, 72 Ardmore St. Licensed eat-in and take-out evening-only pizzeria – but more renowned for its pool table and lively bar.

White House Café & Bar, 33 Dunmore St (☎03/443 9595). One of Wanaka's best: a classy yet casual restaurant in a flamboyantly nautical blue and white open-plan house with a sunny patio (or a raging fire in winter). The cuisine is Mediterranean with strong Maghrebi and Middle Eastern leanings, accompanied by wonderful fresh breads and great strong coffee. Mains are around $16–24, and can be washed down with something from the extensive wine list, all available by the glass. The desserts are sensational. Licensed.

Listings

Bike rental Good Sports, Dunmore St (03/443 7966), rent some very flash machines for $50 a day, though there are others at $30 & $25. Mountain Bikes Unlimited, 99 Ardmore St (☎03/443 7882), also rent out the latest off-road machines for around $35 a day ($20 per half day) during the summer season, complete with a local map indicating prime mountain-biking routes. Less exalted

WINTER IN WANAKA

May signifies the end of the summer season, and Wanaka immediately starts gearing up for winter. Mountain-bike rental shops switch to ski rental (see "Listings", below), watersports instructors don their salopettes, pot-bellied stoves replace parasols at restaurants, and frequent shuttle buses run up to the ski fields, calling at the hotels, hostels and sports shops along the way. Reports on snow conditions can be heard on the local radio at around 6.45am, and shops around town post up the morning's report in their windows – you can't miss them. If you plan to drive up to the ski fields, you'll need tyre chains, which can be rented at petrol stations in Wanaka.

CARDRONA

Cardrona Ski Resort (☎03/443 7341, *www.cardrona.co.nz*) sprawls over three basins on the southeastern slopes of the 1934-metre Mount Cardrona, the 12km unsealed access road branching off 24km south of Wanaka and just short of the hamlet of Cardrona. Predominantly a family-oriented field – they run a junior ski school and a créche – Cardrona is noted for dry snow and an abundance of gentle **runs** ideally suited to beginners and intermediates. Currently there are two quads, a double chair and learner tows, giving a maximum vertical descent of 390m and, though there is little extreme terrain, snowboarders have the run of four half-pipes. As you would expect, there's a full programme of lessons, ski packages and gear rental, plus full restaurant and bar facilities. Beginners can spend the day on the learner field for less than half the $58 adult **lift pass**.

Through most of the long season (June to early October), you'll need snow chains to negotiate the access road which drops you at the base facilities halfway up the field. Non-drivers can get **buses** from Wanaka, and from Queenstown, an hour and a half away.

Cardrona is unique in offering **accommodation** actually on the mountain – in luxury, fully self-contained three-bedroom apartments sleeping six for around $400 (☎03/443 7341).

TREBLE CONE

More experienced skiers tend to frequent the excellent steep slopes of **Treble Cone** (☎03/443 7443, *www.new-zealand.com/treblecone*), 20km west of Wanaka, where additional snow-making equipment has extended the season, which now lasts from mid-June to early October. Its appeal lies in open uncrowded slopes, spectacularly located high above Lake Wanaka, and a full 610 vertical metres of skiing, served by New Zealand's first detachable six-seater chair, a couple of T-bars and a learner tow. The **terrain** is very

specimens are available across the road at Lakeland Adventures, Main Wharf (☎03/443 7495), for $6 an hour or $25 a day. The bargain deal is from the YHA, 181 Upton St (☎ & fax 03/443 7405), which rents out basic bikes for $20 a day to all-comers.

Buses Atomic (☎03/442 8178) run to Christchurch, Dunedin, Invercargill and Greymouth; Catch-a-Bus (☎03/471 4103) runs to Dunedin; InterCity (☎03/442 5628) stop in Wanaka on the Queenstown to Franz Josef and Queenstown to Christchurch runs, and go to Dunedin; and Southern Link Shuttles (☎03/358 8355) run to Christchurch.

Camping and outdoor equipment Good Sports, Dunmore St (☎03/443 7966), rents out fishing tackle ($10 a day), hiker tents ($10 a day), alpine tents ($15 a day) and just about everything else imaginable for use in the outdoors.

Car rental Aspiring Car Rentals (☎03/443 7883) have cars for around $50 a day, with unlimited kilometres and insurance, but don't allow drop-offs; Queenstown-based Apex (☎0800/531 111) do allow one-way rentals and rates start at $45 a day.

Internet Fast machines and lively musical accompaniment at *Wanaka Web*, upstairs at 3 Helwick St (☎03/443 7429, *from_wanaka@hotmail.com*; daily 9am–9pm).

Medical treatment Wanaka Medical Centre, 39 Russell St (☎03/443 7811).

Pharmacy Wanaka Pharmacy, 33 Helwick St (☎03/443 8000).

varied with moguls, powder runs, gully runs and plenty of natural and created half-pipes; the limited extent of wide, groomed slopes makes it hard work for beginners, but snowboarders will have a ball. Day **lift passes** go for $58 and there's a first-timer's package (skiers $42, boarders $60) including a lower lift pass, rental and instruction.

Lessons, gear rental and food are all on tap, and the field is easily reached along a 7km toll-free access road. Morning **buses** leave from Wanaka, and a shuttle bus takes skiers from the start of the access road on Mount Aspiring Road up to the tows.

WAIORAU NORDIC SKI AREA

With so many Kiwi skiers committed to downhill, it comes as a surprise to discover the **Waiorau Snow Farm** (☎03/443 7542), a Nordic ski area across the valley from Cardrona, some 24km south of Wanaka, then 13km up a winding dirt road. At around $20 for access to the field and $15 for ski rental, it is a relatively inexpensive way to get on the snow; and Nordic skiing – essentially tramping on skis – is beginning to catch on. From July to September, exponents negotiate the 55km of marked and groomed Nordic trails designed to cater to beginners and experts in both the Nordic and telemark disciplines. The ski school caters to all levels with improvers' clinics and children's programmes run throughout the season, though more frequently at weekends.

HELI-SKIING

No one is going to fool you into believing that **heli-skiing** is cheap, but there's no other way of getting to runs of up to 1200 vertical metres across virgin snow on any of six mountain ranges. From June to October, Harris Mountains Heli-skiing (☎03/442 6722, fax 441 8563, *www.new-zealand.com/hmh, hmhres@heliski.co.nz*), New Zealand's biggest heli-skiing operator, offers almost 400 different runs on 150 peaks – mainly in the Harris Mountains between Queenstown's Crown Range and Wanaka's Mount Aspiring National Park.

Strong intermediate and **advanced skiers** generally get the most out of the experience, though those with more limited skills can still participate provided they meet the minimum standard determined by an ability questionnaire. **Conditions** are more critical than at the ski fields, but on average there's heli-skiing on seventy percent of days during winter, typically in four- to five-day weather windows separated by storms. Of the multitude of packages, the most popular have to be "The Classic" ($655), with four runs in a day, and "Maximum Vertical" ($830), comprising seven runs for advanced skiers only; **bookings** should be made well in advance and accompanied by a substantial deposit (around 40 percent).

Police Helwick St (☎03/4437272).

Post office The post office at 39 Ardmore St (☎03/443 8211) has poste restante facilities.

Ski rental Harris Mountain Heliskiing, 99 Ardmore St (☎0800/684 468), and Racers Edge, 99 Ardmore St (☎03/443 7882), rent out skis and snowboards for $25–42 per day, and also run a ski tuning and repair service – as does Good Sports on Dunmore St (☎03/443 7966).

Taxis Wanaka Taxis (☎03/443 7999).

Around Wanaka

Wanaka is the only town of any size within a huge area of western Central Otago, and the only resort with easy access to tramps in the **Mount Aspiring National Park**. Consequently, it's a popular base for exploring the surrounding countryside, principally the open and mountainous areas to the north and west, the Haast Pass road over to the West Coast (see p.736), and the tortuous **Cardrona Road**, the most direct route to Queenstown.

The Cardrona Valley

Though designated a state highway (SH89), the **Crown Range Road** through the **Cardrona Valley** from Wanaka to Queenstown is one of New Zealand's highest public roads, reaching an **altitude** of 1120m, and many consider it little more than a track: caravans are banned and car-rental agencies forbid travel over one unsealed twenty-kilometre section. On a fine day, however, its twists and precipitous drops present no more of a problem than any other dirt road in New Zealand. The effort expended is rewarded by a shorter if slower alternative route from Wanaka to Queenstown – 70km as against 120km by SH6 – and a drive past the detritus of the valley's gold-mining heyday. Note that work is underway to tarmac the whole thing; a project due for completion by 2002.

Rumours of William Fox's unwitting discovery of gold in the Arrow River at Arrowtown in 1862 sparked a frenzy of activity. Prospectors spread far and wide, quick-

---

WALKS IN THE MATUKITUKI VALLEY

The DOC's *Matukituki Valley Tracks* and *Rees–Dart Track* leaflets ($1 each) are recommended for these walks, along with the 1:150,000 *Mount Aspiring National Park* map which has a 1:80,000 detail on the back that's perfect for the Cascade Saddle Route.

These walks can be tackled by relatively fit and experienced trampers; all times and distances given are one way, and remember that any reference to the left or right bank of a river assumes you're facing downstream. The climatic differences in the park are extreme, and the half-metre of rain that falls each year in the Matukituki Valley is no indication of the six metres that fall on the western side of the park; as ever, go prepared.

Several huts in this area are owned by the New Zealand Alpine Club (NZAC) but are open to all.

RASPBERRY CREEK TO ASPIRING HUT

The popular day walk from **Raspberry Creek to Aspiring Hut** (9km; 2hr 30min–3hr; 100m ascent) starts along a 4WD track which climbs gently from the Raspberry Creek car park beside the western branch of the Matukituki River, only heading away from the river to avoid bluffs en route to Downs Creek, from where you get fabulous views up to the Rob Roy Glacier and Mount Avalanche. Bridal Veil Falls is only a brief distraction before **Cascade Hut** (NZAC; 4 bunks; $8), which is usually locked. You can gain access through the DOC in Wanaka, but it is barely worth the trouble as it is followed thirty minutes later by the relatively luxurious stone-built **Aspiring Hut** (NZAC; 26 bunks; Nov–April $16 with gas; May–Oct $8 without), a common base camp for mountaineers off to the peaks around Mount Aspiring, which is wonderfully framed by the hut's picture windows.

ROB ROY VALLEY

The **Rob Roy Valley Walk** (6km; 2hr 30min; 400m ascent) is shorter and steeper than the walk to Aspiring Hut but just as spectacular, striking through some magnificent alpine scenery, snowfields and glaciers. From the Raspberry Creek car park, follow the right bank of the Matukituki for fifteen minutes to a swingbridge; cross to the left bank of the Rob Roy stream, which cuts through a small gorge into the beech forest. Gradually the woods give way to alpine vegetation – and the Rob Roy glacier nosing down into the head of the valley.

ASPIRING HUT TO THE HEAD OF THE VALLEY

An excellent day out from Aspiring Hut involves exploring the headwaters of the Matukituki River to the north. The **Aspiring Hut to Pearl Flat** (4km; 1hr 30min; 100m ascent) stretch follows the still-broad river as it weaves in and out of the bush to Pearl ly moving north along the Crown Range and stumbling into the Cardrona Valley, where **gold** was discovered later that year. Five years on, the Europeans legged it to the new fields on the West Coast, leaving the dregs to Chinese immigrants, who themselves had drifted away by 1870.

From Wanaka the road is currently sealed for the first 26km, past the Cardrona and Waiorau Nordic ski area access roads (see "Winter in Wanaka" box on pp.790–91) to the few cottages and long-forgotten cemetery that make up the hamlet of **Cardrona**. Here, the *Cardrona Hotel* (see "Accommodation", p.782) stands in a state of arrested decay. Built in 1868, it survived the floods of 1878 that destroyed most of the old town, battling on until 1961. After years of neglect it was reopened in 1984, with its original facade and a completely renovated interior opening onto a great beer garden; it's now a popular watering hole for skiers in winter, and a good spot for bar and restaurant meals ($10–20) at any time.

South from here, the surfaced section ends, heralding 20km of twisting dirt road through grassy flanks of bald, mica-studded hills to a great viewpoint overlooking

Flat. From **Pearl Flat to the head of the valley** (3.5km; 1hr 30min; 250m ascent) the path follows the right bank, crosses a huge avalanche chute off the side of Mount Barff and climbs high above the river through cottonwood and into open country. Scott Rock Bivvy, marked on some maps, is little more than a sheltering rock 50m east of the river and reached by a sometimes tricky ford.

An alternative, initially following the same route, goes from **Aspiring Hut to French Ridge Hut** (9km; 4hr; 1000m ascent); the new **French Ridge Hut** (NZAC; 20 bunks; $10) has great mountain views but is usually only below the snowline from December to March.

CASCADE SADDLE ROUTE

The most challenging and most satisfying of the local tramps connects the Matukituki Valley to the Rees–Dart Circuit centred on Glenorchy (see p.778), via the arduous **Cascade Saddle Route**, (4–5 days one way) a magnificent alpine crossing with fine panoramic views of the Dart Glacier and the Barrier Range. Long stretches of exposed high country and a finishing point 150km (by road) from the start mean that the route is not one to be undertaken lightly, though it is usually possible to **send your excess gear ahead** to Queenstown with Wanaka Connexions (☎0800/879 926), who charge $10 per bag. Cascade Saddle can only be negotiated without specialized mountaineering equipment for around four months a year (typically Dec–March), and requires sound route-finding skills, totally waterproof clothing and a compass, while a tent gives you the option of breaking the longest day by spending a night in the alpine meadows at the saddle.

The first part of the route follows the track from **Raspberry Creek to Aspiring Hut** (9km; 2hr 30min–3hr; 100m ascent – see description opposite). From **Aspiring Hut to Dart Hut** (13km; 8–11hr; 1350m ascent) views of Mount Aspiring improve as you rise above the tree line onto the steep tussock and snowgrass ridge above. The route is now marked by orange snow poles which lead you to a steel pylon (1835m) that marks the top of the ridge, down to Cascade Creek and across it before climbing gently to the meadows around Cascade Saddle (1500m); four to six hours so far. Non-campers will have to press on another four or five hours to the somewhat oversubscribed Dart Hut, some 500m lower down, along the upper **Dart Valley**. The initial steep descent beside snow poles is treacherous when wet, but on a warm afternoon enjoys expansive views towards the mouth of the rubble-topped Dart Glacier, where chunks of ice periodically crash into the milky river that surges beneath it. In 1914, the terminus of the glacier had crept to within a kilometre of Dart Hut, but it is retreating an average of 50m a year and could all but disappear within eighty years. After following lateral moraine, rounding bluffs and fording streams, you eventually reach the **Dart Hut** (Cat 2; $10; 20 bunks; see also box on p.744), from where it is two days to Glenorchy, following either the Dart or Rees river valleys.

Queenstown and Lake Wakatipu. Here the tarmac resumes, just in time for the steep switchback down towards SH6 and Queenstown.

The Matukituki Valley and Mount Aspiring National Park

The **Matukituki Valley** is very much Wanaka's outdoor playground, a 60km tentacle reaching from the parched Otago landscapes around Lake Wanaka to the steep alpine skirts of Mount Aspiring, which at 3030m is New Zealand's highest mountain outside the Mount Cook National Park. Extensive high-country stations run sheep on the riverside meadows, briefly glimpsed by skiers bound for Treble Cone, rock climbers making for the roadside crags, Matukituki-bound kayakers, and trampers and moun-taineers hot-footing it to the **Mount Aspiring National Park**.

The park, first mooted in 1935 but not created until 1964, is one of the country's largest, extending from the Haast Pass (where there are tramps around Makarora, see p.738) in the north, to the head of Lake Wakatipu (where the Rees–Dart Track and parts of the Routeburn track fall within its bounds, see p.776) in the south. The pyra-midal Mount Aspiring undoubtedly forms the centrepiece of the park, rising with clas-sical beauty over the ice-smoothed, broad valleys and creaking glaciers. It was first climbed in 1909 using heavy hemp rope and none of the modern climbing hardware used by today's mountaineers, who still treat the mountain as one of the grails of Kiwi mountaineering ambition. Travelling along Mount Aspiring Road beside the Matukituki River, the peak hoves into view just outside Wanaka, and remains tantaliz-ingly present all the way to the **Raspberry Creek**, where a car park and public toilets mark the start of a number of magnificent tramps (see box on pp.792–3) into the heart of the park.

Buses operated by Mount Aspiring Express (☎03/443 8422; $25 one way, $45 return), and Alpine Shuttles (☎03/443 7966, *info@good-sports.co.nz;* $25 one way, $45 return) run 55km along Mount Aspiring Road to the national park's main trailhead at Raspberry Creek. Both also run a charter service, which gives you greater flexibility and works out cheaper if you can get at least five people together.

Towards the West Coast: Lake Hawea and Hawea

Mountain-backed **Lake Hawea**, immediately east of Lake Wanaka, receives a fraction of the attention of its western neighbour. With its milky, azure waters this might seem sur-prising, but much of its appeal was shorn away in 1958 with the completion of a small dam, which raised the lake level by twenty metres, in the process drowning the lake's beaches and gently shelving shoreline. Nevertheless, the lake is still popular with anglers intent on bagging landlocked rainbow and brown trout, and salmon. Otherwise there is little reason to spend time here – except to recharge your batteries in the peace and quiet of **HAWEA**, a village that clings to the lake's southern shore 15km northeast of Wanaka. The Lake Hawea Store (Mon–Sat 8am–7pm, Sun 9am–7pm), right in the cen-tre of the village, sells one-day fishing licences ($13) and can put you in touch with local angling experts; expect to pay $300–400 a day for fly-fishing guides.

If you stay, you'll find **camping** and basic **accommodation** in the cabins of the spa-cious, leafy *Lake Hawea Motor Camp*, SH6 (☎ & fax 03/443 1767; tent sites $10, cabins & flats ②–④) right by the lakeshore. The *Lake Hawea Hotel*, 1 Capell Ave (☎03/443 1224, fax 443 1024; dorms ①, motel units ⑤), is optimally sited for uninterrupted lake and mountain views; the backpacker-style lodge has pleasant four-bunk dorms com-plete with bedding, and self-catering facilities. There are decent, fully equipped units a kilometre east of the Hawea store at *Glenruth Lakeview Motel*, 45 Lakeview Terrace (☎03/443 1440, fax 443 1709; ④), while the best of the **B&Bs** is at 4 Bodkin St

(☎03/443 1343; ④), where a couple of balconied rooms tucked atop a craft-filled A-frame boast fine mountain views.

Eating is best done in the B&Bs if that's where you are staying; otherwise, make for the substantial bar meals and beer garden at the *Lake Hawea Hotel* or the takeaway and small café at the Lake Hawea Store.

The Central Otago goldfields

Though Queenstown's gold-rush heritage has largely been swamped by adventure tourism, the mining past remains the main attraction of the **Central Otago goldfields**, a historically rich but now almost deserted region covering much of the country east of the Queenstown–Wanaka axis to the coast at Dunedin. This barren, rugged and peculiarly beautiful high-country hinterland is where, from the 1860s to the end of the century, gold was panned from the streambeds, dredged from the deeper rivers, and eventually mined and blasted from the land. Small-time panners still extract a little "colour" from the streams and a few commercial mines still operate, but for the most part the gold has turned its back on the country it built. The landscape is now littered with abandoned mines, perilous shafts and scattered bits of mysterious-looking machinery, while shingle banks in the rivers occasionally reveal the remains of huge dredges, or the detritus of hare-brained schemes to divert the waters and reveal the gold-bearing riverbed.

Towns which boomed in the 1860s were mostly moribund by the early years of the twentieth century, but a few either struggled on as way-stations between the coast and the farmlands of the interior, or developed into prosperous service towns for the stone-fruit orchards which thrive in the region's crisp, dry winters and searingly hot summers. A shortage of water to irrigate these fertile lands was subsequently addressed by building a couple of controversial hydro dams on the Clutha River, drowning many of the orchards in the process.

Many of the significant locales in the gold country fall under the auspices of the DOC's **Otago Goldfields Park**, which encompasses a score of diverse sites scattered throughout the region – all of which are listed in the free *Otago Goldfields Heritage Highway* leaflet, available from local visitor centres. When out exploring, **take precautions**: deep shafts and heavy machinery are potentially hazardous, so at recognized sites, keep to marked paths and heed safety barriers; elsewhere tread extremely carefully.

The reconstructed nineteenth-century boom town at **Cromwell** probably won't delay you long, but the town is a good jumping-off point for the former mining settlements of **Bannockburn** and **Bendigo**. Cromwell's Lake Dunstan is actually a reservoir backed up behind a dam, adjacent to the peaceful town of **Clyde**, now an attractive knot of restaurants and guest houses. **Alexandra** acts mainly as a service town at the fork of two roads penetrating deep into the less-visited part of the gold county: SH85 heads northeast onto the **Maniototo** Plain, skirting the dilapidated former gold towns of **St Bathan's** and **Naseby** on the way to workaday **Ranfurly**, and the only accessible working mine at **Macreas Flat**; while SH8 dives southeast towards the coast through dull **Roxburgh** and **Lawrence**, where the gold rush initially started.

Major **bus** and shuttle companies run fairly regular services along SH8 between Queenstown and Dunedin, and Catch-A-Bus (☎03/471 4103) run a once-daily service from Wanaka through the Maniototo, but to really explore this region you need your own vehicle.

Some history

New Zealand's greatest gold rush kicked off in 1861 when Gabriel Read, an Australian who had previously worked the Californian fields, unearthed flakes of the precious

GOLD FROM DIRT

The classic image of the felt-hatted old-timer **panning** merrily beside a stream is only part of the story of gold extraction, but it's a true enough depiction of the first couple of years of the Otago gold rush. Initially all a miner needed was a pick and shovel, a pan, and preferably a special wooden box known as a "rocker" for washing the alluvial gravel. Periodic droughts lowered the river levels to reveal unworked banks, but as the easily accessible gravel beds were worked out, all manner of ingenious schemes were devised to gain access to fresh raw material. The most common technique was to divert the river, and some far-fetched schemes were hatched, especially on the Shotover River: steel sheets were driven into the river beds with some success, landslides induced to temporarily dam the flow, and a tunnel was bored through a bluff.

When pickings got thinner miners turned their attentions to the more tightly packed banks of the gorges. Hillside dams were constructed and water was piped under pressure to **sluicing** guns that blasted the auriferous gravel free, ready for processing either by traditional hand-panning or its mechanical equivalent, where "riffle plates" caught the fine gravel and carpet-like matting trapped the fine flakes of gold. Eventually the scale of these operations put individual miners out of business and many pressed on to fresh fields.

To get at otherwise inaccessible gravel stock, larger companies began building **gold dredges**, great clanking behemoths anchored to the riverbanks but floating free on the river. Buckets scooped out the river bottom, then the dredge processed the gravel and spat the "tailings" out of the back to pile up along the riversides.

Otago's alluvial gold starts its life underground embedded in reefs of quartz, and when economic returns from the rivers waned, miners sought the mother lode. **Reef quartz mining** required a considerable investment in machinery and whole towns sprang up to tunnel, hack out the ore and haul it on sledges to the stamper batteries. Here, a series of water-driven (and later steam-powered) hammers would pulverize the rock, which was then passed over copper plates smeared with mercury, and onto gold-catching blankets, before the remains were washed into the berdan – a special kind of cast-iron bowl. Gold was then separated from the mercury, a process subsequently made more efficient with the use of cyanide.

metal beside the Tuapeka River, south of Lawrence. Within weeks Dunedin had all but emptied and thousands were camping out on the **Tuapeka Goldfield** around Gabriels Gully. The excitement at Tuapeka soon fizzled out, although by the winter of 1862 Californian prospectors Horatio Hartley and Christopher Reilly teased their first flakes out of the Clutha River, bagging a 40kg haul in three months. This sparked off an even greater gold rush, this time centred on Cromwell, which mushroomed as wagon trains made their way over the rough muddy trails from the coast into the interior. Tent cities sprung up, soon to be replaced by more permanent buildings as merchants moved in founding banks, hotels, shops, bars and brothels. Later in 1862, Thomas Arthur and Harry Redfern struck lucky at what is now Arthur's Point on the Shotover River, sparking a mass exodus for the fresh fields of what soon became known as "the richest river in the world". Miners flooded into Skipper's Canyon, but a few months later some of the heat was taken from its banks by discoveries on the Fox River near Arrowtown, the last of the major gold towns to be built and still the best preserved. Within a few years, returns had dwindled and many headed off to investigate reports of richer finds on the West Coast. As fortunes waned and traders saw their profits diminishing, Chinese miners were co-opted to pick over the tailings (discarded bits of rock and gravel) left behind by Europeans, and were occasionally allowed to work unwanted claims.

Though the boom and bust cycle was as rapid here as in gold country elsewhere, some form of mining continued for the best part of forty years, and the profits fuelled a South Island economy which, for a time at least, dominated New Zealand's exchequer.

Dunedin's economy boomed, and the golden bounty funded the majority of that city's grand civic buildings.

Many claims were eventually abandoned not for lack of gold but because of harsh winters, famine, war, a dip in the gold price, lack of sluicing water, or just disinterest. Although returns are far from spectacular, there are still people out there eking out a living from gold mining; stakes are still claimed and you'll find small- and medium-scale operations all over the province. There's very little appliance of science and despite a fair bit of sophisticated machinery, these are very much backyard operations where instinct counts for much and fancy mining theories not at all. Bigger capital-intensive companies occasionally gauge the area's potential, and as one mining engineer pithily put it, "there's still a shitload of gold out there".

Cromwell and around

East of Arrowtown, SH6 runs for 40km through the scenic Kawarau Gorge, past the Goldfields Mining Centre (see overleaf), to **CROMWELL**, a deracinated town with its gold-mining roots waterlogged below the shimmering surface of the **Lake Dunstan** reservoir. Formed by the Clyde Dam 20km downstream (see p.799), Lake Dunstan swamped much of Cromwell's historic core, and the present-day town centre is uninspiringly modern. Civic boosters hope that the crisp, dry climate and inchoate waterborne leisure facilities will lure visitors, but on current evidence they don't have a hope: for the moment Cromwell is a soulless place only marginally viable as a base for exploring the gold diggings hereabouts and a couple of young wineries producing impressive vintages.

Soon after Hartley and Reilly's 1862 discovery of **gold** beside the Clutha River, a settlement sprouted at "The Junction" at the fork of the Kawarau and Clutha rivers. Local stories tell that it was later renamed when a government survey party dubbed it Cromwell to spite local Irish immigrant workers. Miners low on provisions planted the first fruit trees in the region, little expecting that Cromwell would become the centre of the Otago orchard belt. Its location, further from the sea than any other town in New Zealand, dictates an extreme temperature range – hot and arid in summer with still, cool, dry winters – making it perfect for growing dripping, toothsome **stone fruit**.

Tour buses disgorge their load at the half-dozen fruit stalls beside SH8, which skirts Cromwell passing the giant glass fibre fruity confection by The Mall. The combined visitor centre (see below) and **museum** (donations welcome) is packed full of gold-mining memorabilia, together with material on the construction of Clyde Dam. Free leaflets outline the self-guided **Cromwell Tour**, mind-numbingly dull but for the section around **Old Cromwell Town** (unrestricted entry), a kind of historic reserve on Melmore Terrace, where Lake Dunstan now laps the old shopfronts. In the mid-1970s when the Clyde Dam was planned and the death knell sounded for the heart of old Cromwell, the preservation instinct kicked in, but in the wrong gear. Cromwell missed a perfect opportunity to preserve an 1870s town as it was in the 1970s and opted instead for a dull "Historic Town" re-creation. A dozen buildings due to be submerged were dismantled stone by stone and have now been rebuilt on the water's edge and house tacky tourist shops. **Aquatic activities** are still in their infancy here, currently geared only towards people bringing their own tackle; though you can take a **lake cruise** (noon–1pm, $12; 5.30–7.30pm, $15) from the wharf by Cromwell Old Town.

Practicalities

Queenstown- or Wanaka-bound **bus** travellers may well have to change in Cromwell, using the stop outside the petrol station on Murray Terrace right by The Mall, Cromwell's civic centre and home to the **visitor centre** (daily 10am–4pm; ☎03/445 0212, fax 445 1649), which provides an abundance of leaflets on the gold region.

The cheapest **place to stay** is at the *Cromwell Holiday Park*, 1 Alpha St (☎03/445 0164, fax 445 0431, *cromwell.holiday.prk@xtra.co.nz*), which has tent sites for $18, and a range of cabins, flats and motel units (②–④). Across town, there's the low-cost *Anderson Park Motel*, Gair Avenue (☎03/445 0321, fax 445 1523; ③–④), and for a few dollars more you can stay by the water at *Gateway Motel*, 45 Alpha St (☎03/445 0385, fax 445 1855; ④). About the only homestay around is at *Cottage Gardens*, 3 Alpha St (☎ & fax 03/445 0628, *eco@xtra.co.nz*; ④), surrounded by an orchard, yet right in town.

The Mall has several places for reasonable **meals**, though *The Ferryman Family Restaurant and Bar* (☎03/445 0607) on Melrose Terrace in "Old Cromwell Town" has most atmosphere.

Around Cromwell

The appropriate response to the lack of diversions in Cromwell is to get out and explore the remains of the gold-country diggings. Hype is reserved for the **Goldfields Mining Centre** (☎03/445 1038, *goldfields@xtra.co.nz*; daily 9am–5.30pm; $14), approached by footbridge over the brooding Kawarau 7km west of Cromwell on SH6. The extensive site occupies a longstanding though not especially lucrative alluvial mining site where ground-sluicing eventually gave way to Californian-style water jets used to loosen the shingle beds. Museum pieces are stations on a partly guided tour, or you can view the lot on gentle guided horseback rides ($30). Though this was an authentic site, there is an overriding staginess about the whole affair; the stamper battery has been brought in, a turbine was recovered from the river before Lake Dunstan filled and the Chinese Village was constructed as a film set in the early 1990s. As well as the usual opportunity to extract a flake or two you can sample the only Otago-based jetboat ride which actually negotiates rapids: Goldfields Jet (☎0800/111 038; $65), which runs thirty-minute trips on the Kawarau just below the site. A short distance upstream from the Goldfields site the small **Roaring Meg** power station marks both an important rapid run by sledgers and river surfers, and the "**natural bridge**", a point where the river narrows into a twisting gorge below cliffs which almost touch. Maori moa hunters and nineteenth-century gold men used the narrows as their main crossing point until ferries and bridges were constructed elsewhere.

Dedicated ruin-hounds should call in at the visitor centre in Cromwell and pick up the *Cromwell and District: Guide to Walks and Outings* leaflet which details minor gold sites within a few minutes' drive of Cromwell. Pioneering spirits can head out to remote clusters of cottage foundations such as those in the Carrick Range or the Nevis Valley (both south of Cromwell), but for most the best bet is **BANNOCKBURN**, a scattered hamlet 9km southwest of Cromwell which has the *Bannockburn Domain Motor Camp* (☎03/445 1450; tents $6), the *Cairnmuir Camp* (☎ & fax 03/445 1956; $8), down by Lake Dunstan and the *Bannockburn Hotel*. Once home to two thousand people, this tortured landscape now serves to illustrate the effect of gold-mining operations on the landscape. A two-hour **self-guided trail** (unrestricted entry except for lambing season, Aug 20 to Oct 20) starts 1.5km along Felton road and weaves around huts, tail-races sluicing and tunnelling operations following numbered stakes. In the last decade, the warm, north-facing slopes towards the end of Felton Road have been planted with grapes, their fermented end product available for sampling at two of Central Otago's finest **wineries**: *Felton Road* (☎03/445 0885, *www.nz-wine.co.nz/felton.road*; Nov–April daily 10am–5pm; May–Oct Mon–Fri 10am–5pm), which has tasting for $4 (refundable with purchase), and *Olssens* (☎03/445 1716; daily 10am–4pm), where you can taste (also $4) then buy a bottle or two and sit outside consuming the picnic you've brought with you.

If venturing slightly further afield, consider the quartz-mining district of **BENDIGO**, 15km north of Cromwell towards the Lindis Pass, and its acolytes Logantown and Welshtown. None comprises much more than a few scattered remains and deep mine shafts, but a (careful) amble among the ruins makes a fine way to pass a summer evening.

Clyde

SH8 cuts southeast from Cromwell through 20km of the bleak and windswept **Cromwell Gorge**, hugging the banks of Lake Dunstan through what used to be New Zealand's most fertile apricot-growing country. The orchards are now all submerged below the waters of the lake, which are held back by the dam at **CLYDE**. The tiny associated town, peacefully situated off the main highway, languished for a number of years but is newly resurgent as a sybaritic retreat. Notwithstanding a few minor museums, there is nothing much to distract you from lounging around some excellent places to stay and dining in a small but perfectly formed cluster of great cafés and restaurants.

Clyde's streets are lined with ornate stone buildings and simple cottages left over from the gold-mining days of the 1860s. Originally known as Dunstan, the town sprang up just downriver from the spot where Hartley and Reilly made their big find in 1862. As tens of thousands of fortune-seekers flooded in from Dunedin and Lawrence, it quickly became the centre of the Dunstan goldfields, but by 1864 waning fortunes and swift river currents forced out the miners in favour of river dredges.

Since the mid-1980s, the town has been dominated by the giant grey hydroelectric **Clyde Dam**, 1km north of town on SH8, which generates five percent of New Zealand's power and provides water for irrigation. Initially controversial, the dam is nevertheless considered something of an engineering marvel, with special "slip joints" providing the dam wall with flexibility in case of earth tremors.

Clyde's other attractions are limited to the panoramic views from the **Clyde Lookout** hill (500m from town; 30min walk) and three small but well-kept museums within easy walking distance of one another. The 1864 stone courthouse on Blyth Street now operates as the **Clyde Museum** (☎03/449 2092; Tues–Sun 2–4pm or by arrangement; $1), worth a peek for its intriguing coverage of Clyde's Great Gold Robbery of 1870. One George Rennie made off with £13,000 in bullion and banknotes, but his horse was so weighed down with the gold that he left a trail of bags hidden behind rocks at intervals. Unfortunately the co-conspirator for whom this trail had been intended had already ratted on Rennie to the police, and the ill-fated villain was easily tracked down and arrested. The **Briar Herb Factory Complex**, corner of Fraser Street and Fache Street (Tues–Sun 2–4pm; $2), was established in the 1930s as New Zealand's first herb factory, and thrived for several decades, making use of the common thyme which still grows wild hereabouts, with entire hillsides flowering purple throughout November. The factory closed in the 1970s but lives on as an exhibition space, housing well-maintained displays of drying trays, presses and home-made machines used for processing the herbs. Other parts of the factory are given over to horse-drawn vehicles, a rabbiter's hut and an early hospital full of ghoulish medical instruments. The former Clyde Railway Station next door houses the **Station Museum** (Sat & Sun 2–4pm; $1), enabling rail fanatics to pore over its varied collection of well-kept locomotives.

Practicalities

Pre-booked InterCity and various shuttle **buses** stop in Clyde on demand, pulling up on the main Sunderland Street, which is where you'll find the majority of the good **places to stay and eat**. Those on a tight budget will want to stay at *Hartley Arms*, 25 Sunderland St (☎ & fax 03/449 2700; dorms ①, room ②), a small and cosy backpackers partly built into Clyde's original gold assay office. Dorms have four bunks and there are doubles made up with sheets and towels. With a fuller wallet, stay at the relaxing and extremely atmospheric *Olivers Lodge & Restaurant*, 34 Sunderland St (☎03/449 2860, fax 449 2862; ⑦–⑧), which has a range of individually styled luxury rooms – one with a huge bathroom fashioned like a Turkish bath – in rustic rural-style buildings that were once part of a large general store catering for the gold-miners. Alternatively there's *Dunstan House*, 29 Sunderland St (☎03/449 2295, *dunstanhouse @xtra.co.nz*; ⑤), a boutique B&B in a fine house dating from 1900, which offers spacious comfortable rooms and a wraparound veranda on the first floor; and *Clyde Holiday and Sporting Complex*, Whitby Street (☎03/449 2713; tent & powered sites $8–9, vans and cabin ②), a pleasant **campsite**, surrounding a cricket ground with a fully self-contained cabin and several on-site caravans, plus a swimming pool and book exchange.

Lunch on a fine day is best taken in the gardens at *Olivers*, which also has an excellent and characterful, award-winning **restaurant** serving breakfast and wholesome lunches (both around $12–14) and dinners ($20–27; book ahead especially at weekends), featuring the likes of lamb and kumara gateau in red wine and thyme jus. Once unchallenged, *Olivers* cuisine is now at least matched by that across the road at *Blues Bank*, 31 Sunderland St (closed Mon–Wed; licensed & BYO), which dishes up wonderful Cajun and Creole plates – many named after the legendary blues players that also provide the decorative theme. Tuck into Creole chilli crabs ($20) or Muddy Waters mussels ($10) selected from menus encased in old record covers. There's entertainment, such as live music or comedy, most Saturday nights. Cheaper pub-style snacks can be obtained 300m away at the attractive *Post Office Café*, on the corner of Blyth and Matau streets, built into the former 1865 post office and with a bar serving a delicious ale, "Post Office Dark", and a garden out the back.

Alexandra and around

A large white clockface – visible from as far away as 5km – looms out of the cliff which backs **ALEXANDRA** (affectionately known as "Alex"), 10km southeast of Clyde. Alexandra sprang up during the 1862 gold rush, and flourished for four frenzied years before settling into decline, although the gold-dredging boom at the end of the century breathed some life back into the town. Now, a prosperous service town for the fruit-growing heartland of Central Otago, it's the largest place for some distance, and its modest clutch of sights and stark mountain scenery may well persuade you to stop, particularly if your visit coincides with the longstanding **Alexandra Blossom Festival**, held on the fourth weekend in September.

A huge waterwheel marks Alexandra's main point of interest, the **Alexandra Museum and Art Gallery** on the corner of Walton Street and Thomson Street (Mon–Sat 11am–5pm, Sun 1–4pm; donations welcome), which houses exhibitions on the glory years of the 1890s, along with an entertaining display on the sorry tale of rabbits, which were introduced into the area in 1909 and did what rabbits do – so well that they soon became a major menace throughout the South Island. To combat the problem, the town holds an Easter Bunny Shoot every year, and hunters from all over New Zealand congregate on Good Friday to slaughter as many as they can.

In the early years, the only way across the Manuherikia River was by unstable punt, but in 1879 the town built the **Shaky Bridge**, a suspension **footbridge** – originally wide enough for wagons but since narrowed – now crossed to reach a **lookout point** (1.5km; 30min one way) high above the town on Tucker Hill, which affords great views of the whole area.

With its long hours of hot sun, the region is now gaining a reputation for its wines. **Black Ridge Vineyard**, Conroys Road, in an unlikely setting amid black schist 6km southwest of Alex (☎ 03/449 2059; daily 10am–5pm; free tasting), produces award-winning wines from the world's most southerly vineyard, and **William Hill Vineyard**,

2km west of Alex on Dunstan Road (☎03/448 8436; tastings Sat & Sun 11am–5pm, sales daily Nov–April), also produces high-quality whites; pick up the free *Central Otago Wine Trail* leaflet from the visitor centre (see below), which locates and briefly describes the region's wineries.

Activities

Alex makes a good base from which to explore some impressive mountain ranges and the Roxburgh Gorge, either on a guided tour or under your own steam. This is a great area for **mountain biking**, with plenty of trails to tackle on your own or with a trail guide recommended by the visitor centre. You can rent a mountain bike from MCS Services, 21 Shannon St (☎03/448 8048), or Henderson Cycles, 17 Limerick St (☎03/448 8917); both charge around $15 for a half day, $22 for a full day. Several operators run **tours** from Alex into the surrounding mountain ranges: you can go **horse trekking** in the thyme-scented hills of the Dunstan Trail (1hr; $20), with longer treks by arrangement (☎03/449 2445 evenings or 7.30–8am); or try a **4WD safari** up the Dunstan Mountains, the Old Man Range or other remote gold-mining areas, with John Douglas (☎03/448 7474, or through the visitor centre; around $35 for half day, $50 full day), who also organizes day or night **rabbit shooting** for up to three people at a time (half-day daytime shoot $40–70, depending on numbers; full-day $65–130 per person; 3hr night-time shoot $45–80). Alternatively, the reasonably fit can try a one-day guided trip paddling a **Canadian canoe** down the Roxburgh Gorge and mountain biking back, with Central Outdoor Adventures (☎03/448 8048; Oct–April; 3 people maximum; around $90 per person). During the winter months there's ice skating on local lakes, cross-country skiing and trips by snow **skidoo** into the mountains (for more information, contact the visitor centre).

Practicalities

InterCity **buses** drop off at the monument at the intersection of Tarbert Street and Centennial Avenue; while Catch-a-Bus offer a door-to-door service. Atomic and Southern Link **shuttles** both stop outside the **visitor centre**, 22 Centennial Ave (Mon–Fri 9am–5pm, Sat & Sun 10am–3pm; ☎03/448 9515, fax 448 9516, *www.tco.org .nz, info@tco.org.nz*), which has leaflets ($0.50) on a number of walks in the local mountains, and the *Mountain Biking* pamphlet detailing five local trails that are open all year. You can also book here for guided 4WD tours of the surrounding rugged terrain (see "Activities", above). The **post office**, 66 Tarbert St (☎03/448 7500) has poste restante facilities; and there's **Internet** access at the library, corner of Skird and Tarbert streets, and *Smith City Cyber Café*, Limerick Street (both open standard business hours).

There's plenty of low-cost **accommodation** in Alexandra, including the *Two Bob Backpackers*, 4 Dunorling St (☎03/448 8152, fax 448 5131, *www.nzsouth.co.nz/twobobs, twobobs@clear.net.nz*; dorms ①, rooms ②), an associate YHA hostel, located in a quiet spot overlooking the Clutha, a five-minute stroll from the centre of town. Among the **motels**, try the soothing *Alexandra Garden Court*, Manuherikia Road (☎ & fax 03/448 8295; ④), a fifteen-minute walk from the centre, with six fully self-contained units and a swimming pool set in extensive landscaped gardens; or the slightly more central, small and friendly *Kiwi Motel*, 115 Centennial Ave (☎03/448 8258, fax 448 6201; ④). The French provincial-style *Rocky Range Lodge*, 2km south of town, signposted off SH8 (☎ & fax 03/448 6150, ☎0800/153 293, *info@rockyrange.co.nz*; ⑧), is the luxury pick, perched high on a hill amid schist outcrops with stunning panoramic views; dinner can be arranged for an extra $50. **Campers** need to head for the *Alexandra Holiday Park* on Manuherikia Road/SH85 (☎03/448 8297, fax 448 8294; huts ①, cabins ②), a large well-kept and tree-sheltered site offering tent sites for $8.50, single-bed huts and cabins, as well as mountain bikes for rent; or the pleasant *Pine Lodge Holiday Camp*, 31 Ngapara

St (☎03/448 8861, fax 448 8276; tent sites $9, flats ③, motel units ④), beside a deer park; both are fifteen minutes' walk from the centre.

The best places to **eat** hereabouts are in Clyde, 8km to the north (see p.799); in town go for the licensed *Briar & Thyme*, 26 Centennial Ave (book for dinner ☎03/448 9189; Oct–April daily; May–Sept Tues–Sat), which specializes in classy lunches like camembert and vegetable turnovers or oven-baked blue cod (around $10 each), as well as elegant dinners ($15–25), in a comfortable historic house with a wine bar. For something more low-key try the *Red Brick*, in the Supervalue car park on the corner of Limerick Street and Ennis Street, a mellow café, licensed and open daily for a good range of lunch ($10–20) and dinner ($20–25) dishes, plus great desserts. Fans of quality burgers and seafood at low prices should eat at the nautically themed *Fish & Ships*, 73 Centennial Ave (☎03/448 5444; closed Mon & Tues), which does the best greasies in town to eat in or take out.

North of Alex: The Maniototo Plain

The most interesting route to the east coast from Alexandra is through the **Maniototo**, a generic name for the flat high country shared by three shallow valleys and the low craggy ranges that separate them. Despite easy road access, the Maniototo seems a world apart, largely ignored by foreign visitors, though it is a common summertime destination for Dunedinites who appreciate the dry climate and the quality of the light some 500 metres up.

Predictably, Europeans first came to the area in search of gold. They found it near **Naseby**, but returns quickly declined and farming on the plains became more rewarding. This was especially true when **railway** developers looking for the easiest route from Dunedin to Alexandra chose a way up the Taieri Gorge (see p.652) and across the Maniototo. The line arrived in **Ranfurly** in 1898 and that soon took over from Naseby as the area's main administrative centre, an honour held to this day. Passenger trains ran through the Maniototo until 1990, but by the end of 1991 all the track had been pulled up; the route has now been fashioned into the **Otago Central Rail Trail** (see box, opposite).

The main road through the Maniototo is SH85 from Alexandra to Palmerston, which is fast, largely straight and paved, and usually known as "The Pigroot"; it began life as the easiest route from the east coast to the Central Otago Goldfields. Scattered on the way are a handful of old gold-mining communities, among them **St Bathans**, **Naseby** and **Ranfurly**, each worth a brief visit for their laid-back atmosphere, calm seclusion and subtle reminders of how greed transforms the land. In between you'll see dozens of small cottages, many abandoned – a testament to the harsh life in these parts.

These days the highway also provides access to a rugged route further northeast to the Waitaki Valley (see p.637), via Dansey's Pass. The only public transport through these parts is the Catch-a-Bus service (☎03/471 4103; daily except Sat) between Dunedin and Wanaka which leaves Dunedin at 8am arriving in Wanaka around noon and then setting back at 1pm.

Omakau, Ophir and St Bathans

Heading northeast from Alexandra you are immediately into the high country plain passing through inconsequential hamlets until you reach the twin settlements of **Omakau** and **Ophir** after 20km. These are mainly of interest for those on the Otago Central Rail Trail and in need of accommodation: try the *Omakau Domain Camping Ground*, Alton St, Omakau (☎03/447 3814; tents $8), or *Ophir Lodge Backpackers*, 1 Macdonald St, Ophir (☎ & fax 03/447 3339, *blgaler@xtra.co.nz*; Sept–May; dorms ①, rooms ②), a small, comfortable and well set-up hostel a couple of kilometres from the trail.

OTAGO CENTRAL RAIL TRAIL

One of the finest ways to explore the Maniototo is on the **Otago Central Rail Trail** (*www.hike.org/walks/Otago-Central-Rail.html*), a relatively little-known 150km route – open to walkers, bicycles and horses – from Clyde to Middlemarch and passing through almost all the towns of importance with the exception of St Bathan's and Naseby.

A mountain bike is definitely the way to go (some sections are rough), but there are currently no rental facilities nearby, so you'll need to obtain one from Queenstown, Wanaka or Dunedin, or bring you own. Walkers are better advised to tackle shorter sections through gorges with plenty of tunnels and viaducts, avoiding the long flat bits: go for the stretch between Lauder and Auripo in the northern section, or the run from Daisybank to Hyde in the east. Both are around 10km, though unless you are prepared to hitch you'll have to hike back; remember to take a torch for the tunnels.

The route is fully outlined in one overall *Otago Central Rail Trail* leaflet (\$0.50) and a series of six section leaflets (\$0.50 each).

The first place with genuine appeal is the minute yet strangely attractive former gold town of **ST BATHANS**, 80km north of Alexandra and accessed 17km along a mostly scaled loop road from Becks. St Bathans began life as a boom town called Dunstan Creek in 1863, following a gold strike at the foot of Mount St Bathans. Within six months two or three hundred miners were working the area, and the tent town comprised twenty stores, four pubs and a bank. The population peaked at 2000, but when the gold ran out in the 1930s, everything went with it. These days it's virtually a ghost town with just three permanent residents and a straggle of ancient buildings strung in a crooked line along a single road. Two of the residents manage the atmospheric 1882 *Vulcan Hotel* (☎03/447 3629; bunks ①, rooms ③), where local farmers and the occasional visitor prop up the old wooden bar, which serves *St Bathans Gold*, a single malt bottled on the premises. The pub offers good cheap snacks and dinners, as well as simple B&B accommodation, though be warned that the place is haunted; doubters should book Room 1.

The prettiest thing about the area is the striking **Blue Lake** right beside the town, where mineral-rich water has flooded a crater left by the merciless sluicing of Kildare Hill, which used to be 120m high until it was entirely washed away. A short track leads from the *Vulcan* to a vantage point over the intensely azure lake, now used for water-skiing, swimming and picnics.

Just up the street from the lake and the hotel, the former post office is once again performing that role as part of Despatches, a kind of mini-museum-cum-Victorian-gift shop that also books **horse riding** with St Bathans Horse Treks (☎ & fax 03/447 3512): rides range from \$30 for a couple of hours to \$180 for an overnight jaunt sleeping in a musterer's hut.

Apart from the hotel, the only other **accommodation** hereabouts is the *Constable Cottage and Gaol* (☎ & fax 03/447 3558, *lauderdale@xtra.co.nz*; gaol ⑤, cottage ⑥), a self-contained former police house and its gaol let separately or together: all meals can be provided by prior arrangement.

Naseby

The small settlement of **NASEBY**, 25km east of St Bathans and 14km off SH85, clings to the Maniototo Plain some 600m above sea level. Surrounding the town, the dark-green swathe of **Naseby Forest** stands out from the tussock-covered hills to the north and the farmland plains to the south. Managed for its exotic timber – mainly European larches, Douglas firs and pines – it is the highest forest of its kind on the South Island. A number of pleasant picnic spots and forest **walks** (750m–3km one way; 30min–90min;

or a circuit walk of 10km, 6hr) are easily accessible from Naseby, signposted through-out the forest with times, distances and destinations, and also listed in the *Naseby Forest* leaflet and map available free from the Timberlands HQ in the middle of town on Derwent Street (Mon–Fri 9am–4pm; ☎03/444 9995). To witness the effects of former sluicing at their most dramatic, follow the **One Tree Hill Track** (1.6km; 1hr return), starting only five minutes' walk north of the Timberlands HQ, which snakes uphill along the eastern side of Hogburn Gully, past dramatic honey-coloured cliffs entirely carved by water; a free sheet on the walk is available from the visitor centre.

At its 4000-strong peak in 1865, Naseby was the largest gold-mining town on the Maniototo, but today numbers have dropped to around 150. It functions as a quiet hol-iday town in summer and the country's centre for the Scottish sport of curling (a sort of bowls on ice played on a local pond) in winter, but is little more than a collection of small houses (many of them originally built by miners from sun-dried mud brick), with a shop, a garage, a couple of hotels, a café, a great campsite and a good pub. There are also a swimming dam, an impressive ice rink for winter use, and a couple of tiny muse-ums, both at the junction of Earne Street and Leven Street. The **Maniototo Early Settlers Museum** (Nov–May Tues–Sun 1.30–3.30pm; $2) features a large number of black-and-white photos of past residents' lives alongside a small collection of items left by Chinese miners, while the **Jubilee Museum** (daily 10am–5pm; $1 token available from the general store across the street) houses the remains of an old watchmaker's shop together with displays on the local gold rush of the 1860s and 1870s plus the his-tory of the town since then. On the northwestern outskirts of town, just outside the for-est boundary and about ten minutes' walk from the centre, is the **swimming dam**, a popular cooling-off spot in summer, surrounded by mature Douglas fir and larch trees. The **Maniototo Ice Rink** (early June to mid-Aug; $10 including skate rental) at the southern end of town on Channel Road is New Zealand's largest outdoor rink, and is a popular venue for skating, ice hockey and particularly curling. If you happen to catch the season, pop along armed with the *Spectators Guide to Curling* leaflet, available free from the Ranfurly visitor centre; or join in. Curling equipment is available for rent ($5 for two hours plus $6 for a stone and broom).

If you want to break your journey here, there's **accommodation** at the *Ancient Briton* pub in Leven Street (☎03/444 9992; dorms ①, rooms ④), which has a number of neat, good-quality motel units, a backpackers and power sites ($10), all in a quiet spot out the back. The pub serves breakfast for around $10 and hearty cheap dinners in enormous portions. There's also the pretty and very tranquil *Naseby Larchview Camping Park* (☎ & fax 03/444 9904; tent and powered sites $9, cabins & vans ②–③), in the forest about five minutes' walk from town; and the *Monkey Puzzle House*, corner of Derwent and Oughter streets (☎ & fax 03/444 9985; dinner, bed and breakfast ⑥), a comfortable if somewhat chintzy B&B with guest-share bathrooms, a lounge full of Victoriana and free use of skates in winter.

The *Stables Café* on Earne Street is good for **snacks** for under $10, to eat in or take-away, and simple dinners for around $10 but it opens only sporadically and you might be better off settling for Devonshire teas at the *Monkey Puzzle House* (Fri–Mon 11am–4pm).

Dansey's Pass

The metalled Kyeburn Diggings Road, running east out of Naseby, continues as a nar-row barren and beautiful route climbing northeast across the Kakanui Mountains via **Dansey's Pass** (about 40km from Naseby), to eventually emerge in the Waitaki Valley, where SH83 gives access to Mount Cook in the west and the coast in the east. Though reasonably well maintained, the route is sometimes closed in summer and always unsafe in winter, so check in Naseby before setting out. Old gold workings are visible from the roadside, where water jets from sluices have distorted the schist and tussock landscape, leaving rock dramatically exposed.

At Kyeburn Diggings, 16km from Naseby, you'll come across the charming **Dansey's Pass Coach Inn** (☎ & fax 03/444 9048, *www.danseyspass.co.nz*; ⑥), a comfortable lodge at the foot of the pass but in the middle of nowhere, built from local schist stone in 1862 and the only remnant of a 2000-strong gold-rush community. The stonemason was reputedly paid a pint of beer for each stone laid. The inn offers good beer, affordable lunches and fairly pricey dinners, as well as nicely modernized en-suite accommodation, which is booked up most weekends throughout the year. They also rent out mountain bikes ($8 per hour, $24 a half day), and in winter will take folk cross-country skiing up at the pass. There's **budget accommodation** at the far end of the route, about 15km north of the pass itself, at the small and quiet *Dansey's Pass Holiday Camp* (☎03/431 2564, fax 431 2560; tent & powered sites $8.50 & $9, cabins ②), down by the riverside.

Ranfurly

Back on SH85 and 5km beyond the Naseby turn-off lies the compact town of **RANFURLY**, the largest settlement on the Maniototo Plain, though with precious little to show for it except for a few places to stay and eat. The elegant **former train station** on Charlemont Street East has a free audio-visual show on the region and pictorial displays tracing the history of the town and the Otago Central Railway. In summer, anyone with a 4WD or high-clearance vehicle can set out from here to explore part of the magnificent **Old Dunstan Road** (unsafe May–Sept), the original route to the Central Otago goldfields before the Pigroot was opened. Traversing the Rock and Pillar and Lammerlaw ranges fills you with admiration for those gold prospectors who guided their horse-drawn drays and bullock wagons through some of the harshest land in the country, all for the sake of a dream. From Ranfurly head 20km south to Patearoa and from there a further 25km to Paerau (aka Styx), where a 50km section of the Old Dunstan Road begins its gruelling journey to Clarks Junction and the easier SH87 heads towards Dunedin.

Next door to the former train station, the **visitor centre**, 5 Charlemont St E (Christmas–Jan Mon–Fri 9am–4.30pm, Sat & Sun 10am–3pm; Feb–Christmas closed weekends; ☎ & fax 03/444 9970, *maniototo.vic@xtra.co.nz*) stocks leaflets on the whole district and can offer further advice on **accommodation**. Opposite the visitor centre there's the large colonial *Ranfurly Lion Hotel* (☎ & fax 03/444 9140; dorms ①, rooms ③–④), with a range of single and double rooms (some en-suite) plus a pleasant and very cheap backpackers across the road. There's a bar, a good but fairly cheap restaurant, and guests get free use of a spa pool. The clean and sheltered *Ranfurly Motor Camp*, Reade Street, off Pery Street, two minutes' walk from the town centre (☎03/444 9144; tent sites $9, dorms ①, cabins ②, tourist flats ③), has a covered swimming pool. About ten minutes' walk west of the centre, in a park-like setting, is the small and quiet *Ranfurly Motel*, Davis Avenue, off Caulfield Street (☎ & fax 03/444 9383; ④). Twelve kilometres east from Ranfurly, on the road to the tiny settlement of Waipiata and close to the rail trail, is *Peter's Farm Hostel* (☎03/444 9083; Dec–April; tent sites $9, dorms ①, rooms ②), a comfortable and very relaxing farm with free use of bikes, kayaks, fishing rods and gold pans; plus several good walks nearby. Phone ahead to enquire about winter opening, to get directions and for a free pick-up from Ranfurly. Talk nicely to Peter and he may let you use the small electricity-free cabin with a gas cooker and fabulous views, located in the nearby Rock and Pillar Range.

The best **eating** in town is at the BYO *Korner Shop* on Northland Street (SH85), which does meals throughout the day and good coffee.

Macraes Gold Mine Middlemarch and SH85 to Dunedin

At Kyeburn, 15km east of Ranfurly, the slow **route to Dunedin** (SH87) branches south off SH85 and twists through the eastern Maniototo, a barren yet scenic landscape squeezed between the towering Rock and Pillar Range and the Taieri River. Fifty kilometres south of Kyeburn you'll reach the tiny and decaying community of **Middlemarch**, the Sunday-only terminus of the **Taieri Gorge Railway**, which makes a spectacular two-hour run between here and Dunedin (see p.652 for details). Anyone planning to tackle the Otago Central Rail Trail from east to west should definitely consider starting by riding the railway either to Middlemarch or to **Pukerangi** (the weekday turn-around point), 18km to the south. Either way you can spend the first night in Middlemarch. Opposite the station at 5 Snow Ave you'll find **accommodation** at *Shannon-Lea* (☎ & fax 03/464 3762, *alistermdl@xtraco.nz*; bunks ①, room ③, en suite ④), a house converted into a combined hostel and lodge; enquire at the shop on the main street. Alternatively, cross the tracks to *Blind Billy's Holiday Camp*, Miro Street (☎03/464 3355, fax 464 3322, *www.middlemarch.co.nz/blind_billys.html*, *blindbillys @xtra.co.nz*; tent sites $8, dorms ①, cabin & vans ②, unit ④), a campsite with cooking facilities in a converted railway carriage and seats outdoors beside the piano. There are also simple dorms, a cabin, a couple of basic on-site vans and an old-fashioned but spacious two-bedroom motel unit.

The most renowned of Otago's operating gold mines, the huge opencast **Macraes Gold Mine**, lies on windswept hills between Ranfurly and Palmerston and can be visited on a two-hour tour (☎03/465 2400; $10) which also takes in a historic reserve and a fully operational stamper battery. Bookings are essential and there is a minimum charge of $70, making visits prohibitive except for groups. Tours leave from *Stanley's Hotel* at Macraes Flat, most quickly reached by following SH85 63km east from Ranfurly and cutting 17km west just before Dunback. Viewing platforms allow you to see the gold-processing plant and the earth-moving equipment at work in the mining pit, but it's not especially fascinating. Should you want to **eat or stay** in the area, the historic and cheap *Stanley's Hotel* (☎ & fax 03/465 2400; B&B ④), another schist-stone construction, has a restaurant and bar, a few rooms with shared bathrooms, and a swimming pool.

Back on SH85 it's a further 14km from Dunback to Palmerston, where SH1 heads south to Dunedin and north towards Oamaru.

Southeast along SH8: Alexandra to Dunedin, via Roxburgh

The fastest route from Alexandra to the coast is SH8, partly because it's a shorter road than SH85, but also because there are fewer enticing stop-offs en route. The road follows the meandering course of the Clutha River, passing through rugged hill country between the Old Man and Lammerlaw ranges to the east, and the Knobby Blue Mountain range to the west. Along the way are a couple of mildly interesting gold towns, Roxburgh and Lawrence, both served by the major **bus** companies and **shuttles** (notably Atomic Shuttle and Catch-a-Bus) running between Queenstown or Alexandra and Dunedin.

Roxburgh and Lawrence

Thirteen kilometres south of Alexandra you pass through the ironically named **Fruitlands**, a tiny settlement where orchards were once planted in the hope that they'd flourish, only to fail and be replaced by grazing sheep. From the ridge to the west of the road you get a good view of the 27-metre-tall **Old Man Rock**, an extraordinary stone obelisk from which the Old Man Range takes its name. A characterful reminder of the gold-mining days, the roadside **Fruitlands Gallery** (daily 10am–5pm), occupies a restored stone pub of 1866 and functions as a fully licensed and BYO café exhibiting local arts and crafts.

Some 15km further on, a signposted turn-off leads to an **observation point** high above the immense **Roxburgh Dam** and power station, which, when completed in

1956, was New Zealand's most massive, and is still only pushed into second place by its cousin upriver at Clyde. From the lookout you get a great view over the shimmering turquoise of Lake Roxburgh, which backs up for over 30km.

Eight kilometres south of the dam, and hemmed in by orchards, farmland and open-cast coal mines, the bland former gold town of **ROXBURGH** occupies the flat western bank of the Clutha River at the foot of a precipitous hillside, in turn dominated by the parched Umbrella Mountains further west. Soon after the discovery of gold here in 1862, Roxburgh turned its attention to fruit growing. The vast orchards now yield bountiful crops of peaches, apricots, apples, raspberries and strawberries, all harvested by an annual influx of seasonal pickers; the season's surplus is sold from a phalanx of roadside stalls from early December through to May. Roxburgh is one of the only towns of significant size between Alexandra and Dunedin, and there are a couple of budget places to stay: the pool equipped *Roxburgh Family Motor Camp*, 11 Teviot St (☎03/446 8093; tent sites $8, dorms ①, cabins ②), in a quiet spot near the town centre; and the central *Villa Rose*, 79 Scotland St (☎03/446 8402; dorms ①, rooms ②), a backpackers in a villa equipped with dorms and several doubles, and frequented by orchard workers. For more luxury, continue 8km south along SH8 to *The Seed Farm* (☎03/446 6824, fax 446 6024; ⑤), a stone-built former hostelry with very comfortable en-suite B&B rooms (one with spa bath), and a **restaurant** serving the best food for some distance at moderate prices (lunches daily in summer and winter weekends; dinner by reservation).

From Roxburgh SH8 runs 24km south to **Raes Junction** (where SH90 spurs off southwest to Tapanui and Gore, see p.673), and continues 26km to **LAWRENCE**, Otago's original gold town. It's hard to believe that this sleepy farming town, with its population barely nudging 550, was once the scene of frenetic activity, as 12,000 gold-seekers scrambled to try their luck in the gold-rich Gabriels Gully, discovered by Gabriel Read on May 23, 1861 (see p.796). This short-lived boom (it was over in barely a year) is recalled in a scattering of Victorian buildings, hastily constructed in a variety of materials and styles.

The combined **visitor centre** and **Goldfields Museum** on Ross Place/SH8 (☎03/485 9222; Mon–Fri 9am–4.30pm, Sat & Sun 10am–4pm) brings something of those heady days to life through imaginative displays, rents out gold pans ($5 per day), and dispenses information on the town. An occasionally steep road walk to **Gabriels Gully** (8.5km round trip; 2.5hr return) is signposted nearby and leads through old gold workings before returning along a ridge with broad views of the town and its surroundings. Along the way the **Pick and Shovel Monument** commemorates Read and the pioneer miners, and a noticeboard illustrates how the area would have looked in its gold-mining heyday. A climb up the steep rise of **Jacob's Ladder** gives a good view of the gully, long since filled with tailings that reach nearly 20m in depth. From here the road follows the ridge, dips into the gully once more and returns to town.

If you are just passing through you may be satisfied with something to **eat** from one of the tearooms along the single main street, or more exalted fare from the smart new *Jazzed on Java* café, 26 Ross Place, which serves imaginative lunches, great coffee and has **Internet** access. For budget **accommodation** head for *Oban Guest House*, 1 Oban St (☎ & fax 03/485 9259, *obanhouse@xtra.co.nz*; dorms ①, rooms ②), a pleasant backpackers in a big old house; or the creekside *Gold Park Motor Camp*, 1km south of the main road on Harrington Street (☎03/485 9850; tents $12 per site, cabins ②), is a fairly basic campsite with cabins in a picturesque setting. Bed and breakfast can be sought just south of town on SH8 at *Marama* (☎ & fax 03/485 9638, *marama.k@xtra.co.nz*; ③–④) where there are two units which can be treated as self-contained or B&B. Guests have use of the tennis court, bikes fishing rods and even golf clubs.

From Lawrence it's another 33km southeast to the junction with SH1 on the east coast, which strikes north towards Dunedin or south to Balclutha (see p.666).

travel details

The following lists the direct scheduled **bus** services in the area and doesn't include the scores of tour buses which ply the Queenstown to Milford Sound route daily – see the relevant accounts for details of these.

Apart from scheduled services to the South Island's main centres, most **flights** are geared towards the lucrative Milford Sound market (see p.820), with nearly a dozen fiercely competitive companies flying out of Wanaka and Queenstown daily.

Buses

Alexandra to: Lawrence (8–10 daily; 1hr 15min); Queenstown (8–10 daily; 1hr 30min); Dunedin (7–9 daily; 3hr).

Arrowtown to: Queenstown (10 daily; 40min).

Lawrence to: Alexandra (8–10 daily; 1hr 15min); Cromwell (8–10 daily; 1hr 45min); Dunedin (6–8 daily; 1hr 20min)

Cromwell to: Alexandra (8-10 daily; 30min); Lawrence (8-10 daily; 1hr 45min); Queenstown (10 daily; 1hr); Wanaka (4 daily; 45–60min).

Glenorchy to: Queenstown (3–7 daily; 1hr).

Queenstown to: Alexandra (7-9 daily; 1hr 30min); Arrowtown (10 daily; 40min); Christchurch (6-7 daily; 7hr–9hr); Cromwell (7-9 daily; 1hr); Dunedin (6-8 daily; 4–5hr); Franz Joseph Glacier (1 daily; 8hr); Glenorchy (3–7 daily; 1hr); Invercargill (2-3 daily; 2hr 30min-5hr); Kingston (1-2 daily; 45min); Milford Sound (2 daily; 5hr 15min); Mount Cook (1 daily; 4hr); Te Anau (2 daily; 2hr 15min); Wanaka (1 daily; 1hr 45min).

Wanaka to: Christchurch (3-4 daily; 6hr 20min-9hr 20min); Cromwell (4 daily; 45min–1hr); Dunedin (2 daily; 4hr 15min); Queenstown (1 daily; 1hr 45min); Ranfurly (1 daily; 2hr).

Flights

Queenstown to: Auckland (3-4 daily; 2hr 30min); Christchurch (4-6 daily; 50min); Milford Sound (5 daily; 35min); Mount Cook (1 daily; 40min); Te Anau (3 daily; 30min); Wanaka (3 daily; 20min).

Wanaka to: Queenstown (3 daily; 20min).

CHAPTER FOURTEEN

FIORDLAND

For all New Zealand's scenic grandeur, no single region quite matches the concentration of stupendous landscapes found in its southwestern corner. Almost the entirety of **Fiordland** falls within the generous boundaries of the Fiordland National Park, a land of superlatives, boasting New Zealand's two deepest lakes, its highest rainfall and some of the world's rarest birds. This hasn't gone unnoticed at the United Nations, which has gathered pretty much the whole region — along with the Mount Aspiring National Park and parts of south Westland and the Mount Cook area — into the **Te Wahipounamu World Heritage Area**.

The **Fiordland National Park**, New Zealand's largest, stretches from Martin's Bay, once the site of New Zealand's remotest settlement, to the southern forests of Waitutu and Preservation Inlet where early gold prospectors set up a couple of short-lived towns. The 12,500 square kilometres of the park embraces breathtaking scenery, a raw and heroic landscape with deep, icy and mountain-fringed lakes in the east and a western coastline of fourteen hairline fiords gouged out over the last two million years by glaciers creaking off the tail of the Southern Alps.

Maori legend tells how the **fiords** were formed at the hands of the great god Tu-to-rakiwhanoa (see box on p.812), while scientific explanations point to a complex underlying geology, which evolved over the last 500 million years. When thick layers of seabed sediment were compressed and heated deep within the earth's crust, hard crystalline granite, gneiss and schist were formed. As the land and sea levels rose and fell, layers of softer sandstone and limestone were overlayed; during glacial periods, great ice sheets deepened the valleys and flattened their bases to create the classic U-shape, invaded by the sea lapping at their mouths.

After a few days in the inhospitable conditions created by Fiordland's copious rainfall and pestilent **sandflies** (*namu*), you'll appreciate why there is little evidence of permanent **Maori settlement** in these parts, though they certainly spent summers hunting here and passed through in search of greenstone (*pounamu*). **Cook** was equally suspicious of Fiordland when, in 1770, he sailed up the coast on his first voyage to New Zealand. Anchorages were hard to come by: the glowering sky put him off entering Dusky Sound; slight, shifting winds hardly encouraged entry into what he dubbed Doubtful Harbour; and, uncharacteristically, he missed Milford Sound altogether.

ACCOMMODATION PRICES

Accommodation listed in this guide has been categorized into one of nine price bands, as set out below. The rates quoted represent the **cheapest available** double or twin **room** – except for category ①, which are per-person rates for a dorm bed. Note that fees for **tent sites** and **DOC huts** (quoted in dollars) are also per-person, unless otherwise stated.

① under $20 per person	④ $60–80	⑦ $140–180
② under $40 per room	⑤ $80–100	⑧ $180–240
③ $40–60	⑥ $100–140	⑨ over $240

For more on accommodation, see p.34.

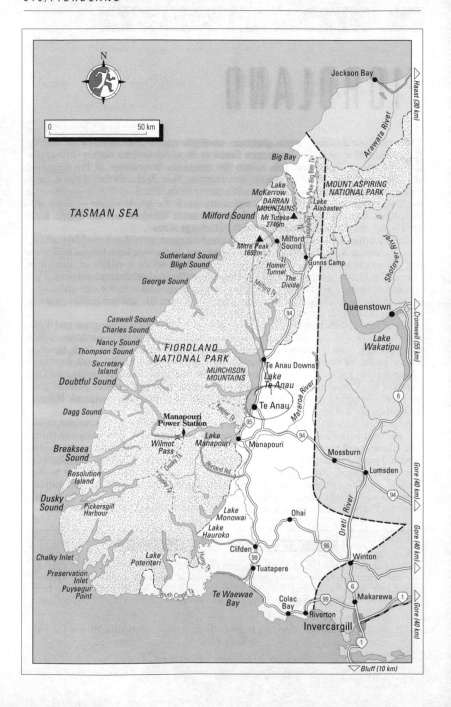

Paradoxically, for a region that's now the preserve of hardy trampers and a few anglers, the southern fiords region was once the best-charted in the country. Cook returned in 1773, after four months battling the southern oceans, and spent five weeks in Dusky Sound. His midshipman, George Vancouver, returned in 1791, with the first bloodthirsty sealers and whalers hot on his heels. Over the mountains, **Europeans** seized, or paid a pittance for, land on the eastern shores of lake Te Anau and Manapouri for the meagre grazing it offered, while **explorers** headed for the interior. More egotistical than their seafaring kin, they conferred their own names on the passes, waterfalls and valleys they came across – Donald Sutherland lent his name to New Zealand's highest waterfall and Quentin McKinnon scaled the Mackinnon Pass (but failed to persuade cartographers to spell his name correctly).

One feature of Fiordland you can't miss is the **rain**: the region is sodden for much of the year. Milford Sound is particularly favoured, being deluged with up to seven metres of rainfall a year – the second-highest in the world (after the mountains of Tahiti). Fortunately the area's settlements are in a relative rain shadow and receive less than half the precipitation of the coast. Despite its frequent soakings, **Milford Sound** sees a concentration of noisy traveller activity and is undoubtedly the most popular destination: wherever you look, ribbons of water plunge from hanging valleys directly into the fiords, where colonies of red and black coral grow and dolphins, fur seals and Fiordland crested penguins gambol. Many visitors on a flying visit from Queenstown see little else of Fiordland, but a greater sense of remoteness is gained by driving along the dramatically scenic **Milford Road** between the sound and the lakeside town of **Te Anau**. Better still, trudge here along the **Milford Track**, widely promoted as the "finest walk in the world", though others in the region – the **Hollyford Track**, the **Kepler Track** and the **Dusky Track** – constantly threaten to steal this title. A second lakeside town, **Manapouri**, is the springboard for trips to the West Arm hydroelectric power station, **Doubtful Sound** and the isolated fiords to the south. From Manapouri, the Southern Scenic Route winds through the western quarter of Southland through minor towns such as **Tuatapere**, a base for exploration of the **Waitutu Tracks** along the southwestern coast of the South Island.

Almost all **buses** in Fiordland ply the corridor from Queenstown through Te Anau to Milford Sound: most are tour buses (in various guises), stopping at scenic spots and regaling passengers with a jocular commentary, but others are scheduled services that disgorge trampers at the **trailheads**. Elsewhere, services are skeletal. Drivers are well disposed to giving **lifts**, though the Milford Road from Te Anau to Milford Sound is notoriously fallow ground for hitchers and, bearing in mind the number of diversions along the way, teaming up with like-minded souls and renting a car for the day, or joining a tour bus, is a much better bet. The only **flights** you are likely to take are the scenic jaunts from Milford Sound to Te Anau or Queenstown, although others do exist.

Te Anau

The growing town of **TE ANAU** straggles along the shores of its eponymous lake, one of New Zealand's deepest and most beautiful. To the west, the lake's watery fingers claw deep into bush-cloaked mountains so remote that their most celebrated inhabitant, the takahe (see box on p.816), was thought extinct for half a century. Civilization of sorts can be found on the lake's eastern side, predominantly in Te Anau, which has set itself up in recent years as a viable alternative to Queenstown because it is a more convenient access point to Milford Sound, Doubtful Sound, the scenic walks, lakes and mountains. The town is the major way station on the route to Milford Sound and serves as a base and recuperation spot for the numerous **tramps**, including several of the most famous and worthwhile in the country. Top of most people's list is the Milford Track,

TU-TO-RAKIWHANOA AND TE NAMU

Fiordland came into being when the great god **Tu-to-Rakiwhanoa** worked with his axe to carve the rough gashes of the southern fiords around Preservation Inlet and Dusky Sound, leaving Resolution and Secretary islands where his feet stood. His technique improved further north, where he formed the more sharply defined lines of Nancy Sound, Caswell Sound and, the most famous of all, Milford Sound (Piopiotahi), the summit of Tu's skill.

After creating this spectacular landscape, Tu was visited by Te-Hine-nui-to-po, the goddess of death, who feared that the vision created by Tu was so wonderful that people may wish to live in Piopiotahi forever. To remind humans of their mortality, she liberated *namu*, or **sandflies**. The place of this liberation, Te Namu-a-Te-Hine-nui-te-po, at the end of the Milford Track, is now known as Sandfly Point. And the pesky critters have certainly had the desired effect. In 1773, when James Cook entered Dusky Sound, he was already familiar with the sandfly:

The most mischievous animal here is the small black sandfly which are exceedingly numerous and are so troublesome that they exceed everything of the kind I ever met with, wherever they light they cause swelling and such an intolerable itching that it is not possible to refrain from scratching and at last ends in ulcers like the small Pox. The almost continual rain may be reckoned another inconvenience attending this Bay.

which is reached across the lake from here, as is the newer **Kepler Track**. To the north, the Milford Road passes The Key, the western end of the Routeburn, Greenstone and Caples tracks (see p.774), and beyond that there's the Hollyford Valley and its tramp to the Tasman Sea.

Arrival, information and transport

Buses either drop off around town or stop on the town's main shopping and restaurant street, known as Town Centre. The **visitor centre**, at the junction of Town Centre and Lake Front Drive (daily: Oct–March 8am–5pm; April–Sept 8.30am–5pm; ☎03/249 8900, *teanau1@fiordlandtravel.co.nz*), is part of the offices of **Fiordland Travel** (☎03/249 7416 & 0800/656 501), who run the visitor centre on Sundays and Mondays, and operate a number of cruises on Lake Te Anau, Lake Manapouri and Milford Sound. The **Fiordland National Park visitor centre** is 500m south along Lake Front Drive (daily: Dec–Feb 8am–8pm; March–April 8am–6pm; April–Oct 9am–4pm; Oct–Dec 8am–5pm; ☎03/249 7921, fax 249 7613, *www.fiordland.org.nz, fiordlandvc@doc.govt.nz*), and has a **Great Walks Booking Desk** (☎03/249 8514, fax 249 8515; July–late April 9am–4.30pm; Oct–Dec 8am–5pm), as well as plenty of general information. From here, the DOC run an excellent summer programme of hour-long evening talks ($3) plus half-day ($7–35), full-day ($40–85), evening ($30), overnight to Deep Cove ($120), conservation-themed trips, all of which need to be booked in advance. Bev's Tramping Gear Hire, 16 Homer St (May–Oct daily 9am–1pm & 5pm–7pm or by arrangement; ☎ & fax 03/249 7389) is the place to **rent** any **gear** you need: individual items are charged by the day, or you can save a few dollars with special packages aimed at Great Walks trampers.

Getting around Te Anau is no problem: everywhere in town is easily walkable, and there's a plethora of transport to the various trailheads. If you yearn for pedals, though, **bikes** can often be rented from your accommodation or, failing that, from Fiordland Mini Golf & Bike Hire, 7 Mokonui St (☎03/249 7211; $20 half day, $25 per day), whose tandems ($8 an hour) make exploring fun. For ranging slightly further afield (Manapouri springs to mind), local taxis/shuttles may fill the gap (**Te Anau**

Taxi and Tours ☎03/249 7777). Alternatively you can hire a **car**, though financially speaking you're almost certainly better with an organized trip. Rent-a-Dent (☎03/249 8363; $95 per day) does a good 24-hour deal aimed primarily at Milford Sound trippers, while the Mount Cook Te Anau Travel Office and Information Centre, Lake Front Drive, diagonally opposite the Fiordland Travel Visitor Centre (daily 8am–6pm; ☎03/249 7516, fax 249 7518) are a Hertz agent offering cars at similar rates; the latter doubles as the Manapouri Airport check-in desk and booking centre for onward travel and trips.

Accommodation

Good motels string the length of Lake Front Drive, while slightly more downmarket places line Quintin Drive a block back. There are also a number of reasonable budget options and a few good B&Bs. At more expensive places, **rates** tend to drop dramatically between June and August, and may be negotiable in the shoulder seasons (mid-April to May & Sept).

Hotels and motels

Alpenhorn Motel, 35–37 Quintin Drive (☎ & fax 03/249 7147). Well-priced concrete-block motel with full kitchen, in-house video and courtesy pick-up. ⑤–⑥.

Arran Motel, 64 Quintin Drive (☎ & fax 03/249 8826). Motel cum B&B with attractive en-suite rooms, some cooking facilities and the added bonus of either a cooked or continental breakfast, plus courtesy car to and from the local transport options. ⑤.

Campbell Autolodge, 42–44 Lake Front Drive (☎03/249 7546, fax 249 7814). Quite attractive place with lake views and flower-bedecked one-bedroom units, each with bath, shower and full kitchen, microwave, TV and phone. Bargain rates June–Aug, rest of the year. ⑤–⑦.

Edgewater XL Motel, 52 Lake Front Drive (☎03/249 7258, fax 249 8099). Fairly basic waterfront motel with one- and two-bedroom units, full kitchen, TV, barbecue and free use of canoes. ⑤–⑥.

Explorer Motor Lodge, 6 Cleddau St (☎03/249 7156, fax 249 7149). These spacious studios and one-bedroom units come complete with microwaves. The decor is slightly faded and quirky, with walls at weird angles. Discounts during the off-season. ⑤–⑦.

Lakefront Lodge, 58 Lake Front Drive (☎ & fax 03/249 7728, *anne@lakefront.co.nz*). Brand-new, luxurious motel units, some with spa bath and all with every convenience, including room service. Prices drop considerably outside the Oct–April season. ⑥–⑦.

B&Bs and homestays

House of Wood, 44 Moana Crescent (☎03/249 8404, fax 249 7676). Four tastefully decorated, modern rooms, one with bathroom, make up this fine homestay, which takes its design cues from an alpine chalet. Guests share the welcoming hosts' cosy lounge and it is only two minutes' walk from the town centre. ⑤–⑥.

Kepler Cottage, William Steven Rd off the Te Anau, Manapouri Highway, just a couple of kilometres from town (☎03/249 7185, fax 249 7186, *kepler@teanau.co.nz*). A very comfortable modern, rural homestay on the edge of the town limits, with plenty of space and friendly hosts. ⑤.

Bob & Nancy Marshall, 13 Fergus Square (☎ & fax 03/249 8241). Pleasant, peaceful homestay rooms and a self-contained apartment five minutes' walk from town. Cooked breakfast is accompanied by fresh home-made bread and dinners are available by prior arrangement. Homestay ⑤, apartment ⑥.

The Cat's Whiskers, 2 Lake Front Drive (☎ & fax 03/249 8112). Excellent and very welcoming lakeside guesthouse with three pleasantly decorated en-suite rooms: one with a bath, and all with TV and full cooked breakfast. ⑦.

Hostels and campsites

Fiordland Holiday Park, Milford Rd, 2km east (☎ & fax 03/249 7059, *fiordland.holiday.park@xtra .co.nz*). Small attractive site with a range of well-priced cabins and tourist flats. A courtesy bus does

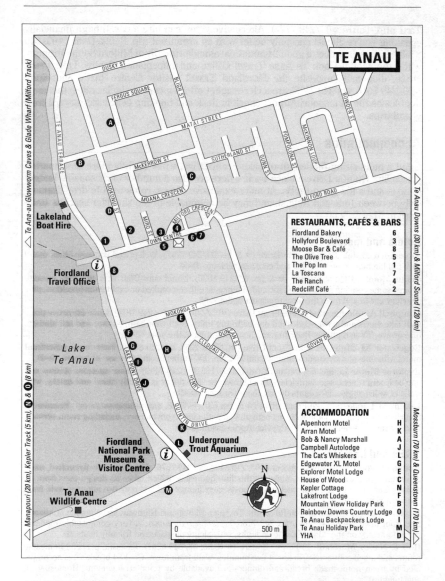

TE ANAU

Te Ana-au Glowworm Caves & Glade Wharf (Milford Track)

Te Anau Downs (30 km) & Milford Sound (120 km)

Mossburn (70 km) & Queenstown (170 km)

Manapouri (20 km), Kepler Track (5 km), ⓝ & ⓞ *(8 km)*

Lakeland
Boat Hire

Fiordland
Travel Office

*Lake
Te Anau*

Fiordland
National Park
Museum &
Visitor Centre

Te Anau
Wildlife Centre

Underground
Trout Aquarium

DUSKY ST

FERGUS SQUARE

BLIGH ST

MATAI STREET

BOWDEN ST

MCKERROW ST

SUTHERLAND ST

GUNN S

POMPOLONA ST

MCKINNON LODGE

MOANA CRESCENT

MILFORD ROAD

MILFORD CRESCENT

MIRO ST

MOKONUI ST

TE ANAU TERRACE

TOWN CENTRE

MOKOROA ST

BOWEN ST

DUNCAN ST

CLEDDAU ST

GOVAN DR

LAKE FRONT DRIVE

HENRY ST

QUINTIN DRIVE

N

0   500 m

RESTAURANTS, CAFÉS & BARS	
Fiordland Bakery	6
Hollyford Boulevard	3
Moose Bar & Café	8
The Olive Tree	5
The Pop Inn	1
La Toscana	7
The Ranch	4
Redcliff Café	2

ACCOMMODATION	
Alpenhorn Motel	H
Arran Motel	K
Bob & Nancy Marshall	A
Campbell Autolodge	J
The Cat's Whiskers	L
Edgewater XL Motel	G
Explorer Motel Lodge	E
House of Wood	C
Kepler Cottage	N
Lakefront Lodge	F
Mountain View Holiday Park	B
Rainbow Downs Country Lodge	O
Te Anau Backpackers Lodge	I
Te Anau Holiday Park	M
YHA	D

daily Kepler Track drop-offs and there's free gear storage. Tent & powered sites $7, cabins & flats ②–③.

Mountain View Holiday Park, 128 Te Anau Terrace (☎ & fax 03/249 7462). Cramped, central park that's most in demand for its fine on-site accommodation. Tent & powered sites $10, cabins & units ②–④.

Rainbow Downs Country Lodge, Mount Yorke Rd, 8km south at Rainbow Reach (☎ & fax 03/249 8006). En-suite units with excellent views in a lovely lodge hand-built from natural timbers and with a licensed à la carte restaurant and bar on site. Horse trekking along the Waiau River is also available. Dorms ①, rooms ③.

Te Anau Backpackers Lodge, 48 Lake Front Drive (☎03/249 7713, fax 249 8319, *hostel@xtra .co.nz*). Shabby former motel saved by a friendly atmosphere and small dorms, mostly with their own bathroom and kitchen. They're well set up for trampers, being five minutes' walk from the DOC office; what's more, pots and cutlery are available on free loan, gear is stored at no charge, and baggage can be sent on to Queenstown for about $5 per piece. As well as dorms, there are nice doubles and free use of shonky bikes. Dorms ①, rooms ③.

Te Anau Holiday Park, Manapouri Rd, 1km south (☎03/249 7457, fax 249 7536). Te Anau's largest site, with spacious camping areas, dorms, and a range of cabins and units. There are also basic bikes for rent ($5 per hour), a sauna ($5 for 30min) and the *Jintz* bar and grill (Oct–April) to keep you fed and amused. Tent sites $10, powered sites $11, dorms ①, cabins ②, motel units ⑥.

YHA, Mokonui St, (☎ & fax 03/249 7847, *yhatanau@yha.org.nz*), within one block of the lake and Town Centre. This modern comfortable hostel is now the best place to stay in town because it has been moved about 1km towards the centre and turned into a two-storey building with large dorms, double rooms, free gear storage and a lawn for camping. Tent sites $10, dorms ①, rooms ③.

Sights and activities

There is little in Te Anau itself to distract you from simply admiring the scenery across the lake and taking gentle strolls along its shore. Ten minutes' walk south, a statue of Milford Track explorer Quintin McKinnon heralds the Fiordland National Park visitor centre (daily: Dec–Feb 8am–8pm; March–April 8am–6pm; April–Oct 9am–4pm; Oct–Dec 8am–5pm), where a short video (20min; $3) introduces the **Fiordland National Park Visitor Centre and Museum** (same hours; free), with its fascinating displays on the construction of the Homer Tunnel and the undersea life of the national park, including an eighteenth-century cannon salvaged from Dusky Sound.

Across the road you can drop $1 in a turnstile to view the dismal tank of fish which masquerades as the **Underground Trout Aquarium**, or stroll on to the **Lake Henry Walk** in the Ivor Wilson Park planted with native and exotic trees (about 20min circular walk). Once back at the visitor centre head a kilometre or so along the Te Anau lakeside path to the DOC's **Te Anau Wildlife Centre**, 178 Manapouri Rd (unrestricted entry; $1 donation box), where you can amble through the park-like setting and see parakeets, morepork and other bush birds, notably the takahe in specially constructed enclosures (see box overleaf for more on the centre's ground-breaking work). If you're feeling particularly energetic then follow the path past the control gates at Dock Bay and head up along the shores of Lake Te Anau toward Brod Bay (1hr 30min one way, or water taxi to the bay and walk back ☎03/249 8364; $15); or better still in the opposite direction along the Waiau River, past the Balloon Loop, dropping in at the wetland viewing platform (for twitchers) and on to the Shallow Bay Hut (where you can use the toilets), overlooking Lake Manapouri (about 17km; 4hr one way), and return by taxi (see p.813).

Te Anau's main paying attraction is the **Te An-au Glow Worm Caves** (guided tours only: Sept–May daily 2pm & 8.15pm; June–Aug daily 2pm & 6.45pm; around 2hr 30min; $39–44), although even this is rather ad hoc and old-fashioned in its approach, with obtrusive concrete gangways and exposed electrical junction boxes obstructing the views. True, there are a couple of nice waterfalls and the glow-worm grotto is impressive, but its main appeal lies in its ability to occupy long evenings in Te Anau stopping you spending all your cash in the local bars. A thirty-minute boat trip takes you across to the western side of Lake Te Anau where you are herded into a visitor centre and taken through the caves in small groups on punts, spending thirty minutes in a 200-metre length of the Aurora cave system which tunnels under the Murchison Mountains.

A fairly recent addition to activities from the town is the **Highride 4xWheeler Adventure** (☎03/249 8599 & 0800/822 882 or book at the visitor centre), a three-hour guided tour, including the shuttle from Te Anau, that takes in the high backcountry and includes some stunning views of lakes Manapouri and Te Anau. No experience is

---

THE TAKAHE

For half a century the flightless blue-green **takahe** (*Notornis mantelli*) was thought to be extinct. These plump, turkey-like birds – close relatives of the ubiquitous pukeko – were once common throughout New Zealand. By the time Maori arrived, however, their territory had become restricted to the southern extremities of the South Island. When Europeans came, only a few were spotted by early settlers in Fiordland. No sightings were recorded after 1898; the few trampers and ornithologists who claimed to have seen its tracks or heard the takahe's call in remote Fiordland valleys were dismissed as cranks.

One keen birder, **Geoffrey Orbell**, pieced together the sketchy evidence and concentrated his search on the 500 square kilometres of the **Murchison Mountains**, a virtual island surrounded on three sides by the western arms of Lake Te Anau and on the fourth by the Main Divide. In 1948, he was rewarded with the first takahe sighting in fifty years. However, the few remaining birds seemed doomed: deer were merrily chomping their way through the grasses on which the takahe relied. Culling of the deer population averted the immediate crisis and management programmes brought takahe numbers to 160 by the early 1990s, but a couple of harsh winters and a plague of stoats have since knocked them back by about a third.

Meanwhile, studies at the **Burwood Bush** rearing facility (closed to the public), in the Red Tussock Conservation Area east of Te Anau, have shown that takahe often lay three eggs but seldom manage to raise more than one chick. DOC officers now enter the Murchison Mountains each November to manipulate the **egg quota** so that each pair has only one viable egg to hatch. Any "surplus" eggs are removed to Burwood Bush, where rearing techniques pioneered here and at the **Te Anau Wildlife Centre** (see previous page) are employed to raise takahe for release back into the wild. Taped takahe noises encourage the chicks to hatch; then, to prevent them imprinting on their carers, the chicks are fed using **hand puppets** designed to look like adult takahe. And to help them hold their own against marauding stoats, young birds have their defensive instincts reawoken by watching DOC "Punch and Judy" shows, featuring stuffed stoats and juvenile takahe glove puppets.

Fear of having all their eggs in one basket has prompted the DOC to establish several takahe populations on predator-free **sanctuary islands** – Maud Island in the Marlborough Sounds, Mana Island and Kapiti Island (both northwest of Wellington), and Tiritiri Matangi in Auckland's Hauraki Gulf – where the birds appear to be breeding well.

---

necessary but make sure you feel confident on your bike before you agree to get under way on the trip proper ($148; 2 daily).

In Te Anau the **Tawaki Dive Company**, 44 Caswell St (☎ & fax 03/249 9006, *sarahdave@tawakidive.co.nz*) offer one of the more exciting and rewarding **scuba** trips (for those who have PADI or SSI dive qualification) in Milford Sound, as well as four to five day PADI courses. The beauty of diving in the Sounds is that the layer of tannin-stained fresh water on top of the sea water blocks out much of the light, making creatures and plants, used to certain conditions, suppose they are deeper than they actually are, thus enabling the divers to see them (visibility can be 10m easily) without having to plumb the extreme depths. Some of the rarities in Milford Sound's confined catchment area are black coral (white but with a black skeleton), brachiopods (living dinosaurs), purple and white nudribranchs, scarlet wrasse and telescope fish (trips from Te Anau $220, full day; lunch $10; maximum 4; plus opportunities to explore the Milford–Te Anau Rd on the return journey).

Lake cruises and flights

Having exhausted the possibilities on shore, it pays to get **cruising** on the lake. If you're going tramping, this can best be accomplished en route to the start of the Kepler or Milford tracks (see below & p.824). The operators who provide trailhead transport also provide a number of other trips. Sinbad Cruises (☎03/249 7106) run the usual to Milford and Kepler and scenic cruises of the lake ($45), evening cruises ($45), overnight specials ($55) and Mount Luxmore Hut day walks on the Kepler ($25) all on the idiosyncratic, home-made ketch *Manuska*, under the captaincy of Murray – a chatty, rough and ready, knowledgeable, lake-version of the typical Kiwi bushman. Fiordland Travel (☎0800/656 501) have acquired the old Bluff-Stewart Island ferry, a powerful catamaran, which does drop-offs and cruises, including a trip for day walkers on the Milford Track ($105) in association with Trips'n'Tramps (☎03/249 7081, *trips@teanau.co.nz*). Fiordland Travel also offer guided trips on the Eglinton River in little "river bugs", one-person inflatable rafts, lasting 4hr, about 2hr in the water ($79). Fiordland Wilderness Experiences (☎03/249 7700 & 0800/200 434, fax 249 7768, *fiordland.sea.kayak@clear.net.nz*) will get you paddling either on guided trips or independently (**kayak rental** about $45 a day) on lakes Te Anau or Manapouri as well as their more spectacular trips to Doubtful, Milford and Dusky sounds. Their one-day guided trip ($90) on Te Anau or Manapouri offers manageable paddling and stunning views at an easily attainable level. Lakeland Boat Hire, The Boat Hire Wharf, Te Anau Terrace between Dusky Street and Matai Street (☎03/249 8364), operate a water taxi to the Brod Bay on the Kepler Track for walkers ($15 one way, $25 return) and **rent** out small **catamarans** ($25; 1hr), **pedaloes** or **canoes** for a gentle tootle along the banks in the summer (around $15; 1hr).

For an aerial view of southern Fiordland or a quick route to the track heads, try **fixed-wing flights** with Waterwings Airways, Lake Front Drive (☎03/249 7405, fax 249 7939), who run float planes into Supper Cove and fly just about anywhere – from local runs (10min; $43) to Kepler Track overflights (20min; $80), Milford Sound overflights ($187), Doubtful Sound overflights (40min; $153), and a fly'n'boat option which involves jetboating down the Waiau River to Lake Manapouri and then flying back to Te Anau via the hidden lakes. Air Fiordland (☎03/249 7505, fax 03/249 7080) use more conventional planes and concentrate more on Milford Sound, offering various combinations of flights, bus rides, kayak trips and cruises, as well as trips over Doubtful Sound, Mount Aspiring and Lake Wanaka ($150–225).

The waterside helipad of Southern Lakes Helicopters, Lake Front Drive (☎03/249 7167, fax 249 7267, *slheli@teanau.co.nz*), launches several **helicopter flights** (from $90) and flights to Milford, Doubtful and Dusky sounds with landings in a narrow canyon known as Campbell's Kingdom or on snow high in the hills. They're also responsible for the **Triple Buzz** ($100–155), a flight/walk/cruise combination taking you over the lake to Mount Luxmore Hut or Forest Burn, both on the Kepler Track, followed by a downhill walk to Brod Bay and a boat ride back to Te Anau. Fiordland Helicopters (☎03/249 7575, fax 249 7595, *fiord.heli@xtra.co.nz*) offer a variety of scenic trips from Te Anau (ten minutes to over an hour) and track transport, with prices depending on numbers.

The Kepler Track

The **Kepler Track** (67km; 3–4 days), finished in 1988, was intended to take some of the load off the Milford and Routeburn tracks. Tracing a wide loop through the Kepler Mountains on the western side of Lake Te Anau, the track takes in one full day of exposed sub-Alpine ridge walking and some lovely virgin beech forest, and has the added advantage of being easily accessible (on foot if you are keen) from Te Anau. Throughout its length it is well graded and maintained but the long haul up to Mount Luxmore Hut makes this a strenuous tramp, and sections can be closed after snowfalls. The DOC's *Kepler Track* leaflet ($1) is adequate, but for more detailed information, consult the 1:50,000 *Kepler Track Trackmap*.

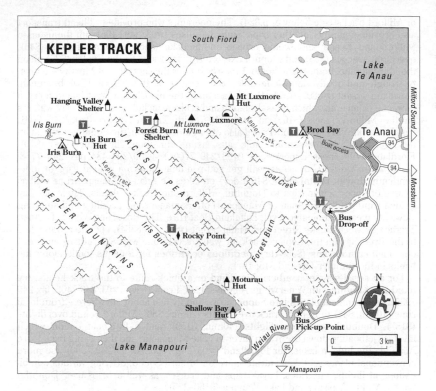

Access and accommodation

The Kepler Track is one of the Great Walks and through the summer season (Nov to mid-April) its three main **huts** ($15, $20 if purchased on the track, 3-night package $40) – Mount Luxmore (60 bunks), Iris Burn (60 bunks) and Moturau (40 bunks) – all come with a warden, gas rings and flush toilets. You don't need to book specific nights in particular huts, but a Great Walks hut **pass** for the required number of nights must be bought in advance from the Great Walks Booking Desks in Te Anau, Glenorchy or Queenstown. During the winter, these huts lose their warden and their gas rings and revert to Category 3 ($5). In addition there is the simple Shallow Bay Hut ($5), just off the track beside Lake Manapouri.

Camping ($6, $8 if bought on the track) is permitted at only two places, Brod Bay and Iris Burn, making for one very short and two very long days – assuming you walk the track anti-clockwise – but getting the bulk of the climbing over with on the first long day.

Trailhead transport

It is possible to start the Kepler from Te Anau, but most people avoid the 5km walk around the southern end of Lake Te Anau by taking the Fiordland Tracknet **shuttle bus** (☎03/249 7777; mid-Oct to April; $5), which picks up at accommodation around town at 8.30am and 9.30am and drops off at the Control Gates, the source of the Waiau River. On the return leg, most trampers stop 11km short of the Control Gates at the swingbridge over the Waiau's Rainbow Reach. Fiordland Tracknet pick up here at 10am, 3pm and 5pm and charge $8 back to Te Anau.

You can skip another 5km of lakeside walking by cutting across Lake Te Anau to Brod Bay: Lakeland Boat Hire (☎03/249 8364) operate an early boat departing from the Te Anau wharf at 8.30am and 9.30am; and Sinbad Cruises (☎03/249 7106) sail the *Manuska* across at 9am. Both services charge $15.

The route

If you're setting out from Te Anau, head south along Lake Front Drive, then right, following the lakeshore and taking the first right to the Control Gates. From the **Control Gates to Brod Bay** (5.5km; 1hr–1hr 30min; flat) the track follows the lakeshore around Dock Bay and over Coal Creek, passing through predominantly beech and kamahi forests but with a fine stand of tree ferns. Brod Bay has good swimming off a sandy beach and makes a lovely place to camp. Non-campers must press on from **Brod Bay to Mount Luxmore Hut** (8.5km; 3–4hr; 880m ascent), following a signpost midway along the beach. The path climbs fairly steeply for a couple of hours to limestone bluffs, from where it is almost another hour to the bushline and fine views over Te Anau and Manapouri lakes and the surrounding mountains. The hut is almost an hour from the bushline.

With the hard ascent done, the section from **Mount Luxmore Hut to Iris Burn Hut** (19km; 5–6hr; 300m ascent, 900m descent) is testing but OK by comparison. Overall it makes a long day, and this is an exposed, high-level section where any hint of bad weather should be treated seriously. The track climbs to just below the summit of Mount Luxmore (from where you can scramble up to the 1471m peak), then descends to Forest Burn Shelter before following a ridge to Hanging Valley Shelter and turning sharply south to trace another open ridge towards Iris Burn. The Iris Burn is reached by zigzagging west into the forested Hanging Valley then following the stream to the hut and campsite in a large tussock clearing.

The track from **Iris Burn Hut to Moturau Hut** (17km; 4–6hr; 300m descent) starts behind the Iris Burn Hut and makes a steady descent through beech forest and riverside clearings beside Iris Burn. About halfway you pass toilets at Rocky Point, then enter a short gorge before hugging the river for several magical kilometres. Just before Iris Burn spills into Lake Manapouri, the track swings east and skirts Shallow Bay to the pleasant lakeside Moturau Hut. The hut is seldom full since some trampers prefer the simpler and older **Shallow Bay Hut** (Cat 4; free; 6 bunks) about forty minutes further on, while others continue from **Moturau Hut to Rainbow Reach** (6km; 1hr 30min; flat) through gentle beech forest to catch the last shuttle bus.

Walkers who persevere with the final stretch along the Waiau River from **Rainbow Reach to the Control Gates** (11km; 2–3hr; negligible ascent) are in for an easy forest walk with opportunities for fishing and swimming.

Eating and drinking

Diners have little culinary genius to look forward to in Te Anau, with a couple of café exceptions, but there are plenty of **no-frills places** selling decent food at reasonable prices, either in the many bars and restaurants within the tourist hotels or the more mundane, purpose-built eateries. The **drinking** picture is much the same, and entertainment is mostly BYO.

Fiordland Bakery, Town Centre, about 10m from *La Toscana*. Produces some excellent bread for the tracks (lasting 3–4 days), particularly the four-grain which includes flax seeds. The bakery café also offers a generous all-day breakfast (around $7). Mon–Sat 7am–4pm.

Hollyford Boulevard, Town Centre. Reasonably priced pseudo-American burger and grills joint which, under threat of litigation, was forced to change its name from the infinitely more catchy Planet Hollyford. Licensed.

Kepler's Family Restaurant, Town Centre. This down-home family restaurant offers succulent open burgers with fries ($9–15), grills and lovely seafood mains ($19–25). Licensed.

Moose Bar & Café, Lake Front Drive. Standard pub meals for lunch and dinner, enlivened by the bar atmosphere and busy at weekends.

The Olive Tree Café, 52 Town Centre. Licensed and open all day this stylish café produces some tangy Greek salads, light omelettes, work-a-day pizzas and some filling and imaginative main meals all for under $20.

The Pop Inn, 92 Tenau Terrace. A lakeside café that opens early with cheap bagels, home-made muffins and pies and an endless supply of chips, as well as cooked breakfasts. They also do snack boxes for trips and offer Internet access.

The Ranch, Milford Rd. Rumbustious place for expensive but expansive ribs and grills; better as a lively place to drink.

Redcliff Café, 12 Mokonui St (☎03/249 7431). Highly regarded evening favourite serving a limited but excellent range of modern Kiwi variations on Pacific Rim cuisine, and in quantities to satisfy trampers' appetites. Their imaginative warm salads are a speciality. The cosy bar area acts as a local meeting spot and is a good place to drop by for a coffee. Licensed.

La Toscana, 108 Town Centre. Reasonable Italian restaurant that tries hard to please with a wide range of good pizza and pasta dishes. Licensed & BYO, plus takeaway.

Milford Sound and around

Milford Sound is the most northerly and most celebrated of Fiordland's fifteen fiords, with vertical sides towering 1200m above the sea and waterfalls plunging from hanging valleys. While many of the other fiords approach Milford for their spectacular **beauty**, none come close for **accessibility** which has perhaps in recent years been its downfall. Before the road was pushed through in 1952 visitors had to arrive by boat or walk the much-lauded **Milford Track** to reach the head of the fiord, but the opening of the Homer Tunnel paved the way for the phalanx of tourist buses that disgorge patrons onto fiord cruises. The tiny little airport hardly seems to rest for a second as planes buzz angrily in and out, while all day in the summer and around the middle of the day during spring and winter, the crowds can certainly detract from the grandeur of the spot – but don't let that, or anything else for that matter, put you off. Even torrential rain adds to the atmosphere of this magical place, as an ethereal mist descends, periodically lifting to reveal the waterfalls at their thunderous best.

Like the other sounds, Milford is a drowned glacial rather than a river valley, making it technically a fiord. Maori know it as **Piopiotahi** ("the single thrush"), and attribute its creation to the god Tu-to-rakiwhanoa, who was called away before he could carve a route into the interior, leaving high rock walls. These precipitous routes are now known as the Homer and Mackinnon passes, but were probably first used by Maori who came here to collect *pounamu*. The first European to sail into Piopiotahi was probably sealer John Grono who, in 1823, named the fiord Milford Haven after his home port in south Wales. The main river flowing into the Welsh Milford was the Cleddau, so naturally the river at the head of the fiord took that name too.

The earliest settler was Scot **Donald Sutherland**, who arrived with his dog, John O'Groat, in 1877; he promptly set a series of thatched huts beside the freshwater basin of what he called the "City of Milford", funding his explorations by guiding the small number of visitors who had heard tell of the scenic wonder hereabouts. By 1890 Sutherland had married a Dunedin widow, Elizabeth Samuel, and together they built a twelve-room hotel to serve the growing number of steamer passengers – "ashfelters" (city dwellers) and "shadow catchers" (photographers) – who flocked to admire the beauty of his remote home and to walk the newly opened Milford Track.

The predations of today's influx of visitors and the operation of a small fishing fleet have necessitated strategies to preserve the fiord's **fragile ecosystem**. Like all fiords, Milford Sound has an Entrance Sill at its mouth, in this case only 70m below the surface as compared to the deepest point of almost 450m. This effectively cuts off much of

---

SHEEP STATIONS, MONORAILS AND SOGGY ROADS

A visit to **Milford Sound** is undoubtedly one of the highlights of most visitors' South Island experience. For most, the **journey** to this remote spot is half the enjoyment, but tour operators catering to short-stay-must-see tourists are constantly on the lookout for new ways to get punters in and out quickly. Milford Sound's topography largely prevents much greater development of the airport, so developers have concentrated on two **hare-brained schemes**: shortening the Queenstown to Milford journey by means of a monorail; and linking the Hollyford Valley with Jackson Bay and Haast to the north. If either of these schemes goes ahead, the dynamics of the whole region will be drastically changed.

The **monorail** plan was originally mooted by the Ngai Tahu *iwi*, which claims land rights over much of the Greenstone Valley, the shortest route from Queenstown to The Divide, just 40km east of Milford Sound. An alliance of greenies and outdoor enthusiasts – recognizable from their bumper stickers proclaiming "Hands off the Greenstone Valley" – raised enough public concern to force the shelving of the plans in 1994. But by 1996 a **second** and more feasible **proposal**, again backed by the Ngai Tahu, was on the table: a $120-million state-of-the-art monorail would link Mount Nicholas Station, at the southwestern crook of Lake Wakatipu, with the Milford Road 50km north of Te Anau, via the Von and Mararoa valleys. Detractors claim that the inconvenience of transferring between catamaran, monorail and bus would offset any time gains, while investors still need to obtain consent for a 30-kilometre section of the route which passes through the DOC-managed Snowdon State Forest. For every supporter of the venture in Queenstown, there is an opponent in Te Anau – a town that relies as heavily on Milford-bound traffic for its livelihood as Queenstown does on its jetboating, bungy-jumping reputation.

The **road proposal** seems less likely to go ahead. The current **Hollyford Valley Road** was approved in 1936, but only 16km of it were built as a spur off the SH94 to Milford. Between the Hollyford end of this spur and existing roads around Jackson Bay lie around 80km of valley floor, across which a new toll-road could be constructed. In its favour, the route is generally flat, but the region is prone to extreme flooding. In this case it is business people in Queenstown who oppose the plans, fearing that tourists would travel the West Coast, see Milford Sound and visit Queenstown briefly – if at all.

---

the natural recirculation of water and hinders mixing of sea water and the vast quantities of fresh water that pour into the fiord. The less-dense tannin-stained fresh, surface layer (up to 10m deep) builds up, further diminishing the penetration of light, which is already reduced by the all-day shadow cast by the fiord walls. The result is a relatively barren inter-tidal zone that protects a narrow – but wonderfully rich and extremely fragile – band of light-shy red and black **corals**; these normally grow only at much greater depths, but thrive here in the dark conditions. Unfortunately, Milford's fishing fleet use crayfish pots, which tend to shear off anything that grows on the fiord's walls. A marine reserve has been set up along the northeastern shore, where all such activity is prohibited, but really this is far too small and conservation groups are campaigning for its extension.

The road to Milford Sound

The 120-kilometre road from Te Anau to Milford Sound has to be one of the world's finest, though this hasn't stopped folk from hatching outlandish plans to circumvent it (see box above). This two-hour drive can easily take a day if you grab every photo opportunity. Anywhere else the initial drive beside Lake Te Anau would be considered obscenely scenic, but it is nothing compared to the Eglinton Valley, where the road penetrates into steeper, bush-clad mountains and winds through a sub-alpine wonderland

THE HOLLYFORD TRACK

The DOC's Hollyford Valley *leaflet ($1) is fine for following the track, though the 1:75,000* Hollyford Track Trackmap *is more detailed.*

The **Hollyford Track** (54 km; 4 days) is long, but mostly flat, following Fiordland's longest valley from the end of the Hollyford Valley road to Martins Bay. The track suffers from being essentially a **one-way tramp**, requiring four days' backtracking – unless you're flash enough to fly out from the airstrip at Martins Bay or tough enough to continue around a long, difficult and remote loop known as the **Big Bay–Pyke route** (9–10 days total; consult the DOC's *Big Bay–Pyke Route* leaflet for details). The joy of the Hollyford is not in the sense of achievement that comes from scaling alpine passes, but in the appreciation of the dramatic mountain **scenery** and the kahikatea, rimu and matai **bush** with an understorey of wineberry, fuchsia and ferns. At Martins Bay, Long Reef has a resident **fur seal** colony, and from September to December you might spot rare Fiordland crested **penguins** (*tawaki*) nesting among the scrub and rocks.

Trampers who hate carrying a big pack, prefer more comfortable lodgings and having hearty meals cooked for them should consider a **guided walk** with Hollyford Valley Walk, PO Box 360, Queenstown (☎03/442 3760 & 0800/832 226): small groups are led by knowledgeable guides, and nights are spent at the relatively luxurious Martins Bay Lodge and the simpler Pyke Lodge (3–4 days plus fly-out $1190–1470); those in a mad rush can even fly from Queenstown, see the seal colonies, jetboat upriver for a night at the Martins Bay Lodge and fly back to Queenstown for around $400.

ACCOMMODATION AND ACCESS

The six Category 3 DOC **huts** ($5) are each equipped with platform bunks, mattresses, water and toilets and do not need to be booked, though hut tickets or an annual hut pass should be bought in advance.

Buses on the Te Anau–Milford run will drop off at Marian Corner, where the Hollyford and Milford roads part company, or head down to the end of the Hollyford Road, by arrangement. Hollyford Track (☎03/249 9080 & 0800/832 226) run most mornings between November and May, to the Road End, as does Fiordland Tracknet (☎03/249

to the bare rock walls of the seemingly impassable head of the Hollyford River. The Homer Tunnel then cuts through to the steep Cleddau Valley, the home straight down to Milford Sound.

Maori parties must have long used this route on their way to seek *pounamu* at Anita Bay on Milford Sound, but no road existed until two hundred unemployment-relief workers with shovels and wheelbarrows were put on the job in 1929. The greatest challenge was to puncture the headwall of the Hollyford Valley: work on the 1200-metre-long **Homer Tunnel** began in 1935, but was badly planned from the start. Working at a one-in-ten downhill gradient, the builders soon hit water and were forced to pump out continuously; a pilot tunnel allowing the water to drain westwards was finished in 1948 – when the whole project was relegated to the too-hard basket until 1952. After a concerted push, the road was finally completed in 1953, and officially inaugurated the following year, opening up Milford Sound to road traffic for the first time.

Despite recent improvements, such as passing bays for buses, the tunnel remains **rough-hewn**, forbiddingly dark and is often choked with diesel fumes (which make the headlights of oncoming vehicles appear to change from red to yellow to white). The sub-alpine section of the road is one of the world's most **avalanche-prone**. Since the last death on the road, in 1984, there has been a sophisticated avalanche-monitoring system in place and, if necessary, explosives are dropped from helicopters to loosen dangerous accumulations of snow while the road is closed. This mostly happens between May and November, when motorists are required to carry chains (available

7777) from mid-October to April; both charge $35, or $30 to the Hollyford Road turn-off, leaving an extra 16km to tramp. Hollyford Track also operate **flights** (which must be pre-booked) to and from Martins Bay or the Hollyford Airstrip (both $280); or, since many people fly out from Martins Bay, you can fly standby from Milford Sound – and walk the track in reverse – for under $95. Both Air Fiordland (☎03/249 7505; $280 for two) and Milford Sound Helicopters (☎03/249 7845; $535 for four) offer the same services to the bay and airstrip.

Finally, you can avoid most of the long day's walk beside the attractive but samey Lake McKerrow with Hollyford Track's **jetboat service** (4–7 people; $65 each for four or more) to the head of Lake McKerrow; if you're really pushed for time, a similarly priced run up the Hollyford River can further reduce the walk by a day.

THE ROUTE

The track from **Road End to Hidden Falls Hut** (9km; 2hr 30min–3hr; negligible ascent) follows a disused section of road which soon crumbles into a track with some riverbank walking to the Hidden Falls Hut (20 bunks). Keen walkers will probably want to push on from **Hidden Falls Hut to Alabaster Hut** (11km; 3–4hr; 100m ascent) through ribbonwood and beech to Little Homer Saddle and past Little Homer Falls. From **Alabaster Hut to Demon Trail Hut** (13km; 3–4hr; negligible ascent), you soon pass a side track to the nicely sited McKerrow Island Hut (20 bunks), before continuing beside Lake Alabaster to Demon Trail Hut (12 bunks). The section from **Demon Trail Hut to Hokuri Hut** (10km; 5–6hr; 100m ascent) is probably the toughest on the walk, following the shore of Lake McKerrow on rough ground with some tricky stream crossings, to Hokuri Hut (12 bunks). The path continues from **Hokuri Hut to Martins Bay Hut** (11km; 4–5hr; negligible ascent), by way of the scant remains of Jamestown, a cattle-ranching settlement that prospered briefly in the 1870s. Passing the small airstrip served by Hollyford Track's flights, you'll stumble across some of the dozen dwellings that comprise Martins Bay; no one lives here permanently, but they are used by opportunistic whitebaiters and hunters. Continuing parallel to Martins Bay, and occasionally glimpsing the Hollyford River through wind-shorn trees, you reach the new Martins Bay Hut (20 bunks).

from service stations in Te Anau for around $25). Whatever the season, drivers should bear in mind that there is heavy bus traffic, which tends to be Milford-bound from around 11am to noon and Te Anau-bound between 3 and 5pm. Apart from the store in the Hollyford Valley, 8km off your route, there is nowhere to buy **food** until you reach Milford, so be prepared. Also, buying petrol at Milford is an exercise in throwing money away so fill up your car before you start your journey.

Along the road there are a dozen simple DOC **campsites** ($5), almost all with giardia-free stream water, long-drop toilets and fireplaces. Two are between Te Anau and Te Anau Downs, and the remaining ten pack into the next 50km, either on the grassy flats of the Eglinton Valley or in the bush nearby. Mackay Creek, Totara Creek and East Branch Eglinton, all around 55km north of Te Anau, are particularly good.

Heading north from Te Anau, there's little reason to stop in the first 30km to **Te Anau Downs Harbour**, where boats stop off en route to the start of the Milford Track. The road then cuts east away from the lake, before veering north into the **Eglinton Valley** through occasional stands of silver, red and mountain beech interspersed with open flats of red tussock grass. Surprisingly in a national park, these plains are grazed, an anomaly resulting from longstanding leases which had to be honoured. The mountains that hem in the valley are picturesquely reflected in the roadside **Mirror Lakes**, if its not too windy, 56km north of Te Anau, just before you hit the underwhelming **Avenue of the Disappearing Mountain** where the road slopes up, creating the illusion of the mountain ahead growing smaller as you approach.

As you get nearer to the head of the valley the road steepens to **The Divide**, at 532m the lowest east–west crossing of the Southern Alps. From the car park, with its toilets and walkers' shelter, you can walk to **Key Summit** (919m; 2–3hr return) for fine panoramic views over three valley systems. For those travelling by bus, a noticeboard details the times of passing services (Kiwi Discovery come through at roughly 11.20am Milford-bound & 4pm Te Anau-bound; ☎03/442 7340 & 0800/505 504), though it's best to **book a pick-up beforehand**. Pressing on towards Milford, you descend into the valley of the Hollyford River, which is best seen from a popular viewpoint just before the Hollyford Road shoots off north. The Milford Road continues west towards the Hollyford's source, a huge glacial cirque in which an Alpine Club hut marks the start of a walk to the Gertrude Saddle (4hr return), where you'll be rewarded by great views of the Darran Mountains and Mount Tutoko (2756m), Fiordland's highest point.

A kilometre further on, the **Homer Tunnel**, home of many curious kea, forges through the rock, emerging at the top of a long switchback down to the Cleddau River. Roughly 10km on from the tunnel all buses stop at **The Chasm**, while their passengers stroll (15min return) to the near-vertical rapids where the Cleddau has scoured out a deep, narrow channel. Tantalizing glimpses through the foliage reveal sculpted rocks hollowed out by churning stones or tortured into free-standing ribs that resemble flying buttresses.

The Hollyford Valley

The Milford Road drops down from The Divide into the Hollyford Valley, which runs 80km from its headwaters in the Darran Mountains north to the Tasman Sea at Martins Bay. A 16km spur road (originally planned to reach Haast – see box on p.821) provides access to the Hollyford Track (see box on pp.822–23) and a couple of other diversions. The first of these is a walk or more of a scramble to **Lake Marian** (5km return; 2–3hr; 400m ascent), which starts 1km along the Hollyford Valley spur road and climbs to a beautiful alpine lake, passing some wonderful cataracts (30–40min return) where boardwalks are cantilevered out from the rock wall.

The only settlement is 8km along the valley road at **Gunns Rest**, home to the idiosyncratic, knowledgeable and entertaining Murray Gunn, who operates a shop (daily 8.30am–8pm) packed with all you need for tramping and a lot more besides: postcards, good books, maps, some rare greenstone (Bowenite Tangiwai) and souvenirs. Murray also runs the *Hollyford Camp* (no phone; bunks ①, rooms ②), a huddle of simple old 1930s cabins which served as married family's quarters for the long-suffering road-builders. Each cabin has a double room and a four-berth bunk room, linked by a kitchen/lounge area equipped with a coal-burning range and cold water supply. The **museum** (shop hours; $1, free to *Hollyford Camp* guests) is yet another Murray Gunn venture – a collection of photos, pioneer artefacts and some interesting paraphernalia relating to the building of the Milford road and the Homer Tunnel, the one-time community at Martins Bay, and the devastating floods that periodically afflict the region.

The road runs 8km beyond Gunns Camp to the Road End – the beginning of the Hollyford Track and a shorter walk to **Humboldt Falls** (20–30min return), a three-step cascade leaping some two hundred metres and apparently the highest falls near a road in Australasia.

The Milford Track

More than any other Great Walk, the Milford Track has become a Kiwi **icon** and it sometimes seems that walking it is the dream of every New Zealander. Unlike other major tramps where foreigners, and particularly Europeans, predominate, Kiwis are in the majority here.

Its exalted **reputation** is partly accidental and partly historical. It seems likely that southern Maori paced the Arthur and Clinton valleys in search of *pounamu*, but there is little direct evidence. The first Europeans to explore this section of Fiordland were Scotsmen **Donald Sutherland** and **John Mackay** who, in 1880, blazed a trail up the Arthur Valley from Milford Sound. The story goes that while working their way up the valley they came upon the magnificent Mackay Falls and tossed a coin to decide who would name it, on the understanding that the loser would name the next waterfall. Mackay won the toss but rued his good fortune when, days later, they stumbled across the much more famous and lofty Sutherland Falls. They may well have climbed the adjacent Mackinnon Pass, but the honour of naming it went to **Quintin McKinnon** who, with his companion Ernest Mitchell, reached it in 1888 after having been commissioned by the Otago Chief Surveyor, C. W. Adams, to cut a path up the Clinton Valley.

The route was finally pushed through in mid-October 1888 and the **first tourists** came through the next year, guided by McKinnon. The greatest fillip came in 1908 when a writer submitted her account of the Milford Track to the editor of London's *Spectator*. She had declared it "A Notable Walk" but, in a fit of editorial hyperbole, the editor retitled the piece "The Finest Walk in the World". From 1903 until 1966 the **government**, through its Tourist Hotel Corporation (THC), held a **monopoly** on the track, allowing only guided walkers; the huts were supplied by a team of packhorses, which weren't finally retired until 1969.

Wider **public access** was only achieved after the Otago Tramping Club challenged the government's policy by tramping the Milford in 1964. Huts were built in 1966 and the first independent parties came through later that year.

Preliminaries – and maps

The **Milford Track** (54km; 4 days) has become a victim of its own **hype**. There is no doubt that it is a wonderful route through some of Fiordland's finest scenery, but many trampers disparage it as over-regimented, expensive, and not especially varied, while other complaints focus on the huts, which are badly spaced and lurk below the tree line among the sandflies. While these criticisms aren't unfounded – the tramp costs $200 in hut and transport **fees** alone – the track is extremely well managed and maintained, the huts are clean and unobtrusive, and, because everyone's going in the same direction, you can go all day without seeing a soul. The Milford is also **tougher** than many people expect, packing the only hard climb and a dash for the boat at Milford Sound into the last two days. Nevertheless, almost anyone of any age can walk the track, though the DOC recommends that unfit aspirants build up to it over 6–8 weeks. As the Mackinnon Pass can only be crossed when avalanche conditions do not prevail check the likely weather at the DOC office before you start out.

The DOC's *Milford Track* **leaflet** (provided free when you book – see below), is adequate for route-finding, though the 1:75,000 *Milford Track Trackmap* provides much more information. The 1:250,000 *Fiordland National Park* **map** is too small a scale to be of much use.

Booking and accommodation

Independent walkers tackling the Milford Track during the November to mid-April tramping season are subject to a rigid system of advance-booking **accommodation passes** – use the DOC's Great Walks Booking Desks in Queenstown, Glenorchy and Te Anau – for the three special category huts. Bookings are made for specific days and you can only walk the track from south to north, spending the first night at Clinton Forks Hut, the second at Mintaro Hut and the third at Dumpling Hut. No backtracking or second nights are allowed and there is strictly **no camping**. **Numbers** are

limited to forty per day, so you'll need to book as far ahead as possible (a month or more if you are adaptable, six months if you need a specific departure date or are part of a large group), but this does have the huge advantage that you are guaranteed a bed. Huts all have wardens and are equipped with flush toilets, running (but not drinking) water, heaters and gas rings, but not pans and plates; the **cost** is $105 for the three nights, and family discounts of thirty percent apply throughout the season. **Credit-card** phone or mail **bookings** are taken for the following season from July 1 and can be made through the Great Walks Booking Desk, the DOC, PO Box 29, Te Anau (Nov–April daily 9am–4.30pm; May–Oct Mon–Fri 9am–4.30pm; ☎03/249 8514, fax 249 8515, *greatwalksbooking@doc.govt.nz*); pick up your accommodation passes from Te Anau before 11.30am on the day of departure. If the track is closed due to bad weather or track conditions, full refunds are made but new bookings can only be taken if there is space.

Outside the season the huts revert to Category 3 ($5). They are unstaffed with heating but no clothes-drying or cooking facilities; bookings are not required and annual hut passes are valid.

Trailhead transport

The initial stretch of the Milford Track is a doddle and you'll find a late start is a good way of avoiding just hanging about at the first hut full of unbearable anticipation at the prospect of the next day. Both ends of the Milford Track can only be realistically approached **by boat**. There are several possibilities, but all must be arranged and paid for before, or at the same time as, accommodation passes are issued. Most independent walkers catch the 1.15pm bus ($11) from outside the Mount Cook Landlines office in Te Anau, which meets the *Fiordland Express* launch (Nov to mid-April; $43; Fiordland Travel) at Te Anau Downs, 30km north of Te Anau. The launch departs at 2pm for the journey across Lake Te Anau (1hr 45min) to the start of the track at Glade Wharf. At the Milford end of the track, the majority catch either the 2pm or the 3pm *Anita Bay* launch from Sandfly Point (Nov to mid-April; $22) for the journey to Milford Sound (20min). **Buses** back to Te Anau can be picked up at 3pm and 5pm (3hr; $35).

Other operators offer different ways to approach and leave the track. They can all be booked individually, but most have combined to marginally undercut the total price you'd pay for independent arrangements. Probably the best way to start from Te Anau is on the *Manuska*, a wooden ketch run by Sinbad Cruises (10.30am; 5–6hr; $55; ☎03/249 7106), which **sails** under canvas whenever possible to Glade Wharf. A package deal costs $99, including a short **paddle** back from Sandfly Point with Rosco's Milford Sound Sea Kayaks ($20 when booked separately; ☎03/249 8840) and a bus from Milford to Te Anau. Sea Kayak Fiordland meet track walkers and give them some paddling on the sound before mini-busing them back to Te Anau (☎03/249 7700, *fiordland.sea.kayak@clear.net.nz*; $49).

If money is no object, you can **fly** in to Glade Wharf with Waterwings Floatplane (☎03/249 7405; $176) or one of the several companies who fly out of Milford Sound, Te Anau or Queenstown.

Guided walks

For many years, the only way to walk the Milford Track was on a **guided walk**. Some would argue that this is still the case, with just your personal effects to carry and comfortable beds to sleep in. Accommodation is in clean, plain huts which aren't exactly luxurious, but do boast hot showers, duvets on the bunks, three-course dinners with wine and cooked breakfasts. Staff prepare the huts, cook the meals, make up the lunches and tidy up after you. All you have to do is walk, but there's a price to pay for all this pampering.

The **Milford Track Guided Walk**, PO Box 185, Te Anau (Nov to mid-April; ☎03/441 1138 & 0800/659 255, fax 441 1124, *mtinfo@milfordtrack. co.nz*) is a six-night, five-day affair and costs $1590, or $895 on standby at the office. For that you get an introductory talk with dinner and a night at the *Te Anau Travel Centre*, transport to the trailhead, accommodation and food on the track, a night at the *Milford Sound Hotel* (used only for this purpose) a cruise and a return bus ride to Te Anau.

Anyone wanting a taste of the track without having to walk more than a couple of kilometres can stay overnight at **Glade House**, the first of the guided walkers' huts on the track. Bus and boat transport are scheduled to leave time to explore the Clinton River and eat a three-course dinner – all for $190 (book through Milford Track Guided Walk).

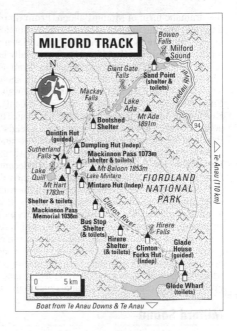

The route

The track starts at the head of Lake Te Anau and follows the Clinton River into the heart of the mountains, climbing over the spectacular Mackinnon Pass before tracing the Arthur River to Milford Sound.

The first day is a doddle. **Glade Wharf to Clinton Forks Hut** (8km; 2hr; 50m ascent) starts along a 2km 4WD track which serves Glade House. The path then crosses a long swingbridge to the right bank of the gentle, meandering Clinton River; keen anglers can spend an hour or two fishing for trout in the deep pools. The track runs through dense beech forest, only occasionally giving glimpses of the mountains ahead beyond Clinton Forks Hut.

From **Clinton Forks Hut to Mintaro Hut** (13.5km; 4–5hr; 350m ascent), the track follows the right bank of the Clinton River to its source, Lake Mintaro, right by the Mintaro Hut. Again this is easy going, and, by the time you reach a short side track to Hidden Lake, the Mackinnon Pass should be visible ahead. The track steepens a little to Bus Stop Shelter, then flattens out to Pompolona Hut. From here it's a further hour to Mintaro Hut where, if it looks like it will be a good sunset, it pays to drop your pack and head up the Mackinnon Pass.

The walk so far does nothing to prepare you for the day from **Mintaro Hut to Dumpling Hut** (14km; 5–6hr; 550m ascent, 1030m descent). Though the surface of the broad path is firm and well graded, bushwalking neophytes will find the haul up to Mackinnon Pass (1hr 30min–2hr) very strenuous. Long breath-catching pauses provide an opportunity to admire the wonderful alpine scenery, notably the headwall of the Clinton Valley, a sheer glacial cirque of grey granite. As the bush drops away behind you, the slope eases to the saddle at Mackinnon Pass, a great place to eat lunch, though you'll have the company of kea and the incessant buzzing of pleasure flights from Milford. A memorial to McKinnon and Mitchell marks the low-point of the saddle, from where the path turns east and climbs to a shelter (with toilets and a gas ring) just below the dramatic form of Mount Balloon. From there it is all downhill, and steeply too, initially skirting the flank of Mount Balloon then following a recent re-routing of the path beside the picturesque Roaring Burn and down to the Arthur River. The confluence is marked by **Quintin Hut**, which was originally built by the Union Steamship Company as an overnight shelter for sightseers from Milford visiting the Sutherland Falls. Though it remains a private hut, toilets and shelter are provided for independent walkers – who mostly dump their packs for the walk to the base of the 560m **Sutherland Falls** (4km; 1hr–1hr 30min return; 50m ascent), the highest in New Zealand. Quintin Hut has an airstrip and anyone with $50 to spare can take a **scenic flight** (minimum 4 people; 20min) to view Lake Quill (which feeds the Sutherland Falls), the Mackinnon Pass and the Clinton Valley. Dumpling Hut is another hour's walk from Quintin Hut.

After a tiring third day, you're in for an early start and a steady walk from **Dumpling Hut to Sandfly Point** (18km; 5–6hr; 125m decent) to meet your launch or kayak at 2pm. After rain this can be a magnificent walk, as the valley walls stream with waterfalls and the Arthur River is in spate. The track follows the tumbling river for a couple of hours to the Boatshed (toilets), before crossing the Arthur River on a swingbridge and cutting inland to the magnificent MacKay Falls. More a steep cascade than a waterfall, they are much smaller than the Sutherland Falls but equally impressive, particularly after rain. Don't miss Bell Rock, a water-hollowed boulder that you can crawl inside. The track subsequently follows Lake Ada, created by a landslip 900 years ago, and named by Sutherland after his Scottish girlfriend. A small lunch shelter midway along its shore heralds Giant Gate Falls, which are best viewed from the swingbridge that crosses the river at the foot of the falls. From here it is roughly an hour and a half to the shelter at Sandfly Point.

Milford Sound

After all the superlatives feted on Milford Sound, initial impressions can be a little deflating. The smattering of buildings that comprise the small settlement are hardly in keeping with such magnificent surroundings and the best of the fiord can only really be seen from the water. Nevertheless, it is a fine spot on the edge of a basin where the Cleddau and Arthur rivers surge into the fiord, and the whole scene is dominated by the triangular glaciated pinnacle of **Mitre Peak** (1694m), named for its resemblance to a bishop's mitre when viewed from this angle.

Arrival and getting around

The most worthwhile way to get here, and the one which conveys the greatest sense of place, is to **walk** the **Milford Track** (see p.824), though **drivers** and **cyclists** do get the freedom to stop, sightsee and camp at the numerous basic campsites along the dramatic road from Te Anau (see p.821). Failing either of those, you can **fly**, hop on a **bus**, or do a combination of both, often with a cruise on the fiord thrown in (see box on pp.830–31 for a rundown of the options).

There isn't much to Milford Sound. The airport, fishing harbour, new cruise terminal, post office and an extremely expensive petrol station are scattered along the shore. Though they are not more than a few hundred metres apart, there is a sporadic free **shuttle bus** connecting them all.

Accommodation and eating

The only **place to stay** in town is *Milford Sound Lodge* (☎ & fax 03/249 8071, *milford.sound.lodge@xtra.co.nz*; tent sites $10, dorms ①, rooms ②–③), under ambitious management which is slowly turning this once unappealing dump into a really worthwhile stopping point on the approach to Milford Sound, almost 2km from the wharf and linked to it by a courtesy bus. Thrown-in extras, like talks and slideshows on plants and animals, are part of the attraction, as is a vastly improved café with low prices. Unfortunately the *THC Milford Sound Hotel* is now closed to the public and used only by the people who do the expensive guided Milford Track trips.

Eating in Milford isn't as easy as it should be and certainly not of the standard you'd expect in an international destination. *Milford Sound Lodge* sells filling meals for under $10 and is the only place to buy groceries – at inflated prices, due to transport costs. The expensive *Lobster Pot Restaurant*, serves hefty main courses at around $20 plus, snackier lunches from $10, and a huge breakfast for around $10; in bad weather, their lounge, with its picture windows and open fire, makes a good place to bide your time over a coffee (when it's open), watching the weather sweeping along the fiord. There is also the spartan, unappealling *Milford* **pub** next door, which does pies and toasted sandwiches, and the basic *Mitre Peak Café* (daily: Nov–March 8.30am–5.30pm; April–Oct 9am–4pm), which sadly follows the usual Kiwi tearoom tradition.

Around Milford

You are pretty much surrounded by water here, and you should waste little time before getting out on it. If tales of his pioneering days have inspired you, pay homage at **Donald Sutherland's grave**, hidden among the staff accommodation behind the pub. Otherwise, there's a five-minute stroll up to a **lookout** behind the *THC Hotel*, or a boardwalk and track beside the cruise terminal leads to the 160m **Lady Bowen Falls** (15min return), named after the wife of George Bowen, New Zealand's governor in the 1860s. Though most impressive in spate, when the upturned lip sends a spume out across the fiord, the falls are worth the walk at any time to observe the village's source of water and hydroelectricity. Three old graves at the foot of the falls guard the remains of nineteenth-century sealers and whalers.

The only other sight attached to terra firma is the **Milford Sound Underwater Observatory**, which can be visited as part of a cruise run either by Red Boat Cruises or Fiordland Travel ($59; see box overleaf), or by shuttle (☎03/249 7400; 9.15am–5pm; $35, subject to availability). It's a floating platform moored to a sheer rock wall in Harrison Cove, part of the marine reserve about a third of the way along the fiord. A series of explanatory panels on the surface prepare you for the main attraction, a spiral staircase which takes you nine metres down through the relatively lifeless freshwater surface layer to a circular gallery where windows look out into the briny heart of the fiord. Sharks and seals have been known to swim by, but most of the action happens immediately outside in window-box "gardens", which have been specially grown from locally gathered **coral** and plant species. Lights pick out colourful fish, tubeworms, sea fans, huge starfish and rare red and black coral (see p.816). This might all sound a little naff – but unless you're an experienced diver, this is the only chance you'll get to see these corals, which elsewhere in the world grow only at depths greater than forty metres. Cruises only stop for around twenty minutes, which isn't really long enough, so if you're really interested, a water taxi's your best bet.

Seeing the fiord: cruises, kayaks and flights

Dramatic though it is, the view from the shore of Milford Sound pales beside the incomparable spectacle from the water, with waterfalls plunging hundreds of metres into the fiord. It is still difficult to grasp the heroic scale of the place, unless your visit coincides with that of one of the great cruise liners – even these formidable vessels are totally dwarfed by the cascades and cliff faces.

The majority of cruises explore the full 22km of Milford Sound, all calling at waterfalls, the seal colony, and overhanging rock faces; at Fairy Falls, boats nose up to the base of the fall, while suitably attired passengers are encouraged to edge out onto the bowsprit and collect a cup of water. Longer trips sometimes anchor in Anita Bay (*Te-Wahi-Takiwai*, "the place of Takiwai"), a former greenstone-gathering place at the fiord's mouth, but still sheltered from the wrath of the Tasman Sea. In short, having come this far, it's essential to get out on the water by some means or other – even if it means putting up with corny cruise commentaries. There are three main options, all of which should be booked a few days in advance: a two- to four-hour cruise around the fiord, an overnight cruise, or kayaking. All boats leave from an incongruous, cavernous new building at the wharf.

Two large companies and one single-boat operator run **cruises on the fiord**. Red Boat Cruises (☎03/249 7926 & 0800/657 444) operate five well-appointed boats, some carrying several hundred passengers and all bombarding you with a running commentary. Most cruises go to the Tasman Sea (2–6 daily; 1hr 45min; $44), but the longer **cruise to the observatory** (daily 12.25pm; 2hr 30min; $59) is preferable, taking you out to the mouth of the fiord and returning to Harrison Cove for a quick look at the underwater observatory. Fiordland Travel (☎03/442 7500) run similar cruises to the Tasman Sea (2–4 daily; 1hr 45min; $44–47) and longer ones on the *Milford Wanderer* (Oct–April 2 daily; 2hr 30min; $49) and an observatory cruise ($59). The smaller company is Mitre Peak Cruises (☎03/249 8110 & 0800/744 633, *in @milfordsound.org*), who operate a smaller more intimate boat and run out to St Annes

---

TRIPS TO MILFORD SOUND

As **Milford Sound** is on most visitors' itineraries, there's no shortage of operators willing to get you there from almost anywhere in the country. **From Queenstown**, a stream of luxury **buses** make the tiring four-to-five-hour drive via **Te Anau** to Milford, complete with frequent photo-opportunity stops and a relentless commentary, decanting their passengers for a cruise on the fiord then running them back again. Trips **from Te Anau** involve the middle (and most interesting) section of Queenstown-based trips and are appreciably shorter, generally taking a leisurely eight rather than a hurried twelve hours. Most tours also include a **cruise** on the sound once you get there – see above for a run-down of the various vessels that ply its waters.

FROM TE ANAU

The **cheapest** trips are those which don't include cruises – good value if you're going kayaking: try the track-transport specialists Fiordland Tracknet (☎03/249 7777; Nov–May), who will get you there and back for $35, but you'll have to put up with detours to the trailheads. The big boys such as Fiordland Travel (☎03/249 7416 & 0800/656 510, *reservations@fiordlandtravel.co.nz*), InterCity (☎03/249 7559 & 0800/731 711), Milford Explorer (☎03/249 7516 & 0800/800 904) and Red Boat Cruises (☎03/441 1137 & 0800/657 444, *teanau.travel@xtra.co.nz*), all run luxury **bus and cruise** packages for $80–95, though there are small reductions for backpackers and substantial standby **discounts** outside the peak season.

The **most interesting** possibilities include trips with Fiordland Wilderness Experiences (☎03/249 7700; $90), involving four hours' kayaking on the fiord; Kiwi Discovery (☎03/442 9792 & 0800/100 792; $89), with a bus and boat ride; Topline Tours (☎03/249 8059), who offer a luxury little bus and then cruise or walk followed either by a plane or bus trip back ($55–105), and Trips 'n' Tramps (☎03/249 7081 & 0800/305 805, *trips@teanau.co.nz*; $98), concentrating on relaxed short bushwalks along the way before usually meeting up with the *Milford Wanderer*.

FROM QUEENSTOWN

Trips typically start between 7am and 8am and seldom get back before 8pm. Many shy away from such a long day and opt instead for a package involving the forty-minute point ($48), a combination trip including the observatory ($68) or an afternoon **cruise to the Tasman Sea** ($43).

Fiordland Travel run backpacker-orientated **overnight trips** on the *Milford Wanderer* (Oct–April daily 5pm–9am; $135), a motor-driven, seventy-berth replica of a sailing scow with cosmetic sails. It makes an impressive sight as it ploughs along the fiord to Anita Bay for some fishing, canoeing and bushwalking before spending the night in Harrison Cove. On-board accommodation is somewhat institutional, with cramped four-bunk rooms equipped with sheets, sleeping bags and towels, but a hearty three-course evening meal is served (drinks extra). They also run a smaller overnighter aboard the MV *Friendship*, a more intimate experience including dinner and breakfast, kayaking and cruising, and walking ($135).

Fine though the cruises are, the elemental nature of Milford Sound can best be appreciated without the throb of an engine. The best **kayaking** is with Fiordland Wilderness Experiences who run full-day, guided trips on Milford Sound, with an ecological slant (☎03/249 7700 & 0800/200 434, *fiordland.sea.kayak@clear.net.nz*; $75 from Milford, $95 from Te Anau). Alternatively, Rosco's Milford Sound Sea Kayaks (☎03/249 8840) offer an extensive range of kayaking trips taking single and double sea kayaks to Harrison Cove and Sandfly Point (mid-Oct to mid-April; $75–225). Both companies organize transport from Te Anau and will pick up trampers coming off the Routeburn, Greenstone or Caples tracks at The Divide.

flight to Milford's small airfield, a **cruise** and a **return flight** or better still travelling from Te Anau. A good compromise is to combine the two: flying there and bussing back is the most economical option (from around $199 with Kiwi Discovery; ☎03/442 7340), since flights back are oversubscribed by people who have booked a bus/cruise/bus trip but simply can't face the return journey, sending prices up to nearer the $260 mark, maximum $335. Travellers locked into the Kiwi Experience or Magic Bus circuit have to pay extra to do the Milford Sound leg; if you can get a group of four or five together, you can get here as cheaply, and with greater flexibility, by renting a car from Queenstown (see p.763).

Prices for the **bus/cruise/bus trips** kick off at $119–199 with Kiwi Discovery and Kiwi Experience (☎03/442 9708) both run comparable trips on smaller buses; but, best value of all, the BBQ Bus (☎03/442 1045; $145) run full-day trips, with stops for short bushwalks and a barbecue in the Hollyford Valley. More upmarket tours using air-conditioned vehicles, complete with prerecorded multilingual commentary, are offered by several companies, including Fiordland Travel (☎03/442 7500 & 0800/656 503; $160), whose unusual wedge-profiled coaches give the best all-round views. Fiordland Travel also run the best trip for those with a couple of days to explore Milford. The backpacker-orientated **Milford Backroad Adventure** (mid-Oct to March Mon, Wed & Fri; $245), which takes the early sailing across Lake Wakatipu on the TSS *Earnslaw* (see p.754), then a minibus along 80km of dirt roads through the Walter Peak and Mount Nicholas high-country stations and on up the scenic Von Valley to Mavora Lakes (see p.780). The bus eventually meets SH94 and continues through Te Anau to Milford Sound in time to catch the *Milford Wanderer* for its overnight sailing. The return journey the following morning is generally broken by a brew up at Mavora Lakes, before catching the early-evening *Earnslaw* sailing back to Queenstown.

Magnificent though it is, the Milford road scenery is upstaged by the aerial views of the top end of Lake Wakatipu and the Routeburn and Greenstone tracks from the **flights to Milford**. Mount Cook Airlines do a four-hour fly/cruise/fly package for $256; other operators include Air Fiordland (☎03/442 3404), Air Wakatipu (☎03/442 4148), and Milford Sound Scenic Flights (☎03/442 3065 & 0800/101 767). Any flights overflying the Olivine Ice Plateau and the Red Hills are likely to be more spectacular.

Scenic **flights** over Fiordland's magnificent alpine terrain are run by numerous companies. Mount Cook Airlines (☎0800/800 737) are typical, running flights to the mouth of the sound (10min; around $50), Sutherland Falls (20min; $80) and a grand tour (Oct–March only; 40min; $135). Milford Sound Helicopters (☎03/249 8384), offer a circuit of Mitre peak (10min; $100), a jaunt to Sutherland Falls (30min; $175) and a Grand Tour (55min; $300).

Manapouri and the southern fiords

There is no shortage of contenders for the title of New Zealand's most beautiful lake, and sloshing 178m above sea level, **Lake Manapouri** is definitely among them, with its long and indented bush-clad shoreline contorted into three distinct arms. The lake has a vast catchment area, guzzling all the water that flows down the Upper Waiau River from Lake Te Anau and unwittingly creating a massive hydroelectric generating capacity – something which almost led to its downfall.

The one good thing to come from the hydroelectric project has been the opening up of **Doubtful Sound**, following the construction of the Wilmot Pass supply road. What was previously the preserve of the odd yacht and a few deerstalkers and trampers is now accessible to anyone prepared to take a boat across Lake Manapouri and a drive

---

A TALE OF ELECTRICITY, ALUMINIUM AND BRICKBATS

Lake Manapouri's **hydroelectric** potential had long been recognized, but nothing was done to realize it until the 1950s. Consolidated Zinc Pty of Australia wanted to smelt their Queensland bauxite into **aluminium** – a tremendously power-hungry process – as cheaply as possible, and their beady eyes alighted upon **Lake Manapouri**. They approached the New Zealand government, who agreed to build a power station on the lake, at taxpayers' expense, while Consolidated Zinc's subsidiary Comalco built a smelter at Tiwai Point, near Bluff, 170km to the southeast.

The scheme entailed blocking the lake's natural outlet into the Lower Waiau River and chiselling out a **vast powerhouse** 200m underground beside Lake Manapouri's West Arm, where the flow would be diverted down a 10km tailrace tunnel to Deep Cove on Doubtful Sound. By the time the fledgling **environmental movement** had rallied its supporters, the scheme was well under way, but the government underestimated the anger that would be unleashed by its secondary plan to boost water storage and power production by raising the water level in the lake by 12m. The threat to the natural beauty of the lake sparked **national protests**, culminating in the presentation to parliament of a 265,000-signature petition, after which the plan was reluctantly dropped. The full saga is recounted in Neville Peat's book *Manapouri Saved* (see "Books" in Contexts, p.881).

The **West Arm Power Station** took eight years to build. Completed in 1971, it remains one of the most ambitious projects ever carried out in New Zealand. Eighty percent of its output goes straight to the **smelter** – which consumes something like fifteen percent of all the electricity used in the country, and yet Comalco are charged only a third of what domestic users pay. It is widely perceived to be an unnecessary drain on the country's resources and every time a new power station is proposed, the cry goes up for the plug to be pulled on the smelter. Nevertheless, a second parallel tailrace tunnel is now being drilled to **increase** the station's **capacity** which has only ever been six sevenths of what was originally intended. The most likely explanation is that the engineers got their sums wrong and then realized if they ever did run at full power the turbine chamber would flood. Meanwhile locals are keeping an eye on the project as its budget spirals out of control; they fear that to try and recuperate lost money the government will agree to another smelting plant or something even less environmentally friendly.

over the Wilmot Pass. Costs are unavoidably high and you need to be self-sufficient (no burger joints or corner shops here), but any inconvenience is easily outweighed by glorious isolation and pristine beauty. Wildlife is a major attraction, not least the resident pod of bottlenose dolphins, who frequently come to play around ships' bows and gleefully cavort near kayakers. Fur seals slather the outer islands, Fiordland crested penguins come to breed here in October and November, and the bush, which comes right down to the water's edge, is alive with kaka, kiwi and other rare bird species.

Cook spotted Doubtful Sound in 1770 but didn't enter as he was "doubtful" of his ability to sail out again in the face of winds buffeted by the steep-walled fiord. The breeze was more favourable for the joint leaders of a Spanish expedition, Malaspina and Bauza, who in February 1793 sailed in and named Febrero Point, Malaspina Reach and Bauza Island.

In fact, Cook seemed more interested in **Dusky Sound**, 40km south, where he spent five weeks on his second voyage in 1773, while his crew recovered from an arduous crossing of the Southern Ocean. At Pickersgill Harbour, Cook endeavoured to ward off scurvy by using manuka leaves to brew a kind of "spruce beer" which, helped along with a touch of brandy, apparently tasted like champagne; obviously, the captain hadn't supped champagne for some time. On Astronomer's Point nearby, it is still possible to see where Cook's astronomer had trees felled so he could get an accurate fix on the stars; not far from here is the site where 1790s castaways built the first European-style house and boat in New Zealand. Marooned by the fiord's waters, Pigeon Island shelters the ruins of a house built by Richard Henry, who battled from 1894 to 1908 to save endangered native birds from introduced stoats and rats.

Manapouri

The scattered community of **MANAPOURI**, 20km south of Te Anau, drapes itself prettily around the shores of the lake of the same name which, in the 1960s became a cause célèbre for conservationists opposed to the raising of the lake level as part of the massive West Arm hydroelectric power scheme (see box opposite). With the power station complete, the lake left at its original level and the passage of three decades, there is little tangible evidence of the passions that once threatened the community's cohesion, but scratch below the surface and you'll find a lingering antipathy between economic rationalists and environmentalists.

Arrival and information

To get to Manapouri without your own transport, hop on the Spitfire Shuttle (contact Fiordland Travel ☎03/249 7416), which leaves Te Anau at 8.30am and returns from Manapouri around 3pm as part of the Te Anau to Invercargill return run, or try the Fiordland Travel buses ($5.50 each way) plying the West Arm and Doubtful Sound runs, who'll take you if their cruise passengers don't fill the bus.

The road from Te Anau reaches Manapouri as Cathedral Drive and then becomes Waiau Street, passing almost everything of interest on the way to the offices of Fiordland Travel, Pearl Harbour (daily: Nov–Feb 8am–8pm; March–Oct 8am–4pm; ☎03/249 6602 & 0800/656 502, fax 249 6603), the closest thing the village has to an information centre, and the jumping-off point for lake cruises. The sole shop and the post office both occupy the same building as the *Cathedral Café* on Cathedral Drive – find one and you've found the lot.

Accommodation and eating

There is a reasonable selection of **places to stay** in Manapouri (see overleaf) but not much choice for **eating** – so, if you are staying at a B&B that provides food, take advantage of it. Failing that, the *Manapouri Motor Inn* now houses the *Beehive Café* which dishes out generous if uninspired café fare while the bar offers ordinary meals ($10–20). Your best bet is the *Cathedral Café*, Cathedral Drive (☎03/249 6619), which serves teas and snacks, but also stays open for $15 evening meals until 8pm, later if you make a reservation.

The Cottage, Waiau St (☎03/249 6838 & 0800/677 866). Attractive en-suite rooms in a cutesy house with a cottage garden close to the wharf. Continental breakfast is included, cooked is $5 extra, and $25 dinners are available. ④.

Deep Cove Hostel, Deep Cove, Doubtful Sound (☎03/249 6602). This two- and four-bed bunkroom accommodation overlooking Doubtful Sound is available only during school holidays. There are mattresses, all eating and cooking utensils and good hot showers, but the nearest place to buy food is Manapouri, so bring everything you'll need. The one-way fare with Fiordland Travel's Doubtful Sound service from Manapouri is $50. ①.

Manapouri Glade Motel and Motor Park, Murrell Ave (☎03/249 6623). Appealingly old-fashioned, peaceful and neatly tended motor park located right where the Waiau River meets the lake. Tent and powered sites go for $8.50. Cabins ③, motel units ④.

Manapouri Lake View Motels and Motor Park, 50 Manapouri–Te Anau Highway, 1km from the wharf (☎03/249 6624). Fully equipped motor park with spa and swimming pool and excellent vistas. Tent and powered sites cost around $8.50 or there are cabins and units. Cabins ②–③, motel units ④–⑤.

Murrell's Grandview House, 7 Murrell Ave (☎ & fax 03/249 6642; reservations essential). The finest of Manapouri's B&Bs, this wide-verandaed house was built in 1889 by the present owner's grandfather. Gracious rooms and spacious grounds exude a country-sports ambience. Swanky dinners making the most of local ingredients go for $50. ⑨ plus breakfast

Possum Lodge Manapouri Backpackers, Cathedral Drive (☎ & fax 03/249 6660). Well organized, friendly, very homely and centrally placed, catering to only a dozen or so guests in a tastefully renovated house overlooking the lake. Beds are in small dorms or doubles, and all have free use of the well-stocked kitchen, comfortable lounge warmed by a log-burning stove, and bikes. They'll even pick you up from Te Anau if you've booked in advance. Dorms ①, rooms ②.

Ruth and Lance Shaw, 1 Home St (☎ & fax 03/249 6600). Self-contained flat let by the folk who operate Fiordland Ecology Holidays. Continental breakfast is included. ④.

Around town

The several dozen houses that constitute Manapouri cluster at the outlet of the Waiau River, which the hydroelectric shenanigans have turned into a narrow arm of the lake now known as Pearl Harbour.

Apart from cruises and kayak trips (see below), the only thing to do in Manapouri is to saunter along some of the **walking trails** detailed in the DOC's *Manapouri Tracks* leaflet ($1, from some accommodation and the Fiordland Travel office). On the Manapouri side there's the **Pearl Harbour to Fraser's Beach** trail (45min), which follows an easy track through lakeshore beech forest with fantails and silvereye flitting about the thin understorey. For all the other tracks, you'll need to rent yourself a row boat to get across the Waiau River: Adventure Charters (☎03/249 6626; daily 8am–6pm), at the Mobil station on Waiau Street, are happy to oblige. Boats cost $5 per person per day, or you can pay another $3 each and stay on the other side overnight, either camping or in one of the two DOC huts (both Category 3; $5).

The most frequently walked is the **Circle Track** (3hr loop; 7km; 330m ascent) initially contouring west around the lake then turning southeast to climb the ridge up to a point with stupendous views over the lake then north back the to start.

The lake: cruises and kayaking

Most of the lake cruises are operated by Fiordland Travel (☎03/249 6602 & 0800/656 502), who run four-hour trips across Lake Manapouri to the impressive, if controversial **West Arm Power Station** (1 daily; $46 ex-Manapouri, $56 ex-Te Anau); work on a second tailrace over the next few years is likely to disrupt tour schedules, so check the latest with Fiordland Travel. The ride across the lake terminates at a visitor centre, which highlights the European "discovery" of Fiordland, its flora and fauna and, more predictably, the construction of the power station. A bus then takes you down a narrow, 2km-long tunnel to a viewing platform in the Machine Hall. All you can see are the exposed sections of seven turbines, but there's an interesting model of the whole system and some panels assaulting you with yet more statistics; read quickly before you're whisked back to the bus for the return trip.

For greater independence, you'll need **kayak rental**: Adventure Charters (☎03/249 6626; daily 8am–6pm) rent reasonable-quality single and double sea kayaks for $40 per day, $35 overnight; or Fiordland Wilderness Experiences, 66 Quintin Drive, Te Anau (☎03/249 7700), rent out better boats for about the same.

The southern fiords

To fully appreciate the beauty and sense the isolation of the **southern fiords**, you really need to spend a few days among them, travelling either by boat or kayak. If time is limited, plump for a full-day trip to Doubtful Sound; with more time to spare, a few days weaving between these mystical waterways is an unforgettable experience.

Fiordland Travel run a full-day trip to **Doubtful Sound** (☎03/249 6602 & 0800/656 502; 1 daily; $160 ex Manapouri, $171 ex Te Anau; lunch $15 extra; and an overnight cruise $260): after the inevitable power-station treatment on Lake Manapouri, you're transferred onto a bus for the 20km ride over Wilmot Pass – the costliest stretch of road in the country and completely unconnected to any other road – to Deep Cove, where the tailrace tunnel spews out vast quantities of lake water. Here you board a three-hour cruise to the mouth of the fiord, where fur seals loll on the rocks, and into Hall Arm, where bottlenose dolphins often congregate.

For a more in-depth encounter with the fiords, join one of the superb multi-day trips organized by Fiordland Ecology Holidays (☎03/249 6600, *eco@xtra.co.nz*; 3–7 days; $165 per day). The **motor-sailer** *Breaksea Girl* is skippered by Lance Shaw, who spent twelve years running the DOC's research vessel in these waters and holds passionate views on the non-extractive use of the fiords. Fishing is out and, though snorkelling and scuba diving are in, care is taken to minimize the impact on this fragile environment. Trips typically take in **Doubtful**, **Dusky** and **Breaksea** sounds, spending time with dolphins and seals and calling at places frequented by Cook and by turn-of-the-century bird conservationist Richard Henry. A worthy alternative to cruising is to take a research holiday (run by Fiordland Ecology Holidays), monitoring skinks and weevils, short- and long-tailed bats and native birds on Breaksea and the surrounding small islands (no experience required; around $925 for 5 days).

A similar ethical vein flavours the energetic and excellent **kayaking trips** run by Fiordland Wilderness Experiences (☎03/249 7700, *fiordland.sea.kayak@clear.net.nz*), who sometimes run joint trips with Fiordland Ecology Holidays which enable kayakers to reach unsullied waters by hitching a ride aboard the *Breaksea Girl* (around $200 per day). Otherwise, their regular guided trips involve the usual bus ride from Te Anau, boat ride from Manapouri, 4WD trek over the Wilmot Pass and then idyllic kayaking on the almost silent Doubtful Sound and camping out in one of its spectacular remote arms where they have set up comfortable, ecologically-minded, camping sites. On day two you'll be paddling and sailing back with a satisfied glow (Tues, Sat & most Thurs departures; 2 days for $245). For an even more remote alternative there are also 3–5 day guided trips at $90 a day and freedom rentals for experienced paddlers. Adventure Charters offer a variation on the theme with cruise and kayak options on the Sound (☎03/249 6626, *information@fiordlandadventure.co.nz*; 2 days for $219; 1 day for $159), involving sitting in their boat *Adventurer I* and then kayaking along either behind or in front of it.

THE DUSKY TRACK

The DOC's Dusky Track leaflet ($1) *is the best single resource for this walk, though tricky route finding makes the 1:50,000* Wilmot (S148) *and* Heath (S157) *maps invaluable adjuncts.*

At its most extensive, the **Dusky Track** is one of the **longest** and **most remote** tracks in New Zealand. The high cost of transportation and the commitment involved make it one of the least-walked tracks, but anyone with sufficient experience and stamina shouldn't miss this opportunity to walk from one of New Zealand's largest lakes (Manapouri) to its longest fiord (Dusky Sound).

There are three basic elements, each following a major river valley and connecting to form an inverted Y. Any two of these can be combined to make a tramp of **four to six days**, or all three can be attempted in **eight to ten days**. On a tramp of this length it is especially important to have plenty of spare food and stove fuel in case of bad weather or flooding. In **summer**, be prepared for a lot of stream crossings and precarious walkwires to negotiate. In **winter** you can also expect snow and ice, which often render the track impassable, though you will be advised of conditions when you **notify** either the Tuatapere or Te Anau DOC office of your **intentions**; remember to **check in** on your return from the track.

ACCOMMODATION AND ACCESS

There is no need to book **huts** on the Dusky, all eight huts are Category 3 ($5) and operate on a first-come-first-served basis. All have twelve bunks (except the 6-bunk West Arm Hut), tank water and long-drop toilets; only Halfway Hut lacks mattresses.

There are four ways of tackling the track: walk in from Lake Hauroko, via Supper Cove and on to Lake Manapouri; doing it the other way round; flying in to Supper Cove and walking out to Manapouri (ignoring Lake Hauroko) or doing this in reverse. Most trampers enter the region by boat across Lake Hauroko with Lake Hauroko Tours (☎03/226 6681; Nov–April Mon & Thurs at 9am; $50), who'll also drive you in from Tuatapere (see p.838). For walkers coming in the opposite direction, pick-ups from Hauroko Burn Hut are on the same days at noon, but must be confirmed in advance.

During the **winter months** (May–Sept), the *Milford Wanderer* (☎03/249 6602 & 0800/656 502) leaves its beat on Milford Sound and indulges in some leisurely cruises around the southern fiords: prices range from $360 for a three-day jaunt to $1295 for a week-long saunter around Preservation Inlet, Dusky, Doubtful and Breaksea sounds.

The Southern Scenic Route

The vast majority of visitors to Te Anau and Manapouri retrace their steps to Queenstown and miss out on the fringe country, where the fertile sheep paddocks of Southland butt up against the remote country of the Fiordland National Park. The minor towns of the region are linked by the understated **Southern Scenic Route**, small roads where mobs of sheep are likely to be the biggest cause of traffic problems. From Te Anau it runs via Manapouri to SH99, following the valley of the Waiau River to the cave-pocked limestone country around **Clifden**. A minor road cuts west to Lake Hauroko, access point to both the Dusky Track and the Hump Track, while the

The **eastern continuation** of the Southern Scenic Route through the Catlins to Dunedin is covered in Chapter Eleven, starting on p.665.

From Lake Hauroko, it's three days' walk to Loch Maree Hut, which is poised at the junction of the three "legs". Some trampers then turn west to **Supper Cove** (1 day) and **fly out** (or in) with Waterwings Airways' scheduled service (☎03/249 7405; Nov–April daily 11am; $162), while others head north to **West Arm** (3 days) to pick up the daily Fiordland Travel **launch** across Lake Manapouri (☎03/249 6602 & 0800/656 502; $50), also worth confirming in advance.

THE ROUTE

You won't want to hang around the Hauroko Burn Hut, and mid-morning boat drop-offs leave you plenty of time to walk from **Hauroko Burn Hut to Halfway Hut** (12km; 4–6hr), following Hauroko Burn as it runs through a short gorge and gradually steepens to Halfway Hut. The second day from **Halfway Hut to Lake Roe Hut** (7km; 3–5hr) goes easily for a couple of hours then climbs above the bushline and follows snow poles to the magnificently sited Lake Roe Hut. On the third day, from **Lake Roe Hut to Loch Maree Hut** (10km; 4–6hr), the track veers west along the tops of the Pleasant Range, with spectacular views to Dusky Sound, before descending very steeply to Loch Maree Hut.

Trampers wishing to walk from **Loch Maree Hut to Supper Cove Hut** (12km; 6hr) continue west from Loch Maree following the Seaforth River. At low tide, the last rough section of track can be avoided by cutting across the flats to Supper Cove Hut – where it is traditional to take out the dinghy and fish for your supper. Anyone not flying out has to retrace their steps to Loch Maree Hut.

From **Loch Maree Hut to Kintail Hut** (11km; 4–5hr), you follow the Seaforth River upstream on fairly difficult ground that can be boggy and becomes impassable when the river is high. The next day, the route from **Kintail Hut to Upper Spey Hut** (7km; 5–6hr) involves a steep ascent to the scenic sub-alpine Centre Pass, then an equally precipitous descent to Upper Spey Hut. The last day takes you fairly painlessly from **Upper Spey Hut to West Arm Hut** (11km; 4–5hr), down the Spey River to the Wilmot Pass road between West Arm and Doubtful Sound. Forty minutes' walk brings you to the wharf at West Arm – hopefully in time to catch the last launch (usually at around 4.30pm). Otherwise you'll have to spend the night at West Arm Hut 200m east of the power-station visitor centre.

Southern Scenic Route continues south through the small service town of **Tuatapere** to estuary-side little **Riverton** and on to Invercargill.

Spitfire shuttle **buses** do the trip through Manapouri, Tuatapere and Riverton on Saturday (☎03/249 7505, *ek@spitfire.co.nz*; 8.30am from Te Anau, arriving at Invercargill around 11am; $34), they also do track drop-offs and pick-ups for all the road accessed tracks including the Dusky, making a few stops along the way.

Borland Road and Lake Monowai

Some 35km south of Manapouri, **Borland/Lake Monowai Road** cuts west to Lake Manapouri's South Arm. Built in 1963, it provides hunting, fishing, mountain-biking and tramping access to a huge swathe of untouched country south of Lake Manapouri.

Passing the dam which controls the flow of water from Lake Manapouri down the Waiau River, the road runs 12km to the *Monowai River Lodge* (☎ & fax 03/225 5191, freephone 0800/877 222; dorms ①, rooms ③), a superb lagoonside retreat geared to both the rod-and-gun set and backpackers. The fully self-contained lodge – complete with piano – sleeps twelve, and when not booked by groups, individual rooms are rented out; failing that, there are beds in rustic but comfortable bunkhouses. The lodge also operates Fiordland Adventures (same phone & fax numbers), offering mountain bikes for rent ($25 per day), 4WD trips and advice on walks off Borland/Lake Monowai Road.

Immediately past the lodge, a spur runs 6km to **Lake Monowai**, the water level of which was artificially raised as part of an early, small-scale hydro scheme in 1925. The scars can still be seen on its shores, where there's a primitive **campsite** ($2) with long-drop toilets and barbecues. Monowai is a popular for fishing – mostly done from boats to avoid snagging lines in the submerged skeletons of drowned trees. Back on Borland Road it is another 4km west to *Borland Lodge* (☎03/225 5464; ①), a youth adventure centre where you can stay in twin chalets (bring your own bedding). They also rent out reasonably priced tents and stoves to those wanting to explore the excellent **walking** country and huts hereabouts, all detailed in the DOC's *Lake Monowai/Borland Road* leaflet ($1).

Beyond *Borland Lodge*, the increasingly narrow, steep and landslip-prone road can be driven another 40km to **Lake Manapouri's South Arm**, where there is a shelter and toilets (Oct–May; key from the DOC in Tuatapere or Te Anau). Close to the end of the road, a spur (open to trampers only) leads 15km over the Percy Saddle to **West Arm** and eventually to Doubtful Sound.

Clifden and Lake Hauroko

Back at the junction with the main highway, it is 32km further south to **CLIFDEN**, barely a town at all but of some interest for the historic **Clifden Suspension Bridge**, one of the longest in the South Island, built over the Waiau River in 1899 and in use until the 1970s. The north abutment overshadows a free campsite and barbecue area. Clifden most likely gets its name from low cliffs made of the same limestone that is riddled with the **Clifden Caves** (unrestricted access, signposted off Clifden Gorge Road), where Maori once camped on summer foraging trips. Suitably equipped with torches and treading carefully, you can explore the stalactite and glow-worm grottos at your leisure, using ladders installed in the steepest sections.

Languishing at the end of a dirt road, 30km west of Clifden, **Lake Hauroko** is New Zealand's deepest lake (462m). Low bush-clad hills surround the lake, leaving it open to the "sounding winds" immortalized in its name. There are no facilities at First Bay, the road end, just a primitive campsite midway between Clifden and Lake Hauroko and, at the north end of the lake, the Hauroko Burn Hut (accessible by boat, or on foot via the Dusky Track – see p.836).

To explore the lake and its environs, call the Wairaurahiri Jet (☎03/236 1137) or Wairaurahiri Wilderness Jet (☎03/225 8174 & 0800/270 556), both of which run day-trips across Lake Hauroko, followed by **jetboating** 27km of the Grade III Wairaurahiri River down to the coast, and exploring the bush around Percy Burn. Transport can be arranged from Tuatapere (see below) or Clifden, and trips are priced by the boat-load ($400 for up to 3 people, $500 for 4 or 5).

Tuatapere and around

Two sawmills and one feeble stand of beech and podocarp forest is the only evidence that **TUATAPERE**, on the banks of the Waiau River 14km south of Clifden, could once have justified its epithet of "The Hole in the Forest". As the largest town in southwestern Southland, the "sausage capital" of the area makes a good geographical though otherwise poor base for exploring the very southern limits of Fiordland.

The Town

Maori legend records the great war canoe Takitimu being wrecked on the Waiau River bar at Te Waewae Bay some six hundred years ago. Maori set up summer foraging camps along the river and used these as way-stations on the route to the *pounamu*

THE WAITUTU TRACKS

The map on the DOC's Waitutu Tracks *leaflet ($1) is adequate for these walks.*

The Waitutu Tracks is the combined name for two historic paths that slice through the largest area of lowland rainforest in New Zealand: the predominantly easy-going and well graded **South Coast Track** from Bluecliffs Beach on Te Waewae Bay southwest to Big River, and the tougher **Hump Track** which rises above the bushline en route from Bluecliffs Beach to Lake Hauroko. For **history** buffs, the South Coast Track in particular is one of the country's most interesting. The route follows a portion of the 100km track cut in 1896 to link Orepuki, 18km southeast of Tuatapere, with Cromarty and Te Oneroa, gold-mining settlements in the southernmost fiord of Preservation Inlet. This paved the way for wood cutters, who arrived en masse in the 1920s. Logs were transported to the mills on tramways, which crossed the burns and gullies on **viaducts** built of Australian hardwood – four of the finest have been faithfully restored, including the one over Percy Burn that spans 125m.

Bluecliffs Beach **trailhead access** is by road from Tuatapere with Lake Hauroko Tours (☎03/226 6681; $30) or by jetboat (Wairaurahiri Jet ☎03/225 8318; or Wairaurahiri Wilderness Jet ☎03/225 8174). Expect to take **a week** to explore all of the South Coast Track; it takes the best part of four days to reach Big River and you'll just have to turn around and walk back, unless you prearrange a **jetboat** out of Wairaurahiri Hut. A popular alternative is to make a **three-day excursion**, staying at Port Craig Hut for two nights and exploring the environs on the second day. Three huts (Cat 3; $5), spaced four to seven hours' walk apart, provide **accommodation** on the South Coast Track and camping is free. Following the accidental razing of the Hump Hut in 1994, the Hump Track has only one hut (Cat 3; $5), around nine hours' walk from Bluecliffs Beach.

THE SOUTH COAST TRACK

The first day's walk is typically **Bluecliffs Beach to Port Craig Hut** (20km; 5–7hr; negligible ascent), a relatively easy walk following either the old logging road or, tide permitting, the beach – which should shave an hour off your walking time. On the section from **Port Craig Hut to Wairaurahiri Hut** (16km; 4–6hr; 200m ascent) the track follows the old tramway, crossing all four of the restored viaducts, before dropping down to the Wairaurahiri River. The path from **Wairaurahiri Hut to Waitutu Hut** (13km, 4–6hr; negligible ascent) largely follows the coastal flats across Maori land. Fit trampers with camping equipment might want to continue from **Waitutu Hut to Big River** (12km; 5–7hr; negligible ascent), the boundary of Fiordland National Park and the end of the track; note that there are no facilities of any kind at Big River. It's also worth remembering that this track gets quite muddy if there's rain.

THE HUMP TRACK

The lack of huts makes camping equipment a real boon on the Hump Track. From **Bluecliffs Beach to Teal Bay Hut** (17km; 9–10hr; 600m ascent, 300m descent), you pick up the old logging road for about 7km to the remains of an old hut and a path branching north. This gradually climbs a ridge, which is followed for around five hours to the site of the burned-out Hump Hut, just below the bushline. The track soon ascends into open country; follow the ill-defined path and the line of orange snow poles, keeping an eye out for a large marker where the path cuts left into the bush and follows another ridge down to the Teal Bay Hut, on the shore of Lake Hauroko. The track from **Teal Bay Hut to Hauroko car park** (18km; 9hr; 300m ascent) hauls steeply up a spur to a ridge that runs parallel to Lake Hauroko for 7km, then descends to Second Bay, which is followed eastwards. The final stretch climbs a headland to First Bay before following an easy shoreline path to the finish, where there is a very basic shelter.

fields around Milford Sound, but it wasn't until European **pioneers** arrived around 1885 that Tuatapere came into being. By 1909 the **railway** had arrived from

Invercargill, bringing with it increasingly sophisticated steam-powered haulers that made short work of clearing the surrounding bushland. More recently, foresters' attention shifted west to the fringes of the Fiordland National Park where, in the 1970s, the Maori owners proposed clear felling stands of rimu. Environmentalists prevailed upon the Conservation Minister who eventually, in 1996, agreed to pay compensation in return for a sustainable management policy. The bush's last stand – a riverside clump of beech, kahikatea and totara on the Domain – forms one station on the **Tuatapere Walkway**, a 5km stroll around town guided by a leaflet from the DOC. If you want to see a rose-coloured version of pioneer history then try out the local museum next to the visitor centre (daily 9am–5pm; free) where the displays are well presented if one-sided.

Practicalities

For such a small town, Tuatapere is thinly spread. The riverside town centre holds a **DOC office**, 21 Orawai Rd (not open to the public) and the Tuatapere **visitor centre**, 18 Orawai Rd (daily 9am–5pm; ☎03/226 6399), which is open to the public although the staff are very unhelpful.

The only **accommodation** of note is the *Five Mountains Holiday Park and Hump Track Backpackers*, 14 Clifden Rd (☎03/226 6418) with cheap, very basic units (②), a primitive bunkhouse (①), and a spacious, if ill-equipped, camping area ($6).

The best **eating** around, and that's not saying much, is to be found at the *South Coast Café*, on the corner of Clifden Road and Half Mile Road (☎03/226 6665), which displays some moa bones found on Goldie Hill in a glass case, in a corridor on the way to the toilet. The other alternatives are to settle for a bar snack at the *Waiau Hotel*, 47 Main St, or go to the butchers, 75 Main St (Mon–Fri 8am–12.30pm & 1.30–5pm) for some of their famous sausages (a mutton and beef mix) and then head out of town in search of a stove.

Around Tuatapere

There is no reason to spend much time in Tuatapere itself, though you might use it as a base for jetboat trips on Lake Hauroko (see p.838) or as a springboard for **Te Waewae Bay**, a large bite out of the Southland coastline 10km to the south where Hector's dolphins frequently frolic and the occasional southern right whale drifts past. **Bluecliffs Beach**, at its western end, 28km from Tuatapere, is the start of the South Coast Track (see box on previous page).

Colac Bay and Riverton

South of Tuatapere, SH99 follows the wind-ravaged cliffs behind the wide and moody Te Waewae Bay, where fierce southerlies have sculpted some much-photographed macrocarpa trees into compact forms not unlike giant broccoli. Beyond the small town of Orepuki, the road cuts inland, regaining the sea 45km southeast of Tuatapere, at the quiet community of **Colac Bay** – a name eighteenth-century whalers derived from the name of the local Maori chief, Korako. Swimming aside, there's little reason to stop here, and you might as well press on a further 12km to **RIVERTON** (*Aparima*), one of the country's oldest settlements. Used by whalers from New South Wales as early as the last decade of the eighteenth century, the town was formally established in 1836 by another whaler, John Howell – who is also credited with kick-starting New Zealand's now formidable sheep-farming industry. The town also boasts a proliferation of somewhat shambolic Art Deco buildings.

Strung along a spit between the sea and the Jacob's River Estuary (actually the mouth of the Aparima and Pourakino rivers), where fishing boats still harbour, Riverton has a relaxed almost comatose feel that might just lull you into staying for a day or so.

The town is trying to pitch itself as some kind of paua capital, with a giant paua shell at the eastern entrance to town, buildings painted in shell-like colours, plans to inlay the streets with bits of shell and, should you be in need of any, shops selling the shells by the score. You should reserve an hour for the interesting local history and hoard of knick-knacks in the **Early Settlers Museum**, 172 Palmerston St (☎03/234 8520; daily 2–4pm; gold coin donation requested). Otherwise, you'll have to seek diversion on the water: one-hour scenic and historic rides up the Pourakino River are offered by Pourakino Jet Boat Tours (☎03/224 6130; around $65); or let one of the many boat charters take you out trout or saltwater **fishing** (check at the visitor centre to see which ones are awake).

Local **information**, including a leaflet detailing leisurely beach and hilltop walks, is available in the Riverton Visitor Information Centre (Nov–Feb daily 9.30am–4.30pm; March–Oct Mon–Fri, same times), on the corner of Palmerston Street and Princess Street, where friendly and helpful staff will tell you more than you ever wanted to know about the town and the area.

Easily the best **place to stay** is *The Riverton Rock*, at 136 Palmerston St (☎03/234 8886 & 0800/248 886, fax 234 8816), where beautifully decorated but expensive, standard (③) and en-suite (④), rooms occupy a recently renovated 1870s building, and there's also a bunkroom $21 a bunk; campervans can park outside for $24, and everyone gets to use the well-equipped kitchen area and spacious, comfortable lounge overlooking the lagoon. If they're full, make for the *Riverton Caravan Park and Holiday Homes* on Roy Street (☎03/234 8526; tent sites $7.50, bunkhouse ①, cottages & chalets ②–③). Of the limited range of **places to eat**, the most appealing is the *Nostalgia Country Café*, 108 Palmerston St (closed winter weekday evenings), which is good for coffee, light meals and predominantly seafood specials.

Beyond Riverton, SH99 heads into the hinterland of Invercargill, 40km away.

travel details

Buses

From Manapouri to: Clifden (1 weekly; 1hr 30min); Te Anau (2 daily; 20min); Riverton (1 weekly; 5hr); Tuatapere (1 weekly; 3hr).

From Milford Sound to: Te Anau (2–5 daily; 2hr 15min); The Divide (2–5 daily; 1hr 30min); Queenstown (2 daily; 5hr 15min).

From Te Anau to: Dunedin (1 daily; 5hr); Manapouri (2 daily; 20min); Milford Sound (2–5 daily; 2hr 15min); Invercargill (2 daily; 3hr); Manapouri (2 daily; 20min); Queenstown (3–5 daily; 2hr 15min); Te Anau Downs (2 daily

Nov–April; 30min); The Divide (2–5 daily; 1hr 20min).

From The Divide to: Milford Sound (2–5 daily; 1hr 30min); Te Anau (2–5 daily; 1hr 20min).

From Tuatapere to: Invercargill (1 weekly; 2hr 30min); Riverton (1 weekly; 1hr 30min).

Flights

From Milford Sound to: Queenstown (5–20 daily; 35min).

From Te Anau to: Queenstown (3 daily; 30min).

THE
CONTEXTS

A BRIEF HISTORY

White New Zealanders have long thought of their country as a model of humanitarian colonization. Most Maori take a different view, however, informed by generations of their ancestors witnessing the theft of land and erosion of rights that were guaranteed by a treaty with the white man. Schoolroom histories have long been faithful to the European view, even to the point of influencing Maori mythology, but in the last couple of decades revisionist historians have largely discredited what many New Zealanders know as fact. Much that is presented as tradition, on deeper investigation turns out to be late nineteenth-century scholarship, often the product of historians who bent what they heard to fit their theories and, in the worst cases, even destroyed evidence. What follows is inextricably interwoven with Maori legend and can be understood more fully with reference to the section on *Maoritanga* (see p.859).

PRE-EUROPEAN HISTORY

Humans from southeast Asia first started exploring the South Pacific around five thousand years ago, gradually evolving a distinct culture as they filtered down through the islands of the Indonesian archipelago. A thousand years of progressive island hopping got them as far as Tonga and Samoa, where a distinctly Polynesian society continued to evolve, the people honing their seafaring skills and navigational skills to the point where lengthy sea journeys were possible. Around a thousand years ago, Polynesian culture reached its classical apotheosis in the Society Islands, a group west of Tahiti. This was almost certainly the hub for a series of migrations heading southwest across thousands of kilometres of open ocean, past the Cook Islands, eventually striking land in what is now known as **New Zealand** (*Aotearoa*).

It is thought that the first of these Polynesian people, the ancestors of modern **Maori**, arrived in double-hulled canoes between 1000 and 1100 AD, as a result of a migration that was planned to the extent that they took with them the *kuri* (dog) and food plants such as taro (a starchy tuber), yam and kumara (sweet potato). It seems likely that there were several migrations and there may have even been two-way traffic, although archeological evidence points to a cessation of contact well before 1500 AD. The widely believed story of a legendary "Great Fleet" of seven canoes arriving in 1350 AD seems most likely to be the product of a fanciful Victorian adaptation of Maori oral history, which has been readopted into contemporary Maori legend.

Arriving Polynesians found a land so much colder than their tropical home that many of the crops and plants they brought with them wouldn't grow. Fortunately there was an abundance of large quarry in the form of marine life and flightless birds, particularly in the South Island, where most settled. The people of this **Archaic Period** are often misleadingly known as "Moa Hunters" and while some undoubtedly lived off these birds, they didn't exist in other areas. By 1300, settlements had been established all around the coast, but it was only later that there is evidence of horticulture, possibly supporting the contention that there was a later migration bringing plants for cultivation. On the other hand, it may just signal the beginning of successful year-round food storage allowing a settled living pattern rather than the short-lived campsites used by earlier hunters. Whichever is the case, this marks the beginning of the **Classic period** when *kainga* (villages) grew up close to the kumara grounds, often supported by pa (fortified villages) where the people could retreat when under attack. As tasks became more specialized and hunting and horticulture began to take up less time, the arts – particularly carving and weaving (see p.862 – began to flourish and warfare became endemic, digs revealing an armoury of *mere*, *patu* and *taiaha* (fighting clubs) not found earlier. The decline of easily caught birdlife and the relative ease of growing kumara in the warmer North Island marked the beginning of a northward population shift, to the extent that when the Europeans arrived, ninety-five percent of the population was located in the North Island, mostly in the northern reaches, with coastal settlements reaching down to Hawke's Bay and Wanganui.

EUROPEAN CONTACT AND THE MAORI RESPONSE

Ever since Europeans had ventured across the oceans and "discovered" other continents, many were convinced of the existence of a *terra australia incognita*, an unknown southern land thought necessary to counterbalance the northern continents. In 1642, the Dutch East India Company, keen to dominate any trade with this new continent, sent Dutchman **Abel Tasman** to the southern oceans where he became the first European to catch sight of the South Island of *Aotearoa*. He anchored in Golden Bay, where a small boat being rowed between Tasman's two ships was intercepted by a Maori war canoe and four sailors were killed. Without setting foot on land Tasman turned tail and fled up the west coast of the North Island and went on to add Tonga and Fiji to European maps. He named *Aotearoa* "Staten Landt" later renamed Nieuw Zeeland after the Dutch maritime province.

New Zealand was ignored for over a century until 1769 when Yorkshireman **James Cook** sailed his *Endeavour* into the Pacific to observe the passage of Venus across the sun. He continued west arriving at "the Eastern side of the Land discover'd by Tasman" where he observed the "Genius, Temper, Disposition and Number of the Natives" and meticulously charted the coastline – the only significant errors were to show Banks Peninsula as an island and Stewart Island as a peninsula – and encouraged his botanists, Banks and Solander, to collect numerous samples.

Cook and his crew found Maori a sophisticated people with a highly formalized social structure and an impressive ability to turn stone and wood into fabulously carved canoes, weapons and meeting houses – and yet they were tied to Stone Age technology, with no wheels, roads, metalwork, pottery or animal husbandry. Cook found them aggressive, surly and little inclined to trade, but after an initial unfortunate encounter near Gisborne (see p.391) and another off Cape Kidnappers, near Napier (see p.405), he managed to strike up friendly and constructive relations with the "Indians". These "Indians" now found that their tribal allegiance was not enough to differentiate them from the Europeans and subsequently began calling themselves *maori* (meaning "normal" or "not distinctive") while referring to the newcomers as *pakeha* ("foreign").

Offshore from the Coromandel Peninsula, Cook deviated from instructions and unfurled the British flag, claiming formal possession without the consent of Maori, but was still allowed to return twice in 1772 and 1776. The French were also interested in New Zealand, and on his first voyage Cook had passed **Jean Francois Marie de Surville** in a storm without either knowing of the other's presence. Two years later, **Marion du Fresne** spent five amicable weeks around the Bay of Islands, before most of his crew were killed, probably after inadvertently transgressing some *tapu* (taboo).

The establishment of the Botany Bay penal colony in neighbouring Australia aroused the first commercial interest in New Zealand and from the 1790s to the 1830s New Zealand was very much part of the Australian frontier. By 1830 the coast was dotted with semi-permanent **sealing** communities which, within thirty years, had almost clubbed the seals into extinction. Meanwhile the British navy was rapidly felling giant kauri trees for its ships' masts, while others were busy supplying Sydney shipbuilders. By the 1820s **whalers** had moved in, basing themselves at Kororareka (now Russell, in the Bay of Islands), where they could recruit Maori crew and provision their ships. This combination of rough whalers, escaped convicts from Australia and all manner of miscreants and adventurers combined to turn Russell into "the Hellhole of the Pacific", a lawless place populated by what Darwin, on his visit in 1835, found to be "the very refuse of Society".

Before long, the Maori way of life had been entirely disrupted. Maori were quick to understand the importance of guns and **inter-tribal fighting** soon broke out on a scale never seen before. Hongi Hika from Ngapuhi *iwi* of the Bay of Islands was the first chief to acquire firearms in 1821, adding 300 muskets to his stock by trading the gifts showered on him by London society when he was presented to George IV as an "equal". Vowing to emulate the supreme power of the imperial king, he set about subduing much of the North Island, using the often badly maintained and inexpertly aimed guns to rattle the enemy, who were then slaughtered with the traditional *mere*. Warriors abandoned the old fighting season – the lulls between hunting and tending the crops – and set off to settle old scores, resulting in a massive loss of life. The quest for new territory fuelled the actions of Ngati Toa's **Te Rauparaha** (see p.219), who soon controlled the southern half of the North Island.

The huge demand for firearms drove Maori to sell the best of their food, relocating to unhealthy areas close to flax swamps, where flax production could be increased. Even highly valued tribal treasures – *pounamu* (greenstone) clubs and the preserved heads of chiefs taken in battle – were traded. Poor living conditions allowed European **diseases** to sweep through the Maori population time and again, while alcohol and tobacco abuse became widespread, Maori women were prostituted to *pakeha* sailors, and the tribal structure began to crumble.

Into this scene stepped the **missionaries** in 1814, the brutal New South Wales magistrate, **Samuel Marsden**, arriving in the Bay of Islands a transformed man with a mission to bring Christianity and "civilization" to Maori, and to save the souls of the sealers and whalers. Subsequently Anglicans, Wesleyans and Catholics all set up missions throughout the North Island, playing a significant role in protecting Maori from the worst of the exploitation and campaigning in both London and Sydney for more policing of *pakeha* actions. In return, they destroyed fine artworks considered too sexually explicit and demanded that Maori abandon cannibalism and slavery; in short Maori were expected to trade in their *Maoritanga* and become Brown Europeans. By the 1830s, self-confidence and the belief in Maori ways was in rapid decline: the *tohunga* (priest) was powerless over new European diseases which could often be cured by the missionaries, and Maori

had started to believe the *pakeha*, who were convinced that the Maori race was dying out. They felt they needed help.

THE PUSH FOR COLONIZATION

Despite Cook's "discoverer's" claim in 1769, imperial cartographers had never marked New Zealand as a British possession and it was with some reluctance – informed by the perception of an over-extended empire only marginally under control – that New South Wales law was nominally extended to New Zealand in 1817. The effect was minimal; the New South Wales governor had no official representation on this side of the Tasman and was powerless to act. Unimpressed, by 1831 a small group of northern Maori chiefs decided to petition the British monarch to become a "friend and the guardian of these islands", a letter that was later used to justify Britain's intervention.

Britain's response was to send the pompous and less-than-competent **James Busby** as British Resident in 1833, with a brief to encourage trade, stay on good terms with the missionaries and Maori, and apprehend escaped convicts for return to Sydney. Feeling that New Zealand was becoming a drain on the colony's economy, the New South Wales governor, Bourke, withheld guns and troops, and Busby was unable to enforce his will. Busby was also duped by the madness of Baron de Thierry, a Brit of French parents, who claimed he had bought most of the Hokianga district from Hongi Hika and styled himself the "sovereign chief of New Zealand", ostensibly to save Maori from the degradation he foresaw under British dominion. In a panic, Busby misguidedly persuaded 35 northern chiefs to proclaim themselves as the **"United Tribes of New Zealand"** in 1835. As far as the Foreign Office was concerned, this allowed Britain to disclaim responsibility for the actions of its subjects.

By the late 1830s there were around two thousand *pakeha* in New Zealand, the largest concentration around Kororareka in the Bay of Islands, where there were often up to thirty ships at anchor. Most were British, but French Catholics were consolidating their tentative toehold, and in 1839 James Clendon was appointed American consul. Meanwhile, land speculators and colonists were taking an interest for the first time. The Australian emancipationist, William Charles Wentworth,

THE TREATY OF WAITANGI: IN ENGLISH AND MAORI

The main points set out in the **English treaty** are as follows.

• The chiefs cede sovereignty of New Zealand to the Queen of England.

• The Queen guarantees the chiefs the "full exclusive and undisturbed possession of their Lands and Estates Forests Fisheries and other properties which they may collectively or individually possess".

• The Crown retains the right of pre-emption over Maori lands.

• The Queen extends the rights and privileges of British subjects to Maori.

However, the **Maori translation** presents numerous possibilities for misunderstanding, since Maori is a more idiomatic and metaphorical language, where words can take on several different meanings. The main points of contention are as follows.

The preamble of the English version cites the main **objectives** of the treaty being to protect Maori interests, to provide for British settlement and to set up a government to maintain peace and order. On the other hand, the main thrust of the Maori version is that the all-important rank and status of the chiefs and tribes will be maintained.

In the Maori version, the concept of **sovereignty** is translated as *kawanatanga* (governorship), a word Maori linked to their experience of the toothless reign of British Resident James Busby. It seems unlikely that the chiefs realized just what they were giving away.

In the Maori text, the Crown guaranteed the *tangata whenua* (people of the land) the possession of their properties for as long as they wished to keep them. In English this was expressed in terms of **individual rights** over property. This is perhaps the most wilful mistranslation and, in practice, there were long periods when Maori were coerced into selling their **land**, and when they refused, lands were simply taken.

Pre-emption was translated as *hokonga* – a term simply meaning "buying and selling", with no explanation of the Crown's exclusive right to buy Maori land, which was clearly spelled out in the English version. This has resulted in considerable friction over Maori being unable to sell any land that the government didn't want, even if they had a buyer.

The implications of British **citizenship** may not have been well understood: it is not clear whether Maori realized they would be bound by British law.

had "bought" the South Island and Stewart Island for a few hundred pounds (the largest private land deal in history, subsequently quashed by government order) and British settlers were already setting sail. The British admiralty finally began to take notice when it became apparent that the Australian convict settlements, originally intended simply as an out-of-sight, out-of-mind solution to their bulging prisons, looked set to become a valuable possession.

It was a combination of these pressures and Busby's continual exaggeration of the Maori inability to control their own affairs that goaded the British government into action. The result was the 1840 **Treaty of Waitangi** (see box above, and also p.448), a document that purported to guarantee continued Maori control of their lands, rights and possessions in return for their loss of sovereignty, a concept poorly understood by Maori. The annexed lands became a dependency of New South Wales until New Zealand was declared a separate colony a year later.

SETTLEMENT AND THE EARLY PIONEERS

Even before the Treaty was signed, there were moves to found a settlement in Port Nicholson, the site of Wellington, on behalf of the **New Zealand Company**. This was the brainchild of **Edward Gibbon Wakefield**, who desperately wanted to stem American-style egalitarianism and hoped to use New Zealand as the proving ground for his theory of "scientific colonization". This involved preserving the English squire-and-yokel class structure by encouraging the settlement of a cross-section of English society, though without the "dregs" at the bottom. It was supposed to be a self-regulating system, whereby the company would buy large tracts of land cheaply from the government then charge a price low enough to encourage the relatively wealthy to invest, yet high enough to prevent labourers from becoming landowners. The revenue from land sales was then to fund the transportation of cheap labour to work the land, but the system ended up encouraging absentee landlordism as English "gentlemen", arriving to find somewhere altogether more rugged and less refined than they had been promised, hot-footed it to Australia or America.

Between 1839 and 1843 the New Zealand Company dispatched nearly 19,000 settlers and established them in **"planned settlements"** in Wellington, Wanganui, Nelson and New Plymouth. This was the core of *pakeha* immigration, the only substantial non-Wakefield settlement being **Auckland**, a scruffy collection of waterside shacks which, to the horror of New Zealand Company officials, became the capital after the signing of the Treaty of Waitangi. Maori welfare and social justice had no place in all this, despite the precarious position of *pakeha* settlements, which were nothing but tiny enclaves in a country still under Maori control. Transgressing the protocols of the local *iwi* was likely to have graver implications than offending the *pakeha* government.

The company couldn't buy land direct from Maori, but the government bought up huge tracts and sold it on, often for ten or twenty times what they paid for it. Maori must have been well aware that they were being swindled and could have negotiated better prices themselves, but sold almost the whole of the South Island in a number of large blocks. Some was bought by two more organizations expounding the Wakefield principle: the dour Free Church of Scotland founded **Dunedin** in 1848, while the Canterbury Association established **Christchurch** in 1850, fashioning it English, Anglo-Catholic and conservative. In 1850 the New Zealand Company foundered, leaving well-established settlements which, subject to the hard realities of colonial life, had failed to conform to Wakefield's lofty theories and were filled with sturdy workers from labouring and lower middle-class backgrounds.

In 1852 New Zealand achieved self-government and set about dividing the country into six **provinces** – Auckland, New Plymouth, Wellington, Nelson, Canterbury and Otago – which took over land sales and encouraged migrants with free passage, land grants and guaranteed employment on road construction schemes. The same people drawn to the

Wakefield settlements heeded the call, hoping for a better life away from the oppression and drudgery of working-class Britain. The new towns were alive with ambitious folk prepared to work hard to realize their high expectations, but many felt stymied by the low-quality land they were able to buy. At this point Maori still held the best land and were doing quite nicely growing potatoes and wheat for both local consumption and export to Australia, where the Victorian gold rush had created a huge demand. *Pakeha* were barely able to compete, and with the slump in export prices in the mid-1850s, many looked to pastoralism. The Crown helped out by halving the price of land, allowing poorer settlers to become landowners but simultaneously paving the way for the creation of huge pastoral runs and putting further pressure on Maori to sell land.

MAORI DISCONTENT AND THE NEW ZEALAND WARS

The first five years after the signing of the Treaty were a disaster, first under governor Hobson then under the ineffectual FitzRoy. Relations between Maori and *pakeha* began to deteriorate immediately, as the capital was moved from Kororareka to Auckland and duties were imposed in the Bay of Islands. The consequent loss of trade from passing ships precipitated the first tangible expression of dissent, a famous series of incidents involving the Ngapuhi leader **Hone Heke**, who repeatedly felled the most fundamental symbol of British authority, the flagstaff at Russell (see p.173). The situation was normalized to some degree by the appointment of **George Grey**, the most able of New Zealand's governors and a man who did more than anyone else to shape the country's early years. He was economical with the truth and despotic, but possessed the intelligence to use his deceit in a most effective (and often benign) way. As Maori began to adapt their culture to accommodate *pakeha* in a way that few other native peoples have – selling their crops, operating flour mills and running coastal shipping – Grey encouraged the process by establishing mission schools, erecting hospitals where Maori could get free treatment, and providing employment on public works. In short, he did what he could to uphold the spirit of the Treaty, thereby gaining enormous respect among Maori. Sadly, he failed to set up any

850/CONTEXTS

mechanism to perpetuate his policies after he left for the governorship of Cape Town in 1853. Under New Zealand's constitution, enacted in 1852, Maori were excluded from political decision-making and prevented from setting up their own form of government; although British subjects in name, they had few of the practical benefits and yet were increasingly expected to comply with British law.

By now it was clear that Maori had been duped by the Treaty of Waitangi: one chief explained that they thought they were transferring the "shadow of the land" while "the substance of the land remains with us", and yet he now conceded "the substance of the land goes to the Europeans, the shadow only will be our portion". Growing **resistance** to land sales came at a time when settler communities were expanding and demanding to buy huge tracts of pastoral land. With improved communications *pakeha* became more self-reliant and dismissive of Maori, who progressively began to lose faith in the government and fell back on traditional methods of handling their affairs. Self-government had given landowners the vote, but since Maori didn't hold individual titles to their land they were denied suffrage. Maori and *pakeha* aspirations seemed completely at odds and there was a growing sense of betrayal, which helped to replace tribal animosities with a tenuous unity. In 1854, a month before New Zealand's first parliament, Maori held inter-tribal meetings to discuss a response to the degradation of their culture and the rapid loss of their land. The eventual upshot was the 1858 election of the ageing **Te Wherowhero**, head chief of the Waikatos, as the Maori "King", the leader of the **King Movement** behind which Maori could rally to hold back the flood of *pakeha* settlement. Initially just the Waikato and central North Island *iwi* supported the King, but soon Taranaki and some Hawke's Bay *iwi* joined in a loose federation united in vowing not to sell any more land. This brave attempt to challenge the changes forced upon them gave Maori a sense of purpose and brought with it a resurgence of ancient customs such as tattooing. While some radical Maori wanted to completely rid the country of the white menace, most were moderates and made peaceful overtures that *pakeha* chose to regard as rebellious.

By now, most settlers felt that the Treaty of Waitangi had no validity whatsoever and sided with the land sellers to drive the government to repress the Maori landholders. There had been minor skirmishes over land throughout the country, but matters came to a head in 1860, when the government used troops to enforce a bogus purchase of land at Waitara, near New Plymouth. The fighting was temporarily confined to Taranaki but soon spread to consume the whole of the North Island in the **New Zealand Wars**, once known by *pakeha* as the Maori Wars and by Maori as *te riri pakeha* (white man's anger). Maori were divided: most of the supporters of the King movement, particularly the Waikatos, traced their *whakapapa* (genealogy) back to the Tainui canoe and some others chose this opportunity to settle old grievances by siding with the government against their traditional enemies. Through the early 1860s the number of *pakeha* troops was tripled to around 3000, providing an effective force against Maori who failed to adopt a co-ordinated strategy. The warrior ethic meant there was no place for more effective guerrilla tactics, except in the east of the North Island, where **Te Kooti** (see box, p.401) kept the government troops on the run. Elsewhere Maori frequently faced off against ranked artillery and, though there were notable successes, the final result was inevitable. Fighting had abated by the end of the 1860s but peace wasn't finally declared until 1881, when the Maori fastness of the "King Country" (an area south of Hamilton which still goes by that title) was finally opened up to *pakeha* once again.

British soldiers had been lured into service with offers of land and free passage and, as a further affront to defeated Maori, many of them were settled in the solidly Maori Waikato. Much of the most fertile land was **confiscated** – in the Waikato, the Bay of Plenty and Taranaki – with little regard to the owners' allegiances during the conflict. By 1862 the Crown had relinquished its right of pre-emption and individuals could buy land directly from Maori, who were forced to limit the stated ownership first to ten individuals and later to just one owner. With their collective power smashed, there was little resistance to voracious land agents luring Maori into debt then offering to buy their land to save them.

Throughout this period, Maori tradition was ignored by settlers and an Anglo-Saxon world view came to dominate all aspects of New

Zealand life; by 1871 the Maori language was no longer used for teaching in schools. A defeated people were widely thought to be close to extinction: Anthony Trollope in 1872 wrote "There is scope for poetry in their past history. There is room for philanthropy as to their present condition. But in regard to their future – there is hardly a place for hope."

Meanwhile, as the New Zealand Wars raged in the North Island, **gold fever** had struck the South. Flakes had been found near Queenstown in 1861 and the initial rushes soon spread to later finds along the West Coast. For the best part of a decade, gold was New Zealand's major export, but the gold provinces never had a major influence on the rest of the country, nor does the gold era retain the legendary status it does in California and Victoria. The major effect was on population distribution: by 1858 the shrinking Maori population had been outstripped by the rapidly swelling horde of *pakeha* settlers, a number which doubled during the first three years of the gold rush, most settling in the South Island where relations with Maori played a much smaller part. The South Island prospered, with both Christchurch and Dunedin consolidating their roles, serving the surrounding farms and more distant sheep stations. Dunedin became the largest town in the country, the influx of the "New Iniquity" radically changing the city's staunch front of the "Old Identity".

CONSOLIDATION AND SOCIAL REFORM

The 1870s were dominated by the policies of **Julius Vogel**, an able Treasurer who started a programme of borrowing on a massive scale to fund public works. Within a decade what had previously been a land of scattered towns in separately governed provinces was transformed into an single country unified by improved roads, an expanding rail system, 7000 kilometres of telegraph wires and numerous public institutions. Almost all the remaining farmable land was bought up or leased from Maori and acclimatization societies sprang up with the express aim of anglicizing the New Zealand countryside and improving **farming**. New Zealand quickly began to realize the agricultural expectation created by fertile soils, a temperate climate and relatively high rainfall. Arable farming was mostly abandoned and pastoralism was taking hold, particularly among those rich

enough to afford to buy and ship the stock. With no extensive market close enough to make perishable produce profitable, **wool** became the main export item, stimulated by the development of the Corriedale sheep, a Romney-Lincoln cross with a long fleece. Wool continued as the mainstay until 1882, when the first refrigerated shipment left for Britain, signalling a turning point in the New Zealand economy and the establishment of New Zealand as Britain's offshore larder, a role it maintained until the 1970s.

From 1879 until 1896 New Zealand went into the "long depression", mostly overseen by the conservative "Continuous Ministry" – the last government composed of colonial gentry. During this time **trade unionism** began to influence the political scene and bolstered the Liberal Pact (a Liberal and Labour alliance), which, in 1890, wrested power from those who had controlled the country for two decades and ushered in an era of unprecedented social change. Its first leader, **John Ballance**, firmly believed in state intervention and installed **William Pember Reeves**, probably New Zealand's most radically socialist MP, as his Minister of Labour. Reeves was instrumental in pushing through sweeping reforms to working hours and factory conditions that were so progressive that no further changes were made to labour laws until 1936. On his own initiative, with no apparent demand from workers, he introduced the world's first **compulsory arbitration system**, which went on to award numerous wage rises, so increasing the national prosperity. He had become too radical for most of his colleagues, however, and only remained in office until 1896. When Ballance died in 1892 he was replaced by **Richard "King Dick" Seddon**, a blunt Lancastrian who became, along with Grey, one of the country's greatest, if least democratic, leaders. Following Ballance's lead he introduced a graduated income tax and repealed property tax, hoping to break up some of the large estates (something eventually achieved much later, as technological changes made dairying and mixed farming more prosperous). New Zealand was already being tagged the "social laboratory of the world", but more was to come.

In 1893, New Zealand was the first nation in the world to enact full **female suffrage**, undoubtedly in line with the liberal thinking of the time, but apparently an accident nonetheless. The story goes that Seddon let an amendment to an electoral reform bill pass on the assumption that it would be rejected by the Legislative Council (an upper house which survived until 1950), thus diverting the ill will of suffragists. Others contend that female suffrage was approved not for any free-thinking liberal principle but in response to the powerful quasi-religious temperance movement, which hoped to "purify and improve the tone of our politics", effectively giving married couples double the vote of the single man who was often seen as a drunken layabout. In 1898 Seddon further astonished the world by weathering a ninety-hour continuous debate to squeeze through legislation guaranteeing an **old age pension**. Fabian Beatrice Webb, in New Zealand that same year, allowed that "it is delightful to see a country with no millionaires and hardly any slums".

By early this century, the radical impetus had faded along with the memory of the 1880s depression, and *pakeha* could rest easy in the knowledge that their standard of living was one of the highest in the world. But things were not so rosy for Maori, whose numbers had dropped from an estimated 200,000 at Cook's first visit to a low of 42,000 in 1896. However, as resistance to European diseases grew, numbers started rising, accompanied by a new confidence buoyed by the rise of Maori parliamentary leadership. **Apirana Ngata**, **Maui Pomare** and Te Rangi Hiroa (**Peter Buck**) were all products of Te Aute College, an Anglican school for Maori, and all were committed to working within the administrative and legislative framework of government, convinced that the survival of *Maoritanga* depended on shedding those aspects of the traditional lifestyle that impeded their acceptance of the modern world.

Seddon died in 1906 and the flame went out of the Liberal torch, though the party was to stay in power another six years. This era saw the rise of the "**Red Feds**", international socialists of the Red Federation who began to organize Kiwi labour. They rejected the arbitration system that had kept wage rises below the level of inflation and prevented strikes for a decade, and encouraged **strikes**, the longest at Blackball (see p.698) on the West Coast, where prime movers in the formation of the Federation of Miners, and subsequently the Federation of Labour, led a three-month stoppage.

The 1912 election was won by William Massey's Reform Party, with the support of the farmers or "cow cockies". Allegiances were now substantially polarized and 1912 and 1913 saw bitter fighting at a series of strikes at the gold mines of Waihi, the docks at Timaru and the wharves of Auckland. As workers opposed to the arbitration system withdrew their labour, the owners organized scab labour, while the hostile Farmers' Union recruited mounted "specials" to add to the government force of "special constables". All were protected by naval and military forces as they decisively smashed the Red Feds. The Prime Minister even handed out medals to strike-breaking dairy farmers. Further domestic conflict was only averted by the outbreak of war.

COMING OF AGE: 1916-1945

Though New Zealand had started off as an unwanted sibling of Mother England, it had soon transformed itself into a devoted daughter who could be relied upon in times of crisis. New Zealand had supported Britain in South Africa at the end of the nineteenth century and was now called upon to do the same in **World War I**. Locally born *pakeha* now outnumbered immigrants and, in 1907, New Zealand had traded its self-governing colony status for that of a Dominion, giving it control over its foreign policy; but the rising sense of nationalism didn't dilute a patriotism for the motherland far in excess of its filial duty. Altogether ten percent of the population were involved in the war effort, 100,000 fighting in the trenches of Gallipoli and elsewhere. Seventeen thousand failed to return, more than were lost in Belgium, a battleground with six times the population.

At home, the **Temperance Movement** was back in action, attempting to curb vice in the army brought on by the demon drink. Plebiscites in 1911, 1914 and 1919 narrowly averted national prohibition but the "wowsers" succeeded to the point that from 1917 pubs would close at 6pm for the duration of the war. Six o'clock closing entered the statute books in 1918: not until 1967 did its repeal end half a century of the "**Six o'clock swill**", an hour or so of frenetic after-work consumption in which the ability to tank down as much beer as possible was raised to an art form. This probably did more to hinder New Zealand's social development than anything else: pubs began to look more like lavatories, which could be hosed down after closing, and the predilection for quantity over quality encouraged breweries to churn out dreadful watery brews.

The wartime boom economy continued until around 1920 as Britain's demand for food remained high. Things looked rosy, especially for *pakeha* returned servicemen, who were rehabilitated on newly acquired farmland; in contrast, Maori returned servicemen got nothing. These highly mortgaged and inexperienced farmers began to suffer with the rapid drop in produce prices in the early 1920s, fostering a sense of insecurity which pervaded the country. Political leadership was weak and yet New Zealand continued to grow with ongoing improvements in infrastructure – hydroelectric dams and roads – and enormous improvements in farming techniques, such as the application of superphosphate fertilizers, sophisticated milking machines and tractors. New Zealand remained a prosperous nation but was ill prepared for the **Great Depression**, when the Wall Street Crash sent shock waves through the country. The already high national debt skyrocketed as export income dropped and the Reform government cut pensions, health care and public works' expenditure. The budget was balanced at the cost of producing huge numbers of unemployed. Prime Minister Forbes dictated "no pay without work" and sent thousands of men to primitive rural relief camps for unnecessary tasks such as planting trees and draining swamps in return for a pittance. With the knowledge of the prosperous years to come it is hard to conjure the image of lines of ragged men awaiting their relief money, malnourished children in schools and former soldiers panhandling in the streets.

Throughout the 1920s the Labour Party had gradually watered down some of its socialist policies in an attempt to woo the middle-ground voter. In 1935 they were swept to power and ushered in New Zealand's second era of massive social change, picking up where Seddon left off. Labour's leader **Michael Joseph Savage** felt that "Social Justice must be the guiding principle and economic organization must adapt itself to social needs", a sentiment translated by a contemporary commentator as aiming "to turn capitalism quite painlessly into a nicer sort of capitalism which will eventually become indistinguishable from socialism".

State socialism was out, but "Red Feds" still held half the cabinet posts. Salaries reduced during the depression were restored; public works programmes were rekindled, with workers on full pay rather than "relief"; income was redistributed through graduated taxation; and in two rapid bursts of legislation Labour built the model **Welfare State**, the first in the world and the most comprehensive and integrated. State houses were built and let at low rental, pensions were increased, a national health service provided free medicines and health care, and family benefits supplemented the income of those with children.

Maori welfare was also on the agenda and there were moves to raise their living standards to the *pakeha* level, partly achieved by increasing pensions and unemployment payments. Much of the best land had by now been sold off but legal changes paved the way for Maori land to be farmed using *pakeha* agricultural methods, while maintaining communal ownership. In return, the newly formed **Ratana Party**, who held all four of the Maori Parliamentary seats, supported Labour, keeping them in office until 1949.

New Zealand's perception of its world position changed dramatically in 1941 when the Japanese bombed Pearl Harbor. The country was forced to recognize its position half a globe away from Britain and in the military sphere of America. As in World War I, large numbers of troops were called up, amounting to a third of the male labour force, but casualties were fewer and on the home front the economy continued to boom. Foreign wars aside, by the 1940s New Zealand was the world's most prosperous country, with a fabulous quality of life and the comfortable bed of the Welfare State to fall back on.

MORE YEARS OF PROSPERITY

The Reform Party and the remnants of the Liberals eventually combined to form the **National Party** which, in 1949 wrested power from Labour. With McCarthyite rhetoric, National branded the more militant unionists as Communists and succeeded in breaking much of the power of the unions during the violent and emotional **1951 Waterfront dispute** – variously described as a strike and a lock-out. From the late 1940s until the mid-1980s, National became New Zealand's natural party of government, disturbed only by two three-year stints with Labour in power. The conservatism always bubbling under had now found its expression. Most were happy with the government's strong-arm tactics, which emasculated the militant unions and the country settled down to what novelist C.K. Stead viewed as the Kiwi ideal: "to live in a country with fresh air, an open landscape and plenty of sunshine; and to own a house, car, refrigerator, washing machine, *bach*, launch, fibre-glass rod, golf clubs, and so on." While the egalitarian myth still perpetuated by many Kiwis may never have existed, by most measures New Zealand's wealth was evenly spread, with few truly rich and relatively few poor.

The exception at least in economic terms were Maori, many now migrating in huge numbers to the cities, especially Auckland, responding to the urban labour shortages and good wages after World War II. By the 1970s the deracination of urban Maori was creating social unrest which, left unchannelled, resulted in high Maori unemployment and a disproportionate representation in prisons. Increasing contact between Maori and Europeans exposed weaknesses in the *pakeha* belief that the country's race relations were the best in the world. *Pakehas* took great pride in Maori bravery, skill, generosity and good humour, but were unable to set aside the discrimination which kept Maoris out of professional jobs.

On the economic front the major changes took place under **Walter Nash**'s 1957–60 Labour government, when New Zealand embarked on a programme designed to relieve the country's dependence on exports. A steel rolling mill, oil refinery, gin distillery and glass factory were all set up and an aluminium industry was encouraged by the prospect of cheap power from hydroelectric project on Lake Manapouri (see box, p.832). When **Keith Holyoake** took over at the helm of the next National government, Britain was still by far New Zealand's biggest export market but was making overtures to the economically isolationist European Common Market. New Zealand was becoming aware that Britain was no longer the guardian she once was. This was equally true in the **military** sphere, where New Zealand began to court its Pacific allies, signing the anti-Communist SEATO (South-East Asia Treaty Organization) document, and the ANZUS pact, which provided for mutual defence of Australia, New Zealand and the US.

DITHERING IN THE FACE OF ADVERSITY 1972-1984

In a landslide victory, the third **Labour government** took control in 1972. Again it was to only last a single three-year term, largely due to the difficulties of having to deal with international events beyond its control. Most fundamental was the long-expected entry of Britain into the Common Market. Some other export markets had been found but New Zealand still felt betrayed. Later the same year oil prices quadrupled in a few months and the treasury found itself with mounting fuel bills and decreasing export receipts. The government borrowed heavily but couldn't avoid electoral defeat in 1975 by National's obstreperous and pugnacious **Robert "Piggy" Muldoon**, who denounced Labour's borrowing and then outdid them. In short order New Zealand had dreadful domestic and foreign debt, unemployment was the highest for decades, and the unthinkable was happening – the standard of living was falling. People began to leave in their thousands and the "brain drain" almost reached crisis point. Muldoon's solution was to **"Think Big"** a catch-all term for a number of capital-intensive petrochemical projects designed to utilize New Zealand's abundant natural gas to produce ammonia, urea fertilizer, methanol and synthetic petrol. Though undoubtedly self-aggrandizing it made little economic sense. Rather than use local technology and labour to convert New Zealand vehicles to run on compressed natural gas (a system already up and running), Muldoon chose to pay international corporations to design and build huge prefabricated processing plants which were then shipped to New Zealand for assembly, mostly around New Plymouth.

Factory outfalls often jeopardized traditional Maori shellfish beds, and where once *iwi* would have accepted this as inevitable, a new spirit of protest saw them win significant concessions. Throughout the mid-1970s Maori began to question the philosophy of *pakeha* life and looked to the Treaty of Waitangi (see box, p.848) to correct the grievances that were aired at occupations of traditional land at Bastion Point in Auckland (see p.94), and Raglan, and through a petition delivered to parliament after a march across the North Island.

Maori also found expression in the formation of **gangs** – Black Power, the Mongrel Mob and the bike-oriented Highway 61 – along the lines graphically depicted in Lee Tamahori's film *Once Were Warriors*, which was originally written about south Auckland life in the 1970s. Fortified suburban homes still exist and such gangs continue to be influential among Maori youth, a position now being positively exploited to bring wayward Maori youth back into the fold.

Race relations were never Muldoon's strong suit and when large numbers of illegal **Polynesian immigrants** from south Pacific islands – particularly Tonga, Samoa and the Cook Islands – started arriving in Auckland he responded by instructing the police to conduct random street checks for "over-stayers", many of whom were deported. Muldoon opted for a completely hands-off approach when it came to sporting contacts with South Africa and in 1976 let the pig-headed rugby administrators send an All Black team over to play racially selected South African teams. African nations responded by boycotting the Montreal Olympics, putting New Zealand in the unusual position of being an international pariah. New Zealand signed the 1977 Gleneagles Agreement requiring it to "vigorously combat the evil of apartheid" and yet in 1981 the New Zealand Rugby Union courted a **Springbok Tour**, which sparked New Zealand's greatest civil disturbance since the labour riots of the 1920s.

MODERN NEW ZEALAND: A MATURING NATION

Muldoon's big-spending economic policies were widely perceived to be unsuccessful, and when he called a snap election in 1984, Labour were returned to power under **David Lange**. Just as National had eschewed traditional right-wing economics in favour of a "managed economy", Labour now changed tactics, addressing the massive economic problems by shunning the traditional left-of-centre approach. Instead, they grasped the baton of Thatcherite economics and sprinted off with it. Under Finance Minister Roger Douglas's **Rogernomics**, the dollar was devalued by twenty percent, exchange controls were abolished, tariffs slashed, the maximum income tax rate was halved, a Goods and Services Tax was introduced, Air New Zealand and the Bank of New Zealand were privatized, and state benefits were cut. Unemployment

doubled to twelve percent, a quarter of manufacturing jobs were lost, and the moderately well-off benefited at the expense of the poor; nevertheless, market forces and enterprise culture had come to stay. As one of the world's most regulated economies became one of the most deregulated, the longstanding belief that the state should provide for those least able to help themselves was cast aside.

In other spheres Labour's views weren't so right-wing. One of Lange's first acts was to refuse US ships entry to New Zealand ports unless they declared that they were nuclear-free. The Americans would do nothing of the sort and withdrew support for New Zealand's defence safety net, the **ANZUS** pact. Most of the country backed Lange on this but were less sure about his overtures towards Maori who, for the first time since the middle of the nineteenth century, got legal recognition for the Treaty of Waitangi. Now, Maori grievances dating back to 1840 could be addressed.

The rise in apparent income under Rogernomics created consumer confidence and the economy boomed until the **stock market crash** of 1987, which hit New Zealand especially hard. The country went into freefall and all confidence in the reforms was lost. Labour's position, consolidated in the 1987 election, now became untenable, and in the 1990 election National's **Jim Bolger** took the helm. Throughout the deep recession National continued Labour's free-market reforms, cutting welfare programmes (a policy dubbed "Ruthanasia" after its perpetrator Ruth Richardson) and extracting teeth from the unions by passing the Employment Contracts Act, which established the pattern of individual workplaces coming to their own agreements on wages and conditions. By the middle of the 1990s the economy had improved dramatically and what for a time had been considered a foolhardy experiment was seen by monetarists as a model for open economies the world over. Meanwhile, the gap between the rich and the poor continues to widen and New Zealand's classless society is increasingly exposed for the myth it always was.

While many have relished the good life, those at the bottom of the pile have suffered. In her resignation speech, **Cath Tizard**, the most popular and charismatic Governor-General New Zealand has had for years, levelled a thinly veiled attack at the government for its record on health care, but succeeded only in raising anti-monarchist hackles at her vice-regal intervention. Nonetheless, the kind of **republican rabble-rousing** championed across the Tasman in recent years largely falls on deaf ears in *Aotearoa*, where, despite the maturing of the nation in the last decade or so, and a progressive realignment with the Pacific and Asia, most seem happy to maintain links with Britain.

Ever since New Zealand achieved self-government from Britain in 1852, it had maintained a first-past-the-post Westminster style of parliament, with the exception of the scrapping of the upper house in 1950 and the provision for four (later five, and now six) Maori seats. Maori can chose to vote for their general or Maori candidate but not both. Through the late 1980s and early 1990s both parties had promised electoral reform and, in the depths of the recession in 1993, New Zealand voted for Mixed Member Proportional representation (MMP), a system which purports to give smaller parties an opportunity to have some say. In the two **MMP elections** since then, this has certainly proved to be the case. In 1996, National and Labour shared the majority of the vote, but the balance of power was held by **New Zealand First**, a new Maori-dominated party headed by former National MP, **Winston Peters**, who shaped their policies of reducing Asian immigration, increasing government spending and accountability, and getting long-term unemployed back to work. They eventually formed a coalition with National under Jim Bolger and introduced a new Maori spirit in parliament, with far more Maori MPs than ever before and maiden speeches received with a *waiata* (song) from their *whanau* (extended family group) in the public gallery. Unfortunately, most were political neophytes and NZ First self-destructed in short order after a spate of scandals. Bolger's poor handling of the situation saw his support

wane, and his attendance at a Commonwealth leaders' conference left the field open for a palace coup, in which **Jenny Shipley** became New Zealand's first female prime minister. Her brand of right-wing economics and more liberal social views succeeded in holding the coalition together but failed to bolster the polls on the lead up to the 1999 election. Suddenly, out of left-field came the **Green Party**, long-sidelined but newly resurgent under MMP. The vagaries of the MMP system meant that, on a nail-biting election night, the Greens were teetering between getting no seats at all and racking up six seats, a tally they eventually achieved with the counting of special votes. They formed a government with Labour and the Alliance, and sent New Zealand's first Rastafarian MP to parliament, one **Nandor Tanczos**. Resplendent in waist-length dreads and a new hemp suit he has become both a bogeyman for the opposition and something of a hero to disenfranchised youth. As if the political landscape weren't topsy-turvy enough, the staunchly conservative Wairarapa district returned the world's first transgender MP, Carterton's former mayor, **Georgina Beyer**.

Nine years in opposition left Labour (the senior coalition partner) with a considerable agenda for change, and they haven't held back. Logging of beech forests on the West Coast has been stopped, the Employment Contracts Act has been replaced by more worker-friendly legislation, and they've unilaterally abolished knighthoods. Support remains strong, but some are already voicing doubts about how long the honeymoon period can last.

Meanwhile, *Maoritanga* looks set to play an ever increasing role in the life of all New Zealanders as Maori consolidate the gains of the past few years. In the twenty-first century the number of New Zealanders who consider themselves Maori may well surpass the number of *pakeha*, and it remains to be seen just how significant that will be.

CHRONOLOGY OF NEW ZEALAND HISTORY

c. 1000AD   Arrival of first **Polynesians**.

c.1350   Mythical arrival of the "Great Fleet" from Hawaiki.

1642   Dutchman **Abel Tasman** sails past the West Coast but doesn't land.

1769   Englishman **James Cook** circumnavigates both main islands and makes first constructive contact.

1772   French sailor **Marion du Fresne** and 26 of his men killed in the Bay of Islands.

1809   Whangaroa Maori attack the *Boyd*; most of the crew killed.

1814   Arrival of **Samuel Marsden**, the first Christian missionary.

1830s   Sealing and whaling stations dotted around the coast.

1833   James Busby installed as British Resident at Waitangi.

1835   Independence of the United Tribes of NZ proclaimed.

1840   **Treaty of Waitangi** signed; capital moved from Kororareka to Auckland.

1840s   Cities of Auckland, Christchurch, Dunedin, Nelson, New Plymouth, Wanganui and Wellington all established.

1852   NZ becomes a self-governing colony divided into six provinces.

1858   Settlers outnumber Maori.

1860–65   **Land Wars** between *pakeha* and Maori.

1860s   Major gold rushes in the South Island.

1865   Capital moved from Auckland to Wellington.

1867   Maori men given the vote.

1870s   **Wool** established as the mainstay of the NZ economy.

1876   Abolition of provincial governments. Power centralized in Wellington.

1882   First **refrigerated meat shipment** to Europe. Lamb becomes increasingly important.

1890   NZ becomes "social laboratory" with introduction of compulsory arbitration and graduated income tax.

1893   Full **women's suffrage**; a world first.

1898   Old-age pension introduced.

1910s   Rise of organized labour under the socialist Red Federation. Strikes at Blackball, Waihi and Auckland.

1914–18   NZ takes part in WWI with terrible loss of life.

1917   **Temperance Movement** gets pubs closed after 6pm. Only repealed in 1967.

1920s   Initial prosperity evaporates as the Great Depression takes hold.

1935   M.J. Savage's Labour government ushers in the world's first **Welfare State** with free health service, family benefits, state housing and increased pensions.

1941   Bombing of Pearl Harbor and WWII begins NZ's military realignment with the Pacific region.

1947   New Zealand becomes fully independent from Britain.

1950   Parliament's upper house abolished.

1951   NZ joins **ANZUS** military pact with the US and Australia.

1950s   NZ comfortable as one of the world's most prosperous nations.

1957–60   Infrastructure improvements: steel mill, oil refinery, and numerous hydro-electric power stations built or planned.

1960s   Start of **immigration from Pacific Islands**. Major **urbanization of Maori** population.

1972–75   Third Labour government. NZ economy struggles to cope with huge oil price hikes and Britain's entry into the Common Market.

1975   **Waitangi Tribunal** established to consider Maori land claims.

1975–84	National's Robert "Piggy" Muldoon tries to borrow NZ out of trouble, investing heavily in ill-considered petro-chemical projects.
1976	African nations boycott Montreal Olympics because of NZ's rugby contacts with South Africa.
1977	NZ signs Gleneagles Agreement banning sporting ties with South Africa.
1981	**Springbok Tour**. Massive protests as a racially selected South African rugby team tours NZ.
1983	NZ signs Closer Economic Relations (CER) Treaty with Australia.
1984	The "Hikoi" land march brings Maori grievances into political focus.
1984	Labour regains power under David Lange. Widespread privatization and deregulation of NZ's protectionist economy. Refusal to allow American nuclear warships into NZ ports severely strains US/NZ relations.

1985	French secret service agents bomb Greenpeace flagship the *Rainbow Warrior* in Auckland Harbour.
1987	New Zealand becomes a **Nuclear-Free Zone**.
1987	Stock market crash devastates NZ economy.
1990–96	Jim Bolger leads National government, pressing on with Labour's free-market reforms and further dismantling the welfare state.
1996	First **MMP election** returns an alliance of National and NZ First.
1997	Jenny Shipley ousts Bolger to become NZ's first woman Prime Minister.
1999	Labour regain power under Jenny Shipley in coalition with the Alliance and the Green Party. The Greens' Nandor Tanczos installed as NZ's first Rastafarian MP and Labour's Georgina Beyer becomes the world's first transgender MP.

MAORITANGA

When the pakeha first came to this Island, the first thing he taught the Maori was Christianity. They made parsons and priests of several members of the Maori race, and they taught these persons to look up and pray; and while they were looking up the pakehas took away our land.

Mahuta, the son of the Maori King
Tawhiao, addressing the New Zealand
Legislative Council in 1903.

The term **Maoritanga** embodies Maori lifestyle and culture – it is the Maori way of doing things, embracing social structure, ethics, customs, legends and art, as well as language (see p.882). In the Anglo-European dominated society that New Zealand has always been, and to a large extent still is, it has been easy to see Maori culture as harping back to some fond-remembered idyll of the past, but *Maoritanga* has remained very much alive, and in the last couple of decades has seen a dramatic resurgence. By most measures, Maori make up over ten percent of New Zealand's population, but Maori–*pakeha* marriage since the early nineteenth century has left a complex inter-racial pool; many third- or fourth-generation *pakeha* can claim a Maori forebear or two, and some contend that there are no full-blooded Maori left. Maori ancestry remains the foundation of Maoridom, but a sense of Maori belonging has become a question of cultural identity as much as bloodlines.

Until very recently, white New Zealanders liked to promote the image of the two races living in harmony as one people, citing scenes of Maori and *pakeha* elbow to elbow at the bar and Maori rugby players in the scrum alongside their *pakeha* brothers. *Pakeha* prided themselves on successful integration that seemed a world away from the apartheid of South Africa or the virtual genocide exacted on North American and Australian aboriginal peoples; after all, Maori could claim all the benefits of *pakeha* plus dedicated seats in parliament, extra university grants and various other concessions. Yet this denied the undercurrent of Maori dissatisfaction over their treatment since the arrival of the first Europeans; the policy of **assimilation** relied entirely on Maori conforming to the *pakeha* way of doing things and made

no concession to *Maoritanga*. Maori adapted incredibly quickly to *pakeha* ways but were rewarded with the loss of their **land**. It is impossible to overestimate the importance of this: Maori spirituality invests every tree, every hill and every bay with a kind of supernatural life of its own, drawn from past events and the actions of the ancestors. It is by no means fanciful to equate the loss of land with the diminution of Maori life-force; little surprise, then, that much of the spirit went out of Maori people.

It is only really in the 1980s and 1990s that the *pakeha* paternal view has been challenged, with the country reacting by adopting **biculturalism**. As Maori rediscover their heritage and *pakeha* open their eyes to what has been around them for generations, knowledge of *Maoritanga* and some understanding of the language is seen as desirable and even advantageous. The government has increasingly channelled resources towards the "flax roots" of Maoridom, fostering a rapid take-up in the learning of Maori language, a resurgence in interest in Maori arts and crafts and a growing pride in Maoridom. At the same time, Maori have won back customary rights to fisheries and resources, and parcels of land have been returned to Maori ownership. Nonetheless, there is a sense in some quarters that Maori are only getting as much as the *pakeha*-dominated government feels it is prepared to give back.

For many *pakeha*, however, there is considerable unease over what is perceived as the government's soft stance on Treaty of Waitangi land claims (see box on p.848). Some envisage a future where Maori will own the land (including private land not currently up for redistribution under Treaty claims), will reclaim the rights granted them by the Treaty, and will have more influence than *pakeha*. Quite frankly, they're afraid. So far, reaction to the strengthening Maori hand in this climate of conciliation has only been voiced quietly, and just how this scenario will pan out remains to be seen. True power-sharing and biculturalism seems a long way off, and Maori aspirations for "sovereignty" – a separate Maori government and judiciary – look far-fetched at present, but the Maori juggernaut is moving fast.

MAORI LEGEND

Maori culture remains highly oral, with chants, storytelling and oratory central to ceremonial and daily life. This was doubly so when Europeans arrived and first recorded the traditions and legends normally passed down verbally. Different tribal groups often had different sets of stories, or at least variations on common themes, but European historians with pet theories to promote often distorted the stories they heard and even destroyed conflicting evidence, creating their own Maori folklore. This generalizing trend served the purpose of creating a common Maori identity, and many of the stories have been accepted back into the Maori tradition, leaving a patchwork of authentic and bowdlerized legends. Nonetheless, there are fixed themes common to most.

CREATION

From the primal nothingness of **Te Kore** sprang **Ranginui** the sky father and **Papatuanuku** the earth mother. They had numerous offspring, principally the major gods: **Haumia Tiketike**, the god of the fern root and food from the forest; **Rongo**, the god of the kumara and cultivation; **Tu Matauenga**, the god of war; **Tangaroa**, the god of the oceans and sealife; **Tawhirimatea**, the god of the winds; and **Tane Mahuta**, the god of the forests. Through long centuries of darkness the brothers argued over whether to separate their parents and create light. Tawhirimatea opposed the idea and fled to the skies where his anger is manifested in thunder and lightning, while Tane Mahuta succeeded in parting the two, breaking their primal embrace and allowing life to flourish. Rangi's tears filled the oceans and even now it is their grief which brings the dew, mist and rain.

Having created the creatures of the sea, the air and the land, the gods turned their attentions to humans and, realizing that they were all male, had to create a female. They fashioned clay into a form resembling their mother and the responsibility again fell to **Tane**, who breathed life into the nostrils of the first woman, the Dawn Maiden, **Hinetitama**. It is from their union that the whole human race is descended.

MAUI THE TRICKSTER AND KUPE THE NAVIGATOR

Maori mythology is littered with half-human demigods, and none is more celebrated than **Maui-Tikitiki-a-Taranga**, whose exploits are legend throughout Polynesia. With an armoury of spells, guile and boundless mischief, Maui gained a reputation as a trickster, using his abilities to turn any situation to his advantage. Equipped with the powerful magic jawbone of his grandmother, he set about taming his world, believing himself invincible. He even took on **the sun**, which had taken to passing so swiftly through the heavens that the people had no time to tend their fields before it disappeared back into its fiery pit. Maui vowed to solve the problem and, with the aid of his older brothers, plaited super-strong ropes which they tied across the sun's pit before dawn. As the sun rose into the net, Maui set upon the sun with his magic jawbone, beating him and imploring him not to go so fast. The sun was weakening rapidly and, in return for his release, agreed to do as Maui asked.

In the New Zealand context, Maui's master work was the creation of **Aotearoa**. With his reputation for mischief, Maui's brothers would often leave him behind when they went fishing, but one morning he stowed away under the seats. Far out at sea he revealed himself, promising to improve their recent poor catch. Maui egged them on until they were well beyond the normal fishing grounds before dropping anchor. In no time at all Maui's brothers filled their canoe with fish, but Maui still had some fishing to do. They scorned his hook (secretly armed with a chip of his grandmother's jawbone) and wouldn't lend him any bait, so Maui struck his own nose and smeared the hook with his own blood. Soon he had hooked a fabulous fish which, as it broke the surface, could be seen stretching into the distance all around them. Chanting an incantation, Maui got the fish to lie quietly on the surface where it became the North Island, known as *Te ika a Maui*, the fish of Maui. As Maui went off to make an offering to the gods, his brothers began to cut up the fish and eat it, hacking mountains and valleys into the surface. To fit in with the legend, the South Island is often called *Te waka a Maui*, the canoe of Maui, and Stewart Island is the anchor, *Te punga o te waka a Maui*.

With more historical veracity, Maori trace their ancestry back to **Hawaiki**, the semi-legendary source of the Polynesian diaspora, for which the Society Islands and the Cook Islands are the most likely candidates. According to legend, the first visitor to *Aotearoa*'s shores was

Kupe, the great Polynesian navigator. In one version of the tale he was determined to kill a great octopus that kept robbing his bait; drawn ever further out to sea in pursuit, he finally reached landfall on the uninhabited shores of *Aotearoa*, the "land of the long white cloud". He named numerous features of the land, then returned to Hawaiki with instructions on how to retrace his voyage.

SOCIAL STRUCTURE AND CUSTOMS

Maori society remains **tribal** to a large extent, though the deracination resulting from the widespread move from the tribal homelands to the cities has eroded some of the closer ties. In urban situations the finer points of *Maoritanga* are having to be re-discovered, but the basic tenets remain strong and formal protocol still reigns for ceremonies as diverse as funeral wakes, meetings and Maori exhibition openings.

The most fundamental and tightest division in Maori society is the extended family or **whanau** (literally "birthing"), which extends from immediate relatives to cousins, uncles and nieces several times removed. A dozen or so *whanau* jointly form a localized sub-tribe or **hapu** (literally "gestation or pregnancy"), perhaps the most important tribal group, comprising dozens of extended families of common descent. *Hapu* were originally economically autonomous and today continue to conduct communal activities, typically through their marae (see p.862). Neighbouring *hapu* are likely to belong to the same tribe or **iwi** (literally "bones"), a looser association of several thousand Maori spread over a fairly large geographical area. The thirty-odd major *iwi* are even more tenuously linked by their common ancestry traced back to semi-legendary canoes, or *waka*. In troubled times, especially during the eighteenth-century New Zealand Wars, *iwi* from the same *waka* would band together for protection. Together these are the **tangata whenua** (literally "the people of the land"), a term that may refer to Maori people as a whole, or just to one *hapu* if local concerns are being aired.

The literal meanings of *whanau*, *hapu* and *iwi* can be viewed as a metaphor for the Maori view of their relationship with their ancestors or **tupuna**, who are considered to exist through their genetic inheritors; the past is very much a part of the present. Evidence of this is seen in the respect accorded the **whakapapa**, an individual's genealogy tracing descent from the gods via one of the migratory *waka* and through the *tupuna*. The *whakapapa* is often recited at length on formal occasions such as **hui** (meetings).

Maori traditional life is informed by the parallel notions of **tapu** (taboo) and **noa** (mundane, not *tapu*). These are not superstition but a belief system designed to impose a code of conduct: transgressing *tapu* brings ostracism and ill fortune and is thought to cause sickness. Objects, places, actions and even people can be *tapu*, demanding extra respect – for example, the body parts of a chief, especially the head; menstruating women; sacred items to do with ritual; earrings, pendants and hair combs; burial sites; and the knowledge contained in the *whakapapa* are all *tapu*. There is a practical aspect too, with the productivity of fishing grounds and forests traditionally maintained by imposing *tapu* at critical times. The direct opposite of *tapu* is *noa*, a term applied to ordinary items which, by implication, are considered safe; a new building is *tapu* until a special ceremony renders it *noa*.

People, animals and artefacts, whether *tapu* or *noa*, possess **mauri** (life force), **wairau** (spirit) and **mana**, a term loosely translated as prestige, but embodying wider concepts of power, influence and charisma. Birthright brings with it a degree of *mana* which can then be augmented through battle or brave deeds, and lost through inaction or defeat. Wartime cannibalism was partly ritual but by eating an enemy's heart a warrior absorbed his *mauri*; likewise personal effects gain *mana* from association with the *mana* of their owner, accruing more as they are passed down to descendants. Any slight on the *mana* of an individual was felt by the whole *hapu*, which must then exact **utu** (a need to balance any action with an equal reaction), a compunction which often led to bloody feuds, sometime escalating to war and further enhancing the *mana* of the victors. *Pakeha* found this a hard concept to grasp and deeds which they considered deceitful or treacherous could be correct in Maori terms.

The responsibility for determining *tapu* fell to the **tohunga** (priest or expert), the most exalted of many specialists in *Maoritanga*, who is conversant with tribal history, sacred lore and the *whakapapa*, and considered to be the earthly presence of the power of the gods

MARAE

The rituals of *hapu* life – *hui*, **tangi** (funeral wakes) and **powhiri** (formal welcomes) – are conducted on the **marae**, a kind of combined community, cultural and drop-in centre (and much more), where the cultural values, protocols, customs and vitality of *Maoritanga* find their fullest expression. Strictly, a marae is simply a courtyard, but the term is often applied to the whole complex, comprising the **whare runanga** (meeting house, or *whare nui*), *whare manuhiri* (house for visitors), *whare kai* (eating house) and possibly even an old-fashioned **pataka** (raised storehouse). Marae belonging to one or more *hapu* are found all over the country, though they're concentrated in rural areas where a larger number of Maori live. In recent years, pan-tribal urban marae have started up, partly to help wayward Maori youth find their roots but also to cope with the growing awareness of *Maoritanga* on the part of urban Maori, many of whom have lost their *whakapapa*.

Visitors, whether Maori or *pakeha*, may not enter marae uninvited, so unless you have Maori friends, you're only likely to visit on a commercially run **tour**. Invited guests are expected to provide some form of **koha** (donation) towards the upkeep of the marae, but this is included in tour fees. Remember that the marae is sacred and due reverence must be accorded the **kawa** (protocols) governing behaviour. There's no need to feel intimidated, though, as you aren't expected to know *kawa* and will be instructed as to what is required of you.

Following long tradition, **manuhiri** (visitors) approaching the marae are ritually challenged to determine friendly intent. This **wero** might involve a fearsome warrior (often the teenager you see driving away after the show) bearing down on you with twirling **taiaha** (long club), flickering tongue and bulging eyes. The women then make the **karanga** (welcoming call), which is followed by their *powhiri* (sung welcome), which breaks the *tapu* and acts as a prelude to ceremonial touching of noses or **hongi**, binding the *manuhiri* and the *tangata whenua* both physically and spiritually. On commercial trips, the welcoming ceremony is followed by a concert comprising songs, dances and chants, and a **hangi** (a feast cooked in an earth oven).

ARTS AND CRAFTS

Although the origins of **Maori art** lie in the traditions of eastern Polynesia, over half a millennium of isolated development has resulted in a unique richness and diversity. Eastern Polynesia has no suitable clay, so Maori forebears had already lost the skills of pottery and focused their talents on wood, stone and weaving, occasionally using naturalistic designs but most often the highly **stylized forms** that make Maori art unmistakable.

As with other *taonga* (treasures), many superb examples were taken out of the country by Victorian and later collectors, but there is a determined move on the part of *iwi* and the Department of Maori Affairs to restore as many *taonga* as possible to New Zealand, including over a hundred severed heads which are scattered through museums all over the world.

WOOD CARVING

Maori handiwork finds its greatest expression in **wood carving**, a discipline applied with as much care to a water bailer or ornamental comb as it is to the pinnacles of Maori creativity, *waka* (canoes) and *whare whakairo* (carved houses).

The earliest examples of wood carving feature the sparse, rectilinear styles of ancient eastern Polynesia, but by the fifteenth century these had been replaced by the cursive style still employed by more traditional carvers today. In the Northland forests, kauri wood was used, but in the rest of the country the durable yet easily worked totara was the material of choice. Carvers worked with shells and sharp stones in the earliest times, but the artist's scope increased dramatically with the invention of tools fashioned from **pounamu** (greenstone, a form of jade; see box on p.722), and again with the transition to steel tools. Some would say that the quality of the work declined with the coming of the Europeans: not just through the demand for quickly executed "tourist art", but as a consequence of pressure to remove the phallic imagery that the missionaries considered obscene. As early as 1844, carving had been abandoned altogether in areas with a strong missionary presence, and it continued to decline into the early years of the twentieth century, when Maori pride was at its lowest ebb. By the end of the 1920s the situation had become so lamentable that Maori parliamentarian Apirana Ngata established Rotorua's pan-tribal **Maori Arts and Crafts Institute**, viewed as the foundation on which *Maoritanga* could be rebuilt, and still the guardian of what is now a much more secure art.

The role of a carver has always been a highly respected one, with seasoned and skilled exponents having the status of *tohunga* and travelling the country both to carve and to teach. The work is a *tapu* activity and *noa* objects must be kept away – cooked food is not allowed near, and carvers have to brush away shavings rather than blow them – though women, previously banned, have now become carvers.

Maori carving exhibits a distinctive **style**, not just in its visual elements but in the approach to the material. Typically, relief forms are determinedly hewn from a single piece of wood with no concession to the natural forms, shapes and blemishes of the material. There is no attempt to represent perspective and while landscapes are represented, they are not actually depicted – figures stand alone. Unadorned wood is rare, carvers creating a stylistic rather than symbolic bed of swirling spirals, curving organic forms based on fern roots or sea shells, and interlocking latticework. Superimposed on this are the key elements, often inlaid with paua shell. The most common is the ancestor figure, the **hei tiki**, a grotesquely distorted, writhing human form, either male, female or of indeterminate gender, often stylized to the point of unrecognizability except for the challenge of a protruding tongue and the threat of a hand-held *mere*. Almost as common are the mythical *manaia*, a beaked birdlike form, often with an almost human profile. Secondary motifs such as the *pakake* (whale) and *moko* (lizard) also occur.

While the same level of craftsmanship was applied to all manner of tools, weapons and ornaments, it reached its most exalted expression in *waka taua* (**war canoes**), sleek and formidable vessels that were the focus of community pride and endeavour. Gunwales, bailers and paddles would all be fabulously decorated, but the most detailed work was reserved for the prow and sternpost, usually a matrix of spirals interwoven with *manaia* figures. As guns and the European presence altered the balance of tribal warfare in the 1860s, the *waka taua*

was superseded in importance by the *whare whakairo* (**carved meeting house**). Originally the chief's residence, the *whare* gradually adopted the symbolism of the *waka* – some even incorporated wood from *waka*. Each meeting house could be seen as the tangible manifestation of the *whakapapa*, usually representing a synthesis of the ancestors: the ridge-pole is the backbone; the rafters form the ribs, enclosing the belly of the interior; the gable figure is the head; and the barge boards represent arms, often decorated with finger-like decoration. Inside, all wooden surfaces are carved and the spaces filled intricate woven panels known as *tukutuku*.

GREENSTONE CARVING

When not using wood, Maori carvers work in **pounamu** (greenstone). In pre-European times complex trade routes developed to supply Maori throughout the land from the sources on the West Coast and in Fiordland; the South Island even became known as *Te Wai Pounamu*, the Water of Jade. The stone was fashioned into adzes, chisels and clubs for hand-to-hand combat; tools which soon took on a ritual significance and demanded decoration. *Pounamu's* hardness dictates a more restrained carving style and *mere* and *patu* in particular tend to be only partly worked, leaving large sweeping surfaces ending in a flourish of delicate swirls. Ornamental pieces range from simple drop pendants worn as earrings or neck decoration, to *hei tiki*, worn as a breast pendant and, for women, serving as a fertility charm and talisman for easy childbirth. Like other personal items, especially those worn close to the body, an heirloom *tiki* possesses the *mana* of the ancestors and absorbs the wearer's *mana*, becoming *tapu*.

TATTOOING

A stylistic extension of the carver's craft is exhibited in *moko*, an ornamental and ceremonial form of **tattooing** that largely died out with European contact. Women would have *moko* just on the lips and chin, but high-ranking men often had their faces completely covered, along with their buttocks and thighs; the greater the extent and intricacy of the *moko*, the greater the status. A symmetrical pattern of the traditional elements – crescents, spirals, fern-root and other organic forms – were painfully gouged into the flesh with an *uhi* (chisel) and mallet, then soot rubbed into the open wound. In the last decade or so the tradition of full-face *moko* has been revived both as an identification with *Maoritanga* and as an art form in its own right; since 1999, *moko* artists have been eligible for government funding through the Creative New Zealand organisation.

WEAVING AND CLOTHING

While men were busy carving, the women dedicated themselves to weaving and the production of clothing. When Polynesians first arrived in these cool, damp islands their paper mulberry plants didn't thrive and they were forced to look for alternatives. In time, they found *harakeke* (New Zealand **flax**), which became the foundation of all Maori fibre-work. The strong, pliable fibres were used as fishing lines and cordage for lashing axe-heads onto hafts, and most importantly for protection from the elements and floor matting. With the arrival of the *pakeha*, Maori quickly adopted European clothes, but they continued to wear cloaks on formal occasions and these now constitute the basis of contemporary design.

Flax will grow on marshy land all over the country and so the long, spindly leaves were almost always on hand. They were used in something close to their raw form for *raranga* (plaiting) into *kete*, handle-less baskets used for collecting shellfish and kumara, triangular canoe sails, sandals and *whariki*, patterned floor mats still used in meeting houses. For finer work, the flax must be treated by trimming, soaking and beating, a laborious process that produces a wonderfully strong and pliable fibre. Most fibre is used in its natural form, but Maori design requires some **colouring**: black is achieved by soaking in a dilute extract of the bark from a *hinau* tree then rubbing with a black swamp sediment known as *paru*; the red-brown range of colours requires boiling in a dye derived from the bark of the *tanekaha* tree then fixed by rolling in hot ashes; and the less popular yellow tint is produced from the bark of the Coprosma species. Economic necessity and consideration for the tree species concerned have seen the introduction of synthetic dyes, but traditional dyes are still used whenever possible.

Natural and coloured fibres are both used in *whatu kakahu* (**cloak-weaving**), the crowning achievement of Maori women's art, the finest cloaks ranking alongside the most prized *taonga*; the immense war canoe now in the Auckland Museum was once exchanged for a particularly fine cloak. The technique is sometimes referred to as finger-weaving as no loom is used, the women working downwards from a base warp strung between two sticks. Complex weaving techniques are employed to produce a huge array of different textures, often decorated with *taniko* (coloured borders), cord tags tacked onto the cloth at intervals and, most impressive of all, **feathers**. Feather cloaks (*kahu hururu*) don't appear to have been common before European contact, though heroic tales often feature key players in iridescent garments undoubtedly made from bird feathers. The appeal of the bright yellow feathers of the *huia* probably saw to its demise, and most other brightly coloured birds are now too rare to use for cloaks, so new feather cloaks are very rarely made. Existing examples have become the most prestigious of garments, and you'll come across some fine examples in museums, the base cloth often completely covered by a dense layer of kiwi feathers bordered by zig-zag patterns of tui, native pigeon and even parakeet feathers. More robust *para* (rain capes) were made using the water-repellent leaves of the cabbage tree, and a form of coarse canvas which could reportedly resist spear thrusts was used for *pukupuku* (war cloaks). Some *pukupuku* were turned into *kahu kuri* (dog-skin cloaks) with the addition of strips of dog skin, arranged vertically so that the natural fur colours produced distinctive patterns.

As with other aspects of *Maoritanga*, weaving and plaiting have seen a resurgence. Cloaks are still an important element of formal occasions, whether on the marae for *hui* and *tangi*, or elsewhere for receiving academic or state honours. Old forms are reproduced directly, and also raided as inspiration for contemporary designs, which interpret traditional elements in the light of modern fashion, sometimes incorporating non-traditional colours and designs.

THE HAKA AND MAORI DANCE

Opposing rugby teams quiver as the New Zealand All Blacks perform the ferocious, thigh-slapping, foot-stomping, tongue-poking, eye-bulging chant *Ka mate, Ka mate, Ka ora, Ka ora* (It is death, it is death, It is life, it is life), from the intimidating Te Rauparaha Haka. This is just the best known of many posture dances (often wrongly referred to as war dances) designed to demonstrate the fitness and prowess of warriors. It was composed by Te Rauparaha himself (see p.219) as he lay in a kumara pit trying to avoid detection by his enemies. Its use by what are often predominantly *pakeha* sides might seem inappropriate, but it is so entrenched that there was considerable backlash when in 1996 the All Black coach suggested the haka may be changed to mollify southern Maori who were decimated by Te Rauparaha.

At commercial **Maori concerts** (predominantly in Rotorua but also in Christchurch, Queenstown and elsewhere) there will always be some form of haka, usually the Te Rauparaha version, which is almost always performed by men. Though women aren't excluded from the haka, they normally concentrate on **poi dances**, where balls of *raupo* (bulrush) attached to the end of strings are swung around

in rhythmic movements originally designed to improve co-ordination and dexterity.

The drums of eastern Polynesia don't appear to have made it to New Zealand, and both chants and the haka go unaccompanied. To the traditional bone flute, *pakeha* added the guitar, which now accompanies **waiata** (songs), relatively modern creations whose impact comes as much from the tone and rhythm as from the lyrics (which you probably won't understand anyway). The impassioned delivery can seem at odds with music that's often based on Victorian hymns: perhaps the most well known are *Pokarekare ana* and *Haere Ra*, both post-European contact creations. Outside the tourist concert party, Maori music has developed enormously in recent years to the point where there are tribal and Maori language music stations almost exclusively playing music written and performed by Maori, often rap and hip-hop with a Pacific twist.

WILDLIFE AND THE NATURAL ENVIRONMENT

New Zealand is still perceived as a green and pleasant land, as it has been by many thousands of immigrants, first from the Polynesian Islands, then Europe and now the Pacific rim of Asia. Although relatively small it boasts an enormous diversity: unspoiled sub-tropical forest, rich volcanic basins (and volcanoes), mud-pools and geysers, intricate and rugged coastline with golden sand beaches and spectacular alpine regions. This diverse landscape supports an extraordinary variety of animals and plant life, with almost ninety percent of the flora not found anywhere else in the world. Thanks to the efforts of a vociferous minority, since the late 1800s, examples of the many habitats, plants and wildlife are still easily accessible, protected within national parks and scenic reserves. For more on green issues, see p.873.

BEGINNINGS

Land has existed in the vicinity of New Zealand for most of the last 500 million years: the earliest rocks found in the country are thought to have originated in the continental forelands of Australia and Antarctica, part of Gondwanaland, the massive continent to which New Zealand belonged. The oceanic islands were created by continental drift, the movement of the large plates that form the earth's crust, which created a distinct island arc and oceanic trench about 100 million years ago.

Roughly 26 million years ago, the land that makes up New Zealand rose further from the sea, and the landscape you see today was formed by **volcanic** activity and continuous movement along fault lines, particularly the Alpine Fault of the South Island. The essential geology of the two islands is different: the North Island is at the edge of two tectonic plates, where one has slid beneath the other, resulting in prolific volcanic activity; the South Island is the site of two tectonic plates crashing into each other, causing rapid **mountain** building. Today New Zealand experiences about four hundred **earthquakes** every year, roughly a quarter of them strong enough to be noticeable. The volcanoes on the North Island, some still impressively active (the last eruption was Ruapehu in 1996), extend from the Bay of Plenty to the dormant volcanic cone of Mount Taranaki on the West Coast.

Isolated from man and other mammals, New Zealand would have been the perfect place to study the **evolution** of species. It's hardly surprising that so many botanists considered the oceanic islands as laboratories where they could perfect their theories. The country was separated from all other land masses for so long that, uniquely, **birds** occupied the position in the food chain usually held by mammals. Darwinism would suggest that with no predators the birds became fearless, learning to walk amid the dense bush, gradually becoming flightless and growing in size. If allowed to develop unhindered, perhaps they would have evolved into a serious competitor to mammals, but their perfect adaptation to the environment brought their downfall with the arrival of man and other aggressive, fast-moving mammals.

No ground-based mammals colonized the islands until Maori gave rats and dogs passage in their canoes, possibly in about 1000 AD although some theories suggest earlier. Maori were also responsible for hunting the large, flightless **moa** into extinction, and clearing great swathes of **bush** with fire. At that time both islands were almost entirely covered in dense **forest** composed of over a hundred species of tree, the floor carpeted by moss and lichen with a thick tangled undergrowth of tree fern, some species over ten metres high. Amongst the trees and ferns were twining creepers, nikau palms and palm lilies, all intermingled and forming an impenetrable bush alive with native birds.

The changes to the land brought by Maori pale in comparison with the incursions of the Europeans. Right from Cook's first exploratory visits, when he brought with him the pig, the sheep and the potato, Europeans tampered with the delicate balance of New Zealand in an attempt to turn it into a "New England". In the early 1800s whalers and sealers bloodied the coastal waters, while logging campaigns cleared vast swathes of native trees, leaving land suitable only for grazing cattle; later, gold prospectors diverted streams and carved chunks out of hillsides. Perhaps the greatest environmental changes were made by immigrant farmers, who had introduced over fifty species of **mammal** to New Zealand by the start of World War I, including rabbits, weasels, mountain goats, cats, dogs, frogs, mice, possums and wallabies. These animals decimated native animal and plant life in the increasing competition for food. Imported plants, such as blackberry, pine and gorse, had just as much effect: allowed to grow wild, they choked and destroyed hundreds of unique plants vital to the ecology of the islands.

THE COAST, ISLANDS AND SEA

New Zealand's indented coastline, battered by the Tasman Sea and the Pacific Ocean, is a meeting place of warm and cold currents, which makes for an environment suited to an enormous variety of **fish**. **Tropical** fish species such as barracuda, marlin, sharks and tuna are attracted by the warm currents, locally populated by **hoki**, **kahawai**, **snapper**, **orange roughy** and **trevally**. The cold Antarctic currents bring blue and red **cod**, blue and red **moki**, and fish that can tolerate a considerable range of water temperatures, such as the **tarakihi**, **grouper** and **bass**, all avidly sought after by an army of weekend anglers.

Many people visit New Zealand with the express intention of seeing the sea mammals that grace the waters, and most leave satisfied. The rare **humpback whale** is an occasional visitor to the shores of Kaikoura and Cook Strait,

while **sperm whales** are common year round in the deep sea trench near Kaikoura. **Orca** are seen regularly wherever there are dolphins, seals and other whales, namely Banks Peninsula, Kaikoura, Dunedin, Stewart Island, the Marlborough Sounds, Cook Strait, the Bay of Plenty and the Bay of Islands. One frequent visitor is the **pilot whale**: up to 200 pass by Farewell Spit each year and some strand themselves there. Despite the efforts of the locals to refloat them, a few die nearly every year. Pilot whales are also seen in Cook Strait and the Bay of Plenty.

Common dolphins congregate all year round in the Bay of Plenty, Bay of Islands and around the Coromandel Peninsula. Of the three other species seen in New Zealand, **bottlenose** dolphins hang around Kaikoura and Whakatane most of the year, while **dusky** dolphins, the most playful, can be spotted near the shore of the Marlborough Sounds and Kaikoura, from October to May. At any time of year you might get small schools of tiny **Hector's** dolphins accompanying your boat around Banks Peninsula, the Catlins and as far down as Invercargill.

Until recently there were few opportunities to see the Hooker's (now called New Zealand) **sea lion** except on remote Antarctic islands; now these rare animals with their round noses and deep, wet eyes are appearing once more around the Catlins and Otago Peninsula. If you do see them, though, be careful: they bite and can move fast over short distances, so don't go any closer than ten metres and avoid getting between them and the sea. The larger New Zealand **fur seal** is in much greater abundance around the coast, easily spotted basking on rocks or sand and gracefully turning in the waters, their broader, pointy heads popping above the surface. You're most likely to come across them in the Sugar Loaf Marine Reserve, the Northland Coast, the Bay of Plenty, near Kaikoura, the Otago Peninsula and in Abel Tasman National Park. Both seals and sea lions can become aggressive during the breeding season (Dec–Feb), so remember to keep your distance (at least 30m) at these times. If you are lucky enough to visit the Nuggets in the Catlins, you may be rewarded by a sighting of one of the few **elephant seals** still breeding on the New Zealand coast; more extensive colonies exist on the offshore islands.

Also drawn by the fish-rich waters of the coast are a number of visiting and native seabirds, the most famous being the graceful and solitary **royal albatross**, found on the Otago Peninsula, and, just offshore, the smaller **wandering albatross**. A far more common sight are **little blue penguins**, which you're almost guaranteed to see on any boat journey, all year round. The large **yellow-eyed penguin** is confined to parts of the east coast of the South Island, from Christchurch to the Catlins, while the **Fiordland crested penguin** with its thick yellow eyebrows is rarely seen outside Fiordland and Stewart Island. Other common sea birds include **gannets**, their yellow heads and white bodies unmistakable as they dive from great heights into shoals of fish; and **cormorants** and **shags** (mostly grey or black), usually congregating on cliffs and rocky shores. On and around islands you're also likely to see the **sooty shearwater**, *titi* (also known as "mutton birds"), while the black **oystercatchers** and the black and white **variable oystercatchers**, both with orange cigar beaks and stooping gait, can be spotted searching in pairs for food on the foreshore almost everywhere.

THE HIGHLANDS

Thanks to the impact of introduced species on the environment (see previous page), to really appreciate the picture that greeted first the Maori and then the European immigrants, you need to visit one of New Zealand's many scenic reserves or national parks. In the Tongariro, Whanganui, Taranaki, Nelson Lakes, Arthur's Pass and Mount Cook national parks, all **highland forest** areas, **tawhairauriki** (mountain beech) grow close to the top of the tree line, straight trees up to 20m high, with sharp dark leaves and little red flowers. Also at high altitudes, often in mixed stands, are **tawhai** (silver beech), whose grey trunks grow up to 30m. Slightly lower altitudes are favoured by the other members of the beech family, the black and red varieties. Often mixed in with them is the thin, straggly **manuka** (tea tree), which grows in both Alpine regions and on seashores.

New Zealand has five hundred species of flowering alpine plant that grow nowhere else in the world. Most famous are the large white mountain daisies, **Mount Cook lilies** – the largest in the world, and a white-flowered

yellow-centred member of the buttercup family. Another interesting plant found on the high ground of the South Island is the **vegetable sheep**, a white hairy plant that grows low along the ground and, at a great distance, could just about be mistaken for grazing sheep.

One of the oldest of New Zealand's unique creatures inhabits caves and rock crevices above the snow line: the **weta** (also known as the "Mount Cook flea"), an insect that has changed little in 190 million years. There are several species, the most impressive being the giant weta, which is the heaviest insect in the world, weighing up to 71g and about the size of a small thrush. Weta aren't dangerous, despite their vicious-looking mandibles (they're said to have been the model for Ridley Scott's *Alien*). Though weta also inhabit the bush, they're hard to spot and you're most likely to see them in museums and zoos.

The red-beaked, green **takahe**, a close relative of the more common pukeko, is one of the most famous of the country's flightless birds. Thought to have been extinct until 1948, its survival is currently in the hands of the DOC, who have set up protection programmes in a few highland regions (see p.142). Another highland forest bird to watch out for is the **New Zealand falcon** or bush hawk, seen sometimes in the north of the North Island and more often in the high country of the Southern Alps, Fiordland and the forests of Westland. It has a heavily flecked breast, chestnut thighs and a pointed head.

New Zealand boasts the only flightless **parrot** in the world, the green and blue, nocturnal **kakapo**. Once widespread, it's now very rare and predominantly seen in the forests and lowlands of Fiordland. You're much more likely to come across the **kea**, regarded as the only truly alpine parrot in the world (see p.607), though its range encompasses both lowland and highland forests. Known for killing sheep (an alleged recently acquired habit), making off with people's possessions and then ripping them apart or eating them, the kea is green with distinctive orange patches on the underside of its wings and a crimson abdomen. Finally, of the smaller birds in the sub-alpine areas, the yellow and green **rock wren** and the **rifleman**, a tiny green and blue bird with spiralling flight, are commonly seen in the high forests of the South Island.

THE LOWLANDS

These days the majority of New Zealand is covered by grazing land, grasslands and plains that are dominated by tall and low **tussock**. Fortunately, there remains a great variety of native trees in the **mid to lowland forests** of Northland, the Coromandel Peninsula, along the west coasts of both islands, around Wellington and on Stewart Island. There are also sixty different endemic native flowering plants in lowland areas, whose blooms mostly range from white to yellow, their relative lack of colour due to the fact that there were no bees to cross-pollinate until the Europeans arrived. Much colour in gardens, parks and mixed forest comes from introduced species such as roses, azaleas and rhododendrons.

New Zealand's best-known tree, the **kauri**, is found in mixed lowland forest, particularly in Northland (see p.189). With a lifespan of two to four thousand years, this magnificent king of the forest rises to thirty metres, two-thirds of its height being straight, branchless trunk. Maori canoe-builders treat the kauri with great reverence and have always enacted solemn ceremonies before hacking them down for transformation into giant canoes; European shipbuilders coveted the trees for making ocean-going traders and warships. The tree is also the source of the kauri gum, dug from ancient forests and exported in the late nineteenth and early twentieth century.

Open spaces along forest edges and river banks are often alive with tui (see p.871) sucking nectar from golden clusters of **kowhai**, the national flower, which hangs from an eponymous tree whose wood was once fashioned into Maori canoe paddles and adze handles. Another useful tree, the **maire** stands up to 20m tall and is covered with whitish bark, thick narrow leaves and tiny pink flowers that look like open umbrellas. Its wood is heavy and close-grained, ideal for war clubs, and when burned it gives off very little smoke. Now quite rare, the 30m **matai** was also once used by Maori as a source of timber for canoe prows and by settlers for buildings; it can be identified by a thick, dark grey bark that flakes off.

North of Banks Peninsula and on the North Island grows New Zealand's only native **palm**, the **nikau**, whose slender branchless stem bears shiny leaves of up to 30cm, long pink spiky flowers and red fruit. Early European settlers used to use the berries as pellets in the absence of ammunition.

The **pohutukawa** is an irregularly branched 20m tree found as far south as Otago, seen in forests around the coast and at lake edges. Bearing bright crimson blossoms from November to January, it's often known as "New Zealand's Christmas tree". Another well-known red-blooming tree is the gnarled **rata**, found in quantity in South Island forests and in ones and twos around the North Island. It starts out life as a climber, its windblown seeds establishing it high in other trees, and then its aerial roots gradually take over the host, eventually draining it of life.

One native pine which was heavily milled for its timber and yet is still widespread throughout mixed forests is the majestic **rimu** (red pine), growing to 50–60m with small green flowers, red cones and tiny green or black fruit. Charcoal from rimu used to be mixed with oil and rubbed into tattoo incisions.

A common shade-loving tree found in stands in the forests is the **tawa**, with a long, thin blackish trunk and spear-shaped leaves. The tree produces black berries which, although initially unpleasant, develop a better flavour some time after picking. Also common throughout the country's mixed forests is the **totara**, which usually lives for a thousand years and was often used by Maori to make war canoes. The tree's thick brown bark was also used: it peels in long lengths, suitable for weaving baskets.

The **ti kouka** grows beneath the forest canopy, usually in moist areas and often along the edges of farmland. These 10- to 20m trees with long, thin grey trunks and spear-shaped leaves are also known as "cabbage trees", a reference to the shoots that were eaten by Captain Cook and his men. The tree also produces hundreds of white flowers in spectacular clusters. Below, on the forest floor grow an enormous variety of **ferns**, many of them hard to tell apart. The most famous, adopted as a national emblem, is the **ponga** (silver fern). Reaching about 10m in height, it has long fronds that are dull green on top and silvery white underneath.

LOWLAND WILDLIFE

Next to the sea, the mid to lowland forests contain the broadest range of **wildlife**. One of the country's oldest inhabitants is the **tuatara**, a

KIWI

The **kiwi** is a member of the ratite family, which includes the ostrich, emu, rhea, cassowary and the long-extinct moa, and if action is not taken soon the kiwi will join the moa on the list of **terminated** animals. A stout muscular bird, shy and nocturnal, which inhabits the forest floor. Sadly there are probably fewer than 15,000 wild birds left in the country and currently the numbers are going down, not up. It sleeps for up to twenty hours a day, which probably explains why it normally lives to the age of 20 or 25. The females are bigger than the males and lay huge eggs, equivalent to around a fifth of their body weight. After eighty days, the eggs hatch and the chicks live off the rich yolk; neither parent feeds them and they emerge from the nest totally independent.

The kiwi is one of the few birds in the world with a well-developed sense of **smell**. At night you might hear them snuffling around in the dark, using the nostrils at the end of their bill to detect earthworms, beetles, cicada larvae, spiders and also koura (freshwater crayfish), berries and the occasional frog. Armed also with sensitive bristles at the base of its bill and a highly developed sense of hearing, the kiwi can detect other birds and animals on its territory and will readily attack them with its claws.

The **Brown Kiwi** (*Apteryx australis*), the largest species, is famous for its big nose, bad temper and for being a tough fighter against intruders on their territory. They live in a wide range of vegetation, including exotic forests and rough farmland on the North Island. In 1993 the **Tokoeka** or *Okarito Brown*, which is almost identical, was identified as a separate species. Inhabiting the South Island and Stewart Island, the southern tokoeka are the most communal of the kiwi family and can be seen poking about along the tideline within a few metres of one another. A subspecies, the **Haast Tokoeka**, are found only in Fiordland.

The **Little Spotted Kiwi** or *Kiwi Pukupuku* (*Apteryx owenii*) is the smallest and rarest of the kiwi, found on only six offshore islands, including Kapiti Island. Predators and land clearance are largely responsible for the low numbers, although a programme to remove predators from the offshore islands has seen their fortunes revive. This species is mellow and docile by nature and pairs often share daytime shelter, going their separate ways to feed, grunting to one another as they pass. Little Spotted Kiwi rarely probe for food, instead finding prey on the ground or in the forest litter. In spring, during courtship, birds stand with bills crossed and pointing downwards while shuffling around each other, grunting, for up to twenty minutes. The best time to hear them is just after dark from high points around an island. Listen carefully for the male's shrill whistle and the female's gentle purr.

Great Spotted Kiwi or *Roa* (*Apteryx haastii*) inhabit regions of snow-covered peaks, herb fields, with rocky outcrops, valleys of red tussock and mountains clothed in beech forest and alpine scrub. Their severe living conditions account for the many legends that surround them. Early European explorers told stories of remote kiwi the size of a turkey with powerful spurs on its legs, whose call was louder than any other of the species. Their harsh home has also helped preserve these big handsome birds, keeping them safe from the pigs, dogs and stoats that have killed so many other kiwi species.

Should you want to help save these symbols of New Zealand you can make a **donation** of $2 direct to the Department of Conservation, Royal Forests and Birds Protection Society and Bank of New Zealand programme.

lizard-like reptile dating back at least 260 million years, making it, to all intents and purposes, a mini dinosaur. It's nocturnal so you're unlikely to see one in the wild, although they have been reintroduced to many pest-free offshore islands – your best chance of spotting one is in a zoo or kiwi house. Tuatara are about sixty centimetres in length and live for over a hundred years, feeding off insects, small mammals and birds' eggs.

New Zealand's national bird, the flightless **kiwi** (see box above) is also mostly found in the mid to lowland forests. It has been on the endangered list for many years, and these days the only place you're likely to see one in the wild is on Stewart Island; however, they can be seen in specially designed kiwi houses all over the country, such as Otorohanga (see p.220) and Napier (see p.405). Of the other flightless birds in New Zealand the most common is the **weka**, which has four subspecies found in a variety of habitats throughout the country. The North Island bird flourishes in Poverty Bay and has been reintroduced around Auckland and in the forests. The South Island bird is found on the west coast of the South Island and Fiordland; and the bluff weka has thrived on the Chatham Islands and is being reintroduced in Canterbury. The last sub-species is ever present on Stewart Island. The bird is slimmer than the kiwi, and dark brown with marked golden flecks, especially on the heavily streaked breast. Like the kiwi, the weka grubs around at dusk but can be seen regularly during the day: many are bold enough to approach trampers and take titbits from their hands. The bird's whistle is a loud and distinctive "kooo-li".

The **kaka** is a member of the parrot family and closely related to the kea, though it does not venture from its favoured lowland forest environments in Northland, around Nelson, the Marlborough Sounds, the West Coast and Stewart Island. You can recognize the bird by its colour: bronze with a crimson belly and underside of the tail and wings.

When walking among the forests of New Zealand, it is not unusual to hear the cry of the **morepork**, an owl that's named after the distinctive sound of its call. A small brown bird, it sometimes appears in town and city gardens. Alongside the morepork is the distinct musical "mackmacko" of the **bellbird**, a shy green and blue, curve-billed bird. In contrast, the **fantail**, another common forest dweller, is more likely to be seen than heard, constantly opening and closing the tail that gives it its name. Often flying alongside walkers on trails, the bird is not keeping you company but feeding on the insects you disturb.

The **tui**, with its white throat and mostly green and purple velvet-like body, is renowned for mimicking the calls of other birds and the copious consumption of nectar and fruit. Its song has greater range than the bellbird and contains some rather unmusical squeaks, croaks and strangled utterances. Just as noisy is the **saddleback**, a rare but pretty bird, mostly black except for a tan-coloured saddle, whose chattering call welcomes you if you stumble into its patch of the forest. The thrush-sized saddleback belongs to the endemic family of wattle birds, of which the North Island kokako is also a member — see below.

Among the smaller birds regularly glimpsed as they flit around the forest the most distinctive are the **robin** family, which range from black with a cream or yellow breast to all black,

depending how on far south you have travelled. They have a prolonged and distinctive song lasting for up to thirty minutes with only brief pauses for breath.

The New Zealand pigeon, the **kereru**, was a favourite Maori food but these days it is prohibited to kill and eat them. It is a very ancient New Zealand species, which seems to have no relatives elsewhere. A handsome large bird with metallic green, purple and bronze colouring and a pure white breast, you'll often see it flashing along in the low-lying forests. Another of New Zealand's oldest birds is the rare **kokako**, an abysmal flyer that lives around the Pureora Forest, Little Barrier Island (see p.143) and Rotorua (see p.269). If you're lucky you'll see it grouchily walking around the forest floor or climbing trees for another crack at flying, or catch a glimpse of its distinctive bright blue wattle.

RIVERS, LAKES AND WETLANDS

New Zealand is riddled with **rivers**, most of them short and flowing rapidly down to the sea. There are some slower, meandering rivers on the east coast of the South Island, however, which create for a unique environment. The braided rivers in Canterbury and the Waitaki/Mackenzie Basin have distinctive wide shingle beds and multiple channels, providing a breeding ground for many birds, insects, fish and plants. Numerous **lakes** provide rich habitats for fish and birds; many of New Zealand's **wetlands**, on the other hand, have been drained for agriculture and property development, although some areas are preserved as national parks and scenic reserves. It's in low wetland areas that you're likely to come across the tallest of the native trees, the **kahikatea** (white pine), which reaches over 60m. There's a particularly fine stand in the central western North Island close to Te Awamutu.

One bird you're bound to see in the vicinity of a lake is the takahe's closest relative, the **pukeko**, a bird which is still in the process of losing the power of flight. The pukeko is mostly dark and mid-blue with large feet and an orange beak, and lets out a high-pitched screech if disturbed.

New Zealand is renowned for its great freshwater fishing, with massive brown and rainbow **trout** and **salmon** swarming through the fast-flowing streams. All introduced species, these fish have adapted so well to their conditions that they grow much larger here than elsewhere in the world; as a result, many native species have been driven out. Another delicacy commonly found in New Zealand's waters are native **eels**, much loved by Maori who built complicated eel traps along many rivers.

Keeping the fishermen company along the river banks of the Mackenzie country and Canterbury are **black stilt** or *kaki*, one of the world's rarest wading birds. A thin black bird with round eyes and long red legs, the stilt is incredibly shy – if you do see one in the wild, keep well away. Usually found in swamps and beside riverbeds, the best place to see them is in the specially created reserve near Twizel (see p.631). A slightly more adaptable member of the family is the **common pied stilt**, a black and white bird that has been more successful in resisting the attentions of introduced mammals, particularly feral cats.

Another inhabitant of the Canterbury braided riverbank is the **wrybill**. This small white and grey bird uses its unique bent bill to turn over stones or pull out crustaceans from mud. In winter the species migrates to Auckland and the mudflats of Kaipara, Manukau and the Firth of Thames. The wrybill's close cousin, the **banded dotterel**, favours the sides of rivers, lakes, open land with sparse vegetation and coastal lagoons and beaches. It is a small brown and white bird with a dark or black band around its neck and breeds only in New Zealand, though it does briefly migrate to Australia.

The **blue duck** is one of four endemic species with no close relatives anywhere in the world. Its Maori name, *Whio*, is a near perfect representation of the male bird's call. You can spot it by its blue-grey plumage, with chestnut on both breast and flanks; it also has an unusual bill with a black flexible membrane along each side, and beady yellow eyes. Mountainous areas are where it makes its home, preferring the swift mountain streams and approaching the coast only where the mountains are close to the sea. Unfortunately this is now an endangered species, preyed upon by mammals and forced to compete for food with the salmon and trout in the rivers.

GREEN ISSUES

The fact that New Zealand is, at least by European standards, apparently both clean and green is more by accident than design, a result of its isolation and relatively short human history. And although many New Zealanders are trying to preserve the country's environment, their efforts are often hampered by a vacillating government and the paramount interests of big business – wildlife has had to pay the price for some short-sighted and flagrant profiteering.

Traditionally meat, wool and dairy products have been New Zealand's main exports, but today a greater proportion is made up of forestry, machinery, aluminium and chemicals, all of which take their toll on the environment in terms of land usage, pollution and energy demands. Today none of the animals or crops and few of the trees harvested are endemic to New Zealand: the countryside is a confusion of native, European and Australian birds, exotic and indigenous trees, and a profusion of plants and animals from each hemisphere. Since human habitation began, forty-three indigenous birds have been consigned to the ranks of the extinct, and New Zealand now accounts for eleven percent of the world's endangered bird species.

LAND-USAGE

People came to New Zealand to build a new life in a green land and visitors today arrive with many romantic images in mind. With a population of only 3.6 million, you would expect human interference to be limited but the country is in fact one of the most bizarre ecological disasters in the history of man. **Forest cover** has been reduced from about 85 percent since human colonization, while nearly three-quarters of the land area is given over to the production of food and commercial forestry, the latter essential to the national economy. Most of the trees are quick-growing **radiata pine**, an American species introduced because it is more profitable

POSSUMS

During 1837–40 the first **Australian brushtail opossums** (*Trichosurus vulpecula*, more commonly known as **possums**) were introduced and liberated in New Zealand by private individuals and Acclimatization Societies wanting to establish a fur industry. Up until 1930 the spread of these nocturnal marsupials was accelerated by further releases, both authorized and illegal, of New Zealand-bred stock.

As early as the 1890s people were advocating control because the potential for damage to orchards and gardens was becoming evident. However, in 1920 a Professor of Botany and Zoology at the then Victoria University College of Wellington released a report supporting the possum, and stating that the harm to native forests was negligible. There followed a series of ineffective regulations until 1947, when heavier penalties for harbouring and liberating opossums were brought into effect and all restrictions on the trapping or killing of possums were cancelled. Finally, in 1951, a control measure was introduced – a bounty of 2s 6d a head to be paid on all killed possums from which skins had not been taken – a scheme that continued until 1960.

Possums number in excess of 70 million, even pushing sheep into second place, and it is thought that they currently munch their way through 21,000 tonnes of vegetation every day. They are also carriers of bovine TB, an added menace to the dairy, beef and deer industries. They pose a threat to the survival of native bush and to the indigenous fauna that rely on the tree fruits and flowers for food, to say nothing of the eating of eggs and killing of chicks.

Most travellers will encounter possums either when walking the tracks or when driving. Road kill possum is know colloquially as "road pizza": the relatively cute-looking, furry little creatures engender an almost pathological hatred in even the most mild mannered Kiwis who will swerve all over the road in order to run them over. Many believe a return to the old possum hunter days would provide the best solution to the problem with hunters getting a few dollars for each pelt and creating employment. The Department of Conservation continue with the controversial policy of poisoning which in the past has led to casualties amongst non-targeted bird species. But whatever the solution it is clear that if the possums are allowed to continue unchecked they will turn New Zealand into a barren wasteland.

than any native variety; these days just ten percent of native forest remains.

The increase in demand for forestry- and wet-land goes unabated, even though commercial timber milling turns areas into virtual lunar deserts dotted with tree stumps. A by-product is added air pollution from fume-spitting, eighteen-wheeler logging trucks. And despite a sustained programme to eradicate them, pests like **possums**, wild deer, goats and rabbits pose a serious threat to the country's economic welfare.

POLLUTION

Influenced by commerce, past governments have favoured some decidedly unfriendly environmental policies, although the recently elected Labour coalition is now trying to redress the balance. Despite a record of admirable moral stands, such as banning ships and submarines carrying nuclear warheads from its shores (see p.855), governments have usually managed to disregard environmental initiatives related to **air pollution** and **industrial emissions**. New Zealand has the second worst record for CO2 emissions in the OECD. Although it's perceived abroad as a country with enviably clean air, the quality of air in many cities, if measured, is shocking (check out Christchurch in the winter), and there have been massive increases in asthma and other respiratory problems amongst the young. Greenpeace rates the pollution from the Tasman pulp and paper mill in Kawerau as one of the country's worst problems. The mill is apparently responsible for the largest discharge of toxic organochlorine chemicals in the country and the nearby Tawera River has been contaminated by some of the most harmful chemicals known to man. New Zealand also scores badly on waste disposal and the monitoring of chemical usage and contaminated sites – with 700 potentially contaminated sites, it is on a par with the USA. Every day more than a billion litres of **sewage** and **industrial waste** is discharged into rivers and the sea.

Further short-sightedness is sadly evident in the use of intensive **farming** techniques and the massive amounts of **phosphates** piled onto soil that has been heavily exploited this century. Some rivers and lakes, in regions such as the Waikato, are either polluted by high nitrate levels or have few natural features left. Thankfully there is a strong groundswell of informed opinion leaning towards organic smallholdings that become increasingly profitable with the rising consumer demand for natural, untreated food. Recently the food industry has introduced a carefully monitored "eco-label", where rigorous standards provide an independent endorsement of the quality of food production. However more recently the Americans have been bullying New Zealand, with threats of trade sanctions, into accepting genetically modified crops and products.

ENERGY

New Zealand is about 70 percent energy self-sufficient, but the known reserves of gas and oil are thought to be good for only another twenty to thirty years and coal will also run out sometime in the next century. Demand for energy is currently on the increase, thanks to energy intensive processes like aluminium smelting (near Invercargill) and the Taranaki petrochemical industry, together with a general increase in energy demand of 57 percent, despite only a 17 percent population rise over the last 25 years.

Although the nation is surrounded by sea water and buffeted by high winds, the efforts to exploit **alternative power sources** have been token at best with the recent Palmerston North wind-farm being a notable exception (see p.259). **Hydroelectricity** is, on the face of it, an environmentally friendly way of coping with the demands for power from an ever increasing population, but the flooding of unique environments to create lakes and grand dams has destroyed numerous natural habitats. Perhaps the most important environments at risk are the riverbanks, where threatened species of birds live, nest and feed.

PRESERVING THE ENVIRONMENT

Much of New Zealand is utilized for farming and forestry, and land constantly swallowed up by urban sprawl, so what remains of pre-colonized New Zealand is under increased pressure.

Although not enough was done, as early as the 1880s it was realized that humans were having a detrimental effect on the land and that measures needed to be taken to preserve the environment. Pressure was exerted by the eco warriors of the time to conserve the forest, wetlands and volcanic areas by gazetting them as **national parks**. In this way, native flora and fauna could be preserved, encouraging regeneration and restocking. In 1887 Te Heuheu Tukino IV (Horonuku) set the ball rolling by giving the nucleus of the Tongariro National Park to the nation, in order to preserve the integrity of a venerated tribal area. The newest national park is the Kahurangi, formed in 1996 to ensure the preservation of an area of great natural beauty at the northwestern tip of the South Island.

A further effort to take back land and alleviate pressure on the national parks has seen the creation of small **scenic reserves** or managed areas, zones given over to preserving or regenerating native bush. There are hundreds of them dotted around the country, each concerned with regenerating a particular aspect of the local environment so that it can sustain native fauna. The process requires great vigilance as the stands grow slowly and are constantly under threat from development and introduced animals. It takes at least a hundred years for the bush to grow to maturity.

In another positive step, the Department of Conservation has made efforts to clear pests from **offshore islands**, in order to trans-locate endangered native species and ensure their survival. The creation of these environmental sanctuaries/havens saves many animals and plants from extinction and provides an opportunity to build up numbers of species on the brink of oblivion. Once the native birds become familiar with their new environment they become less fearful and allow their curiosity full rein, inspecting visitors at close quarters – just as they would have done when Maori first arrived over a thousand years ago.

BOOKS

Kiwis are avid readers, and almost equally keen writers, producing more glossy picture books and wildlife guides than you would think possible. Some excellent novels have come out of New Zealand too, despite the tiny home readership and the great difficulty of breaking into the international market.

Almost all of the following titles can be easily found in bookstores. Where two publishers are given, these refer to UK and US publishers respectively; titles that are published only in New Zealand are denoted NZ. Note that Hodder Headline titles are published by Hodder Moa Becket in New Zealand.

TRAVEL AND IMPRESSIONS

Mark Lawson, *The Battle for Room Service: Journeys to all the Safe Places* (Picador). On the basis that Timaru is rumoured to be the most activity-challenged city in New Zealand, itself the world's most differently-interesting place, Lawson selects this modest South Island city as the first port of call, and first chapter, of his wonderfully entertaining world tour of such dull places.

Austin Mitchell, *The Half-gallon, Quarter-acre, Pavlova Paradise* (OUP). A humorous and insightful vision of 1960s New Zealand as seen through the eyes of a British Labour MP and self-declared Kiwi commentator. Though wildly out of date, in many ways the lifestyles and values he describes still have the ring of truth, and the book stands as a measure of how much New Zealand has progressed, and at the same time how little.

Paul Theroux, *The Happy Isles of Oceania* (Penguin). Another misanthropic diatribe from Mr Theroux, and one which really put Kiwi noses out of joint. This time he kicks off in New Zealand and subsequently rides a clutch of hobby-horses through the Pacific. Some worthwhile observations on trekking in the South Island and a little historical context on the Polynesian migrations go some way towards saving the book.

HISTORY, SOCIETY AND POLITICS

James Belich, *The New Zealand Wars* (Penguin). An extraordinary, well-researched, and in-depth demolition job on the received version of the course and outcome of the colonial wars, which re-examines the Victorian and Maori interpretation of the conflict. A book for committed historians and those fanatically interested in the subject, since it gives more detail than most people will ever need to know.

Alistair Campbell, *Maori Legends* (Viking Sevenseas, NZ). A brief retelling of selected stories in an accessible way with some evocative illustrations.

R.D. Crosby, *The Musket Wars* (Reed). An account of the massive upsurge in inter-*iwi* conflict before the start of European colonization, that was exacerbated by the introduction of the musket and led to the death of 23 percent of the Maori population, a proportion far greater than that of Russian casualties in World War II.

A.K. Grant, *Corridors of Pua* (Hazard Press, NZ). A light-hearted look at the turbulent and fraught political history of the country from 1984 to the introduction of MMP.

Tom Hewnham, *By Batons and Barbed Wire* (o/p). A harrowing account of the 1981 Springbok Tour of New Zealand that stirred up more social hatred than any other event and proved conclusively that there is more to New Zealand society than just a bunch of good blokes and "Hail fellow well met".

Hineani Melbourne, *Maori Sovereignty: The Maori Perspective* (Hodder Headline); and its companion volume *Maori Sovereignty: The Pakeha Perspective* by **Carol Archie** (Hodder Headline). Everyone from grass-roots activists to statesmen get a voice in these two volumes, one airing the widely divergent Maori visions of sovereignty, the other covering the equally disparate *pakeha* view on the subject. They assume a fairly good understanding of Maori structures and recent New Zealand history, but are highly instructive nonetheless.

Claudia Orange, *The Story of the Treaty* (Bridget Williams Books, NZ). A concise, illustrated exploration of the history and myths behind what many believe to be the most important document in New Zealand history, the Treaty of Waitangi. Well written but probably more than the casual traveller needs to know. Much the same criticism applies to the author's *The Treaty of Waitangi* (Allen & Unwin, NZ), which covers the lead-up to the signing, and the treaty's first sixty years.

Margaret Orbell, *A concise Encyclopaedia of Maori Myth and Legend* (Canterbury University Press, NZ). A fairly comprehensive rundown on many tales and their backgrounds that rewards perseverance even though it's a little dry.

Jock Phillips, *A Man's Country? The Image of the Pakeha Male* (Penguin). Recently updated version of a classic treatise on mateship and the Kiwi bloke. This thorough exploration ranges through the formative pioneering years, rugby, wartime camaraderie, the development of the family-man ideal and now includes Nineties man. It comes to life with the partial dismantling of the stereotype in the light of developments of the last twenty years.

Keith Sinclair, *The History of New Zealand* (Penguin). A highly readable general history of New Zealand with comprehensive coverage of the social factors that have shaped the country, as well as the prime movers. Maori oral history gets a brief and informative look-in, and there's plenty on uneasy Maori–*pakeha* relations, but it's not been updated to take into account recent political changes and the Maori renaissance.

D.C. Starzecka (ed), *Maori Art and Culture* (British Museum Press). A kind of Maori culture primer, with concise and interesting coverage of Maori history, culture, social structure, carving and weaving, spiced up by excellent colour photos of artefacts from the British Museum's collection.

Ross Wiseman, *The Spanish Discovery of New Zealand in 1576* (Discovery Press, NZ). Wiseman puts the case for pre-Abel Tasman European discovery based on wreckage from ships, Spanish-sounding Maori names and a clutch of other circumstantial but convincing evidence.

FICTION

Barbara Anderson, *All the Nice Girls* (Vintage, NZ). A short, insightful comedy of manners-cum-romance about a naval officer's wife who goes off the rails in 1960s Auckland, by a writer known for her clarity and vibrancy.

Anonymous, *The Spin* (Hodder Headline). Allegedly written by a government insider, hence the anonymity. Though Kiwis were shocked at the antics of barely disguised current politicians, it's all pretty tame by world standards, and only mildly revealing about the behaviour of elected representatives behind closed doors.

Graeme Aitken, *Fifty Ways of Saying Fabulous* (Headline). An extremely funny book about burgeoning homosexuality in a young farm boy, who lives in a world where he is expected to clean up muck and play rugby. Brilliant and touching, but it loses its way in the final third and serves up an anticlimactic ending.

Eric Beardsley, *Blackball 08* (Collins, NZ). Entertaining and fairly accurate historical novel set in the West Coast coal-mining town of Blackball during New Zealand's longest ever labour dispute.

Graham Billing, *Forbrush and the Penguins* (Oxford University Press, NZ). Described as the first serious novel to come out of Antarctica, it is the compelling description of one man's lonely vigil over a colony of penguins and the relationship he develops with them. Well worth the effort.

Samuel Butler, *Erewhon* (Penguin). Gulliver's Travels-style journey to a utopian land, initially set in the Canterbury high country (where Butler ran a sheep station) but increasingly devoted to a satirical critique of mid-Victorian Britain.

Catherine Chigey, *In a Fishbone Church* (Victoria University Press, NZ). A high-minded, broad-ranging novel spanning physical borders and time, learning about the past and dealing with it, maybe, by focusing on one family.

Ian Cross, *The God Boy* (Penguin). This first and only novel of note from Ian Cross is widely considered to be New Zealand's equivalent to *Catcher in The Rye*. It concerns a young boy trapped between two parents who hate each other and describes the violent consequences of this situation.

Barry Crump, *A Good Keen Man; Hang on a Minute Mate; Bastards I Have Met; Forty Yarns and a Song* (Hodder Headline). Just a few of the many New Zealand bushman books by the Kiwi equivalent of Banjo Patterson, who writes with great humour, tenderness and style about the male-dominated world of hunting, shooting, fishing, drinking, and telling tall stories. Worth reading for a picture of a New Zealand and a lifestyle that have now largely disappeared.

Sigrid Crump, *Bushwoman* (Reed Books, NZ). Light, fresh and highly evocative account of a young German woman's solo travels on foot in New Zealand's backcountry during the 1960s and 70s. Infusing each page with her deep love of the Kiwi bush and fiercely independent spirit, Barry Crump's sister-in-law leaves you full of admiration.

Alan Duff, *Once Were Warriors* (Virago/Random House). A shocking and violent book in the social realism, kitchen-sink drama style, set in 1970s south Auckland and adapted in the 1990s for Lee Tamahori's film of the same name. At its heart are good intentions concerning the predicament of urban Maori, but at times this is a clumsy book with an oddly upbeat ending. Duff has recently published a sequel, *What Becomes of the Broken Hearted* (Virago/Random House).

Denis Edwards, *Connor is Free* (Penguin). A pretty run-of-the-mill thriller, but it will divert you during long bus, train or plane journeys.

Fiona Farrell, *Six Clever Girls Who Became Famous Women* (Penguin). A second novel of some quality and style has the girls of the title reunited in mid-life to confront what they have achieved and come to terms with their present and the possibilities of the future.

Janet Frame, *An Angel at My Table* (Random House). Though undoubtedly one of New Zealand's most accomplished novelists, Frame is perhaps best known for this three-volume autobiography, dramatized in Jane Campion's film which, with wit and a self-effacing honesty, gives a wonderful insight into both the author and her environment. Her superb novels and short stories use humour alongside highly disturbing combinations of events and characters to overthrow readers' preconceptions. For starters, try *Faces in the Water, Living in the Maniototo, Scented Gardens for the Blind,* and *Owls Do Cry* (all The Women's Press).

Maurice Gee, *Crime Story; Going West; Prowlers, The Plumb Trilogy* (Penguin). These

from an underrated but highly talented writer. Despite the misleadingly light titles, Gee's focus is social realism, taking an unflinching, powerful look at motivation and unravelling relationships.

Patricia Grace, *Potiki* (Penguin). Poignant and poetic tale of a Maori community redefining itself through a blend of traditional and modern values, while its land is threatened by coastal development. Exquisite writing by an outstanding author who ranks among the finest in New Zealand today. She has also written several other novels and short-story collections.

Peter Hawes, *Leapfrog with Unicorns* (Vintage Press, NZ) and *Tasman's Lay* (Hazard Press, NZ). Two from the unsung hero, cult figure and probably only member of the absurdist movement in New Zealand, who writes with great energy, wit and surprising discipline about almost anything that takes his fancy. It's not much of a secret that Peter is also **W.P. Hearst** who has written the not-to-be-missed *Inca Girls Aren't Easy* (Vintage), a series of joyous, sad and slippery tales.

Keri Hulme, *The Bone People* (Picador). Celebrated winner of the 1985 Booker Prize, and a wonderful first novel set along the wild beaches of the South Island's West Coast. Mysticism, myth and earthy reality are transformed into a haunting tale peopled with richly drawn characters.

Witi Ihimaera, *Bulibasha – King of the Gypsies* (Penguin). The best introduction to one of the country's finest Maori authors. A rollicking good read, energetically exploring the life of a rebellious teenager in 1950s rural New Zealand, where two mighty sheep-shearing families are locked in battle. It's an intense look at adolescence, cultural choices, family ties and the abuse of power, culminating in a masterful twist. Look out also for the excellent *The Matriarch* (Penguin) by the same author.

Phil Kawana, *Dead Jazz Guys* (Huia Publishers, NZ). A relatively new kid on the block, writing short stories about the young urban Maori, family, drugs and sex. Poignant and intelligent writing in a collection of mixed quality.

Fiona Kidman, *The Book of Secrets* (Picador). Historical novel tracing one family's heritage through the reclusive granddaughter of a Scot who left the highlands with commanding preacher Norman McLeod, eventually ending up in Northland's Waipu.

Elizabeth Knox, *The Vintner's Luck* (Victoria University Press). A very curious book indeed that for no very good reason became an international best seller, all about "a man, his vineyard, love, wine and angels."

Shonagh Koea, *The Grandiflora Tree* (Penguin). A savagely witty yet deeply moving study of the conventions of widowhood, with a peculiar love story thrown in. First novel from a journalist and short-story writer renowned for her astringent humour.

Katherine Mansfield, *The Collected Stories of Katherine Mansfield* (Penguin). All 73 short stories sit alongside 15 unfinished fragments in this 780-page tome. Concise yet penetrating examinations of human behaviour in apparently trivial situations, often transmitting a painfully pessimistic view of the world, and startlingly modern for their time.

Ngaio Marsh, *Opening Night*; *Artists in Crime*; *Vintage Murder* (Fontana). Just a selection from the doyenne of New Zealand crime fiction. Since 1934 she has been airing her anglophile sensibilities and killing off innumerable individuals in the name of entertainment, before solving the crimes with Inspector Allen. Perfect mindless reading matter for planes, trains and buses.

Ronald Hugh Morrieson, *Came a Hot Friday* (OUP). Superb account of the idiosyncrasies of country folk and the two smart spielers who enter their lives, in a comedy thriller focusing on crime and sex in a small country town.

John Mulgan, *Man Alone* (Penguin). Seminal and soberly written boy's-own novel about one man's restless and peripatetic times working the New Zealand back blocks between the wars, as the country lurched from its pioneering days into the modern world. First published in 1939, it is often regarded as one of the first truly Kiwi novels and had a huge influence on New Zealand writing, its evocation of the Kiwi male quickly becoming an archetype.

Vincent O'Sullivan, *Let the River Stand* (Penguin). Deftly conjuring the minutiae of homestead and rural school life in a Waikato farming community of the 1930s, Sullivan weaves disparate tales around the life of his gawky antihero, Alex. Tragic, humorous and captivating. *Believers to the Bright Coast* (Penguin) is O'Sullivan's disappointing follow-up and little more than an impenetrable confusion repeating the themes and obsessions of the first.

Emily Perkins, *Not Her Real Name* (Picador). Sub-Mansfield short-story writer who inexplicably picked up an award for this. Though lacking the subtlety and incisiveness of the master, this uneven collection shows some promise. Sadly, however, this promise subsequently failed to materialize in her first novel, *Leave Before You Go* (Picador).

Frank Sargeson, *The Stories of Frank Sargeson* (Penguin). Though not well-known outside New Zealand, Sargeson is a giant of Kiwi literature. His writing, from the 1930s to the 1980s, is incisive and sharply observed, at its best in dialogue, which is always true to the meter of New Zealand speech. This work brings together some of his finest short stories. *Once is Enough*, *More than Enough* and *Never Enough!* (all Penguin) make up the complete autobiography of a man sometimes even more colourful than his characters; **Michael King** has written a fine biography, *Frank Sargeson: A Life* (Viking).

Maurice Shadbolt, *Strangers and Journeys* (Hodder/Atheneum). On publication in 1972 this became a defining novel in New Zealand's literary ascendancy and its sense of nationhood, putting Shadbolt in the same league as Australia's Patrick White. A tale of two families of finely wrought characters, whose lives interweave through three generations. Very New Zealand, very human and not overly epic. Later works, which have consolidated Shadbolt's reputation, include *Mondays Warriors*, *Season of the Jew* and *The House of Strife* (Hodder/Atheneum).

C.K. Stead, *The Singing Whakapapa* (Penguin). Highly regarded author of many books and critical essays who is sadly little known outside New Zealand and Australia. A combination of a powerful historical novel about an early missionary, and a dissatisfied modern descendant who is searching for meaning in his own life by exploring the past. An excellent and engaging read. His 1998 collection of short stories, *The Blinde Blonde with Candles in her Hair*, was less critically acclaimed, but still entertaining and readable.

Paul Thomas, *Old School Tie* (Hodder Headline). Smart thriller with some neat comedic touches but a bit clichéd, just like his last book *Inside Dope* (Hodder Headline), and lacking any really sympathetic characters. Another relaxing read, ideal while waiting for a bus.

Damien Wilkins, *The Miserables* (Faber). One of the best novels to come out of New Zealand, shorn of much of the colonial baggage of many writers. It is surprisingly mature for a first novel, sharply evoking middle-class New Zealand life from the 1960s to the 1980s through finely wrought characters.

ANTHOLOGIES

Fergus Barrowman (ed), *The Picador Book of Contemporary New Zealand Fiction* (Picador). A good combination of extracts and short stories from most of the best living writers in the country.

Warwick Brown, *100 New Zealand Paintings* (Godwit Publishing, NZ). As the title suggests, with some excellent reproductions and a good bit of information.

Warwick Brown, *100 New Zealand Artists* (Godwit Publishing, NZ). The companion to the above but also allowing room for sculptors, printmakers, photographers and graphic artists.

Bill Manhire (ed), *100 New Zealand Poems* (Godwit Publishing, NZ). A very manageable selection of Kiwi verse which provides an excellent introduction to the poetry of the nation.

C.K. Stead (ed), *Contemporary South Pacific Stories* (Faber and Faber). A great collection from authors as diverse as European Kiwi, Maori, Fijian-Indian, Samoan, Tongan and Cook Islanders, with a brilliant introduction.

Ian Wedde and Harvey McQueen (eds), *The Penguin Book of New Zealand Verse* (Penguin). A comprehensive collection of verse from the earliest European settlers to contemporary poets, and an excellent introduction to Kiwi poetry; highlights are works by James K. Baxter, Janet Frame, C.K. Stead, Sam Hunt, Keri Hulme, Hirini Melbourne, and Apirana Taylor.

REFERENCE AND SPECIALIST GUIDES

Rosemary George, *The Wines of New Zealand* (Faber and Faber). Entertaining and informative look at New Zealand's most important wine regions, the history, the people and the product.

Les Hill & Graeme Marshall, *Images of Silver* (The Halcyon Press, NZ). Inspirational fishing picture book with great shots of anglers in action all over the country.

John Kent, *North Island Trout Fishing Guide* and *South Island Trout Fishing Guide* (Reed, NZ). Laden with information on access, seasons and fishing style, and illustrated with maps of the more important rivers.

Terry Sturm (ed), *The Oxford History of New Zealand Literature* (Oxford University Press). A massive and comprehensive guide to non-fiction, novels, plays and poems by a variety of academics, which is fascinating for anyone with an academic interest in the subject but otherwise as dry as an old stick.

J & J Thomas, *The New Zealand Bed & Breakfast Book* (Moonshine Press, NZ). Annually updated listing of member B&Bs, homestays and farmstays, covering almost 1000 places all over the country. The guide is available from bookshops or direct from Moonshine Press, PO Box 41022, Eastbourne, Wellington (☎ & fax 04/562 7667), for NZ$20, though the larger car-rental firms often supply customers with a free copy. Bear in mind that entries are submitted by the owners, so a little reading between the lines is advisable.

Vic Williams, *The Penguin New Zealand Wine Guide 1999–2000* (Penguin). A comprehensive breakdown of over 1200 wines from the land of the long white cloud that will keep you interested and turn you into a big fan, if you are not already.

FLORA, FAUNA AND THE ENVIRONMENT

D.H. Brathwaite, *Native Birds of New Zealand* (Caxton Press, NZ). Brilliant colour photographs and lots of information pinpointing thirty rare birds that, with a little effort and some patience, you can observe while travelling around.

Andrew Crowe, *Which Native Tree?* (Viking Pacific, NZ). Great little book, ideal for identification of New Zealand's common native trees – though not tree ferns – with diagrams of tree shape, photos of leaves and fruit, and an idea of geographic extent.

John Dawson, *New Zealand Coast and Mountain Plants* (Victoria University Press, NZ). A luxuriant book filled with colourful and unusual illustrations.

Susanne & John Hill, *Richard Henry of Resolution Island* (John McIndoe, NZ).

Comprehensive and very readable account of a man widely regarded as New Zealand's first conservationist. The book serves as a potted history of this underpopulated area of Fiordland, peopled by many of the key explorers.

Geoff Moon, *The Reed Field Guide to New Zealand Birds* (Reed, NZ). Excellent colour reference book, with ample detail for species identification.

Geoff Moon, *The Reed Field Guide to New Zealand Wildlife* (Reed, NZ). Separate chapters, stuffed with colour photos, cover forest, open country, the coast and offshore islands, but facts are too thin on the ground for it to succeed as a reference work.

Rod Morris & Hal Smith, *Wild South: Saving New Zealand's Endangered Birds* (Century Huchinson/TVNZ). A fascinating companion volume to a 1980s TV series following a band of dedicated individuals trying to preserve a dozen of New Zealand's wonderfully exotic bird species, including the kiwi, kakapo, takahe and kea.

Murdoch Riley, *New Zealand Trees and Ferns* (Viking Sevenseas, NZ). An excellent, pocket-size guide with colour illustrations identifying the most often seen trees and ferns.

Neville Peat, *Manapouri Saved* (Longacre Press, NZ). Full and heartening coverage of one of New Zealand's earliest environmental battles when, in the 1960s, a petition signed by ten percent of the country succeeded in persuading the government to cancel its hydroelectric plans for Lake Manapouri.

TRAMPING

Moir's Guide (NZ Alpine Club, NZ). Probably the most comprehensive guide to tramping in the South Island. It is divided into two volumes: North, covering hikes between Lake Ohau and Lake Wakatipu; and South, which concentrates on walks around the southern lakes and fjords including the Kepler Tracks, plus the less popular Dusky and George Sound tracks.

Pearl Hewson, *New Zealand's Great Walks* (Hodder Headline). Pearl is a no-nonsense DOC Officer working out of the Wellington Office and what she doesn't know about the Great Walks isn't worth knowing. This is a practical, concise guide which concentrates her experiences into a useful aid to trampers.

Mark Pickering, *Wild Walks* (Shoal Bay Press, NZ). Sixty short and easily accessible walks on the North Island, mixed in with historical anecdotes and precise descriptions of the local environment.

Philip Temple, *BP Pocket Tramping Guides* (BP). A series of inexpensive, lightweight paperback guides giving handy and informative track notes, with information on the history, flora and fauna, for the major New Zealand tramps. Titles cover the Routeburn, Milford, Copland, Hollyford and Abel Tasman tracks.

CYCLING AND ADVENTURE SPORTS

Mike Bhana, *New Zealand Surfing Guide* (Reed, NZ). Pragmatic handbook to the numerous prime surf spots around the New Zealand coast, with details on access, transport, the best wind and tide conditions and expected swells.

Graham Charles, *New Zealand Whitewater: 120 Great Kayaking Runs* (Craig Potton, NZ). An indispensable, comprehensive and entertaining guide to New Zealand's most important kayaking rivers. River maps and details on access are supplemented by quick reference panels with grades, timings, and handy tips like which rapids not to even think about running.

Bruce Ringer, *New Zealand by Bike* (The Mountaineers, NZ). The definitive Kiwi cycle touring guide with 14 regional tours (with many side-trips) which can all be knitted together into a greater whole. Plenty of maps and altitude profile diagrams.

Marty Sharp, *A Guide to the Ski Areas on New Zealand* (Random House). Exactly what you'd expect, with full descriptions of the fields complete with tow plans and information on access, local towns and ski rental.

Ken Sibly and Mark Wilson, *4 Wheel-drive South Island* (Shoal Bay Press, NZ). A book for adventurous drivers who know how to use their off-road vehicles, covering seventy public, but treacherous, roads.

Paul Simon and Jonathan Kennett, *Classic New Zealand Mountain Bike Rides* (Kennett Bros, NZ). All you need to know about off-road biking in New Zealand with details of over four hundred rides. Paul Simon runs the *www. mountainbike.co.nz* site.

LANGUAGE: KIWI ENGLISH AND MAORI

English and te reo Maori, the Maori language, share joint status as New Zealand's official languages, but on a day-to-day basis all you'll need is English, or its colourful Kiwi variant. All Maori speak English fluently, often slipping in numerous Maori terms which in time become part of everyday Kiwi parlance. You may find television, radio and newspaper articles – especially those relating to Maori affairs – initially confusing without a basic grounding, but with the aid of our glossary (see p.885) you'll soon find yourself using Maori terms all the time. A basic knowledge of Maori pronunciation will make you more comprehensible and some understanding of the roots of place names can be helpful. You'll need to become something of an expert, though, to appreciate much of the wonderful oral history, and stories told through waiata (songs), but learning a few key terms will enhance any Maori cultural events you may attend.

To many Brits and North Americans, **Kiwi English** is barely distinguishable from its trans-Tasman cousin, "Strine", sharing much of the same lexicon of slang terms, but with an accent marginally closer in tone to South African English. Australians have no trouble distinguishing the two accents, repeatedly highlighting the vowel shift which turns "bat" into "bet", makes "yes" sound like "yis" and causes "fish" come out as

"fush". This vowel contortion is carried to new levels in remoter country areas, but there is really very little regional variation, only Otago and Southland – the southern quarter of the South Island – distinguishing themselves with a rolled "r", courtesy of their predominantly Scottish founders. Throughout the land, Kiwis add an upward inflection to statements, making them sound like questions; most are not, and to highlight those that are, some add the interrogative "eh?" to the end of the sentence, a trait most evident in the North Island, especially among Maori.

MAORI

For the 50,000 native speakers and 100,000 who speak it as a second tongue, Maori is very much a living language, gaining strength all the time as both Maori and *pakeha* increasingly appreciate the cultural value of *te reo*, a language central to *Maoritanga* and forming the basis of a huge body of magnificent songs, chants and legends, lent a poetic quality by its hypnotic and lilting rhythms.

Maori is a member of the Polynesian group of languages and shares both grammar and vocabulary with those spoken throughout most of the South Pacific. Similarities are so pronounced that Tupaia, a Tahitian crew member on Captain Cook's first Pacific voyage in 1769, was able to communicate freely with the *Aotearoa* Maori they encountered. The Treaty of Waitangi was written in both English and Maori, but *te reo* soon began to lose ground to the point where, by the late nineteenth century, its use was proscribed in schools. Maori parents keen for their offspring to do well in the *pakeha* world frequently promoted the use of English, and Maori declined further, exacerbated by the mid-twentieth-century migration to the cities. Though never on the brink of extinction, the language reached its nadir in the 1970s when perhaps only ten percent of Maori could speak their language fluently. The tide began to turn towards the end of the decade with the inception of *kohanga reo* **pre-schools** (literally "language nests") where *Maoritanga* is taught and activities are conducted in Maori. Originally a Maori initiative, it has now crossed over and *pakeha* parents are increasingly introducing their kids to biculturalism at an early age. Fortunate *kohanga reo* graduates can progress to the small number of state-funded Maori-language primary schools known as *kura kaupapa*. For decades, Maori has

MAORI PLACE NAMES

The following is a list of some of the most common words and elements you will see in town and place names throughout New Zealand. A.W. Reed's *A Dictionary of Maori Place Names* (Reed) gives more detailed coverage of the same field.

AO	Cloud.	**PAE**	Ridge.
ARA	Road or path.	**PAPA**	Flat, earth, floor.
AWA	River or valley.	**PATERE**	Chants.
HAU	Wind.	**PUKE**	Hill.
IKA	Fish.	**PUNA**	Spring.
ITI	Small.	**RAKI**	North.
KAI	Food, or eat.	**RANGI**	Sky.
KAINGA	Home, village.	**ROA**	Long, high.
KARE	Rippling.	**ROTO**	Lake.
KINO	Bad.	**RUA**	Hole, cave, pit, two.
MA	White, clear.	**RUNGA**	Top.
MANGA	Stream.	**TAHU**	Light.
MANU	Bird.	**TAI**	Sea.
MATA	Headland.	**TANE**	Man.
MAUNGA	Mountain.	**TAPU**	Sacred.
MIHI	Speeches.	**TARA**	Peak.
MOANA	Sea, lake.	**TE**	The.
MOTU	Island or anything isolated.	**TOMO**	Cave.
MURI	End.	**WAI**	Water.
NUI	Big.	**WAKA**	Canoe.
O	The place of.	**WHANGA**	Bay, body of water.
ONE	Sand, beach.	**WHENUA**	Land or country.
PA	Fortified settlement.		

been taught as an option in secondary schools, and there are now two state-funded tertiary institutions operated by Maori, offering graduate programmes in Maori studies.

The success of these programmes has bred a young generation of Maori speakers frequently far more fluent than their parents who, shamed by the loss of their heritage, are beginning to attend Maori evening classes. Legal parity means that Maori is now finding its way into officialdom too, with government departments all adopting Maori names in recent years and many government and council documents being printed in both languages. The increasing knowledge and awareness has spawned Maori TV and radio broadcasts, notably the nightly news, *Te Karere*.

In your day-to-day dealings you won't need **to speak Maori**, though both native speakers and *pakeha* may well greet you with *kia ora* (hi, hello), or less commonly *haere mai* (welcome). On ceremonial occasions, such as marae visits, you'll hear the more formal greeting *tena koe* (said to one person) or *tena koutou katoa* (to a group).

Maori words used in place names are listed in the box above, while those in common use are listed in the general glossary (see p.885). If you are interested in learning a little more, the best handy reference is Patricia Tauroa's *The Collins Maori Phrase Book* (HarperCollins; $15) which has helpful notes on pronunciation, handy phrases and a useful Maori–English and English–Maori vocabulary.

PRONUNCIATION

Laziness and arrogance have combined to give *pakeha* – and consequently most visitors – a distorted impression of Maori pronunciation, which is usually mutated into an Anglicized form. Until the 1970s there was little attempt to get it right, but with the rise in Maori consciousness through the 1980s and 1990s, coupled with a sense of political correctness, most *pakeha* now make some attempt at Maori pronunciation. As a visitor you will probably get away with just about anything, but by sticking to a few simple rules and keeping your ears open, the apparently unfathomable place names will soon trip off your tongue. The key to **pronunciation** is in knowing where to split long compound words; scanning the place name elements in the box (see previous page) should help a great deal, and it is worth remembering that all syllables end in a vowel. Each syllable is then stressed equally, so that, for example, Waikaremoana comes out as a flat Wai-ka-re-mo-ana. The other trick for the unwary is that Maori words don't take an "s" to form a plural, so you'll find many plural nouns in this book – kiwi, tui, kauri, Maori – in what appears to be a singular form; about the only exception is Kiwis (as people), a Maori word wholly adopted into English.

Maori was solely a spoken language before the arrival of British and French missionaries in the early nineteenth century, who transcribed it using only fifteen letters of the Roman alphabet. The five **vowels** come in long and short forms; the long form is sometimes signified in print by a macron – a flat bar above the letter – but usually it is simply a case of learning by experience which sound to use. When two vowels appear together they are both pronounced, though substantially run together. For example, "Maori" should be written with a macron on the "a" and be pronounced with the first two vowels separate, turning the commonly used but incorrect "Mow-ree" into something more like "Maao-ri".

The eight **consonants**, **h**, **k**, **m**, **n**, **p**, **r**, **t** and **w**, are pronounced much as they are in English. Finally, there are two digraphs: **ng**, pronounced much as in "sing", and **wh**, which sounds either like an aspirated "f" as in "off", or like the "wh" in "why", depending on who is saying what and in which part of the country.

GLOSSARY OF KIWI TERMS, PHRASES AND SLANG

ACC Accident Compensation Commission.

ANZAC Australian and New Zealand Army Corps; every town in New Zealand has a memorial to ANZAC casualties from both world wars.

Aotearoa Maori for New Zealand, the land of the long white cloud.

Ariki Supreme chief of an *iwi*.

Bach (pronounced "batch") Holiday home, originally a bachelor pad at work camps and now something of a Kiwi institution that can be anything from shack to palatial waterside residence.

Back-blocks Remote areas.

Biddy-bid A burr-bearing bush (from Maori *piripiri*).

Blat Travel at great speed.

Bludger Someone who doesn't pull their weight or pay their way, a sponger.

Boomer Excellent.

Bro Brother, term of endearment widely used by Maori.

Captain Cooker Wild pig, probably descended from pigs released in the Marlborough Sounds on Cook's first voyage.

Chilly bin Insulated cool box for carrying picnic supplies and beer to the beach or cricket match.

Chook Chicken.

Choice Fantastic.

Chuddy Chewing gum, also "chutty".

Chunder Vomit.

Coaster (Ex-) resident of the West Coast of the South Island.

Cocky Farmer, comes in "Cow" and "Sheep" variants.

Crib South Island name for a bach.

Cuz or **Cuzzy** Short for cousin, see "bro".

Dag Wag or entertaining character.

Dairy Corner shop selling just about everything, open seven days and sometimes 24 hours.

Dally Semi-derogatory name for descendants of Dalmatian immigrants from the Balkans.

Dob in Reporting one's friends and neighbours to the police; there is currently a dobber's charter encouraging drivers to report one another for dangerous driving.

Docket Receipt.

Domain Grassy reserve, open to the public.

Fizz boat Small powerboat.

Flicks Cinema, movie theatre.

Flog Steal.

Footie Rugby, usually union rather than league, never soccer.

Freezing works Slaughter house.

Give it a burl Try it.

Godzone New Zealand, short for "God's own country".

Gorse in your pocket To be slow to pay your share.

Good as (gold) First rate, excellent.

Good on ya Expression of approbation or encouragement, frequently appended with "mate".

Greasies Takeaway food, especially fish and chips.

Greenstone A type of nephrite jade known in Maori as *pounamu*.

Haka Maori dance performed in threatening fashion before All Black rugby games.

Handle Large glass of beer.

Hangi Maori feast cooked in an earth oven (see p.862).

Hapu Maori sub-tribal unit. Several make up an *iwi*.

Hard case See "dag".

Hard yacker Hard work.

Hollywood A faked or exaggerated sporting injury used to gain advantage.

Hongi Maori greeting, performed by pressing noses together.

Hoon Lout, yob or delinquent.

Hori Offensive word for a Maori.

Hui Maori gathering or conference.

Iwi Largest of Maori tribal groupings.

Jandals Ubiquitous Kiwi footwear, thongs or flip-flops.

Jug Litre of beer.

Kai Maori word for food, used in general parlance.

Kaimoana Seafood.

Karanga Call for visitors to come forward on a marae.

Kaumatua Maori elders, old people.

Kawa-Marae Etiquette or protocol on a marae.

Kete Traditional basket made of plaited flax that is seeing something of a resurgence in popularity.

Kiore Polynesian rat.

Koha Donation.

Kohanga Reo Pre-school Maori language immersion (literally "language nest").

Kumara Sweet potato.

Kuri Polynesian dog, now extinct.

Lay-by Practice of putting a deposit on goods until they can be fully paid for.

Log of wood Slang for the Ranfurly Shield, New Zealand rugby's greatest prize.

Mana Maori term indicating status, esteem, prestige or authority, and in wide use among all Kiwis.

Manaia Stylized bird or lizard forms used extensively in Maori carving.

Manchester Linen section of a department store and its contents.

Manuhiri Guest or visitor, particularly to a marae.

Maoritanga Maori culture and custom, the Maori way of doing things.

Marae Literally "courtyard" but much more. Place for conducting ceremonies in front of a meeting house. Also a general term for a settlement centred on the meeting house.

Mauri Life force or life principle.

Mere War club, usually of greenstone.

Metalled Graded road surface of loose stones found all over rural New Zealand.

MMP Mixed member proportional representation – New Zealand's new electoral system.

Moko Old form of tattooing on body and face that has seen a resurgence among Maori gang members.

Ngati Tribal prefix meaning the descendants or people of. Also *Ngai* and *Ati*.

No fear Expression indicating refusal or disagreement.

OE Overseas experience, usually a year spent abroad by Kiwis in their early twenties.

Pa Fortified village of yore, now usually an abandoned terraced hillside.

Paddock Field.

Pakeha A non-Maori, usually white and not usually expressed with derogatory intent. Literally "foreign" though it can also be translated as "flea" or "pest". It may also be a corruption of *pakepakeha*, which are mythical human-like beings with fair skins.

Pashing Kissing or snogging.

Patu Short fighting club

Paua Abalone, a type of shellfish with a wonderful iridescent shell.

Pavlova Meringue dessert with a fruit and cream topping.

Pike out To chicken out or give up.

Piss Beer.

Pissed Drunk.

Piss head Drunkard.

Plunkett rooms Childcare centre.

Poms Folk from Britain; not necessarily offensive.

Powhiri Traditional welcome onto a marae.

Puckerooed Broken. Derived from the Maori for broken, *pakaru*.

Puku Maori for stomach, often used as a term of endearment for someone amply endowed.

Queen Street farmer City businessman owning rural property.

Ranch slider Sliding glass door giving onto the garden or decking.

Rangatira General term for a Maori chief.

Rapt Well-pleased.

Rattle your dags Hurry up.

Root Vulgar term for sex.

Rooted To be very tired or beyond repair, as in "she's rooted mate" – your car is irreparable.

Rough as guts Uncouth, roughly made or operating badly, as in "she's running rough as guts, mate".

Scroggin Trail mix, essentially nuts and raisins.

Sealed road Bitumen-surfaced road.

Section Block of land usually surrounding a house.

She'll be right Everything will work out fine.

Shoot through To leave suddenly.

Shout To buy a round of drinks or generally to treat folk.

Skull To knock back beer quickly.

Slutted Greatly annoyed.

Smoko Tea break.

Snarler, **snag** Sausage.

Spinner A jerk.

Squiz A look, as in "Give us a squiz".

Station wagon Estate car.

Stoked Very pleased.

Taiaha Long-handled club.

Tall poppy Someone who excels. "Cutting down tall poppies" is to bring overachievers back to earth – every Kiwi's perceived duty.

Tane Man.

Tangata whenua The people of the land, local or original inhabitants.

Tangi Mourning or funeral.

Taniwha Fearsome water spirit of Maori legend.

Taonga Treasures, prized possessions.

Tapu Forbidden or taboo. Frequently refers to sacred land.

Te reo Maori Maori language.

Tiki Maori pendant depicting a distorted human figure.

Tiki tour Guided tour.

Togs Swimming costume.

Tohunga Maori priests, experts in *Maoritanga*.

Tukutuku Knotted latticework panels decorating the inside of a meeting house.

Tupuna Ancestors; of great spiritual importance to Maori.

Ute Car-sized pick-up truck, short for "utility".

Varsity University.

Wahine Woman.

Waiata Maori action songs.

Wairau Spirit.

Waratah Stake, a term used to describe snow poles on tramps.

Waka Maori canoe.

Wero Challenge before entering a marae.

Whakapapa Family tree or genealogical relationship.

Whanau Extended family group.

Whare Maori for a house.

Whare runanga Meeting house.

Whare whakairo Carved house.

Within cooee Within reach.

Wop-wops Remote areas.

Yahoo To be or act like a lout.

INDEX

Stay in touch with us!

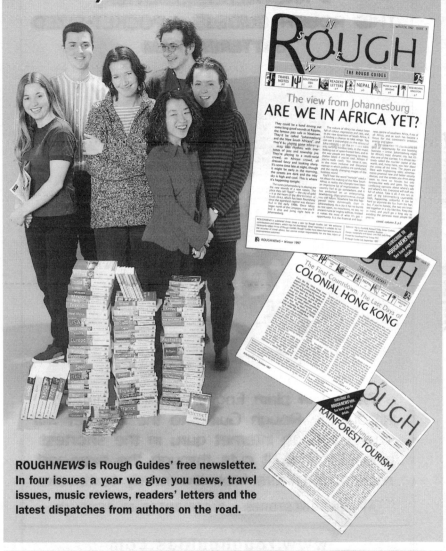

ROUGH*NEWS* is Rough Guides' free newsletter.
In four issues a year we give you news, travel
issues, music reviews, readers' letters and the
latest dispatches from authors on the road.

I would like to receive ROUGH*NEWS*: please put me on your free mailing list.

NAME . . . .

ADDRESS . . . .

Please clip or photocopy and send to: Rough Guides, 62–70 Shorts Gardens, London WC2H 9AH,
England or Rough Guides, 375 Hudson Street, New York, NY 10014, USA.

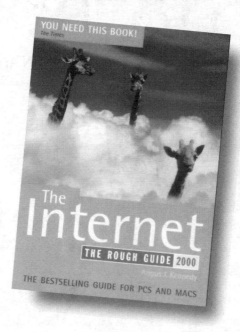

ROUGH GUIDES: Travel

Amsterdam
Andalucia
Australia

Austria
Bali & Lombok
Barcelona
Belgium &
　Luxembourg
Belize
Berlin
Brazil
Britain
Brittany &
　Normandy
Bulgaria
California
Canada
Central America
Chile
China
Corfu & the
　Ionian Islands
Corsica
Costa Rica
Crete
Croatia
Cyprus
Czech & Slovak
　Republics
Dodecanese &
　the East Aegean

Dominican
　Republic
Ecuador
Egypt
England
Europe
Florida
France
French Hotels &
　Restaurants
　1999
Germany
Goa
Greece
Greek Islands
Guatemala
Hawaii
Holland
Hong Kong &
　Macau
Hungary
India
Indonesia
Ireland
Israel & the
　Palestinian
　Territories
Italy
Jamaica
Japan
Jordan

Kenya
Lake District
Laos
London
Los Angeles
Malaysia,
　Singapore &
　Brunei
Mallorca &
　Menorca
Maya World
Mexico
Morocco
Moscow
Nepal
New England
New York
New Zealand
Norway
Pacific Northwest
Paris
Peru
Poland
Portugal
Prague
Provence & the
　Côte d'Azur
The Pyrenees
Rhodes & the
　Dodecanese
Romania

St Petersburg
San Francisco
Sardinia
Scandinavia
Scotland
Scottish
　Highlands &
　Islands
Sicily
Singapore
South Africa
South India
Southwest USA
Spain
Sweden
Switzerland
Syria

Thailand
Trinidad &
　Tobago
Tunisia
Turkey
Tuscany &
　Umbria
USA
Venice
Vienna
Vietnam
Wales
Washington DC
West Africa
Zimbabwe &
　Botswana

AVAILABLE AT ALL GOOD BOOKSHOPS

ROUGH GUIDES: Mini Guides, Travel Specials and Phrasebooks

MINI GUIDES

Antigua
Bangkok
Barbados
Big Island of
  Hawaii
Boston
Brussels
Budapest

Dublin
Edinburgh
Florence
Honolulu
Jerusalem
Lisbon
London
  Restaurants
Madrid
Maui
Melbourne
New Orleans
Rome
Seattle
St Lucia

Sydney
Tokyo
Toronto

TRAVEL SPECIALS

First-Time Asia
First-Time
  Europe
Women Travel

PHRASEBOOKS

Czech
Dutch

Egyptian Arabic
European
French
German
Greek
Hindi & Urdu
Hungarian
Indonesian
Italian
Japanese

Mandarin
  Chinese
Mexican
  Spanish
Polish
Portuguese
Russian
Spanish
Swahili
Thai
Turkish
Vietnamese

ROUGH GUIDES:
Reference and Music CDs

REFERENCE
Classical Music
Classical:
  100 Essential CDs
Drum'n'bass
House Music
Jazz
Music USA

Opera
Opera:
  100 Essential CDs
Reggae
Reggae:
  100 Essential CDs
Rock
Rock:
  100 Essential CDs
Techno
World Music
World Music:
  100 Essential CDs
English Football
European Football

Internet
Millennium

ROUGH GUIDE MUSIC CDs
Music of the
  Andes
Australian
  Aboriginal
Brazilian Music
Cajun & Zydeco

Classic Jazz
Music of
  Colombia
Cuban Music
Eastern Europe

Music of Egypt
English Roots
  Music
Flamenco
India & Pakistan
Irish Music
Music of Japan
Kenya & Tanzania
Native American
North African
Music of Portugal

Reggae
Salsa
Scottish Music
South African
  Music
Music of Spain
Tango
Tex-Mex
West African
  Music
World Music
World Music Vol 2
Music of
  Zimbabwe

DOING NEW ZEALAND?

- 58 great locations – in central urban areas or set in stunning scenery off the beaten track, you choose!

- Twin, double, family and shared rooms available.

- Hot showers, laundry and kitchen facilities.

- No duties, no curfews and 24 hour access for guests.

- Member discounts on travel and activities.

- Friendly, professional staff ready to help you with information, activities and transport.

You can purchase a range of travel and accommodation packages before you go – 14, 21 or 28 nights with YHA, together with various transport options including backpackers' bus, rental cars, travel pass or 3 day City Discovery Pass.

You can also book directly through YHA New Zealand. For further information, please contact YHA New Zealand's national office. Phone: +64 (3) 379 9970
　　　　　　Fax:　　+64 (3) 365 4476
　　　　　　E-mail: info@yha.org.nz
Check out our website at
　　　　http://www.yha.org.nz

HOSTELLING
INTERNATIONAL
YHA NEW ZEALAND